Insurance Law for Common Interest Communities

SECOND EDITION

Condominiums, Cooperatives, and Homeowners Associations

Francine L. Semaya
Douglas Scott MacGregor
Kelly A. Prichett

AMERICAN BAR ASSOCIATION
Real Property, Trust and Estate Law Section

Cover design by Andrew Alcala

Printed in the United States of America.

27 26 25 24 23   5 4 3 2 1

A catalog record for this book is available from the Library of Congress.

For my aunt, Faye Feldman, of blessed memory, who encouraged my love for books—fiction and non-fiction—who I feel certain is very proud of my accomplishments.

✳

For Jeri Klimowicz, an insurance professional whose understanding of insurance for condominium and homeowners associations is exceeded only by her patience in fielding questions. Happy retirement!

CONTENTS

Chapters 2 through 8 are available online at https://ambar.org/ILCIC.

Chapter 12 is available online at https://ambar.org/ILCIC.

CHAPTER 13

ABOUT THE AUTHORS

Francine L. Semaya

Francine L. Semaya is a New York licensed attorney with a practice in insurance regulation, reinsurance, insurance insolvency, and transactional matters. Since July 2010, she has served as a legal and insurance regulatory consultant. She previously chaired the insurance regulatory and transactional group of two international law firms. She performs legal and compliance audits and serves as an expert witness. Ms. Semaya was named a "2009 Woman to Watch" by *Business Insurance* magazine. Active in several professional organizations, Ms. Semaya is a past president of the International Association of Insurance Receivers. She is a longtime member of the American Bar Association's Tort Trial and Insurance Practice Section (TIPS), where she has assumed various leadership roles. Ms. Semaya is on the Board of Directors of the Insurance Federation of New York. She is also a member of the New York City Bar's Insurance Law Committee and is a past member of the Practising Law Institute's Insurance Law Advisory Board. Ms. Semaya also serves on a number of non-profit boards. She is a frequent lecturer, has authored numerous articles, and has served as editor of both legal and insurance trade publications and books for, among others, National Underwriter Property & Casualty, Best's Review, American Bar Association, Practising Law Institute, and others on topics pertaining to insurance regulatory, reinsurance, insolvency law, and common interest communities. She is often called upon to organize and chair seminars and programs of significance to the insurance industry.

Douglas Scott MacGregor

Douglas Scott MacGregor earned his law degree from the University of Florida, Levin College of Law and a Master of Social Work from the University of South Florida. He has written more than 20 legal treatises, focusing on the law of common interest communities including Florida Condominium Law and Colorado Community Association Law. For many years, he has been the update author for two of the seminal works on common interest community law: Patrick J. Rohan, *Home Owners Associations and Planned Unit Developments: Law and Practice*

(Matthew Bender) and Patrick J. Rohan & Melvin A. Reskin, *Cooperative Housing Law and Practice* (Mathew Bender). Mr. MacGregor has also been an update author for *Appleman on Insurance Law* (Matthew Bender) for over 20 years and in 2016 wrote the chapter for that treatise on flood insurance, the first comprehensive treatment of that topic to be published.

Kelly A. Prichett

Kelly A. Prichett earned her legal degree from George Washington University Law School and studied as an undergraduate at the University of California, Santa Cruz where she earned a bachelor's degree in the study of linguistics. She has practiced law in the areas of real property and trusts and estates, and she has edited numerous scholarly legal articles and treatises, and non-legal subjects including self-help, weight management, novels, children's books, and disaster recovery. Ms. Prichett is currently licensed to practice in California.

PREFACE

We first met in the fall of 2013 when Fran was working on two chapters on guaranty funds for the *New Appleman on Insurance Law Library Edition* and she needed a collaborator with extensive research and writing experience. Doug, having written more than 20 legal treatises, had that experience. Bob Lopatin, who was Fran's editor on the project and Doug's on others, put us together. From the moment we started working together, we knew we were a good team. Fran's ability to understand and explain complex insurance law and regulatory issues and Doug's ability to reduce it to writing were complimentary. We knew we wanted to work on another, larger project together, but what? The answer was immediately obvious to the both of us. For nearly 40 years, Doug has researched and written principally about the law of common interest communities—condominiums, homeowners associations, and cooperatives—producing seven treatises on the subject. Fran, on the other hand, is a practicing attorney and consultant who tackles some of the most challenging regulatory and insolvency matters as well as frequently lecturing on and authoring chapters and articles in legal and insurance trade publications about insurance regulatory, reinsurance, and insolvency law. We knew there was no treatise on the insurance concerns of common interest communities and that, in fact, little had been written on the subject at all despite its importance to those communities. We also knew that our combined backgrounds and expertise were what was required to fill that gap.

We began in the summer of 2014 to outline the goals for this book. Before we started to write, we collected every case we could find that discussed insurance and common interest communities. We also assembled files containing applicable state statutes, typical policies issued to common interest communities, and any article or portion of a treatise that we could locate that touched on our topic. Our goal was to produce a comprehensive treatise that would accomplish two objectives. First, we wanted to create a single source for associations, for their attorneys and community association managers, and for the insurance professionals that work with them to use as a reference, a book that would explain what they needed to know about insurance in general. Our second objective was to address comprehensively the unique insurance issues that arise for common interest communities. It took much longer than we expected. We finished the last chapter in October of 2017. During the three years of research and writing, we spent countless hours reading cases, statutes, and policies. Doug prepared drafts, and we then poured over every word together. The benefit of our two very different backgrounds was immediately obvious. Many of the questions we encountered as we read cases and deconstructed policies could be answered only when debated between a person with a deep knowledge of insurance and another with an equal understanding of community association law. This was a daunting and challenging task, but together we came up with the right answers.

We decided to publish this treatise ourselves, not an easy feat, and we recognized we needed help. We turned to Kelly Prichett, whose experience in journalism, law practice, and legal publishing was a perfect fit and we knew was invaluable. She had guided others on the path to self-publishing, so we were happy to have her help. She has ably guided us through many a minefield and, through her questions, comments, and careful editing of the text immeasurably improved the final product. Kelly's insight often made us reflect on our goals, insuring we were not straying from our outline. In some cases, with her help we altered those goals, and that enhanced the work product. Without her guidance, we would still be lost in the weeds.

The law is not static or always certain. Its interpretations can vary from lawyer to lawyer and judge to judge. It is constantly evolving. As you read this, insurers are revising policy language, legislators are amending statutes, and courts are handing down cases, sometimes overturning previous holdings on the very same issues. We continue to pour over the new data and plan to prepare an annual update that will keep you, the reader, informed of changes in the insurance law affecting common interest communities.

Francine Semaya
Douglas MacGregor

GUIDE TO ACRONYMS

ACC	anti-concurrent causation
ACCORD	Association for Cooperative Operations Research and Development
ACV	actual cash value
ALI	American Law Institute
ALTA	American Land Title Insurance
ASC	area of special consideration
BFE	base flood elevation
BPP	Building and Personal Property Coverage Form
CAC	Condominium Association Coverage Form
CAI	Community Associations Institute
CAM	community association manager
CC&Rs	Covenants, Conditions and Restrictions
CGL	commercial general liability policy
CIC	common interest community
CIRM	Community Insurance and Risk Management Specialist
D&O	directors and officers policy
DFS	department of financial services
DIC	differences in conditions policy
DORE	doctrine of reasonable expectations
DWL	defense within limits
E&O	errors and omissions policy
EAJA	Equal Access to Justice Act
EFP	excess flood policy
ERISA	Employment Retirement Income Security Act
EUO	Examination Under Oath
FAIR	Fair Access to Insurance Requirement
FEMA	Federal Emergency Management Agency
FHA	Federal Housing Authority

FHBM	Flood Hazard Boundary Map
FIRM	Flood Insurance Rate Map
FLA	Fidelity Law Association
HOA	homeowners association
ICC	increased cost of compliance or increased cost of coverage
IRMI	International Risk Management Institute
ISO	Insurance Services Office
LOMR	Letter of Map Revision
MRECA	Model Real Estate Cooperative Act
NAIC	National Association of Insurance Commissioners
NCCUSL	National Conference of Commissioners on Uniform State Laws
NFIA	National Flood Insurance Act
NFIP	National Flood Insurance Program
NPMOLIP	Non-Profit Management and Organization Liability Insurance Policy
PCOH	products-completed operations hazard
POA	property owners association
PRP	preferred risk policy
RCV	replacement cost value
RCBAP	Residential Condominium Building Association Policy
SFIP	Standard Flood Insurance Policy
SFHA	special flood hazard areas
SIC	standard industrial classification
SIR	self-insured retention
SLR	severe repetitive loss property
SMP	special multi-peril policy
TCPA	Telephone Consumer Protection Act
UCA	Uniform Condominium Act
UCIOA	Uniform Common Interest Ownership Act
UCL	Uniform Law Commission
UP	United Policyholders
UPA	Uniform Planned Community Act
VA	Veterans Administration
WYO	Write Your Own Program

Chapter 1
Introduction

§ 1.01 Purpose of This Treatise

[1] Background

Prior to World War II, common interest communities were rare. One form of common interest community, the housing cooperative, first appeared in the late 19th century, and by the roaring 1920s, cooperatives were found in 16 cities and were the most popular form of "community housing" in the immediate post-war era.[1] The homeowners association (HOA) also has a long history. One of the earliest was formed in the mid-19th century in Boston. It had many of the features now associated with HOAs: common area maintenance, assessments for common expenses, and use regulations.[2] It was not, however, until the post-war boom in suburban development that HOAs began to become popular. Condominiums existed in Puerto Rico in the 1950s but did not arrive on the mainland United States in their present form until the Federal Housing Administration (FHA) adopted a Model Act in the 1960s based on which all 50 states adopted enabling legislation for the formation of condominiums. In the last quarter of the 20th century, common interest communities spread rapidly across the landscape with condominiums and HOAs replacing housing cooperatives as the most popular form. Statistics compiled by the Community Association Institute (CAI) reveal that the number of common interest communities grew from approximately 10,000 in 1970 to 342,000 in 2016.[3] CAI estimates that just under 70 million Americans—over 21 percent of the population—reside in a common interest community. Additionally, units in condominium and townhouse associations have become increasingly popular as vacation homes in states such as Colorado and Vermont and winter residences across the Sunbelt. The exponential growth

1. 2 Rohan & Reskin, *Real Estate Transactions: Cooperative Housing: Law and Practice—Forms*, § 1.02[1] (Matthew Bender 2017).

2. 6 Rohan, *Real Estate Transactions: Home Owner Associations and Planned Unit Developments—Law and Practice: Forms*, § 2.04[2] (Matthew Bender 2017)

3. *See* https://www.caionline.org/AboutCommunityAssociations/Pages/StatisticalInformation.aspx.

in common interest communities spawned the development of a new profession: community association management. It also led to a specialty law practice: community association law. There are a number of other professionals, including some insurance brokers, who work exclusively to meet the needs of common interest communities.

[2] Unique Issues of the Common Interest Community

Common interest community associations manage and maintain common property through elected governing boards. One of their most important functions is to obtain insurance to protect the community against liability and property damage. For many associations, annual insurance premiums are collectively their largest single expenditure. Yet, association governing boards and the professionals that serve them often know little about their insurance needs or the contents of the policies they purchase to meet those needs. The resources providing information on insurance for common interest communities are limited. Indeed, the leading treatises on insurance law barely mention common interest communities. The purpose of this treatise is to provide a comprehensive guide to that law. In three parts, this treatise provides a comprehensive survey of a wide range of issues: everything from the insurance requirements imposed on associations by law or community documents to how standard insurance policy language affects associations. This treatise has been created for the unique needs of common interest ownership. Below is an overview of the three parts.

§ 1.02 Part One: Primers for Professionals

Part One of the treatise consists of two "primer" chapters. The first—Chapter 2—is titled "Insurance Primer for Common Interest Community Professionals." It is intended to provide a basic understanding of the business and law of insurance for association attorneys and community association managers, but it can also serve to educate association governing board members about the basics of insurance.

Chapter 3 is titled "A Primer on Common Interest Communities for Insurance Professionals." Its purpose is to provide lawyers who specialize in insurance law and professionals in the insurance industry—agents, brokers, adjusters, and others—with a basic understanding of the terminology of common interest communities and how they function. The primer for common interest community professionals begins by describing how insurance is regulated by the states. It also explains how to determine the insurance needs of a common interest community. Those needs are met through working with an agent or broker, and the chapter provides a brief description of their role and responsibilities. The chapter then discusses the importance of insurance applications. A key to understanding insurance is knowing the meaning of key terms used in the industry. A section on insurance terminology offers definitions of excess and umbrella insurance, Difference in Conditions policies, deductibles, exclusions, loss assessment coverage, coinsurance clauses, and subrogation. Many common interest communities finance their premium payments, so another section describes premium financing. Properly filing and pursuing a claim is critical to obtaining an adequate settlement from the insurer; therefore, a section on that topic addresses the notice of claim, reservation of rights by the insurer, investigation of claims by insurers—including site visits, requests for documents, examinations under oath, and working with adjusters—selection of defense counsel, and insurance trustees.

The authors strongly believe that common interest communities will benefit from establishing an insurance committee whose members focus on the insurance needs of the community. For this reason, a section is devoted to discussing the membership and function of these committees. Finally, the chapter ends with a review of some of the resources available to policyholders to better understand insurance.

The primer on common interest communities for insurance professionals, found in Chapter 3, starts with a discussion on the importance of insurance to common interest communities. That is followed by an explanation of the types of common interest communities. It distinguishes between the three basic types of common interest communities—condominiums, cooperatives, and homeowner associations—and discusses the variety of communities that can come under the broad umbrella of the term "homeowners association." Another section provides key definitions and discusses the importance of those definitions to understanding the functions of common interest community associations.

Associations are governed by documents; accordingly, the treatise provides a section explaining the types of documents that govern associations and how they differ, depending on the type of common interest community. When an insurance broker is evaluating the insurance requirements of an association or an attorney is representing an association in a claim against an insurer, it is useful to have a basic understanding of how associations operate, so one section is devoted to issues of governance and the role of professional managers. The broker and attorney equally need to understand that state law as well as the governing documents of an association may impose duties regarding insurance on their governing boards, and for that reason there is a section explaining the duty of the board to obtain and regularly review insurance coverage.

Common interest communities are, in effect, "mini-governments" and, therefore, either state law or the governing documents often mandate that governing board meetings be open to the members of the association. This can present problems for insurance professionals. A section of Chapter 3 explains open meeting requirements and when boards can meet in executive session. Working with dysfunctional associations can be a nightmare for attorneys and insurance professionals alike and, therefore, a section is devoted to helping them to identify and avoid these associations. To understand the potential civil liability in an association, one needs to know something about the law governing the liability of the association, governing board members, and individual association members. The extent of possible liability can affect the association's coverage needs and, therefore, one section in Chapter 3 discusses those issues. Finally, the chapter ends with a bibliography of treatises on common interest community law, including a list of state-specific works.

§ 1.03 Part Two: Sources of Insurance Requirements

Part Two of the treatise consists of four chapters on the sources of insurance requirements for common interest communities. The first chapter collects the statutory insurance requirements for common interest communities of all 50 states, the District of Columbia, Puerto Rico, and the Virgin Islands. The second chapter discusses the Fannie Mae and Freddie Mac guidelines and the requirements of government agencies. The next chapter concerns the insurance mandates typically found in common interest community governing documents and in contracts that associations enter. Finally, the last of the four chapters reviews the insurance requirements of the various uniform acts and the Restatement (Third) on Property: Servitudes.

The key chapter in Part Two is Chapter 5. It contains the insurance requirements in each state's enabling legislation. It explains that all states have enacted condominium legislation and that these laws require condominium associations to obtain and maintain certain insurance coverages. However, very few states have legislation specifically designed to govern homeowners associations, with Florida[4] and California[5] being notable exceptions. Seven other states govern homeowners associations through a version of the Uniform Common Interest Ownership Act, which has extensive insurance requirements. The housing cooperative is the least common of the types of common interest communities, and only a handful of states have laws specifically designed to govern it.[6] However, because a cooperative is almost always incorporated, it should be possible to form one in any state under its non-profit corporation laws, which will generally address indemnification of officers and directors and possibly the authority of the corporation to maintain director's and officer's insurance.

4. Fla. Stat. §§ 720.301, *et seq.*

5. Cal. Civ. Code §§ 4000, *et seq.*

6. *See, e.g.*, Fla. Stat. §§ 719.101, *et seq.*; N.J. Stat. §§ 46:8D-1, *et seq.*; N.Y. Co-op. Corp. §§ 1, *et seq.*

§ 1.04 Part Three: Policies

Part Three of the treatise devotes six chapters to addressing policies that should commonly be obtained by common interest community associations:

- Commercial property insurance (Chapter 10),
- Boiler and machinery or equipment breakdown insurance (Chapter 11),
- Flood insurance (Chapter 12),
- Commercial general liability insurance (Chapter 13),
- Directors and officers liability insurance (Chapter 14), and
- Crime/fidelity insurance (Chapter 15).

Each of these chapters explains the contents of the typical association policy and highlights unique challenges common interest communities face in maintaining adequate coverage. The chapters are annotated with cases analyzing issues from the particular perspective of common interest community associations and their residents. A key feature of these chapters is an "Association Policy Content Checklist" that can help associations evaluate their coverage.

An introductory chapter to Part Three—Chapter 9—describes the roles of designated directors and insurance committees and insurance professionals in obtaining the necessary coverage. This chapter explains how coverages are classified and the need for an annual insurance review. It also has a brief overview of workers' compensation insurance and corrects the mistaken belief that associations need such coverage only if they have employees. The chapter also discusses three other types of insurance coverage that common interest community associations need to consider:

- Law enforcement liability (LEL) coverage,
- Garage keepers legal liability coverage, and
- Pollution or environmental liability coverage.

Finally, the chapter explains package policies that may combine property, liability, and other coverages.

Chapter 2

Insurance Primer for Common Interest Community Professionals

This chapter can be found online at https://ambar.org/ILCIC.

Chapter 3

A Primer on Common Interest Communities for Insurance Professionals

This chapter can be found online at https://ambar.org/ILCIC.

Chapter 4

Sources of Insurance Requirements: Introduction

This chapter can be found online at https://ambar.org/ILCIC.

Chapter 5

Sources of Insurance Requirements: State Statutes

This chapter can be found online at https://ambar.org/ILCIC.

Chapter 6

Sources of Insurance Requirements: Fannie Mae, Freddie Mac, and Federal Agencies

This chapter can be found online at https://ambar.org/ILCIC.

Chapter 7

Sources of Insurance Requirements: Common Interest Community Documents and Contracts

This chapter can be found online at https://ambar.org/ILCIC.

Chapter 8

Sources of Insurance Requirements: Uniform Acts and Restatement

This chapter can be found online at https://ambar.org/ILCIC.

Chapter 9

Introduction to Part Three: The Policies

§ 9.01 The Scope of Part Three and Insurance Basics

Part Three of this treatise includes six chapters. Each chapter addresses a form of insurance coverage that should commonly be obtained by common interest community (CIC) associations: commercial property insurance (Chapter 10); boiler and machinery or equipment breakdown insurance (Chapter 11); flood insurance (Chapter 12); commercial general liability insurance (Chapter 13); directors and officers liability insurance (Chapter 14); and crime/fidelity insurance (Chapter 15). At the end of all but one of these chapters is an "Association Policy Content Checklist." These checklists can aid the association in reviewing its coverage either when a new policy is being considered or when an existing policy is being reviewed. There is no checklist for the flood insurance chapter because there is only one flood policy—the Standard Flood Insurance Policy (SFIP)—issued by the Federal Emergency Management Agency (FEMA), and no changes can be made to it.

Obtaining and maintaining adequate insurance coverage is one of the most important responsibilities of an association governing board. Moreover, the association generally has an obligation to obtain and maintain adequate coverage. The collective premiums for the various coverages usually represent a significant portion of an association's annual budget. In many states, at least some of the six coverage types discussed in Part Three of the treatise are mandated by statute. Additionally, the association governing documents often impose an obligation to obtain certain coverages. Fannie Mae and Freddie Mac guidelines may require an association to obtain some or all of the six types of coverage, and failure to do so will likely result in the inability of unit purchasers to obtain mortgages or share loans in the case of a cooperative apartment. Finally, members of association governing boards generally have a fiduciary duty to act in the best interests of the association and that includes obtaining adequate insurance for the association.

Despite the importance of, and necessity for, proper insurance coverage, the members of association governing boards often know little about insurance in general and less about the existing coverage or coverage needs of the association. Board members are almost always volunteers who have work and family responsibilities. Service on the governing board is a part-time responsibility. Some board members are also officers with specific duties. A board collectively has the duty to adopt an annual budget, manage association funds, adopt and enforce rules, and oversee the maintenance of the property. Insurance can easily take a back seat to these other obligations. For that reason, the authors strongly recommend boards take two actions: establish a person or panel responsible for insurance and obtain the services of an insurance professional.[1]

[1] Designated Directors and Recommended Composition of Insurance Committees

In all but the smallest associations, governing boards consist of at least five members (directors). The boards in larger associations may have seven or eleven members. Typically, there are four officers: President, Vice President, Secretary, and Treasurer. That means there is at least one board member who does not have designated duties. Additionally, the Vice President usually has limited responsibilities. Thus, either the Vice President or a non-officer board member could be assigned responsibility for the association's insurance. The responsibilities that would come with that post can be extensive. They include becoming familiar with the association's insurance needs, assisting the insurance broker in filling out applications, reviewing proffered coverage with the broker, reporting to the board, and acting on behalf of the association when a claim arises.

NOTE: These responsibilities may be too much for one person to handle, especially if the designated director has little knowledge of insurance. For that reason, the authors recommend that associations create an insurance committee with the designated director as chair.

In most communities, there will be a resident who is, or was before retiring, employed in some aspect of the insurance industry. That person is an obvious choice for the committee. There are, however, other residents whose participation on the committee will be beneficial. Owners of small businesses necessarily have to acquire a working understanding of insurance. Employees of larger businesses who have responsibility for risk management also generally learn quite a bit about insurance. Finally, many communities have a resident who is a practicing or retired attorney. Even an attorney whose practice does not involve insurance will be a valuable addition to an insurance committee because of the critical thinking required in any field of law practice and because an insurance policy is a contract and every attorney has a basic understanding of contract law.

1. For notes on guidance for brokers, agents, and insurers, see Chapter 2.

If an association designates a director for insurance and/or creates an insurance committee, it needs to establish clear direction to them in writing. What are the responsibilities of the director or committee? What are they permitted to do on behalf of the association, and what are they prohibited from doing? The procedure and lines of authority become especially important when the insurance contract is being considered. For example, will the board give general guidance to the designated director or committee along with a grant of authority to reach an agreement on behalf of the association, or must the director or committee bring the proposal to the board for a formal vote? It is important that the broker understand the limits of the authority of anyone representing the association.

When a designated director or insurance committee reviews existing policies, it is likely that concerns will be uncovered. Changes may need to be made to the policy on renewal, or the association may need to seek coverage from a different carrier. The designated director or committee needs to begin working on these issues with the association's insurance broker well ahead of the renewal date of the policy. It can take time to address coverage questions. The broker needs time to explore available options. If he or she needs to seek proposals from other companies, he or she has to receive a response from those companies, examine the proposed coverage, and discuss it with the association representatives.[2]

[2] Insurance Professionals

The party through whom one obtains an insurance policy is known broadly as a "producer." The average layperson has little or no understanding of insurance and relies heavily on a producer. A producer may be an "agent" or a "broker." The general public uses these terms interchangeably; however, in the insurance industry, and in law, they have specific meanings.[3] An "agent" represents the insurance company.[4] The agent may be an employee of a particular company, may have a contract to work exclusively for one company, or may have contracts with several insurers.[5] A "broker" is independent and usually is considered the representative of the insured.[6] The broker is not limited to obtaining coverage from a single company.

2. See also related discussion in § 2.15.

3. *But see* UBS Fin. Servs. v. Thompson, 94 A.3d 176 (Md. App. 2014) (Maryland eliminated distinction between terms "insurance agent" and "insurance broker").

4. American Way Cellular, Inc. v. Travelers Property Casualty Co. of America, 216 Cal. App. 4th 1040, 1052, 157 Cal. Rptr. 3d 385, 395 (2013) ("insurance agent" represents insurer under employment by it).

5. *See, e.g.*, Ramirez v. State Farm Mut. Auto. Ins. Co., 2016 U.S. Dist. LEXIS 5245 (N.D. Ind. Jan. 15, 2016).

6. *See, e.g.*, American Way Cellular, Inc. v. Travelers Property Casualty Co. of America, 216 Cal. App. 4th 1040, 1052, 157 Cal. Rptr. 3d 385, 394–95 (2013) ("insurance broker" acts as middleman between insured and insurer, soliciting insurance from public under no employment from any special company; unlike agent, broker does not act for insurer, and insurer is not liable for broker's acts or omissions). *See also* Ga. Cas. & Sur. Co. v. Valley Wood, Inc., 336 Ga. App. 795 (2016).

Producers, whether agents or brokers, generally have no duty to anticipate the needs of their customers, to advise them about the adequacy of coverage obtained, or to inform them of optional coverage that may be available.[7] Conversely, the applicants for coverage have an obligation to specify the coverage and terms they require.[8] When applicants for insurance request specific coverage, courts usually hold the agent or broker has a duty of reasonable care to procure that coverage,[9] as long as the applicants have *agreed* to obtain that particular coverage.[10] Courts will find a duty to advise if the insured can show a "special relationship" between the parties.[11] Failure of an agent or broker to exercise the required care may result in liability.[12] However, agents or brokers have been held

7. *See* Emerson Elec. Co. v. Marsh & McLennan Cos., 362 S.W.3d 7, 13 (Mo. 2012) (neither agents nor brokers have duty to advise insured on its insurance needs or on availability of particular coverage, unless they specifically agree to do so); Houck v. State Farm Fire & Cas. Ins. Co., 366 S.C. 7, 12, 620 S.E.2d 326, 330 (S.C. 2005) (generally agent has no duty to advise insured at point of application, absent express or implied undertaking to do so); Baggett v. Summerlin Ins. & Realty, Inc., 354 N.C. 347, 554 S.E.2d 336 (2001) (agent did not have duty to point out exclusions in written policy where those exclusions did not negate particular coverage specifically requested by plaintiffs).

8. City Blueprint & Supply Co. v. Boggio, 3 So. 3d 62, 65–66 (La. App. 2008); Sinex v. Wallis, 611 A.2d 31, 33 (Del. Super. 1991); Kenyon v. Larsen, 205 Neb. 209, 217, 286 N.W.2d 759, 784 (1980).

9. Star Spa Servs. v. Robert G. Turano Ins. Agency, Inc., 595 F. Supp. 2d 519 (M.D. Pa. 2009). *See also* Traina Enters. v. Cord & Wilburn, Inc. Ins. Agency, 289 Ga. App. 833, 838, 658 S.E.2d 460, 464 (2008) (jury could find agent negligently misrepresented extent of coverage where insured requested renewal of existing policy that included vital coverage for particular business, agent told insured renewal policy had been obtained, agent expressly noted that coverage sought was included in renewal policy, and agent did not advise insured of change noted in coverage letter received from insurer).

10. *See, e.g.*, Avery v. Diedrich, 301 Wis. 2d 693, 734 N.W.2d 159 (2007). *See generally* Pollack, *Homeowner Association Managers, Agents and Officers Beware—Check Insurance Requirements to Avoid Lawsuits From Individual Members!!* (June 2016), available at: http://www.condominiuminsurancelaw.com/2016/06/articles/insurance/homeowner-association-managers-agents-and-officers-beware-check-insurance-requirements-to-avoid-lawsuits-from-individual-members/#more (by working with broker and requesting that broker procure policy that satisfies requirements of governing documents, association can go great lengths towards meeting its insurance obligations).

11. *See* Tiara Condo. Ass'n v. Marsh, USA, Inc., 991 F. Supp. 2d 1271, 1281 (S.D. Fla. 2014) (exception to general rule of no duty to advise applies when broker encourages and engages in "special relationship" with client, thereby triggering enhanced duty of care to advise client about amount of coverage prudently needed to meet its complete insurance needs; evidence of special relationship includes representations by broker about its expertise and about breadth of coverage obtained, length and depth of relationship, extent of broker's involvement in client's decision-making about insurance needs, information volunteered by broker about insurance needs, and payment of additional compensation for advisory services); Schweitzer v. Am. Family Mut. Ins. Co., 16 N.E.3d 982 (Ind. App. 2014); Garnerville Holding Co. v. Kaye Ins. Assocs., 309 A.D.2d 541, 765 N.Y.S.2d 317 (2003), *app. den.*, 780 N.Y.S.2d 311, 2 N.Y.3d 705, 812 N.E.2d 1261 (2004).

12. *See, e.g.*, Sitaram, Inc. v. Bryan Ins. Agency, Inc., 104 So. 3d 524 (La. App.), *writ den.*, 103 So. 3d 375 (La. 2012); Seascape of Hickory Point Condo. Ass'n v. Associated Ins. Servs., 443 So. 2d 488 (Fla. 2d DCA 1984) (where condominium association contacted broker seeking to purchase insurance to cover its seawall in event of storm damage, but was told seawall insurance was not available, only to discover after suffering loss that coverage was available, court held association sufficiently

not to be liable for failure to procure coverage mandated by common interest community laws.[13] In other words, common interest community associations need to take responsibility to identify their insurance requirements and gain the knowledge needed to ask pertinent questions about any proposed coverage. That is yet another reason why an insurance committee can be of great value to the association governing board.

The common interest community will want to engage a broker to find it the best policy from among a number of insurance carriers. However, the CIC needs more than just any broker. As one expert notes, insurance for common interest communities is a "niche market"—a specialty—and the association needs to work with a broker who specializes in it.[14] One way to find a broker who has the requisite knowledge is to look for one with the Community Insurance & Risk Management Specialist Designation from the Community Associations Institute. The designation is available to brokers with five years' experience as a practitioner in the community association insurance industry.

Associations typically obtain all, or nearly all, their policies through a single broker. However, they need to keep in mind that even a broker with considerable experience in insurance for common interest communities may have limited knowledge about some of the more specialized coverages, for example, Flood and Crime/Fidelity insurance. Flood insurance in particular is different from other types of coverage, and associations seeking it should consider employing a broker who specializes in it. For other specialized coverages, the association should make sure that the company for which the broker works employs persons who have knowledge of those types of coverages and in particular the specific needs of common interest communities.

---

alleged relationship between parties from which it could be said broker owed duty to exercise reasonable care in rendering advice on insurance matters because broker held itself out as professional insurance planner, had served association's insurance needs for several years, and association sought specific advice). *See also* Anthony v. Indep. Ins. Advisors, Inc., 56 V.I. 516 (2012) (association sued brokers and others over procurement of policy from insurer who was declared insolvent less than one month after policy was obtained and four months before property was damaged by hurricane and parties reached settlement). *Compare* Garcia v. Omaha Prop. & Cas. Ins. Co., 933 F. Supp. 1064, 1070 (S.D. Fla. 1995), *aff'd*, 95 F.3d 58 (11th Cir. 1996) (regardless of any duty on agent, there is no liability for negligence in failing to procure coverage that is unavailable).

13. *See, e.g.*, Royal Glen Condo. Ass'n v. S.T. Neswold & Assocs., 385 Ill. Dec. 137, 18 N.E.3d 137 (Ill. App. 2014) (where Illinois law provided no policy was to be issued to or renewed for condominium associations unless it met statutory requirements, that law imposed obligations on condominium associations and their boards, not on insurance producers; statute did not impose duty on association's insurance broker giving rise to statutory cause of action).

14. Stoeckert, *The Insurance Puzzle; Making Sense of Premiums and Policies* (Cooperator, Apr. 2012), available at: http://cooperator.com/articles/2418/1/The-Insurance-Puzzle/Page1.html. *See also* Hennessey, *Condominium Management*, 48 St. John's L. Rev. 1064, 1070 (1974) (insuring condominiums creates more difficult problems than many insurance agents and most businesspeople appreciate and, therefore, association is well advised to employ knowledgeable and experienced insurance broker who will be able to recommend best and most economical policies that provide requisite coverage).

[3] Annual Insurance Review

The policies obtained by a common interest community association will typically have a one-, two-, or three-year term after which they are usually renewed with the same insurance company. The underlying data on which coverage is based is often not static, and neither are the policies. Even though a policy is renewed with the same company, the policy language may change. There are several reasons for the changes. First, insurance is heavily regulated by the states, and new legislation may mandate changes in policy language. Second, court decisions interpreting policy language may lead to changes in wording. Third, the insurance industry is constantly reevaluating risks and examining evolving ones, leading to revisions in policy language. Finally, even though a renewal policy itself may be identical to the one it replaces, endorsements that were not in the prior policy may be added, and ones that were in it may be subtracted. For that reason, an association needs to review its coverage with its broker annually. An insurance committee with knowledgeable members is the ideal panel to conduct this review.

The annual insurance review is often referred to as an insurance or premium audit. However, it is important to realize that these are terms of art in the industry. They are defined as an ". . . audit of the exposure basis for an insurance policy (i.e., payroll, sales, or vehicle count) after the end of a policy period to determine the actual (audited) exposure for the purpose of making a final calculation of the premium . . . ."[15] Whether it is called an annual review or audit, this assessment should include several components.

First, an inquiry should be sent to the association counsel asking if any statutory changes or judicial decisions over the previous year are relevant to the association's insurance coverage. Association attorneys should keep in mind that applicable statutes may be found in the pertinent common interest community enabling legislation or the state Insurance Code, and the rules of the state insurance regulatory agency may also be relevant. Next, the governing documents should be reviewed as a reminder of what coverages they require and to make sure they are consistent with any changes in the law.[16] This part of the review may lead the association to realize that amendments to the governing documents are necessary.

A third part of the review is an examination of the data on which coverages are based. This can be accomplished by examining the Declaration Pages for the various policies. For example, property coverages are generally based on the value of the property covered. Do those figures reflect the current value of the property? Have there been recent additions or improvements to any structures, or are any planned? Finally, the existing policies need to be reviewed with the

---

15. *See* https://www.irmi.com/term/insurance-definitions/premium-audit.

16. *See* http://www.condoassociation.com/blog/tabid/19257/bid/72227/Condo-Association-Insurance-Annual-Review.aspx.

association broker. Generally, the association wants to make sure its coverages remain adequate. Some specific questions to ask the broker are whether the association is eligible for any premium discounts offered by the various insurance companies and whether any changes are anticipated when the policy renews.[17] Additionally, if there have been claims against a policy in the past year, the association should discuss the affect they might have on that policy. Prior claims can impact coverage and premium rates and even whether an insurer is willing to underwrite a policy for the upcoming year.

§ 9.02 Classification of Coverage

The types of coverage a common interest community requires come under two broad headings based on the protected interest: first-party and third-party coverage. First-party insurance indemnifies the insured for a loss suffered directly by that insured while third-party insurance protects the insured from liability to third parties injured by the conduct of the insured.[18] For governing board members unfamiliar with insurance, an easy way to explain the distinction is to point to the car insurance almost all of them will have. Everyone understands that if they are in an automobile accident and are liable for an injury to another driver or to another vehicle, their insurance company will pay for the loss. That is third-party coverage. Automobile owners also generally recognize that if the policy includes comprehensive coverage—meaning the policy contains what most people call "collision"—their insurance company will pay for the damages to their vehicle. That is first-party coverage. Automobile policies combine first- and third-party coverages. The various commercial policies that are obtained by common interest communities, however, *generally* provide either first-party or third-party coverage, but not both, although there are exceptions.

Common interest community policies can also be classified as property or liability coverage. As discussed below, there are policies that cover different types of association property against loss and others that cover the liability of the organization or individuals in it.

§ 9.03 Property Policies

There are four types of property policies that the typical common interest community association needs to obtain: commercial property, boiler and machinery or equipment breakdown, crime/fidelity, and flood.

Every association requires coverage by a commercial property policy. The standard commercial property insurance policy provides that the insurer will pay

17. *See* http://www.naic.org/documents/consumer_alert_home_insurance_checkup.htm.

18. *See* 1 Jeffrey E. Thomas, *New Appleman on Insurance Law Library Edition* § 1.08[3] (Matthew Bender 2016).

for "direct physical loss of or damage to" covered property—real or personal[19]—at the premises described on the Declarations Page of the policy caused by or resulting from any covered cause of loss.[20] A "cause of loss" is a "risk,"—for example, fire or windstorm. The causes of loss are described in a causes of loss form incorporated into the policy. Chapter 10 discusses commercial property insurance.

Boiler and machinery or equipment breakdown policies provide coverage for damage to *covered items* from an accident or breakdown and damage to *other property* of the insured caused by an accident to those covered items.[21] "Covered items" typically include boilers, generators, engines, pumps, compressors,[22] and turbines and refrigeration and air conditioning equipment.[23] Electronic business equipment—fax machines, copiers, and telephone systems—can also be covered.[24] Of particular note for common interest communities is that elevators,[25] sprinklers,[26] and security systems[27] may be covered. These policies address a "gap" in the coverage provided by commercial property policies. For example, if a fire in a building damages equipment that provides air conditioning to common areas, it is probably covered by the commercial property policy, but if a malfunction in an air conditioning unit causes it to catch fire, the damage is usually not covered by that policy. Boiler and machinery coverage is addressed in Chapter 11.

Crime/fidelity insurance—sometimes referred to as a "fidelity bond"[28]—may also be called "employee dishonesty" insurance. These policies are designed to

---

19. Basically, real property means buildings and structures while personal property means contents or equipment.

20. *See, e.g.*, ISO Form CP 00 17 06 07, § A; ISO Form CP 00 10 06 07, § A.

21. *Boiler & Machinery Insurance/Equipment Breakdown Insurance What Is Covered by Boiler & Machinery Coverage?*, available at: http://www.brunswickcompanies.com/ci-boiler-machinery-equipment-breakdown-insurance.html.

22. *See, e.g.*, New York Underwriters Ins. Co. v. Coffman, 540 S.W.2d 445 (Tex. Civ. App.—Fort Worth, 1976) (coverage for breakdown of air conditioning compressor).

23. O'Connor, *Construction Law: Recent Issues in Property Coverage*, 34 Wm. Mitchell L. Rev. 177, 202 (2007).

24. Tapia, *Equipment Breakdown Coverage: Not Your Father's Boiler & Machinery Insurance* (Insurance Journal 2000), available at: http://www.insurancejournal.com/magazines/features/2000/11/27/21234.htm. *See also Equipment Breakdown Insurance FAQ*, available at: http://eqgroup.com/Equipment-Breakdown.htm (equipment breakdown insurance covers many types of equipment including modern office equipment).

25. Barnes, *Understanding Your Insurance Policy's Fine-Print: What You Need to Know about Riders* (Cooperator, Aug. 2013), available at: http://cooperator.com/article/understanding-your-insurance-policys-fine-pri.

26. Iannucci, *Insurance Products What's Available, What's Recommended* (Cooperator, Aug. 2006), available at: http://cooperator.com/article/insurance-products.

27. Geberer, *Covering the Gaps Specialty Insurance* (Cooperator, Aug. 2009), available at: http://cooperator.com/article/covering-the-gaps.

28. Although the term "fidelity bond" today refers to an insurance policy, historically it was a "suretyship," a three-party agreement in which the surety guarantees to one party the honesty of another party. One can still obtain a fidelity bond that is a suretyship. Nowack, *We've Been Robbed!*,

indemnify the insured against a loss that arises from a lack of integrity, fidelity, or honesty of employees or others who hold positions of trust.[29] The most common claims under this coverage are for "employee theft," with "employee" being broadly defined to include officers and directors when the insured is a corporation. The commercial property policy may provide coverage for theft generally but will typically exclude coverage for criminal or dishonest acts by an employee or anyone to whom the insured entrusts property. Therefore, the crime/fidelity insurance plugs a hole in the coverage of the commercial property policy. Crime/fidelity insurance is discussed in Chapter 15.

Boiler and machinery and crime/fidelity insurance can be added by endorsement to the commercial property policy. That is rarely the case with flood insurance. Flood insurance, as the name implies, provides coverage for a single risk: losses caused by a flood. Commercial property policies typically exclude coverage for flood damage. A separate policy has to be obtained, and when property is located in an area with a high risk for flooding, that coverage almost always has to be obtained through the National Flood Insurance Program (NFIP). The NFIP policy is called the Standard Flood Insurance Policy, and it is considered in Chapter 12.

§ 9.04 Liability Policies

The basic liability policy that every common interest community association must secure is the commercial general liability (CGL) policy. Coverage under a CGL policy typically includes bodily injury, property damage, personal and advertising injury, and medical payments. The coverage is for injury to others for which the policyholder is responsible. Thus, the property damage coverage insures against liability for damage to the property of others for which the insured is liable, not damage to the property of the insured. "Personal and advertising injury" covers injuries suffered by a third party arising out of offenses such as false arrest, detention, imprisonment, malicious prosecution, wrongful eviction, invasion of the right of private occupancy, or slander.[30] CGL coverage is discussed in Chapter 13. Generally, the CGL policy protects the association from liability, but it provides only limited coverage for its officers and directors. That gap in coverage is filled by directors and officers (D&O) liability insurance. Generally, D&O insurance covers good faith errors and omissions and negligence and is broken

available at: https://www.southernpropertymgt.com/editor_upload/File/Board%20Resources/We_ve_Been_Robbed.pdf (noting that because fidelity bond is guarantee of payment, it is expensive and requires investigation of each of "bonded" person). *See generally* 10 Jeffrey E. Thomas, *New Appleman on Insurance Law Library Edition* §§ 110.01[1], [6][b] (Matthew Bender 2016).

29. Resolution Trust Corp. v. Moskowitz, 845 F. Supp. 247, 250 (D.N.J. 1994); Bralko Holdings, Ltd. v. Insurance Co. of North America, 193 Mich. App. 157, 162, 483 N.W.2d 929, 931 (1992); Ronnau v. Caravan Int'l Corp., 205 Kan. 154, 158, 468 P.2d 118, 122 (Kan. 1970).

30. *See, e.g.*, CG 00 01 12 07, § V.14.

down into two parts: personal coverage that reimburses individual directors and officers and reimbursement of the corporation for legally valid indemnification payments made to directors and officers for covered losses. D&O policies are considered in Chapter 14.

§ 9.05 Other Coverages

There are many other forms of insurance coverage that a common interest community might need. A few of these are discussed briefly below. It is important for an association to provide its broker with a thorough description of the community, of any employees, and of the activities that take place within it for the broker to determine its coverage needs.

[1] Workers' Compensation Insurance

Workers' compensation laws vary from state to state, but generally they require employers to fund potential claims through private insurance, a state fund insurance, or in some states self-insurance. Under these laws, employees are compensated for lost wages and medical expenses while employers are immunized from any additional liability for covered injuries. In other words, in exchange for guaranteed benefits, the employee loses all common-law rights to sue his or her employer for damages.[31] As the leading treatise on workers' compensation explains, the typical state law has as a basic operating principle that employees are automatically entitled to certain benefits whenever they suffer an injury in an accident that arises out of and in the course of their employment.[32] Insurance coverage under the state laws generally falls into one of three categories: full coverage statutes that generally require that all policies have to cover the employer's full liability, modified full coverage statutes under which coverage may be limited to liabilities incurred by a particular class of business or business carried on at a specified location, and statutes that do not expressly treat policy construction.[33] Because of the differences in state law, common interest communities need to consult with a knowledgeable insurance broker to determine what is required of them and what coverage is available to them.

The inevitable question from directors of common interest community governing boards is, if we do not have any employees, why do we need workers' compensation insurance? One reason may be that the governing documents may require it. The usual answer to the question, however, is that when the association hires an independent contractor, if that contractor fails to maintain the required insurance, an injured employee of the contractor may be able to collect from the

31. Ainslie et al., *Business Insurance Law and Practice Guide* § 13.01 (Matthew Bender 2016).
32. 1 Lex K. Larson, *Larson's Workers' Compensation* § 1.01 (rev. ed., Matthew Bender 2016).
33. Ainslie et al., *Business Insurance Law and Practice Guide* § 13.03[1] (Matthew Bender 2016).

association.[34] If the association has its own workers' compensation policy, it will generally cover both any employees of the association and any uninsured contractor's employee.

NOTE: One mistake associations make is assuming that because they always insist on a certificate of workers' compensation insurance from any independent contractor they hire, they do not need their own policy. However, the certificate shows only that the contractor *had* insurance, not that the policy remains in effect.[35] Some unscrupulous contractors may secure coverage in order to obtain a job and then cancel or fail to renew the policy.[36]

Finally, just because the parties to a contract describe workers as independent contractors does not mean they have that status for purposes or workers' compensation laws. Because the meaning of "independent contractor" varies from state to state, associations should obtain guidance from their attorneys about the law in their particular state.

Workers' compensation insurance may also cover "volunteer" workers. It is not uncommon for residents in a common interest community to perform some maintenance tasks—landscaping, changing light bulbs, or making small repairs—to save the association some money.[37] If one of these volunteers is injured, a workers' compensation policy may cover his or her medical expenses and possibly lost wages.[38] However, the coverage may not be available or may prove too

34. Kitchin, *Workers Compensation Insurance* (Association Times 2005).

35. Generally, the governing board or management company should get a certificate that shows dates of coverage and, close to expiration, seek an updated certificate. *See generally* Payne, *Of Course You Don't Need Workers' Compensation Insurance —Or Do You?* (2012), available at: http://www.cohoalaw.com/governance-of-course-you-dont-need-workers-compensation-insurance-or-do-you.html (even when contract between association and contractor requires contractor to carry workers' compensation insurance and provide proof of it to association before beginning work, policy could lapse while work is being performed or be cancelled by contractor or "proof" of insurance could be fraudulent); Kitchin, *Workers Compensation Insurance* (Association Times 2005) (proof from contractor of workers' compensation insurance in form of certificate of insurance offers no guarantee that coverage will remain in effect beyond date it was issued). *But see* Odenthal, *Workers' Compensation: What Your Board-Management Team Should Know* (New England Condominium, Aug. 2016), available at: https://newenglandcondo.com/article/workers-compensation/full (if association is careful to get certificates of insurance from contractors and association itself does not have any employees, then workers' compensation insurance is not *required*).

36. White, *The Residential Condominium Association and Workers Compensation: Is Your Association Protected?* (Jan. 2017), available at: http://www.condo-owner.com/alabama-insurance-blog/2017/01/the-residential-condominium-association-and-workers-compensation/.

37. Humphrey, *HOA Insurance Matters: Do You Need Workers' Compensation Insurance Just to Cover Volunteers?* (2009), available at: https://www.hoaleader.com/public/263.cfm.

38. *The Importance of Workers Compensation for Condominium, Townhome, and Homeowner Associations*, available at: http://www.totins.com/img/~www.totins.com/workerscomp.pdf (workers' compensation policy can cover losses for any non-compensated volunteers of association—board or committee members—if properly endorsed).

expensive to obtain.[39] Where the coverage is available, an association may be able to obtain a "minimum premium workers' compensation policy," under which the association represents that it has no employees needing coverage and the policy provides coverage for injured volunteers.[40] Associations should be aware that in some states there are policies—other than workers' compensation—specifically designed to cover volunteer accidents.[41]

[2] Law Enforcement Liability Coverage

A law enforcement liability (LEL) policy is typically issued to protect law enforcement officials, but it may also provide coverage for those who formulate policies governing law enforcement when their actions are excluded from other liability coverages.[42] This coverage may be necessary for a common interest community association that provides community security. LEL coverage is highly specialized, and brokers who work with associations likely have limited familiarity with it. If that is the case, an association should ask the broker to seek the assistance of a colleague with knowledge of LEL coverage. The coverage is rarely a part of the package of policies provided to associations, so if an association wants it, it will need to specifically request it and make sure it is included. Because it is a special form of coverage, errors can occur. For example, an Arkansas property owners association and an insurer agreed the coverage would be excluded because another carrier already provided it. Nonetheless, when the policy was issued, it failed to exclude the coverage. An association law enforcement officer and the association were sued after an altercation between that officer and two residents of the community. The insurer sought, and was granted, reformation

---

39. Bond, *Confused Over Insurance? Five Common Questions* (Association Times 2010) (coverage for volunteers under workers' compensation policy can be expensive and is typically not offered by most carriers).

40. Adams, *HOAs and Condo Associations Might Consider Workers' Compensation Policy* (2014) (minimum premium workers' compensation policy endorsed with volunteer rider will cover volunteers for injuries sustained while performing their activities subject to Florida's workers' compensation law and can also provide coverage for uninsured contractors working on behalf of association); Humphrey, *HOA Insurance Matters: Do You Need Workers' Compensation Insurance Just to Cover Volunteers?* (2009), available at: https://www.hoaleader.com/public/263.cfm (asserting that cost of these policies is about $1,200 a year, and association needs to make business decision whether that cost is cheaper than three hours of a lawyer's time or first five hours of defending any lawsuit). *See also* White, *The Residential Condominium Association and Workers Compensation: Is Your Association Protected?* (Jan. 2017), available at: http://www.condo-owner.com/alabama-insurance-blog/2017/01/the-residential-condominium-association-and-workers-compensation/ (associations can carry "minimum premium" or "if any" workers' compensation policy).

41. Adams, *HOAs and Condo Associations Might Consider Workers' Compensation Policy* (2014) (Volunteer Accident Policy covers volunteers injured during volunteer activities along with accidental death/disability coverage, depending on carrier); Bond, *Confused Over Insurance? Five Common Questions* (Association Times 2010) (policies specifically written for volunteers tend to be extremely affordable and provide coverage for hundreds of volunteers within any given year).

42. *See* 4 Jeffrey E. Thomas, *New Appleman on Insurance Law Library Edition* § 33.01 (LexisNexis 2023).

based on mutual mistake. The policy was reformed to exclude the LEL coverage and, therefore, the insurer had no duty to defend or indemnify.[43]

[3] Garage Keepers Legal Liability

Associations that offer convenience services for unit owners or guests—valet parking—or that operate a parking facility open to the public may need what is called "garage keepers legal liability coverage." It provides liability and garage keepers coverage. The former is a type of automobile liability insurance that covers accidents resulting from "garage operations," while the latter is quasi-property insurance that covers property in the possession of the insured as a bailee.[44] Because the term "garage operations" is typically defined as an activity necessary or incidental to a garage business, the liability portion of the policy usually covers more than just automobile accidents.[45] However, it generally does not cover a vehicle owned by the association. Coverage for vehicles owned by the association has to be obtained under a commercial automobile policy.[46]

[4] Pollution Liability

Commercial general liability policies exclude coverage for pollution-related liability.[47] The governing boards of common interest communities may take little note of the exclusion, thinking pollution liability is a concern for industry, not residential communities. However, experts warn that associations need to understand that almost anything considered an irritant or contaminant—including pesticides and pool chemicals—can be construed as a pollutant.[48] One way to understand the scope of the pollution exclusion is to forget about "pollution" in the usual sense. As one expert in the insurance field explains, the easiest way to think of the pollution exclusion is that it can apply to a *contaminant* and, therefore, if there is something that could contaminate something else, the pollution exclusion could apply.[49] Indeed, suits against associations often concern substances

---

43. Harleysville Worchester Ins. Co. v. Diamondhead Prop. Owners Ass'n, 741 F.3d 1336 (8th Cir. 2014).

44. 2 *New Appleman Law of Liability Insurance* § 11.01 (rev. ed., Matthew Bender 2023). *See generally* O'Connor, *Garage Liability of Garagekeepers? That is the Question* (Insurance Journal 2014), available at: http://www.insurancejournal.com/magazines/features/2014/02/10/319390.htm; Treese & Rosenberry, *Insurance: How Community Associations Protect Themselves*, at 38 (CAI Press 2013).

45. 2 *New Appleman Law of Liability Insurance* § 11.02[1] (rev. ed., Matthew Bender 2016).

46. Treese & Rosenberry, *Insurance: How Community Associations Protect Themselves*, at 38 (CAI Press 2013).

47. *See* §§ 13.03[4][e], 13.06[7][h], *infra*.

48. Treese & Rosenberry, *Insurance: How Community Associations Protect Themselves*, at 48 (CAI Press 2013).

49. Connelly, *How Much Do You Know About Pollution Exclusions?* (Independent Agent, Feb. 2015), available at: https://www.iamagazine.com/markets/how-much-do-you-know-about-pollution-exclusions.

not considered to be "traditional" pollutants.[50] Therefore, associations should explore purchasing an environmental liability policy with a broker.

§ 9.06 Package Coverage

Associations need to be aware that new programs are being developed by insurers with packages of policies that may combine property, liability, and other coverages.[51] For example, one insurer has created what it calls "V3 CAPP+," a package program for condominiums, homeowners associations, and cooperatives.[52] It is a multi-line policy designed to insure the property, fidelity/crime loss, general liability, and directors and officers. The package is intended to make it easier for the governing boards of community associations to "buy one policy that addresses all of the typical exposures they encounter." It is enhanced to include key property sublimits that address machinery and equipment breakdown, employee dishonesty, landscaping, and elevator collision. It was initially available in 20 states, including California, Illinois, and New York, but not Florida or Texas. When offered a package that bundles coverages, an association should ask if it includes basic property, liability, umbrella, building ordinance, sewer backup, boiler and machinery, crime, terrorism, lead paint and mold, non-owned-hired auto, assault and battery, and directors and officers insurance.[53] Package coverage may be as good as, or better than, coverage obtained by separate policies from different companies. However, as is always the case when purchasing any insurance, the association needs to carefully review the proffered coverage with its broker to make sure it meets the association's needs. While these packages are designed for residential common interest communities, some communities may have coverage requirements that are different from the typical CIC. When purchasing a package policy, associations should be aware of how deductibles are applied. There may be different deductibles for each type of coverage or perhaps an aggregate under the entire policy. The limits of coverage should also be examined. Is there an overall aggregate limit, or does each type of coverage have separate limits?

---

50. First Specialty Ins. Corp. v. GRS Mgmt. Assocs., 2009 U.S. Dist. LEXIS 72708 (S.D. Fla. 2009) (homeowners association sued after swimmer contracted viral infection from contaminants in water of community pool).

51. *See, e.g.*, Alexander v. Nat'l Fire Ins., 454 F.3d 214, 218 (3d Cir. Pa. 2006) (condominium association maintained insurance policy that provided it both first-party property coverage and third-party general liability coverage); Willing v. Cmty. Ass'n Underwriters of Am., Inc., 2007 U.S. Dist. LEXIS 48543 (W.D. Wash. July 5, 2007) (condominium policy included first party property insurance for physical damage to building and structures and third-party liability); Far Northwest Dev. Co., LLC v. Cmty. Ass'n of Underwriters of Am., Inc., 2006 U.S. Dist. LEXIS 79033 (W.D. Wash. Oct. 30, 2006) (policy issued to association contained property coverage and general liability insurance coverage).

52. *See V3 Launches Community Association Package Program* (Insurance Journal, May 27, 2015), available at: http://www.insurancejournal.com/news/national/2015/05/27/369573.htm.

53. Green, *Shopping for Insurance; What Do Boards Need to Know?* (Cooperator, Aug. 2011).

Chapter 10

Commercial Property Insurance

§ 10.01 Introduction

For most common interest communities (CICs), the commercial property insurance policy represents their single largest insurance expenditure. In fact, especially for CICs in coastal hurricane-prone areas, it may be their largest annual expenditure,[1] sometimes equaling as much as 20 percent of their annual budget. Yet, CIC governing boards often have limited familiarity with their property coverage.[2] The odds are, no one on the board has read the policy.[3] That does not distinguish CICs from other policyholders. Courts recognize that "insurance contracts are not typically read or reviewed by the insured."[4] That is because of at least two impediments. First, property policies, with their many forms and

1. Lent, *The ABC's of Insuring Your Co-op or Condo; Common Terms and Options for Insurance* (Cooperator, Aug. 2014), available at: http://cooperator.com/articles/2818/1/The-ABCs-of-Insuring-Your-Co-op-or-Condo/Page1.html (insurance is number one budgeted item for common interest communities).

2. *See, e.g.*, Blanch, *Community Association Boards Need to Know and Understand the Exclusions and Requirements in Their Association Insurance Policies* (Apr. 28, 2014), available at: https://www.floridahoalawyerblog.com/community-association-boards-n/ (attorney specializing in community association law finds that associations often acquire policies with little thought about their provisions other than costs of premiums). In *Doheny Park Terrace Homeowners Ass'n, Inc. v. Truck Ins. Exchange*, 132 Cal. App. 4th 1076, 34 Cal. Rptr. 3d 157 (2005), an association attempted to avoid application of a suit limitation provision by arguing it was run by a volunteer governing board no member of which had the training to assess property damage. The association said it had relied on the insurer's assessment of its damages because no one on the board knew or had reason to believe the insurer's analysis of the cost to repair that damage was wrong or that it was misrepresenting any facts. The appellate court said that while those claims might test the limits of its credulity were it sitting as a trier of fact, it could not say that the alleged explanation for an eight-year delay in submitting a claim, as a matter of law, precluded a finding of reasonable reliance by the association that would prevent the insurer from invoking the suit limitation clause. Association governing boards should not expect to be granted that degree of favor by courts in general.

3. *See, e.g.*, Emmer, *Handling Deductibles and Uninsured Losses*, Common Ground (CAI Nov./Dec. 1988) (frequently, first time governing board looks closely at policy is when loss occurs).

4. Bromfeld v. Harleysville Ins. Cos., 298 N.J. Super. 62, 75, 688 A.2d 1114, 1120 (1997).

endorsements, can be voluminous.[5] Second, policies are complex and recondite.[6] As the federal Fifth Circuit Court of Appeals noted, "inclusions and exclusions of an insurance policy do not always embroider a neat design."[7] The California Supreme Court described one policyholder as being "'unhappily surrounded by concentric circles of uncertainty.'"[8]

Those circles of uncertainty likely also surround the two professionals most CICs employ. The first is the association attorney. He or she has likely never seen the association property policy—except possibly if there is a claim—and if the association attorney does see it, he or she probably does not understand it. The second is the community association manager (CAM) for whom insurance coverage is typically part of his or her training. He or she will have a basic understanding of insurance for common interest communities, but ordinarily it is just enough to be able to communicate with an insurance agent or broker. In almost all circumstances, it is a broker in whom the association resides trust to obtain the necessary insurance. That trust is not always well placed. As in any other profession, some brokers are excellent, while others are mediocre. Moreover, property insurance for common interest communities is an area of specialty. The broker who is very knowledgeable about homeowner's insurance may know little or nothing about the particular needs of a CIC. It is, therefore, incumbent on the governing board to seek out a professional—a broker—who specializes in obtaining coverage for CICs. A broker represents no particular insurance carrier, but acts as an intermediary between the insured and the carrier.[9]

As one commentator acknowledges, building insurance is complicated, but he also urges governing board members to take the insurance seriously because

5. *See, e.g.*, Piankatank River Golf Club, Inc. v. Selective Ins. Co., 2009 U.S. Dist. LEXIS 31724, at *4 (E.D. Va. Apr. 15, 2009) (commercial property insurance policy at issue was 222 pages in length).

6. Bromfeld v. Harleysville Ins. Cos., 298 N.J. Super. 62, 75, 688 A.2d 1114, 1120 (1997) (understanding of insurance policies is often impeded by complex terminology used in standardized forms). *See also* Piankatank River Golf Club, Inc. v. Selective Ins. Co., 2009 U.S. Dist. LEXIS 31724, at *4 (E.D. Va. Apr. 15, 2009) (insurance policy was "certainly not a model of clarity" but was model of unfortunate state to which insurers and their state regulatory agencies have brought many policies with broad articulations of coverage reduced by definitions of property not covered, covered causes of loss, and exclusions all of which are reflected in forms made applicable merely by reference and without any real effort to set forth simply and plainly how various sections, exclusions, or endorsements relate to each other). *See generally* Helveston, *Judicial Deregulation of Consumer Markets*, 36 Cardozo L. Rev. 1739, 1755 (2015) (complexity of insurance policies makes it incredibly difficult for consumers to determine coverage provided by different policies and, consequently, increases chance that there will be mismatch between their desired coverage and actual coverage).

7. Peach State Uniform Service, Inc. v. American Ins. Co., 507 F.2d 996, 1000 (5th Cir. 1975).

8. Gray v. Zurich Ins. Co., 65 Cal. 2d 263, 273 (1966).

9. American Way Cellular, Inc. v. Travelers Property Casualty Co. of America, 216 Cal. App. 4th 1040, 1052, 157 Cal. Rptr. 3d 385, 394 (2013).

having the right kinds and correct amounts of coverage is critical to the financial and physical well-being of the community.[10]

§ 10.02 Insurable Interest and Common Interest Community Associations

Before an entity, including a common interest community, can obtain property insurance in its name, it must have an insurable interest in that property. The insurable interest of common interest communities is clear in some instances and murky in others.[11]

[1] The Concept of "Insurable Interest"

Ordinarily, to obtain insurance coverage, one must have an interest in the property that is to be insured.[12] This "insurable interest doctrine" was first adopted by the British Parliament and has existed for nearly 300 years.[13] The purpose of the doctrine is to prevent use of insurance for gambling or wagering.[14] In a property policy, the interest of the insured may be fee ownership, but other interests will also suffice.[15] For example, mortgagees and tenants may have an insurable interest in real property they do not own.[16]

In many states the insurable interest doctrine has been codified. For example, in New York, a statute provides that

> No contract or policy of insurance on property made or issued in this state, or made or issued upon any property in this state, shall be enforceable except for the benefit of some person having an insurable interest in

10. Stoeckert, *The Insurance Puzzle: Making Sense of Premiums and Policies* (Cooperator, Apr. 2012), available at: http://cooperator.com/articles/2418/1/The-Insurance-Puzzle/Page1.html.

11. *See generally* MacGregor, *The Increasing Complexity of Condominium Property Insurance*, 57, 68–72; New Appleman on Insurance: Current Critical Issues in Insurance Law (Spring 2012).

12. *See, e.g.*, Washington Fire Relief Ass'n v. Albro, 137 Wash. 31, 241 P. 356 (1925) (one cannot insure for his or her own benefit property of another in which he or she has no interest).

13. *See* 1 Jeffrey E. Thomas, *New Appleman on Insurance Law Library Edition* § 1.05[3] (Matthew Bender 2017).

14. *See, e.g.*, Gossett v. Farmers Ins. Co., 133 Wn. 2d 954, 948 P.2d 1264 (1997).

15. *See* Cassadei v. Nationwide Mut. Fire Ins. Co., 21 A.D.3d 681, 799 N.Y.S.2d 687 (2005) (ownership not required to create insurable interest); Gossett v. Farmers Ins. Co., 133 Wn. 2d 954, 948 P.2d 1264 (1997) (legal title to property not dispositive of insurable interest).

16. *See, e.g.*, CLS Mtg., Inc. v. Bruno, 86 Wn. App. 390, 937 P.2d 1106 (1997) (original mortgagee clearly had insurable interest when it held promissory note and Deed of Trust); Sigola Mfg., Inc. v. Dairyland Ins. Co., 124 A.D.2d 654, 508 N.Y.S.2d 38 (1986) (tenant may have insurable interest, especially where tenant has agreed to return premises to lessor in good condition or has agreed to keep premises insured). *See also* Technical Land, Inc. v. Firemen's Ins. Co., 756 A.2d 439 (D.C. 2000) (interests other than those based on legal or equitable title can be insurable); Boston Ins. Co. v. Beckett, 91 Idaho 220, 419 P.2d 475 (1966) (mere right to use property may provide insurable interest).

> the property insured. In this article, "insurable interest" shall include any lawful and substantial economic interest in the safety or preservation of property from loss, destruction or pecuniary damage.[17]

Similar language is found in the insurance codes of many states.[18] The critical words in those statutes are *substantial economic interest*. This can mean any legal or equitable interest.[19] An insurable interest in property can exist for anyone who derives pecuniary benefit or advantage from its preservation or suffers pecuniary loss or damage from its destruction, termination, or injury.[20] However, simply paying premiums,[21] acting as the agent of the property owner,[22] or managing property[23] does not give rise to a substantial economic interest.

[2] Condominiums

Determining insurable interest in condominiums requires an understanding of the different types of property in a condominium. There are general common elements, limited common elements, units, improvements made or fixtures attached to common elements or units, and personal property of either the association or the unit owners. It is also possible, although not common, for an association to have an interest in real property that is not part of the common elements. The common elements, whether general or limited, are by definition owned by the

17. NY CLS Ins. § 3401.

18. *See, e.g.*, Fla. Stat. § 627.405(2) ("insurable interest" means any actual, lawful, and substantial economic interest in safety or preservation of subject of insurance free from loss, destruction, or pecuniary damage or impairment); Tex. Ins. Code § 2210.201 (under Texas Windstorm Insurance Association statutes, "insurable interest" includes any lawful and substantial economic interest in safety or preservation of property from loss, destruction, or pecuniary damage); Va. Code Ann. § 38.2-303(A) ("insurable interest" means any lawful and substantial economic interest in safety or preservation of subject of insurance free from loss, destruction, or pecuniary damage); Rev. Code Wash. § 48.18.040(2) (insurable interest means any lawful and substantial economic interest in safety or preservation of subject of insurance free from loss, destruction, or pecuniary damage). *Compare* Cal. Ins. Code § 281 (every interest in property, or any relation thereto, or liability in respect thereof, of such nature that contemplated peril might directly damnify insured, is an insurable interest).

19. *See* CLS Mtg., Inc. v. Bruno, 86 Wn. App. 390, 937 P.2d 1106 (1997).

20. CLS Mtg., Inc. v. Bruno, 86 Wn. App. 390, 937 P.2d 1106 (1997) (insurable interest in property can arise when one would profit or enjoy advantage from it or would suffer loss from its destruction); Sauer v. Vigilant Ins. Co., 102 Misc. 2d 243, 423 N.Y.S.2d 138 (1979). *See generally* Cozen, *Insuring Real Property*, § 10.04[1] (Matthew Bender & Co. 2015) (generally, insurable interest exists when party has either real or beneficial title to property or can be damaged by loss or benefited by gain).

21. Gossett v. Farmers Ins. Co., 133 Wn. 2d 954, 948 P.2d 1264 (1997) (paying premiums does not give rise to insurable interest where ownership lies elsewhere).

22. CLS Mtg., Inc. v. Bruno, 86 Wn. App. 390, 937 P.2d 1106 (1997) (status of agent for owner of property does not give "substantial economic interest").

23. Judge v. Travelers Ins. Co., 262 A.D.2d 983, 692 N.Y.S.2d 288 (1999).

unit owners of a condominium as tenants in common.[24] The general common elements are available for use of all those owners, while the limited common elements are reserved for the use of fewer than all owners, although usually only one. Balconies, patios, storage units, and parking spaces are typical limited common elements.

The units are owned by the individual residents in fee. When an association has an interest in real property that is not part of the common elements, it would likely be recreational areas that either are owned by the association or in which the association is the lessee in a long-term lease. As a comment to the Uniform Common Interest Ownership Act (UCIOA) observes, in a condominium, all the real estate subject to the Declaration, other than the units, is a part of the common elements, and real estate that is not subject to the Declaration is neither a unit nor a common element. Thus, a condominium association could acquire in its own name title to real estate that is physically located outside the condominium boundaries and that would not automatically become a common element.[25]

---

24. *See* Uniform Condominium Act § 1-130, Comment 5 (unless ownership interest in common elements is vested in owners of units, project is not a condominium). This aspect of the condominium concept of ownership is apparently lost on many courts, leading to some confusion. A host of Florida federal courts have described the common elements or the property as a whole as being *owned* by the association. *See* Crystal Colony Condo. Ass'n v. Aspen Specialty Ins. Co., 2014 U.S. Dist. LEXIS 39543 (S.D. Fla. Mar. 21, 2014) (association is owner of condominium property); Raintree Vill. Condo. No. 11 Ass'n v. Great Am. Ins. Co., 2013 U.S. Dist. LEXIS 134907 (M.D. Fla. Sept. 20, 2013) (association owns condominium); Seagate Towers Condo. Ass'n v. QBE Ins. Corp., 2012 U.S. Dist. LEXIS 188462 (S.D. Fla. Nov. 16, 2012) (association owns and operates condominium); Palma Vista Condo. Ass'n of Hillsborough County v. Nationwide Mut. Fire Ins. Co., 2010 U.S. Dist. LEXIS 118262 (M.D. Fla. Oct. 7, 2010) (association owns residential condominium complex); Beverly Hills Condo. 1-12 v. Aspen Specialty Ins. Co., 2007 U.S. Dist. LEXIS 28999 (S.D. Fla. Jan. 31, 2007) (association owns condominium complex); Longpoint Condo. Ass'n v. Allstate Ins. Co., 2005 U.S. Dist. LEXIS 43917 (N.D. Fla. June 1, 2005) (common areas owned by association). Courts in other jurisdiction have made the same error. *See* Harbor House Condominium Ass'n v. Massachusetts Bay Ins. Co., 915 F.2d 316 (7th Cir. 1990) (association owned common areas of condominium building); Ass'n of Apt. Owners of Imperial Plaza v. Fireman's Fund Ins. Co., 2013 U.S. Dist. LEXIS 69933 (D. Haw. May 16, 2013) (association owned building covered by insurance policy); Pioneer Tower Owners Ass'n v. State Farm Fire & Cas. Co., 880 N.Y.S.2d 885, 12 N.Y.3d 302, 908 N.E.2d 875 (2009) (describing plaintiff association as owner of condominium apartment building); Admiral Indem. v. Onetti, 2008 N.Y. Misc. LEXIS 10946 (2008) (describing insured as condominium association that owns common areas of building); Sunbreaker Condominium Ass'n v. Travelers Ins. Co., 79 Wn. App. 368, 370, 901 P.2d 1079, 1080 (1995) (describing association as owner of condominium building).

25. Uniform Common Interest Ownership Act § 1-103, comment 7. *See also* Rosenberry & Sproul, *A Comparison of California Common Interest Development Law and the Uniform Common Interest Ownership Act*, 38 Santa Clara L. Rev. 1009, 1022 (1998) (UCIOA specifically provides that association may own property that is not part of common scheme and not subject to Act). The comment suggests that property within the condominium boundaries would automatically become part of the common elements. What if the association acquires title to an individual unit by, for example, foreclosing its lien or exercising a right to first refusal? Does that unit become part of the common elements, or is it owned outright by the association? *Consider* Coakley Bay Condominium

Clearly, the association has an insurable interest in any property it owns in its own name, and the unit owners have an insurable interest in their individual units.[26] Who has an insurable interest in the common elements is less clear. The association does not own the common property and ordinarily has no present interest in it.[27] The unit owners, on the other hand, as tenants in common of the common elements, would seem to have an insurable interest in that property.[28] The few courts that have commented appear to agree.[29]

If the unit owners have an insurable interest in the common property and the condominium association has no property interest in it, does it have any insurable

---

Ass'n v. Continental Ins. Co., 770 F. Supp. 1046 (D.V.I. 1991), where the association was described as the owner of some of the individual units. The opinion does not say how the association came to be the owner of those units, but it does say that the insurer agreed it was liable under a property policy issued to the association to provide coverage for damage to their interiors, but not for damage to the interiors of units owned by individual unit owners. The Uniform Common Interest Ownership Act defines "common elements" in a condominium or cooperative as "all portions of the common interest community other than the units." Uniform Common Interest Ownership Act § 1-103(6)(A)(i). If that definition were to apply to the association in *Coakley Bay*, when it acquired individual units would they not by definition still be units and, therefore, not common elements?

26. Perlet, *Condominium Property Insurance*, 9 Forum 685, 697 (1974) (fee owner of individual unit has obvious insurable interest in that unit).

27. Condominium associations do have at least one form of interest in the commonly owned property. By statutes and covenants they have a lien on individual units for payment of assessments they levy to provide for maintenance for the project. *See, e.g.*, Colo. Rev. Stat. § 38-33.3-316(1); Fla. Stat. § 718.116(5). A unit includes an undivided share of the common property; therefore, the lien envelopes common property. There are important differences, however, between a mortgage—or other encumbrances—and an association lien for assessments. A mortgagor owes a current debt to the mortgagee. The condominium unit owner, however, owes the association nothing until an assessment is levied. Also, if a mortgagee forecloses on property other than a condominium unit, it can convey it as it wishes. If the association forecloses its lien, the undivided interest in the common property comes with the unit, but the association cannot convey that interest separate from the unit. The purchaser of the unit also obtains an undivided share of the common elements.

28. Cozen, *Insuring Real Property*, § 10.04[1] (Matthew Bender & Co. 2015) (strong argument could be made that unit owners have insurable interest beyond their individual unit because they have ownership interest in common property, albeit undivided interest, and additionally, to extent association insurance on common areas is insufficient to cover costs of repair, unit owners themselves might be liable for shortage). *But see In re* Sports Shinko (Florida) Co., 333 B.R. 483 (Bankr. M.D. Fla. 2005). In that case, the debtor owned the majority of the condominium units in a golf and tennis resort that it operated. The association sought an order from the bankruptcy court for payment of expenditures—including over $30,000 for building insurance—it had made to maintain the common areas after the bankruptcy petition was filed. In an assertion that went unchallenged by the court, the bankruptcy trustee contended she "did not even have an insurable interest in the condominiums' common areas, since the estate was simply the owner of individual condominium units."

29. *See* Messick, Schoenleber & Miller Associates v. Atlantic Mutual Insurance Co., 218 N.J. Super. 395, 527 A.2d 946 (1987) (all owners owned proportionate share of common elements and, therefore, had insurable interest in them); Craig v. Sandy Creek Condominium Ass'n, Inc., 2009 N.C. App. LEXIS 766, *aff'd*, 197 N.C. App. 628, 680 S.E.2d 272 (2009) (unless otherwise excluded from coverage, individual residents as owners of units, part owners of common areas, and members of association had insurable interest).

interest? It does have a duty to maintain the common elements, and under the condominium legislation in most states—and also generally under the condominium documents—it has a responsibility to maintain insurance on the common property. As noted above, one does not have an insurable interest in property by virtue of acting as the agent of a property owner. A condominium association might be described as the agent of the unit owners. It manages and maintains the common property and directly pays insurance premiums, but it has no ownership interest in the common property and would incur no direct loss if it is destroyed. Based on that depiction, one commentator concluded many years ago that a condominium association has no insurable interest in the common property.[30]

Doubts about the extent to which condominium associations have an insurable interest in common elements have occasionally arisen. Idaho, for example, felt compelled to state in its Condominium Act that an association has an insurable interest.[31] The issue, however, has rarely been mentioned by courts, suggesting parties do not often raise it. The few cases in which the question has been mentioned have not directly addressed it. For example, in a California case, condominium unit owners insisted the association, not being an owner, had no insurable interest in the project. The court responded that the assertion would come as a surprise to both the association and its insurer, which, respectively, paid thousands of dollars in premiums and nearly $2 million in loss benefits. The court tersely said that as the insurer had paid benefits to the association, the unit owners were not entitled to contest the insurability of the association's interest and it did not need to explore the rationale of that insurable interest.[32]

As the California court observed, condominium associations routinely insure their common elements and pay their premiums without any question of insurable interest being raised by insurers. There appears to be an all but unspoken understanding that associations have an insurable interest by virtue of legislation or binding covenants.[33] In most states a condominium association is explicitly granted the authority to insure the common property, and in many states

30. *See* Perlet, *Condominium Property Insurance*, 9 Forum 685, 696 (1974) (association is mere agent of owners and has no direct insurable interest in property of principal).

31. Idaho Code § 55-1517 (management body has authority and *insurable interest* to insure project or any portion thereof against loss or damage by fire or other hazard or casualty). *See also* Perlet, *Condominium Property Insurance*, 9 Forum 685, 695–97 (1974).

32. Countrywide Home Loans, Inc. v. Tutungi, 66 Cal. App. 4th 727, 731, 78 Cal. Rptr. 2d 203, 205 (1998). In what appears to be the only other case where the question of the association's insurable interest was raised, it was not addressed. Lauer v. Chamale Cover, ___ F. Supp. 2d ___, 2006 U.S. Dist. LEXIS 66287 (E.D. La., Sept. 18, 2006) (plaintiff unit owner argued that she and other condominium owners who belong to association had the only insurable interests).

33. *See generally* Cozen, *Insuring Real Property*, § 10.04[1] (Matthew Bender & Co. 2015) (condominium association generally has insurable interest in buildings, excluding those portions that are solely owned by unit owners, and further has insurable interest in all appurtenant structures and facilities).

it is required to do so. Additionally, most condominium Declarations—which are almost always recorded and considered covenants running with the land—require or authorize associations to maintain insurance on the common elements, and associations also have a duty, or at least the authority, to maintain, repair, and replace the common elements.[34] It can be inferred that these duties give the association a "substantial economic interest" in the common property. Moreover, the documents can be viewed as a contractual risk transfer that provides the association with an insurable interest.[35]

If an insurable interest is created by either legislation or recorded documents, is that interest circumscribed by the extent of the authority granted? Courts seem to imply that is the case. For example, a California court stated that an association's insurable interest applied only to the common areas of the condominium property and not to the interior portions of the individual units.[36] California law, unlike the UCIOA, does not require the association to provide coverage for attached units. A Florida court said that to require an association to insure jacuzzis, trellises, and elaborate screen enclosures on outdoor patios that were purchased, installed, could be removed, and were usable only by individual unit owners would make it responsible for insuring property in which it apparently has no insurable interest.[37]

A far more problematic question is raised with regard to individual units. As discussed below, a growing number of states, following the lead of the Uniform Acts, are requiring, or at least authorizing, associations to insure the individual units, although not any improvements to, or personal property in, those units. Clearly, an association has no ownership interest in the units, nor does it have responsibility for maintenance of those units. The basis for an association to have an insurable interest in the units is unclear.[38] However, when a statute or the documents impose an insurance obligation on the association, it would constitute a contractual risk transfer that should provide the necessary insurable interest.

---

34. Rosenberry & Treese, *Purchasing Insurance for the Common Interest Community*, 27 Wake Forest Law Rev. 397, 406 (1992) (insurable interest can exist in form of covenants that require condominium associations to maintain property).

35. "Contractual risk transfer" is defined as "[t]he use of contractual obligations such as indemnity and exculpatory agreements, waivers of recovery rights, and insurance requirements to pass along to others what would otherwise be one's own risks of loss." *See* https://www.irmi.com/glossary?terms=contractual+risk+transfer&ancestors=x159873.

36. Chateau Chamberay Homeowners Ass'n v. Associated Internat. Ins. Co., 90 Cal. App. 4th 335, 340, 108 Cal. Rptr. 2d 776, 779, n.2 (2001).

37. Costa Del Sol Ass'n v. Dep't of Bus. & Prof'l Regulation, Div. of Fla. Land Sales, Condos., & Mobile Homes, 987 So. 2d 734, 736 (Fla. 3d DCA 2008).

38. Kerr, *Condominium-Statutory Implementation*, 38 St. John's L. Rev. 1, 25 (1963) (if association obtains blanket coverage for entire building, there no question over coverage, except possibility of existence of insurable interest).

[3] Cooperatives

There should be little question that a cooperative has an insurable interest in the property. In the typical residential cooperative, a corporation owns all the real property, including fixtures, and the residents have an interest in the corporation evidenced by a share or shares of stock. They also have a lease interest in an apartment by virtue of what is called a proprietary lease or an occupancy agreement. The corporation is in effect a landlord and has the same right as any landlord to insure its property. The residents are tenant/shareholders. Their right and obligation to maintain property insurance may be largely determined by the terms of the proprietary lease. They might be said to have no insurable interest in the real property; however, unlike an ordinary tenant, their interests are intermingled with those of the corporation.[39] A shareholder may have an insurable interest in corporate assets, but that interest would likely be limited to any deficiency in the coverage obtained by the corporation.[40]

[4] Homeowners Associations

Generally, by definition, a homeowners association owns the common property.[41] Thus, the association clearly has an insurable interest in that property. A homeowners association may be required by statute or its documents to insure individual residences especially where units are attached.[42] There would then be a contractual transfer of risk that should provide the basis for an insurable interest.[43]

---

39. 2 Rohan & Reskin, *Real Estate Transactions: Cooperative Housing Law and Practice—Forms*, § 12.01 (Matthew Bender 2016).

40. 2 Rohan & Reskin, *Real Estate Transactions: Cooperative Housing Law and Practice—Forms*, § 12.02[2][g] (Matthew Bender 2016).

41. *See* Uniform Common Interest Ownership Act § 1-103(6)(A)(ii) (in planned community common elements means any real estate owned or leased by association). A comment to the Uniform Act explains that in a planned community, if real estate is subject to the Declaration, and thus within the planned community, it meets the definition of a common element, and if real estate is not within the planned community, title may be held by the association, but it is not a common element unless the Declaration is amended to incorporate that real estate as part of the real estate subject to the Declaration. Uniform Common Interest Ownership Act § 1-103, comment 7.

42. *See, e.g.*, Uniform Common Interest Ownership Act § 3-113(b) (in building that contains units divided by horizontal boundaries described in Declaration, or vertical boundaries that comprise common walls between units, property insurance must, to extent reasonably available, include units, but need not include improvements and betterments installed by unit owners).

43. *See* Treese & Rosenberry, *Insurance: How Community Associations Protect Themselves*, at 14 (CAI Press 2013) (insurable interest in planned community—as opposed to condominium or cooperative—may be based on covenants allowing association to purchase blanket coverage or requiring it to maintain exteriors of private residences); Williams, *Property & Casualty Insurance/Townhome Insurance* (May 2009) (where documents authorize homeowners association to purchase master casualty policy covering all buildings, they created "contractual risk transfer" in which risk of insuring property was transferred to HOA; asserting that insuring total property—including townhomes—under common policy is acceptable provided it's done correctly and clear lines are drawn between "corporate" and personal responsibility).

[5] Community Association Management Companies

A community association management company may be listed on a property policy as the named insured.[44] The apparent purpose of doing so is to obtain lower premiums based on the large portfolio of properties the company manages.[45] A management company, however, ordinarily has no insurable interest in the property it manages.[46]

The problem that lack of insurable interest presents is illustrated in a case decided by the federal Eleventh Circuit Court of Appeals.[47] In that case, a Florida company served as property manager for three apartment complexes in which it had no ownership interest. It was compensated for its management services with a percentage of the gross income generated by the apartment complexes. The named insured on the policies providing coverage for those properties was the management company. The buildings were damaged in a hurricane, and the management company submitted a claim. The insurer contended the insurable interest of the management company was limited to its revenue stream—the percentage of gross income—from the complexes. The management company countered that it had a contractual obligation to procure insurance and that obligation created an insurable interest. The court noted that under Florida law, a property insurance contract is enforceable only when, at the time of loss, the insured has an insurable interest in the covered property. The court acknowledged that an insured need not own property to have an insurable interest. It did not decide whether an obligation to procure insurance would create an insurable interest because it found no such obligation imposed on the property management company. In any event, the court held that the only injury the company could have

44. *See, e.g.*, Equinox on the Battenkill Mgmt. Ass'n v. Phila. Indem. Ins. Co., 125 A.3d 893 (Vt. 2015) (policy was between management association that managed condominium complex and insurer; court found possibility of coverage for condominium property and question of insurable interest was not raised); Belaire at Boca, LLC v. Ass'ns Ins. Agency, Inc., 2007 U.S. Dist. LEXIS 55252 (S.D. Fla. July 31, 2007) (property management company placed as named insured on policy insuring condominium property). *See also* DiMillo v. Travelers Prop. Cas. Co. of Am., 789 F. Supp. 2d 194, 197 (D. Me. 2011) (named insureds were association and its property manager); Shoreline Towers Condo. Owners Ass'n v. Zurich Am. Ins. Co., 196 F. Supp. 2d 1210 (S.D. Ala. 2002) (general management company for condominium association was named insured and association was listed in named insured endorsement).

45. Harris, *Is Your Association Properly Named On Your Insurance Policy?* (Apr. 10, 2014), available at: http://www.condominiuminsurancelaw.com/2014/04/articles/condominium-associations/is-your-association-properly-named-on-your-insurance-policy/. *See also* Belaire at Boca, LLC v. Ass'ns Ins. Agency, Inc., 2007 U.S. Dist. LEXIS 55252 (S.D. Fla. July 31, 2007) (where cobroker on insurance contract was affiliated with property management company, it was able to deliver lower cost insurance by bundling association's policy with all other properties of management company).

46. *See* Treese & Rosenberry, *Insurance: How Community Associations Protect Themselves*, at 15 (CAI Press 2013).

47. Banta Props. v. Arch Specialty Ins. Co., 553 Fed. Appx. 908 (11th Cir. 2014).

suffered from the impairment or destruction of the apartment complexes was loss of revenue—that is, its percentage share of the gross income. Therefore, its insurable interest was limited to that potential loss of revenue.

As one commentator has observed, even though the Eleventh Circuit did not address whether an obligation to procure insurance might itself create an insurable interest, the arguments raised by the insurer should cause common interest community associations to review their policies because if the property owner is not listed as the named insured, insurers may refuse to pay a claim.[48] If, upon review of the policy, the association finds its community association management company is listed as the named insured, it should consult the association attorney who in turn should probably seek the opinion of an attorney who specializes in insurance law.

§ 10.03 Association's Obligation to Obtain Property Insurance

In a great many states *condominium* associations are required to purchase property insurance. For example, Florida[49] and Texas[50] specifically require condominium associations to maintain property insurance. Some states leave the matter to the documents or the direction of the unit owners. For example, the New York Condominium Act does not require insurance but does obligate the governing board—board of managers—to insure the building against loss or damage by fire and other hazards as required by the Declaration, the bylaws, or a majority of the unit owners.[51] In a few states, for instance California,[52] the pertinent legislation makes no mention of an insurance requirement. Illinois is an anomaly in that its law appears to neither specifically authorize nor mandate purchase of property or general liability insurance.[53] When state law contains a requirement that an association maintain property insurance, it is important to determine the extent of the required coverage. For example, under the Uniform Condominium Act,

48. Harris, *Is Your Association Properly Named On Your Insurance Policy?* (Apr. 10, 2014), available at: http://www.condominiuminsurancelaw.com/2014/04/articles/condominium-associations/is-your-association-properly-named-on-your-insurance-policy.

49. Fla. Stat. § 718.111(11)(d) (association must use "best efforts" to obtain and maintain adequate property insurance).

50. Tex. Prop. Code § 82.111(a).

51. N.Y. Real Prop. Law § 339-bb.

52. Rosenberry & Sproul, *A Comparison of California Common Interest Development Law and the Uniform Common Interest Ownership Act*, 38 Santa Clara L. Rev. 1009, 1065 (1998) (California Davis-Stirling Common Interest Development Act does not require community associations to maintain insurance).

53. *But see* Royal Glen Condo. Ass'n v. S.T. Neswold & Assocs., 385 Ill. Dec. 137, 18 N.E.3d 137 (2014) (when sections of Illinois Condominium Property Act are read together, it is clear legislature intended that board of managers has duty to obtain adequate and appropriate insurance coverage).

when a building contains units with horizontal boundaries—that is, "stacked" units—that are described in the Declaration, the property insurance must, to the extent reasonably available, include *the units*, but need not include improvements and betterments installed by unit owners.[54]

Seventeen states have statutes specifically governing homeowners associations: California, Florida, Georgia, Hawaii, Illinois, Indiana, Kansas, Louisiana, Maryland, New Mexico, North Carolina, Ohio, Oregon, Pennsylvania, Texas, Virginia, and Washington. Of those, the laws of Kansas, North Carolina, Ohio, Oregon, and Pennsylvania address property insurance. Under the Kansas Townhouse Ownership Act, the Declaration *must* require each individual townhouse owner to maintain fire and "extended coverage" insurance and *may* require the governing board of the association to obtain and maintain the insurance under one blanket fire and extended coverage policy.[55] The Oregon Planned Community Act requires homeowners associations to obtain and maintain property coverage with premiums as a common expense.[56] The Planned Community Acts of North Carolina, Ohio, and Pennsylvania all obligate associations to maintain property insurance, to the extent reasonably available, beginning no later than the first conveyance of a lot or unit to a person other than a declarant.[57]

Few states have laws governing cooperatives, other than as corporations. Notable exceptions are Florida, New York, Pennsylvania, and Virginia. The New York law has no property insurance mandate. Florida requires cooperative associations to use their "best efforts" to obtain and maintain "adequate insurance" to protect the association property.[58] Pennsylvania and Virginia provide that beginning no later than the first conveyance of a cooperative interest to a person other than a declarant, the cooperative association has to maintain property insurance, to the extent reasonably available.[59]

In the states that have adopted the Uniform Common Interest Ownership Act, common interest communities, including condominiums, cooperatives, and homeowners associations, have to insure "against risks of direct physical loss commonly insured against."[60]

Even where there is no statutory obligation to maintain property insurance, the common interest community documents often impose that responsibility on associations. In a condominium, the obligation may be stated in the Declaration

54. Uniform Condominium Act § 3-113(b).
55. Kan. Stat. Ann. § 58-3712.
56. Or. Rev. Stat. § 94.675(2).
57. N.C. Gen. Stat. § 47F-3-113(a); Ohio Rev. Code Ann. § 5312.06(B); 68 Pa. Cons. Stat. § 5312(a).
58. Fla. Stat. § 719.104(3).
59. 68 Pa. Cons. Stat. § 4313(a); Va. Code § 55-470(A).
60. Uniform Common Interest Ownership Act § 3-113(a)(1) (2008).

of Condominium[61] or the bylaws.[62] In a homeowners association, the Covenants, Conditions, and Restrictions (CC&Rs) are where a property insurance requirement is likely to be found.[63] In a cooperative, either the bylaws or the proprietary lease may compel the cooperative corporation to insure the property. Documents may merely permit the association to provide insurance, in which case they impose no requirement on it.[64]

Sometimes there will be both a requirement for property insurance in the documents and a statute. The two need to be carefully compared to identify any inconsistencies. As a general rule, the documents may supplement, but not contradict, any statutory mandate.[65] One expert cautions that the governing documents are not always easy to understand and, therefore, an association should work with its lawyer when necessary to make sure the governing board members are fully aware of the duties and obligations of the association.[66]

In some respects, the question of whether a common interest community is required by statute or its documents to maintain property insurance is academic because most will come under the property insurance requirements of Fannie Mae and Freddie Mac.[67] Those two governmentally sponsored entities dominate the secondary mortgage market. Effectively, failure to meet their property insurance coverage requirements will prevent those wishing to purchase a home in the community from obtaining a mortgage.

Discharging the property insurance obligation requires "careful attention to changing values, and knowledge of policies available and endorsements that can be secured."[68] Sometimes, the governing board will either fail to maintain insurance as required by statute or the documents, or obtain less than the required

61. *See, e.g.*, Willows Condo. Owners Ass'n v. Kraus, 467 S.W.3d 312 (Mo. App. 2015); Royal Bahamian Ass'n v. QBE Ins. Corp., 750 F. Supp. 2d 1346, 1358 (S.D. Fla. 2010); Association of Unit Owners of Inn of Seventh Mountain v. Gruenfeld, 277 Ore. 259, 560 P.2d 641 (1977).

62. *See, e.g.*, Pac. Indem. Co. v. Deming, 140 F. Supp. 3d 152 (D. Mass. 2015), *rev'd on other grounds*, 828 F.3d 19 (1st Cir. 2016); Onetti v. Gatsby Condominium, 111 A.D.3d 496, 975 N.Y.S.2d 27 (2013); Anderson v. Council of Gables, 404 Md. 560, 564, 948 A.2d 11, 13 (2008).

63. *See, e.g.*, Palacin v. Allstate Ins. Co., 119 Cal. App. 4th 855, 859, 14 Cal. Rptr. 3d 731, 732 (2004).

64. Bosch v. Cedar Vill. Townhomes Homeowners Ass'n, 2011 Tex. App. LEXIS 804 (Tex. App.—Houston 1st Dist., Feb. 3, 2011) (where Declaration stated that association "may" provide fire insurance without imposing requirement to do so, it did not create duty for association to insure individual unit).

65. *See, e.g.*, Hill v. Promenade E. Condo. Ass'n, 2009 Me. Super. LEXIS 14 (Me. Super. Ct. Jan. 12, 2009) (statutory insurance requirement could not be varied or waived in bylaws).

66. Pollack, *Homeowner Association Managers, Agents and Officers Beware—Check Insurance Requirements to Avoid Lawsuits From Individual Members!!* (June 2016), available at: http://www.condominiuminsurancelaw.com/2016/06/articles/insurance/homeowner-association-managers-agents-and-officers-beware-check-insurance-requirements-to-avoid-lawsuits-from-individual-members/#more.

67. For discussion of Fannie Mae and Freddie Mac, see generally Chapter 6, *infra*.

68. Hennessey, *Condominium Management*, 48 St. John's L. Rev. 1064, 1070 (1974).

coverage. Are either the association or the individual members of the governing board liable for that failure? Individual members of a governing board probably cannot be held personally liable, absent a crime, fraud, self-dealing, or unjust enrichment.[69] An association cannot be held liable when it has met the letter of any insurance mandate.[70] The association will probably be held to have fulfilled its duty by a good faith effort to obtain coverage, for example, by contacting an insurance broker to procure insurance.[71] In any event, language in the governing documents typically excludes liability for all but acts that are willful or in bad faith.[72] Nonetheless, occasionally associations have been successfully sued for failing to obtain the required coverage.[73]

69. *See, e.g.*, Munder v. Circle One Condominium, Inc., 596 So. 2d 144 (Fla. 4th DCA 1992) (developer-director was found to have breached fiduciary duty by failing to renew fire insurance on clubhouse, but court did not hold director personally liable).

70. *See* State Farm Fire & Cas. Co. v. Chardonnay Vill. Condo. Ass'n, 171 So. 3d 301 (La. App. 2015) (where Louisiana law required association to maintain property insurance on units, but that it could notify unit owners in writing that insurance was not available, fact that association's established policy clearly stated that it would *not* be responsible for any interior damage to individual units provided plaintiff unit owner with sufficient notice that association was not maintaining insurance coverage on her unit). *See also* Roberts v. Nine Island Ave. Condo. Ass'n, 126 So. 3d 286 (Fla. 3d DCA 2011), where unit owners brought an action against the association for failure to keep the marina and docks insured. These features were "limited common elements," and the documents, according to the court, only required insurance to be maintained on the common elements. Further, the Declaration made a distinction between common elements and limited common elements in its description of the property. Therefore, the court held the association was not required by the terms of the Declaration to purchase and carry coverage for the marina and boat docks. The problem with the court's conclusion is that generally, and specifically under Florida law, limited common elements are simply a subset of common elements. They are common elements owned by all the unit owners in common but reserved for the use of fewer than all the unit owners.

71. *See* Breedy-Fryson v. Towne Estates Condo. Owners Ass'n, 2010 Del. Ch. LEXIS 37 (Del. Ch. Feb. 25, 2010) (where association failed to obtain property insurance for full replacement value as required by governing documents, action against it and board members was dismissed because under governing documents liability was limited to willful acts or those in bad faith and association appeared to have acted in good faith by attempting to procure adequate insurance and by hiring broker as advisor on adequate amount of insurance coverage needed); Acevedo v. Town 'N Country Condominium, Section I, Bd. of Mgrs., 51 A.D.3d 603, 857 N.Y.S.2d 691 (2008) (where board allegedly breached its fiduciary duty by failing to obtain sufficient fire insurance, court found that under business judgment rule, judicial inquiry into actions of board is prohibited as long as it acts for purpose of community within its authority and in good faith; board met its prima facie burden by establishing that it acted in good faith, within its authority, and for the benefit of community when it retained broker to procure insurance sufficient to cover full replacement of buildings to extent obtainable).

72. *See* 6A Rohan, *Real Estate Transactions: Home Owner Associations and Planned Unit Developments—Law and Practice: Forms*, § 7A.07[1][a] (Matthew Bender 2016).

73. *See, e.g.*, Promenade E. Condo. Ass'n, 2009 Me. Super. LEXIS 14 (Me. Super. Ct. Jan. 12, 2009). *See also* Parkside at Mt. Shadows Owners Ass'n v. Travelers Cas. & Sur. Co. of Am., 2015 U.S. Dist. LEXIS 81988 (D. Colo. June 24, 2015) (in prior action, individual owners sued homeowners association board of directors claiming they failed to procure adequate property insurance coverage and noting that one director distributed letter admitting association chose not to carry insurance for damaged property). *And see* Bennett v. Plantations East Condo. Ass'n, 2010 Del. Ch. LEXIS 181 (July 20, 2010), *app. dis.*, 44 A.3d 921 (Del. 2012) (unit owner brought claim alleging

§ 10.04 The Property Insurance Coverage Search

Whether a common interest community is newly formed and seeking its initial coverage or an existing community is looking for a new carrier or substantial changes in its existing coverage,[74] the search for property insurance coverage is one of the most important duties of the association governing board. One commentator observes that it is absolutely necessary for insurance to be a priority for an association governing board and that decisions about it should be made in the best interest of the owners, not what board members personally would do, because insuring the property is the fiduciary responsibility of board members.[75] Yet many governing boards pay little attention to the process.[76] Some leave it entirely to professionals: the community association manager and an insurance broker. However, those persons may or may not have the specialized knowledge required to make good decisions for the association. The starting point for the governing board, therefore, is assessing the professional assistance available to it. One way to accomplish that is to appoint a member of the board of directors or an insurance committee to handle the process.[77]

[1] The Role of the Community Association Managers

Common interest communities may turn to their CAM to take the lead in finding them property insurance coverage. That is a reasonable decision because generally CAMs have some knowledge of the types of insurance their clients require,

---

association failed to maintain sufficient insurance as required under Declaration, but action was dismissed for lack of jurisdiction). *See generally* Pollack, *Homeowner Association Managers, Agents and Officers Beware—Check Insurance Requirements to Avoid Lawsuits From Individual Members!!* (June 2016), available at: http://www.condominiuminsurancelaw.com/2016/06/articles/insurance/homeowner-association-managers-agents-and-officers-beware-check-insurance-requirements-to-avoid-lawsuits-from-individual-members/#more (where there is no coverage for loss to common area because of negligence by association governing board, association can be subject to lawsuits brought by individual members to recoup costs necessary to repair property based on enforcement of association's duties and obligations under governing documents).

74. The association should regularly revisit its property insurance and look for better coverage or premium savings. Policies and the coverage they offer do change and, as one commentator notes, so do rates and the governing board should make sure it is getting the best deal available. Green, *Shopping for Insurance; What Do Boards Need to Know?* (Cooperator, Aug. 2011), available at: http://cooperator.com/articles/2298/1/Shopping-for-Insurance/Page1.html.

75. Lent, *The ABC's of Insuring Your Co-op or Condo; Common Terms and Options for Insurance* (Cooperator, Aug. 2014), available at: http://cooperator.com/articles/2818/1/The-ABCs-of-Insuring-Your-Co-op-or-Condo/Page1.html.

76. Meskin, *A Funny Thing Happened on the Way to the Bank: Fraud in the Community Association* (Katzman & Korr: Legal News Tailored for Community Associations 2008) (associations are often run by volunteers, some with no experience in running a business or management, and others with too little time to devote and, thus, associations and their boards are often ready to let others handle their responsibilities).

77. *See Understanding Homeowner Association Insurance*, available at: http://www.hindmansanchez.com/resources/article/understanding-homeowner-association-insurance.

certainly more than a great many members of association governing boards. In states that license CAMs, knowledge of insurance is part of the educational requirements or of the licensure exam.[78] Most states do not require CAMs to be licensed, but many managers obtain certification through the Community Association Managers International Certification Board. Its basic certification is the Certified Manager of Community Associations (CMCA). The CMCA certification exam tests a number of areas of knowledge, including risk management and insurance. Managers who are neither licensed nor hold a certification likely have some knowledge of insurance gained through experience.

Despite any knowledge and experience a CAM may have, the association should not leave the task of working with an insurance broker to obtain property coverage wholly to the manager. As one expert cautions, delegation of insurance responsibility to someone who is not an insurance professional may be a breach of the duty of the governing board.[79] In any event, the governing documents or statutes commonly place the responsibility to obtain insurance coverage on the association, and the governing board is the body charged with carrying out the duties of the association. Nonetheless, there is at least one case in which an association successfully sued a manager for breach of contract for failure to renew insurance.[80] That, however, does not preclude a court finding that the governing board also failed to carry out its duties.

All that notwithstanding, in some cases managers may have statutory authority to obtain property insurance for *condominium* associations because of a curious provision in the original condominium legislation of 13 states—Connecticut,[81]

---

78. *See, e.g.*, 4 Colo. Code Regs. § 725-7(A-3)(2) (applicant must successfully complete course of study in financial, risk, and facilities management); Fla. Admin. Code § 61E14-1.001(2)(d) (prelicensure education must include insurance matters relating to community associations); Fla. Admin. Code § 61E14-4.001(3)(b) (continuing education must include instruction on insurance and financial management topics relating to community association management).

79. Meskin, *The Community Association Insurance Puzzle: What Boards MUST DO and MUST AVOID to Assemble the Puzzle*, at 14 (Community Association Living, CAI Austin 2012) (noting that management agreements generally require association to indemnify management company and, therefore, if management company commits error regarding insurance, it is probably not accountable to association; error and omissions policies issued to management companies usually expressly exclude claims arising out of insurance issues).

80. Waterpointe I Prop. Owner's Ass'n v. Paragon, Inc., 342 S.C. 454, 536 S.E.2d 878 (Ct. App. 2000). In *Paragon*, the management contract provided that the manager would assist the governing board in acquiring insurance policies for the association as outlined in the Condominium Documents. It also said that the association could delegate to the manager its sole and exclusive authority to obtain bids for, contract to purchase, and actually purchase any insurance. Although the manager undertook that responsibility, it failed to renew the association's flood insurance. The association suffered a flood loss of $126,000.00 and sued the manager for that amount in a breach of contract action. The lower court awarded the association $79,703.86. The award was less than the loss apparently because the court determined a portion of the loss would not have been covered by the insurance. The appellate court affirmed.

81. Conn. Gen. Stat. § 47-83 (1963 Connecticut Unit Ownership Act); Conn. Gen. Stat. § 47-83 (Connecticut Condominium Act of 1976).

Kansas,[82] Maine,[83] Minnesota,[84] Missouri,[85] Montana,[86] New Hampshire,[87] New Mexico,[88] North Carolina,[89] Rhode Island,[90] Utah,[91] Vermont,[92] and Washington[93]—the District of Columbia,[94] and the Virgin Islands[95] concerning managers and insurance. These laws generally provide that the "manager"—or board of directors—has the authority to, and must, obtain insurance for the property. Often the mandate is triggered by a requirement in the governing documents, the direction of lenders, or the majority of unit owners. The statutes usually do not define "manager,"[96] although several suggest by implication that the term refers to a community association manager.[97] With the exception of Kansas and Montana, all of the 13 states and the District of Columbia either adopted the Uniform Condominium Act or Uniform Common Interest Ownership Act, or borrowed heavily from them in replacing their original condominium legislation. The Uniform Acts omit that reference to the manager obtaining property insurance. Depending on the wording of the Uniform Act as adopted by a particular

82. Kan. Stat. Ann. § 58-3125.
83. Me. Rev. Stat. tit. 33, § 563.
84. Minn. Stat. § 515.25.
85. Mo. Rev. Stat. § 448.120.
86. Mont. Code § 70-23-612(1).
87. N.H. Rev. Stat. Ann. § 479-A:24.
88. N.M. Stat. Ann. § 47-7-28(A).
89. N.C. Gen. Stat. § 47A-24.
90. R.I. Gen. Laws § 34-36-29.
91. Utah Code Ann. § 57-8-29(1).
92. Vt. Stat. Ann. tit. 27, § 1325.
93. Wash. Rev. Code § 64.32.220.
94. D.C. Code § 42-2020.
95. V.I. Code Ann. tit. 28, § 924. *See* Anthony v. Indep. Ins. Advisors, Inc., 56 V.I. 516, 532 (2012) (association has right under statute to purchase and maintain insurance coverage over common areas).
96. The Montana Unit Ownership Act is an exception. It defines "manager" as the "manager, board of managers, or other person in charge of the administration of or managing the property." Mont. Code § 70-23-102(10). A commentary observes the peculiarity of this definition and its potential for confusion because condominiums are nearly always governed by a board of directors, which is never referred to as a "manager." These boards usually hire another entity as the "manager." The commentary notes the odd definition of manager raises questions about whether obligations imposed on a manager are imposed on the hired manager or the board. The author says it becomes clear that those duties are imposed on the board when one discovers the definition of manager is a relic of the Puerto Rican statute. Natelson, *Condominiums, Reform, and the Unit Ownership Act*, 58 Mont. L. Rev. 495, 503 (1997). The act also says that the "board may engage the services of a manager or managing agent." Mont. Code § 70-23-308(1). That certainly suggests that the manager is separate from the board.
97. The term "manager" probably refers to a professional manager—usually called a community association manager (CAM)—because of statutes that say the bylaws may provide for whether or not the board may engage the services of a manager or managing agent. *See, e.g.*, Kan. Stat. Ann. § 58-3119(a); Minn. Stat. § 515.19, subd. 1(a); N.H. Rev. Stat. Ann. § 479-A:18(I); R.I. Gen. Laws § 34-36-16(1).

state, the earlier condominium legislation may still apply to condominiums created pursuant to it.

The governing board should pair a member of the board with the manager to provide assistance or additional information when needed and to monitor the process. Having a board member actively participating in the process on behalf of the board demonstrates that the board is endeavoring to carry out its responsibility to obtain adequate property coverage. Before an application is submitted to an insurer, the full governing board should review the proposed coverage and the contents of the application. The governing board should remember that when the manager is its agent, it will generally be bound by the actions of the manager on behalf of the association.[98] For example, where a manager signed an application that did not mention a prior claim by the association, despite the fact that she asserted she had no knowledge of that claim, her signature on the application constituted a failure by the association to disclose the information pertaining to its earlier loss because she was signing on its behalf.[99]

[2] The Role of the Insurance Broker

The general public uses the terms "agent" and "broker" interchangeably; however, in the insurance industry, and in law, they have specific meanings.[100] An "agent" represents the insurance company.[101] The agent may be an employee of a particular company, may have a contract to work exclusively for one company, or may have contracts with several insurers.[102] A "broker" is independent and usually is considered the agent of the insured.[103] The broker is not limited to obtaining coverage from a single company. The common interest community will want to engage a broker to find it the best policy from among a number of insurance carriers. However, the CIC needs more than just any broker. As one expert notes, insurance for common interest communities is a "niche market"—a

98. *See, e.g.*, Biscayne Cove Condo. Ass'n v. QBE Ins. Corp., 971 F. Supp. 2d 1121, 1126 (S.D. Fla. 2013).

99. Towers Condo. Ass'n v. C.E. Brathwaite & Assocs., 40 V.I. 33 (1999).

100. *But see* UBS Fin. Servs. v. Thompson, 94 A.3d 176 (Md. App. 2014) (Maryland eliminated distinction between terms "insurance agent" and "insurance broker").

101. American Way Cellular, Inc. v. Travelers Property Casualty Co. of America, 216 Cal. App. 4th 1040, 1052, 157 Cal. Rptr. 3d 385, 395 (2013) ("insurance agent" represents insurer under employment by it).

102. *See, e.g.*, Ramirez v. State Farm Mut. Auto. Ins. Co., 2016 U.S. Dist. LEXIS 5245 (N.D. Ind. Jan. 15, 2016).

103. *See, e.g.*, American Way Cellular, Inc. v. Travelers Property Casualty Co. of America, 216 Cal. App. 4th 1040, 1052, 157 Cal. Rptr. 3d 385, 394–95 (2013) ("insurance broker" acts as middleman between insured and the insurer, soliciting insurance from public under no employment from any special company; unlike agent, broker does not act for insurer, and insurer is not liable for broker's acts or omissions). *See also* Ga. Cas. & Sur. Co. v. Valley Wood, Inc., 336 Ga. App. 795 (2016).

specialty—and the association needs to work with a broker who specializes in it.[104] One way to find a broker who has the requisite knowledge is to look for one with the Community Insurance & Risk Management Specialist Designation from the Community Associations Institute. The designation is available to brokers with five years' experience as a practitioner in the community association insurance industry.

Finding the right broker can be a challenge. The community association manager or association attorney is probably familiar with brokers who specialize in working with common interest communities. Another source of names of area brokers who specialize in CICs is board members of other nearby associations. Commentators recommend comparing the services of at least three insurance brokers.[105] Another observer agrees that governing boards should interview several brokers and engage the one they believe will best represent them.[106] When the designated director or insurance committee interviews brokers, it will also want to determine the services the broker routinely provides. For example, will the broker participate in an annual review of the association's coverage? Later, the director or committee will compare the coverage the brokers offer to obtain. It should be remembered that typically, one broker obtains all or nearly all of the various policies—property, flood, equipment breakdown, general liability, directors and officers—for the association.

[3] Gathering Information Needed by the Broker

For insurance brokers to obtain a quote on property insurance coverage, there is certain information they will need and for which they will likely ask at the outset.[107] The association representative should gather this information in advance. This basic information is set forth below.

---

104. Stoeckert, *The Insurance Puzzle; Making Sense of Premiums and Policies* (Cooperator, Apr. 2012), available at: http://cooperator.com/articles/2418/1/The-Insurance-Puzzle/Page1.html. *See also* Hennessey, *Condominium Management*, 48 St. John's L. Rev. 1064, 1070 (1974) (insuring condominiums creates more difficult problems than many insurance agents and most business people appreciate and, therefore, association is well advised to employ knowledgeable and experienced insurance broker who will be able to recommend best and most economical policies that provide requisite coverage).

105. Green, *Shopping for Insurance; What Do Boards Need to Know?* (Cooperator, Aug. 2011); *Understanding Homeowner Association Insurance*, available at: http://www.hindmansanchez.com/resources/article/understanding-homeowner-association-insurance (it is customary to get two or three bids or proposals from different brokers before acquiring policy).

106. Lent, *The ABC's of Insuring Your Co-op or Condo; Common Terms and Options for Insurance* (Cooperator, Aug. 2014), available at: http://cooperator.com/articles/2818/1/The-ABCs-of-Insuring-Your-Co-op-or-Condo/Page1.html.

107. *See generally* Green, *Shopping for Insurance; What Do Boards Need to Know?* (Cooperator, Aug. 2011), available at: http://cooperator.com/articles/2298/1/Shopping-for-Insurance/Page1.html; *The Complete Guide to Condo Association Master Insurance*, available at: http://www.lakesideatpleasantmtn.com/uploads/8/6/7/8/8678493/condomasterpolicyebook.pdf.

- The community documents.[108]
- The *official* name of the common interest community. Remember that the community may have a name by which it is commonly known, but that may not be the legal name, which is what the insurer needs. For a condominium, the legal name will be found in the recorded Declaration of Condominium. The legal name of a homeowners association will be stated in the recorded Covenants, Conditions, and Restrictions. A cooperative is almost always incorporated, and its legal name will be found in the articles of incorporation, sometimes known as the Charter.
- The form of common interest community. This would seem to be an item of information that does not require research or confirmation, and yet it does. A community might be governed by a homeowners association but be in the condominium form of ownership. The word "condominium" is sometimes used generically to refer to any community with attached units. The documents need to be checked to confirm the form that the common interest community takes. If there is any doubt, an attorney should be consulted.
- The property address. The insurer needs to know the address of the property to be insured, not its mailing address or the address of its management company.
- Type of construction. The carrier will want to know how the building is constructed, for example, of brick or wood frame.
- The year of construction.
- Property improvements and renovations. Insurers want to know whether the building has a new roof, whether windows have been replaced, or whether the plumbing, heating, and electrical systems have been updated. The insurer should be told about any "green" improvements.[109] In an older

108. *See* Pollack, *Homeowner Association Managers, Agents and Officers Beware—Check Insurance Requirements to Avoid Lawsuits From Individual Members!!* (June 2016), available at: http://www.condominiuminsurancelaw.com/2016/06/articles/insurance/homeowner-association-managers-agents-and-officers-beware-check-insurance-requirements-to-avoid-lawsuits-from-individual-members/#more (association needs to show its governing documents to broker). *See also* Breedy-Fryson v. Towne Estates Condo. Owners Ass'n, 2010 Del. Ch. LEXIS 37 (Del. Ch. Feb. 25, 2010) (unit owners sued association when insurance coverage proved inadequate, alleging broker could not properly advise association on proper amount of coverage because broker was not provided with "code of regulations" that provided for operation, management, and administration of community).

109. It is especially important to inform the broker of any "green updates," as these are often able to better stand up to weather perils and may earn a reduction in the premium. Additionally, some carriers offer "green" insurance for environmentally friendly installations, for example solar panels. Barnes, *Understanding Your Insurance Policy's Fine-Print; What You Need to Know about Riders* (Cooperator, Aug. 2013), available at: http://cooperator.com/articles/2651/1/Understanding-Your-Insurance-Policy039s-Fine-Print/Page1.html.

building, no one, including the manager, may know about any updates and the association records may need to be checked.

- The number of units in the building. This means the total number of units, not just those occupied.
- The number of stories in the building.
- A site plan.
- The entire total interior square footage of the building, including all of the units and common areas.
- The amount of coverage sought, which ordinarily will be the replacement cost of the building. Ultimately this will be determined by an appraisal; however, at this point in the process, an approximation should be sufficient. The professional manager can probably help with that estimate.[110]
- Photographs of the exterior of the property taken from a few different angles.
- A copy of the Declarations Pages of any current insurance.
- Information on prior claims.[111]
- Information about any building violations and evidence of their correction.

The common interest community association should consider changes that can be made to the property that will make it more attractive to insurers and enable the association to garner lower premiums. One insurance agency that focuses on property insurance for commercial buildings offers some suggestions of improvements to consider.[112] These include hard-wired smoke detectors used in conjunction with battery backups, code-compliant elevators, and fire doors equipped with appropriate panic hardware. It is also important to have portable fire extinguishers and sprinkler systems inspected. Additionally, brokers can describe improvements for which specific insurers will offer premium discounts.

[4] Evaluating the Proposed Policy

Experts recommend that associations review an insurance policy with its broker after the policy has been issued to ensure it will meet the needs of the

110. *See* Breedy-Fryson v. Towne Estates Condo. Owners Ass'n, 2010 Del. Ch. LEXIS 37 (Del. Ch. Feb. 25, 2010) (unit owners sued association when insurance coverage proved inadequate, alleging broker could not properly advise association on proper amount of coverage because manager did not provide broker with replacement value for property).

111. A loss history, or "loss runs," report for the property can generally be obtained from the previous insurer. *The Complete Guide to Condo Association Master Insurance*, available at: http://www.lakesideatpleasantmtn.com/uploads/8/6/7/8/8678493/condomasterpolicyebook.pdf.

112. *See 10 Ways to Make a Building More Attractive to an Insurance Company* (Oct. 20, 2014), available at: http://www.trustevergreen.com/blog/2014/10/10-ways-to-make-a-building-more-attractive-to-an-insurance-company/#more-772.

association.[113] The entire board should review the proposed coverage.[114] Better yet, the association should have an insurance committee of knowledgeable residents review the proposal with the governing board present. Whoever worked with the broker—whether the manager or an association member—may make a report, but it is best to meet directly with the broker. Generally, brokers will be only too happy to meet with the board. Usually all the policies, other than flood, are bundled together with the property policy so the premiums are considerable and so too is the broker's commission. He or she has an incentive to "seal the deal." When the association is comparing policies from different brokers or different policies from the same broker, it should not automatically select the least expensive policy. The less expensive policy may omit needed coverage or contain other detrimental limitations.[115] One expert recommends that associations inquire about the insurance carrier rating.[116] There are several companies that rate the financial strength of insurers: A. M. Best Company,[117] Demotech, Inc.,[118] and Standard & Poor's.[119] It is important to keep in mind that Fannie Mae and Freddie Mac have minimum ratings that they require of the carrier providing the association's property coverage before they will purchase a mortgage on an individual home or unit in a common interest community.

---

113. *See, e.g.*, Pollack, *Homeowner Association Managers, Agents and Officers Beware—Check Insurance Requirements to Avoid Lawsuits From Individual Members!!* (June 2016), available at: http://www.condominiuminsurancelaw.com/2016/06/articles/insurance/homeowner-association-managers-agents-and-officers-beware-check-insurance-requirements-to-avoid-lawsuits-from-individual-members/#more.

114. Even if the governing board delegates responsibility for procuring insurance to one of its members and the coverage turns out to be inadequate, neither the board nor its individual members is likely to be liable. For example, in *Breedy-Fryson v. Towne Estates Condo. Owners Ass'n*, 2010 Del. Ch. LEXIS 37 (Del. Ch. Feb. 25, 2010), unit owners sued the association and contended it was remiss in securing adequate insurance coverage because it allowed one governing board member to work with its broker and bind it to a policy without first holding a meeting to review the policy. The court responded that it is not unusual for a board to divide up primary responsibilities for certain tasks among its members and that even if the delegation could be regarded as negligent, it did not constitute the willful misconduct or bad faith required under the governing documents to hold the board liable.

115. It is important to compare coverages, as some carriers will automatically include some extra coverages, while others make every additional coverage optional. *The Complete Guide to Condo Association Master Insurance*, available at: http://www.lakesideatpleasantmtn.com/uploads/8/6/7/8/8678493/condomasterpolicyebook.pdf.

116. Green, *Shopping for Insurance; What Do Boards Need to Know?* (Cooperator, Aug. 2011).

117. *See* http://www.ambest.com. *See also Understanding Homeowner Association Insurance*, available at: http://www.hindmansanchez.com/resources/article/understanding-homeowner-association-insurance (if there is some doubt about liquidity or stability of insurance company, applicant can ask broker to check it out in latest "Best Report," which rates insurance companies based on their financial strength and their overall conduct of business).

118. *See* http://www.demotech.com.

119. *See* http://www.standardandpoors.com.

[a] Questions about the Policy

The broker should be asked about particulars of the coverage. What real and personal property does the policy *not* cover? What is the total limit of coverage? Is it sufficient to avoid triggering any coinsurance clause?[120] Are there any sub-limits? What is the deductible? Are there separate deductibles for certain perils (for example, windstorms or earthquakes)? What do any endorsements add to or subtract from the standard coverage? Does any package bundling property insurance with other coverages include liability, umbrella, flood and quake, building ordinance, sewer backup, boiler & machinery, crime, terrorism, lead paint and mold, non-owned-hired auto, assault and battery, and directors and officers (D&O) insurance?[121]

[b] Surplus Lines Insurers

Because coverage for common interest communities is a specialty coverage, it is often underwritten by surplus lines insurers. A surplus lines insurer is also known as a non-admitted insurer. U.S. non-admitted insurers have to be licensed in at least one state, their home state. The solvency of the insurer is, therefore, regulated by its home state. Surplus lines insurers play an important role by providing insurance in hard-to-place markets. In Florida, for example, it is not uncommon for CIC insurance coverage to be more available in the surplus lines market than insurance issued by admitted companies. A full analysis of surplus lines insurance is beyond the scope of this treatise.[122] It is important to remember that if the policy is issued by a surplus lines insurer and if that insurer should be placed in receivership, then there is no guaranty fund coverage. Every state has a guaranty fund that pays covered claims when a licensed insurer is insolvent. The front page and Declarations Page of the policy will have an explanation either printed or stamped. Florida law, for instance, requires the following disclaimer to be written or stamped on the first page of the policy: "This insurance is issued pursuant to

120. It is also important to determine the source of the limit. Is it based on a recent actual appraisal, or is it taken from a prior policy, in which case it could be out of date and undervalue the insured property.

121. Green, *Shopping for Insurance; What Do Boards Need to Know?* (Cooperator, Aug. 2011).

122. The International Risk Management Institute glossary says that surplus lines insurance "[r]efers to coverage lines that need not be filed with state insurance departments as a condition of being able to offer coverage. The types of risks typically insured in the surplus lines insurance markets can usually be categorized as risks with adverse loss experience, unusual risks, and those for which there is a shortage of capacity within the standard market." https://www.irmi.com/term/insurance-definitions/surplus-lines-insurance. The National Association of Professional Surplus Lines Offices (NAPSLO) is a professional trade association representing the surplus lines industry and the wholesale insurance distribution system. It describes surplus lines insurers as the "safety value" of the insurance industry. They fill needs for coverage by insuring risks declined by the underwriting and pricing processes of standard insurance carriers and act as an effective supplement to the standard market. *See* http://www.napslo.org/.

the Florida Surplus Lines law. Persons insured by Surplus Lines carriers do not have the protection of the Florida Insurance Guaranty Act to the extent of any right of recovery for the obligation of an insolvent unlicensed insurer."[123]

§ 10.05 Duties of Agents and Brokers

While the association may place heavy reliance on the skill and knowledge of the broker, the broker's obligations to the association, or any insured, are circumscribed by long-standing principles of agency. The broker has limited responsibilities to the insured.

[1] Obtaining Requested Coverage

The average layperson has little or no understanding of insurance and relies heavily on the assistance of an insurance agent or broker. Yet, agents and brokers generally have no duty to anticipate the needs of their customers, to advise them about the adequacy of coverage obtained, or to inform them of optional coverage that may be available.[124] Conversely, the applicant for coverage has an obligation to specify the coverage and terms he or she requires.[125] When an applicant for insurance requests specific coverage, courts usually hold the agent or broker has a duty of reasonable care to procure that coverage,[126] as long as he or she has *agreed* to obtain that particular coverage.[127] Courts will find a duty to advise if

---

123. Fla. Stat. § 626.924(1).

124. *See* Emerson Elec. Co. v. Marsh & McLennan Cos., 362 S.W.3d 7, 13 (Mo. 2012) (neither agents nor brokers have duty to advise insured on its insurance needs or on availability of particular coverage, unless they specifically agree to do so); Houck v. State Farm Fire & Cas. Ins. Co., 366 S.C. 7, 12, 620 S.E.2d 326, 330 (S.C. 2005) (generally agent has no duty to advise insured at point of application, absent express or implied undertaking to do so); Baggett v. Summerlin Ins. & Realty, Inc., 354 N.C. 347, 554 S.E.2d 336 (2001) (agent did not have duty to point out exclusions in written policy where those exclusions did not negate particular coverage specifically requested by plaintiffs).

125. City Blueprint & Supply Co. v. Boggio, 3 So. 3d 62, 65–66 (La. App. 2008); Sinex v. Wallis, 611 A.2d 31, 33 (Del. Super. 1991); Kenyon v. Larsen, 205 Neb. 209, 217, 286 N.W.2d 759, 784 (1980).

126. Star Spa Servs. v. Robert G. Turano Ins. Agency, Inc., 595 F. Supp. 2d 519 (M.D. Pa. 2009). *See also* Traina Enters. v. Cord & Wilburn, Inc. Ins. Agency, 289 Ga. App. 833, 838, 658 S.E.2d 460, 464 (2008) (jury could find agent negligently misrepresented extent of coverage where insured requested renewal of existing policy that included vital coverage for particular business, agent told insured renewal policy had been obtained, agent expressly noted that coverage sought was included in renewal policy, and agent did not advise insured of change noted in coverage letter received from insurer).

127. *See, e.g.*, Avery v. Diedrich, 301 Wis. 2d 693, 734 N.W.2d 159 (2007). *See generally* Pollack, *Homeowner Association Managers, Agents and Officers Beware—Check Insurance Requirements to Avoid Lawsuits From Individual Members!!* (June 2016), available at: http://www.condominium insurancelaw.com/2016/06/articles/insurance/homeowner-association-managers-agents-and-offi cers-beware-check-insurance-requirements-to-avoid-lawsuits-from-individual-members/#more

the insured can show a "special relationship" between the parties.[128] Failure of an agent or broker to exercise the required care may result in liability.[129] However, agents or brokers have been held not to be liable for failure to procure coverage mandated by common interest community laws.[130]

Before an association can attempt to hold an agent or broker liable, it must determine who the agent or broker is. That may not be as obvious as it might seem, especially in the case of large common interest communities where complex coverage issues may result in a number of parties taking part in obtaining insurance. For example, in one case a broker for a condominium association contacted an entity that described itself as an "insurance wholesaler." It asserted that its role was as an intermediary between insurance agents and insurance companies. Nonetheless, its name was listed as the "agent" on the policy premium invoices.[131]

(by working with broker and requesting that broker procure policy that satisfies requirements of governing documents, association can go great lengths toward meeting its insurance obligations).

128. *See* Tiara Condo. Ass'n v. Marsh, USA, Inc., 991 F. Supp. 2d 1271, 1281 (S.D. Fla. 2014) (exception to general rule of no duty to advise applies when broker encourages and engages in "special relationship" with client, thereby triggering enhanced duty of care to advise client about amount of coverage prudently needed to meet its complete insurance needs; evidence of special relationship includes representations by broker about its expertise and about breadth of coverage obtained, length and depth of relationship, extent of broker's involvement in client's decision making about insurance needs, information volunteered by broker about insurance needs, and payment of additional compensation for advisory services); Schweitzer v. Am. Family Mut. Ins. Co., 16 N.E.3d 982 (Ind. App. 2014); Garnerville Holding Co. v. Kaye Ins. Assocs., 309 A.D.2d 541, 765 N.Y.S.2d 317 (2003), *app. den.*, 780 N.Y.S.2d 311, 2 N.Y.3d 705, 812 N.E.2d 1261 (2004).

129. *See, e.g.*, Sitaram, Inc. v. Bryan Ins. Agency, Inc., 104 So. 3d 524 (La. App.), *writ den.*, 103 So. 3d 375 (La. 2012); Seascape of Hickory Point Condo. Ass'n v. Associated Ins. Servs., 443 So. 2d 488 (Fla. 2d DCA 1984) (where condominium association contacted broker seeking to purchase insurance to cover its seawall in event of storm damage, but was told seawall insurance was not available, only to discover after suffering loss that coverage was available, court held association sufficiently alleged relationship between parties from which it could be said broker owed duty to exercise reasonable care in rendering advice on insurance matters because broker held itself out as professional insurance planner and had served association's insurance needs for several years, and association sought specific advice). *See also* Anthony v. Indep. Ins. Advisors, Inc., 56 V.I. 516 (2012) (association sued brokers and others over procurement of policy from insurer who was declared insolvent less than one month after policy was obtained and four months before property was damaged by hurricane and parties reached settlement). *Compare* Garcia v. Omaha Prop. & Cas. Ins. Co., 933 F. Supp. 1064, 1070 (S.D. Fla. 1995), *aff'd*, 95 F.3d 58 (11th Cir. 1996) (regardless of any duty on agent, there is no liability for negligence in failing to procure coverage that is unavailable).

130. *See, e.g.*, Royal Glen Condo. Ass'n v. S.T. Neswold & Assocs., 385 Ill. Dec. 137, 18 N.E.3d 137 (Ill. App. 2014) (where Illinois law provided no policy was to be issued to or renewed for condominium associations unless it met statutory requirements, that law imposed obligations on condominium associations and their boards, not on insurance producers; statute did not impose duty on association's insurance broker, giving rise to statutory cause of action).

131. Humphries v. Metropolitan Prop. & Cas. Ins. Co., 2016 N.Y. Misc. LEXIS 89 (Jan. 8, 2016). The association in *Humphries* attempted to sue the so called "insurance wholesaler," claiming it breached its common-law duty to obtain proper coverage. The wholesaler averred that was not an insurance agent and did not provide recommendations to either insurance agents or insureds. It appeared that the broker submitted an application on behalf of the association, however, the court

When an individual resident suffers a loss that is not compensated by the association insurer, can he or she bring an action against the agent for failure to obtain sufficient coverage? In a New York case a condominium unit owner whose unit was destroyed by fire sued the broker who obtained property coverage for the association. The broker contended it had a contractual relationship with the association, not the individual unit owners, and therefore, it was not in privity with the plaintiffs and could not be sued by them. Generally, the broker would owe no duty to one with whom it is not in privity of contract. The unit owner, however, argued there was privity because the governing board for the association acted as the agent for the unit owners in procuring insurance. The court did not agree and also rejected the assertion that the unit owner was an intended third-party beneficiary of the coverage.[132]

[2] Agency Billed Premiums

Common interest community governing board members unfamiliar with commercial insurance are often surprised to find that, unlike their automobile or homeowners insurance, which usually can be paid in installments, the entire premium for commercial property insurance has to be paid in advance. This is because commercial property insurance is "agency billed." That means the insurance company bills the association's broker for the full policy premium, and the broker then has to bill the association.[133] The broker typically has 30 to 90 days to pay the carrier. If it does not—either because of an oversight or because it purposefully holds the money—the insurer may issue a notice of cancellation. When this happens, it is probably time to find a new broker.

NOTE: To avoid any oversight by the broker, the association may want to contact the broker 30 days after making a payment to ask if the payment has been forwarded to the carrier.

§ 10.06 Duty of Community Association Managers to Obtain Coverage

It is not uncommon for common interest communities to delegate the responsibility for selection of insurance coverage to property management companies,[134]

concluded that did not preclude the possibility that the wholesaler had direct contact with the association and, therefore, the court refused to grant its motion to dismiss.

132. Mira v. Scottsdale Ins. Co., 2013 N.Y. Misc. LEXIS 5739 (Nov. 29, 2013).

133. http://www.trustevergreen.com/blog/2011/05/condo-coop-and-hoa-master-insurance-premium.

134. Breslau & O'Connor, *Subrogating Losses in Common Interest Communities*, at 12, available at: https://www.cozen.com/admin/files/publications/Breslau.pdf.

often called community association managers (CAMs). The members of the governing board should consider, however, that delegation of insurance responsibility to someone who is not an insurance professional may be a breach of their duties to the association.[135]

Any duty of the CAM to obtain insurance will likely be stated in the management agreement between the parties. What is the liability of the CAM for failure to exercise that duty properly? In a New York case, because of an error made over a decade earlier and uncorrected in the ensuing years, the original application misstated the square footage of the property. The association alleged that the failure of its manager to submit accurate information was a breach of its contractual duty to keep the property fully insured. The management company contended it was the responsibility of the insurance broker to obtain proper insurance. However, after reviewing the management contract, the court disagreed with the CAM and added that even if the responsibility for obtaining insurance coverage had been delegated to a broker, the CAM could be liable to the association because an agent is generally responsible to its principal—here, the association—for the conduct of a subagent, that is, the broker.[136]

A management company cannot be held to any greater duty than it contracts to provide. For example, a management agreement between a company and a condominium association provided the company would furnish whatever information the condominium association requested for the purpose of establishing the placement of insurance coverage and would aid and cooperate "in every reasonable way with respect to such insurance and any loss thereunder." That, concluded a court, did not obligate the management company to act as an advisor to the association on issues of insurance.[137] Moreover, where unit owners sued the company for failing to provide necessary information to the association's broker, the court found no liability because the complaint did not allege that the association asked the manager to furnish any information and all the management agreement required was that the manager furnish any information requested of it.[138]

---

135. Meskin, *The Community Association Insurance Puzzle: What Boards MUST DO and MUST AVOID to Assemble the Puzzle*, at 14 (Community Association Living, CAI Austin 2012) (noting that management agreements generally require association to indemnify management company and, therefore, if management company commits error regarding insurance it is probably not accountable to association; error and omissions policies issued to management companies usually expressly exclude claims arising out of insurance issues).

136. Lexington Vil. Condominium v. Scottsdale Ins. Co., 2013 N.Y. Misc. LEXIS 5745 (Nov. 29, 2013), *aff'd*, 2016 N.Y. App. Div. LEXIS 664 (Feb. 3, 2016).

137. Absent a duty to act as insurance advisor, the management company could not, said the court, be faulted for not providing advice. The court added that property managers should be able to rely on the agreed upon scope of duties when pricing their services.

138. Breedy-Fryson v. Towne Estates Condo. Owners Ass'n, 2010 Del. Ch. LEXIS 37 (Del. Ch. Feb. 25, 2010).

§ 10.07 The Policy Generally

The policy provided for residential common interest communities is generally called a commercial property policy. That might cause confusion for members of the governing board of a residential community because they may not think they operate a business. However, a *commercial* property policy is the correct one for a CIC.[139] Sometimes state common interest community legislation or a community's governing documents will refer to "casualty" or "hazard" insurance.[140] A property policy provides that coverage.

The basic and widely used commercial property policy was developed by the Insurance Services Office (ISO) and is called the Building and Personal Property Coverage Form (BPP).[141] A CIC will generally be provided with either that form[142] or the more particular Condominium Association Coverage Form (CAC).[143] As the name suggests, the CAC is tailored to the needs of condominium associations, but it might be employed for other types of associations,[144] particularly those that are functionally condominiums, that is, they have property owned by all the residents as tenants in common.[145]

---

139. One case that adds to any confusion is *Citizens Prop. Ins. Corp. v. Galeria Villas Condo. Ass'n*, 48 So. 3d 188, 190 (Fla. 3d DCA 2010), in which the court said that the condominium association obtained a "homeowners' insurance policy" issued by the carrier. What the court meant by a "homeowners' insurance policy" is unclear, but the typical homeowner's policy defines the "insured location" as the "residence premises." ISO Form HO 00 03 05 11, § A.6. It then defined "residence premises" as the one-family dwelling where the named insured resides, the two-, three-, or four-family dwelling where the named insured resides in at least one of the family units, or that part of any other building where the named insured resides and that is shown as the "residence premises." ISO Form HO 00 03 05 11, § A.11.

140. *See, e.g.*, N.D. Cent. Code § 47-04.1-07(1); S.D. Codified Laws § 43-15A-11(6). *See also Understanding Homeowner Association Insurance*, available at: http://www.hindmansanchez.com/resources/article/understanding-homeowner-association-insurance (casualty insurance is broad term used to describe property insurance).

141. *See* ISO Form CP 00 10 06 07.

142. *See, e.g.*, GlenBrook Patiohome, Owners Ass'n v. Lexington Ins. Co., 2011 U.S. Dist. LEXIS 14556 (S.D. Tex. Feb. 14, 2011) (referencing ISO Form CP 00 10). *Compare* Chateau Vill. N. Condo. Ass'n v. Am. Family Mut. Ins. Co., 170 F. Supp. 3d 1349 (D. Colo. 2016) ("Business Owners Policy" issued to condominium association).

143. *See* ISO Form CP 00 17 06 07. A condominium association might be issued a BPP. *See, e.g.*, Windward on Lake Conway Condo. Ass'n v. United Nat'l Ins. Co., 2015 U.S. Dist. LEXIS 153915 (M.D. Fla. Nov. 13, 2015) (describing association policy as Building and Personal Property Coverage Form, CP 00 10). Prior to the early 1970s when the Insurance Services Office (ISO) formulated standard master policies, there was some confusion over insurance for condominium associations. The ISO adopted several forms to which one will occasionally see reference in older cases. Rohan, Reskin & Sanchirico, *Recent Developments in the Field of Insurance for Condominium Projects*, 48 St. John's L. Rev. 1084, 1086 (1974). *See, e.g.*, SMP Condominium-Additional Policy Provisions MLB-29 reproduced in its entirety at pages 1094–97 in the appendix to the article.

144. The CAC would be used for an association whose bylaws say the association is responsible for insuring exterior portions of a building, for example, a roof.

145. *See, e.g.*, Huntingdon Ridge Townhouse Homeowners Ass'n v. QBE Ins. Corp., 2009 U.S. Dist. LEXIS 108558 (M.D. Tenn. Nov. 20, 2009) (floor trusses were integral part of foundation

The BPP and CAC are cited throughout this chapter. While they are largely similar, there are small specific differences,[146] and those are noted. Associations should be aware that new non-ISO policies are being developed by insurers, and some of those policies may combine property, liability, and other coverages.[147]

[1] Causes of Loss Forms

The basic policy form is supplemented with one of three Commercial Property Causes of Loss Forms: Special Form, Basic Form, or Broad Form. In a few states a particular form is required by statute.[148] The Special Form provides all-risk coverage.[149] As the name suggests, it covers any risk of direct physical loss

and, thus, were "common elements" under association bylaws and covenants, which required association to pay for repairs to common elements; noting that association had "condominium association insurance policy" from insurer). *See also* Vision I Homeowners Ass'n v. Aspen Specialty Ins. Co., 643 F. Supp. 2d 1356, 1359 (S.D. Fla. 2009) (homeowners association asserted that it was undisputed its insurance was a condominium policy while insurer stated policy was for a homeowners association).

146. *See Condominium Association Coverage Form* (Summit Business Media, 2013) (Condominium Association Coverage Form—CP 00 17—is identical in most respects to Building and Personal Property Coverage Form—CP 00 10—except in those places where special language is needed to adapt coverage to special needs of condominium association).

147. *See, e.g.*, Alexander v. Nat'l Fire Ins., 454 F.3d 214, 218 (3d Cir. Pa. 2006) (condominium association maintained insurance policy that provided it both first-party property coverage and third-party general liability coverage); Willing v. Cmty. Ass'n Underwriters of Am., Inc., 2007 U.S. Dist. LEXIS 48543 (W.D. Wash. July 5, 2007) (condominium policy included first-party property insurance for physical damage to the building and structures and third-party liability); Far Northwest Dev. Co., LLC v. Cmty. Ass'n of Underwriters of Am., Inc., 2006 U.S. Dist. LEXIS 79033 (W.D. Wash. Oct. 30, 2006) (policy issued to association contained property coverage and general liability insurance coverage). *See also V3 Launches Community Association Package Program* (Insurance Journal, May 27, 2015), available at: http://www.insurancejournal.com/news/national/2015/05/27/369573.htm. The article describes what it calls "V3 CAPP+," a package program for condominiums, homeowners associations, and cooperatives. It is a multi-line policy designed to insure the property, fidelity/crime loss, general liability, and directors and officers. The package is intended to make it easier for the governing boards of community associations to "buy one policy that addresses all of the typical exposures they encounter." It is enhanced to include key property sublimits that address machinery and equipment breakdown, employee dishonesty, landscaping, and elevator collision. It was initially available in 20 states including California, Illinois, and New York, but not Florida or Texas.

148. *See* Colo. Rev. Stat. 38-33.3-313(1)(a) (common interest community policy must be for broad form covered causes of loss); Haw. Rev. Stat. § 514B-143(a)(1) (condominium property insurance has to provide coverage for special form causes of loss); 765 Ill. Comp. Stat. 605/12(a)(1) (condominium property insurance coverage must be for special form causes of loss); Minn. Stat. § 515B.3-113(a)(1) (common interest community policy must be for broad form covered causes of loss); N.J. Stat. § 46:8B-14(d) (condominium association has to maintain coverage against loss by fire or other casualties normally covered under broad form fire and extended coverage insurance policies).

149. *See* ISO Form CP 10 30 06 07. All-risk coverage is common for CICs. *See, e.g.*, Buczek v. Contl. Cas. Ins. Co., 378 F.3d 284 (3d Cir. 2004); Biscayne Cove Condo. Ass'n v. QBE Ins. Corp., 951 F. Supp. 2d 1292, 1303 (S.D. Fla. 2013) (noting policy was Causes of Loss—Special Form CP 10 30 04 02); Ass'n of Apt. Owners of Imperial Plaza v. Fireman's Fund Ins. Co., 939 F. Supp. 2d

unless specifically excluded or limited by the policy.[150] All risk, however, does not mean "all loss." Coverage extends only to *fortuitous* losses, meaning occurring by chance or without deliberate intention.[151]

The Basic Form provides coverage for 11 named perils.[152] The Broad Form adds to the list of covered perils.[153] It is easy to determine which causes of loss form is incorporated into the policy. At the beginning of the Declarations Page—which precedes the policy—there is a section that says the policy consists of certain coverage parts. Below that it will specify the coverage cause of loss by saying special, broad, or basic. The practical difference between *all-risk* and *named perils* coverage is that in the case of the latter, the insured has the burden to show that

1059, 1061 (D. Haw. 2013) (insurer issued all-risks insurance policy to association); Seward Park Hous. Corp. v. Greater N.Y. Mut. Ins. Co., 43 A.D.3d 23, 836 N.Y.S.2d 99 (2007); DePasquale v. American Cas. Co. of Reading, PA, Inc., 764 A.2d 180 (R.I. 2000); Island Breakers v. Highlands Underwriters Ins. Co., 665 So. 2d 1084 (Fla. 3d DCA 1995) (condominium buildings were covered by commercial all-risk property insurance policy); Magnolia Square Homeowners Ass'n v. Safeco Ins. Co., 221 Cal. App. 3d 1049, 1054, 271 Cal. Rptr. 1, 2 (1990) (insurer provided coverage for association under all-risk property insurance policy); Tex-La Properties v. South State Ins. Co., 514 So. 2d 707 (La. App. 1987). *See also* Pheasantbrook Home Owners Ass'n v. Travelers Indem. Co., 2016 U.S. Dist. LEXIS 8414 (D. Utah Jan. 25, 2016); Raintree Vill. Condo. No. 11 Ass'n v. Great Am. Ins. Co., 2013 U.S. Dist. LEXIS 134907 (M.D. Fla. Sept. 20, 2013); Royal Marco Point 1 Condo. Ass'n v. QBE Ins. Corp., 2007 U.S. Dist. LEXIS 60940 (M.D. Fla. Aug. 14, 2007); Beverly Hills Condominium 1-12, Inc. v. Aspen Specialty Ins. Co., 2007 U.S. Dist. LEXIS 28999 (S.D. Fla. Jan. 31, 2007).

150. Steamboat Dev. Corp. v. Bacjac Indus., Inc., 701 P.2d 127 (Colo. App. 1985) (all-risk policy is special type of coverage extending to risks not usually covered under other insurance, and recovery is allowed for all losses, other than those resulting from willful or fraudulent act of insured, unless policy contains specific provision expressly excluding particular loss from coverage). *See also* Buczek v. Cont'l Cas. Ins. Co., 378 F.3d 284, 287 (3d Cir. 2004) (all-risks insurance is special type of insurance extending to risks not usually contemplated, and generally allows recovery for all fortuitous losses, unless policy contains specific exclusion expressly excluding loss from coverage); Amitie One Condo. Ass'n v. Nationwide Prop. & Cas. Ins. Co., 2010 U.S. Dist. LEXIS 129103 (M.D. Pa. Dec. 7, 2010) (where policy provided that covered causes of loss were risks of direct physical loss unless excluded or limited, policy language clearly indicated coverage for all losses to covered property that were not limited or excluded and policy, therefore, was all risk); Beverly Hills Condo. 1-12 v. Aspen Specialty Ins. Co., 2007 U.S. Dist. LEXIS 28999 (S.D. Fla. Jan. 31, 2007) (policy was "all-risk" policy that specifically covered hurricanes and hurricane force winds). The fact that the Condominium Association Coverage Form says the carrier will pay for direct physical loss of or damage to covered property caused by or resulting from *any* covered cause of loss does not make it an all-risk policy. The word "any" modifies "covered cause of loss," and the only way to read that clause is to understand that the insurer will pay for damage to property, when that damage was due to a specifically and explicitly named cause of loss, covered in the policy. To determine what losses are covered, one has to examine the covered cause of loss section of the policy. Where that section listed 11 discrete covered perils, the policy specified which perils were covered and it was a named perils policy. Royale Green Condo. Ass'n v. Aspen Specialty Ins. Co., 2009 U.S. Dist. LEXIS 24349 (S.D. Fla. Mar. 24, 2009).

151. Cozen, *Insuring Real Property*, § 2.02[2][b] (Matthew Bender & Co. 2015).

152. *See, e.g.*, ISO form CP 10 10 06 07.

153. *See, e.g.*, ISO form CP 10 20 06 07.

any loss was caused by one of the *named* perils,[154] after which the insurer has the burden to show one of the exclusions applies.[155] Under all-risk coverage, the insured is relieved of its burden, but the carrier is not.[156]

[2] Commercial Property Conditions Endorsement

There are a host of endorsements that may be added to the BPP or CAC. One that is always appended is the Commercial Property Conditions Endorsement.[157] It includes provisions voiding the policy for concealment, misrepresentation, or fraud by the insured, contractually limiting the time within suit may be filed against the insurer, and the "other insurance" clause that explains the results when there is any other insurance that is subject to the same plan, terms, conditions, and provisions.

[3] Standard Property Policy

A third policy that may be issued to common interest communities is the Standard Property Policy.[158] The principle difference between the Standard Property Policy and other commercial property policies is that it does not need to be supplemented with a causes of loss form or conditions endorsement. The causes of loss and conditions are included. Otherwise, the Standard Property Policy and BPP are very similar. If the insured opts for all the available causes of loss under the Standard Property Policy, it will be largely comparable to the Basic Form causes of loss. A generic Condominium Association Changes Endorsement can be added to the policy to adapt it to the particular needs of condominium

---

154. *See* Royale Green Condo. Ass'n v. Aspen Specialty Ins. Co., 2009 U.S. Dist. LEXIS 24349 (S.D. Fla. Mar. 24, 2009) (in named perils policy insured has burden of proving that damage occurred by covered cause).

155. *See, e.g.*, Burton v. State Farm Fire & Casualty Co., 533 F.2d 177, 178 (5th Cir. 1976) (under Alabama law insurance company is charged with burden of proving that particular loss falls within exclusionary clause of policy); Reynolds v. Shelter Mut. Ins. Co., 313 Ark. 145, 152, 852 S.W.2d 799, 803 (1993) (if insurer claims damages are excluded under its policy, it has burden of so proving, but that burden is not placed on insurer until insured has first made prima facie case that damages are covered under policy).

156. *See* Ass'n of Apt. Owners of Imperial Plaza v. Fireman's Fund Ins. Co., 939 F. Supp. 2d 1059, 1070 (D. Haw. 2013) (unlike specific peril policy, under all-risk policy insured does not have to prove peril proximately causing his or her loss was covered; policy covers all risks save those specifically excluded, and insurer has burden to prove that peril that proximately caused loss was specifically excluded from coverage of policy). *See also* Amitie One Condo. Ass'n v. Nationwide Prop. & Cas. Ins. Co., 2010 U.S. Dist. LEXIS 129103 (M.D. Pa. Dec. 7, 2010) (where policy was all risk, all association needed to show in its prima facie coverage case was that covered property suffered some type of fortuitous damage, after which burden shifts to insurer to establish applicable exception to coverage); Royale Green Condo. Ass'n v. Aspen Specialty Ins. Co., 2009 U.S. Dist. LEXIS 24349 (S.D. Fla. Mar. 24, 2009) (under all-risks policy, insured must prove only that damage to property occurred while policy was in effect, with burden then shifting to insurer to prove loss arose from cause excluded under policy).

157. *See, e.g.*, ISO Form CP 00 90 07 88.

158. *See, e.g.*, ISO Form CP 00 99 10 90.

associations and unit owners.[159] There are also state-specific endorsements to the policy that serve the same purpose.[160] The Standard Property Policy, with a Condominium Association Changes Endorsement, is used by some states in state-sponsored property insurance programs.[161]

[4] Omissions from Coverage

The BPP, CAC, and Standard Property Policy forms cover only loss of or damage to *property* at the premises described on the Declarations Page by any covered cause of loss. They do not cover *liability*, and certain types of property coverage are excluded, most notably equipment breakdown and flood. However, policies have been developed and are available to CICs that do provide general liability coverage and directors and officers liability coverage.[162] For example, one insurer has a multi-line policy specifically designed for common interest communities that provides general liability, directors and officers, and property coverage, including machinery and equipment breakdown coverage.[163] Additionally, an increasing number of carriers offer equipment breakdown coverage as an endorsement to a commercial property policy.[164] Currently it is difficult to obtain flood coverage as

---

159. *See, e.g.*, ISO form CP 17 99 06 95 (Commercial Property; Condominium Association Changes—Standard Property Policy); ISO Form CP 01 99 01 91 (Commercial Property; Condominium Association Coverage Condominium Law Provisions).

160. *See, e.g.*, ISO Form CP 01 39 10 12 (Connecticut Changes—Condominium Association Coverage—Condominium Law Provisions); ISO Form CP 01 48 10 12 (Texas Changes—Condominium Association Coverage—Condominium Law Provisions).

161. *See, e.g.*, the Illinois Fair Plan (https://www.illinoisfairplan.com/producers/commercial policyforms) and the North Carolina NCJUA-FAIR Plan and NCIUA-Coastal Property Insurance Pool (http://www.ncjua-nciua.org/html/forms.htm).

162. *See, e.g.*, Audubon Hill S. Condo. Ass'n v. Cmty. Ass'n Underwriters of Am., 82 Mass. App. Ct. 461, 463, 975 N.E.2d 458, 462, n.2 (2012) (policy covered property, premises liability, and loss or injury caused by acts or omissions of association directors and officers). *See also* Alexander v. Nat'l Fire Ins., 454 F.3d 214, 218 (3d Cir. 2006) (condominium association maintained policy providing both first-party property coverage and third-party general liability coverage); Chateau Vill. North Condo. Ass'n v. Am. Family Mut. Ins. Co., 2015 U.S. Dist. LEXIS 28411 (D. Colo. Mar. 9, 2015) (association purchased commercial property and liability insurance policy); Huntingdon Ridge Townhouse Homeowners Ass'n v. QBE Ins. Corp., 2009 U.S. Dist. LEXIS 108558 (M.D. Tenn. Nov. 20, 2009) (policy provided both property and D&O coverage).

163. *See V3 Launches Community Association Package Program* (Insurance Journal, May 27, 2015), available at: http://www.insurancejournal.com/news/national/2015/05/27/369573.htm (discussing multi-line policy package insuring property, crime, general liability and directors and officers for condominium and homeowner associations and cooperative apartments).

164. *See, e.g.*, Nat'l Union Fire Ins. Co. v. Travelers Indem. Co., 210 F. Supp. 2d 479 (S.D.N.Y. 2002) (property all-risk policy included Boiler and Machinery Endorsement that provided coverage for certain specified causes of loss that would otherwise be excluded under property coverage form); Litho Color, Inc. v. Pacific Emplrs. Ins. Co., 98 Wn. App. 286, 289, 991 P.2d 638, 640 (1999) (Boiler and Machinery endorsement to commercial property insurance policy). *See also* Nationwide Mut. Ins. Co. v. CG Stony Point Townhomes, LLC, 2015 U.S. Dist. LEXIS 5682 (E.D. Va. Jan. 15, 2015) (equipment breakdown secondary coverage).

an endorsement to a commercial property policy, especially if the property is in an area with a high risk for flooding.[165]

[5] Group Policies and Risk Pooling

The high cost of commercial property insurance would seem to make alternatives to traditional insurance—risk pooling and group coverage—attractive for common interest communities. However, as discussed below, a number of roadblocks effectively preclude these alternatives.

[a] Risk Pooling

State common interest community legislation typically requires associations to obtain property insurance. While these laws do not explicitly rule out self-insurance, their clear intent is to obligate associations to obtain coverage through an insurance company. Two states, however, specifically authorize "risk pooling" by common interest communities. Illinois has enacted a law entitled the Condominium and Common Interest Community Risk Pooling Trust Act.[166] It permits the governing boards of two or more condominium or common interest community associations to establish a trust fund to provide protection of the participating associations against the risk of financial loss because of damage to, destruction of, or loss of property.[167] The Florida Condominium Act allows an association, or group of associations, to provide adequate property insurance through a self-insurance fund and permits an association to provide property insurance coverage for a group of at least three communities created and operating under the Act or the laws governing cooperatives, homeowners associations, or timeshare estates, by obtaining and maintaining for those communities insurance sufficient to cover an amount equal to the probable maximum loss for the communities for a 250-year windstorm event.[168] According to the Florida Office of Insurance

165. Flood coverage is available through the National Flood Insurance Program. See Chapter 12.

166. 765 Ill. Comp. Stat. 605/12.1.

167. 765 Ill. Comp. Stat. 605/12.1(b). The trust fund has to be established and amended by a written instrument filed with and approved by the Director of Insurance before becoming effective. For an association to be a beneficiary of a trust fund, it has to be incorporated under the laws of Illinois. Trust funds are authorized to indemnify the association beneficiaries against the risk of loss from damage, destruction, or loss to property or imposition of legal liability as required or authorized under the Act or the association Declaration. Risks assumed by a trust fund may be pooled and shared with other trust funds established under the Act.

168. Fla. Stat. § 718.111(11)(a). A policy or program providing coverage may not be issued or renewed unless it has been reviewed and approved by the Office of Insurance Regulation. The review and approval has to include approval of the policy and related forms, approval of the rates, a determination that the approved loss model was accurately and appropriately applied to the insured structures to determine the 250-year probable maximum loss, and a determination that complete and accurate disclosure of all material provisions were provided to unit owners before execution of the agreement by the association.

Regulation, the Act seems to allow for insurance risk pooling arrangements, but none have existed in the state over the last decade.

"Reciprocal insurance exchanges" are a form of risk pooling. One commentary says that the "community association field is host to some large" reciprocal exchanges.[169] These exchanges are made up of entities known as subscribers that share risk in a plan administrated by an attorney in fact.[170]

[b] Group Policies

A policy that insures more than one common interest community would seem to be a way of obtaining the potential benefits of risk spreading without resorting to pooled self-insurance. These master or group policies are typically written in the name of a community association management company. They have the potential to offer lower premiums, but they also present pitfalls. One expert commentary identifies some of these: lack of insurable interest in the management company that could void the coverage, a loss in one community could affect all of them, coverage will likely not conform to the requirements of the governing documents, and the way the limits of coverage are structured could cause the association to be underinsured.[171]

The Office of General Counsel of the New York Department of Insurance was asked to issue an opinion on the legality of these arrangements. The question was whether an authorized property insurer could issue a group policy insuring unrelated cooperatives and the for-profit management company that managed them. The office said that would violate New York insurance law. A group policy can be written in New York for homogeneous groups of not-for-profit organizations that have been formed for purposes *other than obtaining insurance*. The inclusion of a single for-profit entity would disqualify the group from eligibility for group coverage; however, if the management company were not an insured, said the opinion, a "group" of qualifying not-for-profit cooperative organizations could obtain coverage on a group basis.[172] The opinion adds that there are circumstances in which an insurer may issue a single policy with a first named insured and additional insureds and that policy is not considered a "group policy" when the insurer issues a single policy with a first named insured and additional insureds in regard to, *inter alia*, shared interests, provided those shared interests exist among all additional insureds. For property insurance, "shared interests" means insurable interest in the additional insured's property, including

169. Treese & Rosenberry, *Insurance: How Community Associations Protect Themselves*, at 2 (CAI Press 2013).

170. https://en.wikipedia.org/wiki/Reciprocal_inter-insurance_exchange.

171. Treese & Rosenberry, *Insurance: How Community Associations Protect Themselves*, at 15 (CAI Press 2013).

172. OGC Opinion No: 00-05-02 (May 5, 2000) (New York Department of Insurance General Counsel Opinion).

legal interest in or control of that property, so that physical loss or damage to it may result in pecuniary loss to the first-named insured. The opinion concludes that the cooperatives at issue were unrelated, and hence would not have the requisite shared interests.

[c] Fannie Mae Requirements

The discussion of self-insurance or group policies is rendered largely academic by the requirements of Fannie Mae because in a common interest community that does not meet those requirements, mortgages will be effectively unavailable. Self-insurance or risk pooling is prohibited because, unless Fannie Mae approves an alternative arrangement in advance, the blanket property policy for condominium, cooperative, and planned unit development (PUD) projects has to be written by a carrier that meets prescribed rating requirements.[173] Further, Fannie Mae generally does not permit master/blanket insurance policies that provide coverage for multiple unaffiliated projects in a single policy.[174] It explains that the complexity of these policies can make it difficult to understand the terms of coverage and create operational risk for associations. The term "affiliated projects" means those that are under the same master association or share the use of common facilities that are owned either individually or as part of a master association or development, and those lacking these characteristics, even if they are managed by the same management company, are not considered to be affiliated projects.

[6] State-Sponsored Insurance

The path for state-sponsored property insurance programs was paved in 1968 by federal legislation passed in that year.[175] Under that law, states could enact fair access to insurance requirements (FAIR) plans.[176] These programs were state-subsidized insurers of "last resort" for those too "high risk" to obtain insurance in the voluntary market.[177] They have proven to be particularly important to

173. Fannie Mae Single Family Selling Guide § B7-3-01 (Nov. 3, 2015).

174. https://selling-guide.fanniemae.com/Selling-Guide/Origination-thru-Closing/Subpart-B7-Insurance/Chapter-B7-3-Property-and-Flood-Insurance/There are exceptions. *See* § 9.02[2], *supra*. *See also Fannie Mae Single Family Selling Guide* § B7-3-03 (Dec. 14, 2022) (acceptable property policies have to provide coverage for either individual project or multiple *affiliated* projects).

175. 12 U.S.C. §§ 1749bbb, *et seq*. The popular name of the legislation was the Urban Property Protection and Riot Reinsurance Act of 1968. It was amended by the National Insurance Development Act of 1975. *See* P.L. 94-13, 89 Stat. 69 (Apr. 8, 1975).

176. Firemen's Ins. Co. v. Washington, 483 F.2d 1323, 1330 (1973). *See also* Ondera, *Testing the Waters: The South Carolina Coastal Captive Insurance Act as Part of a Multifaceted Approach to the Coastal Insurance Conundrum*, 59 S.C. L. Rev. 599 (2008).

177. Randlett, *Fair Access to Insurance Requirements: Do "FAIR" Property Insurance Premiums for Individual Coastal Property Owners in Massachusetts Equate with Fairness to the Greater Market?*, 15 Ocean & Coastal L.J. 127, 135 (2010).

residents of coastal states prone to major storms.[178] The federal program ended decades ago,[179] but over 30 states and the District of Columbia still have FAIR plans.[180] The possibility of encountering state-sponsored property insurance is increased by the fact that some of the best-known programs are in three of the five largest states: California,[181] Florida,[182] and Texas.[183] A discussion of these plans is beyond the scope of this treatise, but much has been written about them elsewhere.[184] There are two things associations should know about these plans. First, the policies obtained under them may be standard ISO property forms or may be other policy forms.[185] Second, questions may arise about the extent to which a policyholder may bring suit under a state-sponsored insurance program. That is because in general, governments have "sovereign immunity," meaning they cannot be sued. That proscription generally does not apply to breach of contract actions, and states have adopted tort claims acts that waive their immunity in certain circumstances for non-contract actions. The FAIR program legislation itself may address the right of policyholders to bring suit. To determine their rights under a FAIR program policy, associations need to consult with their insurance broker and attorney.

---

178. Randlett, *Fair Access to Insurance Requirements: Do "FAIR" Property Insurance Premiums for Individual Coastal Property Owners in Massachusetts Equate with Fairness to the Greater Market?*, 15 Ocean & Coastal L.J. 127, 135 (2010).

179. Gilmore, *Insurance Redlining & the Fair Housing Act: The Lost Opportunity of* Mackey v. Nationwide Insurance Companies, 34 Cath. U.L. Rev. 563, 579 (1985) (program terminated on Nov. 30, 1983).

180. Randlett, *Fair Access to Insurance Requirements: Do "FAIR" Property Insurance Premiums for Individual Coastal Property Owners in Massachusetts Equate with Fairness to the Greater Market?*, 15 Ocean & Coastal L.J. 127, 135 (2010); Ondera, *Testing the Waters: The South Carolina Coastal Captive Insurance Act as Part of a Multifaceted Approach to the Coastal Insurance Conundrum*, 59 S.C. L. Rev. 599 (2008); Gilmore, *Insurance Redlining & the Fair Housing Act: The Lost Opportunity of Mackey v. Nationwide Insurance Companies*, 34 Cath. U.L. Rev. 563, 579 (1985).

181. *See* Cal. Ins. Code §§ 10089.5, *et seq.* (California Earthquake Authority).

182. *See* Fla. Stat. § 627.351(6) (Citizens Property Insurance Corporation).

183. *See* Tex. Ins. Code §§ 2210.001, *et seq.* (Texas Windstorm Insurance Association).

184. *See* MacGregor, *An Overview of Seven State-Sponsored Property Insurance Programs*, 45–110; New Appleman on Insurance: Current Critical Issues in Insurance Law (Fall 2011); Randlett, *Fair Access to Insurance Requirements: Do "FAIR" Property Insurance Premiums for Individual Coastal Property Owners in Massachusetts Equate with Fairness to the Greater Market?*, 15 Ocean & Coastal L.J. 127 (2010); Ondera, *Testing the Waters: The South Carolina Coastal Captive Insurance Act as Part of a Multifaceted Approach to the Coastal Insurance Conundrum*, 59 S.C. L. Rev. 599 (2008); Burner, DeLargy & McCandless, *Reforming the Texas Windstorm Insurance Association: The Politics and Policy of Catastrophe Risk Sharing*, 19 F.O.R.C.J. 16 (2008); Graditor, *Responsibility for the Restoration of the Hurricane Insurance Industry: Business Proposal or State Solution?*, 31 Nova L. Rev. 527 (2007).

185. *See* Prahl, *Protective Safeguards Endorsements—Issues and Implications*, available at: http://adjustersinternational.com/publications/adjusting-today/vacancy-occupancy-clauses-protective-safeguards-endorsements/7/ (Standard Fire Policy [SFP] used prior to mid-1980s appears in many state FAIR plan policies).

[7] Retaining Expired Policies

Common interest communities often dispose of old documents in their files on a periodic basis. This process may be initiated by the community association management company and may even be one of the services the contract between it and the association provides. When the documents are culled, should the association retain old property policies?

Typically, a commercial property policy has a term of one year and sometimes two years.[186] However, potentially covered losses can appear months or years after the precipitating incident. For occurrence policies, claims can be made after the policy period ends; the claims process will be easier if the association maintains records of the policies it has previously had in place, the name of the carrier, and the time period of each policy.

When an association sues an insurer, it has the initial burden of showing coverage,[187] and that is more difficult to do without the policy. It is often held that a copy of the policy needs to be attached to the complaint in a suit against the insurer,[188] although where the policy cannot be produced courts generally will allow evidence of its contents to be introduced.[189] Gathering and introducing that evidence takes time and is an additional expenditure. Clearly, it is best if the

---

186. *See, e.g.*, Holden Manor Homeowners Ass'n v. Safeco Ins. Co. of Am., 2016 U.S. Dist. LEXIS 78821 (W.D. Wash. June 16, 2016) (policy that covered association was effective Aug. 27, 1980, to Aug. 27, 1982); Ass'n of Unit Owners v. State Farm Fire & Cas. Co., 670 F. Supp. 2d 1156 (D. Or. 2009) (property policy was effective Jan. 1, 2005, through Jan. 1, 2007).

187. *See, e.g.*, Borough of Sayreville v. Bellefonte Ins. Co., 320 N.J. Super. 598, 605, 728 A.2d 225, 228 (1998); Gold Fields Am. Corp. v. Aetna Cas. & Sur. Co., 173 Misc. 2d 901, 904, 661 N.Y.S.2d 948, 950 (1997) (policyholder has burden of proof on issue of existence of policy and its terms; where policyholder asserts it has lost policy, problem is for policyholder to address).

188. *See, e.g.*, Karaskiewicz v. Allstate Ins. Co. (*In re* Am. Arbitration Ass'n Arbitration), 109 Ill. App. 2d 370, 372, 248 N.E.2d 756, 758 (1969) (remanded to lower court with directions to strike complaint for failure to attach copy of insurance contract); State Farm Mut. Auto. Ins. Co. v. Jones, 98 Ga. App. 46, 56, 104 S.E.2d 725, 733 (1958) (pleadings in action against insurer required that copy of policy be attached or that petition allege language contained in policy).

189. *See, e.g.*, Rubenstein v. Royal Ins. Co. of Am., 44 Mass. App. Ct. 842, 846, 694 N.E.2d 381, 384 (1998) (existence of insurance policy is generally proven by documentary evidence; that policy has been lost or destroyed does not mean that its existence and contents may not be reconstructed from business records, underwriter's folios, or billings of insurer to insured); Borough of Sayreville v. Bellefonte Ins. Co., 320 N.J. Super. 598, 605, 728 A.2d 225, 228 (1998) (nothing in record suggested missing policies were different from others issued later that were available); Fraser v. Metropolitan Life Ins. Co., 165 Wash. 667, 669, 5 P.2d 978, 980 (1931) (where evidence was introduced that policy had been lost or mislaid and could not be found, form of policy was offered and received into evidence as testimony showed it was same form of policy as had been issued to insured). *See generally* Jones, *No Policy, No Problem? How Insureds Are Finding Coverage Even Though They Can't Find Their Policies*, 50 Drake L. Rev. 611 (2002). The author notes that claims for breach of insurance agreements are based on allegations of a breach of a written contract and much of the information to complete the policy is unique to the specific insured: coverage limits, locations for which coverage is provided, and the period during which coverage exists. The written contract is, therefore, critical to determining the existence and scope of coverage.

association can produce the actual policy.[190] Thus, there is nothing to be gained by disposing of old policies, and there may be a benefit to retaining them.

One expert recommends keeping expired copies policies for at least five years after their expiration and preferably ten years.[191] Here is another reason for the association to have an insurance committee or governing board member designated to be responsible for insurance matters. That committee or board member can make sure expired policies are properly stored.

Record retrieval is as important as record retention. The association may have retained expired policies, but if no one can find them, they may as well have been destroyed. An expert asserts that it is the responsibility of the governing board to assure that records are adequately maintained.[192] As many associations were established long before the advent of digital records, in cases where hard copies are the only form of record, the association should have a storage facility for important documents that is separate from any facility maintained by the management company, and it should not be in the home or garage of a member of the association but in an area accessible to future board members, either an off-site leased facility or a segregated and secure area that is part of the common areas of the community, for example, a clubhouse. It is also important that there be an index or cataloging system that makes it easy to find a specific document in the collection of retained material.

Record retention and retrieval can be made easier in the age of electronic documents. Newer documents are typically readily available in electronic formats. Older documents can be scanned to create an electronic copy. That copy can be kept on the association computer with a backup retained on a flash drive. CAMs often scan the insurance policies issued to the associations they manage and post them along with other documents on a website so that members of the association can view them. The association can retain the electronic copy of the policies each year. Storage of hardcopies of policies is a challenge as collectively the various policies can total several hundred pages each year. Electronic copies take up little space, but some of the same cautions that apply to hardcopies also apply to electronic ones. The sole electronic copy should not be in the possession

190. One problem is that a court may allow use of a sample policy of the type that was apparently issued by the carrier at the time the policy in question was issued. *See, e.g.*, Gold Fields Am. Corp. v. Aetna Cas. & Sur. Co., 173 Misc. 2d 901, 906, 661 N.Y.S.2d 948, 951 (1997) (courts have permitted use of specimen policies to show what terms of policy at issue were). That policy, however, will not contain the information on the Declarations Page that may be critically important, for example, the limits of insurance. Additionally, use of a sample policy will not help determine the specific endorsements that were a part of the actual policy.

191. Wick, *Record Retention Means Future Protection*, Common Ground (CAI July/Aug. 1990).

192. https://pl.cpa/publication/records-retention-guide.

of the management company. The association should have its own copy. When the electronic copies are on a flash drive, they should be kept in a common area, not in the home of a board member.

§ 10.08 The Application

The application form will likely be an Association for Cooperative Operations Research and Development (ACORD) form used for commercial insurance applications.[193] The basic application will ask for some of this information:

- the first named insured;
- mailing address of the first named insured;
- whether the first named insured is a corporation, limited liability company, non-profit organization, or trust;
- any other named insureds;
- location of the premises;
- whether the named insured owns the building, is a tenant, or has some other interest in the building;
- the number of square feet the named insured occupies and the number of square feet open to the public;
- a description of the operation of the named insured;
- whether the nature of the business is "condominiums," but not whether the insured is a cooperative or homeowners association;
- whether any policy or coverage has been declined, cancelled, or not renewed during the preceding three years;
- whether any past losses or claims relate to sexual abuse, discrimination, or negligent hiring;
- whether any applicant has been indicted or convicted for a crime of fraud, bribery, or arson;
- whether there are any uncorrected fire or safety code violations;
- whether the applicant has had a foreclosure, repossession, or bankruptcy in the previous five years;
- whether there has been a judgment or lien in the previous five years;
- prior carrier information; and
- the loss history.[194]

---

193. ACORD stands for Association for Cooperative Operations Research and Development. It is a global, non-profit organization serving the insurance and related industries that, among other things, publishes standardized forms. https://www.acord.org/about/Pages/default.aspx. These forms have been described as the "gold standard" and are widely used by agencies.

194. *See* ACORD 125 (2013/01).

The first question for common interest communities to answer with regard to insurance applications is who will contact the broker to make the application and sign it? It may be an officer of the CIC[195] or the CAM. In many cases the manager will be the person best equipped to answer the questions on the application; however, if the CAM represents the CIC, the governing board should obtain a copy of the application and review it for accuracy.[196] The CAM may have provided incorrect information to the agent,[197] or the agent may have obtained inaccurate data from a prior application.[198]

The contents of the application—or omissions from it—are important because the insurer will base decisions on it,[199] and misrepresentations in the application may be a basis for the insurer to deny coverage or, more importantly, rescind the policy.[200] Generally, an insurer has no duty to investigate the

---

195. In a curious argument, an association contended an application was "blank" because it was never signed by it, but only its agent. Therefore, it argued, any misrepresentations in the application could not be attributed to it. The application was signed by the president of the association. The court characterized the association's contention as raising "troubling agency concerns," by which it probably meant that the association could only act through its agents and the authority of the president of an organization to bind it is not generally a matter of dispute. Thus, the court found that any misrepresentation in the application was "squarely and unequivocally" that of the association. Caribbean I Owners' Ass'n v. Great Am. Ins. Co., 600 F. Supp. 2d 1228 (S.D. Ala. 2009).

196. The governing board should remember that the manager is its agent, and it will, therefore, generally be bound by the actions of the manager on behalf of the association. *See, e.g.*, Biscayne Cove Condo. Ass'n v. QBE Ins. Corp., 971 F. Supp. 2d 1121, 1126 (S.D. Fla. 2013).

197. *See, e.g.*, Towers Condo. Ass'n v. C.E. Brathwaite & Assocs., 40 V.I. 33 (1999) (manager signed application prepared by broker without providing any additional information; application lacked information about prior claim, and manager professed to have no awareness of that prior claim).

198. *See, e.g.*, Lexington Vil. Condominium v. Scottsdale Ins. Co., 2013 N.Y. Misc. LEXIS 5745 (Nov. 29, 2013), *aff'd*, 2016 N.Y. App. Div. LEXIS 664 (Feb. 3, 2016), where the agent included building square footage on an application obtained from an application for the prior policy and that information later proved to be incorrect.

199. For example, one commentary explains that information about the property will be provided to the underwriter for the insurer who will enter the data into a Cost Estimator System that calculates an estimated Replacement Cost Value. *Confused over Insurance? Five Common Questions* (Association Times 2010), available at: http://associationtimes.associaliving.com/2010/11/confuse-doverinsurancefivecommonquestions/. Obviously, if the data the underwriter receives from the association is inaccurate, so too will be the estimate.

200. *See, e.g.*, Towers Condo. Ass'n v. C.E. Brathwaite & Assocs., 40 V.I. 33 (1999), where a representative of the condominium signed an application the agent filled in based on information previously supplied. The agent allegedly did not ask if the condominium had suffered any losses in the interim, which in fact it had. The insurer refused coverage because the failure to disclose that loss on the application constituted a material misrepresentation by the condominium association. The court said that when the association representative signed the application, it constituted a failure by the association to disclose information pertaining to its prior loss. However, an issue of material fact remained as to whether the agent was negligent in its handling of the application and whether the association had an obligation to ascertain whether the information given was current and accurate as of the date the application was signed. Additionally, there was also an issue of fact regarding whether the failure to disclose was made with intent to deceive.

statements on application and to verify their accuracy; instead, the insured has a duty to divulge fully all he or she knows.[201]

NOTE: When coverage is obtained from a particular carrier and then renewed year after year, the application may have been filled out many years ago.[202] That presents a potential problem for common interest communities because, with turnover in the membership of the governing board, no board member may know what information is in the application and whether it was accurate originally or remains accurate.

The issue of possible misstatements on an application is illustrated by an Alabama condominium case. The building had minor water intrusion problems soon after it was built, and those and other construction issues led it to sue the builder. In neither its original application nor renewal applications did the association reveal the leaks or the litigation. Several years later the building was seriously damaged by a hurricane. The insurer refused to pay, and the association sued it for breach of contract. The insurer defended by asserting that material omissions in the application and renewal processes entitled it to rescind the policy as a matter of law. Fortunately for the association, the court said no questions or instructions in the applications specifically prompted an applicant to enumerate all known construction defects or maintenance problems in the building, to set forth the history of water intrusion, or to disclose whether it was or had previously been involved in litigation with the builder over alleged construction defects. The insurer countered that the application asked the applicant to enter all claims or losses or occurrences that may have given rise to claims for the previous five years. The court, however, found it was not obvious, as a matter of law, that "claims or losses" would encompass the information at issue, and given the ambiguities in the application it could not find as a matter of law that the failure of the association to disclose the construction defects and maintenance issues as "claims or losses" amounted to a misrepresentation or omission supporting rescission.[203]

NOTE: One question that does not appear on applications is, what requirements do your governing documents contain regarding property coverage? The savvy broker will be aware that there may be requirements in the documents and will want copies of them. Nonetheless, when applying for coverage, the association should provide copies of the pertinent document provisions to the broker and discuss with him or her obtaining coverage that conforms to the document mandates.

201. American Way Cellular, Inc. v. Travelers Property Casualty Co. of America, 216 Cal. App. 4th 1040, 1050–51, 157 Cal. Rptr. 3d 385, 394 (2013).

202. Lexington Vil. Condominium v. Scottsdale Ins. Co., 2013 N.Y. Misc. LEXIS 5745 (Nov. 29, 2013), *aff'd*, 2016 N.Y. App. Div. LEXIS 664 (Feb. 3, 2016) (application over decade old).

203. Caribbean I Owners' Ass'n v. Great Am. Ins. Co., 600 F. Supp. 2d 1228 (S.D. Ala. 2009).

§ 10.09 Binders or Temporary Insurance

A binder is a contract for temporary insurance that is not itself an insurance policy but that provides interim insurance from the date of an application until either the policy is issued or the carrier declines to provide coverage.[204] A document that meets the requirements for a binder does not necessarily need to be called a binder to be enforceable as one.[205] Generally, the binder includes the provisions of the policy that ordinarily would be issued by the insurance company.[206] Sometimes the binder will expressly incorporate by reference the terms of the policy to be issued.[207] To avoid any doubt about temporary coverage, the insured should ask the broker to explain the coverage that will be in place until the policy is issued. In any event, it is important to have the policy issued as quickly as possible.

§ 10.10 Premium Financing

Property insurance premiums can be substantial. The policy is usually "agency billed," meaning the entire premium has to be paid up-front, rather than in installments.[208] This presents a dilemma for common interest communities, almost all of which receive all, or a substantial portion, of their income from assessments paid by their residents on a monthly, or perhaps a quarterly, basis. If the CIC starts out without the funds to pay for the initial property insurance premium, they usually remain behind, unable to set aside enough money to pay the insurance bill when it becomes due. The solution is premium financing.

A "premium finance agreement" is one in which an insured contracts with a premium finance company for that company to pay the amount advanced to the insurer or broker for payment of premiums on the policy.[209] The insured then pays the premium finance company, usually in monthly installments.[210]

---

204. United States v. Renzi, 769 F.3d 731, 753–54 (9th Cir. 2014) (binders give insured temporary coverage while application for policy is being processed or while formal policy is being prepared); Coastal Hardware & Rental Co., LLC v. Certain Underwriters at Lloyds, London, 120 So. 3d 1017, 1023 (Miss. App. 2013).

205. Chicago Title Ins. Co. v. AMZ Ins. Services, Inc., 188 Cal. App. 4th 401, 115 Cal. Rptr. 3d 707 (2010).

206. Hershaw v. Farm & City Ins. Co., 32 Kan. App. 2d 684, 694, 87 P.3d 360, 367 (2004) (binder should include provisions of policy that ordinarily would have been issued).

207. Alea London, Ltd. v. Bono-Soltysiak Enters., 186 S.W.3d 403, 410 (Mo. App. 2006).

208. Green, *Shopping for Insurance; What Do Boards Need to Know?* (Cooperator, Aug. 2011). *See also* http://www.trustevergreen.com/blog/2011/05/condo-coop-and-hoa-master-insurance-premium (condominium, cooperative, or HOA master policy is agency billed, meaning carrier bills insurance broker full policy premium; broker has to bill client association and usually has 30 to 90 days to pay full premium to carrier).

209. KMJ Servs. v. Hood, 115 So. 3d 34 (La. App. 2013).

210. Mangram, *Insurance Premium Financing; a Great Solution for Condo and Homeowner Associations*, available at: www.flcaj.com/pdfdocs/insurance premium.pdf (insurance premium financing allows association to pay premium over equal installments within 11 months).

There are several disadvantages to premium financing. First, the premium finance company does not ordinarily pay the entire premium. The association still has to pay a portion—typically 20 percent—of the bill itself.[211] Second, like other lenders, the premium finance company charges interest on the money it loans and it can be substantial; even in a low interest rate market it can be as high as 10 percent.[212] A third problem with a premium financing arrangement is that the agreement will invariably grant the company a power of attorney allowing it to cancel the policy if it is not paid.[213] Thus, if the association's management company or accountant fails to issue the monthly check, or the check is sent but the finance company does nt receive it or properly record its receipt, the policy could be cancelled without the association knowing of the cancellation. That should not happen, because premium finance companies are heavily regulated and state laws require them to notify the insured of their intent to cancel a policy.[214] However, not everything that is supposed to happen actually happens. The fact that the association has remedies against the premium finance company is cold comfort if it has to litigate to obtain compensation for a loss that occurred after the policy was cancelled.[215]

Because of the disadvantages of premium financing, associations may want to free themselves of it. One way to do that would be a one-time special

211. Green, *Shopping for Insurance; What Do Boards Need to Know?* (Cooperator, Aug. 2011).

212. One large insurance agency that specializes in coverage for commercial buildings says financing companies bill monthly or quarterly with a 6 to 10 percent interest rate. *See* http://www.trustevergreen.com/blog/2011/05/condo-coop-and-hoa-master-insurance-premium. A commentary agrees that 6 to 10 percent is the usual range of rates. Green, *Shopping for Insurance; What Do Boards Need to Know?* (Cooperator, Aug. 2011). Other observers are more hopeful, estimating typical insurance premium financing rates at between 2 and 6 percent. Mangram, *Insurance Premium Financing; a Great Solution for Condo and Homeowner Associations*, available at: www.flcaj.com/pdf docs/insurance premium.pdf.

213. *Consider* Western States Land & Cattle Co. v. Lexington Ins. Co., 459 N.W.2d 429 (S.D. 1990) (cancellation by agent of insured—including premium financing agency—is cancellation by insured and not by insurer, so statutory restrictions on cancellation by *insurer* would not apply).

214. *See, e.g.*, Fla. Stat. § 627.848(1)(a)1 (not less than ten days' written notice must be mailed to each insured shown on premium finance agreement of intent of premium finance company to cancel insurance contract unless defaulted installment payment is received within ten days); 215 Ill. Comp. Stat. 5/513a11(b) (not less than ten days' written notice must be mailed to named insured of intent of premium finance company to cancel insurance contract unless default is cured within ten-day period); N.Y. Bank Law § 576(1)(a) (no insurance contract may be cancelled pursuant to premium finance agreement unless not less than ten days' written notice is mailed to insured at his or her last known address as shown on records of premium finance agency of intent of that agency to cancel insurance contract unless default is cured within that ten-day period and at least three days for mailing of notice is added to ten-day notice; copy of notice of intent to cancel must also be mailed to insurance agent or broker).

215. *See, e.g.*, Fla. Stat. § 627.848(1)(f) (if insurance contract is cancelled by insurer on receipt of copy of cancellation notice from premium finance company, and if premium finance company failed to provide notice to insured, insured has cause of action against premium finance company for damages caused by that failure to provide notice).

assessment that would collect the funds needed to pay the entire premium up front.[216] After that, the regular assessments can include a proportionate share of the premium so that the association will always have enough to pay the premium when it becomes due.

§ 10.11 Declarations Page

The Declarations Page—also known as the Declarations, the "dec page," or the "dec sheet"—is a part of the policy. Despite the name, in a commercial property policy it is usually *several* pages of critical information. The information typically found on the Declarations Page includes the duration of the policy and its inception date,[217] the policy number, the name of the insurer, the broker's name, the name of the insured, the "business" description of the insured, the mailing address of the insured, a description of the premises, a list of forms and endorsements, the premium amount, the deductible, the amount of coverage or limit of liability, and optional coverages.

When the association receives the policy, it is advisable for the governing board or any insurance committee to review it for accuracy. The board or committee should make sure, for example, that the name of the association is its legal name and that the premises intended to be covered are accurately described.

[1] Named Insured

In a common interest community, the named insured would typically be the association or, in the case of a cooperative, the corporation that owns the building. The name of the insured as it appears on the Declarations Page should be the legal name of the association in the governing documents, not a name by which it is popularly known.[218] It is also important in a CIC to take into account any layers of associations. For example, a community may consist of several condominium or townhouse associations, a recreation association, and a master or umbrella association, all with similar sounding names.[219] Each of these will have

216. Should the association decide to set aside funds to cover a future premium payment, there may be tax consequences. This topic is beyond the scope of this treatise. The association should consult the association attorney or accountant.

217. Typically, the term of a property policy is one year, but it can be longer. *See, e.g.*, Holden Manor Homeowners Ass'n v. Safeco Ins. Co. of Am., 2016 U.S. Dist. LEXIS 78821 (W.D. Wash. June 16, 2016) (two-year term).

218. *Consider* Far Northwest Dev. Co., LLC v. Cmty. Ass'n of Underwriters of Am., Inc., 2006 U.S. Dist. LEXIS 79033 (W.D. Wash. Oct. 30, 2006), where the policy was issued to the "Somerset Village Townhomes Condominium," rather than the association. It was argued that the condominium was merely a building and, therefore, not a legal entity capable of owning anything. The court found it clear that the intent of the parties was to provide coverage to the association and, therefore, the association was the named insured regardless of the Declarations Page.

219. *See, e.g.*, Certain Underwriters at Lloyd's v. Am. Family Mut. Ins. Co., 2007 U.S. Dist. LEXIS 66599 (D. Colo. Sept. 10, 2007), where property policies were issued by two different

distinct responsibilities and property interests spelled out in their respective governing documents. It is important to determine that the Declarations Page lists the proper association as the named insured.[220]

NOTE: Sometimes the community association management company is listed on a property policy as the named insured.[221] A management company, however, ordinarily has no insurable interest in the property it manages,[222] but commentators warn that while a management company can be added as an additional insured, they should never be listed first in the *named insured* section.[223]

One question that arises is whether the members of the association—or tenant/shareholders in the case of a cooperative—are additional insureds. In general, the fact that an association is the named insured does not mean its members are automatically additional insureds.[224] The status of members of the association is a topic about which there is considerable debate.[225] The governing documents and the law of the state where the association is located are two factors that can

---

insurers. One policy was for the "Washington Park Townhouse Association," and the other was for the "Washington Park Swim & Tennis Townhome Association." The court noted that although the named insured in each policy was different, the parties agreed that the insured under each policy was the same.

220. Note that courts may look beyond the actual name listed on the Declarations Page to the intent of the parties. *See, e.g.*, El-Ad 250 West LLC v. Zurich Am. Ins. Co., 2016 N.Y. Misc. LEXIS 1239, 2016 NY Slip Op. 30595(U) (N.Y. Sup. Ct. Mar. 30, 2016) (if policy inaccurately recites party for whom it was intended, that coverage for subject risk would be available, that intended insured could receive coverage, despite not being named in policy; equitable reformation of policy could be employed to correct obvious inadvertent misidentification of named insured).

221. *See, e.g.*, Equinox on the Battenkill Mgmt. Ass'n v. Phila. Indem. Ins. Co., 125 A.3d 893 (Vt. 2015) (policy was between management association that managed condominium complex and insurer; court found possibility of coverage for condominium property and question of insurable interest was not raised); Belaire at Boca, LLC v. Ass'ns Ins. Agency, Inc., 2007 U.S. Dist. LEXIS 55252 (S.D. Fla. July 31, 2007) (property management company placed as named insured on policy insuring condominium property). *See also* DiMillo v. Travelers Prop. Cas. Co. of Am., 789 F. Supp. 2d 194, 197 (D. Me. 2011) (named insureds were association and its property manager); Shoreline Towers Condo. Owners Ass'n v. Zurich Am. Ins. Co., 196 F. Supp. 2d 1210 (S.D. Ala. 2002) (general management company for condominium association was named insured and association was listed in named insured endorsement).

222. *See* Treese & Rosenberry, *Insurance: How Community Associations Protect Themselves*, at 15 (CAI Press 2013).

223. *Property Manager as Named Insured on Condominium Policy* (Apr. 2014) (first named insured on policy controls it and gets paid first).

224. Ryan v. Travelers Indem. Co., 2013 U.S. Dist. LEXIS 91539, at *10 (E.D. Cal. June 27, 2013).

225. *Compare* Peters v. Lexington Ins. Co., 836 F. Supp. 2d 1117 (D. Haw. 2011) (language under which some property in individual units was covered by association policy did not state that those unit owners thereby become insureds) *with* Craig v. Sandy Creek Condominium Ass'n, Inc., 2009 N.C. App. LEXIS 766, *aff'd*, 197 N.C. App. 628, 680 S.E.2d 272 (June 16, 2009) (North Carolina law required association to purchase insurance as trustee for each unit owner and did not impose "absurd requirement" that every unit owner be named individually as insured; named

determine the status of the members of the association. An association could wait for a court to weigh the factors and reach a decision, or more prudently, it could ask the insurer to state its position.

Mortgagees of individual owners may also want to be additional insureds on the association policy. A mortgagee has obvious rights that it wants to protect, but typically those rights are protected by statute and/or the governing documents.[226] Experts assert that mortgagees of owners should not also be additional insureds under the association policy and that the mortgagee should be satisfied with a Certificate of Insurance proving the existence of the coverage.[227]

[2] Description of Premises

The premises may simply be described by the address of the association. Where the property consists of more than one building and the association intends all of them to be insured under the policy, it is important to determine if the description of the premises is adequate to accomplish the intended purpose.[228] If there

---

insured was association, and it was composed of everyone who owned any interest in a condominium unit).

226. *See, e.g.*, Uniform Common Interest Ownership Act § 2-119(a) (Declaration may require that all or specified number or percentage of lenders who hold security interests encumbering units or who have extended credit to association have to approve specified actions of unit owners or association as condition to effectiveness of those actions); Uniform Common Interest Ownership Act § 3-113(e) (insurance trustee or association must hold any insurance proceeds in trust for association, unit owners, and lien holders as their interests may appear); Uniform Common Interest Ownership Act § 3-113(g) (insurers must issue certificates or memoranda of insurance on "request made in a record," to any unit owner or holder of security interest).

227. *See* https://www.iamagazine.com/strategies/read/2016/05/20/condo-associations-and-additional-insureds-who-belongs-on-the-policy.

228. *See* Cozen, *Insuring Real Property*, § 2.05[1] (Matthew Bender & Co. 2015) (because description of covered property will limit coverage to described premises, it is important that description is accurate; if insured premises contains more than one building, particular buildings for which coverage applies must be clearly delineated and failure to use care in specifying building or buildings to be covered may result in no coverage). *See, e.g.*, JJD Assocs. of Palm Beach, Ltd. v. Am. Empire Surplus Lines Ins. Co., 2011 U.S. Dist. LEXIS 134878 (S.D. Fla. Nov. 22, 2011), where the insured premises was a shopping center that included seven subproperties. Some of the seven subproperties were adjoined, while others were detached. One of them suffered a loss, and the insurer invoked the vacancy clause. The parties disagreed over whether "building" in the vacancy clause referred to each premises individually or the shopping center as a whole. The court examined the Declarations Page and found that under "description of premises," building was used in a potentially ambiguous way. It referred to premises numbered one through seven but in each case referred only to "Bldg. No. 1." That, said the court, made it unclear whether "Bldg. No. 1" indicated a single building on each of premises one through seven or that each of the seven premises were constituents of a building identified as building number one. The court resolved the dilemma by holding that "building," as used throughout the policy, referred to each premises individually and noted that the ordinary use of the term "building" would rarely include a group of premises not all of which were bounded by the same walls and roof. *Compare* Park Place Apts., L.L.C. v. Farmers Union Mut. Ins. Co., 358 Mont. 394, 403, 247 P.3d 236, 241 (2010) (insurer disputed whether policy covered carport because it was not listed under "insured premises" section on Declarations Page, but court decided insurer's interpretation skipped over "at the premises" in definition of covered property and that a more

is any doubt about the accuracy of the description, the association should seek clarification. There is nothing wrong with seeking a written explanation or a revised Declarations Page from the insurer.

[3] Coverage Amount

The Declarations Page will list the coverage limit. It is important to determine the source and accuracy of this figure.[229] Is it based on a current appraisal?[230] Did the insurer calculate it using a formula it employs for per-square-foot construction costs?[231] Does it reflect unique features of the property that affect its value? There can be serious consequences for the association if the property is underinsured.[232]

[4] Premiums

Simply put, a premium is the consideration one pays for insurance protection or coverage.[233] The policy itself generally says little about the premium, and nothing about how much it is or how it is determined. The Declarations Page lists the amount of the premium as well as any additional premium for additional coverage—and also establishes the legal significance of the premium by a statement reading something like, "in return for the payment of the premium, and subject to all the terms of this policy, the carrier agrees to provide the insurance as stated in the policy."

reasonable interpretation was that coverage extended to all buildings and structures that were at premises described on Declarations Page).

229. Treese, *Risk Management Essential to Insurance Plan* (CAI 1995) (association must accurately determine insurable replacement cost of its property, and purchasing an appraisal is excellent method of obtaining those values). One commentary warns that real estate appraisals, reserve studies, and unit values should never be used to calculate the Replacement Cost Value for a community. *Confused Over Insurance? Five Common Questions* (Association Times 2010), available at: http://associationtimes.associaliving.com/2010/11/confusedoverinsurancefivecommonquestions/.

230. *See Confused Over Insurance? Five Common Questions* (Association Times 2010), available at: http://associationtimes.associaliving.com/2010/11/confusedoverinsurancefivecommonquestions/ (many appraisal firms guarantee their appraisals for three to five years, and association can contact firm once a year prior to renewal and update it on any changes or additions).

231. *See Massachusetts Condominium Law*, § 5.1.4(f) (3rd ed. MCLE, Inc., 2008 & Supp. 2009, 2015) (for smaller structures carriers usually use per-square-foot construction cost figure based on their experience and studies).

232. The cost of an appraisal can be considerable. When a common interest community has multiple buildings with common floor plans, one commentary suggests there is the potential for substantial savings as the appraisal company can simply value the different building floor plans and the association can extrapolate those values among the other common buildings. *Confused Over Insurance? Five Common Questions* (Association Times 2010), available at: http://associationtimes.associaliving.com/2010/11/confusedoverinsurancefivecommonquestions/.

233. State Farm Mut. Auto. Ins. Co. v. United States, 200 F. Supp. 324 (S.D. Ill. 1961), *rev'd on other grounds*, 314 F.2d 363 (7th Cir. 1963) (insurance premium may be defined as agreed price for assuming and carrying the risk, consideration paid insurer for undertaking to indemnify insured against specified peril); Brownsville Fabrics, Inc. v. Gulf Ins. Co., 550 S.W.2d 332, 338 (Tex. Civ. App.—Corpus Christi 1977).

[a] Calculation of the Premium Amount

For commercial property insurance, the premium is based on several factors in addition to the value of the property insured.[234] These include:

- Square footage. The size of the insured premises is one factor in determining the premium.[235]
- Construction. The materials of which the building is constructed—their resistance to fire or wind—is a consideration in setting the premium.[236]
- Building age. Older buildings may be susceptible to certain types of damage—for example, fires as a result of old electrical wiring—and, therefore, more costly to insure,[237] whereas newer buildings or ones with recent upgrades of wiring, plumbing, or HVAC systems will generally be less costly.[238]
- Occupancy. The use of the premises is a factor in the cost of the premium, and for mixed-use common interest communities where the policy covers higher risk uses, for example, restaurants or clubs, the rate may be higher than for a purely residential community.
- Protection. Security measures—sprinklers, smoke detectors, alarms—can be a basis for a lower premium.[239]
- Geography. The location of the premises relates to a number of factors, including availability of urban firefighting, vulnerability to crime and vandalism, proximity of high-risk uses, and environmental risks such as tornadoes or earthquakes.
- Loss experience.[240] Past losses are usually considered by insurers in setting rates.[241]

---

234. *See generally* California Department of Insurance, *Commercial Guide*, available at: http://www.insurance.ca.gov/01-consumers/105-type/95-guides/09-comm/commercialguide.cfm#howarecommercial.

235. *See* Geare, *How Are Commercial Property Insurance Rates Determined?*, available at: https://www.quora.com/How-are-commercial-property-insurance-rates-determined (noting that large structures are individually rated while smaller ones are organized into various categories that are rated as a class). *See also* http://www.insureon.com/products/property-insurance/factors-that-affect-cost/.

236. https://www.nationwide.com/property-insurance-rates.jsp.

237. http://www.insureon.com/products/property-insurance/factors-that-affect-cost/.

238. https://www.nationwide.com/property-insurance-rates.jsp.

239. http://www.insureon.com/products/property-insurance/factors-that-affect-cost/; https://www.nationwide.com/property-insurance-rates.jsp.

240. *See, e.g.*, Oak Hills Highlands Ass'n v. Levasseur, 21 Neb. Ct. App. 889, 845 N.W.2d 590 (2014) (association's annual insurance premium increased from $39,120 to $65,325, which association contended was increase of $15,648 for claim related to fire and $10,557 increase as result of statewide increase for all condominiums).

241. Geare, *How Are Commercial Property Insurance Rates Determined?*, available at: https://www.quora.com/How-are-commercial-property-insurance-rates-determined.

These are just some of the factors that are considered by insurers in establishing premium rates. In general, the premium for commercial property insurance is set by multiplying the value of the building and its contents times a value associated with the level of risk.[242] However, rating formulas for commercial property coverage can also be quite complex, and it behooves an association governing board to discuss with its broker how the policy premium is calculated.[243]

There are factors that affect rates over which the association has control. These include the amount of the deductible—the higher the deductible, the lower the rate—and discounts that may be available for certain improvements made to the property. Higher deductibles are not best for every association, and the costs of improvements may not justify any discount, but both at least merit exploration.

[b] Allocation of the Premium to Association Members

An aspect to insurance premiums that has nothing to do with the policy, but is of critical importance to common interest community associations and their members, is the allocation of the cost of the premium to those members. Typically, the premium is a common expense allocated to the members based on a formula in the governing documents. Indeed, associations are often specifically required by law to allocate the cost of insurance premiums as a common expense.[244]

There are three formulas for allocating common expenses. They can be divided equally among the units, or they can be allocated based on either the size or value of units. The first two methods generally do not accurately represent the risk. The insurer bases the premium on the total value of the property insured; however, even if all the units are identical, some will have a greater fair market value than others. For example, in a townhouse community, end units may command a higher price than interior ones. In a mid- or high-rise building, a unit on the highest floor that has a desirable view will generally have a higher market value than the identical unit on the lowest floor. If all these units are assessed on either an equal or square footage basis, the cost of the property insurance will not be fairly allocated. On the other hand, if the common expense is allocated based on the value of units, the distribution of insurance expenses is, at least in theory, fairer. If that valuation is derived from the original selling price set by the developer and all the units increase in value uniformly over time, the allocation may well be fair. That, however, may well not occur. The market for certain types of

---

242. https://www.nationwide.com/property-insurance-rates.jsp. *See also* California Department of Insurance, *Commercial Guide*, available at: http://www.insurance.ca.gov/01-consumers/105-type/95-guides/09-comm/commercialguide.cfm#howarecommercial (premium is calculated by simple formula: rate × exposure = premium).

243. California Department of Insurance, *Commercial Guide*, available at: http://www.insurance.ca.gov/01-consumers/105-type/95-guides/09-comm/commercialguide.cfm#howarecommercial.

244. *See, e.g.*, Colo. Rev. Stat. § 38-33.3-313(13); Fla. Stat. § 719.107(1)(e); Ind. Code § 32-25-8-9(a).

units may cause them to increase in price faster than other units, and those with substantial renovations will be more valuable than those with none.

No matter the method of allocating common expenses, in some instances, the association may be able to divorce the premium expense from the common expense. The Uniform Common Interest Ownership Act and the laws of some states[245] allow the costs of premiums to be allocated on the basis of risk.[246] The governing documents of some common interest communities also permit that approach.[247] The challenge for the association is to develop a method of fairly determining that risk. Generally, one would expect the courts to defer to the business judgement of the association in making that determination; however, if the allocation is patently arbitrary or selectively applied, it could be struck down.

§ 10.12 Basic Coverage

The standard commercial property insurance policy provides that the insurer will pay for "direct physical loss of or damage to" covered property at the premises described on the Declarations Page caused by or resulting from any covered cause of loss.[248] The causes of loss are described in one of three causes of loss forms—the Special Form, Basic Form, or Broad Form—that is incorporated into the policy. Policies do not define "direct physical loss or damage." Generally, courts say a "direct loss" is one proximately caused by an insured peril and that the term is intended to exclude loss by an intervening force.[249] The phrase "direct physical loss or damage" has been interpreted to mean that an insured has to demonstrate

245. *See, e.g.*, N.Y. Real Prop. Law § 339-bb (insurance premiums are common expense, but in charging it to unit owners "consideration may be given to the higher premium rates on some units than on others"). *See also* N.Y. Real Prop. Law § 339-m.

246. Uniform Common Interest Ownership Act § 3-115(c)(3) (1982) (to extent *required* by Declaration, costs of insurance *must be assessed* in proportion to risk).

247. *See, e.g.*, Carriage Park Assoc. v. Emanuel, 2003 Conn. Super. LEXIS 416 (Feb. 6, 2003) (Declaration provided that any insurance premium increase attributable to particular unit by virtue of activities in or construction of that unit would be assessed against it); BRT Prop. Group v. Willow Springs Condo. Ass'n, 1996 Conn. Super. LEXIS 2615 (Conn. Super. Ct. Oct. 9, 1996) (bylaws provided that unit owner would be assessed when premium increase was attributable to either "activities in" or construction of that particular unit). *See also Massachusetts Condominium Law* (MCLE, Inc. 2nd ed. 2008 & Supp. 2009, 2015) (sample cooperative proprietary lease provides that if, by reason of occupancy or use of apartment by lessee, rate of fire insurance on building or any apartment, or contents of either, increases, lessee is liable for additional insurance premiums incurred by lessor or any lessee or lessees of apartments in building on all policies so affected).

248. *See, e.g.*, ISO Form CP 00 17 06 07, § A; ISO Form CP 00 10 06 07, § A.

249. *See* Advance Cable Co., LLC v. Cincinnati Ins. Co., LLC, 788 F.3d 743, 746 (7th Cir. 2015) (although policy does not elaborate on meaning of "direct," common sense suggests it is meant to exclude situations in which intervening force plays some role in damage); Southall v. Farm Bureau Mut. Ins. Co., 276 Ark. 58, 60, 632 S.W.2d 420, 422 (Ark. 1982) (direct loss is one proximately caused by hazard insured against). *See also* Crestview Country Club, Inc. v. St. Paul Guardian Ins. Co., 321 F. Supp. 2d 260 (D. Mass. 2004) (intangible damage did not count as direct physical loss or damage).

that an event had a direct impact and proximately caused a loss that is related to the physical matter of the property.[250] "Physical" loss is a distinct, demonstrable, and physical alteration of the property.[251] Thus, where a condominium constructed a temporary parking lot to replace a collapsed parking deck, the court found that the insurer was obligated to pay for construction of a new structure to replace the damaged one, but that the temporary parking spaces did not fall within the categories of either "physical loss of" or "damage to" the parking deck and the insurer did not have to pay the cost of the temporary construction.[252]

Coverage applies only to a loss to covered property at the premises described on the Declarations Page. Thus, where there is more than one building at the premises, it is critical to determine which ones are covered.[253] Experts recommend that all buildings on the premises need to be delineated.[254]

[1] Covered Property

Commercial property policies list the property covered. Covered property means the building or structure described on the Declarations Page, business personal property located in or on that building or structure, and personal property of others in the care, custody, or control of the insured and located in or on that building or structure, as potentially limited by the section of the policy on property not covered.[255]

[a] Building

Property policies do not define the word "building." There does not appear to be a single accepted definition of the term,[256] but it is not confined to structures of any particular size or shape.[257] One court has said the word "building" embraces "structures of many and varied character, for occupation, habitation, storage of

250. Ass'n of Apt. Owners of Imperial Plaza v. Fireman's Fund Ins. Co., 939 F. Supp. 2d 1059, 1070 (D. Haw. 2013).

251. *See* Port Auth. of N.Y. & N.J. v. Affiliated FM Ins. Co., 311 F.3d 226, 235 (3d Cir. 2002). *See also* Advance Cable Co., LLC v. Cincinnati Ins. Co., LLC, 788 F.3d 743 (7th Cir. 2015) (denting by hail changed physical characteristics of roof and satisfied language of policy regarding "physical" loss).

252. Pepper Mill Condo. Ass'n v. Hartford Fire Ins. Co., 71 Pa. D. & C. 4th 54 (Pa. Dist. 2005).

253. *See, e.g.*, TWBC III, Inc. v. Certain Underwriters at Lloyd's London, 323 N.J. Super. 60, 731 A.2d 1228 (1999) (where property consisted of nightclub and beach club in two separate buildings and application described premises as "beach club seasonal operation," only beach club was covered by policy).

254. Cozen, *Insuring Real Property*, § 2.05[1] (Matthew Bender & Co. 2015) (because description of covered property will limit coverage to described premises, it is important that description is accurate; if insured premises contains more than one building, particular buildings for which coverage applies must be clearly delineated and failure to use care in specifying building or buildings to be covered may result in no coverage).

255. *See* ISO Form CP 00 17 06 07, § A.1; ISO Form CP 00 10 06 07, § A.1.

256. Great Eastern Casualty Co. v. Blackwelder, 21 Ga. App. 586, 590, 94 S.E. 843, 845 (1918).

257. University City v. Home Fire & Marine Ins. Co., 114 F.2d 288, 296 (8th Cir. 1940).

goods, shelter, and *for other useful purposes.*"[258] To avoid any uncertainty, a common interest community should ask whether a particular structure constitutes a building. For example, an apartment building had, as do many common interest communities, a detached carport. The court said it was doubtful that a carport would be considered a "building" as the term is generally thought to refer to a walled, roofed structure.[259] Nonetheless, the court found the carport was covered under the policy because, while it was not physically attached to the apartment building, it was located very close to it and it seemed logical that the carport was considered an "add-on to the apartment building."[260] Clearly it would have been preferable to get a definitive decision from the insurer when the policy was first issued.

[i] Building and Personal Property Coverage Form

The Building and Personal Property Coverage Form provides that "building" means the building or structure described on the Declarations Page, including certain prescribed components.[261] Those components are:

- Completed additions.[262]
- Fixtures, including outdoor fixtures.[263]
- Permanently installed machinery and equipment.
- Personal property owned by the named insured that is used to maintain or service the building or structure or its premises, including fire-extinguish-

---

258. Great Eastern Casualty Co. v. Blackwelder, 21 Ga. App. 586, 590, 94 S.E. 843, 845 (1918).

259. Park Place Apts., L.L.C. v. Farmers Union Mut. Ins. Co., 358 Mont. 394, 247 P.3d 236 (2010).

260. Park Place Apts., L.L.C. v. Farmers Union Mut. Ins. Co., 358 Mont. 394, 403, 247 P.3d 236, 242 (2010).

261. ISO Form CP 00 10 06 07, § A.1.a. *See* University City v. Home Fire & Marine Ins. Co., 114 F.2d 288, 297 (8th Cir. 1940) (general rule is that insurance contract on "building" covers all inseparable and constituent parts of insured building).

262. *Consider* Ormond Country Club v. James River Ins. Co., 2008 U.S. Dist. LEXIS 25250 (E.D. La. Mar. 27, 2008) (rejecting argument that tennis courts and fence around them should be considered "completed additions" because they were not a part of any building listed on Declarations Page; no showing of substantial connection of use of clubhouse and of swimming pool that would render it structural part—as completed addition—of insured clubhouse).

263. The policy does not define "outdoor fixtures, but they would not include any property listed in the policy as not covered. Sioux City Country Club v. Cincinnati Ins. Co., 2004 U.S. Dist. LEXIS 12833 (N.D. Iowa June 22, 2004) (term "outdoor fixtures" is not defined in policy, but as policy identifies types of property that are specifically not covered, if item of damaged property is specifically identified in policy as not being covered, then that specific identification would control over general term "outdoor fixtures"). *See also* Ormond Country Club v. James River Ins. Co., 2008 U.S. Dist. LEXIS 25250 (E.D. La. Mar. 27, 2008) (rejecting argument that tennis courts and fence around them should be considered "outdoor fixtures" because they were not a part of any building listed in the Declarations Page; no showing of substantial connection of use of clubhouse and of swimming pool that would render it structural part—as outdoor fixture—of insured clubhouse).

ing equipment, outdoor furniture, floor coverings, and appliances used for refrigerating, ventilating, cooking, dishwashing, or laundering.
- Additions under construction, alterations and repairs to the building or structure and materials, equipment, supplies and temporary structures, on or within 100 feet of the described premises, used for making additions, alterations or repairs to the building or structure if not covered by other insurance.

[ii] Condominium Association Coverage Form

The Condominium Association Coverage Form differs from the BPP. It defines the "building" as the building or structure described on the Declarations Page and including certain prescribed components, but not including personal property owned by, used by, or in the care, custody, or control of a unit owner, except for certain prescribed property contained within a unit, regardless of ownership, if the association is required to insure it.[264] There are typically five separate components that are included as part of the building:

- Completed additions.[265]
- Fixtures, *outside of individual units*, including outdoor fixtures.[266]
- Permanently installed machinery and equipment.
- Personal property owned by the insured used to maintain or service the building or structure or its premises, including fire-extinguishing equipment, outdoor furniture, floor coverings, and appliances used for refrigerating, ventilating, cooking, dishwashing, or laundering that are *not contained* within individual units.[267]

---

264. CP 00 17 06 07, § A.1.a.

265. *Consider* Ormond Country Club v. James River Ins. Co., 2008 U.S. Dist. LEXIS 25250 (E.D. La. Mar. 27, 2008) (rejecting argument that tennis courts and fence around them should be considered "completed additions" because they were not a part of any building listed in the Declarations Page; no showing of substantial connection of use of clubhouse and of swimming pool that would render it structural part—as completed addition—of insured clubhouse).

266. The BPP omits the phrase "outside of individual units," but otherwise the language is identical to that of the Condominium Association Coverage Form. The policy does not define "outdoor fixtures," but they would not include any property listed in the policy as not covered. Sioux City Country Club v. Cincinnati Ins. Co., 2004 U.S. Dist. LEXIS 12833 (N.D. Iowa June 22, 2004) (term "outdoor fixtures" is not defined in policy, but as policy identifies types of property that are specifically not covered, if item of damaged property is specifically identified in policy as not being covered, then that specific identification would control over general term "outdoor fixtures").

267. The Condominium Association Coverage Form adds the phrase "that are not contained within individual units" to the comparable language of the BPP. *See* Costa Del Sol Ass'n v. Dep't of Bus. & Prof'l Regulation, Div. of Fla. Land Sales, Condos., & Mobile Homes, 987 So. 2d 734 (Fla. 3d DCA 2008) (jacuzzis, trellises, and elaborate screen enclosures purchased, installed, subject to removal, and usable only by individual unit owners were not "condominium property" that had to be insured by association merely because they were located on patio outside, rather than inside, individual unit).

- Additions under construction, alterations and repairs to the building or structure and materials, equipment, supplies, and temporary structures, on or within 100 feet of the described premises, used for making additions, alterations or repairs to the building or structure, if not covered by other insurance.

The Condominium Association Coverage Form adds a sixth set of components to the meaning of building. These are fixtures, improvements, and alterations that are a part of the building or structure *and* appliances, such as those used for refrigerating, ventilating, cooking, dishwashing, laundering, security, or housekeeping *contained within a unit*, regardless of ownership, if the "Condominium Association Agreement" requires the association to insure them.[268] This addition means that, for example, lighting fixtures, built-in cabinets or bookshelves, or an appliance that an individual unit owner has installed is covered by the association policy if the "Condominium Association Agreement" requires that the association insure that property.[269]

That the policy may cover identified components contained within the individual units does not mean, at least according to one court, that those individual unit owners become insureds who may bring claims against the insurer on their own.[270]

[A] "Condominium Association Agreements"

The policy uses, but does not define, the term "Condominium Association Agreement." There is no document in common interest community law known as a Condominium Association Agreement. Presumably the policy refers to any agreement that binds the association to insure any of the identified components. This

268. Where the documents merely permit the association to provide insurance, they impose no requirement on it. Bosch v. Cedar Vill. Townhomes Homeowners Ass'n, 2011 Tex. App. LEXIS 804 (Tex. App.—Houston 1st Dist., Feb. 3, 2011) (where Declaration stated that association "may" provide fire insurance without imposing requirement to do so, it did not create duty for association to insure individual unit). One commentator notes that it is common for builders, within local building code guidelines, to place wall-to-wall carpeting over plywood floors and treat them as finished floors and to supply lighting fixtures, kitchen counters, and cabinets, dishwashers, stoves, and refrigerators, and customary bathroom fixtures, but for bylaws to make unit owners responsible for replacing those items. Based on that requirement, insurance company adjusters often tell individual owners that they, not the carrier, are responsible for replacing the items. Rohan, *Preparing Community Associations for the Twenty-First Century: Anticipating the Legal Problems and Possible Solutions*, 73 St. John's L. Rev. 3, 27 (1999). As can be seen from the policy language, in the case of the CAC policy, the adjuster would be patently wrong.

269. *Condominium Association Coverage Form* (Summit Business Media, 2013). In *Bosch v. Cedar Vill. Townhomes Homeowners Ass'n*, 2011 Tex. App. LEXIS 804 (Tex. App.—Houston 1st Dist., Feb. 3, 2011), the Declaration of Condominium—presumably a "condominium agreement"—provided that the unit owners could obtain insurance for their own benefit and identified the components that would be covered by that insurance. The court rejected the argument of a unit owner that the Declaration, therefore, required the association to insure all components not identified as the insurance responsibility of the unit owners.

270. Peters v. Lexington Ins. Co., 836 F. Supp. 2d 1117 (D. Haw. 2011).

could be the condominium Declaration—sometimes called the master deed or master lease[271]—and/or any articles of incorporation and association bylaws.[272] One authority on condominium law says it is not clear what the term "agreement" means for purposes of the policy, but that arguably, it could mean all of the governing documents—the Declaration of Condominium, articles of incorporation, bylaws, rules, and board resolutions—and that the governing board would be required to interpret the term "agreement" and decide what that agreement requires regarding insurance coverage.[273]

One of the only cases that appears to have mentioned a "Condominium Association Agreement" suggests it means the "governing documents and bylaws,"[274] and governing documents should include the Declaration and articles of incorporation. If the association is required by state law to insure any of the identified components, but no mention of that obligation is made in any of the condominium documents, does the applicable statute constitute a "Condominium Association Agreement" for purposes of the policy? That would appear to be exactly the position taken by the only court to have addressed the question.[275]

[B] State-Specific Endorsements

For some states, there is an endorsement that modifies the Condominium Association Coverage Form. For example, an endorsement for Florida condominiums, while largely the same as the Condominium Association Coverage Form, has a somewhat different list of building components.[276] The endorsement says "building" means the building or structure described on the Declarations Page. It includes items on the Condominium Association Coverage Form: fixtures,

271. The District of Columbia once used the term "plat of condominium subdivision." D.C. Code § 42-2002(9). The Virginia Condominium Act uses the term "condominium instruments to refer to the declaration, bylaws, and plats and plans." Va. Code § 55-79.45.

272. The obligation to insure any of the identified components could be stated in board adopted rules. Would that be a "Condominium Association Agreement"? The rules are usually unilaterally adopted by the governing board but might be considered an "agreement" as the Declaration or bylaws likely obligate the unit owners to obey board adopted rules.

273. Rohan & Reskin, *Condominium Law and Practice: Forms*, § 49.04 (Matthew Bender 2007).

274. *See* Mayfair House Ass'n v. QBE Ins. Corp., 2008 U.S. Dist. LEXIS 66456 (S.D. Fla. Aug. 29, 2008).

275. *See* Royal Bahamian Ass'n v. QBE Ins. Corp., 750 F. Supp. 2d 1346 (S.D. Fla. 2010). For the court in *Royal Bahamian* the question was whether the association policy provided coverage for windows and sliding glass doors in the units. The court noted that the Florida Condominium Act "allocates responsibility for insuring sliding windows and glass doors to the association" and that the policy provides coverage for any portion of the condominium property the association is required to insure under the Condominium Association Agreement. The court then concluded that because the association was obligated under the statute to insure windows and glass doors and they were portions of the condominium property, they were covered by the policy.

276. ISO Form CP 01 91 02 10 (Florida Changes—Residential Condominium Associations). *See, e.g.*, Mayfair House Ass'n v. QBE Ins. Corp., 2008 U.S. Dist. LEXIS 66456 (S.D. Fla. Aug. 29, 2008) (components of building were more specifically defined in policy endorsement Form CP 01 91 01 04).

outside of individual units, including outdoor fixtures; permanently installed machinery and equipment; personal property owned by the named insured used to maintain or service the building or structure or its premises, including fire-extinguishing equipment, outdoor furniture floor coverings, and appliances used for refrigerating, ventilating, cooking, dishwashing, or laundering that are not contained within individual units; and materials, equipment, supplies, and temporary structures, on or within 100 feet of the described premises, used for making additions, alterations, or repairs to the building or structure, if not covered by other insurance. From that point it is different from the Condominium Association Coverage Form. It includes as part of the building additions; alterations and repairs; air conditioning and heating equipment, including air conditioning compressors, used to service the building or structure, including individual units and limited common elements; any other portion of the condominium property located outside of individual units; and additional property as described in a schedule or on the Declarations Page.

The differences between the Condominium Association Coverage Form and the Georgia endorsement are even greater.[277] The first four components included in the "building" are the same as the Condominium Association Coverage Form: completed additions; fixtures, outside of individual units, including outdoor fixtures; permanently installed machinery and equipment; and personal property owned by the insured used to maintain or service the building or structure or its premises, including fire-extinguishing equipment, outdoor furniture, floor coverings, and appliances used for refrigerating, ventilating, cooking, dishwashing, or laundering that are not contained within individual units. The sixth component is also the same as in the Condominium Association Coverage Form: additions under construction, alterations and repairs to the building or structure, and materials, equipment, supplies and temporary structures, on or within 100 feet of the described premises, used for making additions, alterations, or repairs to the building or structure if not covered by other insurance. The endorsement then deviates from the Condominium Association Coverage Form with three categories of components that are included in the building.

First, the endorsement includes in the building, regardless of the boundaries of the condominium units; all portions of the building that are common elements, including limited common elements; all foundations;[278] roofs and roof structures; exterior walls, including windows and doors and their framing; and all convertible space within the building, meaning a portion of the building that may be converted into one or more condominium units or common elements in accordance with the Georgia Condominium Act.

277. ISO Form CP 01 67 02 09 (Georgia Changes—Condominium Associations).

278. The endorsement says that as foundations are considered covered property, they are removed from the section on "Property Not Covered" in the policy.

Next, included in the building are fixtures, improvements, and alterations that are a part of the building or structure and appliances, for example those used for security or housekeeping that are contained within a unit, regardless of ownership, if the Condominium Association Agreement requires the association to insure it.

Finally, the endorsement lists categories of components that are included in the building with respect to each condominium unit, regardless of who is responsible for maintaining them under the Condominium Association Agreement. These include an HVAC system serving a condominium unit and all sheetrock and plaster board comprising the walls and ceilings of a condominium unit.

Additionally, floors and subfloors, walls, ceiling and floor coverings, plumbing and electrical lines and fixtures, built-in cabinetry and fixtures, and appliances used for refrigeration, cooking, dishwashing, and laundry within a condominium unit are included when they are of the type and quality initially installed, or replacements of like kind and quality in accordance with the original plans and specifications or as they existed at the time the unit was initially conveyed, if the original plans and specifications are not available. However, coverage for unfinished shell units conveyed as such by a declarant[279] applies only with respect to those portions of a unit constructed by the declarant, unless the Declaration[280] provided by the declarant provides otherwise. If, however, an unfinished shell unit has not been conveyed at the time of an insured loss, the coverage provided applies to the unit as it existed at the time of that loss.

Generally, the building does not include personal property owned by, used by, or in the care, custody, or control of a unit owner except for personal property listed in the last two sections of the provision describing the building, which are those items listed in the Condominium Association Agreement that the association is required to insure and items with respect to each condominium unit, regardless of who is responsible for maintaining them under the Condominium Association Agreement.

These endorsements illustrate the need to carefully check the policy for exactly what it—and any endorsements to it—includes as part of the building. The association might have its broker and an association representative walk through the premises and identify specific items to be included by endorsement if not otherwise listed.

279. "Declarant" has the same meanings as in the Georgia Condominium Act. *See* Ga. Code Ann. § 44-3-71(13).

280. "Declaration" has the same meanings as in the Georgia Condominium Act. *See* Ga. Code Ann. § 44-3-71(14).

[iii] Commercial Property Standard Property Policy

There is a Standard Property Policy that may be used to provide property coverage.[281] A generic "Condominium Association Changes" endorsement can be added to it to adapt the policy to the particular needs of condominium associations and unit owners.[282] There are also state-specific endorsements to the Standard Property Policy that serve the same purpose. When either endorsement is added to the policy, the section on building coverage is replaced with a list of six building components. Under the generic endorsement, building means the building or structure described on the Declarations Page, including these components:

- Completed additions;[283]
- Fixtures, outside of individual units, including outdoor fixtures;[284]
- Permanently installed machinery and equipment;
- Personal property owned by the named insured that is used to maintain or service the building or structure or its premises, including fire-extinguishing equipment, outdoor furniture, floor coverings, and appliances used for refrigeration, ventilating, cooking, dishwashing, or laundering *not contained within individual units*;[285]
- Additions under construction, alterations, and repairs to the building or structure and materials, equipment and supplies, and temporary structures, on or within 100 feet of the described premises, used for making

281. *See, e.g.*, ISO Form CP 00 99 10 90.

282. *See, e.g.*, ISO form CP 17 99 06 95 (Commercial Property; Condominium Association Changes—Standard Property Policy); ISO Form CP 01 99 01 91 (Commercial Property; Condominium Association Coverage Condominium Law Provisions).

283. *Consider* Ormond Country Club v. James River Ins. Co., 2008 U.S. Dist. LEXIS 25250 (E.D. La. Mar. 27, 2008) (rejecting argument that tennis courts and fence around them should be considered "completed additions" because they were not a part of any building listed in the Declarations Page; no showing of substantial connection of use of clubhouse and of swimming pool that would render it structural part—as completed addition—of insured clubhouse).

284. The policy does not define "outdoor fixtures," but they would not include any property listed in the policy as not covered. Sioux City Country Club v. Cincinnati Ins. Co., 2004 U.S. Dist. LEXIS 12833 (N.D. Iowa June 22, 2004) (term "outdoor fixtures" is not defined in policy, but as policy identifies types of property that are specifically not covered, if item of damaged property is specifically identified in policy as not being covered, then that specific identification would control over general term "outdoor fixtures"). *See also* Ormond Country Club v. James River Ins. Co., 2008 U.S. Dist. LEXIS 25250 (E.D. La. Mar. 27, 2008) (rejecting argument that tennis courts and fence around them should be considered "outdoor fixtures" because they were not a part of any building listed in the Declarations Page; no showing of substantial connection of use of clubhouse and of swimming pool that would render it structural part—as outdoor fixture—of insured clubhouse).

285. *See, e.g.*, Allegrino v. Conway E & S, Inc., 2010 U.S. Dist. LEXIS 109317 (W.D. Pa. Oct. 14, 2010) (general meaning of "personal property used to maintain or service the building" is personal property used to care for building, to continue its productivity, or to repair it; equipment intended to be used to operate search engine business was to be used for business purposes rather than to service or maintain building and was not, therefore, equipment covered by policy).

additions, alterations, or repairs to the building or structure if not covered by other insurance; and

- Fixtures, improvements, and alterations that are a part of the building or structure and appliances, such as those used for refrigerating, ventilating, cooking, dishwashing, laundering, security or housekeeping *contained within a unit*, regardless of ownership, if the Condominium Association Agreement requires the named insured to insure it.

Finally, "building" does not include personal property owned by, used by, or in the care, custody, or control of a unit owner except for fixtures, improvements, and alterations that are a part of the building or structure and appliances, such as those used for refrigerating, ventilating, cooking, dishwashing, laundering, security, or housekeeping contained within a unit.

Connecticut and Texas are two states for which there are specific endorsements to the Standard Property Policy. They are entitled "Connecticut Changes—Condominium Association Coverage—Condominium Law Provisions"[286] and "Texas Changes—Condominium Association Coverage—Condominium Law Provisions."[287] Those endorsements are the same as the generic Condominium Association Changes Endorsement.

The Standard Property Policy with a Condominium Association Changes Endorsement is used by some states in state-sponsored property insurance programs, rather than either the Building and Personal Property Coverage Form or the Condominium Association Coverage Form.[288]

The net effect of the endorsement is to make the building section of the Standard Property Policy read the same as that of the Condominium Association Coverage Form.

[b] Business Personal Property

Both the BPP and the CAC provide coverage for "business personal property." "Personal property" has been variously defined as any movable or intangible thing subject to ownership and not classified as real property,[289] property of a personal

286. ISO Form CP 01 39 10 12 (Connecticut Changes—Condominium Association Coverage—Condominium Law Provisions).

287. ISO Form CP 01 48 10 12 (Texas Changes—Condominium Association Coverage—Condominium Law Provisions).

288. *See, e.g.*, the Illinois Fair plan (https://www.illinoisfairplan.com/producers/commercialpolicyforms) and the North Carolina NCJUA-FAIR Plan and NCIUA-Coastal Property Insurance Pool (http://www.ncjua-nciua.org/html/forms.htm).

289. Riverside-Quindaro Bend Levee Dist. v. Mo. Am. Water Co., 117 S.W.3d 140, 157 (Mo. App. 2003) (quoting *Black's Law Dictionary* and finding that buried utility line constituted personal property because it was movable piece of property that did not constitute real property). *See also* Southwest Airlines Co. v. Ariz. Dep't of Revenue, 217 Ariz. 451, 456, 175 P.3d 700, 704 (Ariz. App. 2008) (under Arizona law personal property is defined as property of every kind, both tangible and intangible, not included in term "real estate").

or movable nature as opposed to that of a local or immovable character,[290] and "'money, goods, and movable chattels.'"[291] "Business personal property" has been called a catchall phrase intended to include items of a business nature not otherwise covered under another category in a policy of insurance.[292] These definitions are significant because while the BPP describes specific types of business personal property, for instance furniture and machinery, it also includes as business personal property "all other personal property owned by the named insured and used in its business.[293] The definition of "personal property" is even more important under the CAC where the description of personal property is even broader that in the BPP.

While older policy forms speak simply of the personal property of the insured, the current CAC mirrors the BPP in using the term "business personal property." Is a residential condominium in business? Is it accurate to describe its personal property as "business property"? Some residential condominium associations may be said to be "in business" to the extent they lease condominium property or facilities to third parties or make condominium property or facilities available to non-residents for a fee. However, all residential communities can be said to be in the "business" of "governing a condominium association."[294] Experts agree, therefore, that use of the term "business personal property" in policies is not likely to be problematic.[295]

Generally, the covered business personal property has to be located in or on the building described on the Declarations Page or in the open—or in a vehicle—within 100 feet of the described premises. This policy language can give rise to confusion. For example, an insured moved personal business property to a warehouse within 100 feet of the furniture store in which it was previously located. A few days later the property that had been moved was destroyed by fire. The insurer denied coverage because, it said, the policy only covered personal property within 100 feet of the described premises when that personal property was "in the open," not when it was in another building. The court, however, found the policy language to be ambiguous and, therefore, construed it favorably for the insured.[296] In another case, business personal property was stolen from a truck

290. Lowrance v. Lowrance, 95 Ind. App. 345, 357–58, 182 N.E. 273, 277 (1932) (quoting *Black's Law Dictionary*).

291. Best Friends Pet Care, Inc. v. Design Learned, Inc., 77 Conn. App. 167, 182, 823 A.2d 329, 337, n.16 (2003) (quoting *Ballentine's Law Dictionary*).

292. Harrod v. Farmland Mut. Ins. Co., 346 F.3d 1184, 1186 (8th Cir. Ark. 2003).

293. ISO Form CP 00 10 06 07, § A.1.b.(4).

294. Olde Colonial Vill. v. Millers Mut. Ins., 2002 Del. Super. LEXIS 341 (Del. Super. Ct. May 17, 2002) (observing that association was in "business" of "governing a condominium association," and its operations presumably included adopting bylaws, enforcing rules, keeping books, providing ordinary maintenance, and hiring and supervising necessary help).

295. *Condominium Association Coverage Form* (Summit Business Media, 2013).

296. Bituminous Casualty Corp. v. Harris, 372 So. 2d 342 (Ala. App.), *cert den.*, 372 So. 2d 345 (Ala. 1979). The insurer refused coverage because it contended the insured property had to be in

parked in a shopping center parking lot almost 300 feet from the entrance to one of the premises described on the Declarations Page, but less than 100 feet from other buildings in the shopping center. The parking lot was a common area to which the insured had certain legal rights under a lease. The court held the policy was not ambiguous and expressly stated that it covered business personal property in or on the premises described on the Declarations Page or within 100 feet of it. The shopping center common area parking lot was not that described premises and, therefore, there was no coverage for the stolen property.[297]

The business personal property sections of the BPP and CAC Forms are different, and those differences are explained below.

[i] Building and Personal Property Coverage Form

The Building and Personal Property Coverage Form provides coverage for certain prescribed business personal property of the named insured that is located in or on the building described on the Declarations Page or in the open—or in a vehicle—within 100 feet of the described premises, unless otherwise specified on the Declarations Page or a "Separation of Coverage form."[298] The prescribed personal property is

- Furniture and fixtures;
- Machinery and equipment;
- Stock;[299]
- All other personal property owned by the named insured and used in its business;
- Labor, materials, or services furnished or arranged by the named insured on personal property of others;
- The use interest of the named insured as tenant in improvements and betterments;[300] and

---

the open *and* within 100 feet of the described premises to be insured. The court rejected that interpretation of the policy and found for the insured. It said that under a rational and practical reading of the policy, there was coverage if the property was in or on the described building, was in the open on the described premises, or was within 100 feet of the described premises.

297. Evergreen Nat'l Indem. Co. v. Tan It All, Inc., 111 S.W.3d 669 (Tex. App.—Austin 2003).

298. ISO Form CP 00 10 06 07, § A.1.b. In some versions of the BPP, the reference to a "Separation of Coverage Form" may be omitted and the prescribed distance may be 100 feet of the building or structure or within 100 feet of the premises described on the Declarations Page, whichever distance is greater.

299. "Stock" is defined as "merchandise held in storage or for sale, raw materials and in-process or finished goods, including supplies used in their packing or shipping." ISO Form CP 00 10 10 00, § H.2.

300. Improvements and betterments are fixtures, alterations, installations, or additions made part of the building or structure the named insured occupies but does not own and that the named insured acquired or made at its expense but cannot legally remove.

- Leased personal property for which the named insured has a contractual responsibility to insure, unless otherwise provided for under the "Personal Property of Others" section of the policy.

[ii] Condominium Association Coverage Form

The Condominium Association Coverage Form provides that certain prescribed "business personal property" of the insured located in or on the building described on the Declarations Page or in the open—or in a vehicle—within 100 feet of the described premises is covered property.[301] The list of prescribed personal property is quite different from that in the BPP. The specifically listed business personal property is:

- Personal property owned by the insured association or owned indivisibly by all unit owners;[302]
- The interest of the insured association in the labor, materials, or services furnished or arranged by it on personal property of others;
- Leased personal property for which the insured association has a contractual responsibility to insure, unless otherwise provided for under coverage for personal property of others.

The business personal property of the association *does not include* personal property owned only by a unit owner.[303]

[c] Personal Property of Others

Commercial property policies provide coverage for the personal property of others that is in the care, custody, or control of the insured and located in or on the building described on the Declarations Page or in the open—or in a vehicle—within 100 feet of the described premises,[304] although the payment for loss of or damage to personal property of others by the insurer will only be for the account of the owner of the property.[305]

---

301. ISO Form CP 00 17 06 07, § A.1.b.

302. The phrase "owned indivisibly by all unit owners" is evidently intended to refer to personal property that constitutes part of the condominium common elements and is, therefore, owned by all the unit owners as tenants in common.

303. *See, e.g.*, Hayne v. Woodridge Condos., 957 So. 2d 804, 809 (La. App., 2007) (association policy did not indicate that unit owners were entitled to individual coverage for their personal losses, for example, rental income and in fact, it specifically excluded from coverage personal property and/or business property of individual owners).

304. *Consider* Villa D'Orleans Condo. Ass'n v. Pac. Ins. Co., 2008 U.S. Dist. LEXIS 41171 (E.D. La. May 22, 2008), where the court apparently accepted the argument that appliances—dishwashers, ranges, and refrigerators—in damaged condominium units were covered as property of others in the described building and within the care, custody, or control of the association. The court at least refused to grant summary judgment to the insurer.

305. ISO Form CP 00 10 06 07, § A.1.c; ISO Form CP 00 17 06 07, § A.1.c.

[2] Loss of Business and Maintenance Fee Income

Neither the Building and Personal Property Coverage nor Condominium Association Coverage Forms provides coverage for business income or lost maintenance fee income. There are policies that furnish that coverage. For example, one policy covers loss of an association's business and maintenance fee income that is the direct result of a direct covered loss that results in either the necessary interruption of the association's described *condominium* operations or the described premises being rendered incapable of being occupied.[306] There are also standard endorsements that add business income coverage.[307]

[a] Maintenance Fee Income

Coverage for loss of an association's maintenance fee income is available in some policies or by endorsement. In one policy, coverage is also provided if the loss is the result of access to the described premises being prohibited by order of any civil authority providing the order is the result of a fortuitous direct physical loss to property at a premises other than the described premises caused by an applicable covered cause of loss.[308] Specifically, the policy covers a loss by the association of assessments and/or maintenance fees that would have been paid under the Condominium Association Agreement by the unit owners to the extent that those fees would otherwise have been earned or incurred by the association's condominium operations had the direct covered loss not occurred. There is also coverage for the association's loss of rent from tenant occupancies and continuing expenses that are the obligation of tenants, under written leases, but that

---

306. MSO Policy Form MCP 014 10 07. *But see* http://www.mcleckie.com/Travelers_Product_Guide_5-2-2011.pdf, where the company says coverage for maintenance fees is included in the Business Income and Extra Expense coverage of its policy. It explains that these fees consist of the regular payments made to the insured association by unit owners. Apparently, there is no comparable coverage for homeowners associations or other non-condominium planned communities. Treese & Rosenberry, *Insurance: How Community Associations Protect Themselves*, at 53 (CAI Press 2013). *And see* GlenBrook Patiohome, Owners Ass'n v. Lexington Ins. Co., 2011 U.S. Dist. LEXIS 14556 (S.D. Tex. Feb. 14, 2011) (insurer issued "Real and Personal Property, Business Interruption Insurance" to association).

307. *See, e.g.*, ISO Form CP 00 30 10 91. There are Business Income endorsements with and without extra expense coverage. "Extra expense" means the necessary expenses incurred by the insured during the "period of restoration" that would not have been incurred if there had been no direct physical loss or damage to the property.

308. MSO Policy Form MCP 014 10 07. Apparently, there is no comparable coverage for homeowners associations or other non-condominium planned communities. Treese & Rosenberry, *Insurance: How Community Associations Protect Themselves*, at 53 (CAI Press 2013). *But see* GlenBrook Patiohome, Owners Ass'n v. Lexington Ins. Co., 2011 U.S. Dist. LEXIS 14556 (S.D. Tex. Feb. 14, 2011) (insurer issued "Real and Personal Property, Business Interruption Insurance" to association).

become the obligation of the association because of the direct covered loss.[309] Generally, this coverage would not be available to unit owners who are lessors of their units.[310]

Some experts recommend lost maintenance fee income coverage.[311] However, a common interest community should consult the association attorney before asking its broker to obtain the coverage because under applicable statutes and the governing documents, individual owners may be required to pay maintenance assessments even if their units are rendered uninhabitable. When that is the case, the association would suffer no deficiency from a covered cause of loss,[312] and the insurer would almost certainly deny any claim. Residential cooperatives are in most cases an exception. The units in a cooperative are generally occupied pursuant to a proprietary lease under which the "rent" abates if the unit is uninhabitable. Cooperatives, therefore, generally need rent loss coverage—which is available by endorsement[313]—to avoid a loss of income needed to operate the building when some units have been damaged.

[b] Business Income

Some associations may own and/or operate business enterprises—for example, a country club with a restaurant and golf course or parking garages—that generate income from residents and perhaps from non-residents as well. If the income is significant, these associations may want to have coverage for their loss. The typical policy language provides the insurer will pay for actual loss of business income sustained by the insured from the "necessary suspension" of its "operations"—meaning the business activities of the insured occurring at the described

---

309. *How to Insure Your Condominiums Income* (Feb. 4, 2013) (when association owns unit for which it collects rent, rent loss coverage could cover loss if there is covered claim and unit is damaged and uninhabitable).

310. *See, e.g.*, Elkins v. QBE Ins. Corp., 2011 U.S. Dist. LEXIS 43314 (W.D. Wash. Apr. 21, 2011) (where association policy provided coverage for loss of *community* income, including loss of rent or lease payments because of suspension of operations of association during "period of restoration," community meant named insured—association—and, therefore, individual unit rent income was not community income).

311. *See, e.g.*, *How to Insure Your Condominiums Income* (Feb. 4, 2013) (by purchasing maintenance fee insurance association can look to insurer to pick up uncollected fees due to covered loss to unit); Iannucci, *Insurance Products What's Available, What's Recommended* (Cooperator, Aug. 2006), available at: http://cooperator.com/article/insurance-products (Loss of Maintenance policy reimburses building for loss of fees or rent when something happens to unit).

312. In other words, if a unit owner refuses to pay his or her assessments because he or she cannot occupy the unit, the loss to the association would be caused by the volitional act of the unit owner, not the peril that damaged the unit. The unit owner remains liable for the assessments, and the association has effective means to collect those assessments.

313. *See* § 10.36[2][f], *infra*.

premises[314]—during a "period of restoration."[315] "Business income" is defined as the net profit or loss before income taxes that would have been earned or incurred and continuing normal operating expenses, including payroll.[316] The coverage may or may not include what is called "extra expense" coverage. That additional coverage encompasses the *necessary* expenses incurred during a "period of restoration" that would not have been incurred had there been no direct physical loss or damage to property.[317] One court explained that extra expense coverage includes expenses "incurred to maintain business operations beyond normal coverage."[318] In the example of a country club with a golf course, covered extra expenses might include the cost of renting temporary buildings and facilities—for example, portable buildings for office use and portable toilets—during the time the clubhouse building is uninhabitable.[319] A finance charge on a line of credit used for rebuilding might also be considered an extra expense.[320] However, the cost of relocating residents of a common interest community has been held not to be an extra expense of an association because while the association helpfully took the chore on itself and organized evacuation of the property after serious structural defects were discovered, it was not in the business of providing housing and moving expenses for its residents when it bought its insurance.[321]

---

314. *See, e.g.*, ISO Form CP 00 30 10 91, § G.2. The "business" of a common interest community association is governance, including adopting bylaws, enforcing rules, keeping books, providing ordinary maintenance to the building and grounds, and hiring and supervising necessary help. Olde Colonial Vill. v. Millers Mut. Ins., 2002 Del. Super. LEXIS 341 (Del. Super. Ct. May 17, 2002). It is critical to determine the scope of the "described premises." For example, a Louisiana country club was damaged by Hurricane Katrina. It had coverage for business interruption, but only its club house, not its golf course, was listed on the Declarations Page. Therefore, the court held that losses attributable to closure of the golf course were not covered. Ormond Country Club v. James River Ins. Co., 2008 U.S. Dist. LEXIS 25250 (E.D. La. Mar. 27, 2008).

315. *See, e.g.*, ISO Form CP 00 30 10 91, § A. The suspension has to be caused by direct physical loss of, or damage to, property at the premises described on the Declarations Page, including personal property in the open, or in a vehicle within 100 feet, caused by or resulting from any covered cause of loss. Note that policies typically require the insured to resume operations as quickly as possible, and if it does not, the insurer will only pay based on the length of time it would have taken to resume operations as quickly as possible. ISO Form CP 00 30 10 91, § D.4.d.

316. *See, e.g.*, ISO Form CP 00 30 10 91, § A.1.

317. *See, e.g.*, ISO Form CP 00 30 10 91, § A.3.a.

318. Detroit Edison Co. v. Protection Mut. Ins. Co., 134 F.3d 790, 792, n.3 (6th Cir. 1998).

319. *See* Olde Colonial Vill. v. Millers Mut. Ins., 2002 Del. Super. LEXIS 341 (Del. Super. Ct. May 17, 2002) (stating in *dicta* that "extra expense" of renting temporary office while association building was rendered uninhabitable would be covered).

320. Seward Park Hous. Corp. v. Greater N.Y. Mut. Ins. Co., 43 A.D.3d 23, 28–29, 836 N.Y.S.2d 99, 102 (2007) (line of credit allowed insured to rebuild garage and resume receiving rental income).

321. Olde Colonial Vill. v. Millers Mut. Ins., 2002 Del. Super. LEXIS 341 (Del. Super. Ct. May 17, 2002) (association was not entitled to reimbursement for any relocation expenses except its own). *See also* Hill v. Promenade E. Condo. Ass'n, 2009 Me. Super. LEXIS 14 (Me. Super. Ct. Jan. 12, 2009) (association's statutory obligation to insure units did not require it to pay for temporary replacement housing). *Compare* Three Palms Pointe, Inc. v. State Farm Fire & Cas. Co., 250 F.

[3] Property Not Covered

Property policies list property that is *not covered.* This list is separate from the exclusions that in the BPP and CAC are found in the causes of loss form added to the policy. The "property not covered" clause is not, therefore, a list of exclusions, although courts sometimes refer to the items on the list as exclusions.[322] The distinction is important because the insurer has the burden to show an exclusion applies, while the insured has the burden of showing initial coverage that would include showing—when challenged—that property for which a claim has been submitted is *not* on the "property not covered" list. The list of property that is not covered property is essentially the same for the BPP and the CAC.[323] Under both policies, covered property does not include:

- Accounts, bills, currency, food stamps, or other evidences of debt, money, notes, or securities;[324]
- Animals, unless owned by others and boarded by the named insured;[325]
- Automobiles held for sale;
- Bridges, roadways, walks, patios, or other paved surfaces;
- Contraband, or property in the course of illegal transportation or trade;
- The cost of excavations, grading, backfilling, or filling;[326]
- Foundations of buildings, structures, machinery, or boilers if their foundations are below the lowest basement floor or, if there is no basement, below the surface of the ground;
- Land—including land on which the property is located—water, growing crops, or lawns;
- Personal property while airborne or waterborne;
- Bulkheads, pilings,[327] piers, wharves, or docks;

Supp. 2d 1357 (M.D. Fla. 2003), *aff'd*, 362 F.3d 1317 (11th Cir. 2004) (cost of relocating residents was necessary and direct result of construction and repair process and covered under policy; noting policy failed to exclude coverage for, or costs of, personal relocation expenses).

322. *See, e.g.*, Opperman v. Heritage Mut. Ins. Co., 566 N.W.2d 487 (S.D. 1997); Strand v. State Farm Ins. Co., 34 Ohio App. 3d 97, 517 N.E.2d 265 (1986). *See also* Snow Lake Shores Prop. Owners Corp. v. United States Fid. & Guar., 1994 U.S. Dist. LEXIS 21145 (N.D. Miss. Aug. 23, 1994).

323. *See* ISO Form CP 00 10 06 07, § A.2; ISO Form CP 00 17 06 07, § A.2.

324. The policies both provide that lottery tickets held for sale are not securities.

325. The BPP adds that covered property does not include animals if owned by the named insured, only as "stock" while inside of buildings. ISO Form CP 00 10 06 07, § A.2.b.

326. *See, e.g.*, Sioux City Country Club v. Cincinnati Ins. Co., 2004 U.S. Dist. LEXIS 12833 (N.D. Iowa June 22, 2004) (graded slope was "land," and repairing it would involve excavation, grading, backfilling, or filling and, therefore, graded slope was not covered under policy).

327. *See, e.g.*, Buczek v. Cont'l Cas. Ins. Co., 378 F.3d 284, 290 (3d Cir. 2004) (pilings served as foundation for building, and language of policy clearly excluded both foundations and "pilings" as covered property).

- Property that is covered under the association property policy or any other policy[328] in which it is more specifically described, except for the excess of the amount due, whether the named insured can collect on it or not, from that other insurance;
- Retaining walls that are not part of a building;
- Underground pipes, flues, or drains;[329] and
- Vehicles or self-propelled machines—including aircraft or watercraft—that are licensed for use on public roads or are operated principally away from the described premises.[330]

The BPP adds that covered property does not include the cost to research, replace, or restore information on "valuable" papers and records, including those that exist on electronic or magnetic media, except as provided in the coverage extensions.[331] The CAC has a similar but more extensive provision. It provides that covered property does not include the cost to replace or restore information on valuable papers and records, including those that exist as electronic data, and that "valuable papers and records" include, but are not limited to, proprietary information, books of account, deeds, manuscripts, abstracts, drawings, and card index systems.[332] It then directs the insured to refer to the coverage extension for Valuable Papers and Records (Other Than Electronic Data) for limited coverage for valuable papers and records other than those that exist as electronic data.[333]

328. The CAC says, "this [meaning the association policy] or any other policy," while the BPP policy says, "another coverage form of this or any other policy." One commentary notes that the difference apparently reflects the blending of commercial coverage with personal coverage found in the HO 00 06, which is the condominium homeowner's policy, and the concern that condominium unit owners more likely understand the HO 00 06 to be "policy of insurance" rather than a "coverage form." *Condominium Association Coverage Form* (Summit Business Media, 2013).

329. *See, e.g.*, Sioux City Country Club v. Cincinnati Ins. Co., 2004 U.S. Dist. LEXIS 12833 (N.D. Iowa June 22, 2004) (underground drainage system beneath parking lot fit squarely within definition of "underground pipes, flues, and drains").

330. This part does not apply to vehicles or self-propelled machines or autos the named insured manufactures or warehouses or to vehicles or self-propelled machines, other than autos, the named insured holds for sale; rowboats or canoes out of water at the described premises; or trailers, but only to the extent provided for in the coverage extension for non-owned detached trailers. *Consider* Opperman v. Heritage Mut. Ins. Co., 566 N.W.2d 487 (S.D. 1997) (expansive interpretation of "warehouse" would conceivably cover vehicle insured might have chosen to put in building for repairs, but that hardly fit within risk parties contemplated).

331. ISO Form CP 00 10 06 07, § A.2.n.

332. ISO Form CP 00 10 06 07, § A.2.o. *See* Barlow, Massmann, Alexander & Schreibman, *Condominium Insurance Coverage Guide* at 148 (2d ed. National Underwriter Co., 2016) (broadly worded definition of "valuable papers" means insureds may need specialized coverage).

333. ISO Form CP 00 10 06 07, § A.2.o. Note that other versions of the BPP may have the identical language. *See* ISO Form CP 00 10 10 12, § A.2.o.

Additionally, the CAC provides that covered property does not include electronic data, except as provided under Additional Coverages—Electronic Data.[334] The policy defines "electronic data" as information, facts, or computer programs[335] stored as or on, created or used on, or transmitted to or from computer software—including systems and applications software—on hard or floppy disks, CD-ROMs, tapes, drives, cells, data processing devices, or any other repositories of computer software that are used with electronically controlled equipment. Given the broad definition of "electronic data," associations that are concerned about the possibility of a substantial loss to electronic data should consider a specialized policy to provide the coverage needed.[336]

Finally, both policies provide that the section on Property Not Covered does not apply to certain prescribed property while outside of buildings.[337] That property is grain, hay, straw, or other crops and fences;[338] radio or television antennas—including satellite dishes—and their lead-in wiring, masts, or towers; and trees, shrubs, or plants—other than "stock" of trees, shrubs or plants[339]—all except as provided in the coverage extensions.

Some of the property listed as not covered will be of particular concern to common interest communities. For example, some common interest communities have their own streets, sidewalks, patios in recreational areas, and water, sewer, and storm water pipes. Most have a paved parking lot. Thus, the elimination of coverage for roadways, walks, patios, other paved surfaces, underground pipes, flues, and drains can be significant. For example, a pipe in the water system of a condominium property broke. The repair required extensive digging in a paved parking lot, replacement of the broken water line, and landscaping. The insurer

334. ISO Form CP 00 17 06 07, § A.2.n. There are versions of the BPP that also list "electronic data" as property not covered. Under those policies there is an exception if there is coverage under the section titled "Additional Coverage, Electronic Data." Electronic data is defined as information, facts, or computer programs stored as or on, created or used on, or transmitted to or from computer software—including systems and applications software—on hard or floppy disks, CD-ROMs, tapes, drives, cells, data processing devices, or any other repositories of computer software used with electronically controlled equipment. "Computer programs" means a set of related electronic instructions that direct the operations and functions of a computer or device connected to it, and that enable the computer or device to receive, process, store, retrieve, or send data. This provision on electronic data does not apply to the named insured's "stock" of prepackaged software, or to electronic data that is integrated in and operates or controls the building's elevator, lighting, heating, ventilation, air conditioning, or security system. *See* ISO Form CP 00 10 10 12, § A.2.n.

335. "Computer programs" means a set of related electronic instructions that direct the operations and functions of a computer or device connected to it, and that enable the computer or device to receive, process, store, retrieve, or send data.

336. Barlow, Massmann, Alexander & Schreibman, *Condominium Insurance Coverage Guide* at 148 (2d ed. National Underwriter Co., 2016).

337. *See* ISO Form CP 00 10 06 07, § A.2.p; ISO Form CP 00 17 06 07, § A.2.q.

338. *Consider* Seward Park Hous. Corp. v. Greater N.Y. Mut. Ins. Co., 43 A.D.3d 23, 836 N.Y.S.2d 99 (2007) (fence affixed to parking garage did not fall within definition of property not covered).

339. The BPP adds an exception for "trees, shrubs or plants" that are part of a *vegetated roof*.

denied a claim for the loss and the court agreed. It cited the fact that the definition of "property not covered" included bridges, roadways, walks, patios or other paved surfaces, the cost of excavations, grading, backfilling or filling, land, and underground pipes, and the insured acknowledged that the broken pipe resulted in damage to a parking lot and a landscaped area.[340] Similarly, when the parking garage of a residential cooperative collapsed, an appellate court vacated the portion of an award allocated for underground pipes, trenching, trees, lawns, shrubs, and excavations, but allowed the award for losses to paved surfaces affixed to the parking garage itself, apparently considering that paved surface not to be an "other paved surface" but a component of the building.[341]

Many common interest communities have tennis, racquetball, or basketball courts on their property. They should take note of a case in which a federal court determined that tennis courts are "paved surfaces" and, therefore, not covered property.[342] A CIC may also operate a golf course. Golf courses are not covered property because they constitute land.[343] Finally, waterfront communities often have docks. A "dock" has been defined as an area of water used for reception of ships.[344] A dock in a CIC may be a limited common element reserved for the use of one association member, or it may be part of a marina in which dock space is available to all the owners, commonly for a fee under a lease. A dock is clearly not covered property, and neither for that matter are bulkheads, pilings, piers, or wharves.[345]

---

340. DePasquale v. American Cas. Co. of Reading, PA, Inc., 764 A.2d 180 (R.I. 2000). *See also* Chalmette Retail Ctr., L.L.C. v. Lafayette Ins. Co., 974 So. 2d 822 (La. App. 2008) (if parking lot were paved, it would clearly be excluded from coverage by provision on "other paved surfaces"; however, even if it were not paved, it would be excluded under provision on land); Snow Lake Shores Prop. Owners Corp. v. United States Fid. & Guar., 1994 U.S. Dist. LEXIS 21145 (N.D. Miss. Aug. 23, 1994) (insurer denied coverage for collapsed spillway because it was not covered property under provision including "bridges, roadways, walks, patios or other paved surfaces" under definition of property not covered; denying summary judgment to insurer because of ambiguity created by supplemental coverage for "water system").

341. Seward Park Hous. Corp. v. Greater N.Y. Mut. Ins. Co., 43 A.D.3d 23, 836 N.Y.S.2d 99 (2007). One portion of the garage in *Seward Park* had no soil or grass on top, but was paved and used for above-ground parking. That is apparently the paved surface for which the court allowed the loss. Another portion of the garage was covered with two to three feet of soil and a lawn used as a recreational area. There was also a system of drainage pipes that directed water absorbed by the soil away from the garage. The landscaped area and drainage pipes would appear to be the underground pipes, trees, lawns, and shrubs to which the court referred.

342. Sioux City Country Club v. Cincinnati Ins. Co., 2004 U.S. Dist. LEXIS 12833 (N.D. Iowa June 22, 2004) (rejecting argument by insured that there was ambiguity concerning whether tennis courts were "paved surfaces" and not covered property or "outdoor fixtures" because they were central part of operations of country club and, therefore, covered as component of building).

343. Ormond Country Club v. James River Ins. Co., 2008 U.S. Dist. LEXIS 25250 (E.D. La. Mar. 27, 2008).

344. Global Ship Sys., LLC v. Cont'l Cas. Co., 292 Ga. App. 214, 217, 663 S.E.2d 826, 829 (2008).

345. Global Ship Sys., LLC v. Cont'l Cas. Co., 292 Ga. App. 214, 217, 663 S.E.2d 826, 829 (2008) (finding marine railway to be a dock as it was area of water used for reception of ships and,

Some CICs may have "vehicles or self-propelled machines" for the use of residents. Under both the BPP and CAC, these are not covered if they are licensed for use on public roads or are operated principally away from the described premises. Thus, vehicles operated on the insured premises may be covered if not otherwise excluded.[346] Thus, if an association has scooters for disabled residents or golf carts for use of employees or residents to move about the property, they would not fit under the definition of "property not covered." However, if the scooter or golf cart is used principally *off the premises* and is only temporarily on the premises at the time of a loss, there is no coverage.[347]

§ 10.13 Scope of Coverage under the Association Policy

The most basic question about a property insurance policy in a common interest community is, what does it cover? In a cooperative, the answer is easy. The cooperative corporation owns all the real property and insures it. The residents—tenant/shareholders—insure the personal property that they own, and the corporation insures any personal property it owns.[348] In a homeowners association the answer can also be straightforward where there is a clear demarcation between the property—real and personal—owned by the association and by the individual

therefore, within meaning of "dock" for purposes of provision on property not covered); Catucci v. Greenwich Ins. Co., 37 A.D.3d 513, 830 N.Y.S.2d 281 (2007) (where outdoor concrete deck abutting waterway used to load and unload shipping containers collapsed, insurer denied coverage because, *inter alia*, under section of policy titled "Property Not Covered," bulkheads, pilings, piers, wharves, or docks were excluded).

346. *See* Strand v. State Farm Ins. Co., 34 Ohio App. 3d 97, 517 N.E.2d 265 (1986). *Strand* concerned a homeowner's policy where the "property not covered" language is different. Typically, those policies provide that motor-propelled vehicles or machines are not covered property unless they are used solely for service of the insured location and not licensed for use on public highways. In *Strand* a three-wheel all-terrain vehicle (ATV) was stolen from the insured home. The insurer argued that "service to the insured location" meant the exception was intended to apply to lawnmowers, rototillers, and snowblowers, machines that perform a useful task. The court rejected that contention and found the word "service" to be ambiguous. It concluded that an ATV, despite the fact that it is often thought of as a recreational vehicle, could and had been used in "service to the insured location" when the residents used the ATV for errands and inspecting the property. It is interesting that the court made note of the fact that it is a "common sight" to see golf carts used around buildings with large grounds where there may be a number of employees traveling about on golf carts.

347. Opperman v. Heritage Mut. Ins. Co., 566 N.W.2d 487 (S.D. 1997) (where front-end loader ordinarily used at gravel pits several miles away, but on insured premises for overhaul, was damaged when that building burned was vehicle operated principally away from described premises and not covered).

348. *See, e.g.*, Dudey, *Multi-Family Complexes (Apartment and Condo): An In-Depth Look at Insuring the Many Exposures and Losses* at 7 (2009), available at: http://adjustersinternational.com/publications/adjusting-today/multi-family-complexes-insuring-exposures-and-losses/0/ (noting that cooperative apartments and rental apartments have similar insurance needs that are not nearly as complex as condominiums and with only a few differences; in both cases, residents insure only their own personal property).

residents, respectively, for example in a neighborhood of traditional single-family detached homes where the association owns only recreational facilities and buildings. Matters become more complex when there are attached units or the association is effectively a condominium meaning the residents collectively own as tenants in common all the property other than their individual homes.

In condominiums, the question of property insurance has presented questions and confusion.[349] These have been resolved by one of three ways of dividing the insurance responsibility. Initially, condominiums employed what is called the "bare walls" approach.[350] The condominium association insured the common elements—the property owned by the unit owners as tenants in common—on behalf of the unit owners, and each unit owner insured his or her individual unit. The unit owners paid the premium for the association policy through an assessment levied by the association. This was called "bare walls" coverage because each unit is in effect a "box of air" and the association coverage excluded wallpaper, paint, finished surfaces, cabinets, and fixtures in units.[351] The bare walls approach is problematic because of the difficulty in distinguishing units from common elements. In response to that predicament, "single entity" coverage was developed.[352] Under that approach, units and common elements are treated as one and the association insures common elements and units—including *original* fixtures—but not any improvements to the units or personal property in them.[353] A third approach is called "all inclusive" or "all in." Under that concept, the

349. Nitschke, *Is Your Condominium Unit Properly Insured?* (Association Times Feb. 2010) (condominium unit owners believe association policy covers their personal losses); Kenyon, *Insuring the Condominium*, 19 Prac. Law. 13 (1973) (overlapping coverage or gaps in it can result from separate ownership of units); Rohan, *Preparing Community Associations for the Twenty-First Century: Anticipating the Legal Problems and Possible Solutions*, 73 St. John's L. Rev. 3, 25 (1999) (imprecise condominium statutes caused lawsuits over whether windows and doors were common elements covered by association policy or were part of units and, therefore, covered by unit owner's carrier). *See also* Van der Merwe, *A Comparative Study of the Distribution of Ownership Rights in Property in an Apartment or Condominium Scheme in Common Law, Civil Law and Mixed Law Systems*, 31 Ga. J. Int'l & Comp. L. 101 (2002); Rohan, *Disruption of the Condominium Venture: The Problems of Casualty Loss and Insurance*, 64 Colum. L. Rev. 1045 (1964).

350. Dudey, *Multi-Family Complexes (Apartment and Condo): An In-Depth Look at Insuring the Many Exposures and Losses* at 6 (2009), available at: http://adjustersinternational.com/publications/adjusting-today/multi-family-complexes-insuring-exposures-and-losses/0/ ("bare walls" concept was widely used during early days of condominium development).

351. Rosenberry & Treese, *Purchasing Insurance for the Common Interest Community*, 27 Wake Forest Law Rev. 397, 413 (1992); Perlet, *Condominium Property Insurance*, 9 Forum 685, 702–03 (1974).

352. Dudey, *Multi-Family Complexes (Apartment and Condo): An In-Depth Look at Insuring the Many Exposures and Losses* at 6 (2009), available at: http://adjustersinternational.com/publica tions/adjusting-today/multi-family-complexes-insuring-exposures-and-losses/0/ ("bare walls" concept has largely been superseded by association coverage of all property originally included in unit with unit owner insuring any additions he or she has made).

353. Rosenberry & Treese, *Purchasing Insurance for the Common Interest Community*, 27 Wake Forest Law Rev. 397, 413 (1992); Perlet, *Condominium Property Insurance*, 9 Forum 685, 703 (1974).

association in effect insures all the real property—fixtures and improvements—and individual unit owners need coverage only for their personal property.[354] Not surprisingly, all in coverage may be more costly.[355]

The variety of ways associations could seek to insure the property could present a problem for insurance carriers. However, they have devised an elegant solution. The CAC, as discussed below, ties the building coverage to the insurance responsibility of the association described in the governing documents.[356] While the CAC is designed for condominium associations, it may be used to insure homeowners associations in some cases.

There are circumstances in which the dichotomy between units and common elements should not matter. For example, where a contractor for a condominium association entered a unit and destroyed its floor in order to work on a common crawlspace, the court said the unit owner did not have to pay for a new floor even though the insurer for the association never agreed to pay for work in individual units.[357]

[1] The Applicable Policy Language

The Condominium Association Coverage Form provides that the insured "building" includes fixtures, improvements,[358] alterations, and certain appliances[359] that are a part of the building or structure contained within a unit—regardless of

354. Rosenberry & Treese, *Purchasing Insurance for the Common Interest Community*, 27 Wake Forest Law Rev. 397, 413 (1992) (an "all in" coverage is similar to single entity but also covers all improvements made by unit owners).

355. Orlando, *Changes to Insurance Requirements for Condominium Associations*, 2010-R-0378 (Office of Legislative Research, Sept. 27, 2010) (changing association coverage from "single entity" to "all in" may increase premiums 6 to 10 percent).

356. *Compare* Royale Green Condo. Ass'n v. Aspen Specialty Ins. Co., 2009 U.S. Dist. LEXIS 24349 (S.D. Fla. Mar. 24, 2009) (policy did not incorporate bylaws; although both bylaws and Florida statutes required association to obtain hazard insurance, it does not follow that once coverage is obtained, bylaws are automatically included within coverage and even if bylaws were included within policy, they did not specify scope of coverage for individual condominium units).

357. Olde Colonial Vill. Condo. Council v. Millers Mut. Ins. Co., 2002 Del. Super. LEXIS 42 (Del. Super. Ct. Jan. 28, 2002) (association was entitled to reimbursement for any money it paid to cover damage caused to condominium unit by reconstruction of common area, including repairing or replacing subflooring, hardwood floors, ceramic tiles, sheet goods, and carpet as well as plumbing, drywall, carpentry, and painting).

358. *See* Pinnacle Port Community Ass'n v. Orenstein, 952 F.2d 375, 378 (11th Cir. 1992) (work on walls not intended to enhance assumed value of property, but to restore walls to their original watertight state, was repair, not improvement); Hillsboro Island House Condominium Apartments, Inc. v. Town of Hillsboro Beach, 263 So. 2d 209, 213 (Fla. 1972) (improvement is valuable addition to property that is more than repair or replacement).

359. The policy says the building included appliances, "such as those used for refrigerating, ventilating, cooking, dishwashing, laundering, security or housekeeping." ISO Form CP 00 17 06 07, § A.1.a.(6).(b). It adds that "building" does not include personal property owned by, used by, or in the care, custody, or control of a unit owner except for fixtures, improvements, alterations that are a part of the building or structure, and appliances.

ownership—if the "Condominium Association Agreement" requires the association to insure them.[360] In several states, this language is modified by an endorsement. For example, in Florida, an endorsement omits the appliances in a unit.[361] A Georgia endorsement is far more extensive. First, it defines building to include fixtures, improvements, and alterations that are a part of the building or structure and appliances "such as those used for security or housekeeping" that are contained within a unit, regardless of ownership, if the Condominium Association Agreement requires the association to insure them.[362] It then adds a list of components considered to be part of the "building" regardless of who is responsible for maintaining them under the Condominium Association Agreement. These are the HVAC system serving a condominium unit; all sheetrock and plaster board comprising the walls and ceilings of a condominium unit; and additional items within a unit of the type and quality initially installed, or replacements of them of like kind and quality in accordance with the original plans and specifications or as they existed at the time the unit was initially conveyed, if the original plans and specifications are not available.[363] These items are floors and subfloors; wall, ceiling, and floor coverings; plumbing and electrical lines and fixtures; built-in cabinetry and fixtures; and appliances used for refrigeration, cooking, dishwashing, and laundry.[364]

Neither the CAC nor these endorsements defines "Condominium Association Agreement," and there is no document in common interest community law

---

360. ISO Form CP 00 17 06 07, § A.1.a.(6).(a). *See, e.g.*, Bennett v. USAA Cas. Ins. Co., 2013 Del. Super. LEXIS 46 (Del. Super. Ct. Feb. 15, 2013).

361. *See* ISO Form CP 01 91 07 10, § A.1.h. (Florida Changes–Residential Condominium Associations). *Compare* ISO Form CP 01 82 11 13, §§ A.1.a.(6), (7) (Utah Changes–Condominium Associations) (building includes fixtures, improvements and alterations that are part of building or structure, and appliances, such as those used for refrigerating, ventilating, cooking, dishwashing, laundering, security, or housekeeping contained within unit, regardless of ownership, if Condominium Association Agreement requires association to insure them and any fixture, improvement, or "betterment" installed at any time to unit or to limited common area associated with unit, whether installed in original construction or in any remodel or later alteration, including floor covering, cabinet, light fixture, electrical fixture, heating or plumbing fixture, paint, wall covering, window, and any other item permanently part of or affixed to unit or to limited common element associated with unit). A "betterment" is an improvement to real property that renders it better than mere repairs would do. *The Law Dictionary* (Anderson Publishing Co. 2002).

362. ISO Form CP 01 67 02 09, § A.1.a.(7) (Georgia Changes–Condominium Associations).

363. ISO Form CP 01 67 02 09, § A.1.a.(8) (Georgia Changes–Condominium Associations).

364. Note that for these items coverage for unfinished shell units conveyed as such by the declarant applies only to those portions of the units constructed by the declarant, unless the Declaration provided by the declarant provides otherwise; however, if an unfinished shell unit has not been conveyed at the time of an insured loss, the coverage applies to the unit as it existed at the time of that loss. Some policies may have additional limitations on coverage for components in a unit. For example, the court in *Bennett v. USAA Cas. Ins. Co.*, 2013 Del. Super. LEXIS 46 (Del. Super. Ct. Feb. 15, 2013) quoted policy language that said "building" did not include electrical fixtures, appliances, air conditioner or heating equipment, water heaters, or built-in cabinets located within an individual unit and which the *unit owner is required to repair or replace.*

known as a Condominium Association Agreement.[365] The courts appear to presume the term means the "governing documents and by-laws,"[366] and governing documents should include the Declaration and articles of incorporation.[367]

The CAC also does not define "fixtures," "improvements," or "alterations." The word "fixture" refers to something that, by reason of its "annexation to real property and adaptation to continuing use in connection with the realty, is considered a part of the realty."[368] An "alteration" changes the form of something so that it is different, but its identity is not destroyed.[369]

An "improvement" is an addition or change that makes something better or more valuable.[370] One article on condominium insurance says the improvements to a unit generally include cabinets, floor coverings, paneling, electrical fixtures, interior partition walls, air conditioning units, and possibly paint, wallpaper, and "other decorating."[371] "Improvements" may not always be obvious. If, for example, a unit owner removes walls in her unit to join two small bedrooms or to create an "open floor plan" in the kitchen and living room area, is that an improvement? Consider a scenario in which the unit is seriously damaged in a fire and then acquired by a new owner, possibly a foreclosing mortgagee. If the new owner wants to restore the unit to its original condition, are those reconstruction costs covered by the association policy? The insurer might contend the removal of walls was an excluded unit owner improvement while the new owner may characterize the removal as having diminished the value of the unit and, therefore, it was not an improvement.

---

365. One authority on condominium law says it is not clear what the term "agreement" means for purposes of the policy, but that arguably, it could mean all of the governing documents—the Declaration of Condominium, articles of incorporation, bylaws, rules, and board resolutions—and that the governing board would be required to interpret the term "agreement" and decide what that agreement requires regarding insurance coverage. Rohan & Reskin, *Condominium Law and Practice: Forms*, § 49.04 (Matthew Bender 2007).

366. *See* Mayfair House Ass'n v. QBE Ins. Corp., 2008 U.S. Dist. LEXIS 66456 (S.D. Fla. Aug. 29, 2008).

367. Royal Bahamian Ass'n v. QBE Ins. Corp., 750 F. Supp. 2d 1346 (S.D. Fla. 2010) (reference to "Condominium Association Agreement" incorporated Declaration into policy).

368. *See* http://www.dictionary.com/browse/fixtures. *See also Ballentine's Law Dictionary* (LexisNexis 2010) (something physically annexed or constructively affixed to realty, thus, becoming accessory to it and part and parcel of it).

369. *Ballentine's Law Dictionary* (LexisNexis 2010).

370. *See* http://www.merriam-webster.com/dictionary/improvement. *See also Ballentine's Law Dictionary* (LexisNexis 2010) (anything that enhances value of real property permanently and is either original construction or substantial reconstruction as opposed to repair); http://legal-dictionary.thefreedictionary.com/Improvements.

371. Perlet, *Condominium Property Insurance*, 9 Forum 685, 692 (1974). The author contends that the law of fixtures has in a sense been imported into condominium law; however, unlike in the landlord and tenant context, the title to an addition to a condominium unit that constitutes a fixture does not pass to the association. The unit owner owns the addition and can remove or change it.

[2] The Significance of the Policy Language

The significance of specific policy language, and of endorsements modifying the principal policy, is illustrated by a 25-year-old decision out of the Virgin Islands.[372] In that case the interiors of individual condominium units were damaged in a hurricane. The association made a claim for that damage. The claim was denied. The policy was a form commonly used at the time for condominium associations called a "Special Multi-Peril Policy." The coverage under that policy was actually similar to that under the Condominium Association Coverage Form commonly used today. Coverage was provided for fixtures, improvements, and alterations comprising a part of the building and refrigerators, air conditioners, cooking ranges, dishwashers, and clothes washers and dryers contained within units and owned by the association or a unit owner. The parties agreed that the policy provided coverage of fixtures, improvements, alterations, and certain appliances in individual units. However, an endorsement first eliminated coverage for any fixtures, improvements, alterations, or named appliances, then added it back but only for common property. Therefore, the court held that under the endorsement, coverage extended only to property owned in common and not to the interior of individually owned units.

[3] The Meaning of the Association's "Insurance Responsibility"

The insurance responsibility of the association is determined by the documents.[373] Tying policy coverage to the insurance responsibilities of the association as stated in the documents might appear to simplify the question of what the association policy covers. Unfortunately, that may not be the case. For example, sometimes the question of whether the association is even required to obtain any property insurance may be determined by a vote of the unit owners.[374] In that case the insurance responsibility of the association may be found in the association minutes if the documents were not amended to reflect a unit owner-imposed obligation. Sometimes coverage issues are left to the association governing board, and then one needs to examine its minutes to determine what, if anything, the board has decided about insuring the property. These decisions having been dictated by the governing documents should arguably meet the CAC requirement for

---

372. Coakley Bay Condominium Ass'n v. Continental Ins. Co., 770 F. Supp. 1046 (D.V.I. 1991).

373. *See, e.g.*, Kelly, Messick, Schoenleber & Miller Associates v. Atlantic Mut. Ins. Co., 218 N.J. Super. 395, 527 A.2d 946 (1987) (responsibility of obtaining insurance coverage for all common elements was delegated to association in documents and, therefore, policy of insurer that provided coverage to owner of multiple units for resale did not, nor was it intended to, provide coverage for common element central heating system).

374. Kan. Stat. Ann. § 58-3125 (manager of board of directors, if required by Declaration, bylaws, or majority of apartment owners, has authority to, and shall, obtain insurance for property); N.Y. Real Prop. § 339-bb (board of managers must, if required by Declaration, bylaws, or majority of unit owners, insure building against loss or damage by fire and other hazards).

coverage, but it would be wise in those circumstances to explore the issue with the insurer when the policy is initially obtained.

The governing documents—the "Condominium Association Agreement"—may not be a model of clarity. The documents are generally drafted by a developer's counsel who specializes in construction rather than community association law. In older projects the documents may be cursory and fail to adequately address insurance issues. Sometimes both the Declaration and the bylaws will have provisions on insurance, and they may conflict. If they do, the Declaration generally governs because it is usually recorded and considered a covenant running with the land.[375] If the Declaration and bylaws do not conflict, then the latter supplement the former. There can also be conflicts between the documents and state law. In some states the Declaration can actually *annul* the statutory property insurance provisions.[376] Generally, however, if there is a conflict, state law governs.[377] In states that have adopted one of the Uniform Acts, the provisions of the act cannot be varied by agreement and rights conferred by it cannot be waived.[378] In non–Uniform Act states, there is generally a statute that either says every condominium is subject to the provisions of the enabling legislation[379] or prescribes the contents of the Declaration, but permits it to contain any other provisions that are not inconsistent with the enabling legislation.[380] Thus, to accurately determine the insurance responsibilities of an association requires a review of the state enabling legislation and the governing documents and possibly the rules and regulations and the minutes of the governing board or the association.

[a] The Leading Case

Florida has the most extensive case law on condominiums, and the decisions of its courts have long been cited and viewed as persuasive by courts of other jurisdictions. Therefore, it is reasonable to conclude that the leading case on this question should be the Florida decision relied on by other Florida courts. That case is *Mayfair House Ass'n v. QBE Ins. Corp.*[381] The insurer in *Mayfair* denied

375. *See, e.g.*, Good v. Bear Canyon Ranch Ass'n, 160 P.3d 251 (Colo. Ct. App. 2007); Pepe v. Whispering Sands Condominium Ass'n, 351 So. 2d 755 (Fla. 2d DCA 1997); St. Paul Fed. Bank for Sav. v. Wesby, 149 Ill. App. 3d 1059, 103 Ill. Dec. 390, 501 N.E.2d 707 (1986). Sometimes, however, bylaws are recorded, and that may give them equal status with the Declaration.

376. *See, e.g.*, Haw. Rev. Stat. § 514B-143(a)(1)(A) (associations required to purchase property insurance for common elements, unless Declaration or bylaws provide otherwise); Ohio Rev. Code Ann. § 5311.16 (governing board has to obtain fire and extended coverage insurance for condominium property if Declaration or bylaws do not provide otherwise).

377. Rosenberry & Treese, *Purchasing Insurance for the Common Interest Community*, 27 Wake Forest Law Rev. 397, 401, n.6 (1992).

378. Uniform Common Interest Ownership Act § 1-104 (2008).

379. *See, e.g.*, Fla. Stat. § 718.102.

380. *See, e.g.*, N.J. Stat. § 46:8B-9(m); Haw. Rev. Stat. § 514B-32(a).

381. Mayfair House Ass'n v. QBE Ins. Corp., 2008 U.S. Dist. LEXIS 66456 (S.D. Fla. Aug. 29, 2008).

the association's claim for windstorm damage to exterior windows and sliding glass doors of individual units, and its reasoning directly confronted the heart of the question. It contended those doors and windows were not the insurance responsibility of the association under its governing documents and, therefore, lay outside the grant of the policy coverage. The association conceded that under its documents, the responsibility for maintenance of the windows and doors fell on the unit owners, but it contended that the obligation to *maintain* was not necessarily coextensive with the obligation to *insure* and that it had assumed a responsibility to insure the windows and doors under its governing documents. The court examined the documents and found that the association was required to obtain coverage for the building and all "other insurable improvements upon the land," including all of the units and common elements with certain prescribed exceptions. Exterior glass windows and sliding glass doors, observed the court, were not specifically mentioned in that list of items excepted from the insurance obligations of the association. Thus, the court found that they constituted a "portion of the condominium property" that the association was required to insure and fell within a catch-all definition of a covered "building" component: any other portion of the condominium property if the "Condominium Association Agreement" requires the association to insure it.[382]

In a subsequent case, a Florida court adopted the report and recommendation of a magistrate judge who followed *Mayfair* on the same issue: coverage of windows and sliding glass doors.[383] In that case, the condominium Declaration was not as specific as in *Mayfair*. However, the magistrate judge noted the Declaration provided it should be construed in accordance with the Florida Condominium Act "as amended." A statute in the Condominium Act governing insurance was construed by the judge to obligate condominium associations to provide coverage for windows and doors and, therefore, the Declaration incorporated that obligation by reference.[384] That, in turn, meant that under the catch-all provision of the policy—concerning "portions of the condominium property"—the association was entitled to coverage of its sliding glass doors and windows because, said the judge, an ordinary person would consider them a portion of the

382. In the alternative, the court concluded exterior glass windows and sliding glass doors were fixtures owned by unit owners and located inside individual units, and the policy defined covered property to include fixtures, installations, or additions owned by unit owners and located inside individual units that were either initially installed in accordance with the original plans and specifications, or replacements of like kind or quality as those initially installed, or as existed at the time the unit was initially conveyed if the original plans and specifications were not available.

383. Royal Bahamian Ass'n v. QBE Ins. Corp., 750 F. Supp. 2d 1346 (S.D. Fla. 2010).

384. *See also* Royale Green Condo. Ass'n v. Aspen Specialty Ins. Co., 2009 U.S. Dist. LEXIS 24349 (S.D. Fla. Mar. 24, 2009) (policy adopted statutory language excluding coverage for air conditioning systems servicing individual units and wall coverings, including painting and wallpaper and, therefore, excluded coverage for many features and components of units that would otherwise be covered).

condominium property and the association was obligated to insure them.[385] One caution needs to be raised about the application of statutes. The "as amended" language noted by the court has been interpreted by Florida courts to mean that the parties agreed to include future amendments to the Condominium Act in the Declaration.[386] Without that language, the statutes that govern a particular common interest community are generally those that were in effect when the Declaration was recorded,[387] unless there is a basis for applying those statutes to preexisting documents.

[b] Distinguishing Common Elements from Units

When the Declaration or bylaws—the Condominium Association Agreement—require the association to insure units with certain exceptions, as in the case of *Mayfair*, then it is relatively easy to determine the association's insurance responsibility. However, often the association is required to insure only the "common elements." It then becomes necessary to distinguish common elements from units.[388] It is important to realize that the term "common elements" is defined in

385. Royal Bahamian Ass'n v. QBE Ins. Corp., 750 F. Supp. 2d 1346, 1365 (S.D. Fla. 2010). It is interesting to note that three years later the same carrier faced another claim for windows and sliding glass doors that provide access to individual condominium units, and it conceded in response to interrogatories that they were covered property under the policy. Biscayne Cove Condo. Ass'n v. QBE Ins. Corp., 951 F. Supp. 2d 1292 (S.D. Fla. 2013). *See also* 200 Leslie Condo. Ass'n v. QBE Ins. Corp., 965 F. Supp. 2d 1386, 1391, n.1 (S.D. Fla. 2013), *aff'd*, 616 Fed. Appx. 936 (11th Cir. 2015) (insurer made formal admission that glass windows and sliding glass doors in condominium units were covered property under policy). In another case that year, the carrier, instead of contending there was no coverage for windows and sliding glass doors, first argued that because it had never explicitly denied that windows and sliding glass doors were covered under the policy, the action was not justiciable. In the alternative, it maintained the policy was void in its entirety, and the claim was, therefore, moot. Cypress Chase Condo. Ass'n "A" v. QBE Ins. Corp., 2013 U.S. Dist. LEXIS 40347 (S.D. Fla. Mar. 22, 2013).

386. *See* Kaufman v. Shere, 347 So. 2d 627, 628 (Fla. 3d DCA 1977), *cert. den.*, 355 So. 2d 517 (Fla. 1978). *See also* Century Village, Inc. v. Wellington, E, F, K, L, H, J, M, & G, Condominium Ass'n, 361 So. 2d 128 (Fla. 1978). *Compare* Pudlit 2 Joint Venture, LLP v. Westwood Gardens Homeowners Ass'n, 169 So. 3d 145, 149 (Fla. 4th DCA 2015) (where Declaration provided for automatic amendment to include statutes "required" by plain language of legislation to be adopted, but nothing in language of statute at issue demonstrated it was required to be adopted by Florida homeowners associations, association could not argue that statute as enacted by Florida legislature automatically amended Declaration).

387. *See* § 5.01[4], *supra*. *See generally* Glazer & Goetz, *Florida Community Association Law: Contracts Clause Application in an Ever-Changing Legislative Landscape*, 89 Fla. Bar J. 46 (2015) (recommending that attorney newly hired by common interest community should obtain and review condominium Declaration to determine rights and obligations of client).

388. One early critic of both the "single entity" and "all inclusive" concepts argued that if distinctions between units and common elements presented a problem for "bare walls" coverage, the policy should define those terms. That, he contended, would be preferable to incorporating by reference individual laws of various states or individual Declarations. He concluded there was probably no simple means of insuring the various property interests in condominiums, but that the "bare walls" approach offered the "best coverage to the greatest number." Perlet, *Condominium Property Insurance*, 9 Forum 685, 723 (1973).

state condominium legislation and that it is defined in two ways. The term can be defined inclusively or exclusively. An *inclusive* definition lists specific components that make up the common elements—for example, foundations, halls, stairways—followed by a "catchall" clause of "all other elements rationally of common use."[389] An example of an *exclusive* definition is found in the Uniform Common Interest Ownership Act, which defines the term to mean all portions of a condominium or cooperative *other than the units* or, in a planned community, any real estate owned or leased by the association, *other than a unit*, and in all common interest communities, any other interests in real estate for the benefit of unit owners that are subject to the Declaration.[390] The Declaration will likely include a definition of "common elements"; however, in general, it cannot conflict with the statutory definition. Therefore, one must examine both definitions to distinguish common elements from units. It is also important to be aware that there can be "limited common elements." They are common elements that are reserved for the exclusive use of fewer than all the unit owners, for example, balconies or garage parking spaces. Courts generally recognize that limited common elements are distinguished from other common elements only by use, not by ownership. That is, all common elements are owned by the unit owners as tenants in common, and limited common elements are simply a subset of the common elements restricted as to use. Occasionally, however, courts fail to make that distinction, and, in any event, the governing documents can, and sometimes do, treat limited common elements differently for insurance purposes.

A New Jersey case shows how important the definition of common elements can be to determining insurance responsibilities.[391] The master deed—the equivalent of a Declaration—for the community stated that the association was obligated to insure the common elements of the buildings. The "common elements" were defined to include only common systems and equipment, including mechanical, electrical, plumbing, ventilating, sprinkler, and fire suppression systems that served all units and did not fall within the boundaries of any individual unit. "Units" included all framing, heating, plumbing, ventilating, and air conditioning systems; electrical and cable television wiring; circuit breakers and outlets; and equipment, appliances, and machinery to the extent they served individual units. After a fire damaged the property, the association sought coverage for, *inter alia*, HVAC, electrical, heating, and plumbing systems, which it contended constituted common elements for which it was required to obtain insurance coverage and were "covered equipment" under the terms of its policy. The court first noted that the determination of whether a component was a common element required an examination of both the applicable statute and the master deed and

389. *See, e.g.*, S.C. Code Ann. § 27-31-20(f).

390. Uniform Common Interest Ownership Act § 1-103(6) (2008).

391. Bay Colony Condo. Assoc. v. Scottsdale Ins. Co., 2012 U.S. Dist. LEXIS 182016 (D.N.J. Dec. 26, 2012).

that under New Jersey law, the definition in the master deed had to yield to that in the statute. Based on the statutory and master deed definitions the association argued the buildings' electric, HVAC, plumbing, heating, and framing were common elements for which it was required to obtain insurance coverage. The court did not agree. It said that the statute and master deed made clear that common elements were solely comprised of central power sources that serviced all units and the components for which the association sought coverage solely provided service or transmitted energy to individual condominium units. Coverage, concluded the court, was only provided for "central hubs" of energy. It explained that pursuant to the master deed, if a component was part of a system's central line, then it was considered a common element, but once it broke off from that central line and provided service or energy to an individual unit, it was deemed to be part of the unit. Thus, wiring and piping attributable to individual units were the arteries stemming from the main power sources at the heart of the building.

[4] Consequences of Wrongful Denial of Damage to a Unit

If the association's insurer refuses to pay a claim for damage to a unit, what is the unit owner's recourse? In an Ohio case,[392] a pipe burst in the wall between the garage and interior bathroom of a condominium unit. The court said that a "cursory review" of the association bylaws revealed that the association was required to provide coverage for the loss. The policy, however, had been issued to the developer as the named insured. After the unit owner filed a claim, the developer notified the carrier that it did not want to pursue that claim. Pursuant to that refusal, the carrier closed the claim even though the bylaws assigned to the association, not the developer, the duty to buy insurance. Based on the bylaws, the court found against the insurer. It said the insurer could not reasonably rely on the decision of the developer not to pursue the claim as a basis for refusing to pay the unit owner. It should have been on notice that, to resolve the unit owner's claim, it had to investigate thoroughly the rights of the various parties under the policy. Could it be extrapolated from the holding that if the *association* had refused to pursue the claim, the insurer would have had the same duty and that the unit owner could sue the insurer for breach of contract? Even if the answer to that question is "yes," some courts have held the unit owner has no standing to bring an action against the insurer. Unit owner standing is discussed in another section.[393]

[5] Complications with Unit Owner Improvements

One reason for the association to provide single entity rather than "all inclusive" or "all in" coverage is the problems unit owner improvements can cause.

---

392. Stefano v. Commodore Cove E., Ltd., 145 Ohio App. 3d 290, 762 N.E.2d 1023 (2001).
393. *See* § 10.38[6][c], *infra*.

First, under "all in" coverage, expensive improvements by a few owners can affect the value of the property and the premiums.[394] In contrast, single entity coverage applies to original fixtures but not any improvements to a unit. The unit owner insures those improvements. Unless the association has the original plans and keeps a record of changes made to units over the years, the association and its insurer may not be able to determine whether a component of a unit is an improvement made by the unit owner or an "upgrade" by the developer.[395] Additionally, if the association does not require that unit owners notify it of improvements, it will have no record of them and when a unit is sold, unless the seller informs the buyer of the improvements he or she made, neither the buyer nor the association will know their respective insurance responsibilities.[396] Many associations require unit owners to notify them of proposed improvements and to obtain permission for them from the governing board before the work begins. One reason for this rule is to make sure the work does not impair the integrity of the building or intrude on common property or property of neighbors. Insurance consequences and responsibility are other reasons for associations that have no such rule to consider adopting one.[397] That rule might also be written to relieve

---

394. Skull & Wagner, *Insurance and Damage and Destruction Provisions for Condominiums and Planned Developments*, 11 Cal. Real Prop. J. 18 (1993) (under "all in" coverage, costly improvements by one owner can increase insurance values); Hakala, *Condominium Casualty and Liability Insurance*, 48 St. John's L. Rev. 1112, 1118 (1974) (where unit owners make significant upgrades to units, value of structure could exceed stated limit of policy and insurance proceeds may prove to be far below expected return; to eliminate possibility of detrimental outcome, documents should impose duty on unit owners to notify association of all significant in-unit improvements that may be construed to have become part of structure); Rohan, Reskin & Sanchirico, *Recent Developments in the Field of Insurance for Condominium Projects*, 48 St. John's L. Rev. 1084 (1974) (while one or a few unit owners may be affected by fire or other disaster, unit owner who has installed expensive paneling or other costly improvements may experience greater loss than neighbor whose unit has not been improved to any measurable degree).

395. Perlet, *Condominium Property Insurance*, 9 Forum 685, 707 (1973). When units are sold before construction, it is not unusual for developers to make changes requested by purchasers. Over the years other unit owners may copy those changes. If the association has no record of the changes and when they were made, it will be difficult if not impossible to distinguish the original constriction of a unit from improvements installed later. *See also* Orlando, *Changes to Insurance Requirements for Condominium Associations*, 2010-R-0378 (Office of Legislative Research, Sept. 27, 2010) (one reason to have all-inclusive coverage is that it is often difficult to tell which fixtures were installed by developer and which were installed by unit owners, especially in older units that may have changed ownership several times). *Consider* Conn. Gen. Stat. § 47-255(a) (in common interest communities with more than 12 units, unless association insures all improvements and betterments, it has to prepare and maintain schedule of standard fixtures, improvements, and betterments in units, including any standard wall, floor, and ceiling coverings covered by association policy and provide that schedule to unit owners at least annually so they can coordinate their homeowners coverage with association coverage).

396. Dudey, *Multi-Family Complexes (Apartment and Condo): An In-Depth Look at Insuring the Many Exposures and Losses* at 6 (2009), available at: http://adjustersinternational.com/publications/adjusting-today/multi-family-complexes-insuring-exposures-and-losses/0/.

397. One authority says it is advisable when a unit owner combines units or makes substantial improvements to a unit that details of the changes being made be transmitted to the appropriate

the association of the responsibility to insure improvements of which it has no notice. The association might also seek language in the policy providing that unit owner-installed improvements will not be considered in the value of the structure for coinsurance purposes.[398] The governing documents could also pass increased costs directly to the owners responsible for them.[399]

[6] Areas of Responsibility Policy

An "Areas of Responsibility" policy is a document that establishes guidelines for defining who is responsible for insurance and maintenance.[400] It addresses the dividing line between the association and its residents regarding maintenance and insurance, and it typically lists building components and assigns responsibility to either owners or the association. It can either provide that division of responsibility where the governing documents fail to address it or further refine it where the documents are vague on the topic.

An organization called Regensis—a homeowners association management company—provides a sample Areas of Responsibility policy online.[401] It can be used for condominium associations and adapted for others. An introduction to the policy notes that the policy has to comply with the maintenance and insurance responsibilities found in the governing documents. The governing board can adopt the policy without amending the governing documents,[402] but it would be wise to discuss with the insurer whether, for a condominium insured under a CAC, the policy constitutes a "Condominium Association Agreement." A homeowners association will also want to determine how the insurer will treat any Areas of Responsibility policy. Ideally, the insurer will provide a written explanation of its position.

The sample Areas of Responsibility policy states that the association has the responsibility to insure and maintain the common elements, and its members

---

insurers. Rohan, *Preparing Community Associations for the Twenty-First Century: Anticipating the Legal Problems and Possible Solutions*, 73 St. John's L. Rev. 3, 27, n.71 (1999). However, if the association has no requirement that a unit owner notify it of improvements, it will likely not have the information required to inform an insurer about unit changes.

398. Hakala, *Condominium Casualty and Liability Insurance*, 48 St. John's L. Rev. 1112, 1118 (1974).

399. Skull & Wagner, *Insurance and Damage and Destruction Provisions for Condominiums and Planned Developments*, 11 Cal. Real Prop. J. 18 (1993) (recommending governing documents allow association to pass costs of increased premium cost directly to responsible owner).

400. Thompson, *HOA Insurance Victimization* (Realty Times, June 2012).

401. *See* http://www.regenesis.net/3/policy-areas.htm.

402. There are a number of reasons the board might elect to adopt the Areas of Responsibility policy as board policy rather than amending the documents. Two of those reasons are that, first, amendments to governing documents may require a super-majority of the members of the association—often difficult to achieve—and second, if those documents are recorded, the amendments must also be recorded, and that usually carries a fee. On the other hand, recorded documents provide legal notice.

have the responsibility to insure and maintain their units. It then states that to define the maintenance and insurance responsibilities of the association and the members, the governing board is adopting a Maintenance and Insurance Areas of Responsibility List in the form of a schedule attached to the board policy, and it defines the responsibilities for maintenance and insurance for the listed components.

While an Areas of Responsibility policy can be an effective method of defining insurance responsibilities, it carries legal implications that may not be apparent to the members of the governing board and should be reviewed by the association attorney. One matter the attorney will want to consider is whether the policy is consistent with any applicable statutes or the governing documents. If there is a conflict, the statutes and governing documents would ordinarily take precedence, but it is best not to have a conflict at all as conflicts often have to be resolved by costly litigation.

§ 10.14 Covered Cause of Loss: Risks or Perils

Unlike the Standard Property Policy, homeowner's policies, and other property policies, the Building and Personal Property and Condominium Association Coverage Forms do not include the causes of loss. These are stated in a form added to the BPP and CAC called a causes of loss form, of which there are three: Basic, Broad, and Special. Which form applies can be quickly determined by examining the Declarations Page where, under the "coverage cause of loss," one will find the word basic, broad, or special. The Special Form is all-risk coverage, meaning it covers all risks except those specifically excluded.[403] The Basic Form provides coverage for "named perils," meaning it covers only the risks it specifically lists.[404] The Broad Form also covers named perils, the difference being that its list is slightly longer than that of the Basic Form.[405] A "peril" is simply a specific risk—sometime also called a "hazard"—that can cause damage.[406] The 14 perils covered by the Broad Form causes of loss are discussed below. One should remember that additional perils can be added by endorsement, while stated perils may be eliminated or curtailed by other policy language or an endorsement. Additionally, the BPP and CAC each have an additional coverage section and a coverage extension section.

---

403. *See, e.g.*, ISO Form CP 10 30 04 02. *See also* University of Cincinnati v. Arkwright Mutual Ins. Co., 51 F.3d 1277, 1280 (6th Cir. 1995) (contrasting "all-risk" policies with "named peril" ones).

404. *See, e.g.*, ISO Form CP 10 10 04 02.

405. *See, e.g.*, ISO Form CP 10 20 04 02.

406. Fire Ins. Exchange v. Superior Court, 116 Cal. App. 4th 446, 465, 10 Cal. Rptr. 3d 617, 663, n.13 (Cal. App. 2004) (peril is usually understood as physical force that brings about loss). *See also* Detroit Edison Co. v. Protection Mut. Ins. Co., 134 F.3d 790, 793 (6th Cir. 1998) ("risk" merely signifies peril insured against).

§ 10.15 Named Perils

The "named perils" listed below are the ones that appear in the causes of loss Broad Form. It should be remembered that policies say that the insurer will pay for *direct physical loss of or damage to* covered property caused by or resulting from any covered cause of loss.[407]

[1] Fire

The most basic covered peril is fire.[408] Many things appear simple and straightforward until they become the subject of insurance. Most insureds would say they know what a fire is and that their property policy covers any loss they suffer from a fire. They would be wrong. Property policies do not define the word "fire," and courts have, therefore, come up with a definition. It distinguishes "friendly" from "hostile" fires. For most courts, only the latter are covered. They explain the concept this way: "fire wholly confined to the place where it is intended to be is not a fire within the meaning of a fire insurance policy and damages resulting therefrom are not covered by the contract, but if it escapes its intended place and burns outside its normal confines it becomes a fire within the meaning of the policy and any loss occasioned thereby is compensable."[409] The New Hampshire Supreme Court noted that "hostile fire" has become shorthand for a fire that is accidental in origin and explained that a reasonable person in the position of the insured is barred from recovery under a property policy if he or she willfully fails to prevent the spread of a hostile fire.[410]

---

407. Clouse v. St. Paul Fire & Marine Ins. Co., 152 Neb. 230, 233 40 N.W.2d 820, 823 (1950) ("direct" in phrase "direct loss" means "immediate" or "proximate" as distinguished from "remote" or "incidental"). *See also* Tracy v. Palmetto Fire Ins. Co., 207 Iowa 1042, 1045, 222 N.W. 447, 448 (1928).

408. ISO Form CP 10 20 04 02, § A.1.

409. Owens v. Milwaukee Ins. Co., 125 Ind. App. 208, 212, 123 N.E.2d 645, 646 (1955). *See also* David v. National Union Fire Ins. Co., 206 Pa. Super. 78, 81, 211 A.2d 66, 68, n.1 (1965) ("friendly" fire has been defined as one lighted and contained in usual or ordinary place for fire—furnace, stove, incinerator—and used for the purposes of heating, cooking, manufacturing, or other common and usual everyday purposes); Barcalo Mfg. Co. v. Firemen's Mut. Ins. Co., 24 A.D.2d 55, 57, 263 N.Y.S.2d 807, 809 (1965) (generally, friendly fire is one that is deliberately kindled and remains within designated place while hostile fire is one that has escaped from place or container in which it was intended to remain or one started with or without human agency in place where fire was never expected to be started or maintained); Pappadakis v. Netherlands Fire & Life Ins. Co., 137 Wash. 430, 434, 242 P. 641, 642 (1926) (where fire escaped from its accustomed place—bakery oven—where it was intended to be and heated sprinkler head, causing it to release water and damage property, damage was caused by fire out of place and it was, therefore, hostile fire and one that brought loss within terms of policy).

410. Consoli v. Commonwealth Ins. Co., 97 N.H. 224, 225, 84 A.2d 926, 927 (1951).

Some courts have recognized that a "friendly" fire could "turn hostile" even though "confined to the place where it was intended to be." These courts add to the definition of "friendly fire" that it must not be "excessive" or "uncontrolled."[411] Thus, a fire may effectively become hostile, and the damage its causes be covered, if its size—the heat it generates—becomes greater than would be anticipated.[412]

Because the policy covers direct *physical loss of or damage to* covered property caused by or resulting from any covered cause of loss, coverage is not limited to losses from burning. Losses that are the immediate consequence of a fire also may be covered.[413] Determining when a loss is the "immediate consequence" of a fire can be difficult. Courts have long said that to render a fire the immediate or proximate cause of loss or damage, the insured property need not actually be ignited or consumed by fire.[414] The damage may be caused by smoke, soot, fall of a building, explosion, and even theft as a result of a fire.[415] A loss may be the direct effect of ignition or burning, or efforts to save property by removing it from the danger, destruction of buildings to prevent a fire's spread, or use of water to extinguish the fire.[416] Demolition of an safe building or portion of a building after a fire may be covered as a loss caused by fire.[417]

The difficulty in defining when a loss is caused by a fire means a common interest community governing board should never assume a loss related to a fire is not covered. At a minimum, the association should contact its broker and possibly submit a claim. If the loss is substantial and the broker expresses doubt about coverage or the insurer actually denies the claim, consultation with an attorney who specializes in insurance law should be the next step.

When considering the peril of fire, it is important to determine whether the policy has a Protective Safeguards Endorsement as it adds an exclusion for loss or damage caused by fire when the insured fails to maintain certain protective safeguards, for example a fire suppression system.[418]

---

411. Engel v. Redwood County Farmers Mut. Ins. Co., 281 N.W.2d 331 (Minn. 1979).

412. Bowes v. North Carolina Farm Bureau Mut. Ins. Co., 26 N.C. App. 234, 238, 215 S.E.2d 855, 857, *cert. den.*, 288 N.C. 238, 217 S.E.2d 662 (1975).

413. Cozen, *Insuring Real Property*, § 1.06[7][b][i][A] (Matthew Bender & Co. 2015).

414. Ermentraut v. Girard Fire & Marine Ins. Co., 63 Minn. 305, 308, 65 N.W. 635, 636 (1895).

415. Reliance Ins. Co. v. Naman, 118 Tex. 21, 26–27, 6 S.W.2d 743, 745 (1928).

416. Fogarty v. Fidelity & Casualty Co., 122 Conn. 245, 188 A. 481, 1936 Conn. LEXIS 65 (1937).

417. Frontis v. Milwaukee Ins. Co., 156 Conn. 492, 500, 242 A.2d 749, 753 (1968).

418. *See* § 10.36[1][a], *infra*.

[2] Lightning

Lightning is a standard named peril.[419] Policies do not define it. The New York Court of Appeals, in a case decided over 150 years ago, conceded it was unable to determine "what electricity is," but settled on a dictionary definition of lightning as a sudden discharge of electricity from a cloud to the earth producing a vivid flash of light.[420] Precisely one century later, the Nebraska Supreme Court was more confident of the definition, saying lightning is any sudden and violent discharge of electricity, occurring in course of nature, between positively and negatively electrified bodies, usually developing light, heat, and disruptive force.[421] A more succinct definition is a natural—as opposed to artificial—discharge of electricity from the atmosphere.[422]

It can be difficult to prove that damage was caused by lightning rather than something else.[423] That difficulty is borne out in a case decided by the Florida Supreme Court.[424] The insured homeowner sought coverage for lightning damage. The insurer denied coverage citing an absence of any evidence of lightning in the area of the dwelling or any other facts to support the theory that lightning caused the damage. There were no signs of lightning on any of the trees around the dwelling, but one witness testified that recently there had been a "violent electric storm" nearby and lightning had struck very close to the house. On the other hand, there was evidence of faulty construction. The jury found for the homeowner. The insurer appealed. The court acknowledged the question was close, but concluded a jury question was presented and said it did not "feel authorized" to overthrow a verdict approved by the trial court. The decision reveals that evidence that lightning damaged insured property is problematic, in part because it is an instantaneous event. Frequently, a windstorm is in progress, and the insurer can point to evidence that wind damaged the property.[425] Witnesses can often testify to lightning striking in the vicinity, but can seldom say they saw lightning

419. ISO Form CP 10 20 04 02, § A.2.

420. Babcock v. Montgomery County Mut. Ins. Co., 4 N.Y. 326, 336 (1850).

421. Clouse v. St. Paul Fire & Marine Ins. Co., 152 Neb. 230, 237, 40 N.W.2d 820, 825 (1950).

422. Cozen, *Insuring Real Property*, § 1.06[7][b][i][B] (Matthew Bender & Co. 2015).

423. Beakes v. Phoenix Ins. Co., 143 N.Y. 402, 407, 38 N.E. 453, 454 (1894) (duty of jury in cases involving lightning strike is difficult to perform; where building is shattered by lightning stroke, but not prostrated, and moment later high wind completes work of destruction, it is not easy for insured to prove its case).

424. Caledonian Am. Ins. Co. v. Coe, 76 So. 2d 272 (Fla. 1954).

425. *See, e.g.*, Hartford Fire Ins. Co. v. Cincinnati Ice Mfg. & Cold Storage Co., 9 Ohio App. 403 (1918) (insurer produced weather reports to show damage was caused by wind and argued lightning would necessarily have shown some fusing or burning of the metals or wood; insured contended its loss coincided exactly with stroke of lightning and severe thunder clap testified to by numerous witnesses in immediate vicinity; while difficult question was raised as to cause of loss, issue was one that was peculiarly within province of jury to decide and it decided for insured).

strike and damage the insured property.[426] Thus, the evidence may be purely circumstantial and yet sufficient to support a claim for lightning damage.[427]

When a policy provides coverage against loss or damage caused by lightning, it usually covers all known effects of electricity that come under the general heading of lightning, including all loss or damage that results as a direct and natural consequence of that lightning, even if other incidental agencies might have added to the loss or damage.[428] Thus, in a Georgia case, lightning burned off the valve head of a water pump under a house. That caused water to escape, which in turn caused wooden floors to rise and buckle and suffer mold and mildew damage. The court concluded all the damage was a direct loss by lightning within the meaning of the policy.[429] In another case, fire partially destroyed a building *adjacent* to the insured property. A wall of the damaged building was left standing. Over one month later it collapsed onto the insured building, allegedly because it was struck by lightning. The court said that lightning did not need to strike the insured property for there to be coverage. It concluded that the loss, if from a lightning strike, was an immediate loss from lightning that the parties intended to cover.[430] Finally, a refrigerator was damaged when all circuits breaker switches

---

426. *See* Gelfo v. General Acci. Fire & Life Assurance Corp., 167 So. 2d 31 (Fla. 3d DCA 1964), where lightning allegedly struck a seawall and caused it to collapse. As is often the case, witness descriptions of the point of impact varied. All witnesses testified lightning struck in the "immediate vicinity" of the seawall and that the seawall slid into the water almost immediately following the flash, but none could say that the bolt actually struck the wall and there was no other evidence of a direct strike. The jury found for the policyholder, but the trial court directed a verdict for the insurer and in the alternative ordered a new trial. The appellate court said the evidence was not so clear, convincing, and without conflict as to establish as a matter of law that the insurer was entitled to a verdict. It reversed the directed verdict. On the other hand, it affirmed the order of a new trial. *See also* Clouse v. St. Paul Fire & Marine Ins. Co., 152 Neb. 230, 40 N.W.2d 820 (1950) (where witnesses testified to loud crash of thunder and bright flash of lightning immediately after which insured building collapsed, there was sufficient evidence to support jury verdict for insured).

427. *See, e.g.*, Travelers Indem. Co. v. Jarrett, 369 S.W.2d 653 (Tex. Civ. App.—Waco 1963) (where insured, an electrical engineer, opined that only lightning striking power line could cause sudden surge of excess electricity required to break all circuits to house and power company employee testified there were one or more severe electrical storms in area during relevant period of time and company equipment had apparent lightning damage, appellate court refused to accept insurer's argument on appeal that there was no evidence to support factual findings in lower court concerning lightning as constituting cause of loss); Shields v. Vermont Mut. Fire Ins. Co., 102 Vt. 224, 147 A. 352 (1929) (where neighborhood was visited by electrical storm, accompanied by wind and rain, and insured barn was seen to be standing before storm, but after it, barn was found to be demolished and no witness saw it fall and no fire ensued, testimony about proximity of lightning strike was sufficient for jury to find that lightning and not wind caused loss).

428. Clouse v. St. Paul Fire & Marine Ins. Co., 152 Neb. 230, 233 40 N.W.2d 820, 823 (1950).

429. Atlantic Mut. Fire Ins. Co. v. Chadwick, 115 Ga. App. 850, 156 S.E.2d 182, 183 (1967). *See also* Cummins v. Pennsylvania Fire Ins. Co., 153 Iowa 579, 134 N.W. 79 (1912) (injury to goods from water and debris into which they were precipitated by falling of wall was direct and natural consequence of lightning).

430. Automobile Ins. Co. v. Thomas, 153 Md. 253, 138 A. 33 (1927).

were thrown and, without electricity, the food in the refrigerator spoiled. The insurer argued the damage was caused by putrefied food, a peril not covered, and it was not, therefore, liable to the insured. The court upheld judgment for the insured and said, the food was not an intervening cause but an intermediate link in the chain of causation. The lightning was not merely a remote cause, and the court could not to say the policy did not insure the loss.[431]

[3] Explosion

Commercial property polices provide coverage for "explosion,"[432] including explosion of gases or fuel within a furnace of any fired vessel or within flues or passages through which gases of combustion pass. The cause of loss of explosion does not include loss or damage by rupture, bursting, or operation of pressure relief devices or rupture or bursting by expansion or swelling of the contents of any building or structure, caused by or resulting from water. This coverage needs to be read in conjunction with an equipment breakdown policy,[433] or endorsement as many common interest communities will have equipment—for example, heating and air conditioning systems, water pumps, and backup generators—that are potentially subject to "explosion."

[4] Windstorm

Policies usually group windstorm and hail together, but for purposes of the discussion here they are separated. "Windstorm" is almost universally listed in policies as a covered cause of loss.[434] Typically, policies provide that the peril does not include frost or cold weather, ice (other than hail), snow or sleet, whether driven by wind or not, or loss or damage to the interior of any building or structure, or property inside that building or structure, caused by rain, snow, san, or dust, whether driven by wind or not, unless the building or structure first sustained wind or hail damage to its roof or walls through which the rain, snow, sand, or dust entered.[435]

---

431. Travelers Indem. Co. v. Jarrett, 369 S.W.2d 653 (Tex. Civ. App.—Waco 1963).

432. ISO Form CP 10 20 04 02, § A.3.

433. *See* Chapter 11, *infra.*

434. ISO Form CP 10 20 04 02, § A.4.

435. *See* Dunn v. Scottsdale Ins. Co., 2013 U.S. Dist. LEXIS 107984 (M.D. Pa. Aug. 1, 2013) (coverage would be invoked when structure experienced some type of physical damage covered by policy and, subsequently, precipitation was able to enter interior of structure and cause additional damage). *See also* Divine Motel Grp., LLC v. Rockhill Ins. Co., 2015 U.S. Dist. LEXIS 87789 (M.D. Fla. July 7, 2015) (no coverage where wind-driven rain of tropical storm entered property because of deterioration of roof's weatherproofing system, deficient repairs, inadequate maintenance, leaks under doors, insufficient weatherproofing of air conditioning units, and oversaturation of certain components of concrete walls as wear and tear, decay, and deterioration were specifically excluded causes of loss and policy also excluded loss or damage caused by or resulting from faulty, inadequate, or defective design, specifications, workmanship, repair, construction and maintenance; damages that allowed water to intrude during tropical storm were all specifically

[a] Definition of "Windstorm"

The term "windstorm" is not defined in property polices, and there is some disagreement over its meaning. The primary difference of opinion is over whether a windstorm is one sufficient to damage the insured property or a storm of extraordinary force and violence, instead of merely a wind capable of causing the alleged damage.[436]

For example, the Iowa Supreme Court, relying on a dictionary definition, said a windstorm is one characterized by high wind, but with little or no precipitation.[437] The court went on to say it must be an "outburst of tumultuous force," not an "ordinary gust of wind," no matter how prolonged. The court added that the term takes its meaning measurably from the other words with which it is associated—tornado and cyclone—although the court was quick to add that a windstorm does not need to have either the cyclonic or the twirling or whirling features that usually accompany tornadoes or cyclones, but it has to be more than an ordinary current of air no matter how long it continues.

Some courts say any wind strong and sustained enough to damage insured property is a windstorm.[438] Courts add that a windstorm is a wind of force and velocity sufficient to cause damage to the property if that property is in *reasonable condition.*[439]

A Georgia appellate court rejected the contention that coverage for a windstorm means a policy covers any damage if there was wind sufficient to cause it. It agreed with earlier decisions that a windstorm requires a wind sufficiently violent

---

excluded from coverage, and any resulting damage did not appear to satisfy exception to water intrusion limitation); Royale Green Condo. Ass'n v. Aspen Specialty Ins. Co., 2009 U.S. Dist. LEXIS 24349 (S.D. Fla. Mar. 24, 2009) (where testimony of inspectors conflicted on question of whether components were part of air conditioning system or of roof, it was unclear whether water entered through manmade opening or wind damage; summary judgment for insurer denied); Tropic Sun Towers Condo. Ass'n v. Zurich Am. Ins. Co. of Illinois, 2006 U.S. Dist. LEXIS 89358 (M.D. Fla. Dec. 8, 2006) (where policy prohibited coverage for water damage unless building first sustained damage by covered cause of loss to its roof or walls through which rain entered, question was whether the damage to property was caused by permanent damage to sliding glass doors that allowed water into building or whether that damage to sliding glass doors was only temporary, and therefore not covered); Stufflebean v. Firemen's Fund Ins. Co., 710 S.W.2d 931, 933 (Mo. App. 1986) (where broken gutter caused water to accumulate on porch and then seep into basement, direct force of wind did not cause opening in roof or wall of house through which rainwater entered).

436. Cozen, *Insuring Real Property*, § 1.06[7][b][i][D] (Matthew Bender & Co. 2015).

437. Jordan v. Iowa Mut. Tornado Ins. Co., 151 Iowa 73, 77, 130 N.W. 177, 178 (1911) (blizzard was windstorm).

438. *See* Adams Apple Products Corp. v. National Union Fire Ins. Co., 170 Pa. Super. 269, 275, 85 A.2d 702, 705 (1952) (any wind, strong and sustained enough to damage insured property is "windstorm" within meaning of term as used in policy). *See also* Koory v. Western Casualty & Sur. Co., 153 Ariz. 412, 737 P.2d 388 (1987).

439. *See* Yunker v. Republic-Franklin Ins. Co., 2 Ohio App. 3d 339, 442 N.E.2d 108 (1982); St. Paul Fire & Marine Ins. Co. v. Central Park Mobile Homes, 22 Ariz. App. 557, 560, 529 P.2d 711, 714 (1974).

to be capable of damaging insured property, either by itself or by hurling an object against it and, therefore, it has to be a wind of extraordinary force and violence, tumultuous in character, that injuriously disturbs the insured property.[440]

The determination of whether there is a windstorm is fact driven and ordinarily a question for a jury. For instance, in a case before the Mississippi Supreme Court, an insured property suffered a collapsed wall and fallen roof. The velocity of the wind at a Weather Bureau facility was 21 miles per hour, but the insured property was about three miles away and there was proof tending to show that for any appreciable windstorm damage to the building to have occurred, it would have been necessary to have had a velocity of 35 or 40 miles per hour. The court said the case "presented an issue which was peculiarly for the decision of the jury."[441]

[b] Distinguishing Windstorm Damage from Flood Damage

When property damage occurs in a windstorm accompanied by flooding, the question of concurrent causation arises: was the damage caused by the wind or the water?[442] Damage from flood waters is typically excluded from coverage under property policies while damage from wind is not covered by any flood insurance the policyholder may have. The majority of courts have responded to this dilemma by invoking the "efficient proximate cause" doctrine.[443] Under that doctrine, if two risks contribute to a loss and one is covered and the other excluded, the loss is covered when the covered peril was the efficient, proximate or predominant cause of the loss.[444] Insurers have reacted to that doctrine by adding what is called an "Anti-Concurrent Causation" clause (ACC) to their policies. For the BPP and CAC, the clause is found in the causes of loss form that is added to the policy. The typical wording of the ACC clause says the insurer will not pay for loss or damage caused directly or indirectly by any of the excluded perils and that the loss or damage is excluded regardless of any other cause or event contributing concurrently, or in any sequence, to the loss.[445] While that

---

440. General Ins. Co. v. Davis, 115 Ga. App. 804, 809–10, 156 S.E.2d 112, 115 (1967).

441. New Hampshire Fire Ins. Co. v. Kochton Plywood & Veneer Co., 242 Miss. 169, 175, 134 So. 2d 735, 736–37 (1961).

442. *See generally* Wilson, *A Procedure for Segregating Damages from Wind and Flood Water*, 16 Tex. Tech. Admin. L. J. 141 (2014).

443. Bell, *A Concurrent Mess and a Call for Clarity in First-Party Property Insurance Coverage Analysis*, 18 Conn. Ins. L.J. 73, 79 (2011).

444. VanDine & Norton, *Anti-Concurrent Causation Clauses and Hurricane Relief: Was It Wind or Water?*, 19 S. Carolina Lawyer 18, 20 (2008). *See also* Sunbreaker Condominium Ass'n v. Travelers Ins. Co., 79 Wn. App. 368, 375, 901 P.2d 1079, 1082–83 (1995) (efficient proximate cause rule requires courts to apply insurance contract causation language with reference to efficient proximate cause of the loss, rather than its immediate, physical cause, and effectively imposes liability on insurer for loss efficiently caused by covered peril, even though other, excluded perils contributed to that loss).

445. *See, e.g.*, ISO Form CP 10 30 04 02, § B.1.

language was incorporated into policies at least as early as the 1980s, Hurricane Katrina focused attention on the ACC as insurers invoked it to avoid coverage for gargantuan losses.[446]

Many courts enforce these ACC provisions literally so that if the insurer can identify an event in the chain of causation that is excluded, coverage is denied and if 99 percent of the loss would be covered but 1 percent would be excluded, then coverage for the entire loss can be barred.[447] On the other hand, many other courts invalidate Anti-Concurrent Causation clauses finding them to be a "contractual attempt to dodge apparently immutable doctrinal rules for assessing concurrently caused insurance losses."[448] Some courts hold that for an ACC to apply, the excluded loss has to be a substantial factor or the efficient proximate cause of the loss.[449] California restrains application of the ACC by statute.[450]

A full exploration of the ACC and losses in windstorms accompanied by flooding is beyond the scope of this treatise. Fortunately, it is explored in depth by treatises and journal articles.[451] What common interest community associations need to know when they are hit by both tropical storm force winds and the storm surge they produce is that professional assistance is almost certainly required in preparing a claim. That means an attorney and public adjuster with extensive experience in handling these claims, but also consultants knowledgeable about structural engineering and building construction.[452] The attorney can

446. VanDine & Norton, *Anti-Concurrent Causation Clauses and Hurricane Relief: Was It Wind or Water?*, 19 S. Carolina Lawyer 18, 20 (2008).

447. Bell, *A Concurrent Mess and a Call for Clarity in First-Party Property Insurance Coverage Analysis*, 18 Conn. Ins. L.J. 73, 87 (2011). See also Phillips & Coplen, *Concurrent Causation versus Efficient Proximate Cause in First-Party Property Insurance Coverage Analysis*, 36 Brief 32 (2007), for a state-by-state analysis.

448. Knutsen, *Confusion About Causation in Insurance: Solutions for Catastrophic Losses*, 61 Ala. L. Rev. 957, 996 (2010).

449. Bell, *A Concurrent Mess and a Call for Clarity in First-Party Property Insurance Coverage Analysis*, 18 Conn. Ins. L.J. 73, 88 (2011).

450. Cal. Ins. Code §§ 530, 532.

451. Steven Plitt et al., *Couch on Insurance* §§ 101:39–:60, 150:34–.37 (3d ed. Supp. 2015); Cozen, *Insuring Real Property*, §§ 48.01–.05 (Matthew Bender & Co. 2015). *See also* Wilson, *A Procedure for Segregating Damages From Wind and Flood Water*, 16 Tex. Tech Admin. L.J. 141 (2014); French, *The Ensuing Loss Clause in Insurance Policies: The Forgotten and Misunderstood Antidote to Anti-Concurrent Causation Exclusions*, 13 Nev. L.J. 215 (2012); Bell, *A Concurrent Mess and a Call for Clarity in First-Party Property Insurance Coverage Analysis*, 18 Conn. Ins. L.J. 73 (2011); Knutsen, *Confusion About Causation in Insurance: Solutions for Catastrophic Losses*, 61 Ala. L. Rev. 957 (2010).

452. Any expert needs to be fully qualified in his or her field, and his or her opinion has to be based on more than speculation, otherwise his or her testimony may be inadmissible in court. For example, a condominium association that had been damaged in Superstorm Sandy attempted to introduce into evidence the report of a contractor stating that its loss was from wind, not water. The court noted that what it called the "alleged" expert contractor was a resident of the condominium, and his report consisted of unsupported speculation. The contractor's report was excluded from being introduced into evidence. 151 E. Leaming Ave. Condo Ass'n v. QBE Specialty Ins. Co.,

navigate the complex causation questions and the policy language. The consultants can, by providing empirical evidence of the cause of loss, help the association meet its burden of proving that the claim is covered.[453] However, the cost of establishing causation in these cases is expensive.[454] For the association, the extent of that expense can depend on how the burden of proof is allocated. Generally, an insured has the responsibility to show its claim is covered under the policy and the insurer then has the burden to prove an exclusion applies. If the association has to prove its loss was caused *solely* by wind, its task will likely prove difficult and expensive. On the other hand, courts may impose more of the burden on the insurer to show the loss was caused *in part by water* and, therefore, barred under the flood exclusion.[455]

[5] Hail

Hail is a covered risk.[456] Policies usually group windstorm and hail together, but for purposes of the discussion here, they are separated. Hail does not include frost or cold weather, ice—other than hail—snow, or sleet,[457] whether driven by wind or not or loss or damage to the interior of any building or structure, or the property inside, that is caused by rain, snow, sand, or dust, whether driven by wind or not, unless the building or structure first sustains wind or hail damage to its roof or walls through which the rain, snow, sand, or dust enters. The policy describes conditions that are not hail, but it does not define hail. What then is hail? One court accepted the definition that it is ice pellets in excess of five millimeters.[458] While hail is generally thought of as a phenomenon that occurs during

---

2015 U.S. Dist. LEXIS 79002 (D.N.J. June 18, 2015) (noting numerous deficiencies in report including failure to rule out other potential causes of damage).

453. Field & Carmel, *Evaluating First-Party Property Claims with Multiple Causes Under the Efficient Proximate Cause Doctrine* (ABA Jan. 30, 2012).

454. Knutsen, *Confusion about Causation in Insurance: Solutions for Catastrophic Losses*, 61 Ala. L. Rev. 957, 960 (2010) (questions of concurrent causation are not only difficult to answer but are expensive to answer). The association needs to work closely with an experienced attorney who can determine when and if consultants are needed.

455. VanDine & Norton, *Anti-Concurrent Causation Clauses and Hurricane Relief: Was It Wind or Water?*, 19 S. Carolina Lawyer 18, 23 (2008).

456. ISO Form CP 10 20 04 02, § A.4.

457. Courts have observed the practical difficulty of distinguishing between sleet and certain forms of hail and have, therefore, found that coverage of hail under a policy includes sleet, at least when sleet is not specifically excepted. Evana Plantation, Inc. v. Yorkshire Ins. Co., 214 Miss. 321, 326–29, 58 So. 2d 797, 799–800 (1952) (terms of policy and consideration of meanings of "hail" indicate that it includes "sleet" as one of insured risks). *Accord* Southall v. Farm Bureau Mut. Ins. Co., 276 Ark. 58, 632 S.W.2d 420 (Ark. 1982) (noting that insurer conceded that sleet on the roof of insured chicken house was small hail). *Compare* Commonwealth Lloyds Ins. Co. v. Downs, 853 S.W.2d 104 (Tex. App.—Fort Worth 1993) (finding term "hail" to be ambiguous, but finding where damage was caused by either ice, freezing rain, snow, or sleet, or combination of them, there was no coverage under provision for hail).

458. Home Mut. Fire Ins. Co. v. Jones, 63 Ark. App. 221, 228, 977 S.W.2d 12, 15 (1998).

summer storms, some courts say there is such a thing as winter hail,[459] but others do not agree.[460]

Hail damage is particularly prevalent in the states in the central third of the country. In recent years, common interest communities have made claims for hail damage in Colorado,[461] Illinois,[462] Indiana,[463] Iowa,[464] Ohio,[465] Minnesota,[466] North Dakota,[467] and Texas.[468] The damage is most often to roofs but can also be to windows, siding,[469] and equipment such as HVAC units. Sometimes a building will collapse after an alleged hail storm. In that case, the insurer will generally argue either that the damage was caused by ice—a peril not covered—or that collapse is not a covered peril or is specifically excluded.[470]

Hail can cause denting, but is that a loss if the property is still functional? Insurers argue their policies do not cover dents where the damage is merely cosmetic. In one case the court responded that the insurer was in effect arguing that because the roof was not damaged enough to diminish its function or value, the policy did not require it to pay to replace the roof. However, noted the court, the policy provided the insurer would pay for direct physical loss to covered property

---

459. Evana Plantation, Inc. v. Yorkshire Ins. Co., 214 Miss. 321, 328, 58 So. 2d 797, 800 (1952).

460. Commonwealth Lloyds Ins. Co. v. Downs, 853 S.W.2d 104, 113 (Tex. App.—Fort Worth 1993) (hail is not present in wintertime because it cannot form).

461. *See, e.g.*, Madison Park Townhouses Homeowners Ass'n v. Country Mut. Ins. Co., 2015 U.S. Dist. LEXIS 119090 (D. Colo. Sept. 8, 2015); Laredo Landing Owners Ass'n v. Sequoia Ins. Co., 2015 U.S. Dist. LEXIS 75104 (D. Colo. June 10, 2015); Avalon Condo. Ass'n v. Secura Ins., 2015 U.S. Dist. LEXIS 129373 (D. Colo. Sept. 25, 2015); Edge Constr., LLC v. Owners Ins. Co., 2015 U.S. Dist. LEXIS 85835 (D. Colo. June 29, 2015); Sable Cove Condo. Ass'n v. Owners Ins. Co., 2014 U.S. Dist. LEXIS 124050 (D. Colo. Sept. 5, 2014).

462. Stratford W. Homeowners Ass'n v. Country Mut. Ins. Co., 273 Ill. Dec. 33, 338 Ill. App. 3d 288, 788 N.E.2d 342 (2003).

463. Autumn Glen Homeowners Ass'n v. Travelers Ins. Co., 2015 U.S. Dist. LEXIS 33317 (S.D. Ind. Mar. 18, 2015).

464. N. Glenn Homeowners Ass'n v. State Farm Fire & Cas. Co., 854 N.W.2d 67 (Iowa App. 2014).

465. Bethel Vill. Condo. Ass'n v. Republic-Franklin Ins. Co., 2007 Ohio App. LEXIS 471 (Feb. 8, 2007), *app. den.*, 114 Ohio St. 3d 1427, 868 N.E.2d 681 (2007).

466. *See, e.g.*, Trout Brook South Condo. Ass'n v. Harleysville Worcester Ins. Co., 995 F. Supp. 2d 1035 (D. Minn. 2014); Cedar Bluff Townhome Condo. Ass'n v. Am. Family Mut. Ins. Co., 857 N.W.2d 290 (Minn. 2014). *See also* Condos. of Shenandoah Place v. SECURA Ins., 2016 U.S. Dist. LEXIS 18608 (D. Minn. Feb. 16, 2016); QBE Ins. Corp. v. Twin Homes of French Ridge Homeowners Ass'n, 778 N.W.2d 393 (Minn. App. 2010).

467. First Int'l Bank & Trust v. Peterson, 797 N.W.2d 316 (N.D. 2011).

468. Ridglea Estate Condo. Ass'n v. Lexington Ins. Co., 309 F. Supp. 2d 851 (N.D. Tex. 2004); Spicewood Summit Office Condos. Ass'n v. Am. First Lloyd's Ins. Co., 287 S.W.3d 461 (Tex. App.—Austin 2009).

469. *See, e.g.*, Cedar Bluff Townhome Condo. Ass'n v. Am. Family Mut. Ins. Co., 857 N.W.2d 290 (Minn. 2014).

470. *See, e.g.*, Barton v. Columbia Mut. Casualty Ins. Co., 930 F.2d 1337 (8th Cir. 1991) (policy expressly excluded loss because it was caused directly or indirectly by ice other than hail); Home Mut. Fire Ins. Co. v. Jones, 63 Ark. App. 221, 977 S.W.2d 12 (1998) (insurer denied claim because insured had not purchased "collapse coverage").

from a covered cause of loss which in turn was a risk of direct physical loss, with loss defined as accidental loss or damage. Under the phrase "loss or damage," even without a measurable loss in value or in function, the policy contemplated the possibility that there could still be damage.[471] Finally, there was no exception to the definition of "loss," said the court, for cosmetic damage or any other kind of particular damage.[472] The court found for the insured. It got a new roof. In response to decisions like this one, insurers may consider adding an endorsement excluding coverage for cosmetic damage to roofs.[473]

Frequently, the insurer will only agree to pay for *repair* to a roof damaged by hail, repair primarily meaning replacing damaged shingles or tiles. One court noted that the industry standard is that an adjuster has to find a minimum number of 10 to 12 hail hits within a test square for an insurer to declare a roof a total loss, otherwise the carrier will pay only to repair damaged shingles and other roofing components.[474] That may be the "industry standard," but where there is evidence that there is no guarantee the roof will not leak if only repaired, a court may well find the insured is entitled to have the insurer pay to replace the roof.[475] As that suggests, cases concerning hail damage can be very fact specific. In one Louisiana case, for example, two different adjusters for the carrier found no hail damage to the insured's roof, but two contractors who inspected the roof testified that there was hail damage. The court ruled in favor of the insured because the parties agreed there were leaks in a bedroom and the front porch, the house did not leak before the hail storm, and the residences on each side of the insured property were damaged and their roofs were replaced. In an interesting aside, the court said it knew from personal experience that hail damage is not easily detected.[476]

Another issue that arises is whether the insurer must pay to replace all the tiles or shingles on a roof or siding on a building to maintain consistency in

---

471. *See also* Great Plains Ventures, Inc. v. Liberty Mut. Fire Ins. Co., 2016 U.S. Dist. LEXIS 17751 (D. Kan. Feb. 11, 2016) (phrase "physical loss or damage" in policy provides coverage where cosmetic hail dents physically alter insured property; coverage not limited to decrease in usefulness or function for normal purposes).

472. Advance Cable Co., LLC v. Cincinnati Ins. Co., LLC, 788 F.3d 743 (7th Cir. 2015).

473. *See, e.g.*, ISO Form CP 10 26 10 14 (Commercial Property: West Virginia Exclusion of Cosmetic Damage to Roof Surfacing). The endorsement provides the carrier will not pay for cosmetic damage to roof surfacing caused by wind and/or hail and defines "cosmetic damage" to mean that wind and/or hail caused marring, pitting, or other "superficial damage" that changed the appearance of roof surfacing, but did not prevent the roof from continuing to function as a barrier to entrance of the elements to the extent it did before that cosmetic damage occurred.

474. Autumn Glen Homeowners Ass'n v. Travelers Ins. Co., 2015 U.S. Dist. LEXIS 33317 (S.D. Ind. Mar. 18, 2015).

475. *See, e.g.*, Higginbotham v. New Hampshire Indem. Co., 498 So. 2d 1149 (La. App. 1986), *cert. den.*, 501 So. 2d 236 (La. 1987) (record convinced court that insured homeowners could not be fully compensated for their damage by repairing roof).

476. Van Rossum v. St. Paul Mercury Ins. Co., 147 So. 2d 100 (La. App. 1962).

appearance. Insurers understandably resist paying for replacement of undamaged property. For example, a common interest community in Minnesota consisted of 20 multi-unit residential buildings. All of the buildings were damaged in a hail storm. Some had damage to only a few siding panels while others had more extensive damage to their siding. While replacement panels were available from the same manufacturer, panels of the same color were not. The association contended that all of the siding on all 20 buildings had to be replaced because there would be a color mismatch with existing panels if only the damaged ones were replaced. The association and carrier disagreed over whether policy language providing for replacement of damaged property with other property of comparable material and quality required replacement of all siding, even undamaged siding, to provide a color match. The association argued "comparable material and quality" mandated a color match between the damaged and undamaged panels, and the carrier countered that the policy only required replacement of panels that had actually been damaged.

The court said the plain meaning of "comparable material and quality" is material suitable for matching and, thus, it concluded "on the spectrum of resemblance," the phrase required less than an *identical color match* but a reasonable color match nonetheless. Therefore, the policy required a "reasonable color match" between new and existing siding. Because there was not a reasonable color match available, all the panels would have to be replaced providing the color mismatch constituted a direct physical loss of or damage to covered property as that is what the policy required the insurer to cover. The court decided that because a color mismatch would result from the inability to replace the damaged panels with ones of "comparable material and quality," the covered property—that is, the buildings—sustained direct physical loss. The association was entitled to have all the siding panels on each of its 20 buildings replaced. However, the court concluded by saying that "all storm-related property damage claims present their own facts," warning the reader that different facts—including different policy language—could yield a different result.[477] Indeed in a Kentucky case, the court distinguished the Minnesota decision because the policy in the Minnesota case provided for replacement cost, and in the case before it there was an actual cash value policy. The insurer requested an umpire for appraisal, and the court appointed an umpire but refused to instruct him that cosmetic matching of the siding was required.[478]

In many states, there will be an endorsement to the policy limiting coverage to the actual cash value for roof surfacing even if replacement cost coverage is

477. Cedar Bluff Townhome Condo. Ass'n v. Am. Family Mut. Ins. Co., 857 N.W.2d 290 (Minn. 2014). *See also* Trout Brook South Condominium Association v. Harleysville Worcester Insurance Co., 995 F. Supp. 2d 1035 (D. Minn. 2014).

478. Cincinnati Specialty Underwriters Ins. Co. v. C.F.L.P. 1, LLC, 2015 U.S. Dist. LEXIS 132523 (W.D. Ky. Sept. 30, 2015).

otherwise applicable.[479] Generally, for purposes of the endorsement, roof surfacing refers to shingles, tiles, cladding, metal or synthetic sheeting, or similar materials covering the roof and includes all materials used in securing the roof surface and all materials applied to or under the roof surface for moisture protection, and to roof flashing.

[6] Smoke

Smoke that causes "sudden and accidental"[480] loss or damage is covered under commercial property policies, but not smoke from agricultural smudging or industrial operations.[481] Is "vapor" smoke? Courts disagree on that question.[482]

[7] Aircraft or Vehicles

Coverage for "aircraft or vehicles" is only for physical contact of an aircraft, a spacecraft, a self-propelled missile, a vehicle, or an object thrown up by a vehicle with the described property or with the building or structure containing the described property and includes loss or damage by objects falling from aircraft.[483] There is, however, no coverage for loss or damage caused by or resulting from vehicles owned by the insured or that are operated in the course of the business of the insured.

[8] Riot or Civil Commotion

Riot or civil commotion is a covered peril.[484] It includes acts of striking employees while occupying the described premises and looting that occurs at the time and place of a riot or civil commotion.

---

479. *See* ISO Form CP 10 22 10 12 (Commercial Property: Connecticut Actual Cash Value for Roof Surfacing); ISO Form CP 10 25 11 13 (Commercial Property: Indiana Actual Cash Value for Roof Surfacing); ISO Form CP 10 23 10 12 (Commercial Property: Massachusetts Actual Cash Value for Roof Surfacing); ISO Form CP 10 24 12 13 (Commercial Property: New Hampshire Actual Cash Value for Roof Surfacing); ISO Form CP 10 49 10 12 (Commercial Property: Wyoming Actual Cash Value for Roof Surfacing). *See also* ISO Form CP 10 48 10 12 (Commercial Property: Missouri Limitations on Coverage for Roof Surfacing).

480. *See* Sokoloski v. American West Ins. Co., 294 Mont. 210, 214, 980 P.2d 1043, 1046 (1999) (smoke damage from the candles that occurred over a four- to five-week period was not sudden).

481. ISO Form CP 10 20 04 02, § A.5.

482. *See* United States Fid. & Guar. Co. v. First State Bank & Trust Co., 125 F.3d 680 (8th Cir. 1997) (vapor cloud containing hydrochloric acid that damaged property did not contain any particulate matter and, therefore, did not constitute smoke); K & Lee Corp. v. Scottsdale Ins. Co., 769 F. Supp. 870, 875 (E.D. Pa. 1991), *aff'd*, 953 F.2d 1380 (3d Cir. 1992) (finding no coverage because invisible chemical vapors are not within common usage of term "smoke"). *Compare* Henri's Food Products Co. v. Home Ins. Co., 474 F. Supp. 889, 893 (E.D. Wis. 1979) (accepting that vapor was smoke and thus within policy coverage).

483. ISO Form CP 10 20 04 02, § A.6.

484. ISO Form CP 10 20 04 02, § A.7.

[9] Vandalism

Common interest communities can present tempting targets for vandals. Recreational facilities that are easily accessible and unattended are particularly enticing to mischief-makers. Vandalism is commonly a named peril and is defined as willful and malicious damage to, or destruction of, the described property.[485] Under vandalism coverage, the carrier will not pay for loss or damage caused by or resulting from theft, except for building damage caused by breaking in or exiting of burglars.[486] This exception for loss caused by theft has been the subject of much litigation and raises many questions beyond the scope of this discussion, but it is thoroughly addressed elsewhere.[487]

For an act to be one of vandalism under property policies, it has to be "willful and malicious." That means the act "must have been intentional or in such reckless and wanton disregard of the rights of others as to be the equivalent of intent."[488]

Courts are divided on the question of malice. Some hold the insured has to show intent to damage or destroy the insured property while others adopt a broader definition under which acts done with sufficient reckless and wanton disregard for the rights of the property owner are malicious.[489] The majority of courts adopt the latter definition under which a specific intent to injure or destroy a particular article is not required and it is sufficient that damage of some kind to some property should or could have been expected from the intentional act.[490] For example, where someone uncoupled water pipes and left the water running from the severed connections and the water found its way from one floor of the building to the ground floor that the insured rented and in which it kept the covered property, a New York court rejected the argument that there could be no coverage

485. ISO Form CP 10 20 04 02, § A.8.

486. *Consider* JJD Assocs. of Palm Beach, Ltd. v. Am. Empire Surplus Lines Ins. Co., 2011 U.S. Dist. LEXIS 134878 (S.D. Fla. Nov. 22, 2011) (regardless of "ideal" legal characterization, damage qualified as either theft or vandalism even if those acts were also constituents of act of burglary; property damage was excluded as vandalism and removal of copper wiring was excluded as theft).

487. Witus, *The Paradox of Insurance Coverage for Vandalism But Not Theft*, 56 Wayne L. Rev. 1747 (2010). For example, the author says one significant question is whether there is coverage for a loss incurred when criminals willfully damage a building to take items from it. One might ask, are those criminals thieves or are they vandals?

488. Livaditis v. American Casualty Co., 117 Ga. App. 297, 299, 160 S.E.2d 449, 450 (1968) (malice may be inferred from act of destruction).

489. Burgess Farms v. New Hampshire Ins. Group, 108 Idaho 831, 833–34, 702 P.2d 869, 871–72 (Idaho App. 1985). *See also* Witus, *The Paradox of Insurance Coverage for Vandalism But Not Theft*, 56 Wayne L. Rev. 1747, 1750–51 (2010).

490. Grabowski v. Agricultural Ins. Co., 675 F. Supp. 279 (E.D. Pa. 1987), *aff'd*, 856 F.2d 183 (3d Cir. 1988) (majority, but not universal, rule is that to recover under coverage for vandalism, insured has to show intentional act done by some known or unknown person in conscious or intentional disregard of rights of others in property that was proximate cause of damage to insured property).

because the willfulness and malice were exerted on the plumbing fixtures, not the covered property, which was "distant and out of sight."[491] When there is water damage resulting from vandalism, the insurer may attempt to invoke the standard water exclusion under which the insurer will not pay for loss or damage caused directly or indirectly by water. In a California case, for instance, vandals entered a warehouse and broke a valve on a water-cooled air conditioning unit, allowing water to escape. The water would have drained from the building without serious damage to it, but a burlap bag left in a drain caused the water to back up and damage insured inventory. The insurer denied coverage based on the water damage exclusion, but the court held the specific peril of vandalism set other causes in motion and was the proximate cause of the entire loss.[492]

Property policies almost always have a "vacancy" clause.[493] These clauses generally provide that if a building where loss or damage occurs has been vacant for more than 60 consecutive days before that loss or damage occurs, the insurer will not pay for any loss or damage caused by, *inter alai*, vandalism.[494]

[10] Sprinkler Leakage

Damage from leaking sprinkler systems presents the possibility of significant losses for common interest communities with multi-story buildings.[495] Consider, for example, a four-story building in which over a period of a week or more, all of the units in one stack are unoccupied. Some owners may be on vacation or away on a business trip. A unit may be vacant because the owner has moved, and the unit has yet to be sold. If a sprinkler head malfunctions or a water pipe bursts in the fourth-floor unit in that stack, the water will penetrate the floor and walls until it reaches the ground floor, at which time it may become visible in a hallway outside the ground floor unit. Until that time, a considerable amount of water damage may go undetected. Fortunately, "sprinkler leakage" is a named peril.

The term "sprinkler leakage" means leakage or discharge of any substance from an "automatic sprinkler system,"[496] including collapse of a tank that is part

491. Cresthill Industries, Inc. v. Providence Washington Ins. Co., 53 A.D.2d 488, 385 N.Y.S.2d 797 (1976).

492. Franklin Packaging Co. v. California Union Ins. Co., 171 N.J. Super. 188, 408 A.2d 448 (1979), *cert. den.*, 84 N.J. 434, 420 A.2d 340 (1980).

493. ISO Form CP 00 10 06 07, § E.6; ISO Form CP 00 17 06 07, § E.7.

494. See § 10.31, *infra*, for a discussion on the vacancy clauses.

495. As the federal Fourth Circuit Court of Appeal has noted, when automatic sprinkler systems were developed, and their use encouraged by offers of more favorable fire insurance rates, a new peril was created because, while the systems substantially diminished the risk of loss from fire, they created a new water hazard, because freezing water in the system, heat short of fire, corrosion, and other occurrences could cause a discharge of water. Carva Food Corp. v. Equitable Fire & Marine Ins. Co., 261 F.2d 254, 257 (4th Cir. 1958).

496. *See* Saiz v. Charter Oak Fire Ins. Co., 2007 U.S. Dist. LEXIS 67767 (D. Colo. Sept. 12, 2007) (by plain meaning of term "leak," coverage for sprinkler leakage is for water accidently spilling forth from sprinkler). "Automatic Sprinkler System," under the policy, means any automatic

of that system.[497] If the building or structure containing the automatic sprinkler system is covered property, the insurer will also pay the cost to repair or replace damaged parts of the system if the damage caused sprinkler leakage or was caused by freezing. The insurer will also pay the cost to tear out and replace any part of the building or structure to repair damage to the system that has resulted in sprinkler leakage.

The negligent act of the insured will generally not vitiate the coverage.[498] Where water pressure caused by attempts to fight a fire at a nearby property resulted in a leak in the sprinkler system at the insured premises, there was coverage.[499]

Depending on the policy language, coverage may be provided for loss or damage caused by a leak from an automatic sprinkler system on only the insured premises, even though the system is building wide. Thus, where the insured occupied the second floor of a building and a broken sprinkler on the fifth floor of that building occupied by a third party caused water damage to the insured premises, there was no coverage. The policy insured against a loss from a leak in the automatic sprinkler system "erected in or on that portion of the building occupied by the" insured. The court concluded that the loss that was insured against was one arising from leakage or discharge occurring in the sprinkler on the insured premises—in other words, the portion of the building occupied by the policyholder.[500] This limitation may affect the coverage of a common interest community in a mixed-use building. If, for example, the top floor of a multistory CIC building is a commercial use—perhaps a restaurant—that is separately insured from the residential association below, sprinkler leakage in that portion of the building might not be covered by the association policy.

A standard limitation in property policies provides the insurer will not pay for any loss or damage caused by sprinkler leakage, unless the insured has protected the system against freezing,[501] if the building where loss or damage occurs

---

fire protective or extinguishing system, including connected sprinklers and discharge nozzles, ducts, pipes, valves and fittings, tanks, their component parts and supports, and pumps and private fire protection mains. It also means non-automatic fire protective systems and hydrants, standpipes, and outlets when supplied from an automatic fire protective system.

497. ISO Form CP 10 20 04 02, § A.9.

498. *See* Wertheimer-Swarts Shoe Co. v. United States Casualty Co., 172 Mo. 135, 72 S.W. 635 (1903) (negligence by employee of insured causing damage to sprinkler system did not bar recovery).

499. *See* New York Dock Co. v. Aetna Casualty & Surety Co., 46 N.Y.S.2d 307 (1943) (where pressure exerted by fire engines in pumping water caused break in system, nearby fire was neither direct nor indirect cause of loss).

500. Bottomley v. Royal Ins. Co., 190 Mass. 73, 76 N.E. 463 (1906).

501. Coverage applies even if there has been a leak caused by freezing because all the insured is required to do is "protect" the system against freezing. *See* 7th & Allen Equities v. Hartford Cas. Ins. Co., 2012 U.S. Dist. LEXIS 158081 (E.D. Pa. Nov. 2, 2012) (noting "protect" is undefined and potentially ambiguous). *See also* Saiz v. Charter Oak Fire Ins. Co., 2007 U.S. Dist. LEXIS 67767 (D. Colo. Sept. 12, 2007) (where under policy, sprinkler leakage will be covered if insured

has been vacant for more than 60 consecutive days before that loss or damage occurs.[502] Further, when the policy is issued to the owner or general lessee of a building, "building" means the entire building and a building is vacant unless at least 31 percent of its total square footage is used by the building owner to conduct "customary operations."[503] The policy does not define what it means to "conduct customary operations." In one case an insured building owner rented out space in the building, but for some time only 15 percent of the space was rented to a tenant. The insured argued that because it was attempting to rent the entire property, it was being used for its customary operations. The court did not agree. It said the customary operations of the insured might be leasing buildings, but it did not conduct those customary operations at the property or even operate a leasing office out of the property. Merely showing the property to prospective tenants was not sufficient to establish that it was used for the customary operations of the insured, and, therefore, because less than 31 percent of the property was rented and the insured did not use the property for its customary operations, the property was unambiguously vacant as defined by the policy.[504]

[11] Sinkhole Collapse

"Sinkhole collapse" is typically a named peril. The term means loss or damage caused by sudden sinking or collapse of land into underground empty spaces by the action of water on limestone or dolomite, but it does not include the cost of filling sinkholes or sinking or collapse of land into *human-made* underground cavities.[505] Coverage for sinkhole collapse is an exception to the standard "earth movement" exclusion.[506]

There will be coverage only when a sinkhole causes damage to *covered property*. Thus, sinkhole damage to a parking lot is not covered because policies ordinarily list "paved surfaces" as "property not covered."[507] A structure in a parking lot is not covered unless it is a building or one of the components listed in the

---

has protected system against freezing, cause of leakage is not relevant, and coverage will lie even if leakage was caused by freezing; only issue relevant to limitation is whether insured has taken requisite action).

502. *See* ISO Form CP 00 10 10 12, § E.6.b.(1)(b); ISO Form CP 00 17 06 07, § E.7.b.(1)(b).

503. *See* ISO Form CP 00 10 10 12, § E.6.a.(1)(b); ISO Form CP 00 17 06 07, § E.7.a.(1)(b).

504. 7th & Allen Equities v. Hartford Cas. Ins. Co., 2012 U.S. Dist. LEXIS 158081 (E.D. Pa. Nov. 2, 2012). *See also* Saiz v. Charter Oak Fire Ins. Co., 2007 U.S. Dist. LEXIS 67767 (D. Colo. Sept. 12, 2007) (where under policy, business was identified as "family style restaurant," and insured closed restaurant and used office in building to work on selling building and other properties, building was vacant because premises were not being used for customary operations).

505. ISO Form CP 10 20 04 02, § A.10. *See* El-Ad Grp. v. Northbrook Prop. & Cas. Ins. Co., 2006 U.S. Dist. LEXIS 102038 (D.N.J. Mar. 14, 2006) (no coverage for loss that occurred because of underground void created by soil migration caused by broken sewer pipes as that was man-made event).

506. *See, e.g.*, ISO Form CP 10 30 06 07, § B.1.b.(4).

507. *See, e.g.*, ISO Form CP 00 10 06 07, § A.2.d; ISO Form CP 00 17 06 07, § A.2.d.

policy as part of a covered building.[508] Land, trees, plants, and shrubs are also not covered property.[509]

Sinkholes may be brought on by flooding. Is damage from a sinkhole that develops after flooding covered? The Georgia Supreme Court was asked by the federal Eleventh Circuit Court of Appeals whether an exclusion for damage resulting directly or indirectly from floods bars coverage for damage produced by a sinkhole collapse that was precipitated by a flood.[510] The Georgia court answered that the policy, when read as a whole, did not extend its flood exclusion to the sinkhole coverage and it, therefore, covered damage produced by a sinkhole collapse that was precipitated by a flood.[511]

Coverage is for *sudden* sinking or collapse. A condominium association was denied coverage based on this temporal aspect of the policy language. Cracks developed in one corner of the condominium building, and there was structural damage caused by movement of the foundation. Testing found that the bedrock in the area was weathered and susceptible to voids making sinkholes likely. The insurer concluded the structural problems were caused by sinkhole activity progressing over a period of several years and denied coverage because the policy covered sinkhole damage only if it resulted from sudden collapse. The court held there was no coverage because the "sinking or collapse" of the covered property was not "sudden."[512]

Sinkhole coverage may be affected by state statutes. For instance, Tennessee has a statute that requires the insurer that offers homeowner property insurance to make coverage available for insurable sinkhole losses.[513] The statute also imposes claims investigation standards on the insurer.[514] Florida has a statute that requires insurers to make coverage for sinkhole losses on any structure available to the extent provided in the form to which the coverage attaches and allows the carrier to include a deductible for sinkhole losses in a policy for residential property insurance—which would apply to condominiums—of up to

508. *See also* Mountview Plaza Assocs. v. Main St. Am. Assur. Co., 2013 Conn. Super. LEXIS 2127 (Conn. Super. Ct. Sept. 24, 2013) (no coverage for culvert in parking lot as it was not within policy list of buildings).

509. *See, e.g.*, ISO Form CP 00 10 06 07, §§ A.2.h, q.(2); ISO Form CP 00 17 06 07, §§ A.2.h, q.(2).

510. York Ins. Co. v. Williams Seafood of Albany, Inc., 223 F.3d 1253, 1256 (11th Cir. 2000).

511. York Ins. Co. v. Williams Seafood of Albany, Inc., 273 Ga. 710, 544 S.E.2d 156 (2001).

512. Amitie One Condo. Ass'n v. Nationwide Prop. & Cas. Ins. Co., 2010 U.S. Dist. LEXIS 129103 (M.D. Pa. Dec. 7, 2010).

513. Tenn. Code Ann. § 56-7-130(b). *See generally* McMullen & Mullen, *Sunk: What Protection Does the Sinkhole Statute Offer Your Clients?*, 49 Tenn. B.J. 12 (2013).

514. Tenn. Code Ann. § 56-7-130(d). For example, if an insurer concludes that structural damage to a covered structure is inconsistent with sinkhole activity, before it denies a claim it has to obtain a written certification from an engineer, a professional geologist, or other qualified individual stating that an analysis of sufficient scope was conducted to provide an opinion within a reasonable professional probability on the cause of the observed structural damage and that sinkhole activity did not cause the observed structural damage. Tenn. Code Ann. § 56-7-130(d)(3).

10 percent.[515] These statutes will likely result in endorsements that modify the standard sinkhole coverage.[516]

[12] Volcanic Action

"Volcanic action" is typically a named peril. The term means direct loss or damage that results from eruption of a volcano when that loss or damage is caused by airborne volcanic blast or airborne shock waves, ash, dust or particulate matter, or lava flow.[517] Policies generally provide that all volcanic eruptions that occur within any 168-hour period—one week—constitute a single occurrence. The policy generally does not cover the cost to remove ash, dust, or particulate matter that does not cause direct physical loss or damage to the described property.

[13] Falling Objects

A rarely invoked peril is "falling objects."[518] While insured property is covered for loss or damage by falling objects, the insurer will not pay for loss or damage to personal property in the open or the interior of a building or structure, or property inside them, unless the roof or an outside wall was first damaged by a falling object.

One problem with a claim for damage or loss by a "falling object" is that policies do not define the term. As one court has noted, even applying the plain and ordinary meaning to the term does not help because there are numerous definitions to each word.[519] Nonetheless, the Oklahoma Supreme Court offered the obvious understanding of the term: a falling object possesses the attribute of being freed from suspension or support and drops or descends by the force of gravity.[520] Thus, courts have held that a silo that fell onto an adjacent barn was a falling object,[521] as were objects that fell off one vehicle and hit another.[522]

515. Fla. Stat. § 627.706.

516. In Florida, for example, the standard sinkhole coverage may be eliminated by an endorsement. *See, e.g.*, ISO Form CP 01 25 02 12, § E (Florida Changes). Coverage designed to conform to state requirements may then be added by another endorsement. *See, e.g.*, Heritage Property & Casualty Insurance Company Form HC SLC 08 14 (Florida—Sinkhole Loss Coverage).

517. ISO Form CP 10 20 04 02, § A.11.

518. ISO Form CP 10 20 04 02, § A.12.

519. West American Ins. Co. v. Red Cricket Condo. Ass'n, 2008 U.S. Dist. LEXIS 57154 (D. Idaho July 29, 2008).

520. Concordia Fire Ins. Co. v. Smith, 205 Okla. 344, 345, 237 P.2d 631, 633 (1951). *See also* Pohl v. Commercial Ins. Co., 36 Misc. 2d 173, 232 N.Y.S.2d 92 (1962).

521. Schluckebier v. Arlington Mut. Fire Ins. Co., 8 Wis. 2d 480, 485, 99 N.W.2d 705, 707 (Wis. 1959) (where silo adjacent to insured barn collapsed and damaged barn, fall of silo was certainly impelled by force of gravity and silo constituted "falling body").

522. Pohl v. Commercial Ins. Co., 36 Misc. 2d 173, 176, 232 N.Y.S.2d 92, 95 (1962) (where wheel and tire left ground and fell through space onto insured vehicle, it was "falling object" as ordinary layperson would understand that term); Getzoff v. Piedmont Fire Ins. Co., 203 Misc. 267, 122 N.Y.S.2d 43 (1953) (stone that fell from truck and ultimately came in contact with insured vehicle was "falling object").

Gravity was clearly at work in the damage suffered by a condominium building. A contractor had placed excavated material upslope from the condominium property. The material became saturated by spring runoff, traveled down the mountainside, and struck the rear of the condominium building, collapsing most of the backside concrete wall and continuing through the building and out the garage doors in the front. The association claimed it suffered damage from a falling object. The court said the term "falling object" was "ambiguous in this particular case." It concluded that whether the earth movement was or was not a falling object in the plain sense of the words was a question of fact and, because ambiguities have to be construed against the insurer, it would assume earth movement could be a falling object under the terms of the policy. That assumption is of little precedential value because the court decided the earth movement was excluded as a mudflow or mudslide.[523]

For a common interest community with one or more multi-story buildings, damage can occur when objects are thrown or knocked over from upper floors. Furniture on a balcony, for instance, can cause considerable damage when blown off that balcony. If that damage is not covered as a loss from a windstorm, under what circumstances is there a loss from a falling object? The parameters of coverage may be worth pursuing with the association broker and carrier.

The effect of gravity alone is a necessary, but not sufficient, characteristic of a falling object.[524] Gravity, for example, may have caused one vehicle on a roadway to strike another, but the first vehicle did not fall *onto the other* and was not a falling object.[525]

[14] Weight of Snow, Ice, or Sleet

Property policies may identify the weight of snow, ice, or sleet as a named peril but provide there is no coverage for loss or damage to *personal property* outside of buildings or structures.[526] The particular facts of a claim can be critical to determining whether a loss or damage was caused by the weight of snow, ice, or sleet. For example, after a second heavy snowfall, shingles were dislodged from

---

523. West American Ins. Co. v. Red Cricket Condo. Ass'n, 2008 U.S. Dist. LEXIS 57154 (D. Idaho July 29, 2008). *Compare* Gullett v. St. Paul Fire & Marine Ins. Co., 446 F.2d 1100 (7th Cir. 1971) (where retaining wall gave way, sending rocks crashing down onto insured building, jury found rocks to be falling objects).

524. *See, e.g.*, Nevins v. Essex Owners Corp., 276 A.D.2d 315, 317, 714 N.Y.S.2d 38, 40 (2000), *app. den.*, 723 N.Y.S.2d 132, 96 N.Y.2d 705, 746 N.E.2d 187 (2001) (elevator, sent into descent by injured plaintiff himself, even if his control over descent was interfered with by malfunctioning device, nevertheless was not falling object).

525. Concordia Fire Ins. Co. v. Smith, 205 Okla. 344, 345, 237 P.2d 631, 633 (1951) (where right rear wheel of truck struck side of bridge and impact threw rear end of truck sidewise and into air and left rear wheel of truck struck side of insured automobile in descending motion, although angle from which impact with automobile occurred was downward, truck was not "falling object" within meaning of insurance policy).

526. ISO Form CP 10 20 04 02, § A.13.

the roof of an insured home and water leaked through the roof, damaging the interior. The insurer denied coverage because it said the shingles were dislodged by melting snow, backing up of the melted snow by blocked gutters, and cracking of shingles on the roof as the melted snow would later freeze. The homeowner had a simpler contention: the shingles were dislodged by the weight of snow and ice. The trial and appellate courts agreed with the insured, noting the snow and ice adhered to the shingles that came off the roof as snow and ice slipped off it.[527]

Damages proximately caused by the weight of snow, ice, or sleet generally will be covered. For instance, an accumulation of snow and ice on the roof of a house forced gutters to separate from the side of the house, allowing water to run down the side of the house into the ground next to the foundation, and when the temperature dropped, the water turned to ice that expanded and cracked the foundation of the home. The court found the insurer was liable for the damage under the coverage for the weight of ice, snow, or sleet.[528]

Snow and sleet are weather phenomena, but ice is not necessarily the product of weather. Thus, barring an applicable exclusion, damage or loss from an artificial generation of ice should be covered.[529]

Typically, the language of the policy is succinct. It simply lists "weight of snow, ice or sleet" as one of the causes of loss without further explanation other than to except personal property outside a building or structure. It does not say the weight has to be applied to the property of the insured. That could be significant for common interest communities. For example, in a community of attached townhomes, each unit, including its roof, might be separately owned and insured by individual residents. If snow accumulated on roofs of townhouses and the weight of the snow caused part of a roof to fall onto and damage an adjacent clubhouse owned and insured by the association, the association policy should cover the damage absent an applicable exclusion.

It is important not to confuse coverage for weight of snow, ice, or sleet as a named peril with additional coverage for collapse. The weight of snow, ice, or

527. Nationwide Mut. Fire Ins. Co. v. White, 209 Va. 787, 167 S.E.2d 125 (1969).

528. Nationwide Ins. Co. v. Warren, 675 S.W.2d 402 (Ky. App. 1984). *See also* O'Neill v. State Farm Ins. Co., 1995 U.S. Dist. LEXIS 4790 (E.D. Pa. Apr. 7, 1995) (where weight of ice, snow, and sleet in yard of insured broke ground-level basement windows allowing snow, ice, and water that had accumulated on ground to enter basement, insurer improperly denied coverage for water damage in basement based on water damage exclusion; court found that water damage from melted snow and ice was not encompassed by exclusion, although at trial it would have to be determined how much ice, as opposed to water, entered basement, and how much damage that ice caused).

529. *See* Macheca Transp. Co. v. Phila. Indem. Ins. Co., 649 F.3d 661 (8th Cir. 2011). In *Macheca*, the weight of ice that accumulated on a refrigeration pipe in a warehouse caused it to rupture, fall, and release ammonia, which damaged floors and walls, as well as products stored inside the warehouse. The insurer contended "ice" did not include artificial ice generated in cooling a cold storage facility. The court observed that the fact that "ice" was grouped with "snow" and "sleet" did not necessarily lead to the conclusion the three items were listed together to limit coverage to naturally occurring elements of the weather. It found the insured was entitled to summary judgment on its claim for damage caused by ice.

sleet is not a named peril under the causes of loss Basic Form,[530] as opposed to the Broad Form; however, the policy may provide coverage for collapse caused by a long list of perils, including weight of snow, ice, or sleet. In that event, there is coverage only if there has been a "collapse" as defined by the policy or court interpretation.[531]

Common interest communities may have carports adjacent to individual units. In a Louisiana case, 61 metal carport canopies in a condominium development collapsed during a snow and ice storm. The insurer was required under the policy to pay for the cost of replacing the carports.[532]

[15] Water Damage

Water damage is a covered peril under the Broad Form causes of loss[533] but not the Basic Form, although there is always an exclusion for water,[534] so the coverage for loss or damage caused by water has to be read in conjunction with that exclusion. Water damage as a named peril means accidental discharge or leakage of water or steam as the direct result of the breaking apart or cracking of a plumbing, heating, air conditioning, or other system or appliance that is located on the described premises and that contains water or steam.

It is important to recognize that under the coverage for wind damage, loss or damage to the interior of a building or structure, or property inside that building or structure caused by *rain*, may be covered if the building or structure first sustained wind or hail damage to its roof or walls through which the rain entered.[535]

---

530. ISO Form CP 10 10 04 02.

531. *See, e.g.*, Dreiblatt v. St. Paul Fire & Marine Ins. Co., 264 F.3d 126 (1st Cir. 2001), where a condominium consisted of nine buildings with flat roofs. After a heavy snow storm, the association discovered problems with the roofs; however, the court agreed with the insurer that there was no coverage because no collapse had occurred, as required by the policy.

532. Tex-La Properties v. South State Ins. Co., 514 So. 2d 707 (La. App. 1987).

533. ISO Form CP 10 20 04 02, § A.14.

534. *See* § 10.19[7], *infra*.

535. *See* Dunn v. Scottsdale Ins. Co., 2013 U.S. Dist. LEXIS 107984 (M.D. Pa. Aug. 1, 2013) (coverage would be invoked when structure experienced some type of physical damage covered by policy and, subsequently, precipitation was able to enter interior of structure and cause additional damage). *See also* Divine Motel Grp., LLC v. Rockhill Ins. Co., 2015 U.S. Dist. LEXIS 87789 (M.D. Fla. July 7, 2015) (no coverage where wind-driven rain of tropical storm entered property because of deterioration of roof's weatherproofing system, deficient repairs, inadequate maintenance, leaks under doors, insufficient weatherproofing of air conditioning units, and oversaturation of certain components of concrete walls as wear and tear, decay, and deterioration were specifically excluded causes of loss and policy also excluded loss or damage caused by or resulting from faulty, inadequate, or defective design, specifications, workmanship, repair, construction, and maintenance; damages that allowed water to intrude during tropical storm were all specifically excluded from coverage, and any resulting damage did not appear to satisfy exception to water intrusion limitation); Royale Green Condo. Ass'n v. Aspen Specialty Ins. Co., 2009 U.S. Dist. LEXIS 24349 (S.D. Fla. Mar. 24, 2009) (where testimony of inspectors conflicted on question of whether components were part of air conditioning system or of roof, it was unclear whether water entered through man-made opening or wind damage; summary judgment for insurer denied); Tropic Sun Towers

If the coverage is considered to be wind damage, it may be subject to any policy limitations on wind damage, for example, a separate higher deductible for losses caused by wind. Also, even if the loss would otherwise be covered, the anti-concurrent cause provision would bar coverage for damage caused by water driven by wind in combination with any other excluded force.[536] Thus, one has to examine the water damage exclusion to determine whether a loss is covered.[537]

Water damage does not include discharge or leakage from an automatic sprinkler system, a sump, or related equipment and parts, including overflow because of sump pump failure or excessive volume of water, or roof drains, gutters, downspouts, or similar fixtures or equipment. It also does not include the cost to repair any defect that caused the loss or damage. Loss or damage caused by or resulting from continuous or repeated seepage or leakage of water is not considered water damage, nor is the presence or condensation of humidity, moisture, or vapor that occurs over a period of 14 days or more. Finally, loss or damage caused by or resulting from freezing is not water damage unless the insured does its best to maintain heat in the building or structure or drains the equipment and shuts off the water supply if the heat is not maintained. The phrase "does its best" is not defined, but generally it means reasonable efforts.[538] Note that the language requires the *insured* to do its best to maintain heat. Common interest communities have to be concerned with conduct of others on the property.[539]

Condo. Ass'n v. Zurich Am. Ins. Co. of Illinois, 2006 U.S. Dist. LEXIS 89358 (M.D. Fla. Dec. 8, 2006) (where policy prohibited coverage for water damage unless building first sustained damage by covered cause of loss to its roof or walls through which rain entered, question was whether the damage to property was caused by permanent damage to sliding glass doors that allowed water into building or whether that damage to sliding glass doors was only temporary, and therefore not covered); Stufflebean v. Firemen's Fund Ins. Co., 710 S.W.2d 931, 933 (Mo. App. 1986) (where broken gutter caused water to accumulate on porch and then seep into basement, direct force of wind did not cause opening in roof or wall of house through which rainwater entered).

536. Legacy Condos., Inc. v. Landmark Am. Ins. Co., 2008 U.S. Dist. LEXIS 655 (S.D. Miss. Jan. 4, 2008) (under anti-concurrent cause provision, covered loss is non-compensable when acting concurrently with excluded loss and, therefore, when water driven by wind combines with any other force to cause loss, that loss is not compensable).

537. For instance, in *Legacy Condos., Inc. v. Landmark Am. Ins. Co.*, 2008 U.S. Dist. LEXIS 655 (S.D. Miss. Jan. 4, 2008), the insurer conceded it would have to pay for damage caused by wind/water entering through blown-off roof structures, but argued it did not have to compensate the association for wind-driven rain and/or storm surge spray that entered around undamaged windows and doors as that was barred by the water exclusion. The court observed that if wind or another covered peril caused a breach that allowed both rain and spray to enter and damage the same area, the loss would not be covered under the anti-concurrent cause provision.

538. Auto-Owners Ins. Co. v. Hansen Hous., Inc., 604 N.W.2d 504, 512 (S.D. 2000). *See also* Me. State Props., LLC v. Chubb Custom Ins. Co., 2016 U.S. Dist. LEXIS 89175 (D. Me. July 8, 2016) (obligation to use reasonable efforts to maintain heat in building contemplates that insured will make reasonable efforts).

539. *See, e.g.*, Rolling Green at Whip-Poor-Will Condominium Townhouse Unit Owners Ass'n v. Bank of America, 2016 U.S. Dist. LEXIS 27773 (D.N.H. Mar. 4, 2016) (after association shut off water to vacant unit, agent of mortgagee turned water back on and left heat off without notifying association, after which pipes burst and damaged unit and neighboring properties).

Generally, the association will not be responsible for acts of third parties not under its control.[540]

Where water damage coverage does apply, and the building or structure that contains the system or appliance is covered property, the carrier will pay the cost to tear out and replace any part of the building or structure to repair damage to the system or appliance from which the water or steam escaped, but will not pay the cost to repair any defect that caused the loss or damage.[541] One commentator recommends that unless the water damage is catastrophic, a claim should not be submitted to the association carrier even if the policy provides coverage because leaks in common interest community buildings are common and insurance companies establish rates according to the number of claims filed and the dollars paid. If the association files many small claims, it may jeopardize its insurability.[542]

Water leaks that affect association property or the property of more than one resident are a frequent occurrence in common interest communities. The sources of these leaks may be a common pipe,[543] a pipe wholly within the confines of a single residence,[544] a roof,[545] or an appliance in a unit.[546] The policy definition of water damage includes accidental discharge or leakage of water as the direct result of the *breaking apart or cracking* of a plumbing, heating, air conditioning, or "other system" or appliance that contains water or steam. Thus, if the system or appliance does not break apart or "crack," there is apparently no coverage.[547] Additionally, it would seem that a roof does not qualify as an "other system."[548]

540. Standard Commercial Property Conditions Forms address the issue. *See, e.g.*, ISO Form CP 00 90 07 88, § B (act or neglect of any person other than insured beyond direction or control of insured will not affect this insurance). There are decisions in which courts have refused to impute to the insured the failure of an agent to use reasonable care to maintain heat. Chow v. Merrimack Mut. Fire Ins. Co., 83 Mass. App. Ct. 622, 987 N.E.2d 1275 (2013); International Ins. Co. v. Reid, 400 S.W.2d 939 (Tex. Civ. App.—Beaumont 1966).

541. ISO Form CP 10 20 04 02, § A.14.b.

542. Thompson, *HOA Insurance Victimization* (Realty Times, June 2012).

543. *See, e.g.*, Wagner v. Edlund, 229 S.W.3d 870 (Tex. App. 2007).

544. *See, e.g.*, Cincinnati Ins. Co. v. Greenmont Mut. Hous. Corp., 2014 Ohio App. LEXIS 1922 (May 9, 2014).

545. *See, e.g.*, Doherty v. Admiral's Flagship Condo. Trust, 80 Mass. App. Ct. 104, 951 N.E.2d 936 (2011); Pershad v. Parkchester South Condo., 174 Misc. 2d 92, 662 N.Y.S.2d 993 (1997), *aff'd*, 178 Misc. 2d 788, 683 N.Y.S.2d 708 (1998).

546. *See, e.g.*, Trousdell Vil. Owners Corp. v. Gagliardo, 39 Misc. 3d 1204(A), 969 N.Y.S.2d 807 (2013) (bathtub spout); Schindler v. Baumann, 272 S.W.3d 793 (Tex. App.—Dallas, 2008) (water filtration unit); Aherry v. Regency Ins. Co., 884 So. 2d 175 (Fla. 2d DCA 2004) (washing machine hose); Handler v. 1050 Tenants Corp., 295 A.D.2d 238, 744 N.Y.S.2d 161 (2002) (air conditioner); Antich v. McPartland, 293 A.D.2d 728, 740 N.Y.S.2d 728 (2002) (washing machine hose).

547. *See, e.g.*, Scottsdale Ins. Co. v. Sally Group, LLC, 2012 U.S. Dist. LEXIS 47532 (S.D. Tex. Apr. 3, 2012) (no record evidence that air conditioning system itself leaked or that it broke apart; rather, facts supported insurer's position that the mold was caused by high humidity and condensation due to fact humidifier had been incorrectly assembled).

548. Dunn v. Scottsdale Ins. Co., 2013 U.S. Dist. LEXIS 107984 (M.D. Pa. Aug. 1, 2013) (where insurer noted that damage was not caused by broken pipe or other listed condition, but

Another limitation on coverage is that the system or appliance has to be located on the *described premises*. Ownership of the system or appliance does not appear to be at issue, only its location. A system or appliance that is not situated at the described location—meaning the premises described on the Declarations Page—could not produce a covered cause of loss.

[16] Theft

Theft is not a named peril under either the Basic or Broad Form causes of loss, but is covered under all-risk coverage. Property policies do not define theft. Courts say that when the word "theft" is used in a policy, without definition, "it should be interpreted as liberally as possible to protect the insured."[549] A number of courts have said that theft is synonymous with "larceny," which is the felonious taking and carrying away of the personal goods of another with the intent to steal them.[550] Generally, the intent must be to permanently—as opposed to temporarily—deprive the owner of his or her property.[551] Other courts say that "theft" is broader than larceny and includes any wrongful deprivation of property—including embezzlement—of another.[552]

A condition that applies to theft coverage is that in the event of loss or damage the named insured must see to it that the police are notified if a law may have been broken.[553]

---

from water that entered building through poorly constructed and maintained roof, court said that generally, policy only provided coverage for water damage from leakage from plumbing and heating components).

549. Toms v. Hartford Fire Ins. Co., 146 Ohio St. 39, 43, 63 N.E.2d 909, 911 (1945).

550. Chemstrand Corp. v. Maryland Casualty Co., 266 Ala. 626, 630, 98 So. 2d 1, 4 (1957) (for act to constitute theft or larceny, taking has to be made with felonious intent by taker to deprive owner of property); Downs v. New Jersey Fidelity & Plate Glass Ins. Co., 91 N.J.L. 523, 525, 103 A. 205, 206 (1918) (larceny is felonious taking and carrying away of personal goods of another with intent to steal). *See also* Fidelity & Casualty Co. v. Wathen, 205 Ky. 511, 513, 266 S.W. 4, 5 (1924) (larceny is felonious taking of property of another without his or her consent and against his or her will, with intent to convert it to use of taker).

551. *Ballentine's Law Dictionary* (LexisNexis 2010).

552. Fidelity & Casualty Co. v. Wathen, 205 Ky. 511, 513, 266 S.W. 4, 5 (1924) ("theft" is broader term than "larceny" and includes any wrongful deprivation of property of another). *See also* Long v. Glidden Mut. Ins. Asso., 215 N.W.2d 271, 273 (Iowa 1974) ("theft" has its popular meaning when not defined in policy as word of general and broad connotation covering any wrongful appropriation of another's property to use of taker); Central Surety Fire Corp. v. Williams, 213 Ark. 600, 211 S.W.2d 891 (Ark. 1948); Toms v. Hartford Fire Ins. Co., 146 Ohio St. 39, 43, 63 N.E.2d 909, 911 (1945) ("theft" is of broader scope than "larceny" and comprehends essentially willful taking or appropriation of property by another wrongfully and without justification and with design to hold or make use of that property in violation of rights of its owner and has been construed to include any wrongful deprivation of property of another without claim or color of right, fraudulent, and wrongful taking of the property of another, or taking where natural consequence creates unreasonable risk of permanent loss to owner).

553. CP 00 17 06 07, § E.3.a.(1).

There are a number of limitations on theft coverage in the standard commercial property policy.[554] First, there is no coverage for property that is missing when there is no physical evidence showing what happened to it.[555] That should bar coverage for a "mysterious disappearance."[556] Next, property policies list accounts, bills, currency, food stamps, or other evidences of debt, money, notes, or securities as "property not covered."[557] Coverage is also proscribed for loss of building materials and supplies not attached to the building or structure caused by or resulting from theft.[558] Finally, property policies have a "vacancy" clause providing that if a building where loss or damage occurs has been vacant for more than 60 consecutive days before that loss or damage occurs,[559] the insurer will not pay for any loss or damage caused by, *inter alia*, theft or attempted theft.[560]

There are exclusions to Standard Property Policies that create gaps that may be filled by a fidelity or crime policy. First, there is a broad exclusion for loss or damage caused by, or resulting from, any "dishonest" or criminal act by any

554. *See generally* Shapiro, *Crime and Fidelity Insurance Addresses Growing Risks of Fraud and Theft* (Kibble & Prentice Holding Co.) (under Special Form, coverage is limited to theft of only portion of tangible property, does not include mysterious disappearances, will respond only if there are obvious signs of break-in, and provides no coverage for theft of money and securities).

555. CP 10 30 06 07, § C.1.e. There is also no coverage when the only evidence of loss or damage is a shortage disclosed on taking inventory.

556. Shapiro, *Crime and Fidelity Insurance Addresses Growing Risks of Fraud and Theft* (Kibble & Prentice Holding Co.) (property insurance does not cover mysterious disappearance). *See also* Cozen, *Insuring Real Property*, § 2.04[16] (Matthew Bender & Co. 2015) (all-risk policies exclude coverage for loss of property by unexplained or mysterious disappearance and exclusion may read that policy does not insure against loss caused by unexplained or mysterious disappearance of any property).

557. *See* ISO Form CP 00 10 06 07, § A.2; ISO Form CP 00 17 06 07, § A.2.

558. ISO Form CP 10 30 06 07, § C.1.d.

559. Is the 60 days measured from the beginning of any period of vacancy or from the inception of the policy? In *Travelers Property Casualty Co. of America v. Superior Court*, 215 Cal. App. 4th 561, 576, 155 Cal. Rptr. 3d 459, 471 (2013), the trial court concluded the vacancy limitation did not apply because it required the property to be vacant for 60 days prior to the loss, and 60 days could not have run between when the policy was issued in January and the loss occurred in February. The appellate court acknowledged that some courts have found a vacancy period has to begin at or after policy issuance when it indicates the clause is triggered if the property is vacant beyond a period of 60 days. However, the vacancy clause before the court—which is the same as that found in standard BPP and CAC policies—was different. The time period was backward-looking from the date of the loss and did not implicate the date the policy was issued. *See also* Tazari, LLC v. Am. Family Ins., 2012 Ohio Misc. LEXIS 17 (Ohio C.P. Feb. 7, 2012) (if property has been vacant for 60 days, there is no coverage even if policy has been in effect less than 60 days). In some cases, it may not be clear when the damage or loss "occurred." For example, in *Cent. Mut. Ins. Co. v. KPE First-place Land, LLC*, 271 S.W.3d 454 (Tex. App.—Tyler 2008), the insured discovered on December 31 that some time prior to that thieves had removed copper coils from air conditioning equipment located on the roof of its building. The insurer denied coverage based on the vacancy clause. The insured argued the carrier could not prove the claim for that loss was excluded under the vacancy provision because it could not show the property had been vacant for 60 days at the time the loss "occurred." The court found that "occurred" means when damage happened, not when it was discovered. Therefore, it affirmed summary judgment for the insured.

560. ISO Form CP 00 10 06 07, § E.6.b.(1); ISO Form CP 00 17 06 07, § E.7.b.(1).

officers, managers, employees, directors, trustees, authorized representatives of the named insured, or anyone to whom the named insured entrusts covered property for *any* purpose.[561] Additionally, when property that has been transferred to a person or place outside the described premises based on unauthorized instructions, there is no coverage.[562] If an insured wants coverage in either circumstance, it must be obtained in a stand-alone crime or fidelity policy or endorsement.

§ 10.16 Additional Coverages in Commercial Property Coverage Forms

The BPP and CAC each include six additional coverages.[563] These are debris removal, preservation of property, fire department service charge, pollutant cleanup and removal, increased cost of construction, and electronic data.

[1] Debris Removal

Removal of debris after a casualty can be critical because reconstruction often cannot begin until the debris is cleared away.[564] In general, under a "Debris Removal" clause, the insurer will pay expense incurred by the insured to remove "debris of covered property"[565] caused by or resulting from a covered cause of loss that occurs during the policy period, but only if reported to the insurer *in writing* within 180 days of the date of direct physical loss or damage.[566] One expert commentary notes that under the usual policy language, expenses have to be reported, but not necessarily incurred, within the 180 days and, therefore, the estimate of a contractor given to the insurer for work not yet completed should satisfy the reporting requirement, although there have been cases in which an

---

561. ISO Form ISO Form CP 10 30 06 07, § B.2.h. The exclusion applies whether any of the named actors is acting alone or in collusion with others or whether or not the act occurs during hours of employment. It does not apply to acts of destruction by employees of the named insured, including leased employees, but theft by employees, including leased employees, is not covered.

562. ISO Form CP 10 30 06 07, § C.1.f.

563. *See* ISO Form CP 00 10 06 07, § A.4; ISO Form CP 00 17 06 07, § A.4.

564. Barlow, Massmann, Alexander & Schreibman, *Condominium Insurance Coverage Guide,* at 159 (2d ed. National Underwriter Co., 2016).

565. The debris itself must be "of covered property." *See, e.g.*, Harbor Cmtys., LLC v. Landmark Am. Ins. Co., 2008 U.S. Dist. LEXIS 59179 (S.D. Fla. Aug. 4, 2008). *See also* W.H. Breshears, Inc. v. Federated Mut. Ins. Co., 832 F. Supp. 288 (E.D. Cal. 1993), *aff'd*, 38 F.3d 1219 (9th Cir. 1994) (where vandals broke into premises and caused gasoline to be released from aboveground storage tank on and into ground, debris removal coverage did not apply to costs to extract pollutants from land or water or to remove, restore, or replace polluted land or water as that coverage provided debris removal coverage for debris of covered property).

566. *See, e.g.*, ISO Form CP 00 17 06 07, § A.4.a.(1); ISO Form CP 00 10 06 07, § A.4.a.(1). See Dudey & Malecki, *Debris Removal and Pollution Damage: How These Additional Costs Impact the Property Claim* (Adjusting Today, 2015), available at: http://adjustersinternational.com/publications/adjusting-today/debris-removal-and-pollution-damage/ for an excellent history of the coverage for debris removal and an analysis of the language in the policies cited.

insurer has insisted the work has to have been completed within the 180 days for coverage to apply.[567] Thus, it is recommended that if the 180-day deadline is approaching and the debris removal cannot be completed within the time period, the insured should seek an extension, which, given a good reason for the delay, many insurers will grant.

The costs of demolition attendant in debris removal are not covered,[568] but the expense of repairing property damaged in removing debris may be covered.[569] The policy does not specify that the debris be removed from the premises of the insured for the removal costs to be covered. Thus, courts have found coverage for the cost of removing damaged covered property not located on the premises of the insured.[570] They have also concluded that debris removal encompasses cleanup costs including wages and benefits paid to employees of the insured to carry out that cleanup.[571] Note that "covered property" is not necessarily property owned by the insured. Property policies typically provide coverage for personal property of others that is in the care, custody, or control of the insured.[572]

[a] "Debris" Defined

Policies do not define "debris." Courts have described debris as waste material resulting from the destruction of something.[573] They have found coverage for the

567. Dudey & Malecki, *Debris Removal and Pollution Damage: How These Additional Costs Impact the Property Claim* at 4 (Adjusting Today, 2015), available at: http://adjustersinternational.com/publications/adjusting-today/debris-removal-and-pollution-damage/.

568. Harbor Cmtys., LLC v. Landmark Am. Ins. Co., 2008 U.S. Dist. LEXIS 59179 (S.D. Fla. Aug. 4, 2008) (debris removal does not include demolition costs because demolition entails act of destroying or wrecking, neither of which fits within meaning of removal).

569. Manduca Datsun, Inc. v. Universal Underwriters Ins. Co., 106 Idaho 163, 168, 676 P.2d 1274, 1279 (Idaho App. 1984) (damage to asphalt would be recoverable under Debris Removal clause where most economical way to remove that debris would be by heavy equipment and that would necessarily produce asphalt damage; economic purpose of coverage would be partly or wholly defeated if it did not provide payment for damage necessarily caused by debris removal process itself).

570. Mont. Rail Link v. Lexington Ins. Co., 175 F. Supp. 2d 1248, 1250 (D. Mont. 2001) (where policyholder's rail cars derailed and spilled their contents into river, cost of removing that debris from the river was covered under policy; policy provides no basis for assumption by insurer that debris removal has to be linked with covered real property or premises of the insured). *See also* Stadium Lincoln-Mercury v. Heritage Transp., 160 Ohio App. 3d 128, 826 N.E.2d 332 (Ohio App. 2005) (cost of towing damaged vehicles from scene of accident covered under debris removal clause).

571. Interstate Gourmet Coffee Roasters, Inc. v. Seaco Ins. Co., 59 Mass. App. Ct. 78, 794 N.E.2d 607 (2003).

572. *See, e.g.*, ISO Form CP 00 17 06 07, § A.1.c; ISO Form CP 00 10 06 07, § A.1.c. *See also* Mont. Rail Link v. Lexington Ins. Co., 175 F. Supp. 2d 1248 (D. Mont. 2001) (policy of railroad company covered insured's interest in property of others in care, custody, or control of insured as common carrier, contract carrier, warehouseman, or bailee).

573. Lexington Ins. Co. v. Ryder System, Inc., 142 Ga. App. 36, 37, 234 S.E.2d 839 (1977). *See also* Stadium Lincoln-Mercury v. Heritage Transp., 160 Ohio App. 3d 128, 137, 826 N.E.2d 332, 339 (Ohio App. 2005) (debris is remains of something broken down or destroyed).

cost of removal from the ground of fuel that escaped from underground storage tanks[574] and property in transit damaged by an accident.[575]

[b] Exception for "Pollutants"

The debris removal coverage does not include costs to extract "pollutants" from land or water or remove, restore, or replace polluted land or water.[576] "Pollutants" is defined as any "solid, liquid, gaseous or thermal irritant or contaminant, including smoke, vapor, soot, fumes, acids, alkalis, chemicals and waste."[577]

[c] Increased Costs of Construction Exclusion

In a Montana case, the policy had an exclusion typically found in property policies that barred coverage for any loss or damage caused by or resulting from enforcement of any ordinance or law, either directly or indirectly regulating construction, repair, or demolition of buildings or structures. The insured property was damaged by fire. After the fire, the insured incurred additional costs for removal of materials containing asbestos. Removal of those materials was subject to regulations that increased the cost of removing and disposing of them over that of removing and disposing of ordinary building materials. The insurer argued that coverage for that increase was excluded by the increased cost of compliance exclusion. The Montana Supreme Court did not agree. It concluded the exclusion was clearly inapplicable because the asbestos regulations neither "caused" nor "resulted in" loss or damage to the insured property. Rather, it was the fire that caused the loss or damage.[578] However, the court limited the holding to removal of fire-damaged asbestos and undamaged asbestos that had to be removed to repair damaged materials.

[d] Limits of Coverage

The most the insurer will pay for the total of direct physical loss or damage plus debris removal expense is the limit of insurance applicable to the covered property

---

574. Lexington Ins. Co. v. Ryder System, Inc., 142 Ga. App. 36, 37, 234 S.E.2d 839, 840 (1977) (escaped oil that contaminated surrounding earth was debris, and its removal was compensable because, as oil in storage, it was insured).

575. Mont. Rail Link v. Lexington Ins. Co., 175 F. Supp. 2d 1248 (D. Mont. 2001) (cost of removing and disposing of asphalt and beer cans spilled from derailed railroad cars was covered); Stadium Lincoln-Mercury v. Heritage Transp., 160 Ohio App. 3d 128, 826 N.E.2d 332 (Ohio App. 2005) (damaged cars fit definition of "debris" since they would be broken down remains of original working automobiles and removing them from scene of accident by towing would be removing debris; rejecting arguments by insurer that only clearing broken fragments from highway constituted clearing debris and that vehicles could not be construed as "debris" because they had documented value).

576. *See, e.g.*, ISO Form CP 00 17 06 07, § A.4.a.(2); ISO Form CP 00 10 06 07, § A.4.a.(2).

577. *See, e.g.*, ISO Form CP 00 17 06 07, § H.2; ISO Form CP 00 10 06 07, § H.2. The term "waste" includes materials to be recycled, reconditioned, or reclaimed.

578. Farmers Union Mut. Ins. Co. v. Oakland, 251 Mont. 352, 355, 825 P.2d 554 (Mont. 1992).

that has sustained loss or damage.[579] Additionally, the amount the insurer will pay for debris removal expense is limited to 25 percent of the sum of the deductible plus the amount that it pays for direct physical loss or damage to the covered property that has sustained loss or damage.[580]

The insurer will pay up to an additional $10,000 for debris removal expense, for each location, in any one occurrence of physical loss or damage to covered property, if the total of the actual debris removal expense plus the amount the insurer pays for direct physical loss or damage exceeds the limit of insurance on the covered property that has sustained loss or damage and/or the actual debris removal expense exceeds 25 percent of the sum of the deductible plus the amount that the insurer pays for direct physical loss or damage to the covered property that has sustained loss or damage.[581] Therefore, if one or both of the contingencies applies, the insurer's total payment for direct physical loss or damage and debris removal expense may reach, but will never exceed, the limit of insurance on the covered property that has sustained loss or damage, plus $10,000.[582]

For some common interest communities, the $10,000 cap on debris removal expenses will be insufficient. Additional coverage can be obtained by endorsement. There are ISO endorsements that modify either the Building and Personal Property Coverage Form, the Condominium Association Coverage Form, or the Standard Property Policy.[583] However, as one authority notes, the challenge for the policyholder is to determine how to assess the future costs of debris removal at the outset of the policy when they are unknown and difficult to determine.[584]

[2] Preservation of Property

Property policies pay certain expenses related to protecting covered property. If it is *necessary* for the insured to move covered property from the described premises to preserve it from loss or damage by a covered cause of loss, the insurer will pay for any direct physical loss or damage to that property while it is being moved

579. *See, e.g.*, ISO Form CP 00 17 06 07, § A.4.a.(3).(a); ISO Form CP 00 10 06 07, § A.4.a.(3).(a).

580. *See, e.g.*, ISO Form CP 00 17 06 07, § A.4.a.(3).(b); ISO Form CP 00 10 06 07, § A.4.a.(3).(b).

581. *See, e.g.*, ISO Form CP 00 17 06 07, § A.4.a.(4); ISO Form CP 00 10 06 07, § A.4.a.(4).

582. The ISO Form CP 00 17 06 07 provides examples of how the debris removal coverage is calculated where there is no coinsurance penalty. One expert notes the possibility of ambiguity in the policy language and, to avoid potential disagreement with the carrier over a claim amount, recommends determining the meaning of the coverage language before any need arises. Hayman, *Hurricanes and Windstorm Coverage: Case Studies and Coverages* at 4 (Adjusting Today, 2011), available at: http://adjustersinternational.com/publications/adjusting-today/hurricanes-and-wind storm-coverage/0/.

583. *See, e.g.*, ISO Form CP 04 15 10 00 (Commercial Property: Debris Removal Additional Insurance); ISO Form CP 04 15 06 95 (Commercial Property: Debris Removal Additional Limit of Insurance). Both endorsements increase the coverage to the amount shown on the schedule incorporated into the form).

584. Barlow, Massmann, Alexander & Schreibman, *Condominium Insurance Coverage Guide* at 159 (2d ed. National Underwriter Co., 2016).

or while temporarily stored at another location, but only if the loss or damage occurs within 30 days after the property is first moved.[585] Note that this is *not* coverage for the cost of moving covered property to safety. Also, the coverage only applies when it is *necessary* that the property be moved to preserve it from loss or damage by a covered cause of loss.[586] Thus, the Preservation of Property clause applies when it is necessary to move the covered property, and when the threat to the property is a covered cause of loss. For example, a standard exclusion is for loss or damage caused directly or indirectly by fungus.[587] Damage from fungus, therefore, is not a covered cause of loss, and if the insured has to move property to protect it from fungus, the Preservation of Property clause is inapplicable.

[3] Fire Department Service Charge

Ordinarily under property polices, the insurer will pay a fire department service charge when the fire department is called to save or protect *covered property* from a covered cause of loss.[588] The carrier will pay up to $1,000, unless a higher limit is shown on the Declarations Page, for liability for fire department service charges that are either assumed by contract or agreement before the loss or required by local ordinance. Generally, no deductible applies to this coverage. The insured should be aware that while fire department service charge coverage is a discrete additional coverage in the types of policies typically issued to common interest communities—the Building and Personal Property Coverage Form[589] and the Condominium Association Coverage Form[590]—it may be subsumed under a different additional coverage—most likely a "Protection and Preservation of Property" clause—in other policies and may be broader or narrower than the coverage described above.

[4] Pollutant Cleanup and Removal

Typically, property policies provide that the insurer will pay expenses incurred by the insured to extract "pollutants" from land or water at the described premises if the discharge, dispersal, seepage, migration, release, or escape of those pollutants is caused by or results from a covered cause of loss *occurring during the policy period*.[591] "Pollutants" is defined as any "solid, liquid, gaseous or thermal irritant

585. *See, e.g.*, ISO Form CP 00 17 06 07, § A.4.b; ISO Form CP 00 10 06 07, § A.4.b. There is one small difference between the CAC (CP 00 17) and the BPP. The latter applies when it is necessary to move covered property from the described premises while the CAC says it applies when it necessary *for the insured* to move covered property from the described premises.

586. *See* Buczek v. Cont'l Cas. Ins. Co., 378 F.3d 284 (3d Cir. 2004) (preservation clause provides coverage only in instances where covered cause of loss is implicated).

587. *See, e.g.*, ISO Form CP 10 30 06 07, § B.1.h.

588. *See, e.g.*, ISO Form CP 00 17 06 07, § A.4.c; ISO Form CP 00 10 06 07, § A.4.c.

589. *See, e.g.*, ISO Form CP 00 10 06 07.

590. *See, e.g.*, ISO Form CP 00 17 06 07.

591. *See, e.g.*, ISO Form CP 00 17 06 07, § A.4.d; ISO Form CP 00 10 06 07, § A.4.d.

or contaminant, including smoke, vapor, soot, fumes, acids, alkalis, chemicals and waste."[592] Note that the covered cause of loss that *causes* the discharge, dispersal, seepage, migration, release, or escape of pollutant has to occur during the policy period for the coverage to apply.

This additional coverage does not apply to costs to test for, monitor, or assess the existence, concentration, or effects of pollutants, but the insurer will pay for testing that is performed in the course of extracting the pollutants from the land or water.

The most that will be paid under the Pollution Cleanup and Removal coverage for each described premises is $10,000 for the total of all covered expenses arising out of covered causes of loss occurring during each separate 12-month period of the policy.

[5] Increased Cost of Construction

When buildings are constructed, they are required to meet applicable ordinances and laws then in effect. These directives prescribe standards for construction materials, plumbing, electrical wiring, and the setback of structures from property lines.[593] They may also mandate hurricane impact windows or construction techniques to mitigate earthquake damage. When a building is destroyed, or damaged to a certain extent, reconstruction generally has to meet the ordinance or law requirements that have been adopted since the building was originally constructed. The expense of meeting these requirements can be considerable. Coverage for the increased cost of construction incurred to comply with enforcement of an ordinance or law is a typical additional coverage.[594] It is complex and much litigated. It is often called "ordinance and law" coverage. Policies also usually have an "ordinance or law" or "civil authority" exclusion.[595] The *additional* coverage for increased cost of construction is not subject to the terms of that

592. *See, e.g.*, ISO Form CP 00 17 06 07, § H.2; ISO Form CP 00 10 06 07, § H.2. The term "waste" includes materials to be recycled, reconditioned, or reclaimed.

593. Most of the laws that affect building construction are local ordinances, but state law can also apply. Even federal law can govern construction, most notably the Americans with Disabilities Act (ADA). 42 U.S.C. §§ 12101, *et seq*. That law may even mandate property upgrades to undamaged premises. The law applies to "places of public accommodation," and courts generally hold that residential common interest communities are not places of public accommodation. *See, e.g.*, Champlin v. Sovereign Residential Servs. 2008 U.S. Dist. LEXIS 115274 (M.D. Fla. Apr. 7, 2008); Mabson v. Ass'n of Apt. Owners of Maui Kamaole, 2007 U.S. Dist. LEXIS 59260 (D. Haw. Aug. 13, 2007). If, however, a common interest community operates facilities open to the general public or is a mixed-use project with commercial portions of the property open to the public, the ADA may apply. *See generally* Ransom, *How the Americans with Disabilities Act Affects Residential Community Associations*, 9 Prac. Real Est. Law 55 (1993).

594. *See, e.g.*, ISO Form CP 00 17 06 07, § A.4.e; ISO Form CP 00 10 06 07, § A.4.e.

595. *See, e.g.*, ISO Form CP 10 30 06 07, § B.1.a.

exclusion, to the extent the exclusion would conflict with the provisions of the increased cost of construction coverage.[596]

Typical policy language states that increased cost of construction coverage applies only to buildings to which the "Replacement Cost Optional Coverage" also applies.[597] In other words, under the optional coverage, replacement cost is actually the limit and generally increased costs are covered over the life of the policy; however, if the policy does not include that optional coverage, any increase in construction costs will not be covered if it exceeds the limits of the policy. Note also that increased cost of construction coverage often has its own limit as discussed below.

Policies provide that in the event of damage by a covered cause of loss to a building that is covered property, the insurer will pay the increased costs incurred to comply with enforcement of an ordinance or law in the course of repair, rebuilding, or replacement of *damaged* parts of that property, subject to prescribed limitations.[598] The meaning of "enforcement" can be a source of disagreement between carriers and policyholders. Does "enforcement" mean a written directive? When a building official orally conveys the requirements of an ordinance, does that constitute enforcement?[599]

The ordinances or laws that invoke the coverage are those that regulate construction or repair of buildings or establish zoning or land use requirements at the described premises and that are in force at the time of loss.[600]

[a] Exceptions to Coverage

Under the increased cost of construction coverage, the insurer will not pay any costs because of an ordinance or law with which the insured was required to comply before the loss—even when the building was undamaged—and with which the

596. *See, e.g.*, ISO Form CP 00 17 06 07, § A.4.e.(8); ISO Form CP 00 10 06 07, § A.4.e.(8).

597. *See, e.g.*, ISO Form CP 00 17 06 07, § A.4.e.(1); ISO Form CP 00 10 06 07, § A.4.e.(1).

598. *See, e.g.*, ISO Form CP 00 17 06 07, § A.4.e.(2); ISO Form CP 00 10 06 07, § A.4.e.(2).

599. *Consider* Bischel v. Fire Ins. Exchange, 1 Cal. App. 4th 1168, 177, 2 Cal. Rptr. 2d 575, 581 (Cal. App. 4th Dist. 1991) ("enforcement" means carrying out of mandate or command; municipality carries out mandate or command of municipal code by implementing building standards and withholding permits for construction in violation of those standards). *See also* Lexington Ins. Co. Ins. Co. v. Meadows West Condo Ass'n, 2016 U.S. App. LEXIS 289 (5th Cir. Jan. 6, 2016), where the insurer argued the ordinance at issue did not *require* demolition or regulate repair, but merely gave discretion to the building officials. The building official, exercising that discretion, did not mandate a specific type of repair but instead asked the association to hire a mechanical engineer to design a repair to duct work that caused a fire. The building official also said he was obligated to see that potential fire hazards had been repaired. The repair plans had to be approved by the Planning, Zoning, and Codes Department, and the repair itself was subject to inspection by the fire marshal. Thus, the court concluded the association was required, by law and through application of the applicable ordinance, to remove and replace its duct work, triggering the ordinance or law provision.

600. *See, e.g.*, ISO Form CP 00 17 06 07, § A.4.e.(3); ISO Form CP 00 10 06 07, § A.4.e.(3).

insured failed to comply.[601] For this limitation to apply, the insured must have an opportunity to comply.[602]

The insurer also will not pay for enforcement of any ordinance or law that requires demolition, repair, replacement, reconstruction, remodeling, or remediation of property due to contamination by "pollutants"[603] or the presence, growth, proliferation, spread, or any activity of "fungus,"[604] wet or dry rot or bacteria.[605] Costs associated with enforcement of an ordinance or law requiring any insured *or others* to test for, monitor, clean up, remove, contain, treat, detoxify or neutralize, or in any way respond to, or assess the effects of "pollutants," fungus, wet or dry rot, or bacteria are also not covered.[606]

[b] Limitation on the Amount of Coverage

The most that will be paid under the standard policy for each described building insured under the policy for increased cost of construction is $10,000 or 5 percent of the limit of insurance applicable to that building, whichever is less.[607] If a damaged building is covered under a blanket limit of insurance that applies to more than one building or item of property, the most the carrier will pay for that damaged building is the lesser of $10,000 or 5 percent multiplied by the value of the damaged building at the time of loss multiplied by any applicable coinsurance percentage. Additionally, subject to these limitations, if the building is repaired

601. *See, e.g.*, ISO Form CP 00 17 06 07, § A.4.e.(4); ISO Form CP 00 10 06 07, § A.4.e.(4).

602. *See, e.g.*, Houston Specialty Ins. Co. v. Meadows West Condo Ass'n, 2016 U.S. App. LEXIS 289 (5th Cir. Jan. 6, 2016), where the insurer invoked this exception because an ordinance would have required the association to remedy an unsafe condition after a 2010 fire. The court noted local officials did not identify the unsafe condition until several years later after another fire, and thus, the association could not have failed to comply. Most importantly, the ordinance was not adopted until late 2011 after city officials advised the association of their findings from the 2010 fire but before the cause was identified. Because the ordinance was not in effect at the time of the 2010 fire, the court held the association could not have failed to comply with it.

603. "Pollutants" is defined as any "solid, liquid, gaseous or thermal irritant or contaminant, including smoke, vapor, soot, fumes, acids, alkalis, chemicals and waste." ISO Form CP 00 17 06 07, § H.2; ISO Form CP 00 10 06 07, § H.2. The term "waste" includes materials to be recycled, reconditioned, or reclaimed.

604. "Fungus" is defined as "any type or form of fungus, including mold or mildew, and any mycotoxins, spores, scents or by-products produced or released by fungi." ISO Form CP 00 17 06 07, § H.1; CP 00 10 06 07, § H.1.

605. *See, e.g.*, ISO Form CP 00 17 06 07, § A.4.e.(5).(a); ISO Form CP 00 10 06 07, § A.4.e.(5).(a).

606. *See, e.g.*, ISO Form CP 00 17 06 07, § A.4.e.(5).(b); ISO Form CP 00 10 06 07, § A.4.e.(5).(b).

607. *See, e.g.*, ISO Form CP 00 17 06 07, § A.4.e.(6); ISO Form CP 00 10 06 07, § A.4.e.(6). The limit is illustrated in a case in which a condominium association had to replace a fire alarm panel at the cost of $85,000. The association argued the panel could not be repaired because it was impossible to obtain materials of like kind and quality. The court, however, concluded that the $85,000 reflected the cost of additional work required to ensure that the fire alarm system met code requirements. The policy unequivocally provided that repairs due to code requirements did not fall under the replacement cost provision, and therefore the $10,000 limit applied. Sands on the Ocean Condo. Ass'n v. QBE Ins. Corp., 2009 U.S. Dist. LEXIS 24689 (S.D. Fla., Mar. 23, 2009).

or replaced at the same premises, or if the insured elects to rebuild at another premises, the most the insurer will pay for is the increased cost of construction at the same premises,[608] and if an ordinance or law requires relocation to another premises, the most the insurer will pay is the increased cost of construction at the new premises.[609] The amount payable under the increased cost of construction coverage is additional insurance. Generally, then the policy has to include a line for "additional coverage for construction" coverage. If the insured wants greater coverage than provided by the policy, an endorsement must be obtained with a greater limit on the amount of coverage.[610]

[c] Two-Year Completion Limitation

The insurer will not pay for increased cost of construction until the property is actually repaired or replaced, at the same or another premises and unless the repairs or replacement are made as soon "as reasonably possible" after the loss or damage, but not to exceed two years.[611] During the two years, the carrier may extend the limitation in writing. An insurer may be barred by its actions from enforcing the two-year limitation. For example, in a common interest community damaged by fire in 2003, the local government announced it would enforce the "50% rule" under which if a building was more than 50 percent damaged, any reconstruction or repair had to comply with current building codes. The insurer and association cooperated in trying to convince the local government not to enforce the 50 percent rule and in moving toward replacing the damaged building until mid-2005 when, for the first time, the insurer told the association it would invoke the two-year limitation and deny payment for increased construction cost because the replacement was not completed. The court said that the increased cost of construction coverage then evaporated when, through no fault of its own, the association could not complete the replacement building within two years from the date of loss. The tardy invocation of the two-year clause to avoid liability for an existing coverage constituted forfeiture. The court found the insurer waived the two-year limitation by failing to bring the limitation to the attention of the association despite knowing that the association expected the entire claim

---

608. *See, e.g.*, ISO Form CP 00 17 06 07, § A.4.e.(7).(b); ISO Form CP 00 10 06 07, § A.4.e.(7).(b).

609. *See, e.g.*, ISO Form CP 00 17 06 07, § A.4.e.(7).(c); ISO Form CP 00 10 06 07, § A.4.e.(7).(c).

610. *See, e.g.*, Royal Glen Condo. Ass'n v. S.T. Neswold & Assocs., 385 Ill. Dec. 137, 18 N.E.3d 137 (Ill. App. 2014) (association purchased "Ordinance or Law Coverage" endorsement, with $1 million limit).

611. *See, e.g.*, ISO Form CP 00 17 06 07, § A.4.e.(7).(a); ISO Form CP 00 10 06 07, § A.4.e.(7).(a). *See, e.g.*, Oriole Gardens Condo. Ass'n I v. Aspen Specialty Ins. Co., 875 F. Supp. 2d 1379, 1385 (S.D. Fla. 2012) (insured must first repair or replace damaged property before seeking benefits for increased costs of construction and any repair or replacement generally must be completed within two years; thus, where association conceded that it had not repaired or replaced damaged property even though alleged damage occurred several years earlier, court granted summary judgment to insurer on claim for increased costs of construction).

to be paid and by continued adjustment of the entire claim after the two-year period expired.[612]

Some courts may apply the "prevention doctrine" under which the insurer cannot invoke the two-year limitation where it was the one that frustrated the efforts to make repairs because it did not provide an actual cash value payment when requested to do so and without those funds the insured cannot make the needed repairs.[613]

[d] Other Conditions

The costs addressed in the loss payment and valuation conditions and the replacement cost optional coverage do not include the increased cost attributable to enforcement of an ordinance or law. The amount payable under increased cost of construction coverage is not subject to that limitation.[614]

[e] Coverage by Endorsement

There is a standard endorsement that modifies the Building and Personal Property Coverage and Condominium Association Coverage Forms.[615] Under that endorsement, if a covered cause of loss occurs to covered building property shown on the schedule in the endorsement, the insurer will pay for loss to the *undamaged* portion of the building caused by enforcement of any ordinance or law that requires the demolition of parts of the same property not damaged by a covered cause of loss, regulates construction or repair of buildings or establishes zoning or land use requirements applicable to the described premises, and is in force at the time of loss.[616] This coverage is included within the limit of insurance applicable to the covered building property shown on the Declarations Page and is not additional insurance. In a case involving a New York cooperative, the court said the term "undamaged" refers to a lack of damage from a covered cause of loss.[617]

The meaning of the endorsement language was at issue when a single building in an 18-building condominium property was damaged by fire. The fire originated in the HVAC duct work of a unit. A building official informed the association's property manager that the duct work in the buildings was likely contributing to

612. Axis Surplus Ins. Co. v. Caribbean Beach Club Ass'n, 164 So. 3d 684 (Fla. 2d DCA 2014), *rev. den.*, 171 So. 3d 113 (Fla. 2015).

613. Vision I Homeowners Ass'n v. Aspen Specialty Ins. Co., 674 F. Supp. 2d 1333 (S.D. Fla. 2009) (while association never made repairs, it could still recover because insurer frustrated its efforts to make those repairs).

614. *See, e.g.*, ISO Form CP 00 17 06 07, § A.4.e.(9); ISO Form CP 00 10 06 07, § A.4.e.(9).

615. *See* ISO Form CP 04 05 10 90 (Commercial Property; Ordinance or Law Coverage).

616. *See* ISO Form CP 04 05 10 90, § A.1. There are additional limitations on this coverage. *See* ISO Form CP 04 05 10 90, § C.

617. Seward Park Hous. Corp. v. Greater N.Y. Mut. Ins. Co., 43 A.D.3d 23, 28, 836 N.Y.S.2d 99, 102 (2007).

fires. The association replaced the duct work and sought coverage under the ordinance or law provision. The insurer refused to cover the replacement of the duct work in the 17 undamaged buildings. It contended that the phrase "undamaged portion" meant that the ordinance or law provision applied only to buildings that were damaged in the fire. The court noted that the policy defined "building" as the buildings or other structures at the insured location and, therefore, the singular term "building" referred to all of the buildings at the property and if only one building were damaged by a covered cause of loss, the ordinance or law provision covered all of the buildings at the covered property. In other words, damage to just one building was sufficient to trigger coverage as to all buildings.[618]

If a covered cause of loss occurs to covered building property and a demolition cost limit of insurance is shown in the endorsement schedule, the insurer will pay the cost to demolish and clear the site of undamaged parts of the property caused by enforcement of building, zoning, or land use ordinance or law.[619] The coinsurance additional condition does not apply to demolition cost coverage.

Under the endorsement, if a covered cause of loss occurs to covered building property and an increased cost of construction limit of insurance is shown on the endorsement schedule, the insurer will pay for the increased cost to repair, rebuild, or construct the property caused by enforcement of building, zoning, or land use ordinance or law.[620] If the property is repaired or rebuilt, it has to be intended for similar occupancy as the current property, unless otherwise required by zoning or land use ordinance or law. The insurer will not pay for the increased cost of construction if the building is not repaired or replaced. The coinsurance additional condition does not apply to increased cost of construction coverage.

The carrier will not pay for costs associated with enforcement of any ordinance or law that requires any insured or others to test for, monitor, clean up, remove, contain, treat, detoxify or neutralize, or in any way respond to or assess the effects of "pollutants."[621]

The terms of the endorsement apply separately to each building to which the endorsement applies.[622]

[6] Electronic Data Coverage

A relatively new and evolving additional coverage is for "electronic data."[623] Electronic data is defined as information, facts, or "computer programs" stored as or on, created or used on, or transmitted to or from computer software—including

618. Houston Specialty Ins. Co. v. Meadows West Condo Ass'n, 2016 U.S. App. LEXIS 289 (5th Cir. Jan. 6, 2016).

619. *See* ISO Form CP 04 05 10 90, § A.2. *See* ISO Form CP 04 05 10 90, § D.

620. *See* ISO Form CP 04 05 10 90, § A.3. *See* ISO Form CP 04 05 10 90, § E.

621. *See* ISO Form CP 04 05 10 90, § B.

622. *See* ISO Form CP 04 05 10 90, § F.

623. *See, e.g.*, ISO Form CP 00 17 06 07, § A.4.f; ISO Form CP 00 10 06 07, § A.4.f.

systems and applications software—on hard or floppy disks, CD-ROMs, tapes, drives, cells, data processing devices, or any other repositories of computer software used with electronically controlled equipment.[624]

Under electronic data coverage, an insurer will pay the cost to replace or restore electronic data that has been destroyed or corrupted by a covered cause of loss.[625] To the extent the electronic data is not replaced or restored, any loss is valued at the cost of replacement of the media on which the electronic data was stored with blank media of substantially identical type. Note that this policy language does not actually specify to whom the electronic data belongs or on whose property it is stored. A CAM company often stores electronic data for an association it manages. Some of that data might be contracts to which the association is a party, minutes of its meetings, and copies of its insurance policies. Other data would be the "property" of the association, for example, email between the CAM and third parties concerning the association or accounting documents prepared by the CAM concerning the association's finances. Is there coverage for this electronic data stored by a CAM for the benefit of an association, even if the electronic data does not belong to the association?

The covered causes of loss that apply to business personal property apply to the coverage for electronic data, subject to specified changes.[626] Those changes are as follows:

- If the Causes of Loss—Special Form (that is, all-risk coverage) is part of the policy, the electronic data coverage is limited to the "specified causes of loss" as defined in that form, and collapse as set forth in that form.
- If the Causes of Loss—Broad Form is part of the policy, the electronic data coverage includes collapse as set forth in that form.
- If the causes of loss form is endorsed to add a covered cause of loss, that additional covered cause of loss does not apply to the coverage provided under the electronic data coverage.
- The covered causes of loss include a virus, harmful code or similar instruction introduced into or enacted on a computer system, including electronic data, or a network to which it is connected, designed to damage or destroy any part of the system or disrupt its normal operation; however, there is no coverage for loss or damage caused by or resulting from manipulation of a computer system—including electronic data—by any employee, including a temporary or leased employee, or by an entity retained by or for the

624. *See, e.g.*, ISO Form CP 00 17 06 07, § A.2.n; ISO Form CP 00 10 06 07, § A.2.n. "Computer programs" means a set of related electronic instructions that direct the operations and functions of a computer or device connected to it, that enable the computer or device to receive, process, store, retrieve, or send data.

625. *See, e.g.*, ISO Form CP 00 17 06 07, § A.4.f.(2); ISO Form CP 00 10 06 07, § A.4.f.(2).

626. *See, e.g.*, ISO Form CP 00 17 06 07, § A.4.f.(3); ISO Form CP 00 10 06 07, § A.4.f.(3).

insured to inspect, design, install, modify, maintain, repair, or replace that system.

The most the carrier will pay under the standard electronic data coverage is $2,500 for all loss or damage sustained in any one policy year, regardless of the number of occurrences of loss or damage or the number of premises, locations, or computer systems involved. If a loss payment on the first occurrence does not exhaust the $2,500, then the balance is available for subsequent loss or damage sustained in, but not after, that policy year. When an occurrence begins in one policy year and continues or results in additional loss or damage in a subsequent policy year or years, all loss or damage is deemed to be sustained in the policy year in which the occurrence began.

§ 10.17 Additional Coverages Otherwise Excluded

There are two additional coverages that are otherwise excluded perils. These are "collapse" and "'fungus,' wet rot, dry rot, and bacteria."

[1] Collapse

Generally, coverage for collapse is included when either the Causes of Loss—Broad Form[627] or Causes of Loss—Special Form[628] is made part of the policy. Collapse coverage may also be added or modified by endorsement.[629] The language of a clause covering collapse can vary from form to form. Often the language of these clauses is confusing and circuitous, especially when one attempts to reconcile it with other parts of a policy, particularly the coverage exclusions.[630] To add to the confusion, the meaning of the term has evolved over the years, both as an insured peril and as an exclusion.

There is frequent litigation over collapse coverage and,[631] therefore, it is important for a common interest community to discuss the available coverage with its broker, to determine its desired coverage, and to get an explanation from the broker of the coverage when the policy is issued.

---

627. *See, e.g.*, ISO Form CP 10 20 04 02, § C.

628. *See, e.g.*, ISO Form CP 10 30 06 07, § D.

629. *See, e.g.*, Palma Vista Condo. Ass'n of Hillsborough County v. Nationwide Mut. Fire Ins. Co., 2010 U.S. Dist. LEXIS 118262 (M.D. Fla. Oct. 7, 2010).

630. *See, e.g.*, 130 Slade Condo. Ass'n v. Millers Capital Ins. Co., 2008 U.S. Dist. LEXIS 44182 (D. Md. June 2, 2008), where the court, examining language similar to that in the ISO Form CP 10 30 06 07, referred to it as a "somewhat confusing policy."

631. *See* Doheny West Homeowners' Ass'n v. American Guarantee & Liability Ins. Co., 60 Cal. App. 4th 400, 403, 70 Cal. Rptr. 2d 260, 262 (1997) (it is "perhaps an understatement" to say that collapse coverage has spawned much litigation since its appearance in property policies in 1954).

[a] "Abrupt" Collapse

A typical Causes of Loss—Special Form provides coverage only for "abrupt" collapse,[632] which it defines as "an abrupt falling down or caving in" of a building, or any part of it,[633] with the result that the building or part of it cannot be occupied for its intended purpose.[634] The policy does not define "caving in," but clearly it must be different from "falling down."[635] One court decided it meant "any serious impairment of structural integrity," and that a building "caved in" when a steel supporting column buckled.[636]

[b] Causes of Loss

The carrier will pay for direct physical loss or damage to covered property[637] caused by abrupt collapse of a building or any part of a building insured under the policy or that contains covered property insured under the policy if the collapse is one or more of four prescribed causes:[638]

---

632. Policies may also refer to "sudden" collapse. *See, e.g.*, Ass'n of Unit Owners v. State Farm Fire & Cas. Co., 670 F. Supp. 2d 1156 (D. Or. 2009) (term "sudden" in collapse coverage clause has temporal element and means marked by or manifesting abruptness or haste or made or brought about in short time and, thus, conditions that gradually lead to collapse are excluded; where any collapse resulted from water damage and decay occurring over period of time, collapse was not sudden under terms of policy).

633. *Consider* Council Tower Ass'n v. Axis Specialty Ins. Co., 630 F.3d 725, 728–29 (8th Cir. 2011) ("or any part thereof" obviously refers to "collapse" of part of building, not partial collapse of part or whole of building).

634. *See, e.g.*, ISO Form CP 10 30 06 07, § D.1. *See also* Kings Ridge Cmty. Ass'n v. Sagamore Ins. Co., 98 So. 3d 74, 77 (Fla. 5th DCA 2012) ("abrupt" is defined as characterized by or involving action or change without preparation or warning).

635. An event, however, could meet the definition of both "falling down" and "caving in." Kings Ridge Cmty. Ass'n v. Sagamore Ins. Co., 98 So. 3d 74 (Fla. 5th DCA 2012) (when trusses failed and roof above them deflected downward 12 inches, it met definition of both "falling down" and "caving in").

636. 130 Slade Condo. Ass'n v. Millers Capital Ins. Co., 2008 U.S. Dist. LEXIS 44182 (D. Md. June 2, 2008) (building that buckles three inches down and three inches to south during abrupt event that renders it unsafe and subject to evacuation certainly suffers serious impairment to its structural integrity). *See also* Kings Ridge Cmty. Ass'n v. Sagamore Ins. Co., 98 So. 3d 74 (Fla. 5th DCA 2012) (when trusses failed and roof above them deflected downward 12 inches, it met definition of "caving in").

637. Property policies typically have a list of "Property Not Covered." *See, e.g.*, ISO Form CP 00 10 10 00, § A.2; ISO Form CP 00 17 04 02, § A.2. If property is on that list and not included in the collapse coverage clause, then there would be no coverage for it. *See* Mountview Plaza Assocs. v. Main St. Am. Assur. Co., 2013 Conn. Super. LEXIS 2127 (Conn. Super. Ct. Sept. 24, 2013) (culvert damaged by sinkhole was not building, and there was no coverage for collapse not caused by collapse of building or any part of building); Seward Park Hous. Corp. v. Greater N.Y. Mut. Ins. Co., 43 A.D.3d 23, 33, 836 N.Y.S.2d 99, 106 (2007) (additional coverage for collapse specifically requires that property be "covered property").

638. *See, e.g.*, ISO Form CP 10 30 06 07, § D.2.

- Building decay hidden from view,[639] unless the presence of that decay is known to an insured prior to collapse;[640]
- Insect or vermin damage hidden from view, unless the presence of that damage is known to an insured prior to collapse;
- Use of defective material or methods in construction, remodeling, or renovation if the abrupt collapse occurs *during* the course of construction, remodeling, or renovation; and
- Use of defective material or methods in construction, remodeling, or renovation if the abrupt collapse occurs *after* the construction, remodeling, or renovation is complete, but only if the collapse is caused in part by building decay[641] or insect or vermin damage hidden from view,[642] one or

639. The policy does not define "hidden," but many courts have done so. *See* Sandalwood Condo. Ass'n at Wildwood, Inc. v. Allstate Ins. Co., 294 F. Supp. 2d 1315 (M.D. Fla. 2003) (to show damage was "hidden" requires insured to demonstrate it was not visible and that insured neither knew nor should have known of structural damage with sufficient time to allow for repairs before it reached stage of collapse); Olde Colonial Vill. Condo. Council v. Millers Mut. Ins. Co., 2002 Del. Super. LEXIS 42 (Del. Super. Ct. Jan. 28, 2002) (hidden can mean "out of sight" or "concealed" as opposed to "unknown" and, therefore, assuming council had actual knowledge of decay, that decay could still be characterized as "hidden" because it was out of sight and concealed); Panorama Vill. Condo. Owners Ass'n Bd. of Dirs. v. Allstate Ins. Co., 144 Wn. 2d 130, 141, 159, 26 P.3d 910, 916, 924 (2001) ("hidden" means "out of sight" or concealed; if insurer intends "hidden" to mean "unknown," it must say so and to extent term is ambiguous, it must be construed against the insurer; dissenting judge contended that if "hidden" meant out of sight, insured could simply allow known decay to continue behind walls to point of collapse simply because decay was not visible, so that definition would permit insureds to turn their backs on maintenance problems to keep something hidden); Stamm Theatres, Inc. v. Hartford Casualty Ins. Co., 93 Cal. App. 4th 531, 534, 113 Cal. Rptr. 2d 300, 301 (Cal. App. 2001) (policy covering collapse of building because of hidden decay applied to unexpected failure of wooden roof trusses, with no evidence of rot where policy did not limit scope of term "hidden decay" to organic decay, unless other policy terms limit coverage); Island Breakers v. Highlands Underwriters Ins. Co., 665 So. 2d 1084, 1085, n.1 (Fla. 3d DCA 1995) (Cope, J., concurring) (for purposes of collapse coverage, rust of reinforcing bars embedded inside concrete can constitute hidden decay); Whispering Creek Condominium Owner Ass'n v. Alaska Nat'l Ins. Co., 774 P.2d 176, 181 (Alaska 1989) (distinction between "hidden decay" and "rot" is one without any difference; "decay" and "rot" are synonymous terms; where policy covered collapse caused by "hidden decay," it necessarily covered collapse caused by rot). *See also* Three Palms Pointe, Inc. v. State Farm Fire & Cas. Co., 362 F.3d 1317 (11th Cir. 2004) (although buildings never actually collapsed, insurer agreed that "hidden decay" of buildings constituted "accidental direct physical loss" of property in accordance with terms of policy); 130 Slade Condo. Ass'n v. Millers Capital Ins. Co., 2008 U.S. Dist. LEXIS 44182 (D. Md. June 2, 2008) (declaring that it "strains reason" to suggest that "hidden decay" does not include deterioration from rust).

640. *See* Island Breakers v. Highlands Underwriters Ins. Co., 665 So. 2d 1084, 1086 (Fla. 3d DCA 1995) (Cope, J., concurring) (that cracks were visible does not automatically mean that association knew, or should have known, of interior decay to steel reinforcing bars).

641. *Consider* Beachwalk Homeowners Ass'n v. General Star Indem. Co., 76 Fed. Appx. 494, 2003 U.S. App. LEXIS 18178 (4th Cir. S.C. 2003) (portion of building was built over construction debris pit, which was causing settlement of foundation; court found "decay" to refer to decay that existed in covered property, not in land beneath it).

642. *Consider* West Am. Ins. Co. v. Chateau La Mer II Homeowners Ass'n, 622 So. 2d 1105 (Fla. 1st DCA 1993). The trial court determined there was decay and insect damage that was a

more of the "specified causes of loss," breakage of building glass, weight of people or personal property, or weight of rain that collects on a roof.[643]

The specified causes of loss are usual named perils: fire, lightning, explosion, windstorm or hail, smoke, aircraft or vehicles, riot or civil commotion, vandalism, leakage from fire-extinguishing equipment, sinkhole collapse,[644] volcanic action, falling objects, weight of snow, ice or sleet, and water damage.[645]

There is certain property for which, if an abrupt collapse is caused by one of the causes of loss listed above, the carrier will pay for loss or damage to that property *only* if the loss or damage is a direct result of the abrupt collapse of a building insured under the policy and the property is covered property under the policy.[646] These items are outdoor radio or television antennas including satellite dishes and their lead-in wiring, masts or towers, awnings, gutters and downspouts, yard fixtures, outdoor swimming pools, fences, piers, wharves and docks, beach or diving platforms or appurtenances, retaining walls, and walks, roadways, and other paved surfaces.

[c] Personal Property

If *personal property* abruptly falls down or caves in and the collapse is not the result of abrupt collapse of a building, the carrier will pay for loss or damage to covered property caused by the collapse of personal property only if

- The collapse of personal property was caused by one of the causes of loss listed above.
- The personal property that collapses is inside a building.
- The property that collapses is not one of those items listed above, regardless of whether that kind of property is considered to be personal property or real property.

---

direct result of faulty or inadequate construction and/or plans and/or specifications and/or maintenance. The appellate court found the policy expressly covered loss due to collapse from hidden decay or damage by insects, but remanded for the trial court to determine whether the decay and insect damage was hidden.

643. *Consider* Seward Park Hous. Corp. v. Greater N.Y. Mut. Ins. Co., 43 A.D.3d 23, 28, 836 N.Y.S.2d 99, 102 (2007) (collapse clause does not require that weight of rain be dominant cause of collapse, but unambiguously provides coverage where "weight of rain" is a partial cause of collapse).

644. *See* Amitie One Condo. Ass'n v. Nationwide Prop. & Cas. Ins. Co., 2008 U.S. Dist. LEXIS 60491 (M.D. Pa. Aug. 4, 2008) (although sinkhole activity progressed over many years, court refused to dismiss association's claim for collapse coverage based on insurer's assertion that did not meet definition of *sudden* sinking or collapse of land into underground empty spaces). Subsequently, the court decided there was no material dispute of fact that the sinking or collapse of the covered property was sudden. Amitie One Condo. Ass'n v. Nationwide Prop. & Cas. Ins. Co., 2010 U.S. Dist. LEXIS 129103 (M.D. Pa. Dec. 7, 2010).

645. *See, e.g.*, ISO Form CP 10 30 06 07, § G.2.

646. *See, e.g.*, ISO Form CP 10 30 06 07, § D.4.

This coverage does not apply to personal property if marring and/or scratching is the only damage to it caused by the collapse.[647] It also does not apply to personal property that has not abruptly fallen down or caved in, even if the personal property shows evidence of cracking, bulging, sagging, bending, leaning, settling, shrinkage, or expansion.[648]

[d] Limitations on Coverage

Collapse coverage does not apply to a building or any part of a building in danger of falling down or caving in; a part of a building that is standing, even if it has separated from another part of the building;[649] or a building that is standing or any part of a building that is standing, even if it shows evidence of cracking, bulging, sagging, bending, leaning, settling, shrinkage, or expansion.[650] As one court observed, this language could be seen as narrowing collapse to an event in which a building actually falls down into rubble, but that would render the coverage for "caving in" meaningless.[651]

The collapse coverage will not increase the limits of insurance,[652] and the term "covered cause of loss" includes the additional coverage for collapse described in the clause on collapse.[653] The coverage then is within the standard limits and is not considered an additional coverage over the limit, that is, it must fall within the limits on the Declarations Page.

[e] Exclusions and Collapse Coverage

Determining collapse coverage is further complicated by standard policy exclusions. First, collapse itself is generally excluded, although the exclusion is rendered inapplicable to the extent the coverage is provided under the additional coverage portion of a policy.[654] Under the exclusion, the carrier will not pay for

647. *See, e.g.*, ISO Form CP 10 30 06 07, § D.5.

648. *See, e.g.*, ISO Form CP 10 30 06 07, § D.6.

649. Kings Ridge Cmty. Ass'n v. Sagamore Ins. Co., 98 So. 3d 74 (Fla. 5th DCA 2012) (where trusses failed and roof above them deflected downward 12 inches, "standing" exception did not apply as there was no evidence that ceiling, roof, and trusses separated from another part of building and they were not "standing" because they were no longer at same level, degree, or amount of height that they had previously maintained). *See also* Clark, *What Is a Covered "Collapse" for Insurance Purposes?* (July 13, 2012), available at: http://www.floridahoalawyerblog.com/2012/07/what-is-a-covered-collapse-for.html?utm_source=feedburner&utm_medium=feed&utm_campaign=Feed:+FloridaHoaLawyerBlogCom+%28Florida+HOA+Lawyer+Blog%29.

650. *See, e.g.*, ISO Form CP 10 30 06 07, § D.3. *Consider* Kings Ridge Cmty. Ass'n v. Sagamore Ins. Co., 98 So. 3d 74, 79 (Fla. 5th DCA 2012) (because ceiling, roof, and trusses were by definition not standing, exception did not apply even though roof showed evidence of bending or sagging).

651. 130 Slade Condo. Ass'n v. Millers Capital Ins. Co., 2008 U.S. Dist. LEXIS 44182 (D. Md. June 2, 2008).

652. *See, e.g.*, ISO Form CP 10 30 06 07, § D.7.

653. *See, e.g.*, ISO Form CP 10 30 06 07, § D.8.

654. *See, e.g.*, ISO Form CP 10 30 06 07, § B.2.k.

loss or damage caused by or resulting from collapse of property or any part of the property, including abrupt falling down or caving in; loss of structural integrity, including separation of parts of the property or property in danger of falling down or caving in; or cracking, bulging, sagging, bending, leaning, settling, shrinkage, or expansion as they relate to abrupt falling down or caving in or loss of structural integrity. If, however, collapse results in a covered cause of loss at the described premises, the carrier will pay for the loss or damage caused by that covered cause of loss. Finally, the exclusion does not apply to collapse caused by one or more of the "specified causes of loss," breakage of building glass, weight of rain that collects on a roof, or weight of people or personal property.

Some courts, taking note of the fact that the exclusion does not apply to the extent that coverage is provided under the additional coverage provision, have concluded that the additional collapse coverage is "not modified or qualified by any of the other listed exclusions . . . which appear to apply to the general coverage provisions of the policy instead."[655]

If those other exclusions are applicable, there are quite a few that could bar coverage for collapse. One exclusion common to most property policies is for "earth movement."[656] Among the types of earth movement that are excluded is earth sinking—other than sinkhole collapse—rising, or shifting, including "soil conditions" that cause settling, cracking, or other disarrangement of foundations or other parts of real property. Another common set of exclusions that may be related to collapse are for loss or damage caused by or resulting from rust or other corrosion, decay,[657] deterioration, hidden or latent defect,[658] or any quality

---

655. Kings Ridge Cmty. Ass'n v. Sagamore Ins. Co., 98 So. 3d 74, 79 (Fla. 5th DCA 2012) (at best, collapse exclusion is ambiguous). *See also* 130 Slade Condo. Ass'n v. Millers Capital Ins. Co., 2008 U.S. Dist. LEXIS 44182 (D. Md. June 2, 2008) (exclusion from coverage for collapse except as provided in Additional Coverage for Collapse section indicates that additional collapse coverage is not modified or qualified by any other listed exclusions that apply instead to general coverage provisions). *Compare* West American Ins. Co. v. Red Cricket Condo. Ass'n, 2008 U.S. Dist. LEXIS 57154 (D. Idaho July 29, 2008) (coverage provided for collapse caused by one of listed specified causes of loss remained subject to exclusions, and because mudflows and mudslides were specifically excluded in policy, collapse coverage for falling objects was within specific exclusions listed). *And see* York Ins. Co. v. Williams Seafood of Albany, Inc., 273 Ga. 710, 544 S.E.2d 156 (2001).

656. *See, e.g.*, ISO Form CP 10 30 06 07, § B.1.b.

657. *Consider* Mercer Place Condo. Ass'n v. State Farm Fire & Cas. Co., 104 Wn. App. 597, 605, 17 P.3d 626, 630 (2000), *rev. den.*, 143 Wn. 2d 1023, 25 P.3d 1020 (2001) (policy specifically excludes coverage for damage from hidden decay that has not yet reached point of collapse during policy period and, therefore, collapse that occurs after policy period is specifically excluded from coverage).

658. *See, e.g.*, Seward Park Hous. Corp. v. Greater N.Y. Mut. Ins. Co., 43 A.D.3d 23, 836 N.Y.S.2d 99 (2007) (while insurer argued collapse fell within exclusion for "hidden and latent" defects, it failed to satisfy its burden of establishing that claimed policy exclusion defeated coverage, particularly given express provision of coverage for collapses caused, even in part, by "weight of rain").

in property that causes it to damage or destroy itself,[659] and for settling, cracking, shrinking, or expansion.[660]

These and other exclusions may be invoked by insurers to bar coverage for collapse. To address the labyrinth of coverage and exclusion language, an insured needs an attorney experienced in insurance law.

[f] Traditional Interpretation of Collapse Coverage

The meaning of coverage for collapse has long been a subject of disagreement among the courts.[661] Courts have defined the term in three major ways: actual collapse,[662] imminent collapse, and substantial impairment of structural integrity.[663]

The narrow interpretation of "collapse" has limited it to instances in which a building has fallen down or caved in.[664] Courts adopting this approach have generally considered policies that do not define "collapse."

---

659. *See, e.g.*, ISO Form CP 10 30 06 07, § B.2.d.(2).

660. *See, e.g.*, ISO Form CP 10 30 06 07, § B.2.d.(4). *See also* Beachwalk Homeowners Ass'n v. General Star Indem. Co., 76 Fed. Appx. 494 (4th Cir. 2003). In *Beachwalk* the association experienced structural problems, including cracking of walls and ceilings, sloping of floors and countertops, and misalignment of doors. It was discovered that a portion of the building was built over a construction debris pit, which was causing settlement of the foundation. The court found the exclusion for "settling, cracking, shrinking or expansion" barred coverage because the loss was caused by long term settlement.

661. *See generally* Tarr, Daskam & Baumann, *Insurance Coverage for Collapse Claims: Evolving Standards and Legal Theories*, 35 Tort & Ins. L.J. 57 (1999).

662. This is also called the "rubble-on-the-ground" test. Queen Anne Park Homeowners Ass'n v. State Farm Fire & Cas. Co., 2012 U.S. Dist. LEXIS 59275 (W.D. Wash. Apr. 27, 2012).

663. Queen Anne Park Homeowners Ass'n v. State Farm Fire & Cas. Co., 183 Wn. 2d 485, 491–92, 352 P.3d 790, 794 (2015).

664. *See, e.g.*, Heintz v. United States Fidelity & Guaranty Co., 730 S.W.2d 268, 269 (Mo. App. 1987) (condition of impending collapse is insufficient; there must have been falling down or collapsing of part of building); Sherman v. Safeco Ins. Co., 670 P.2d 16, 17 (Colo. App. 1983) (collapse connotes falling or shrinking together, falling into flattened mass or disorganized state, breaking down, or falling into irregular mass or flattened form); Central Mut. Ins. Co. v. Royal, 269 Ala. 372, 375, 113 So. 2d 680, 683 (1959) (building did not collapse where there was no falling in, no loss of shape, no reduction to flattened form or rubble). *See also* Dreiblatt v. St. Paul Fire & Marine Ins. Co., 264 F.3d 126, 129 (1st Cir. 2001) (under Massachusetts law, collapse has three elements: suddenness, perceptible change in appearance, and completeness; evidence of internal deterioration within roof structure was insufficient given that roof still performed its basic functions). *And see* Mercer Place Condo. Ass'n v. State Farm Fire & Cas. Co., 104 Wn. App. 597, 17 P.3d 626 (2000), *rev. den.*, 143 Wn. 2d 1023, 25 P.3d 1020 (2001) (coverage extends only to those portions of property shown to be in state of collapse during policy period and not to damage not yet in state of collapse during policy period that will eventually reach point of collapse, unless condition causing damage is sooner repaired).

The majority of courts have expanded the definition of collapse beyond "actual collapse" to include "imminent collapse,"[665] thereby taking what has been called the "middle-of-the-road interpretation."[666] "Imminent collapse" has been defined to mean that collapse is likely to happen "without delay."[667] The concept of "imminent" collapse is illustrated in an oft-cited California case where a structural engineer hired by a homeowners association discovered cracking of girders, columns, and wall surfaces in a parking structure. The association made repairs and submitted a claim to its property insurer. The insurer denied the claim because, it said, "collapse" means "actual collapse." The court rejected an interpretation of "collapse" that would provide coverage only if a building fell and exclude coverage for collapse that is inevitable but has not yet taken place. Instead, for there to be coverage the damage has to be sufficient to lead to collapse. Because the trial court correctly found there was no actual or imminent collapse of the association's parking structure, the appellate court affirmed judgment for the insurer.[668]

---

665. *See, e.g.*, Ocean Winds Council of Co-Owners, Inc. v. Auto-Owner Ins. Co., 350 S.C. 268, 565 S.E.2d 306 (S.C. 2002) ("imminent" collapse is most reasonable construction of policy clause covering risks of direct physical loss involving collapse); Whispering Creek Condominium Owner Ass'n v. Alaska Nat'l Ins. Co., 774 P.2d 176, 181 (Alaska 1989) (when condition of building is such that its basic structure or its substantial integrity is materially impaired, it can no longer perform its function, and it is in immediate danger of complete collapse, it is in state of collapse within meaning of collapse provisions of policy). *See also* Equinox on the Battenkill Mgmt. Ass'n v. Phila. Indem. Ins. Co., 125 A.3d 893 (Vt. 2015) (where policy provided coverage for loss caused by or resulting from risks of direct physical loss involving collapse of buildings or any part of buildings, balconies could incur damage from "risk of direct physical loss involving collapse" even where they had not detached and completely fallen away from buildings; risk of direct physical loss involving collapse means risk of imminent collapse).

666. Hilton Head Resort Four Seasons Ctr. Horizontal Prop. Regime Council of Co-Owners, Inc. v. General Star Indem. Co., 357 F. Supp. 2d 885, 888 (D.S.C. 2005).

667. Ocean Winds Council of Co-Owners, Inc. v. Auto-Owner Ins. Co., 350 S.C. 268, 270, 565 S.E.2d 306, 308 (S.C. 2002) (imminent means impending or threatening and requires showing of more than substantial impairment). That collapse could occur as a result of a rare event does not make the possibility of collapse imminent. Buczek v. Cont'l Cas. Ins. Co., 378 F.3d 284, 291 (3d Cir. 2004) (that building was vulnerable to rare threat of 90 mile-per-hour wind did not make threat imminent and could not serve to support finding of collapse). *See also* Siena Del Lago Condo. Ass'n v. Am. Fire & Cas. Co., 2013 U.S. Dist. LEXIS 69308 (W.D. Wash. May 14, 2013), *aff'd*, 2016 U.S. App. LEXIS 7150 (9th Cir. Apr. 20, 2016) (where policy period ended in 2002 and damage was not discovered until 2011, association would be unable to show coverage because it would have to show both substantial impairment and imminent threat of collapse; when almost nine years elapsed between end of coverage and discovery of damage, it could not show *imminent collapse* as matter of law).

668. Doheny West Homeowners' Ass'n v. American Guarantee & Liability Ins. Co., 60 Cal. App. 4th 400, 70 Cal. Rptr. 2d 260 (1997). The court noted that limiting "collapse" to actual collapse would require an insured seeking coverage to neglect repairs and allow a building to fall. That, asserted the court, would not advance the best interests of the insured, the public, or even the insurer.

A variation on imminent collapse provides that the condition of a building together with action by local building officials to condemn and order the evacuation of a building constitute "collapse," even where the building did not fall down.[669]

A minority interpretation of collapse defines it as the material and substantial impairment of the basic structure of a building without any aspect of "imminence."[670] One court has suggested this interpretation is the "modern trend."[671] "Substantial impairment of structural integrity" means substantial impairment of the structural integrity of a building or part of a building that renders the building or part of it unfit for its function or unsafe.[672]

[g] Navigating the Difficult Straits of Collapse Coverage

One cannot rely on the considerable case law interpreting "collapse." One reason for that is that in many states the highest court has not yet issued a definitive ruling. Next, it is an unsettled area of law and courts are open to persuasion.

---

669. Olde Colonial Vill. Condo. Council v. Millers Mut. Ins. Co., 2002 Del. Super. LEXIS 42 (Del. Super. Ct. Jan. 28, 2002) (collapse happened when building inspector declared building unsafe for occupancy; when building was condemned its structural condition was so precarious, it probably would fail completely "at any moment"). *Compare* Huntingdon Ridge Townhouse Homeowners Ass'n v. QBE Ins. Corp., 2009 U.S. Dist. LEXIS 108558 (M.D. Tenn. Nov. 20, 2009) (building structure that is in danger of falling down or caving in is not considered to be in state of collapse even if building has been declared by civil authority or person technically qualified to do so to be in imminent state of collapse).

670. *See, e.g.*, Sandalwood Condo. Ass'n at Wildwood, Inc. v. Allstate Ins. Co., 294 F. Supp. 2d 1315, 1318 (M.D. Fla. 2003) (to constitute "collapse," damage to building need not render it uninhabitable and structure need not be in imminent danger of collapse, rather, damage must substantially impair structural integrity of the building—that is, alter the basic stability or structure of building). *See also* Macheca Transp. Co. v. Phila. Indem. Ins. Co., 649 F.3d 661 669 (8th Cir. 2011) (to define "collapse" as any serious impairment of building or part of structural integrity of building would be more consistent with what average layperson would reasonably understand term to mean).

671. Ocean Winds Council of Co-Owners, Inc. v. Auto-Owner Ins. Co., 350 S.C. 268, 270, 565 S.E.2d 306, 308 (S.C. 2002) (modern trend is to find "collapse" ambiguous and construe it to mean "substantial impairment" of structural integrity of building); Rankin by & Through Rankin v. Generali-United States Branch, 986 S.W.2d 237, 239 (Tenn. App. 1998) (following "modern trend" in holding collapse constitutes substantial impairment of structural integrity of building or any part of building); Beach v. Middlesex Mut. Assurance Co., 205 Conn. 246, 252, 532 A.2d 1297, 1300 (1987) (term "collapse" is sufficiently ambiguous to include coverage for any substantial impairment of structural integrity of building).

672. Queen Anne Park Homeowners Ass'n v. State Farm Fire & Cas. Co., 183 Wn. 2d 485, 487, 352 P.3d 790, 791–92 (2015). *Note* Queen Anne Park Homeowners Ass'n v. State Farm Fire & Cas. Co., 2012 U.S. Dist. LEXIS 59275 (W.D. Wash. Apr. 27, 2012) (although "imminent collapse" has frequently been described as occurring when structural integrity is materially or substantially impaired, those two tests are not necessarily equivalent). *See also* Council Tower Ass'n v. Axis Specialty Ins. Co., 630 F.3d 725, 729 (8th Cir. 2011) (falling of seven out of twenty-six stories of decorative brick veneer did not impair structural integrity and would not constitute collapse).

Changes in policy language can render cases of dubious precedent,[673] and wording of collapse clauses continues to evolve.[674]

There are other factors that make collapse coverage challenging. For example, if collapse is something more than a building falling down or caving in, questions can be raised about precisely when the "collapse" occurred.[675] Thus, in some circumstances coverage may fall under a prior policy or policies.[676] The question of when the contractual suit limitation clause is triggered may be raised.[677]

For common interest communities, the challenge of making a successful collapse coverage claim can be greater than for owners of single-family homes. Many CICs comprise mid-rise or high-rise structures. The engineering and construction techniques for these taller buildings can make it more difficult to assess the causes of apparent structural problems. For that reason, when cracks or spalling—chipping or splintering—are observed, a CIC should give serious consideration to employing a structural engineer, as well as other professionals, to examine the condition of the building.[678] Given the substantial sums of money involved in remedying structural deficiencies and the complexity in ascertaining

673. Recondite alterations in policy language can make significant changes in coverage. *See, e.g.*, Hilton Head Resort Four Seasons Ctr. Horizontal Prop. Regime Council of Co-Owners, Inc. v. General Star Indem. Co., 357 F. Supp. 2d 885, 888 (D.S.C. 2005) (policy covering "risks of direct physical loss involving collapse" appears to cover even threat of loss from collapse, but policy language providing coverage for "direct physical loss or damage to Covered Property, caused by collapse of a building or any part of a building" requires not just threat of collapse, and not just collapse itself, but actual loss or damage caused by collapse).

674. While insurers attempt to amend policy language to respond to court decisions they believe expand coverage beyond what they intended, courts warn that this complex area of coverage produces a possibility of ambiguity that will be construed against the carriers. *See* 130 Slade Condo. Ass'n v. Millers Capital Ins. Co., 2008 U.S. Dist. LEXIS 44182 (D. Md. June 2, 2008) (while insurance companies may be able to qualify or limit collapse coverage in their policies, any remaining ambiguity will be construed against insurer by not requiring that building be reduced to rubble before insured party can invoke coverage).

675. *Consider* Ellis Ct. Apts. v. State Farm, 117 Wn. App. 807, 814, 72 P.3d 1086, 1090 (2003) ("commence" refers to time damage first began, not to when it was discovered); Olde Colonial Vill. Condo. Council v. Millers Mut. Ins. Co., 2002 Del. Super. LEXIS 42 (Del. Super. Ct. Jan. 28, 2002) (trigger of collapse provision is collapse itself, not what led to it). *See also* Queen Anne Park Homeowners Ass'n v. State Farm Fire & Cas. Ins. Co., 633 Fed. Appx. 415 (9th Cir. 2016) (association could not point to any evidence from which reasonable jury could find that parts of its condominiums collapsed over 17 years ago, given that condominiums remained standing).

676. One expert recommends that community association attorneys advise associations to review both current and historic policies to ascertain whether there is collapse coverage. Adams, *Community Associations: 1996 Survey of Florida Law*, 21 Nova L. Rev. 69, 87 (1996).

677. *See, e.g.*, Queen Anne Park Homeowners Ass'n v. State Farm Fire & Cas. Co., 2012 U.S. Dist. LEXIS 59275 (W.D. Wash. Apr. 27, 2012) (collapse might commence during policy period but remain hidden and, therefore, constitute continuing occurrence of loss for some time after policy expires, in which case suit will be timely so long as it is filed within contractual period after decay is revealed).

678. *See generally* Adams, *Community Associations: 1996 Survey of Florida Law*, 21 Nova L. Rev. 69, 87 (1996).

the availability of insurance coverage, hiring highly qualified professionals is almost always worth the expense. Moreover, an engineer's report may be useful to the association in any subsequent coverage disputes.[679]

Finally, a CIC should not rely on its association attorney to advise it on the complex issues that arise in collapse coverage. The association attorney who wishes to avoid malpractice should not offer that advice. This is an area of law that requires an attorney who has special knowledge of and experience with collapse coverage.

[2] "Fungus," Wet Rot, Dry Rot, and Bacteria: Limited Coverage

Commercial property policies typically include additional coverage for "fungus," wet rot, dry rot, and bacteria.[680] This coverage serves to override an exclusion for the same peril. That exclusion does not apply to the extent coverage is provided by this additional coverage "with respect to loss or damage by a cause of loss other than fire or lightning."[681]

Policies do not ordinarily define "wet rot," "dry rot," or "bacteria," but "fungus" is defined as "any type or form of fungus, including mold or mildew, and any mycotoxins, spores, scents or by-products produced or released by fungi."[682]

This coverage applies only when the fungus, wet or dry rot, or bacteria is the result of one or more of the specified causes of loss—explosion; windstorm or hail; smoke; aircraft or vehicles; riot or civil commotion; vandalism; leakage from fire-extinguishing equipment; sinkhole collapse; volcanic action; falling objects; weight of snow, ice, or sleet; or water damage[683]—or flood, if a Flood Coverage Endorsement applies to the affected premises[684]—that occurs during the policy period and only if all reasonable means were used to save and preserve the property from further damage at the time of and after that occurrence.[685]

The carrier will pay for "loss or damage" by fungus, wet or dry rot, or bacteria. The term "loss or damage" means direct physical loss or damage to covered property caused by fungus, wet or dry rot, or bacteria, including the cost of their removal; the expense to tear out and replace any part of the building or other property as needed to gain access to the fungus, wet or dry rot, or bacteria; and the expense of testing performed after removal, repair, replacement or restoration

679. Raintree Vill. Condo. No. 11 Ass'n v. Great Am. Ins. Co., 2013 U.S. Dist. LEXIS 134907 (M.D. Fla. Sept. 20, 2013) (it is axiomatic that in insurance coverage dispute, insured may rely on engineer's report about extent of damage to subject property).

680. *See, e.g.*, CP 10 30 06 07, § E. *See generally* Houser & Bolduan, *Mold: Another Four-Letter Word Every Coverage Attorney Needs to Know*, 38 Tort Trial & Ins. Prac. L.J. 15, 16 (2002).

681. *See, e.g.*, CP 10 30 06 07, § B.1.h.

682. *See, e.g.*, CP 10 30 06 07, § G.1.

683. *See, e.g.*, CP 10 30 06 07, § G.2. Fire and lightning are also specified causes of loss but are specifically excepted. *See* CP 10 30 06 07, § E.1.a.

684. *See, e.g.*, CP 10 30 06 07, § E.1.b.

685. *See, e.g.*, CP 10 30 06 07, § E.1.

of the damaged property is completed, provided there is a reason to believe that fungus, wet or dry rot, or bacteria are present.[686] However, the standard coverage is limited in amount to $15,000 regardless of the number of claims.[687] That amount is the most the carrier will pay for the total of all loss or damage arising out of all occurrences of the specified causes of loss, other than fire or lightning, and flood that take place in a 12-month period beginning with the commencement of the annual policy period. For a particular occurrence of loss that results in fungus, wet or dry rot, or bacteria, the carrier will not pay more than a total of the $15,000 even if the fungus, wet or dry rot, or bacteria continues to be present or active, or recurs, in a later policy period. Thus, as one expert observes, this cap is well below the actual costs of remediating mold, so it behooves an insured to contain any potential for mold by completely removing all wet carpet, drywall, and contents, and drying out the site immediately after exposure.[688] That will help eliminate the potential for mold and protect against unexpected out-of-pocket expenses.

The coverage does not increase the applicable limit of insurance on any covered property, and if a particular occurrence results in loss or damage by fungus, wet or dry rot, or bacteria and other loss or damage, the carrier will not pay more for the total of all loss or damage than the applicable limit of insurance on the affected covered property.[689] If there is covered loss or damage to covered property that is not caused by fungus, wet or dry rot, or bacteria, loss payment will not be limited by the terms of the limited coverage for fungus, wet or dry rot, or bacteria except to the extent any of them causes an increase in the loss. Any increase in the loss is subject to the terms of the limited coverage for fungus, wet or dry rot, or bacteria.

The terms of the limited coverage for fungus, wet or dry rot, or bacteria do not increase or reduce the coverage provided under any additional coverage extension for "Water Damage, Other Liquids, Powder or Molten Material Damage"[690] or under the additional coverage for collapse.[691]

A certain part of the limited coverage applies only if there is Business Income and/or Extra Expense coverage for the described premises and only if

686. *See, e.g.*, CP 10 30 06 07, § E.2.

687. *See, e.g.*, CP 10 30 06 07, § E.3. *Consider* Villa D'Orleans Condo. Ass'n v. Pac. Ins. Co., 2008 U.S. Dist. LEXIS 41171 (E.D. La. May 22, 2008) (where estimate for anti-microbial treatments and mold remediation for five buildings was just under $75,000, insurer contended $15,000 limit applied on per-building basis to each of those five buildings for total of $75,000, but court denied summary judgment to insurer because it found unresolved factual issue about amount for treatment determined by insurer as it failed to show basis for number or how it was calculated).

688. Hayman, *Hurricanes and Windstorm Coverage: Case Studies and Coverages* at 3 (Adjusting Today, 2011), available at: http://adjustersinternational.com/publications/adjusting-today/hurricanes-and-windstorm-coverage/0/.

689. *See, e.g.*, CP 10 30 06 07, § E.4.

690. *See* CP 10 30 06 07, § F.2.

691. *See, e.g.*, CP 10 30 06 07, § E.5.

any "suspension" of "operations" satisfies all terms and conditions of that coverage form.[692] The first loss to come under this limitation is one that resulted in fungus, wet or dry rot, or bacteria and did not in itself necessitate a suspension of operations, but a suspension was necessary because of loss or damage to property caused by fungus, wet or dry rot, or bacteria. In that case, the payment under the Business Income and/or Extra Expense will be limited to the amount of loss and/or expense sustained in a period of not more than 30 days.[693] Next, if a covered suspension of operations was caused by loss or damage other than fungus, wet or dry rot, or bacteria, but remediation of any of them prolonged the "period of restoration," the carrier will pay for loss and/or expense sustained during the delay, regardless of when that delay occurs during the period of restoration, but the coverage is limited to 30 days.[694]

§ 10.18 Coverage Extensions in Commercial Property Coverage Forms

The BPP and CAC each include six coverage extensions.[695] These are for newly acquired or constructed property, personal effects and property of others, valuable papers and records, property off-premises, outdoor property, and non-owned detached trailers. The BPP and CAC provide that the extensions apply to property located in or on the building described on the Declarations Page or in the open—or in a vehicle—within 100 feet of the described premises. If a coinsurance percentage of 80 percent or more is shown on the Declarations Page, the insured may extend the insurance provided to include the extended coverages. The BPP adds the insured may extend the insurance provided to include the extended coverages if a value reporting period symbol is shown on the Declarations Page. These coverage extensions are additional insurance unless otherwise indicated, and the additional condition of coinsurance does not apply to the extensions. In other words, the coinsurance is not applied separately to these additional coverages.

[1] Newly Acquired or Constructed Property

The insured may extend the insurance that applies to "Building" to apply to its new buildings while being built on the described premises and buildings it acquires at locations other than the described premises intended for similar use as the building described on the Declarations Page or use as a warehouse.[696] The

692. *See, e.g.*, CP 10 30 06 07, § E.6.
693. *See, e.g.*, CP 10 30 06 07, § E.6.a. The days need not be consecutive.
694. *See, e.g.*, CP 10 30 06 07, § E.6.b. The days need not be consecutive.
695. *See, e.g.*, ISO Form CP 00 10 06 07, § A.5; ISO Form CP 00 17 06 07, § A.5.
696. *Consider* Dixie Fire Ins. Co. v. Minick, 226 Ky. 498, 500, 11 S.W.2d 141, 142 (1928) (insurance policy does not cover additions to building made after policy was issued, unless it so

most the carrier will pay for loss or damage under this coverage extension is $250,000 at each building.[697]

If the policy covers the business personal property of the insured, it may extend the insurance to apply to business personal property, including property the insured newly acquires,[698] at any location it acquires other than at fairs, trade shows, or exhibitions; property the insured newly acquires, located at its newly constructed or acquired buildings at the location described on the Declarations Page; or business personal property that the insured newly acquires, located at the described premises. The most the carrier will pay for loss or damage under this coverage extension is $100,000 at each building.[699]

For insurance on or at each newly acquired or constructed property, coverage will end with the expiration of the policy, the expiration of 30 days after the insured acquires the property or begins construction of that part of the building that would qualify as covered property, or the insured reports values to the insurer, whichever comes first.

The carrier will charge an additional premium for values reported from the date the insured acquires the property or begins construction of that part of the building that would qualify as covered property.

[2] Personal Effects and Property of Others

It is commonplace for employees to keep personal property on the premises of their place of employment.[700] For that reason, the insured may extend the coverage that applies to its business personal property to personal effects owned by the insured and its officers, partners, members, managers, or employees—but not to loss or damage by theft—and to personal property of others in the care, custody, or control of the insured.[701] The most the insurer will pay for loss or damage

---

provides in express terms or by necessary implication); Arlington Co. v. Colonial Assurance Co., 180 N.Y. 337, 73 N.E. 34 (1905) (word "additions" referred to additions to plant and included new buildings).

697. *See, e.g.*, ISO Form CP 00 10 06 07, § A.5.a; ISO Form CP 00 17 06 07, § A.5.a. There is a slight difference in the language of the policies. The BPP says: "If this policy covers Building, you may extend that insurance . . . ." The CAC states: "You may extend the insurance that applies to Building . . . ."

698. Generally, "acquired" does not mean "acquire an ownership interest." *See, e.g.*, Binnings Equipment Co. v. Travelers Indem. Co., 139 So. 2d 551 (La. App. 1962) (if insurer had intended to limit its exposure to equipment actually *owned* by insured, it could have substituted words "purchased" or "owned" wherever word "acquired" appears or could have simply excluded borrowed or leased equipment). However, the policy may exclude coverage for property not owned by the insured, which would serve to limit the "newly acquired" property provision. *Compare* Wright Constr. Co. v. St. Lawrence Fluorspar, Inc., 254 A.2d 252, 253 (Del. Super. Ct. 1969) ("acquire" generally imports "ownership").

699. *See, e.g.*, ISO Form CP 00 17 06 07, § A.5.a.(2).(a).

700. Barlow, Massmann, Alexander & Schreibman, *Condominium Insurance Coverage Guide* at 166 (2d ed. National Underwriter Co., 2016).

701. *See, e.g.*, ISO Form CP 00 10 06 07, § A.5.b; ISO Form CP 00 17 06 07, § A.5.b.

under this coverage extension is $2,500 at each described premises, and its payment for loss of or damage to personal property of others will be for only the account of the owner of that property.[702]

[3] Valuable Papers and Records Other Than Electronic Data

The insured may extend the insurance that applies to its business personal property to the cost to replace or restore the lost information on valuable papers and records for which duplicates do not exist; however, the coverage extension does not apply to valuable papers and records that exist as electronic data.[703]

If the Causes of Loss—Special Form applies, this extended coverage is limited to the "specified causes of loss" as defined in that form—meaning fire; lightning; explosion; windstorm or hail; smoke; aircraft or vehicles; riot or civil commotion; vandalism; leakage from fire-extinguishing equipment; sinkhole collapse; volcanic action; falling objects; weight of snow, ice, or sleet; and water damage—and collapse as set forth in that form. If, on the other hand, the Causes of Loss—Broad Form applies, the extended coverage includes collapse as set forth in that form.

The most the insurer will pay to replace or restore the lost information is $2,500 at each described premises, unless a higher limit is shown on the Declarations Page. That amount is additional insurance. The carrier will also pay for the cost of blank material for reproducing the records, whether or not duplicates exist, and, when there is a duplicate, for the cost of labor to transcribe or copy the records. The costs of blank material and labor are subject to the applicable limit of insurance on the insured's business personal property and, therefore, coverage of those costs is not additional insurance.

[4] Property Off-Premises

The insured may extend the insurance provided to apply to its covered property while it is away from the described premises, if it is temporarily at a location the insured does not own, lease, or operate, in storage at a location the insured leases, provided the lease was executed after the beginning of the current policy term, or at any fair, trade show, or exhibition.[704] The extended coverage does not apply to property in or on a vehicle or in the care, custody, or control of the insured's salespersons, unless the property is in that care, custody, or control at a fair, trade

702. Barlow, Massmann, Alexander & Schreibman, *Condominium Insurance Coverage Guide* at 167 (2d ed. National Underwriter Co., 2016) (under coverage for "personal property of others" payment for losses would be directly to owner of property).

703. *See, e.g.*, ISO Form CP 00 10 06 07, § A.5.c; ISO Form CP 00 17 06 07, § A.5.c. See ISO Form CP 00 10 06 07, § A.2.n and ISO Form CP 00 17 06 07, § A.2.n for the definition of "electronic data."

704. *See, e.g.*, ISO Form CP 00 10 06 07, § A.5.d; ISO Form CP 00 17 06 07, § A.5.d.

show, or exhibition. Under the standard policy, the most the carrier will pay for loss or damage is $10,000.

[5] Outdoor Property

The policyholder may extend the insurance provided to apply to its outdoor fences, radio and television antennas—including satellite dishes—trees, shrubs, and plants—other than "stock" of trees, shrubs, or plants—including debris removal expense, caused by or resulting from fire, lightning, explosion, riot or civil commotion, or aircraft if they are covered causes of loss.[705] The most the insurer will pay for loss or damage is $1,000, but not more than $250 for any one tree, shrub, or plant. The limits apply to any one occurrence, regardless of the types or number of items lost or damaged in that occurrence.

[6] Non-owned Detached Trailers

The insured may extend the insurance that applies to its business personal property to loss or damage to trailers it does not own, provided the trailer is used in its business and is in its care, custody, or control at the premises described on the Declarations Page, and it has a contractual responsibility to pay for loss or damage to the trailer.[706]

The carrier will not pay for any loss or damage that occurs while the trailer is attached to any motor vehicle or motorized conveyance, whether or not the motor vehicle or motorized conveyance is in motion or during hitching or unhitching operations, or when a trailer becomes accidentally unhitched from a motor vehicle or motorized conveyance.

The most the insurer will pay for loss or damage is $5,000, unless a higher limit is shown on the Declarations Page. This insurance is excess over the amount due, whether the insured can collect on it or not, from any other insurance covering the property.

§ 10.19 Exclusions

In both the BPP[707] and the CAC,[708] the exclusions are found in the applicable causes of loss form. There are three different causes of loss forms—Basic, Broad, and Special—but the principal exclusions are the same in all three. There are eight named principal exclusions, and they are discussed below. These eight exclusions apply whether or not the loss event results in widespread damage or affects a substantial area. The carrier will not pay for loss or damage caused directly

705. *See, e.g.*, ISO Form CP 00 10 06 07, § A.5.e; ISO Form CP 00 17 06 07, § A.5.e.
706. *See, e.g.*, ISO Form CP 00 10 06 07, § A.5.F; ISO Form CP 00 17 06 07, § A.5.F.
707. *See* ISO Form CP 00 10 10 00, § B.
708. *See* ISO Form CP 00 17 04 02, § B.

or indirectly by any of the eight principal exclusions, and the loss or damage is excluded regardless of any other cause or event that contributes concurrently or in any sequence to the loss. This is known as an ACC.

The ACC serves a particular purpose. It responds to imposition of the "efficient proximate cause" doctrine. The majority of courts take the position asserted by the West Virginia Supreme Court that

> when examining whether coverage exists for a loss under a first-party insurance policy when the loss is caused by a combination of covered and specifically excluded risks, the loss is covered if the covered risk was the efficient proximate cause of the loss. No coverage exists for a loss if the covered risk was only a remote cause of the loss, or conversely, if the excluded risk was the efficient proximate cause of the loss. The efficient proximate cause is the risk that sets others in motion. It is not necessarily the last act in a chain of events, nor is it the triggering cause. The efficient proximate cause doctrine looks to the quality of the links in the chain of causation. The efficient proximate cause is the predominating cause of the loss.[709]

An ACC avoids the efficient proximate cause doctrine by excluding a loss if it results from a combination of covered and excluded perils.[710] Note that the ACC applies to the principal exclusions, those found in subsection one of the exclusions section of the policy.[711] It will generally remain applicable when one of the principal exclusions is modified by endorsement.[712]

---

709. Murray v. State Farm Fire & Cas. Co., 203 W. Va. 477, 488, 509 S.E.2d 1, 12 (1998). *See also* Kelly v. Farmers Ins. Co., 281 F. Supp. 2d 1290 (W.D. Okla. 2003); Sunbreaker Condominium Ass'n v. Travelers Ins. Co., 79 Wn. App. 368, 375, 901 P.2d 1079, 1082–83 (1995) (efficient proximate cause rule requires courts to apply insurance contract causation language with reference to efficient proximate cause of loss, rather than its immediate, physical cause and effectively imposes liability on insurer for loss efficiently caused by covered peril, even though other, excluded perils contributed to that loss). *See generally* Steven Plitt et al., *Couch on Insurance* §§ 148.61–.62 (3d ed. Supp. 2015); Bell, *A Concurrent Mess and a Call for Clarity in First-Party Property Insurance Coverage Analysis*, 18 Conn. Ins. L.J. 73 (2011/2012); Smith & Simpson, *Causation in Insurance Law*, 48 S. Tex. L. Rev. 305 (2006).

710. Ass'n of Apt. Owners of Imperial Plaza v. Fireman's Fund Ins. Co., 939 F. Supp. 2d 1059 (D. Haw. 2013). *See also* Ski Chalet Vill. Owners Club, Inc. v. Emplrs. Mut. Cas. Co., 2016 U.S. Dist. LEXIS 161563 (E.D. Tenn. Nov. 22, 2016) (typically, there is coverage where excluded cause of loss and covered cause combine to cause damage; however, insurer may contract around that possibility through "anti-concurrent cause provision" under which there is no coverage for damage that is caused in any manner by excluded cause regardless of any other concurring or contributing causes); High St. Lofts Condo. Ass'n v. Am. Family Mut. Ins. Co., 821 F. Supp. 2d 1235 (D. Colo. 2011) (where street construction by city started in motion damage to building, insurer apparently concluded that earth shifting was one of causes of damage and, by application of anti-concurrent cause term, no damage was, therefore, covered).

711. Barlow, Massmann, Alexander & Schreibman, *Condominium Insurance Coverage Guide* at 153 (2d ed. National Underwriter Co., 2016).

712. *See* Chateau Vill. N. Condo. Ass'n v. Am. Family Mut. Ins. Co., 170 F. Supp. 3d 1349, 1357 (D. Colo. 2016) (ACC language applied to water exclusion that was modified by endorsement to provide coverage for sewer backup and sump overflow).

When the insurer asserts an exclusion as a defense to a suit by the policyholder seeking coverage, a widely accepted principle of insurance law is that the burden of proving the applicability of an exclusion rests with the insurer.[713]

[1] Ordinance or Law

The "ordinance or law" exclusion—sometimes referred to as "civil authority"[714]—eliminates coverage of costs for enforcement of any ordinance or law regulating construction, use, or repair of any property or tearing down any property, including the cost of removing its debris.[715] The exclusion applies when the loss results from an ordinance or law that is enforced,[716] even if the property has not been damaged,[717] or from the increased costs incurred to comply with an ordinance or law in the course of construction, repair, renovation, remodeling, or demolition of property, or removal of its debris, following a physical loss to that property.

A California appellate panel noted that there is a split among courts over whether, after a loss from a covered peril, an insurer is required to pay for code upgrades required to replace lost or damaged property, even if those upgrades provide the insured with something better than he or she originally had and whether a party whose property was non-compliant before the loss deserves a "windfall."[718] Insurers, not surprisingly, protest bearing the cost of providing a "windfall," but one commentator questions why, under replacement coverage, paying to replace a ten-year-old roof with a new one should be less objectionable to insurers than paying to replace a home built under an old building code with a one that complies with current building codes?[719]

Many courts hold the exclusion is unambiguous and deny coverage for any portion of a loss arising from the existence of new building codes. For example, electrical wiring in a home was damaged by lightning. The entire home had to be rewired to meet current codes. Because of the ordinance or law exclusion, the insurer was required to pay only the amount needed to repair the portion of the

---

713. *See, e.g.*, Caribbean I Owners' Ass'n v. Great Am. Ins. Co., 600 F. Supp. 2d 1228, 1246 (S.D. Ala. 2009).

714. Reichert v. State Farm General Ins. Co., 212 Cal. App. 4th 1543, 152 Cal. Rptr. 3d 6 (2012) (predecessor of law or ordinance exclusion was called civil authority exclusion); Spears v. Shelter Mut. Ins. Co., 73 P.3d 865, 867, n.2 (Okla. 2003) (ordinance or law exclusion is also sometimes referred to as civil authority exclusion).

715. *See, e.g.*, ISO Form CP 10 30 06 07, § B.1.a.

716. *See, e.g.*, Reichert v. State Farm General Ins. Co., 212 Cal. App. 4th 1543, 152 Cal. Rptr. 3d 6 (2012) (where insured property was demolished pursuant to enforcement of city of flood plain regulations, law or ordinance exclusion "plainly applied").

717. Sometimes new laws or ordinances require existing properties to be brought "up to code." The cost of compliance would not, under this part of the exclusion, be covered.

718. Reichert v. State Farm General Ins. Co., 212 Cal. App. 4th 1543, 1547–48, 152 Cal. Rptr. 3d 6, 11 (2012) (noting cases may be divided into two "anti-windfall" and "pro-compliant" camps).

719. Wood, *The Insurance Fallout Following Hurricane Andrew: Whether Insurance Companies Are Legally Obligated to Pay for Building Code Upgrades Despite the "Ordinance or Law" Exclusion Contained in Most Homeowners Policies*, 48 U. Miami L. Rev. 949, 952 (1994).

wiring directly damaged by lightning.[720] Similarly, when after a fire, a commercial hotel had to add a sprinkler system pursuant to building codes, the cost of the system was not covered.[721] Finally, two Florida condominiums damaged by the same hurricane sought coverage for complete replacement of their roofs because under the state building code, no more that 25 percent of the total roof area or roof section of an existing building or structure could be repaired, replaced, or recovered in any 12-month period unless the entire existing roofing system or roof section was replaced to conform to code requirements. The ordinance and law exclusion applied, and the insurer was liable only for the cost of repairing the damaged portion of the roofs.[722]

Some courts find ordinance or law exclusions to be ambiguous. For example, the Alaska Supreme Court found a clause containing the standard language to be ambiguous and held that an insurer had to pay the costs of replacing the insured building *with upgrades* mandated by ordinance.[723]

Non-conforming uses are ones that are inconsistent with local ordinances but allowed to continue until a triggering event.[724] For example, a building built before the adoption of building codes may not meet current setback requirements. In many communities, a non-conforming use may not be reconstructed if it suffers damages that exceed 50 percent of its appraised value. In a New Jersey case the local government ordered a non-conforming building to be destroyed after determining that damages it sustained in a fire exceeded 50 percent of its assessed valuation. An appellate court held that, an ordinance and law clause notwithstanding, the building owner was entitled to be compensated by the insurer for a total loss of the property destroyed on an actual cash basis.[725]

There are two legal constructs that, at least in theory, could bar application of the ordinance or law exclusion: the constructive total loss doctrine and valued policy statutes. Under the "constructive total loss" doctrine, when requirements of an ordinance or law exclusion prevent the policyholder from rebuilding or repairing a damaged structure, the loss is considered total, and some courts hold

---

720. Spears v. Shelter Mut. Ins. Co., 73 P.3d 865 (Okla. 2003) (loss should be calculated as if there were no new building codes affecting repair).

721. Prytania Park Hotel v. General Star Indem. Co., 896 F. Supp. 618 (E.D. La. 1995) (when rebuilding laundry room after fire, insured was required by building code to add sprinkler system to that area, but costs arising from enforcement of that building code, even though they arose from the repair after fire, were excluded under plain, unambiguous language of ordinance or law exclusion).

722. El-Ad Residences v. Mt. Hawley Ins. Co., 2010 U.S. Dist. LEXIS 109084 (S.D. Fla. Sept. 28, 2010); Royale Green Condo. Ass'n v. Aspen Specialty Ins. Co., 2009 U.S. Dist. LEXIS 24349 (S.D. Fla. Mar. 24, 2009) (association argued that exclusion applied only to ordinances or laws created *after* effective date of the policy, but court held that exclusion applied to all ordinances and laws, regardless of when they were enacted).

723. Bering Strait Sch. Dist. v. RLI Ins. Co., 873 P.2d 1292 (Alaska 1994).

724. 4 Yokley, *Zoning Law and Practice*, § 22-2 (Matthew Bender 2016).

725. Danzeisen v. Selective Ins. Co. of Am., 298 N.J. Super. 383, 689 A.2d 798 (1997).

the ordinance or law exclusion is inapplicable.[726] Generally, under "valued policy" statutes when there is a total loss, whether it is actual or perhaps even constructive, the policyholder is entitled to collect the face amount of the policy.[727] Courts have held ordinance or law exclusions to be inapplicable when they conflict with a valued policy statute.[728] While many states have valued policy statutes, their wording, and the interpretation accorded that wording, varies.[729]

Finally, there can be some overlap and confusion between the ordinance and law exclusion and the governmental action exclusion that bars coverage for, *inter alia*, destruction of property by order of governmental authority.

[2] Earth Movement

Loss or damage caused directly or indirectly by "earth movement" is generally excluded.[730] Policies ordinarily list four types of earth movement under the exclusion: earthquake, including any earth sinking, rising, or shifting related to

---

726. *See, e.g.*, Lenfest v. Coldwell, 525 F.2d 717, 724 (2d Cir. 1975) (doctrine of "constructive total loss" was designed to alleviate harshness of requirement of actual total loss); Stahlberg v. Travelers Indem. Co., 568 S.W.2d 79, 84 (Mo. App. 1978) (under doctrine of constructive total loss there is total loss if building is so damaged that no substantial remnant remains that prudent uninsured person would use on rebuilding). *See also* Algernon Blair Group, Inc. v. United States Fidelity & Guaranty Co., 821 F.2d 597, (11th Cir. 1987). *But see* Bischel v. Fire Ins. Exchange, 1 Cal. App. 4th 1168, 1178, 2 Cal. Rptr. 2d 575, 581 (1991) (while in many states, ordinance or law exclusion does not apply when ordinance would require entire structure to be replaced, California has not accepted that proposition and instead California courts hold that cost of construction upgrades required by ordinances or laws must be borne by property owner rather than insurer).

727. *See* § 10.38[3], *infra*. *See also* Wood, *The Insurance Fallout Following Hurricane Andrew: Whether Insurance Companies Are Legally Obligated to Pay for Building Code Upgrades Despite the "Ordinance or Law" Exclusion Contained in Most Homeowners Policies*, 48 U. Miami L. Rev. 949, 971 (1994).

728. *See, e.g.*, Hertog v. Milwaukee Mut. Ins. Co., 415 N.W.2d 370, 373 (Minn. App. 1987) (where policy insures direct physical loss and excludes from coverage loss occasioned by any ordinance, courts generally limit exclusionary provision in cases of total loss because it is contrary to valued policy statute); Stevick v. Northwest G. F. Mut. Ins. Co., 281 N.W.2d 60, 63 (N.D. 1979) (whether loss was in fact or in law total, valued policy statute should apply, and insured was entitled to face amount of policy and any policy provision, including ordinance and law exclusion, that prevents insured from showing that loss is in law or in fact total runs directly afoul of clear intent of statute); Stahlberg v. Travelers Indem. Co., 568 S.W.2d 79, 85 (Mo. App. 1978) (generally if repair or reconstruction of damaged building is prohibited by municipal authorities acting under proper authority of law, recovery may be had by insured as for total loss, and exclusionary ordinance and law provision that attempts to limit liability of insurer to less than face value of policy in cases of total loss is contrary to valued policy statute and void). *See generally* Garaffa, *Florida's "Valued Policy Law"—The Eye of the Storm*, 79 Fla. Bar J. 8 (2005).

729. *See, e.g.*, Fla. Stat. § 627.702 (valued policy law); Minn. Stat. § 65A.08, subd. 2; Mo. Rev. Stat. § 379.140 (company not to deny value; full amount of policy to be paid); N.D. Cent. Code, § 26.1-39-05 (face amount of policy to be paid in case of covered loss).

730. *See, e.g.*, ISO Form CP 10 30 06 07, § B.1.b. *See generally* Mattis, *Earthquake and Earth Movement Claims under All-Risk Insurance Policies in the New Madrid Fault Zone*, 21 Mem. St. U. L. Rev. 59 (Fall 1990).

that event; landslide,[731] including any earth sinking, rising, or shifting related to that event; mine subsidence, meaning subsidence of a human-made mine, whether or not mining activity has ceased; earth sinking[732]—other than sinkhole collapse—rising, or shifting, including "soil conditions" that cause settling,[733] cracking, or other disarrangement of foundations or other parts of real property;[734] and volcanic eruption, explosion, or "effusion."[735] Tremors and aftershocks may also be encompassed within the meaning of earth movement.[736]

If one of the enumerated forms of earth movement, other than volcanic eruption, explosion, or effusion, results in fire or explosion, the carrier *will* pay for the loss or damage caused by that fire or explosion. If volcanic eruption, explosion, or "effusion" results in fire, building glass breakage, or "volcanic action,"[737] the carrier will pay for the loss or damage caused by that fire, building glass breakage, or volcanic action.

---

731. *See* Gullett v. St. Paul Fire & Marine Ins. Co., 446 F.2d 1100 (7th Cir. 1971) (where retaining wall gave way, sending rocks crashing down onto insured building, jury could find that what probably happened to earth not a "landslide" if it believed that weakened wall caved in from normal deterioration, prior to earth moving). *Compare* Dupps v. Travelers Ins. Co., 80 F.3d 312 (8th Cir. 1996) (where roof of cave situated above covered property partially collapsed and sent rock down onto that property, earth movement exclusion applied because falling rocks constituted landslide).

732. *See* Audubon Hill S. Condo. Ass'n v. Cmty. Ass'n Underwriters of Am., 82 Mass. App. Ct. 461, 469 975 N.E.2d 458, 465 (2012) (where association's engineer opined that leaking pipe had caused soil changes and earth movement under foundational slab, coverage was barred pursuant to earth movement exclusion). *See also* High St. Lofts Condo. Ass'n v. Am. Family Mut. Ins. Co., 821 F. Supp. 2d 1235, 1241, 1243 (D. Colo. 2011), where the court describes the "earth sinking" portion of the exclusion as "somewhat of an un-grammatical maze." It also noted that only a handful of cases have interpreted this particular policy language, and all of them involved application of subsurface water as the cause of the earth movement giving rise to the property damage. *And see* Piankatank River Golf Club, Inc. v. Selective Ins. Co., 2009 U.S. Dist. LEXIS 31724 (E.D. Va. Apr. 15, 2009) (where tropical storm caused earthen barrier to collapse, reasonable jury could find resulting losses were not within scope of earth movement exclusion; noting neither party argued barrier failed from "sinking" or "rising" of earth).

733. *See* Burton v. State Farm Fire & Casualty Co., 533 F.2d 177, 179 (5th Cir. 1976) ("settling" refers to damage caused by action of structure in response to gradual movement of earth beneath).

734. "Soil conditions" is defined to include contraction, expansion, freezing, thawing, erosion, improperly compacted soil, and the action of water under the ground surface. ISO Form CP 10 20 04 02, § B.1.b.(4).

735. "Effusion" is the act of "pouring forth." *Webster's New Universal Unabridged Dictionary* at 622 (Random House 1966).

736. Barlow, Massmann, Alexander & Schreibman, *Condominium Insurance Coverage Guide* at 152 (2d ed. National Underwriter Co., 2016) (discussing language of 2012 Causes of Loss—Broad Form).

737. "Volcanic action" means direct loss or damage that results from eruption of a volcano when that loss or damage is caused by airborne volcanic blast or airborne shock waves, ash, dust or particulate matter, or lava flow. It is typically a named peril. *See* ISO Form CP 10 20 04 02, § A.11.

One question with which courts wrestle is whether the exclusion applies to earth movement caused by human activity.[738] For example, a lot adjacent to a condominium building was excavated, causing the earth beneath the condominium building to slide away and cracks to appear. The insurer contended the earth movement exclusion applied because the loss was the result of the movement of earth, that is, "sinking" and "shifting" of the earth beneath the building. The condominium association countered that intentional removal of earth by humans is a different kind of event from those listed in the exclusion and that had the insurer wanted excavation to be brought within the exclusion, it could have listed it. The court said the case was a close one, but it could not say the event that caused the loss to the association was unambiguously excluded from coverage and held for the association.[739] Some courts agree,[740] while many others do not.[741]

Deducing the meaning of the earth movement exclusion can be challenging, as revealed in *High St. Lofts Condo. Ass'n v. Am. Family Mut. Ins. Co.*[742] In that case the city government performed road work near the condominium property. Its contractor used a vibrating compactor to compact and set the roadbed. Shortly after work began, the association noticed damage to its building and associated structures, including cracks in walls, sloping of floors, and separation of porches from the building. The insurer refused to pay for the damages, citing the earth movement exclusion. The court concluded that the only potion of the exclusion that was "even arguably" applicable was the one excluding loss or damage for "earth sinking." That part of the exclusion applies when soil conditions cause "settling, cracking or other disarrangement of foundations." The court said there was little doubt that the condominium building suffered "cracking" and "disarrangement of foundations" and that the damage was the result

738. Note that some earth movement exclusions may specifically bar coverage whether the damage was caused by acts of nature or "otherwise." Barlow, Massmann, Alexander & Schreibman, *Condominium Insurance Coverage Guide* at 152 (2d ed. National Underwriter Co., 2016) (discussing 2012 edition of Causes of Loss—Broad Form).

739. Pioneer Tower Owners Ass'n v. State Farm Fire & Cas. Co., 880 N.Y.S.2d 885, 887, 12 N.Y.3d 302, 307, 908 N.E.2d 875, 877 (2009).

740. *See, e.g.*, Wyatt v. Northwestern Mut. Ins. Co., 304 F. Supp. 781, 783 (D. Minn. 1969) (exclusionary clause, if not limited to natural phenomena, at least did not exclude coverage for damage from excavation of contiguous property).

741. *See, e.g.*, Bilotto v. Allied Prop. & Cas. Ins. Co., 79 F. Supp. 3d 660 (W.D. Tex. 2015) (insured contended earth movement exclusion applied only to movement from naturally occurring causes rather than human-made sources, but court found exclusion applicable regardless of whether movement occurred as result of natural or artificial means). *See also* One Place Condo., LLC v. Travelers Prop. Cas. Co. of Am., 2014 U.S. Dist. LEXIS 142025 (N.D. Ill. Oct. 6, 2014), where the court discussed a number of cases in which courts declined the invitation to find ambiguity in the exclusion and to construe the language as meaning that only naturally occurring earth movement was excluded.

742. High St. Lofts Condo. Ass'n v. Am. Family Mut. Ins. Co., 821 F. Supp. 2d 1235 (D. Colo. 2011).

of vibrations transmitted through the ground that would constitute shifting of the earth beneath and around the building foundation. However, it was not clear to the court that the earth movement fell within the mechanisms—for example, freezing, thawing, erosion, or the action of water[743]—contemplated by the exclusion, other than possibly improper compaction of the soil. If the insurer could show that the vibrations damaged the building because the soil under and around the foundation was "improperly compacted," making the property susceptible to damage from vibrations, then, said the court, the exclusion would apparently apply. If, however, the association were able to show the soil was *properly compacted*, and the shifting of the earth from vibrations was not caused in part or whole by compaction defects, then none of the causal agents would be responsible for the earth movement and the exclusion would not apply. The court refused to make the determination of the applicability on the insurer's summary judgment motion.

[3] Governmental Action

A loss or damage caused directly or indirectly by seizure or destruction of property by order of governmental authority is excluded from coverage.[744] However, the carrier will pay for loss or damage caused by or resulting from acts of destruction ordered by governmental authority and taken at the time of a fire to prevent its spread, if that fire would be a covered cause of loss under the policy. One authority says that governmental acts that would trigger the exclusion include seizure of property under a search warrant, confiscation of contraband, and demolition of a condemned building.[745] Where the actions were not actually or apparently reasonably necessary to execute an order or exceed the scope of the order, courts generally find the exclusion to be inapplicable.[746] On the other hand,

743. *Consider* Peach State Uniform Service, Inc. v. American Ins. Co., 507 F.2d 996 (5th Cir. 1975) (term "earth movement" refers only to phenomena related to forces operating within earth itself and not to merely superficial effects of external forces, for example erosion by run-off rainwater). *Compare* Ski Chalet Vill. Owners Club, Inc. v. Emplrs. Mut. Cas. Co., 2016 U.S. Dist. LEXIS 161563 (E.D. Tenn. Nov. 22, 2016) (where ruptured water pipe resulted in subsequent earth movement causing swimming pool to partially drop or shift, because earth movement was "a cause" of damage or loss, there was no coverage regardless of any other contributing or concurrent causes of loss and, therefore, it did not matter that movement resulted from water leaking from burst pipe; "earth movement" exclusion applied).

744. *See, e.g.*, ISO Form CP 10 30 06 07, § B.1.c.

745. 5 Jeffrey E. Thomas, *New Appleman on Insurance Law Library Edition* § 43.02[8][a] (Matthew Bender 2017). *See also* Employers Mut. Casualty Co. v. Nelson, 361 S.W.2d 704 (Tex. 1962) (exclusion did not apply where damage was caused by excavation work done by city adjacent to insured property; exclusion applies to damage brought about by exercise of police power—condemnation of hazardous and unsafe property, zoning regulations—rather than that produced by work contracted for by public authorities).

746. *See, e.g.*, Kao v. Markel Ins. Co., 708 F. Supp. 2d 472, 476 (E.D. Pa. 2010) (order must be both valid and lawfully executed for exclusion to apply; where police officers exceeded scope of

the insured cannot create liability by acting in advance of anticipated action by a civil authority.[747]

The exclusion could apply where authorities are executing a warrant to search the property of a resident in a common interest community or confiscating contraband from a resident and damage is caused to property the association insures.[748] However, a hypothetical posited by a Pennsylvania federal court has relevance for CICs. The court described a scenario in which police obtain a warrant that listed the general address of a large apartment complex without specifying any particular apartment or subunit. The police would not, said the court, have the authority to break down the doors to all of the apartments in a 20-story building at that address and if they did they would not be lawfully executing the warrant they held, and thus not acting by order of governmental authority.[749] That should be distinguished from damage accidentally caused in proper execution of the warrant or damage to property an association insures that was necessary in carrying out the warrant.

[4] Nuclear Hazard

Coverage is excluded for any loss or damage caused directly or indirectly by "nuclear hazard," which means nuclear reaction or radiation, or radioactive contamination, however caused.[750] If, however, the nuclear reaction, radiation, or radioactive contamination results in fire, the carrier will pay for the loss or damage caused by that fire.

---

their authority in executing warrant by impermissibly entering property at address adjacent to one for which warrant was issued, damage done was not by order of governmental authority and was not covered by exclusion). *See also* West Electronics, Inc. v. National Union Fire Ins. Co., 128 B.R. 905 (Bankr. D.N.J. 1991) (finding actions outside scope of IRS authority); Bankers Fire & Marine Ins. Co. v. Bukacek, 271 Ala. 182, 189, 123 So. 2d 157, 163 (1960) (order is not cause of loss, and insurer remains liable when act causing loss is done by mistake and is not act ordered to be done, is not actually or apparently reasonably necessary to execute order, is not one civil authority is authorized by law to do or ordered to be done, or was not in execution of order received but to gratify ill will of actor).

747. Joplin v. National Live Stock Ins. Ass'n, 61 Ore. 544, 122 P. 897 (1912).

748. *See, e.g.*, Alton v. Manufacturers & Merchants Mut. Ins. Co., 416 Mass. 611, 624 N.E.2d 545 (1993) (damage to insured building occupied by tenant that was caused, directly or indirectly, by police in executing legal order of governmental authority—search warrant—excluded from coverage).

749. Kao v. Markel Ins. Co., 708 F. Supp. 2d 472, 478 (E.D. Pa. 2010).

750. *See, e.g.*, ISO Form CP 10 30 06 07, § B.1.d. *See, e.g.*, Falcon Products, Inc. v. Insurance Co. of Pennsylvania, 615 F. Supp. 37 (E.D. Mo. 1985), *aff'd*, 782 F.2d 779 (8th Cir. 1986) (exclusion applied where scrap metal sold and delivered to insured by third party for use in tables to be made by insured had been previously bombarded by radiation).

[5] Utility Services

Under the "utility exclusion" coverage is eliminated for loss or damage caused directly or indirectly by failure of power, communication,[751] water, or other utility service supplied to the described premises, however that failure is caused, if the failure meets one of two conditions.[752] The first condition is that the failure originates away from the described premises. The second condition is that the failure originates at the described premises, but only if that failure involves equipment used to supply the utility service to the described premises from a source *away from the described premises*. Failure of any utility service includes lack of sufficient capacity and reduction in supply.

Loss or damage caused by a surge of power is also excluded if the surge would not have occurred but for an event causing a failure of power. However, if the failure or surge of power, or the failure of communication, water, or other utility service, results in a covered cause of loss, the carrier will pay for the loss or damage caused by that covered cause of loss.

[6] War and Military Action

The carrier will not pay for loss or damage caused directly or indirectly by war or military action.[753] The exclusion encompasses undeclared or civil war; warlike action by a military force, including action in hindering or defending against an actual or expected attack, by any government, sovereign or other authority using military personnel or other agents; and insurrection, rebellion, revolution, usurped power, or action taken by any governmental authority to hinder or defend against any insurrection, rebellion, revolution, or usurped power.

[7] Water

Under the typical commercial property policy, the insurer will not pay for loss or damage caused directly or indirectly by water.[754] "Water" is defined broadly. First, it includes flood,[755] surface water, waves, tides, tidal waves, overflow of any body of water, or their spray, all whether driven by wind or not.[756] Second,

---

751. Communication services include, but are not limited to, service relating to internet access or access to any electronic, cellular, or satellite network.

752. *See, e.g.*, ISO Form CP 10 30 06 07, § B.1.e.

753. *See, e.g.*, ISO Form CP 10 30 06 07, § B.1.f.

754. *See, e.g.*, ISO Form CP 10 30 06 07, § B.1.g.

755. "Flood" is not defined but has been defined by courts. Some courts hold the term includes water from the failure of a dam or levee. *See* Kane v. Royal Ins. Co., 768 P.2d 678, 681 (Colo. 1989) ("flood," though undefined in policy, is not ambiguous, and generally accepted meaning of that term does not distinguish between artificial and natural floods; therefore, damage from large-scale inundation of water when dam failed was excluded flood). Other courts disagree. *See* Barking Dog v. Citizens Ins. Co. of America, 164 N.H. 80, 53 A3d 554 (2012).

756. *See, e.g.*, ISO Form CP 10 30 06 07, § B.1.g.(1).

the term includes "mudslide or mudflow."[757] This is significant because the Federal Emergency Management Agency (FEMA) Standard Flood Insurance Policy definition of "flood" specifically includes "mudflow."[758] In commercial property policies, "water" also includes that which backs up or overflows from a sewer, drain,[759] or sump,[760] and water under the ground surface pressing on, or flowing or seeping through, foundations, walls, floors or paved surfaces, basements, whether paved or not, or doors, windows, or other openings.[761]

If water as defined in the policy results in fire, explosion, or sprinkler leakage, the insurer will pay for the loss or damage caused by that fire, explosion, or sprinkler leakage.

Interpretation and application of the exclusion for water varies greatly from court to court. As just one example, many courts interpret "surface water" to mean only water on the ground,[762] while others conclude that water that accumulates on a roof can be surface water.[763] Because courts interpreting the same language reach widely differing conclusions, it behooves a common interest community to submit a claim for any water damage and, when the damage is significant, to employ experienced professionals who may be able to persuade the carrier that the loss is covered or at least lay the predicate for legal action.

---

757. *See, e.g.*, ISO Form CP 10 30 06 07, § B.1.g.(2). The term "mudflow" is generally not defined in policies but has been defined by courts. *See, e.g.*, West American Ins. Co. v. Red Cricket Condo. Ass'n, 2008 U.S. Dist. LEXIS 57154 (D. Idaho July 29, 2008) (finding term "mudflow" to be unambiguous and that its plain and ordinary meaning is moving mass of soil made fluid by rain or melting snow or soil made fluid by excessive water).

758. General Property Form Standard Flood Insurance Policy, at 2 (June 2014). *See also* 44 C.F.R. § 59.1.

759. Insureds sometimes argue that their damage was caused not by water but by organisms carried into the property by water that backed up from a sewer line; however, courts generally hold that the exclusion applies whether the loss was caused by pure water or by the pollutants contained in the sewage acting concurrently with water. Rodin v. State Farm Fire & Casualty Co., 844 S.W.2d 537 (Mo. App. 1993). *See also* Cardio Diagnostic Imaging, Inc. v. Farmers Ins. Exchange, 212 Cal. App. 4th 69, 150 Cal. Rptr. 3d 798 (2012); Citrano v. Hingham Mut. Fire Ins. Co., 58 Mass. App. Ct. 906, 788 N.E.2d 975 (2003) (rejecting argument that exclusion did not apply because damage was caused by sewage, not water); Newberg v. Commercial Union Ins. Co., 619 N.W.2d 757 (Minn. App. 2000) (plain and ordinary meaning of water damage exclusion includes water containing raw sewage) *Consider* St. Joseph's Condo. Ass'n v. Pac. Ins. Co., 2008 U.S. Dist. LEXIS 86470 (E.D. La. Oct. 24, 2008) (where gutter system overflowed and damaged property, court found "gutter" was synonymous with "drain," and thus, under plain language of policy, damage resulted from excluded cause; finding no reason to distinguish between overflow from above-ground gutter or drain and overflow from underground gutter or drain).

760. *See, e.g.*, ISO Form CP 10 30 06 07, § B.1.g.(3).

761. *See, e.g.*, ISO Form CP 10 30 06 07, § B.1.g.(4).

762. *See, e.g.*, Am. Ins. Co. v. Guest Printing Co., 114 Ga. App. 775,152 S.E.2d 794 (1966). *See also* Chateau Vill. N. Condo. Ass'n v. Am. Family Mut. Ins. Co., 170 F. Supp. 3d 1349, 1358 (D. Colo. 2016) (surface water from runoff of melted snow loses its character as surface water when it is diverted into man-made trenches or enters sewer system).

763. *See, e.g.*, Sherwood Real Estate & Inv. Co. v. Old Colony Ins. Co., 234 So. 2d 445 (La. App. 1970).

NOTE: Because backups or overflows from sewers or drains are excluded but can be a serious problem for common interest communities, a governing board should consider inquiring about an endorsement to the policy adding the coverage.[764]

[8] Fungus, Wet Rot, Dry Rot, and Bacteria

Coverage is excluded for loss or damage caused directly or indirectly by the presence, growth, proliferation, spread, or any activity of "fungus,"[765] wet or dry rot, or bacteria.[766] If, however, "fungus," wet or dry rot, or bacteria results in a "specified cause of loss," the carrier will pay for loss or damage caused by that specified cause of loss.[767] Additionally, some courts have held that the exclusion would preclude coverage for mold occurring naturally or that resulted from a non-covered event, but when mold ensues from water damage, and water damage is covered under the policy, the mold damage is covered despite the exclusion.[768]

The exclusion is inapplicable when "fungus," wet or dry rot, or bacteria results from fire or lightning, or loss or damage by a cause of loss other than fire or lightning, to the extent that coverage is provided by the limited additional coverage under another policy section for "fungus," wet rot, dry rot, and bacteria.[769]

§ 10.20 Additional Exclusions

There are 16 additional exclusions that apply generally. These are (1) electrical arcing, (2) delay, loss of use, or loss of market,[770] (3) smoke, vapor, or gas from agricultural smudging or industrial operations,[771] (4) wear and tear, (5) explosion of certain equipment, (6) seepage or leakage of water or the presence or condensation of humidity and moisture or vapor, (7) material that leaks or flows

764. *See* § 10.36[2][j], *infra.*

765. "Fungus" is defined as any type or form of fungus, including mold or mildew, and any mycotoxins, spores, scents, or by-products produced or released by fungi. CP 10 30 06 07, § G.1.

766. *See, e.g.*, ISO Form CP 10 30 06 07, § B.1.h.

767. The specified causes of loss are fire, lightning, explosion, windstorm or hail, smoke, aircraft or vehicles, riot or civil commotion, vandalism, leakage from fire-extinguishing equipment, sinkhole collapse, volcanic action, falling objects, weight of snow, ice or sleet, or water damage. CP 10 30 06 07, § G.2. "Sinkhole collapse" is defined as the sudden sinking or collapse of land into underground empty spaces created by the action of water on limestone or dolomite. The cost of filling sinkholes or sinking or collapse of land into man-made underground cavities is not included in the sinkhole cause of loss.

768. *See, e.g.*, Boardwalk Condo. Ass'n v. Travelers Indem. Co., 2007 U.S. Dist. LEXIS 48325 (S.D. Cal. July 3, 2007) (where damage was caused by water intrusion, including build-up of condensation and leaks through roof, windows, and fireplaces, damage suffered by association was not loss or damage caused by or resulting from mold).

769. *See, e.g.*, CP 10 30 06 07, § E, as discussed in § 10.18[2], *supra.*

770. *See, e.g.*, CP 10 30 06 07, § B.2.b.

771. *See, e.g.*, CP 10 30 06 07, § B.2.c.

from equipment, (8) dishonest or criminal acts, (9) voluntary parting with any property if induced by fraud, (10) rain, snow, ice, or sleet to personal property in the open,[772] (11) collapse, (12) pollution, (13) neglect by an insured to use all reasonable means to save and preserve property from further damage at and after the time of loss,[773] (14) weather conditions,[774] (15) acts or decisions of any person, group, organization, or governmental body,[775] and (16) faulty planning, design, repair, or maintenance.[776] The carrier will not pay for loss or damage caused by or resulting from any of them.[777] The more significant of these are discussed below. Note that the ACC, which avoids the efficient proximate cause doctrine by excluding a loss if it results from a combination of covered and excluded perils, does not apply to these exclusions.[778]

[1] Electric Arcing

Commercial property polices typically exclude coverage for artificially generated electrical, magnetic, or electromagnetic energy that damages, disturbs, disrupts, or otherwise interferes with any electrical or electronic wire, device, appliance, system or network or device, appliance, system, or network using cellular or satellite technology.[779] These losses should be covered by an equipment breakdown endorsement or stand-alone policy.

Electrical, magnetic, or electromagnetic energy includes, but is not limited to, electrical current, including arcing,[780] electrical charge produced or conducted by a magnetic or electromagnetic field, pulse of electromagnetic energy, or electromagnetic waves or microwaves.

The exclusion provides that the carrier will pay for loss or damage by a resulting fire.[781]

---

772. *See, e.g.*, CP 10 30 06 07, § B.2.j.

773. *See, e.g.*, CP 10 30 06 07, § B.2.m.

774. *See, e.g.*, CP 10 30 06 07, § B.3.a.

775. *See, e.g.*, CP 10 30 06 07, § B.3.b.

776. *See, e.g.*, CP 10 30 06 07, § B.3.c.

777. *See, e.g.*, CP 10 30 06 07, § B.2.

778. Barlow, Massmann, Alexander & Schreibman, *Condominium Insurance Coverage Guide* at 153 (2d ed. National Underwriter Co., 2016).

779. *See, e.g.*, CP 10 30 06 07, § B.2.a.

780. *See* Continental Ins. Co. v. Arkwright Mut. Ins. Co., 102 F.3d 30, 31 (1st Cir. 1996) (energized electrical switching panels came into contact with flood waters, which immediately caused "electrical arcing"—movement of electrons from one point to another—known in lay terms as electrical short circuit); Aetna Ins. Co. v. Getchell Steel Treating Co., 395 F.2d 12, 17 (8th Cir. 1968) (electrical arcing is movement of electrons from one point to another and produces heat and light, but does not involve combustion of matter).

781. *See, e.g.*, Associated Electric Cooperative v. Mutual Boiler & Machinery Ins. Co., 492 F. Supp. 410 (W.D. Mo. 1980). *Compare* Quadrangle Dev. Corp. v. Hartford Ins. Co., 645 A.2d 1074, 1075 (D.C. 1994) (in its common and ordinary usage "fire" indicates presence of flame and where damage to switchboard caused by electric arcing resulted in presence of smoke, but no flame, ensuing loss exception of exclusion did not apply). *See also* Aetna Ins. Co. v. Getchell Steel Treating Co.,

[2] Wear and Tear

Commercial property polices block coverage for normal deterioration or everyday damage of property by excluding coverage for:

- Wear and tear;
- Rust or other corrosion,[782] decay, deterioration, hidden or latent defect,[783] or any quality in property that causes it to damage or destroy itself;[784]
- Smog;
- Settling, cracking, shrinking, or expansion;[785]

---

395 F.2d 12, 15 (8th Cir. 1968) (fire that coexisted with electrical disturbance was covered "ensuing fire" within meaning of policy language; fire does not become ensuing only after termination of electrical disturbance).

782. *See* TRAVCO Ins. Co. v. Ward, 715 F. Supp. 2d 699, 714 (E.D. Va. 2010) (corrosion to metals and metallic surfaces, including air conditioning equipment caused by gases emitted by Chinese drywall, excluded from coverage); Bettigole v. American Employers Ins. Co., 30 Mass. App. Ct. 272, 274, 567 N.E.2d 1259, 1261 (1991) (corrosion is gradual wearing away of substance by chemical action and is not confined to wearing away by "natural" means of weather).

783. Most courts impose a high hurdle for determining that a defect is latent or hidden. *See, e.g.*, City of Burlington v. Hartford Steam Boiler Inspection & Ins. Co., 190 F. Supp. 2d 663, 688 (D. Vt. 2002), *aff'd*, 346 F.3d 70 (2d Cir. Vt. 2003) ("latent defect" means one that is hidden or that could not have been discovered by any known or customary test or examination); Board of Educ. v. International Ins. Co., 292 Ill. App. 3d 14, 20, 684 N.E.2d 978, 983, 225 Ill. Dec. 987 (Ill. App. Ct. 1st Dist. 1997) (for purposes of latent defect exclusion, latent defect means one that is hidden and not readily observable or discoverable to any but most searching examination); Scott v. Continental Ins. Co., 44 Cal. App. 4th 24, 32, 51 Cal. Rptr. 2d 566, 572 (Cal. App. 1996) ("latent defect" is one that is both not readily observable and not discoverable to any but most searching examination). *See also* Caribbean I Owners' Ass'n v. Great Am. Ins. Co., 600 F. Supp. 2d 1228, 1246 (S.D. Ala. 2009) (where insurer argued damage from hurricane was caused by construction defects, but there was record evidence that building sustained wind-driven rain damage during hurricane, that wind-driven rain damage entering through doors, windows, or other openings would not necessarily be product of "hidden or latent defect" that exclusion targets; absent showing by insurer that, as matter of undisputed fact, loss was attributable to construction defects rather than wind-driven rain leaking through doors and windows, summary judgment on basis of "hidden or latent defect" exclusion was inappropriate). *Compare* Neri v. Nationwide Mut. Fire Ins. Co., 719 A.2d 1150, 1154 (R.I. 1998) (latent defect is one that is undiscoverable on reasonable inspection).

784. This "quality in property that causes it to damage or destroy itself" replaces "inherent vice" as a part of the exclusion. The interpretation of "inherent vice" remains useful in understanding the current exclusion language. *See, e.g.*, GTE Corp. v. Allendale Mut. Ins. Co., 372 F.3d 598, 611 (3d Cir. 2004) (inherent vice is defined as any existing defects, diseases, decay, or inherent nature of commodity that will cause it to deteriorate with lapse of time; field code programmed into software that required remediation was excluded inherent vice because it was internal quality that brought about its own problem); Port of Seattle v. Lexington Ins. Co., 111 Wn. App. 901, 910, 48 P.3d 334, 339 (2002) (vice must be inherent in property for which recovery is sought).

785. Application of this exclusion is often fact driven. For example, a New York court concluded in a case where cracks appeared in a condominium building caused by excavation on an adjacent lot that, while it was a close case, the exclusion did not apply. Pioneer Tower Owners Ass'n v. State Farm Fire & Cas. Co., 880 N.Y.S.2d 885, 887, 12 N.Y.3d 302, 308, 908 N.E.2d 875, 877 (2009) (agreeing that settling or cracking exclusion would not be thought by ordinary reader to apply to settling or cracking that is immediate and obvious result of some other event, as in case intentional removal of earth in vicinity of insured building; noting that read literally, exclusion

- Nesting or infestation, or discharge or release of waste products or secretions, by insects, birds, rodents, or other animals;
- Mechanical breakdown, including rupture or bursting caused by centrifugal force—however, if mechanical breakdown results in elevator collision, the carrier will pay for the loss or damage caused by that collision; and
- Losses to personal property caused by dampness or dryness of atmosphere, changes in or extremes of temperature, or marring or scratching.[786]

However, if one of these excluded causes of loss results in a "specified cause of loss"—that is, fire; lightning; explosion; windstorm or hail; smoke; aircraft or vehicles; riot or civil commotion; vandalism; leakage from fire-extinguishing equipment; sinkhole collapse; volcanic action; falling objects; weight of snow, ice, or sleet; or water damage[787]—or building glass breakage, the carrier will pay for the loss or damage caused by that specified cause of loss or building glass breakage.[788]

[3] Explosions

A standard commercial property policy exclusion is for explosion of steam boilers, steam pipes, steam engines, or steam turbines owned or leased by the insured or operated under the control of the insured.[789] If, however, an explosion of any of this equipment results in a fire or combustion explosion, the carrier will pay for the loss or damage caused by that fire or combustion explosion. It will also pay for loss or damage caused by or resulting from explosion of gases or fuel within the furnace of any fired vessel or the flues or passages through which those gases of combustion pass.

[4] Seepage or Leakage

Commercial property policies generally exclude coverage for continuous or repeated seepage or leakage of water, or the presence or condensation of humidity, moisture, or vapor, that occurs over a period of 14 days or more.[790] The exclusion probably does not apply when there has been both a loss caused by continuous or repeated seepage or leakage and another loss by a single unrelated event.[791]

---

would apply where refrigerator fell over and cracked wall, although that cannot have been intent of policy drafters).

786. *See, e.g.*, CP 10 30 06 07, § B.2.d.

787. *See, e.g.*, ISO Form CP 10 30 06 07, § G.2.

788. *See generally* French, *The "Ensuing Loss" Clause in Insurance Policies: The Forgotten and Misunderstood Antidote to Anti-Concurrent Causation Exclusions*, 13 Nev. L.J. 215 (2012).

789. *See, e.g.*, CP 10 30 06 07, § B.2.e.

790. *See, e.g.*, CP 10 30 06 07, § B.2.f.

791. In *Caribbean I Owners' Ass'n v. Great Am. Ins. Co.*, 600 F. Supp. 2d 1228, 1247 (S.D. Ala. 2009), a condominium building had experienced minor leaks around windows and doors

[5] Freezing

When water, other liquids, powder, or molten material leaks or flows from plumbing, heating, air conditioning, or other equipment except fire protective systems and is caused by or results from freezing, it is ordinarily excluded unless the insured "does its best" to maintain heat in the building or structure or drains the equipment and shuts off the supply if the heat is not maintained.[792]

[6] Dishonest or Criminal Acts

Dishonest or criminal act by the insured or any partners, members, officers, managers, employees including leased employees, directors, trustees, authorized representatives of the insured, or anyone to whom the insured entrusts the property for any purpose, acting alone or in collusion with others or whether or not occurring during hours of employment, is excluded.[793] The exclusion does not apply to acts of destruction by employees, including leased employees of the insured, but theft by employees, including leased employees, is not covered.

[7] Voluntary Parting of Property

When an insured or anyone else to whom the insured has entrusted the property voluntarily parts with it, there is no coverage when the parting is induced by any fraudulent scheme, trick, device, or false pretense.[794]

---

for years during rain storms. Then in a hurricane it experienced significant water intrusion. The insurer attempted to invoke the continuous or repeated seepage or leakage condition. The court agreed there was record evidence of repeated seepage or leakage of water into the building well in excess of the required 14-day period. However, the association sought coverage only after the hurricane damages and the court said that for the exclusion to apply, the insurer would have to show that the loss was caused by or resulted from that repeated seepage over time, rather than the singular event of the hurricane. The insurer, said the court, would lump the hurricane water leakage in with the prior water leakage, finding all of it to be a single unified, excluded event. But that reading of the policy would improperly conflate two distinct causes of loss and expand the exclusion beyond the strict, narrow reading required. The exclusion, observed the court, did not state that all water damage was automatically excluded if the building had leaked for more than 14 days. Rather, it excluded coverage for damage caused by continuous or repeated seepage or leakage of water and, in the light most favorable to the association, the evidence was that the damages it claimed were not caused by a continuous or repeated seepage of water, but by the one-time event of a hurricane. If that were true, the exclusion could not apply because the damage was caused by a one-time catastrophic intrusion of wind-driven rain, rather than by the cumulative effects of frequent minor leaks.

792. *See, e.g.*, CP 10 30 06 07, § B.2.g.

793. *See, e.g.*, CP 10 30 06 07, § B.2.h.

794. *See, e.g.*, CP 10 30 06 07, § B.2.i.

[8] Collapse

Collapse is often an additional coverage.[795] However, there is also usually a collapse exclusion.[796] Typically, the exclusion provides it does not apply to the extent that coverage is provided under the "Additional Coverage—Collapse." The exclusion also usually does not apply to collapse caused by breakage of building glass, weight of rain that collects on a roof, weight of people or personal property, or the "specified causes of loss," which generally means fire; lightning; explosion; windstorm or hail; smoke; aircraft or vehicles; riot or civil commotion; vandalism; leakage from fire-extinguishing equipment; sinkhole collapse; volcanic action; falling objects; weight of snow, ice, or sleet; and water damage.

The exclusion defines collapse as any of three conditions of the property or any part of it. Those conditions are:

- An abrupt falling down or caving in;
- Loss of structural integrity, including separation of parts of the property or property in danger of falling down or caving in; and
- Any cracking, bulging, sagging, bending, leaning, settling, shrinkage, or expansion as they relate to an abrupt falling down or caving in or loss of structural integrity.

However, if collapse results in a covered cause of loss at the described premises, the carrier will pay for the loss or damage caused by that covered cause of loss.

[9] Pollutants

A commercial property policy generally excludes coverage for discharge, dispersal, seepage, migration, release, or escape of "pollutants" unless that discharge, dispersal, seepage, migration, release, or escape is itself caused by any of the "specified causes of loss."[797] "Pollutants" is defined as "any solid, liquid, gaseous or thermal irritant or contaminant, including smoke, vapor, soot, fumes, acids, alkalis, chemicals and waste."[798] Generally, the "specified causes of loss" are the usual named perils: fire; lightning; explosion; windstorm or hail; smoke; aircraft or vehicles; riot or civil commotion; vandalism; leakage from fire-extinguishing equipment; sinkhole collapse; volcanic action; falling objects; weight of snow,

---

795. *See, e.g.*, ISO Form CP 10 30 06 07, § D. For more on the subject of collapase generally, see § 10.17[1], *supra*.

796. *See, e.g.*, CP 10 30 06 07, § B.2.k.

797. *See, e.g.*, CP 10 30 06 07, § B.2.l. *See* Nationwide Mut. Ins. Co. v. CG Stony Point Townhomes, LLC, 2015 U.S. Dist. LEXIS 5682 (E.D. Va. Jan. 15, 2015) (claimed damages that resulted from "pollution" emitted from "Chinese Drywall" not covered because of "pollution exclusion").

798. *See, e.g.*, ISO Form CP 00 17 06 07, § H.2. Waste includes materials to be recycled, reconditioned, or reclaimed.

ice, or sleet; and water damage.[799] If the discharge, dispersal, seepage, migration, release, or escape of pollutants results in one of these specified causes of loss, the carrier will pay for the loss or damage caused by that specified cause of loss.[800] Additionally, the exclusion does not apply to damage to glass caused by chemicals applied to the glass.

[10] Weather Conditions, Acts or Decisions, and Faulty Planning or Design

Typically, commercial property policies exclude coverage for three additional perils.[801] The carrier will not pay for loss or damage caused by or resulting from them, but if one of these perils results in a covered cause of loss, the carrier will pay for loss or damage caused by that covered cause of loss.[802]

The first of these excluded perils is "weather conditions."[803] The exclusion applies only if weather conditions contribute in any way with a cause or event excluded by the principal exclusions—ordinance or law, earth movement; governmental action; nuclear hazard; utility services; war and military action; water; and fungus, wet rot, dry rot, and bacteria—to produce the loss or damage. Thus, the weather exclusion is apparently effective only when weather is coupled with any of those named exclusions.[804]

---

799. *See, e.g.*, ISO Form CP 10 30 06 07, § G.2.

800. *Consider* Ass'n of Apt. Owners of Imperial Plaza v. Fireman's Fund Ins. Co., 939 F. Supp. 2d 1059, 1075 (D. Haw. 2013), where the court said that a somewhat similar exception contradicted the anti-concurrent clause language barring coverage and held there was coverage for damage caused by arsenic allegedly caused by moisture infiltration.

801. *See, e.g.*, CP 10 30 06 07, § B.3.

802. The exception is known as coverage for an "ensuing" or "resulting" loss. *See, e.g.*, Ass'n of Apt. Owners of Imperial Plaza v. Fireman's Fund Ins. Co., 939 F. Supp. 2d 1059, 1072 (D. Haw. 2013) (ensuing loss clause operates to carve out exception to policy exclusion; moisture infiltration was covered cause of loss and separate agent that caused damage, even though design defect may have allowed that agent to enter); Five Star Hotels, LLC v. Ins. Co. of Greater N.Y., 2011 U.S. Dist. LEXIS 31313 (S.D.N.Y. Mar. 24, 2011) (leakage from automatic sprinkler system was specifically covered by "ensuing loss provision" and, therefore, not excluded under general exclusion for faulty design or faulty maintenance; policy language made clear that damage resulting from frozen and leaking sprinkler system was covered cause of loss and because of ensuing loss provision, exclusion for faulty design or faulty maintenance did not bar coverage for water damage resulting from frozen sprinkler system); Boardwalk Condo. Ass'n v. Travelers Indem. Co., 2007 U.S. Dist. LEXIS 48325 (S.D. Cal. July 3, 2007) (exception is referred to as "resulting" or "ensuing" loss provision; condensation—covered peril—was hazard or occurrence that caused loss or injury and while *resulting* from excluded peril of lack of ventilation, was new hazard separate and independent from lack of ventilation). *See also* Legal Servs. Plan of E. Mich. v. Citizens Ins. Co. of Am., 2009 Mich. App. LEXIS 954 (Mich. Ct. App. Apr. 30, 2009) (where construction company working for city government removed curb and sidewalk and during rainstorm water flowed off road and into old coal chute in basement of insured property that had become unsealed during construction, that construction activity was act for purposes of "acts or decisions" exclusion; however, insurer would have been required to pay for damage caused by covered cause of loss instead of surface water, which was not covered cause of loss).

803. *See, e.g.*, CP 10 30 06 07, § B.3.a.

804. *See* Sunbreaker Condominium Ass'n v. Travelers Ins. Co., 79 Wn. App. 368, 901 P.2d 1079 (1995) (weather conditions exclusion does not apply to events listed as additional exclusions, and

Next, carriers will not pay for loss or damage caused by or resulting from acts or decisions, including the failure to act or decide, of any person, group, organization, or governmental body.[805] The apparent intent of the exclusion is to bar coverage for a loss that is the result of discretionary actions or decisions. For a common interest community, "any person" could include not only members of the governing board but also the community association manager,[806] residents, employees, and independent contractors working for the association or residents of the community. The language of the exclusion, however, is even broader than that. It excludes coverage for loss or damage caused by or resulting from the acts or decisions or failure to act or decide by anyone, whether affiliated with the CIC or not. Insurers have attempted to apply the exclusion to decisions by a neighboring property owner,[807] the landlord of the insured,[808] and utilities companies,[809] and decisions of governmental authorities.[810] Note that wording of the exclusion does not appear to restrict it to *authorized* acts or decisions. Does the exclusion still apply when a director, community association manager, or resident makes a decision on behalf of the association that he or she is not authorized to make?

The language of the exclusion is so broad that many courts have found it to be ambiguous.[811] One court said that, as the insurer recognized, the exclusion

---

fungus exclusion was one of these in policy at issue). Note that *Sunbreaker* was decided over 20 years ago, and that generally under current polices, fungus is a principal exclusion.

805. *See, e.g.*, CP 10 30 06 07, § B.3.b. Note that some policies have a limitation with similar language. *See, e.g.*, Tento Int'l, Inc. v. State Farm Fire & Cas. Co., 222 F.3d 660, 661 (9th Cir. 2000) (policy had limitation on coverage for any loss consisting of conduct, acts, or decisions, including failure to act or decide, of any person, group, organization, or governmental body whether intentional, wrongful, negligent, or without fault).

806. The governing board should remember that the manager is its agent, and it will, therefore, generally be bound by the actions of the manager on behalf of the association. *See, e.g.*, Biscayne Cove Condo. Ass'n v. QBE Ins. Corp., 971 F. Supp. 2d 1121, 1126 (S.D. Fla. 2013).

807. *See, e.g.*, Jussim v. Massachusetts Bay Ins. Co., 33 Mass. App. Ct. 235, 597 N.E.2d 1379 (1992) (as result of negligent acts of neighboring property owner and oil delivery company, fuel oil was pumped through disconnected fuel delivery line into basement of insured home).

808. Scottsdale Ins. Co. v. Sally Group, LLC, 2012 U.S. Dist. LEXIS 47532 (S.D. Tex. Apr. 3, 2012).

809. *See, e.g.*, Auto-Owners Ins. Co. v. Hansen Hous., Inc., 604 N.W.2d 504 (S.D. 2000).

810. *See, e.g.*, Cytopath Biopsy Lab., Inc. v. United States Fid. & Guar. Co., 6 A.D.3d 300, 774 N.Y.S.2d 710 (2004). *See also* Merrimack Mut. Fire Ins. Co. v. Slater, 22 Mass. L. Rep. 583 (Mass. Super. 2007) (law enforcement).

811. Auto-Owners Ins. Co. v. Hansen Hous., Inc., 604 N.W.2d 504 (S.D. 2000) (insurer denied coverage for damage caused to building as result of power supply being cut off by utilities company; exclusion found inapplicable as proximate cause of loss remained broken water pipes). *See also* Merrimack Mut. Fire Ins. Co. v. Slater, 22 Mass. L. Rep. 583 (Mass. Super. 2007) (where police fired tear gas canisters into home to apprehend armed and mentally ill occupant, damage to property was not excluded as intent of forced entry was not for destruction, confiscation, or seizure and conduct of occupant set in motion chain of events causing losses; any ambiguity in policy language had to be construed in favor of insured); St. Paul Fire & Marine Ins. Co. v. General Injectables & Vaccines, Inc., 2000 U.S. Dist. LEXIS 2597 (W.D. Va. Mar. 3, 2000) (actions occurring after power interruption made loss worse but did not cause it). *Compare* Landmark Hospitality, LLC v. Cont'l Cas., Co., 2002 U.S. Dist. LEXIS 27794 (C.D. Cal. July 2, 2002) (finding acts and decisions

could "not be taken literally. If it were to be so taken, it would exclude coverage from all acts and decisions of any character of all persons, groups, or entities. Such an interpretation would leave the insurance policy practically worthless."[812] Thus, many courts have resisted enforcing the exclusion, although some have applied it to deny coverage.[813]

Finally, coverage is excluded for any loss or damage of part or all of any property on or off the described premises caused by or resulting from faulty, inadequate, or defective planning, zoning, development, surveying, siting, design,[814] specifications, workmanship, repair, construction, renovation, remodeling, grading, compaction, materials used in repair, construction, renovation or remodeling, or maintenance.[815]

§ 10.21 Special Exclusions

There are special exclusions that apply to only specified coverage forms. These are the Business Income and Extra Expense Coverage Forms,[816] Leasehold Interest Coverage Form,[817] and Legal Liability Coverage Form.[818] These coverage forms are ordinarily acquired by businesses and are not, therefore, discussed here.

---

exclusion unambiguous and enforceable; exclusion provision excuses insurer from providing coverage for damages caused by negligence of insured).

812. Jussim v. Massachusetts Bay Ins. Co., 33 Mass. App. Ct. 235, 238–39, 597 N.E.2d 1379, 1382 (1992). *See also* Mettler v. Safeco Ins. Co. of Am., 2013 U.S. Dist. LEXIS 8622 (W.D. Wash. Jan. 22, 2013) (under interpretation of insurer exclusion, any time human or organization of humans had any role in loss, no matter how tangential, policy would exclude coverage); St. Paul Fire & Marine Ins. Co. v. General Injectables & Vaccines, Inc., 2000 U.S. Dist. LEXIS 2597 (W.D. Va. Mar. 3, 2000) (exclusion is overly broad, ambiguous, and irreconcilable with other policy provisions and with very concept of all-risk insurance coverage).

813. *See, e.g.*, Cytopath Biopsy Lab., Inc. v. United States Fid. & Guar. Co., 6 A.D.3d 300, 774 N.Y.S.2d 710 (2004) (there was no coverage for losses claimed resulting from refusal by the authorities to permit resumption of operations until proper permits were obtained and more acceptable ventilation system was installed because of acts and decisions exclusion). *See also* Legal Servs. Plan of E. Mich. v. Citizens Ins. Co. of Am., 2009 Mich. App. LEXIS 954 (Mich. Ct. App. Apr. 30, 2009) (where construction company working for city government removed curb and sidewalk and during rainstorm water flowed off road and into old coal chute in basement of insured property that had become unsealed during construction, because that construction activity constituted "acts" for purposes of exclusion, damage caused by that activity was not covered).

814. *See, e.g.*, Houston Specialty Ins. Co. v. Meadows West Condo Ass'n, 2016 U.S. App. LEXIS 289 (5th Cir. Jan. 6, 2016) (where correspondence between local officials following fire suggested flex duct work was faulty in design, maintenance, or construction at time of loss, those observations could allow reasonable fact-finder to conclude that defect existed in property and exclusion applied).

815. *See, e.g.*, CP 10 30 06 07, § B.3.c.

816. *See, e.g.*, CP 10 30 06 07, § B.4.a.

817. *See, e.g.*, CP 10 30 06 07, § B.4.b.

818. *See, e.g.*, CP 10 30 06 07, § B.4.c.

§ 10.22 Limits of Insurance

The Building and Personal Property Coverage Form and Condominium Association Coverage Form as well as the causes of loss forms all have limitations on coverage. These limitations are clearly noted on the Declarations Page of the policy. The governing board, or its designated insurance committee, should become familiar with the limits of insurance on all policies purchased for the association rather than wait until a loss occurs.

[1] Policy Limitations

The BPP and CAC have an identical "Limits of Insurance" section.[819] It provides that the most the carrier will pay for loss or damage in any *one occurrence* is the applicable limit of insurance shown on the Declarations Page. The most it will pay under the standard forms of those policies for loss or damage to outdoor signs, whether or not the sign is attached to a building, is $2,500 per sign in any one occurrence. The amounts of insurance stated in the additional coverages of the fire department service charge, pollutant cleanup and removal, increased cost of construction, and electronic data apply in accordance with the terms of those coverages and are separate from any limits shown on the Declarations Page for any other coverage. Finally, payments under the Preservation of Property additional coverage will not increase the applicable limit of insurance.

[2] Causes of Loss Form Limitations

The typical commercial property policy causes of loss form limitation section contains a list of limitations that apply to all policy forms and endorsements, unless it is provided otherwise.

[a] Equipment, Building Interior, and Materials

Under one part of a common limitations section, the carrier will not pay for loss of or damage to property as described and limited and will not pay for any loss that is a consequence of loss or damage as described and limited.[820]

[i] Equipment

There is no coverage for loss or damage to steam boilers, steam pipes, steam engines, or steam turbines caused by or resulting from any condition or event inside them.[821] However, the carrier will pay for loss of or damage to that equipment caused by or resulting from an explosion of gases or fuel within the furnace of any fired vessel or within the flues or passages through which the gases

819. *See* ISO Form CP 00 10 06 07, § C.; ISO Form CP 00 17 06 07, § C.
820. *See, e.g.*, CP 10 30 06 07, § C.1.
821. *See, e.g.*, CP 10 30 06 07, § C.1.a.

of combustion pass. This limitation needs to be compared with the exclusion for explosion[822] and any coverage added under equipment breakdown coverage added by an endorsement or provided by a separately purchased stand-alone policy.

There also is no coverage for loss or damage to hot water boilers or other water heating equipment caused by or resulting from any condition or event inside them other than an explosion.[823] Again, coverage for these losses may be added under equipment breakdown coverage provided by an endorsement or stand-alone policy.

[ii] Interior of Structures and Building Materials

Damage to the interior of any building or structure, or to personal property in the building or structure, caused by or resulting from rain, snow, sleet, ice, sand, or dust, whether driven by wind or not, is not covered.[824] However, that damage will be covered if the building or structure first sustains damage by a covered cause of loss to its roof or walls through which the rain, snow, sleet, ice, sand, or dust enters or the loss or damage is caused by or results from thawing of snow, sleet, or ice on the building or structure.

The carrier will not pay for loss of building materials and supplies not attached as part of the building or structure caused by or resulting from theft.[825] The limitation does not apply to building materials and supplies held for sale by the insured, unless they are otherwise insured.

[iii] Property That Is Missing or Transferred

There is no coverage for property that is missing, where the only evidence of the loss or damage is a shortage disclosed on taking inventory or where there is no physical evidence to show what happened to the property.[826] The loss of property that has been transferred to a person or a place outside the described premises on the basis of unauthorized instructions is also not covered.[827]

[b] Specific Personal Property

Commercial property policies ordinarily limit coverage for three categories of property.[828] The carrier will not pay for loss of or damage to the specified types of property unless caused by either the specified causes of loss—the typically named perils—or building glass breakage. The exception applies to only animals

---

822. *See, e.g.*, CP 10 30 06 07, § B.2.e.
823. *See, e.g.*, CP 10 30 06 07, § C.1.b.
824. *See, e.g.*, CP 10 30 06 07, § C.1.c.
825. *See, e.g.*, CP 10 30 06 07, § C.1.d.
826. *See, e.g.*, CP 10 30 06 07, § C.1.e.
827. *See, e.g.*, CP 10 30 06 07, § C.1.f.
828. *See, e.g.*, CP 10 30 06 07, § C.2.

if they are killed or their destruction is made necessary. The limited coverage applies to fragile articles, including statuary, marbles, chinaware, and porcelains, if broken, but the restriction does not apply to glass or containers of property held for sale. There is also limited coverage for builders' machinery, tools, and equipment owned by the insured or entrusted to the insured provided these items are covered property.

The limitation does not apply if the property is located on or within 100 feet of the described premises, unless the premises is insured under the Builders Risk Coverage Form or to Business Income Coverage or to Extra Expense Coverage.

[c] Special Limits

Commercial property policies may place caps on the amount of coverage that is provided for specific types of property.[829] That figure is the total limit for loss of or damage to all property in that category. The special limit applies to any single occurrence of theft, regardless of the types or number of articles that are lost or damaged in that occurrence. The property to which these special limits apply is not the type that a common interest community would ordinarily own.[830]

[d] Escape of Liquid, Powder, or Molten Material

A narrow limitation applies to the cost to repair any defect to a system or appliance from which water, other liquid, powder, or molten material escapes.[831] Under commercial property policies, the carrier will not pay for the cost to repair those defects but will pay the cost to repair or replace damaged parts of fire-extinguishing equipment if the damage results in discharge of any substance from an automatic fire protection system or is directly caused by freezing. The limitation does not apply to Business Income Coverage or to Extra Expense Coverage.

§ 10.23 Deductible

A deductible is applied after a covered loss has been established, and its purpose is to shift some of the covered risk from the insurer to the insured by setting a limit on the value of covered losses below which the carrier is not obligated to pay.[832]

829. *See, e.g.*, CP 10 30 06 07, § C.3.

830. The property includes furs, jewelry, precious alloys or metals, patterns, dies, molds, forms, stamps, tickets, and letters of credit.

831. *See, e.g.*, CP 10 30 06 07, § C.4.

832. Penthouse Owners Ass'n, Inc. v. Certain Underwriters, 612 F.3d 383, 387 (5th Cir. 2010). In *Penthouse* the court rejected the argument that a deductible is a mechanism that increases the risk of the insurer by expanding the scope of coverage, although it conceded "the rare possibility that explicit words of coverage in a deductible, interpreted in the context of the policy as a whole, may establish coverage or an ambiguity. . . ." The policy at issue excluded water damage and stated that water loss or damage was excluded regardless of any other cause of loss or event that contributed concurrently or in any sequence to the loss. That is known as an "anti-concurrent causation

The BPP and CAC have identical sections on deductibles.[833] They provide that in any one occurrence of loss or damage the carrier will first reduce the amount of loss if required by the coinsurance condition or the agreed value optional coverage. If the adjusted amount of loss is less than or equal to the deductible, the insurer will not pay for that loss, but if the adjusted amount of loss exceeds the deductible, it will subtract the deductible from the adjusted amount of loss and pay the resulting amount or the limit of insurance, whichever is less. Additionally, when the occurrence involves loss to more than one item of covered property and separate Limits of Insurance apply, the losses will not be combined in determining application of the deductible. The deductible, however, will be applied only once per occurrence.

Those serving on a common interest community governing board whose knowledge of insurance is limited to their own automobile or homeowner's policy will likely think the deductible is a simple matter. If the association submits a claim, the insurer will subtract the deductible and pay the difference. However, the deductible in a commercial property policy can be quite complicated.

NOTE: CIC board members are often unaware of how the deductible in their policy works. This ignorance can leave them surprised, and the association facing an unexpected cost, when the property suffers significant damage and the deductible is larger than expected. The association that is unprepared will likely then have to levy a special assessment on its residents to pay for the expense. To avoid unpleasant surprises, the governing board should, as a part of an annual insurance audit, have its broker fully explain how the deductible works.

---

[1] Straight Deductible

A "straight deductible" is a set dollar amount. In an ordinary automobile or homeowner's policy it is usually $500 or $1,000, perhaps slightly higher. A commercial property policy typically has a straight deductible as well. The amount can be easily determined by examining the Declarations Page.

CICs may have a deductible that is as little as $1,000 or $2,500, and the governing board members often give it little thought. They should, however, consider that a low deductible results in a higher premium and that it may not make sense

---

clause." An endorsement to the policy added a windstorm deductible that applied to loss or damage "'caused directly or indirectly by windstorm or hail, regardless of any other cause or event that contributes concurrently or in any sequence to the loss or damage.'" The lower court concluded that the language in the endorsement that matched that in the main policy operated as a "reverse anti-concurrent cause clause" that expanded coverage to include any damage caused concurrently or in any sequence to windstorm damage, even if that damage otherwise would not have been covered because of the water damage exclusion. The appellate court disagreed.

833. *See, e.g.*, ISO Form CP 00 17 06 07, § D; ISO Form CP 00 10 06 07, § D.

for a building valued at $20 million to have the same deductible as an automobile worth less than $50,000.

Higher deductibles are available,[834] but the amount an association chooses may be limited by several factors:

- The carrier. Obviously, the deductible can be no higher than the insurance company is willing to accept. The flip side is that the company may *insist* on a deductible that is higher than the association wants,[835] usually because the association has a loss history that makes it a bad risk or because the insurer insists on higher deductibles as a result of its experience with similarly situated risks. Many insurers will negotiate over the deductible, but some may not.
- State law. A few states have limits on the amount of property insurance deductibles.[836] A great many states have adopted the language of the Uniform Common Interest Ownership Act that requires that the total amount of insurance, after application of any deductibles, has to be no less than 80 percent of the actual cash value of the insured property at the time the insurance is bought and at each renewal date.[837] The act also mandates "reasonable deductibles," although not every state that has adopted the act has incorporated that wording.[838]

834. *See, e.g.*, Condos. of Shenandoah Place v. SECURA Ins., 2016 U.S. Dist. LEXIS 18608 (D. Minn. Feb. 16, 2016) (deductible of $5,000 per building); GlenBrook Patiohome, Owners Ass'n v. Lexington Ins. Co., 2011 U.S. Dist. LEXIS 14556 (S.D. Tex. Feb. 14, 2011) ($100,000 deductible); Shoreline Towers Condo. Owners Ass'n v. Zurich Am. Ins. Co., 196 F. Supp. 2d 1210, 1212 (S.D. Ala. 2002) ($40,000 windstorm deductible); Highridge Place Condo. Unit Owner's Ass'n v. Langley, 66 Va. Cir. 185 (2004) ($25,000 deductible for water damage).

835. *See, e.g.*, Anderson v. Council of Gables, 404 Md. 560, 948 A.2d 11 (2008) (associations—"councils"—did not choose deductible amount; rather, insurers dictated it based on cost or as "best option for the price").

836. *See, e.g.*, Fla. Stat. § 718.111(11)(c) (under Florida Condominium Act deductibles must be "consistent with industry standards and prevailing practice for communities of similar size and age" with similar construction and facilities in locale where condominium property is located and may be based on available funds, including reserve accounts, or predetermined assessment authority at time insurance is obtained; governing board is required to establish amount of deductibles based on level of available funds and predetermined assessment authority); Or. Rev. Stat. § 94.675(4) (under Oregon Planned Community Act, notwithstanding provision in Declaration or bylaws that imposes maximum deductible, if governing board determines that it is in best interest of association and unit owners, it may adopt resolution authorizing policy with deductible amount exceeding specified maximum, but not in excess of greater of maximum deductible acceptable to Federal National Mortgage Association or $10,000). *See also* Utah Code Ann. § 57-8a-405(8) (under Utah Community Association Act, deductible amount is not prescribed, but associations are required to set aside amount equal to property insurance deductible or, if that deductible exceeds $10,000, no less than $10,000).

837. Uniform Common Interest Ownership Act § 3-113(a)(1) (2008).

838. Uniform Common Interest Ownership Act § 3-113(a) (2008) (commencing not later than time of first conveyance of unit to person other than declarant, association must maintain property, liability, and fidelity insurance, to extent reasonably available *and subject to reasonable deductibles*).

- Fannie Mae. Under the *Fannie Mae Selling Guide*, the maximum allowable deductible for insurance covering a property—including common elements in a condominium—securing a first mortgage loan is 5 percent of the face amount of the policy.[839]

From a financial standpoint, if the association opts for a high deductible, it should determine where the funds will come from in the event it has a claim and has to absorb the deductible amount. Unless the association sets aside funds in a contingency to cover the cost,[840] or is able to borrow the money, it will have to levy a special assessment,[841] which may prove problematic, particularly if the documents require that any special assessment be approved by a super-majority vote of the governing board or by a vote of the residents themselves, or in some other way limit special assessments.

[2] Named Perils Deductibles

Sometimes there is a separate deductible for a specific peril, referred to as a "split deductible." This deductible will be reflected on the Declarations Page. There are typically two reasons for a separate deductible tied to a particular peril. The first is the loss history of the community. The insurer may impose a higher deductible because prior claims place it in a "high risk" category.[842] The second reason for a split deductible is that there is a relatively high probability of damage from the specified peril. This is most commonly associated with the risks of windstorms,[843]

---

839. *See* Fannie Mae Single Family Selling Guide § B7-3-02 (Dec. 16, 2014).

840. Should the association decide to set aside funds to cover a deductible, there may be tax consequences. This topic is beyond the scope of this treatise. The association should consult the association attorney or accountant. *See generally* Treese, *Community Association Insurance: Losses, Deductibles, Funding Deductibles, Reserves & Federal Tax Implications* § 3 (Feb. 18, 2013), available at: http://communityassociations.net/wp-content/uploads/2013/02/Treese+on+Insurance+Deductibles++Revised+02-18-2013.pdf (if association is eligible to file IRS Form 1120-H, maintaining insurance deductibles as expense line item should not pose direct federal income tax problem because revenue collected to fund line item deductible, by definition, would come from exempt function income).

841. *See, e.g.*, Nationwide Prop. & Cas. Ins. Co. v. DPF Architects, P.C., 792 So. 2d 369, 370, n.1 (Ala. 2000) (after hurricane, association assessed individual unit owners $4,500 to assist with satisfaction of deductible and expenses not covered by policy). If the association assesses unit owners to cover the cost of the deductible, those unit owners may have a federal income tax deduction for a casualty loss. *See* Internal Revenue Service Publication # 547. If residents have a homeowners policy with loss assessment coverage, they can submit a claim to their insurer. Typically, a homeowners policy with loss assessment coverage will pay no more than $2,000.

842. *See, e.g.*, Highridge Place Condo. Unit Owner's Ass'n v. Langley, 66 Va. Cir. 185 (2004) (association was required to obtain policy with $25,000 deductible for water damage as result of earlier claims for water damage that placed association in high-risk category for water damage coverage).

843. *See, e.g.*, Avalon Condo. Ass'n v. Secura Ins., 2015 U.S. Dist. LEXIS 129373 (D. Colo. Sept. 25, 2015) (2 percent wind deductible); Shoreline Towers Condo. Owners Ass'n v. Zurich Am. Ins. Co., 196 F. Supp. 2d 1210, 1212 (S.D. Ala. 2002) ($40,000 windstorm deductible). *See generally* Worley, *Not Your Grandfather's Policy; Changing Times Require a New Look at Condo Insurance*

hurricanes,[844] or earthquakes.[845] One thing to note immediately is that the term "windstorm" is broader than "hurricane," but how much broader depends on the meanings of both terms.

It is critical for a common interest community association to determine and understand the definition of these terms. Unfortunately, they are typically not defined in the policy. The purpose of a split deductible is for the insurer to impose a higher deductible amount for damages caused by the named peril and, therefore, it is to the advantage of the association for the basic deductible to apply to a claim rather than the one attached to a named peril. Consider, for example, a split deductible that applies only to hurricanes. If the meaning of "hurricane" is a storm that has been officially declared as such, then the hurricane deductible should not apply when damage is caused by hurricane force winds in an unnamed storm or when a storm is initially thought to be a hurricane but is officially determined not to be one.[846] In these examples, the deductible would be the lower one generally applied. It is also important to determine how the insurer applies the term. For example, if once again, there is a split deductible that applies only to hurricanes and a weak hurricane causes no damage but produces a tornado that causes considerable damage, does the hurricane deductible apply?

It is common, as discussed below, for these deductibles to be stated as a percentage rather than as a stated amount. It is important to be aware that often there are state-specific named peril deductibles.[847]

(Cooperator, Aug. 2011), available at: http://cooperator.com/articles/2292/1/Not-Your-Grand father039s-Policy/Page1.html.

844. *See, e.g.*, Biscayne Cove Condo. Ass'n v. QBE Ins. Corp., 971 F. Supp. 2d 1121, 1125 (S.D. Fla. 2013) (separate hurricane deductible); Summit Towers Condo. Ass'n v. QBE Ins. Corp., 798 F. Supp. 2d 1311 (S.D. Fla. 2011) (hurricane damage deductible). The "hurricane deductible" was a result of Hurricane Andrew, which hit South Florida in 1992 and both devastated vast swaths of property and also endangered the solvency of insurers. Sometimes the deductible applies to "named storms." *See, e.g.*, ISO Form CP 03 25 10 06 (Commercial Property: Named Storm Percentage Deductible endorsement). "Named storm" is defined in the endorsement as a storm system identified as a tropical storm or hurricane and assigned a name by the National Hurricane Center or the Central Pacific Hurricane Center of the National Weather Service. A named storm begins when a watch or warning is issued for the area in which the affected premises are located and ends 72 hours after the termination of the last watch or warning issued for that area.

845. *See, e.g.*, Cheviot Vista Homeowners Ass'n v. State Farm Fire & Casualty Co., 143 Cal. App. 4th 1486, 50 Cal. Rptr. 3d 1 (2006) (condominium association policy had endorsement for earthquake coverage with 10 percent deductible); Parkview Villas Ass'n, Inc. v. State Farm Fire & Casualty Co., 133 Cal. App. 4th 1197, 1202, 35 Cal. Rptr. 3d 411, 413 (2005) (earthquake coverage was subject to policy limit and per building deductible equal to 10 percent of coverage for each building).

846. For example, after Superstorm Sandy, many regulators had to reinforce to insurers that they could not treat it as a hurricane and apply the steep deductible for hurricanes on claims coming from the storm.

847. *See Hurricane and Windstorm Deductibles* (Insurance Information Institute), available at: http://www.iii.org/issue-update/hurricane-and-windstorm-deductibles. The article offers a state-by-state analysis of hurricane and windstorm deductibles. *See, e.g.*, ISO Form CP 03 27 01 06 (Commercial Property: Florida Hurricane Percentage Deductible—Each Hurricane); ISO Form

[3] Percentage Deductibles

Rather than a stated amount, deductibles may be a percentage of another figure, most commonly the amount of the insurance, the amount of the loss, or the value of the property. Obviously, it is critical to determine to what figure the percentage applies. The percentage will be stated on the Declarations Page. Typically, the percentage is from 1 to 5 percent[848] but can be as high as 10 percent.[849] These percentages can produce enormous deductibles, sometimes as much as one or two million dollars.[850] Some CIC governing boards are caught by surprise by the numbers, either because they are unaware that the policy has a percentage deductible or because they did not "do the math." Their associations may, therefore, be unprepared for the prospect of having a large claim denied because it does not exceed the deductible amount. Supplemental coverage for large deductibles is available,[851] but in many associations the governing boards never even have a discussion about purchasing that coverage.

When the common interest community consists of more than one building, the percentage may apply separately to each building.[852] It is also important to

---

CP 03 26 06 01 (Commercial Property: Mississippi Hurricane Percentage Deductible); ISO Form CP 03 28 04 10 (Commercial Property: North Carolina—Named Storm Percentage Deductible).

848. *See, e.g.*, Avalon Condo. Ass'n v. Secura Ins., 2015 U.S. Dist. LEXIS 129373 (D. Colo. Sept. 25, 2015) (2 percent wind deductible); Citizens Prop. Ins. Corp. v. Mango Hill #6 Condo. Ass'n, 117 So. 3d 1226 (Fla. 3d DCA 2013) (3 percent hurricane deductible); Bliss Mine Rd. Condo. Ass'n v. Nationwide Prop. & Cas. Ins. Co., 11 A.3d 1078 (R.I. 2010) (1 percent of amount of coverage). *See generally* Worley, *Not Your Grandfather's Policy: Changing Times Require a New Look at Condo Insurance* (Chicago Cooperator, 2011), available at: http://chicagocooperator.com/article/not-your-grandfathers-policy (experts say that steepest wind deductibles will top out at 5 percent, and amount association will pay depends on insured value of property and trigger selected by insurance company).

849. *See* Harris, *Is Your Hurricane Deductible and Coinsurance Provision Enforceable?* (Oct. 2010), available at: http://www.condominiuminsurancelaw.com/tags/coinsurance/ (depending on policy and association's choices when purchasing it, hurricane deductible can rise as high as 10 percent). *See also* St. Joseph's Condo. Ass'n v. Pac. Ins. Co., 2008 U.S. Dist. LEXIS 86470 (E.D. La. Oct. 24, 2008) (deductible of 10 percent of total value of insured property); Lincoln Fountain Villas Homeowners Ass'n v. State Farm Fire & Casualty Ins. Co., 136 Cal. App. 4th 999, 39 Cal. Rptr. 3d 345 (2006) (earthquake coverage had 10 percent deductible). *See also* Fla. Stat. § 627.706 (policy for residential property insurance may include deductible amount applicable to sinkhole losses equal to 1, 2, 5, or 10 percent of policy dwelling limits).

850. *See, e.g.*, Summit Towers Condo. Ass'n v. QBE Ins. Corp., 798 F. Supp. 2d 1311 (S.D. Fla. 2011) (hurricane deductible of $1,984,748); Fla. Ins. Guar. Ass'n v. Olympus Ass'n, 34 So. 3d 791 (Fla. 4th DCA 2010) ($2,550,545 in deductibles).

851. *See* Hayman, *Hurricanes and Windstorm Coverage: Case Studies and Coverages* at 2 (Adjusting Today, 2011), available at: http://adjustersinternational.com/publications/adjusting-today/hurricanes-and-windstorm-coverage/0/ (financial impact of percentage deductible can be mitigated by purchase of "buy-back deductible," supplemental coverage that allows policyholder to forfeit paying deductible by opting to pay additional premium). *See, e.g.*, Avalon Condo. Ass'n v. Secura Ins., 2015 U.S. Dist. LEXIS 129373 (D. Colo. Sept. 25, 2015) (association purchased Wind Deductible Buy-Back Coverage).

852. *See, e.g.*, Citizens Prop. Ins. Corp. v. Mango Hill #6 Condo. Ass'n, 117 So. 3d 1226 (Fla. 3d DCA 2013) (hurricane deductible of 3 percent of coverage limit for each building); Parkview

check whether the percentage deductible applies per occurrence or the aggregate of claims during the policy period.

[4] Per Building Deductible

For common interest communities with more than one building, the deductible may apply separately to each building.[853] It is important to determine the parameters of these deductibles. Do they apply to all claims, or only those claims for losses from specific perils?

Questions can also arise over whether the deductible is subtracted from the damages to each building or aggregated.[854] Consider, for instance, a scenario in which a common interest community has ten buildings and there is a $5,000 deductible *per building*. One building has a fire and suffers $49,000 in damages. Will the insurer pay the association $44,000, or will it aggregate the deductibles and deny the loss as less than the total $50,000 deductible? In a different scenario, half the buildings are damaged in a windstorm. Five buildings sustain $9,000 in damages, and the others have no loss. The total loss is $45,000. Will the carrier subtract the deductible from the loss to each building and pay $20,000, or will it aggregate the deductibles and deny the loss as less than the total $50,000 deductible? Finally, consider a scenario in which a sinkhole destroys three buildings but leaves the others with minor damage. The loss for the three buildings is $200,000 each. For the others, the losses are no more than $2,500. If the carrier subtracts the deductible from each building, it will pay nothing for seven buildings and $585,000 for the three buildings that were destroyed. If it aggregates the deductibles, it will pay a total of $550,000.

Villas Ass'n, Inc. v. State Farm Fire & Casualty Co., 133 Cal. App. 4th 1197, 1202, 35 Cal. Rptr. 3d 411, 413 (2005) (earthquake coverage subject to policy limit and per building deductible equal to 10 percent of coverage for each building).

853. Kendall Lakes Townhomes Developers, Inc. v. Agric. Excess & Surplus Lines Ins. Co., 916 So. 2d 12, 13 (Fla. 3d DCA 2005) (policy insured nine buildings against physical loss caused by windstorm, with per building deductible of $7,500); Condos. of Shenandoah Place v. SECURA Ins., 2016 U.S. Dist. LEXIS 18608 (D. Minn. Feb. 16, 2016) ($5,000 deductible for each of 14 condominium buildings applied under policy).

854. *See, e.g.*, Royale Green Condo. Ass'n v. Aspen Specialty Ins. Co., 2008 U.S. Dist. LEXIS 39362 (S.D. Fla. May 14, 2008), where a condominium association had damage to multiple buildings in a hurricane. It argued that the policy should be interpreted as applying a single, one-time-per-occurrence deductible subtracted once from the aggregate assessed damage value of all damaged buildings covered under the policy. The insurer countered that the deductible applied separately to each building, and no payment was required unless the damage to a building exceeded the minimum deductible for that building. The court said a deductible of 5 percent of total insured value (TIV) or $100,000, whichever was greater, applied to each building, per occurrence, with no payment to be made unless the adjusted assessed damage to an *individual* building exceeded the deductible for that building.

NOTE: The resolution of these hypotheticals depends on the precise wording of the policy,[855] but that in turn depends on the policy language being clear enough to avoid doubt about its meaning, which is often not the case. It is incumbent on the association governing board, the manager, or anyone else in charge of insurance, to get a clear understanding of how the deductible applies at the time the policy is purchased rather than wait until a loss occurs.

[5] Calculation of Deductibles

The calculation of a deductible can lead to confusion. For example, in a federal case in Louisiana,[856] the policy provided the deductible was 2 percent of the total scheduled insured values of the items insured that had sustained a loss. The insurer calculated 2 percent of the value of each damaged building in the community and arrived at a figure of just over $78,000. The association calculated the deductible to be a little over $42,000 by excluding the deductibles for buildings whose damages were insufficient to overcome the deductible. The association argued that the minimal damages to those buildings, not the larger deductibles, should be subtracted from the total of the damages recoverable under the policy. The court did not reach the merits of the arguments,[857] but the case demonstrates the type of conflict that can arise. In another case, an insurer claimed a windstorm deductible was calculated by taking 5 percent of the total value of all the structures insured under the policy that included 24 residential buildings. That value was $30,967,930 and, therefore, the insurer said the deductible was $1,548,396.50. The association, however, contended the deductible should be calculated by multiplying 5 percent times the total limit of insurance per occurrence—$5,000,000—or $250,000. The court found for the insurer.[858]

855. *See, e.g.*, State Farm Fla. Ins. Co. v. Seville Place Condo. Ass'n, 2009 Fla. App. LEXIS 15529 (Fla. 3d DCA Oct. 14, 2009) (under hurricane deductible endorsement percentage deductible was to be applied to amount of insurance on each covered building or structure rather than to aggregate amount of loss); Tex-La Properties v. South State Ins. Co., 514 So. 2d 707 (La. App. 1987) (where policy applied $100 deductible separately to each building, up to maximum of $1,000, and more than ten canopies were destroyed, maximum $1,000 deductible was applicable).

856. Villa D'Orleans Condo. Ass'n v. Pac. Ins. Co., 2008 U.S. Dist. LEXIS 41171 (E.D. La. May 22, 2008).

857. The court said the insurer failed to show that the proper method to calculate a deductible could be determined on a motion for summary judgment.

858. Beverly Hills Condominium 1-12, Inc. v. Aspen Specialty Ins. Co., 2007 U.S. Dist. LEXIS 28999 (S.D. Fla. Jan. 31, 2007) (policy provided that "per location" deductible was intended to apply to total insurable values of entire premises, inclusive of all buildings, and was not applicable to series of individual buildings regardless of labeling in statement of values on file with company). *See also* El-Ad Enclave at Miramar Condo. Ass'n v. Mt. Hawley Ins. Co., 752 F. Supp. 2d 1282 (S.D. Fla. 2010), where the policy had a "peril deductible" of 3 percent of total values at risk per building at the time of loss for windstorm or hail. Though the insured property consisted of multiple buildings, the policy only listed $44 million aggregate value for the entire property and did

What cases like these illustrate is that the method of calculating a deductible may not be readily apparent to a policyholder, and it is incumbent on an insured to determine, in consultation with its broker, how the deductible will be calculated *before* a claim arises.

§ 10.24 Insureds Duties in the Event of a Loss

The typical commercial property policy imposes eight duties on the insured in the event of loss or damage to covered property.[859] Failure to comply with these duties may result in denial of a claim. These duties are that the insured must

- Notify the police if a law may have been broken;
- Give the insurer prompt notice of the loss or damage, including a description of the property involved;
- Give the insurer a description of how, when, and where the loss or damage occurred as soon as possible;
- Take all reasonable steps to protect the covered property from further damage, and keep a record of expenses required to protect that property;
- At the request of the insurer, provide it with complete inventories of the damaged and undamaged property, including quantities, costs, values, and the amount of loss claimed;
- Allow the insurer to inspect the property as often as may be reasonably required and examine the books and records of the insured;
- Send the insurer a signed, sworn proof of loss containing the information it requests within 60 days after the insurer requests it; and
- Cooperate with the insurer in the investigation or settlement of the claim.

[1] Timely Notice

The purpose of a notice requirement is to allow the insurer to make a timely and thorough investigation of a claim.[860] It is to the benefit of the insured that the claims process proceeds quickly, albeit deliberatively, because, as one court put

---

not include a separate schedule providing the value of each individual building. The property suffered damage in a hurricane. The insurer said the applicable deductible for the losses claimed was 3 percent of the insured value of each building while the association argued the deductible should be interpreted as 3 percent of the policy limit of $1 million, or $30,000. The court said that based on the plain language of the deductible provision, the only reasonable interpretation was that offered by the insurer.

859. *See* ISO Form CP 00 10 06 07, § E.3.a; ISO Form CP 00 17 06 07, § E.3.a.

860. Mitchell Buick & Oldsmobile Sales, Inc. v. National Dealer Services, Inc., 93 Ill. Dec. 71, 138 Ill. App. 3d 574, 581, 485 N.E.2d 1281, 1286 (1985) (notice provision is not to be considered as technical requirement merely for convenience of insurer, but rather is valid prerequisite for coverage).

it, "[i]nsurance claims are not like fine wines; they do not become better with time."[861]

The typical policy requires the insured to provide the carrier with "prompt" notice of any loss or damage.[862] What is prompt notice? There is no definitive answer.[863] Initially, "prompt" is what the insurer says it is. An objective construction of the term is within a *reasonable* time given the peculiar facts and circumstances of the case.[864] The magnitude of the damage can play a role in determining whether notice was prompt because significant damage should generally be discovered in a short time.[865] Indeed, the insured may have an obligation to make a reasonable effort to discover damage when it has good reason to know it may have occurred.[866]

Certainly, notice provided to the insurer within days of a loss is sufficiently prompt,[867] while notice supplied years after the event causing damage is almost

---

861. Citizens Prop. Ins. Corp. v. Galeria Villas Condo. Ass'n, 48 So. 3d 188, 191, n.6 (Fla. 3d DCA 2010).

862. *See* ISO Form CP 00 10 06 07, § E.3.a.(2); ISO Form CP 00 17 06 07, § E.3.a.(2).

863. *See* Yacht Club on the Intracoastal Condo. Ass'n v. Lexington Ins. Co., 599 Fed. Appx. 875 (11th Cir. 2015) (prompt means "reasonable dispatch" and within reasonable time in view of all of facts and circumstances of particular case; there is no "bright-line" rule setting forth particular period of time beyond which notice cannot be considered prompt; rather, notice several years after occurrence has been found prompt in some cases, but not others; interpretation of prompt may be different when damage is caused by known event, such as hurricane, or when insured was on-site when readily apparent problems developed); Vision I Homeowners Ass'n v. Aspen Specialty Ins. Co., 674 F. Supp. 2d 1333 (S.D. Fla. 2009) (question of whether notice 22 months after loss was "prompt notice" was question of fact for jury precluding summary judgment; insurer created possibility of inherent ambiguity regarding notice by using term "prompt notice" rather than finite term, for example requiring notice within 60 or 90 days from date of loss); Mitchell Buick & Oldsmobile Sales, Inc. v. National Dealer Services, Inc., 93 Ill. Dec. 71, 138 Ill. App. 3d 574, 581, 485 N.E.2d 1281, 1286 (1985) (generally, time within which notice is required is determined by standard of reasonableness based on facts and circumstances of particular case).

864. Kendall Lakes Towers Condo. Ass'n v. Pac. Ins. Co., 2012 U.S. Dist. LEXIS 10749 (S.D. Fla. Jan. 30, 2012). *See also* Ridglea Estate Condo. Ass'n v. Lexington Ins. Co., 309 F. Supp. 2d 851, 857–58 (N.D. Tex. 2004) (under Texas law "prompt notice" or notice "as soon as possible" means within reasonable time from occurrence of event causing loss or damage).

865. *See, e.g.*, Ridglea Estate Condo. Ass'n v. Lexington Ins. Co., 309 F. Supp. 2d 851 (N.D. Tex. 2004) (common sense dictates that if hailstorm damage of $450,000 was sustained, association would, or should, have been aware of damage shortly after storm occurred, certainly within a few months).

866. *See, e.g.*, Ridglea Estate Condo. Ass'n v. Lexington Ins. Co., 2005 U.S. App. LEXIS 16724 (5th Cir. Aug. 10, 2005) (that roof damage might have been difficult to discover on two-story buildings because it was not visible from ground did not excuse late notice given magnitude of hail storm and damage to other portions of property; association should have been aware of likelihood that its roofs had suffered hail damage, and thus, should have had roofs inspected by expert at some reasonable time soon after storm occurred).

867. *See, e.g.*, Biscayne Cove Condo. Ass'n v. QBE Ins. Corp., 971 F. Supp. 2d 1121 (S.D. Fla. 2013) (where hurricane struck on October 24, notice of damage to insured condominium property

surely untimely as a matter of law.[868] On the other hand, even notice supplied months after the event may be accepted by the insurer without question.[869] The company may, however, either deny the claim for failure to provide prompt notice or, more likely, send a "reservation of rights letter" to preserve its right to claim the insured violated the policy by failing to provide prompt notice.[870] The insurer is more likely in most circumstances to reserve its rights rather that outright deny the claim because of the notice-prejudice rule. Under that rule, an untimely notice will not necessarily bar a claim unless the insurer is prejudiced by the delay.[871] In many states the rule is applied to property policies by case law[872] or statute.[873] Some states require the insurer to prove it was prejudiced for late notice to bar a

on October 26 was timely); Summit Towers Condo. Ass'n v. QBE Ins. Corp., 2012 U.S. Dist. LEXIS 188510 (S.D. Fla. Apr. 26, 2012) (insured fully complied with its post-loss obligations as a matter of law when it notified insurer of loss it sustained within ten days of hurricane).

868. *See* Yacht Club on the Intracoastal Condo. Ass'n v. Lexington Ins. Co., 599 Fed. Appx. 875 (11th Cir. 2015) (notice given four years and seven months after hurricane damaged association property was untimely as matter of law).

869. Inlet Condo. Ass'n v. Childress Duffy, Ltd., Inc., 615 Fed. Appx. 533 (11th Cir. 2015) (hurricane made landfall September 5, and association reported its hurricane damage in May of following year). *See also* Cypress Pointe at Lake Orlando Condo. Ass'n v. Mt. Hawley Ins. Co., 2012 U.S. Dist. LEXIS 175268 (M.D. Fla. Nov. 19, 2012) (tropical storm damaged condominium buildings in August, and association reported its loss to insurer in following March).

870. *See, e.g.*, Crystal Colony Condo. Ass'n v. Aspen Specialty Ins. Co., 6 F. Supp. 3d 1295 (S.D. Fla. 2014) (where condominium association waited nearly four months after sustaining damage to its property in hurricane to file claim, insurer sent association "Reserved Rights Letter" reserving right to seek declaratory judgment that association violated terms of policy that required association to give insurer prompt notice of loss or damage).

871. *See, e.g.*, Yacht Club on the Intracoastal Condo. Ass'n v. Lexington Ins. Co., 599 Fed. Appx. 875 (11th Cir. 2015) (that structure sustained additional damage because repairs were not made immediately and that certain repairs were undertaken before filing claim were evidence of prejudicial effect of passage of time and prejudice from inability of insurer to investigate prior to repairs).

872. *See, e.g.*, Ridglea Estate Condo. Ass'n v. Lexington Ins. Co., 2005 U.S. App. LEXIS 16724 (5th Cir. Aug. 10, 2005) (prejudice requirement applies to property insurance policies, and lower court erred in holding that insurer was not required to show prejudice to raise breach of prompt notice provision as defense); Vuarnet Footwear, Inc. v. Sea-Rail Servs. Corp., 334 N.J. Super. 442, 453, 759 A.2d 1230, 1236 (2000) (where questions of notice to insurer are in issue, coverage will not be defeated by untimely notice unless insurer has been prejudiced); Independent Fire Ins. Co. v. NCNB Nat'l Bank, 517 So. 2d 59, 64 (Fla. 1st DCA. 1987) (generally when insurer is entitled to receive notice as condition precedent to maintaining action on claim, violation of that provision will not operate to defeat coverage absent substantial prejudice to insurer).

873. Utah Code Ann. § 31A-21-312(2) (failure to give notice does not bar recovery under policy if insurer fails to show it was prejudiced by that failure); Wis. Stat. § 631.81(1) (provided notice is furnished as soon as reasonably possible and within one year after time it was required by policy, failure to furnish notice within time required by policy does not invalidate or reduce claim unless insurer is prejudiced thereby and it was reasonably possible to meet time limit). *But see* N.Y. Ins. Law § 3402(a)(5).

claim.[874] In others, the insured has to prove the absence of prejudice.[875] Courts will generally leave the question of prejudice to the jury.[876]

[a] Description of the Property Involved

The typical policy language of the notice clause says the prompt notice of the loss is to include "a description of the property involved."[877] The insurer may argue that the notice is inadequate for failure to identify the scope of damages. For example, after a hurricane, a condominium association gave notice of a loss within ten days but did not mention damages to windows and sliding glass doors. Some four years later it sought coverage for the windows and sliding glass doors, resulting in a claim of more than six times that contemplated immediately after the hurricane. The insurer contended that by failing to raise the claim for windows and sliding glass doors until several years later, the association failed to comply with the requirement of timeliness. The court did not agree. It said that the policy did not require the association to submit a notice containing the specificity the insurer suggested, but only to provide notice of the loss or damage and

874. *See, e.g.*, Clementi v. Nationwide Mut. Fire Ins. Co., 16 P.3d 223, 232 (Colo. 2001) (once it has been established that insured has unreasonably provided delayed notice to insurer, insurer may only deny benefits if it can prove by preponderance of evidence that it was prejudiced by that delay); American Continental Ins. Co. v. Phico Ins. Co., 132 N.C. App. 430, 437, 512 S.E.2d 490, 495 (1999) (once insured proves that it acted in good faith, burden shifts to insurer to prove its ability to investigate and defend was materially prejudiced by delay); Weaver v. State Farm Mut. Auto. Ins. Co., 936 S.W.2d 818, 821 (Mo. 1997); Brakeman v. Potomac Ins. Co., 472 Pa. 66, 77, 371 A.2d 193, 198 (1977) (in view of facts that insurance contract is not truly consensual agreement, that what is involved is forfeiture and it is company who chooses to disclaim its obligations under policy, it is more equitable to place burden of showing prejudice on company).

875. *See* Nat'l Publ'g. Co. v. Hartford Fire Ins. Co., 287 Conn. 664, 675, 949 A.2d 1203, 1211 (2008) (burden of establishing lack of prejudice must be borne by insured). *See also* 1500 Coral Towers Condo. Ass'n v. Citizens Prop. Ins. Corp., 112 So. 3d 541 (Fla. 3d 2013) (once presumption of prejudice exists, burden shifts to insured to show that insurer was not prejudiced by late notice); Oriole Gardens Condominiums, III v. Independence Casualty & Surety Company, 2012 U.S. Dist. LEXIS 29100 (S.D. Fla. Mar. 6, 2012) (Florida law provides that failure to give timely notice creates rebuttable presumption of prejudice to insurer, but insured can rebut that presumption by introducing evidence tending to show that insurer was in fact not prejudiced by late notice); Kings Bay Condo. Ass'n v. Citizens Prop. Ins. Corp., 102 So. 3d 732 (Fla. 4th DCA 2012) (where notice of claim was served 29 months after alleged loss, lower court erred in finding that untimely notice barred claim as a matter of law because, while prejudice will be presumed if insured breaches notice provision, insured may rebut presumption by showing that insurer has not been prejudiced by lack of notice).

876. *See, e.g.*, Kendall Lakes Towers Condo. Ass'n v. Pac. Ins. Co., 2012 U.S. Dist. LEXIS 10749 (S.D. Fla. Jan. 30, 2012) (although extended passage of time between loss and notice created very strong inference that investigation and defense of insurer were substantially diminished, nevertheless record contained evidence tending to support that insurer was able to conduct sufficient investigation under circumstances and whether prompt investigation would have enabled insurer to determine cause of damage with greater certainty or to take steps to mitigate damages and, if so, whether insurer was placed at substantial disadvantage as to be prejudiced by delay, presented genuine questions of material fact that could not be resolved on motion for summary judgment).

877. *See* ISO Form CP 00 10 06 07, § E.3.a.(2); ISO Form CP 00 17 06 07, § E.3.a.(2).

no more. The insurer had conflated the notice provision with one requiring a "complete inventory." Under that section an insured must provide an inventory at the request of the insurer. That provision, noted the court, places the onus on the insurer to request an itemization of damages from its insured and, therefore, until the insurer requested a complete inventory, the association was under no obligation to provide one.[878]

The court's ruling is particularly significant for common interest communities that have suffered a loss in a catastrophic natural disaster: a hurricane, tornado, or earthquake. In that event, it may be difficult to adequately survey the full extent of the loss immediately afterward. That may be because the local authorities restrict access to the property, but also because in a larger CIC it may be difficult to safely examine the scope of the loss. The association should, therefore, be able to notify the insurer that it has suffered extensive property damage in a tornado, but that the full extent of the damage cannot yet be determined. Implicit in the court's holding is that this is sufficient to put the insurer on notice to begin its own investigation, which is the exact purpose of the notice clause.[879] Because insurers, by state insurance law, have statutory time frames in which to respond, once notice *is* received, the insurer should begin its investigation.

[b] Supplemental Claim

After a catastrophic event, an insured may initially notify the insurer of a claim although it is not yet aware of all the damages. It may not discover the full extent of the loss until the property is inspected by professionals. For example, a condominium property was damaged by a hurricane in 2005. About three weeks later it notified the insurer of its loss. The insurer inspected the property and determined the damage fell below the deductible. Four years later, the association, through its public adjuster, notified the insurer it wished to reopen the claim and contended it had damages well in excess of the deductible. The insurer argued the association failed to provide prompt notice of its "supplemental claim." The court said there were ambiguities in the notice requirement. Whether the duty to notify only pertained to the initial claim or also imposed a time limit on supplementing a claim was unclear. The policy, said the court, contained no provision delineating

---

878. Summit Towers Condo. Ass'n v. QBE Ins. Corp., 2012 U.S. Dist. LEXIS 188510 (S.D. Fla. Apr. 26, 2012). *Compare* Automobile Ins. Co. v. Thomas, 153 Md. 253, 262–63, 138 A. 33, 37 (1927) (it is incumbent on insured who has peculiar knowledge of facts to show reasons for failure to show ground of claim and to show that it was due to honest mistake or ignorance, and not to concealment).

879. *See, e.g.*, Garden-Aire Vill. South Condo. Ass'n v. QBE Ins. Corp., 591 Fed. Appx. 868 (11th Cir. 2014). The condominium community was damaged by a hurricane on October 24, and it provided the carrier a written notice of loss on October 25, asserting there was damage to the buildings, roofs, windows, and fences. The association could not have known the full extent of the loss the day after the hurricane and could easily have overlooked some damage; nonetheless, an adjuster for the carrier made a preliminary inspection of the property on November 2.

when an insured could submit a revised proof of loss or contest a claim determination. The court refused to grant summary judgment to the insurer.[880] The lesson of the case is that an association should conduct its own investigation as soon as it is safe to do so if, after providing a notice of loss, the insurer finds it has no liability.

An insured may not have to notify the insurer of additional damages, even after a claim is paid. A Florida condominium was damaged by a hurricane in late October of 2005.[881] That same month, the association contacted the insurer to notify it of its loss, identifying roof, building, and glass damage to the property. The insurer's adjuster visited the property shortly thereafter and later estimated the loss at just under $400,000. The insurer paid the claim, minus the deductible, in June of the following year. Four years later, a public adjuster hired by the association prepared a damage estimate. It stated that the amount of damage attributable to the hurricane loss was over $5 million replacement cost value. The association did not submit a supplemental claim or even notify the insurer of the additional claimed damages. Instead, it filed suit against the insurer for breach of the insurance contract based on an alleged failure to properly cover damages stemming from the hurricane loss. The insurer argued recovery under the policy was barred because the association failed to provide timely notice of its claim and failed to fulfill other duties prescribed in the contract. The company pointed to the fact that the association provided no notice of the additional damages before filing suit and argued it was unable to perform a proper investigation of those additional claims because the damages were not brought to its attention before the suit was instituted. The court disagreed. It said that under the plain language of the policy, the association was required to provide prompt notice of any loss or damage and include a description of the property involved. It did so. The insurer had, said the court, a "full and fair" opportunity to investigate the damage and request additional information. It did not request any additional information, and the association was under no obligation to give the insurer notice of the additional claimed damages before filing suit. The court acknowledged that it might not make sense to the insurer that an insured could submit notice of a loss, receive payment for claimed damages, and then years later go to court claiming

880. Oriole Gardens Condominiums, III v. Independence Casualty & Surety Company, 2012 U.S. Dist. LEXIS 29100 (S.D. Fla. Mar. 6, 2012). *See also* Cypress Chase Condo. Ass'n "A" v. QBE Ins. Corp., 2013 U.S. Dist. LEXIS 40347 (S.D. Fla. Mar. 22, 2013) (where association provided notice of its original claim within 48 hours after hurricane damaged property but waited nearly five years to give notice of its supplemental claim, court rejected argument by insurer that association failed to provide prompt notice of loss, noting that notice provision only required that insured notify insurer of loss and describe property, but did not require detailed inventory of loss and another policy provision required that detailed inventory, but only at request of insurer).

881. Ocean View Towers Ass'n v. QBE Ins. Corp., 2011 U.S. Dist. LEXIS 147579 (S.D. Fla. Dec. 22, 2011).

millions of dollars in additional damages, but that, said the court laconically, was not its concern.

Policyholders need to be alert to any endorsement that might restrict supplemental claims. For example, a standard endorsement to the Condominium Association Coverage Form in Florida provides that any claim, supplemental claim, or reopened claim for loss or damage caused by a hurricane or other windstorm is barred unless a notice of claim was given within three years after the hurricane first made landfall or a windstorm other than a hurricane caused the covered damage that is the subject of the claim.[882] The endorsement defines a supplemental claim or reopened claim as an additional claim for recovery for losses from the same hurricane or other windstorm that the insurer has previously adjusted pursuant to the initial claim.

[c] Method of Providing Notice

Policyholders usually provide notice of a loss by calling the broker "agent" that sold them the policy because that is who they know.[883] Generally, however, they do not know whether that "agent" is a representative of insurer or a broker who is their representative.[884] When the policy covers commercial property, the party from whom it was obtained is usually a broker and notice to a broker is not notice to the insurer,[885] while notice to an agent of the insurer is notice to that insurer. Any doubt can be avoided by providing notice directly to the insurer as well as to the agent or broker. It is important for common interest community associations to realize that when the duty of submitting a notice of a claim is delegated to the community association manager, failure of the manager to provide prompt notice of the loss will not excuse late notice.[886]

---

882. ISO Form CP 01 25 02 12, § H(1) (Florida Changes). This provision does not affect any limitation for legal action against the insurer provided in the policy under the "Legal Action Against Us Condition."

883. *Consider* Hilton Head Resort Four Seasons Ctr. Horizontal Prop. Regime Council of Co-Owners, Inc. v. General Star Indem. Co., 357 F. Supp. 2d 885, 886 (D.S.C. 2005) (Council asserted that it notified insurance agency from which it purchased policy several times, to no avail).

884. *See, e.g.*, Mitchell Buick & Oldsmobile Sales, Inc. v. National Dealer Services, Inc., 93 Ill. Dec. 71, 138 Ill. App. 3d 574, 582, 485 N.E.2d 1281, 1287 (1985) (it is generally recognized that broker acts as agent of insured rather than agent of insurance carrier).

885. *See, e.g.*, Southeastern Express Sys. v. Southern Guar. Ins. Co., 224 Ga. App. 697, 700, 482 S.E.2d 433, 435 (1997) (independent insurance agent or broker found to be agent of insured, and notice to that agent did not constitute notice to insurer). *See also* Kendall Lakes Towers Condo. Ass'n v. Pac. Ins. Co., 2012 U.S. Dist. LEXIS 10749 (S.D. Fla. Jan. 30, 2012) (prompt notice to "producing agent"—party hired by insured and acting on its behalf—was not notice to carrier).

886. Ridglea Estate Condo. Ass'n v. Lexington Ins. Co., 2005 U.S. App. LEXIS 16724 (5th Cir. Aug. 10, 2005) (that management neglected to have roofs inspected by expert at some reasonable time soon after hailstorm occurred did not serve to toll prompt notice provision in favor of association); Ridglea Estate Condo. Ass'n v. Lexington Ins. Co., 309 F. Supp. 2d 851 (N.D. Tex. 2004) (that association's manager may have been negligent in discovering damage or engaged in subsequent activities to blame damage on later-occurring storms—perhaps as cover-up for earlier

Often, the policy does not explicitly require that the notice be in *writing*. Under state law, an insurer may not be able to require that notice of claim be provided in writing unless that requirement is specified in the policy or an endorsement.[887] Nonetheless, whether or not the policy mandates written notice, it is always advisable to provide notice in writing. First, written notice creates a record of the action of the insured that may be necessary if the insurer disputes having received prompt notice of the loss. Second, under state law written notice may provide the insured with certain protections.

Written notice need not take any particular form. Usually the policy simply requires notice of the loss or damage including a description of the property. A letter, or series of letters, to the insurer that briefly mentions the event and describes the property that was damaged is sufficient.[888] Email can be used to provide notice, however, if an association does not have its own email address—as is the case with many smaller associations—and if notice is sent by an officer, board member, or the manager, it is a good idea to place a hardcopy of the notice—and the insurer's response—in the association files as board members, officers, and managers change and the association may not be able to access the electronic version of the notice in the future.

There are more formal methods of providing written notice. If, as is usually the case, the insured reports the loss to its broker, the broker will fill out a standard form. That form may be one for a specific company, but more likely it is a generic form published by an organization called the Association for Cooperative Operations Research and Development (ACORD).[889] The agent may fill that form out by hand or in an electronic version. The agent then ordinarily forwards the form to the insured to review for accuracy and a signature. The association can request a hardcopy of the completed form for its records. In an abundance of caution, it can check with the carrier to confirm it has received the form. If it has not, the association can protect its interests by sending a copy of the completed form to the carrier with a cover letter explaining that the association reported

---

negligence—did not work to benefit of association on notice issue). The governing board should remember that the manager is its agent, and it will, therefore, generally be bound by the actions of the manager on behalf of the association. *See, e.g.*, Biscayne Cove Condo. Ass'n v. QBE Ins. Corp., 971 F. Supp. 2d 1121, 1126 (S.D. Fla. 2013).

887. *See, e.g.*, 10 Cal. Code Regs. 2695.5(f).

888. Summit Towers Condo. Ass'n v. QBE Ins. Corp., 2012 U.S. Dist. LEXIS 188510 (S.D. Fla. Apr. 26, 2012) (where condominium association provided two letters to insurer referencing hurricane damage to covered property and included description of property involved—fence, glass, roof fans, roofs, pole lights and possibly other areas—that was all insured was required to do under policy to notify insurer).

889. *See, e.g.*, Biscayne Cove Condo. Ass'n v. QBE Ins. Corp., 971 F. Supp. 2d 1121 (S.D. Fla. 2013) (notice to insurer that association had sustained hurricane loss made through Acord Property Loss Notice form). ACORD, founded in 1970, is a global, non-profit organization serving the insurance and related industries that among other things publishes standardized forms. https://www.acord.org/about/Pages/default.aspx.

the loss to the agent on a particular date and obtained a copy of the attached property loss notice form.

[d] Notice Problems for Common Interest Communities

Providing the notice of loss presents special issues for common interest communities. The first issue is who will provide the notice? In a business of any size there will likely be a person whose job responsibilities include handling insurance claims. That person is probably fairly familiar with the insurance coverage and claims procedures. A common interest community, however, is run by residents who volunteer to serve on the governing board with, in many cases, the assistance of a professional manager. The person who provides the notice will generally be either the manager or an officer of the corporation. Neither the officers nor the manager may have much experience with large insurance claims. It would be advisable for one person to be assigned the responsibility of handling claims and to educate him- or herself on the process. Unfortunately, common interest community officers are often in office for only a few years. For these reasons, the association may turn to the manager to handle a claim. Ordinarily managers have some knowledge of insurance. The association, however, needs to monitor the progress of its claim. It should assign an officer or director to receive copies of all communications to or from the manager concerning the claim.[890]

A second problem for common interest communities is that the volunteer board members likely have little knowledge of building construction, especially of large multi-story structures, and may not recognize the possibility of hidden damage. As a result, association governing boards have occasionally concluded that any property damage is minimal—below the deductible—and decide not to notify the insurer at all, only to discover later that there is significant and costly damage. However, prompt notice is not excused merely because an insured may not be aware of the full extent of damage or believes the damage will not exceed the deductible; instead, notice of a loss that implicates a potential claim must be given.[891]

890. The governing board should remember that the manager is its agent, and it will, therefore, generally be bound by the actions of the manager on behalf of the association. *See, e.g.*, Biscayne Cove Condo. Ass'n v. QBE Ins. Corp., 971 F. Supp. 2d 1121, 1126 (S.D. Fla. 2013).

891. Yacht Club on the Intracoastal Condo. Ass'n v. Lexington Ins. Co., 599 Fed. Appx. 875 (11th Cir. 2015) (that board acknowledged building had suffered damage from hurricane and set aside money were sufficient facts to lead reasonable and prudent person to believe claim for damages would arise and whatever concerns board had about extent of damage and its deductible were not relevant under law); 1500 Coral Towers Condo. Ass'n v. Citizens Prop. Ins. Corp., 112 So. 3d 541 (Fla. 3d 2013) (when policy requires notice, insured must give notice of loss that implicates potential claim without waiting for full extent of damages to become apparent; association was not entitled to wait until it determined on its own that damages exceeded deductible or it ascertained precise cause of damage before giving notice of loss or damage); Kendall Lakes Towers Condo. Ass'n v. Pac. Ins. Co., 2012 U.S. Dist. LEXIS 10749 (S.D. Fla. Jan. 30, 2012) (association was not entitled to wait until it determined on its own that damages exceeded deductible or it ascertained

Finally, the membership on a common interest community governing board can change significantly in a short period of time. Decisions made by earlier boards can be reversed by later boards. Occasionally, a board will submit a claim to the insurer and before the company makes a decision, a newly elected board will decide not to pursue the claim. If the claim is later resubmitted, is the notice late? In one condominium case, notice of a claim was submitted in March, but the claim was withdrawn in September. Over two years later the association again notified the insurer of the claim. The insurer contended that filing, withdrawing, and resubmitting the claim constituted a breach of the prompt notice provision. The court found there was evidence tending to show the insurer was not prejudiced, and it refused to grant summary judgment to it. Whether the notice was prompt was, concluded the court, a question for the jury.[892]

[e] Estimate of the Amount of Loss

One expert in the field of insurance notes that when an insured notifies the insurer of a loss, it is likely to be asked the amount of the loss, but it is not required to provide a dollar estimate at this point in the process.[893] The expert warns that the answer can set the tone for the adjustment. The carrier will establish a reserve for the claim, and if the insured provides an estimate that is less than the actual loss, it will be more difficult to settle at a figure higher than the reserve amount.

[f] Response of the Insurer to Notice

Commercial property policies impose duties on the insured in the event of a loss but do not specify the response of the insurer to notice of a claim. The states, however, mandate that insurers respond promptly to a notice of a claim and handle the claim fairly. For example, under Florida law, after an insurer receives a communication regarding a claim, it generally has to review and acknowledge receipt of that communication within 14 calendar days.[894] The insurer's acknowledgment has to be responsive to the communication, and if that communication constitutes a notification of a claim, unless the acknowledgment reasonably advises the insured that the claim appears not to be covered by the policy, the

---

precise cause of the damage; rather, it was required to give notice of loss or damage, without regard for whether it intended to submit any claim or determined loss was covered under policy; insured must give notice of loss that implicates potential claim without waiting for full extent of damage to become apparent, and good faith belief that damage is trivial or not covered is insufficient to justify non-compliance with notice provision).

892. Palma Vista Condo. Ass'n of Hillsborough County v. Nationwide Mut. Fire Ins. Co., 2010 U.S. Dist. LEXIS 118262 (M.D. Fla. Oct. 7, 2010).

893. Rake, *Property Insurance Claims: Negotiating Unfamiliar Terrain*, at 2 (Adjusting Today, 2010), available at: http://adjustersinternational.com/publications/adjusting-today/property-insurance-claims/0/.

894. Fla. Stat. § 627.70131(1)(a).

acknowledgment has to provide necessary claims forms, and instructions, including an appropriate telephone number.[895] Similarly, California requires that, on receiving notice of a claim, the insurer must immediately, but in no event more than 15 calendar days later, acknowledge receipt to the insured of that notice and provide to the insured the necessary forms, instructions, and reasonable assistance.[896] Often, an insurer will issue a "reservation of rights" letter to protect its right to deny the claim but still continue to investigate before it determines that the claim, in its analysis, is not covered.

Insurance companies are bound to follow these mandates, although in the event of a catastrophic event, they will generally be granted some latitude. If an insurer fails to respond promptly to a notice of claim, the remedy for the insured will vary from state to state. In some states the insured may have a cause of action against the insurer for a statutory violation while in others, only the state regulators have authority to take action for a statutory offense.

[2] Protection of the Covered Property

The property policy will generally require the insured to take all "reasonable steps" to protect the covered property from further damage and to keep a record of expenses necessary to protect it.[897] The policy says these expenses will not increase the limit of insurance. The policy will also require the insured to set the damaged property aside, if feasible, in the best possible order for examination. Finally, under the policy, the insurer will not pay for any subsequent loss or damage that results from a cause of loss that is not a covered cause of loss. This means that the insurer's obligation to reimburse for actions to preserve or protect covered property "does not extend to require reimbursement for prevention of damage to property that is excluded from coverage or for a circumstance that is not a covered cause of loss."[898]

---

895. Fla. Stat. § 627.70131(2).

896. 10 Cal. Code Regs. 2695.5(e).

897. *See* ISO Form CP 00 10 60 07, § E.3.a.(4); ISO Form CP 00 17 06 07, § E.3.a.(4). *See, e.g.*, Higginbotham v. New Hampshire Indem. Co., 498 So. 2d 1149 (La. App. 1986), *cert. den.*, 501 So. 2d 236 (La. 1987) (where trial court held that any later damage suffered because of deterioration of roof was result of failure by insured to have original damage repaired in timely fashion, appellate court did not find that decision so erroneous as to warrant payment for damages sustained after storm where measures could have been taken to reasonably protect premises from further deterioration).

898. Buczek v. Cont'l Cas. Ins. Co., 378 F.3d 284, 293 (3d Cir. 2004) (policy language clearly provides that loss or damage resulting from cause of loss that is not "covered cause of loss" is excluded from coverage). *See also* Ski Chalet Vill. Owners Club, Inc. v. Emplrs. Mut. Cas. Co., 2016 U.S. Dist. LEXIS 161563 (E.D. Tenn. Nov. 22, 2016) (association contended property protection clause included right to recover expenses in connection with protection of covered property; however, court held that provision does not create any coverage but is condition precedent to obtaining coverage for damage to covered property not resulting from excluded cause).

One expert in the insurance field notes that what is practical and reasonable will vary from loss to loss and identifies some of the actions that may need to be taken to protect property after a loss.[899] These include securing the property to prevent looting and to protect it against further damage from the elements, and this may require moving the property to another location. Computer-controlled equipment and other electronics need to be protected from smoke residue, which can corrode electronic components quickly.

[3] Inventory

The insured is generally required to give the carrier, at its request,[900] complete inventories of the damaged and undamaged property, including quantities, costs, values, and the amount of loss claimed.[901] The inventory is not limited to personal property[902] but includes portions of real property, for example, windows and doors[903] and individual units.[904]

[4] Inspection of Property and Examination of Books and Records

Property policies require the insured to allow the insurer to inspect the property proving the loss or damage and examine the books and records of the insured as often as may be reasonably required.[905] Additionally, the insured has to allow the insurer to take samples of damaged and *undamaged* property for inspection, testing, and analysis, and to make copies from its books and records. These obligations probably fall under the "cooperation" clause as well as the specific clause

899. Rake, *Property Insurance Claims: Negotiating Unfamiliar Terrain*, at 2 (Adjusting Today, 2010), available at: http://adjustersinternational.com/publications/adjusting-today/property-insurance-claims/0/.

900. Cypress Chase Condo. Ass'n "A" v. QBE Ins. Corp., 2013 U.S. Dist. LEXIS 40347 (S.D. Fla. Mar. 22, 2013) (policy required that insured provide detailed inventory, but only at request of insurer).

901. *See* ISO Form CP 00 10 06 07, § E.3.a.(5); ISO Form CP 00 17 06 07, § E.3.a.(5). *See, e.g.*, 200 Leslie Condo. Ass'n v. QBE Ins. Corp., 965 F. Supp. 2d 1386 (S.D. Fla. 2013), *aff'd*, 616 Fed. Appx. 936 (11th Cir. 2015) (that neither estimate nor proposal for window replacement identified which components of property were damaged and which were undamaged supported conclusion that insured association failed to comply with inventory requirement).

902. 200 Leslie Condo. Ass'n v. QBE Ins. Corp., 965 F. Supp. 2d 1386, 1401 (S.D. Fla. 2013), *aff'd*, 616 Fed. Appx. 936 (11th Cir. 2015) (rejecting association argument that "inventory" means complete list of items such as property, goods in stock, or contents of building, not building itself).

903. Biscayne Cove Condo. Ass'n v. QBE Ins. Corp., 971 F. Supp. 2d 1121, 1143 (S.D. Fla. 2013).

904. Cypress Chase Condo. Ass'n "A" v. QBE Ins. Corp., 2013 U.S. Dist. LEXIS 40347 (S.D. Fla. Mar. 22, 2013) (where insurer asked association to indicate which units suffered damage to their windows and doors, but association did not prepare any estimate of damaged property, its inventory was insufficient, and it failed to meet inventory requirement).

905. *See* ISO Form CP 00 10 06 07, § E.3.a.(6); ISO Form CP 00 17 06 07, § E.3.a.(6).

concerning inspection of property, books, and records.[906] The association should check its policy for any endorsements that concern property inspection.[907]

[a] Inspection of Property

The CIC is obligated to allow the insurer to inspect the property proving the loss or damage as often as may be reasonably required. Generally, inspections are made with prior notice to the insured. After a catastrophic loss, inspections may occur immediately or, in some cases, after a long wait. The CIC association does not have to permit those inspecting the damage to speak with individual owners, even if their units are inspected.[908] The insured may not, however, limit who inspects the property on behalf of the insurer. For example, a condominium association attempted to deny access to damaged property to a "loss consultant" to the insurer and insisted that the insurer instead have an adjuster inspect the property. The court said in effect that the association could not pick and choose which employees and agents of the insurer carried out its right to inspect the property.[909]

[i] Preserving the Property for Inspection

The CIC must preserve damaged property for the insurer to inspect. For example, in a condominium, building pipes in a rooftop cooling tower burst from freezing temperatures. A company hired on behalf of the association was to remove and store the damaged cooling tower, but instead destroyed it. The insurer disclaimed coverage for the loss, contending the association breached the policy requirement that it maintain and preserve the cooling tower for inspection. The court agreed. The policy imposed an obligation to set damaged property aside for inspection as often as reasonably required to determine whether the loss was covered. That condition, said the court, was clear and unambiguous and constituted an express condition precedent with which the association had to literally comply before it could recover. The insurer never had the opportunity to inspect the damage after the tower was removed and the association breached the policy condition.[910]

---

906. Summit Towers Condo. Ass'n v. QBE Ins. Corp., 2012 U.S. Dist. LEXIS 188510 (S.D. Fla. Apr. 26, 2012) (where parties failed to specify section of policy that required association to provide requested documents, court determined requirement could be set forth in section requiring cooperation with investigation or settlement of claim).

907. *See, e.g.*, ISO Form CP 01 25 02 12, § H(2) (Florida Changes) (any inspection or survey by carrier, or on its behalf, of property that is subject of claim will be conducted with at least 48 hours' notice to insured, but insured may waive that notice).

908. 200 Leslie Condo. Ass'n v. QBE Ins. Corp., 965 F. Supp. 2d 1386, 1398, n.7 (S.D. Fla. 2013), *aff'd*, 616 Fed. Appx. 936 (11th Cir. 2015) (although insurer's inspection team members were not allowed to speak to the individual unit owners, that was not policy requirement).

909. Citizens Prop. Ins. Corp. v. Galeria Villas Condo. Ass'n, 48 So. 3d 188, 191 (Fla. 3d DCA 2010).

910. Seaport Park Condominium v. Greater N.Y. Mut. Ins. Co., 39 A.D.3d 51, 828 N.Y.S.2d 381 (2007).

[ii] Inspection of Individual Units or Apartments

When an insurer seeks to inspect the damaged property, it may ask for access to individual units. In some cases, that will be because the policy provides coverage not only for common areas but also for the units. Even if the policy does not cover units, damage to common elements may be visible only from within a unit. For example, in a multi-story building damaged by an earthquake, load-bearing support columns may traverse the units and they may need to be examined. The association, therefore, needs to obtain entry to the units for the insurer.[911] That may be troublesome. For example, in a Florida case,[912] an insurer requested access to inspect units in a condominium for damage after a hurricane. It was able to gain entry to 75 percent of the units but not the remaining units, including some that were in foreclosure, that were empty for some other reason, or in which the unit owners were uncooperative. The court observed that the blame for the inability to access units appeared to lie chiefly with unit owners, and there was no evidence the association could compel those owners to assist the insurer. Thus, the court found the insurer had not shown as a matter of law that the association materially breached the inspection provision.

The decision is curious. Under Florida law, condominium associations have the irrevocable right of access to each unit during reasonable hours when needed for "maintenance, repair, or replacement of any common elements or of any portion of a unit to be maintained by the association pursuant to the Declaration or as necessary to prevent damage to the common elements or to a unit."[913] It would seem obvious that an inspection by an insurer in preparation for settling a claim that will provide proceeds to repair the property would meet the requirements of the statute. Additionally, Florida law grants discretion to the governing board to enter an abandoned unit to inspect it and adjoining common elements,[914] and a unit is presumed to be abandoned if it is the subject of a foreclosure action.[915] Why the court made no mention of Florida law is unclear. What is clear is that there was no need for the association to compel owners to assist the insurer; the association itself had the statutory authority to provide access to all the units.

The right of a common interest community to gain entry to individual units is not unique to Florida. The UCIOA, for example, provides that generally an association is responsible for maintenance, repair, and replacement of the common elements and that each unit owner has to afford to the association, and to its agents or employees, access through his or her unit when reasonably necessary

---

911. *See, e.g.*, Sunland Vill. Homeowners Ass'n v. State Farm Fire & Cas. Co., 2007 Cal. App. Unpub. LEXIS 3816 (May 14, 2007).

912. Coconut Key Homeowners Ass'n v. Lexington Ins. Co., 649 F. Supp. 2d 1363 (S.D. Fla. 2009).

913. Fla. Stat. § 718.111(5)(a).

914. Fla. Stat. § 718.111(5)(b)1.

915. Fla. Stat. § 718.111(5)(b)1.a.

for those purposes.[916] That grant of access would appear to encompass inspections by insurance carriers. Many states provide a right of access in their *condominium* enabling legislation, although the right may be circumscribed.[917] On the other hand, few states, other than those that have enacted the UCIOA, grant a statutory right of entry for cooperatives or homeowners associations,[918] and the California Davis-Stirling Common Interest Development Act, which governs all types of common interest communities, makes no mention of association access. However, even where there is no statutory grant of access, the governing documents may address the right of an association to have access to units.

In the case of cooperatives, no statutory right may be needed as the cooperative generally owns the entire building and the residents are in effect "tenants." The cooperative corporation is the "landlord" and should have a right of access to its property. Additionally, the proprietary lease or occupancy agreement between each resident and the corporation may enshrine the right of entry, although it may also place limitations on it. In the case of a homeowners association where units are attached, any right of access would probably need to be stated in the documents, and often is.[919] In a homeowners association consisting of detached single-family homes, the need for an inspection by the association insurer would be rare.

[b] Documents: Books and Records

Document production may present problems for residential common interest communities. Operated by volunteers, the association may not maintain an effective filing system. Some documents may never end up in the files. Others may be removed and disposed of as unneeded. Documents may be in the hands of different officers who do not transfer them to the association files. Even if the

916. Uniform Common Interest Ownership Act § 3-107(a).

917. Illinois and New York have fairly broad grants of access. 765 Ill. Comp. Stat. 605/18.4(j) (powers and duties of board of managers include access to each unit from time to time as may be necessary for maintenance, repair, or replacement of any common elements or for making emergency repairs necessary to prevent damage to common elements or to other units); N.Y. Real Prop. Law § 339-i(5) (unit owners have irrevocable right, to be exercised by board of managers, to access to each unit from time to time during reasonable hours to extent necessary for operation of property, or for making emergency repairs necessary to prevent damage to common elements or to another unit or units). Texas, on the other hand, appears to limit the association's access to emergency situations. Tex. Prop. Code § 82.102(a)(16) (unless otherwise provided by Declaration, association, acting through its board, may enter unit for bona fide emergency purposes when conditions present imminent risk of harm or damage to common elements, another unit, or occupants).

918. Fla. Stat. § 719.104(1) (cooperative association has irrevocable right of access to each unit from time to time during reasonable hours when necessary for maintenance, repair, or replacement of any structural components of building or of any mechanical, electrical, or plumbing elements necessary to prevent damage to building or to another unit).

919. *See, e.g.*, Lloyd v. Pier W. Prop. Owners Ass'n, 470 S.W.3d 293, 301 (2015) (bylaws provided that governing board could enter any unit when necessary in connection with maintenance for which board was responsible).

association has good files, the person who maintains them may move away, leaving no one with knowledge of the filing system. At least in theory, if an association has professional management, its files are either in the possession of, or supervised by, the manager. That, however, may not guarantee a thorough filing system. Documents may be discarded or misfiled before the manager ever learns of them. Older—but still needed—files may be purged without the manager's knowledge. In small communities, the manager probably manages many other small projects and may only be on site a few times a month. All this means that a common interest community may be thoroughly unprepared to respond to a request for documents.

Policies generally provide the insurer the right to "examine" books and records and make copies of them. All that should be required of the insured is that it make the books and records available on a reasonable basis. For example, where a CIC association through its president or attorney responded to repeated requests from the adjuster for a large number of documents and offered to make the documents available at the property or the management offices, the insurer treated these offers as unresponsive and took the position that the association failed to respond to its requests to provide access to the requested records and documents. The court did not directly address whether the insured had violated the cooperation requirement but appeared to accept that the insured had fully cooperated.[920]

A mere delay in producing documents may not breach the obligation to allow the insurer to examine the association books and records. For example, an insurer requested that an association produce unit owner files. The association claimed the files were confidential. The insurer offered a confidentiality agreement for any of those files. Almost two years later the insurer was finally granted access to the unit owner files. The court said that summary judgment for the insurer based on failure to allow for examination of the files was unwarranted. The association offered an explanation for not producing the files, and thus the insurer failed to show as a matter of law that the association materially breached. The dispute over examination of the files was for a jury to decide.[921]

Sometimes the number of documents requested runs into the thousands and the association makes an apparent good faith effort to comply with the requests.

---

920. Boardwalk Condo. Ass'n v. Travelers Indem. Co., 2007 U.S. Dist. LEXIS 48325 (S.D. Cal. July 3, 2007).

921. El Dorado Towers Condo. Ass'n v. QBE Ins. Corp., 717 F. Supp. 2d 1311 (S.D. Fla. 2010). *See also* Oriole Gardens Condominiums, III v. Independence Casualty & Surety Company, 2012 U.S. Dist. LEXIS 29100 (S.D. Fla. Mar. 6, 2012) (where record did not indicate what specific documents were outstanding, or whether they were relevant or necessary for insurer to investigate claim and association complied "to a certain degree" with its obligation to produce and disclose documents, there was question of fact for jury as to whether association satisfied its obligation and insurer was, therefore, not entitled to summary judgment for failure of association to comply with obligation to produce and disclose documents).

In one condominium case, the association provided over 39,000 documents to the insurer over roughly a ten-month period. The insurer claimed there were documents that it had not received and that it was seeking still more documents. The court said that even if the insurer had demonstrated a disputed issue of fact as to whether the association provided all requested documents, it offered neither evidence nor argument to establish that it had been substantially prejudiced by any failure to produce documents.[922]

When the insurer's request appears to the association to be excessive or intrusive, it should consult with an experienced insurance law attorney because many courts limit access to books and records by a rule of reasonableness and specificity and will prohibit the insurer from roaming at will through all of the financial records of an insured.[923]

[i] Minutes

One set of documents insurers often request is governing board or association minutes.[924] There is a difference between the minutes of the association and those of the governing board. Governing boards meet regularly, usually once or twice a month. The association is the organization made up of all the residents and ordinarily has one annual meeting at which the members of the governing board are elected. Occasionally there are special association meetings. When an insurer requests minutes, it should specify whether it wants board or association minutes. If the insurer does not specify which minutes it needs, the association representative should seek clarification. It is important to be responsive to the request, but if the association is unsure about the request, it should seek legal guidance on what documents should be produced.

Minutes are relevant to any claim. As one court noted, they may disclose decisions that were made to undertake capital improvements affecting the damaged property, expenses that were incurred to maintain or repair common elements, and the nature and dates of prior damage or repairs.[925]

Minutes can present a problem for common interest communities. Experts warn that the contents of board minutes should be limited.[926] Other than basic introductory information—the name of the organization; the date, time, and place of the meeting; the determination of a quorum; and the announcement of compliance with any meeting notice requirements—the minutes should state

922. Summit Towers Condo. Ass'n v. QBE Ins. Corp., 2012 U.S. Dist. LEXIS 188510 (S.D. Fla. Apr. 26, 2012).

923. *See, e.g.*, Stover v. Aetna Cas. & Sur. Co., 658 F. Supp. 156, 160 (S.D. W. Va. 1987).

924. *See, e.g.*, Oriole Gardens Condominiums, III v. Independence Casualty & Surety Company, 2012 U.S. Dist. LEXIS 29100 (S.D. Fla. Mar. 6, 2012); Citizens Prop. Ins. Corp. v. Galeria Villas Condo. Ass'n, 48 So. 3d 188 (Fla. 3d DCA 2010).

925. Citizens Prop. Ins. Corp. v. Galeria Villas Condo. Ass'n, 48 So. 3d 188 (Fla. 3d DCA 2010).

926. *See, e.g.*, 6A Rohan, *Real Estate Transactions: Home Owner Associations and Planned Unit Developments—Law and Practice: Forms*, § 7A.04[2][c] (Matthew Bender 2016).

no more than the motions made and seconded and the results of the vote on each motion. Nonetheless, well-meaning association secretaries persist in making the minutes a narrative account of the meeting. They include not only the discussion surrounding motions but even discussion that took place without a proper motion having been made. Therein lies danger for the common interest community. Under the rules of evidence, records of regularly conducted business activity are admissible in court as an exception to the hearsay rule.[927] However, before they ever reach a courtroom, the minutes may be examined by the insurer and found to provide a basis for denying a claim, or worse, evidence of fraud. For example, in one case an insurer reviewed board minutes when investigating a claim for earthquake damage and learned that there were prior problems with the property, including land erosion, water intrusion, and tile buckling.[928] In another case, the minutes stated that an earthquake caused "superficial cosmetic damage" and that the insurer's finding of no structural damage and total "incidental damage" falling far short of the deductible was "as expected," suggesting the association agreed with the carrier's assessment.[929] The minutes of a Utah association appeared to suggest the association was attempting to manipulate its claim to force the insurer to pay for full roof replacements where only less expensive repairs may have been required.[930] The lesson for common interest community boards is obvious: never include a narrative discussion in the minutes.

Insurance carriers may not be aware of other documents that may be beneficial to them. For example, some associations produce and post "board reports" or "meeting summaries." When they are prepared by an association board member or director, they may constitute official association records. Similarly, a newsletter that purports to represent the views of the association governing board may also be considered an official record. These reports may be as useful to the insurer as the minutes. The carrier, therefore, when requesting documents should inquire whether the association produces these or similar documents. Associations, on the other hand, should not produce board reports or meeting summaries at all, should make sure any newsletter is "unofficial," and should be careful about the content of any written communication about their claims to unit owners.[931]

927. Uniform Rules of Evidence Act, Rule 803(6). The federal rules and those of the states are similar to the Uniform Act. *See also* Meadows Condo. Ass'n v. Redman, 2009 Conn. Super. LEXIS 2062 (Conn. Super. July 30, 2009) (board minutes should be taken as best evidence of actions actually taken by board).

928. Chateau Chamberay Homeowners Ass'n v. Associated Internat. Ins. Co., 90 Cal. App. 4th 335, 341, 108 Cal. Rptr. 2d 776, 780 (2001).

929. Cheviot Vista Homeowners Ass'n v. State Farm Fire & Casualty Co., 143 Cal. App. 4th 1486, 50 Cal. Rptr. 3d 1 (2006).

930. Pheasantbrook Home Owners Ass'n v. Travelers Indem. Co., 2016 U.S. Dist. LEXIS 8414 (D. Utah Jan. 25, 2016).

931. *See, e.g.*, Encino Park W. Homeowners Ass'n v. Truck Ins. Exch., 2007 Cal. App. Unpub. LEXIS 6354 (Aug. 3, 2007) (memorandum from HOA board of directors to unit owners referring

[ii] Governing Documents and Contracts

An association should anticipate that the insurer will want to inspect its governing documents and possibly contracts to which it is a party. For example, one insurer sought an association's Declaration of Condominium, condominium bylaws, and contracts for property management services for the prior seven years.[932] The association argued these requests were overbroad, ambiguous, and not relevant to adjustment of its claim. The court did not agree. It noted that these documents typically contain information bearing directly on a claim and the respective obligations of the insurer, the insured, and the residents who live within the insured units. The Declaration and bylaws, for example, ordinarily define the insurance and maintenance obligations of the association and unit occupants. Property management contracts are important because they may reveal decisions to undertake capital improvements and efforts to maintain or repair common elements. Additionally, the records might identify individuals with pertinent knowledge who could then be contacted during the investigation of the claim.

Failure to produce the requested documents for inspection may be a basis for denial of a claim. In a subsequent action on that claim, courts will generally be somewhat lenient if the insured has made a reasonable effort to comply—instead of being willfully uncooperative. The court will then usually either stay the action or dismiss it without prejudice to allow belated compliance.[933]

[5] Proofs of Loss

A standard requirement of property policies is that the insured submit a proof of loss. Under basic commercial property policies, the insurer supplies the insured with the proof of loss form and the insured must send the carrier the signed, sworn proof of loss containing the information the insurer requires within 60 days after its request.[934] Generally under that policy language the obligation to provide a proof of loss form is not triggered until the insurer makes the request.[935]

---

to "stylish upgrading that has taken place" used by insurer to prove release signed on behalf of association was not executed under "economic duress").

932. Citizens Prop. Ins. Corp. v. Galeria Villas Condo. Ass'n, 48 So. 3d 188, 191, n.3 (Fla. 3d DCA 2010).

933. *See* El-Ad Enclave at Miramar Condo. Ass'n v. Mt. Hawley Ins. Co., 752 F. Supp. 2d 1282 (S.D. Fla. 2010) (where association "amicably" attempted to coordinate production of documents and inquired whether insurer wanted copies of documents or wanted to inspect them personally and on two occasions parties agreed to dates for inspection of documents, there was disputed fact presented regarding whether association was in compliance with demands for documents; if insured has not demonstrated willful disregard of policy preconditions, courts either stay action or dismiss it without prejudice to allow belated compliance).

934. *See* ISO Form CP 00 10 10 00, § E.3.a.(7); ISO Form CP 00 17 04 02, § E.3.a.(7).

935. *See, e.g.*, Yacht Club on the Intracoastal Condo. Ass'n v. Lexington Ins. Co., 944 F. Supp. 2d 1258, 1261–62 (S.D. Fla. 2013), *aff'd*, 599 Fed. Appx. 8753 (11th Cir. 2015) (policy did not make submission of proof of loss condition precedent to suit; instead, under language of policy, insured association could not sue on policy if it was not in compliance with requirement that it submit

The purpose of a proof of loss provision is to inform the insurer of facts surrounding the loss and to afford it an adequate opportunity to investigate and determine its rights and liabilities before it is obliged to pay.[936] For that reason, substantial compliance with the proof of loss requirement is usually sufficient.[937] Generally, the "notice-prejudice" rule applies to proofs of loss just as it does notices of loss. Thus, when that rule applies, submission of a proof of loss form after the 60-day deadline will not bar the claim unless the insurer was prejudiced by the delay.

[6] Cooperation with the Carrier

A broadly worded post-loss duty imposed on the insured is to cooperate with the carrier in the investigation or settlement of the claim.[938] The purpose of the cooperation clause is to allow the insurer to obtain information about the loss while it is fresh.[939] It serves to guard against collusion and fraud.[940]

The cooperation clause is the last of the duties imposed by policies on insureds in the event of a loss. It is frequently invoked when the insured fails to submit to an examination by the carrier under oath, a topic discussed below,[941] but may apply when the insured fails to comply with any number of its contractual duties under the policy.[942]

Failure to cooperate with the insurer in the investigation of a claim has been held to be a material breach of the contract justifying denial of the claim.[943]

---

proof of loss within 60 days of request by insurer). *Compare* Ocean Harbour S. Condo. Ass'n v. Empire Indem. Ins. Co., 2007 U.S. Dist. LEXIS 25724 (S.D. Fla. Apr. 5, 2007) (failure of insurer to provide proof of loss form did not relieve association of its obligations).

936. *See, e.g.*, Allstate Floridian Ins. Co. v. Farmer, 104 So. 3d 1242, 1246 (Fla. 5th DCA 2012).

937. *See, e.g.*, Allstate Ins. Co. v. Charity, 255 Va. 55, 59, 496 S.E.2d 430, 432 (1998) (where insured did not state dollar amount of loss on proof of loss form, information provided on that form allowed insurer to investigate loss, to determine its liability, and to prevent fraudulent claim and, therefore, proof of loss substantially and reasonably complied with terms of policy and purposes of proof of loss; not knowing dollar amount of claim did not affect ability of insurance company to determine amount of its liability). *See also* Ocean Harbour S. Condo. Ass'n v. Empire Indem. Ins. Co., 2007 U.S. Dist. LEXIS 25724 (S.D. Fla. Apr. 5, 2007) (detailed communication providing adequate notice of claim and definitively establishing particulars of claim, including description of and magnitude of loss, acted as equivalent of delivering proof of loss).

938. *See* ISO Form CP 00 10 06 07, § E.3.a.(8); ISO Form CP 00 17 06 07, § E.3.a.(8).

939. Weissberg v. Royal Ins. Co., 240 A.D.2d 733, 734, 659 N.Y.S.2d 505, 506 (1997).

940. Staples v. Allstate Ins. Co., 176 Wn. 2d 404, 411, 295 P.3d 201, 205 (2013).

941. *See* § 10.25, *infra.*

942. Cozen, *Insuring Real Property*, § 1.07[2] (Matthew Bender & Co. 2015) (failure of insured to perform one of specified actions when required to do so has often been sufficient to prevent recovery pursuant to cooperation clause). *See, e.g.*, Summit Towers Condo. Ass'n v. QBE Ins. Corp., 2012 U.S. Dist. LEXIS 188510 (S.D. Fla. Apr. 26, 2012) (requirement to provide documents to insurer is part of duty to cooperate with the insurer's investigation, otherwise known as "cooperation clause").

943. Akers v. Liberty Mut. Group, 847 F. Supp. 2d 21, 25 (D.D.C. 2012).

Partial cooperation is generally insufficient,[944] although courts have said that if an insured cooperates to "some degree" or explains the failure to comply, then the question of whether the insured materially breached the policy is for the jury.[945] One treatise explains that breach of the duty to cooperate occurs only when the failure to cooperate substantially and materially affects the interest of the carrier in an adverse manner.[946] In one case a condominium association did not follow specific instructions regarding repairs, but as those instructions were not in the policy, the court found a reasonable jury could conclude the association did not fail to cooperate.[947]

The majority rule is that if the carrier denies coverage under the policy, it cannot then require the insured to follow a contractual duty to cooperate because when the insurer first breaches the contract by denying coverage, the insured is no longer bound to cooperate under that agreement.[948]

---

944. Wright v. Farmers Mut., 266 Neb. 802, 669 N.W.2d 462 (2003). *Compare* Avarello v. State Farm Fire & Casualty Co., 208 A.D.2d 483, 616 N.Y.S.2d 796, 797 (1994) (duty of insured under cooperation clause is satisfied by substantial compliance).

945. Curtis v. Tower Hill Prime Ins. Co., 154 So. 3d 1193, 1198 (Fla. 2d DCA 2015).

946. Cozen, *Insuring Real Property*, § 1.07[2] (Matthew Bender & Co. 2015). *See also* Edge Constr., LLC v. Owners Ins. Co., 2015 U.S. Dist. LEXIS 85835 (D. Colo. June 29, 2015) (where during claims process insurer requested information related to whether general contractor overhead and profit was warranted and insured failed to provide that information, refusal to cooperate substantially disadvantaged insurer in material respects as it precluded insurer from learning identities of subcontractors, number of subcontractors and/or trades purportedly used on project, and scope of their work during claims process and that information all went to crux of issue of whether project was complex job warranting extra overhead and profit); Staples v. Allstate Ins. Co., 176 Wn. 2d 404, 411, 295 P.3d 201, 205 (2013) (insured who "substantially and materially" breaches cooperation clause is contractually barred from bringing suit under policy when insurer can show it has been actually prejudiced); Summit Towers Condo. Ass'n v. QBE Ins. Corp., 2012 U.S. Dist. LEXIS 188510 (S.D. Fla. Apr. 26, 2012) (for failure of insured to cooperate to excuse insurer from its policy obligations, it must prove insured failed to cooperate, that lack of cooperation was material, it suffered substantial prejudice, and it exercised diligence and good faith in trying to bring about cooperation). *See also* C-Suzanne Beauty Salon, Ltd. v. General Ins. Co., 574 F.2d 106, 110 (2d Cir. 1978) (New York courts, when construing cooperation clause, hold breach that will defeat recovery cannot be based on technical or unimportant omissions or defects in performance of duty imposed by it, but rather on willful and fraudulent withholding of information).

947. Pheasantbrook Home Owners Ass'n v. Travelers Indem. Co., 2016 U.S. Dist. LEXIS 8414 (D. Utah Jan. 25, 2016) (insured association did not fail to cooperate when it did not consult with insurer prior to authorizing contractor to complete repair work even though communication to insured purportedly instructed it to submit supplemental claims "within three days," policy contained requirement that supplements be submitted within certain time frame, and association ultimately notified insured of need to replace or repair all roofs and of amount it believed those repairs and replacements would cost).

948. Ass'n of Apt. Owners of Imperial Plaza v. Fireman's Fund Ins. Co., 939 F. Supp. 2d 1059, 1065 (D. Haw. 2013) (rationale behind relieving insured from cooperation provision after denial of coverage is that denial exposes insured to financial insecurity that it attempted to avoid by purchasing insurance and that reasoning was especially applicable where association needed to quickly remediate and repair property to prevent spread of arsenic-contaminated water instead of waiting for insurer to decide whether or not to investigate damage).

An insured may initially refuse to respond to a request the insurer makes during its investigation and then, after consulting counsel, offer to comply with the cooperation clause. The Nebraska Supreme Court, however, noted that a later promise to comply can be too late to cure a breach.[949] The lesson for common interest community associations is that if they believe they have a valid reason not to cooperate with the insurer's investigation, rather than pointedly refuse to cooperate, it is time to consult counsel and have the attorney promptly respond to the insurer's request.

§ 10.25 Examination under Oath

A clause allowing the insurer to examine the insured under oath (EUO) is standard in many types of policies, not just property policies.[950] The BPP[951] and the CAC[952] forms have identical language permitting the carrier to examine *any insured* under oath, while not in the presence of any other insured, at times as may be reasonably required, about any matter relating to the insurance or a claim, including the books and records of the insured. Any answers provided at the examination have to be signed by the insured.

The clause is valid and generally enforceable.[953] The purpose of the examination is to determine whether the claim is just and should be paid.[954] More particularly, the examination protects the carrier against fraud by permitting it to probe into the circumstances of the loss.[955] In furtherance of that goal, the insurer can generally inquire about any information *relevant and material* to the claim or

949. Wright v. Farmers Mut., 266 Neb. 802, 808, 669 N.W.2d 462, 467 (2003).

950. *See generally* Knoll, *Examination Under Oath: The Insurance Companies' Best Friend*, 16 Forum 777 (1981).

951. *See* ISO Form CP 00 10 06 07, § E.3.b.

952. *See* ISO Form CP 00 17 06 07, § E.B.3.

953. Gordon v. St. Paul Fire & Marine Ins. Co., 197 Mich. 226, 230, 163 N.W. 956, 957 (1917).

954. Ransom v. Selective Ins. Co., 229 N.J. Super. 43, 46, 550 A.2d 1006, 1007 (1988); Gordon v. St. Paul Fire & Marine Ins. Co., 197 Mich. 226, 230, 163 N.W. 956, 957 (1917) (purpose of examination is to elicit facts based on which company may determine whether it will defend or adjust claim). *See also* Graham, *The Sworn Examination Under Oath in Insurance Investigations*, 26 Los Angeles Lawyer 26 (2003) (examination of an insured may be useful in resolving issues such as valuation of damaged or destroyed property or ascertainment of coverage under policy and if proof of loss is unclear or contains numerous inaccuracies, or fails to provide adequate documentation, EUO proceeding may assist in resolving outstanding questions).

955. Hart v. Mechanics & Traders Ins. Co., 46 F. Supp. 166, 169 (D. La. 1942) (through examination under oath insurer is better able to determine its obligations and to protect itself against false claims).

the insurance.[956] An insured is not required to answer *immaterial* questions.[957] Additionally, the carrier should not use the examination "solely to obtain partial, unfavorable, or inaccurate admissions from a party, to be used in future litigation."[958]

The right of the insurance company to have an *insured* appear for examination under oath is a substantial and important one.[959] Thus, where an insured had disappeared and a petition in involuntary bankruptcy was filed against him, the receiver appointed for the purpose of collecting insurance proceeds could not take the place of the insured at an examination under oath.

The examination may be conducted by an adjuster for the company.[960] More commonly, however, it is handled by an attorney for the carrier and resembles a deposition with the examination transcribed by a court reporter.[961] It is important, therefore, that the association is also represented by an attorney with insurance experience. Even if the officer being examined under oath is an attorney, the association should have outside independent counsel representing its interests.

[1] State Law Applicable to Examinations under Oath

State law may address examinations under oath. Some states mandate that a Standard Property Policy include an examination under oath requirement. For example, Connecticut provides that the standard form of fire insurance policy has to state that the "insured, as often as may be reasonably required . . . submit to examinations under oath by any person named by this Company, and subscribe the same."[962]

---

956. *See, e.g.*, Stover v. Aetna Casualty & Surety Co., 658 F. Supp. 156, 160 (S.D. W. Va. 1987) (insurer has right to examine about any matter material to its liability limited by rule of reasonableness and specificity); Phillips v. Allstate Indem. Co., 156 Md. App. 729, 734, 848 A.2d 681, 689 (2004) (generally during EUO, insurer may conduct searching examination, though all questions should be confined to matters relevant and material to loss that is determined in context of claim and investigation); Southern Guaranty Ins. Co. v. Dean, 252 Miss. 69, 76, 172 So. 2d 553, 556 (1965) (all matters are material in examination of insured that have bearing on insurance and loss). *See also* 200 Leslie Condo. Ass'n v. QBE Ins. Corp., 965 F. Supp. 2d 1386, 1397 (S.D. Fla. 2013), *aff'd*, 616 Fed. Appx. 936 (11th Cir. 2015) (demand for examination under oath of representative with most knowledge about quantum of loss, cause of the loss, maintenance history of buildings, preparation of and support for claim package, repairs/replacement of damaged property and any estimates for them, and whether repair and replacement of windows and sliding glass doors providing access to individual units was responsibility of association or its members presented subject areas of inquiry within scope of EUO clause that permitted examination about any matter relating to policy or claim).

957. Phillips v. Allstate Indem. Co., 156 Md. App. 729, 734, 848 A.2d 681, 689 (2004).

958. Gordon v. St. Paul Fire & Marine Ins. Co., 197 Mich. 226, 230, 163 N.W. 956, 957 (1917).

959. Sims v. Union Assur. Soc., 129 F. 804, 808 (C.C.D. Ga. 1903).

960. Cozen, *Insuring Real Property*, § 2.07[10] (Matthew Bender & Co. 2015).

961. 1 Jeffrey E. Thomas, *New Appleman on Insurance Law Library Edition* § 4.06[4][c] (Matthew Bender 2017).

962. Conn. Gen. Stat. § 38a-307.

California has set forth by statute the rights of insureds when there is an examination under oath, and those rights specifically apply to "policies and endorsements that insure against property damage and are issued to common interest developments or to associations managing common interest developments."[963] Under the California law, the insurer must notify the insured that it has decided to conduct an examination under oath and provide the insured with a copy of the statute.[964] The examination can be conducted only to obtain information relevant and reasonably necessary to process or investigate the claim.[965] The insured has to be given reasonable notice of the EUO, which has to be conducted at a reasonably convenient place and for a reasonable length of time.[966] The insured may be represented by counsel and record the examination proceedings in their entirety.[967] The insured is permitted to make sworn corrections to the transcript so that it accurately reflects the testimony under oath.[968] The insured may assert any objection that can be made in a deposition under state or federal law; however, the statute warns that if as a result of asserting an objection, the insured fails to provide an answer to a material question, and the failure prevents the insurer from being able to determine the extent of loss and validity of the claim, the rights of the insured under the contract may be affected.[969]

[2] Demand for Examination under Oath

The requirement that the insured submit to a sworn examination is not self-executing.[970] The insurer must make a demand on the insured.[971] Generally, the insured need do no more than meet the specifics of that demand.[972] For a demand

963. Cal. Ins. Code § 790.031.
964. Cal. Ins. Code § 2071.1(a)(1).
965. Cal. Ins. Code § 2071.1(a)(2).
966. Cal. Ins. Code § 2071.1(a)(3).
967. Cal. Ins. Code § 2071.1(a)(4). The insurer has to notify the insured that, on request and free of charge, it will provide the insured with a copy of the transcript of the proceedings and an audio or video recording of them, if one exists. Cal. Ins. Code § 2071.1(a)(5).
968. Cal. Ins. Code § 2071.1(a)(5).
969. Cal. Ins. Code § 2071.1(a)(6).
970. Weber v. General Acci. Fire & Life Assurance Corp., 10 Ohio App. 3d 305, 307, 462 N.E.2d 422, 424 (1983).
971. Nicolai v. Transcontinental Ins. Co., 61 Wn. 2d 295, 297, 378 P.2d 287, 288 (1963) (numerous cases hold demand is prerequisite for examination under oath). *See also* C-Suzanne Beauty Salon, Ltd. v. General Ins. Co., 574 F.2d 106 (2d Cir. 1978) (where insurer requested examination and set date for it, but did not further insist on its right to examine insureds and instead appeared to have decided to mark time silently until period for insured to bring suit expired, no proper demand was made).
972. *See, e.g.*, Summit Towers Condo. Ass'n v. QBE Ins. Corp., 2012 U.S. Dist. LEXIS 188510 (S.D. Fla. Apr. 26, 2012) (no dispute of fact existed over whether condominium association complied with demand for EUO where, when association filed suit, it had complied with request for EUO of named individual and there was no pending request to complete that EUO or to take additional EUOs).

by the insurer that the insured submit to an examination under oath to be legally sufficient, it must designate the time and place of the examination and the person before whom the examination is to be conducted; if it lacks that specificity, the defense to an action by the insured under the policy by the insurer that the insured failed to submit to a sworn examination is unavailable to the insurer.[973] The demand may also set out the type of information the insurer expects the insured to be prepared to address.[974] A request for an examination under oath pursuant to the policy has to be made within a reasonable time.[975] Even though compliance with a demand for examination under oath may be a condition to recovery under the policy, where it is impossible for the insured to comply with the condition, or through no fault of the insured, he or she cannot submit to the examination, that failure will not operate to forfeit the policy.[976]

---

973. Weber v. General Acci. Fire & Life Assurance Corp., 10 Ohio App. 3d 305, 307, 462 N.E.2d 422, 424 (1983). In *Weber*, the insurer sent a letter to the attorney for the insured requesting that the insured "'appear for the purpose of taking his examination under oath at a mutually agreeable time and place,'" but no additional communications were made by either party and the sworn examination was never conducted. The court said the notice of the examination under oath was defective in two respects. First, apparently only the attorney received the letter, but because the policy was a contract between the carrier and the insured, fairness required notice to be given to the insured as well as to his attorney. Next, the letter requesting a sworn examination was not reasonably specific, but was couched in precatory language and appeared to shift to the insured the responsibility of arranging the details of the examination. *See also* Roberto v. Hartford Fire Ins. Co., 177 F.2d 811, 815 (7th Cir. 1949) (policy stipulation for examination of insured is valid and performance of it is condition precedent for recovery providing time and place designated for examination are reasonable); Green v. St. Paul Fire & Marine Ins. Co., 691 F. Supp. 700, 703 (S.D.N.Y. 1988) (where no demand was made that former employee of insured corporation appear at specific time and place, he did not breach insurance policy by not appearing); Saft America, Inc. v. Insurance Co. of North America, 155 Ga. App. 500, 271 S.E.2d 641 (1980) (insurer failed to specifically designate time and place for examination as required under its own policy provisions and, therefore, summary judgment in its favor was error); Nicolai v. Transcontinental Ins. Co., 61 Wn. 2d 295, 297, 378 P.2d 287, 288 (1963) (demand must be explicit as to time and place for examination and as to person before whom it should take place).

974. For example a letter to one condominium association letter demanded an examination under oath of the representative with the most knowledge about the quantum of loss, the cause of the loss, the maintenance history of the buildings, preparation of and support for the claim package, repairs/replacement of damaged property and any estimates for them, and whether the repair and replacement of windows and sliding glass doors providing access to individual units was the responsibility of the association or its members. 200 Leslie Condo. Ass'n v. QBE Ins. Corp., 965 F. Supp. 2d 1386, 1397 (S.D. Fla. 2013), *aff'd*, 616 Fed. Appx. 936 (11th Cir. 2015). *See also* Oriole Gardens Condominiums, III v. Independence Casualty & Surety Company, 2012 U.S. Dist. LEXIS 29100 (S.D. Fla. Mar. 6, 2012) (insurer requested that condominium association provide representative for EUO regarding nine areas of inquiry).

975. Beckley v. Otsego County Farmers Cooperative Fire Ins. Co., 3 A.D.2d 190, 195, 159 N.Y.S.2d 270, 275 (1957) (timeliness of demand made almost four months after proofs of loss were filed was a question of fact that could not be determined on motion for summary judgment).

976. Roberto v. Hartford Fire Ins. Co., 177 F.2d 811, 815 (7th Cir. 1949).

[3] Examination of Organizations Generally

Generally, a corporation has an obligation under the policy to produce an officer or officers for examination under oath.[977] Insurers sometimes seek to examine former officers and directors under oath.[978] Courts have decided that failure of a *former* officer, director, or employee to appear for examination does not constitute a breach of the insured corporation's contractual obligation to submit to examination under oath.[979]

When the insured is an entity rather than an individual, carriers generally may demand to examine more than one person in fulfillment of the EUO mandate. Interestingly, however, one court in a condominium case said that even though the policy stated that the insurer was entitled to examine "any insured," it did not require the association to subject itself to more than one examination under oath.[980]

[4] Examination of Common Interest Communities

Policies generally provide that any insured can be required to submit to an examination under oath. Common interest communities are ordinarily organized as non-profit corporations. It is said that because a corporation can act only through its officers and agents, its officers, employees, and agents may be required to submit to examinations under oath.[981] On the other hand, an insurance treatise cautions that the insured, not its counsel or public adjuster,[982] must submit to the

977. New Hampshire Fire Ins. Co. v. Kochton Plywood & Veneer Co., 242 Miss. 169, 176, 134 So. 2d 735, 737 (1961) (stating it was duty of corporation to produce for examination under oath all witnesses who possessed knowledge or information about cause and extent of loss). *See also* Ausch v. St. Paul Fire and Marine Insurance Co., 125 A.D. 2d 43, 511 N.Y.S 2d 919, *app. den.*, 522 N.Y.S.2d 110, 170 N.Y.S.2d 610, 516 N.E.2d 1223 (1987).

978. *See, e.g.*, El Dorado Towers Condo. Ass'n v. QBE Ins. Corp., 717 F. Supp. 2d 1311 (S.D. Fla. 2010) (insurer requested examinations under oath of former members of Board of Directors).

979. *See, e.g.*, Green v. St. Paul Fire & Marine Ins. Co., 691 F. Supp. 700 (S.D.N.Y. 1988) (where corporation was in bankruptcy and insurer contended that it would be useless to examine bankruptcy trustee who had no personal knowledge of claim and that, therefore, it had contractual right to examine former officers, court said policy made no provision for examination of former officers).

980. El Dorado Towers Condo. Ass'n v. QBE Ins. Corp., 717 F. Supp. 2d 1311, 1319 (S.D. Fla. 2010).

981. Cozen, *Insuring Real Property*, § 22.02[1] (Matthew Bender & Co. 2015) (insurance company may request the insured to "cooperate" by making independent contractors voluntarily available for examination); Biller & Schillaci, *The Examination Under Oath—A Connecticut Overview*, 83 Conn. B.J. 289, 318 (2009) (employees and agents of insured may be examined).

982. At least one court has said that an insured has the right to have its public adjuster present at an EUO. Nawaz v. Universal Prop. & Cas. Ins. Co., 91 So. 3d 187, 188–89 (Fla. 4th DCA 2012). In *Nawaz* the policy included the usual condition that the insured submit to an examination under oath while not in the presence of any other "insured." The court noted that the policy defined "insured" as the named insured, and residents of the household of the named insured who are relatives of the named insured or other persons under the age of 21 and in the care of the named insured. A public adjuster, concluded the court, did not fit into the plain language of the definition

examination.[983] The insurer, however, *may* seek to examine the public adjuster under oath. In one case an insurer insisted on examining a condominium association's public adjuster. A federal judge agreed that examination of the public adjuster would have aided the insurer's investigation but declined to conclude that failure to submit the public adjuster for examination under oath constituted a material breach of the policy warranting summary judgment in favor of the insured.[984]

Examination of officers or directors of a common interest community presents problems for both the CIC association and the insurance carrier. First, unlike in a business corporation, officers and directors of a CIC association are volunteers that may devote little time to the affairs of the association and often lack sophistication in commercial matters. They usually rely on the professional manager for guidance in business matters.[985] Second, officers and directors in an association generally serve a two- or three-year term of office. There are associations, especially smaller ones, in which officers and directors serve many consecutive terms, but there are others in which there is a frequent turnover of directors and officers. Officers and directors also may serve only a single term because of the press of responsibilities at home or work, and they often move out of the community. The recall of directors is rare in business corporations but happens with surprising frequency in common interest community associations. Thus, the officers and directors who were serving at the time of a loss may not be serving or even living in the community at the time the insurer wants to conduct an examination under oath.[986] The sitting officers may not have served at the time of loss.[987] The best person available for the examination may not have held any

of "insured" and, therefore, the court found that under the policy the insured was not prohibited from having a public adjuster present during an examination under oath.

983. 1 Jeffrey E. Thomas, *New Appleman on Insurance Law Library Edition* § 4.06[4][c] (Matthew Bender 2017) (insureds are often represented by public adjusters or legal counsel, but insured, and not his or her representative, must submit to examination under oath).

984. El Dorado Towers Condo. Ass'n v. QBE Ins. Corp., 717 F. Supp. 2d 1311, 1320 (S.D. Fla. 2010). *See also* 200 Leslie Condo. Ass'n v. QBE Ins. Corp., 965 F. Supp. 2d 1386 (S.D. Fla. 2013), *aff'd*, 616 Fed. Appx. 936 (11th Cir. 2015) (that association's president rather than its maintenance supervisor appeared for EUO did not constitute concealment by association); Oriole Gardens Condominiums, III v. Independence Casualty & Surety Company, 2012 U.S. Dist. LEXIS 29100 (S.D. Fla. Mar. 6, 2012) (public adjusters for condominium association submitted to EUOs to testify as to alleged damages caused by hurricane).

985. The insurer may seek to examine the manager under oath. *See* El Dorado Towers Condo. Ass'n v. QBE Ins. Corp., 717 F. Supp. 2d 1311 (S.D. Fla. 2010) (insurer requested examinations under oath of property manager).

986. *See, e.g.*, 200 Leslie Condo. Ass'n v. QBE Ins. Corp., 965 F. Supp. 2d 1386, 1397 (S.D. Fla. 2013), *aff'd*, 616 Fed. Appx. 936 (11th Cir. 2015) (while association president at time of hurricane would have been better candidate for EUO, he no longer resided at condominium at time of examination).

987. *See, e.g.*, Garden-Aire Vill. South Condo. Ass'n v. QBE Ins. Corp., 591 Fed. Appx. 868 (11th Cir. 2014) (association property suffered damage from hurricane in 2005 and later produced its president for examination under oath, but he knew virtually nothing about claim, having come

office or even been a resident of the community at the time of the loss.[988] Even if the persons who were serving at the time of the loss are still in office or at least available, it is quite common for them to have little or no knowledge or useful information about the claim.

The association has an obligation to present a knowledgeable person for examination. If the association produces a person who is unable to answer—or fails to prepare for—the questions put forward at the examination under oath, a court may well find that it did not fully comply with the policy requirement that its representative submit to examination about any matter relating to the insurance or the claim.[989] Lack of preparation and knowledge can be so deficient as to constitute a failure to comply with the EUO requirement and constitute a material breach of the policy.[990] For example, a condominium association provided its treasurer for examination under oath. She, however, knew very little about the claim and did nothing to prepare for the EUO. The court said the insurer produced evidence that the treasurer did not fully participate in the EUO and

to association after hurricane and having made no effort to learn even most basic information about it); Oriole Gardens Condominiums, III v. Independence Casualty & Surety Company, 2012 U.S. Dist. LEXIS 29100 (S.D. Fla. Mar. 6, 2012) (association president submitted to EUO but did not possess certain knowledge of information prior to his election); Citizens Prop. Ins. Corp. v. Mango Hill Condo. Ass'n 12, 54 So. 3d 578, 580 (Fla. 3d DCA 2011) (current president of condominium association who was not president when losses were incurred submitted to examination under oath).

988. *See, e.g.*, 1231 Euclid Homeowners Ass'n v. State Farm Fire & Casualty Co., 135 Cal. App. 4th 1008, 1020, 37 Cal. Rptr. 3d 795, 804 (2006) (individual declared to be "person most knowledgeable" during discovery did not even live in community at time of earthquake that cause claimed loss).

989. In one case, for example, the sitting president, who was not in office at the time of the loss, submitted to an examination under oath on behalf of the association. He did not look at any association minutes or records before the EUO, and his only preparation for the examination was a meeting with the association and brief review of the Proof of Loss. Although he did not refuse to answer any of the questions posed, he did not know the answer to many of them. The court found he did not reasonably prepare for the EUO and, therefore, did not adequately respond to the inquiries regarding matters relating to the insurance or the claim as required by the policy and that, therefore, the association did not fully comply with the policy requirement that its representative submit to examination under oath. 200 Leslie Condo. Ass'n v. QBE Ins. Corp., 965 F. Supp. 2d 1386, 1397 (S.D. Fla. 2013), *aff'd*, 616 Fed. Appx. 936 (11th Cir. 2015). *Compare* Vision I Homeowners Ass'n v. Aspen Specialty Ins. Co., 674 F. Supp. 2d 1333 (S.D. Fla. 2009) (where person provided by association for EUO was unable to answer numerous questions, fact that insurer may have had some unanswered questions at conclusion of examination did not mean that examination was insufficient as matter of law to satisfy association's policy obligations and at most created disputed issue of material fact regarding compliance with terms of policy).

990. Biscayne Cove Condo. Ass'n v. QBE Ins. Corp., 971 F. Supp. 2d 1121, 1133 (S.D. Fla. 2013) (rejecting argument that person who testifies in EUO is not obligated to prepare or otherwise have information; where association "purposely presented" two witnesses who were not prepared for EUOs, refusal to produce witness who could respond amounted to willful disregard of post-loss obligation under policy and material breach of policy).

denied summary judgment to the association on the issue of its compliance with the policy mandate.[991]

[5] "Unreasonable" Demands by Insurer

Ideally, an insurer would simply request to examine the most knowledgeable representative of the association.[992] However, some insurers may make what many would consider unreasonable demands for examinations under oath. For example, in one case a condominium association contended it attempted to comply with the under oath examinations provision of the policy by attempting to schedule examinations of its President and several members of its Board of Directors, but objected to the insurer's demand to examine all of the directors and *every unit owner and tenant* of the building. The association argued the demand was unreasonable, overbroad, and contrary to the intent of the policy.[993] The court did not resolve the question. In another common interest community case, the insurer argued it was entitled to request examinations under oath of former directors who were unit owners and thus considered to be "additional insureds" under the policy. This court, too, did not reach the issue of whether any of the directors qualified as additional insureds.[994] If a policy allows the carrier to examine *any insured* under oath—as policies typically do—the resolution of the question of whether the insurer may insist on examining unit owners would require a determination of whether they actually are "insureds" under the policy.

Some insurers may also subject insureds to prolonged examinations on wide-ranging subjects and demand they produce voluminous amounts of documentation at the EUO as a strategy to induce the insured to forfeit a claim or accept a low amount in settlement.[995] Those abuses can be curbed by the presence of the attorney for the association at the examination. Representatives of the association should have counsel for the association attend each EUO.

---

991. Cypress Chase Condo. Ass'n "A" v. QBE Ins. Corp., 2013 U.S. Dist. LEXIS 40347 (S.D. Fla. Mar. 22, 2013) (rejecting by implication arguments of association that insured does not have any duty to acquire information about its claim in preparation for EUO and that in any event insurer had opportunity to collect information on the claim by discovery, which compensated for any deficiencies in testimony at EUO).

992. *See, e.g.*, Caribbean I Owners' Ass'n v. Great Am. Ins. Co., 600 F. Supp. 2d 1228 (S.D. Ala. 2009).

993. Horizons Condo. Ass'n v. QBE Ins. Corp., 2007 U.S. Dist. LEXIS 6091 (M.D. Fla. Jan. 29, 2007).

994. El Dorado Towers Condo. Ass'n v. QBE Ins. Corp., 717 F. Supp. 2d 1311, 1320 (S.D. Fla. 2010). The court did, however, say that even assuming the insurer was entitled to examine unit owners as additional insureds, there is no provision in the policy requiring the association to subject itself to more than one examination under oath.

995. Graham, *The Sworn Examination Under Oath in Insurance Investigations*, 26 Los Angeles Lawyer 26, 27 (2003).

[6] Production of Documents Prior to Examination

Carriers may insist on having certain documents from the insured before proceeding with the EUO. However, the refusal of the insurer to go forward with the examination without those documents does not necessarily constitute refusal of the insured to cooperate with the examination.[996]

[7] Attorneys: Advice about and Presence at the Examination

Sometimes attorneys will advise the insured not to submit to an examination under oath. The fact that the insured does not cooperate with the insurer's investigation on the advice of counsel does not excuse the breach of the policy obligations.[997]

The insured has the right to have its attorney present at an examination under oath.[998] That an insured insists on the presence of counsel does not amount to a refusal to submit to an examination.[999] Courts generally say that counsel for the insured cannot take part or "share" in the examination.[1000] There is some authority that attorneys for an insured may object to any questions put to their client on any legal grounds available.[1001] The consensus, however, is that objections are not permitted.[1002] Nonetheless, in practice the attorney might want to make

996. *See* Kendall Lakes Towers Condo. Ass'n v. Pac. Ins. Co., 2012 U.S. Dist. LEXIS 10749 (S.D. Fla. Jan. 30, 2012). The company claimed the condominium association failed to submit to an EUO. It admitted the association agreed to provide an EUO, but argued the agreement was illusory and that it could not conduct a meaningful examination without first receiving documents it had requested. The court noted that the association provided substantial documentation and information related to its claim. The policy required the insured to cooperate with the insurer and to submit to an EUO, but it did not, said the court, provide the insurer with an "unfettered right to place conditions on the examination."

997. Hanover Ins. Co. v. Cape Cod Custom Home Theater, Inc., 72 Mass. App. Ct. 331, 336, 891 N.E.2d 703, 707 (2008); Evans v. International Ins. Co., 168 A.D.2d 374, 562 N.Y.S.2d 692, 694 (1990).

998. Hart v. Mechanics & Traders Ins. Co., 46 F. Supp. 166, 169 (D. La. 1942); Shelter Ins. Cos. v. Spence, 656 S.W.2d 36, 38 (Tenn. App. 1983); Gross v. United States Fire Ins. Co., 71 Misc. 2d 815, 817, 337 N.Y.S.2d 221, 224 (1972). *See also* Gordon v. St. Paul Fire & Marine Ins. Co., 197 Mich. 226, 230, 163 N.W. 956, 957 (1917) (there can be no reasonable objection to bona fide request that examination be conducted in presence of insured's attorney).

999. Gordon v. St. Paul Fire & Marine Ins. Co., 197 Mich. 226, 231, 163 N.W. 956, 957 (1917).

1000. Hart v. Mechanics & Traders Ins. Co., 46 F. Supp. 166, 169 (D. La. 1942); Shelter Ins. Cos. v. Spence, 656 S.W.2d 36, 39 (Tenn. App. 1983).

1001. Gross v. United States Fire Ins. Co., 71 Misc. 2d 815, 817, 337 N.Y.S.2d 221, 224 (1972).

1002. Cozen, *Insuring Real Property*, § 22.01 (Matthew Bender & Co. 2015) (attorney for insured is not entitled to ask questions of insured or make objections on basis of local rules of civil procedure); Biller & Schillaci, *The Examination Under Oath—A Connecticut Overview*, 83 Conn. B.J. 289, 301 (2009) (attorney for insured can attend examination but theoretically is not allowed to object).

objections to "protect the interests" of the insured, especially when the examiner is asking blatantly irrelevant or harassing questions.[1003]

[8] Consequences of Failure to Comply

The consequences of failure to comply with a demand for examination under oath vary. For some courts, failure to comply merely suspends any right of recovery until the insured does comply, while others hold non-compliance is a bar to recovery, although that prohibition may be softened by either requiring the non-compliance to be willful or requiring the insurer to show it was prejudiced by the failure to comply.[1004] For example, the Second Circuit Court of Appeals has said that while refusal to appear for an examination under oath is a material breach of the contract, a breach defeating recovery cannot be based on technical or unimportant defects in performance; rather, willful and fraudulent withholding of information has to be shown.[1005]

Courts are reluctant to find a forfeiture of rights under insurance policies and may simply order an insured who failed to submit to an EUO to be deposed in the pending litigation over the claim.[1006] Evidence of substantial compliance generally creates a question of fact for the jury and precludes a finding of non-compliance on summary judgment.[1007] A Florida federal court held that

1003. Biller & Schillaci, *The Examination Under Oath—A Connecticut Overview*, 83 Conn. B.J. 289, 318 (2009) (objection will let examiner know attorney for insured will not allow examination to turn into "free-for-all" session; recommending attorney should advise client of limited role during examination as client may believe he or she has been billed for services during which his or her interests were not protected).

1004. DeFranco, *The Penalty for Failing to Submit to an Examination Under Oath*, 38 S. Ill. U. L.J. 261 (2014).

1005. C-Suzanne Beauty Salon, Ltd. v. General Ins. Co., 574 F.2d 106 (2d Cir. 1978). *See also* Thomson v. State Farm Ins. Co., 232 Mich. App. 38, 53, 592 N.W.2d 82, 88–89 (1998) (generally, failure to comply with requirement to submit to EUO is not complete bar to coverage, at least absent willful non-compliance). *See also* Thompson v. West Va. Essential Property Ins. Ass'n, 186 W. Va. 84, 91, 411 S.E.2d 27, 34 (1991) (trial court erred in granting insurer's motion for summary judgment where insurer suffered no substantial prejudice by failure of insured to answer material questions during examination under oath). *Compare* Hanover Ins. Co. v. Cape Cod Custom Home Theater, Inc., 72 Mass. App. Ct. 331, 336, 891 N.E.2d 703, 707 (2008) (willful, unexcused refusal to comply with reasonable request for examination under oath constitutes material breach of condition precedent to insurance contract and discharges insurer's obligations; insurer need not show prejudice in those circumstances).

1006. Pogo Holding Corp. v. New York Property Ins. Underwriting Asso., 73 A.D.2d 605, 422 N.Y.S.2d 123 (1979).

1007. *See, e.g.*, Oriole Gardens Condominiums, III v. Independence Casualty & Surety Company, 2012 U.S. Dist. LEXIS 29100 (S.D. Fla. Mar. 6, 2012). In *Oriole Gardens* the court found the association cooperated to a substantial degree with its obligation to submit to an EUO. It produced its experts, public adjusters, and sitting president for examination. The president serving during the loss was unable to submit for an EUO because of age and illness. The current president had been, before he took office, the person primarily responsible for handling the claim for the association

substantial compliance with an EUO requirement by a condominium association was a condition precedent to suit. Even though nine months had elapsed since the carrier sought an EUO, the court decided that because the non-compliance did not appear to be willful, the proper course was to dismiss the association's action against the insurer without prejudice to allow belated compliance with the EUO requirement.[1008]

If a date is set for an EUO and the insurer subsequently unilaterally cancels the EUO, that should not be grounds for the insurer to claim the insured refused to comply even if the insured files suit to compel appraisal after the EUO date has been set.[1009] Suit to compel appraisal should not be considered tantamount to a refusal by the insured to participate in the EUO.

§ 10.26 Loss Payment

The loss payment clause is largely the same in the BPP and CAC policies.[1010] When there is loss or damage covered by the policy, the insurer has four options.[1011] The insurer will give notice of its intentions within 30 days after receiving a sworn proof of loss.[1012] It can

- Pay the value of lost or damaged property;
- Pay the cost of repairing[1013] or replacing the lost or damaged property;[1014]

---

and was able to answer questions about how the association documented its activities, its business processes, and his personal observations of the condition of the property after the hurricane that damaged it. He did not have knowledge of the physical condition of the property before the hurricane or other information prior to his election to the board in 2008.

1008. Southgate Gardens Condo. Ass'n v. Aspen Specialty Ins. Co., 622 F. Supp. 2d 1332 (S.D. Fla. 2008). *See also* El-Ad Enclave at Miramar Condo. Ass'n v. Mt. Hawley Ins. Co., 752 F. Supp. 2d 1282, 1286 (S.D. Fla. 2010) (if insured has not demonstrated willful disregard of policy preconditions including EUO, courts either stay action or dismiss without prejudice to allow belated compliance); El-Ad Residences v. Mt. Hawley Ins. Co., 2010 U.S. Dist. LEXIS 109084 (S.D. Fla. Sept. 28, 2010) (if insured has not displayed willful disregard of policy preconditions, courts either stay or dismiss pending actions without prejudice to allow belated compliance; that relief was not necessary because association produced requested documents and EUO was taken less than one month after action was filed and, therefore, summary judgment based on non-compliance with policy pre-suit conditions was denied).

1009. Caribbean I Owners' Ass'n v. Great Am. Ins. Co., 600 F. Supp. 2d 1228, 1250 (S.D. Ala. 2009) (suggesting decision might be different if suit were for damages).

1010. ISO Form CP 00 10 06 07, § E.4; ISO Form CP 00 17 06 07, § E.4.

1011. ISO Form CP 00 10 06 07, § E.4.a; ISO Form CP 00 17 06 07, § E.4.a.

1012. ISO Form CP 00 10 06 07, § E.4.c; ISO Form CP 00 17 06 07, § E.4.c.

1013. Where the method employed to repair units in a common interest community rendered them uninhabitable, the relocation expenses of the residents were covered as a necessary and direct result of the construction and repair. On the other hand, if a collapse caused condemnation of the units, there would be no coverage for relocation expenses. Three Palms Pointe, Inc. v. State Farm Fire & Cas. Co., 250 F. Supp. 2d 1357 (M.D. Fla. 2003), *aff'd*, 362 F.3d 1317 (11th Cir. 2004).

1014. The insured generally has the burden of demonstrating the need for replacement instead of repair. *See, e.g.*, Inlet Condo. Ass'n v. Childress Duffy, Ltd., Inc., 615 Fed. Appx. 533 (11th Cir.

- Take all or any part of the property at an agreed or appraised value; or
- Repair, rebuild, or replace the property with other property of "like kind and quality."[1015]

Where an option involves the cost to repair, rebuild, or replace, it does not include any increased cost attributable to enforcement of any ordinance or law regulating the construction, use, or repair of any property.[1016] The carrier will determine the value of lost or damaged property, or the cost of its repair or replacement, in accordance with the terms of the valuation clause or any endorsement that supersedes it.[1017]

[1] Limitations on Loss Payment

The carrier will not pay the insured more than its financial interest in the covered property.[1018] It may adjust losses with the owner of lost or damaged property if that is someone other than the insured and if it does, those payments will satisfy the claims of the insured against the insurer for that property. The insurer will not pay those owners more than their financial interest in the covered property.[1019] The carrier may elect to defend the insured against suits arising from claims of owners of property and will do so at its expense.[1020] If the carrier does make payment or enter into a settlement on behalf of the insured, it should have a release signed by the parties that received the payment or settlement, so that those owners no longer have a claim against the insured for the same loss.

The insurer will pay for covered loss or damage to covered property within 30 days after it receives a sworn proof of loss, if the insured has complied with all of the coverage terms and the parties have reached agreement on the amount

---

2015) (insufficient evidence that any damage required complete replacement of damaged elevators).

1015. *Consider* St. Paul Village Condo. Ass'n v. St. Paul Fire & Marine Ins. Co., 5 Mass. L. Rep. 376 (1996), where the association repaired damaged hardwood floors with wall-to-wall carpeting. The court said the association could either receive the cost of repairing or replacing property or, if it did not replace the damaged property that of similar kind and quality, to receive the actual cash value of the covered, damaged property. If, therefore, carpeting was similar in kind and quality to wood flooring, the association could reasonably expect to receive the amount actually spent to replace the damaged flooring, but if the two materials were not similar in kind and quality, then it could reasonably expect to receive the actual cash value of the damaged wood flooring.

1016. ISO Form CP 00 10 06 07, § E.4.b; ISO Form CP 00 17 06 07, § E.4.b.

1017. *See* § 10.27, *infra.*

1018. ISO Form CP 00 10 06 07, § E.4.d; ISO Form CP 00 17 06 07, § E.4.d. *See* May v. Mid-Century Ins. Co., 151 P.3d 132, 141–42 (Okla. 2006) (policy clause stating insurer would not pay association more than its financial interest in insured property did not mean association was not entitled to indemnity for loss of covered property based on lack of any financial interest in separate property of unit owner; finding no conflict between "financial interest" clause and one allowing insurer to pay association directly for covered loss of unit owner's property as association would receive those funds for benefit of unit owner rather than as indemnity for some covered losses of its own).

1019. ISO Form CP 00 10 06 07, § E.4.e; ISO Form CP 00 17 06 07, § E.4.e.

1020. ISO Form CP 00 10 06 07, § E.4.f; ISO Form CP 00 17 06 07, § E.4.f.

of loss or an appraisal award has been made.[1021] The CAC policy adds that if the insured names an insurance trustee, the carrier will adjust losses with the insured but will pay the insurance trustee, and if it does pay the trustee, those payments will satisfy the claims of the insured against the carrier.[1022] The significance of the reference to an "insurance trustee" is that under the various Uniform Acts, which have been adopted in a number of states, any loss covered by a property policy has to be adjusted with the association, but the insurance proceeds are payable to any insurance trustee designated for that purpose or otherwise to the association.[1023] The insurance trustee or association is required to hold any insurance proceeds in trust for the association, unit owners, and lien holders as their interests may appear. Even in common interest communities not governed by one of the Uniform Acts, the governing documents may provide for an insurance trustee.[1024] The policy language of the CAC protects the insurance company when it pays the policy proceeds to the named trustee. Once the company pays the proceeds to the trustee, any claim the association has for those funds must be brought against the trustee. The policy, it should be noted, says that if the carrier pays a named trustee, those payments "will satisfy your claims" against it. "Your" means the named insured shown on the Declarations Page. Will the policy language, therefore, protect the insurer from a claim by an individual owner?

[2] Party Walls

In settling covered losses involving a "party wall," the carrier will pay a proportion of the loss to the party wall based on the interest of the insured in the wall in proportion to the interest of the owner of the adjoining building.[1025] The policy defines a "party wall" as one that separates, and is common to, adjoining buildings that are owned by different parties. The definition would make the provision

---

1021. ISO Form CP 00 10 06 07, § E.4.g; ISO Form CP 00 17 06 07, § E.4.g. The association should be alert to the possibility that this language may be modified by an endorsement. For example, in *Ocean Harbour S. Condo. Ass'n v. Empire Indem. Ins. Co.*, 2007 U.S. Dist. LEXIS 25724 (S.D. Fla. Apr. 5, 2007), an amendatory endorsement section labeled FLORIDA CHANGES provided that the carrier would pay *within 20 days* after it received a sworn proof of loss and reach written agreement with the insured *or within 30 days* after it receive the sworn proof of loss and there was an entry of a final judgment or filing of an appraisal award with the carrier, provided the insured complied with all the coverage terms.

1022. *See Condominium Association Coverage Form* (Summit Business Media, 2013) (clause reflects common practice among condominiums of naming trustee to act on behalf of unit owners in common on insurance and other financial matters).

1023. *See, e.g.*, Uniform Common Interest Ownership Act § 3-113(e) (1982).

1024. *See, e.g.*, Golomb v. Warwick Condo. Ass'n, 2007 N.J. Super. Unpub. LEXIS 186 (App. Div. Apr. 26, 2007) (governing board appointed insurance trustee pursuant to condominium bylaws). Note that the trustee in *Golomb* may have had less latitude than under the UCIOA, as the court says the trustee issued a report *recommending* the insurance proceeds be held in a reserve account for future use. Under the UCIOA, the trustee would apparently be able to place the proceeds in a reserve account providing it serves the interests of the unit owners and lienholders.

1025. ISO Form CP 00 10 06 07, § E.4.h; ISO Form CP 00 17 06 07, § E.4.h.

applicable when a common interest community shares a party wall with another building that is not part of the CIC, but not to buildings, or portions of them, within a CIC. For example, in a condominium, walls that separate individual units might be thought of as party walls. However, those walls divide the building into units; they do not separate them from another building. In a development of attached townhouses in which those townhouse units are insured under one association policy—as is mandated by the Uniform Common Interest Ownership Act when there are vertical boundaries that make up common walls between units[1026]—the "party walls" would once again divide units under different ownership but would not separate the insured building from a building owned by a different party.

If the insured elects to repair or replace its building and the owner of the adjoining building elects not to repair or replace that building, the insurer will pay its insured the full value of the loss to the party wall, subject to all applicable policy provisions, including Limits of Insurance, the valuation clause, any coinsurance clause, and all other loss payment conditions. Payment by the insurer does not alter any right of subrogation it may have against any entity, including the owner or insurer of the adjoining building, and does not alter the terms of the "Transfer of Rights of Recovery Against Others to Us Condition" in the policy.

[3] "Like Kind and Quality"

One of the options available to the insurer is to repair, rebuild, or replace the property with other property of "like kind and quality."[1027] What is "like kind and quality"?[1028] Courts have not given the phrase an exact and consistent meaning. One definition is that like kind and quality (LKQ) "refers to a condition in property insurance policies that states that the insurer would cover the cost of repairing or replacing a covered loss with property similar to the original in composition and quality."[1029] Many courts say the phrase simply means sufficient to restore property to its pre-loss condition.[1030] In one of the leading cases, a Texas court stated that the words "like kind and quality" do not refer to parts of "like age, use, and condition, or present cash value." The court explained that it may be that parts of like age, use, and condition of the damaged or destroyed parts

1026. *See* Uniform Common Interest Ownership Act § 3-113(b) (2008).

1027. ISO Form CP 00 10 06 07, § E.4.a.(4); ISO Form CP 00 17 06 07, § E.4.a.(4).

1028. *See generally* Farrish, *"Diminished Value" in Automobile Insurance: The Controversy and Its Lessons*, 12 Conn. Ins. L.J. 39 (2005/2006). Although the article is focused on automobile insurance, it is concerned with property damage and has an extensive discussion of the meaning of "like kind and quality."

1029. https://www.insuranceopedia.com/definition/402/like-kind-and-quality-lkq.

1030. *See, e.g.*, Avery v. State Farm Mut. Auto. Ins. Co., 296 Ill. Dec. 448, 216 Ill. 2d 100, 835 N.E.2d 801, 829 (2005).

can be obtained or that they are not practicably obtainable and if it is practicable to use only new parts, the words and meaning of the stipulation would not forbid it.[1031]

An issue that often arises is whether the insured is entitled to replace undamaged portions of a building when those parts of the property will be inconsistent with the portions that are repaired or replaced. The classic example is damage to a roof. When damaged roof shingles are no longer in production, insureds argue that like kind and quality means an entirely new roof, not one with mismatched shingles. A Pennsylvania court said that where the exact shingles that were damaged were no longer available, but shingles of similar color and texture were available, repair of a damaged roof with shingles similar in function, color, and shape to those damaged met the parameters of the policy language.[1032] On the other hand, some of the limestone panels on the façade of a church in the District of Columbia were damaged by an earthquake. The church was concerned that replacement panels would diminish the aesthetic qualities of the exterior because the new, unweathered panels could have noticeably different coloration than the remaining ones. It insisted that the insurer pay for a matching façade. The court agreed with the church and offered a hypothetical in support. Imagine, said the court, that an insurer pays for repairs to a single wall of a room. The paint color in the room—a light blue—is no longer manufactured. If the insurer were to insist on a bright red or even dark blue paint, albeit of the same quality and manufacture, for the one wall, no one, according to the court, would feel the insured had been made whole; "only repainting the whole room would do that," unless the policy had a pertinent exclusion.[1033]

The message of the cases interpreting "like kind and quality" or similar phrases is that the exact policy language and the specific facts of a particular claim can be critically important. Uniformity of appearance is especially important to common interest communities. When an association faces having to

1031. Maryland Motor Car Ins. Co. v. Smith, 254 S.W. 526, 528 (Tex. Civ. App. 1923). *See also* Siegle v. Progressive Consumers Ins. Co., 788 So. 2d 355, 360 (Fla. 4th DCA 2001) (repair with like kind and quality would require property to be restored to good condition with parts, equipment, and workmanship of same essential character, nature, and degree of excellence that previously existed; damaged vehicle may or may not be returned to its pre-accident market value, but return to market value is not what words "repair" with "like kind and quality" commonly connote).

1032. Greene v. United Servs. Auto. Ass'n, 936 A.2d 1178 (Pa. Super. 2007), *app. den.*, 598 Pa. 750, 954 A.2d 577, 2008 Pa. LEXIS 1801 (2008). *See also* Ocean View Towers Ass'n v. QBE Ins. Corp., 2011 U.S. Dist. LEXIS 147579 (S.D. Fla. Dec. 22, 2011) (policy provided coverage only for direct physical loss or damage and did not cover replacement of undamaged property to ensure "matching").

1033. Nat'l Presbyterian Church, Inc. v. GuideOne Mut. Ins. Co., 82 F. Supp. 3d 55, 59 (D.D.C. 2015). *See also* Cedar Bluff Townhome Condo. Ass'n v. Am. Family Mut. Ins. Co., 857 N.W.2d 290 (Minn. 2014) (plain meaning of "comparable material and quality" is material suitable for matching and, thus, phrase required less than identical color match, but reasonable color match nonetheless and because there was no reasonable color match available, all siding panels would have to be replaced).

replace undamaged components to maintain a uniform appearance, it is well advised to consider hiring an experienced public adjuster or insurance attorney early in the process. It is also advisable to have the phrase "like kind and quality" clearly explained in the policy to ensure no misunderstanding. The broker for the insured should seek language that provides for repairs and replacements to meet the standard of "uniformity of appearance."

§ 10.27 Valuation

The valuation clause determines the value of covered property in the event of loss or damage. There are significant differences between the valuation clauses in the BPP and in the CAC.

[1] Actual Cash Value

Both the BPP and CAC provide that the carrier will determine the value of covered property in the event of loss or damage at actual cash value (ACV) as of the time of loss or damage with certain exceptions.[1034] Actual cash value means repair or replacement cost less depreciation.[1035] It may include a contractor's overhead and profit when a contractor would reasonably be used to make repairs.[1036] Sales

1034. ISO Form CP 00 10 06 07, § E.7.a; ISO Form CP 00 17 06 07, § E.8.a. One exception under the BPP is for "stock" sold but not delivered. It will be paid at the selling price less discounts and expenses the insured otherwise would have had. This exception would rarely be applicable to a residential CIC.

1035. *See* Gilderman v. State Farm Ins. Co., 437 Pa. Super. 217, 226, 649 A.2d 941, 945 (1994). *See also* Mazzocki v. State Farm Fire & Cas. Corp., 1 A.D.3d 9, 13, 766 N.Y.S.2d 719, 722 (2003); Ghoman v. New Hampshire Ins. Co., 159 F. Supp. 2d 928, 934 (N.D. Tex. 2001) ("actual cash value" is synonymous with "fair market value," and Texas courts recognize replacement cost less depreciation as accepted method of calculating actual cash value); Elberon Bathing Co. v. Ambassador Ins. Co., 77 N.J. 1, 7, 9, 389 A.2d 439, 442–43 (1978) (appraisal based on replacement cost without consideration of depreciation does not measure actual cash value). *See generally* Parker, *Replacement Cost Coverage: A Legal Primer*, 34 Wake Forest L. Rev. 295 (1999) (actual cash value coverage, commonly referred to as basic coverage, recognizes that insurer is entitled to deduct reasonable depreciation from value of the loss); McCracken, *What Exactly Is Actual Cash Value? Better Yet, How Do You Calculate It?* (IRMI, Dec. 2007), available at: http://www.irmi.com/articles/expert-commentary/what-exactly-is-actual-cash-value (courts have defined ACV in one of three ways: replacement cost minus depreciation, fair market value, or according to "broad evidence" rule that combines first two definitions). Some policies may define "actual cash value" as "replacement cost less a deduction that reflects depreciation, age, condition and obsolescence." In *Whitehouse Condo. Group, LLC v. Cincinnati Ins. Co.*, 569 Fed. Appx. 413 (6th Cir. 2014), the court held that the term "obsolescence" does not include a decline in market value caused by factors external to the property itself.

1036. *See* Mills v. Foremost Ins. Co., 511 F.3d 1300, 1306 (11th Cir. 2008) (majority of courts have determined that actual cash value payment includes general contractor's overhead and profit charges in circumstances where policyholder would be reasonably likely to need general contractor in repairing or replacing damaged property in issue); Tritschler v. Allstate Ins. Co., 213 Ariz. 505, 144 P.3d 519 (Ariz. App. 2006); Gilderman v. State Farm Ins. Co., 437 Pa. Super. 217, 226, 649 A.2d 941, 945 (1994) (repair or replacement costs include any cost that insured is reasonably likely

tax on the value of building supplies will also generally be included in actual cash value.[1037]

A major insurer explains that depreciation is generally calculated by evaluating the replacement cost value of an item and its life expectancy and cautions that condition of an item may also be a factor in the depreciation calculation.[1038] One commentary says that using estimating software based on Internal Revenue Service depreciation rules, the insurance industry has developed depreciation rates for practically every item of property.[1039] The insured can ask for a copy of those depreciation schedules and can also obtain its own depreciation rates and tools and can develop a depreciation schedule for its major possessions before it has to make a claim. One advantage of hiring a public adjuster is that the adjuster will have depreciation schedules that can be used to compute depreciation. If the insured has no public adjuster, there are depreciation schedules available.[1040]

[2] Building Repairs or Replacement

The policies provide that in lieu of actual cash value, if the building limit of insurance satisfies the additional condition, and the coinsurance, and the cost to repair or replace the damaged building property is $2,500 or less, the carrier will pay the cost of building repairs or replacement.[1041] That does not include the increased cost attributable to enforcement of any ordinance or law regulating the construction, use, or repair of any property. Certain property, however, is always valued at the actual cash value even though it is attached to the building. That property is awnings or floor coverings; appliances for refrigerating, ventilating, cooking, dishwashing, or laundering; and outdoor equipment or furniture.

---

to incur in repairing or replacing covered loss and in some instances will include use of general contractor and his or her 20 percent overhead and profit). *Compare* McCracken, *What Exactly Is Actual Cash Value? Better Yet, How Do You Calculate It?* (IRMI, Dec. 2007), available at: http://www.irmi.com/articles/expert-commentary/what-exactly-is-actual-cash-value (noting that when calculating ACV, some insurers start with replacement cost, then deduct depreciation and then deduct another 20 percent for contractor's overhead and profit, but that courts have generally disapproved of that practice).

1037. Mills v. Foremost Ins. Co., 511 F.3d 1300, 1305 (11th Cir. 2008); Ghoman v. New Hampshire Ins. Co., 159 F. Supp. 2d 928, 934 (N.D. Tex. 2001).

1038. *See* https://www.travelers.com/claims/understanding-depreciation.aspx.

1039. *See* http://budgeting.thenest.com/insurance-companies-depreciate-things-24725.html.

1040. For example, a consumer advocacy group called United Policyholders provides a depreciation schedule at its website. *See* https://uphelp.org/wp-content/uploads/2020/09/UP-Depreciation-Schedule.pdf. *See also* http://www.claimspages.com/documents/docs/2001D.pdf.

1041. ISO Form CP 00 10 06 07, § E.7.b; ISO Form CP 00 17 06 07, § E.8.b. *See* Olde Colonial Vill. Condo. Council v. Millers Mut. Ins. Co., 2002 Del. Super. LEXIS 42 (Del. Super. Ct. Jan. 28, 2002) (terms "repair," "replace," and "rebuild" all concern returning something to its pre-loss condition, without improvement).

[3] Glass

As an exception to actual cash value, both policies will pay for glass at the cost of replacement with safety-glazing material *if required by law.*[1042] This clause does not require the carrier to cover the cost of replacement with "impact rated" glass, meaning glass that is high wind impact resistant.[1043]

[4] Tenant Improvements and Betterments

Only the BPP addresses valuation of tenant improvements and betterments.[1044] In general, an "improvement" is a valuable addition to property that is more than a repair or replacement.[1045] One creative definition of "improvements and betterments" is that if one were to turn a unit upside down, whatever falls would be personal property of the tenant, while whatever remains affixed would be improvements and betterments.[1046] The value of tenant improvements and betterments will be determined at actual cash value of the lost or damaged property if the insured makes repairs promptly.[1047] The value will be determined at a proportion of the insured's original cost if the insured does not make repairs promptly.[1048] The proportionate value is determined by multiplying the original cost by the number of days from the loss or damage to the expiration of the lease and dividing that amount by the number of days from the installation of improvements to the expiration of the lease. If the lease contains a renewal option, the expiration of the renewal option period will replace the expiration of the lease. The improvements and betterments will be valued at nothing if someone other than the insured pays for repairs or replacement.

1042. ISO Form CP 00 10 06 07, § E.7.d; ISO Form CP 00 17 06 07, § E.8.c.

1043. *See* Ocean View Towers Ass'n v. QBE Ins. Corp., 2011 U.S. Dist. LEXIS 147579 (S.D. Fla. Dec. 22, 2011). The association argued that under the valuation provision providing coverage for the cost of replacing glass with safety glazing material "as required by law," that in hurricane zones, windows and doors had to be replaced with impact rated glass, which may require windows and doors with safety glazing material. The insurer, however, contended that federal regulation requiring safety glazing on glass made clear that the safety glazing is different from high wind impact resistant glass. The purpose of safety glazing is to reduce or eliminate unreasonable risks of injury or death when glass is broken by human contact rather than by high winds. *See* 16 C.F.R. § 1201.1(a). The court agreed and found that the policy reference to safety glazing glass did not require the carrier to cover the cost of high wind impact resistant glass.

1044. ISO Form CP 00 10 06 07, § E.7.e.

1045. *See* Hillsboro Island House Condominium Apartments, Inc. v. Town of Hillsboro Beach, 263 So. 2d 209, 213 (Fla. 1972). *See also* Pinnacle Port Community Ass'n v. Orenstein, 952 F.2d 375, 378 (11th Cir. 1992) (work on walls not intended to enhance assumed value of property, but to restore walls to their original watertight state, was repair, not improvement).

1046. Lent, *Mind the Gap; Understanding Your Insurance Responsibilities* (Cooperator, Aug. 2012), available at: http://cooperator.com/articles/2461/1/Mind-the-Gap/Page1.html. *See also The Law Dictionary* (Anderson Publishing Co. 2002) ("betterment" is improvement to real property that renders it better than mere repairs would).

1047. ISO Form CP 00 10 06 07, § E.7.e.(1).

1048. ISO Form CP 00 10 06 07, § E.7.e.(2).

§ 10.28 Appraisal

An appraisal provision is a staple of property policies.[1049] Appraisal is a means of alternative dispute resolution designed to resolve differences over the amount owed on an insured loss.[1050] It is favored because it provides a means for prompt resolution of claims and discourages needless lawsuits.[1051] Appraisal is not appropriate when a claim has been denied in its entirety based on lack of coverage.[1052] Policies provide little guidance on the process. Extensive case law has, however, developed on the topic. Some issues that arise are whether appraisal is governed by the law of arbitration, what procedure is available for confirming an appraisal award in court, if an appraisal award can be challenged in court, and whether due process protections have to be afforded to the parties to an appraisal. A comprehensive review of these and other questions about appraisal is beyond the scope of this discussion. Fortunately, there are resources available that focus exclusively on the law of appraisal.[1053]

The appraisal process can prove very beneficial to the insured. For example, in one case concerning damage after a hurricane, the insurer paid only about $23,000 on the claim of a condominium association. The appraisal panel, however, issued an appraisal award totaling over $380,000. The insurer compensated the association for the difference between its initial payment and the appraisal award, and the court concluded that a jury could reasonably find that, given the discrepancy between the two amounts, the insurer acted in bad faith by intentionally "low balling" its calculation of damages.[1054]

1049. Law & Starinovich, *What Is It Worth? A Critical Analysis of Insurance Appraisal*, 13 Conn. Ins. L.J. 291, 292 (2006/2007) (virtually every property insurance policy contains provision specifying appraisal as means of dispute resolution).

1050. Parker, *Understanding the Insurance Policy Appraisal Clause: A Four-Step Program*, 37 U. Tol. L. Rev. 931 (2006). *See also* Smith, *Property Insurance Appraisal: Is Determining Causation Essential to Evaluating the Amount of Loss?*, 2012 J. Disp. Resol. 591, 593 (2012) (purpose of appraisal is to avoid litigation when insurer admits coverage and dispute between parties concerns only amount of value of loss).

1051. Fla. Ins. Guar. Ass'n v. Olympus Ass'n, 34 So. 3d 791, 794 (Fla. 4th DCA 2010).

1052. *See, e.g.*, Oceania I Condo Ass'n v. QBE Ins. Corp., 2011 U.S. Dist. LEXIS 54256 (S.D. Fla. May 20, 2011) (where insurer declared policy void, there was no covered claim and therefore the parties could not disagree over amount of any covered claim and appraisal was not appropriate). *But see* Cypress Chase Condo. Ass'n "A" v. QBE Ins. Corp., 2013 U.S. Dist. LEXIS 40347 (S.D. Fla. Mar. 22, 2013) (*Oceania I* does not imply that suit to compel appraisal automatically fails once insurer denies coverage).

1053. *See* Wilkofsky, *The Law and Procedure of Insurance Appraisal* (3d ed. Ditmas Park Legal Publishing, Ltd., 2014). There are also some excellent law review articles on the topic. *See, e.g.*, Smith, *Property Insurance Appraisal: Is Determining Causation Essential to Evaluating the Amount of Loss?*, 2012 J. Disp. Resol. 591 (2012); Law & Starinovich, *What Is It Worth? A Critical Analysis of Insurance Appraisal*, 13 Conn. Ins. L.J. 291 (2006/2007); Parker, *Understanding the Insurance Policy Appraisal Clause: A Four-Step Program*, 37 U. Tol. L. Rev. 931 (2006).

1054. Fox Haven of Foxfire Condo. IV Ass'n v. Nationwide Mut. Fire Ins. Co., 2015 U.S. Dist. LEXIS 18758 (M.D. Fla. Feb. 17, 2015). The insurer concluded it would cost approximately $87,000 to repair building damage and about $31,000 to repair damage to appurtenant structures

[1] Language of Standard Appraisal Clauses

The language of appraisal clauses has become fairly standardized, although there are some variations in their wording.[1055] They almost all state that if the carrier and policyholder disagree on the value of the property or the amount of loss,[1056] either one may make a written demand for an appraisal of the loss.[1057] The policy language does not require the written demand for appraisement to include a request for appointment of a competent and impartial appraiser, but it is recommended that it do so.[1058] It is also suggested that a formal written notice of demand be sent by registered or certified mail, return receipt requested.[1059]

When the appraisal clause is invoked, each party selects a "competent and impartial" appraiser and they, in turn, select an umpire. If the appraisers selected by the parties cannot agree on an umpire, either may request that the selection be made by a judge of a court having jurisdiction.[1060] Courts may also impose guidelines for the appraisal process.[1061] The appraisers separately state the value of the property and amount of the loss, and if they fail to agree, they submit their differences to the umpire[1062] and a decision agreed to by any two of the three is

such as carports. However, it also decided that only 20 percent of the building damage was a result of the hurricane and after accounting for deductibles and depreciation, it found the association was owed a cash payment of $23,579.25. While finding there was a basis for a bad faith claim, the court nonetheless granted the insurer summary judgment on the association's demand for punitive damages because the evidence could not in its estimation lead a reasonable jury to conclude the insurer knowingly "low balled" property insurance claims as part of its *general business practice.*

1055. *See* Law & Starinovich, *What Is It Worth? A Critical Analysis of Insurance Appraisal*, 13 Conn. Ins. L.J. 291, 295 (2006/2007).

1056. *See* GlenBrook Patiohome, Owners Ass'n v. Lexington Ins. Co., 2011 U.S. Dist. LEXIS 14556 (S.D. Tex. Feb. 14, 2011) (dispute over applying policy terms to covered loss, as opposed to one over amount of covered loss, does not trigger appraisal right).

1057. *See, e.g.*, ISO Form CP 00 10 06 07, § E.2; CP 00 17 06 07, § E.2. when insurers "demand" appraisal, there are some general rules it is suggested they follow. *See* Cozen, *Insuring Real Property*, § 30.03[3][a] (Matthew Bender & Co. 2015) (carrier is probably well advised to phrase demand letter as exercise of right to initiate appraisal proceedings to avoid harshness of "demand" and ambiguity of "request" and to avoid asserting that loss is sum certain).

1058. Parker, *Understanding the Insurance Policy Appraisal Clause: A Four-Step Program*, 37 U. Tol. L. Rev. 931, 944 (2006).

1059. Cozen, *Insuring Real Property*, § 30.03[3][a] (Matthew Bender & Co. 2015).

1060. *See, e.g.*, State Farm Fla. Ins. Co. v. Seville Place Condo. Ass'n, 74 So. 3d 105 (Fla. 3d DCA 2011), *rev. dis.*, 91 So. 3d 133 (Fla. 2012) (noting that trial court ordered parties to appraisal and ultimately appointed neutral umpire to conduct appraisal with each party's designated appraiser).

1061. *See, e.g.*, Auto-Owners Ins. Co. v. Summit Park Townhome Ass'n, 2015 U.S. Dist. LEXIS 120714 (D. Colo. Sept. 10, 2015).

1062. Parker, *Understanding the Insurance Policy Appraisal Clause: A Four-Step Program*, 37 U. Tol. L. Rev. 931, 947 (2006) (policy language does not require appraisers to concur in summoning umpire to settle their differences; whenever disagreement arises between appraisers and that disagreement comes to attention of umpire, latter becomes qualified to act, but where umpire purports to act absent differences between appraisers, any award is invalid).

binding on the parties.[1063] Each party pays its chosen appraiser and bears the other expenses of the appraisal and umpire equally.[1064] Finally, policies state that when there is an appraisal, the carrier retains its right to deny the claim.[1065]

The language of the standard appraisal clause does not address when appraisal has to be invoked, and it would appear that there is no obligation to demand appraisal at the time of the incident at issue, prior to filing suit,[1066] or at any other time.[1067] However, the right to appraisal has to be exercised within a reasonable period, and courts will find an insurer has waived the right to appraisal when it is not timely invoked.[1068]

Policies typically provide in a loss payment clause that the insurer will pay for a covered loss to covered property within a prescribed number of days after it

---

1063. *Consider* Citizens Prop. Ins. Corp. v. Mango Hill #6 Condo. Ass'n, 117 So. 3d 1226, 1227, n.1 (Fla. 3d DCA 2013) (phrase "appraisal award" is misnomer because appraisal panel determines only amount of loss, not entitlement of insured to any damages).

1064. *See* Citizens Prop. Ins. Corp. v. River Oaks Condo. II Ass'n, 190 So. 3d 1110, 1112 (Fla. 2d DCA 2016) (where trial court awarded to association various expenses and fees in appraisal process as taxable costs, appellate court reversed because under policy association was required to pay its own appraiser and bear equal share of umpire and other appraisal expenses). *Compare* Sands on the Ocean Condo. Ass'n v. QBE Ins. Corp., 2012 U.S. Dist. LEXIS 177380 (S.D. Fla., Dec. 14, 2012) (rejecting argument by insurer that because policy provides each party will pay its chosen appraiser and bear appraisal costs, association was not entitled to taxation of costs pursuant to federal rule; governing provision for taxation of costs was rule and statute, not policy).

1065. *See* Paradise Plaza Condo. Ass'n v. Reinsurance Corp., 685 So. 2d 937 (Fla. 3d DCA 1996) (reservation of right to contest coverage does not render damage appraisal clause void for lack of mutuality; when carrier invokes appraisal clause it does not waive its right subsequently to deny coverage under policy).

1066. *See, e.g.*, Laredo Landing Owners Ass'n v. Sequoia Ins. Co., 2015 U.S. Dist. LEXIS 75104 (D. Colo. June 10, 2015) (where insurer first demanded appraisal less than two months after association filed suit against it, and then about five months later moved to compel appraisal, despite fact that parties appeared to discuss propriety of appraisal for some time, insurer continued to assert its right to demand appraisal and, thus, mere assertion by association that experts had been consulted and monies spent was insufficient to establish unreasonable delay or undue prejudice necessary to find insurer waived its rights under appraisal provision). *See also* GlenBrook Patiohome, Owners Ass'n v. Lexington Ins. Co., 2011 U.S. Dist. LEXIS 14556 (S.D. Tex. Feb. 14, 2011) (insurer may compel appraisal after insured files suit, as long as insurer has not otherwise waived right to appraisal).

1067. Royal Marco Point 1 Condo. Ass'n v. QBE Ins. Corp., 2007 U.S. Dist. LEXIS 60940 (M.D. Fla. Aug. 14, 2007) (insurer did not waive right to appraisal because it waited for 512 days to file its motion to compel). *Accord* Bullard Bldg. Condo. Ass'n, Inc. v. Travelers Prop. Cas. Co. of Am., 2006 U.S. Dist. LEXIS 70674 (M.D. Fla. Sept. 25, 2006).

1068. Law & Starinovich, *What Is It Worth? A Critical Analysis of Insurance Appraisal*, 13 Conn. Ins. L.J. 291, 311 (2006/2007). The authors note that some policies specify a time period in which a demand has to be made, for example 60 days after proof of loss, while others do not and questions of waiver then turn on findings of reasonableness and lack of prejudice. *See, e.g.*, GlenBrook Patiohome, Owners Ass'n v. Lexington Ins. Co., 2011 U.S. Dist. LEXIS 14556 (S.D. Tex. Feb. 14, 2011) (contractual right to appraisal may be waived when delay is long enough to show an intention to yield known right; when policy does not specify deadline for demanding appraisal, demand has to be made within reasonable time from point at which insurer is on notice that there is disagreement over amount of damages, that is, point of impasse with insured).

receives the sworn proof of loss if the insured has complied with the policy and an appraisal award has been made.[1069] Even though the policy may also say that the insurer will not pay for losses until they are incurred, the loss payment clause can serve to override that limitation.[1070]

[2] Statutory Requirements

Some states have statutes that govern appraisal. These statutes may mandate that policies contain an appraisal clause and prescribe its contents.[1071] Others set forth a procedure for appointment of an umpire.[1072] Under a Florida statute, insurers are required to notify insureds of the right to participate in a mediation program and if they fail to do so, the insured is not required to submit to or participate in any contractual loss appraisal process of the property loss damage as a precondition to legal action for breach of contract.[1073] In one case an insurer brought an action for appointment of a neutral umpire, but it had failed to notify the insured condominium association of the right to mediation. The association counterclaimed, and the insurer argued any counterclaim was barred because the association had not complied with all the policy terms, specifically the appraisal provision. The association countered that the insurer was not entitled to enforce the appraisal provision of the contract because it never notified it of its right to participate in the mediation program. The court held that pursuant to the statute, the association had the right to bring its counterclaims without having participated in the appraisal process.[1074]

[3] Appraisal Compared to Arbitration

Although appraisal is generally thought to be less formal than arbitration,[1075] many courts treat it as arbitration subject to the state's arbitration laws.[1076] In

---

1069. ISO Form CP 00 17 06 07, § E.4.g.(2).

1070. *See, e.g.*, Three Palms Pointe, Inc. v. State Farm Fire & Cas. Co., 250 F. Supp. 2d 1357, 1365 (M.D. Fla. 2003). *Compare* Fla. Ins. Guar. Ass'n v. Somerset Homeowners Ass'n, 83 So. 3d 850 (Fla. 4th DCA 2011) (rejecting association argument that under doctrine of prevention of performance, it was excused from the contractual obligation to complete repairs before receipt of payment because of delay in payment of appraisal award).

1071. *See, e.g.*, Va. Code § 38.2-2105.

1072. *See, e.g.*, Mass. G. L. c. 175, § 100.

1073. Fla. Stat. § 627.7015(7).

1074. QBE Ins. Corp. v. Dome Condo. Ass'n, 577 F. Supp. 2d 1256 (S.D. Fla. 2008).

1075. Law & Starinovich, *What Is It Worth? A Critical Analysis of Insurance Appraisal*, 13 Conn. Ins. L.J. 291, 298 (2006/2007).

1076. *See, e.g.*, QBE Ins. Corp. v. Twin Homes of French Ridge Homeowners Ass'n, 778 N.W.2d 393, 398 (2010) (appraisal decisions are subject to Minnesota arbitration statutes); Stratford W. Homeowners Ass'n v. Country Mut. Ins. Co., 273 Ill. Dec. 33, 338 Ill. App. 3d 288, 291, 788 N.E.2d 342, 343 (2003) (appraisal provision was essentially arbitration clause and Uniform Arbitration Act applied); Devonwood Condominium Owners Ass'n v. Farmers Ins. Exchange, 162 Cal. App. 4th 1498, 77 Cal. Rptr. 3d 88 (2008) (generally, appraisal award proceedings are subject to arbitration provisions of California Arbitration Act); Louise Gardens of Encino Homeowners'

New York, on the other hand, a statute provides that appraisal is not arbitration.[1077] In a jurisdiction in which appraisal is considered arbitration, the Federal Arbitration Act will govern when the policies involve interstate commerce.[1078] One consequence of an appraisal provision being treated as an agreement to arbitrate is that the procedural and substantive rules applied to arbitration are considerably stricter than those otherwise applicable to appraisal.[1079]

[4] Preconditions to Appraisal

The purpose of an appraisal is to resolve a "disagreement"; therefore, a federal court refused to order appraisal where no disagreement existed between the parties when a condominium association filed the case and failed to demonstrate that the parties met the procedural requirements before it demanded appraisal.[1080] Appraisal is appropriate only if the insured has complied with its post-loss obligations.[1081] An insurer is not obligated to go to an appraisal where the insured fails to comply with its post-loss obligations. Where, for example, a condominium association did not respond to requests from the insurer's adjuster for additional documents and reinspection of the property,

---

Ass'n, Inc. v. Truck Ins. Exchange, Inc., 82 Cal. App. 4th 648, 658, 98 Cal. Rptr. 2d 378, 385 (Cal. App. 2d Dist. 2000) (agreement to conduct appraisal contained in policy of insurance is considered to be arbitration agreement subject to arbitration law). *See also* Laredo Landing Owners Ass'n v. Sequoia Ins. Co., 2015 U.S. Dist. LEXIS 75104 (D. Colo. June 10, 2015) (appraisal process is properly "classified as an arbitration" under Colorado Uniform Arbitration Act); Royal Marco Point 1 Condo. Ass'n v. QBE Ins. Corp., 2007 U.S. Dist. LEXIS 60940 (M.D. Fla. Aug. 14, 2007) (in Florida, appraisal clauses in insurances polices have generally been treated as arbitration provisions). *See generally* Law & Starinovich, *What Is It Worth? A Critical Analysis of Insurance Appraisal*, 13 Conn. Ins. L.J. 291, 297 (2006/2007) (courts often compare appraisal to arbitration, and it may be considered type of arbitration, "akin" to arbitration, or fundamentally different from arbitration).

1077. N.Y. Insurance Law § 3408(c) (appraisal shall proceed pursuant to terms of applicable appraisal clause of insurance policy and not as arbitration).

1078. Law & Starinovich, *What Is It Worth? A Critical Analysis of Insurance Appraisal*, 13 Conn. Ins. L.J. 291, 301 (2006/2007).

1079. Parker, *Understanding the Insurance Policy Appraisal Clause: A Four-Step Program*, 37 U. Tol. L. Rev. 931, 935 (2006).

1080. Cypress Chase Condo. Ass'n "A" v. QBE Ins. Corp., 2011 U.S. Dist. LEXIS 41104 (S.D. Fla. Apr. 15, 2011). *See also* Avila Condo. Ass'n v. QBE Ins. Corp., 2011 U.S. Dist. LEXIS 159461 (S.D. Fla. June 28, 2011) (where "disagreement" between association and insurer was unilateral, it was insufficient to trigger appraisal; complaint was, in essence, first request for appraisal). *Compare* 200 Leslie Condo. Ass'n v. QBE Ins. Corp., 2011 U.S. Dist. LEXIS 65720 (S.D. Fla. June 21, 2011) (at some point complete failure by insurer to respond to assertion of insured contesting valuation by insurer and to demand compliance with pre-appraisal obligations has to act as implicit "disagreement" under policy, otherwise, insurers could always avoid appraisal by simply ignoring demands for it).

1081. Biscayne Cove Condo. Ass'n v. QBE Ins. Corp., 951 F. Supp. 2d 1292, 1301 (S.D. Fla. 2013). *See also* Citizens Prop. Ins. Corp. v. Admiralty House, Inc., 66 So. 3d 342, 344 (Fla. 2d DCA 2011) (before court can compel appraisal, it has to make preliminary determination as to whether demand for appraisal is ripe).

did not submit a proper proof of loss,[1082] and did not submit to an examination under oath, the insurer was not obligated to go to appraisal because the association materially breached the policy by failing to comply with its post-loss obligations.[1083]

[5] Pre-Appraisal Agreement

After the parties decide to submit to appraisal, they may enter into a separate appraisal agreement that may specify the loss to be appraised or may clarify the procedures of the process.[1084] Neither party is obligated to enter such an agreement. "The agreement for an appraisal is found in the policy itself . . ." and no other agreement "is necessary or permissible unless consented to by both parties."[1085]

The parties might also reach a pre-appraisal agreement that settles the amount due and is, in effect, an accord and satisfaction. That should override any appraisal if the agreement is valid and binding. Whether the agreement is enforceable is a question for the court because it raises a claim not encompassed by the appraisal clause and is a one that appraisers are ill-equipped to decide.[1086]

1082. *Compare* Condos. of Shenandoah Place v. SECURA Ins., 2016 U.S. Dist. LEXIS 18608 (D. Minn. Feb. 16, 2016) (insurer provided no case law to support contention that year delay would rise to sufficient prejudicial level as to render appraisal inappropriate and pointed to no policy language specifying specific time period within which insured had to report claim and without more, delay was not prejudicial as matter of law).

1083. Biscayne Cove Condo. Ass'n v. QBE Ins. Corp., 971 F. Supp. 2d 1121 (S.D. Fla. 2013). The court did not determine whether, under Florida law, the insurer had to bear the burden of showing prejudice, but found that in any event the insurer had met that burden. *See also* 200 Leslie Condo. Ass'n v. QBE Ins. Corp., 965 F. Supp. 2d 1386, 1401–02 (S.D. Fla. 2013), *aff'd*, 616 Fed. Appx. 936 (11th Cir. 2015) (before appraisal can be invoked, insured must comply with post-loss conditions; where insured association breached inventory, proof of loss, and examination under oath policy requirements, it had burden to show that insurer was not prejudiced by its failure to comply and because it did not carry its burden of showing prejudice, it could not avoid conditions precedent to appraisal with which it did not comply); Citizens Prop. Ins. Corp. v. Mango Hill Condo. Ass'n 12, 54 So. 3d 578 (Fla. 3d DCA 2011) (insured must comply with all policy post-loss obligations before appraisal clause is triggered; reversing order compelling appraisal and remanding for evidentiary hearing on whether association sufficiently complied with post-loss requirements).

1084. Law & Starinovich, *What Is It Worth? A Critical Analysis of Insurance Appraisal*, 13 Conn. Ins. L.J. 291, 317 (2006/2007) (agreement may provide for hearing to be attended by both appraisers and umpire, for evidence and testimony to be taken, and for submission of preliminary memoranda by parties). *See also* Smith, *Property Insurance Appraisal: Is Determining Causation Essential to Evaluating the Amount of Loss?*, 2012 J. Disp. Resol. 591, 605 (2012) (to avoid limited utility of appraisal, parties can prepare and agree on Memorandum of Appraisal containing questions to be appraised, procedure of appraisal, and any other issues that will facilitate fair and efficient appraisal process).

1085. Pennsylvania Lumbermens Mut. Fire Ins. Co. v. Barfield, 138 F.2d 365, 366 (5th Cir. 1943). *See also* Brethren Mut. Ins. Co. v. Filsinger, 54 Md. App. 357, 364, 458 A.2d 880, 884 (1983).

1086. Citizens Prop. Ins. Corp. v. River Manor Condo. Ass'n, 125 So. 3d 846 (Fla. 4th DCA 2013).

The attorney who represents a common interest community in community association law matters may well be unfamiliar with the issues addressed by a pre-appraisal agreement and the full implications of its contents and should, therefore, consult with an attorney who specializes in insurance matters.

[6] Court-Ordered Appraisal

The appraisal clause is part of the contract between the carrier and policyholder. Therefore, if one party demands appraisal as provided for in the policy and the other party fails to comply, an action to compel compliance can be brought.[1087] The court generally has to determine that post-loss obligations have been met before it can compel appraisal.[1088]

Where an insured litigates other issues, it may waive its right to appraisal. For example, in one case an association litigated a case for 16 months before seeking to stay the litigation and obtain appraisal. The court said a party that fails to seek appraisal within a reasonable time after the beginning of the litigation waives its appraisal right by acting in a manner inconsistent with that right.[1089] In another case, a court denied summary judgment to a condominium association seeking a declaratory judgment that it was entitled to appraisal where the insurer asserted the affirmative defense of fraud, misrepresentation, or concealment. The court said that if the insurer was able to carry its burden of proof on the affirmative defense at trial, the association would not be entitled to appraisal.[1090]

In general, the policyholder has to demand an appraisal before seeking a court order compelling appraisal. The insurer has to be given an opportunity to investigate the claim and adjust its estimate. Without that opportunity, appraisal

---

1087. Smith, *Property Insurance Appraisal: Is Determining Causation Essential to Evaluating the Amount of Loss?*, 2012 J. Disp. Resol. 591, 594 (2012) (if party refuses to enter appraisal, other party may employ courts to compel appraisal; to compel appraisal, demand for it has to be ripe, meaning that parties have complied with post-loss requirements of policy). *See also* Law & Starinovich, *What Is It Worth? A Critical Analysis of Insurance Appraisal*, 13 Conn. Ins. L.J. 291, 312–13 (2006/2007) (parties can generally compel appraisal in jurisdictions that apply arbitration law to appraisal provisions, but rules are not as predictable in those that distinguish between arbitration and appraisal).

1088. Cypress Chase Condo. Ass'n "A" v. QBE Ins. Corp., 2013 U.S. Dist. LEXIS 40347 (S.D. Fla. Mar. 22, 2013) (adequacy of compliance by association with its post-loss obligations had to be determined before court could compel appraisal).

1089. Summit Towers Condo. Ass'n v. QBE Ins. Corp., 2012 U.S. Dist. LEXIS 59504 (S.D. Fla. Apr. 5, 2012) (court found itself "hard pressed to imagine" situation where party could act more inconsistently with right to seek appraisal). *See also* Cypress Pointe at Lake Orlando Condo. Ass'n v. Mt. Hawley Ins. Co., 2012 U.S. Dist. LEXIS 175268 (M.D. Fla. Nov. 19, 2012) (even if insurer admitted coverage, association waived its right to appraisal by engaging in extensive litigation and failing to seek appraisal until roughly three months before trial); Bullard Bldg. Condo. Ass'n, Inc. v. Travelers Prop. Cas. Co. of Am., 2006 U.S. Dist. LEXIS 70674 (M.D. Fla. Sept. 25, 2006) (while right to appraisal may be waived if party maintains position inconsistent with appraisal remedy, considering relatively short time case had been pending, insurer effectively made prompt invocation of its appraisal rights).

1090. Biscayne Cove Condo. Ass'n v. QBE Ins. Corp., 951 F. Supp. 2d 1292 (S.D. Fla. 2013).

is premature. For example, a condominium association filed suit and the following day sent the insurer a letter stating its disagreement with the assessment of its loss and demanding the dispute be resolved through appraisal. The court concluded that the association did not notify its insurer before it filed suit and, therefore, at that time its demand for appraisal was premature. However, the association subsequently filed an amended complaint. In the two years between the time the association demanded an appraisal and it filed its amended complaint, the insurer, said the court, failed to respond to the demand and that satisfied the disagreement prerequisite required to render the appraisal provision operative.[1091]

The appraisal clause may be invoked when there is a *disagreement* between the parties. There has to be a "real difference in fact," arising from an honest effort between the parties to agree.[1092] The policyholder seeking an order compelling appraisal, therefore, may have to establish that there is a disagreement between the parties before a court will order the insurer to comply with the appraisal clause. For example, a condominium association sought a declaration by a court that hurricane damage to its glass windows and sliding glass doors had to be resolved through the appraisal process it had invoked. The insurer argued that because the association never disputed how its claim was handled and the claim for the purported damage to glass windows or sliding glass door had yet to be denied, an actual dispute between the parties had yet to arise. The court noted that the association claimed the insurer *did not consider* glass windows and sliding doors when it determined the amount of the damage. Failure to consider, said the court, is not the same as denial of a claim. Thus, the insurer never received notice of any dispute about coverage for damage to glass windows and sliding glass doors and without a disagreement, the demand for appraisal was premature. The court said an insured has to meet the post-loss obligations stated in the policy before compelling appraisal, although it conceded that at some point, lack of response to an attempt to fulfill those obligations can result in a *de facto* disagreement between the parties.[1093]

1091. Seagate Towers Condo. Ass'n v. QBE Ins. Corp., 2012 U.S. Dist. LEXIS 188462 (S.D. Fla. Nov. 16, 2012). *See also* Biscayne Cove Condo. Ass'n v. QBE Ins. Corp., 2013 U.S. Dist. LEXIS 5194 (S.D. Fla. Jan. 14, 2013).

1092. Wilshire Condo. Ass'n v. QBE Ins. Corp., 2011 U.S. Dist. LEXIS 157457 (S.D. Fla. Sept. 9, 2011). *See also* Garden-Aire Vill. South Condo. Ass'n v. QBE Ins. Corp., 591 Fed. Appx. 868 (11th Cir. 2014) (when association filed suit seeking to compel appraisal, it had no pending claim with insurer and there was no pending disagreement about amount of loss and association, by failing to cooperate in investigation, prevented insurer from reaching agreement on loss; therefore, lower court properly rejected demand for appraisal); Citizens Prop. Ins. Corp. v. Galeria Villas Condo. Ass'n, 48 So. 3d 188 (Fla. 3d DCA 2010) (until conditions—including providing requested documents are met—and insurer has reasonable opportunity to investigate and adjust claim, there is no "disagreement" regarding value of property or amount of loss; only when there is real difference in fact, arising out of actual and honest effort to reach agreement between parties, is appraisal warranted).

1093. Ocean E. Apts., Inc. v. QBE Ins. Corp., 2011 U.S. Dist. LEXIS 157454 (S.D. Fla. Sept. 9, 2011). *See also* 200 Leslie Condo. Ass'n v. QBE Ins. Corp., 2011 U.S. Dist. LEXIS 65720 (S.D.

[7] Competent and Impartial Appraiser

The standard language of appraisal clauses says each party is to select a "competent and impartial" appraiser. Policies do not define "competent." "Competency requires only that individuals have the knowledge and experience to make an intelligent judgment concerning the amount of loss."[1094] It may be developed from extensive experience adjusting or appraising losses.[1095]

Questions are frequently raised about the impartiality of appraisers,[1096] and ironically the very experience that makes one competent to act as an appraiser can arguably be grounds for disqualification because that proficiency will necessarily be gained by working for policyholders or the insurance industry.[1097] Thus, appraisers are challenged based how often they may have worked for the carrier that is a party to the appraisal or the percentage of their income that is derived from that company.[1098]

Another ground for challenging the impartiality of an appraiser is that he or she is remunerated on a contingency basis.[1099] For example, a condominium association hired a public adjuster. The contract between the association and the adjuster allowed the adjuster to collect a percentage of the recovered claim on the policy. The association requested appraisal and nominated the adjuster as its appraiser. The insurer moved to strike, arguing the adjuster lacked impartiality because he had what amounted to a contingency fee–based contract with the

Fla. June 21, 2011) (at some point complete failure by insurer to respond to assertion of insured contesting valuation by insurer and to demand compliance with pre-appraisal obligations has to act as implicit "disagreement" under policy, otherwise, insurers could always avoid appraisal by simply ignoring demands for it). *And see* Wilshire Condo. Ass'n v. QBE Ins. Corp., 2011 U.S. Dist. LEXIS 157457 (S.D. Fla. Sept. 9, 2011), where the court dismissed without prejudice the association's request for a declaratory judgment requiring that the insurer participate in an appraisal, but noting that the insurer had failed to participate with the association to fulfill any post-loss obligations. The court expressed concern that the appraisal process being turned "upside-down" by a situation in which an insured would be unable to invoke appraisal without first completing post-loss obligations, but would be unable to complete those obligations because the insurer chose to never respond to the requests from the insured.

1094. Law & Starinovich, *What Is It Worth? A Critical Analysis of Insurance Appraisal*, 13 Conn. Ins. L.J. 291, 318 (2006/2007).

1095. Parker, *Understanding the Insurance Policy Appraisal Clause: A Four-Step Program*, 37 U. Tol. L. Rev. 931, 939 (2006).

1096. Law & Starinovich, *What Is It Worth? A Critical Analysis of Insurance Appraisal*, 13 Conn. Ins. L.J. 291, 318 (2006/2007)

1097. Parker, *Understanding the Insurance Policy Appraisal Clause: A Four-Step Program*, 37 U. Tol. L. Rev. 931, 939 (2006).

1098. Law & Starinovich, *What Is It Worth? A Critical Analysis of Insurance Appraisal*, 13 Conn. Ins. L.J. 291, 318 (2006/2007).

1099. Parker, *Understanding the Insurance Policy Appraisal Clause: A Four-Step Program*, 37 U. Tol. L. Rev. 931, 942 (2006) (manner in which appraisers are compensated has been fertile soil for issue of whether appraiser is disinterested or impartial, specifically whether payment of appraiser on contingency fee basis constitutes interest that disqualifies appraiser or justifies setting aside award).

association and had, therefore, a financial interest in the outcome and a motive to inflate the amount of the loss. The court agreed and granted the motion.[1100]

Whether a court may remove an umpire is another matter. In a Louisiana federal case, a condominium association argued the umpire was biased and incompetent and should be removed by the court. The court said it was unclear whether it had the authority to remove an umpire during an ongoing appraisal process but that if the court were to take that action, it would be necessary for the association to identify some evidence that the umpire had acted in a biased or prejudiced manner. It had not done so, and furthermore, the umpire had not refused to resolve a dispute but had only declined to determine it in the precise manner the association would have liked. The court concluded that the position of the umpire appeared to be entirely consistent with the appraisal process set forth by the policy, and the process, therefore, had to be permitted to run its course.[1101]

[8] Causation and Appraisal

The typical appraisal clause provides that the process is to be used to resolve disputes over the value of the property or the amount of loss.[1102] Can causation be determined in the process?[1103] The courts are divided over that question, and many are yet to address it.[1104] Generally, courts agree that appraisal may not resolve questions of coverage.[1105] Some also say appraisers may not determine

1100. Chardonnay Vill. Condo. Ass'n v. James River Ins. Co., 2008 U.S. Dist. LEXIS 59989 (E.D. La. Aug. 6, 2008). The court noted that while the contract between the adjuster and the association quoted an hourly rate, it also included an alternative percentage of recovery formula and, therefore, more closely resembled a contingency fee contract that impermissibly renders the adjuster a partial, interested party.

1101. Carriage Court Condo. Owners Ass'n v. State Farm Fire & Cas. Co., 2009 U.S. Dist. LEXIS 51379 (E.D. La. May 28, 2009).

1102. GlenBrook Patiohome, Owners Ass'n v. Lexington Ins. Co., 2011 U.S. Dist. LEXIS 14556 (S.D. Tex. Feb. 14, 2011) (appraiser must decide amount of loss, not construe policy or decide whether insurer should pay).

1103. *See* Law & Starinovich, *What Is It Worth? A Critical Analysis of Insurance Appraisal*, 13 Conn. Ins. L.J. 291, 296 (2006/2007) (whether issues of causation are subject to appraisal is recurring question).

1104. Smith, *Property Insurance Appraisal: Is Determining Causation Essential to Evaluating the Amount of Loss?*, 2012 J. Disp. Resol. 591, 592 (2012). The article provides an appendix with a chart showing the position of each jurisdiction on the question of whether causation can be determined in appraisal.

1105. *See, e.g.*, Auto-Owners Ins. Co. v. Summit Park Townhome Ass'n, 100 F. Supp. 3d 1099 (D. Colo. 2015) (determination of whether policy requires insurer to pay to replace undamaged property in order to achieve visual consistency constitutes coverage issue beyond scope of appraisal although appraisal should address cost of replacing undamaged property to achieve matching and separately calculate and identify disputed costs so that court can either include or exclude them once it has determined whether policy provides coverage); Trout Brook South Condo. Ass'n v. Harleysville Worcester Ins. Co., 995 F. Supp. 2d 1035, 1041 (D. Minn. 2014) (in Minnesota coverage questions are not for appraisers); Citizens Prop. Ins. Corp. v. River Manor Condo. Ass'n, 125 So. 3d 846 (Fla. 4th DCA 2013) (appraisers determine amount of the loss, including calculating cost of repair or replacement of property damaged and ascertaining how much of damage was caused by

causation.[1106] The trend, however, appears to favor allowing causation to be determined in appraisal.[1107] It is important to carefully review the applicable case law in a given jurisdiction because there are nuances.[1108] For example, Florida has developed a "dual-track approach" under which causation is an issue for the court when the insurer maintains there is no covered loss, but when the insurer admits there is at least some covered loss, but disagrees with the insured over the amount of that loss, appraisal is appropriate to determine causation issues.[1109]

---

covered peril as opposed to excluded causes; court decides all coverage matters). *Compare* QBE Ins. Corp. v. Twin Homes of French Ridge Homeowners Ass'n, 778 N.W.2d 393 (Minn. 2010) (finding appraisal panel did not exceed its authority by making improper coverage determination, rather than valuation determination of amount of loss, when it awarded total roof replacement based on wear and tear and unavailability of roofing shingles that were used on original roof).

1106. *See, e.g.*, Caribbean I Owners' Ass'n v. Great Am. Ins. Co., 619 F. Supp. 2d 1178 (S.D. Ala. 2008) (under Alabama law appraisers cannot decide issues of causation; questions of coverage and liability should be decided only by courts, not appraisers; estimate of cost to repair building, including costs related to alleged construction deficiencies from original construction, could not be subject to appraisal). *See generally* Smith, *Property Insurance Appraisal: Is Determining Causation Essential to Evaluating the Amount of Loss?*, 2012 J. Disp. Resol. 591, 597 (2012) (most courts that prohibit appraisal process from determining causation focus on policy language); Parker, *Understanding the Insurance Policy Appraisal Clause: A Four-Step Program*, 37 U. Tol. L. Rev. 931, 946 (2006) (courts construe language of appraisal clauses to preclude appraisers from resolving issues pertaining to coverage, liability, causation, and exclusions).

1107. Auto-Owners Ins. Co. v. Summit Park Townhome Ass'n, 100 F. Supp. 3d 1099 (D. Colo. 2015) (plain meaning of "amount of loss" incorporates concept of causation; one purpose of appraisal is to avoid litigation and encourage settlement, and declining to allow appraisers to consider causation would significantly undermine that purpose); N. Glenn Homeowners Ass'n v. State Farm Fire & Cas. Co., 854 N.W.2d 67 (Iowa App. 2014) (causation is integral part of definition of loss, without consideration of which appraisers cannot perform their assigned function; during appraisal process, appraisers may consider what damage was caused by hail, and what damage was not, or damage with which they are unconcerned, for example, normal wear and tear, and once appraisers conclude their work, issue of coverage may be further litigated and causation determinations by appraisers may be subject to further review by court). *See also* Condos. of Shenandoah Place v. SECURA Ins., 2016 U.S. Dist. LEXIS 18608 (D. Minn. Feb. 16, 2016) (determination of amount of loss under appraisal clause necessarily includes determination of causation). *See generally* Smith, *Property Insurance Appraisal: Is Determining Causation Essential to Evaluating the Amount of Loss?*, 2012 J. Disp. Resol. 591, 599–600 (2012), discussing justifications developed by courts for permitting causation to be determined in appraisal.

1108. *See, e.g.*, N. Glenn Homeowners Ass'n v. State Farm Fire & Cas. Co., 854 N.W.2d 67 (Iowa App. 2014) (judicial determination of coverage need not be made before appraisal is conducted; where party has demanded appraisal, process should go forward with other judicial determinations waiting until after process has been completed). *See also* GlenBrook Patiohome, Owners Ass'n v. Lexington Ins. Co., 2011 U.S. Dist. LEXIS 14556 (S.D. Tex. Feb. 14, 2011) (often, litigation is stayed while appraisal is completed; however, where record made clear that there were issues of both coverage and of loss valuation, part of litigation that involved loss valuation was appropriately stayed and part that involved coverage issues could continue pending appraisal).

1109. *See* Biscayne Cove Condo. Ass'n v. QBE Ins. Corp., 951 F. Supp. 2d 1292, 1301 (S.D. Fla. 2013) (causation is coverage question for court when insurer wholly denies there is covered loss and amount-of-loss question for appraisal panel when insurer admits there is covered loss amount of which is disputed); Three Palms Pointe, Inc. v. State Farm Fire & Cas. Co., 250 F. Supp. 2d 1357, 1365, n.11 (M.D. Fla. 2003) (when insurer admits loss is covered, appraisers can determine cause of damage and amount of loss without judicial review of that decision; however, when insurer

[9] Judicial Confirmation of Appraisal Award

A party make seek judicial confirmation of an appraisal award.[1110] In a Florida federal case, an insurer argued that because the appraisal process is not an arbitration, confirmation of an award is unnecessary. The court responded that although appraisal and arbitration are separate processes, that does not alter the right to confirmation of an appraisal award. However, the court disagreed that it should confirm the appraisal award without addressing issues regarding coverage and the deductible. The award was made without any consideration of the deductible amount or prior payments issued to the insured or any terms, conditions, provisions, or exclusions of the policy. Thus, the award reflected the agreement of the appraisers on the amount owed to the insured based on the evidence of property damage before them and did not reflect the amount owed under the policy. Therefore, the court found the insurer was entitled to challenge coverage as to portions of the appraisal award.[1111]

Where a trial court order provided directions to an umpire, and the umpire failed to follow those directions, an appellate court held that the lower court erred by confirming the appraisal award.[1112]

[10] Challenging an Appraisal Award

In general, it is difficult to challenge an appraisal award as courts prefer not to second-guess appraisers.[1113] Judicial review of an appraisal award is often limited to fraud, corruption, or misconduct that caused an unjust result,[1114] although

---

claims loss is not covered, coverage question must be judicially determined); Fla. Ins. Guar. Ass'n v. Olympus Ass'n, 34 So. 3d 791 (Fla. 4th DCA 2010); Kendall Lakes Townhomes Developers, Inc. v. Agric. Excess & Surplus Lines Ins. Co., 916 So. 2d 12 (Fla. 3d DCA 2005) (although there was large discrepancy between estimates of loss, because insurer had not wholly denied that there was covered loss, causation was amount-of-loss question for appraisal panel, not coverage question that could only be decided by court; it was, therefore, permissible for appraisal panel to decide causation issues when causation was not coverage question, but rather amount-of-loss question). *See generally* Smith, *Property Insurance Appraisal: Is Determining Causation Essential to Evaluating the Amount of Loss?*, 2012 J. Disp. Resol. 591, 603 (2012).

1110. *See, e.g.*, Royal Marco Point 1 Condo. Ass'n v. QBE Ins. Corp., 2008 U.S. Dist. LEXIS 68909 (M.D. Fla. Sept. 10, 2008) (payment of appraisal amount constituted confession of judgment, entitling association to entry of judgment confirming appraisal award).

1111. Sands on the Ocean Condo. Ass'n v. QBE Ins. Corp., 2009 U.S. Dist. LEXIS 24689 (S.D. Fla., Mar. 23, 2009). *See also* Fla. Ins. Guar. Ass'n v. Olympus Ass'n, 34 So. 3d 791 (Fla. 4th DCA 2010) (trial court erred by entering final judgment in favor of association and awarding it amount set forth in appraisal without first deciding issue of coverage liability).

1112. Kendall Lakes Townhomes Developers, Inc. v. Agric. Excess & Surplus Lines Ins. Co., 916 So. 2d 12, 16 (Fla. 3d DCA 2005).

1113. Law & Starinovich, *What Is It Worth? A Critical Analysis of Insurance Appraisal*, 13 Conn. Ins. L.J. 291, 314–15 (2006/2007) (standards to confirm or vacate award may depend on whether particular jurisdiction treats awards in same manner as arbitration awards, for which standards for confirming and vacating them are often well settled).

1114. *See, e.g.*, Three Palms Pointe, Inc. v. State Farm Fire & Cas. Co., 362 F.3d 1317 (11th Cir. 2004) (once award has been made, only defenses that remain for insurer to assert are lack of

courts may also review an award when questions are raised about whether the appraisers have exceeded the scope of their authority.[1115] Courts have also said that violations of policy conditions by the insured may be considered.[1116] Judicial review may be permitted where an appraisal has determined causation.[1117] Occasionally, a mere mistake has been sufficient to vacate an award.[1118]

Questions about the determination of the amount of loss generally must be raised with the appraisers. For example, an insurer claimed that certain items awarded in appraisal were duplicative. The court said it was not the duty of the trial court to ascertain whether the amounts awarded were in fact duplicative; rather, it was incumbent on the insurer to seek clarification and/or modification of the award. An alleged mistake concerning the amount of loss was, pronounced the court, an issue solely within the province of the appraisers.[1119]

What if an award includes payment for losses for which the association is not required to obtain coverage? A court rejected the argument of an insurer that it properly removed amounts from an appraisal award that represented loss to property the unit owners—as opposed to the association—were responsible for insuring pursuant to statute. The court said it did not matter whether the association was statutorily "obligated" to secure coverage for the items the insurer removed from the appraisal because the dispositive issue was whether the policy issued by the insurer *actually* covered them. Because the insurer did not contend that coverage was lacking, the lower court did not err in refusing to entertain the insurer's argument, as the statutory division of responsibility, even if correct, would provide no legal basis for reducing the award.[1120]

---

coverage for entire claim, or violation of one of standard policy conditions, for example, fraud, lack of notice, failure to cooperate).

1115. Parker, *Understanding the Insurance Policy Appraisal Clause: A Four-Step Program*, 37 U. Tol. L. Rev. 931, 946 (2006). *See also* Law & Starinovich, *What Is It Worth? A Critical Analysis of Insurance Appraisal*, 13 Conn. Ins. L.J. 291, 315 (2006/2007) (if appraisers go beyond their scope of authority, award may be challenged). *See, e.g.*, Kendall Lakes Townhomes Developers, Inc. v. Agric. Excess & Surplus Lines Ins. Co., 916 So. 2d 12 (Fla. 3d DCA 2005) (where trial court imposed limitations on duties it granted to umpire, it erred in confirming appraisal award when umpire exceeded those assigned duties).

1116. Three Palms Pointe, Inc. v. State Farm Fire & Cas. Co., 362 F.3d 1317 (11th Cir. 2004) (once award has been made, only defenses that remain for insurer are lack of coverage for entire claim or violation of one of standard policy conditions, for example, fraud, lack of notice, or failure to cooperate).

1117. Smith, *Property Insurance Appraisal: Is Determining Causation Essential to Evaluating the Amount of Loss?*, 2012 J. Disp. Resol. 591, 604 (2012) (some courts allow judicial review of appraisal awards any time panel determines causation).

1118. Law & Starinovich, *What Is It Worth? A Critical Analysis of Insurance Appraisal*, 13 Conn. Ins. L.J. 291, 315 (2006/2007).

1119. Citizens Prop. Ins. Corp. v. River Manor Condo. Ass'n, 125 So. 3d 846 (Fla. 4th DCA 2013).

1120. Citizens Prop. Ins. Corp. v. River Manor Condo. Ass'n, 125 So. 3d 846, 855 (Fla. 4th DCA 2013).

Appraisal clauses ordinarily state that a decision agreed to by any two of the three members of the appraisal panel is binding on the parties.[1121] If the policy language is less definitive, judicial review may depend on whether appraisal is considered binding. For example, a homeowners association participated in an appraisal to determine the amount of loss it suffered in a hailstorm. The policy stated that a written agreement signed by any two of the three panel members would "set the amount of loss." The association disagreed with the appraisal and brought suit against the insurer, which responded that the association was bound by the result of the appraisal. The court, however, said that any waiver of the right to file suit had to be clear and unambiguous and that without language requiring binding appraisal, a policy would be construed as an agreement to submit to non-binding appraisal.[1122]

In a common interest community, is an appraisal decision binding on individual residents? In a Connecticut case, a unit suffered a loss caused by ice damming. The association submitted a claim for coverage of the damage and loss caused by the ice damming to appraisal. The insurer asserted that the appraisal barred suit by the unit owner against it. The court found that the insurer failed to establish that claims by the unit owner for emotional distress as well as other extra contractual claims were the subject of the final appraisal. The unit owner also brought a breach of contract action for failure to provide policy benefits; however, the court opinion does not mention whether that claim was barred by the appraisal.[1123]

§ 10.29 Abandonment

Property policies prohibit abandonment of any property to the insurer.[1124]

§ 10.30 Recovered Property

Both the BPP and CAC have a recovered property clause.[1125] The clause provides that if either the insured or the carrier recovers any property after loss settlement, that party has to give the other one prompt notice. If the carrier recovers the property, at the option of the insured, the property will be returned to the

1121. *See, e.g.*, ISO Form CP 00 10 06 07, § E.2; CP 00 17 06 07, § E.2.

1122. Stratford W. Homeowners Ass'n v. Country Mut. Ins. Co., 273 Ill. Dec. 33, 338 Ill. App. 3d 288, 788 N.E.2d 342 (2003) (nothing in insurance contract indicated that, by participating in appraisal, association was forfeiting its right to seek redress in court; appraisal did not operate as final and binding resolution of dispute over amount of loss and did not foreclose either party from maintaining action in court of law).

1123. McCarthy v. Glenwood Place of Farmington Ass'n, 2016 Conn. Super. LEXIS 274 (Conn. Super. Ct. Feb. 3, 2016).

1124. *See, e.g.*, ISO Form CP 00 10 06 07, § E.1; ISO Form CP 00 17 06 07, § E.1.

1125. *See, e.g.*, ISO Form CP 00 10 06 07, § E.5; ISO Form CP 00 17 06 07, § E.5.

insured. The insured, in turn, has to then return to the insurer the amount it paid for the property. The insurer will still pay recovery expenses and the cost to repair the recovered property, subject to the limit of insurance.

§ 10.31 Vacancy

Both the BPP and CAC have a vacancy clause.[1126] While the clause is found among the loss conditions and is a limitation, not an exclusion, courts may still place the burden on the insurer to show the limitation applies,[1127] treat it as an exclusion, and construe it against the insurer.[1128]

The reason for the vacancy clause is that a vacant or unoccupied structure increases the insurer's loss potential from particular perils because typically no one is tending to the property.[1129] Additionally, when the property is unattended, what might have initially been minor damage—a small leak that causes less damage than the deductible amount—can turn into a major loss. The vacancy clause addresses these concerns but can reduce or even eliminate coverage for an insured common interest community. The clause provides that if a building where loss or damage occurs has been vacant for more than 60 consecutive days before that loss or damage occurs,[1130] the insurer will not pay for any loss or damage caused

---

1126. *See, e.g.*, ISO Form CP 00 10 06 07, § E.6; ISO Form CP 00 17 06 07, § E.7.

1127. *See, e.g.*, TRB Investments, Inc. v. Fireman's Fund Ins. Co., 40 Cal. 4th 19, 50 Cal. Rptr. 3d 597 (2006); Knoff v. United States Fidelity & Guaranty Co., 447 S.W.2d 497, 500–01 (Tex. Civ. App.—Houston 1st Dist., 1969).

1128. *See, e.g.*, Hartford Cas. Ins. v. Mark, 2014 U.S. Dist. LEXIS 10516 (W.D. Wash. Jan. 28, 2014).

1129. Prahl, *Vacancy/Occupancy Clauses in Property Insurance—An Often Overlooked But Significant Limitation*, at 2 (Adjusting Today, 2015), available at: http://adjustersinternational.com/publications/adjusting-today/vacancy-occupancy-clauses-protective-safeguards-endorsements/1/. *See also* Oakdale Mall Assocs. v. Cincinnati Ins. Co., 702 F.3d 1119, 1124 (8th Cir. 2013) (primary purpose of vacancy provision is to reduce risk of loss by requiring physical presence at property to help secure it from vandals and thieves); Kut Suen Lui v. Essex Ins. Co., 2015 Wash. App. LEXIS 725 (Wash. Ct. App. Apr. 6, 2015), *rev. granted*, 84 Wn. 2d 1017, 360 P.3d 819 (2015) (insurers use vacancy provisions to reflect increased risk posed by vacant buildings as they are more susceptible to insurance risks such as fire, trespass, leaks, and other defects that often cause greater damage because they go unnoticed); Vushaj v. Farm Bureau Gen. Ins. Co., 284 Mich. App. 513, 516, 773 N.W.2d 758, 760 (2009), *app. den.*, 485 Mich. 1119, 779 N.W.2d 496 (2010) (vacancy clause protects insurance company from increased risk that accompanies insuring property that has no occupant).

1130. Is the 60 days measured from the beginning of any period of vacancy or from the inception of the policy? In *Travelers Property Casualty Co. of America v. Superior Court*, 215 Cal. App. 4th 561, 576, 155 Cal. Rptr. 3d 459, 471 (2013), the trial court concluded the vacancy limitation did not apply because it required the property to be vacant for 60 days prior to the loss and 60 days could not have run between when the policy was issued in January and the loss occurred in February. The appellate court acknowledged that some courts have found a vacancy period has to begin at or after policy issuance when it indicates the clause is triggered if the property is vacant beyond a period of 60 days. However, the vacancy clause before the court—which is the same as that found in standard BPP and CAC policies—was different. The time period was backward-looking from the date of the loss and did not implicate the date the policy was issued. *See also* Tazari, LLC v. Am.

by vandalism, sprinkler leakage—unless the insured has protected the system against freezing—glass breakage, water damage, theft, or attempted theft.[1131] For losses other than those listed, the carrier will reduce the amount it would otherwise pay for the loss or damage by 15 percent.[1132]

If an association has a policy that is neither a standard BPP nor CAC, it should be alert for other limitations in any vacancy clause. For example, the percentage of reduction for non-named perils might be higher than 15 percent. If the policy generally provides for replacement cost coverage, the vacancy clause might modify that and value any loss at actual cash value.[1133] The vacancy clause in the ISO Standard Property Policy says the carrier will not pay for any loss or damage if the building where the loss or damage occurs has been "vacant" or "unoccupied" for more than 30 consecutive days before that loss or damage if caused by vandalism—when vandalism is a covered cause of loss—or 60 consecutive days before that loss or damage if caused by any other covered cause of loss.[1134] This clause both omits the definition of "vacant" found in the BPP and CAC and also eliminates coverage where the building has been vacant or unoccupied for 60 days before the loss or damage instead of simply reducing it by a percentage.

[1] Definition of a Vacant Building

When the policy is issued to the owner or general lessee of a building, "building" means the entire building. The building is considered vacant unless at least 31 percent of its total square footage is used by the building owner to conduct customary operations.[1135] The building is also considered vacant unless at least 31 percent of its total square footage is rented to a lessee or sublessee and used by them to conduct their "customary operations,"[1136] and/or is used by the building

Family Ins., 2012 Ohio Misc. LEXIS 17 (Ohio C.P. Feb. 7, 2012) (if property has been vacant for 60 days, there is no coverage even if policy has been in effect less than 60 days). In some cases it may not be clear when the damage or loss "occurred." For example, in *Cent. Mut. Ins. Co. v. KPE Firstplace Land, LLC*, 271 S.W.3d 454 (Tex. App.—Tyler 2008), the insured discovered on December 31 that some time prior to that thieves had removed copper coils from air conditioning equipment located on the roof of its building. The insurer denied coverage based on the vacancy clause. The insured argued the carrier could not prove the claim for that loss was excluded under the vacancy provision because it could not show the property had been vacant for 60 days at the time the loss "occurred." The court found that "occurred" means when damage happened, not when it was discovered. Therefore, it affirmed summary judgment for the insured.

1131. ISO Form CP 00 10 06 07, § E.6.b.(1); ISO Form CP 00 17 06 07, § E.7.b.(1).

1132. ISO Form CP 00 10 06 07, § E.6.b.(2); ISO Form CP 00 17 06 07, § E.7.b.(2).

1133. Rico, *Vacancy Provisions in a Property Policy* (May 20, 2015), available at: http://www.assuranceagency.com/blog-post/vacancy-provisions-in-a-property-policy.

1134. *See, e.g.*, ISO Form CP 00 99 10 90, § F.8.

1135. ISO Form CP 00 10 06 07, § E.6.a.(1)(b)(ii); ISO Form CP 00 17 06 07, § E.7.a.(1)(b)(ii). The *intent* of the insured to use the building is generally immaterial. Vushaj v. Farm Bureau Gen. Ins. Co., 284 Mich. App. 513, 519, 773 N.W.2d 762, 760 (2009), *app. den.*, 485 Mich. 1119, 779 N.W.2d 496 (2010).

1136. ISO Form CP 00 10 06 07, § E.6.a.(1)(b)(i); ISO Form CP 00 17 06 07, § E.7.a.(1)(b)(i).

owner to conduct customary operations. Assuming the building "owner" means the common interest community association that is the named insured—which is not actually the case in a condominium[1137] but generally is for cooperatives and homeowners associations[1138]—the vacancy formula raises several questions. First, does "total square footage" include area owned or occupied by individual residents of the community? Second, what are the "customary operations" of a common interest community association? Third, does the square footage in use "by the building owner" include the square footage of occupied residences? The answers to these questions may be critical to determining whether a vacancy clause applies.

Occasionally, a common interest community may share a building with other entities. For example, in an urban area a developer might construct a building and retain ownership of the lower floors to rent as retail stores and offices, and submit the upper floors to condominium ownership. How then is "building" as used in the vacancy clause interpreted? In a Washington case the insured owned a suite in an office building but not the entire building in which the suite was located. The suite was damaged by a sewer backup, and the insurer invoked the vacancy clause. The insured argued that as the owner of only a portion of a building, the definition of "building" as "entire building" did not apply and neither, therefore, did the vacancy clause. The court, however, said the phrase "entire building" referred to the insured premises.[1139]

A federal circuit court discussing a subdivided structure raised a hypothetical relevant to common interest communities. In considering the risks attendant in a single, subdivided structure, the court said it was prompted to ask, "Would a single structure of several rowhouses be one building or multiple buildings? What if the houses were connected through the basement or through first-floor fire doors? Is a single structure divided into multiple condominiums one building or many?"[1140] Its answer was that courts would be hard pressed to find as a matter of law that a particular style of contiguous structure is a single building or multiple buildings and, therefore, each ruling would depend on the specific circumstances of the case, the policy language, and ultimately the intent of the parties to that policy.

One could speculate at length over how courts might treat various structural configurations, but the sensible step to take if there is any doubt is to ask the

1137. *Consider* Travelers Property Casualty Co. of America v. Superior Court, 215 Cal. App. 4th 561, 155 Cal. Rptr. 3d 459 (Cal. App. 2013) (could not reasonably be disputed that insured condominium association was owner of building for purposes of vacancy clause; association's interest in building was, of necessity, more akin to that of owner than tenant).

1138. In that regard, consider *Travelers Property Casualty Co. of America v. Superior Court*, 215 Cal. App. 4th 561, 577, 155 Cal. Rptr. 3d 459, 471, 472, n.18 (2013) (interest of condominium homeowners association in building was more akin to that of owner than tenant).

1139. Hartford Cas. Ins. v. Mark, 2014 U.S. Dist. LEXIS 10516 (W.D. Wash. Jan. 28, 2014).

1140. United Capitol Ins. Co. v. Kapiloff, 155 F.3d 488, 498 (4th Cir. 1998).

insurer to state in writing whether, for purposes of the vacancy clause, it views the CIC as one or more than one building.

[2] The Meaning of "Customary Operations"

Policies do not define "customary operations." Courts will, therefore, look to the ordinary meaning of the phrase based usually on a dictionary definition. In doing so, one court concluded "customary" means "commonly practiced, used, or observed."[1141] Courts also examine the Declarations Page. Typically, the Declarations Page—even one accompanying a Condominium Association Coverage Form—has a space for "business description." Inserted in that space will probably be a description of the form of common interest community the insured constitutes. A court will generally look to the business description to determine the "customary operations" of the insured. For example, where the Declarations Page identified the insured as a "family style restaurant," but the restaurant had closed, and the building was being used as an office to work on selling the building and on other restaurant projects located elsewhere, not preparing and selling food or running a family-style restaurant, the building was vacant because the premises were not being used for customary operations.[1142]

The term "customary operations" lends itself to contrary decisions. A Georgia court said that the customary business activity of the owner of a residential apartment building is leasing of apartments to tenants for profit and, therefore, an insured apartment building would be considered vacant if the required percentage of square footage was not occupied by tenants.[1143] Another court concluded that the fact that premises are available for use is insufficient.[1144] On the

1141. Saiz v. Charter Oak Fire Ins. Co., 299 Fed. Appx. 836 (10th Cir. 2008). *See also* Bedford Internet Office Space, LLC v. Travelers Cas. Ins. Co., 41 F. Supp. 3d 535, 547 (N.D. Tex. 2014).

1142. Saiz v. Charter Oak Fire Ins. Co., 2007 U.S. Dist. LEXIS 67767 (D. Colo. Sept. 12, 2007). *See also* Keren Habinyon Hachudosh D'Rabeinu Yoel v. Phila. Indem. Ins. Co., 2011 U.S. Dist. LEXIS 25172 (E.D.N.Y. Mar. 10, 2011) (although school was used for storage and one teacher/student gathering, that activity could not be reasonably expected to constitute customary operations of school where there were no regular faculty, student body, or teaching and learning taking place).

1143. R&G Investments & Holdings, LLC v. American Family Insurance Company, 2016 Ga. App. LEXIS 331 (June 9, 2016). *See also* Oakdale Mall Assocs. v. Cincinnati Ins. Co., 702 F.3d 1119 (8th Cir. 2013) (posting sign outsides mall advertising available space for rent and seeking out new tenants for unoccupied space did not constitute using property to conduct normal business operations; that mall could be completely vacant but be deemed fully occupied for purposes of vacancy provision if owner simply posted signs outside or advertisement online or in newspaper was unreasonable interpretation, bordering on absurd); 1 West Main St., LLC v. Tower Nat'l Ins. Co., 2016 U.S. Dist. LEXIS 33650 (E.D. Pa. Mar. 15, 2016) (where it was undisputed that less than 20 percent of building was in use for customary operations of leasing space, building was vacant even though owner was willing to lease out unoccupied space).

1144. Holmes v. N.C. Farm Bureau Mut. Ins. Co., 233 N.C. App. 487, 492, 756 S.E.2d 848, 852, *rev. den.*, 367 N.C. 520, 762 S.E.2d 445 (2014) (relevant question regarding vacancy clause is what percentage of total square footage is actually used to conduct customary operations, not what amount could have been used).

other hand, where a building was a rental property made up of three apartments, a storefront, a basement, and a garage, it was not vacant because there was sufficient business personal property on the premises—furnishings, in the three apartments—to conduct the owner's "customary operations" of renting the apartments.[1145]

A Texas court said the mere access to a building or incidental use of it does not constitute "customary operations" and that where there is no electricity or water service, it would be seemingly impossible to conduct business activities at a property, so there could be no customary operations taking place.[1146]

The fact that the property owner has plans to use the property in the future is irrelevant to whether or not a building is vacant 60 days prior to the date of a loss.[1147]

[3] The Vacancy Problem in Common Interest Communities

Does the vacancy clause even apply to residential properties? In a Georgia case an insured argued a vacancy clause had no application to a residential apartment building. The court disagreed and observed that a construction of the vacancy clause that would render it inapplicable as a whole to residential apartment buildings would have the result of reading the provision entirely out of the policy. The court rejected that result.[1148]

The vacancy clause can create particular problems for common interest communities. Consider the following scenario. A condominium is a vacation or seasonal home for its individual unit owners. There are periods during the "off season" when 80 percent of those unit owners are not in residence. During those periods, the association continues its "customary operations" of maintaining the building. The total square footage of the building is 140,000. There are 50 units. Each unit has 2,500 square feet. The common area—including a meeting room office, lobby, and hallways—comprises 15,000 square feet. For the building not to be considered vacant under the policy definition, 43,400 square feet must be used by the association for its "customary operations." If only 10 unit owners were in residence, the maximum number of square feet in use would be 40,000.[1149] Thus,

---

1145. Gallo v. Travelers Prop. Cas., 21 A.D.3d 1379, 1380, 801 N.Y.S.2d 849, 851 (2005).

1146. Bedford Internet Office Space, LLC v. Travelers Cas. Ins. Co., 41 F. Supp. 3d 535, 548 (N.D. Tex. 2014).

1147. Keren Habinyon Hachudosh D'Rabeinu Yoel v. Phila. Indem. Ins. Co., 2011 U.S. Dist. LEXIS 25172 (E.D.N.Y. Mar. 10, 2011).

1148. R&G Investments & Holdings, LLC v. American Family Insurance Company, 2016 Ga. App. LEXIS 331 (June 9, 2016).

1149. When is an individual unit considered to be vacant? *Consider* Vushaj v. Farm Bureau Gen. Ins. Co., 284 Mich. App. 513, 516, 773 N.W.2d 758, 760 (2009), *app. den.*, 485 Mich. 1119, 779 N.W.2d 496 (2010) (vacancy clause may apply even though property is not wholly empty, otherwise fully furnished house would never be considered vacant, even if no one entered it for years, simply because furniture prevented it being "completely empty").

if over any 60-day period no more than 10 unit owners visited the property, the penalties of the vacancy clause could be invoked. Moreover, because the policy says at least 31 percent of its total square footage has to be used by the building owner to conduct its customary operations, unless the occupancy of a unit by a unit owner is included in the computation of use "by the building owner" for customary operations, the building is always vacant for purposes of the vacancy clause.

The result would be entirely different if the common interest community were a cooperative. The individual units in a cooperative are leased to tenant/shareholders. Even if most or all of those tenant/shareholders are not in residence, the cooperative corporation is probably still conducting its "customary operations" of maintaining the building. Moreover, if the "customary operations" of the tenant/shareholders would be maintaining the apartment as a part-time residence, they might all be considered to be carrying on "customary operations" regardless of whether or not they are residing in their apartments. However, the mere fact that a premises is leased is not enough to show that it is not vacant where the tenant has not taken possession.[1150]

When a CIC is made up of separate buildings, it is possible that at some point one of the buildings might be vacant for purposes of the vacancy clause while the others are not. In that instance, it becomes important to determine whether the policy treats the community as one building. That may be determined by how the premises are described on the Declarations Page; however, it would be best to obtain a direct answer from the insurer.[1151]

1150. Bedford Internet Office Space, LLC v. Travelers Cas. Ins. Co., 41 F. Supp. 3d 535, 547 (N.D. Tex. 2014) (that lessee was preparing to operate its business at insured property was not enough to overcome vacancy exclusion).

1151. *See, e.g.*, JJD Assocs. of Palm Beach, Ltd. v. Am. Empire Surplus Lines Ins. Co., 2011 U.S. Dist. LEXIS 134878 (S.D. Fla. Nov. 22, 2011), where the insured premises was a shopping center that included seven subproperties. Some of the seven subproperties were adjoined, while others were detached. One of them suffered a loss, and the insurer invoked the vacancy clause. The parties disagreed over whether "building" in the vacancy clause referred to each premises individually or the shopping center as a whole. If it were the latter, the clause would not apply because the portion of the shopping center that was vacant for 60 days prior to the loss was not at least 31 percent of the entire shopping center. If, however, "building" referred to each of the subdivisions of the shopping center individually, the court said the clause would likely apply because, arguably, at least 69 percent of the premises at issue was vacant for 60 days prior to the loss. The court examined the Declarations Page and found that under "description of premises," building was used in a potentially ambiguous way. It referred to premises numbered one through seven but in each case referred only to "Bldg. No. 1." That, said the court, made it unclear whether "Bldg. No. 1" indicated a single building on each of premises one through seven or that each of the seven premises were constituents of a building identified as building number one. The court resolved the dilemma by holding that "building," as used throughout the policy, referred to each premises individually and noted that the ordinary use of the term "building" would rarely include a group of premises not all of which were bounded by the same walls and roof.

[4] Seasonal Common Interest Communities

Some common interest communities operate exclusively on a seasonal basis and close during the off season. As the customary operations of these seasonal communities is not being carried out during the months they are closed, they would seem to meet the definition of vacant.[1152] The fact that a caretaker may be present during some hours or that maintenance occasionally takes place would not constitute customary operations in a facility otherwise vacant.[1153] These seasonal communities should discuss their coverage and application of the vacancy clause with their broker or the insurer. There is support for the proposition that an insurer that issues a policy with a vacancy clause and knows the insured property is vacant or that the insured is a seasonal operation waives the right to invoke the clause.[1154]

[5] The Vacancy Permit Endorsement

For the CIC that is concerned about application of the vacancy clause, the recourse is to obtain a Vacancy Permit Endorsement. The endorsement can suspend the vacancy clause exclusions, continue coverage for a specified period of time, and negate the 15 percent reduction in coverage for all other perils.[1155] A standard ISO Vacancy Permit Endorsement is available that modifies both the Building and Personal Property Coverage Form and Condominium Association Coverage Form.[1156]

[6] Buildings under Construction or Renovation

Buildings "under" construction or renovation are not, by definition, considered vacant.[1157] Policies generally do not define either "construction" or "renovation."

1152. Prahl, *Vacancy/Occupancy Clauses in Property Insurance—An Often Overlooked but Significant Limitation*, at 3 (Adjusting Today, 2015), available at: http://adjustersinternational.com/publications/adjusting-today/vacancy-occupancy-clauses-protective-safeguards-endorsements/1/.

1153. *See* JJD Assocs. of Palm Beach, Ltd. v. Am. Empire Surplus Lines Ins. Co., 2011 U.S. Dist. LEXIS 134878 (S.D. Fla. Nov. 22, 2011) (sporadic entry into insured building by agent for insured and maintenance personnel would not constitute "customary" operations contemplated by policy and even if those were qualifying uses, they plainly did not occupy requisite 31 percent of premises). *See also* Keren Habinyon Hachudosh D'Rabeinu Yoel v. Phila. Indem. Ins. Co., 2011 U.S. Dist. LEXIS 25172 (E.D.N.Y. Mar. 10, 2011).

1154. *See* McKinney v. Providence Wash. Ins. Co., 144 W. Va. 559, 109 S.E.2d 480 (1959); Bellevue Roller-Mill Co. v. London & L. Fire Ins. Co., 4 Idaho 307, 39 P. 196 (Idaho 1895).

1155. Prahl, *Vacancy/Occupancy Clauses in Property Insurance—An Often Overlooked but Significant Limitation*, at 4 (Adjusting Today, 2015), available at: http://adjustersinternational.com/publications/adjusting-today/vacancy-occupancy-clauses-protective-safeguards-endorsements/1/.

1156. *See, e.g.*, ISO Form CP 04 50 07 88.

1157. ISO Form CP 00 10 06 07, § E.6.a.(2); ISO Form CP 00 17 06 07, § E.7.a.(2). "Under renovation" means more than planning to renovate. 1 West Main St., LLC v. Tower Nat'l Ins. Co., 2016 U.S. Dist. LEXIS 33650 (E.D. Pa. Mar. 15, 2016) (having plans to make changes or repairs

One court cited a dictionary definition of renovation as making changes and repairs to put something back in good condition.[1158] Another acknowledged that there is an appreciable overlap among terms like "repair," "remodeling," and "renovation" and that on a continuum, renovation falls between repair and remodeling.[1159] Be that as it may, interpretation of the "renovation" exception to the vacancy clause limitation has produced mixed results and no little debate.[1160] For example, repairing and reactivating a sprinkler system was not renovation,[1161] while removing a walkway between the insured building and an adjacent property did qualify as renovation.[1162] Even if a precise rule of law could be divined from the cases, it would behoove an association contemplating work that would require vacating a sufficient amount of square footage to possibly trigger the vacancy clause to consult with its broker, or perhaps the insurer directly, to determine whether the renovation exception will apply.

§ 10.32 Loss Conditions Only in Condominium Association Coverage Form

The Condominium Association Coverage Form includes two loss conditions not found in the Building and Personal Property Coverage Form. First the CAC notes that unit owners may have other insurance covering the same property as the association policy. The CAC asserts that the association policy is intended to be primary and not to contribute with the other insurance.[1163] Next, under the CAC, the carrier waives its rights to recover payment from any condominium unit owner that is shown on the Declarations Page.[1164] Note that under the various Uniform Acts, the insurer is required to waive its right to subrogation against

---

does not equate to being "under renovation," especially when permits necessary to make those changes or repairs have not even been sought).

1158. 1 West Main St., LLC v. Tower Nat'l Ins. Co., 2016 U.S. Dist. LEXIS 33650 (E.D. Pa. Mar. 15, 2016) (citing Merriam-Webster Online Dictionary).

1159. Farbman Group v. Travelers Ins. Cos., 2006 U.S. Dist. LEXIS 70199 (E.D. Mich. Sept. 28, 2006).

1160. *See, e.g.*, Farbman Group v. Travelers Ins. Cos., 2006 U.S. Dist. LEXIS 70199 (E.D. Mich. Sept. 28, 2006) (many would consider rewiring, new roof, and "other capital improvements" as examples of "repair" or "remodeling" rather than renovation, depending on precise nature and purpose of work being done).

1161. Suder-Benore Co., Ltd. v. Motorists Mut. Ins. Co., 995 N.E.2d 1279 (Ohio App. 2013), *app. den.*, 138 Ohio St. 3d 1414, 3 N.E.3d 1216 (2014).

1162. Farbman Group v. Travelers Ins. Cos., 2006 U.S. Dist. LEXIS 70199 (E.D. Mich. Sept. 28, 2006).

1163. ISO Form CP 00 17 06 07, § E.6.

1164. ISO Form CP 00 17 06 07, § E.9.

any unit owner—not just one shown on the Declarations Page—or member of his or her household.[1165]

§ 10.33 Coinsurance

One clause of which associations may not be aware is the coinsurance provision.[1166] Both the BPP and CAC have identical coinsurance clauses.[1167] The Texas Supreme Court explained coinsurance clauses nearly a century ago. It said that these clauses in effect require insureds to "maintain insurance on each item of property insured equal to its actual cash value, or a certain percentage thereof, and failing to do so make [them] an insurer to the extent of the deficiency," and require them as "co-insurer to" bear their proportionate part of loss on each item.[1168] The purpose of the clause is to encourage the policyholder to carry a reasonable amount of insurance—usually 80 percent, sometimes more[1169]—in relation to the full value of the property, and if the proper amount of insurance is not carried, the policyholder shares in the loss above the deductible amount.[1170] The resulting reduction in coverage is a disadvantage to the insured, while an advantage of the coinsurance clause is that higher coinsurance provisions reduce premiums.[1171]

1165. *See, e.g.*, Uniform Condominium Act § 3-113(d)(2).

1166. Harris, *Failing to Obtain Regular Appraisals Can Hurt Associations after a Large Loss* (July 2010), available at: http://www.condominiuminsurancelaw.com/tags/coinsurance/.

1167. ISO Form CP 00 10 06 07, § F.1; ISO Form CP 00 17 06 07, § F.1. These clauses are rarely the subject of litigation. One decision addressing a coinsurance clause in a FEMA flood insurance policy (SFIP) is *Penthouse Owners Assoc. v. Certain Underwriters at Lloyd's, London*, 2011 U.S. Dist. LEXIS 147289 (S.D. Miss. Dec. 21, 2011). The language of the coinsurance clause in the BPP, CAC, and SFIP is identical, so the *Penthouse* decision should be of persuasive value.

1168. Commercial Union Assurance Co. v. Preston, 115 Tex. 351, 358, 282 S.W. 563, 566 (Tex. 1926).

1169. *See* Marker, *Condominium Insurance Law: The Policyholders Advocate* (Feb. 2011), available at: http://www.condominiuminsurancelaw.com/tags/coinsurance/ (coinsurance clause provides that property must be insured for specific percentage, usually 80% to 100% of its value); Harris, *Failing to Obtain Regular Appraisals Can Hurt Associations after a Large Loss* (July 2010), available at: http://www.condominiuminsurancelaw.com/tags/coinsurance/ (coinsurance provisions come in all shapes and sizes, but most common are 80, 90, and 100 percent coinsurance provisions).

1170. Residences at Bay Point Condo. Ass'n v. Std. Fire Ins. Co., 41 F. Supp. 3d 427, 429 (D.N.J. 2014) *See also* Regency of Palm Beach, Inc. v. QBE Ins. Corp., 2009 U.S. Dist. LEXIS 75929, at *9, n.2 (S.D. Fla. Aug. 25, 2009) (coinsurance clause is insurance policy provision that requires property owner to carry separate insurance up to amount stated in policy to qualify for full coverage). *See generally* Cozen, *Insuring Real Property*, § 1.06[5] (Matthew Bender & Co. 2015).

1171. Harris, *Failing to Obtain Regular Appraisals Can Hurt Associations After a Large Loss* (July 2010), available at: http://www.condominiuminsurancelaw.com/tags/coinsurance/. A premium rate reduction may be mandated by state law. *See, e.g.*, Mo. Rev. Stat. § 379.160.3 (when coinsurance clause is attached to any policy, reduction in rate has to be given in accordance with coinsurance credits filed as part of public rating record in office of director of Department of Insurance).

[1] How the Coinsurance Clause Is Applied

The coinsurance clause provides that if a coinsurance percentage is shown on the Declarations Page, the insurer will not pay the full amount of any loss if, *at the time of the loss*,[1172] the value of covered property multiplied by the coinsurance percentage is greater than the limit of insurance for the property.[1173] Instead, the insurer determines the most it will pay by a formula set forth in the policy. It multiplies the value of covered property at the time of loss by the coinsurance percentage, divides the limit of insurance of the property by that product, multiplies the total amount of loss—before application of any deductible—by that result, and subtracts the deductible from that product. It will then pay the amount determined by the formula or the limit of insurance, whichever is less.[1174] If one limit of insurance applies to two or more separate items, the coinsurance clause applies to the total of all property to which the limit applies.[1175] If the coinsurance percentage is not satisfied, the *insured* has to make up the difference,[1176] but if it is met, then the entire loss is paid up to the limits of insurance.[1177] Helpfully, the policies provide examples to illustrate how the formula works.[1178] Associations should be aware that occasionally the insurer will not enforce the coinsurance penalty.[1179]

[2] Avoiding Application of the Coinsurance Clause

To avoid application of the coinsurance clause, associations should periodically review their policies to determine if they are subject to a coinsurance percentage

---

1172. The adequacy test is performed at the time of the loss. Barlow, Massmann, Alexander & Schreibman, *Condominium Insurance Coverage Guide* at 175 (2d ed. National Underwriter Co., 2016).

1173. *Consider* Penthouse Owners Assoc. v. Certain Underwriters at Lloyd's, London, 2011 U.S. Dist. LEXIS 147289 (S.D. Miss. Dec. 21, 2011) (phrase "total amount of loss" means whole or complete amount of loss to each of three buildings comprising condominium community).

1174. ISO Form CP 00 10 06 07, § F.1.a; ISO Form CP 00 17 06 07, § F.1.a.

1175. ISO Form CP 00 10 06 07, § F.1.b; ISO Form CP 00 17 06 07, § F.1.b.

1176. Marker, *Condominium Insurance Law: The Policyholders Advocate* (Feb. 2011), available at: http://www.condominiuminsurancelaw.com/tags/coinsurance/ (insurer can shift part of risk of loss back to policyholder if property is not insured to certain ratio of value of property at time of loss; if value of property times coinsurance percentage is greater than limit of insurance for property, then insurer may apply coinsurance "penalty" and may not have to pay full value of that loss).

1177. Cozen, *Insuring Real Property*, § 1.06[5] (Matthew Bender & Co. 2015).

1178. One commentator provides an example of the operation of a 100 percent coinsurance provision with $100,000 worth of property insurance purchased but a replacement cost value of the property of $200,000. In that case the insurer would only be liable for 50 percent of the loss and thus, if there was a loss of $100,000, the insurer would only be required to pay $50,000 because the property was only insured to 50 percent of its replacement cost value. Harris, *Failing to Obtain Regular Appraisals Can Hurt Associations after a Large Loss* (July 2010), available at: http://www.condominiuminsurancelaw.com/tags/coinsurance/.

1179. *See, e.g.*, Buckley Towers Condo., Inc. v. QBE Ins. Corp., 2008 U.S. Dist. LEXIS 56195 (S.D. Fla. June 17, 2008) (regarding issues related to coinsurance provision, insurer stipulated that it would not seek to enforce coinsurance penalty).

and to make sure they are adequately insured for the value of the property according to any coinsurance percentage.[1180] An association needs periodic reappraisals of the value of the property and needs to be aware of any significant remodeling by individual owners that affects that value.[1181] Additionally, inflation guard coverage automatically increases the limit of insurance by an agreed inflation factor and can protect the association from the consequences of a coinsurance clause.[1182] The association can also elect an "agreed value" option—if it is available in the policy—which replaces the coinsurance clause,[1183] or in the alternative, an Agreed Amount Endorsement can be added to the policy to delete or waive the coinsurance penalties.[1184]

A commentary highlights a problem that can occur in a homeowners association insured under the BPP.[1185] In a hypothetical, a ten-unit townhouse building has a replacement cost of $200,000 per unit and a total insured value of $2 million. The governing documents require the association to insure a portion of the building amounting to $120,000 per unit, while individual owners have to insure carpet, interior paint, wallpaper, appliances, cabinets, bath tubs, showers, interior doors, sliding glass doors, and interior non-load-bearing walls constituting $80,000 per unit. Under the standard BPP, all building items are covered, even those the bylaws make the responsibility of individual owners. If coverage is for ten times $120,000, the association will suffer the coinsurance penalty when it makes a claim because the policy does not meet the minimum under an 80 percent coinsurance clause of $1.6 million. That the documents state that individual owners have to insure certain building components does not, says the commentary, affect that fact that those items are still covered property under the BPP policy. Thus, to avoid the coinsurance penalty the association policy has to be endorsed with an "Additional Property Not Covered" rider containing a description of the property not covered.[1186]

1180. Marker, *Condominium Insurance Law: The Policyholders Advocate* (Feb. 2011), available at: http://www.condominiuminsurancelaw.com/tags/coinsurance/; Harris, *Failing to Obtain Regular Appraisals Can Hurt Associations After a Large Loss* (July 2010), available at: http://www.condominiuminsurancelaw.com/tags/coinsurance/.

1181. Hakala, *Condominium Casualty and Liability Insurance*, 48 St. John's L. Rev. 1112, 1118 (1974) (noting that particularly in conversion buildings where owners tend to do significant in-unit remodeling, cases arise where value of structure exceeds stated limit of policy by 20 percent or more).

1182. Cozen, *Insuring Real Property*, § 1.06[5] (Matthew Bender & Co. 2015).

1183. *See* § 10.34[1], *infra*.

1184. Treese, *Risk Management Essential to Insurance Plan* (CAI 1995).

1185. Quoted in Williams, *Property & Casualty Insurance/Townhome Insurance* (May 2009).

1186. *See, e.g.*, ISO Form CP 14 20 11 91. The form is an endorsement that can be added to the Building and Personal Property Coverage Form, the Condominium Association Coverage Form, or the Standard Property Policy. It has a schedule listing specific types of property. If an "X" is shown in a box to the left of each specific type of property, that property is added to the list of "Property Not Covered" under the policy. None of the listed types of property would appear to be unit components, but the endorsement also provides that information required to complete the

[3] Lenders Coinsurance Clause Requirements

Associations are often told that lenders will not make loans to buyers wishing to purchase homes in the community unless the coinsurance is set at 100 percent. That assumes that a lender actually examines the association policy before committing to make a loan. A lender does not need to examine the entire policy to ascertain the coinsurance percentage as it is listed on the Declarations Page. However, whether lenders have adequate procedures and staff to track insurance requirements is open to question. To the extent a lender insists on 100 percent coinsurance, its decision may be based on a misunderstanding of the coinsurance clause.[1187] Lenders may believe that if the coinsurance is set at 100 percent, their collateral has the maximum protection. It can be argued that the opposite is the case. Because the coinsurance clause is a penalty that reduces the amount the insurer will pay on a claim, a 100 percent coinsurance clause has the effect of forcing the association to pay a larger portion of repair expenses out-of-pocket. The money to pay for the repairs will generally come from either a special assessment on the association members or from reserves. Buyers may be reluctant to purchase homes in communities with a history of large special assessments. They may also be wary of communities with small amounts in reserve. In any event, if an association draws on reserves to make repairs—assuming it is legally permitted to do so[1188]—its financial soundness is diminished, at least until the reserve fund is replenished. Thus, the lender that insists on 100 percent coinsurance may actually impair its collateral.

§ 10.34 Optional Coverages

The BPP and CAC both provide for the same three optional coverages.[1189] These optional coverages are provided if they are shown on the Declarations Page. The optional coverages apply separately to each item.

---

schedule, if not shown on the endorsement, will be shown on the Declarations Page. Apparently then the building components for which the association members have a responsibility under the governing documents to insure can be listed on the Declarations Page.

1187. *See* Harris, *Failing to Obtain Regular Appraisals Can Hurt Associations After a Large Loss* (July 2010), available at: http://www.condominiuminsurancelaw.com/tags/coinsurance/ (if association policy includes coinsurance provision, it should be between 80 and 90 percent and having 100 percent coinsurance penalty is almost never recommended).

1188. The association may be restricted in how it uses reserves by either statute or the governing documents.

1189. *See* ISO Form CP 00 10 06 07, § G; ISO Form CP 00 17 06 07, § G.

[1] Agreed Value

If the insured selects, and the insurer agrees to, the "agreed value" option, it replaces the Coinsurance clause.[1190] The selection is shown on the Declarations Page. The coinsurance provision then does not apply to covered property to which the optional agreed value coverage applies, and the carrier will pay no more for loss of or damage to that property than the proportion that the limit of insurance for the property bears to the agreed value shown for it on the Declarations Page.[1191] If the expiration date for the agreed value coverage shown on the Declarations Page is not extended, then the Coinsurance provision is reinstated and the agreed value coverage expires.[1192] Agreed value coverage applies only to loss or damage that occurs on or after the effective date of the coverage and before the agreed value expiration date shown on the Declaration Page or the policy expiration date, whichever occurs first.[1193] The policy may require the insured to verify the values chosen by documentation at the inception of the policy and at each renewal.[1194]

[2] Inflation Guard

Inflation guard coverage automatically increases the limit of insurance shown on the Declarations Page by an agreed inflation factor and protects an insured from the consequences of a Coinsurance clause or limit of insurance when there is a loss in the middle of the term of a policy.[1195] It allows the carrier to automatically change the policy limit during the policy period and on each subsequent renewal generally by a predetermined percentage.[1196] When the coverage is available, Fannie Mae requires it,[1197] and so too may the governing documents of a particular common interest community.[1198]

1190. Barlow, Massmann, Alexander & Schreibman, *Condominium Insurance Coverage Guide* at 177 (2d ed. National Underwriter Co., 2016).

1191. *See* ISO Form CP 00 10 06 07, § G.1.a; ISO Form CP 00 17 06 07, § G.1.a. *See generally* Cozen, *Insuring Real Property*, § 1.06[5] (Matthew Bender & Co. 2015).

1192. *See* ISO Form CP 00 10 06 07, § G.1.b; ISO Form CP 00 17 06 07, § G.1.b.

1193. *See* ISO Form CP 00 10 06 07, § G.1.c; ISO Form CP 00 17 06 07, § G.1.c.

1194. Barlow, Massmann, Alexander & Schreibman, *Condominium Insurance Coverage Guide* at 177 (2d ed. National Underwriter Co., 2016).

1195. Cozen, *Insuring Real Property*, § 1.06[5] (Matthew Bender & Co. 2015).

1196. *A Massachusetts Guide to Understanding the Insurance Policy Covering Your Home*, p. 8 (Massachusetts Division of Insurance, June 2007) (inflation guard endorsement allows insurer to automatically change policy limit during policy period and on each subsequent renewal policy by predetermined percentage, for example, 2, 4, 6, or 8 percent).

1197. *See* § 6.02[6][e], *supra*.

1198. The documents may simply require that coverage be reviewed annually and adjusted to provide the coverage the association deems prudent, and obtaining inflation guard coverage would fulfill that mandate. *See, e.g.*, Gonzalez v. DeBerry, 2011 Cal. App. Unpub. LEXIS 5533 (2011) (CC&Rs required that all policies be reviewed at least annually and adjusted, if necessary, to provide coverage and protection as association might deem prudent or as reasonably required by any first mortgagee).

Under inflation guard coverage, the limit of insurance for property to which it applies will automatically increase by the annual percentage shown on the Declarations Page.[1199] The amount of that increase is determined by taking the limit of insurance that applied on the most recent of the policy inception date, the policy anniversary date, or any other policy change amending the limit of insurance and multiplying it by the percentage of annual increase (expressed as a decimal) shown on the Declarations Page; that result is then multiplied by the number of days since the beginning of the current policy year or the effective date of the most recent policy change amending the limit of insurance, divided by 365.[1200]

If a common interest community policy includes inflation guard protection, it is important to check the Declarations Page to determine the percentage by which the limit of insurance is being increased. It may be as high as 10 percent, which may be excessive or inadequate depending on the local real estate market.

[3] Replacement Cost

When the replacement cost coverage option is elected, coverage without deduction for depreciation replaces "actual cash value" in the loss condition section of the policy.[1201] It is important to realize that replacement cost coverage may be mandated. Fannie Mae requires that property insurance for properties securing loans delivered to it has to provide for claims to be settled on a replacement cost basis.[1202] In a few states, replacement cost coverage is required by law.[1203] The governing documents of common interest communities often specifically require that the association obtain replacement cost coverage.[1204]

1199. *See* ISO Form CP 00 10 06 07, § G.2.a; ISO Form CP 00 17 06 07, § G.2.a.

1200. *See* ISO Form CP 00 10 06 07, § G.2.b; ISO Form CP 00 17 06 07, § G.2.b.

1201. *See* ISO Form CP 00 10 06 07, § G.3.a; ISO Form CP 00 17 06 07, § G.3.a. *See* Summit Towers Condo. Ass'n v. QBE Ins. Corp., 2012 U.S. Dist. LEXIS 80881 (S.D. Fla. May 29, 2012) (replacement cost coverage under § G.3, when purchased by insured, supersedes actual cash value provision of § E.8). *See generally* Prum, *The Next Green Issue: Considering Property Insurance for the Green Building*, 7 Va. L. & Bus. Rev. 421, 436–38 (2013).

1202. *See* § 6.02[6], *supra*. *See also* Boucher, *Co-Insurance for Condominiums . . . What??* (Mar. 2014), available at: https://activerain.com/blogsview/4386779/co-insurance-for-condominiums---what-- (if association tries to save money by opting for 80 percent coinsurance policy, it would eliminate conventional and FHA financing options within project, having negative impact on property values).

1203. *See, e.g.*, Colo. Rev. Stat. 38-33.3-313(1)(a); Fla. Stat. § 718.111(11)(a); Haw. Rev. Stat. § 514B-143(a); 765 Ill. Comp. Stat. 605/12(a); Minn. Stat. § 515.25.

1204. *See, e.g.*, Royal Bahamian Ass'n v. QBE Ins. Corp., 750 F. Supp. 2d 1346, 1358 (S.D. Fla. 2010) (association must obtain fire and extended coverage insurance and vandalism and malicious mischief insurance in amount equal to maximum insurable replacement value, as determined annually by governing board); Roberts v. Nine Island Ave. Condo. Ass'n, 126 So. 3d 286, 288–89 (Fla. 3d DCA 2011) (association must purchase and carry casualty insurance coverage for building and other improvements in amount equal to maximum insurance replacement value as determined annually by governing board); Anderson v. Council of Gables, 404 Md. 560, 575, 948 A.2d 11, 15 (2008) (association must obtain and maintain casualty or physical damage insurance in amount equal to full replacement value of condominium); Countrywide Home Loans, Inc. v. Tutungi, 66

Under the BPP and CAC, replacement cost coverage does not apply to "personal property of others," contents of a residence, or works of art, antiques, etchings, pictures, statuary, marbles, bronzes, porcelains, and "bric-a-brac."[1205]

There is one significant difference between the BPP and CAC policy forms. Under the latter, personal property owned indivisibly by all unit owners and fixtures, improvements and alterations that are a part of the building, or structure and appliances—for example, those used for refrigerating, ventilating, cooking, dishwashing, laundering, security, or housekeeping—contained within a unit, regardless of ownership, if the "Condominium Association Agreement" requires the association to insure them,[1206] are not considered to be the personal property of others.[1207] On the other hand, the BPP provides that tenant improvements and betterments are not considered to be the personal property of others.

Both policies provide that the insured may make a claim for loss or damage covered by the policy on an actual cash value basis instead of on a replacement cost basis, but that the insured may still make a claim for the additional replacement cost coverage if the insured notifies the carrier of the intent to do so within 180 days after the loss or damage.[1208] Under the replacement cost coverage, replacement is the "default" method for determining the value of the covered property and, therefore, if the insured makes no election to receive actual cash value, it does not have to notify the carrier that it wants to make a claim for replacement cost.[1209]

The practice is for the insurer to determine both actual cash value and full replacement cost and withhold the difference between those figures as depreciation until the insured actually repairs or replaces the damage.[1210] Thus,

Cal. App. 4th 727, 730, 78 Cal. Rptr. 2d 203, 204 (1998) (CC&Rs required association to carry replacement cost insurance policy).

1205. *See* ISO Form CP 00 10 06 07, § G.3.b; ISO Form CP 00 17 06 07, § G.3.b. Note that the BPP adds "stock" to the list of exceptions unless the "including stock option" is shown on the Declarations Page.

1206. The policy does not define "Condominium Association Agreement," but it apparently refers to the governing documents.

1207. Barlow, Massmann, Alexander & Schreibman, *Condominium Insurance Coverage Guide* at 178 (2d ed. National Underwriter Co., 2016) (property owned indivisibly by all unit owners is not personal property of others and is subject to replacement cost coverage).

1208. *See* ISO Form CP 00 10 06 07, § G.3.c; ISO Form CP 00 17 06 07, § G.3.c. *See also* Oriole Gardens Condo. Ass'n I v. Aspen Specialty Ins. Co., 875 F. Supp. 2d 1379, 1384 (S.D. Fla. 2012) (untimely notice—more than four years after the date of loss—barred replacement cost claim); Vision I Homeowners Ass'n v. Aspen Specialty Ins. Co., 674 F. Supp. 2d 1333, 1343 (S.D. Fla. 2009) (failure by association to notify insurer of its intention to seek RCV coverage until well after 180 days provided for in policy—whether calculating 180-day time period from the date of loss or date association provided its first notice of loss to insurer—barred RCV claim).

1209. Madison Park Townhouses Homeowners Ass'n v. Country Mut. Ins. Co., 2015 U.S. Dist. LEXIS 119090 (D. Colo. Sept. 8, 2015) (insurer opted to pay ACV benefits, but association never accepted nor cashed the checks; finding provision for election of actual cash value inapplicable).

1210. Goff v. State Farm Fla. Ins. Co., 999 So. 2d 684, 690 (Fla. 2d DCA 2008).

replacement cost payments are not made on an "upfront" basis.[1211] The carrier will not pay on a replacement cost basis for any loss or damage until that lost or damaged property is *actually* repaired or replaced,[1212] and the repairs or replacement have to be made *as soon as reasonably possible* after the loss or damage.[1213] The policy does not define "as soon as reasonably possible," and at least one court has found the phrase ambiguous.[1214] The fact that the insured may lack the financial ability to perform the work does not change the fact that completion of repairs remains a prerequisite to payment.[1215]

The BPP adds that in the case of tenant improvements and betterments, if the conditions that the lost or damaged property be actually repaired or replaced and the repairs or replacement be made *as soon as reasonably possible* after the

---

1211. Madison Park Townhouses Homeowners Ass'n v. Country Mut. Ins. Co., 2015 U.S. Dist. LEXIS 119090 (D. Colo. Sept. 8, 2015); Ocean View Towers Ass'n v. QBE Ins. Corp., 2011 U.S. Dist. LEXIS 147579 (S.D. Fla. Dec. 22, 2011) (policy plainly provides RCV coverage only after lost or damaged property is actually repaired or replaced and, thus, where repairs have yet to occur, policy did not afford RCV coverage); Legacy Condos., Inc. v. Landmark Am. Ins. Co., 2008 U.S. Dist. LEXIS 655 (S.D. Miss. Jan. 4, 2008) (under replacement cost provision, insurer was not obligated to compensate association until lost or damaged property was actually repaired or replaced and unless those repairs or replacements were made as soon as reasonably possible after loss or damage; repairs actually made render estimates for those same repairs irrelevant).

1212. *See* Oriole Gardens Condo. Ass'n I v. Aspen Specialty Ins. Co., 875 F. Supp. 2d 1379, 1384 (S.D. Fla. 2012) (replacement cost claim failed because association had not repaired or replaced most of allegedly damaged property, even though six and a half years had passed since date of loss); Goff v. State Farm Fla. Ins. Co., 999 So. 2d 684, 690 (Fla. 2d DCA 2008) (under replacement cost policy, following loss, both actual cash value and full replacement cost are determined and difference between those figures is withheld as depreciation until insured actually repairs or replaces damaged structure). *See also* Edge Constr., LLC v. Owners Ins. Co., 2015 U.S. Dist. LEXIS 85835 (D. Colo. June 29, 2015) (recoverable depreciation is difference between replacement cost value and actual cost value).

1213. *See* ISO Form CP 00 10 06 07, § G.3.d; ISO Form CP 00 17 06 07, § G.3.d. *See, e.g.*, Hilton Head Resort Four Seasons Ctr. Horizontal Prop. Regime Council of Co-Owners, Inc. v. General Star Indem. Co., 357 F. Supp. 2d 885, 888–89 (D.S.C. 2005) (insured elected replacement cost coverage in excess policy covering damages exceeding $1 million; where no repairs had been made to damaged roofs during policy period and insured failed to demonstrate that it had paid repair or replacement costs in amount exceeding $1 million, no duties on part of insurer arose under contract of insurance). Absent this condition, an increase in the cost of construction material during a delay in repair or replacement could cause costs to balloon, something for which the insurer understandably wants to avoid payment. Barlow, Massmann, Alexander & Schreibman, *Condominium Insurance Coverage Guide* at 179 (2d ed. National Underwriter Co., 2016).

1214. *See* Madison Park Townhouses Homeowners Ass'n v. Country Mut. Ins. Co., 2015 U.S. Dist. LEXIS 119090 (D. Colo. Sept. 8, 2015) (meaning of "unless the repairs or replacement are made as soon as reasonably possible after the loss or damage" is not defined in policy and is ambiguous as to when, exactly, insured has to have repairs or replacement completed before becoming entitled to RCV benefits; whether time period is "as soon as reasonably possible" involves questions of fact that have to be resolved by jury).

1215. Oriole Gardens Condo. Ass'n I v. Aspen Specialty Ins. Co., 875 F. Supp. 2d 1379, 1385 (S.D. Fla. 2012). *See also* Buckley Towers Condo., Inc. v. QBE Ins. Corp., 395 F. App'x 659 (11th Cir. 2010) (prevention of performance argument, if accepted, would impermissibly rewrite contract).

loss or damage are met, the value of those improvements and betterments will be determined as a proportion of the original cost of the insured, as set forth in the valuation loss condition of the policy, and the carrier will not pay for loss or damage to tenant improvements and betterments if others pay for repairs or replacement.[1216]

The insurer will not pay more for loss or damage on a replacement cost basis than the lesser of the limit of insurance applicable to the lost or damaged property, the cost to replace the lost or damaged property with other property of comparable material and quality and used for the same purpose, or the amount actually spent that is necessary to repair or replace the lost or damaged property.[1217] When a building is rebuilt at a new premises, the cost to replace the lost or damaged property with other property of comparable material and quality and used for the same purpose is limited to the cost that would have been incurred if the building had been rebuilt at the original premises. The meaning of "comparable material and quality" is a source of disagreement. Does it require the insurer to pay to replace undamaged property—for example, roof tiles or siding—to maintain a uniform appearance? Courts have said the plain meaning of "comparable material and quality" is material suitable for matching and, thus, "on the spectrum of resemblance," the phrase requires less than an *identical color match*, but a reasonable color match nonetheless. One court decided that because a color mismatch would result from the inability to replace the damaged siding panels with ones of "comparable material and quality," the covered property—that is, the buildings—sustained direct physical loss. The insured condominium association was entitled to have all the siding panels on each of its buildings replaced. However, the court concluded by saying that "all storm-related property damage claims present their own facts," warning the reader that different facts—including different policy language—could yield a different result.[1218]

1216. *See* ISO Form CP 00 10 06 07, §§ G.3.d.(3), (4).

1217. *See* ISO Form CP 00 10 06 07, § G.3.e; ISO Form CP 00 17 06 07, § G.3.e. *See also* Villa D'Orleans Condo. Ass'n v. Pac. Ins. Co., 2008 U.S. Dist. LEXIS 41171 (E.D. La. May 22, 2008) (where public adjuster's estimate includes markup for overhead and profit at rate of 31 percent, but general contractor who actually performed work for association charged nothing for overhead and only 10 percent for profit, under terms of policy providing carrier would not pay more than amount actually spent that was necessary to repair or replace lost or damaged property, insured association could recover no more than what it actually paid to repair covered damage). *Compare* Chateau Argonne Condo. Ass'n v. State Farm Ins. Co., 2008 U.S. Dist. LEXIS 70917 (E.D. La. Sept. 18, 2008) (insured association made initial repairs, apparently paid for by insurer, but subsequently received updated repair estimate and challenged proposed valuation of insurer; insurer argued it should not be liable for any amount greater than that already spent on repairs, but court denied summary judgment to insurer and held it was possible that insurer may have paid for only portion of necessary repairs and that there were genuine issues of fact remaining as to total cost of repairs and whether insurer might be liable for additional expenses).

1218. Cedar Bluff Townhome Condo. Ass'n v. Am. Family Mut. Ins. Co., 857 N.W.2d 290 (Minn. 2014). The property in *Cedar Bluff* consisted of 20 multi-unit residential buildings. All of the buildings were damaged in a hail storm. Some had damage to only a few siding panels while

The cost of repair or replacement does not include the increased cost attributable to enforcement of any ordinance or law regulating the construction, use or repair of any property.[1219]

The replacement cost coverage can be extended to the personal property of others if that coverage is shown on the Declarations Page.[1220]

§ 10.35 Commercial Property Conditions

Both a Building and Personal Property Coverage Form and a Condominium Association Coverage Form will have attached another form titled "Commercial Property Conditions."[1221] This form addresses nine conditions: fraud by the insured; control of the property, insurance under two or more coverages, legal actions against the carrier, revisions to the policy broadening coverage, bailees, other insurance, policy period and coverage territory, and transfer of rights of recovery against others.

[1] Concealment, Misrepresentation, or Fraud

The policy specifically provides that it is void in any case of fraud by the insured as it relates to the policy at any time. It is also void if the insured or any "other insured," at any time, intentionally conceals or misrepresents a material fact concerning the policy, the covered property, the interest of the insured in the covered

---

others had more extensive damage to their siding. Replacement panels were available from the same manufacturer, but panels of the same color were not. The association contended all of the siding on all 20 buildings had to be replaced because there would be a color mismatch with existing panels if only the damaged ones were replaced. The association and carrier disagreed over whether policy language providing for replacement of damaged property with other property of comparable material and quality required replacement of all siding, even undamaged siding, to provide a color match. The association argued "comparable material and quality" mandated a color match between the damaged and undamaged panels, and the carrier countered that the policy only required replacement of panels that had actually been damaged. The court found that the policy required a "reasonable color match" between new and existing siding. Because there was not a reasonable color match available, all the panels would have to be replaced providing the color mismatch constituted a direct physical loss of or damage to covered property as that is what the policy required the insurer to cover. *Accord* Trout Brook South Condo. Ass'n v. Harleysville Worcester Ins. Co., 995 F. Supp. 2d 1035 (D. Minn. 2014) (where policy required insurer to cover cost of repair or replacement with similar materials for same use and purpose or to repair, replace, or rebuild property with material of like kind and quality to extent practicable, terms "similar materials" and "material of like kind and quality" could not be defined, as matter of law, to preclude consideration of color; rather, jury would have to determine whether policy obligated insurer to pay for matching shingles).

1219. *See* ISO Form CP 00 10 06 07, § G.3.f; ISO Form CP 00 17 06 07, § G.3.f. *See, e.g.*, Ocean View Towers Ass'n v. QBE Ins. Corp., 2011 U.S. Dist. LEXIS 147579 (S.D. Fla. Dec. 22, 2011) (carrier was not required under replacement cost provision to pay cost of replacing glass with impact rated glass as required by building code).

1220. *See* ISO Form CP 00 10 06 07, § G.4; ISO Form CP 00 17 06 07, § G.4.

1221. *See, e.g.*, ISO Form CP 00 90 07 88.

property, or a claim under the policy:[1222] The clause is often invoked based on statements in a proof of loss.[1223] To prevail under the clause, the insurer must show more than a false statement; it must prove the insured made a false statement of fact known by the insured to be false at the time it was made.[1224] That an initial estimate may far exceed the amount of loss stated on the proof of loss may be evidence of overstating the loss, but that does not alone show the insured made any material misrepresentations or committed fraud.[1225]

Failure to disclose pertinent information in a proof of loss may be the basis for finding fraud or concealment. For example, in a Florida condominium case, an insurer alleged the association failed to disclose in a supplemental proof of loss that roofing repairs and replacements had been made after a hurricane at a cost substantially less than what the claim represented, and that the association knew the true cost of the replaced roofs at the time the supplemental claim was made but failed to disclose it or even that the roof repairs had already been made. The court found the insurer adequately alleged with particularity that the association intentionally concealed material facts during the course of the claims process to obtain a greater recovery on the policy.[1226]

Statements made at an examination of the insured under oath might also be the basis for invoking the fraud or concealment clause; however, the mere

---

1222. *See, e.g.*, ISO Form CP 00 90 07 88, § A.

1223. *See, e.g.*, Cypress Chase Condo. Ass'n "A" v. QBE Ins. Corp., 2013 U.S. Dist. LEXIS 40347 (S.D. Fla. Mar. 22, 2013), where the insurer argued the association either recklessly or intentionally submitted an inflated claim for hurricane damage in its proof of loss statement. Specifically, it contended the adjuster for the association based his estimate on an "improper extrapolation" of the building damages and that the claim was overstated by inclusion of the replacement costs of windows and sliding glass doors that were not damaged by the hurricane. The association responded that it never misled the insurer but only refused to respond to "pretextual requests" for information. The court said the insurer's fraud and concealment defense depended on whether the association submitted the proof of loss statement in good faith. The court found there was a disputed issue of material fact as to whether the association attempted to defraud the insurer and denied summary judgment to the insurer on its affirmative defense of fraud and concealment.

1224. *See* 200 Leslie Condo. Ass'n v. QBE Ins. Corp., 965 F. Supp. 2d 1386 (S.D. Fla. 2013), *aff'd*, 616 Fed. Appx. 936 (11th Cir. 2015) (insurer failed to meet its burden of proving fraud and concealment by association where representative of association who signed proof of loss testified that he relied on information provided him and expertise of professionals in concluding information in proof of loss was realistic and truthful).

1225. El-Ad Residences v. Mt. Hawley Ins. Co., 2010 U.S. Dist. LEXIS 109084 (S.D. Fla. Sept. 28, 2010). In *El-Ad Residences* there were what the court characterized as "some troubling facts" regarding the submission by an association of an estimate that was for more than twice the amount stated in the proof of loss. The court said although there was evidence supporting the allegation that the initial estimate was overstated, the insurer had not provided any evidence demonstrating which specific portions, if any, of the estimate were intentionally overstated and had not proved that the difference between the estimate and proof of loss could be attributed to intentional misrepresentations of fact.

1226. Nova Hills Villas Condo. Ass'n v. Aspen Specialty Ins. Co., 2008 U.S. Dist. LEXIS 3972 (S.D. Fla. Jan. 21, 2008).

fact the insured did not reasonably prepare for the EUO and, therefore, did not adequately respond to inquiries is insufficient to show fraud or concealment.[1227]

[2] Control of the Insured

A standard clause provides that any act or neglect of any person other than the insured beyond the direction or control of the insured will not affect the insurance. Further, the breach of any condition of the policy at any one or more locations will not affect coverage at any location where, at the time of loss or damage, the breach of condition does not exist.[1228]

The first thing to note about this clause is that it discusses any act or neglect of any person other than *you*. Commercial property policies provide that "you" refers to the named insured shown of the Declarations Page. Courts have held that the named insured includes any additional insured.[1229] When that is the case, if the members of the association are considered additional insureds, the clause *could* be read to say, "Any act or neglect of any person other than the association or its members beyond the direction or control of the association or its members will not affect this insurance." That would defeat the purpose of the control clause.[1230]

The next thing to observe is that the clause says the operable act or neglect "will not affect this insurance." What does "affect" the insurance mean? A Michigan appellate court is one of the few to address that language. That court concluded the act of another person outside the control of the insured is not a basis to grant coverage, nor is it a reason to deny coverage; rather, the court has to look to the terms of the policy to determine if any particular loss is covered and if the loss is specifically excluded, there is no coverage.[1231] In other words, the "control" clause does not override a specific exclusion. Finally, courts have held that the

1227. 200 Leslie Condo. Ass'n v. QBE Ins. Corp., 965 F. Supp. 2d 1386 (S.D. Fla. 2013), *aff'd*, 616 Fed. Appx. 936 (11th Cir. 2015).

1228. *See, e.g.*, ISO Form CP 00 90 07 88, § B.

1229. *See* K & W Builders v. Merchants & Bus. Men's Mut. Ins. Co., 255 Va. 5, 10, 495 S.E.2d 473, 476 (1998). *See also* Sentience Studio, LLC v. Travelers Ins. Co., 102 Fed. Appx. 77 (9th Cir. 2004) (pursuant to "control" clause, insurer could not deny coverage to innocent coinsureds based on exclusion and to extent coinsured may be exempted from exclusion under innocent coinsured doctrine, there would be no reason why third-party beneficiary should not be similarly exempted).

1230. Hakala, *Condominium Casualty and Liability Insurance*, 48 St. John's L. Rev. 1112, 1117 (1974) (provision in association policy stating that its coverage will be unaffected by act or neglect of any person if that conduct is beyond knowledge or control of association prevents insurer from arguing that act of owner increasing danger to property should invalidate entire coverage).

1231. Torres Hillsdale Country Cheese v. Auto-Owners Ins. Co., 2013 Mich. App. LEXIS 1547 (2013) (exclusions clearly denied recovery for any loss caused by government seizure of covered property as well as any loss caused by decision of governmental body and, therefore, where state agency seized contaminated and uncontaminated product, there was no coverage for loss of uncontaminated product because act of agency was outside control of insured). *But see* Sentience Studio, LLC v. Travelers Ins. Co., 102 Fed. Appx. 77 (9th Cir. 2004).

fact that the control provision might appear to conflict with specific exclusions does not create an ambiguity.[1232]

One obvious question for a common interest community association is, who is under its control: employees, contractors, the community association manager, members of the association? The policy does not define "control." Courts have said the word is synonymous with management, authority to direct, restrict, regulate, govern, or administer.[1233] Certainly a CIC manages and has authority to direct anyone it directly employs. It would have some authority to direct parties with which it contracts—including the community association manager—by virtue of the agreement between the parties. It could be said that members of a CIC control it, rather than the other way around, by virtue of their right to amend the governing documents, to elect the governing board, and, where authorized by statute or the documents, to remove members of the governing board. On the other hand, an association ordinarily has specific authority to direct, restrict, regulate, and govern its members. Associations generally are given authority in the governing documents to enforce any restrictions on members found in those documents and to adopt rules governing the conduct of their members. As one example, in CICs with attached units, leaks from one unit causing damage to common property and other units are a common problem. In response, governing boards often adopt rules to prevent leaks—for example, requiring shut-off valves on washing machine hoses and that water be turned off to a unit that is vacant more than a few days. Are unit owners subject to these rules under the "direction or control" of the association? There does not appear to be any reported decision addressing the question. An association may want to raise the issue with its insurer.[1234]

1232. K & W Builders v. Merchants & Bus. Men's Mut. Ins. Co., 255 Va. 5, 11, 495 S.E.2d 473, 477 (1998) (where act or neglect in question was not attributed to person or entity other than named insured and additional insured, control of property provision did not apply, and there was no ambiguity concerning question of whether fraud clause or dishonest acts exclusion negated coverage for all insureds based on acts of any coinsured). *See also* Traders & Gen. Ins. Co. v. Freeman, 81 F. Supp. 2d 1070, 1077 (D. Or. 1999) (control of property condition did not create ambiguity).

1233. Halldin v. Usher, 315 P.2d 418, 424 (Cal. App. 1957) ("control" is synonymous with management, authority to direct, superintend, restrict, regulate, govern, administer, or oversee); Wolffe v. Loeb, 98 Ala. 426, 432–33, 13 So. 744, 746 (1893), *overruled on other grounds*, Hillens v. Brinsfield, 108 Ala. 605, 18 So. 604, 1895 Ala. LEXIS 18 (1895) ("control" means to check, restrain, govern, have under command, and authority over). *Consider* Am. Econ. Ins. v. Camera Mart, Inc., 2006 U.S. Dist. LEXIS 66433 (E.D. Ark. Sept. 15, 2006) (where officer and stockholder of closely held corporation allegedly had exclusive control over its financial and business decisions and managed it on daily basis, if corporation through that person committed arson, the act in that circumstance would not be beyond control of corporation).

1234. The fact someone at the company ventures a definition of "control" will almost certainly not bind the insurer if the question is in litigation. If an association wants a definitive definition of the term, it must obtain an endorsement to the policy.

[3] Insurance under Two or More Coverages

Policies provide that if two or more of the coverages under the policy apply to the same loss or damage, the insurer will not pay more than the actual amount of the loss or damage.[1235]

[4] Legal Action against the Carrier

Typically, policies include two provisions related to actions against the insurer. The first is that compliance with the policy is a precondition to any legal action. The second is a contractual limitation on the time within any action must be brought.

[a] Policy Compliance

Policies typically state that *no one* may bring a legal action against the insurer under the policy unless there has been full compliance with all of the terms of the policy.[1236]

The wording of the compliance clause has significance for residents of common interest communities. Sometimes residents believe they have a loss covered by the association policy, but either the association refuses to make a claim or the insurer refuses to pay it. The individual resident may then bring suit against the insurer. The compliance clause does not say the named insured may not sue the insurer without first complying with the policy terms; it says *no one* may. Apparently then, the individual resident has to comply with all the policy terms as a precondition to suing the insurer.

[b] Contractual Limitation

The typical commercial property policy provides that *no one* may bring an action against the insurer under the policy unless it is brought within a prescribed time

1235. *See, e.g.*, ISO Form CP 00 90 07 88, § C.

1236. ISO Form CP 00 90 07 88, § D.1. *See, e.g.*, Horizons Condo. Ass'n v. QBE Ins. Corp., 2007 U.S. Dist. LEXIS 6091 (M.D. Fla. Jan. 29, 2007) (where association allegedly failed to produce all records relating to its claim or allowed insurer to conduct any requested examinations under oath and its proof of loss allegedly contained errors, court said that while total failure to comply with policy provisions made prerequisite to suit under policy may constitute breach precluding recovery from insurer as matter of law, if insured cooperates to some degree or provides explanation for its non-compliance, fact question is presented for resolution by jury); Ridglea Estate Condo. Ass'n v. Lexington Ins. Co., 309 F. Supp. 2d 851, 859 (N.D. Tex. 2004) (where association conceded that, under provision requiring full compliance with all of terms of policy before legal action could be brought, compliance with notice requirements were conditions precedent and it would have to know that its contention that insurer was required to show prejudice from failure to give required notices before benefiting from that failure was patently without merit). *See also* Ocean View Towers Ass'n v. QBE Ins. Corp., 2011 U.S. Dist. LEXIS 147579 (S.D. Fla. Dec. 22, 2011).

period after the date on which the direct physical loss or damage occurred.[1237] The prescribed period is usually either one or two years[1238] but may be extended by endorsement.[1239] The limit may be less than any applicable statute of limitations.[1240] Generally, the insured must show that its action meets the contractual limitation.[1241]

1237. *See, e.g.*, ISO Form CP 00 90 07 88, § D.2 (two-year limitation). *See* Panorama Vill. Condo. Owners Ass'n Bd. of Dirs. v. Allstate Ins. Co., 144 Wn. 2d 130, 26 P.3d 910 (2001), where the court interpreted "after a loss occurs" to suggest a policyholder has to bring any action for coverage within one year subsequent to or succeeding the loss. This, said the court, is to be distinguished from a contract that requires an action to be brought within a prescribed period "after the inception of a loss." That type of suit limitation requires the policyholder to bring an action within a time certain subsequent to the *beginning* of the loss. *See also* Holden Manor Homeowners Ass'n v. Safeco Ins. Co. of Am., 2016 U.S. Dist. LEXIS 78821 (W.D. Wash. June 16, 2016) (where alleged loss was hidden damage from wind-driven rain because of faulty construction, and that loss had been present since completion of construction in 1979, suit filed in 2015 was not time-barred as decay was not exposed until 2014); Eagle Harbour Condo. Ass'n v. Allstate Ins. Co., 2016 U.S. Dist. LEXIS 15791 (W.D. Wash. Feb. 9, 2016) (loss did not "occur" until association knew about system-wide failure of building envelopes; policy could have limited insurer's liability by providing inception clause, but it did not); Queen Anne Park Homeowners Ass'n v. State Farm Fire & Cas. Co., 2012 U.S. Dist. LEXIS 59275 (W.D. Wash. Apr. 27, 2012) (collapse might commence during policy period but remain hidden and, therefore, constitute continuing occurrence of loss, for some time after policy expires, in which case suit will be timely so long as it is filed within contractual period after decay is revealed); 815 Park Ave. Owners v. Fireman's Ins. Co., 225 A.D.2d 350, 639 N.Y.S.2d 325 (1996), *app. den.*, 647 N.Y.S.2d 713, 88 N.Y.2d 808, 670 N.E.2d 1345 (1996) (where contractual period of limitation in policy required that suit against the insurer be commenced within two years after loss occurs, limitation period would not be measured from date related litigation by tenant/shareholder over loss might be concluded as that measure would only be proper where policy provides coverage against loss or damage for which insured may be held legally liable as opposed to first-party property coverage; if court were to assume that the tenant did not resume occupancy of apartment until March 1991, that was last month in which covered rent loss was sustained and commencement of action against insurer in July 1993 was, therefore, untimely with respect to rent-loss claim).

1238. *See, e.g.*, Winding Hills Condo. Ass'n, Inc. v. North Am. Specialty Ins. Co., 332 N.J. Super. 85, 752 A.2d 837 (2000), where the insured had several policies, some with a two-year limitation and others with a one-year limitation.

1239. *See, e.g.*, ISO Form IL 01 75 09 07 (Florida Changes—Legal Action Against Us), providing that any legal action against the insurer involving direct physical loss or damage to property has to be brought within five years from the date the loss occurs.

1240. Bethel Vill. Condo. Ass'n v. Republic-Franklin Ins. Co., 2007 Ohio App. LEXIS 471 (Feb. 8, 2007), *app. den.*, 114 Ohio St. 3d 1427, 868 N.E.2d 681 (2007). Sometimes the prescribed limitation will be modified by stating that if the law of the state in which the policy is issued allows more than that prescribed period, that longer period of time will apply. In 1515–1519 Lakeview Blvd. Condo. Ass'n v. State Farm Fire & Cas. Co., 2001 Wash. App. LEXIS 429 (Wash. Ct. App. Mar. 12, 2001), *rev. den.*, 144 Wn. 2d 1012, 31 P.3d 1184 (2001), the association argued the language deferring to state law rendered the suit limitation clause ambiguous. The court disagreed. It said the average person would conclude that the suit limitation clause controlled unless a state statute *specifically* extended the minimum period, rather than the fact that the state has a general statute of limitations on breaches of contract that happens to be longer than the contractual limitation period.

1241. *See, e.g.*, Ass'n of Unit Owners v. State Farm Fire & Cas. Co., 670 F. Supp. 2d 1156 (D. Or. 2009) (while inception of loss would begin at point of collapse, not point of decay, association

Policies do not define the phrase "direct physical loss or damage," but that does not allow an insured to make the date a claim is denied as the time when the damage occurred. For example, the property of a common interest community was damaged in a hail storm in April of 2003. The association argued its damage occurred when the insurer notified it in February 2004 that it would not pay for installation of ice guards. The court did not agree. It found that the damage occurred in the hail storm and, therefore, the association action against the insurer filed in February 2006 was barred by the two-year contractual limitation.[1242]

To prevent insurers from delaying a decision on a claim until the limitation period has expired, many courts hold the limitation period is tolled from the time the insured provides notice of its claim or submits a proof of loss and the time the insurer denies coverage of the claim.[1243] However, the fact that the insured does not discover the *full extent* of its damages during the limitation period does not toll it.[1244] For example, a California homeowners association suffered damage in the 1994 Northridge earthquake. It immediately submitted a claim to the insurer. The carrier denied the claim because its inspection showed the damages did not exceed the deductible. However, eight years later a professional inspection of the property obtained by the association revealed damage that exceeded the deductible. The association sued the carrier, which raised the contractual limitation as a defense. The court said that once any damage becomes reasonably apparent, the limitation period begins to run, even if the full extent of the damage is unknown.

---

failed to present specific facts showing that instance of loss occurred after date on which contractual limitation began to run and, therefore, it could not show that it brought suit within two years after occurrence of loss to meet that condition of coverage).

1242. Bethel Vill. Condo. Ass'n v. Republic-Franklin Ins. Co., 2007 Ohio App. LEXIS 471 (Feb. 8, 2007), *app. den.*, 114 Ohio St. 3d 1427, 868 N.E.2d 681 (2007).

1243. *See, e.g.*, Doheny Park Terrace Homeowners Ass'n, Inc. v. Truck Ins. Exchange, 132 Cal. App. 4th 1076, 34 Cal. Rptr. 3d 157 (2005) (running of limitation period may be tolled during period that insurer is considering claim); Clark v. Truck Ins. Exch., 95 Nev. 544, 546, 598 P.2d 628, 629 (1979) (limitation will be tolled from time insured gave notice of loss until insurer formally denies liability); Peloso v. Hartford Fire Ins. Co., 56 N.J. 514, 521, 267 A.2d 498, 502 (1970) (limitation was tolled while parties negotiated and did not begin to run again until insureds were notified in writing that liability was denied). *See generally* Council, *Equitable Tolling Revisited in Michigan: The Dangerous Abolition of a Necessary Insurance Doctrine*, 54 Wayne L. Rev. 1389 (2008).

1244. *See* Magnolia Square Homeowners Ass'n v. Safeco Ins. Co., 221 Cal. App. 3d 1049, 271 Cal. Rptr. 1 (1990) (where association claimed loss did not occur until May 1986 when its experts cut open walls and discovered structural defects, but it was on notice over one year earlier of sufficient damage to warrant further investigation and it could have discovered extent of loss through exercise of reasonable diligence, action brought in 1987 was barred by one-year contractual limitation). *Compare* Winding Hills Condo. Ass'n, Inc. v. North Am. Specialty Ins. Co., 332 N.J. Super. 85, 752 A.2d 837 (2000), where the association hired an engineering consultant that discovered structural deficiencies in 1989. An extensive report was completed and delivered to the association in January 1991. It explained that deficiencies in the on-site drainage system had led to structural failures of the foundation footings. The court said that arguably the association should have been charged with notice of the loss as early as 1989 when the foundation problems were first reported to it, but agreed with the trial court that the loss could have been no later than the delivery to plaintiff of the January report.

The association, noted the court, knew there had been enough damage to warrant notifying the insurer, and that started the running of the limitation period in which to commence an action. The association argued the running of the limitations period should be equitably tolled because the insurer never sent it a formal written unequivocal letter of denial. However, the court said that when the insurer told the association that the damages did not exceed the deductible, the practical effect of that communication was a specific unequivocal denial.[1245]

While generally the parties may contract for a limitations period that is less than the applicable statute of limitations, state law may prohibit reducing the statutory limitations period. For example, under Florida law, a cause of action for breach of an insurance contract accrues when the insurer denies the claim, not when the loss occurs. By statute, the limitations period for breach of contract actions is five years, and any contractual provision reducing that period is void.[1246] Thus, a contractual limitation requiring actions to be filed within five years of the date of loss shortened the limitations period and was unenforceable.[1247] Texas has a law under which a limitations period that is shorter than two years is void. A limitation requiring any action to be brought within two years and one day after the date on which direct physical loss or damage occurred, but also providing no action could be brought unless there had been full compliance with all the terms of the policy, violated the Texas statute because "full compliance" with the post-loss obligations clause had the practical effect of providing a period in which to file suit that was less than two years.[1248]

[5] Liberalization

A "liberalization" clause says that if the insurer adopts any revision that would broaden the coverage without an additional premium within 45 days prior to or during the policy period, the broadened coverage will immediately apply.[1249]

[6] Bailees

A "bailment" is the delivery of personal property by one person—the bailor—to another—the bailee—in trust for a specific purpose, subject to a contract, either

1245. Doheny Park Terrace Homeowners Ass'n, Inc. v. Truck Ins. Exchange, 132 Cal. App. 4th 1076, 34 Cal. Rptr. 3d 157 (2005) (tolling period ends on unconditional denial of claim in writing, and it does not matter that denial does not specifically use that word; request for reconsideration of claim will not extend time to sue).

1246. Fla. Stat. § 95.03.

1247. Palma Vista Condo. Ass'n of Hillsborough County v. Nationwide Mut. Fire Ins. Co., 2010 U.S. Dist. LEXIS 118262 (M.D. Fla. Oct. 7, 2010).

1248. Spicewood Summit Office Condos. Ass'n v. Am. First Lloyd's Ins. Co., 287 S.W.3d 461 (Tex. App.—Austin 2009).

1249. *See, e.g.*, ISO Form CP 00 90 07 88, § E.

express or implied, that the bailee will faithfully execute the trust.[1250] Bailments that a common interest community might encounter could involve delivery of property to another to be repaired or stored. A standard condition of commercial property polices provides that no person or organization, other than the insured who has custody of the covered property, may benefit from the coverage of the policy.[1251] Thus, the typical association policy will not cover its personal property while in the custody of a bailee. The association, therefore, needs to determine whether the bailee has insurance that covers the property while it is in the possession of the bailee. Generally, the liability of a bailee for loss or damage to the goods in its possession is measured by a standard of ordinary care; in other words, the bailor can recover from the bailee in a negligence action for damage to, or the loss of, the property if the bailee fails to exercise ordinary care.[1252] That is of little help to the CIC if the property is lost or damaged in an event in which the bailee was not negligent—for example, a tornado, earthquake, or flood—or the bailee is insolvent.

[7] Other Insurance

Under "other insurance" clauses, if an insured has another policy subject to the same plan, terms, conditions, and provisions, the insurer will pay its share of the covered loss or damage that is the proportion that the applicable limit of insurance bears to the limits of insurance of all insurance covering on the same basis.[1253] If there is any other insurance that covers the same loss or damage, the insurer will pay only for the amount of covered loss or damage in excess of the amount due from that other insurance, whether the insured can collect on it or not, but will not pay more than the applicable limit of insurance.[1254]

1250. *Ballentine's Law Dictionary* (LexisNexis 2010).

1251. *See, e.g.*, ISO Form CP 00 90 07 88, § F. *See* Seeley v. State Farm Fire & Cas. Co., 2016 Conn. Super. LEXIS 972 (Conn. Super. Ct. May 3, 2016) ("No Benefit to Bailee" provision not intended to negate any enforceable rights of unit owners).

1252. Helmholz, *Bailment Theories and the Liability of Bailees: The Elusive Uniform Standard of Reasonable Care*, 41 U. Kansas Law Rev. 97 (1992).

1253. *See, e.g.*, ISO Form CP 00 90 07 88, § G.1.

1254. *See, e.g.*, ISO Form CP 00 90 07 88, § G.2. *See* Certain Underwriters at Lloyd's v. Am. Family Mut. Ins. Co., 2007 U.S. Dist. LEXIS 66599 (D. Colo. Sept. 10, 2007), in which two insurers issued property policies to the same common interest community association. The policy of the first insurer included both subsections of section G on other insurance. The second insurer had no *pro rata* clause, but instead only an excess insurance provision stating that if there was other insurance covering the same loss or damage, it would pay only for the amount of covered loss or damage in excess of the amount due from that other insurance. The court held that when there are two policies, each with an excess provision, by operation of Colorado law, they are deemed repugnant and each insurer is obligated to pay its *pro rata* share of the loss. Thus, regardless of whether the *pro rata* clause in the Lloyd's policy applied, each insurer was required to provide benefits on a *pro rata* basis.

[8] Policy Period and Coverage Territory

A standard condition in commercial property policies states that the carrier covers loss or damage *commencing* during the policy period shown on the Declarations Page and within the coverage territory, which is the United States of America—including its territories and possessions—Puerto Rico, and Canada.[1255] Generally, the insured has the burden to establish specific facts to show a loss commencing during that policy period. Thus, where an expert for a condominium association denied that it was possible to prove when the purported collapse of structural members of the building occurred, the association did not, and, according to its own expert, could not identify a specific instance of collapse that occurred during the policy period and the court would have to assume, based on speculative probability, a structural member fell into pieces during that period. That was a leap, the court said, it should not take.[1256]

[9] Subrogation: Transfer of Rights of Recovery to the Carrier

Commercial property policies contain a clause titled "Transfer of Rights of Recovery Against Others" that is a subrogation provision.[1257] It provides that if anyone to or for whom the insurer makes payment under the policy has rights to recover damages from another, those rights are transferred to the insurer to the extent of its payment.[1258] The person or organization receiving the payment is required to do everything necessary to secure the rights of the insurer and is prohibited from doing anything after a loss to impair those rights. The insured, however, may waive his or her rights against another party in writing *before a loss* to his or her covered property or income.

After a loss to covered property or income, the insured may only waive rights against another party in writing if, at time of loss, that party is someone insured by the policy, a business firm owned or controlled by the insured or that owns or controls the insured, or the *tenant* of the insured. This does not restrict the insurance for the insured. Thus, if the insured waives its rights against one of the specified third parties, the insurance remains in place, but it will not apply if one of those named parties was seeking to recover from its own carrier or another person.

1255. ISO Form CP 00 90 07 88, § H. *See, e.g.*, Ridglea Estate Condo. Ass'n v. Lexington Ins. Co., 309 F. Supp. 2d 851, 859–60 (N.D. Tex. 2004) (court was "inclined to agree" that insurer would not be liable for hail damage resulting from storm that occurred during effective period of its policy unless damage resulting from that storm manifested itself during policy period).

1256. Ass'n of Unit Owners v. State Farm Fire & Cas. Co., 670 F. Supp. 2d 1156 (D. Or. 2009).

1257. *Condominium Association Coverage Form* (Summit Business Media, 2013).

1258. *See, e.g.*, ISO Form CP 00 90 07 88, § I. *Consider* May v. Mid-Century Ins. Co., 151 P.3d 132, 142 (Okla. 2006) (although policy may allow insurer to bring subrogation claim in name of unit owner, that does not provide unit owner with standing as express third-party beneficiary of policy to bring bad faith claim against insurer as under policy insurer owed no duty of any kind to owner and its claim against third-party tortfeasor would neither create contractual duty in favor of unit owner nor invest her with right to claim against insurer).

[a] Subrogation and Common Interest Communities

In common interest communities, waivers of subrogation serve the goal of preventing litigation between unit owners, and between unit owners and the governing board.[1259] To that end, under the UCIOA, and in the CIC legislation of many states, every property policy is required to provide that the insurer waives its right to subrogation under the policy against any unit owner or member of his or her household.[1260] Commentary to the Uniform Act notes that the waiver appears consistent with traditional insurance practice in which a homeowner is not held liable by his or her insurer for his or her own negligence. If the house is damaged, the carrier is required to pay the cost of rebuilding. On the other hand, the commentary notes that in common interest communities, the association suffers from the risk of a careless resident whose risky behavior incurs no consequences to him or her, but may result in dramatic increases in premiums for the association, or even in cancellation of the policy.[1261] The UCIOA addresses this threat by providing that if damage to a unit or other part of the community is caused by the willful misconduct or *gross* negligence of any unit owner or guest or invitee of a unit owner, the association may assess that expense exclusively against that owner's unit, even if it maintains insurance for that damage or common expense.[1262] A commentary to that provision explains that it authorizes a charge-back despite the mandated waiver of subrogation rights and, therefore, an association could choose not to submit a claim under its policy and instead proceed directly against the unit owner for the entire cost of the repair, including any amount that would otherwise be paid from the deductible.[1263]

[b] Waiver and Condominium Unit Owners

The standard Subrogation clause is modified in the Condominium Association Coverage Form by another clause called "Waiver of Rights of Recovery" in which the insurer waives it rights to recover payment from any unit owner shown on the Declarations Page for damage to insured property for which the insurer has paid the association.[1264] Unit owners are rarely "shown on the Declarations Page" by name or in any other direct fashion. Indeed, the typical commercial property policy Declarations Page does not have a designated space for that purpose. So, what does "shown on the Declarations Page" mean? The apparent position taken

---

1259. Pac. Indem. Co. v. Deming, 140 F. Supp. 3d 152 (D. Mass. 2015), *rev'd on other grounds*, 828 F.3d 19 (1st Cir. 2016).

1260. Uniform Common Interest Ownership Act § 3-113(d)(2) (2008).

1261. Uniform Common Interest Ownership Act § 3-113 (2008), comment 2.

1262. Uniform Common Interest Ownership Act § 3-115(e) (2008). *See also* Uniform Common Interest Ownership Act § 3-115(c)(3) (to extent required by Declaration, costs of insurance have to be assessed in proportion to risk).

1263. Uniform Common Interest Ownership Act § 3-115 (2008), comment 6.

1264. *See, e.g.*, ISO Form CP 00 17 06 07, § E.9. *See also Condominium Association Coverage Form* (Summit Business Media, 2013).

by insurers is that when the Declarations Page identifies the association as the named insured, one then looks to the association governing documents. If those documents prescribe that the name of the insured will be the association "and the unit owners without naming them"—or similar language—then the unit owners are in effect "shown on the Declarations Page." There does not appear to be an appellate court ruling on this matter, so it is probably advisable to provide the insurer with the insurance provisions in the governing documents and ask that the governing documents be attached to and become part of the policy, which would ensure that the named insured is clearly identified.

This Waiver of Rights of Recovery clause may be further modified in some states by endorsement. For example, a standard Utah endorsement to the Condominium Association Coverage Form provides that the insurer waives its rights to recover payment from a person residing with a unit owner, if the unit owner resides in the unit, and any unit owner of the condominium shown on the Declarations Page.[1265] The language of standard endorsements in Connecticut, Maryland, Minnesota, and Texas are different from that of Utah. Those endorsements say that the carrier waives its rights to recover payment against any unit owner described on the Declarations Page, including the developer, and members of his or her household, the association, and members of the board of directors for acts or omissions within the scope of their duties for the insured, but reserves its rights to recover from the developer damages for which the developer may be held liable in the capacity of a developer.[1266] The purpose of these endorsements is to conform the policy language to state law, although it should be noted that in none of these three states does the applicable law limit the waiver to unit owners *shown on a Declarations Page*.

[c] Waiver of Subrogation by Association Documents

When an insured waives the right to subrogation, that waiver also bars the insurer's rights to recover against a negligent third party because an insurer takes nothing more by way of subrogation than its insured had.[1267] Typical policy language provides that the insured may waive rights to recover damages against another party in writing before a loss.[1268] In the case of a common interest community,

1265. ISO Form CP 01 82 11 13, § B (Commercial Property: Utah Changes—Condominium Associations).

1266. ISO Form CP 01 39 10 12, § F (Commercial Property: Connecticut Changes—Condominium Association Coverage—Condominium Law Provisions); ISO Form CP 17 03 10 09, § B (Commercial Property: Maryland Changes—Condominium Additional Provisions); ISO Form CP 01 06 02 96, § B (Commercial Property: Minnesota Changes—Condominiums); ISO Form CP 01 48 10 12, § E (Commercial Property: Texas Changes—Condominium Association Coverage—Condominium Law Provisions).

1267. Pac. Indem. Co. v. Deming, 140 F. Supp. 3d 152 (D. Mass. 2015).

1268. *See, e.g.*, ISO Form CP 00 90 07 88, § I ("Transfer of Rights of Recovery Against Others to Us").

that written waiver can take the form of language in the governing documents.[1269] Thus, when the policy contains that typical language, courts examine the CIC documents to determine whether an association's insurer may recover an amount it paid to the association from a resident of the community.

Some courts hold that where the CIC documents *require* that policies waive subrogation by the insurer as to any claims against the association or the individual owners, it constitutes the required written waiver before a loss. For example, a condominium unit owner allegedly was negligent in maintaining a unit, allowing pipes to freeze and burst. The association's insurer paid for the resulting damage and sought subrogation from the unit owner. The rules of the condominium provided that all policies would contain a waiver of subrogation by the insurer as to any claims against a unit owner. The court found that the association waived its right of subrogation against the unit owner and the insurer could not have a right of subrogation greater than that of its insured.[1270]

In contrast, in a case decided by the First Circuit Court of Appeals, the bylaws required that condominium unit owners obtain their own property coverage and that the coverage include a waiver of subrogation. A unit owner obtained a policy, but it lacked a waiver. That unit owner suffered a substantial loss when a tenant fell asleep after turning on the bathtub faucets in the master bathroom and the water overflowed. The insurer for the unit owner paid that claim and sought subrogation against the tenant. The court said the bylaws did not constitute a waiver and the insurer for the unit owner could bring an action against the tenant for subrogation.[1271]

1269. *See generally* Breslau & O'Connor, *Subrogating Losses in Common Interest Communities*, available at: https://www.cozen.com/admin/files/publications/Breslau.pdf.

1270. Scottsdale Ins. Co. v. Schell Props., LLC, 2015 Del. Super. LEXIS 399 (Del. Super. Ct. Aug. 5, 2015). *See also* New York Mar. & Gen. Ins. Co. v. 320 Parsonage Lane, LLC, 2016 N.Y. Misc. LEXIS 2148 (June 8, 2016) (granting dismissal of subrogation action by association insurer to residents of condominium who argued association waived right to subrogation though bylaws requiring it to obtain and maintain coverage for physical damage and to waive subrogation; rejecting argument of insurer that bylaws did not evidence waiver of right to subrogation as they showed only what association was required to do, not whether it complied); Admiral Indem. Co. v. Delins, 2012 N.Y. Misc. LEXIS 1321 (Mar. 19, 2012) (condominium bylaws required all policies of physical damage insurance to contain waivers of subrogation and insurer seeking subrogation against unit owner argued bylaws did not waive subrogation, but instead deferred that issue to controlling insurance policies; court noted insurer failed to provide copy of policy and held bylaws provided for waiver of subrogation claims for any amounts that would benefit owners and, therefore, insurer could not maintain subrogation action).

1271. Pac. Indem. Co. v. Deming, 828 F.3d 19, 25 (1st Cir. 2016). *See also* Cmty. Ass'n Underwriters of Am. v. McGillick, 2010 U.S. Dist. LEXIS 138198 (D.N.J. Dec. 13, 2010), where the court considered bylaws that required policies of physical damage insurance issued to a condominium association to contain waivers of subrogation. The policy at issue, however, contained no waiver. A fire started at the unit of the defendant unit owners and spread to other portions of the community. The insurer paid the claim and subrogated to the association's claim against the unit owners. The unit owners argued the insurer was barred from suing them because of the waiver of subrogation in the bylaws. The court said the insurer was not a party to the bylaws but would inherit the

Sometimes the governing documents will require the association to use its "best efforts" to obtain a waiver of subrogation. Courts have held that although the standard policy language does not automatically waive subrogation rights, the intent expressed by a "best efforts" clause meets the policy condition for the association to waive its rights to recovery against another party.[1272] Even though a "best efforts" mandate does not actually require the association to *succeed* in obtaining a waiver of subrogation in the policy, courts have said it does obligate the use of best efforts to do so and the insurer—having stepped into the shoes of its insured—cannot, therefore, maintain a subrogation action unless *its insured* lived up to its obligation.[1273] Conversely, in one case where condominium bylaws required waivers of subrogation "to the extent obtainable," it was held that the bylaw merely authorized waiver but did not constitute one.[1274]

When common interest communities are obliged to obtain waivers of subrogation in their policies, failure to do so may subject them to liability to a resident who is injured—that is, has to reimburse the association insurer—by that failure.[1275]

---

association's claims under the bylaws as a subrogee. Only by stepping into the shoes of the insured by virtue of subrogation, noted the court, did the insurer become a party to bylaws that required waiver of that subrogation. The court then concluded that any alleged breach by the association in failing to waive subrogation did not preclude the insurer's suit.

1272. Insurance Co. of Greater N.Y. v. Rusmussen, 2015 N.Y. Misc. LEXIS 2722 (July 22, 2015) (where proprietary lease stated cooperative association would use its best efforts to obtain provision in all insurance policies carried by it waiving right of subrogation against tenant/shareholders, and it and tenant/shareholders entered into that lease before fire that caused damage at issue, lease met all requirements of "Transfer of Rights of Recover Against Others to Us" clause of policy).

1273. Greater New York Mut. Ins. Co. v. Nasarre, 2009 N.Y. Misc. LEXIS 5926 (2009). In *Nasarre* a tenant/shareholder in a cooperative building allegedly caused water damage that the cooperative corporation's insurer paid for. The insurer sought to recover the amount it paid from the tenant/shareholder. The proprietary lease provided the corporation would use its *best efforts* to obtain a provision in all its policies waiving the right of subrogation against the tenant. The corporation's policy, however, had no waiver and, said the court, the lease did not by its terms contain a waiver. However, the corporation breached the lease by failing to use its best efforts to waive subrogation in its policy and, held the court, a breach of an agreement to obtain a waiver of subrogation in a policy prevents the *insurer* from maintaining a subrogation action. The court added that the breaching party could be directly liable for its failure to obtain the waiver.

1274. Admiral Indem. v. Onetti, 2008 N.Y. Misc. LEXIS 10946 (2008) (where condominium bylaws provided that all policies of physical damage insurance had to contain "to the extent obtainable" waivers of subrogation, bylaws only authorized waiver of subrogation but did not constitute actual waiver of subrogation).

1275. Greater New York Mut. Ins. Co. v. Nasarre, 2009 N.Y. Misc. LEXIS 5926 (2009) (if cooperative association failed to obtain waiver, it could be directly liable for that failure). *See also* Cmty. Ass'n Underwriters of Am. v. McGillick, 2010 U.S. Dist. LEXIS 138198 (D.N.J. Dec. 13, 2010) (unit owners could counterclaim for breach of contract for alleged breach by association in failing to waive subrogation).

§ 10.36 Endorsements

An "endorsement"—also called a "rider"—is a separate form attached to a policy that modifies it. An endorsement may add to, or exclude from, coverage provided in the main policy or change some other aspect of the policy. It is generally said that an endorsement is subject to, and governed by, all relevant terms of the primary policy unless otherwise stated.[1276] The typical commercial property policy will have a number of endorsements. Some of these will be added by the insurer to address a particular risk. Others may be added to respond to a request for specific coverage not found in the policy. Many endorsements are necessary to conform the policy to state law. These may address substantive issues (for example, coverage for a specific peril like sinkholes) or procedural matters (for instance, the process for cancellation or non-renewal of the policy). Some endorsements may be broad and encompass several different parts of the primary policy, while others can be very narrow, excluding coverage for a specific risk in only a single jurisdiction.[1277]

The insured can determine which endorsements have been added to the policy by examining the Declarations Page where there will be a section headed "forms and endorsements made a part of the policy at time of issue" or "this policy is comprised of the following forms and endorsements." All of the various forms and endorsements that make up the policy will then be listed. Unfortunately, they will probably be listed by a series of identifying letters and numbers rather than a descriptive title. When that is the case, the association should ask the broker from whom the policy was obtained for a list of the endorsements by descriptive title and for an explanation of the import of the various endorsements before the policy is finalized or the premium is paid so that at the time of purchase the association clearly understands which endorsements are part of the policy, and what purpose they serve.

[1] Additional Exclusions from Coverage

Two endorsements that may be added to the policy and that may limit its coverage are the innocent-sounding Protective Safeguards Endorsement and the Sprinkler Leakage Exclusion Endorsement. Either has the potential to leave a common

1276. LCS Corr. Servs. v. Lexington Ins. Co., 800 F.3d 664 (5th Cir. 2015); Penthouse Owners Ass'n, Inc. v. Certain Underwriters, 612 F.3d 383, 386 (5th Cir. 2010) (endorsement controls policy insofar as it enlarges, modifies, or restricts terms of policy, and if there is any conflict between it and policy, endorsement controls in construing contract expressly where provisions of endorsement are more specific); Transcon. Ins. Co. v. Wash. Pub. Utils. Dist. Util. Sys., 111 Wn. 2d 452, 462, 760 P.2d 337 (1988).

1277. *See, e.g.*, ISO Form CP 01 46 08 94 (Commercial Property—Arizona Changes) (modifies Building and Personal Property Coverage Form and Condominium Association Coverage Form to make fire department service charge inapplicable).

interest community with a large uninsured loss. Discovering one of these two "sleeper" policy modifications would alone justify the time a governing board might spend reviewing its property policy with its broker.

[a] Protective Safeguards

The Protective Safeguard Endorsement (PSE) has an innocent-sounding name, but it can cost the unwary insured coverage for a loss.[1278] It does, however, have one benefit for the insured, and that is that many insurers offer a discount when the endorsement is attached.[1279] At the same time, a PSE can have negative consequences for the policyholder, and for that reason, associations may want to consider asking the insurer to remove it if they find it attached to their policy.[1280] However, that may not be an option with the insurer. For example, when a common interest community has a facility that operates as a restaurant, the insurer is very likely to insist on including the endorsement.[1281]

The language of these endorsements may vary with the carrier, and that language will determine the obligations and extent of coverage of the insured. Some PSEs, as is the case with the ISO endorsement discussed below, add an exclusion for fire, but others may exclude coverage for other perils—for example, theft or vandalism—or suspend all coverage while protective safeguards are not being maintained.[1282] On the other hand, there are policies that will, if protective safeguards are not maintained, merely limit the amount the insurer will pay for a loss.[1283]

1278. Rico, *Does Your Policy Have a Protective Safeguards Endorsement?* (Apr. 1, 2015), available at: http://www.assuranceagency.com/blog-post/does-your-policy-have-a-protective-safeguards-endorsement.

1279. Prahl, *Protective Safeguards Endorsements—Issues and Implications*, available at: http://adjustersinternational.com/publications/adjusting-today/vacancy-occupancy-clauses-protective-safeguards-endorsements/7/.

1280. One commentator notes that when a commercial building is equipped with a protective safeguard device, underwriters will usually attach a PSE to the policy. Prahl, *Protective Safeguards Endorsements—Issues and Implications*, available at: http://adjustersinternational.com/publications/adjusting-today/vacancy-occupancy-clauses-protective-safeguards-endorsements/7/.

1281. *See* Three Monkeys Rest. Inc. v. Cortland Ins. Agency, Inc., 2014 N.Y. Misc. LEXIS 5013 (Nov. 18, 2014) (quoting attorney and licensed insurance broker as stating endorsement is common requirement imposed by insurance companies as a condition for property insurance coverage for restaurants, due to risk of fire from grills and deep fryers).

1282. *See, e.g.*, Landmark Am. Ins. Co. v. Green Lantern Roadhouse LLC, 2009 U.S. Dist. LEXIS 12211 (S.D. Ill. Feb. 18, 2009) (policy provided carrier would not pay for loss or damage caused by or resulting from theft if, prior to that theft, insured knew of any suspension or impairment in any protective safeguard and failed to notify carrier or failed to maintain any protective safeguard in complete working order); Coos Head Timber Co. v. Unigard Indem. Co., 73 Ore. App. 598, 600, 699 P.2d 1143, 1144 (1985), *overruled on other grounds*, Kabban v. Mackin, 104 Ore. App. 422, 801 P.2d 883 (1990); SFI, Inc. v. United States Fire Ins. Co., 453 F. Supp. 502 (M.D. La. 1978) (failure to maintain alarm suspended insurance).

1283. *See, e.g.*, Prendergast v. Pac. Ins. Co., 2012 U.S. Dist. LEXIS 43084 (W.D.N.Y. Mar. 28, 2012) (under policy, carrier would not pay more than $60,000 for covered loss caused by or

[i] Language of Standard Endorsement

Under an ISO Protective Safeguards Endorsement,[1284] the insured is required to maintain protective devices or services listed on a schedule as a condition of the insurance.[1285] The burden will likely be on the insured to show compliance.[1286]

There are five named protective safeguards to which the endorsement applies.[1287] They can be listed by symbol on the schedule. There is one catch-all symbol—"P-9"—for any system specifically described on the schedule. The five named protective devices are:

- An automatic sprinkler system,[1288]
- An automatic fire alarm that protects the entire building and that is connected to a central station or reports to a public or private fire alarm station,[1289]
- A security service with a recording system or watch clock that makes hourly rounds covering the entire building when the premises are not in operation,[1290]
- A service contract with a privately owned fire department that provides fire protection service to the described premises,[1291] and
- An automatic commercial cooking exhaust and extinguishing system.[1292]

A wide variety of protective safeguards may be listed under the catch-all category, for example, a contract with a security company or private fire department,

---

resulting from burglary or theft if, prior to that burglary or theft, insured failed to keep applicable protective safeguard in complete working order).

1284. *See* ISO Form CP 04 11 10 12. *See also* ISO Form IL 04 15 04 98.

1285. ISO Form CP 04 11 10 12, § A.1.

1286. American Way Cellular, Inc. v. Travelers Property Casualty Co. of America, 216 Cal. App. 4th 1040, 1054, 157 Cal. Rptr. 3d 385,396 (2013) (compliance with Protective Safeguards Endorsement was condition precedent to coverage); Versai Mgmt. Corp. v. Landmark Am. Ins. Corp., 2013 U.S. Dist. LEXIS 24370 (E.D. La. Feb. 22, 2013) (insured had burden to put forward facts proving that it satisfied this condition precedent).

1287. ISO Form CP 04 11 10 12, § A.2.

1288. An automatic sprinkler system includes related supervisory services. Its symbol is "P-1." An automatic sprinkler system means any automatic fire protective or -extinguishing system, including connected sprinklers and discharge nozzles, ducts, pipes, valves and fittings, tanks, their component parts and supports, and pumps and private fire protection mains. When supplied from an automatic fire protective system it means non-automatic fire protective systems and hydrants, standpipes, and outlets.

1289. The symbol is "P-2."

1290. The symbol is "P-3."

1291. The symbol is "P-4."

1292. The symbol is "P-5." The system is one installed on cooking appliances that has a hood, grease removal device, duct system, and wet chemical fire-extinguishing equipment.

fencing and security,[1293] burglar alarms,[1294] fire extinguishers,[1295] and smoke detectors.[1296] There also may be mandates or prohibitions listed.[1297]

The endorsement adds an exclusion to the causes of loss form or to the Standard Property Policy, whichever is applicable. Under that exclusion, the carrier will not pay for loss or damage caused by or resulting from fire[1298] if prior to it, the insured either knew of any suspension or impairment in any protective safeguard listed on the schedule and failed to notify the carrier of that fact or failed to maintain any listed protective safeguard over which the insured had control in "complete working order."[1299] Additionally, if part of an Automatic Sprinkler System or Automatic Commercial Cooking Exhaust and Extinguishing System is shut off because of breakage, leakage, freezing conditions, or opening of sprinkler heads, the insured does not need to notify the carrier if the insured can restore full protection within 48 hours.[1300]

[ii] Meaning of "Maintained" and "Good Working Order"

The standard ISO and other endorsements use the word "maintain" twice: once in the opening "conditions" clause and again in the Exclusion clause. That can lead to no little confusion.[1301] For example, a New York federal court interpreting the ISO language concluded that the word "maintain" was "hopelessly ambigu-

---

1293. *See, e.g.*, Versai Mgmt. Corp. v. Landmark Am. Ins. Corp., 2013 U.S. Dist. LEXIS 24370 (E.D. La. Feb. 22, 2013) (schedule stated, "Fenced with Security").

1294. SFI, Inc. v. United States Fire Ins. Co., 453 F. Supp. 502 (M.D. La. 1978). *See also* Prendergast v. Pac. Ins. Co., 2012 U.S. Dist. LEXIS 43084 (W.D.N.Y. Mar. 28, 2012).

1295. Colony Ins. Co. v. Peterson, 2012 U.S. Dist. LEXIS 70830 (M.D.N.C. May 22, 2012).

1296. *See, e.g.*, Sagar Megh Corp. v. United Nat'l Ins. Co., 2013 U.S. Dist. LEXIS 159338 (N.D. Ill. Nov. 6, 2013).

1297. *See, e.g.*, Versai Mgmt. Corp. v. Landmark Am. Ins. Corp., 2013 U.S. Dist. LEXIS 24370 (E.D. La. Feb. 22, 2013) (schedule stated, "No Aluminum Wiring"); Colony Ins. Co. v. Peterson, 2012 U.S. Dist. LEXIS 70830 (M.D.N.C. May 22, 2012) (all utilities must remain on and functioning).

1298. The endorsement exclusion cannot, therefore, be a basis for denying coverage when another peril is the cause of loss. *See, e.g.*, Anghel v. Utica Mut. Ins. Co., 127 A.D.3d 897, 7 N.Y.S.3d 390 (2015) (where Protective Safeguard Endorsement related only to fire loss, it did not provide any basis for denial of claim for flood loss).

1299. ISO Form CP 04 11 10 12, § B.

1300. *See* Schwarz & Schwarz of Va., L.L.C. v. Certain Underwriters at Lloyd's, 2009 U.S. Dist. LEXIS 80625 (W.D. Va. Aug. 31, 2009) ("restore full protection" has temporal component—that sprinkler system is providing protection at all times—if insured cannot restore full protection within 48 hours, it has to notify insurer). *See also* Lake States Ins. Co. v. River City Metal Prods., 2004 Mich. App. LEXIS 2040 (Mich. App. July 29, 2004) (rejecting argument that notification was not necessary because, although system was shut down for 19 days before fire struck, insured could have fixed it within 48 hours if it had chosen to do so).

1301. *But see* Yera, Inc. v. Travelers Cas. Ins. Co. of Am., 2014 Pa. Super. Unpub. LEXIS 1267 (2014) (within context of policy, meaning of "maintain" is clear: insured is required to have safeguard device in place and under exclusion section, insured is required to keep required safeguard system in complete working order; policy used word "maintain" in two instances, and specific context of each use leaves meaning of word clear).

ous" and, construing it favorably for the insured, found that it required only that the insured keep an automatic sprinkler system in place on the premises, but did not require the insured to ensure that the water in the system did not freeze or even that the insured maintained its sprinkler system in working order.[1302] In contrast, the exclusion applies when the safeguard exists but the insured has failed to maintain it in working order.[1303] Similarly, where a policy said that "protections provided for the safety of the insured property shall be maintained in good order," and a sprinkler system failed to function because a valve that controlled water flow into it from a tank was closed, making it impossible for water to enter the system, and the tank was empty because of leaks, the court found the insured failed to maintain the sprinkler system in good order and coverage was denied.[1304] Failure to maintain may also mean failure to upgrade a deficient system.[1305]

1302. Five Star Hotels, LLC v. Ins. Co. of Greater N.Y., 2011 U.S. Dist. LEXIS 31313 (S.D.N.Y. Mar. 24, 2011). *See also* French King Realty Inc. v. Interstate Fire & Cas. Co., 79 Mass. App. Ct. 653, 948 N.E.2d 1244 (2011) (insured did not breach condition because it had fire suppression system in place, even though it was antiquated, could no longer be serviced, was labeled non-compliant, and had to be replaced); Breton, LLC v. Graphic Arts Mut. Ins. Co., 2009 U.S. Dist. LEXIS 104846 (E.D. Va. Nov. 10, 2009); Cent. Mut. Ins. Co. v. Ycaw5, 2011 Ohio Misc. LEXIS 12499 (Jan. 4, 2011) (condition precedent to coverage providing that insured maintain a sprinkler system was satisfied once system was installed and in working order and fact that water supply valve was inadvertently closed after sprinkler system was in place and operational did not breach any threshold obligation). *Compare* SFI, Inc. v. United States Fire Ins. Co., 453 F. Supp. 502, 505 (M.D. La. 1978) (contention that protective safeguards clause required system only to be in working order but not "on" was interpretation "too narrow" for court to accept); American Way Cellular, Inc. v. Travelers Property Casualty Co. of America, 216 Cal. App. 4th 1040, 157 Cal. Rptr. 3d 385 (2013) (where application for coverage stated property had sprinkler system, but no sprinkler system was in place and policy required insured to maintain protective devices or services listed, one of which was an automatic sprinkler system, insured was required to have "functioning, operational sprinkler system" and was, therefore, precluded from coverage for failure to maintain automatic sprinkler system as required). *See generally* Cozen, *Insuring Real Property*, § 2.07[16][b][iii] (Matthew Bender & Co. 2015) (majority of courts have found that requirement that insured maintain protective safeguards as condition of insurance is not ambiguous).

1303. *See, e.g.*, Cent. Mut. Ins. Co. v. Ycaw5, 2011 Ohio Misc. LEXIS 12499 (Jan. 4, 2011).

1304. Star Varifoam Corp. v. Buffalo Reinsurance Co., 64 N.C. App. 306, 307 S.E.2d 194 (1983), *rev. den.*, 310 N.C. 154, 311 S.E.2d 294 (1984). *See also* Goldstein v. Fidelity & Guar. Ins. Underwriters, 86 F.3d 749 (7th Cir. 1996) (where policy provided insurer would not pay for loss or damage caused by or resulting from fire if insured failed to maintain automatic sprinkler system over which insured had control, in complete working order, and sprinkler system was not in working order at time of fire, coverage was properly denied). *But see* Breton, LLC v. Graphic Arts Mut. Ins. Co., 446 Fed. App'x 598 (4th Cir. 2011) (where Protective Safeguards Endorsement provided insurer would not pay for loss caused by or resulting from fire if insured failed to maintain any listed protective safeguard in complete working order and, after fire, investigation revealed that valve controlling supply of water to sprinkler heads was in closed position, rendering automatic sprinkler system inoperable, court nonetheless found insured was only required to keep sprinkler system in place and endorsement did not bar coverage).

1305. French King Realty Inc. v. Interstate Fire & Cas. Co., 79 Mass. App. Ct. 653, 948 N.E.2d 1244 (2011) (where fire suppression system could no longer be serviced, parts for it were no longer available, and building inspector refused to issue certificate of inspection because system was non-compliant and needed to be upgraded, insured was required to take steps to bring system

Typically, when an endorsement requires a protective system to be maintained in good working order, it refers to a system over which the insured is in "complete control."[1306] It should be noted that under the language of many of these endorsements, not only water damage from an improperly maintained automatic sprinkler system[1307] but also damage from a fire the system was intended to suppress might be barred.

A concern for common interest communities is that residents or visitors may tamper with a protective safeguard. Generally, under the language of the typical policy, the association may be absolved of the obligation to maintain a protective safeguard in working order if it is not in the association's control. For example, does the association have control over safeguards—sprinklers or smoke detectors—that are located in individual residences? Initially, the answer might appear to be no, but consider that the association may have a right of access to individual units and that it may require residents in the governing documents or by rule to maintain a protective safeguard or report its malfunction. In any event, if an association is aware of the potential for tampering, it may be required to take reasonable precautions to shield a protective safeguard from tampering.[1308]

[iii] Notice of Suspension or Impairment

In general, a PSE requires an insured who knows of any suspension or impairment in any protective safeguard to notify the carrier or lose coverage.[1309] Additionally, a PSE usually requires the insured to notify the carrier if part of the automatic sprinkler system is shut off because of breakage, leakage, freezing conditions, or opening of sprinkler heads; however, notification is generally not necessary if the insured can restore full protection within 48 hours. Additionally, an endorsement may provide that the insurer will not pay for loss or damages caused

---

into compliance and failure to do so meant insured failed to maintain system in complete working order).

1306. Does "control" mean "physical control" or "legal control"? One court found that unclear and, therefore, ambiguous. It construed "control" to mean physical control. A landlord, then, did not have physical control. Breton, LLC v. Graphic Arts Mut. Ins. Co., 446 Fed. App'x 598 (4th Cir. 2011). *Breton* probably has no implications for residential cooperatives because in *Breton*, the landlord surrendered complete control to the premises, including the sprinkler system. While the residents in a cooperative are "tenants," the documents—most likely the proprietary lease or occupancy agreement—will invariably grant the cooperative corporation access to the apartments to make repairs.

1307. *See, e.g.*, Five Star Hotels, LLC v. Ins. Co. of Greater N.Y., 2011 U.S. Dist. LEXIS 31313 (S.D.N.Y. Mar. 24, 2011) (insurer denied coverage for water damage caused by frozen and ruptured sprinkler system because insured allegedly failed to provide adequate heat to stairwells housing sprinkler system in violation of Protective Safeguards Endorsement).

1308. *See, e.g.*, Sagar Megh Corp. v. United Nat'l Ins. Co., 2013 U.S. Dist. LEXIS 159338 (N.D. Ill. Nov. 6, 2013) (where motel knew guests would remove batteries from smoke detectors, it may have breached its duty by failing to incorporate additional safeguards, such as construction of mesh or wire cages around smoke detectors, to prevent motel guests from tampering with them).

1309. *See generally* Cozen, *Insuring Real Property*, § 2.07[16][c] (Matthew Bender & Co. 2015).

by or resulting from fire if, prior to the fire, the insured knew of any suspension or impairment in the automatic sprinkler system and failed to notify the insurer of that fact.[1310] Thus, if the insured knowingly turns off or suspends the sprinkler system, even for routine maintenance, and does not notify the carrier, a loss caused by fire during the suspension can be denied.[1311]

[iv] Inspections

Will regular inspections by a licensed service provider—a good idea in any event—suffice to meet the obligations imposed by the endorsement? How often should the system be inspected?[1312] The CIC association should maintain records of inspections, any reports provided to it by the company making the inspection, and evidence of any repairs made. Should the insurer invoke the Protective Safeguards Endorsement to deny coverage, these records would likely serve to convince a court that the association has complied with the mandates of the endorsement.[1313] However, the fact that the insured has a contract with a professional will not necessarily relieve it of the responsibility to maintain the system in complete working order.[1314]

[v] Automatic Sprinkler System

When a common interest community has an automatic sprinkler system, it is likely an underwriter will attach a Protective Safeguards Endorsement. A CIC should attempt to establish what is required for it to comply with the endorsement. The insurer may offer some guidelines.

Sprinkler systems in a common interest community will generally be found in both the common areas and individual units. For that reason, the association

---

1310. *See, e.g.*, ISO Form BP 04 30 01 06, § B.1 (carrier will not pay for loss or damages caused by or resulting from fire if, prior to fire, insured knew of any suspension or impairment in any scheduled protective safeguard and failed to notify carrier of that fact). Thus, failure to notify the insurer of even a temporary impairment suspends coverage until the protection is restored. https://www.irmi.com/term/insurance-definitions/protective-safeguards-endorsement.

1311. Rico, *Does Your Policy Have a Protective Safeguards Endorsement?* (Apr. 1, 2015), available at: http://www.assuranceagency.com/blog-post/does-your-policy-have-a-protective-safeguards-endorsement.

1312. *See* Breton, LLC v. Graphic Arts Mut. Ins. Co., 446 Fed. App'x 598 (4th Cir. 2011) (court noted policy did not indicate how frequently any purportedly required inspections had to take place, what components of system would need to be examined during any inspection, or how rapidly defects revealed during an inspection had to be repaired).

1313. While one commentary recommends an insured should keep detailed records of the nature, timing, and results of maintenance activities, it cautions that it is not clear that maintenance efforts will be sufficient to satisfy requirements of a Protective Safeguards Endorsement if a maintenance failure at a single, critical time leads to a system failure, but agrees that an insured is in a stronger position if a consistent pattern of maintenance can be shown. Calvin & Ferrell, *Protective Safeguards Endorsements to Property Insurance Policies May Pose Unanticipated Risks for Landlords, Tenants and Others* (Aug. 1, 2009).

1314. Cozen, *Insuring Real Property*, § 2.07[16][d] (Matthew Bender & Co. 2015).

should monitor alterations made by the owners. Many associations require an owner who proposes modifications to his or her unit to have an alteration agreement with the association. That agreement can address the status of the part of the sprinkler system within the unit. It may be necessary to amend the community documents to specifically address this issue and clearly grant the association the authority to review renovation plans and to assure that it has notice of any suspension of sprinklers in a unit during renovation.

A CIC should also have in place a policy under which any shut down or suspension of the sprinkler system is immediately reported to its insurance broker who should then notify the carrier.[1315] It is wise for that notification to be in writing and, in case the broker fails to forward the notice to the insurer, for a copy of the notification to be sent to the insurer. That can easily be accomplished by email. Even if the initial notification is made orally, a follow up email can be sent.

Sometimes it may be necessary to permanently cap a sprinkler head. The association should notify the insurer of that action, as capping even a small number of sprinkler heads can result in a denial of coverage.

[b] Sprinkler Leakage

Damage or loss caused by sprinkler leakage is a named peril generally covered in commercial property policies.[1316] The potential loss from sprinkler leakage is great and, therefore, it should come as no surprise that insurers may add a specific exclusion for that risk, especially in buildings with older systems. There is a standard form that adds sprinkler leakage as an exclusion to the applicable causes of loss form and defines it as leakage or discharge of any substance from an automatic sprinkler system, including collapse of a tank that is part of that system.[1317]

As part of a long list of endorsements, the sprinkler leakage exclusion can easily go unnoticed. This is yet another reason to have an annual insurance audit and review the policy with the broker, specifically examining the topics addressed by the endorsements. If a there is a sprinkler leakage exclusion, the association should not simply accept it. The broker can be asked to contact the insurer to ask if the exclusion will be removed. The insurer may agree unconditionally or may require routine inspections and maintenance of the system.

1315. Rico, *Does Your Policy Have a Protective Safeguards Endorsement?* (Apr. 1, 2015), available at: http://www.assuranceagency.com/blog-post/does-your-policy-have-a-protective-safeguards-endorsement.

1316. ISO Form CP 10 20 04 02, § A.9.

1317. ISO Form CP 10 56 06 95, § A. The form contains a number of other modifications that bear close examination.

[2] Added Coverage

There is a wide variety of endorsements from which a common interest community governing board might choose to add coverage. Some of these—like the Green Upgrades endorsement—are a nice addition to the association coverage, while others—especially the Joint or Disputed Loss endorsement—are essential in certain circumstances and superfluous in others.

[a] Additional Covered Property

Commercial property policies typically include a list of property *not* covered.[1318] Some of the property components that are not covered and may be of concern to common interest communities are roadways, walks, patios, or other paved surfaces; building foundations;[1319] bulkheads, pilings, piers, wharves, or docks; retaining walls that are not part of a building; underground pipes; flues or drains; land; and the cost of excavations, grading, backfilling, or filling. There are a number of endorsements that modify the Building and Personal Property Coverage, Condominium Association Coverage, and Standard Property Policy forms to address these components. The most basic is the Commercial Property Additional Covered Property endorsement.[1320] It is essentially a blank form listing property withdrawn from "Property Not Covered" and added to "Covered Property."[1321] There is also an Additional Building Property endorsement in which additional building property described on a schedule or the Declarations Page is deemed added to the description of "building."[1322] Finally, the Outdoor

1318. *See* ISO Form CP 00 10 06 07, § A.2; ISO Form CP 00 17 06 07, § A.2. See § 10.12[3], *supra*, for a discussion of this topic.

1319. As one observer notes, foundations can be severely damaged and the cost to tear up, remove, and replace them can be very expensive. Boggs, *Three Commercial Property Endorsements Every Client Should Have* (July 27, 2009), available at: http://www.mynewmarkets.com/articles/102464/three-commercial-property-endorsements-every-client-should-have.

1320. *See, e.g.*, ISO Form CP 14 10 06 95.

1321. There are some state specific versions of the endorsement. For example, ISO Form CP 14 12 10 12, titled Commercial Property: Virginia Changes—Additional Covered Property, has a schedule of the "Property Not Covered" under the policy and then when an "X" is marked next to any property component on the schedule, it is withdrawn from "Property Not Covered" and added to "Covered Property."

1322. *See, e.g.*, ISO Form CP 14 15 07 88. One commentary notes that unless the distinction between "building" and "business personal property" is clear up front, the issue might be subject to interpretation after a loss. It adds that anytime property can be covered as a "building," the insured should take advantage of that classification for two reasons. First, the rate is lower for "building" than for business personal property. Second, if the insured includes some property under the building limits, but the carrier considers it business personal property when adjusting the loss, the coinsurance penalty could be invoked. Boggs, *Three Commercial Property Endorsements Every Client Should Have* (July 27, 2009), available at: http://www.mynewmarkets.com/articles/102464/three-commercial-property-endorsements-every-client-should-have.

Trees, Shrubs and Plants,[1323] Outside Signs,[1324] Radio or Television Antennas,[1325] and Leased Property[1326] endorsements extend coverage to the extent it is otherwise not provided.

[b] Earthquake

A standard exclusion is for loss or damage caused directly or indirectly by "earth movement."[1327] Thus, damage from earthquakes is excluded. While only a small percentage of the world's earthquakes happen in the United States, roughly 90 percent of Americans live in seismically active areas.[1328] Earthquake damage is, therefore, a significant risk for property owners, including common interest communities. One way to add coverage for earthquakes is through a Difference in Conditions (DIC) policy. Indeed, commentators say that one of the primary uses of a DIC policy is to cover earthquake losses.[1329] When that is the purpose the DIC policy serves, it is important to note that the policy says separate limits of coverage are shown on the Declarations Page for earthquake damage.[1330] Coverage can also be obtained as an endorsement to a standard commercial property policy.

[i] Causes of Loss—Earthquake Form

The ISO Commercial Property Causes of Loss—Earthquake Form provides that when "Earthquake" is shown on the Declarations Page, covered causes of loss means earthquake and volcanic eruption—that is, explosion or effusion of a

---

1323. *See, e.g.*, ISO Form CP 14 30 10 00. Under the endorsement, outdoor trees, shrubs, and plants at locations described in the endorsement schedule are added to Covered Property and deleted from Property Not Covered.

1324. *See, e.g.*, ISO Form CP 14 40 10 00. Under the endorsement, outside signs (other than signs attached to buildings) described in the endorsement schedule are deleted from Property Not Covered, but the carrier will not pay for loss or damage caused by or resulting from dampness or dryness of atmosphere; changes in or extremes of temperature; marring or scratching; or rain, snow, ice, or sleet.

1325. *See, e.g.*, ISO Form CP 14 50 10 00. Under the endorsement, radio or television antennas (including satellite dishes) and their lead-in wiring, masts, or towers, as described in the endorsement schedule, are added to Covered Property and deleted from Property Not Covered.

1326. *See, e.g.*, ISO Form CP 14 60 07 88. The endorsement provides that Business Personal Property is revised to include personal property of others in the care, custody, or control of the insured under written leases, as described in the endorsement schedule or the Declarations Page.

1327. *See, e.g.*, ISO Form CP 10 30 06 07, § B.1.b.

1328. Prahl, *Earthquake Insurance: What's Your Exposure?* at 1 (Adjusting Today, 2011), available at: http://adjustersinternational.com/publications/adjusting-today/earthquake-insurance/0/.

1329. Prahl, *Difference in Conditions Coverage: What Is It and Who Needs It?* at 3 (Adjusting Today, 2012), available at: http://adjustersinternational.com/publications/adjusting-today/difference-in-conditions-coverage/0/. *See also* Cozen, *Insuring Real Property*, § 12.03 [4] (Matthew Bender & Co. 2015) (DIC insurance may be used to add earthquake coverage to Basic Property Coverage Forms that do not provide coverage for earthquake loss).

1330. *See, e.g.*, ISO Form IH 00 80 09 09, § C.1.

volcano.[1331] Under the coverage, all earthquake shocks or volcanic eruptions that occur within any 168-hour period constitute a single event and the expiration of the policy does not reduce that 168-hour period.

The Earthquake Form has five basic exclusions: ordinance or law, governmental action,[1332] nuclear hazard,[1333] off-premises services,[1334] and war and military action. The insurer will not pay for loss or damage caused directly or indirectly by any of these, and the loss or damage is excluded regardless of any other cause or event that contributes concurrently or in any sequence to the loss.[1335]

The carrier also will not pay for loss or damage caused by or resulting from artificially generated electrical current, including electric arcing, that disturbs electrical devices, appliances, or wires; fire; explosion, other than volcanic explosion; landslide; mine subsidence; tidal wave; flood; mudslide or mudflow, even if attributable to an earthquake or volcanic eruption; or any earthquake or volcanic eruption that begins before the inception of the insurance.[1336] There is also a specific limitation on coverage for loss of or damage to exterior masonry veneer on wood frame walls.[1337]

The Earthquake Form has a percentage deductible—which can be as high as 10 or 20 percent[1338]—and there are nuances in its application that the insured should review with the broker.[1339] Finally, for specified coverage forms the

1331. *See, e.g.*, ISO Form CP 10 40 10 91.

1332. "Governmental action" means seizure or destruction of property by order of governmental authority.

1333. "Nuclear hazard" means nuclear reaction or radiation, or radioactive contamination, however caused.

1334. "Off-premises services" means failure of power or other utility service supplied to the described premises, however that failure is caused when it occurs away from the described premises. However, if loss or damage by a covered cause of loss results, the carrier will pay for that resulting loss or damage.

1335. *See, e.g.*, ISO Form CP 10 40 10 91, § B.1.

1336. *See, e.g.*, ISO Form CP 10 40 10 91, § B.2.

1337. *See, e.g.*, ISO Form CP 10 40 10 91, § C.

1338. *See, e.g.*, Cheviot Vista Homeowners Ass'n v. State Farm Fire & Cas. Co., 2006 Cal. App. Unpub. LEXIS 8327 (Sept. 20, 2006) (condominium association policy with endorsement for earthquake coverage had limit of coverage for damage caused by earthquake of $2,612,398, with 10 percent deductible).

1339. *See, e.g.*, ISO Form CP 10 40 10 91, § D. *See generally* Prahl, *Earthquake Insurance: What's Your Exposure?* at 4 (Adjusting Today, 2011), available at: http://adjustersinternational.com/publications/adjusting-today/earthquake-insurance/0/. The author explains that the deductible provisions apply to each earthquake or volcanic eruption and that separate deductibles are calculated and applied to each building, to personal property at each building, and to personal property in the open. They are calculated separately and applied even if two or more buildings sustain damage, personal property at two or more buildings sustains damage, or a building and the personal property in it sustain damage. If there is damage from another cause in addition to from an earthquake and that other cause is covered through an exception to the earth movement exclusion in the primary policy, then the earthquake deductible is the only one taken and it will be significantly higher than the one in the primary policy.

Earthquake Form provides that for buildings over four stories in height, the carrier will only pay for loss sustained after the first 168 hours after direct physical loss or damage caused by or resulting from earthquake or volcanic eruption.[1340]

[ii] California

California, with its propensity for earthquakes, presents distinctive challenges for common interest communities. First, earthquake coverage can be prohibitively expensive and in any event, insurers will often not provide coverage for full replacement cost.[1341] Second, under California law, "[n]o policy of residential property insurance may be issued or delivered . . . by any insurer unless the named insured is offered coverage for loss or damage caused by the peril of earthquake . . . ."[1342] The phrase "residential property insurance" means a policy insuring individually owned residential structures of not more than four dwelling units and individually owned condominium units.[1343] There is no requirement under California law that an insurer provide earthquake insurance to cover the common areas of a condominium association, and that extends to the common areas in a homeowners association owned by the association and a building owned by a cooperative corporation.[1344]

The California Earthquake Authority (CEA)—created by the state—provides most earthquake insurance in California, although policies are not bought directly from the CEA but from insurance companies that are members of it.[1345] The policies themselves are provided by the CEA. One of them is called the "Basic Earthquake Policy—Common Interest Development."[1346] That policy has optional loss assessment coverage with limits up to $100,000. Under the coverage,

1340. Under another version of the Earthquake Form the carrier will pay only for loss sustained after the first 168 hours after direct physical loss or damage caused by or resulting from earthquake or volcanic eruption, and the deductible is applicable only to buildings over four stories in height. ISO Form CP 10 40 07 88.

1341. Pender, *Condo Owners on Shaky Ground* (San Francisco Chronicle May 2010), available at: http://www.consumerwatchdog.org/story/condo-owners-shaky-ground. The author refers to one property manager who estimates that earthquake coverage doubles the cost of insurance for common interest communities. In one townhome community, according to the manager, $5 million worth of coverage was obtained for $55,000 a year.

1342. Cal. Ins. Code § 10081.

1343. Cal. Ins. Code § 10087(a).

1344. Marina Green Homeowners Ass'n v. State Farm Fire & Casualty Co., 25 Cal. App. 4th 200, 204–05, 30 Cal. Rptr. 2d 364, 366–67 (1994) (applicable California statute refers to interests in spaces inside condominium's structure and plain meaning of term "policy of residential property insurance" includes policy covering interest of individual in space of each unit, and presumably in contents and fixtures within that space, but not interest of joint owners in structure; statute also does not include policies covering structures held through other forms of joint ownership, for example, cooperatives or tenancies-in-common). *Accord* Foothill Village Homeowners Ass'n v. Bishop, 68 Cal. App. 4th 1364, 1377, 81 Cal. Rptr. 2d 195, 204 (1999).

1345. *See* http://www.insurance.ca.gov/01-consumers/105-type/95-guides/03-res/eq-ins.cfm.

1346. *BEQ-6B* (2020 revision), available at: https://www.earthquakeauthority.com/California-Earthquake-Insurance-Policies/Policy-Samples/Condo/Condo-Unit-Policy-Sample.

the policyholder's share of any assessment charged by the association against all property owners in the common interest development is covered if three requirements are satisfied.[1347] Those three requirements are that the insured has a legal obligation to pay the amounts assessed against him or her by the association and the assessment is properly and legally made as a result of a loss directly caused by an earthquake that begins during the policy period as part of a seismic event that begins during the policy period; the assessment is not made as a result of a loss specified in "Losses Not Covered"[1348] and the assessment is made as a result of a loss to structures or other real property; and the property is owned by all members of the association of owners collectively, by the association itself, by the policyholder, or any combination of them. Another provision under the Loss Assessment Coverage clause covers reduction in the value of the policyholder's ownership interest. This provides coverage if two requirements are satisfied for reduction in the value of the ownership interest in the dwelling unit *and* the common interest development if there is physical loss to structures or other real property at the development directly caused by an earthquake and the association

1347. Note that were an association to require owners to obtain an earthquake policy with loss assessment coverage, it would in effect acquire some coverage for the common areas. If the association has insurance, it might well be able to cover its deductible in that manner.

1348. The losses not covered include those that arise out of loss or damage to land, detached garages, outbuildings, structures other than residential structures, or fences and masonry fences and walls that are not integral to the stability of the residential structure containing the dwelling unit or integral to the stability of other residential structures at the common interest development; awnings and patio coverings, carports, or their support structures; antennas or satellite dishes, or to any towers, brackets, or attachments that support or secure them; decorative or artistic features of any property at the common interest development; exterior masonry veneer; plaster, to the extent the cost to repair or replace it exceeds the value of its replacement with sheetrock or drywall; exterior water supply systems including, but not limited to, irrigation systems, sprinkler systems, and water reclamation systems; underground structures or equipment located outside the perimeter of the dwelling unit foundation; walkways, driveways, decks, or patios, except that portion of them necessary for and regularly used for ingress to and or egress from the residential structure containing the dwelling unit by pedestrian or non-ambulatory occupants of that residential structure; fences, bulkheads, piers, and outside walls, including retaining walls; landscaping, trees, shrubs, lawns, or plants; and swimming pools, spas, and hot tubs. Certain assessments are considered losses not covered. The first is an assessment that does not relate directly to reconstruction of structures or other real property damaged or destroyed as a direct result of an earthquake that begins during the policy period as part of a seismic event that begins during the policy period. Second, assessments for the purpose of improving, bettering, or updating covered property to a condition or status better or more costly than the condition and status of the property as it existed immediately preceding the earthquake causing loss to the property are not covered losses, except for those resulting from the cost of reconstruction to bring the property up to local residential building code standards in effect on the date of the earthquake as required as part of the approval of the reconstruction permit process. Finally, assessments that follow or relate in any way to payment or distribution to the policyholder, or any other member of the association, of capital or assets of the association are not covered losses, unless the payment or distribution of capital is made as a result of a loss that is directly caused by an earthquake and is made for the purpose of payment or reimbursement for the repair or replacement of covered loss to property at the common interest development.

elects not to repair or replace that property or is permanently prevented by a government authority or court order from repairing or replacing it.

[c] Loss of Utilities

Under the standard "utility exclusion," coverage is generally eliminated for loss or damage caused directly or indirectly by power surge or failure of power, communication, water, or other utility service supplied to the described premises.[1349] There are endorsements that may modify the Building and Personal Property Coverage and Condominium Association Coverage Forms and that add back coverage. For example, the Utility Services—Direct Damage endorsement provides that the carrier will pay for loss of or damage to covered property described on a schedule caused by the interruption of service—water, communication, and power supply services—to the described premises if the interruption results from direct physical loss or damage by a covered cause of loss.[1350] Under some endorsements, the additional coverage may apply only after a prescribed period of time—for example, from 4 up to 72 hours—has elapsed.[1351]

[d] Vacancy Permit

A vacancy clause is a standard provision in commercial property policies.[1352] The clause provides that if a building where loss or damage occurs has been vacant for more than 60 consecutive days before that loss or damage occurs, the insurer will not pay for any loss or damage caused by vandalism; sprinkler leakage, unless the insured has protected the system against freezing; glass breakage; water damage; theft; or attempted theft, and for losses caused by other perils, and the carrier will reduce the amount it would otherwise pay for the loss or damage by 15 percent.[1353] An endorsement can suspend the vacancy clause exclusions, continue coverage for a specified period of time, and negate the 15 percent reduction in coverage for all other perils.[1354] A standard ISO Vacancy Permit Endorsement is available that modifies both the Building and Personal Property Coverage Form and the Condominium Association Coverage Form.[1355]

1349. *See, e.g.*, ISO Form CP 10 30 06 07, § B.1.e.

1350. ISO Form CP 04 17 06 95. Under the Off-Premises Power Failure—Direct Damage Form (ISO Form CP 04 17 07 88), the carrier will pay for loss of or damage to covered property caused by interruption of service—water, communication, and power supply services—to the described premises if the interruption results from direct physical loss or damage by a covered cause of loss.

1351. Hayman, *Hurricanes and Windstorm Coverage: Case Studies and Coverages* at 8 (Adjusting Today, 2011), available at: http://adjustersinternational.com/publications/adjusting-today/hurricanes-and-windstorm-coverage/0/.

1352. *See, e.g.*, ISO Form CP 00 10 06 07, § E.6; ISO Form CP 00 17 06 07, § E.7.

1353. ISO Form CP 00 10 06 07, § E.6.b.(2); ISO Form CP 00 17 06 07, § E.7.b.(2).

1354. Prahl, *Vacancy/Occupancy Clauses in Property Insurance—An Often Overlooked But Significant Limitation*, at 4 (Adjusting Today, 2015), available at: http://adjustersinternational.com/publications/adjusting-today/vacancy-occupancy-clauses-protective-safeguards-endorsements/1/.

1355. *See, e.g.*, ISO Form CP 04 50 07 88.

[e] Joint or Disputed Loss

When an association has a stand-alone Boiler and Machinery or Equipment Breakdown policy, a loss could trigger—or appear to trigger—both that policy and the commercial property policy. To address the potential dispute between carriers, policies may have a "Joint or Disputed Loss" clause. The clause requires the carriers to pay the insured for the disputed loss once the policy provisions are met without holding the insured hostage while they contest the amount of liability each has for the loss.[1356] While the Boiler and Machinery policy likely includes the clause, commercial property policies often do not. However, for the insured to benefit, both policies have to contain the provision.[1357]

There is a standard ISO endorsement that modifies the insurance provided under commercial property coverage.[1358] It says it is intended to facilitate payment of insurance proceeds when both a boiler and machinery and the commercial property policy are in effect, damage occurs to covered property insured by both policies, and there is disagreement between the insurers over whether there is coverage or the amount of loss to be paid, if any, by each carrier under its own policy.[1359]

The endorsement does not apply if both insurers do not admit to any liability and neither contends that coverage applies under the other policy.[1360] The provisions of the endorsement apply only if the boiler and machinery policy carried by the named insured, insuring the covered property, contains a similar provision at the time of the loss or damage, with substantially the same requirements, procedures, and conditions; the damage to the covered property was caused by a loss for which both carriers admit to some liability for payment under their respective policies; and the total amount of loss is agreed to by the insured and the two carriers.[1361]

If the conditions of the endorsement are satisfied, each carrier will pay, after a written request by the insured, the entire amount of loss it has agreed as being covered, if any, by its policy and one-half the amount of the loss that is in dispute.[1362] Acceptance by the insured of sums paid under the endorsement does

---

1356. Ark. Power & Light Co. v. Hartford Steam Boiler Inspection & Ins. Co., 257 F.3d 853, 855 (8th Cir. 2001) (clause provides means for insured to receive prompt payment when two or more insurers with potentially overlapping coverages disagree as to cause of loss).

1357. Boggs, *Three Commercial Property Endorsements Every Client Should Have* (July 27, 2009), available at: http://www.mynewmarkets.com/articles/102464/three-commercial-property-endorsements-every-client-should-have. *See also* Austin, *Equipment Breakdown—More Than Just Boiler and Machinery* (IRMI 2011), available at: http://www.irmi.com/articles/expert-commentary/equipment-breakdown (joint loss agreement should be requested to be made part of any property policy when equipment breakdown coverage is provided by monoline policy).

1358. ISO Form CP 12 70 09 96.

1359. ISO Form CP 12 70 09 96, § A.

1360. ISO Form CP 12 70 09 96, § B.

1361. ISO Form CP 12 70 09 96, § C.

1362. ISO Form CP 12 70 09 96, § D.

not alter, waive, or surrender any other rights against the commercial property insurer.[1363]

The endorsement provides for arbitration. When both carriers admit to some liability under their respective policies and they agree to submit their differences to arbitration, they will determine the amount each will pay the insured and pay it within 90 days.[1364] Otherwise, the carriers agree to submit their differences to arbitration within 90 days after payment of the loss under the terms of the endorsement.[1365] The insured agrees to cooperate with any arbitration procedures.[1366]

Under the endorsement, the insurer found responsible for the greater percentage of the ultimate loss has to return the excess contribution to the other carrier; additionally, the insurer found responsible for the greater portion of the loss has to pay liquidated damages to the other carrier on the amount of the excess contribution of that insurer.[1367] Arbitration expenses are not part of the excess contribution for which liquidated damages are calculated, and arbitration expenses are to be apportioned between the carriers on the same basis that the ultimate loss is apportioned.

[f] Rent Loss

Generally, under the proprietary lease in a residential cooperative, the "rent" paid by a shareholder/tenant is abated during any time his or her unit—apartment—is uninhabitable.[1368] There is no ISO endorsement form that specifically addresses rent loss.[1369] Rent loss coverage may be found in the property policy,[1370] but it is often added as part of a Business Income endorsement. For example, the Business Income (and Extra Expense) Coverage Form includes the option to incorporate "rental value" in the term business income, and to limit the meaning of business income to rental value only.[1371] The latter would limit the endorsement to rent loss coverage. "Rental value" is defined as the total anticipated rental income from tenant occupancy of the premises described on the Declarations Page as furnished and equipped by the insured and the amount of all charges that

---

1363. ISO Form CP 12 70 09 96, § D.6.

1364. ISO Form CP 12 70 09 96, § E.1.

1365. ISO Form CP 12 70 09 96, § E.2.

1366. ISO Form CP 12 70 09 96, § E.3.

1367. ISO Form CP 12 70 09 96, § F.

1368. 2 Rohan & Reskin, *Real Estate Transactions: Cooperative Housing Law and Practice—Forms* § 12.02[2][b] (Matthew Bender 2016). *See also* Iannucci, *Insurance Products What's Available, What's Recommended* (Cooperator, Aug. 2006), available at: http://cooperator.com/article/insurance-products.

1369. Meislik, *What Would Rent Insurance Be If There Were Such a Thing*? (May 12, 2013), available at: http://www.retailrealestatelaw.com/archives/1822.

1370. *See, e.g.*, 815 Park Ave. Owners v. Fireman's Ins. Co., 225 A.D.2d 350, 639 N.Y.S.2d 325 (1996), *app. den.*, 647 N.Y.S.2d 713, 88 N.Y.2d 808, 670 N.E.2d 1345 (1996) (property damage afforded by section one of policy included additional coverage for lost rent).

1371. ISO Form CP 00 30 06 95, § A.

are the legal obligation of the tenants that would otherwise be obligations of the insured and the fair rental value of any portion of the described premises that is occupied by the insured.[1372]

Under the endorsement, the carrier will pay for the actual loss of business income sustained by the insured because of the necessary suspension of its "operations" during the "period of restoration."[1373] Any loss of "rental value" has to be caused by direct physical loss or damage at the described premises caused by or resulting from any covered cause of loss.[1374] In other words, there is no coverage when a tenant/shareholder is merely in default or his or her share loan is in foreclosure or where the cooperative defaults in performance of its leasehold obligation to maintain premises in a habitable condition.[1375] Additionally, the coverage is provided to the named insured; therefore, if a tenant/shareholder sublets his or her unit, he or she will probably not be able to have any loss in rent he or she sustains covered by the endorsement.[1376] Finally, the amount of rent recovered would be based on the amount being paid at the time, not any planned increase unless the landlord is able to show there was going to be an increase in

---

1372. ISO Form CP 00 30 06 95, § G.5. Coverage for "fair rental value of any portion of the described premises occupied by the insured," explains one commentator, is provided on the theory that the insured would be taking temporary, replacement space elsewhere. Meislik, *What Would Rent Insurance Be If There Were Such a Thing*? (May 12, 2013), available at: http://www.retailrealestatelaw.com/archives/1822.

1373. Limiting recovery to the "actual loss sustained" means the amount by which the rental value is actually reduced minus expenses and charges that do not necessarily continue during the period of untenantability. Ainslie et al., *Business Insurance Law and Practice Guide* § 5.03[2][f] (Matthew Bender & Company, Inc. 2015). Generally, the coverage ends at the point restoration would have been completed had the landlord been diligent. Meislik, *What Would Rent Insurance Be If There Were Such a Thing*? (May 12, 2013), available at: http://www.retailrealestatelaw.com/archives/1822.

1374. ISO Form CP 00 30 06 95, § A.3.d.

1375. *See* 815 Park Ave. Owners v. Fireman's Ins. Co., 225 A.D.2d 350, 639 N.Y.S.2d 325 (1996), *app. den.*, 647 N.Y.S.2d 713, 88 N.Y.2d 808, 670 N.E.2d 1345 (1996) (where policy rent loss provision applied to loss of rents caused by perils insured against damaging or destroying, during policy period, real or personal property and provided reimbursement for actual loss sustained by insured resulting from necessary untenantability for only length of time as would be required with exercise of due diligence and dispatch to rebuild, repair, or replace damaged or destroyed property, coverage was limited to rent loss resulting from period during which apartment could not be occupied because of covered casualty and ensuing repairs and could not be read as extending coverage to breach of the statutory warranty of habitability by cooperative resulting in impairment of value of premises; coverage did not extend to default by cooperative in performance of its implicit leasehold obligation, imposed by law, to maintain premises in habitable condition).

1376. *See* Elkins v. QBE Ins. Corp., 2011 U.S. Dist. LEXIS 43314 (W.D. Wash. Apr. 21, 2011). In *Elkins* the owners of units in an office condominium sought to recover insurance proceeds for loss of rental income to their units that were damaged in a fire. The association policy covered loss of "community income," including loss of rent or of lease payments, caused by the suspension of the association's operations. The court said the policy as a whole limited use of the term "community" to the named insured—the association—and, therefore, it did not provide insurance for loss of rent to the individual unit owners.

rent by, for example, producing notices already sent to tenants of an impending increase.[1377]

The Business Income endorsement is lengthy and complex. The "rental value" component is especially thorny.[1378] It is important, therefore, to review it carefully with the insurance broker to assess the scope of, and limitations on, its coverage.

[g] Increased Cost of "Green" Upgrades

If an association wishes to replace damage to its property with "green" upgrades and have the cost covered by its property insurer, it needs to obtain a Commercial Property Increased Cost of Loss and Related Expenses for Green Upgrades endorsement.[1379] It modifies both the Building and Personal Property Coverage and Condominium Association Coverage Forms and defines "green" as "enhanced energy efficiency or use of environmentally-preferable, sustainable materials, products or methods in design, construction, manufacture or operation. . . ."[1380] The endorsement is lengthy and complex and before deciding whether to obtain it, the association governing board should discuss the coverage it provides and the limitations it imposes with its broker. As explained by one commentary, the endorsement provides that when a covered building sustains a loss, the carrier is obligated to repair or replace it with "materials and products recognized by a third-party verification organization or governmental entity that sets a standard related to green products and practices."[1381]

Green buildings offer advantages and disadvantages. On the one hand, valuing the cost of the new technologies can be challenging and it is more difficult to avoid being underinsured at the time of a loss or being charged too much for the premium; on the other hand, there is a widespread belief that green buildings are better physical risks than traditional ones and as a result, some insurers are offering substantial premium discounts, some as high as 40 percent.[1382]

[h] Expenses of Community Association Manager

When the property of a common interest community association suffers significant damage, the community association manager is often called on to help with

1377. *Business Income, Rent Increase Included in Business Income Calculation?* (Summit Business Media, 2013).

1378. Meislik, *What Would Rent Insurance Be If There Were Such a Thing*? (May 12, 2013), available at: http://www.retailrealestatelaw.com/archives/1822.

1379. *See* ISO Form CP 04 02 09 09.

1380. ISO Form CP 04 02 09 09, § A.3. *See generally* Prum, *Green Buildings, High Performance Buildings, and Sustainable Construction: Does It Really Matter What We Call Them?*, 21 Vill. Envt'l L.J. 1 (2010).

1381. Prum, *The Next Green Issue: Considering Property Insurance for the Green Building*, 7 Va. L. & Bus. Rev. 421, 438 (2013).

1382. Wells, *It's Not Easy Being Green; But It's Profitable* (Apr. 21, 2009), available at: http://www.insurancejournal.com/news/national/2009/04/21/99798.htm.

the claim and with coordinating reconstruction. If the CAM bills for the extra hours expended, can the association recoup that expense from the insurer? There are endorsements that can be added to the policy that may allow recovery of those expenses.

One carrier has a Property Manager Expense Coverage endorsement that specifically modifies the Condominium Association Coverage Form.[1383] It provides that the carrier will pay up to $2,500 for expenses incurred by a property manager listed on a Property Manager Schedule due to direct physical loss of or damage to covered property caused by or resulting from a covered cause of loss. It defines "expense" as all reasonable expenses incurred by the property manager to assist the named insured in the investigation or settlement of any *non-litigation* claim. The definition of property manager would encompass the typical CAM. The endorsement has a special deductible of $250 and provides that no other deductible applies to the coverage it provides.

Expenses of a CAM in investigating or settling a claim or coordinating reconstruction might also be covered under a standard Business Income (and Extra Expense) Coverage Form.[1384] That, at least, is the opinion of one expert in the insurance field.[1385] Insurers, however, do not necessarily agree. If an association wants coverage for extra expenses of its CAM, it should discuss that desire with its broker and be sure the carrier agrees that those expenses are indeed covered under the selected endorsement.

[i] Employee Dishonesty

The Standard Property Policy excludes coverage for loss or damage caused by, or resulting from, any "dishonest" or criminal act by any officers, managers, employees, directors, trustees, authorized representatives of the named insured, or anyone to whom the named insured entrusts covered property for *any* purpose.[1386] Yet, under the law in a number of states, common interest community associations are required to have this form of theft coverage.[1387] Moreover, Fannie Mae requires common interest community associations to have blanket fidelity/crime insurance coverage for anyone who either handles or is responsible for funds that

1383. *See* Aspen American Insurance Company Form BCP 0012 09 11.

1384. *See, e.g.*, ISO Form CP 00 30 04 02.

1385. Claverol, *Are Property Manager's Fees Recoverable?—Understanding Business Interruption Claims* (2010), available at: http://www.propertyinsurancecoveragelaw.com/2010/12/articles/commercial-insurance-claims/are-property-managers-fees-recoverable-understanding-business-interruption-claims-part-52/.

1386. ISO Form ISO Form CP 10 30 06 07, § B.2.h. The exclusion applies whether any of the named actors is acting alone or in collusion with others or whether or not the act occurs during hours of employment. It does not apply to acts of destruction by employees of the named insured, including leased employees, but theft by employees, including leased employees, is not covered.

1387. *See* § 15.01[5][b], *infra*.

it holds or administers, whether or not that individual receives compensation for services, including coverage for a management agent.[1388]

To meet its obligation, an association must purchase either a stand-alone crime/fidelity policy or an employee dishonesty or employee theft endorsement. Some insurers offer employee dishonesty coverage as an optional addition to their policy. An endorsement may cover only employee dishonesty or theft,[1389] while the typical stand-alone policy is more comprehensive and generally provides coverage for losses other than those caused by the acts of employees. Whether the coverage obtained is by way of a stand-alone policy or an endorsement, the definition of employee has to be expanded to include officers, directors, volunteers, and community association managers.

[j] Sewer Backup and Sump Overflow

Standard commercial property policies exclude coverage for loss or damage caused directly or indirectly by "water," and included within the definition of that term is water that backs up or overflows from a sewer, drain, or sump.[1390] Sewer backups are a growing problem generally[1391] and can be a significant predicament for common interest communities, especially for multi-story buildings. When a pipe is blocked on the lowest level, waste water from all the floors above can overflow into units or common elements on the lowest level. Thus, experts recommend that common interest communities obtain sewer backup coverage.[1392]

Sewer backup coverage is available from companies that insure common interest communities.[1393] Associations interested in obtaining it should discuss their needs with their insurance broker. Typically, endorsements provide coverage for direct physical loss or damage to covered property caused by or resulting from either water or waterborne material that backs up through or overflows or is otherwise discharged from a sewer or drain or that overflows or is otherwise

1388. Fannie Mae Single Family Selling Guide § B7-4-02 (Mar. 29, 2016).

1389. *See* Mansion Hills Condo. Ass'n v. Am. Family Mut. Ins. Co., 62 S.W.3d 633, 635 (Mo. App. 2001) (association had policy of business and property insurance and, for additional premium, separate endorsement was included that provided for employee dishonesty coverage). *See, e.g.*, American Resources Insurance Company Form CP-AR-01 (Commercial Property Enhancement Endorsement), available at: https://www.aric.cc/forms/uw/Property%20Enhancement%20Form.pdf; Markel Insurance Company Form MCP 038 (Commercial Property Select Extension Endorsement), available at: https://www.markelinsurance.com/~/media/specialty/agents-sales-materials/forms/mcp038.pdf?la=en.

1390. *See, e.g.*, ISO Form CP 10 30 06 07, § B.1.g.

1391. The Civil Engineering Research Foundation reports that the number of backed up sewers is increasing at a rate of about 3 percent annually. *See* http://www.iii.org/article/sewer-backup from the Insurance Information Institute.

1392. Barnes, *Understanding Your Insurance Policy's Fine-Print; What You Need to Know about Riders* (Cooperator, Aug. 2013), available at: http://cooperator.com/articles/2651/1/Understanding-Your-Insurance-Policy039s-Fine-Print/Page1.html.

1393. *See, e.g.*, Travelers Condominium Business Owners policy as described at: http://www.independentagent.com/SiteAssets/TFT/Ads/AdDocs/CondoPac.pdf.

discharged from a sump, sump pump, or related equipment, even if the overflow or discharge results from mechanical breakdown of the sump pump or its related equipment.[1394] There are two important conditions of which the association should be aware. First, coverage will likely be excluded when the association fails to keep a sump pump or its related equipment in proper working condition or to perform routine maintenance or repair required to keep a sewer or drain free from obstructions.[1395] Second, the endorsement often has its own limit of liability—typically $5,000—which may, or may not, be adequate for the association's needs.[1396]

Sewer backups can occur for a variety of reasons,[1397] but one cause is flooding that forces water up and out of sewer pipes. Flood damage is generally excluded in property policies, and under an Anti-Concurrent Causation clause, an insurer will not pay for loss or damage caused directly or indirectly by a covered loss when an excluded loss contributes concurrently or in any sequence to that loss. The ACC can apply to sewer backup coverage added by endorsement. For example, condominium property was damaged by both surface and ground water that seeped through doors and foundation areas and by water that backed up and overflowed from toilets and bathtub drains. The association had a sewer backup endorsement, but the insurer denied coverage based on the ACC. The association argued, in effect, that the ACC applied only to the water exclusion in the original policy, not the endorsement that replaced that exclusion with added coverage. The court, however, concluded that there was no reason why the ACC should not apply to the language of the replacement exclusion in the same manner that it applied to the original language.[1398] One commentator recommends that when there is damage that was potentially caused by a sewer or drain backup, the policyholder should immediately employ a contractor to obtain video evidence of

---

1394. *See, e.g.*, ISO Form BP 04 53 07 13, § A. Note that the insurer will generally not pay the cost of repairing or replacing a sump pump or its related equipment if there is a mechanical breakdown. An association should discuss with its broker the parameters of coverage for the sump pump under any boiler and machinery or equipment breakdown policy or endorsement. *See* Chapter 11, *infra*.

1395. *See, e.g.*, ISO Form BP 04 53 07 13, § B. If an association has a sump pump, it should be aware that there may be no coverage for a sump pump failure caused by or resulting from failure of power, unless the policy is endorsed to cover a power failure that affects the described premises. The association needs to discuss with its brokers whether this endorsement is included or needs to be added.

1396. *See, e.g.*, ISO Form BP 04 53 07 13, § C. Under this ISO endorsement, the most the insurer will pay for the coverage for all direct physical loss or damage to covered property is $5,000 per location, unless a different Covered Property Annual Aggregate Limit of Insurance is shown on a schedule that is part of the endorsement.

1397. Identified causes of sewer backups include aging sewer systems, combined stormwater and sewage pipelines, and tree roots. *See* http://www.iii.org/article/sewer-backup from the Insurance Information Institute.

1398. Chateau Vill. N. Condo. Ass'n v. Am. Family Mut. Ins. Co., 170 F. Supp. 3d 1349 (D. Colo. 2016).

any sewer and drain blockage.[1399] The insured is thus armed with some evidence if the insurer later argues that some chain of causation included flooding.

When obtaining sewer backup coverage, the association should discuss the parameters of coverage with the broker. It should determine if there are circumstances in which the offered endorsement will preclude coverage when a blockage is in pipes for which the association has no maintenance responsibility.[1400] It should also establish what damages to individual units the association endorsement will not cover. It should then alert the members of the association to discuss any possible gaps in coverage that would need to be addressed by their homeowner's insurance with their own insurance agents.[1401] Typically, homeowner's policies do not cover sewer backups, but an endorsement can be added to them to provide the additional protection.[1402]

§ 10.37 Difference in Conditions Policies

A common interest community will often have as a part of its package of policies a Difference in Conditions policy. Unless the governing board holds a regular insurance audit with its broker or has a knowledgeable insurance committee, it is likely no one in the community has heard of its DIC policy or knows what it is. Even if the broker discusses the DIC with the board or committee, given the enormous amount of information to survey, he or she probably says little about the policy and the board or committee members likely remember even less. However, a DIC policy is an important, in some cases critical, part of the property coverage of a CIC.

In most states, DIC insurance is a "non-filed class of inland marine insurance"[1403] and is typically provided by a surplus lines carrier. Surplus lines

---

1399. *See* https://uphelp.org/claim-guidance-publications/cautionary-coverage-tales-from-the-trenches-sewer-drain-backup/.

1400. It is important to recognize that building owners are generally responsible for any sewer "laterals" that connect its sewer system to main lines in the street. Barnes, *Understanding Your Insurance Policy's Fine-Print; What You Need to Know about Riders* (Cooperator, Aug. 2013), available at: http://cooperator.com/articles/2651/1/Understanding-Your-Insurance-Policy039s-Fine-Print/Page1.html.

1401. Associations need to be careful not to offer any advice or to interpret the association policy for the unit owners.

1402. Barnes, *Understanding Your Insurance Policy's Fine-Print; What You Need to Know about Riders* (Cooperator, Aug. 2013), available at: http://cooperator.com/articles/2651/1/Understanding-Your-Insurance-Policy039s-Fine-Print/Page1.html (sewer backups are not covered under typical homeowner's policy or flood insurance, and coverage has to be purchased either as separate product or endorsement to homeowner's policy).

1403. Prahl, *Difference in Conditions Coverage: What Is It and Who Needs It?* at 2 (Adjusting Today, 2012), available at: http://adjustersinternational.com/publications/adjusting-today/difference-in-conditions-coverage/0/.

insurance provides coverage for difficult-to-insure risks that may otherwise be uninsurable.[1404]

A surplus lines carrier, also known as a non-admitted insurer, is licensed in its domiciliary state or, if a non-U.S. carrier, in its home country, but is not licensed in the individual states where it is covering risks. A full discussion of surplus lines insurers is beyond the scope of this treatise but is important because often they are the only type of insurer that can write unusual or high-risk coverages. A surplus lines insurer is subject to less regulation than licensed, admitted carriers.[1405] The insurer does not have to file policy forms or rates with state insurance departments for approval.[1406] Therefore, policies issued by surplus lines insurers may not have all the protections afforded policyholders by state regulation,[1407] and if the surplus lines insurer becomes insolvent, losses covered by the insurer are not covered by state guaranty funds.[1408]

[1] Difference in Conditions Insurance Defined

A DIC policy is a form of property insurance obtained in conjunction with an underlying commercial property policy.[1409] The National Association of Insurance Commissioners defines difference in conditions insurance as a "special form of open-peril coverage written in conjunction with basic fire coverage and designed to provide protection against losses not reimbursed under the standard fire forms."[1410]

The most common use of DIC policies is to provide coverage for catastrophic perils, for example, floods or earthquakes, that are ordinarily excluded in standard coverage forms or to provide additional limits of coverage for specific perils.[1411] The policy may thus be used to write coverage excess over the primary

---

1404. TWBC III, Inc. v. Certain Underwriters at Lloyd's London, 323 N.J. Super. 60, 61, 731 A.2d 1228, 1230 (1999).

1405. 1 Jeffrey E. Thomas, *New Appleman on Insurance Law Library Edition* § 1.06[8] (Matthew Bender 2017).

1406. Prahl, *Difference in Conditions Coverage: What Is It and Who Needs It?* at 2 (Adjusting Today, 2012), available at: http://adjustersinternational.com/publications/adjusting-today/difference-in-conditions-coverage/0/.

1407. Lent, *The ABC's of Insuring Your Co-op or Condo; Common Terms and Options for Insurance* (Cooperator, Aug. 2014), available at: http://cooperator.com/articles/2818/1/The-ABCs-of-Insuring-Your-Co-op-or-Condo/Page1.html (while admitted carrier will be in compliance with state regulations, adding additional element of security for policyholders, admitted carrier is not always better than non-admitted one, underscoring need for thorough vetting of proposed insurer before signing agreement).

1408. There is one exception: the New Jersey Surplus Lines Guaranty Fund.

1409. Prahl, *Difference in Conditions Coverage: What Is It and Who Needs It?* at 1 (Adjusting Today, 2012), available at: http://adjustersinternational.com/publications/adjusting-today/difference-in-conditions-coverage/0/.

1410. *See* http://www.naic.org/consumer_glossary.htm#D.

1411. *Difference in Conditions Policies* (Summit Business Media, 2012).

limit.[1412] Indeed, a commonly used DIC policy supplements a property policy by providing coverage excluded in the underlying policy and can also be used to provide excess coverage for a type of loss covered by the underlying policy.[1413] When a policy is "excess," it provides coverage only after a loss exceeds the maximum limit of that underlying policy.[1414]

While DIC coverage is usually thought of as provided by a stand-alone policy issued by a different carrier than the one that issued the primary property policy, the primary carrier may include that coverage in its primary policy[1415] or may issue a separate DIC policy.[1416]

[2] The Policy

A DIC policy can take several forms. It can be an "all-risk" primary coverage form excluding perils being provided by a standard policy,[1417] a specified peril primary coverage form,[1418] or an excess property form with the underlying policies scheduled and standard causes of loss excluded. [1419]

For large businesses with complex insurance needs and the potential for large losses, a DIC policy is often written as a separate, non-standard form

---

1412. Prahl, *Difference in Conditions Coverage: What Is It and Who Needs It?* at 2 (Adjusting Today, 2012), available at: http://adjustersinternational.com/publications/adjusting-today/difference-in-conditions-coverage/0/.

1413. *Difference in Conditions Policies* (Summit Business Media, 2012).

1414. *See, e.g.*, Vision I Homeowners Ass'n v. Aspen Specialty Ins. Co., 674 F. Supp. 2d 1328, 1331–32 (S.D. Fla. 2009) (liability of excess insurer kicks in only after primary policy is exhausted, but that does not preclude insured from bringing lawsuit against excess carrier before primary policy is exhausted or dictate judgment on claims as matter of law; exhaustion provision merely created condition precedent to liability, not to litigation).

1415. *See, e.g.*, Great Am. Ins. Co. v. Towers of Quayside No. 4 Condo. Ass'n, 2015 U.S. Dist. LEXIS 150358 (S.D. Fla. Nov. 4, 2015) (carrier issued property insurance policy that included Difference in Conditions Coverage Form); St. Paul Village Condo. Ass'n v. St. Paul Fire & Marine Ins. Co., 5 Mass. L. Rep. 376 (1996) (Difference in Conditions coverage was included in property insurance policy).

1416. *See, e.g.*, Samia Cos. v. United States Fire Ins. Co., 789 So. 2d 706, 708 (La. App.), *writ den.*, 799 So. 2d 1145 (La. 2001) (insurer issued commercial property coverage policy to insured and in following month issued inland marine policy that included Difference in Conditions coverage).

1417. *See, e.g.*, Falcon Products, Inc. v. Insurance Co. of Pennsylvania, 615 F. Supp. 37 (E.D. Mo. 1985), *aff'd*, 782 F.2d 779 (8th Cir. 1986) (Difference in Conditions property insurance insured against all risks of direct physical loss or damage to personal property).

1418. Under this policy only the listed perils are to be covered. For example, a DIC policy could be drafted solely to cover flood or earthquake, in which case it is limited to only the listed perils and a loss arising from any other peril would be excluded.

1419. *Difference in Conditions Policies* (Summit Business Media, 2012). When the DIC policy takes the form of excess coverage, it provides additional limits of insurance only for causes of loss limited on the standard policy. This combines an excess property form with a DIC form to fulfill needed limits of coverage for specific perils.

or a "manuscript policy."[1420] "Non-standard" means the carrier drafts its own form.[1421] A "manuscript policy" is one drafted for a particular insured for a particular risk.[1422] It is possible that an especially large common interest community may have a non-standard or manuscript policy, but the ordinary CIC will probably have a standard ISO "Differences in Conditions Coverage Form" known as a "commercial inland marine" policy.[1423]

[a] Key Differences between DIC and Primary Policies

The language of the ISO DIC policy parallels that of the types of primary property policies with which a CIC is most likely to be provided. There are, however, important differences. One distinction that may be important to a business, but probably not to a CIC, is that business personal property is covered while in transit as well as in or on the described building.[1424] The more important difference for CICs is found in the exclusions. The ISO DIC policy is "all risk," meaning it covers all causes of loss except those specifically excluded.[1425] Thus, if the underlying property policy only covers specifically named perils, the DIC offers expanded coverage. If the underlying property policy is also "all risk," as is frequently the case for CICs, the DIC exclusions have to be compared to those in the underlying commercial property policy. Losses excluded in the commercial property policy, but not excluded in the DIC, will then ordinarily be covered by the DIC.[1426]

[b] Exclusions

The first thing to observe about the DIC exclusions in the ISO policy is that the carrier will not pay for loss or damage caused by or resulting from fire, lightning, windstorm, hail, or any other cause of loss covered by the underlying policy or policies.[1427] Fire, lightning, windstorm, and hail are covered causes of loss in any

1420. Cozen, *Insuring Real Property*, § 12.03 [4] (Matthew Bender & Co. 2015). *See, e.g.*, Falcon Products, Inc. v. Insurance Co. of Pennsylvania, 615 F. Supp. 37 (E.D. Mo. 1985), *aff'd*, 782 F.2d 779 (8th Cir. 1986) (Difference in Conditions policy covered all risks of direct physical loss or damage to personal property owned or acquired by insured while on premises occupied by plaintiff in Mexico).

1421. *Difference in Conditions Policies* (Summit Business Media, 2012).

1422. *See* 1 Jeffrey E. Thomas, *New Appleman on Insurance Law Library Edition* § 1.07[9] (Matthew Bender 2023).

1423. *See, e.g.*, ISO Form IH 00 80 12 11.

1424. *Difference in Conditions Policies* (Summit Business Media, 2012).

1425. *See, e.g.*, ISO Form IH 00 80 09 09, § A.3.

1426. Prahl, *Difference in Conditions Coverage: What Is It and Who Needs It?* at 3 (Adjusting Today, 2012), available at: http://adjustersinternational.com/publications/adjusting-today/difference-in-conditions-coverage/0/.

1427. *See, e.g.*, St. Paul Village Condo. Ass'n v. St. Paul Fire & Marine Ins. Co., 5 Mass. L. Rep. 376 (1996) (insurer argued DIC coverage did not apply to association's loss because that loss was

commercial property policy whether it is an all-risk or named peril policy. Obviously, when the underlying policy is all risk, a peril can be covered though not named. For the purposes of the "any other cause of loss covered by the underlying policy" exclusion in the DIC policy, a peril need not be precisely defined in the underlying policy to be excluded by the DIC exclusion. One court explained that where the peril of theft was covered by the underlying policy, not because it is precisely defined in that policy, but rather because it was *not excluded* by it, theft fell within the definition of "perils" under that policy because it was a covered cause of loss and could then be excluded by the DIC policy.[1428]

The second and more important observation is that the DIC list of exclusions *does not* include "water" or "earth movement," although settling, cracking, shrinkage, and expansion are excluded[1429]—coverage for which is almost always barred in a commercial property policy. That is why commentators say that the primary use of a DIC policy is to cover flood and earthquake losses.[1430] When that is the purpose the DIC policy serves, it is important to note that the policy says separate limits of coverage are shown on the Declarations Page for earthquake and water damage.[1431]

[c] Underlying Insurance

The ISO DIC policy specifically addresses the underlying coverage. It provides that the insurance afforded by underlying policies described on the Declarations Page "will be maintained" for the full term of the DIC policy, and as each underlying policy expires, the insured will renew it at limits and for causes of loss equal to or greater than those of the expiring policy.[1432] If the insured fails to meet these

---

covered under primary coverage and by its terms, DIC coverage only included certain causes of physical loss or damage that were not covered under primary coverage).

1428. Siena Del Lago Condo. Ass'n v. Am. Fire & Cas. Co., 2013 U.S. Dist. LEXIS 69308 (W.D. Wash. May 14, 2013), *aff'd*, 2016 U.S. App. LEXIS 7150 (9th Cir. Apr. 20, 2016). The court held that as the peril of wind-driven rain was not listed as one of the exclusions in the underlying policy, it was insured against as a covered cause of loss and, therefore, in turn excluded by the DIC exclusion. The DIC exclusionary language in *Siena Del Lago* was somewhat different from that found in the ISO DIC policy. The exclusionary clause in the Washington case said the policy did not insure against other perils as "defined and limited" under policies insuring against perils carried by the insured under any other more specific insurance in the name of the insured. The court found that the policy excluded a peril to the extent that peril was limited by the underlying policy or policies, not to the extent coverage or loss was generally limited by a limiting condition, for example, one limiting coverage to damage commencing during the policy period.

1429. *See, e.g.*, ISO Form IH 00 80 09 09, § B.2.g.

1430. Prahl, *Difference in Conditions Coverage: What Is It and Who Needs It?* at 3 (Adjusting Today, 2012), available at: http://adjustersinternational.com/publications/adjusting-today/difference-in-conditions-coverage/0/. *See also* Cozen, *Insuring Real Property*, § 12.03 [4] (Matthew Bender & Co. 2015) (DIC insurance may be used to add earthquake coverage to Basic Property Coverage Forms that do not provide coverage for earthquake loss).

1431. *See, e.g.*, ISO Form IH 00 80 09 09, § C.1.

1432. *See, e.g.*, ISO Form IH 00 80 09 09, § E.2.a.(1).

obligations, the DIC carrier will pay only to the extent it would have paid had the insured complied.[1433] In other words, the DIC policy does not drop down to cover a dollar one loss but will continue to be only an excess policy over the primary policy, even if the primary policy is not renewed or if the primary policy insurer is insolvent and not able to pay losses under the primary policy.

The DIC policy presupposes that the Declarations Page will list or describe the underlying property policies. However, it may not do so. On receiving the Declarations Page, the policyholder should look for that list or description and, if there is none, should insist on an amended Declarations Page containing that information so that the policyholder knows which policies it is obligated to maintain.

[d] Other Insurance

Because there is a possibility for duplication of coverage between underlying policies and the DIC policy, special attention needs to be given to the "other insurance clauses" of all these policies.[1434] Typically, neither the ISO Differences in Condition Coverage Form nor the commonly used commercial property coverage forms contains an "other insurance" clause. These clauses are found in a separate form. Attached to the commercial property policy will be a form titled "Commercial Property Conditions."[1435] The ISO DIC employs a "Commercial Inland Marine Conditions" form for the same purpose.[1436] The ISO language of these forms is identical. It provides that if the insured has other insurance that is subject to the same plan, terms, conditions, and provisions as the insurance under "this Coverage Part," the insurer will pay its share of the covered loss or damage that is the proportion that the applicable limit of insurance under "this Coverage Part" bears to the limits of insurance of all policies covering on the same basis.[1437] Additionally, if there is other insurance covering the same loss or damage, other than that described above, the carrier will pay only for the amount of covered loss or damage that exceeds the amount due from that other insurance, whether the insured can collect on it or not, and will not pay more than the applicable limit of insurance.[1438] One expert commentary states that the commercial property policy other insurance clause should state that it is primary, and the DIC policy should specify it is excess over other insurance and will not be considered contributing insurance if there is duplication of coverage.[1439]

1433. *See, e.g.*, ISO Form IH 00 80 09 09, § E.2.a.(2).
1434. *Difference in Conditions Policies* (Summit Business Media, 2012).
1435. *See, e.g.*, ISO Form CP 00 90 07 08.
1436. *See, e.g.*, ISO Form CM 00 01 09 04.
1437. *See, e.g.*, ISO Form CP 00 90 07 08, § G.1; Form CM 00 01 09 04, § F.1.
1438. *See, e.g.*, ISO Form CP 00 90 07 08, § G.2; Form CM 00 01 09 04, § F.2.
1439. *Difference in Conditions Policies* (Summit Business Media, 2012).

[e] Deductibles

In general, DIC policies have higher deductibles because they are often targeted to catastrophic losses, not frequent small ones.[1440] However, even if the base deductible is comparable to that in the underlying commercial property policy, a DIC policy likely will contain separate and higher deductibles for flood and earthquake.[1441] Additionally, some DIC policies may include payment for only a percentage of the loss above the deductible[1442] or may use percentage deductibles that can vary from 2 to 5 percent of the value of the property, not of the loss.[1443] If the CIC has more than one building, it is important to determine whether the deductible applies to the entire property or separately to each building. The latter is to the association's advantage. Consider a common interest community that consists of five buildings each valued at $1 million. If there is a 5 percent deductible applied on a per building basis and one building is damaged, the deductible is $50,000. If, however, the 5 percent applies to the entire property but only one building is damaged, the deductible is $250,000.

[f] Coinsurance

In general, a Coinsurance clause limits the loss payment when at the time of a loss, the value of covered property multiplied by the coinsurance percentage—typically 80 percent—shown for it on the Declarations Page is greater than the limit of insurance for the property. These clauses are typically included in the commercial property policies issued to CICs;[1444] however, they apply only if a coinsurance percentage is shown on the Declarations Page. DIC policies ordinarily have no coinsurance clause.[1445] This is so because a DIC policy may provide coverage at limits less than the full value of the property.[1446]

1440. *Difference in Conditions Policies* (Summit Business Media, 2012).

1441. Prahl, *Difference in Conditions Coverage: What Is It and Who Needs It?* at 7 (Adjusting Today, 2012), available at: http://adjustersinternational.com/publications/adjusting-today/difference-in-conditions-coverage/0/.

1442. *Difference in Conditions Policies* (Summit Business Media, 2012).

1443. Prahl, *Difference in Conditions Coverage: What Is It and Who Needs It?* at 7 (Adjusting Today, 2012), available at: http://adjustersinternational.com/publications/adjusting-today/difference-in-conditions-coverage/0/.

1444. *See, e.g.*, ISO Form CP 00 10 06 07, § F.1; CP 00 17 06 07, § F.1.

1445. *Difference in Conditions Policies* (Summit Business Media, 2012); Prahl, *Difference in Conditions Coverage: What Is It and Who Needs It?* at 5 (Adjusting Today, 2012), available at: http://adjustersinternational.com/publications/adjusting-today/difference-in-conditions-coverage/0/.

1446. Prahl, *Difference in Conditions Coverage: What Is It and Who Needs It?* at 5 (Adjusting Today, 2012), available at: http://adjustersinternational.com/publications/adjusting-today/difference-in-conditions-coverage/0/.

[g] Joint/Disputed Loss Agreement

There are circumstances in which a loss might be partially covered by both the commercial property policy and the DIC policy. Any time there is a potential overlap in coverage, the two carriers may dispute their liability, leaving the insured uncompensated until the disagreement is resolved. This problem can be addressed by a "joint/disputed loss agreement endorsement." Ordinarily, this provision requires carriers to pay the insured for the disputed loss once the policy provisions are met so that the insured does not have to wait while the carriers contest the amount of liability each has for the loss.[1447] For this protection to be effective, the commercial property and DIC policies have to include a joint or disputed loss provision that are substantially the same.[1448] Unfortunately, joint/disputed loss agreement endorsements are commonly omitted—whether intentionally or inadvertently—from one or both policies.

[h] Protective Safeguards

The ISO DIC policy has a clause that says that the insured has to maintain the protective safeguards it said were in effect at the location when the coverage was initiated.[1449] Further, if the insured fails to maintain those protective safeguards in working condition and in operation when the insured is "closed for business," the coverage for which the protective safeguards apply is automatically suspended and the suspension lasts until the equipment or services are back in operation. The policy refers to safeguards "stated by you [the insured] to be in effect," but it does not say where the insured may have made that statement or to whom. It may be in the application, which becomes part of the policy. However, the open-ended language of the policy does not preclude a statement made in an email to the insurance broker, minutes of the board of directors, a communication to community residents, or even a written or oral statement to a third party from constituting the statement of safeguards in effect. However, in most instances, this "extrinsic evidence" will not be admissible to determine the terms of the policy. There may, however, be extenuating circumstances when extrinsic statements may be given consideration by the courts.

1447. Boggs, *Three Commercial Property Endorsements Every Client Should Have* (July 27, 2009), available at: http://www.mynewmarkets.com/articles/102464/three-commercial-property-endorsements-every-client-should-have. *See also* Ark. Power & Light Co. v. Hartford Steam Boiler Inspection & Ins. Co., 257 F.3d 853, 855 (8th Cir. 2001) (clause provides means for insured to receive prompt payment when two or more insurers with potentially overlapping coverages disagree as to cause of loss).

1448. Prahl, *Difference in Conditions Coverage: What Is It and Who Needs It?* at 6–7 (Adjusting Today, 2012), available at: http://adjustersinternational.com/publications/adjusting-today/difference-in-conditions-coverage/0/.

1449. *See, e.g.*, ISO Form IH 00 80 09 09, § E.2.c.

Also, unlike the standard Protective Safeguard Endorsement added to a commercial property policy, the ISO DIC policy does not identify any safeguards. Typically that endorsement identifies the safeguards as an automatic sprinkler system, automatic fire alarm, security service, service contract with a privately owned fire department providing fire protection service, and any protective system described on a schedule.[1450] Given the potential for confusion created by a protective safeguard clause like that in the ISO DIC policy, an association may want to work with the insurance broker to develop a list of protective safeguards in effect and ask the insurer to confirm that the list contains the safeguards the insurer considers to be governed by the safeguard clause.

There is good reason for caution when the policy has a protective safeguard clause, as where policy language calls for the insured to maintain a protective safeguard in "good order" or "working order" and it fails to function, some courts will hold that the insured failed to maintain the system in good or working order and coverage will be denied, even though the insured may have had no warning of a problem.[1451]

[i] Forms Containing Additional Conditions

Typically, a DIC coverage form has two additional important forms that are made a part of the policy. The first is a "Common Policy Conditions" form.[1452] It addresses matters like the right of either party to cancel the policy, the right of the insurer to audit the books and records of the insured, the right of the insurer to inspect the property, and a limitation on the transfer of rights and duties of the insured under the policy. The second critical form is a "Conditions" form, which in the case of the ISO DIC policy will probably be the "Commercial Inland Marine Conditions" form.[1453] That form contains loss conditions. These include abandonment of property, the appraisal process, duties of the insured in the event of a loss, the insurer's loss payment procedures, other insurance, the procedure in the event of recovered property, and the transfer of the right of recovery against others to the insurer. The form will also consist of general conditions, including preconditions for bringing suit against the carrier and valuation of the property.

[3] Flood Coverage and Difference in Conditions Insurance

In theory, a DIC policy will cover flood loss or damage because it is an all-risk policy and omits the usual exclusion for "water." The ISO DIC policy defines water damage as, *inter alia*, flood, surface water, waves, tides, tidal water, overflow

---

1450. *See, e.g.*, ISO Form IL 04 15 04 98.

1451. Goldstein v. Fidelity & Guar. Ins. Underwriters, 86 F.3d 749 (7th Cir. 1996); Star Varifoam Corp. v. Buffalo Reinsurance Co., 64 N.C. App. 306, 307 S.E.2d 194 (1983), *rev. den.*, 310 N.C. 154, 311 S.E.2d 294 (1984).

1452. *See, e.g.*, ISO Form IL 00 17 11 98.

1453. *See, e.g.*, ISO Form CM 00 01 09 04.

of any body of water, mudslide, mudflow, and water that backs up or overflows from a sewer or drain.[1454] This largely parallels the definition of water, an excluded peril, in the typical commercial property policy where the term includes flood, surface water, waves, tides, tidal waves, overflow of any body of water, mudslide or mudflow,[1455] and water that backs up or overflows from a sewer, drain, or sump.[1456] It should be noted that some DIC policies may define flood as overflowing of normal boundaries of water, and that definition would not provide coverage for flooding from surface water derived from rain or melting snow that follows no defined course as it flows over the ground.[1457]

Private carriers rarely cover flood losses when a property is located in an area at high risk for flooding. For that reason, it is highly likely there will be an endorsement to the DIC adding "water" as an exclusion. The definition of water in the exclusion will likely be identical to that in the underlying commercial property policy, but possibly omitting "water that backs up or overflows from a sewer, drain, or sump." Thus, for a common interest community that is at a high risk for flood damage, the only coverage available will be that offered by FEMA through the National Flood Insurance Program (NFIP). Most private insurers do not offer their own flood insurance, so even CICs located in areas with a low risk of flooding may not be able to obtain private coverage. The one exception may be excess coverage.

The Standard Flood Insurance Policy (SFIP) of the NFIP provides limited coverage. Generally, for CICs other than certain condominiums, the maximum building coverage will be $500,000. For condominiums that qualify for the Residential Condominium Building Association Policy (RCBAP) of the SFIP, the maximum coverage is $250,000 times the number of units, but not to exceed the replacement cost of the building.[1458] Coverage of contents is also limited and is not included within the building coverage; it has to be separately purchased.

The SFIP coverage limitations mean that many CICs are underinsured for flood loss, although they often appear to be unaware of that fact. The $500,000 maximum building coverage will clearly be inadequate for many homeowners associations and residential cooperatives. The RCBAP coverage may appear adequate on its face—especially in a multi-story building where any damage may be expected to be confined to the lowest levels—but may not be. Thus, excess coverage is strongly recommended.

1454. *See, e.g.*, ISO Form IH 00 80 09 09, § G.4.

1455. This is significant because "mudslide or mudflow" are included in the FEMA Standard Flood Insurance Policy definition of "flood."

1456. *See, e.g.*, ISO Form CP 10 30 06 07, § B.1.g.

1457. *Difference in Conditions Policies* (Summit Business Media, 2012); Prahl, *Difference in Conditions Coverage: What Is It and Who Needs It?* at 5 (Adjusting Today, 2012), available at: http://adjustersinternational.com/publications/adjusting-today/difference-in-conditions-coverage/0/.

1458. 44 C.F.R. § 61.6(b).

When the association is seeking to add flood coverage through a DIC policy, it is important to establish that there is no coinsurance clause, otherwise coverage would have to be purchased with limits equal to the total value of the property insured. This would result in a limit sufficient to insure only property on lower floors that would be the property normally subject to flooding, which can be purchased without the danger of an underinsurance penalty.[1459]

Typically, a DIC policy contains separate limits for flood coverage.[1460] For example, the ISO DIC policy says separate limits of coverage are shown on the Declarations Page for water damage.[1461]

[4] Understanding the DIC Policy and Securing the Desired Coverage

Experts agree that a DIC policy has to be carefully reviewed. It and the commercial property policy need to be examined side by side to be sure the language dovetails.[1462] However, insurance policies in general, and DIC policies in particular, are prolix and difficult to comprehend. The recommended comparison of the commercial property and DIC policies is a challenging task. The governing board, or any insurance committee, should work with an experienced insurance broker who is knowledgeable about DIC and property coverage.

A CIC needs to be sure that any DIC policy it obtains provides the desired coverage. When coverage is sought for a specific purpose—for example, excess flood coverage—a written request to the broker describing in some detail the needs of the association may be helpful in holding the broker to account for negligent failure to procure the requested coverage. Generally, an applicant for insurance cannot depend on a broker to anticipate its needs or to advise it about optional coverage—like a DIC policy—that may be available.[1463] When, however,

1459. Difference in Conditions Policies (44 Business Media, 2012); Prahl, *Difference in Conditions Coverage: What Is It and Who Needs It?* at 5 (Adjusting Today, 2012), available at: http://adjustersinternational.com/publications/adjusting-today/difference-in-conditions-coverage/0/.

1460. Prahl, *Difference in Conditions Coverage: What Is It and Who Needs It?* at 6 (Adjusting Today, 2012), available at: http://adjustersinternational.com/publications/adjusting-today/difference-in-conditions-coverage/0/.

1461. *See, e.g.*, ISO Form IH 00 80 09 09, § C.1.

1462. Prahl, *Difference in Conditions Coverage: What Is It and Who Needs It?* at 6 (Adjusting Today, 2012), available at: http://adjustersinternational.com/publications/adjusting-today/difference-in-conditions-coverage/0/.

1463. *See, e.g.*, Houck v. State Farm Fire & Cas. Ins. Co., 366 S.C. 7, 12, 620 S.E.2d 326, 330 (S.C. 2005); Garnerville Holding Co. v. Kaye Ins. Assocs., 309 A.D.2d 541, 765 N.Y.S.2d 317 (2003), *app. den.*, 780 N.Y.S.2d 311, 2 N.Y.3d 705, 812 N.E.2d 1261 (2004); Baggett v. Summerlin Ins. & Realty, Inc., 354 N.C. 347, 554 S.E.2d 336 (2001). *See also* Zinsel Co. v. J. Everett Eaves, Inc., La. App. 99-691, 749 So. 2d 798 (La. App. 1999), where the insured property owner suffered a $300,000 underinsured flood loss. It sued its long-term insurance agent alleging, *inter alia*, that the agent was derelict in not informing it of the availability of DIC insurance. The court held that if the insured had obtained the maximum coverage available to it under a FEMA flood policy, the limits of that policy would have been sufficient to cover the loss and any DIC policy would not have been invoked; therefore, it was irrelevant whether the agent advised the insured of DIC coverage or not.

an applicant for insurance requests specific coverage, courts usually hold that a duty of reasonable care to procure that coverage arises,[1464] provided the broker agrees to procure the requested coverage.[1465] On the other hand, courts may also find that had the policyholder "been diligent" in inspecting the policy when issued, any insufficiencies in coverage could have been discovered and corrected.[1466]

§ 10.38 Commercial Property Insurance Claims and Settlements

There are some unique aspects to property insurance claims, especially when the claimant is a common interest community, that merit examination. The most fundamental information to know about claims is that the burden is on the insured to initiate and support its claim. That is, it has to comply with the duties the policy imposes in the event of a claim and show it has a loss.[1467] For example, while an insurer may have a duty to investigate a claim presented to it, where an association refused to give its insurer permission to inspect all the individual units

---

1464. *See, e.g.*, Travelers Property Casualty Co. of America v. Superior Court, 215 Cal. App. 4th 561, 578, 155 Cal. Rptr. 3d 459, 474 (2013) (brokers owe limited duty to their clients to use reasonable care, diligence, and judgment in procuring insurance requested by insured); Sullivan v. State Farm & Cas. Co, 2006 U.S. Dist. LEXIS 55295 (E.D. La. July 26, 2006) (where insureds requested contents coverage in SFIP, but did not receive it, court found they alleged viable cause of action against agent); Nicol v. Auto-Owners Ins. Co., 2006 U.S. Dist. LEXIS 9502 (D. Minn. Mar. 8, 2006) (agent owed insured duty to act with reasonable care, skill, and diligence in procuring and maintaining flood insurance; where insured requested coverage for two buildings, but policy covered only one, insured properly alleged negligence claim against agent). *Consider* Star Spa Servs. v. Robert G. Turano Ins. Agency, Inc., 595 F. Supp. 2d 519 (M.D. Pa. 2009) (agent could be liable for failing to procure flood insurance that would provide coverage that would not be provided by SFIP); Maher v. Ins. Underwriters, Ltd., 2008 U.S. Dist. LEXIS 2650 (E.D. La. Jan. 14, 2008) (where insured claimed she asked agent to adequately insure her home and to increase coverage of existing NFIP flood coverage, where increased coverage did not take immediate effect because of 30-day waiting period, she stated claim against agent for negligent procurement sufficient to survive motion to dismiss as private flood insurance may have been available, perhaps without waiting period).

1465. Avery v. Diedrich, 2007 WI 80, 301 Wis. 2d 693, 734 N.W.2d 159 (2007) (insurance agent does not have duty to procure requested insurance coverage until there is agreement that agent will do so).

1466. Samia Cos. v. United States Fire Ins. Co., 789 So. 2d 706 (La. App.), *writ den.*, 799 So. 2d 1145 (La. 2001).

1467. *See, e.g.*, Harbor House Condominium Ass'n v. Massachusetts Bay Ins. Co., 915 F.2d 316 (7th Cir. 1990) (burden was on association to prove extent and amount of its damages to reasonable degree of certainty and, having failed to do so, it was precluded from recovering any amount in excess of that already received); 1231 Euclid Homeowners Ass'n v. State Farm Fire & Casualty Co., 135 Cal. App. 4th 1008, 37 Cal. Rptr. 3d 795, 802–03 (2006) (where association notified insurer of claim, but its president subsequently advised insurer that claim for which notice had previously been given was withdrawn, voluntary withdrawal of claim arguably had same legal consequence as failure to file any claim at all; if after filing claim, association failed or refused to provide information necessary to adjust claim, insurer could not be faulted for closing its file; insurer had every justification to conclude association had independently determined that whatever damage its building may have sustained, it did not exceed policy deductible).

in the project, any failure by the insurer to thoroughly investigate the claim was considered to be the result of the association's actions.[1468]

Before an insured can bring suit against the insurer for breach of contract for failure to pay a claim, the insurer generally must have actually denied the claim. For instance, in one case an association contended its insurer failed to consider damage to glass windows and sliding glass doors that provided access to individual condominium units. The court said that in the phrases "did not consider" and "denied coverage," there is a distinction with a significant difference as the latter establishes a dispute or actual controversy over a coverage position, but the former is facially vague and could merely indicate an oversight by the insurer. Because the insurer had not taken an adverse position to the association's loss, no justiciable dispute was presented.[1469] Taking an "adverse" position does not necessarily mean, however, an explicit denial of a claim. For example, an association submitted a claim for hurricane damages, and over three years after the loss the insurer had not provided any estimate of damages; adjusted, paid, or settled the claim; and/or even denied coverage. That failure, said a federal court, was sufficient for the association to infer the existence of a dispute about its right to coverage under the policy.[1470]

Another important consideration with property damage is that the association needs to take steps to contain and mitigate the loss. The property policy will generally require the insured to take all "reasonable steps" to protect the covered property from further damage and to keep a record of expenses necessary to protect it.[1471] When a loss is reported, the insurer will generally ask if precautions

---

1468. Sunland Vill. Homeowners Ass'n v. State Farm Fire & Cas. Co., 2007 Cal. App. Unpub. LEXIS 3816 (May 14, 2007).

1469. Wilshire Condo. Ass'n v. QBE Ins. Corp., 2011 U.S. Dist. LEXIS 157457 (S.D. Fla. Sept. 9, 2011).

1470. Regency of Palm Beach, Inc. v. QBE Ins. Corp., 2009 U.S. Dist. LEXIS 75929 (S.D. Fla. Aug. 25, 2009). *See also* Cypress Chase Condo. Ass'n "A" v. QBE Ins. Corp., 2013 U.S. Dist. LEXIS 40347 (S.D. Fla. Mar. 22, 2013) (insurer argued claim was not justiciable because it had never explicitly denied that windows and sliding glass doors were covered under policy and, therefore, there was no dispute between parties regarding coverage, but court rejected that argument, finding that longstanding failure of insurer to take any position on coverage amounted to de facto denial of coverage); Quadomain Condo. Ass'n v. QBE Ins. Corp., 2007 U.S. Dist. LEXIS 34972, 20 Fla. L. Weekly Fed. D 870 (S.D. Fla. May 14, 2007) (where association filed claim alleging wind and water damage to property in excess of $2.8 million and insurer inspected damages, but had not paid claim and parties disagree as to extent of damage covered under policy, association adequately pled actual controversy as it had submitted its claim for damages, and insurer had yet to investigate, adjust, pay, and/or settle it). *Compare* Townhouses of Highland Beach Condo. Ass'n v. QBE Ins. Corp., 504 F. Supp. 2d 1307 (S.D. Fla. 2007).

1471. *See* ISO Form CP 00 10 60 07, § E.3.a.(4); ISO Form CP 00 17 06 07, § E.3.a.(4). *See, e.g.*, Higginbotham v. New Hampshire Indem. Co., 498 So. 2d 1149 (La. App. 1986), *cert. den.*, 501 So. 2d 236 (La. 1987) (where trial court held that any later damage suffered because of deterioration of roof was result of failure by insured to have original damage repaired in timely fashion, appellate court did not find that decision so erroneous as to warrant payment for damages sustained

have been taken to prevent further damage.[1472] For example, if the building has suffered water damage from a leaking pipe, the association not only needs to have the water shut off until the pipe is repaired but also should bring in a restoration service. It is wise to document the steps taken to mitigate the damage. It is also important to take pictures of the damage before mitigation and restoration steps are taken to create a record to provide the insurer as part of the proof of loss.

One feature of common interest communities is that because they are governed by an elected board, the position of the association on a claim can change. In one case, for example, an association battled its insurer for years over a sinkhole claim while the insurer dragged its feet. Then the unit owners elected a new board that was, as the court put it, "inexplicably hostile to the sinkhole claim." To further confuse matters, the board that had vigorously pursued the claim was later restored to office.[1473] Insurers need to be prepared to deal with these changes, as they can seriously affect the carrier. For instance, an association and insurer might be amicably resolving a claim when a new, more aggressive board is elected. The insurer that believed it was close to settling the claim could suddenly find itself facing a newly hired attorney who is threatening litigation and implying it has acted in bad faith.

A question that arises when damage is minor is whether the association should file a claim at all. As one commentator observes, small claims can look bad on the association's record and the policy might not be renewed or the premiums raised.[1474] Another expert asserts that one large claim, for example, a fluke fire, is less problematic than five or six water damage claims because insurers become concerned about repetition and the likelihood of problems in the building.[1475] Of course, if the policy requires that the insured report all claims no matter how insignificant they might appear, the decision is made for the association.[1476]

[1] Professional Assistance

Property claims for common interest communities can be substantial. Once it has submitted a claim, therefore, the association can expect the insurer to take its potential liability very seriously. If the association hopes to achieve a reasonable settlement when the property has suffered significant damage, it should consider employing experts to assist it, starting with a reputable public adjuster. A

after storm where measures could have been taken to reasonably protect premises from further deterioration).

1472. Langston, *So You Have an Insurance Claim?* (Association Times 2009).

1473. Citizens Prop. Ins. Corp. v. River Oaks Condo. II Ass'n, 190 So. 3d 1110 (Fla. 2d DCA 2016).

1474. Langston, *So You Have an Insurance Claim?* (Association Times 2009). The author says if it is not clear whether a claim will exceed the deductible, it is all right to report it.

1475. Olear, *To Claim, or Not to Claim? The Insurance Dilemma* (Cooperator, Aug. 2014), available at: https://cooperatornews.com/article/to-claim-or-not-to-claim.

1476. Langston, *So You Have an Insurance Claim?* (Association Times 2009).

common interest community certainly has the right to assign an agent to act on its behalf in settling a claim.[1477]

Some of the most valuable assistance can be provided by a "public adjuster." The role of these professionals is to help the insured evaluate the claim and negotiate with the carrier on behalf of the insured. Public adjusters are required by states to be licensed. It is always important to check the status of that license, but after a natural disaster, public adjusters may travel from far away and that makes it all the more imperative to check license status and references in the state where the association is located before signing a retainer contract. It is important to be aware that after catastrophic losses states permit non-resident licensed public adjusters to provide their services in the non-licensed state. Often, emergency temporary licenses are issued to these non-resident licensed public adjusters. Even though the association has hired a public adjuster, and perhaps other professionals, to deal with its claim, for a large claim it should consider appointing a claim management team—which could be an existing insurance committee—to help retrieve and organize any information needed to support the claim and monitor the work of the professionals the association has employed.[1478] The need to monitor the progress of a claim is illustrated by a tragic case in Florida. A high-rise condominium building in the upscale community of Naples suffered extensive damage in a hurricane. The association submitted a claim of some 2,500 pages for over $20 million. The claim was prepared by "experts," and board members

1477. Stall v. State Farm Fire & Cas. Co., 995 So. 2d 670 (La. App. 2008). In *Stall* a New Orleans company was in the business of restoring historic properties to be used as hotels or residential properties. It converted a building into a condominium and managed it. It had a single policy insuring properties it had restored, including the condominium, which was damaged in Hurricane Katrina. The restoration company filed a claim with the insurer. The insurer paid the claim, and the proceeds were allocated by a public adjuster among the covered properties including the condominium. The condominium association, as trustee on behalf of the unit owners, then divided its share of the insurance proceeds among the individual owners that had sustained damages. A unit owner, dissatisfied with her share, sued the association, claiming it had improperly abdicated its role in settling the claim to the restoration company and had no authority to appoint an agent to act on its behalf to resolve the claim. More specifically, she argued the association did not receive all of the insurance proceeds to which it was entitled and that hindered her ability to repair her condominium unit. The court also noted that pursuant to the condominium Declaration, the association, as trustee for each unit owner, had specific authority to adjust all claims and losses with any carrier providing property coverage. The association assigned the responsibility to the restoration company, its manager. The court observed that the plaintiff did not assert that the association failed to act in the best interests of the association and its members by appointing the restoration company to negotiate the settlement and that the company, as the manager of the property and holder of the policy, was clearly knowledgeable about the damage, structural requirements, and other factors required to assess financial needs as part of the settlement. As one does not breach a fiduciary duty by acting in the best interest of the organization, the plaintiff had no cause of action against the association.

1478. Rake, *Property Insurance Claims: Negotiating Unfamiliar Terrain*, at 3 (Adjusting Today, 2010), available at: http://adjustersinternational.com/publications/adjusting-today/property-insurance-claims/0/.

apparently never reviewed it. The insurer accused the association of inflating its claim and paid nothing. Its decision was upheld in court, and the association was forced to assess unit owners more than $100,000 each to pay for the repairs.[1479]

If an association elects to forego professional representation, it should formally notify the insurer of the association's contact person and agree, as the insurer will no doubt insist, that the insurer will not have to respond to questions from other residents.[1480]

[2] Valuing Building Loss

One expert in the field of insurance notes that if a loss includes building damages, the insurer will probably employ a contractor to measure the damage, but that there is considerable subjectivity in defining the scope of damages and there are often sizable discrepancies between estimates.[1481] There may also be differences between the recommended repair and the policy coverage. For example, that expert says the policy might entitle the insured to collect for the cost to replace plaster, but the contractor for the insurer could recommend installation of drywall. Even if the insured replaces the plaster with drywall, it might choose to collect for the value of the plaster and use the savings elsewhere in the building. Discovering these opportunities is one reason to employ a public adjuster and other professionals. Another benefit of professional assistance is the help they can bring in determining depreciation when the coverage is based on actual cash value.

Another expert notes that one problem that can arise when individual homes in a common interest community are damaged and then restored under the association policy is that the homeowner may take the opportunity to upgrade the quality of the replacement items. The insurer will not cover the cost of the upgrades, so if the association hires a contractor to make the repairs, it needs to determine how to pass the cost of any upgrades onto the homeowner.[1482] The

1479. Layden, *Monaco Beach Club Residents Sue Condo Association Over Hurricane Wilma Damages* (Naples News Apr. 21, 2011). Unit owners brought suit against the governing board members who were in office when the claim was in process, alleging, *inter alia*, breach of fiduciary duty, negligence, and fraud. Unfortunately for the unit owners, suits against board members personally are rarely successful.

1480. For example, in one case the association representative informed the adjuster for the insurer that she would be the contact person for her homeowners association for purposes of handling the claim. The insurer confirmed this agreement in a letter to her in which it stressed that it would be unable to respond to each individual unit owner, but would address any questions she might have and asked her to advise members of her association to direct inquiries through her. 1231 Euclid Homeowners Ass'n v. State Farm Fire & Casualty Co., 135 Cal. App. 4th 1008, 1012, 37 Cal. Rptr. 3d 795, 798, n.5 (2006).

1481. Rake, *Property Insurance Claims: Negotiating Unfamiliar Terrain*, at 4 (Adjusting Today, 2010), available at: http://adjustersinternational.com/publications/adjusting-today/property-insurance-claims/0/.

1482. Langston, *So You Have an Insurance Claim?* (Association Times 2009).

same expert warns of cost overruns that result in the contractor's price coming in higher than the adjuster has allowed. She recommends asking the insurer's adjustor to determine if the numbers can be recalculated based on what the contractor needs to charge. There may have been a "hold-back" by the insurer on the claim for just that eventuality.

[3] Valued Policy Statutes

A number of states have what are called "valued policy" statutes.[1483] These statutes relieve the insured of the burden of proving the full value of the insured property when it is totally destroyed.[1484] Generally, under these laws, on the total loss of an insured building, the insurer is required to pay the face value of the policy instead of the actual cash value or replacement cost. Thus, the value definitively fixed in the policy by the parties at its inception is conclusive on the question of the value of the insured property when there is a total loss.[1485]

Valued policy statutes vary from state to state and may be limited in their application to specific types of property,[1486] policies, or causes of loss. For example, the Texas statute applies to total loss by fire of property insured under a fire insurance policy,[1487] while the comparable Florida law applies to the total loss of any building "insured by any insurer as to a covered peril."[1488]

The statutes usually do not define "total loss." Courts have given the phrase different interpretations. The analyses courts apply to decide whether a damaged building is a total loss include the "identity" test, the "restoration" test, and whether the building was a "constructive" total loss.[1489] The Georgia Supreme Court has said that a structure is "wholly destroyed" when it would cost more to repair than to replace it.[1490] The Texas Supreme Court said many years ago that whether a building is an actual total loss depends on whether "a reasonably

1483. *See generally* Conway, *As Hurricanes End, Legal Storms Begin: The Insurance Battle under State Valued Policy Laws*, 24 Ga. St. U.L. Rev. 1043 (2008). The policy itself may provide that it is "agreed" or "stated" value. *See* § 10.34[1], *supra*.

1484. Cozen, *Insuring Real Property*, § 27.03 (Matthew Bender & Co, 2015).

1485. Cozen, *Insuring Real Property*, § 27.02 (Matthew Bender & Co. 2015).

1486. *See, e.g.*, Ga. Code Ann. § 33-32-5(a) (whenever any policy insuring specifically described *one or two family residential building* or structure against loss by fire and building or structure is wholly destroyed by fire without fraudulent or criminal fault on part of insured, amount of insurance set forth in policy relative to that building or structure must be taken conclusively to be value of property).

1487. Tex. Ins. Code § 862.053(a).

1488. Fla. Stat. § 627.702(1)(a). *Compare* Ore. Rev. Code Ann. § 3929.25 (building or structure insured against loss or damage by fire or lightning).

1489. Conway, *As Hurricanes End, Legal Storms Begin: The Insurance Battle under State Valued Policy Laws*, 24 Ga. St. U.L. Rev. 1043, 1049 (2008).

1490. Georgia Farm Bureau Mut. Ins. Co. v. Brown, 192 Ga. App. 504, 508, 385 S.E. 2d 87, 90 (1986) (evidence showing that it would cost more to repair house than to replace it and photographs showing house was substantially gutted by fire found sufficient to support conclusion that house was "wholly destroyed by fire" as contemplated by statute).

prudent owner, uninsured, desiring to rebuild, would have used the remnant for restoring the building."[1491] In Florida, the state's highest court has said that "total loss" means a building has lost its identity and specific character as a building, and becomes so far disintegrated that it cannot be possibly designated as a building, even though some part remains standing.[1492]

Two issues regarding valued policy laws are the applicability of ordinance and law exclusions and ACCs. Many courts have held that ordinance or law exclusions are inapplicable when they conflict with a valued policy statute.[1493] There is less clarity on the applicability of an ACC.[1494]

When a common interest community association suffers a catastrophic loss that might be governed by a valued policy law, the association would be wise to employ experienced professionals—an insurance attorney and public adjuster—early in the process to steer it through the difficult legal straits it will confront.

[4] The Role of the Community Association Manager

The community association manager may well be the point person for dealing with an event that damages the property. One consideration for the manager is that the time he or she spends addressing the problem and handling the claim should be documented as it may be reimbursable under the policy.[1495]

Associations may delegate much of the responsibility for handling claims to their community association managers. The manager may be qualified to take on that role, but the governing board should still state explicitly the parameters of the manager's authority, record those limitations in writing—which may be stated in the management agreement—and communicate them to the manager

1491. Glens Falls Ins. Co. v. Peters, 386 S.W. 2d 529, 531 (Tex. 1965).

1492. Lafayette Fire Ins. Co. v. Camnitz, 111 Fla. 556, 560, 149 So. 653, 654 (1933). *See also* Citizens Prop. Ins. Corp. v. Hamilton, 43 So. 3d 746 (Fla. 1st DCA 2010).

1493. *See, e.g.*, Hertog v. Milwaukee Mut. Ins. Co., 415 N.W.2d 370, 373 (Minn. App. 1987) (where policy insures direct physical loss and excludes from coverage loss occasioned by any ordinance, courts generally limit exclusionary provision in cases of total loss because it is contrary to valued policy statute); Stevick v. Northwest G. F. Mut. Ins. Co., 281 N.W.2d 60, 63 (N.D. 1979) (whether loss was in fact or in law total, valued policy statute should apply and insured was entitled to face amount of policy and any policy provision, including ordinance and law exclusion, that prevents insured from showing that loss is in law or in fact total runs directly afoul of clear intent of statute); Stahlberg v. Travelers Indem. Co., 568 S.W.2d 79, 85 (Mo. App. 1978) (generally if repair or reconstruction of damaged building is prohibited by municipal authorities acting under proper authority of law, recovery may be had by insured for total loss and exclusionary ordinance and law provision that attempts to limit liability of insurer to less than face value of policy in cases of total loss is contrary to valued policy statute and void). *See generally* Garaffa, *Florida's "Valued Policy Law"—The Eye of the Storm*, 79 Fla. Bar J. 8 (2005).

1494. Conway, *As Hurricanes End, Legal Storms Begin: The Insurance Battle Under State Valued Policy Laws*, 24 Ga. St. U.L. Rev. 1043, 1059 (2008) (noting many states have yet to address the question).

1495. *See* § 10.36[2][h], *infra*. *See also* Langston, *So You Have an Insurance Claim?* (Association Times 2009).

and the insurer. The governing board, for instance, should retain the sole authority to agree to any settlement amount and to approve any release. If the manager has actual or apparent authority to act for the association, his or her actions will usually be binding on the board.[1496] Additionally, a designated board member, the full board, or an insurance committee should monitor the process of the claim and receive regular reports from the manager. At the same time, the board should be prepared to call a special meeting to provide any guidance the manager seeks.[1497]

[5] Releases

With limited exceptions—one being fraud in the inducement—when an association signs a release proffered by the insurer in exchange for a settlement of its claim, the release is binding.[1498]

A common interest community governing board is made up of volunteers with varying degrees of business sophistication, and it acts through agents who may be officer/board members, a professional manager, or others. It is, therefore, incumbent on the board to establish, before it submits a claim, who is authorized to sign a release. Absent duress, undue influence, or fraud in the inducement, the association will generally be bound by a release signed on its behalf by someone

1496. *See, e.g.*, Crystal Colony Condo. Ass'n v. Aspen Specialty Ins. Co., 6 F. Supp. 3d 1295 (S.D. Fla. 2014) (where manager signed release on behalf of association despite believing proceeds received were inadequate, but signed to receive payment and speed up damage repair process, release was based on valid consideration of forbearance from pursing future legal action and was, therefore, binding on association); Shoreline Towers Condo. Owners Ass'n v. Zurich Am. Ins. Co., 196 F. Supp. 2d 1210 (S.D. Ala. 2002) (under management agreement, manager had authority to handle all insurance matters on behalf of condominium association, including placing or keeping in force all insurance, adjusting all claims, delivering releases on payment of claims, receiving any insurance proceeds on behalf of association, and exercising all rights of insured; pursuant to that management agreement, manager had actual authority to sign binding release on behalf of association).

1497. For example, in one case the manager asked the insurer not to issue payment until he had discussed the claim with the association board. One month later, the insurer had received no communication from the association and sent a letter informing the association that the claim was being closed without payment and that the association had 24 months from the date of loss to pursue the claim. Madison Park Townhouses Homeowners Ass'n v. Country Mut. Ins. Co., 2015 U.S. Dist. LEXIS 119090 (D. Colo. Sept. 8, 2015). Association governing boards often meet no more than once a month. It may have been that the governing board had not yet met to discuss the claim with the manager before the month expired. In any event, the failure of the board to meet promptly and give the manager guidance delayed the processing of the claim.

1498. *See, e.g.*, Bonita Villas Condo. Ass'n v. Empire Indem. Ins. Co., 2010 U.S. Dist. LEXIS 62868 (S.D. Fla. June 22, 2010). The insurer offered to settle a claim for about $1 million less than the association sought. The association signed a release as a condition of settlement. Eighteen months later the association sued the insurer. It alleged it was coerced into releasing its claim because the insurer purportedly said that otherwise the claim would be the subject of "long protracted and expensive litigation" that would take years to resolve. The court dismissed the action, finding the release was binding.

having actual or apparent authority.[1499] For example, in *Continuum Condo. Ass'n v. Mt. Hawley Ins. Co.*,[1500] the association president apparently signed a broad agreement that released the insurer from any and all actions, causes of action, claims, and demands whatsoever for all loss and damages arising from a particular hurricane. The association subsequently contended the release was fraudulent, that it had never authorized the release, and that it was never signed by the president. It alleged, therefore, that it never settled all of its claims with the insurer and that it was entitled to payment for a disputed portion of its claim. The case was resolved on other grounds, but it illustrates the need for associations to determine how releases are to be handled before they are proffered.

[6] Dissatisfied Unit Owners

When the association policy covers property of association members, there is the potential for conflict between them as well as between a member and the insurer. What happens if the resolution of a claim made by the association is not to the satisfaction of an individual owner? Can that owner sue either the association or the insurer?

[a] Claims against the Association

Initially, if a unit owner is dissatisfied with the way in which the association has handled a claim, any action probably has to be brought against the association, rather than against the members of the board of directors individually who made the contested decisions on behalf of the association.[1501] Broadly worded governing documents may bind the owners to any settlement reached by the association.[1502]

1499. *See, e.g.*, Encino Park W. Homeowners Ass'n v. Truck Ins. Exch., 2007 Cal. App. Unpub. LEXIS 6354 (Aug. 3, 2007). *See also* Oriole Gardens Condo. Ass'n I v. Aspen Specialty Ins. Co., 875 F. Supp. 2d 1379 (S.D. Fla. 2012) (where association president represented it in connection with insurance claim and association did not dispute that president was fully authorized to handle claim on its behalf, it was bound by document signed by him though form was presented to him by insurer and he had neither attorney nor public adjuster to assist him; court treated claim as foreclosed by accord and satisfaction).

1500. Continuum Condo. Ass'n v. Mt. Hawley Ins. Co., 2011 U.S. Dist. LEXIS 58693 (S.D. Fla. June 1, 2011). *See generally* Marker, *Condominium Insurance Law: The Policyholders Advocate* (June 2011), available at: http://www.condominiuminsurancelaw.com/tags/release/.

1501. *See, e.g.*, Perlow v. Goldberg, 700 So. 2d 148 (Fla. 3d DCA 1997), where unit owners alleged a breach of fiduciary duty by the directors in failing to properly administer insurance proceeds. The court held that the directors could not be held liable in their individual capacity absent crimes, fraud, self-dealing, willful misconduct, or unjust enrichment. At most, the directors were negligent in failing to properly administer insurance funds and their actions or omissions were insufficient to impose personal liability.

1502. *See* Anthony v. Indep. Ins. Advisors, Inc., 56 V.I. 516, 534 (2012) (where under governing documents governing board had exclusive right to bind association and unit owners in respect to all matters affecting insurance carried by association, including settlement of loss claim, unit owner was bound by settlement reached by association with broker in procurement litigation).

Courts are divided on the question of whether a unit owner can sue the association over its handling of a claim. Where the loss is to the plaintiff's own unit, courts have allowed these suits to proceed.[1503] On the other hand, where the action was based more broadly on the handling of a claim, Louisiana courts have said the action had to be brought as a derivate claim—that is, on behalf of the association—rather than as an individual action.[1504]

[b] Claims against Insurer

The member of an insured association faces barriers to having the insurance company respond to his or her ostensibly covered loss. First, can the member file a claim with the association's insurer? Second, if the insurer denies the claim, can the member sue the insurer for breach of contract?

[i] Duty of Insurer to Investigate Scope of Coverage

An Ohio appellate court imposed on an insurer the duty to determine whether a unit owner was entitled to coverage under an association policy.[1505] The unit owner suffered damage when a pipe burst. The association's insurer opened a claims file, but the developer, the named insured who evidently had not yet transferred control of the association to the unit owners, notified the insurer it did not wish to pursue the claim. The insurer closed the file and refused to pay on the claim. The court said that because the policy related to a condominium and involved different parties with defined rights and responsibilities, the insurer should have been on notice that, to resolve the claim, it had to thoroughly investigate the rights of the various parties under the policy. The bylaws revealed that the association was required to buy insurance to cover the claim. The insurer

1503. *See, e.g.*, King v. Casa Grande Condo. Ass'n, 416 Fed. Appx. 363 (5th Cir. 2011) (remanding to lower court to determine which costs claimed by unit owners for damage to their unit, if any, would have been covered by policy but for association's negligence in failing to assiduously pursue claim on their behalf); McLean v. Vision Mgmt., LLC, 2012 Conn. Super. LEXIS 2351 (Conn. Super. Ct. Sept. 17, 2012) (where unit owner alleged association and management company either neglected or refused to submit claim for her losses, court refused to dismiss action seeking writ of mandamus ordering association to place claim through carrier for alleged damages in her unit); Moshyedi v. Council of Unit Owners of Annapolis Rd. Med. Ctr. Condo., 132 Md. App. 184, 752 A.2d 279 (2000) (finding that where association received funds from its carrier for damage to individual units and association president directed contractor to perform only limited work on appellant's unit, association failed to fulfill its obligation under bylaws to arrange for prompt repair or to pay for needed restoration of unit).

1504. Stall v. Bakery Condo. Ass'n, 66 So. 3d 1112 (La. App. 2011) (where unit owner alleged association and its president improperly delegated authority to manager to negotiate settlement, unit owner had no right of action because she would have had to sue as shareholder—derivative suit—rather than as individual); Stall v. State Farm Fire & Cas. Co., 995 So. 2d 670 (La. App. 2008) (where association had improperly abdicated its role in settling claim, alleged injury would be to corporation and not plaintiff directly and even if she had suffered indirect loss, claim would have had to have been asserted derivatively and not individually).

1505. Stefano v. Commodore Cove E., Ltd., 145 Ohio App. 3d 290, 762 N.E.2d 1023 (2001).

closed the claim, observed the court, because the developer, as the named insured, refused to pursue it even though the bylaws assigned to the association, not the developer, the duty to buy insurance. The policy itself provided that the insurer could cancel it only after prior notice to the named insured and each unit owner to whom a certificate of insurance had been issued. Thus, the bylaws and policy indicated that the insurer could not reasonably rely on the developer's decision not to pursue the claim as a basis for refusing to pay. When the claim was made, concluded the court, the insurer should have known that it had to determine the identity of the named insured and whether, under the policy, other persons or entities could file a claim.

[ii] Association Claim Submitted to Appraisal

If the association submits a claim to appraisal, is the loss of an individual unit owner barred? In one case the named insured, a condominium association in which the plaintiff was a unit owner, submitted a claim for coverage to a final appraisal. The insurer argued the appraisal was binding on the plaintiff, but the court found that the damages she claimed were not confined to those that were the subject of the appraisal and refused to dismiss her claim against the insurer.[1506]

[c] Standing of Unit Owners to Sue Association Insurer

A basic rule of contract law is that to bring an action for breach of a contract, one must be a party to that contract, or perhaps a "third party beneficiary" of it. Thus, when individual owners sue the association's property insurer, the carrier almost invariably raises as a defense lack of standing[1507]—the plaintiff is not a party to the contract. This defense has met with mixed results.

[i] Status of Owners as Insureds

The earliest case to discuss the right of residents of a common interest community to sue the association's insurer appears to be *Gantman v. United Pacific Ins. Co.*[1508] It concerned a homeowners association that owned and insured the

---

1506. McCarthy v. Glenwood Place of Farmington Ass'n, 2016 Conn. Super. LEXIS 274 (Conn. Super. Ct. Feb. 3, 2016).

1507. In some cases, however, in which individual owners sue the insurer for the association, it appears that standing is not raised. *See, e.g.*, Stephan v. Transportation Insurance Co., 140 Fed. Appx. 340 (3d Cir. 2005); Buczek v. Cont'l Cas. Ins. Co., 378 F.3d 284 (3d Cir. 2004); Humphries v. Metropolitan Prop. & Cas. Ins. Co., 2016 N.Y. Misc. LEXIS 89 (Jan. 8, 2016). The question of standing is complex enough to leave insurers confused. *See, e.g.*, Stefano v. Commodore Cove E., Ltd., 145 Ohio App. 3d 290, 294–95, 762 N.E.2d 1023, 1026 (2001) (insurer advised unit owner that only governing board of association could, under bylaws and policy, file claim and, in unit owner's action against it, insurer moved for summary judgment stating unit owner had no right to file claim on policy, yet employee of insurer concluded that under bylaws, policy provisions, and relevant state law, unit owner could pursue claim for property damage independent of named insured's refusal to submit claim).

1508. Gantman v. United Pacific Ins. Co., 232 Cal. App. 3d 1560, 284 Cal. Rptr. 188 (1991).

common area. Its Declaration specifically barred individual owners from separately insuring their residences and provided that each owner was deemed to have appointed the association as attorney in fact to act in all matters concerning a master insurance policy. Roofs in the community leaked, and the association submitted a claim for only a portion of the roofs. Unit owners sued the insurer over the other portions of the roofs, none of which they owned. The court held the plaintiffs lacked standing to bring an action based on policies purchased by and issued to the association under which they were not insureds.[1509]

A North Carolina court reached a different conclusion.[1510] Under that state's Uniform Act, the condominium association obtained property insurance covering individual units. The plaintiff owned a unit damaged by a fire that started in an adjacent unit. The association's insurer refused to cover property losses to the interior of the plaintiff's unit. The plaintiff sued the insurer, which predictably argued lack of standing. The court, however, concluded the plaintiff was insured under the policy and, therefore, had standing to sue on it. North Carolina law, explained the court, required associations to purchase insurance as trustee for each unit owner. It did not impose the "absurd requirement" that every unit owner be named individually as an insured. The named insured was the association, and it was comprised of everyone who owned any interest in a condominium unit. The plaintiff, as a member of the association, held the court, was in effect a named insured. Courts in Connecticut, another Uniform Act state, have reached the same result and applied it whether the issue was damage to common elements or improvements and betterments to a particular unit.[1511] A federal court in Maine, on the other hand, found that state's condominium law, which is based on the Uniform Condominium Act, does not grant unit owners standing to bring claims against the association's insurer.[1512] Courts in non–Uniform Act

1509. *See also* Peters v. Lexington Ins. Co., 836 F. Supp. 2d 1117 (D. Haw. 2011) (where policy insured only association and not individual unit owners, unit owners lack standing to assert breach of insurance agreement; language under which some property in individual units was covered by association policy did not state that those unit owners thereby become insureds who could bring claims against insurer on their own); Stall v. State Farm Fire & Cas. Co., 995 So. 2d 670 (La. App. 2008); Calloway v. St. Paul Fire & Marine Ins., 2000 Mass. App. Div. 85 (2000) (where it was clear that policy was between insurer and condominium trust—association—and bylaws that created and defined relationship of unit owners and trustees plainly placed responsibility for casualty insurance with trustees, summary judgment in favor of insurer was appropriate). *And see* Elkins v. QBE Ins. Corp., 2011 U.S. Dist. LEXIS 43314 (W.D. Wash. Apr. 21, 2011) (that individual condominium unit owners benefited from repair of their units does not support argument that they are entitled to directly recover under policy).

1510. Craig v. Sandy Creek Condominium Ass'n, Inc., 2009 N.C. App. LEXIS 766, *aff'd*, 197 N.C. App. 628, 680 S.E.2d 272 (June 16, 2009).

1511. *See* Boyle v. Apple Hill Condo. Ass'n, 2014 Conn. Super. LEXIS 3191 (Conn. Super. Ct. Dec. 29, 2014) (under Connecticut Common Interest Ownership Act, unit owners had standing as insureds both as to common elements and improvements and betterments).

1512. DiMillo v. Travelers Prop. Cas. Co. of Am., 789 F. Supp. 2d 194, 207 (D. Me. 2011).

states, however, have allowed unit owners to pursue actions against their association's insurer.[1513]

Occasionally an owner may have standing independent of any status as an insured. For example, a condominium in South Florida suffered extensive damage in a hurricane that struck in October of 2005. The insurer allegedly dragged its feet, and the association claim was unresolved until February of 2009 when a jury awarded it nearly $20 million. Unit owners sued the insurer alleging that because of its "dilatory practices," they were forced to abandon their uninhabitable and unmarketable units, which were subsequently foreclosed on. They alleged a statutory claim for bad faith. The insurer moved to dismiss the action arguing the plaintiffs were not entitled to relief under the statute because they failed to allege any damages and they were never insured by it. The court's laconic response was "[n]either argument persuades." It said the plaintiffs alleged damages caused by the dilatory processing of the claim and, even though they were not themselves insureds, the statutory remedy was not limited to insureds but allowed all persons damaged by enumerated acts of an insurer to seek redress.[1514] A California court came to a different conclusion on similar facts.[1515] The policy in that case covered the common areas but not individual condominium units owned by the plaintiffs. The association made a claim for damages caused by the Northridge earthquake and ultimately recovered an award in arbitration. The individual unit owners were unable to repair their units before the common elements were repaired, and they incurred the expense of other living arrangements and suffered significant diminution in the value of their units. They sued the insurer for "negligent acts and omissions," arguing the additional expenses would not have been incurred had the insurer timely and fully performed its obligations under the policy.[1516]

1513. *See, e.g.*, Allday v. Newpark Square I Office Condo. Ass'n, 113 So. 3d 346 (2013) (disagreeing with argument of insurer for association that unit owner lacked standing to pursue any claims against it because he was not named insured); Rosenberg v. Truck Insurance Exchange, 2003 Cal. App. Unpub. LEXIS 4148 (Apr. 25, 2003) (where complaint by unit owner contended that association insurer represented that policy fully covered earthquake damage to her unit, it alleged she had basis for standing as an insured; that policy provided coverage for property owned exclusively by individual unit owners, allowed insurer to negotiate directly with unit owners to adjust their claims, provided primary coverage for unit owners, waived insurer's right of subrogation, and provided that all insureds could file claims as if separate policy had been issued to each would also support unit owner's standing to sue for breach of contract). *And see* First Int'l Bank & Trust v. Peterson, 797 N.W.2d 316, 321 (N.D. 2011) (in dispute over insurance proceeds, because members of association had standing to sue insurer in their own right, association met requirements for associational standing).

1514. Benson v. QBE Ins. Corp., 61 F. Supp. 3d 1277 (S.D. Fla. 2014). *See also* Sable Cove Condo. Ass'n v. Owners Ins. Co., 2014 U.S. Dist. LEXIS 124050 (D. Colo. Sept. 5, 2014) (contractor assigned right by insured association to receive overhead and profit could bring statutory bad faith action against insurer).

1515. Adelman v. Associated International Ins. Co., 108 Cal. Rptr. 2d 788, 90 Cal. App. 4th 352 (2001).

1516. The plaintiffs, said the court, raised a novel issue: "may an insurer be subject to liability to a noninsured third party for the negligent performance of its indemnity obligations to the

The plaintiffs claimed a personal economic interest in prompt performance by the insurance company of its policy obligations. The court, however, found for the company. Among the reasons offered by the court for its decision was that while the insured association would not be able to recover for mere negligence but was limited to a breach of contract remedy, if it ruled for the plaintiffs, who were *not* insured parties, they would recover for negligence and, thus, have greater rights than the law grants to an insured party.

In an unpublished California decision, a unit owner sued the association's insurer alleging it committed fraud against her and made negligent misrepresentations to her about coverage under the association policy for her loss. The court said standing to sue based on these causes of action was independent of standing to sue on the policy.[1517]

[ii] Third-Party Beneficiary Status

When a contract is formed for the benefit of another, it confers on that party—the "third party beneficiary"—the power to enforce the agreement.[1518] The Restatement of Contracts states a contractual promise imposes an obligation on a promisor to an *intended* beneficiary to perform that promise and that "[u]nless otherwise agreed between promisor and promisee, a beneficiary of a promise is an intended beneficiary if recognition of a right to performance in the beneficiary is appropriate to effectuate the intention of the parties and either . . . the performance of the promise will satisfy an obligation of the promisee to pay money to the beneficiary; or . . . the circumstances indicate that the promisee intends to give the beneficiary the benefit of the promised performance."[1519]

---

named insured based upon allegations that there is a 'special relationship' between the insurer and the third party . . . ?" The plaintiffs did not claim to be parties to the association policy and did not seek recovery for breach of contract or for any alleged bad faith under the policy. Instead, they attempted to recover for damages allegedly sustained as a direct and proximate result of a breach of a duty of reasonable care they asserted was owed to them.

1517. Rosenberg v. Truck Insurance Exchange, 2003 Cal. App. Unpub. LEXIS 4148 (Apr. 25, 2003). The unit owner alleged the insurer represented to her that damage to her unit was fully covered under the policy and that it would restore and repair her condominium unit. These representations were false, she contended, because the insurer never intended to pay her the insurance benefits to which she was entitled. The court said that as the unit owner was the person to whom the representations were made and who justifiably relied on them to her detriment, she was the real party in interest whose rights allegedly were violated under the substantive law of fraud and negligent misrepresentation.

1518. *Corbin on Contracts*, § 44.1 (Matthew Bender & Company, Inc. 2011).

1519. Restatement (Second) of Contracts § 302(1). An "incidental beneficiary" is by definition not an intended one. Restatement (Second) of Contracts § 302(2). *See, e.g.*, Mira v. Scottsdale Ins. Co., 2013 N.Y. Misc. LEXIS 5739 (Nov. 29, 2013) (where plaintiff unit owner was not named as insured, nor was there any reference in policy to plaintiff or to any of unit owners, plaintiff had to demonstrate parties to insurance contract intended that he be more than mere incidental beneficiary and plaintiff failed to do so; while bylaws required board of managers to procure fire insurance at expense of unit owners and appointed board of managers as agent for each unit owner, plaintiff failed to show bylaws were admissible extrinsic proof to interpret meaning of policy or that insurer

In common interest communities, the individual owners clearly benefit from the promise of the insurer to pay the association, the named insured. Even if the policy does not cover individual units, the individual owners have an interest in the property insured. In a condominium, the unit owners own the insured common property as tenants in common. In a housing cooperative, the tenant/shareholders own the corporation that owns all the real property. Even in a homeowners association where the association owns and insures real property in its own name, the individual owners are members of that association. In all three forms of common interest ownership, the owners actually pay the premiums through assessments levied by the association. Does the association then intend to give the owners the benefit of the promised performance?[1520]

The *Gantman* decision discussed above rejected third-party beneficiary status for the residents of a homeowner association. A number of courts have concurred with that conclusion.[1521] Others, however, have disagreed. For example, a Connecticut court, relying on the language of the association policy, rejected the insurer's argument that condominium unit owners were mere incidental beneficiaries of the policy and instead held that they were third-party beneficiaries with standing to bring an action for breach of contract even though only the association was named as an insured.[1522] The court also cited as significant, policy

---

was bound by them). Some confusion about the Restatement remains. Does it require both parties to intend to confer third-party rights, or is the intent of the promisee sufficient? Corbin concludes that under the Restatement the right to performance is determined by intent of both contracting parties *and* the promisee to benefit the third party. *Corbin on Contracts*, § 44.1 (Matthew Bender & Company Inc., 2011).

1520. *Consider* Ryan v. Travelers Indem. Co., 2013 U.S. Dist. LEXIS 91539 (E.D. Cal. June 27, 2013) (mere fact that policy is purchased by homeowners association with dues paid by individual members, or even that it is purchased to benefit those members, is insufficient to establish that individual members are intended beneficiaries; where named insured is an entity, its members, shareholders, or owners have no standing to bring direct claim against insurer despite fact they would clearly gain under policy, as they are not intended beneficiaries and their potential benefits are merely incidental and "incidental beneficiaries" do not have standing to sue under insurance contracts).

1521. *See, e.g.*, Ryan v. Travelers Indem. Co., 2013 U.S. Dist. LEXIS 91539 (E.D. Cal. June 27, 2013); DiMillo v. Travelers Prop. Cas. Co. of Am., 789 F. Supp. 2d 194 (D. Me. 2011) (finding no evidence that granting enforceable benefit to plaintiff unit owner would effectuate intentions of parties despite fact that as member of association he paid for insurance and that it covered all units); Stall v. State Farm Fire & Cas. Co., 995 So. 2d 670 (La. App. 2008); May v. Mid-Century Ins. Co., 151 P.3d 132 (Okla. 2006) (loss payment clause gave insurer exclusive choice to settle covered losses directly with unit owners or with association for account of unit owners and expressed intent to confer solely on insurer power to regard all contractual obligations due under policy as extending to named insured specifically negated existence of any enforceable obligation in favor of unit owners *qua* third-party beneficiaries; no obligation may be imposed on promisor in favor of third party if contract expressly relieves that promisor of liability to that third party, and unit owner was thus contractually deprived of any right to assert bad faith tort claim against insurer).

1522. O'Connor v. QBE Ins. Corp., 2015 Conn. Super. LEXIS 553 (Conn. Super. Ct. Mar. 12, 2015) (distinguishing *Gantman* where unit owners were suing for damage to shared feature—roofs—from case before it in which plaintiffs were suing for damage to their individual unit). *See*

language under which covered property included units that were defined as portions of the real property, designated for separate ownership and occupancy.[1523] In contrast, a federal judge in Hawaii said that policy language under which some property in individual units was covered if the Condominium Association Agreement required the association to provide insurance did not give unit owners standing to sue.[1524] Taking it a step further, a California federal court refused to consider association documents at all as a basis for determining whether an individual owner was an insured because they were not incorporated into the policy that "controlled the outcome of the claim."[1525]

[iii] Individual Owners as Assignees of Association

If an owner can obtain an assignment of the association's rights under the policy, then generally he or she will have standing to bring a claim. Some policies have an explicit prohibition on assignment. Two of the policies that are often issued to common interest communities—the BPP and CAC—do not prohibit assignments, although it is possible an endorsement could be added to bar assignments. A common interest community may also have an ISO Standard Property Policy, and it has a clause that says the rights and duties of the named insured under the policy may not be transferred without the written consent of the insurer.[1526]

The language prohibiting the transfer of the rights and duties of the insured without the insurer's consent is interpreted by most courts to prohibit only assignments without consent *before* a loss, not those after one. The reason for the distinction is that before a loss the insurer might be unwilling to underwrite a risk for a party with whom it did not contract, but after the loss the right that is transferred is to receive the insurance proceeds and it should not matter to whom the

---

also Seeley v. State Farm Fire & Cas. Co., 2016 Conn. Super. LEXIS 972 (Conn. Super. Ct. May 3, 2016) (that association property insurance policy expressly covered individual units and was primary with respect to any coverage obtained by unit owners gave them at least colorable claim to be third-party beneficiaries of policy); Boyle v. Apple Hill Condo. Ass'n, 2014 Conn. Super. LEXIS 3191 (Conn. Super. Ct. Dec. 29, 2014) (under Connecticut Common Interest Ownership Act, unit owners had standing as third-party beneficiaries to association policy); Rosenberg v. Truck Insurance Exchange, 2003 Cal. App. Unpub. LEXIS 4148 (Apr. 25, 2003) (where complaint by unit owner contended that association insurer represented that policy fully covered earthquake damage to her unit, it alleged she had basis for standing as intended beneficiary; that policy provided coverage for property owned exclusively by individual unit owners, allowed insurer to negotiate directly with unit owners to adjust their claims, provided primary coverage for unit owners, waived insurer's right of subrogation, and provided that all insureds could file claims as if separate policy had been issued to each would also support unit owner's standing to sue for breach of contract).

1523. The court also noted the Declarations Page stated the policy provided coverage for "twenty-four three-story frame condominium buildings containing eighty residential units."

1524. Peters v. Lexington Ins. Co., 836 F. Supp. 2d 1117 (D. Haw. 2011).

1525. Ryan v. Travelers Indem. Co., 2013 U.S. Dist. LEXIS 91539 (E.D. Cal. June 27, 2013).

1526. ISO Form CP 00 99 10 90 § E.6.

insurer pays a claim that it is obliged to pay.[1527] There is, however, a minority position, most prominently adhered to in Texas, in which non-assignment clauses are enforced even for assignments made post-loss.[1528] Interestingly, in one of the only cases to consider application of a non-assignment clause where a common interest community assigned the right to receive insurance proceeds from its insurer, a Maine federal court followed that minority rule.[1529]

It should be remembered that in any transfer of rights, the assignor—the party making the assignment—can transfer no more rights to the assignee—the party receiving the assignment—than the assignor itself had.[1530] Additionally, once the assignment has been effected, the assignor loses whatever rights it assigned.[1531]

§ 10.39 Avoiding Unnecessary Claims

Avoiding unnecessary claims is vital to protecting the association from the potential for increased premiums or the refusal of the insurer to renew the policy. There are common losses that can be prevented by a risk management plan. For example, in multi-story buildings, water leaks are commonplace and often preventable.[1532] A major source of property insurance claims is fire damage, which

---

1527. Sable Cove Condo. Ass'n v. Owners Ins. Co., 2014 U.S. Dist. LEXIS 124050 (D. Colo. Sept. 5, 2014) (association validly assigned to contractor right to receive overhead and profit as part of insurance proceeds; right to receive money due or to become due under existing contract may be assigned, even though contract itself may not be assignable). *See also* Edgewood Manor Apt. Homes LLC v. RSUI Indem. Co., 782 F. Supp. 2d 716, 735 (E.D. Wis. 2011) (right to receive money due or to become due under contract may be assigned even though contract itself may not be assignable; contract to pay money may be assigned by person to whom money is payable, unless there is something in terms of contract manifesting intent of parties that it may not be assigned); Antal's Restaurant v. Lumbermen's Mut. Cas. Co., 680 A.2d 1386, 1388 (D.C. 1996).

1528. *See* Keller Founds., Inc. v. Wausau Underwriters Ins. Co., 626 F.3d 871, 874 (5th Cir. 2010).

1529. DiMillo v. Travelers Prop. Cas. Co. of Am., 789 F. Supp. 2d 194, 205 (D. Me. 2011) (under non-assignment clause it was unambiguous that association could not transfer its rights and duties under policy without insurer's written consent; one claiming contractual rights as assignee has burden of proof on issue of assignment, and unit owner failed to respond to insurer's argument that non-assignment clause applied to preclude his having standing to sue insurer for insurance proceeds).

1530. *See generally* Cozen, *Insuring Real Property*, § 23.04[9] (Matthew Bender & Co. 2015) (effect of transfer is to allow assignee same rights to collect policy proceeds as insured-assignor had).

1531. *See* Sable Cove Condo. Ass'n v. Owners Ins. Co., 2014 U.S. Dist. LEXIS 124050 (D. Colo. Sept. 5, 2014) (association that assigned rights to insurance proceeds lost right to bring action for breach of contract against insurer).

1532. *See generally* Heft, *15 Preventable Homeowners' Insurance Claims and How to Avoid Them* (Dec. 2016), available at: http://www.propertycasualty360.com/2016/12/19/15-preventable-homeowners-insurance-claims-and-how?eNL=585aab50160ba08a768434c8&utm_source=PC360_ClaimsConnection&utm_medium=EMC-Email_editorial&t=catastrophe-restoration&utm

can be caused by faulty wiring and open flame cooking. Common interest community governing boards have rule-making authority and can use it to address these preventable mishaps. For instance, burst washing machine water hoses are a significant source of water damage. Many associations require installation of shut-off valves[1533]—so that water to washing machines is off except when they are in use—and steel reinforced hoses to reduce the possibility of hose failures when washing machines are being used. Associations may also bar use of grills on balconies or patios and impose maintenance regimes for fireplaces and heaters. Finally, in areas subject to hurricanes, some associations mandate impact resistant windows or hurricane shutters in multi-story buildings. These requirements can prevent a great deal of damage that association policies may cover, including consequential damage to common elements when storm force winds and rain enter a building through a window in an individual unit that has broken out.

An experienced community association manager should be able to assist a governing board in identifying building risks and crafting preventative measures. Any rules drafted to address prevention should be reviewed by the association attorney to make sure they are clear and enforceable. Well-drafted documents may help an association avoid having to make a claim. For example, a rule might require residents to have an annual HVAC inspection. If a resident fails to comply and a breakdown in his or her unit damages the common elements, the governing documents may allow the association to recover from the resident rather than filing a claim with its insurer.

§ 10.40 Disposition of Insurance Proceeds

The disposition of insurance proceeds in common interest communities can present some unique problems. Who receives any insurance proceeds, the use to which they must be put, and the circumstances under which they may be distributed to individual owners or lienholders will be governed by applicable statutes or the common interest community documents, or a combination of both.

[1] Statutes and Governing Documents

The various Uniform Acts have specific requirements for disposition of proceeds. For example, the UCIOA provides that any loss covered by the property policy has to be adjusted with the association, but the insurance proceeds are payable

---

_campaign=12212016&page=5&page_all=1. The author identifies washing machines, loose toilets, refrigerator water supply lines, and water heaters as sources of damaging water leaks and offers maintenance suggestions to prevent them.

1533. *See* Ruickoldt, *How Automatic Shut-Off Water Systems Are Changing Homeowners' Claims: Learn Tools That Can Mitigate Water Damage* (Sept. 2016), available at: http://www.propertycasualty360.com/2016/09/29/how-automatic-shut-off-water-systems-are-changing?slreturn=1482504297.

to any insurance trustee designated for that purpose, or otherwise to the association, not to any holder of a security interest.[1534] The trustee or association has to hold proceeds in trust for the association, unit owners, and lien holders, as their interests may appear. Generally, the proceeds have to be disbursed first for repair or replacement of the damaged property.[1535] The association, unit owners, and lien holders are not entitled to receive payment of any portion of those proceeds unless there is a surplus after the property has been completely repaired or replaced, or the common interest community is terminated. Commentary to the UCIOA explains that unless a decision is made not to rebuild, any available insurance proceeds have to be used for repairs,[1536] and that distribution of insurance proceeds to lenders is barred until the intended purpose of the insurance has been met.[1537] This prevents a mortgagee from preempting insurance proceeds and applying them to any mortgage debt.[1538]

Another subsection of the UCIOA provides that if an entire common interest community is not repaired or replaced, the insurance proceeds attributable to the damaged common elements have to be used to restore the damaged area to a condition compatible with the remainder of the community.[1539] Then, except to the extent that others will be distributees, the insurance proceeds attributable to units and limited common elements that *are not* repaired or replaced have to be distributed to the owners of those units and the owners of the units to which those limited common elements were allocated, or to lien holders, as their interests may appear. Then, the remainder of the proceeds have to be distributed to *all* the unit owners or lien holders, as their interests may appear, in a condominium, in proportion to the common element interests of all the units, and in a cooperative or planned community, in proportion to the common expense liabilities of all the units.[1540]

For *condominiums*, some non–Uniform Act states have similar requirements,[1541] and a number of states simply provide that damage to or destruction of the

1534. Uniform Common Interest Ownership Act § 3-113(e).

1535. Note that the insurer may agree to pay insurance proceeds directly to a contractor making repairs to the property. *See, e.g.*, Lifetime Constr., L.L.C. v. Lake Marina Tower Condo. Ass'n, 117 So. 3d 109 (La. App. 2013) (insurer and association, acting through its president, reached agreement under which insurance proceeds would be paid directly to contractor for initial demolition and rebuild work).

1536. Uniform Common Interest Ownership Act § 3-113, comment 10. The comment adds that it is significant that insurance proceeds may not be paid to any mortgagee or other outside party. This assures the proceeds are available for any repairs or restoration to the common interest community that may be required.

1537. Uniform Common Interest Ownership Act § 2-119, comment 5.

1538. Hakala, *Condominium Casualty and Liability Insurance*, 48 St. John's L. Rev. 1112, 1114–15 (1974).

1539. Uniform Common Interest Ownership Act § 3-113(i)(1).

1540. Uniform Common Interest Ownership Act § 3-113(i)(2).

1541. *See, e.g.*, 765 Ill. Comp. Stat. 605/12(g) (Illinois Condominium Property Act); Kan. Stat. Ann. § 58-3712 (Kansas Townhouse Ownership Act).

building has to be promptly repaired and reconstructed using the proceeds of insurance, if any, on the building for that purpose.[1542] In contrast, Florida law says little about insurance proceeds other than in the event a condominium is terminated.[1543]

Disposition of insurance proceeds may also be addressed by the governing documents of a common interest community. Often the documents will require that insurance proceeds are to be disbursed first for the repair or restoration of the damaged property.[1544] Some require the governing board to appoint an insurance trustee to receive insurance proceeds.[1545] Others specifically protect lenders by providing them a veto over the use of insurance proceeds.[1546]

Because of the variety of possible statutory and document-based requirements governing insurance proceeds, it is critical for the association to examine its own documents and the applicable state law *before* it receives insurance proceeds. If there is any doubt as to the requirements of the documents or an applicable statute, or there is a conflict between them, the association should consult with its legal counsel before proceeding with receipt or disposition of the proceeds.

1542. *See, e.g.*, N.J. Stat. § 46:8B-3(d)(vii) (New Jersey Condominium Act); N.Y. Real Prop. Law § 339-cc(1) (New York Condominium Act); Ohio Rev. Code Ann. § 5311.14(A) (Ohio Condominium Property Act).

1543. A plan for termination must specify any interests of the respective unit owners in insurance proceeds not used for repair or reconstruction at the time of termination and, unless the Declaration expressly addresses the distribution of insurance proceeds, the plan may apportion those proceeds pursuant to any statutorily prescribed method. Fla. Stat. § 718.117(10)(e). After approval, the governing board is required to collect and receive insurance proceeds for the association. Fla. Stat. § 718.117(6)(h).

1544. *See, e.g.*, Willows Condo. Owners Ass'n v. Kraus, 467 S.W.3d 312, 315 (Mo. App. 2015). *See also* Hakala, *Condominium Casualty and Liability Insurance*, 48 St. John's L. Rev. 1112, 1115 (1974) (Declaration must, to guard against threat of pre-emption, provide that no portion of insurance proceeds are to be applied to payment of any unit owner's mortgage indebtedness unless, after extensive damage to structure, association decides not to repair or rebuild; efficiency of that provision can be assured by additional directive requiring all insurance proceeds to be paid to independent financial institution acting as trustee for association, with trustees then disbursing funds directly to contractors performing restoration work).

1545. *See, e.g.*, Mountain Top Condo. Ass'n v. Dave Stabbert Master Builder, Inc., 72 F.3d 361 (3d Cir. 1995) (bylaws required board to appoint insurance trustee to approve adjustment of any loss and to receive all insurance proceeds for losses in excess of $50,000).

1546. *See, e.g.*, Foothill Village Homeowners Ass'n v. Bishop, 68 Cal. App. 4th 1364, 1375, 81 Cal. Rptr. 2d 195, 202 (1999) (CC&Rs provided that unless 75 percent of lenders gave written approval, neither association nor individual owners could use hazard insurance proceeds for losses to any properties within project—whether units or common area—for other than repair, replacement, or reconstruction except as provided by statute in case of substantial loss); National Title Ins. Co. v. Lakeshore 1 Condo. Ass'n, 691 So. 2d 1104, 1105 (Fla. 3d DCA 1997) (Declaration provided that any insurance proceeds not used for reconstruction were to be distributed to unit owners and their mortgagees as their interests appeared and that if there were mortgagee endorsement for any unit, unit owner's share of insurance proceeds was to be held in trust for mortgagee who had no right to determine whether or not damaged property would be reconstructed).

[2] Policy Provisions

The CAC specifically addresses insurance trustees, while the BPP does not. The CAC says that if the association names an insurance trustee, the carrier will adjust losses with the association but will pay the insurance trustee and that if it pays the trustee, the payments will satisfy the association's claims against the carrier.[1547] When a Standard Property Policy is used for a common interest community, there is a generic or state-specific endorsement that can be added that says the same thing.[1548] It is important to be alert to endorsements that have different language and may affect distribution of insurance proceeds.[1549]

It is possible for there to be an endorsement that provides for payment of insurance proceeds to a "loss payee."[1550] An insurer that pays an association in contravention of a loss payee endorsement may be found to be in breach of contract.[1551] On the other hand where an endorsement was added to an association

---

1547. ISO Form CP 00 17 06 07, § E.4.g.

1548. *See, e.g.*, ISO Form CP 17 99 03 87, § C (Condominium Association Coverage endorsement of Standard Property Policy); ISO Form CP 01 99 10 90, § E (Condominium Association Coverage Condominium Law Provisions; endorsement of Standard Property Policy). *See also* ISO Form CP 01 39 10 12, § E (Connecticut Changes—Condominium Association Coverage—Condominium Law Provisions; endorsement of Standard Property Policy); ISO Form CP 17 97 07 10, § C (Florida Changes—Residential Condominium Associations —Standard Property Policy); ISO Form CP 17 01 02 09, § C (Georgia Changes—Condominium Associations—Standard Property Policy); ISO Form CP 17 04 10 09 § D (Maryland Changes—Condominium Association Coverage Condominium Law Provisions; endorsement of Standard Property Policy); ISO Form CP 01 95 10 90, § D.g (Minnesota Condominium Association Coverage Condominium Law Provisions; endorsement of Standard Property Policy); ISO Form CP 17 99 02 00, § C (Condominium Association Changes—Standard Property Policy—Oregon); ISO Form CP 01 48 10 12, § D (Texas Changes—Condominium Association Coverage—Condominium Law Provisions; endorsement of Standard Property Policy); ISO Form CP 17 05 11 13 § C (Utah—Condominium Association Changes—Standard Property Policy).

1549. *See, e.g.*, ISO Form CP 01 01 01 12, § C.4.b (Kansas Changes; Townhouse Associations) (providing that carrier will pay for covered loss of or damage to buildings or structures to insurance trustee for benefit of each townhouse owner, holder of each first mortgage, and association as interests may appear and as shown in townhouse Declaration); ISO Form CP 01 03 02 98, § B (Massachusetts Changes—Condominiums; endorsement to Condominium Association Coverage Form Condominium Association Changes—Standard Property Policy) (adding that mortgage holder appoints insurance trustee for owners or coowners of condominium who will act on all matters dealing with loss or damage to buildings or structures and have right to receive loss payment due to mortgage holder and execute full release on behalf of mortgage holder).

1550. *See, e.g.*, ISO Form CP 12 18 06 95 (Loss Payable Provisions; endorsement of Building and Personal Property Coverage Form, Builders' Risk Coverage Form, Condominium Association Coverage Form, Condominium Commercial Unit Owners Coverage Form, and Standard Property Policy) (providing insurer will adjust losses with named insured and pay any claim for loss or damage jointly to named insured and named loss payee, "as interests may appear").

1551. *See, e.g.*, Lexington Ins. Co. v. Covest, Ltd., 1996 Tex. App. LEXIS 1427 (Tex. App.—Houston 1st Dist. Apr. 11, 1996), where the named insureds were a condominium and property owners' association. An endorsement provided that any loss due to the insured under the policy was to be held payable to a mortgage servicing company—loss payee—acting as agent for unit mortgagees. The insurer paid a claim to the insureds, and the loss payee objected. The court said

policy naming unit mortgagees as loss payees and the insurer later issued a check payable to the association and the loss payees, one of whom refused to endorse it, a court said that particular loss payee had no right to use the endorsement as a means to control how the association, as statutory trustee, used insurance proceeds to rebuild and repair the units.[1552]

[3] Unit Owners and Proceeds

The members of a common interest community have an interest in insurance proceeds. When managing those proceeds for its owners, an association has a fiduciary duty to use reasonable care.[1553] The members of the association, however, may want the proceeds managed by an independent insurance trustee. The governing board would almost certainly have the authority to appoint a trustee—other than the association—but may well not want to do so. If members of the association want there to be an independent trustee, the governing documents will probably have to address the issue. Some documents may do so, but in many cases they will need to be amended. An amendment might mandate an independent trustee in all circumstances or allow the membership to vote to require an independent trustee when the board refuses to do so.

When the association policy covers damage to units, the insurer will pay the association for any claim. Are the individual unit owners entitled to the insurance proceeds attributable to their units? As discussed above, the UCIOA addresses that question, but what if there is no statutory language like that in the UCIOA that is applicable? Generally, it can be said that the association holds insurance

---

the servicing agent was an authorized agent for the mortgagees and under the endorsement itself became a mortgagee to whom the insurer owed a separate duty under the policy. The insurer contended that the servicing agent had to demonstrate some interest before it was entitled to receive any of the proceeds and, as it did not file a proof of loss statement separately from the condominium owners, it did not show its interest. The court rejected that argument because the policy required the *insured* to file a proof of loss—which they did—but contained no such requirement for the loss payee. The court held there was a contract between the insurer and the servicing agent that required the insurer to pay the insurance proceeds to the servicing agent as loss payee, and the insurer breached that contract by issuing a check payable to the association rather than the servicing agent.

1552. Mahogany Run Condo. Ass'n v. ICG Realty Mgmt. Corp., 1999 U.S. Dist. LEXIS 2005, 40 V.I. 404 (1999). The applicable statute said associations were to insure the property against loss in their name as trustee for each of the owners. An association, said the court, therefore had a statutory right to receive insurance proceeds and determine how best to use them, and the mortgagee of a condominium unit ceded control over the use of the proceeds from a claim to the association no matter what endorsements in favor of mortgagees might be added to the policy obtained by the association.

1553. *See, e.g.*, Mahogany Run Condominium Assoc., Inc. v. ICG Realty Mgmt. Corp. (*In re* Icon Inv. Trust No. 1), 2001 Bankr. LEXIS 2153 (Bankr. D.V.I. Jan. 9, 2001) (condominium governing board had fiduciary duty to unit owners regarding insurance proceeds and breached that duty by failure to commence permanent repairs within reasonable time after loss).

proceeds for the benefit of the owners.[1554] However, the language of the governing documents may dictate the outcome. For example, in a California case, condominium units were damaged by a leak in a unit above. The association submitted a claim to its insurer and received just over $28,000. The association allocated roughly half of that amount to one particular unit. The association sued that unit owner because he allegedly denied it access to his unit. He counterclaimed seeking a portion of the proceeds allocated to his unit. The governing documents said that insurance proceeds were to be used by the association for repair or replacement of the property for which the insurance was carried and authorized distribution of insurance proceeds to an owner if a decision were made not to rebuild or repair. The court found for the association because it concluded the language on use of insurance proceeds for repair or replacement made no mention of payment of proceeds to individual owners and that provision was controlling.[1555]

While typically the insurer would pay insurance proceeds to the association which in turn would either pay for repairs or reimburse owners for payments they made to make repairs, an insurer might issue a check directly to a unit owner. Associations, however, should probably seek to remain as intermediary between the insurer and its members because when insurers deal directly with individual owners, it can lead to problems. For example, in one case damage to a garage in a common interest community restricted use by a resident of his assigned garage space. The insurer told him it would issue a check to him for repairs to the garage, but another resident who apparently had administrative duties for the association called the adjuster and had the check issued to her. She then refused to forward the check to the neighbor who had suffered the loss. He sued her for conversion—in effect, civil theft—and the court found the plaintiff pleaded a valid cause of action.[1556] The facts of the case are unusual, but it does illustrate that it would be better for the proceeds to be given to the association and then distributed subject to the usual financial safeguards the association employs.

If a unit owner is dissatisfied with how the association administers the proceeds, he or she may be able to sue it,[1557] but generally not the individual members

1554. Foothill Village Homeowners Ass'n v. Bishop, 68 Cal. App. 4th 1364, 81 Cal. Rptr. 2d 195 (1999).

1555. Montecito Condo. Homeowner's Ass'n v. Rahmanizad, 2009 Cal. App. Unpub. LEXIS 561 (Jan. 23, 2009).

1556. Seaphus v. Lilly, 691 F. Supp. 127 (N.D. Ill. 1988).

1557. *See, e.g.*, Peters v. Lexington Ins. Co., 836 F. Supp. 2d 1117 (D. Haw. 2011) (if unit owners believed insurer breached insurance agreement, they had no standing to sue it, but were not left without any remedy as, if they believed association had not been vigorous enough in pursuing claims, their dispute "may well be with" association); Moshyedi v. Council of Unit Owners of Annapolis Rd. Med. Ctr. Condo., 132 Md. App. 184, 752 A.2d 279 (2000) (where association received funds from its carrier for damage to individual units and association president directed contractor to perform only limited work on appellant's unit and appellant repaired unit, lower court should have directed that insurance proceeds paid to association specifically for repair of appellant's unit be remitted to appellant). *See also* Mountain Top Condo. Ass'n v. Dave Stabbert

of the board of directors absent some misconduct: fraud, self-dealing, willful misconduct, or unjust enrichment.[1558]

In a Georgia case,[1559] the unit owned by the plaintiffs was flooded from above, evidently as a result of the negligence of the owners of that other unit. The property insurer for the association paid the plaintiffs $10,000 for damages to their unit and personal property. They claimed damage of twice that amount and sued their neighbors. The jury granted the plaintiffs a verdict, but the court offset it by the amount of the insurance proceeds. The appellate court overruled that decision. It said that the plaintiff's recovery was not based on the liability of the other owners but on the right of the plaintiffs to collect for property damage as an insured under the association's duty to restore the damaged property of that insured. Moreover, any part of the assessments the defendants paid to the association to fund the blanket property insurance were paid by them for their *own property damage rights for their own condominium*, not for property damage coverage of another owner's unit and certainly not for their tort liability to another owner. Thus, the trial court erred in granting the defendants a setoff to their tort liability in the amount paid by the association's insurer for the property damage.

[4] Former Unit Owners and Proceeds

A former unit owner may be entitled to a share of insurance proceeds where he or she paid an assessment that was levied to pay for repairs pending possible settlement with the insurer.[1560]

[5] Surplus Proceeds

As noted above, the Uniform Acts address distribution of surplus funds. Surplus funds are those proceeds that exceed the amount needed to make repairs to the property. Some state condominium acts also address surplus funds, at least in the

---

Master Builder, Inc., 72 F.3d 361 (3d Cir. 1995) (where association and contractors were involved in litigation over quality of reconstruction work and any settlement between parties could have depleted remaining insurance funds deposited in registry of court and allocated for repairing damage to condominium property, unit owners were permitted to intervene because they had right to participate in any proceeding that could result in disbursement of those funds other than to duly appointed independent trustee); Cambridge Mut. Fire Ins. Co. v. 1347–49 N. Sedgwick Condo. Ass'n, 2013 U.S. Dist. LEXIS 9750 (N.D. Ill. Jan. 23, 2013) (unit owner sued condominium association for unjust enrichment and conversion where association refused to forward to unit owner funds from association property insurer that were intended to reimburse unit owner for damages to its unit).

1558. *See* Perlow v. Goldberg, 700 So. 2d 148 (Fla. 3d DCA 1997).

1559. Powers v. Jones, 185 Ga. App. 859, 366 S.E.2d 234 (1988).

1560. Golomb v. Warwick Condo. Ass'n, 2007 N.J. Super. Unpub. LEXIS 186 (Apr. 26, 2007) (if special assessment were viewed as loan pending receipt by association of insurance proceeds, statutory obligation of association to distribute proceeds to unit owners would not be discharged by sale of unit; association might have provided in its documents that insurance proceeds need not be used to repair covered loss).

case of termination of the regime.[1561] Courts look to those statutes to determine who is entitled to surplus insurance proceeds. The governing documents may also play a role in a court's decision. For example, in *Willows Condo. Owners Ass'n v. Kraus*,[1562] one building of a multi-building condominium community was destroyed by fire. After reconstruction of the building was completed, the association had over $500,000 in insurance proceeds remaining. It took the position that those surplus insurance funds should be distributed to all the unit owners, not just those owning units in the building that had suffered the loss. The unit owners in that building disagreed. The Declaration provided that insurance proceeds were to be disbursed first for the repair or restoration of the damaged property, and unit owners were not entitled to receive any portion of the proceeds unless there was a surplus after the property had been completely repaired or restored, or the condominium was terminated. The court held that because all of the unit owners would have had to bear any shortfall as a common expense if the damaged building could not have been fully reconstructed using only the insurance proceeds, the "unit owners" entitled to receive payment of any surplus of proceeds after repair or reconstruction were *all of the unit owners*.

[6] Mortgagees

Anyone holding a security interest in any part of a common interest community property has an obvious concern in the disposition of insurance proceeds. Who has what interest in those proceeds requires an examination of a variety of documents.

[a] Policy Obligations of Insurer

The BPP and CAC have identical mortgage holder clauses. They first provide that the carrier will pay for covered loss of or damage to buildings or structures to each mortgage holder shown on the Declarations Page in their order of

1561. *See, e.g.*, 765 Ill. Comp. Stat. 605/14(1) (where insurance proceeds are insufficient to reconstruct building and property is subjected to action for partition, net proceeds of sale and property insurance are considered one fund and must be divided among all unit owners in percentage equal to percentage of undivided interest owned by each owner in property, after first paying out of respective shares of unit owners, to extent sufficient for purpose, all liens on *undivided interest* in property owned by each unit owner); Wis. Stat. § 703.18(2)(b) (if condominium is damaged to an extent that is more than available insurance proceeds, it is subject to an action for partition in which case net proceeds of sale together with any net insurance proceeds are then considered as one fund to be divided among all unit owners in proportion to their percentage interests in common elements and distributed in accordance with priority of interests in each unit).

1562. Willows Condo. Owners Ass'n v. Kraus, 467 S.W.3d 312 (Mo. App. 2015). The court noted that if the insurance proceeds had been insufficient for reconstruction, under the Declaration all unit owners would be required to share the shortfall. The unit owners from the damaged building raised a statutory argument based on the Uniform Condominium Act, but the court responded that as the condominium was created in July 1983, the UCA did not apply.

precedence, as their interests may appear.[1563] Additionally, the policies provide that a mortgage holder has the right to receive loss payment even if it has started foreclosure or similar action on the building or structure.[1564] Next, if the carrier denies the association's claim because of its acts or because it has failed to comply with the terms of the policy, the mortgage holder still has the right to receive loss payment if it pays any premium due that the association has failed to pay; submits a signed, sworn proof of loss within 60 days after receiving notice from the carrier of the failure of the association to do so; and has notified the carrier of any change in ownership or occupancy or substantial change in risk known to it.[1565] Finally, if the insurance company pays a mortgage holder for any loss or damage and denies payment to the association because of its acts or failure to comply with the terms of the policy, the mortgage holder's rights under the mortgage will be transferred to the company to the extent of the amount it pays and the mortgage holder's right to recover the full amount of its claim will not be impaired.[1566]

[b] Obligations of Association to Unit Owner Mortgagees

The holders of individual unit mortgages—or, in the case of a cooperative, share loans—have an obvious interest in any property insurance proceeds. The obligations of the common interest community association to the mortgagees of unit owners can be found in any applicable statutes, in the governing documents, and in the loan documents. For example, in *Foothill Village Homeowners Ass'n v.*

1563. *See* ISO Form CP 00 10 06 07, § F.2.b; ISO Form CP 00 17 06 07, § F.2.b. In some cases, mortgagees of individual units may be added as "additional insureds" to the association policy. *See, e.g.*, DiMillo v. Travelers Prop. Cas. Co. of Am., 789 F. Supp. 2d 194 (D. Me. 2011). *Consider* First Int'l Bank & Trust v. Peterson, 797 N.W.2d 316 (N.D. 2011). In *Peterson*, a hail storm damaged a condominium development in which the developer had sold only 10 of the 50 units. It submitted a claim that the insurer valued at $215,000. One month after the storm, the construction lender initiated foreclosure proceedings on the 40 units owned by the developer and subsequently purchased the units at a foreclosure sale. About six months later, the insurer issued a settlement check made payable to the developer and the lender. The lender brought an action against the developer and insurer seeking a declaration that the insurance proceeds should be paid to it. By the time the lender brought suit, control of the association had been transferred to the unit owners. The court concluded that had the developer remained solvent, under the terms of the condominium governing documents, it would have had a duty, as the entity controlling the association, to use the insurance proceeds to repair any damage from the storm. Although it no longer controlled the association, its successor—the unit owner-controlled association—was entitled to the insurance proceeds.

1564. *See* ISO Form CP 00 10 06 07, § F.2.c; ISO Form CP 00 17 06 07, § F.2.c.

1565. *See* ISO Form CP 00 10 06 07, § F.2.d; ISO Form CP 00 17 06 07, § F.2.d. All of the policy terms then apply directly to the mortgage holder.

1566. *See* ISO Form CP 00 10 06 07, § F.2.e; ISO Form CP 00 17 06 07, § F.2.e. At its option, the insurer may pay to the mortgage holder the whole principal on the mortgage plus any accrued interest, in which case the mortgage and note will be transferred to the insurer and the insured will pay its remaining mortgage debt to the insurer.

Bishop,[1567] a condominium association received more than $2 million for earthquake damage. The unit owners voted not to rebuild, and the question before the court was should the insurance proceeds go to a lender or to the individual unit owners? The court sided with the unit owners because the lender never required the purchase of insurance nor explicitly included in any of its loan documents a requirement that it share in the proceeds of any insurance.

Does that interest of mortgagees extend to requiring the association to properly manage those proceeds? A Florida court answered yes.[1568] In the case, a condominium project was severely damaged in a hurricane. The association received a substantial sum from its insurer but spent it all without completing reconstruction. The plaintiff mortgagee foreclosed on two units and subsequently sued the association for dissipation of the insurance proceeds in which it claimed an interest. It contended the association negligently administered the proceeds, and the association responded that if it owed a duty to anyone it was solely to the unit owners, not the mortgagee. However, the court held that having undertaken to manage the proceeds on behalf of unit owners and mortgagees, the association owed a mortgagee a duty to use reasonable care in management of those proceeds. The court noted that the association did not own the insurance proceeds, but was managing them on behalf of the owners and mortgagees pursuant to the authority granted by the Declaration. Once the association decided to reconstruct the property using the insurance proceeds, said the court, it assumed the duty of care commensurate with the enterprise it embarked on and the "obvious duty of care when managing funds for others is to use reasonable care to avoid depletion through negligent management or mismanagement." The mortgagee had a legally protected interest in the proceeds for two reasons. First, Florida law recognizes the interest of a mortgagee in any insurance proceeds derived from insurance that protects its interest in the insured property;[1569] second, the terms of the Declaration reflected the understanding that rights of unit owners are

---

1567. Foothill Village Homeowners Ass'n v. Bishop, 68 Cal. App. 4th 1364, 81 Cal. Rptr. 2d 195 (1999).

1568. National Title Ins. Co. v. Lakeshore 1 Condo. Ass'n, 691 So. 2d 1104 (Fla. 3d DCA 1997). *See also* Mahogany Run Condominium Assoc., Inc. v. ICG Realty Mgmt. Corp. (*In re* Icon Inv. Trust No. 1), 2001 Bankr. LEXIS 2153 (Bankr. D.V.I. Jan. 9, 2001) (where trust owned units and suffered loss of rents when association breached fiduciary duty by failing to timely repair units, mortgagee of trust was granted damages).

1569. The court noted that under Florida law, a mortgagee has an equitable lien on insurance proceeds, but that under the terms of the Declaration, it was prohibited from accessing those proceeds and had to accede to association management and control of them, rendering the lien unenforceable. National Title Ins. Co. v. Lakeshore 1 Condo. Ass'n, 691 So. 2d 1104, 1107, n.3 (Fla. 3d DCA 1997). If neither the Declaration nor any applicable statute limited the lien, the mortgagee could have enforced it. Note that under the UCIOA, any loss covered by the property policy has to be adjusted with the association, but the insurance proceeds are payable to any insurance trustee and not to any holder of a security interest. The proceeds have to be disbursed first for the repair or replacement of the damaged property, and the association, unit owners, and lien holders are not entitled to receive payment of any portion of the proceeds unless there is a surplus after the

commonly subject to a mortgage interest. The court concluded that the association purchased insurance to protect the interests of unit owners and mortgagees in the insured property, the plaintiff mortgagee had an interest in the insurance proceeds, and therefore, the invasion of that interest was actionable.

[c] Rights of Mortgagees after Foreclosure

Generally, a lender that forecloses on a unit and obtains title to it would be treated as any other unit owner for purposes of distribution of insurance proceeds.[1570] It should be entitled to the same rights as any other unit owner but no greater rights by virtue of having previously been the mortgagee of a unit.

§ 10.41 Association Policy Content Checklist

When the association reviews its property coverage, the checklist below provides some important questions it should ask about that coverage.

- ☐ Does the association have an insurable interest in the property it seeks to insure? See § 10.02.
- ☐ Is the community association management company the named insured? See § 10.02[5].
- ☐ Does the association have the information it will need to apply for coverage? See § 10.04[3].
- ☐ Is the policy provided by a surplus lines carrier? See § 10.04[4][b].
- ☐ How are the premiums calculated and paid? See §§ 10.05[2], 10.10, 10.11[4].
- ☐ Which causes of loss form is incorporated into the policy? See § 10.07[1].

---

property has been completely repaired or replaced, or the common interest community is terminated. Uniform Common Interest Ownership Act § 3-113(e).

1570. Countrywide Home Loans, Inc. v. Tutungi, 66 Cal. App. 4th 727, 78 Cal. Rptr. 2d 203 (1998). In *Tutungi* the association received proceeds after the Northridge earthquake from its carrier that were insufficient to repair the project. Under the CC&Rs the individual owners could decide to proceed with repairs by special assessment or to distribute the insurance proceeds to themselves proportionally, subject to the rights of any mortgagees. They decided to do the latter. A lender that had foreclosed on a unit claimed a share of the proceeds because it succeeded to the borrowers' position as a member of the association. The court agreed with the lender that as successor owner of the foreclosed unit, it also succeeded to membership in the association. Therefore, as owner and association member when the decision to divide the proceeds was made, the lender was entitled to the association's distribution to members.

- ☐ Is coverage provided by a group policy or risk pooling? See § 10.07[5].
- ☐ How is the association listed on the Declarations Page? See § 10.11[1].
- ☐ What is the meaning of "building" in the policy? See § 10.12[1][a].
- ☐ Does the policy cover loss of maintenance fee income? See § 10.12[2][a].
- ☐ Does the policy cover loss of business income? See § 10.12[2][b].
- ☐ Are there components of association property that are listed in the policy as not covered, and does the association want them covered? See § 10.12[3].
- ☐ Does the policy cover both common areas and any property of association members? See § 10.13.
- ☐ Does the association know what improvements individual owners have made to their property, and are those improvements covered under the association policy? See § 10.13[5].
- ☐ Does the association have an "Areas of Responsibility" policy and how does it affect the coverage? See § 10.13[6].
- ☐ If the policy provides additional coverage for debris removal, fire department service charges, pollutant cleanup and removal, increased cost of construction, and electronic data, are any specific limits to the amount of coverage adequate to the needs of the association? See § 10.16.
- ☐ Is the debris removal coverage adequate? See § 10.16[1].
- ☐ Is there increased cost of construction coverage and is it adequate? See §§ 10.16[5], 10.19[1]
- ☐ Does the association need electronic data coverage? See § 10.16[6].
- ☐ What is the extent of the coverage for collapse? See §§ 10.17[1], 10.20[8].
- ☐ Does the association need coverage for outdoor property? See § 10.18[5].
- ☐ In what circumstances is there coverage for earth movement? See §§ 10.18[2], 10.36[2][b].
- ☐ In what circumstances is there coverage for water damage? See § 10.18[7]. Does the association need coverage for sewer backups? If so, an endorsement probably needs to be added to the policy. See § 10.36[2][j].

- ☐ How does the deductible work? Are there any separate deductibles for specific risks—for example, windstorms or earthquakes—and are there percentage deductibles? See § 10.23.
- ☐ If there is more than one building that is insured, does the deductible apply separately to each one? See § 10.23[4].
- ☐ What are the requirements for giving the insurer a notice of loss? See § 10.24[1].
- ☐ Under what circumstances must the association allow the insurer to inspect the property, including the individual homes or units, and to what extent must the association allow the insurer to inspect its books and records? See § 10.24[4].
- ☐ What does the association have to do to comply with the policy requirement to submit to an examination under oath? See § 10.25.
- ☐ What does the policy say about payment for losses involving party walls, and how does that apply to a common interest community association where units have shared walls? See § 10.26[2].
- ☐ How is the lost or damaged property valued? See § 10.27.
- ☐ How does the appraisal process work? See § 10.28.
- ☐ How does the policy vacancy clause apply to a common interest community in which there are unoccupied units? See §§ 10.31, 10.36[2][d].
- ☐ Does a coinsurance clause apply, and how does it work? See § 10.33.
- ☐ Does the policy include inflation guard coverage or an Agreed Amount clause or endorsement to ameliorate or eliminate the negative effects of any coinsurance clause? If the policy includes inflation guard protection, is the percentage by which the limit of insurance is being increased excessive or inadequate for the local real estate market? See §§ 10.33[2], 10.34[1], 10.34[2].
- ☐ Does the policy provide actual cash value or replacement cost coverage? See § 10.34[3].
- ☐ Are residents considered "under the control" of the association for purposes of the clause providing that any act or neglect of any person other than the insured beyond the direction or control of the insured will not affect the insurance? See § 10.35[2].

- ☐ Have the association documents waived subrogation? See § 10.35[9][c].
- ☐ Is a Protective Safeguards Endorsement added to the policy? See 10.36[1][a].
- ☐ If the association has a stand-alone boiler and machinery or equipment breakdown policy with another insurer, does the property policy have a Joint or Disputed Loss clause? See § 10.36[2][e].
- ☐ If the common interest community is a residential cooperative, is there a rent loss endorsement? See § 10.36[2][f].
- ☐ Are expenses for which the community association manager bills the association when the manager handles a covered loss also covered under the policy? See § 10.36[2][h].
- ☐ Does the policy include an endorsement covering theft by employees, officers, directors, and the manager? See § 10.36[2][i].
- ☐ Does the association have a Difference in Conditions policy in addition to the commercial property policy, and if so, what coverage does it provide? See § 10.37.
- ☐ If there is a Difference in Conditions policy in addition to a commercial property policy, how do the Other Insurance clauses of the two policies relate? See § 10.37[2][d].
- ☐ Does any Difference in Conditions policy provide flood coverage? See § 10.37[3].
- ☐ Is there a "Valued Policy" statute in the state in which the association is located, and if so, how does it affect claims under the policy? See § 10.38[3].

Chapter 11

Boiler and Machinery or Equipment Breakdown Insurance

§ 11.01 Introduction and History

Boiler and machinery coverage is a specialized form of insurance that has existed since 1866.[1] In that year the Hartford Steam Boiler Inspection and Insurance Company (HSB) was founded.[2] In the mid-19th century steam powered the expanding industrial revolution.[3] Steam power drove an economic explosion but also led to actual and dangerous explosions. They occurred at the rate of almost one every four days.[4] The Hartford, Connecticut, Polytechnic Club took an interest in the problem. They concluded that inspections would increase boiler safety and insurance would serve as an incentive to inspections and would be a guarantee of quality inspections. Out of that, HSB and its boiler and machinery policy were born. The company remains the industry leader today.[5] It continues to offer boiler and machinery coverage and inspections of the equipment it insures,[6] and it also reinsures other carriers that offer the coverage.[7]

1. Malecki, *Equipment Breakdown Coverage: This Oft-Misunderstood Coverage is a Necessity for Many Clients*, available at: http://www.roughnotes.com/rnmagazine/2008/march08/03p114.htm.

2. http://www.munichre.com/HSB/hsb-history/index.html.

3. Tapia, *Equipment Breakdown Coverage: Not Your Father's Boiler & Machinery Insurance* (Insurance Journal 2000), available at: http://www.insurancejournal.com/magazines/features/2000/11/27/21234.htm.

4. http://www.munichre.com/HSB/hsb-history/index.html.

5. Va. Apple Storage, Inc. v. Ins. Ctr. of Winchester, Inc., 1997 Va. Cir. LEXIS 740 (Apr. 11, 1997) (premier boiler and machinery coverage insurance company in the United States is Hartford Steam Boiler Inspection and Insurance Company). *See also* Malecki, *Equipment Breakdown Insurance: Too Important to Ignore!*, at 3 (Adjusting Today, 2009), available at: http://adjustersinternational.com/publications/adjusting-today/equipment-breakdown-insurance/1/ (for larger risks, HSB is undoubtedly predominate insurer).

6. HSB has over 1,200 engineers, inspectors, and technical personnel around the globe. http://www.munichre.com/HSB/about-hsb/index.html.

7. Austin, *Equipment Breakdown—More Than Just Boiler and Machinery* (IRMI 2011), available at: http://www.irmi.com/articles/expert-commentary/equipment-breakdown (HSB is major

While HSB remains a going concern, the business it started has changed dramatically since it began. In fact, the term "boiler and machinery" insurance is an anachronism.[8] Today the coverage is called "equipment breakdown," and modern policies cover much more than boilers and production machinery.[9] The equipment that is typically covered includes boilers, generators, engines, pumps, compressors,[10] turbines, and refrigeration and air conditioning equipment.[11] Electronic business equipment—fax machines, copiers, and telephone systems—can also be covered.[12] Of particular note for common interest communities is that elevators,[13] sprinklers,[14] and security systems[15] may also be covered.

The insurance industry is a paradox. It can respond quickly to changes in society while hanging on to archaic terminology. Thus, while the experts want us to believe "boiler and machinery" insurance is a term out of use,[16] it is still widely employed and insurance professionals, including agents and brokers, continue to

---

insurer of equipment breakdown coverage as both a primary insurer or as reinsurer of primary insurer when that insurer does not have underwriting or claim expertise needed to provide direct coverage); Malecki, *Equipment Breakdown Insurance: Too Important to Ignore!*, at 3 (Adjusting Today, 2009), available at: http://adjustersinternational.com/publications/adjusting-today/equipment-breakdown-insurance/1/ (some insurers that offer equipment breakdown coverage have HSB reinsure their accounts). A reinsurer provides insurance to the carrier that issues the policy. It is not in privity with the policyholder who, with very limited exceptions, cannot therefore sue the reinsurer. *See, e.g.*, Litho Color, Inc. v. Pacific Emplrs. Ins. Co., 98 Wn. App. 286, 991 P.2d 638 (1999).

8. Malecki, *Equipment Breakdown Insurance: Too Important to Ignore!*, at 1 (Adjusting Today, 2009), available at: http://adjustersinternational.com/publications/adjusting-today/equipment-breakdown-insurance/1/.

9. Tapia, *Equipment Breakdown Coverage: Not Your Father's Boiler & Machinery Insurance* (Insurance Journal 2000), available at: http://www.insurancejournal.com/magazines/features/2000/11/27/21234.htm (equipment breakdown coverage is modern-day descendant of what has been traditionally referred to as boiler and machinery insurance).

10. *See, e.g.*, New York Underwriters Ins. Co. v. Coffman, 540 S.W.2d 445 (Tex. Civ. App.—Fort Worth, 1976) (coverage for breakdown of air conditioning compressor).

11. O'Connor, *Construction Law: Recent Issues in Property Coverage*, 34 Wm. Mitchell L. Rev. 177, 202 (2007).

12. Tapia, *Equipment Breakdown Coverage: Not Your Father's Boiler & Machinery Insurance* (Insurance Journal 2000), available at: http://www.insurancejournal.com/magazines/features/2000/11/27/21234.htm. *See also Equipment Breakdown Insurance FAQ*, available at: http://eqgroup.com/Equipment-Breakdown.htm (equipment breakdown insurance covers many types of equipment including modern office equipment).

13. Barnes, *Understanding Your Insurance Policy's Fine-Print: What You Need to Know about Riders* (Cooperator, Aug. 2013), available at: http://cooperator.com/article/understanding-your-insurance-policys-fine-pri.

14. Iannucci, *Insurance Products What's Available, What's Recommended* (Cooperator, Aug. 2006), available at: http://cooperator.com/article/insurance-products.

15. Geberer, *Covering the Gaps Specialty Insurance* (Cooperator, Aug. 2009), available at: http://cooperator.com/article/covering-the-gaps.

16. *See, e.g.*, Malecki, *Equipment Breakdown Coverage: This Oft-Misunderstood Coverage is a Necessity for Many Clients*, available at: http://www.roughnotes.com/rnmagazine/2008/march08/03p114.htm (boiler and machinery insurance no longer exists; the new term is equipment breakdown insurance).

refer to equipment breakdown coverage as "boiler and machinery" or "B&M" for short. In fact, although some carriers began using the term "equipment breakdown" in the 1990s, the Insurance Services Office (ISO) that provides hundreds of standardized policies and endorsements for the insurance industry only began using the modern appellation in 2006.[17]

No matter what phrase is used to refer to the coverage, it is highly specialized,[18] offered by a limited number of carriers,[19] and not widely understood,[20] even by otherwise knowledgeable agents and brokers.[21] Therefore, it is incumbent on the insured to be sure the agent understands the coverage and to seek clarification directly from the insurer if necessary. Basically, B&M is a form of property insurance covering named perils,[22] rather than all risks.[23] Ordinarily it covers losses to "covered equipment" and consequential damage to other property as well as losses related to a breakdown to the covered equipment, for example, business loss and expenses of recovering from a breakdown.

NOTE: Probably the single most important caution about the coverage that can be conveyed is that the language of the various available policies varies greatly, and endorsements can change that language significantly. An insured needs to carefully review that language with the broker to determine the extent of the coverage provided and to seek clarification.

17. Malecki, *Equipment Breakdown Insurance: Too Important to Ignore!*, at 1 (Adjusting Today, 2009), available at: http://adjustersinternational.com/publications/adjusting-today/equipment-breakdown-insurance/1/.

18. O'Connor, *Construction Law: Recent Issues in Property Coverage*, 34 Wm. Mitchell L. Rev. 177, 202 (2007) (boiler and machinery insurance coverage is special type of property insurance).

19. Tapia, *Equipment Breakdown Coverage: Not Your Father's Boiler & Machinery Insurance* (Insurance Journal 2000), available at: http://www.insurancejournal.com/magazines/features/2000/11/27/21234.htm (more than 200 companies offer equipment breakdown coverage).

20. Austin, *Equipment Breakdown—More Than Just Boiler and Machinery* (IRMI 2011), available at: http://www.irmi.com/articles/expert-commentary/equipment-breakdown; Malecki, *Equipment Breakdown Insurance: Too Important to Ignore!*, at 6 (Adjusting Today, 2009), available at: http://adjustersinternational.com/publications/adjusting-today/equipment-breakdown-insurance/1/ (equipment breakdown coverage ranks high among more exotic and frequently misunderstood property and casualty coverages); Malecki, *Equipment Breakdown Coverage: This Oft-Misunderstood Coverage is a Necessity for Many Clients*, available at: http://www.roughnotes.com/rnmagazine/2008/march08/03p114.htm.

21. Tapia, *Equipment Breakdown Coverage: Not Your Father's Boiler & Machinery Insurance* (Insurance Journal 2000), available at: http://www.insurancejournal.com/magazines/features/2000/11/27/21234.htm (many agents, brokers, and buyers may not understand equipment breakdown coverage).

22. Austin, *Equipment Breakdown—More Than Just Boiler and Machinery* (IRMI 2011), available at: http://www.irmi.com/articles/expert-commentary/equipment-breakdown.

23. Stone Container Corp. v. Hartford Steam Boiler Inspection & Ins. Co., 165 F.3d 1157, 1161 (7th Cir. 1999).

§ 11.02 Covering a "Gap" in Commercial Property Insurance

An insured may wonder if mechanical equipment is not covered by a commercial property policy. The answer is, yes, it is. The equipment is covered either as contents or, if permanently installed, then as part of the building. However, the coverage under the commercial property policy is usually for losses caused by external events—for example, fire, vandalism, windstorm—as set forth in the policy.[24] Moreover, typically the policy will specifically exclude coverage for mechanical breakdown, including rupture or bursting caused by centrifugal force,[25] and explosion of steam boilers, steam pipes, steam engines, or steam turbines owned or leased by the insured.[26] That does not mean that property policies never cover equipment breakdown. Some comprehensive all-risk property policies specifically incorporate boiler and machinery coverage;[27] however, a common interest community (CIC) is unlikely to have that type of policy.

A CIC may have a commercial property insurance policy that excludes coverage for mechanical breakdown. It will probably not, however, define "mechanical breakdown." Courts interpret the term to mean "a functional defect in the moving parts of the equipment which causes the latter to cease functioning or to function improperly."[28] Additionally, as an exclusion, it is usually narrowly

---

24. Austin, *Equipment Breakdown—More Than Just Boiler and Machinery* (IRMI 2011), available at: http://www.irmi.com/articles/expert-commentary/equipment-breakdown. *See also Equipment Breakdown Insurance FAQ*, available at: http://eqgroup.com/Equipment-Breakdown.htm (property insurance covers many standard perils, such as fire, but even "all risk" property coverage was not designed to pay for equipment accidents from unique causes of equipment failure—short circuits, centrifugal force, or mechanical breakdown—and equipment breakdown coverage is specially designed to pay for damage caused by these risks).

25. *See, e.g.*, ISO Form CP 10 10 04 02, § B.2.e.

26. *See, e.g.*, ISO Form CP 10 10 04 02, § B.2.d. *See generally* Boggs, *Three Commercial Property Endorsements Every Client Should Have* (July 27, 2009), available at: http://www.mynewmarkets.com/articles/102464/three-commercial-property-endorsements-every-client-should-have (equipment breakdown protection fills several causes of loss gaps present in commercial property policy, for example, losses to HVAC and telephone equipment caused by power surge, explosion of steam pipes, boilers). *See also* Continental Ins. Co. v. Acadia Ins. Co., 974 F. Supp. 371, 374 (D. Vt. 1997) (hazards associated with boilers and production machinery are often excluded from general insurance policies).

27. 5 Jeffery E. Thomas, *New Appleman on Insurance Law Library Edition* § 51.01[2][c][i] (LexisNexis 2023). The coverage may also be added by an endorsement. *See, e.g.*, St. Mary's Area Water Auth. v. St. Paul Fire & Marine Ins. Co., 2007 U.S. Dist. LEXIS 34814 (M.D. Pa. May 11, 2007) (policy provided coverage for mechanical breakdown in endorsement added to it).

28. National Investors Fire & Casualty Co. v. Preddy, 248 Ark. 320, 322, 451 S.W.2d 457, 458 (Ark. 1970). The court gave as an example when the thermostat on a motor vehicle sticks, it is mechanical trouble, but when a tire goes flat, it is simply tire trouble. *See also* Lake Charles Harbor & Terminal Dist. v. Imperial Casualty & Indem. Co., 670 F. Supp. 189 (W.D. La. 1987); Standard Structural Steel Co. v. Bethlehem Steel Corp., 597 F. Supp. 164 (D. Conn. 1984).

construed to restrict it to losses "arising from internal or inherent deficiency or defect, rather than from any external cause."[29]

The insurer generally has no responsibility to fill that gap in coverage usually left when the insured has only a commercial policy that excludes coverage for mechanical breakdown. In one Federal Circuit Court of Appeals case, the insured contended the insurer misrepresented the scope of its coverage and failed to disclose that gap. The court held the insurer had no duty to disclose the existence of a gap in coverage to the insured.[30] Rather, the insured had the burden of knowing the contents of its policies, and non-disclosure provides no basis for insurer liability.

§ 11.03 Service Contracts and Warranties

Most equipment will come with a warranty, and common interest communities often purchase service or maintenance contracts for their equipment. Warranties and service contracts, however, do not cover many of the common causes of equipment breakdowns. A maintenance contract will provide routine service but will not pay for damage caused by operator error, the origin of over 35 percent of equipment breakdowns.[31] Additionally, neither warranties nor maintenance contracts pay for business interruption or income loss resulting from breakdown, damage to surrounding property, or extra expenses to restore operations.

§ 11.04 Available Policies

Initially, boiler and machinery coverage was available only as a stand-alone policy. The policy covered losses excluded by a commercial property policy. Insurers continue to offer the coverage in a stand-alone policy,[32] but an increasing number of carriers offer it either as an endorsement to a commercial property policy[33] or

---

29. Caldwell v. Transportation Ins. Co., 234 Va. 639, 644, 364 S.E.2d 1, 3 (1988) (if exclusion were interpreted broadly, it might be found to exclude losses arising from external causes as well as from inherent defect and would have effect of excluding from coverage almost every imaginable loss resulting in failure of equipment to function).

30. Commonwealth Ins. Co. v. Stone Container Corp., 351 F.3d 774 (7th Cir. 2003).

31. *Equipment Breakdown Insurance FAQ*, available at: http://eqgroup.com/Equipment-Breakdown.htm.

32. *See* Malecki, *Equipment Breakdown Insurance: Too Important to Ignore!*, at 2 (Adjusting Today, 2009), available at: http://adjustersinternational.com/publications/adjusting-today/equipment-breakdown-insurance/1/ (equipment breakdown coverage commonly is written under separate policy).

33. *See, e.g.*, Nat'l Union Fire Ins. Co. v. Travelers Indem. Co., 210 F. Supp. 2d 479 (S.D.N.Y. 2002) (property all-risk policy included Boiler and Machinery Endorsement that provided coverage for certain specified causes of loss that would otherwise be excluded under property coverage form); Litho Color, Inc. v. Pacific Emplrs. Ins. Co., 98 Wn. App. 286, 289, 991 P.2d 638, 640 (1999)

as part of a package of comprehensive property coverage.[34] At least one insurer has a multi-line policy specifically designed for common interest communities that provides general liability, directors and officers, and property coverage. The property component includes machinery and equipment breakdown insurance.[35]

To determine what coverage is in place, an expert advises that one should first look for a separate policy titled either "equipment breakdown" or something similar, or even the "archaic term" boiler and machinery. If coverage is embedded in a property policy, one has to look to the Declarations Page to determine whether it refers to equipment breakdown or boiler and machinery or whether sublimits are listed for the coverage. If the Declarations Page is unclear, then one has to read the policy to ascertain whether coverage is within the policy—embedded—or added by endorsement. An endorsement will generally remove any applicable exclusion, "adding back" coverage otherwise excluded.[36] When equipment breakdown coverage is added by an endorsement, other exclusions in the main policy will still apply unless the endorsement specifically negates them.[37]

(Boiler and Machinery Endorsement to commercial property insurance policy); Rorer Group v. Insurance Co. of N. Am., 440 Pa. Super. 69, 655 A.2d 123 (1995) (Boiler and Machinery Endorsement to all-risk policy). *See also* Scottsdale Ins. Co. v. Sally Group, LLC, 2012 U.S. Dist. LEXIS 47532 (S.D. Tex. Apr. 3, 2012) (Commercial Property Conditions Form with Equipment Breakdown Coverage Endorsement).

34. *See, e.g.*, Commonwealth Ins. Co. v. Stone Container Corp., 351 F.3d 774, 776 (7th Cir. 2003) (single all-risk policy included boiler and machinery coverage); Detroit Edison Co. v. Protection Mut. Ins. Co., 134 F.3d 790, 793 (6th Cir. 1998) (insured obtained comprehensive property insurance form developed to replace boiler/machinery forms on which insured objects had been listed individually); Fairhaven Power Co. v. Hartford Steam Boiler Inspection & Ins. Co., 1995 U.S. Dist. LEXIS 21733 (N.D. Cal. June 2, 1995) (section B of property policy was titled "boiler and machinery"). *See also* Nationwide Mut. Ins. Co. v. CG Stony Point Townhomes, LLC, 2015 U.S. Dist. LEXIS 5682 (E.D. Va. Jan. 15, 2015) ("Equipment Breakdown" secondary coverage). *See generally* Austin, *Equipment Breakdown—More Than Just Boiler and Machinery* (IRMI 2011), available at: http://www.irmi.com/articles/expert-commentary/equipment-breakdown (equipment breakdown insurance can be found in property insurance policy when coverage is embedded into policy form); Tapia, *Equipment Breakdown Coverage: Not Your Father's Boiler & Machinery Insurance* (Insurance Journal 2000), available at: http://www.insurancejournal.com/magazines/features/2000/11/27/21234.htm (of 200 companies currently offering equipment breakdown coverage, perhaps only a dozen offer it on monoline basis).

35. *See V3 Launches Community Association Package Program* (Insurance Journal, May 27, 2015), available at: http://www.insurancejournal.com/news/national/2015/05/27/369573.htm. *See also* Geberer, *Covering the Gaps Specialty Insurance* (Cooperator, Aug. 2009), available at: http://cooperator.com/article/covering-the-gaps (separate B&M policy can be written but can also be included in typical property policy for condominium or cooperative development).

36. Austin, *Equipment Breakdown—More Than Just Boiler and Machinery* (IRMI 2011), available at: http://www.irmi.com/articles/expert-commentary/equipment-breakdown.

37. Rorer Group v. Insurance Co. of N. Am., 440 Pa. Super. 69, 73–74, 655 A.2d 123, 125 (1995) (where endorsement extended coverage and abrogated exclusions as to certain perils, for example, explosion, mechanical breakdown, electrical injury, and rupture or bursting, and added cracking to coverage—even though cracking was never previously excluded—but did not address exclusions in policy regarding corrosion or latent defects, it could not abrogate or modify those exclusions).

§ 11.05 Common Interest Communities and Equipment Breakdown Coverage

In some states, the requirement that common interest community associations obtain equipment breakdown insurance will be addressed by statute, and for some associations coverage will be required by the governing documents. However, many associations will need to procure equipment breakdown coverage because Fannie Mae requires it when there is central heating or cooling equipment.[38] Even if the Fannie Mae requirement does not apply, associations should consider having the coverage because the cost of equipment breakdown can be substantial. Associations need to survey their property to determine what equipment needs coverage.

[1] Requirement to Obtain Coverage

Two states specifically mention equipment breakdown insurance in legislation governing condominiums. The Illinois Condominium Property Act says the declaration *may* require the association to carry any insurance including, *inter alia*, equipment breakdown that the board of directors considers appropriate.[39] Hawaii's Condominium Property Act provides that the Declaration, bylaws, or governing board may require the association to carry any insurance—including for equipment breakdown—the governing board considers appropriate.[40] Of course, the documents of any common interest community may require an association to obtain equipment breakdown coverage regardless of any statutory authorization.

A number of states have adopted the Uniform Common Interest Ownership Act, which governs all types of CICs. The act does not mention equipment breakdown coverage but does require associations to maintain, to the extent "reasonably available," property insurance on the common elements insuring against all risks of direct physical loss "commonly insured."[41] Equipment breakdown is not one of the perils ordinarily covered in a commercial property policy;[42] in fact, it is typically excluded in those policies. On the other hand, it is coverage that is recommended by experts,[43] and it is not unusual for insurance agents to advise CICs

---

38. For discussion on Fannie Mae and Freddie Mac requirements, see generally Chapter 6.
39. 765 Ill. Comp. Stat. 605/12(d).
40. Haw. Rev. Stat. § 514B-143(e).
41. Uniform Common Interest Ownership Act § 3-113(a)(1).
42. For discussion of applicability of commercial property policy as it relates to CICs, see § 10.7.
43. Hanna & Van Atta, *California Common Interest Developments* § 20:13 (Thompson Reuters 2015) (boiler and machinery coverage is particularly important for projects that have complex heating and elevator systems); Barnes, *Understanding Your Insurance Policy's Fine-Print: What You Need to Know about Riders* (Cooperator, Aug. 2013), available at: http://cooperator.com/article/understanding-your-insurance-policys-fine-pri. *Compare* Geberer, *Covering the Gaps Specialty*

to obtain equipment breakdown insurance. That the agent recommends the coverage does not necessarily obligate a CIC to purchase it. Generally, under what is called the "business judgment" rule a decision of a CIC governing board is not open to question—or second-guessing by courts—unless there is a showing of fraud, self-dealing, dishonesty or incompetency.[44] However, the rule has not been applied to CICs in some jurisdictions,[45] and courts generally require boards to "act in reasonable manner,"[46] or to "exercise due care,"[47] before applying the rule. Thus, if a board decides not to obtain B&M coverage, it would be wise to notify the association attorney of that decision. Reliance on the opinion of counsel can be a basis for finding a decision of a CIC board to be reasonable.[48]

Counsel and the governing board should keep in mind that the losses covered by a boiler and machinery or equipment breakdown policy can be considerable. One insurer provides the example of a high-rise apartment complex—which could very well be a condominium or housing cooperative—that is heated by a large steam boiler in which a safety relief valve fails, creating excessive pressure that causes an explosion, with the cost of the boiler replacement, and surrounding building damage, totaling $500,000.[49] HSB offers another example. An apartment building has an air conditioning motor burn out and in 90-plus degree temperatures rents "spot coolers" that have to be set up, resulting in property damage of over $83,000 and extra expense—overtime to get the motor back on line—of almost $17,000 for a total loss of over $100,000. If the CIC has no coverage for either loss, it will have to assess the individual owners who may explore whether the governing board is liable for failing to obtain coverage. In the second scenario, the residents may react as much to the discomfort as to the assessment.

From a practical standpoint, many common interest communities will have to obtain coverage because Fannie Mae requires it before it will purchase or securitize mortgages. The *Fannie Mae Selling Guide* says a Boiler and Machinery/Equipment Breakdown Endorsement is required for condominiums, cooperatives,

---

Insurance (Cooperator, Aug. 2009), available at: http://cooperator.com/article/covering-the-gaps (suggesting that governing boards "might take a look at" equipment breakdown coverage).

44. *See, e.g.*, Garcia v. Crescent Plaza Condominium Ass'n, Inc., 813 So. 2d 975 (Fla. 2d DCA 2002); Lamden v. LaJolla Shores Condo. Homeowners Ass'n, 21 Cal. 4th 249, 87 Cal. Rptr. 2d 237, 980 P.2d 940 (1999); Levandusky v. One Fifth Ave. Corp., 554 N.Y.S.2d 807, 75 N.Y.2d 530, 553 N.E.2d 1317 (1990); Schwarzmann v. Association of Apt. Owners of Bridgehaven, 655 P.2d 1177 (Wash. App. 1982).

45. *See, e.g.*, Johnson v. Hobson, 505 A.2d 1313, 1317 n.7 (D.C. App. 1986); Noble v. Murphy, 34 Mass. App. Ct. 452, 612 N.E.2d 266, 271 n.7 (1993).

46. Garcia v. Crescent Plaza Condominium Ass'n, Inc., 813 So. 2d 975 (Fla. 2d DCA 2002).

47. Wolinsky v. Kadison, 370 Ill. Dec. 205, 987 N.E.2d 971 (2013).

48. *See, e.g.*, Bennett v. Weimar, 975 P.2d 691 (Alaska 1999).

49. *Boiler & Machinery Insurance/Equipment Breakdown Insurance What is Covered by Boiler & Machinery Coverage?*, available at: http://www.brunswickcompanies.com/ci-boiler-machinery-equipment-breakdown-insurance.html.

and planned unit developments if they have central heating or cooling.[50] A Mechanical Breakdown Endorsement in a master hazard insurance policy meets the requirement for a Steam Boiler and Machinery Coverage Endorsement. Fannie Mae will accept a separate stand-alone boiler and machinery policy instead of an endorsement to the commercial property policy. The *Fannie Mae Selling Guide* does not define "central heating or cooling." The phrase probably refers to a system that provides heating or cooling to common areas but could mean systems that heat or cool the individual units. Fannie Mae says the coverage should provide for the insurer's minimum liability per accident to at least equal the lesser of $2 million or the insurable value of the building or buildings housing the boiler or machinery.

[2] Acquiring the Coverage That Is Needed

One commentary notes that equipment breakdown protection is generally provided when an association has central heating and air conditioning units; however, a policy might also include coverage on swimming pool heaters, pumps and filters, and water pumps in high-rise buildings.[51] Other equipment, for example elevators or backup generators, may also need coverage. Therefore, before meeting with its broker to discuss the insurance, an association should create an inventory of all equipment owned, leased, or in the possession of the common interest community or owned or leased by the unit owners as tenants in common, including boilers, water heaters, air conditioning and heating systems, water pumps, backup generators, elevators, fire suppression/sprinkler systems, pool pumps and heaters, irrigation systems,[52] and electronic business equipment. Available policies may not cover all of these items,[53] but the association needs to determine what can be covered and what uninsured losses it may have to absorb.

Another consideration for associations is the coverage limit, that is, the maximum amount the insurer will pay for a loss. Typically, policies provide on the Declarations Page for a total aggregate limit and individual limits for specific losses, for example, utility interruption or increased cost of construction. One expert asserts that the insured has to assume a catastrophic loss from an explosion and

---

50. Fannie Mae Single Family Selling Guide § B7-3-03 (Dec. 14, 2022).

51. Rohan, Reskin & Sanchirico, *Recent Developments in the Field of Insurance for Condominium Projects*, 48 St. John's L. Rev. 1084, 1090 (1974).

52. *See Irrigation System and Steam Boiler Policy* (Summit Business Media, 2013).

53. Even central heating and air conditioning systems (HVAC) might not be covered by some policies. *See, e.g.*, Bay Colony Condo. Assoc. v. Scottsdale Ins. Co., 2012 U.S. Dist. LEXIS 182016 (D.N.J. Dec. 26, 2012) (association claimed HVAC, heating, and electric systems constituted equipment covered by policy, but court asserted that those items could *conceivably* fall within definition of covered equipment because they generated, transmitted, and/or used energy). *Compare* Nationwide Mut. Ins. Co. v. CG Stony Point Townhomes, LLC, 2015 U.S. Dist. LEXIS 5682 (E.D. Va. Jan. 15, 2015) (court found that it appeared undisputed that accident to covered equipment was defined in manner that would generally include "mechanical breakdown" of HVAC system).

the possible complete destruction of a building and, therefore, the overall limit has to be sufficient to replace or repair any direct damage loss.[54] The aggregate limit should then be at least the total value of the building.

§ 11.06 Declarations Page

The Declarations Page is a critical part of the policy. As a part of any insurance audit, it should be carefully reviewed with the broker. This is important because policies often cross-reference to the Declarations Page.[55] Also, some policies list the covered equipment, or "objects," on the Declarations Page,[56] although others have a definition of covered equipment in the policy definitions section,[57] and some have separate "schedules" attached to the policy that list the covered equipment.[58] Because the coverage is based on an accident or breakdown to covered equipment or objects, it is essential to determine what is encompassed within those terms.[59]

---

54. Austin, *Equipment Breakdown—More Than Just Boiler and Machinery* (IRMI 2011), available at: http://www.irmi.com/articles/expert-commentary/equipment-breakdown.

55. *See* Malecki, *Equipment Breakdown Insurance: Too Important to Ignore!*, at 6 (Adjusting Today, 2009), available at: http://adjustersinternational.com/publications/adjusting-today/equipment-breakdown-insurance/1/ (equipment breakdown Declarations Page is important part of policy, and data on it should be checked carefully to make sure it is correct and complete as there are references to data shown on it throughout other portions of policy and any errors or omissions on it can be damaging to intended coverage).

56. *See, e.g.*, Pioneer Chlor Alkali Co. v. Royal Indem. Co., 879 S.W.2d 920, 925, n.1 (Tex. App.—Houston 14th Dist., 1994) ("object" was equipment shown on Declarations Page). *See also* ISO Form BM 00 25 02 91, § F.2 ("object" means equipment shown in Declarations). The policy adds that a full description of specific object categories is found in the "Object Definitions endorsement" attached to the coverage form.

57. *See, e.g.*, ISO Form BM 00 20 07 01; HSB Freestyle Policy Form 6671 (10/2002).

58. *See, e.g.*, Foote Mineral Co. v. Maryland Casualty Co., 173 F. Supp. 925 (D. Tenn. 1959), *aff'd*, 277 F.2d 452 (6th Cir. 1960), *cert. den.*, 364 U.S. 818, 81 S. Ct. 49, 5 L. Ed. 2d 48 (1960) (policy provided coverage against loss by accident of objects described in detail on two schedules); Good Canning Co. v. London Guarantee & Acci. Co., 128 F. Supp. 778, 781 (D. Ark. 1955); Enosburg Falls v. Hartford Steam Boiler Inspection & Ins. Co., 117 Vt. 114, 85 A.2d 577 (1952) (objects were set forth in separate schedules each describing different items of equipment, and many types of accidents were provided for in coverage); Senn Products Corp. v. Hartford Steam Boiler Inspection & Ins. Co., 180 Misc. 675, 41 N.Y.S.2d 133 (1943) ("objects" insured were described in schedules attached to policy).

59. *See, e.g.*, Hartford Steam Boiler Inspection & Ins. Co. v. Kleinman, 293 S.W. 894 (Tex. App. 1927) (while fire box and chimney were parts of heating plant, they were not parts of boiler described in policy as equipment covered and because explosions occurred in fire box and chimney from gas there accumulated, resulting damage was not protected by policy). *See also* Bay Colony Condo. Assoc. v. Scottsdale Ins. Co., 2012 U.S. Dist. LEXIS 182016 (D.N.J. Dec. 26, 2012), where the policy defined "covered property" to include permanently installed machinery and equipment and further provided that equipment would only be covered if it generated, transmitted, or used energy or, during normal usage, operated under vacuum or pressure. It also stated that "sewer piping" and "water piping" were excluded from the definition of "covered equipment." The court

A great deal of important information is contained on the Declarations Page. This is revealed by an examination of the standard ISO "Equipment Breakdown Protection Coverage Form Declarations" document.[60] The first items of information on any Declarations Page are the named insured and its mailing address.[61] For common interest communities, these are not always routine matters. It is always important that the official legal name of the CIC be listed, not a name by which it is commonly known or that of a larger community of which it is part.[62] Similarly, the mailing address needs to be the one at which it actually receives mail, whether that is the address of the community association manager or a Post Office box. The Declarations Page—or a separate schedule—will also state the policy period, which is often one year but may be for a longer period.[63] The ISO form shows the termination of the policy as 12:01 a.m. Standard time at the stated mailing address. The covered premises or location will be stated on the Declarations Page or a separate schedule. It is imperative that the description of the location of the covered premises be accurate because policies will refer to equipment "at a location described in the Declarations,"[64] or "located at the premises described in the Declarations."[65] However, in most policies there will be an errors and omissions clause under which coverage applies for loss that

found that it was clear and unambiguous the plumbing system of the condominium building was not equipment covered by the policy. The court conceded the HVAC, heating, and electric systems of the building could conceivably constitute equipment covered by the policy because they would generate, transmit, and/or use energy. An association would certainly want more than "conceivable" coverage. The case illustrates the need to identify the specific equipment the policy covers. *Compare* Nationwide Mut. Ins. Co. v. CG Stony Point Townhomes, LLC, 2015 U.S. Dist. LEXIS 5682 (E.D. Va. Jan. 15, 2015) (court found that it appeared undisputed that accident to covered equipment was defined by in manner that would generally include "mechanical breakdown" of HVAC system).

60. ISO Form BM DS 07 07 01.

61. For a complete overview of the Declarations Page, see § 2.10.

62. *Consider* Far Northwest Dev. Co., LLC v. Cmty. Ass'n of Underwriters of Am., Inc., 2006 U.S. Dist. LEXIS 79033 (W.D. Wash. Oct. 30, 2006), where the policy was issued to the "Somerset Village Townhomes Condominium," rather than the association. It was argued that the condominium was merely a building and, therefore, not a legal entity capable of owning anything. The court found that the clear intent of the parties was to provide coverage to the association and, therefore, the association was the named insured regardless of the Declarations Page. *See also* Beauvallon Condo. Ass'n v. Granite State Ins. Co., 2011 U.S. Dist. LEXIS 69606 (D. Colo. June 29, 2011) (association established that it was named insured under policies where insurer acknowledged designation of named insured as "Beauvallon Homeowners Association" was scrivener's error and endorsements had been executed to correct that error).

63. Sometimes the policy term is three years. *See, e.g.*, Cyclops Corp. v. Home Ins. Co., 352 F. Supp. 931 (W.D. Pa. 1973); Pioneer Chlor Alkali Co. v. Royal Indem. Co., 879 S.W.2d 920 (Tex. App.—Houston 14th Dist., 1994); Good Canning Co. v. London Guarantee & Acci. Co., 128 F. Supp. 778 (D. Ark. 1955); Withington Co. v. Maryland Casualty Co., 75 R.I. 297, 65 A.2d 710 (1949).

64. HSB Freestyle Policy Form 6671 (10/2002) § A.1.b. (definition of equipment).

65. ISO Form BM 00 20 07 01, § A.2.a. (property damage coverage).

would not otherwise be paid because of an error or unintentional omission in the description of the insured property or any error resulting in the failure to include any premises owned or occupied by the named insured at the inception of the policy.[66] Travelers, one of the major insurers providing equipment breakdown insurance, has a policy in which the clause is called "error in description" and provides the carrier will pay for a loss covered by the policy if that loss is otherwise not payable solely because of an unintentional error or omission in the description of a location as insured.[67]

The Declarations Page also lists the available coverages and will usually include limits for them based on monetary amounts[68] or a time period. If nothing is shown for a particular coverage, then that coverage is not provided. The ISO Equipment Breakdown Protection Coverage Form provides the listed coverages that are provided if either a limit or the word "included" is shown for that coverage.[69] The Travelers policy says that coverage is provided if a limit, the word "included," or *other coverage indicator* is shown on the Declarations Page.[70] When a coverage is "included," the limit for it is part of the base limit or total limit per breakdown.[71]

The ISO Declarations form lists coverage limits for ammonia contamination, consequential loss, data and media, hazardous substance, and water damage. It also provides for recording a business income report date, the business income annual value, and business income coinsurance percentage. Most Declarations Pages will allow optional coverages—for example, diagnostic equipment or production machines—to be shown as included. They also usually identify conditions applicable to the deductible. On the ISO Declarations form the listed deductibles are preceded by an explanation that a deductible applies only when an amount, hours, days, or the word "included" is shown for a particular coverage. Additionally, if the word "included" is shown, the deductible for that coverage is part of the "combined deductible." Generally, deductibles apply separately for each applicable coverage unless one is shown as "combined," in which case the carrier will subtract the combined deductible amount from the total amount of any loss

66. Malecki, *Equipment Breakdown Insurance: Too Important to Ignore!*, at 4 (Adjusting Today, 2009), available at: http://adjustersinternational.com/publications/adjusting-today/equipment-breakdown-insurance/1/.

67. Travelers EnergyMax 21, § A.2.h.

68. The monetary limit is a ceiling. The insurer may determine a loss to be less than the limit of coverage and only pay that amount. *Boiler and Machinery Coverage Form* (Summit Business Media, 2013).

69. ISO Form BM 00 20 07 01, § A.2.

70. Travelers EnergyMax 21, § A.2.

71. Malecki, *Equipment Breakdown Insurance: Too Important to Ignore!*, at 5 (Adjusting Today, 2009), available at: http://adjustersinternational.com/publications/adjusting-today/equipment-breakdown-insurance/1/ (if $500,000 base limit is selected and other coverages are designated in Declarations as being included, coverage will hinge on how much is left after paying for damage to property named insured owns or has in its care, custody, or control).

to which the combined deductible applies.[72] The deductibles for property damage and spoilage are listed in dollar amounts while those for business income,[73] extra expense, and utility interruption are stated in terms of hours or days. Finally, the ISO Declarations form provides for recording additional insureds, mortgage holders, loss payees, and their addresses.

§ 11.07 Coverage

Boiler and machinery or equipment breakdown coverage includes damage to *covered items* from an accident or breakdown and damage to the *other property* of the insured caused by an accident to those covered items.[74] The general rule is that factual disputes over whether a loss is within the coverage of a policy of boiler and machinery insurance are for the jury to determine.[75]

[1] Covered Cause of Loss—Accident

Traditionally, in boiler and machinery policies the covered cause of loss is an "accident." Indeed, the phrase "sudden and accidental," so familiar in the insurance industry, was borrowed from boiler and machinery insurance policies,[76] where it had been used for many years before finding its way into other policies.[77] Despite the fact that "accident" has been used for many years and has been construed by many courts, the precise way in which it is defined in a contract is critical to coverage.[78]

---

72. ISO Form BM 00 20 07 01, § D.1.a.

73. *See* Austin, *Equipment Breakdown—More Than Just Boiler and Machinery* (IRMI 2011), available at: http://www.irmi.com/articles/expert-commentary/equipment-breakdown (business income coverage may be subject to an average daily value (ADV) deductible that is based on number of days that business income would have been earned during period of interruption had no accident occurred and can be significant and likely much greater in amount than direct damage deductible).

74. *Boiler & Machinery Insurance/Equipment Breakdown Insurance What is Covered by Boiler & Machinery Coverage?*, available at: http://www.brunswickcompanies.com/ci-boiler-machinery-equipment-breakdown-insurance.html.

75. Welders Supply, Inc. v. American Employers' Ins. Co., 342 F.2d 972, 974 (6th Cir. 1965).

76. Guiliano, *The Sudden and Accidental Exception to the Pollution Exclusion Solution?*, 13 Temp. Envtl. L. & Tech. J. 261 (1994).

77. Hamel, *The 1970 Pollution Exclusion in Comprehensive General Liability Policies: Reasons for Interpretations in Favor of Coverage in 1996 and Beyond*, 34 Duq. L. Rev. 1083, 1094 (1996).

78. *See, e.g.*, Rueckert Meat Co. v. Hartford Steam Boiler, Inspection & Ins. Co., 368 S.W.2d 914 (Mo. App. 1963), where the policy defined "accident" as the sudden and accidental tearing asunder of the object caused by *pressure of contents therein*. In the case, ammonia gas escaped through a hole in the shell of a refrigeration system. There had been a short of electricity in a coil, which started boring the hole. The insurer contended the loss was caused not by pressure from within but by the burning and melting of the metal because of the short. The court agreed and said the predominant efficient cause of the loss was the electrical arcing and not a sudden accidental tearing asunder of any part of the refrigeration system caused by pressure of the contents in it.

[a] Typical Policy Language

The ISO Boiler and Machinery Coverage Form provides that a covered cause of loss is an accident to an "object" listed on the Declarations Page.[79] The policy definition of "object" reiterates that an object is the equipment shown on the Declarations Page.[80] The policy defines "accident" as a "sudden and accidental breakdown"[81] of an object, or part of one.[82] The "breakdown" does not necessarily have to be shown by direct physical evidence. An inference may support the determination of an accident. For example, where a cooling system malfunctioned allegedly because of a defective "O" ring, but there was no physical evidence of any defect, the fact that the system worked "perfectly" after the "O" ring was replaced allowed the inference to arise that there was indeed a defective "O" ring.[83]

The ISO Boiler and Machinery Coverage Form adds that when a breakdown happens it has to be *manifested* by physical damage to the object, damage requiring repair or replacement.[84] "Manifest," according to one court, does not

79. ISO Form BM 00 25 02 91, § A.2. *See* Malecki, *Equipment Breakdown Insurance: Too Important to Ignore!*, at 2 (Adjusting Today, 2009), available at: http://adjustersinternational.com/publications/adjusting-today/equipment-breakdown-insurance/1/ ("object" is term that has its genesis with boiler and machinery policies and refers to general category of equipment covered and defined in more precise terms of what "object" included). The policy definition of a specific object can determine the liability of the insurer. For example, in *Norfolk & W. R. Co. v. Royal Indemnity Co.*, 257 F. 849 (D. Pa. 1919), the term "boiler" was defined to encompass "'all connecting pipes and fittings up to and including the valve nearest the boiler.'" There was a rupture of a "whistle pipe," which was beyond the whistle valve, and that was the valve of that pipe nearest the boiler. The court found that the rupture occurred beyond the physical limits of what the insurer undertook to insure against steam pressure.

80. ISO Form BM 00 25 02 91, § F.2. The policy adds that a full description of specific object categories is found in the "Object Definitions endorsement" attached to the coverage form. Note that some policies may define the term "object" rather than cross-reference the Declarations Page. That definition can be ambiguous and subject to construction in favor of the insured. *See* Lakeshore Marine, Inc. v. Hartford Acc. & Indem. Co., 164 Ga. App. 417, 296 S.E.2d 418 (1982).

81. Can a breakdown be the result of an external cause, for example, a power surge? *See* Nat'l Union Fire Ins. Co. v. Travelers Indem. Co., 210 F. Supp. 2d 479 (S.D.N.Y. 2002) (damage to insured's property from power surge allegedly caused by vandalism to off-premises transformer owned by utility company constituted "breakdown" as used in definition of "accident" as term should be construed broadly to include internal damage resulting from *external* causes).

82. *See generally* Hoey, *The Meaning of "Accident" in Boiler and Machinery Insurance and New Developments in Underwriting*, 19 Forum 467 (1984) (boiler and machinery policies once had varying definitions of accident depending on type of object insured, but in early 1960s uniform and concise definition of accident was adopted by many insurers).

83. Commercial Union Ins. Co. v. F.R.P. Co., 172 Ga. App. 244, 249-50, 322 S.E.2d 915, 920 (1984).

84. ISO Form BM 00 25 02 91, § F.1. *See* Hoey, *The Meaning of "Accident" in Boiler and Machinery Insurance and New Developments in Underwriting*, 19 Forum 467, 468 (1984) (where accident is defined to mean sudden and accidental damage to object, or part thereof, that necessitates repair or replacement to object or part thereof, only damage rather than breakdown of object is required to meet definition). *Consider* Good Canning Co. v. London Guarantee & Acci. Co., 128 F. Supp.

mean "discovered" by the insured. Something manifests, said the court, when there are "observable signs of an underlying event or causative factor," but it is not required that the observer understand or comprehend those causative connections. In other words, an insured may be aware of problems with covered equipment but unaware that physical damage requiring repair or replacement has manifested.[85] In that case, a crack progressed for over a year before the equipment seized and failed. That failure occurred after the policy terminated, but the court found coverage, in effect concluding that the breakdown was the crack that had "manifested" previously.[86] The court may be correct in its interpretation of "manifest," but doesn't manifest describe the nature of the "breakdown"? In other words, shouldn't the equipment have to fail—breakdown as *evidenced* by physical damage—for there to be coverage? Has there been a breakdown while the equipment is operating even though an undiscovered flaw will inevitably cause the equipment to fail at some time in the future?

An overlooked portion of many definitions of accident is the part requiring that any damage necessitate "repair or replacement." Equipment can cease to function, but no repair or replacement is required. For example, where a fan stopped functioning because it iced over, the insurer argued there was no accident because the fan required no repair, only defrosting.[87]

The ISO policy also provides that an object has to be "in use" or "connected ready for use" at the specified location—meaning the location specified in the policy—at the time of the accident.[88] The phrase "in use" has been construed to mean an object is "being used for the purpose for which it was designed."[89]

778, 788 (D. Ark. 1955) (that 42-inch brick wall was moved approximately six inches by occurrence was almost conclusive proof that damage was caused by pressure of steam or water in boiler and was result of *sudden* occurrence).

85. Zurich Am. Ins. v. Emplrs Ins. Co., 2005 U.S. Dist. LEXIS 47947 (W.D. Wash. July 25, 2005) (coverage was triggered because crack was showing itself—manifesting—through operational and maintenance problems during policy period even though insured was unaware of its existence until equipment seized; policy required that breakdown manifest itself, but did not say to whom or require that insured understand connection between breakdown—crack—and evidence of breakdown).

86. *Compare* New England Gas & Electric Ass'n v. Ocean Acc. & Guarantee Corp., 330 Mass. 640, 656, 116 N.E.2d 671, 681 (1953) (injury arising from use of property during policy term is not removed from coverage merely because condition that caused that injury *antedated* policy).

87. Associated Freezers v. Fireman's Fund Ins. Co., 1996 Tex. App. LEXIS 98 (Tex. App.—Houston 1st Dist., Jan. 11, 1996) (insurer argued that where fan iced over and ceased operating, there was no accident as fan did not need to be repaired or "replaced, but only defrosted").

88. ISO Form BM 00 25 02 91, § A.2.

89. Foote Mineral Co. v. Maryland Casualty Co., 173 F. Supp. 925, 930 (D. Tenn. 1959), *aff'd*, 277 F.2d 452 (6th Cir. 1960), *cert. den.*, 364 U.S. 818, 81 S. Ct. 49, 5 L. Ed. 2d 48 (1960) (generator was not in use when it was under repair and not producing direct current, purpose for which it was designed).

The widely used HSB policy says a covered cause of loss is an "accident" and that without an accident, there is no equipment breakdown coverage.[90] The HSB policy goes on to define "accident" as a "fortuitous event" causing direct[91] physical damage to "covered equipment."[92] "Covered equipment," unless otherwise specified on the Declarations Page, means equipment that generates, transmits, or uses energy, including electronic communications and data processing equipment, or that, during normal usage, operates under vacuum or pressure, other than the weight of its contents.[93] Generally, the equipment has to be at a location described on the Declarations Page and owned or leased by the named insured or operated under the control of the named insured.[94] However, unlike the ISO policy, the HSB policy does not require the equipment to be "in use."[95]

While the HSB policy is based on the ISO form, it adds that an accident must be one of six specified events:

- Mechanical breakdown, including rupture[96] or bursting caused by centrifugal force;
- Artificially generated electrical current, including electrical arcing, damaging electrical devices, appliances, or wire;

90. HSB Freestyle Policy Form 6671 (10/2002) § A.1.

91. *See* Dixie Pine Products Co. v. Maryland Casualty Co., 133 F.2d 583, 585 (5th Cir. 1943) (it is well settled that "direct cause" is ordinarily synonymous in legal intendment with "proximate cause"); Central Louisiana Electric Co. v. Westinghouse Electric Corp., 579 So. 2d 981, 985, n.8 (La. 1991) ("direct" as used in contract insuring against direct loss or damages means immediate or proximate as distinguished from remote). *See also* Hartford Steam Boiler Inspection & Ins. Co. v. Sonneborn, 96 Md. 616, 54 A. 610 (1903) (where boiler exploded and released steam that melted sprinkler heads allowing water to escape and damage merchandise belonging to insured, policy provided coverage for water damage as active and efficient cause that released water was clearly heat from explosion, and not intervention of any new and independent agency).

92. HSB Freestyle Policy Form 6671 (10/2002) § A.1.a.

93. HSB Freestyle Policy Form 6671 (10/2002) § A.1.b.(1).

94. HSB Freestyle Policy Form 6671 (10/2002) § A.1.b.(2).

95. There are 13 items that are explicitly excepted from the definition of "covered equipment," including buried vessels or piping, waste, drainage or sewer piping, piping, valves or fittings forming part of a sprinkler or fire suppression system, and water piping not part of a closed loop used to conduct heat or cooling from a boiler or refrigeration or air conditioning system. HSB Freestyle Policy Form 6671 (10/2002) §§ G.8.b.(5)–(8).

96. *See* Cleveland Drop Forge Co. v. Travelers' Indem. Co., 114 Ohio St. 549, 151 N.E. 671 (1926) (breaking apart of boiler head, in which rivets were sprung, constituted "rupture" within meaning of policy for which insurer was liable); Louisville College of Dentistry v. Hartford Steam Boiler Inspection & Ins. Co., 185 Ky. 778, 215 S.W. 941 (1919) (where irregular, semicircular opening developed in casting on front of boiler, there was sufficient evidence of rupture as defined in policy). *See also* Travellers Indem. Co. v. B & B Ice & Coal Co., 248 Ky. 443, 446, 58 S.W.2d 640, 641 (1933) (it is not indispensably essential that sudden rupture be accompanied by extremely loud noise).

- Explosion, but not a combustion explosion, of steam boilers, piping, engines, or turbines;
- An event inside steam boilers, pipes,[97] engines, or turbines that damages them;
- An event inside a hot water boiler or other water heating equipment that damages them; or
- Bursting, cracking,[98] or splitting.[99]

One authority notes that this list of "perils" can be a starting point for determining equipment breakdown exposure and that while an insured may not have a "boiler and machinery" exposure, there may still be insurable equipment breakdown exposures, whether electrical arcing or mechanical breakdown of HVAC or refrigeration equipment.[100]

All these policies require the equipment malfunction to result from an accident, and thus chronic failures of equipment attributable to age are not covered.[101] Also not covered are losses caused by design, construction, or installation defects.[102]

[b] Occurrences Defined Not to Be Accidents

Many policies list occurrences that are, by definition, *not accidents*. For example, the ISO policy lists seven occurrences that are not accidents, including depletion,

---

97. *Consider* Kropp Forge Co. v. Globe Indem. Co., 275 F.2d 539, 542 (7th Cir. 1960) (where steam under pressure injected into steam line induces heat that in turn results in damage to line, it must follow that steam pressure, rather than heat, is dominant efficient cause of accident and resulting damage).

98. *See* Sam Braman & Son v. Hartford Steam Boiler Inspection & Ins. Co., 9 Ohio Misc. 203, 222 N.E.2d 456 (Ohio C.P. 1966) (noting that original meaning of "crack" was "break" and concluding that in context of policy in question term meant incomplete separation or fissuring caused by concealed or inherent defects in material, or negligence in operation of machinery, or both together, but finding it would be unreasonable to extend coverage to negligent opening of valve, not in course of operation).

99. HSB Freestyle Policy Form 6671 (10/2002) §§ A.1.a.(1)–(6). *Consider* Bay Colony Condo. Assoc. v. Scottsdale Ins. Co., 2012 U.S. Dist. LEXIS 182016 (D.N.J. Dec. 26, 2012) (where policy contained similar list of events giving rise to accident and damage for which coverage was sought solely resulted from fire, damage was not result of accident and was not covered despite lack of fire exclusion).

100. Austin, *Equipment Breakdown—More Than Just Boiler and Machinery* (IRMI 2011), available at: http://www.irmi.com/articles/expert-commentary/equipment-breakdown.

101. O'Connor, *Construction Law: Recent Issues in Property Coverage*, 34 Wm. Mitchell L. Rev. 177, 202 (2007). *See also* Barnes, *Understanding Your Insurance Policy's Fine-Print: What You Need to Know about Riders* (Cooperator, Aug. 2013), available at: http://cooperator.com/article/understanding-your-insurance-policys-fine-pri (no policy covers equipment wear-and-tear).

102. Scottsdale Ins. Co. v. Sally Group, LLC, 2012 U.S. Dist. LEXIS 47532 (S.D. Tex. Apr. 3, 2012).

deterioration,[103] corrosion,[104] erosion, wear and tear,[105] and breakdown of electronic computer or electronic data processing equipment.[106] The HSB policy also lists occurrences that are not accidents no matter how they are caused and regardless of whether the condition or event is normal and expected or unusual and unexpected. These include depletion; deterioration; rust; corrosion; erosion; settling; wear and tear; any gradually developing condition; and any defect, programming error, programming limitation, computer virus, malicious code, loss of "data," loss of access, loss of use, loss of functionality, or other condition within or involving "data" or "media."[107] Some policies may add that the functioning of any safety or protective device is not an accident.[108] The fact that a safety or protective device is triggered or employed does not necessarily mean, however, that there was no accident as there is a question of causation. For example, in one case the temperature of chemicals that were mixed to produce the product of the insured was supposed to be reduced by pumping methanol into a tank; however, the system malfunctioned, allowing the temperature to rise sharply, which triggered a safety valve to release the chemicals. They were lost as a result, and the insured made a claim for the lost product. The insurer invoked the exclusion for function of a safety or protective device. The court, however, found that the chemicals were already rendered useless at the time they were vented through the safety device and the loss was caused by the malfunction of the cooling system. That the chemicals were removed from the reaction tank via a safety device did not, concluded the court, change the cause of their loss.[109]

That named occurrences are not considered to be accidents does not necessarily mean that an accident cannot result from one of them. For example, in a Georgia case, the policy clearly precluded corrosion from being an accident. Corrosion around metal surrounding a valve seat led to chlorine escaping a tank—a covered object—at a rapid velocity, causing considerable damage to

103. *See, e.g.*, 515 Assocs. LLC v. Travelers Indem. Co., 160 Fed. Appx. 147 (3d Cir. 2005) (no coverage where old and deteriorating condition of elevators was identified as cause of breakdown; elevators had, according to expert, long outlasted their life expectancy). *See also* Daybreak Foods v. Western Nat'l Mut. Ins. Co., 508 N.W.2d 231 (Minn. App. 1993) (no coverage where failure was caused by deterioration or leakage).

104. *See, e.g.*, Central Louisiana Electric Co. v. Westinghouse Electric Corp., 579 So. 2d 981 (La. 1991) (because corrosion pitting formed gradually and was predictable and known event associated with particular turbine generator blade configuration, it could not be considered sudden and accidental occurrence).

105. *See, e.g.*, Louis Meyers & Son, Inc. v. Affiliated F M Ins. Co., 424 F.2d 471 (2d Cir. 1970) (accidental discharge of water from sprinkler system was not covered because leakage resulted from deterioration of materials due to corrosion or wear and tear, occurrences that were expressly excepted from definition of accident).

106. ISO Form BM 00 25 02 91, §§ F.1.a, b & e.

107. HSB Freestyle Policy Form 6671 (10/2002) § G.1.1.b.(1)–(3).

108. 515 Assocs. LLC v. Travelers Indem. Co., 160 Fed. Appx. 147 (3d Cir. 2005); Simkins Industries, Inc. v. Lexington Ins. Co., 42 Md. App. 396, 401 A.2d 181 (1979).

109. Commercial Union Ins. Co. v. F.R.P. Co., 172 Ga. App. 244, 322 S.E.2d 915 (1984).

the premises and its contents. The court said no express policy language excluded coverage for a sudden and accidental breakdown of an object resulting from, at least in part, corrosion. Thus, the court held the loss was covered under the terms of the policy.[110] The Louisiana Supreme Court agreed that when corrosion directly causes a sudden and accidental occurrence that in turn directly causes damage, that damage is covered because its proximate cause was a covered risk—an accident—while corrosion was only an indirect cause.[111] The court offered an example. A specific blade in a turbine generator that fractured as a result of corrosion would not be covered because corrosion would be the direct cause of that fracture and corrosion was excepted from the definition of accident. However, any "downstream damage" that occurred to surrounding machinery from the fractured blade would be covered because the damage would be directly caused by an accident—the fracturing of the blade—rather than by corrosion, which would be the more remote indirect cause.

Some policies may modify the list of occurrences that are defined as not being accidents by stating that these occurrences are not accidents "unless a sudden and accidental breakdown ensues." According to one court, that clause only means that the existence of deterioration "does not bar a claim if an unrelated unexpected and unintended breakdown occurs, and that a breakdown due to natural deterioration cannot be 'unexpected' from the insured's perspective."[112]

[c] Interpretation of "Accident" and "Sudden"

Some courts say that coverage for an accident is determined without reference to causation,[113] and thus, while the roots of an event may be a gradual process, the

110. Lakeshore Marine, Inc. v. Hartford Acc. & Indem. Co., 164 Ga. App. 417, 422, 296 S.E.2d 418, 422 (1982) (had insurer intended to exclude coverage of sudden and accidental breakdown of object resulting from corrosion, more apt and definitive language would undoubtedly have been used). *Lakeshore* has been referred to as an "anomalous" case on the issue of causation. *See* Cozen, *Insuring Real Property*, § 5.09 (Matthew Bender & Co., 2015). *See also* Resorts International, Inc. v. American Home Assurance Co., 311 So. 2d 806 (Fla. 3d DCA 1975) (insurer properly denied coverage for failure of newly installed air-conditioning system on grounds that it resulted from corrosion).

111. Central Louisiana Electric Co. v. Westinghouse Electric Corp., 579 So. 2d 981, 987 (La. 1991). *See also* Pioneer Chlor Alkali Co. v. Royal Indem. Co., 879 S.W.2d 920 (Tex. App.—Houston 14th Dist., 1994) (agreeing that while policy definition of accident excluded corrosion, it did not exclude sudden and accidental breakdown caused by corrosion); Riefflin v. Hartford Steam Boiler Inspection & Ins. Co., 164 Mont. 287, 293, 521 P.2d 675, 678 (Mont. 1974) (internal boiler scaling problem was not an accident under usual meaning of term as defined in policy; however, cracking of boiler sections caused by scale buildup was accident covered by policy).

112. 515 Assocs. LLC v. Travelers Indem. Co., 160 Fed. Appx. 147, 151 (3d Cir. 2005) (rejecting interpretation that modifying clause means that if equipment wears out, it should be replaced, but if before replacement it breaks down, there is coverage).

113. Cyclops Corp. v. Home Ins. Co., 352 F. Supp. 931, 936 (W.D. Pa. 1973) (definition of accident does not require any consideration of term cause). *See also* New England Gas & Electric Ass'n v. Ocean Acc. & Guarantee Corp., 330 Mass. 640, 651, 116 N.E.2d 671, 679 (1953) (words

event itself may still be sudden and an "accident."[114] In other words, there is no temporal element to the term "accident."[115] Indeed, as one judge noted, except in cases of *manufactured* defects, machinery defects almost always trace back to deterioration of critical parts and, therefore, to hold that once there is deterioration there can be no accident leads to an absurd result in which coverage under a boiler and machinery policy would be almost completely precluded.[116] Other courts hold that a "sudden" event has to occur over a short period of time.[117] While an event may be sudden "if viewed entirely in isolation," it is not an accident if it was the final manifestation of a gradual process.[118] Mere discovery that covered equipment has developed a flaw in what may have been a progressive process does not constitute an accident.[119]

"sudden and accidental" describe result and do not refer to any means by which that result has been brought about).

114. Community Federal Sav. & Loan Ass'n v. Hartford Steam Boiler Inspection & Ins. Co., 580 F. Supp. 1170, 1173 (E.D. Mo. 1984) (mechanical breakdown was sudden and accidental, even though cause might not have been); Anderson & Middleton Lumber Co. v. Lumbermen's Mut. Cas. Co., 53 Wn. 2d 404, 333 P.2d 938 (1959) (while breaking or cracking may have been gradual process that went on over period of from one day to three weeks, sudden break occurred within meaning of policy as break was unforeseen and unexpected); New England Gas & Electric Ass'n v. Ocean Acc. & Guarantee Corp., 330 Mass. 640, 653, 116 N.E.2d 671, 680 (1953) (it is enough if mechanical breakdown itself is sudden; damage must be sudden, but cause need not be); Detroit Lakes v. Travelers Indem. Co., 201 Minn. 26, 28, 275 N.W. 371, 372 (1937) (though factors of causation may have been gradual and even slow in operation, where portion of turbine steam engine became deformed and cracked by expansion, rupturing itself doubtless was sudden, at least in its beginning); Travellers Indem. Co. v. B & B Ice & Coal Co., 248 Ky. 443, 446, 58 S.W.2d 640, 641 (1933) (explosion was sudden where it was reasonably certain that its proximate cause was assembling of deposit of some sort of substance from its operation and force of heat preventing equal distribution of heat). *See also* Preferred Mut. Ins. Co. v. Travelers Cos., 127 F.3d 136 (1st Cir. 1997) (where leaky fuel pump seal allowed oil to enter burner tube where it caught fire, causing melting and damage to line and further release of oil, leaking was breakdown or accident).

115. *See, e.g.*, Hamel, *The 1970 Pollution Exclusion in Comprehensive General Liability Policies: Reasons for Interpretations in Favor of Coverage in 1996 and Beyond*, 34 Duq. L. Rev. 1083, 1094 (1996) ("sudden and accidental" have been interpreted by courts to simply mean "unexpected and unintended," with no temporal element). *See also* Pioneer Chlor Alkali Co. v. Royal Indem. Co., 879 S.W.2d 920 (Tex. App.—Houston 14th Dist., 1994) (definitions of sudden and accidental have to do with surprise and lack of foreseeability, not time).

116. Daybreak Foods v. Western Nat'l Mut. Ins. Co., 508 N.W.2d 231, 234 (Minn. App. 1993) (Crippen, J. dissenting).

117. Fairhaven Power Co. v. Hartford Steam Boiler Inspection & Ins. Co., 1995 U.S. Dist. LEXIS 21733 (N.D. Cal. June 2, 1995) ("sudden" event must occur over relatively short period of time).

118. Daybreak Foods v. Western Nat'l Mut. Ins. Co., 508 N.W.2d 231, 234 (Minn. App. 1993) (where rubber valve gasket fractured as result of deterioration or leakage, there was no "accident"). *See also* Fairhaven Power Co. v. Hartford Steam Boiler Inspection & Ins. Co., 1995 U.S. Dist. LEXIS 21733 (N.D. Cal. June 2, 1995) (as stress corrosion is invariably gradual phenomenon, it would not constitute an "accident").

119. *See, e.g.*, Senn Products Corp. v. Hartford Steam Boiler Inspection & Ins. Co., 180 Misc. 675, 41 N.Y.S.2d 133 (1943) (discovery of bulge or distortion in boiler that had been in normal use for great number of years, where nothing had happened up to that time to attract attention, and

Courts also take into consideration that an event is unforeseen.[120] Thus, improper adjustment of equipment would not bar coverage where the damage was unintended and could not have been reasonably anticipated.[121] One commentator has contended in response to that holding that it may be argued that even if the insured had no actual knowledge or warning of potential damage, it may still not be sudden as the test should not be subjective, but objective: whether the insured could or should reasonably have anticipated the damage.[122] On the other hand, in an unreported decision, the federal Third Circuit said that "whether or not a leak—allegedly the cause of the loss—was expected is not indicative of whether the loss was 'sudden and accidental.'"[123] The case involved a glass melting furnace that developed a leak that turned into a catastrophic event in which molten glass was spewed, causing severe damage to the furnace and other equipment. The trial court held the insured expected the incident because there had been previous leaks and the furnace manager had expressed concern about the risk of another leak. The appellate court, however, said there were factual issues about exactly what the insured expected. In particular, the anticipated severity of those leaks was in dispute and thus, there were factual issues regarding what risks of loss and damage the insured expected. The appellate court raised an important point: covered equipment often experiences problems requiring repair or at least monitoring before an accident occurs. The fact that the insured is aware its equipment is not perfect does not mean it expected that equipment to break down in a particular way.[124]

without any explanation of when it occurred—whether suddenly or progressively—or satisfactory proof of how it occurred or what its cause was, fell far short of establishing accident occurred).

120. *See, e.g.*, Associated Freezers v. Fireman's Fund Ins. Co., 1996 Tex. App. LEXIS 98 (Tex. App.—Houston 1st Dist., Jan. 11, 1996) (where insured was aware that fan had iced over and ceased operating on other occasions and plant engineer had unfrozen it on prior occasions, and to his knowledge, out of all cooler fans he checked, it was the only one that had ever frozen up, and mounting brackets on fan were changed to facilitate future removal of ice, it could not be said that future interruptions to fan from ice accumulations were unexpected or unforeseen and, therefore, accidental).

121. New England Gas & Electric Ass'n v. Ocean Acc. & Guarantee Corp., 330 Mass. 640, 116 N.E.2d 671 (1953) (accident is unexpected, undesigned, and unintended happening or mishap; improper adjustment of equipment did not bring damage outside of coverage; finding it difficult to see how damage—cracking of spindle—could have been reasonably anticipated and concluding it was an accident).

122. Hoey, *The Meaning of "Accident" in Boiler and Machinery Insurance and New Developments in Underwriting*, 19 Forum 467, 469 (1984).

123. United States Fire Ins. Co. v. Kelman Bottles, 538 Fed. Appx. 175, 181 (3d Cir. 2013).

124. *See also* St. Paul Fire & Marine Ins. Co. v. General Injectables & Vaccines, Inc., 2000 U.S. Dist. LEXIS 2597 (W.D. Va. Mar. 3, 2000) (equipment had failed on five prior occasions in prior year, but never resulted in losses; although insured may have had reason to believe equipment might fail sometime in future, it did not know that it would fail during policy period, or that failure inevitably would cause particular damage that occurred).

Generally, whether there has been an "accident" is a jury question.[125] As the word "sudden" is part of the definition of "accident," a coverage term, the burden is on the insured to show the alleged accident was sudden.[126]

[2] Covered Cause of Loss—Breakdown

Some policies do not use the word "accident" in defining a covered cause of loss. For example, the ISO Equipment Breakdown Protection Coverage Form says that a covered cause of loss is a breakdown to covered equipment.[127] The policy then defines "breakdown" to mean a prescribed direct physical loss causing damage to covered equipment and requiring its repair or replacement.[128] "Covered equipment" is defined by way of inclusion and exclusion.[129] It includes equipment built to operate under internal pressure or vacuum, electrical or mechanical equipment used in generation, transmission, or use of energy, communication, and computer equipment,[130] and any of this equipment that is owned by a utility and used solely to supply utility services to the premises of the named insured.[131] Except for that utility equipment, the covered equipment has to be located at a premises described on the Declarations Page and be owned, leased, or operated under the control of the named insured.[132] There are 12 items that are specifically

---

125. Food Source, Inc. v. Zurich Ins. Co., 751 S.W.2d 596, 598 (Tex. App.—Dallas 1988) (whether breaking of gear constituted "accident" as defined in policy was question of 'fact for jury to decide).

126. Fairhaven Power Co. v. Hartford Steam Boiler Inspection & Ins. Co., 1995 U.S. Dist. LEXIS 21733 (N.D. Cal. June 2, 1995).

127. ISO Form BM 00 20 07 01, § A.1. *Consider* St. Mary's Area Water Auth. v. St. Paul Fire & Marine Ins. Co., 472 F. Supp. 2d 630 (M.D. Pa. 2007) (it is not necessarily true that mechanical breakdown only results from internal causes).

128. ISO Form BM 00 20 07 01, § F.1. *See also* Connie's Constr. Co. v. Continental Western Ins. Co., 227 N.W.2d 204 (Iowa 1975) (mechanical breakdown means functional defect in moving parts of machinery that causes it to operate improperly or cease operating). Some policies do not define "breakdown." *See, e.g.*, Zurich Am. Ins. v. Emplrs Ins. Co., 2005 U.S. Dist. LEXIS 47947 (W.D. Wash. July 25, 2005) (where "breakdown" was not defined in policy court said term generally encompasses any defect in or failure of equipment that causes it to cease functioning or to function improperly); Fairhaven Power Co. v. Hartford Steam Boiler Inspection & Ins. Co., 1995 U.S. Dist. LEXIS 21733 (N.D. Cal. June 2, 1995) (where policy did not define "breakdown," court found term to be ambiguous and construed it in favor of insured, rejecting insurer's contention that term required that disabling problem had to arise while machine was operating rather than being tested).

129. ISO Form BM 00 20 07 01, § F.6.

130. Computer equipment is the insured's programmable electronic equipment used to store, retrieve, and process data and associated peripheral equipment providing communication, including input and output functions—for example, printing—or auxiliary functions, including data transmission, but does not include data or media. ISO Form BM 00 20 07 01, § F.5.

131. ISO Form BM 00 20 07 01, § F.6.a. If, however, the policy provides utility interruption coverage, then utility equipment supplying services to the premises of the named insured is not included in the definition of covered equipment.

132. This exception does not apply to certain prescribed coverages.

excluded from the definition of covered equipment.[133] Examples are media,[134] vessels, piping and other equipment buried below ground,[135] and vehicles, aircraft, self-propelled equipment, or floating vessels.[136]

A popular policy that tracks the ISO language lists three malfunctions that constitute breakdowns: failure of pressure or vacuum equipment; mechanical failure, including rupture[137] or bursting caused by centrifugal force; and electrical failure, including arcing.[138] Some policies have a definition of breakdown that is similar to that of accident. For example, a policy discussed in one case defined the term to mean sudden and accidental direct physical loss to covered equipment that manifests itself by physical damage, requiring its repair or replacement.[139] As an observer notes, a dictionary definition of "breakdown" includes being rendered inoperative by breakage or wear, or wearing out,[140] but if the reason for a breakdown is wear, the insured should not expect coverage.[141]

[3] Coverage Provided

The coverage provided by the policies extends beyond the repair or replacement of the covered equipment. The policies pay for other loss or damage—in other words, consequential loss or damages—that is a direct result of a covered cause of loss. If the insured cannot show that direct result, there is no coverage. In other words, there is no coverage if the consequential loss does not result from an accident to, or breakdown of, an object or covered equipment.[142] Thus, where the

---

133. ISO Form BM 00 20 07 01, § F.6.b.

134. ISO Form BM 00 20 07 01, § F.6.b.(1). "Media" means electronic data processing or storage media, for example, films, tapes, discs, drums, or cells. ISO Form BM 00 20 07 01, § F.11.

135. ISO Form BM 00 20 07 01, § F.6.b.(6).

136. ISO Form BM 00 20 07 01, § F.6.b.(8).

137. *See* Cleveland Drop Forge Co. v. Travelers' Indem. Co., 114 Ohio St. 549, 151 N.E. 671 (1926) (breaking apart of boiler head, in which rivets were sprung, constituted "rupture" within meaning of policy for which insurer was liable); Louisville College of Dentistry v. Hartford Steam Boiler Inspection & Ins. Co., 185 Ky. 778, 215 S.W. 941 (1919) (where irregular, semicircular opening developed in casting on front of boiler, there was sufficient evidence it was rupture as defined in policy). *See also* Travellers Indem. Co. v. B & B Ice & Coal Co., 248 Ky. 443, 446, 58 S.W.2d 640, 641 (1933) (it is not indispensably essential that sudden rupture be accompanied by extremely loud noise).

138. Travelers EnergyMax 21, § F.1.

139. Cowiche Growers, Inc. v. Cont'l Cas. Co., 2010 U.S. Dist. LEXIS 113140 (E.D. Wash. Oct. 25, 2010).

140. *See, e.g.*, *Webster's New Universal Unabridged Dictionary* at 257 (Random House, 1966).

141. Malecki, *Equipment Breakdown Coverage: This Oft-Misunderstood Coverage is a Necessity for Many Clients*, available at: http://www.roughnotes.com/rnmagazine/2008/march08/03p114.htm (under ISO equipment breakdown form, if through wear and tear there is direct physical loss that causes damage to covered equipment requiring its repair or replacement, coverage will apply, but if through wear and tear or corrosion equipment simply stops functioning, no coverage should be expected).

142. Withington Co. v. Maryland Casualty Co., 75 R.I. 297, 65 A.2d 710 (1949) (if damaged equipment was not considered to be an object covered by policy, consequential damage caused by

covered equipment was an air conditioning unit and a terminal board had to be replaced to return the air conditioner to working order but there was no evidence the terminal board was damaged by the accident, there was no coverage for the cost of the replacement.[143] On the other hand, after sand and silt was found in a turbine, an insured sought to recover the cost of opening up the turbine, taking it apart, cleaning it, and reassembling it. The insured contended a steam line running from the turbine across a river had been broken off and that allowed sand and silt to pour through the broken pipe into the turbine. The court said there was sufficient evidence from which the jury could have found the turbine damage was the *direct result* of the accident that broke the steam pipes and permitted mud or debris to enter.[144]

The specific categories of loss or damage vary from policy to policy. The categories most pertinent to common interest communities are discussed below. Note that in policies that define a covered cause of loss as an accident, the policy may explicitly restrict payment to the portion of a loss, damage, or expense that is solely attributable to the "accident."[145]

[a] Property Damage

Policies generally provide that the insurer will pay for direct or physical damage to "covered property" that is located at the premises described on the Declarations Page at the time of the accident or breakdown.[146] It is important to note that policies provide for payment of damage to covered *property* only when there is a covered cause of loss that is a breakdown to covered *equipment*.[147] One has to look to the policy to determine which equipment is covered.

"Covered property" is usually defined as property owned by the named insured or in the "care, custody or control" of the named insured and for which it is legally liable.[148] That language was undoubtedly included to address prop-

its explosion could not be basis for recovery under that policy).

143. Cafritz Co. v. Employers Commercial Union Ins. Co., 309 A.2d 302 (D.C. 1973).

144. Simkins Industries, Inc. v. Lexington Ins. Co., 42 Md. App. 396, 412, 401 A.2d 181, 190 (1979).

145. HSB Freestyle Policy Form 6671 (10/2002) § A.2.

146. *See* ISO Form BM 00 20 07 01, § A.2.a; HSB Freestyle Policy Form 6671 (10/2002) § A.2.a. The definition of "covered property" might be given more specificity. For example, one policy defined the term to include "permanently installed machinery and equipment" in the building or structure. Bay Colony Condo. Assoc. v. Scottsdale Ins. Co., 2012 U.S. Dist. LEXIS 182016 (D.N.J. Dec. 26, 2012).

147. *See* ISO Form BM 00 20 07 01, §§ A.1, A.2.a; Travelers EnergyMax 21, § A.1. *See, e.g.*, Hartford Steam Boiler Inspection & Ins. Co. v. Kleinman, 293 S.W. 894 (Tex. App. 1927) (while fire box and chimney were parts of heating plant, they were not parts of boiler described in policy as equipment covered and because explosions occurred in fire box and chimney from gas there accumulated, resulting damage was not protected by policy).

148. ISO Form BM 00 25 02 91, § A.1; HSB Freestyle Policy Form 6671 (10/2002) § G.9.a. An insured could be "legally liable" by implication, not just by an express agreement.

erty in the "care, custody or control" of the named insured as lessee or perhaps bailor. It can, however, take on new meaning in the case of a common interest community in which commonly owned property—that is, property owned by all the residents of the community as tenants in common—is generally the responsibility of the governing association.[149]

The HSB policy adds a list of property that is *not* considered "covered property," including accounts, bills, currency, deeds or other evidences of debt, money, notes or securities, fine art, land,[150] trees, shrubs, or plants.[151]

[b] Expediting Expenses

This coverage may be called a "mitigating cost" provision and is automatically included in some policies while it needs to be specifically selected, and for an additional cost, in others.[152] For damaged covered property—meaning property owned by the named insured or in the care, custody, or control of the named insured and for which it is legally liable—the insurer will pay the "reasonable" extra cost to make temporary repairs and expedite permanent repairs or permanent replacement of damaged property.[153] Under that language, the expediting expense coverage does not cover temporary *replacement*. The coverage is for repair, and temporarily replacing damaged property is not repairing it temporarily.[154] However, the policy language may be broader.

149. In *R.D. Offutt Co. v. Lexington Ins. Co.*, 494 F.3d 668, 675 (8th Cir. 2007), the insurer raised an argument that could have relevance to a common interest community. The insured had sought coverage for expenses it incurred to avoid losses by tenants for which it would have been legally responsible. The insurer argued the boiler and machinery policy was a first-party property policy, rather than a third-party liability policy, designed to protect loss or damage to property owned by the policyholder rather than to reimburse it against liability to a third party. Thus, the expenses in question were not covered because they were incurred to avoid liability to third-party tenants. The court rejected the argument, saying the insurer had pointed to no authority convincing it that intent or purpose of an insured should inform its coverage analysis. Note that the coverage in question arose under an expediting expenses clause.

150. A policy may also have an exclusion under which it does not cover loss or damage to land. *See, e.g.*, St. Paul Fire & Marine Ins. Co. v. Protection Mut. Ins. Co., 664 F. Supp. 328 (N.D. Ill. 1987).

151. HSB Freestyle Policy Form 6671 (10/2002) § G.9.b.

152. Malecki, *Equipment Breakdown Insurance: Too Important to Ignore!*, at 10 (Adjusting Today, 2009), available at: http://adjustersinternational.com/publications/adjusting-today/equipment-breakdown-insurance/1/.

153. *See* ISO Form BM 00 20 07 01, § A.2.b; HSB Freestyle Policy Form 6671 (10/2002) § A.2.k.

154. Detroit Edison Co. v. Protection Mut. Ins. Co., 134 F.3d 790 (6th Cir. 1998) (installation of temporary transformer constituted neither "temporary repair" of damaged transformer nor expediting of permanent repair or replacement of damaged transformer; expediting expense clauses differentiate between "repair" and "replacement" insofar as permanent repairs and replacements are concerned). In *Detroit Edison* the chief underwriter for the carrier testified that expediting expense coverage would obligate the policy to pay the additional cost to "fly in" new permanent equipment or the extra cost of temporary repair. *Accord* Cincinnati Gas & Elec. Co. v. Hartford Steam Boiler Inspection & Ins. Co., 2008 U.S. Dist. LEXIS 29569 (S.D. Ohio Apr. 9, 2008).

In one of the leading cases,[155] the policy provided coverage for the "reasonable extra cost of temporary repair and/or replacement and/or expediting the repair and/or replacement" of damaged property insured under the policy. The insured leased land for farming and was obligated to provide the tenants with water. Failure of a switchgear that controlled the supply of electricity to a pump cut its water pumping capacity in half. The failure had to be addressed immediately to prevent crops from dying. As a permanent replacement of the switchgear would take weeks or even months, the insured rented portable generators and bought diesel fuel to supply them. It sought coverage for those expenses. The insurer contended the rented generators and diesel fuel did not temporarily repair or replace the switchgear. The court said the question was whether "replacement" meant an exact replacement—temporarily replacing the damaged switchgear with a working one—or a functional replacement. The court concluded the meaning of "replace" was broad enough to include substitution of the damaged switchgear with generators and fuel.[156]

[c] Extra Expense

As a commentator notes, expediting expense and extra expense coverage can be confused.[157] One court explained that extra expense coverage is more "expansive" than expediting expense coverage and covers expenses "incurred to maintain business operations beyond normal coverage."[158]

The HSB policy provides that the carrier will pay the reasonable and necessary "extra expense" to operate the business of the insured during the "period of restoration."[159] It defines "extra expense" as the additional cost incurred by the insured to operate its business over and above the cost it normally would have incurred to operate the business during the same period had no "accident" occurred.[160] The "period of restoration" is the interval of time that begins at the time of the "accident" and continues until the earlier of the date the physical

155. R.D. Offutt Co. v. Lexington Ins. Co., 494 F.3d 668 (8th Cir. 2007) (distinguishing *Detroit Edison* where policy covered only "temporary repair").

156. The policy also had an exclusion sometimes found for loss or damage to growing crops. The trial court decided the exclusion did not apply because it barred coverage for physical loss or damage to crops, not costs incurred to replace covered property to save or protect crops. The appellate court agreed.

157. Malecki, *Equipment Breakdown Insurance: Too Important to Ignore!*, at 10 (Adjusting Today, 2009), available at: http://adjustersinternational.com/publications/adjusting-today/equipment-breakdown-insurance/1/.

158. Detroit Edison Co. v. Protection Mut. Ins. Co., 134 F.3d 790, 792, n.3 (6th Cir. 1998).

159. HSB Freestyle Policy Form 6671 (10/2002) § A.2.d. *See also* ISO Form BM 00 20 07 01, § A.2.c (Business Income and Extra Expense—Extra Expense Only). *And see* ISO Form BM 15 34 09 88 (Boiler and Machinery Extra Expense Values Worksheet). The worksheet provides information to the insurer about estimated extra expenses needed over and above normal if alternate facilities or equipment are used.

160. HSB Freestyle Policy Form 6671 (10/2002) § G.12.

damage to the "covered equipment" is repaired or replaced or on which the damage could have been repaired or replaced with the exercise of due diligence and dispatch, plus any number of days shown on the Declarations Page for "Extended Period of Restoration."[161] The HSB policy provides what has been called "pure extra expense insurance."[162] Generally, it is needed by businesses—for example, hospitals or banks—that must continue to operate after an accident or mechanical breakdown. The same applies to residential common interest communities that may need to obtain substitute power, heating, or cooling. A common interest community association might also be able to recover for the "extra expense" of renting a temporary office when its building is rendered uninhabitable.[163] One commentary urges careful consideration of the limit of coverage for extra expenses because these costs can be greater than the direct damage.[164] The limit for extra expenses can be found on the Declarations Page. An association needs to evaluate initially and for each renewal whether the stated limit is sufficient.

Another type of extra expense coverage is, according to one commentator, actually more appropriately called "expenses to reduce loss" coverage and is available only when business income coverage is not accompanied by extra expense coverage.[165] It pays any necessary expenses incurred to reduce the business income loss but only to the extent the expenses incurred reduce the business income loss.

[d] Ordinance and Law

Ordinance and law coverage is protection against the increased cost of complying with building requirements. It applies when an "accident" damages a building that is "covered property"—meaning property owned by the named insured or in the care, custody, or control of the named insured and for which it is legally liable—and the loss is increased by an ordinance or law that regulates construction or repair of buildings, including "building utilities," is in force at the time of the "accident" and is not addressed under demolition or hazardous substances

161. HSB Freestyle Policy Form 6671 (10/2002) § G.19.

162. Malecki, *Equipment Breakdown Insurance: Too Important to Ignore!*, at 10 (Adjusting Today, 2009), available at: http://adjustersinternational.com/publications/adjusting-today/equipment-breakdown-insurance/1/.

163. *See* Olde Colonial Vill. v. Millers Mut. Ins., 2002 Del. Super. LEXIS 341 (Del. Super. Ct. May 17, 2002). Note that *Millers* concerned an "extra expense" provision in a *property* policy; however, the language of the clause the court interpreted was similar to that found in boiler and machinery or equipment breakdown policies.

164. Austin, *Equipment Breakdown—More Than Just Boiler and Machinery* (IRMI 2011), available at: http://www.irmi.com/articles/expert-commentary/equipment-breakdown (increased operating expenses may be significant, perhaps even greater than direct damage if equipment damaged or destroyed will require long lead time for parts and/or repair).

165. Malecki, *Equipment Breakdown Insurance: Too Important to Ignore!*, at 10 (Adjusting Today, 2009), available at: http://adjustersinternational.com/publications/adjusting-today/equipment-breakdown-insurance/1/.

coverage.[166] A typical policy pays for the actual and necessary cost to repair or reconstruct the damaged portions of the building and to bring undamaged portions of the building into compliance with the ordinance or law.[167] Additional costs are those beyond what would have been payable under the policy had the pertinent ordinance or law not been in force at the time of the accident.[168]

Some policies have both an ordinance and law coverage clause and an ordinance and law exclusion clause. Obviously, these two clauses need to be read in conjunction with one another. Often, the coverage clause will state that it applies despite the exclusion.[169]

The Travelers Equipment Breakdown Policy includes some specific limitations on the coverage.[170] Under it the insurer will not pay for demolition or site clearing until undamaged portions of the building or structures are actually demolished. It will also not pay for any increase in loss until the damaged or destroyed buildings are actually either rebuilt or replaced and approved by the applicable regulatory agency. Losses from any ordinance, law, rule, regulation, or ruling with which the insured was required to comply before the loss, even if the building was undamaged, and with which the insured failed to comply are not covered. There is no coverage for an increase in loss that exceeds the amount needed to meet the minimum requirement of any ordinance, law, rule, regulation, or ruling at the time of the breakdown.[171] Any increase in loss that results from a substance declared by any governmental agency to be hazardous to health or the environment is not covered under the policy.[172] One obvious example would be the cost of removing asbestos.

Finally, under the Travelers policy, if the building or structure is damaged by a breakdown covered by the policy and there is other uncovered physical damage and the building damage in its entirety results in enforcement of an ordinance, law, rule, regulation, or ruling, the insurer will not pay the total amount of the

---

166. HSB Freestyle Policy Form 6671 (10/2002) § A.2.j.(1). *See also* ISO Form BM 00 20 07 01, A.3.g. The ISO policy also has an ordinance and law exclusion. ISO Form BM 00 20 07 01, § B.1.

167. HSB Freestyle Policy Form 6671 (10/2002) § A.2.j.(2).

168. HSB Freestyle Policy Form 6671 (10/2002) § A.2.j.(3).

169. *See, e.g.*, ISO Form BM 00 20 07 01, § A.2.g; Travelers EnergyMax 21, § A.2.k. *See also* Malecki, *Equipment Breakdown Insurance: Too Important to Ignore!*, at 4 (Adjusting Today, 2009), available at: http://adjustersinternational.com/publications/adjusting-today/equipment-breakdown-insurance/1/ (ordinance or law coverage applies despite ordinance or law exclusion otherwise applicable).

170. Travelers EnergyMax 21, § A.2.k.(2).

171. In other words, if the insured decides to go beyond the minimum requirements, it does so at its own expense. For example, if an ordinance requires two entrance and exit ramps, but the insured wants to construct three ramps, the insurer will only pay for the two that are required. *Boiler and Machinery Coverage Form* (Summit Business Media, 2012).

172. The policyholder should, however, consider that there may be coverage under its commercial property policy.

loss but only the proportion that the covered breakdown loss bears to the total physical loss.[173]

[e] Demolition

Demolition coverage may be separately listed or may be included within "Ordinance and Law" coverage, which ordinarily covers repair or reconstruction.[174]

Demolition coverage generally applies if an "accident" damages a building that is "covered property"—meaning property owned by the named insured or in the care, custody, or control of the named insured and for which it is legally liable—and the loss is increased by an ordinance or law that requires demolition of a building that is otherwise reparable, is in force at the time of the accident, and is not addressed under any hazardous substances coverage.[175]

Demolition coverage usually pays two types of additional costs to comply with a pertinent ordinance or law. These are the actual and necessary costs to demolish and clear the site of the undamaged parts of the building and to reconstruct the undamaged parts of the building.[176] "Additional costs" mean those beyond what would have been payable under the policy had no pertinent ordinance or law been in force at the time of the accident.[177]

[f] Data Restoration

The HSB policy pays for the "reasonable and necessary" cost to research, replace, or restore lost "data."[178] "Data" is defined as "information or instructions stored in digital code capable of being processed by machinery."[179] When there is also business income and/or extra expense coverage, the policy also pays for "loss and expense" as defined under those coverages during the restoration process; however, the amount is subject to the data restoration limit shown on the Declarations Page.[180]

The Traveler Equipment Breakdown Policy has optional "data or media" coverage. The policy defines "data" as programmed and recorded material stored on media and programming records used for electronic data processing,

173. Travelers EnergyMax 21, § A.2.k.(3).

174. Travelers EnergyMax 21, § A.2.k.

175. HSB Freestyle Policy Form 6671 (10/2002) § A.2.i.(1). The policy also pays for loss and expense as defined under Business Income coverage and Extra Expense coverage that is the result the increased cost of meeting an applicable ordinance or law if that coverage is otherwise applicable under the policy. This coverage is included within and subject to any demolition limit. HSB Freestyle Policy Form 6671 (10/2002) § A.2.i.(4).

176. HSB Freestyle Policy Form 6671 (10/2002) § A.2.i.(2).

177. HSB Freestyle Policy Form 6671 (10/2002) § A.2.i.(3).

178. HSB Freestyle Policy Form 6671 (10/2002) § A.2.h.(1).

179. HSB Freestyle Policy Form 6671 (10/2002) § G.10.

180. HSB Freestyle Policy Form 6671 (10/2002) § A.2.h.(2).

or electronically controlled equipment.[181] "Media" refers to electronic data or processing or storage material, for example, films, tapes, discs, drums, or cells. The policy says that if the insured purchases "data or media" coverage, has also selected business income and/or extra expense coverage, and media is damaged or data is lost or corrupted as a direct result of a breakdown to covered equipment, it will pay the actual loss of business income or extra expenses while it is necessary to research, recreate, replace, or restore damaged media or lost or corrupted data and reprogram instructions used in any covered computer equipment.[182] There is, however, no coverage for any data or media that cannot be replaced, recreated, or restored.

If data restoration is not included in the policy, a common interest community should give consideration to adding it if it stores critical information, especially financial records, electronically. In many states,[183] CICs are required to retain certain information and make it available to unit owners for inspection. The ability to meet that mandate is another consideration in determining whether to obtain data restoration coverage.

[g] Business Income

Business income coverage pays for lost earnings.[184] It represents a significant amount of the losses paid by the typical carrier.[185] "Business income" means the aggregate of net income—meaning net profit or loss before income taxes—that would have been earned or incurred and continuing normal operating expenses

181. Travelers EnergyMax 21, § F.9.

182. Travelers EnergyMax 21, § A.2.g.

183. *See, e.g.*, Cal. Civ. Code § 5205(a) (association must make association records available for inspection and copying by member of association); Fla. Stat. §§ 720.303(4) & (5) (homeowners association required to maintain official records of association for seven years and that must be made available to owner for inspection or photocopying); 765 Ill. Comp. Stat. § 605/19 (association must keep and maintain prescribed records, or true and complete copies of them, at association principal office and any member of association has right to inspect, examine, and make copies of those records); N.Y. Real P. § 339-w (governing board must keep detailed, accurate records of receipts and expenditures arising from operation of property that must be available for examination by unit owners). *See also* Uniform Common Interest Ownership Act § 3-118 (association must retain prescribed records and make them available for examination and copying by unit owners).

184. *See, e.g.*, Detroit Edison Co. v. Protection Mut. Ins. Co., 134 F.3d 790, 792, n.3 (6th Cir. 1998) (business interruption insurance covers loss of earnings due to loss of either sales or production).

185. Tapia, *Equipment Breakdown Coverage: Not Your Father's Boiler & Machinery Insurance* (Insurance Journal 2000), available at: http://www.insurancejournal.com/magazines/features/2000/11/27/21234.htm (as much as 50 percent of all losses one carrier pays have some business interruption component to them). *See also* Austin, *Equipment Breakdown—More Than Just Boiler and Machinery* (IRMI 2011), available at: http://www.irmi.com/articles/expert-commentary/equipment-breakdown (loss of income may be significant, perhaps even greater than direct damage if equipment damaged or destroyed will require long lead time for parts and/or repair).

incurred, including employee payroll.[186] Many policies will pay for *actual loss* of business income during the "period of restoration" that results directly from the necessary total or partial interruption of the business,[187] and any *necessary expenses* incurred during that period to reduce the amount of loss to the extent they do not exceed the amount of loss that otherwise would have been payable.[188] The insured generally has the burden of proving the loss with reasonable certainty,[189] and that the interruption was necessary.[190]

The term "period of restoration" in the HSB policy means the period of time beginning at the time of the "accident" and continuing until the earlier of the date the physical damage to covered equipment is repaired or replaced or on which that damage could have been repaired or replaced with the exercise of "due diligence and dispatch," plus the number of days, if any, shown in the Declarations for Extended Period of Restoration.[191] The ISO Equipment Breakdown Protection Coverage Form defines the term somewhat differently. It says the period of restoration is the period of time that begins at the time of the breakdown, or 24 hours before the insurer receives notice of it, whichever is later, and ends five consecutive days after the date when the damaged property at the described premises is repaired or replaced with "reasonable speed and similar quality."[192]

Policies that provide business income coverage usually say that in determining the amount of payment, the insurer will consider the actual experience of the business before the "accident" and the probable experience the insured would have had without it.[193] Use of the phrase "actual experience" would allow the

---

186. HSB Freestyle Policy Form 6671 (10/2002) § G.5; ISO Form BM 00 20 07 01, § F.2. *Consider* New York Underwriters Ins. Co. v. Coffman, 540 S.W.2d 445, 452–53 (Tex. Civ. App.—Fort Worth, 1976) (policy was designed to provide coverage for all kinds of businesses with daily sales or production—including motels, hotels, retail establishments, and factories—and it was obvious the company intended to insure for loss of rental income of apartments).

187. HSB Freestyle Policy Form 6671 (10/2002) § A.2.c.(1).

188. *See, e.g.*, HSB Freestyle Policy Form 6671 (10/2002) § A.2.c.(2); ISO Form BM 00 20 07 01, § A.2.c. Another form of business interruption is "valued coverage" in which the insured receives a specified amount whether or not there is an actual loss of earnings; however, a *per diem* limit of liability usually applies along with limits on the number of days for which coverage is provided and per accident. Cozen, *Insuring Real Property*, § 5.07[1] (Matthew Bender & Co., 2015).

189. Jacobs Press v. Hartford Steam Boiler Inspection & Ins. Co., 1997 U.S. App. LEXIS 3769 (4th Cir. Mar. 4, 1997) (insured had burden of proving its business interruption loss claim strictly in accordance with policy terms and had to do so with reasonable certainty and without duplication as between "actual loss" and "extra expense" components of business interruption loss provision).

190. *See* Anderson & Middleton Lumber Co. v. Lumbermen's Mut. Cas. Co., 53 Wn. 2d 404, 410, 333 P.2d 938, 942 (1959), where the policy required that, as a condition of qualifying for *per diem* loss of business payments, the insured had to use "diligence and dispatch" in obtaining and installing replacement equipment. The court said the insured had the burden of showing that, with the use of diligence and dispatch, it was necessary for its business to remain closed for the time period claimed.

191. HSB Freestyle Policy Form 6671 (10/2002) § G.19.

192. ISO Form BM 00 20 07 01, § F.13.

193. HSB Freestyle Policy Form 6671 (10/2002) § A.2.c.(3).

insurer to insist that the insured produce evidence of its income. Additionally, where a business returns to partial operation, recovery may be based on the percentage of operation.[194]

The policies generally do not define either "business" or "income." A "business" is "an occupation, profession, or trade."[195] A dictionary definition of "income" is "the monetary payment received for goods or services or from other sources, as rents or investments."[196] A residential common interest community is not engaged in an occupation, profession, or trade.[197] The revenue it uses to pay its expenses—the common expenses that benefit all the residents—is derived from assessments it levies on the members of the CIC association. That revenue is more like a tax than revenues received for goods or services or rent or investment income. Indeed, Congress realized that it would be unfair to tax these revenues as the association is simply collecting money from its members to pay expenses on their behalf. Therefore, a CIC can elect to be treated as an exempt homeowners association. If it meets the applicable criteria, its membership dues, fees, or assessments are "exempt function income" and are not taxed.[198] CICs can have income that is taxable and meets the dictionary definition of "income." Often it is a small amount and received from lessees of association property or interest earned on funds in bank accounts. Some CICs, however, earn considerable rental income. For example, mid- or high-rise buildings may rent space on their roofs for communication antennae. The CIC may use this income for operating expenses, and its loss could impose a considerable financial hardship. If the shortfall is the result of a covered cause of loss, it should be covered by a business income clause even if it does not meet the definition of "business income."

[h] Utility Interruption

Some policies provide "utility interruption" coverage, which may require an additional premium.[199] When the insured has coverage for business income, extra expense, or spoilage damage, the utility interruption clause extends them

194. *See, e.g.*, Simkins Industries, Inc. v. Lexington Ins. Co., 42 Md. App. 396, 401 A.2d 181 (1979).

195. *Webster's New Universal Unabridged Dictionary* at 283 (Random House, 1966).

196. *Webster's New Universal Unabridged Dictionary* at 967 (Random House, 1966).

197. *Consider* Olde Colonial Vill. v. Millers Mut. Ins., 2002 Del. Super. LEXIS 341 (Del. Super. Ct. May 17, 2002), a property insurance case. The association sought "extra expense" coverage for the cost of relocating evacuated residents after the building was condemned as dangerous. The court, in finding the association was not entitled to reimbursement for any relocation expenses other than its own, observed that the association was in the "business" of "governing a condominium association," and its operations presumably included adopting bylaws, enforcing rules, keeping books, providing ordinary maintenance, and hiring and supervising necessary help.

198. 26 U.S.C. § 528.

199. *See, e.g.*, Kips Bay Endoscopy Ctr., PLLC v. Travelers Indem. Co., 2015 U.S. Dist. LEXIS 96957 (S.D.N.Y. July 24, 2015) (insureds purportedly paid additional premium to specifically include "utility failure" as covered cause of loss).

to include loss resulting from the interruption of utility services.[200] Conditions are placed on that coverage extension. In the Travelers policy, there are four conditions:

- The interruption must be the direct result of a breakdown—as defined by the policy—to covered equipment—again, as defined by the policy—owned, operated, or controlled by the local utility.
- That equipment has to be located more than 500 feet from the insured premises.
- The equipment has to be used to supply air conditioning, communication services, electric power, gas, heating, refrigeration, steam, water, or waste treatment to the insured premises.
- The interruption to the insured premises has to last at least the length of time shown on the Declarations Page—probably 12 or 24 hours—before coverage begins.[201]

In addition to the time limitation, a separate deductible will probably apply to the utility interruption coverage. If that deductible is large—for example, $10,000 or $25,000—a utility interruption loss may not exceed the deductible for the typical common interest community. Thus, if the coverage is only available for an additional premium and the CIC is unable, or unwilling, to pay for coverage with a lower deductible, the cost of that coverage may not be worth the possible benefit.

The Travelers policy also has a specific exclusion applicable to utility interruption coverage. It excludes any loss resulting from aircraft; civil commotion; collapse; freezing caused by cold weather; impact of aircraft, missiles, or vehicles; lightning; molten material; objects falling from aircraft or missiles; riot, smoke; vandalism; vehicles; weight of snow, ice, or sleet; acts of sabotage; or deliberate acts of load shedding by the supplying or distributing utility whether or not coverage for that cause of loss is provided by another policy or a self-insurance risk retention plan.[202]

[i] Errors and Omissions

An errors and omission clause is not so much a provision of coverage as a restoration of coverage that would have been in effect but for an error or omission—that is an unintentional, honest mistake—by the insured. For example, the ISO Equipment Breakdown Protection Coverage Form provides that the carrier will pay for a loss or damage that would not otherwise be payable because of any error or unintentional omission in the description or location of the insured

200. *See, e.g.*, ISO Form BM 00 20 07 01, § A.2.e.

201. Travelers EnergyMax 21, § A.2.d.

202. Travelers EnergyMax 21, § B.18. The exclusion adds that it applies to all resulting direct or indirect loss.

property, or in any subsequent amendments, any failure by error to include any premises owned or occupied by the insured at the inception date, or any error or unintentional omission by the insured that results in cancellation of any insured premises.[203] A condition of the coverage extension is that the insured report any errors or omissions on discovery. The errors and omission clause does not, however, extend coverage where the insured fails to obtain desired coverage or fails to provide information related to it that renders it ineffective.[204]

§ 11.08 Exclusions

The typical policy excludes perils commonly excluded in commercial property policies: earth movement, water, nuclear hazard, war or military action, and mold.[205] It may also contain a variety of exclusions unique to equipment breakdown coverage. Some of these are an accident to covered equipment while being tested; lack or excess of power, light, heat, steam, or refrigeration; and breakdown caused directly or indirectly by hail or windstorm, and deliberate acts, including vandalism, malicious mischief, and sabotage. As in other forms of insurance, the insured must initially show that the policy provides coverage after which the insurer has the burden to show that the specific language of the policy excludes coverage for the loss.[206] As is also generally the rule in insurance law, courts will construe an ambiguous exclusion against the carrier and find coverage.[207]

When reading the exclusions, it is important to examine the prefatory language. The ISO Equipment Breakdown Protection Coverage Form says the insurer will not pay for loss or damage caused directly or indirectly by any of the excluded perils, that the loss or damage is excluded regardless of any other cause

203. ISO Form BM 00 20 07 01, § A.2.h.

204. *See Boiler and Machinery Coverage Form* (Summit Business Media, 2012).

205. Malecki, *Equipment Breakdown Insurance: Too Important to Ignore!*, at 5 (Adjusting Today, 2009), available at: http://adjustersinternational.com/publications/adjusting-today/equipment-breakdown-insurance/1/ (of 21 exclusions in ISO form EB 00 20, about six apply because those losses can be handled by property insurance and others apply unless coverages are selected under policy). A standard endorsement adds windstorm or hail, smoke, aircraft or vehicles, riot or civil commotion, and vandalism to the list of exclusions. ISO Form BM 99 39 07 90.

206. Leprino Foods Co. v. Factory Mut. Ins. Co., 453 F.3d 1281, 1287 (10th Cir. 2006) (insurer must establish that exclusion applies and is not subject to any other reasonable interpretation); Fire Ins. Exch. & Farmers Ins. Exch. v. Pring-Wilson, 831 F. Supp. 2d 493, 506 (D. Mass. 2011).

207. *See, e.g.*, St. Paul Fire & Marine Ins. Co. v. Compaq Computer Corp., 539 F.3d 809, 819 (8th Cir. 2008) (courts construing exclusionary clauses have to adopt construction urged by insured as long as that construction is not unreasonable); Boyd & Stevenson Coal Co. v. Dir., OWCP, 407 F.3d 663, 668–69 (4th Cir. 2005) (general principle of contract law is that exclusionary language in contract will be construed against insurer); National Union Fire Ins. Co. v. Hudson Energy Co., 811 S.W.2d 552, 555 (Tex. 1991) (exceptions or limitations on liability are strictly construed against insurer and in favor of insured); St. Paul Fire & Marine Ins. Co. v. S.L. Nusbaum & Co., 227 Va. 407, 411, 316 S.E.2d 734, 736 (1984) (language in policy purporting to exclude certain events from coverage will be construed most strongly against insurer).

or event that contributes concurrently or in any sequence to it, and that the exclusions apply whether or not widespread damage results or a substantial area is affected.[208] The HSB policy provides the carrier will not pay for any excluded loss, damage, or expense, even though any other cause or event contributes concurrently or in any sequence, or caused directly or indirectly by any of the excluded perils, whether or not caused by or resulting from an "accident."[209]

Under the "efficient proximate cause" doctrine as applied to property coverage, when a loss is caused by a combination of covered and excluded perils, there is coverage if the covered peril was the efficient proximate cause of the loss.[210] In response, insurers add "anti-concurrent cause" language to their policies, which defeats operation of the efficient proximate cause rule.[211] An example of that language is the "concurrently or in any sequence" wording that is found in both the ISO and HSB policies as discussed above. In most states, that language will negate the "efficient proximate cause" doctrine.[212] However, in a couple of states—notably California and North Dakota—courts hold, based on applicable statutes, that an insurer may not contractually preclude coverage when the efficient proximate cause of a loss is a covered peril.[213] Additionally, the concurrent

---

208. ISO Form BM 00 20 07 01, § B. *See* Hartford Steam Boiler Inspection & Ins. Co. v. Quantum Chem. Corp., 1996 U.S. Dist. LEXIS 17551 (N.D. Ill. Nov. 12, 1996) (under concurrent cause provision loss is not covered so long as any cause of loss is excluded).

209. HSB Freestyle Policy Form 6671 (10/2002) § B.

210. *See, e.g.*, Kelly v. Farmers Ins. Co., 281 F. Supp. 2d 1290, 1296 (W.D. Okla. 2003) (efficient proximate cause doctrine applies only when two or more identifiable causes, at least one of which is covered under policy and at least one of which is excluded, contribute to single property loss; if insured successfully demonstrates that proximate cause of loss is covered, entire loss is covered notwithstanding that event in chain of causation was specifically excluded from coverage); Murray v. State Farm Fire & Cas. Co., 203 W. Va. 477, 487, 509 S.E.2d 1, 11 (1998) (when loss is caused by combination of covered and specifically excluded risks, loss is covered if covered risk was proximate cause of loss). *See also* American Steam Boiler Ins. Co. v. Chicago Sugar Ref. Co., 57 F. 294, 301–02 (7th Cir. 1892) (where loss by fire was not covered and fire caused explosion, entire result was traceable to fire in kilns as efficient cause; that explosion would not have happened if fire had been better managed and door of kiln been kept closed did not matter as attendants, while perhaps not choosing best and safest method of extinguishing flames, acted in good faith) *See generally* Bell, *A Concurrent Mess and a Call for Clarity in First-Party Property Insurance Coverage Analysis*, 18 Conn. Ins. L.J. 73 (2011/2012).

211. *See* St. Mary's Area Water Auth. v. St. Paul Fire & Marine Ins. Co., 472 F. Supp. 2d 630, 636 (M.D. Pa. 2007) (an anti-concurrent cause clause defeats operation of efficient proximate cause rule).

212. *See, e.g.*, Preferred Mut. Ins. Co. v. Travelers Cos., 955 F. Supp. 9, 11–12 (D. Mass. 1997) (under "chain of events" rule, insured would recover for otherwise excluded loss if efficient proximate cause of that loss was covered; however, where preamble provides policy did not apply to losses resulting directly or indirectly from particular proximate cause, chain of events rule was avoided and liability was effectively excluded without regard to efficient proximate cause).

213. *See, e.g.*, W. Nat'l Mut. Ins. Co. v. Univ. of N.D., 643 N.W.2d 4 (N.D. 2002), where the court noted that pursuant to "anti-concurrent cause" language some courts have held the parties are free to contract out of the efficient proximate cause doctrine, but North Dakota has statutorily adopted that doctrine and, therefore, a property insurer may not contractually preclude coverage when the efficient proximate cause of a loss is a covered peril.

clause does not apply where there was no "concurrent" or other "contributing" cause of the loss at issue.[214]

[1] Explosion

The original purpose of what is today often called equipment breakdown insurance was to protect from the risk of boiler explosion or catastrophic failure.[215] Therefore, it is somewhat surprising to find that modern policies have an explosion exclusion. These exclusions, however, do not eliminate all coverage for explosions; rather, they limit it. The purpose is to avoid an overlap in coverage with the commercial property policy. The policy language of these exclusions varies.

The HSB policy is rather straightforward. It excludes coverage for damage or expense caused directly or indirectly by a "combustion explosion," or any other explosion, except of steam boilers, steam piping, steam engines, or steam turbines, whether or not caused by or resulting from an "accident."[216] In an Illinois case a court considered language in a different HSB boiler and machinery policy. There was an exception from the explosion exclusion for a loss "caused by or resulting from an explosion of an 'object' of a kind described." A list of seven specific objects followed. The incident at issue was the explosion of a steel tank called a "pulp digester." The question then was whether the pulp digester was "of a kind" listed on the catalog of objects that were excepted from the exclusion. The court concluded that pulp digesters were "a kind of object, but not one of the kinds in the list."[217] The lesson for policyholders is that they should establish—and make sure it is explicit in the policy—before an accident or breakdown which equipment is covered by the policy and which is excluded.

The Travelers policy has a more involved provision. It excludes coverage for explosion generally, and then states it will pay for direct loss or damage by an explosion of a steam boiler, electric steam generator, steam piping, steam turbine, steam engine, gas turbine, or any other moving or rotating machinery (when the

---

214. Hartford Steam Boiler Inspection & Ins. Co. v. Quantum Chem. Corp., 1996 U.S. Dist. LEXIS 17551 (N.D. Ill. Nov. 12, 1996) (purpose of concurrent cause provision is to eliminate need for expensive factual inquiry; however, it is not meant to give insurer undeserved protection where loss was complete before excluded peril occurred but to preclude need for determining how much damage was done by covered peril when both covered and uncovered peril contribute to loss; if equipment failed beyond repair as result of crack before it exploded, concurrent cause provision would be inapplicable because loss was complete before explosion occurred; however, if crack caused damage that could have been repaired, then explosion clearly destroyed repairable equipment and would have to be regarded as concurrent or contributing cause of loss).

215. 5 Jeffery E. Thomas, *New Appleman on Insurance Law Library Edition* § 51.01[2][a] (LexisNexis 2023).

216. HSB Freestyle Policy Form 6671 (10/2002) § B.1.a.

217. Stone Container Corp. v. Hartford Steam Boiler Inspection & Ins. Co., 165 F.3d 1157, 1161 (7th Cir. 1999) (distinction between fired and unfired pressure vessels helps to resolve question as these are two different kinds of pressure vessel with one including steam boilers, but not pulp digesters, and other including pulp digesters but not steam boilers).

explosion is caused by centrifugal force or mechanical breakdown) unless otherwise excluded.[218] There are then two additional explosion exclusions. One is for combustion explosions, including those resulting in a breakdown, occurring at the same time as a breakdown, or ensuing from a breakdown.[219] A "breakdown" is failure of pressure or vacuum equipment; mechanical failure, including rupture[220] or bursting caused by centrifugal force; and electrical failure, including arcing, resulting physical damage requiring repair or replacement.[221] A second specific exclusion is for an explosion within the furnace of a chemical recovery boiler or the gas passages from the furnace to the atmosphere.[222]

The ISO Boiler and Machinery Coverage Form generally excludes a loss caused by or resulting from an explosion, but it does cover losses caused by or resulting from an explosion of a *covered object*.[223] It also excludes coverage for an explosion that occurs at the same time as an accident or ensues from an accident,[224] or that is of gas or unconsumed fuel within the furnace of a boiler or fired vessel or within the passages from that furnace to the atmosphere.[225]

One problem with any exclusion for explosions is that the term is not easily defined[226] and is generally not defined by policies. The usual definition of the term is a violent bursting, or expansion, with noise, following sudden production

218. Travelers EnergyMax 21, § B.6.

219. Travelers EnergyMax 21, § B.7.

220. *See* Cleveland Drop Forge Co. v. Travelers' Indem. Co., 114 Ohio St. 549, 151 N.E. 671 (1926) (breaking apart of boiler head, in which rivets were sprung, constituted "rupture" within meaning of policy for which insurer was liable); Louisville College of Dentistry v. Hartford Steam Boiler Inspection & Ins. Co., 185 Ky. 778, 215 S.W. 941 (1919) (where irregular, semicircular opening developed in casting on front of boiler, there was sufficient evidence it was rupture as defined in policy). *See also* Travellers Indem. Co. v. B & B Ice & Coal Co., 248 Ky. 443, 446, 58 S.W.2d 640, 641 (1933) (it is not indispensably essential that sudden rupture be accompanied by extremely loud noise).

221. Travelers EnergyMax 21, § F.1.

222. Travelers EnergyMax 21, § B.8.

223. ISO Form BM 00 25 02 91, § B.4.a. The exclusion can be modified by endorsement. *See* ISO Form BM 99 40 06 95. The endorsement provides the insurer will pay for direct loss or damage caused by an explosion of one of the "objects" specified in the endorsement if it is covered by the policy and described on an "object definitions" endorsement that is a part of the policy and that is not otherwise excluded.

224. ISO Form BM 00 25 02 91, § B.4.b.

225. ISO Form BM 00 25 02 91, § B.4.c.

226. Julius Hyman & Co. v. American Motorists Ins. Co., 136 F. Supp. 830, 833–34 (D. Colo. 1955) (exact line between explosion and something less is not susceptible of very exact measure or definition, and terms "accident" as defined by policies and "explosion" as commonly understood are not necessarily synonymous); Bower v. Aetna Ins. Co., 54 F. Supp. 897, 898 (D. Tex. 1944) ("explosion" is variously used and is not term that admits of exact definition and has no fixed and definite meaning, either in ordinary speech or in law, and seems to be general term unlimited in its application); Crombie & Co. v. Employers' Fire Ins. Co., 250 S.W.2d 472, 474 (Tex. App. 1952) (generally "explosion" does not admit of definite definition, having no fixed and definite meaning in ordinary speech or in law). *Compare* Hartford Steam Boiler Inspection & Ins. Co. v. Quantum Chem. Corp., 1996 U.S. Dist. LEXIS 17551 (N.D. Ill. Nov. 12, 1996) (rejecting argument that "explosion" has no generally accepted meaning).

of great pressure, but every sudden tearing asunder from pressure from within is not an explosion.[227] In the final analysis, courts give the word its "ordinary-language meaning."[228]

[2] Fire

All equipment breakdown policies exclude coverage for fire. The reason for the exclusion is that all commercial property policies cover losses from fire. The specific exclusion may be short and to the point.[229] It may also specifically exclude coverage for loss from smoke from a fire,[230] or for a fire that occurs at the same time as an accident or ensues from one.[231] Courts interpret a fire that occurs at the same time as an accident to mean a "hostile fire" and find the exclusion inapplicable if a fire is not hostile.[232] A fire is not hostile when it is required for operation of the equipment and is the ordinary fire required for its operation.[233] As

---

227. Hartford Fire Ins. Co. v. Empire Coal Min. Co., 30 F.2d 794, 798 (8th Cir. 1929) (usual elements characteristic of explosion are sudden and rapid combustion, great expansion of air, and sharp noise or report). *See also* Pre-Cast Concrete Products, Inc. v. Home Ins. Co., 417 F.2d 1323, 1326 (7th Cir. 1969); Bower v. Aetna Ins. Co., 54 F. Supp. 897, 898 (D. Tex. 1944) (noting that authorities make "explosion" synonymous with "bursting"). *Compare* Crombie & Co. v. Employers' Fire Ins. Co., 250 S.W.2d 472, 475 (Tex. App. 1952) (that there was corrosion and erosion preceding blowing or exploding of packing around valve stem mattered little if at all; insurance coverage was to protect against weaknesses and breakdowns, and evidence supported finding there was explosion of ammonia, even though intensity or degree was much less than in "great eruptions").

228. *See* Stone Container Corp. v. Hartford Steam Boiler Inspection & Ins. Co., 165 F.3d 1157, 1160 (7th Cir. 1999) (case law gives word "explosion," when it appears without definition in insurance contract, its ordinary-language meaning). *See also* Hartford Steam Boiler Inspection & Ins. Co. v. Quantum Chem. Corp., 1996 U.S. Dist. LEXIS 17551 (N.D. Ill. Nov. 12, 1996) (plain meaning of "explosion" covered incident in which sudden increase in pressure caused object to rupture and release its contents).

229. *See, e.g.*, Travelers EnergyMax 21, § B.7. *See also* American Steam Boiler Ins. Co. v. Chicago Sugar Ref. Co., 57 F. 294, 299 (7th Cir. 1892) (there was no provision in policy for insurance against fire and coverage would, at best, rest on inference and construction and to guard against any possible construction or inference express provision barred indemnity for "any loss or damage by fire resulting from any cause whatever").

230. HSB Freestyle Policy Form 6671 (10/2002) § B.1.a.(1).

231. ISO Form BM 00 25 02 91, § B.4.b. *Consider* Associated Electric Cooperative v. Mutual Boiler & Machinery Ins. Co., 492 F. Supp. 410 (W.D. Mo. 1980) (exclusion does not require that each separate piece of equipment be damaged by fire, but only that fire ensue).

232. *See, e.g.*, Good Canning Co. v. London Guarantee & Acci. Co., 128 F. Supp. 778, 788 (D. Ark. 1955) (insurer argued damage to boiler was caused directly by fire under it that became "hostile fire" because of lack of sufficient water in boiler, and therefore loss was excluded; however, court found damage was from pressure of steam or water in boiler and, since exclusion applied only to hostile fires and damage was not caused by hostile fire, exclusion was inapplicable); First Nat'l Bank v. Royal Indem. Co., 193 Iowa 221, 186 N.W. 934 (1922) ("fire" as used in policy has no reference to fire under boiler, without which it could not be operated or used, but rather to what may be called "hostile fire," thus emphasizing to policyholder that insurer assumes no risk of fire hazard from any outside source).

233. *See, e.g.*, Dixie Pine Products Co. v. Maryland Casualty Co., 133 F.2d 583, 585 (5th Cir. 1943) (where accident occurred in normal course of operations, and risk incident to escape of

one court observed, the exception for fire is in the "nature of a notice or warning to the property owner" that the insurer is "not assuming the risk of ordinary fire hazard, but confines its liability to those risks which pertain directly and immediately to the maintenance, operation, and use" of equipment for its designed purposes.[234]

The exclusion, therefore, applies to fires that originate *outside* the covered equipment.[235] In a case involving a fire in the boiler room of a condominium, the first sentence of the fire exclusion was nearly identical to that in the ISO Boiler and Machinery Coverage Form: "Fire or combustion explosion that occurs at the same time as an 'accident' or that ensues from an 'accident.'" The fire allegedly occurred when a leaky seal in a fuel pump that supplied oil to a burner that heated the boiler allowed oil to be propelled into a burner tube where it caught fire. The fire caused melting that allowed the burner to fall, damaging the oil line and releasing oil that caught fire and burned. The court said the leak in the pump was an accident to an object and, therefore, the burning of the fuel supply "ensued" from an accident and was plainly excluded. The second sentence of the exclusion provided that with regard to *electrical equipment* that formed part of an "object"—that is, covered equipment—coverage for any fire or explosion outside that object that occurred at the same time as an "accident" or ensued from one was excluded.[236] This portion of the exclusion was inapplicable because the fire did not occur as a result of the failure of any electrical equipment, or as the court laconically offered, to characterize the pump as electrical would be nonsense.

The Arkansas Supreme Court followed that decision in a case in which a plant was damaged by fire when an ammonia filter ruptured on an icemaker, leading to the escape of liquid ammonia that entered the control panel of one of the ice machines and exploded. The entire plant was heavily damaged in the ensuing fire. The policy excluded coverage for fire or explosion outside the equipment—the ice machine—that occurred at the same time as, or ensued from, a sudden and accidental breakdown of that equipment. The court said the filter

---

highly explosive solvent was hazard insured against and explosion resulting from contact of solvent with fire was reaction as certain as "laws of chemistry," that explosion was touched off by fire is of no significance, as it was "friendly fire" confined to burning in boiler, place where parties contemplated it should be); Holmes v. Employers' Liability Assurance Corp., 70 Ohio App. 239, 259, 43 N.E.2d 746, 754 (1941) (normal fire in firebox under boiler would not be hostile fire, but where fire is operated in manner or under conditions that it gets out of control and develops extreme heat, it must then be considered hostile). *See also* St. John v. American Mut. Fire & Marine Ins. Co., 11 N.Y. 516, 518 (1854) (where fire is applied by design, as in culinary and several manufacturing processes, and loss occurs in consequence of overheating or other misapplication of fire to subject on which it was intended to operate, and injury is limited to that particular subject, damage is not considered loss by fire).

234. First Nat'l Bank v. Royal Indem. Co., 193 Iowa 221, 229, 186 N.W. 934, 937–38 (1922).

235. *Consider* St. John v. American Mut. Fire & Marine Ins. Co., 11 N.Y. 516 (1854).

236. Preferred Mut. Ins. Co. v. Travelers Cos., 127 F.3d 136, 138 (1st Cir. 1997).

rupture was an accident to covered equipment and the fire was *outside* of it.[237] The dissent raised an important point. The policy exclusion did not say whether the fire or explosion had to *originate* outside the covered equipment for the exclusion to apply, or merely *occur* outside it. It was undisputed that the explosion and fire originated *inside* the ice machine. The dissenting judge called the exclusion language "confusing and muddled." The exclusionary language in the case before the court, as well as in the condominium boiler room case, could be read as denying coverage only for explosions or fires that *originate* outside of the covered equipment. By accepting the broader interpretation of the insurer, the majority was placing its imprimatur on one interpretation of the "highly questionable exclusionary language."[238]

An exclusion may be modified in its application to specific equipment. For example, in one case the policy said that for any electrical equipment forming a part of an object, it excluded losses caused by or resulting from fire or explosion *outside* the object occurring at the same time as an accident or ensuing from an accident. The argument was put forward, but not specifically addressed by the court, that by excluding fires or explosions outside of the object, the policy implicitly provided coverage for fires or explosions originating *within* the object.[239]

The fact that a boiler and machinery policy may provide coverage for some fire-related losses does not make it fire insurance.[240]

[3] Deterioration, Corrosion, and Wear and Tear

Some policies may eliminate coverage for deterioration, corrosion, erosion, and wear and tear by specifically excluding them from the definition of "accident."[241] Other policies have an explicit exclusion.[242] The exclusion will ordinarily be prefaced by the statement that the carrier will not pay for loss or damage *caused* directly or indirectly by one of the excepted conditions. To obtain benefit of the exclusion, the insurer has to do more than put forward evidence of one of the

237. Ratliff Enters., Inc. v. American Emplrs. Ins. Co., 334 Ark. 547, 975 S.W.2d 837 (1998).

238. Ratliff Enters., Inc. v. American Emplrs. Ins. Co., 334 Ark. 547, 557, 975 S.W.2d 837, 843 (1998) (Brown, J. dissenting).

239. Continental Ins. Co. v. Acadia Ins. Co., 974 F. Supp. 371 (D. Vt. 1997).

240. Enosburg Falls v. Hartford Steam Boiler Inspection & Ins. Co., 117 Vt. 114, 123, 85 A.2d 577, 583 (1952) (where policy narrowly limited loss by fire to within object resulting from accident and insured against many kinds of damage other than fire, it afforded insurance of specified, particular, definite, and restricted kind and was not general fire insurance policy as to generator).

241. *See, e.g.*, HSB Freestyle Policy Form 6671 (10/2002) § B.1.b.(1) (depletion, deterioration, rust, corrosion, erosion, settling, and wear and tear are not accidents).

242. *See, e.g.*, ISO Form BM 00 20 07 01, § B.11 (excluding coverage for depletion, deterioration, corrosion, erosion, or wear and tear); Travelers EnergyMax 21, § B.12 (excluding coverage for depletion, deterioration, corrosion, erosion, wear and tear, rust, fungus, decay, wet or dry rot, and mold).

excepted conditions; it must show the condition caused damage, whether directly or indirectly.[243]

A policy may add that, while the carrier will not pay for a loss caused by an excepted condition, if a breakdown occurs, the policy will pay the resulting loss or damage.[244] Policies do not define deterioration, corrosion, erosion, or wear and tear. Those terms have, however, been frequently construed by courts. In one well known B&M case a federal court said that the "terms 'depletion,' 'deterioration,' 'corrosion' and 'erosion' . . . in common understanding can mean no more than the action of normally expected elements of stress, friction, and the daily traumas of its life to the object during its normal life expectancy."[245] Where chemical action of sulfuric acid caused holes to appear in steel, a court called that corrosion.[246] Another court, relying on the *Webster's Dictionary*, called corrosion a gradual wearing away or disintegration by a chemical process, for example, the rusting of iron.[247] "Wear and tear" has been defined as the "ordinary and natural deterioration or abrasion" an object experiences by expected contacts between its component parts and outside objects during the period of its natural life expectancy.[248]

[4] Water/Flood

Some policies merely exclude "flood," although they do not define it.[249] Most policies exclude water and define that to include flood.[250] These policies bar coverage for three categories of water:

243. J.O.B. Invs., LLC v. Gootee Servs., LLC, 908 F. Supp. 2d 771 (E.D. La. 2012) (insurer cannot merely put forth evidence that air conditioning unit was corroded; rather, policy exclusion is triggered only if corrosion caused damage, whether directly or indirectly).

244. ISO Form BM 00 20 07 01, § B.11. *See also* Travelers EnergyMax 21, § B.12 (if "breakdown" ensues, carrier will pay ensuing loss or damage not otherwise excluded).

245. Cyclops Corp. v. Home Ins. Co., 352 F. Supp. 931, 936 (W.D. Pa. 1973).

246. Arkwright-Boston Mfrs. Mut. Ins. Co. v. Wausau Paper Mills Co., 818 F.2d 591 (7th Cir. 1987) (where steel was eaten away or diminished by chemical action of sulfuric acid to point that holes appeared, corrosion was cause; speed at which corrosion took place was not relevant to whether it fell under corrosion exclusion).

247. Lakeshore Marine, Inc. v. Hartford Acc. & Indem. Co., 164 Ga. App. 417, 296 S.E.2d 418 (1982).

248. Cyclops Corp. v. Home Ins. Co., 352 F. Supp. 931, 936 (W.D. Pa. 1973) (modifiers "ordinary" or "natural" add nothing to commonly understood meaning of "wear and tear," and their use is "typical lawyer's redundancy").

249. ISO Form BM 00 25 02 91, § B.4.g.

250. *See, e.g.*, HSB Freestyle Policy Form 6671 (10/2002) § B.1.f; ISO Form BM 00 20 07 01, § B.3; Travelers EnergyMax 21, § B.3.

- Flood, surface water,[251] waves, tides, tidal waves, overflow of any body of water, or spray from any of them, and all whether or not driven by wind;[252]
- Mudslides or mudflow;[253] and
- Water damage from backup of sewer,[254] drains, or drainage piping.[255]

Some policies add a fourth category: water damage caused by discharge or leakage of sprinkler systems or domestic water piping.[256] There is often a separate exclusion for water or other means employed to extinguish a fire, even when the attempt is unsuccessful.[257] Where fire damage is covered, the loss is not necessarily excluded because there was also water damage caused by efforts to extinguish the fire.[258]

A policy may have exceptions to the water/flood exclusion. The HSB policy will pay for the amount actually spent to dry out electrical "covered equipment," subject to the applicable deductible, but will not pay more than the actual cash value[259] or to replace the equipment or for any other loss, damage, or expense.[260] The ISO Boiler and Machinery Coverage Form provides that if an "accident"

251. *See* State v. N.D. State Univ., 694 N.W.2d 225 (2005) (interpreting HSB policy; finding surface water is not limited to water whose flow has not been altered in any way by paved surfaces, buildings, or other structures).

252. The Travelers policy adds "tsunami." Travelers EnergyMax 21, § B.3.

253. Mudslides and mudflow are covered by the Standard Flood Insurance Policy. *See* General Property Form Standard Flood Insurance Policy, at 2 (June 2014); Residential Condominium Building Association Policy Standard Flood Insurance Policy, at 2 (June 2014). The SFIP defines "mudflow" as a river of liquid and flowing mud on the surfaces of normally dry land areas, as when earth is carried by a current of water." General Property Form Standard Flood Insurance Policy, at 5 (June 2014); Residential Condominium Building Association Policy Standard Flood Insurance Policy, at 5 (June 2014).

254. There may be coverage where this exclusion is omitted. *See, e.g.*, W. Nat'l Mut. Ins. Co. v. Univ. of N.D., 643 N.W.2d 4 (N.D. 2002) (where boiler and machinery policy did not explicitly exclude coverage for sewer backup, insurer conceded it provided that coverage).

255. The HSB policy excludes water that backs up or overflows from a sewer, drain, or sump. HSB Freestyle Policy Form 6671 (10/2002) § B.1.f.(3).

256. ISO Form BM 00 20 07 01, § B.3.d. The Travelers policy adds sewer piping. Travelers EnergyMax 21, § B.3.d.

257. *See, e.g.*, ISO Form BM 00 25 02 91, § B.4.e; Travelers EnergyMax 21, § B.10.

258. Jacobs Press v. Hartford Steam Boiler Inspection & Ins. Co., 1997 U.S. App. LEXIS 3769 (4th Cir. Mar. 4, 1997) (where insurer conceded fire inside printing press could have caused loss, even in part, fire could have been deemed responsible for entire loss and jury could fairly conclude it rendered printing press, though perhaps usable to some extent, essentially undependable thereafter, whether or not there was also water damage in form of rust).

259. *See* Travellers Indem. Co. v. B & B Ice & Coal Co., 248 Ky. 448, 446, 58 S.W.2d 640, 642 (1933) (term "cash value" means price boiler would bring when offered for sale by one who desires to sell, but is not compelled to do so, and is bought by one who desires to purchase, but is not compelled to do so).

260. HSB Freestyle Policy Form 6671 (10/2002) § B.1.f.

results from a flood, the carrier will pay for "direct damage"[261] to covered property caused by that accident.[262] For example, river flooding swept trees downstream, and the trees struck steam pipes belonging to the insured that crossed the river. The insurer conceded that the breaking of those pipes, though caused by flooding, was an accident within the meaning of its policy.[263]

The reason for excluding flood damage is that coverage for it is available under a FEMA Standard Flood Insurance Policy (SFIP). The building coverage portion of the SFIP specifically covers central air conditioners, elevator equipment, fire-extinguishing apparatus, fire sprinkler systems, walk-in freezers, furnace pumps and machinery for operating pumps, and ventilating equipment.[264] The SFIP in some cases excludes coverage for lower levels or basements, but even then, it specifically covers:

- Central air conditioners;
- Electrical junction and circuit breaker boxes;
- Elevators, dumbwaiters, and related equipment, except for related equipment installed below the base flood elevation after September 30, 1987;
- Fuel tanks and the fuel in them;
- Furnaces and hot water heaters;
- Heat pumps;
- Pumps and tanks used in solar energy systems;
- Sump pumps; and
- Well water tanks and pumps.

The purpose of this list, when read in conjunction with the comparable list in Coverage B of the SFIP for personal property, is to give a clear picture as to what items are insured as fixtures, machinery, and equipment under Coverage A of the SFIP for the building, and what items are insured as personal property under Coverage B.[265] Coverage B must be separately purchased, and it generally covers personal property inside the fully enclosed insured building[266] against

261. *See* Preferred Mut. Ins. Co. v. Travelers Cos., 955 F. Supp. 9, 11 (D. Mass. 1997) (noting lack of definition of "direct damage").

262. ISO Form BM 00 25 02 91, § B.4.g.

263. Simkins Industries, Inc. v. Lexington Ins. Co., 42 Md. App. 396, 401 A.2d 181 (1979) (silt and sand that entered turbines through broken pipes constituted "direct damage").

264. General Property Form Standard Flood Insurance Policy, at 7–8 (June 2014); Residential Condominium Building Association Policy Standard Flood Insurance Policy, at 7 (June 2014).

265. Studio Frames, Ltd. v. Std. Fire Ins. Co., 483 F.3d 239, 246 (4th Cir. 2007).

266. *See* Riverside Bldg. Supply, Inc. v. Federal Emergency Management Agency, 723 F.2d 1159 (4th Cir. 1983) (where property was stored in "umbrella building," which had no walls and consisted of roof supported by columns, payment properly refused on ground there was no authority to insure as "contents" were not located in enclosed building).

direct physical loss by or from flood.[267] Under the General Property Form SFIP, the personal property must be either owned solely by the insured,[268] or in the case of a condominium, owned solely by the condominium association and used exclusively in the conduct of the business affairs of the association or owned in common by the unit owners of the association.[269] There is a SFIP called the Residential Condominium Building Association Policy, and under it the personal property has to either be owned by the unit owners of the association in common, meaning property in which each unit owner has an undivided ownership interest, or owned solely by the association and used exclusively in the "conduct of the business affairs" of the association.[270]

[5] Earth Movement

While the language varies, almost all policies exclude coverage for "earth movement." The HSB policy excludes coverage for loss or damage caused directly or indirectly by earth movement, whether natural or human-made, *including, but not limited to*, earthquakes, shocks, tremors, subsidence, landslides, rock falls, earth sinking, sinkhole collapse, or tsunamis.[271] The ISO Boiler and Machinery Coverage Form excludes coverage for accidents caused directly or indirectly by earth movement, *including, but not limited to*, earthquakes, landslides, mudslides, subsidence, or volcanic eruptions.[272] Both policies provide that their exclusion is not limited to the specifically named earth movements. One authority notes that it is unclear whether some of these exclusions only apply to "natural movement" or also include "human movement."[273]

In one case, instead of an earth movement exclusion, the policy provided that the breakdown of any structure or foundation supporting a covered object or any part of it was not an accident and therefore not covered.[274] The policyholder was a company that owned a fish processing plant that stood along the waterfront of a bay. An enormous earthquake set off massive submarine slides.

---

267. General Property Form Standard Flood Insurance Policy, at 11 (June 2014); Residential Condominium Building Association Policy Standard Flood Insurance Policy, at 10 (June 2014).

268. *See* Cardon Prop. No. 4, LLC v. Fid. Nat'l Indem. Ins. Co., 58 F. Supp. 3d 645, 655 (E.D. La. 2014) (insured cannot recover for personal property that it did not own at time of loss).

269. General Property Form Standard Flood Insurance Policy, at 11 (June 2014).

270. Residential Condominium Building Association Policy Standard Flood Insurance Policy, at 10 (June 2014).

271. HSB Freestyle Policy Form 6671 (10/2002) § B.1.c.

272. ISO Form BM 00 25 02 91, § B.4.i.

273. Malecki, *Equipment Breakdown Insurance: Too Important to Ignore!*, at 5 (Adjusting Today, 2009), available at: http://adjustersinternational.com/publications/adjusting-today/equipment-breakdown-insurance/1/.

274. Fidelity & Casualty Co. v. Halibut Producers Cooperative, 73 Wn. 2d 153, 154, 437 P.2d 182, 183 (1968).

The plant plunged into the bay. The company claimed coverage under its boiler and machinery insurance policy, and the insurer sought a declaration that that it was not obligated to pay for the losses. The trial court ruled that if the damage to the covered objects was caused by a seismic wave and it occurred before the breakdown of any structure or foundation supporting those objects, there was an "accidental breakdown" within the meaning of the policy and the losses were covered. The jury, however, found that the damage was caused by earth slides before the seismic wave. Therefore, there was no coverage. The appellate court affirmed.

[6] Ordinance or Law

An ordinance or law exclusion is common to all forms of property insurance. The ostensible purpose of the exclusion is to prevent the insurer from providing the insured with a windfall: property rendered more valuable than that which was damaged or destroyed by virtue of meeting the mandates of an ordinance or law.[275] Many policies provide some ordinance or law coverage but limit it by exclusion, while others simply exclude it. An example of the latter is the ISO Boiler and Machinery Coverage Form. It provides that the carrier will not pay for any "increase in loss" caused by or resulting from enforcement of an ordinance, law, regulation, rule, or ruling regulating or restricting repair, replacement, alteration, use, operation, construction, or installation.[276] The exclusion may also apply to the cost of cleanup or disposal of covered property[277] and the cost of a study required by government officials as a precondition of returning to operations.[278]

Under the HSB policy the carrier will not pay for loss, damage, or expense caused directly or indirectly by enforcement of, or change in, any ordinance, law, regulation, rule, or ruling regulating or restricting repair, replacement, alteration, use, operation, construction, or installation, except as specifically provided otherwise in the coverage section of the policy.[279]

---

275. Wood, *The Insurance Fallout Following Hurricane Andrew: Whether Insurance Companies Are Legally Obligated to Pay for Building Code Upgrades Despite the "Ordinance or Law" Exclusion Contained in Most Homeowners Policies*, 48 U. Miami L. Rev. 949, 951 (1994).

276. ISO Form BM 00 25 02 91, § B.1. Increase in loss includes expenses incurred beyond those for which the carrier would have paid if no substance declared to be hazardous to health by a governmental agency had been involved in the "accident." *See also* Hartford Steam Boiler Inspection & Ins. Co. v. Quantum Chem. Corp., 1996 U.S. Dist. LEXIS 17551 (N.D. Ill. Nov. 12, 1996) (use of word "increase" makes clear that exclusion is meant to apply even in situations where loss has occurred and insured must take additional action related to that loss to comply).

277. Travelers EnergyMax 21, § B.1.

278. Hartford Steam Boiler Inspection & Ins. Co. v. Quantum Chem. Corp., 1996 U.S. Dist. LEXIS 17551 (N.D. Ill. Nov. 12, 1996) (provision would not apply to costs of study based on insured's own reasonable safety concerns).

279. HSB Freestyle Policy Form 6671 (10/2002) § B.1.b.

There is ordinarily nothing in an ordinance and law exclusion that limits it to laws or rulings of authorities related to the permitting process for the replacement of damaged property.[280]

[7] Perils Covered by Other Insurance

Most equipment breakdown policies exclude coverage caused by certain prescribed causes of loss if coverage for it is provided by another policy whether or not collectible. Thus, if there is no other policy, the loss may be covered. The exclusion may apply when there is a self-insurance risk retention plan.[281] The HSB policy exclusion applies whether or not the other policy provides the same coverage or scope of coverage.[282] The prescribed causes of loss vary from policy to policy. The ISO Equipment Breakdown Protection Coverage Form excludes breakdowns caused by aircraft or vehicles; freezing from cold weather; lightning; sinkhole collapse; smoke; riot; civil commotion or vandalism; or the weight of snow, ice, or sleet.[283] The Travelers policy excludes breakdowns caused directly or indirectly by aircraft; civil commotion; collapse; freezing caused by cold weather; impact by a missile, aircraft, or vehicle; lightning; molten material; objects falling from aircraft or missiles; riot; smoke; vandalism; vehicles; and the weight of snow, ice, or sleet.[284] The HSB policy will not pay for accidents caused by or resulting from falling objects; weight of snow, ice, or sleet; water damage (meaning discharge or leakage of water or steam as the direct result of breaking apart or cracking of any part of a system or appliance containing water or steam); collapse; glass breakage; freezing caused by cold weather; and discharge of molten material from equipment, including the heat from that discharged material.[285] However, when the excluded peril happens at a location not described on the Declarations Page and causes an electrical surge or other "electrical disturbance," and other prescribed requirements are met, the exclusion does not apply.[286]

The specific language of an "other insurance" clause can be critical. For example, an insured business suffered a fire when a circuit breaker malfunctioned

280. Hartford Steam Boiler Inspection & Ins. Co. v. Quantum Chem. Corp., 1996 U.S. Dist. LEXIS 17551 (N.D. Ill. Nov. 12, 1996).

281. Travelers EnergyMax 21, § B.14.

282. HSB Freestyle Policy Form 6671 (10/2002) § B.3.

283. ISO Form BM 00 20 07 01, § B.12.

284. Travelers EnergyMax 21, § B.14.

285. HSB Freestyle Policy Form 6671 (10/2002) § B.3.

286. HSB Freestyle Policy Form 6671 (10/2002) § B.4. For the exception to the exclusion to apply, the surge or disturbance must have been transmitted through utility service transmission lines to a described location; at that location, the surge or disturbance has to have resulted in an "accident" to "covered equipment" owned or operated under the control of the insured or the landlord of the insured; and, the loss, damage, or expense caused by the surge or disturbance must not be a covered cause of loss under another coverage part or policy of insurance, whether collectible or not, and without regard to whether or not the other coverage part or policy of insurance provides the same coverage or scope of coverage.

and arced. The property insurer argued the boiler and machinery carrier should pay the full fire loss. It pointed to an exclusion in its policy that said it would not cover property "more specifically insured in whole or in part by any other insurance," but would cover the amount in excess of the amount due from that more specific insurance. The court said that although the boiler and machinery policy "more specifically insured," it did not more specifically insure *property*. To the contrary, it more specifically insured against a particular peril: fire or explosion outside of the circuit breaker or other covered object.[287]

In an earlier case,[288] the policy of the property insurer provided it did not cover any property or interest specifically insured by the owner "against similar liabilities in whole or in part." An equipment breakdown policy covered a specific generator against loss or damage by fire within it, resulting from a breakdown, but not by fire outside it whether resulting from breakdown or any other cause. There was a fire inside the generator that resulted from a breakdown, and the equipment breakdown carrier conceded the loss was almost entirely within the provisions of its policy. It brought an action, however, to recover the part of the loss for which it paid that it argued was not covered. The defendant property insurer relied on the "specifically insured" exclusion. The court found that the equipment breakdown policy constituted specific insurance within the meaning of the exclusion and held that liability for the loss was excluded from coverage by the defendant's policy. In contrast, an equipment breakdown policy provided that if at the time of an accident covered by the policy there was other similar, valid, and collectible insurance against damage to property, the insured could not recover from the equipment breakdown carrier any greater proportion of the loss than the equipment breakdown coverage bore to the whole amount of the other insurance. There was a breakdown of an elevator motor covered by the equipment breakdown policy, and that breakdown was accompanied by a fire that seriously injured the motor but did not extend beyond its housing. The equipment breakdown carrier, relying on the exclusion, denied coverage for the damage resulting from the fire and argued the fire insurance carrier was responsible for that loss. The court, however, decided that the phrase "other similar insurance" referred to other policies that had the same specific coverage, not those having general coverage.[289]

In another case, lightning struck and damaged an electrical transformer on the property of the insured, who had both property and boiler and machinery policies. The former had an "excess clause" under which it provided coverage for

287. Continental Ins. Co. v. Acadia Ins. Co., 974 F. Supp. 371, 373 (D. Vt. 1997).

288. Hartford Steam Boiler Inspection & Ins. Co. v. Firemen's Mut. Ins. Co., 110 Conn. 332, 148 A. 135 (1930).

289. Kanawha Inv. Co. v. Hartford Steam Boiler Inspection & Ins. Co., 107 W. Va. 555, 149 S.E. 605 (1929) (special protection from loss and damage from injury by fire in machine has to be deemed particular purpose of equipment breakdown insurance, otherwise there would be no justification for it).

loss to property, *not including* property that was covered under another coverage form of the property policy itself, or any other policy, in which it is more specifically described, except for the excess of the amount due whether or not the insured could collect it. The boiler and machinery policy, on the other hand, excluded coverage for loss caused by or resulting from lightning if coverage for that cause of loss was provided by another policy of the insured. The court said that when an excess clause and an exclusion—or non-liability clause—conflict, the latter is not given effect because the policy containing the excess clause does not constitute "other available insurance" within the meaning of the exclusion.[290]

[8] Neglect

Some policies require the insured to protect covered property by excluding coverage where the insured fails or neglects to use all reasonable means to protect or to save and preserve covered property from damage after an "accident"[291] or at and after the time of the loss.[292] The exclusion is not applicable where the evidence is of negligence before an accident.[293]

[9] Equipment Being Repaired or Tested

Some policies exclude coverage when covered equipment is being tested or repaired. The language of the exclusion may specify specific types of testing[294] or may refer to testing generally.[295] In a Tennessee case, the policy provided the carrier would not be liable for loss from an accident to any object while undergoing an insulation breakdown test, or while being repaired or "dried out."[296] A generator exploded while a part was being ground to remove grooving, scarring, and

290. Utica Mut. Ins. Co. v. Travelers Ins. Co., 213 A.D.2d 983, 624 N.Y.S.2d 485 (1995). *Compare* Monroe Guar. Ins. Co. v. Hartford Steam Boiler Inspection & Ins. Co., 2000 Ohio App. LEXIS 1456 (Mar. 31, 2000) (where *both property and boiler and machinery policies contained excess clauses* disclaiming primary liability when there was other insurance covering same loss and boiler and machinery policy excluded coverage for lightning if coverage for that cause of loss was provided by another policy, property insurer was primarily liable for loss because it afforded coverage for lightning as cause of loss).

291. HSB Freestyle Policy Form 6671 (10/2002) § B.1.g.

292. ISO Form BM 00 20 07 01, § B.19; Travelers EnergyMax 21, § B.20.

293. Maryland Casualty Co. v. Neiman-Marcus Co., 186 F.2d 140, 142 Cir. 1951) (finding untenable contention that claimed negligence of insured in not keeping exhaust fan running and not sooner discovering escape of ammonia and protecting against its consequences was intermediate controlling and self-sufficient intervening cause; no evidence of failure after accident to take all necessary precautions to minimize its results).

294. *See* ISO Form BM 00 20 07 01, § B.9 (excluding damage to covered equipment undergoing pressure or electrical test).

295. *See* ISO Form BM 00 25 02 91, § B.4.h (excluding accident to any object while being tested).

296. Foote Mineral Co. v. Maryland Casualty Co., 173 F. Supp. 925 (D. Tenn. 1959), *aff'd*, 277 F.2d 452 (6th Cir. 1960), *cert. den.*, 364 U.S. 818, 81 S. Ct. 49, 5 L. Ed. 2d 48 (1960).

pitting that was a natural result of use of the generator and had to be addressed periodically. The insured contended the generator was undergoing preventive maintenance at the time of the accident, not repairs. The court, however, employing the meaning of "repair" it said the ordinary person ascribes to the term, found the generator was being repaired at the time of the accident and the repair exclusion precluded recovery for the loss. The court noted that "maintenance" has been construed to include repair and that if "repair" had a restrictive meaning in the particular industry, the burden was on the plaintiff to prove it.

[10] Lack of Power

Policies may exclude coverage for loss or damage caused directly or indirectly by lack of or excess of power, light, heat, steam, or refrigeration except as provided by business income coverage, extra expense, coverage, utility interruption, and/or spoilage damage coverage.[297] These exclusions have been found unambiguous and applicable to consequences of a loss of power. For example, a four-hour power failure resulted in three compressors on the insured's building being exposed to snow and freezing temperatures and damaged beyond repair. The insured argued the immediate and proximate cause of its loss was below freezing temperatures and therefore contended that the policy provided coverage for its loss because damage from freezing was not expressly excluded from coverage. The court did not agree. The policy excluded damage from loss of power and heat, and the court could thus reasonably assume the exclusion extended to what would follow if power and heat were lost in freezing weather.[298]

§ 11.09 Limits of Insurance

All policies include a section on limits of insurance. The limits vary from policy to policy. One limitation common to all policies provides the carrier will pay no more for one accident or one breakdown than the amount shown as the limit on the Declarations Page.[299] The limitation then depends on the definition of "one accident" or "one breakdown." The definitions vary slightly. The HSB policy simply says that "one accident" means all "accidents" that occur at the same time from the same event and adds that if an "accident" causes other "accidents," all

297. *See, e.g.*, Travelers EnergyMax 21, § B.17.

298. Sawyer Fruit & Vegetable Co-operative Corp. v. Lumbermens Mut. Casualty Co., 73 Ill. Dec. 1, 117 Ill. App. 3d 407, 453 N.E.2d 826 (Ill. App. 1983).

299. *See, e.g.*, ISO Form BM 00 25 02 91, § C.1; HSB Freestyle Policy Form 6671 (10/2002) § C.1. According to an analysis of the ISO Equipment Breakdown Protection Coverage Form, the amount of the limit per breakdown chosen by the insured is the most the insurer will pay for any one breakdown, even though the various coverage parts purchased exceed that limit. At the same time, the chosen limit for any specific coverage is the most the insurer will pay in any one breakdown for that loss. *Boiler and Machinery Coverage Form* (Summit Business Media, 2013).

of them will be considered as "one accident."[300] The language of the Boiler and Machinery Coverage Form is nearly identical whether defining one accident or breakdown. It provides that if an initial "accident" or "breakdown" causes other "accidents" or "breakdowns," all of them will be considered one "accident" or "breakdown," and all "accidents" or "breakdowns" at any single location that manifest themselves at the same time and are the result—or, in the case of policies styled equipment breakdown protection, the direct result[301]—of the same cause will be considered one "accident" or "breakdown." [302]

Under the HSB policy, and many others, the limit of the insurance for each individual coverage—for example, property damage, business income, extra expense, data restoration, ordinance or law, expediting expense—from loss, damage, or expense arising from any "one accident" is the amount indicated *for that coverage* on the Declarations Page. Those limits, says the policy, "are a part of, and not in addition to, the Equipment Breakdown Limit."[303] Thus, the amount of the limit per breakdown is the most the insurer will pay for any one breakdown, even though the various coverage parts purchased exceed that limit while at the same time, the chosen limit for any specific coverage is the most the insurer will pay in any one breakdown for that loss.[304] If a coverage is shown on the Declarations Page as "included," it is provided *up to the remaining amount* of the equipment breakdown limit, and if no limit is shown for a coverage,[305] or a coverage is shown as "Excluded," it is considered to have a limit of $0.[306] Finally, if two or more coverage limits apply to the same loss or a portion of the same loss, the carrier will pay only the smallest of the applicable limits for that loss or portion of it. In other words, if the insured has a loss under one of the specific individual coverages and all or part of it is not covered because the applicable coverage is excluded or has a limit that is less than the amount of the loss, the carrier will not pay the *remaining amount* of that loss under any other coverage.[307]

---

300. HSB Freestyle Policy Form 6671 (10/2002) § F.17. *Consider* Hartford Steam Boiler Inspection & Ins. Co. v. Pabst Brewing Co., 201 F. 617 (7th Cir. 1912) (where three of a battery of boilers exploded in distinct succession, not concurrently, and policy limited insurer's liability for loss resulting from any one explosion, limitation applied as primary explosion occurred in one boiler followed by explosion of two others plainly attributable to first and, under doctrine of proximate cause, one explosion was cause of contract liability).

301. ISO Form BM 00 20 07 01, § F.12. *See also* Travelers EnergyMax 21, § F.14.

302. ISO Form BM 00 25 02 91, § F.3.

303. HSB Freestyle Policy Form 6671 (10/2002) § C.2.a. If an amount of time is shown, the coverage continues for no more than that amount of time *immediately* following the "accident."

304. *Boiler and Machinery Coverage Form* (Summit Business Media, 2013).

305. *See, e.g.*, Malecki, *Equipment Breakdown Insurance: Too Important to Ignore!*, at 5 (Adjusting Today, 2009), available at: http://adjustersinternational.com/publications/adjusting-today/equipment-breakdown-insurance/1/ (if $500,000 base limit is selected and other coverages are designated in declarations as being included, coverage will hinge on how much is left after paying for damage to property named insured owns or has in its care, custody, or control).

306. HSB Freestyle Policy Form 6671 (10/2002) § C.2.a.

307. HSB Freestyle Policy Form 6671 (10/2002) § C.2.b.

Note that the ISO Boiler and Machinery Coverage Form refers to direct damage[308] to *covered property* resulting from one accident while the other policies limit payment to one accident or breakdown and define accident or breakdown as a physical loss to covered *equipment*.

Policies also generally include hazardous substances and ammonia contamination limitations.[309] For example, the Travelers policy says the most the carrier will pay for contamination by ammonia or damage, contamination, or pollution by a hazardous substance of covered property as a direct result of a breakdown of covered equipment is the amount on the Declarations Page under coverage limitations, and that those limits are part of, not in addition to, the limit for property damage.[310]

§ 11.10 Deductibles

The amount of the deductible will be stated on the Declarations Page. The deductible may be a stated amount or a percentage of loss. There may be a single deductible, or a different deductible amount may apply to different causes of loss.

The insured needs to examine the policy language to determine how the deductible is applied. The deductible clause may be brief. For example, the ISO Boiler and Machinery Coverage Form provides that the carrier will not pay for loss or damage resulting from any "one accident" until it exceeds the stated deductible.[311] Under the policy, if an initial "accident" causes others, they are all considered to be "one accident," and all accidents at any one location that manifest at the same time and result from the same cause are also considered one accident.[312] Once the amount of loss or damage exceeds the deductible, the carrier will pay up to the applicable limit of insurance; however, if more than

---

308. *See* Preferred Mut. Ins. Co. v. Travelers Cos., 955 F. Supp. 9, 11 (D. Mass. 1997) (noting lack of definition of "direct damage").

309. ISO Form BM 00 25 02 91, § C.2.b & c; HSB Freestyle Policy Form 6671 (10/2002) § C.4.a & b.

310. Travelers EnergyMax 21, § C.4. The policy also provides that if covered property is contaminated by a hazardous substance as a direct result of a breakdown of covered equipment, the insurer will pay for additional expenses incurred to clean up, repair, replace, or dispose of that property. Travelers EnergyMax 21, § C.4.b. In *Nationwide Mut. Ins. Co. v. CG Stony Point Townhomes, LLC*, 2015 U.S. Dist. LEXIS 5682 (E.D. Va. Jan. 15, 2015), the insurer conceded that secondary damages that resulted from an accident to covered equipment were generally covered, but argued that because the undisputed facts demonstrated that a breakdown of HVAC systems did not, in turn, cause any additional damages or release a hazardous substance leading to additional damages, there was no coverage under the equipment breakdown provisions of the policy. The court granted summary judgment to the insurer. In *dicta*, the court opined that if an HVAC system broke down, and the breakdown caused the release of a hazardous substance, for example, Freon, the hazardous substances subclause would operate to provide coverage for damages caused by the Freon despite a pollution exclusion.

311. ISO Form BM 00 25 02 91, § D.

312. ISO Form BM 00 25 02 91, § F.3.

one "object"—meaning the equipment shown on the Declarations Page[313]—is involved in one accident, then only the highest deductible applies.[314]

Ordinarily, the deductible is applied to damages or loss associated with a specific accident or breakdown. Thus, where the same object or covered equipment suffers a series of accidents or breakdowns, the deductible will apply to each one.[315]

The ISO Equipment Breakdown Protection Coverage Form contains a lengthier deductible clause.[316] It has two subsections. The first addresses application of deductibles, and the second concerns determination of deductibles. Under that first subsection of that deductible clause, the policy states that the carrier will not pay for loss or damage that results from any "one breakdown"[317] until the amount of covered loss or damage exceeds the deductible for each applicable coverage after which it will pay the amount of covered loss or damage that exceeds the deductible, up to the applicable limit of insurance.[318] Additionally, a deductible applies separately for each applicable coverage unless either it is shown on the Declarations Page as combined for any of the coverages, in which case the carrier will first subtract the combined deductible amount from the total amount of any loss to which the combined deductible applies,[319] or more than one piece of "covered equipment" is involved in one breakdown, in which case only one deductible, that being the highest, applies for each of the applicable coverages.[320]

The policy then describes how the various types of deductibles are applied.[321] The Declarations Page will state the type of deductible, and there will typically be more than one type, with different types applying to different coverages. The types are dollar, time, multiple of daily value, percentage of loss, and maximum or minimum.[322] Dollar coverage is a specific stated dollar amount, and it will likely apply to property damage. The policy simply states that if the Declarations Page

313. ISO Form BM 00 25 02 91, § F.2.

314. ISO Form BM 00 25 02 91, § D.

315. *See* Community Federal Sav. & Loan Ass'n v. Hartford Steam Boiler Inspection & Ins. Co., 580 F. Supp. 1170, 1173 (E.D. Mo. 1984) (where air conditioning unit was covered equipment and suffered series of failures and repairs over six-month period, insurer was entitled to make policy deduction for each failure).

316. *See generally* Malecki, *Equipment Breakdown Insurance: Too Important to Ignore!*, at 7 (Adjusting Today, 2009), available at: http://adjustersinternational.com/publications/adjusting-today/equipment-breakdown-insurance/1/.

317. A "breakdown" is a prescribed direct physical loss causing damage to covered equipment. ISO Form BM 00 20 07 01, § F.1. "One breakdown" means that if an initial one causes others, all will be considered one breakdown and all breakdowns at any one premises that manifest themselves at the same time and are the direct result of the same cause are considered to be one breakdown. ISO Form BM 00 20 07 01, § F.12.

318. ISO Form BM 00 20 07 01, § D.1.

319. ISO Form BM 00 20 07 01, § D.1.a.

320. ISO Form BM 00 20 07 01, § D.1.a.

321. ISO Form BM 00 20 07 01, § D.2.

322. Another type of deductible is "multiple per unit." *See* Travelers EnergyMax 21, § D.2.b.

shows a dollar deductible, the carrier will first subtract the deductible amount from any loss it would otherwise pay.[323] The "time deductible" is often applied to business income or extra expense coverage. It is stated in hours—often 24—or days and has the effect of compelling the insured to bear the full loss for the initial stated period. If there is a time deductible, the policy says the insurer will not be liable for any loss under the coverage to which the time deductible applies that occurs during that specified time period *immediately following* a breakdown.[324] When the deductible is stated as a percentage of loss, the policy provides the carrier will not be liable for the stated percentage of the gross amount of loss or damage—before the applicable deductible or coinsurance—insured under the applicable coverage.[325]

§ 11.11 Conditions

Boiler and machinery policies include many conditions, some familiar and some unique to the form of coverage. The conditions frequently found address abandonment, additional insureds, appraisal, bankruptcy, coinsurance, concealment, misrepresentation or fraud, defense of the insured, duties in the event of loss or damage, insurance under two or more coverages, joint or disputed loss, legal actions against the carrier, liberalization, loss payable, mortgage holders, bailees, other insurance, policy period and coverage territory, the carrier's privilege to adjust with the owner, reducing the loss, suspension, the transfer of rights of recovery against others to the carrier, and valuation.

In addition to the conditions stated in the policy itself, a "common policy conditions" form will be included with the policy. It addresses cancellation,[326]

323. ISO Form BM 00 20 07 01, § D.2.a.

324. ISO Form BM 00 20 07 01, § D.2.b. *See also* Austin, *Equipment Breakdown—More Than Just Boiler and Machinery* (IRMI 2011), available at: http://www.irmi.com/articles/expert-commentary/equipment-breakdown (business income coverage may be subject to an average daily value (ADV) deductible that is based on number of days that business income would have been earned during period of interruption had no accident occurred and can be significant and likely much greater in amount than direct damage deductible).

325. ISO Form BM 00 20 07 01, § D.2.d.

326. *See, e.g.*, ISO Form IL 00 17 11 98, § A. Under this clause, the first named insured may cancel the policy by mailing or delivering advance written notice of cancellation to the insurer. The insurer may cancel the policy by mailing or delivering written notice of cancellation to the first named insured at least ten days before the effective date of cancellation if the cancellation is for non-payment of the premium or 30 days before the effective date of cancellation if it is for any other reason. The insurer will mail or deliver notice to the first named insured's last mailing address known to it. Notice of cancellation will state the effective date of cancellation, and the policy period will end on that date. If the policy is cancelled, the insurer will send the first named insured any premium refund due and if the insurer cancels, the refund will be *pro rata*, but if the insured cancels, the refund may be less than *pro rata*. Cancellation is effective even if the insurer has not made or offered a refund. Finally, if notice is mailed, proof of mailing is sufficient proof of notice. These requirements and procedures are substantially changed by state law and regulation in virtually every state. In order to determine the cancellation laws and procedures that the insurer

changes to the policy,[327] examination of the books and records of the named insured,[328] inspections and surveys by the insurer,[329] premiums,[330] and the transfer by the named insured of its rights and duties under the policy.[331] Travelers uses a common policy conditions form that adds that, in case there was any doubt, the term "equipment breakdown" means boiler and machinery and vice versa.[332]

---

must follow in each state, one has to examine and become familiar with the state-specific cancellation and non-renewal endorsement attached to the policy.

327. *See, e.g.*, ISO Form IL 00 17 11 98, B. The changes clause provides that the policy contains all the agreements between the parties about the insurance, but the first named insured may make changes in the terms of the policy with the consent of the insurer, and the terms can be amended or waived only by endorsement issued by the insurer and made a part of the policy.

328. *See, e.g.*, ISO Form IL 00 17 11 98, C. This clause allows the insurance company to examine and audit the books and records of the named insured as they relate to the policy at any time during the policy period and up to three years subsequently.

329. *See, e.g.*, ISO Form IL 00 17 11 98, D. Under the inspections and surveys clause, the insurer has the right to make inspections and surveys at any time, give reports to the named insured on the conditions it finds, and recommend changes; however, the clause does not obligate the insurer to make any inspections, surveys, reports, or recommendations, and any of those actions that the insurer does undertake relate only to insurability and the premiums to be charged. The clause emphasizes that the insurer does not make safety inspections and does not undertake to perform the duty of any person or organization to provide for health or safety of workers or the public. It also does not warrant that conditions are safe, healthful, or in compliance with laws, regulations, codes, or standards. There is an exception for any inspections, surveys, reports, or recommendations the insurer may make about certification under state or municipal statutes, ordinances, or regulations of boilers, pressure vessels, or elevators. The provisions of the inspections and surveys clause apply to any rating, advisory, rate service, or similar organization that makes insurance inspections, surveys, reports, or recommendations. *See* Clarendon Am. Ins. Co. v. Bayside Rest., LLC, 567 F. Supp. 2d 1379, 1388 (M.D. Fla. 2008) (language of condition is clear: insured is not to rely on inspection conducted by third party at behest of insurer).

330. *See, e.g.*, ISO Form IL 00 17 11 98, E. This condition provides that the first named insured is responsible for payment of all premiums and will be the payee for any return premiums the insurer pays.

331. *See, e.g.*, ISO Form IL 00 17 11 98, F. This clause prohibits the insured for transferring its rights and duties under the policy without written consent of the insurer except in the case of death of an individual named insured. An issue over which courts are divided is whether the clause prohibits assignment of claims. The majority rule is that an anti-assignment clause "is unenforceable once an insured occurrence takes place because at that point the insured is entitled to recovery under the policy; that right is a chose in action; a chose in action is a form of personal property; the anti-assignment provision amounts to a restraint upon the alienation of this property right; and, a restraint upon the alienation of property is in opposition to public policy." Wehr Constructors, Inc. v. Assur. Co. of Am., 384 S.W.3d 680, 682–83 (Ky. 2012). *See also* 1200 Grand St. Condo. Ass'n v. 1200 Grand St. Urban Renewal LLC (*In re* Tarragon Corp.), 2013 Bankr. LEXIS 1676 (Bankr. D.N.J. Apr. 16, 2013) (where rights were assigned to association by consent order only assignment that could have occurred was assignment of claim, not general rights under policy; association would not incur actual loss until judgment fixed amount). The minority view—followed most notably in Texas—is that no assignments are allowed without the consent of the insurer. *See* Keller Founds., Inc. v. Wausau Underwriters Ins. Co., 626 F.3d 871, 875 (5th Cir. 2010). *See also* Bambrick, *In re Katrina Canal Breaches Litigation: The Louisiana Supreme Court Defies the Majority in Upholding Prohibitions on Postloss Assignments of Insurance Policies*, 86 Tul. L. Rev. 1345 (2012).

332. Travelers Form IL T0 01 01 07, § G.

[1] Duties in the Event of Loss or Damage

All insurance policies impose post-loss duties on insureds. Equipment breakdown policies are no exception. Typically, these policies require the insured to see to it that certain steps are taken in the event of loss or damage to covered property.[333] These steps are:

- Give the carrier prompt notice of the loss or damage, including a description of the property involved.[334]
- Act to reduce the loss, damage, or expense, if possible.[335]
- Allow the carrier a reasonable time and opportunity to examine the property and premises before repair or replacement or before physical evidence of the accident is removed, while still taking whatever measures are necessary for protection from further damage.[336]
- Make no statement that will assume any obligation or admit any liability for any loss, damage, or expense for which the carrier may be liable without the consent of the carrier.[337]
- Promptly send the carrier any legal papers or notices received concerning the loss, damage, or expense.[338]
- Permit the carrier to inspect the property, premises, and records of the insured as often as may be reasonably required, and also allow it to take

---

333. HSB Freestyle Policy Form 6671 (10/2002) § E.6; Travelers EnergyMax 21, § E.1.d.

334. HSB Freestyle Policy Form 6671 (10/2002) § E.6.a. State law will often modify specific notice requirements. *See, e.g.*, New York Underwriters Ins. Co. v. Coffman, 540 S.W.2d 445 (Tex. Civ. App.—Fort Worth, 1976) (requirement that notice be given to home office or to Houston office was void and unenforceable as in violation of state statute; giving notice within 16 days of occurrence met requirement that it be given as soon as practicable).

335. HSB Freestyle Policy Form 6671 (10/2002) § E.6.b. The steps the insured must take are to protect property from further damage; resume business, partially or completely at the location of loss or at another location; make up lost business within a reasonable amount of time; use merchandise or other property available; use property or services of others; and salvage the damaged property.

336. HSB Freestyle Policy Form 6671 (10/2002) § E.6.c. *Consider* New York Underwriters Ins. Co. v. Coffman, 540 S.W.2d 445 (Tex. Civ. App.—Fort Worth, 1976). In *Coffman* the policy required the insurer to have a reasonable time and opportunity to examine the property and the premises before repairs were undertaken or physical evidence of the accident was removed, except for protection or salvage. The insured property was a residential apartment complex. In the middle of summer, the air conditioning system for the entire complex failed because a compressor broke down. Restoring the air conditioning was urgent. The insureds hired a repair company that removed the old compressor and a motor from the premises without their knowledge or permission and took the compressor to a salvage yard where it was put in storage and kept intact. It was inspected there by a representative of the insurer. The court noted machinery was not repaired, but was replaced, and was removed for salvage, to a salvage yard where it was stored intact. The insured did not violate the inspection provision of the policy.

337. HSB Freestyle Policy Form 6671 (10/2002) § E.6.d.

338. HSB Freestyle Policy Form 6671 (10/2002) § E.6.e.

samples of damaged and undamaged property for inspection, testing, and analysis, and to make copies from the books and records of the insured.[339]
- Permit the carrier, if it so requests, to examine the insured and any of its agents, employees, and representatives under oath.[340]
- Send the carrier, within 60 days after its request, a signed, sworn proof of loss containing the information it requests.[341]
- Cooperate with the carrier in its investigation and settlement of the claim.[342]

The HSB policy adds that it is the responsibility of the insured, at its expense, to provide the carrier with documentation demonstrating that the loss, damage, or expense was the result of an "accident" covered under the policy and calculating the dollar amount of the loss, damage, and expense the insured contends is covered.[343] Failure to comply with the prescribed duties in the event of loss or damage can result in denial of a claim.[344]

[2] Reducing the Loss

Policies impose obligations on the insured after a breakdown or accident.[345] These include resuming business partially or completely; making up for lost business within a reasonable period of time; and making use of every reasonable means to reduce or avert loss, including using the property or services of others.[346] These

339. HSB Freestyle Policy Form 6671 (10/2002) § E.6.f.

340. HSB Freestyle Policy Form 6671 (10/2002) § E.6.g. The policy says the carrier may examine any insured under oath while not in the presence of any other insured and that the examination may be at any time reasonably required, may be about any matter relating to the insurance, the loss, damage, or expense, or claim, including, but not limited to, the books and records of the insured, and may be recorded by any methods chosen by the carrier.

341. HSB Freestyle Policy Form 6671 (10/2002) § E.6.h.

342. HSB Freestyle Policy Form 6671 (10/2002) § E.6.i.

343. HSB Freestyle Policy Form 6671 (10/2002) § E.8. The responsibility to demonstrate that the loss, damage, or expense was the result of an "accident" covered under the policy applies whether or not the possible "accident" occurred at the premises of the insured or involved its equipment.

344. *See, e.g.*, Riefflin v. Hartford Steam Boiler Inspection & Ins. Co., 164 Mont. 287, 293, 521 P.2d 675, 678 (Mont. 1974) (trial court correctly ruled that failure by insureds to submit notification of accident and proof of loss as soon as practicable barred any claims for reimbursement; insureds could not claim "substantial compliance" with policy requirements as they filed nothing for nearly two years and fact that insurer may have known of problems with boiler did not relieve insured of responsibility to give notice and submit proof of loss).

345. *Consider* Anderson & Middleton Lumber Co. v. Lumbermen's Mut. Cas. Co., 53 Wn. 2d 404, 333 P.2d 938 (1959), where under the policy it was the duty of the insured to use "diligence and dispatch and all reasonable means" to resume business. The court said the insured had the burden to show that, with the use of diligence and dispatch, it was required to have its business shut down for the period of time claimed.

346. Travelers EnergyMax 21, § E.1.i. *See also* ISO Form BM 00 20 07 01, § E.1.j.

responsibilities may be incorporated into the clause on the duties of the insured in the event of loss or damage.[347]

Any obligation to use every reasonable means to reduce or avert loss does not mean the insured can replace damaged with upgraded, more expensive equipment at the insurer's expense because that is the quickest way to return safely to normal operations.[348]

[3] Valuation

All policies have a valuation clause. These clauses may be detailed and specific or broad and lacking in precision. They attempt to determine how the insurer will respond to a loss. Generally, policies prescribe that for damaged covered property, the carrier will pay the lesser of the cost to repair the damaged property,[349] the cost to replace it,[350] or the amount actually spent that was necessary to repair or replace it.[351] For example, the standard ISO policy provides the insurer will determine the value of covered property based on the cost to repair, rebuild, or replace the damaged property with property of the same kind, capacity, size, or quality on the same or another site, whichever is the less costly, or the cost actually and necessarily spent to repair, rebuild, or replace on the same or another site, whichever is the less costly, except that the insurer will not pay for damaged property that is obsolete and useless to the insured.[352] The HSB policy adds that

347. *See, e.g.*, HSB Freestyle Policy Form 6671 (10/2002) § E.6.b. requiring the insured to protect property from further damage; resume business, partially or completely at the location of loss or at another location; make up lost business within a reasonable amount of time; use merchandise or other property available; use property or services of others; and salvage the damaged property.

348. Hartford Steam Boiler Inspection & Ins. Co. v. Quantum Chem. Corp., 1996 U.S. Dist. LEXIS 17551 (N.D. Ill. Nov. 12, 1996).

349. If the insurer initially directs the insured to repair rather than replace covered equipment, it may subsequently have to pay to replace it if there is another covered cause of loss. Community Federal Sav. & Loan Ass'n v. Hartford Steam Boiler Inspection & Ins. Co., 580 F. Supp. 1170 (E.D. Mo. 1984).

350. *Consider* Va. Apple Storage, Inc. v. Ins. Ctr. of Winchester, Inc., 1997 Va. Cir. LEXIS 740 (Apr. 11, 1997) (not every loss embraced by coverage terms of boiler and machinery policy occurs for item of property for which there is established market in which to determine replacement costs at time of loss; character of damaged property determines appropriate method of evaluation used to determine replacement costs, and appraisers frequently testify based on market, cost, or income method of valuation).

351. *See, e.g.*, HSB Freestyle Policy Form 6671 (10/2002) § E.10.a. Note that the Travelers policy says the carrier will pay the amount the insured spent to repair or replace covered property directly or indirectly damaged by a breakdown to covered equipment, but the payment will be the lesser of the three options. Travelers EnergyMax 21, § E.1.1.(1).

352. ISO Form BM 00 20 07 01, § E.1.1. A commentary notes that the policy provides for replacement cost recovery of damaged property and that when replacement cost insurance is not desired, an endorsement has to be added to delete the property damage valuation clause of the policy. *Boiler and Machinery Coverage Form* (Summit Business Media, 2013). The endorsement is ISO Form BM 99 59 07 01 (Equipment Breakdown: Actual Cash Value). It provides the insurer will pay the amount spent to repair or replace covered property directly damaged by a breakdown.

the amount of the payment will be based on the most cost-effective means to replace the function, capacity, and remaining useful life of the damaged property and that may include use of generic, used, or reconditioned parts, equipment, or property.[353] Other provisions of valuation clauses vary from policy to policy.

When the policy says the carrier will pay the lesser of the cost to repair or replace, and the former is less, the insured cannot recover replacement cost merely because repair was impractical.[354]

Many policies address payment for replacing *covered equipment*—as opposed to covered property—with more efficient equipment. For example, the HSB policy provides that generally the *insured* has to pay the extra cost of replacing damaged property with property of a better kind or quality or of a different size or capacity;[355] however, if "covered equipment" requires replacement because of an "accident," the carrier will pay the additional cost to replace it if the carrier agrees it is better for the environment, safer for people, or more energy efficient than the equipment being replaced.[356] The carrier, however, will not pay more than 125 percent of what the cost would have been to replace with like kind and quality and will not pay to increase the size or capacity of the equipment. The Travelers policy has a "new generation coverage clause" that serves a similar purpose. The policy says that if covered equipment cannot be repaired or the repair cost exceeds the replacement cost and the damage to it equals or exceeds 100 percent of its actual cash value, the insured may elect to replace the damaged covered equipment with a "newer generation covered equipment" of the same capacity. The insurer will then pay up to 25 percent more than covered equipment of like kind, quality, and capacity would have cost at the time of the breakdown.[357] Finally, with the exception of the new generation coverage, the *insured* is required to pay the extra cost of replacing damaged property with that of a better kind or quality or larger capacity,[358] although where no replacement equipment of like kind is on the market, the insurer may be obliged to pay the cost to purchase the available equipment that most nearly approximates that being replaced even if it

---

353. HSB Freestyle Policy Form 6671 (10/2002) § E.10.b.

354. New York Underwriters Ins. Co. v. Coffman, 540 S.W.2d 445 (Tex. Civ. App.—Fort Worth, 1976) (where insured replaced air conditioner compressor and jury found reasonable cost to replace compressor with equipment of like kind, capacity, size, and quality was $8,500, court did not err in awarding cost of repairs of $6,500 rather than cost of replacement).

355. *See, e.g.*, HSB Freestyle Policy Form 6671 (10/2002) § E.10.c. *See also* Hartford Steam Boiler Inspection & Ins. Co. v. Quantum Chem. Corp., 1996 U.S. Dist. LEXIS 17551 (N.D. Ill. Nov. 12, 1996) (whether physical differences between damaged equipment and replacement caused latter equipment to be not of "like kind" was factual question).

356. *See, e.g.*, HSB Freestyle Policy Form 6671 (10/2002) § E.10.d. The provision only applies to property damage coverage, to any property valued on an actual cash value basis, or to the replacement of component parts and does not increase any of the applicable limits.

357. Travelers EnergyMax 21, § E.1.1.(3).

358. Travelers EnergyMax 21, § E.1.1.(4).

results in the insured receiving an "upgrade" and even though the policy has no "new generation" clause.[359]

Under the HSB policy *any property* that does not currently serve a useful or necessary function for the insured,[360] any *covered property* the insured does not repair or replace within 24 months after the date of the "accident," and any *covered property* for which actual cash value coverage is specified on the Declarations Page will be valued on an actual cash value basis, which includes deductions for depreciation.[361] Policies generally do not define "actual cash value."[362]

Another common feature of valuation clauses concerns property held for sale by the insured. When prescribed conditions are met, property held for sale by the insured will be valued at the sales price as if no loss or damage had occurred, minus discounts and expenses that would have applied.[363] The "held for sale" provision should not apply to common interest communities because the first condition is generally that the property was manufactured by the insured.

Other property-specific valuation formulations apply to "data" and "media,"[364] air conditioning or refrigeration equipment that uses refrigerant containing chlorofluorocarbon substances,[365] and spoilage.[366]

---

359. *See* Hartford Steam Boiler Inspection & Ins. Co. v. Quantum Chem. Corp., 1996 U.S. Dist. LEXIS 17551 (N.D. Ill. Nov. 12, 1996).

360. *Compare* Malecki, *Equipment Breakdown Insurance: Too Important to Ignore!*, at 8 (Adjusting Today, 2009), available at: http://adjustersinternational.com/publications/adjusting-today/equipment-breakdown-insurance/1/ (insurer will not pay for any damaged property considered obsolete and useless to insured).

361. HSB Freestyle Policy Form 6671 (10/2002) § E.10.e.

362. *See* Travellers Indem. Co. v. B & B Ice & Coal Co., 248 Ky. 448, 446, 58 S.W.2d 640, 642 (1933) (term "cash value" means price boiler would bring when offered for sale by one who desires to sell, but is not compelled to do so, and is bought by one who desires to purchase, but is not compelled to do so).

363. *See, e.g.*, HSB Freestyle Policy Form 6671 (10/2002) § E.10.f; Travelers EnergyMax 21, § E.1.1.(7).

364. ISO Form BM 00 20 07 01, § E.1.1 (carrier will not pay for "data" or "media" it determines is not or cannot be replaced with data or media of like kind and quality or property of similar functional use); Travelers EnergyMax 21, § E.1.1.(8) (insurer will pay for replacement cost for loss to damaged "data" or "media" that are mass produced and commercially available and otherwise for cost of blank material for reproducing records and labor to transcribe or copy records when duplicate exists).

365. HSB Freestyle Policy Form 6671 (10/2002) § E.10.h (equipment that uses refrigerant containing CFC will be valued at cost to do the least expensive of repair or replace damaged property and replace any lost CFC refrigerant, repair damaged property, retrofit system to accept non-CFC refrigerant and charge system with non-CFC refrigerant, or replace system with one using non-CFC refrigerant).

366. Travelers EnergyMax 21, § E.1.1.(9).

Any recovery should be reduced by the salvage value of damaged property,[367] and the policy may address salvage value.[368]

Many policies provide that if any damaged covered property—generally meaning property owned by the named insured or in the "care, custody or control" of the named insured and for which it is legally liable—is protected by an extended warranty, maintenance contract, or service contract and the warranty or contract becomes void or unusable because of a breakdown, the insurer will reimburse the insured for the unused costs of non-refundable, non-transferable warranties or contracts.[369] This coverage may be of particular value to common interest communities. An individual homeowner or business may forego extended warranties or service contracts. A CIC association, however, has responsibility for property in which others have an interest, either through ownership as tenants in common of common property or through an interest in the association. The governing board will, therefore, be likely to obtain service contracts, especially for major components like heating and cooling systems, elevators, back-up generators, and water pumps. Reimbursement for unusable service contracts could be a part of a loss payment; however, the CIC would almost certainly be required to produce the contracts before obtaining reimbursement. Therefore, it is important to keep copies of those contracts in a safe location to prevent their being destroyed in a catastrophic loss.

Finally, a standard policy clause provides that if two or more of the coverages apply to the same loss or damage, the insurer will not pay more than the actual amount of the loss or damage.[370] This is described as an "anti-stacking" clause under which even if the policyholder has chosen more than one coverage that could apply to the same loss, the insured cannot stack two or more coverage amounts and be paid more than the actual amount of loss suffered.[371]

---

367. Jacobs Press v. Hartford Steam Boiler Inspection & Ins. Co., 1997 U.S. App. LEXIS 3769 (4th Cir. Mar. 4, 1997) (any verdict against carrier for damage to covered equipment would have to give credit for salvage value).

368. *See, e.g.*, Travelers EnergyMax 21, § E.9 (when, in connection with any loss any salvage or recovery is received after payment for that loss, amount of loss will be refigured on basis on which it would have been settled had amount of salvage or recovery been known at time loss was originally determined).

369. ISO Form BM 00 20 07 01, § E.1.1.(3); Travelers EnergyMax 21, § E.1.1.(5). Note that the Travelers policy provides coverage when the damaged covered property is "intended for your use." *See generally* Malecki, *Equipment Breakdown Insurance: Too Important to Ignore!*, at 8 (Adjusting Today, 2009), available at: http://adjustersinternational.com/publications/adjusting-today/equipment-breakdown-insurance/1/.

370. BM 00 20 07 01, § E.1.e.

371. *Boiler and Machinery Coverage Form* (Summit Business Media, 2013).

[4] Appraisal

Many, but not all,[372] policies contain an appraisal clause. These clauses typically provide that if the insurer and insured disagree on the value of the property or amount of loss, either one may make written demand for an appraisal of the loss; however, if there is an appraisal, the insurer retains its right to deny the claim.[373]

[5] Coinsurance

Some policies have a "coinsurance" provision that has the effect of limiting the amount the carrier will pay on a claim. The Declarations Page will identify the coverages subject to coinsurance. When coinsurance applies, the HSB policy says the carrier will not pay the full amount of any loss if the value of the property subject to the coverage at the time of the accident multiplied by the coinsurance percentage on the Declarations Page is greater than the applicable limit.[374] Instead, the most the carrier will pay is determined by using a mathematical formula stated in the policy.

The HSB policy also has a business income coverage coinsurance clause that applies unless the Declarations Page states otherwise.[375] Under that clause the carrier will not pay the full amount of any business income loss if the "business income actual annual value"[376] is greater than the "business income estimated annual value"[377] at the time of the "accident." Instead, the most the carrier will pay is determined by using a mathematical formula stated in the policy.

[6] Joint or Disputed Loss

Try as they might, those who draft policy language may not succeed in making the exclusions of commercial property policies dovetail perfectly with the

372. *See, e.g.*, ISO Form BM 00 25 02 91; HSB Freestyle Policy Form 6671 (10/2002).

373. ISO Form BM 00 20 07 01, § E.1.b.

374. HSB Freestyle Policy Form 6671 (10/2002) § E.4.a.

375. HSB Freestyle Policy Form 6671 (10/2002) § E.3. *See also* ISO Form BM 00 20 07 01, § E.1.m; Travelers EnergyMax 21, § E.1.n. *And see* Austin, *Equipment Breakdown—More Than Just Boiler and Machinery* (IRMI 2011), available at: http://www.irmi.com/articles/expert-commentary/equipment-breakdown (because business income coverage may be subject to coinsurance clause, additional due diligence is required to assure that proper values have been submitted).

376. The phrase "business income actual annual value" is defined as the business income for the current fiscal year that would have been earned had no accident occurred. The policy says that in calculating that amount, the carrier will take into account the actual experience of the business before the accident and the probable experience the insured would have had without it. HSB Freestyle Policy Form 6671 (10/2002) § G.6.

377. The phrase "business income estimated annual value" is defined as the anticipated business income reported to the carrier and shown on the Declarations Page. If no value is shown, the estimated annual value will be the most recent report of anticipated business income values on file with the carrier. HSB Freestyle Policy Form 6671 (10/2002) § G.7.

coverage of equipment breakdown policies.[378] One loss, therefore, could trigger—or appear to trigger—both policies.[379] If a dispute arises between carriers, payment will likely be delayed to the detriment of the insured.[380] Some policies have a "joint or disputed loss" clause, also sometimes called a loss adjustment clause.[381] The purpose of the clause is to facilitate payment of the insurance proceeds when there are both commercial property and equipment breakdown policies in effect, damage occurs to covered property covered by both of them, and the insurers disagree over coverage.[382] The clause requires the carriers to pay the insured for the disputed loss once the policy provisions are met without holding the insured hostage while they contest the amount of liability each has for the loss.[383]

While a "joint or disputed loss" or "loss adjustment" clause is a standard part of many policies, it can also be added to an equipment breakdown policy by an endorsement.[384] As discussed below, whether the language is in the main policy

---

378. Austin, *Equipment Breakdown—More Than Just Boiler and Machinery* (IRMI 2011), available at: http://www.irmi.com/articles/expert-commentary/equipment-breakdown (even when policies are carefully crafted to dovetail coverage, loss disagreements may arise as to which policy insurer believes should cover loss).

379. Boggs, *Three Commercial Property Endorsements Every Client Should Have* (July 27, 2009), available at: http://www.mynewmarkets.com/articles/102464/three-commercial-property-endorsements-every-client-should-have.

380. Austin, *Equipment Breakdown—More Than Just Boiler and Machinery* (IRMI 2011), available at: http://www.irmi.com/articles/expert-commentary/equipment-breakdown (coverage disagreements inhibiting ability of insured to receive funds to timely repair damage and seek coverage for lost income and increased operating expenses are fairly common); Boggs, *Three Commercial Property Endorsements Every Client Should Have* (July 27, 2009), available at: http://www.mynewmarkets.com/articles/102464/three-commercial-property-endorsements-every-client-should-have (with two carriers involved, there is a possibility that any loss payment will be delayed as carriers attempt to piece together incident and decide which carrier should pay bulk of claim).

381. *See* Ark. Power & Light Co. v. Hartford Steam Boiler Inspection & Ins. Co., 257 F.3d 853, 855 (8th Cir. 2001) (loss adjustment endorsement is also referred to as joint loss agreement); Hartford Steam Boiler Inspection & Ins. Co. v. Underwriters at Lloyd's & Cos. Collective, 271 Conn. 474, 857 A.2d 893 (2004), *cert. den.*, 544 U.S. 974, 125 S. Ct. 1826, 161 L. Ed. 2d 723 (2005) (both policies contained "Loss Adjustment Endorsements"); Arcadian Corp. v. Olin Corp., 698 So. 2d 9 (La. App. 1997), *writ. den.*, 827 So. 2d 1174 (La. 2002) (policies contained loss adjustment endorsements that allowed insured to receive payments under them even when insurers were unable to agree as to which policy provided coverage for particular incident).

382. Travelers EnergyMax 21, § E.3.a.

383. Boggs, *Three Commercial Property Endorsements Every Client Should Have* (July 27, 2009), available at: http://www.mynewmarkets.com/articles/102464/three-commercial-property-endorsements-every-client-should-have. *See also* Ark. Power & Light Co. v. Hartford Steam Boiler Inspection & Ins. Co., 257 F.3d 853, 855 (8th Cir. 2001) (clause provides means for insured to receive prompt payment when two or more insurers with potentially overlapping coverages disagree as to cause of loss).

384. *See, e.g.*, ISO Form BM 99 42 02 91; ISO Form BM 99 43 09 96. *See also* Ark. Power & Light Co. v. Hartford Steam Boiler Inspection & Ins. Co., 257 F.3d 853, 855 (8th Cir. 2001) (commercial all-risk property and boiler and machinery policies both contained loss adjustment *endorsements*); Arcadian Corp. v. Olin Corp., 698 So. 2d 9 (La. App. 1997), *writ. den.*, 827 So. 2d 1174 (La. 2002).

or added by endorsement, the commercial property policy must have comparable language for the purpose to be achieved.

[a] Substantive Provisions of the Clause

The joint or disputed loss clause does not apply if both carriers do not admit to any liability and neither contends coverage applies under the other's policy.[385] Under the Travelers policy, the clause does apply when the commercial property policy insuring the covered property has a similar clause at the time of the loss or damage with substantially the same requirements, procedures, and conditions and the damage was caused by a loss for which both carriers admit to some liability or there is disagreement between the carriers over whether the damage was caused by a covered cause of loss in their policies, or over the extent of participation of the policies in a loss insured against partially or wholly by any or both policies.[386] If these conditions are met, each carrier will, after written request by the insured, pay the entire amount of loss they have agreed is covered by their respective policies and one-half of the amount of the loss that is in dispute.[387] The Travelers policy has some additional conditions. One is that the carrier will not pay a share of the amount in disagreement in excess of the amount payable under the equivalent provision of the commercial property policy. Another condition is that the carrier will not pay more than the amount it would have paid had there been no commercial property policy in effect at the time of the loss, and in no event will it pay more than the limit of insurance shown on the Declarations Page.

When there is more than one commercial property carrier—for example, a carrier providing primary coverage and another providing excess coverage,[388] or even several carriers[389]—they share responsibility for one-half of the disputed amount.[390] A joint or disputed loss clause may provide that the amount in dispute is to be reduced by the highest deductible contained in any of the policies.[391] The

385. Travelers EnergyMax 21, § E.3.b; ISO Form BM 00 20 07 01, § E.3.b.

386. Travelers EnergyMax 21, § E.3.c.

387. Travelers EnergyMax 21, § E.3.d.

388. Note that if the excess policy is "follow the form" of the primary policy, it would include the joint or disputed loss or loss adjustment clause, otherwise one would need to be added to the excess policy.

389. *See, e.g.*, Ark. Power & Light Co. v. Hartford Steam Boiler Inspection & Ins. Co., 257 F.3d 853 (8th Cir. 2001) (insured had single boiler and machinery policy and all-risk property insurance provided by six carriers).

390. Ordinarily, the all-risk insurers would divide their one-half according to a *pro rata* share based on their policy coverages.

391. *See, e.g.*, Arcadian Corp. v. Olin Corp., 698 So. 2d 9 (La. App. 1997), *writ. den.*, 827 So. 2d 1174 (La. 2002) (where insured claimed total loss of $27,663,543 and all-risk policies contained deductibles of $500,000 and boiler and machinery policy provided for deductible of $1,750,000, after subtracting latter as highest deductible, insurers were obligated to insured for $25,913,543.00, with each *type of insurance* owing one-half of that amount pursuant to terms of loss adjustment endorsements).

same condition may be found in a joint loss deductible clause or endorsement. For example, in one case the endorsement provided that if there were a "combined loss"—defined as one covered by both the boiler and machinery policy and the property policy—the highest applicable deductible would be used. The loss adjustment endorsement provided the payment of the boiler and machinery carrier was limited to the minimum amount remaining payable under either policy. The commercial property policy had a $5 million deductible while the boiler and machinery policy had only a $250,000 deductible. The carriers applied the higher deductible. The insured sued for the difference. The court said that with a $5,000,000 deductible, the amount remaining payable for the property carrier was approximately $23,000,000, whereas with a $250,000 deductible, the amount remaining payable for the boiler and machinery carrier would be over $27,000,000 and, therefore, under the plain language of loss adjustment endorsement, the "minimum amount remaining payable" was the amount determined using the $5,000,000 deductible.[392]

Acceptance of sums paid under the condition does not waive any other rights against the carrier that issued the equipment breakdown policy.[393] Payment by the insurers and acceptance by the insured constitute an agreement between the insurers to proceed with arbitration, and the insured agrees to participate, but not intervene in, the arbitration.[394] The ISO Equipment Breakdown Protection Coverage Form adds that the insurer found responsible for the greater percentage of the ultimate loss has to return the excess contribution to the other carrier and that the insurer found responsible for the greater portion of the loss has to pay liquidated damages to the other on the amount of that other insurer's excess contribution.[395]

Arguably, a suit by the insurers against a third party to which they are subrogated should not be brought until after the arbitration because the apportionment will ultimately determine the loss of each insurer, and if the whole loss is borne by one insurer, the other has no interest in pursuing the claim against the third party. However, where no evidence was presented that any court had ordered arbitration, a Louisiana appellate court ruled a suit against a third party could proceed.[396]

---

392. Ark. Power & Light Co. v. Hartford Steam Boiler Inspection & Ins. Co., 257 F.3d 853 (8th Cir. 2001).

393. Travelers EnergyMax 21, § E.3.d.(6).

394. Travelers EnergyMax 21, § E.3.e.

395. ISO Form BM 00 20 07 01, § E.3.f. Arbitration expenses are not part of the excess contribution for which liquidated damages are calculated, but are to be apportioned between the carriers on the same basis that the ultimate loss is apportioned.

396. Arcadian Corp. v. Olin Corp., 698 So. 2d 9 (La. App. 1997), *writ. den.*, 827 So. 2d 1174 (La. 2002).

[b] Need for a Comparable Clause in the Property Policy

While the equipment breakdown policy may include a joint or disputed loss clause, commercial property policies often do not.[397] However, for the insured to benefit from a joint or disputed loss agreement, both policies have to contain the provision.[398] Unless the same insurer provides both the general commercial property coverage and equipment breakdown insurance,[399] by way of, for example, a combined commercial property/equipment breakdown policy,[400] the agreement will have to be added to the commercial property policy by endorsement, which should be available for no additional premium.[401] There is a standard ISO endorsement form that can be appended to a commercial property policy.

It is important for policyholders to realize that equipment breakdown insurance is specialized coverage about which some agents may have little knowledge.[402] They may obtain a policy for the insured that has no joint loss agreement or may fail to obtain a comparable endorsement for the commercial property policy. If a common interest community wants the advantage of a joint loss agreement, it should specifically request it and verify its inclusion when policies are issued. Determining whether both policies contain joint loss agreement language should also be a standard part of any regular insurance audit.

[c] ISO Endorsement

There is an ISO endorsement that modifies the insurance provided under commercial property coverage.[403] The endorsement says it is intended to facilitate payment of insurance proceeds when both a boiler and machinery and the commercial property policy are in effect, damage occurs to covered property insured

397. Austin, *Equipment Breakdown—More Than Just Boiler and Machinery* (IRMI 2011), available at: http://www.irmi.com/articles/expert-commentary/equipment-breakdown (joint loss agreement should be requested to be made part of any property policy when equipment breakdown coverage is provided by monoline policy).

398. Boggs, *Three Commercial Property Endorsements Every Client Should Have* (July 27, 2009), available at: http://www.mynewmarkets.com/articles/102464/three-commercial-property-endorsements-every-client-should-have.

399. Malecki, *Equipment Breakdown Insurance: Too Important to Ignore!*, at 8 (Adjusting Today, 2009), available at: http://adjustersinternational.com/publications/adjusting-today/equipment-breakdown-insurance/1/.

400. Boggs, *Three Commercial Property Endorsements Every Client Should Have* (July 27, 2009), available at: http://www.mynewmarkets.com/articles/102464/three-commercial-property-endorsements-every-client-should-have.

401. Austin, *Equipment Breakdown—More Than Just Boiler and Machinery* (IRMI 2011), available at: http://www.irmi.com/articles/expert-commentary/equipment-breakdown.

402. *See, e.g.*, Tapia, *Equipment Breakdown Coverage: Not Your Father's Boiler & Machinery Insurance* (Insurance Journal 2000), available at: http://www.insurancejournal.com/magazines/features/2000/11/27/21234.htm (coverage is area of insurance about which many agents remain uninformed in comparison to other commercial insurance).

403. ISO Form CP 12 70 09 96.

by both policies, and there is disagreement between the insurers over whether there is coverage or the amount of loss to be paid, if any, by each carrier under its own policy.[404]

The endorsement does not apply if both insurers do not admit to any liability and neither contends that coverage applies under the other policy.[405] The provisions of the endorsement apply only if the boiler and machinery or equipment breakdown policy carried by the named insured, insuring the covered property, contains a similar provision at the time of the loss or damage, with substantially the same requirements, procedures, and conditions; the damage to the covered property was caused by a loss for which both carriers admit to some liability for payment under their respective policies; and the total amount of loss is agreed to by the insured and the two carriers.[406]

If the conditions of the endorsement are satisfied, each carrier will pay, after a written request by the insured, the entire amount of loss it has agreed as being covered, if any, by its policy and one-half the amount of the loss that is in disagreement.[407] Acceptance by the insured of sums paid under the endorsement does not alter, waive, or surrender any other rights against the commercial property insurer.[408]

The endorsement provides for arbitration. When both carriers admit to some liability under their respective policies and they agree to submit their differences to arbitration, they will determine the amount each will pay the insured and pay it within 90 days.[409] Otherwise, the carriers agree to submit their differences to arbitration within 90 days after payment of the loss under the terms of the endorsement.[410] The insured agrees to cooperate with any arbitration procedures.[411]

Under the endorsement, the insurer found responsible for the greater percentage of the ultimate loss has to return the excess contribution to the other carrier and additionally, the insurer found responsible for the greater portion of the loss has to pay liquidated damages to the other carrier on the amount of the excess contribution of that insurer.[412] Arbitration expenses are not part of the excess contribution for which liquidated damages are calculated, and arbitration expenses are to be apportioned between the carriers on the same basis that the ultimate loss is apportioned.

---

404. ISO Form CP 12 70 09 96, § A.
405. ISO Form CP 12 70 09 96, § B.
406. ISO Form CP 12 70 09 96, § C.
407. ISO Form CP 12 70 09 96, § D.
408. ISO Form CP 12 70 09 96, § D.6.
409. ISO Form CP 12 70 09 96, § E.1.
410. ISO Form CP 12 70 09 96, § E.2.
411. ISO Form CP 12 70 09 96, § E.3.
412. ISO Form CP 12 70 09 96, § F.

[7] Carrier's Privilege to Adjust with the Owner

A customary policy condition concerns property of others in the care, custody, or control of the insured. Policies generally provide that in the event of loss, damage, or expense involving that property, the carrier has the right to settle with the *owner* of the property and settlement will satisfy any claim of the insured against the carrier.[413]

[8] Defense of the Insured

Policies generally provide that the carrier has the right—but not the obligation—to defend the insured against suits that arise from claims of owners of property in the care, custody, or control of the insured and that the defense will be at the carrier's expense.[414] Some policies are more specific. The Travelers equipment breakdown policy provides that the carrier has the right and duty to defend the insured when there is damage to property of another in the care, custody, or control of the insured for which the insured is legally liable and that was caused by a breakdown to covered equipment.[415] The policy adds that if a claim or suit is brought against the insured alleging it is liable, the insurer may either settle the claim or suit or defend it while reserving the right to settle at any point.[416]

[9] Transfer of Rights of Recovery against Others to the Carrier

A standard policy provision, known as the "subrogation clause," addresses the transfer of rights of recovery to the insurer.[417] The ISO Boiler and Machinery Coverage Form includes the basic version of the clause. It provides that if any person or organization to or for whom the insurer makes payment has rights to recover damages from another, those rights are transferred to the insurer to the extent of its payment and the person or organization is required do everything necessary to secure rights of the insurer and must not do anything after loss to impair those rights.[418] The HSB policy adds that before an accident the insured

413. HSB Freestyle Policy Form 6671 (10/2002) § F.12; ISO Form BM 00 20 07 01, § E.1.i..

414. HSB Freestyle Policy Form 6671 (10/2002) § E.5; ISO Form BM 00 20 07 01, § E.1.c. *See generally Boiler and Machinery Coverage Form* (Summit Business Media, 2013) (defense condition is placed in policy because property of others for which insured is legally liable is considered covered property and breakdown of covered equipment of insured could easily damage property of others and lead to lawsuit against insured).

415. Travelers EnergyMax 21, § E.1.c.(1).

416. Travelers EnergyMax 21, § E.1.c.(2).

417. *Boiler and Machinery Coverage Form* (Summit Business Media, 2013) (transfer of rights clause is standard simplified language subrogation clause retaining for insurer right of recovery against other parties when payment is made under coverage and requiring that person or organization to or for whom insurer makes payment do everything necessary to secure rights of insurer and do nothing after loss to impair them).

418. ISO Form BM 00 25 02 91, § E.1.f.

may waive its rights against another party in writing.[419] After an accident the insured may only waive those rights if at the time of the accident the other party is someone insured by the policy or a business firm owned or controlled by the insured or that owns or controls the insured. The policy does not define "business firm," but should the term apply to a common interest community, it must be borne in mind that where a community has layers of associations, one or more associations may control another. For example, two separate condominium associations may control a homeowners association that has the responsibility for maintaining roads or a property owners association that manages recreational amenities.

If a policy allows the named insured to waive rights to recovery after a loss when the party receiving the waiver is a *tenant* of the named insured, the waiver has implications for residential *cooperatives*.

[10] Suspension

Suspension clauses apply when covered equipment is found to be in, or exposed to, a "dangerous condition." Policies do not define "dangerous condition," but whenever one is found, any representative of the insurer can suspend the insurance against loss from a "breakdown" to that "covered equipment."[420] The suspension is usually put into effect by delivering or mailing a written notice of suspension to the last known address of the insured or the address where the covered equipment is located.[421] The fact that delivery of the notice to the address where the equipment is located is considered sufficient should give a common interest community governing board pause. Some CICs do not receive mail at the place where they are located. Mail is delivered to a post office box or the office of the community association manager. The policy, however, uses the term "delivery," suggesting the notice could be left at the location of the equipment in question. The CIC should consider requesting that any notice be sent to the manager with a copy to the agent, as a notice left at the property might not reach a board member.[422]

Once a suspension goes into effect, the insurance can only be reinstated by an endorsement for that covered equipment.[423] When the insurance is suspended, the insured will get a *pro rata* refund of the premium for that covered equipment for the period of suspension; however, suspension is effective even if the insurer has not yet made or offered that refund.[424]

419. HSB Freestyle Policy Form 6671 (10/2002) § F.14.
420. ISO Form BM 00 20 07 01, § E.2.i.
421. HSB Freestyle Policy Form 6671 (10/2002) § F.13.
422. The association could also ask that a copy of the notice be sent to either the association president or the chair of any insurance committee.
423. ISO Form BM 00 20 07 01, § E.2.i.
424. HSB Freestyle Policy Form 6671 (10/2002) § F.13.

§ 11.12 Endorsements

Endorsements add to, subtract from, or modify the provisions in the main policy. There are a great many possible endorsements of a boiler and machinery or equipment breakdown policy. Many of them will have application to operation of a manufacturing or business concern. One endorsement that may be applied to a common interest community concerns valuation. It may be denominated "actual cash value" or "repair or replacement." It deletes the property damage valuation clause and substitutes language that provides the carrier will pay the amount the insured spends to repair or replace covered property directly damaged by a breakdown and that valuation of that property will be as of the time of the breakdown; however, the carrier will not pay for damaged property that is obsolete and useless to the insured.[425] Another endorsement a CIC might want to consider adds coverage for bodily injury.[426] Under the endorsement, the carrier will pay sums the insured becomes legally obligated to pay as damages, including for care and loss of services because of bodily injury and sickness, disease, or death resulting from bodily injury for a bodily injury caused as a result of an "accident" to an "object" while it is in use or connected ready for use.[427] The coverage does not apply to any obligation for which the insured or one of its insurers may be liable under any workers' compensation, disability benefits, or unemployment compensation or any similar law.[428] Any coverage under the endorsement is excess insurance over any valid and collectible insurance available to the insured.[429]

Many states have statutes or regulations that impose requirements on insurers. In those states an endorsement will automatically be added to the policy to conform its contents to the applicable state law. An endorsement may concern the time limits on contractual performance. For example, a North Carolina endorsement extends the time period for submission of a proof of loss when a disaster is declared.[430] Other endorsements address a variety of substantive issues. A Wisconsin endorsement provides that any provision of the coverage part in conflict with a state statute or rule is considered amended to conform to that statute or

---

425. ISO Form BM 99 59 07 01. *Consider* Cafritz Co. v. Employers Commercial Union Ins. Co., 309 A.2d 302 (D.C. 1973) (endorsement providing loss meant amount actually expended by insured to repair or replace property shifted ultimate burden of persuasion to insurer, it being at most sufficient to establish, *prima facie*, extent of loss).

426. ISO Form BM 99 27 11 85.

427. ISO Form BM 99 27 11 85, § A. *Consider* Hartford Steam Boiler Inspection & Ins. Co. v. Cochran Oil Mill & Ginnery Co., 26 Ga. App. 288, 105 S.E. 856 (1921) (where there was policy of employer's liability and boiler and machinery policy, former was specific and latter, providing coverage primarily for injury to property and only secondarily for personal injury caused by boiler explosion, was general and, therefore, liability of carrier issuing latter was secondary, attaching only after exhaustion of policy issued by former).

428. ISO Form BM 99 27 11 85, § B.4.a.

429. ISO Form BM 99 27 11 85, § D.

430. ISO Form BM 01 01 07 01.

rule.[431] Some impose an entirely new obligation on the carrier. Under a New York endorsement, an insurer must provide its written estimate of damages to real property on request.[432] There are even state-specific endorsements that add a joint or disputed loss agreement to the policy, and these may vary slightly from state to state.[433]

Often, endorsements and riders are automatically included with a policy. However, insureds sometimes specifically request an endorsement or a change to one.[434] That request should be made in writing and specify the purpose the insured is seeking to achieve. The insured should carefully review the language of that endorsement and, if necessary, seek clarification, again in writing. Caution is advisable in these circumstances because when an insured has sought a specific change to a policy, courts may dispense with the usual rule of construction in which policy language is construed against the insurer and treat the endorsement language as contractual terms for which the parties bargained.[435]

§ 11.13 Claims

The basic responsibilities of the insured when making a claim under a boiler and machinery or equipment breakdown policy are the same as under any property policy: give the carrier prompt notice of the loss or damage, allow the carrier a reasonable time and opportunity to examine the property, submit to Examination Under Oath, send the carrier a signed, sworn proof of loss containing the information it requests, and cooperate with the carrier in its investigation and settlement of the claim.[436]

However, it is important for the insured to understand that the damage to covered equipment that triggers coverage can raise challenging technical issues. If a potential claim is substantial, the insured should consider employing a public

431. ISO Form BM 01 04 06 95. The endorsement also makes some specific changes. It deletes, for example, the legal action against the insurer clause and modifies the concealment, misrepresentation or fraud condition.

432. ISO Form BM 01 37 05 02.

433. *See, e.g.*, ISO Form BM 01 29 12 97 (Rhode Island changes—Joint or Disputed Loss Agreement); ISO Form BM 01 32 12 98 (Texas changes—Joint or Disputed Loss Agreement).

434. Note that if the policy has to be filed and approved by the state Department of Insurance, only approved endorsements may be issued. The same is not true for a manuscript policy—a non-standard policy—or one written by a surplus lines carrier.

435. *See, e.g.*, Cyclops Corp. v. Home Ins. Co., 352 F. Supp. 931, 933 (W.D. Pa. 1973) (because parties bargained for endorsement, usual presumption of construing terms of policy most strongly against insurer would not apply; where prior endorsement contained requirements that were excluded, the court was "better informed" as to what was intended by new endorsement). *See also* Cincinnati Gas & Elec. Co. v. Hartford Steam Boiler Inspection & Ins. Co., 2008 U.S. Dist. LEXIS 29569 (S.D. Ohio Apr. 9, 2008) (where parties were sophisticated business entities represented by experienced insurance brokers, all capable of bargaining with specificity and experience, appropriate course for court was to determine intent of parties as to meaning of endorsement).

436. *See, e.g.*, HSB Freestyle Policy Form 6671 (10/2002) § E.6.

adjuster and/or insurance counsel with experience in equipment breakdown claims. An engineer with particular expertise may be required, and the public adjuster or attorney with experience in the field should know the type of expert needed and the names of those qualified to provide that expertise.

Equipment breakdown claims may implicate both a boiler and machinery and commercial property policy. The insured will likely need assistance in understanding which policy provides coverage for specific losses. The limitations and exclusions of the boiler and machinery or equipment breakdown policy add an additional layer of complexity. As one commentator observes, expert-intensive analysis may be required "to appropriately navigate the boiler and machinery claim process and get to the recovery phase."[437] When both commercial property and boiler and machinery or equipment breakdown carriers are involved, any loss payment may be delayed as they attempt to piece together the incident and decide which of them should pay the bulk of the claim.[438] Unless both policies have a "joint or disputed loss" clause, the insured will have to front the costs of the loss. This can be problematic for common interest communities. Some CICs have a small contingency fund but not the hundreds of thousands of dollars that may be needed. A well-managed CIC will have reserve funds for replacing major components, and those funds may total several hundred thousand dollars, but there are often statutory and document restrictions on the use of reserve funds that may limit their direct expenditure or use as collateral for a loan. Generally, a CIC will have the ability to levy special assessments on its members, but again, applicable statutes or the documents may impose restrictions on special assessments. For example, a vote of the unit owners may be required. Even if the governing board is authorized to levy a special assessment, it can be weeks or months before the funds are received by the association. Thus, where one or both policies lack a "joint or disputed loss" clause and there is a substantial loss, it is critical to have the professional assistance of a public adjuster and insurance attorney who are able to negotiate on behalf of the named insured with the insurers.

§ 11.14 Successive Insurers

Equipment can suffer an initial accident or breakdown and then, after being repaired at the insurer's direction—rather than replaced—suffer subsequent accidents or breakdowns. What happens when the insurer is changed during that series of equipment failures? In a Missouri case the motor of an air conditioning unit chiller suffered a mechanical breakdown that was sudden and accidental.

437. Marker, *Breaking Down Boiler and Machinery Coverage* (2015), available at: http://www.propertyinsurancecoveragelaw.com/tags/boiler-and-machinery-coverage/.

438. Boggs, *Three Commercial Property Endorsements Every Client Should Have* (July 27, 2009), available at: http://www.mynewmarkets.com/articles/102464/three-commercial-property-endorsements-every-client-should-have.

The motor was an "object" as defined by the policy. Two days later the insured cancelled the policy and obtained a new policy with a different carrier. The first insurer directed the insured to repair the motor and treated the repair as a covered loss. Less than one month later the motor failed again and then two more times over the ensuing several months. The court noted that an effectively repaired motor could have been expected to have a substantial lifetime; however, even assuming the subsequent breakdowns were proximately caused by ineffective repair, those "accidents" occurred when the first policy was no longer in effect and, thus, that insurer was not liable for the loss.[439]

Covered equipment could also have an undiscovered defect during the coverage period of policy that results in a breakdown during a subsequent policy period. What if different carriers provide the coverage for each period? In a Washington case, a forging press seized and required extensive repairs the day after the policy of one insurer terminated and that of another carrier went into effect. The crack that led to the seizure had been in progress, but undiscovered, for over a year before the equipment failed. The court found coverage under the first policy. The policy provided that at the time of the breakdown, it had to manifest itself by physical damage to the covered equipment that required repair or replacement.[440] The court found that the crack had manifested itself during the policy period through operational and maintenance problems with the equipment. Therefore, the court found the necessary prerequisites for the second insurer to obtain equitable contribution.[441]

The fact that it may not be immediately clear which policy provides coverage argues in favor of retaining expired policies. Indeed, one expert recommends keeping expired copies of policies for at least five years after their expiration and preferably ten years.[442] When an association sues an insurer, it has the initial

439. Community Federal Sav. & Loan Ass'n v. Hartford Steam Boiler Inspection & Ins. Co., 580 F. Supp. 1170 (E.D. Mo. 1984) (first policy had expired by dates of subsequent breakdowns and policy issued to insureds by second carrier covered three subsequent failures as each mechanical breakdown was sudden and accidental). *See also* Resorts International, Inc. v. American Home Assurance Co., 311 So. 2d 806 (Fla. 3d DCA 1975).

440. The result in the case might have been different had the policy used the term "accident" rather than "breakdown," in which case the seizure may have been the accident.

441. Zurich Am. Ins. v. Emplrs Ins. Co., 2005 U.S. Dist. LEXIS 47947 (W.D. Wash. July 25, 2005). An interesting question arose in the case. The two insurers disagreed over the interpretation of the policy issued by the first carrier. Ordinarily ambiguities are resolved against the drafter-insurer and in favor of the insured. The court said that when a coverage dispute arises between two insurers, the party claiming coverage stands in the place of the insured. Therefore, since the second carrier contended the loss was covered by the policy of the first carrier, the second insurer was entitled to a favorable interpretation of any ambiguities.

442. Wick, *Record Retention Means Future Protection*, Common Ground (CAI July/Aug 1990). *See also* Porter, *Records Retention Guide for Homeowners Associations* (CAI Ledger Quarterly 1990) (retention of insurance policies and claims paid records is board administrative decision; recommending retaining claims paid records for five years).

burden of showing coverage,[443] and that is more difficult to do without the policy. It is often held that a copy of the policy needs to be attached to the complaint in a suit against the insurer,[444] although where the policy cannot be produced, courts generally will allow evidence of its contents to be introduced.[445] Gathering and introducing that evidence takes time and is an additional expenditure. Clearly, it is best if the association can produce the actual policy.[446] Thus, there is nothing to be gained by disposing of old policies, and there may be a benefit to retaining them.

Record retrieval is as important as record retention. The association may have retained expired policies, but if no one can find them, they may as well have been destroyed. An expert asserts that it is the responsibility of the governing board to assure that records are adequately maintained.[447] The association should have a storage facility for important documents that is separate from any facility maintained by the management company and should not be in the home or garage of a member of the association, but in an area accessible to future board members,

---

443. *See, e.g.*, Borough of Sayreville v. Bellefonte Ins. Co., 320 N.J. Super. 598, 605, 728 A.2d 225, 228 (1998); Gold Fields Am. Corp. v. Aetna Cas. & Sur. Co., 173 Misc. 2d 901, 904, 661 N.Y.S.2d 948, 950 (1997) (policyholder has burden of proof on issue of existence of policy and its terms; where policyholder asserts it has lost policy, problem is for policyholder to address).

444. *See, e.g.*, Karaskiewicz v. Allstate Ins. Co. (*In re* Am. Arbitration Ass'n Arbitration), 109 Ill. App. 2d 370, 372, 248 N.E.2d 756, 758 (1969) (remanded to lower court with directions to strike complaint for failure to attach copy of insurance contract); State Farm Mut. Auto. Ins. Co. v. Jones, 98 Ga. App. 46, 56, 104 S.E.2d 725, 733 (1958) (pleadings in action against insurer required that copy of policy be attached or that petition allege language contained in policy).

445. *See, e.g.*, Rubenstein v. Royal Ins. Co. of Am., 44 Mass. App. Ct. 842, 846, 694 N.E.2d 381, 384 (1998) (existence of insurance policy is generally proven by documentary evidence; that policy has been lost or destroyed does not mean that its existence and contents may not be reconstructed from business records, underwriter's folios, or billings of insurer to insured); Borough of Sayreville v. Bellefonte Ins. Co., 320 N.J. Super. 598, 605, 728 A.2d 225, 228 (1998) (nothing in record suggested missing policies were different from others issued later that were available); Fraser v. Metropolitan Life Ins. Co., 165 Wash. 667, 669, 5 P.2d 978, 980 (1931) (where evidence was introduced that policy had been lost or mislaid and could not be found, form of policy was offered and received into evidence as testimony showed it was same form of policy as had been issued to insured). *See generally* Jones, *No Policy, No Problem? How Insureds are Finding Coverage Even Though They Can't Find Their Policies*, 50 Drake L. Rev. 611 (2002). The author notes that claims for breach of insurance agreements are based on allegations of a breach of a written contract and much of the information to complete the policy is unique to the specific insured: coverage limits, locations for which coverage is provided, and the period during which coverage exists. The written contract is, therefore, critical to determining the existence and scope of coverage.

446. One problem is that a court may allow use of a sample policy of the type that was apparently issued by the carrier at the time the policy in question was issued. *See, e.g.*, Gold Fields Am. Corp. v. Aetna Cas. & Sur. Co., 173 Misc. 2d 901, 906, 661 N.Y.S.2d 948, 951 (1997) (courts have permitted use of specimen policies to show what terms of policy at issue were). That policy, however, will not contain the information on the Declarations Page that may be critically important, for example, the limits of insurance. Additionally, use of a sample policy will not help determine the specific endorsements that were a part of the actual policy.

447. Porter, *Records Retention Guide for Homeowners Associations* (CAI Ledger Quarterly 1990).

either an offsite leased facility or a segregated and secure area that is part of the common areas of the community—for example, a clubhouse. It is also important that there be an index or cataloging system that makes it easy to find a specific document in the collection of retained material.

Record retention and retrieval can be made easier in the age of electronic documents. Documents can be scanned to create an electronic copy. That copy can be kept on the association computer with a backup retained on a flash drive. Community association managers often scan the insurance policies issued to the associations they manage and post them along with other documents on a website so that members of the association can view them. The association can retain the electronic copy of the policies each year. Storage of hardcopies of policies is a challenge as collectively the various policies can total several hundred pages each year. Electronic copies take up little space, but some of the same cautions that apply to hardcopies also apply to electronic ones. The sole electronic copy should not be the possession of the management company. The association should have its own copy. When the electronic copies are on a flash drive, they should be kept in a common area, not in the home of a board member.

§ 11.15 Association Checklists

When a common interest community applies for a policy of equipment breakdown or boiler and machinery insurance, there are a number of actions it should take.

- ☐ Create an inventory of all equipment owned, leased, or in the possession of the common interest community or owned or leased by the unit owners as tenants in common including boilers, water heaters, air conditioning and heating systems, water pumps, backup generators, elevators, fire suppression/sprinkler systems, pool pumps and heaters, irrigation systems, and electronic business equipment. See § 11.05[2].
- ☐ Submit the inventory to the insurance agent or a representative of the insurer to determine which equipment is covered by the policy. See § 11.05[2].
- ☐ Determine if both the equipment breakdown and commercial property policies contain joint or disputed loss provisions. See § 11.11[6].
- ☐ Review the Declarations Page with the insurance agent when the policy is first issued and at each renewal. See § 11.06.

- [ ] If the association has income other than from individual owners—assessments in a condominium or homeowners association or rent in a cooperative—find out whether the policy covers loss of that income and under what circumstances. See § 11.07[3][g].
- [ ] When the policy provides that damaged covered property is protected by an extended warranty, maintenance contract, or service contract and the warranty or contract becomes void or unusable because of a breakdown, the insurer will reimburse the insured for the unused costs of non-refundable, non-transferable warranties or contracts; the association needs to be sure to retain those warranties or contracts and keep them in a safe location to prevent their being destroyed in a catastrophic loss. See § 11.11[3].
- [ ] The inventory should be reviewed as part of an annual insurance audit, and the information obtained by the other actions should be confirmed as part of that review. When there is a potential claim, there are other actions required. See §§ 11.11[1], 11.13.
- [ ] Immediately notify the equipment breakdown and commercial property carriers.
- [ ] If anyone was injured, also notify the commercial general liability and workers' compensation carriers.
- [ ] At the same time as the carriers are notified, also notify the association attorney and the community association manager.
- [ ] From this point forward, provide the attorney with copies of all correspondence between the association and the insurer. Forward a written summation of any oral discussion with a representative of the insurer to the attorney. Be sure to include the date and time of the discussion and the names and titles of the parties to the discussion.
- [ ] Determine when any of the carriers will conduct an inspection, and identify a member of the governing board who, together with the CAM, will be present at the inspection.
- [ ] Have the CAM take notes at the inspection. From those notes, a letter can be sent to the insurer memorializing the pertinent statements of the person who inspects the property.
- [ ] If a carrier requests an examination of anyone under oath, contact the attorney for advice.

- ☐ When the insurer requests a written proof of loss and the claim could be substantial, consider employing a public adjuster to assist in preparing the proof of loss and assisting in the claims process.
- ☐ If the claim will include any extra or expediting expense, meticulously document the amount of, and necessity for, each expenditure or loss.
- ☐ If additional expenditures are required to comply with any ordinance or law, obtain a copy of that ordinance or law and, if there is any doubt about its application, obtain a written opinion from the enforcement official or board. Be aware that in some states, there may be statutory building or equipment requirements applicable to common interest communities. Because policies may not cover an increase in loss that exceeds the amount needed to meet the minimum requirement, determine whether a variance or other exception is available.
- ☐ If all, or a portion, of a substantial claim is denied, work with the association counsel to identify an experienced insurance attorney to represent the association.

Chapter 12

Flood Insurance

This chapter can be found online at https://ambar.org/ILCIC.

Chapter 13

Commercial General Liability Insurance

§ 13.01 Introduction

Commercial general liability insurance—sometimes referred to as "public liability"—is known by the acronym "CGL." The precursor of today's standard CGL contract was promulgated in 1940.[1] Up until 1986, CGL stood for comprehensive general liability,[2] and one still sees the phrase used today. For example, common interest community (CIC) laws in at least four states require associations to maintain "comprehensive general liability insurance."[3]

Even though a common interest community is completely residential, a *commercial* general liability policy is the correct policy for it.[4] Most CGL insurance is written on standardized forms developed by the Insurances Services Office, Inc. (ISO).[5] Thus, insurers will generally provide a CIC association with the current ISO Commercial General Liability Coverage Form.[6] Some carriers are

1. Am. Family Mut. Ins. Co. v. Am. Girl, Inc., 268 Wis. 2d 16, 33, 673 N.W.2d 65, 74 (2004).
2. Boston Gas Co. v. Century Indem. Co., 454 Mass. 337, 910 N.E.2d 290, 293 n.3 (2009).
3. La. Rev. Stat. § 9:1123.112(A) (beginning no later than first conveyance of unit to person other than declarant, association must maintain, to extent reasonably available, comprehensive general liability insurance); Md. Code Ann., Real Prop. § 11-114 (a)(2) (governing council must maintain comprehensive general liability insurance, including medical payments insurance, in amount determined by council, but not less than any amount specified in declaration or bylaws); Minn. Stat. § 515A.3-112(a) (beginning no later than first conveyance of unit to person other than declarant, association must maintain, to extent reasonably available, comprehensive general liability insurance); 68 Pa. Cons. Stat. § 3312(a) (beginning no later than first conveyance of unit to person other than declarant, association must maintain, to extent reasonably available, liability insurance, and any comprehensive general liability insurance carried by association may have deductible provision).
4. If a common interest community is non-residential, it likely will be issued a Business Owners Liability Coverage Form. *See, e.g.*, Cambridge Mut. Fire Ins. Co. v. 1347-49 N. Sedgwick Condo. Ass'n, 2013 U.S. Dist. LEXIS 9750 (N.D. Ill. Jan. 23, 2013). An example of that form is ISO Form BP 00 06 01 97.
5. Am. Family Mut. Ins. Co. v. Am. Girl, Inc., 268 Wis. 2d 16, 33, 673 N.W.2d 65, 74 (2004).
6. *See, e.g.*, ISO Form CG 00 01 12 07.

developing packages for CICs that combine property and liability coverage, possibly including both CGL and directors and officers coverage.[7]

Commercial general liability insurance is an essential component of risk management for common interest communities. CICs are subject to incurring liability from a wide variety of incidents. A CIC association can find itself facing a lawsuit for damages when someone slips and falls in its lobby, suffers an injury or drowns in its swimming pool, is defamed at a board meeting, or is attacked by a criminal in the association parking lot. It is important to recognize that CGL coverage is not just for any ultimate damages judgment that might be rendered against the association. It also provides coverage for defense costs. Generally, coverage for defense costs is in addition to the limits of liability under the policy, although some policies include defense costs in the limits of liability. The carrier's duty to defend may be the more important part of the coverage for an association. Liability coverage is vital to protecting a policyholder from large money judgments. Many associations, however, will not be subject to a major claim. On the other hand, an association may lose a minor lawsuit and have defense costs that far exceed the damages it has to pay.[8] Even when an association prevails in a lawsuit, it can incur substantial expenses in the process.[9]

[1] Association's Obligation to Obtain Liability Insurance

In some cases, the association will be required by statute to obtain and maintain commercial general liability insurance. For example, under the Uniform Common Interest Ownership Act (UCIOA), associations have to maintain commercial

7. *See, e.g.*, Riverdale Peaks Homeowners Ass'n v. Auto-Owners Ins. Co., 2012 U.S. Dist. LEXIS 54180 (D. Colo. Apr. 18, 2012) (association policy contained CGL coverage form with Habitational Association Directors and Officers Liability Endorsement, D&O endorsement, that provided coverage for liability arising from errors and omissions, negligent acts, and breaches of duty related to activities of officers or directors); Alexander v. Nat'l Fire Ins., 454 F.3d 214, 218 (3d Cir. Pa. 2006) (condominium association maintained insurance policy that provided it both first-party property coverage and third-party general liability coverage); Willing v. Cmty. Ass'n Underwriters of Am., Inc., 2007 U.S. Dist. LEXIS 48543 (W.D. Wash. July 5, 2007) (condominium policy included first-party property insurance for physical damage to the building and structures and third-party liability); Far Northwest Dev. Co., LLC v. Cmty. Ass'n of Underwriters of Am., Inc., 2006 U.S. Dist. LEXIS 79033 (W.D. Wash. Oct. 30, 2006) (policy issued to association contained property coverage and general liability insurance coverage). *See also* BRT Prop. Group v. Willow Springs Condo. Ass'n, 1996 Conn. Super. LEXIS 2615 (Conn. Super. Oct. 9, 1996) (association obtained liability insurance including directors and officers liability coverage).

8. Pine Cone Harbour Condo. Ass'n v. Nationwide Mut. Ins. Co., 1993 U.S. Dist. LEXIS 21429 (W.D. Va. Oct. 19, 1993), *aff'd*, 30 F.3d 130 (4th Cir. 1994) (underlying suit against association was settled for relatively small amount; however, association incurred substantial legal fees in its defense of action for which insurer disclaimed liability and refused to defend).

9. Jerry, *The Insurer's Right to Reimbursement of Defense Costs*, 42 Ariz. L. Rev. 13 (2000) (as percentage of total claims costs, expense of providing defenses to insureds is considerable and according to industry data, approximately 14 percent of expenditures on claims is attributable to defense costs).

general liability insurance, including medical payments coverage, in an amount determined by the governing board—but not less than any amount specified in the Declaration—covering all occurrences commonly insured against for bodily injury, and property damage arising out of or in connection with the use, ownership, or maintenance of the common elements and, in cooperatives, also of all units.[10] The other Uniform Acts have the same requirement. In non-Uniform Act states, only a few states require CGL coverage.

[a] State Law

The absence of a statutory requirement to maintain liability insurance is demonstrated by the laws of the five largest states. The common interest community laws of California,[11] Florida,[12] Illinois,[13] and New York[14] do not require commercial general liability insurance. Texas is the exception. It has adopted the Uniform Condominium Act, which requires condominium associations to maintain commercial general liability insurance that includes medical payments insurance.[15] Texas also has statutes governing property owners' associations under which

10. Uniform Common Interest Ownership Act § 3-113(a)(2).

11. Rosenberry & Sproul, *A Comparison of California Common Interest Development Law and the Uniform Common Interest Ownership Act*, 38 Santa Clara L. Rev. 1009 (1998) (while California Davis-Stirling Act requires association to disclose coverage it has and to maintain insurance if it wishes to gain limited immunity for it owners, directors, and officers, it does not require associations to maintain insurance; fiduciary duty directors and officers owe association presumably includes obligation to buy both property and liability insurance when it is reasonable to do so).

12. The Florida Condominium Act simply authorizes associations to obtain and maintain liability insurance for directors and officers, insurance for the benefit of association employees, and flood insurance for common elements, association property, and units. Fla. Stat. § 718.111(11)(e). Florida also has acts governing cooperatives and homeowners associations, but they do not mandate commercial general liability insurance.

13. Neither the Illinois Common Interest Community Association Act—765 Ill. Comp. Stat. 160/1-1, *et seq.*—nor the Illinois Condominium Property Act 765 Ill. Comp. Stat. 605/1, *et seq.*—appear to specifically authorize or mandate purchase of general liability insurance. *But see* Royal Glen Condo. Ass'n v. S.T. Neswold & Assocs., 385 Ill. Dec. 137, 18 N.E.3d 137 (2014) (when §§ 12 and 18.4(f) of Condominium Property Act are read together, it is clear legislature intended that board of managers has duty to obtain adequate and appropriate insurance coverage as set forth in § 12).

14. The New York Condominium Act does not require insurance. *See* Brenner, *Recent Development in New York Law: Despite the Ruling in Pekelnaya v. Allyn, The Area of Law Regarding Individual Unit Owners' Liability Stemming from a Defect in the Condominium's Common Elements Still Requires Legislative Action*, 81 St. John's L. Rev. 729, 733 (2007) (New York has not adopted any form of statute either mandating that condominium board obtain adequate liability insurance or imposing liability on individual condominium unit owners). The New York Cooperative Corporations Law makes no mention of insurance.

15. Tex. Prop. Code § 82.111(a)(2). The coverage has to be in an amount determined by the governing board, but not less than any amount specified in the declaration. It must cover all occurrences commonly insured against for death, bodily injury, and property damage arising out of or in connection with the use, ownership, or maintenance of the common elements.

associations generally are *authorized* to purchase the insurance and fidelity bonds that the governing board considers appropriate or necessary.[16]

In most non-Uniform Act states, there is no requirement that a common interest community maintain commercial general liability insurance. Notable exceptions are found in the condominium legislation of Georgia,[17] Hawaii,[18] Indiana,[19] Maryland,[20] New Jersey,[21] Ohio,[22] Utah,[23] and Wisconsin.[24] The Ohio

16. Tex. Prop. Code § 204.010(a)(15) (authorization may be changed by restrictions, articles of incorporation, or bylaws); Tex. Prop. Code § 215.005(17) (applicable to "master mixed-use" property owners' associations).

17. The Georgia Condominium Act requires associations to obtain commercial general liability coverage that includes bodily injury and property damage of at least $1 million for a single occurrence and $2 million aggregate. Ga. Code §§ 44-3-107(a)(2), (b).

18. Under the Hawaii condominium law, unless the declaration or bylaws provide otherwise, the association is required to purchase, and at all times maintain, property insurance and commercial general liability insurance. Haw. Rev. Stat. § 514B-143(a). The commercial general liability insurance must provide coverage against claims and liabilities arising in connection with the ownership, existence, use, or management of the property and be in a minimum amount of $1 million, or a greater amount deemed sufficient in the judgment of the governing board. Haw. Rev. Stat. § 514B-143(a)(2).

19. Indiana law requires a condominium association to purchase a "master liability policy" in an amount required by the bylaws, the declaration, or revised from time to time by a decision of the board of directors. Ind. Code § 32-25-8-9(a)(2), formerly Ind. Code § 32-1-6-18.

20. Under the Maryland Condominium Act, the governing council—association—has to maintain comprehensive general liability insurance, including medical payments insurance, in an amount determined by the council, but not less than any amount specified in the declaration or bylaws. It has to cover occurrences "commonly insured against" for death, bodily injury, and property damage that arise out of, or in connection with, the use, ownership, or maintenance of the common elements. Md. Code Ann., Real Prop. § 11-114 (a)(2).

21. The New Jersey Condominium Act requires associations to maintain liability coverage for personal injury and death for accidents that occur in the limited or general common elements. The coverage must also provide for the defense of any actions brought because of injury or death to a person, or damage to property that occurs in the common elements and not arising by reason of any act or negligence of any individual unit owner. N.J. Stat. § 46:8B-14(e). Note that the Act does not actually define "general common elements." It only defines "common elements" and "limited common elements."

22. The Ohio Condominium Property Act requires the governing board, unless the declaration *or bylaws* provide otherwise, to purchase liability coverage. Ohio Rev. Code Ann. § 5311.16.

23. The Utah Condominium Ownership Act requires an association to maintain, to the extent reasonably available, liability coverage beginning no later than the day on which the first unit is conveyed to a person other than a declarant and an association has to maintain, to the extent reasonably available, liability insurance covering all occurrences commonly insured against for death, bodily injury, and property damage that arise out of or in connection with the use, ownership, or maintenance of the common areas and facilities. Utah Code Ann. § 57-8-43(3). The policy must be in an amount determined by the governing board, but not less than any amount specified in the declaration or bylaws. Utah Code Ann. § 57-8-43 (10)(b).

24. Wisconsin Condominium Ownership Act requires associations to obtain a liability policy covering all claims "commonly insured against." Wis. Stat. § 703.17(1).

Planned Community Law,[25] Oregon Planned Community Act,[26] and Utah Community Association Act[27] also have CGL requirements.

[b] Governing Documents

The governing documents of a common interest community may address liability insurance. In some cases, there will be a brief statement requiring the association to maintain liability coverage.[28] In other cases, the documents may contain broader requirements.[29] They may mandate "public liability insurance" or "comprehensive general liability insurance." The latter is the term once used to describe what is today called commercial general liability insurance. Whether the coverage is described as "public liability" or "comprehensive general liability," a standard commercial general liability policy should suffice to meet the mandate.

---

25. Under the Ohio Planned Community Law, associations are authorized, through their boards of directors, to purchase insurance and fidelity bonds the directors consider "appropriate and necessary." Ohio Rev. Code Ann. § 5312.06(D)(16).

26. Under the Oregon Planned Community Act, which governs homeowners associations and applies to "planned communities," associations have to obtain and maintain public liability coverage, with premiums as a common expense. Or. Rev. Stat. § 94.675(2). All the statute says about the public liability policy is that it has to cover all common property and all damage or injury caused by the negligence of the association. Or. Rev. Stat. § 94.675(1)(b).

27. Under the Utah Community Association Act an association has to maintain property and liability insurance, to the extent reasonably available, beginning no later than the day on which the first lot is conveyed to a person other than a declarant, and the association has to maintain liability insurance covering all occurrences commonly insured against for death, bodily injury, and property damage arising out of or in connection with the use, ownership, or maintenance of the common areas. Utah Code Ann. § 57-8a-403(1). The liability policy has to be in an amount determined by the board, but not less than an amount specified in the declaration or bylaws. Utah Code Ann. § 57-8a-406(2).

28. *See, e.g.*, Cuiyun Qian v. Toll Bros. Inc., 223 N.J. 124, 121 A.3d 363 (2015) (association was required, by its bylaws, to maintain liability insurance for accidents occurring within property of community); Lloyd v. Pier W. Prop. Owners Ass'n, 470 S.W.3d 293 (Ark. App. 2015) (bylaw required insurance policy to be acquired to insure board of administration and unit owners against any liability); DiPasquale v. Costas, 186 Ohio App. 3d 121, 156, 926 N.E.2d 682, 710, *app. den.*, 126 Ohio St. 3d 1513, 930 N.E.2d 332 (2010) (Declaration provided that as common expense, association was required to insure itself, governing board, all unit owners and occupants, and all other persons lawfully in possession or control of any part of the condominium property against liability for bodily injury, disease, illness, or death and for injury to or destruction of property occurring on, in or about, or arising from common elements); BRT Prop. Group v. Willow Springs Condo. Ass'n, 1996 Conn. Super. LEXIS 2615 (Conn. Super. Oct. 9, 1996) (Condominium Declaration stated association was required to maintain liability insurance).

29. AOAO Queen Emma Gardens v. Wai Hung Ma, 2013 Haw. App. LEXIS 192 (Haw. Ct. App. Apr. 5, 2013) (bylaws required association to procure and maintain policies liability insurance to insure governing board, association, each apartment owner, managing agent, and other employees of association against claims for personal injury, death, property damage, and such broader coverage as board determined, arising out of condition of property or activities thereon, under ISO Commercial General Liability form providing combined single limit coverage of not less than $2 million or any higher limits as board might from time to time establish with due regard to then prevailing prudent business practice in the state and as reasonably adequate for association's protection).

[c] Fannie Mae Requirements

Even if neither the applicable common interest community legislation nor the governing documents require commercial general liability insurance, Fannie Mae does, and that requirement is effectively binding on common interest community associations. Fannie Mae requires liability insurance for all condominium and cooperative projects, with some exceptions.[30] The association or cooperative corporation has to maintain a commercial general liability insurance policy for the entire project, including all common areas and elements, public ways, and any other areas that are under its supervision. The policy also has to cover commercial spaces owned by the association or cooperative corporation, even if they are leased to others. The policy has to provide coverage for bodily injury and property damage that result from the operation, maintenance, or use of the project's common areas and elements. It must be in the amount of at least $1 million for bodily injury and property damage for any single occurrence.

If the policy does not include severability of interest or separation of insureds in its terms, Fannie Mae requires a specific endorsement to preclude the insurer from denying a unit owner's claim because of negligent acts of the association or cooperative corporation or of other unit owners. The policy has to include a provision that calls for at least ten days' written notice to the association or insurance trustee before it can be cancelled or substantially modified for any reason.

[d] Consequences of Failing to Procure Liability Insurance

If the association fails to secure liability coverage, it may be subject to suit by its members.[31] The financial consequences for the association can be substantial.[32]

The association whose policy does not meet statutory requirements may attempt to shift the resulting loss to the carrier. For example, in a South Carolina case, a unit owner brought a claim against the association that was barred by an exclusion to the policy. The association argued the exclusion did not comport

30. Fannie Mae Single Family Selling Guide, § B7-4-01 (Aug. 30, 2016).

31. For example, in *AOAO Queen Emma Gardens v. Wai Hung Ma*, 2013 Haw. App. LEXIS 192 (Haw. Ct. App. Apr. 5, 2013), the bylaws required the association to procure and maintain a policy of liability insurance to insure the association and each apartment owner against claims for personal injury, death, property damage, and any broader coverage as the governing board determined arising out of the condition of the property or activities on it. A member of the association sued it arguing the policy should include areas reserved for the exclusive use or occupancy of the individual owners. The plaintiff asked the court to require the association to procure the requisite coverage and reimburse him for any costs incurred as a result of underinsurance. The association contended the bylaws only require it to provide coverage to the unit owners for damages arising out of the use of the common elements. A lower court found against the unit owner, but an appellate court said the lower court erred because the intent of the parties was essential to resolve the ambiguity of the language of the bylaws, and that intent remained to be determined.

32. *See, e.g.*, Henning v. Contl. Cas. Co., 254 F.3d 1291 (11th Cir. 2001) (unit owner and association settled her claim for negligent failure to obtain proper liability insurance and association consented to judgment against it of $225,000).

with a statute requiring associations to obtain insurance and that, therefore, the court should not enforce the exclusion because the insurer issued a policy that did not comply with the statutory obligation to properly insure the association against risks. The court was unmoved. It said that it was the responsibility of the *association* to obtain coverage. It failed, "presumably by mistake, to properly do so" and, therefore, the question was not whether the exclusion should be enforced, but who should bear the consequences of the mistake. The court stated unequivocally that the association, as the party responsible for obtaining adequate insurance, ought to bear the consequences of that failure.[33] It would seem logical that the same principle should apply when the association fails to obtain the coverage mandated by its bylaws.

[e] Locating and Obtaining the Proper Coverage

Common interest communities need a procedure for assuring that the commercial general liability coverage they obtain meets their needs and also any statutory requirements or the mandates of the documents. One way to accomplish this is to appoint a member of the board of directors or an insurance committee to investigate the association's requirements and the coverage available.[34] Almost all carriers will offer coverage under the exact same basic standard commercial general liability policy. In liability coverage, the devil is most certainly in the details. Those details are in the limits of coverage and the endorsements added to the policy. Some endorsements will be automatically added to the policy by the insurer, either to meet state law requirements or to reduce its risk. There are, however, endorsements the association needs or will want to have added to the policy to meet its specific requirements. The designated director or insurance committee will need to discuss the peculiar circumstances of the association with a person knowledgeable about insurance. That person is broadly referred to as an insurance producer and finding him or her is the first task.

The general public uses the terms "agent" and "broker" interchangeably; however, in the insurance industry, and in law, they have specific meanings.[35] An "agent" represents the insurance company. The agent may be an employee of a particular company, may have a contract to work exclusively for one company, or may have contracts with several insurers.[36] A "broker" is independent and usually is considered the agent of the insured.[37] The broker is not limited to obtaining

33. Northfield Ins. Co. v. Evian HPR, 2002 U.S. Dist. LEXIS 26684 (D.S.C. Aug. 27, 2002), *aff'd*, 2003 U.S. App. LEXIS 14064 (4th Cir. 2003).

34. *See Understanding Homeowner Association Insurance*, available at: http://www.hindmansanchez.com/resources/article/understanding-homeowner-association-insurance.

35. *But see* UBS Fin. Servs. v. Thompson, 94 A.3d 176 (Md. App. 2014) (Maryland eliminated distinction between terms "insurance agent" and "insurance broker").

36. *See, e.g.*, Ramirez v. State Farm Mut. Auto. Ins. Co., 2016 U.S. Dist. LEXIS 5245 (N.D. Ind. Jan. 15, 2016).

37. *See, e.g.*, Ga. Cas. & Sur. Co. v. Valley Wood, Inc., 336 Ga. App. 795 (2016).

coverage from a single company. The association needs a broker who will find it the best coverage available. Insurance for common interest communities is a "niche market"—a specialty—and the association needs to work with a broker who specializes in it.[38] One way to find a broker who has the requisite knowledge is to look for one with the Community Insurance & Risk Management Specialist Designation from the Community Associations Institute. The designation is available to brokers with five years' experience as a practitioner in the community association insurance industry. It is generally recommended that associations interview at least two or three brokers.[39] It is critically important to assess whether the broker is one that will actively protect the interests of the association.[40] When the designated director or insurance committee interviews brokers, it will also want to determine the services the broker routinely provides. For example, will the broker participate in an annual review of the association's coverage? Later, the director or committee will compare the coverage the brokers offer to obtain. It should be remembered that typically, one broker obtains all or nearly all of the various policies—property, flood, equipment breakdown, general liability, directors and officers, fiduciary/crime—for an association.

When a broker presents the association with a policy to consider, the designated director or insurance committee should discuss with the broker how

38. Stoeckert, *The Insurance Puzzle; Making Sense of Premiums and Policies* (Cooperator, Apr. 2012), available at: http://cooperator.com/articles/2418/1/The-Insurance-Puzzle/Page1.html; *Understanding Homeowner Association Insurance*, available at: http://www.hindmansanchez.com/resources/article/understanding-homeowner-association-insurance (association should only work with broker who is experienced in handling association insurance, and one way to determine that is to ask about level of experience of broker and how many associations he or she currently insures). *See also* Hennessey, *Condominium Management*, 48 St. John's L. Rev. 1064, 1070 (1974) (insuring condominiums creates more difficult problems than many insurance agents and most business people appreciate and, therefore, association is well advised to employ knowledgeable and experienced insurance broker who will be able to recommend best and most economical policies that provide requisite coverage).

39. Lent, *The ABC's of Insuring Your Co-op or Condo; Common Terms and Options for Insurance* (Cooperator, Aug. 2014), available at: http://cooperator.com/articles/2818/1/The-ABCs-of-Insuring-Your-Co-op-or-Condo/Page1.html; *Understanding Homeowner Association Insurance*, available at: http://www.hindmansanchez.com/resources/article/understanding-homeowner-association-insurance (it is customary to get two or three bids or proposals from different brokers before acquiring policy). *See also* Green, *Shopping for Insurance; What Do Boards Need to Know?* (Cooperator, Aug. 2011) (recommending comparing services of at least three insurance brokers).

40. The facts of one case illustrate a particularly egregious example of a broker that failed to properly protect the interests of its client. The broker secured a CGL policy for a homeowners association. Shortly after renewal of the policy, the insurer added two endorsements to it that reduced the coverage without notifying the broker or the association. An underwriter subsequently sent copies of the endorsements to the broker, and the broker admitted it had copies of both endorsements in its office files, but its spokesperson could not recall if copies had been sent to the association and acknowledged he had not spoken to anyone at the association about the endorsements. National Fire & Marine Ins. Co. v. Hoene Springs Improvement Ass'n, 889 F. Supp. 362, 365–66 (E.D. Mo. 1995). Fortunately for the association, the court in effect refused to enforce the endorsements.

that policy meets the association's particular coverage needs. It is also important that the broker establish the liquidity or stability of the proposed carrier. That is determined from the rating the insurance company is given by the various rating agencies, along with review and analysis of the financial statements filed with the insurance departments where the insurer is licensed.

Because coverage for common interest communities is a specialty coverage, it is often underwritten by surplus lines insurers. A surplus lines insurer is also known as a non-admitted insurer. U.S. non-admitted insurers have to be licensed in at least one state, their home state. The solvency of the insurer is, therefore, regulated by its home state. Surplus lines insurers play an important role by providing insurance in hard-to-place markets. In Florida, for example, it is not uncommon for CIC insurance coverage to be more available in the surplus lines market than insurance issued by admitted companies. A full analysis of surplus lines insurance is beyond the scope of this treatise.[41] It is important to remember that if the policy is issued by a surplus lines insurer and if that insurer should be placed in receivership, then there is no guaranty fund coverage. Every state has a guaranty fund that pays claims when a licensed insurer is insolvent. The front page and Declarations Page of the policy will have an explanation. Florida law, for instance, requires the following disclaimer to be written or stamped on the first page of the policy: "This insurance is issued pursuant to the Florida Surplus Lines law. Persons insured by Surplus Lines carriers do not have the protection of the Florida Insurance Guaranty Act to the extent of any right of recovery for the obligation of an insolvent unlicensed insurer."[42]

[2] The Application

The first question for common interest communities to answer with regard to insurance applications is who will contact the agent or broker to make the application and sign it? It may be an officer of the CIC[43] or the community association manager (CAM). In many cases the manager will be the person best equipped to

---

41. The International Risk Management Institute glossary says that surplus lines insurance "[r]efers to coverage lines that need not be filed with state insurance departments as a condition of being able to offer coverage. The types of risks typically insured in the surplus lines insurance markets can usually be categorized as risks with adverse loss experience, unusual risks, and those for which there is a shortage of capacity within the standard market." https://www.irmi.com/term/insurance-definitions/surplus-lines-insurance.

42. Fla. Stat. § 626.924(1).

43. In a curious argument, an association contended an application was "blank" because it was never signed by it, but only its agent. Therefore, it argued, any misrepresentations in the application could not be attributed to it. The application was signed by the president of the association. The court characterized the association's contention as raising "troubling agency concerns," by which it probably meant that the association could only act through its agents and the authority of the president of an organization to bind it is not generally a matter of dispute. The court found that any misrepresentation in the application was "squarely and unequivocally" that of the association. Caribbean I Owners' Ass'n v. Great Am. Ins. Co., 600 F. Supp. 2d 1228 (S.D. Ala. 2009).

answer the questions on the application; however, if the CAM represents the CIC, the governing board should obtain a copy of the application and review it for accuracy.[44] The CAM may have provided incorrect information to the broker,[45] or the broker may have obtained inaccurate data from a prior application.

The application is of primary importance as it becomes part of the policy once issued. The contents of the application—or omissions from it—are important because misrepresentations in the application may be a basis for the insurer to deny coverage or rescind the policy.[46] When coverage is obtained from a particular carrier and then renewed year after year, the application may have been completed many years ago.[47] That presents a potential problem for common interest communities because, with turnover in the membership of the governing board, no board member may know what information is in the application and whether it was accurate originally, or remains accurate. It is advisable to review and update the application for each renewal year.

The application form will likely be two Association for Cooperative Operations Research and Development (ACORD) forms used for commercial insurance applications.[48] Some of the information for which the basic application will ask is the first named insured; mailing address of the first named insured; whether the first named insured is a corporation, limited liability company, non-profit organization, or trust; any other named insureds; location of the premises; whether the

44. The governing board should remember that the manger is its agent, and it will, therefore, generally be bound by the actions of the manager on behalf of the association. *See, e.g.*, Biscayne Cove Condo. Ass'n v. QBE Ins. Corp., 971 F. Supp. 2d 1121, 1126 (S.D. Fla. 2013).

45. *See, e.g.*, Towers Condo. Ass'n v. C.E. Brathwaite & Assocs., 40 V.I. 33 (1999) (manager signed application prepared by broker without providing any additional information; application lacked information about prior claim, and manager professed to have no awareness of that prior claim).

46. *See, e.g.*, Towers Condo. Ass'n v. C.E. Brathwaite & Assocs., 40 V.I. 33 (1999), where a representative of the condominium signed an application the agent filled in based on information previously supplied. The agent allegedly did not ask if the condominium had suffered any losses in the interim, which in fact it had. The insurer refused coverage because the failure to disclose that loss on the application constituted a material misrepresentation by the condominium association. The court said that when the association representative signed the application, it constituted a failure by the association to disclose information pertaining to its prior loss. However, an issue of material fact remained as to whether the agent was negligent in its handling of the application and whether the association had an obligation to ascertain whether the information given was current and accurate as of the date the application was signed. Additionally, there was also an issue of fact regarding whether the failure to disclose was made with intent to deceive. Note that the policy provides that by accepting it, the insured agrees that the statements in the Declarations are accurate and complete, they are based on representations made by the insured to the carrier, and the carrier issued the policy in reliance on those representations of the insured. ISO Form CG 00 01 12 07, § IV.6.

47. Lexington Vil. Condominium v. Scottsdale Ins. Co., 2013 N.Y. Misc. LEXIS 5745 (Nov. 29, 2013), *aff'd*, 2016 N.Y. App. Div. LEXIS 664 (Feb. 3, 2016) (application over decade old).

48. ACORD stands for Association for Cooperative Operations Research and Development. It is a global, non-profit organization serving the insurance and related industries that, among other things, publishes standardized forms. https://www.acord.org/about/Pages/default.aspx. These forms have been described as the "gold standard" and are widely used by agencies.

named insured owns the building, is a tenant, or has some other interest in the building; the number of square feet the named insured occupies and the number of square feet open to the public; a description of the operation of the named insured; whether the nature of the business is "condominiums," but not whether the insured is a cooperative or homeowners association (HOA); whether any policy or coverage has been declined, cancelled, or not renewed during the preceding three years; whether any past losses or claims relate to sexual abuse, discrimination, or negligent hiring; whether any applicant has been indicted or convicted for a crime of fraud, bribery, or arson; whether there are any uncorrected fire or safety code violations; whether the applicant has had a foreclosure, repossession, or bankruptcy in the previous five years; whether there has been a judgment or lien in the previous five years; prior carrier information; and the loss history.[49]

The commercial general liability application form asks additional questions, many of which can only be answered by the broker. Others will need to be addressed by the association's representative. For example, does the applicant install, service, or demonstrate products? Are there any guarantees, warranties, or hold harmless agreements? Does the applicant rent or loan equipment to others? Are parking facilities owned or rented, and is a fee charged for parking? Are recreational facilities provided? Are there any lodging operations? Is there a swimming pool on the premises? Are social activities or athletic teams sponsored? Are structural alterations or demolition contemplated? Are employees leased to or from other employers? Are there day care facilities? Have crimes occurred or been attempted in the previous three years? And is there a formal written safety and security policy?[50]

Instead of the second ACORD form there is a Condominium or Homeowners Association General Liability Application that is often used. It asks basic information about the age of the association, the number and type of units, the number of stories, and whether the buildings have sprinklers or are fire resistive. It enquires about the number of swimming pools, whether any diving boards are over one meter in height, if rules are posted, whether any pools are fenced, whether gates are self-closing and locking, and whether there are any lifeguards. It also asks for the number of parks, clubhouses, saunas, spas, baseball parks, volleyball courts, tennis courts, basketball courts, racquetball courts, playgrounds, ice skating areas, boat docks, boat rentals, and dams. It asks if there are any lakes, their size in acreage, and if swimming is allowed. The application enquires about any waterworks/sewage treatment/disposal facilities and if the association is responsible for maintenance of roads and if so how many miles of road. Next, the application queries whether there are horse or bike trails and if so how many miles of trails there are. It also asks whether there is a master association that provides group common areas for individual associations and whether there are

49. *See* ACORD 125 (2013/01).
50. *See* ACORD 126 (2011/09).

security guards on the premises, how many, whether they are armed or unarmed, and whether they are directly employed by the association is another group of questions. Finally, the application asks about "special events," although it does not explain what would constitute a special event.[51]

As can be seen, the ability to correctly address the various questions requires a considerable knowledge of the community. The association needs to be certain that whoever provides the information to the broker has that knowledge. Because residents, officers and directors, and managers change over time—sometimes quite frequently—it may be that no one person, or no one at all, has sufficient information. For that reason, it is wise for the entire governing board to review the application at a meeting open to the residents. A former board member in attendance may have information not known to the sitting board members or the current manager.

One question that does not appear on applications is, what requirements do your governing documents contain regarding liability coverage? The savvy broker will be aware that there may be requirements in the documents and will want copies of them. Nonetheless, when applying for coverage, the association should provide copies of the pertinent document provisions to the broker and discuss with him or her obtaining coverage that conforms to the document mandates.

When the commercial general liability policy is renewed with the same carrier year after year, the application may become outdated. The governing board should consider making a brief review of the original application part of an annual insurance audit with its broker. For example, five years after the application was submitted, the association may for the first time be considering structural alterations to an aging building. In the three years preceding the application, no crimes may have been attempted or committed, but one may have occurred several years later. Perhaps the association had a pool installed since it first applied for coverage. By reviewing the application questions on an annual basis, the governing board will be able to call these changes to the attention of the broker and avoid having the insurer claim it was not informed of information material to the risk.

51. Associations might need to obtain special events insurance. It is a breed of CGL coverage that, among other things, can provide coverage for an event holder that enters into a lease agreement for a venue at which an event is held requiring it to indemnify the lessor. Baker & Whitescarver, *What's So Special About Special Event Insurance?* (Insurance Journal 2009), available at: http://www.insurancejournal.com/magazines/features/2009/04/06/158019.htm. A sample policy can be seen at the Philadelphia Insurance Companies (PHLY) website. *See* https://www.phly.com/Files/SpecialEventsPolicy-Non-SportingEvents31-6907.pdf. It uses a standard commercial general liability policy—ISO Form CG 00 01 04 13—with a non-ISO endorsement that limits coverage to specified events listed on a schedule. It includes a number of other endorsements. Some are standard ISO forms, and others are not.

[3] Binders or Temporary Insurance

A binder is a contract for temporary insurance that is not itself an insurance policy but that provides interim insurance from the date of an application until either the policy is issued or the carrier declines to provide coverage.[52] A document that meets the requirements for a binder does not necessarily need to be called a binder to be enforceable as one.[53] Generally, the binder includes the provisions of the policy that ordinarily would be issued by the insurance company.[54] Sometimes the binder will expressly incorporate by reference the terms of the policy to be issued.[55] To avoid any doubt about temporary coverage, the insured should ask the broker to explain the coverage that will be in place until the policy is issued. In any event, it is important to have the policy issued as quickly as possible.

[4] Declarations Page

At the beginning of the policy are pages denominated the Common Policy Declarations, also known as the Declarations Page, "dec page," or "dec sheet." The Declarations state essential terms of the policy in abbreviated form.[56] To a large extent, the data in the Declarations is based on information supplied by the insured in its application for coverage. The policy provides that by accepting it, the insured agrees that the statements in the Declarations are accurate and complete, they are based on representations made by the insured to the carrier, and the carrier issued the policy in reliance on those representations of the insured.[57] This is significant because the basic rule of law is that if one party is induced to enter a contract by a fraudulent or material misrepresentation by the other party, and the first party was justified in his or her reliance, the contract is "voidable,"[58] meaning the contract is not void but can be rendered void. Of course, insurance law is rarely that simple. The general rule has been modified in many states. For example, in some states the insurer may be required to show *intent* to deceive or defraud before it can avoid the policy, while in others fraud

52. United States v. Renzi, 769 F.3d 731, 753–54 (9th Cir. 2014) (binders give insured temporary coverage while application for policy is being processed or while formal policy is being prepared); Coastal Hardware & Rental Co., LLC v. Certain Underwriters at Lloyds, London, 120 So. 3d 1017, 1023 (Miss. App. 2013).

53. Chicago Title Ins. Co. v. AMZ Ins. Services, Inc., 188 Cal. App. 4th 401, 115 Cal. Rptr. 3d 707 (2010).

54. Hershaw v. Farm & City Ins. Co., 32 Kan. App. 2d 684, 694, 87 P.3d 360, 367 (2004) (binder should include provisions of policy that ordinarily would have been issued).

55. Alea London, Ltd. v. Bono-Soltysiak Enters., 186 S.W.3d 403, 410 (Mo. App. 2006).

56. Midwestern Indem. Co. v. Brooks, 779 F.3d 540 (8th Cir. 2015) (terms stated on Declarations Page are subject to refinement and definition in body of policy).

57. *See, e.g.*, ISO Form CG 00 01 12 07, § IV.6.

58. Restatement (Second) of Contracts, § 164(1).

or a misrepresentation that is without intent to deceive but *material* to the risk of loss is sufficient.[59] Whether a matter is material and whether the insurer justifiably relied on it are much litigated questions and beyond the scope of this discussion. If an association wants to know the law in its particular state, it needs to consult an attorney, but the principal thing an association needs to know is that the governing board should carefully scrutinize the Declarations—and the application on which it is based—to insure the information on them is accurate. Anything that might not be completely accurate should be called to the attention of the broker. It is far better to have a discussion about possible inaccuracies at the outset than to engage in costly litigation later.

Some basic information can be located in the Declarations: the name of the insurer, the policy number, the policy term, and the premium. The form of the insured—limited liability company, partnership, organization/corporation—will be identified as will the "business description," for example, homeowners association or condominium association.

At the outset, the named insured and its mailing address will be listed. In a common interest community, the named insured would typically be the association or, in the case of a cooperative, the corporation that owns the building. The name of the insured as it appears in the Declarations should be the legal name of the association in the governing documents, not a name by which it is popularly known.[60] It is also important in a CIC to take into account any layers of associations. For example, a community may consist of several condominium or townhouse associations, a recreation association, and a master or umbrella association, all with similar sounding names.[61] Each of these will have distinct responsibilities spelled out in their respective governing documents. It is important to determine that the proper association is listed as named insured in the Declarations.

Sometimes the policy will be issued to the management company with it as the named insured and the association as an additional insured or additional

---

59. *See generally* 4 *New Appleman Law of Liability Insurance* § 38.03 (Matthew Bender, 2016).

60. *Consider* Far Northwest Dev. Co., LLC v. Cmty. Ass'n of Underwriters of Am., Inc., 2006 U.S. Dist. LEXIS 79033 (W.D. Wash. Oct. 30, 2006), where the policy was issued to the "Somerset Village Townhomes Condominium," rather than the association. It was argued that the condominium was merely a building and, therefore, not a legal entity capable of owning anything. The court found it clear that the intent of the parties was to provide coverage to the association and, therefore, the association was the named insured regardless of the Declarations Page. *See also* Beauvallon Condo. Ass'n v. Granite State Ins. Co., 2011 U.S. Dist. LEXIS 69606 (D. Colo. June 29, 2011) (association established that it was named insured under CGL policies where insurer acknowledged designation of named insured as "Beauvallon Homeowners Association" was scrivener's error and endorsements had been executed to correct that error).

61. *Consider* State Farm Fire & Cas. Co. v. Beck's Branch, Inc., 2016 U.S. Dist. LEXIS 22836 (W.D. Tenn. Feb. 25, 2016) (insureds were Beck's Branch, Inc., River Breeze Estates Associates, LLC, Riverbreeze at Becks Branch Homeowner's Association Inc, River Breeze Estates Homeowners Association, River Breeze Estates at Beck's Branch Homeowners Association, Inc.).

named insured.[62] The entity listed first on the Declarations Page as an insured is known as the first named insured or primary named insured.[63] Generally, the standard CGL policy grants equal status to the named insured shown in the Declarations and *any other person or organization qualifying* as a named insured under the policy. However, the *first* named insured has rights and responsibilities that do not apply to other named insureds. For example, if the carrier cancels the policy,[64] or refuses to renew it,[65] it is required to give notice, but generally only to the first named insured.[66] There is also a difference between being an additional insured and an additional *named* insured.[67] If the association is not the named insured on the Declarations Page, it needs to discuss with the broker, and possibly the association attorney, its precise status.

The Declarations contain the limits of insurance. This is the most that the insurer will pay in the event of a covered loss under the policy. Ordinarily there are six specific limits listed: the general aggregate limit, products-completed operations aggregate limit, personal and advertising injury limit, each occurrence limit, damage to premises rented to the named insured limit, and medical expense limit. Some policies may add a "professional incident" limit. For common interest communities, the general aggregate limit is often $1 or $2 million.[68] That may sound like a substantial amount of coverage but could well turn out to be insufficient.[69] One commentator recommends that policyholders attempt to have the aggregate limit deleted or raised as high as possible.[70] In the alternative, excess insurance

62. *See, e.g.*, Phila. Indem. Ins. Co. v. Yachtsman's Inn Condo Ass'n, 595 F. Supp. 2d 1319, 1320 (S.D. Fla. 2009) (commercial general liability policy was issued to management company as named insured with separate endorsement naming condominium association as additional named insured).

63. https://www.irmi.com/online/insurance-glossary/terms/f/first-named-insured.aspx.

64. *See* IL 00 17 11 98, § A.2.

65. *See* ISO Form CG 00 01 12 07, § IV.9.

66. Typically, notices of cancellation or nonrenewal have to be mailed or delivered anywhere from at least ten to sixty days before the effective date of cancellation or expiration of the policy. If the notice only goes to the management company, there will necessarily be some delay in receipt of notice by the association.

67. *See generally* Pomerantz, *Recognizing the Unique Status of Additional Named Insureds*, 53 Fordham L. Rev. 117, 138–39 (1984).

68. *See, e.g.*, Boggs, *Understanding Legal Liability for Condominium Association and Unit Owners* (2011), available at: http://www.mynewmarkets.com/articles/180950/understanding-legal-liability-for-condominium-association-and-unit-owners; Berding, *Exposed!? What Protects an Individual Homeowner from a Catastrophic Judgment Against Her Community Association?*, available at: https://www.berding-weil.com/articles/what-protects-homeowner-from-judgment-against-hoa.php#:~:text=Property%20owners%20within%20a%20community%20association%20are%20protected,and%20the%20CGL%20policy%20of%20the%20association%20itself. *See also* Dover Lake Park v. Scottsdale Ins. Co., 2003 Ohio App. LEXIS 2973 (June 25, 2003) (commercial general liability policy specified liability limits of $1 million per occurrence). Note that the general aggregate limit may be specified by state law. *See, e.g.*, Ga. Code § 44-3-107; Haw. Rev. Stat. § 514B-143.

69. *See, e.g.*, Pekelnaya v. Allyn, 25 A.D.3d 111, 808 N.Y.S.2d 590 (2005) (damages expected to exceed $2 million in liability insurance carried by association).

70. *See* Treese, *Risk Management Essential to Insurance Plan* (CAI 1995).

can be obtained.[71] The personal and advertising injury and each occurrence limits will typically be $500,000 or $1,000,000. The damage to premises rented to the named insured limit is ordinarily $100,000, while the medical expense limit is usually just $5,000.

[5] Premiums and Deductibles

Premiums vary greatly with risk and location. For many common interest communities, the commercial general liability policy represents a relatively small expenditure. For example, for a homeowners association in Missouri, the premium was less than $2,000.[72] On the other hand, in a Connecticut condominium the combined premium for CGL and directors and officers liability coverage was over $23,000.[73]

[a] Calculation of Premium

The standard policy says that the carrier will compute all premiums in accordance with its rules and rates.[74] Typically, the company will calculate the premium based in part on the number of units in the community by multiplying a rate per unit by the number of units. The premium may also include charges for common halls based on the area and streets based on the number of miles. The portion of the premium for coverage of swimming pools is ordinarily based on the number of pools. A flat charge is assessed for non-owned and hired automobiles coverage.

The standard CGL policy provides that the premium shown as an "advance premium" is only a deposit, and at the close of each audit period the insurer will compute the earned premium for that period and send a notice to the first named insured of any amount due.[75] The policy requires the first named insured to keep records of the information needed for premium computation and to send copies of those records when the carrier requests them.[76] These premium audit provisions have been held to be unambiguous and enforceable. For example, an athletic club paid an initial advance premium of just under $9,000 for the first year and an advance premium of just over $8,000 on renewal of the policy. The

71. *See* § 13.01[6], *infra.*

72. *See* National Fire & Marine Ins. Co. v. Hoene Springs Improvement Ass'n, 889 F. Supp. 362, 364–65 (E.D. Mo. 1995) (initial CGL policy issued to homeowners association had premium of $1,600, including $500 for special events coverage, and renewal policy had premium of $1,975, including $600 for special events coverage).

73. *See* BRT Prop. Group v. Willow Springs Condo. Ass'n, 1996 Conn. Super. LEXIS 2615 (Conn. Super. Oct. 9, 1996) (association obtained liability insurance including directors and officers liability coverage for $23,369).

74. *See, e.g.*, ISO Form CG 00 01 12 07, § IV.5.a.

75. *See, e.g.*, ISO Form CG 00 01 12 07, § IV.5.b. The due date for audit and retrospective premiums is the date shown on the bill as the due date. If the sum of the advance and audit premiums paid is greater than the earned premium, the carrier will return the excess to the first named insured.

76. *See, e.g.*, ISO Form CG 00 01 12 07, § IV.5.c.

insurer conducted audits for both policy terms that revealed the club had been underbilled about $23,500 because it had underestimated the potential exposure to the insurer.[77] The club refused to pay and argued the policy was ambiguous because the Declarations made no mention of an additional premium. The court held the premium audit provision was unambiguous and the club was properly subject to an audit for the purpose of ascertaining the actual exposure of liability and any additional premiums due and owing to the insurer.[78]

The typical common interest community association will generally not be subject to a premium audit because the premium is based on fixed criteria: number of units, area of common elements, and number of swimming pools. Ordinarily the criteria subject to audit are the payroll and sales of the insured.[79] Commercial policyholders estimate these numbers at the commencement of a policy period, and the purpose of the audit is to determine whether the actual payroll or sales are greater or less than what was estimated. These determinations would usually be inapplicable to a residential common interest community. An exception would be for an association that operates a facility—for example, a clubhouse—that has an employee payroll and generates revenues from the sale of food and beverages and perhaps club monogrammed goods.

[b] Allocation of the Cost of Premiums to Association Members

Typically, insurance premiums are a line item in the association annual budget. The association then levies an assessment—usually paid on a monthly basis—against its members to cover the amount budgeted for its annual expenses based on each member's share of the common expenses. However, under the Uniform Common Interest Ownership Act (UCIOA)—and the law of many states[80]—to the extent *required* by the governing documents of an association, the costs of insurance *have to be assessed* in proportion to risk.[81] In other words, an association can charge an individual owner who is responsible for an increase in the cost

77. There was evidence that the information supplied by the club to the insurer was that its gross receipts for the health club associated with the business were $150,000, but from the audits, the insurer learned the estimates of gross receipts totaled more than $500,000.

78. Capitol Indem. Corp. v. North Hills Athletic Club, 182 Wis. 2d 511, 514 N.W.2d 879 (Wis. App. 1994).

79. *See, e.g.*, *Premium Audit Guide* (Patriot Ins. Co.), available at: https://www.patriotinsuranceco.com/wp-content/uploads/sites/2/2017/10/pi-2017-audit-guide.pdf. *Commercial General Liability Insurance; What is a Premium Audit?* (Texas Dep't of Insurance 2010), available at: http://www.tdi.texas.gov/pubs/pc/pcgenliab.html.

80. *See, e.g.*, Code of Ala. § 35-8A-315(c)(3); Mo. Rev. Stat. § 448.3-115.3(3); Neb. Rev. Stat. § 76-873(c)(3).

81. Uniform Common Interest Ownership Act § 3-115(c)(3). *Consider* Carriage Park Assoc. v. Emanuel, 2003 Conn. Super. LEXIS 416 (Feb. 6, 2003) (where insurer refused to renew policy citing losses attributable to two units and replacement policy resulted in substantial increase, association could not assess increased insurance premiums against particular units as right to do so was conditioned on increased *prospective* risk not previous claim).

of coverage. Unfortunately, the Act does not explain how "proportion to risk" is determined.

Sometimes the increased risk is easy to determine. For example, a condominium in Connecticut, a state that has adopted the UCIOA, had a provision in its documents stating that unit owners would be assessed when a premium increase was attributable to either "activities in" or "construction of" their unit. A partnership owned a substantial number of the units in the community and rented them to residential tenants. The association's liability insurer cancelled its policy because almost half the units were investor/rental units not occupied by a unit owner. The association obtained substitute coverage, but at an increased premium. It assessed the added insurance expense against the non-owner-occupied units. The partnership challenged the assessment, but the court said that by assessing the incremental increase in insurance costs to the units that were non-owner occupied, the association "properly assessed the costs of insurance in proportion to the risk." The court noted that the cancellation notice specifically stated the policy was terminated for one reason, the large number and high percentage of non-owner-occupied units. Thus, the incremental increase in insurance coverage costs was solely attributable to those unit owners who rent out their units, and rental activity created an increased risk of loss.[82]

It may not always be easy to accurately attribute an increase in premiums to the activities of specific members of the association. Associations that want to assess the costs of insurance in proportion to risk in those circumstances should confer with the association attorney to establish a defensible basis for allocating premium expenses to fewer than all its members.

[c] Deductible

Commercial general liability policies issued to common interest community associations generally have no deductible. Deductibles serve to reduce the premium because the potential liability to the insurer is diminished. For most associations, the cost of a CGL policy is relatively small so there is no need for a deductible. In some cases, a particular association may present an increased risk for a carrier and it will charge a higher than usual premium. In that case, a deductible can be added to the policy by endorsement.[83] That deductible is likely to be rather small.

The standard deductible endorsement contains a schedule on which is listed the amount of the deductible or deductibles, whether it is applied on a per claim

82. BRT Prop. Group v. Willow Springs Condo. Ass'n, 1996 Conn. Super. LEXIS 2615 (Conn. Super. Oct. 9, 1996).

83. *See, e.g.*, ISO Form CG 03 00 01 96. The association could also have a policy with a self-insured retention ("SIR") endorsement. A SIR is a stated amount for which the insured is responsible—that is, it "self-insures." There are differences between a SIR and a deductible. For example, generally the party that has self-insured is responsible for defense of a claim within the SIR limit. However, there are variations, and if the policy has a SIR endorsement, the association needs to discuss its parameters with its broker.

or per occurrence basis, and whether there are any limitations on its application. If there are no limitations, the deductibles apply to damages for all bodily injury and property damage, however caused, and the carrier's obligation under the bodily injury and property damage liability coverages to pay damages on behalf of the named insured applies only to the amount of damages that exceed the deductible amounts stated in the schedule.[84]

The CGL for most common interest community associations will contain an endorsement making its members additional insureds. If the carrier pays a claim on behalf of an association member, who is responsible for paying the deductible amount? Courts generally look at the language of the standard deductible endorsement—which says that *you*, meaning the named insured, have to promptly reimburse the carrier for the part of the deductible amount it paid—and conclude that because "you" refers to the named insured, the named insured is the party responsible for paying the deductible.[85] However, the governing documents for an association may grant it the possibility of recouping the deductible from the member responsible for the claim. If an association wants to employ a clause in its documents for that purpose, it should confer with its attorney to determine whether the document language will support that action and, perhaps more important, whether there is some basis for it to recover any costs and attorney's fees expended in pursuing that recovery. Because CGL deductibles for associations are often rather small, the cost of recovery could easily exceed the deductible amount, making it impractical to bring an action to recover the deductible without also recovering its fees and costs.

84. *See, e.g.*, ISO Form CG 03 00 01 96, § A. The endorsement provides that the terms of the policy, including those regarding the right and duty of the carrier to defend the insured against any suits seeking the damages specified in the endorsement and the duties of the insured in the event of an occurrence, claim, or suit, apply regardless of application of the deductible amount. *See* ISO Form CG 03 00 01 96, § C. The insurer may pay any part or all of the deductible amount to settle a claim or suit and, on notification of the action taken, the insured must promptly reimburse the insurer for the part of the deductible amount paid by the insurer. *See* ISO Form CG 03 00 01 96, § D.

85. Hartford Accident & Indem. Co. v. U.S. Natural Resources, 897 F. Supp. 466, 473 (D. Or. 1995) (plain language of CGL policy imposes burden of reimbursing deductible on party qualifying as named insured, and not on those qualifying as "persons insured," "insured," or "additional persons insured"). *See also* Select Build Ill., LLC v. Ace Am. Ins. Co., 2015 U.S. Dist. LEXIS 156878 (N.D. Ill. Nov. 16, 2015); Barletta Heavy Div., Inc. v. Layne Christensen Co., 2011 U.S. Dist. LEXIS 40045, at *25, n.8 (D. Mass. Apr. 13, 2011) (language of deductible endorsement goes to issue of which party—policyholder or additional insured—would have obligation to insurer to pay deductible, and courts that have addressed that question have generally determined that policyholder has that obligation; that obligation to pay insurer for any deductibles owed falls to policyholder supports conclusion that deductible is responsibility of policyholder and not additional insured). *And see* Continental Casualty Co. v. Campbell Design Group, 914 S.W.2d 43 (Mo. App. 1996) (officers of insured corporation while also insureds under policy were not liable under terms of policy for deductible amount because neither was a party to insurance contract and language in contract to which they were not parties could not bind them).

[6] Excess Policy

The typical commercial general liability policy issued to a common interest community association provides either $1 or $2 million in total coverage. Judgments, however, can easily exceed that amount. The members of the governing board of an association may be under the illusion that because the association is a non-profit entity composed of homeowners, it cannot be subject to a substantial judgment against it. A Colorado court dismissed that idea, saying that the existence and amount of the liability insurance of a non-profit organization provide no basis for limiting a judgment against it.[86] Therefore, to protect itself adequately, an association needs excess coverage. Generally, excess liability insurance merely provides an increase in the limit of insurance over the amount provided by the underlying CGL policy, as opposed to an umbrella policy that may provide both an increased limit of insurance and differences in coverage.[87] It is not uncommon for the excess coverage to be issued by the insurer that issued the underlying or primary coverage. That raises a concern. If that insurer goes insolvent, the association has no coverage. It will have to rely on the state guaranty fund to pay a claim, and the fund generally does not pay the full amount the primary insurer would have. If the excess and primary insurer are the same company, the fund may or may not pay under both policies.

[7] Certificates of Insurance

A certificate of insurance is simply evidence of the existence of a policy.[88] It is not an insurance policy,[89] does not create legal obligations,[90] and in fact is not even a contract.[91] Common interest community associations often ask for certificates of insurance from those with whom they contract for services for two reasons: first,

---

86. Wycoff v. Grace Cmty. Church, 251 P.3d 1260 (Colo. App. 2010).

87. *Excess Liability Insurance and Umbrella Insurance for Homeowner Associations*, available at: http://dandavisins.com/excess-liabilityumbrella/.

88. 10 Ellicott Square Court Corp. v. Mt. Valley Indem. Co., 634 F.3d 112, 122 (2d Cir. 2010) (under New York contract law certificate of insurance is merely evidence of contract for insurance). *But see* Gushin v. Whispering Hills Condominium I, 2010 N.Y. Misc. LEXIS 6440 (Dec. 15, 2010) (where condominium association claimed company with which it had snow removal contract failed to procure insurance on its behalf, court said that certificate of insurance did not establish issue of fact as to whether insurance coverage existed and gave no weight to certificate of insurance).

89. Sevenson Envtl. Servs., Inc. v. Sirius Am. Ins. Co., 74 A.D.3d 1751, 1753, 902 N.Y.S.2d 279, 280 (2010) (certificate of insurance, by itself, does not confer insurance coverage); Am. Family Ins. Co. v. Globe Am. Cas. Co., 774 N.E.2d 932, 939 (Ind. App. 2002) (purpose of certificate of insurance is to inform its recipient that insurance has been obtained, but certificate is not equivalent of insurance policy). *See also* 10 Ellicott Square Court Corp. v. Mt. Valley Indem. Co., 634 F.3d 112, 122 (2d Cir. 2010) (certificate of insurance is not contract to insure).

90. G.E. Tignall & Co. v. Reliance Nat'l Ins. Co., 102 F. Supp. 2d 300, 304 (D. Md. 2000) (certificate alone does not create coverage or legal duties).

91. Clarendon Am. Ins. Co. v. Aargus Sec. Sys., 312 Ill. Dec. 544, 374 Ill. App. 3d 591, 597, 870 N.E.2d 988, 993 (2007) (certificates of insurance are not contracts).

to assure themselves that the service provider is properly insured and second, if the contract between the parties requires that the association be named as an additional insured on the policies of the service provider,[92] the association can determine whether it has that status by examining the certificate.

A certificate of insurance for liability coverage is usually in the form of the standard certificate of liability insurance from the ACORD Corporation.[93] This certificate contains two disclaimers. First, at the top of the form, in all capitals, it states that it is issued as a matter of information only, confers no rights on the certificate holder, does not affirmatively or negatively amend, extend, or alter the coverage afforded by the policy, and does not constitute a contract between the issuing insurers, authorized representative or producer, and the certificate holder. Second, it states that if the certificate holder is an additional insured, the policy has to have additional insured provisions or be endorsed and if subrogation is waived, subject to the terms and conditions of the policy, an endorsement may be required and any statement in the certificate confers no rights to the certificate holder in lieu of an endorsement. Additionally, at the end of the certificate it states that should the policy be cancelled before its expiration date, notice will be delivered in accordance with the policy provisions. The standard commercial general liability policy provides that the insurer may cancel the policy by mailing or delivering *written* notice of cancellation to the *first named insured*;[94] thus, if an association is an additional insured, unless the policy is modified to require notice to additional insureds, the association will not be provided notice by the insurer of the cancellation.[95]

Certificates of insurance are important in common interest communities in at least three respects. First, in some states if the insurer for the association issues a certificate of insurance to individual owners or lienholders, it incurs additional obligations. Second, an association may require that workers who make alterations to individual residences be insured, and the certificate provides proof that requirement has been met. Finally, certificates of insurance are important for an association to obtain when it contracts for services with third parties.

92. *See generally* Mehta, *Additional Insured Status in Construction Contracts and Moral Hazard*, 3 Conn. Ins. L.J. 169 (1996/1997); Pomerantz, *Recognizing the Unique Status of Additional Named Insureds*, 53 Fordham L. Rev. 117 (1984).

93. *See* ACORD 25 (2016/03).

94. *See, e.g.*, IL 00 17 11 98, § A.2.

95. *See, e.g.*, Pinnacol Assur. v. Hoff, 375 P.3d 1214 (2016) (workers' compensation carrier had no obligation to notify non-insured holder of certificate of insurance when policy evidenced by that certificate was cancelled because plain language of certificate promised only that notice would be delivered in accordance with provisions of policy and policy contained no promise to give notice to certificate holders).

[a] Residents and Lienholders

The UCIOA requires insurers to issue certificates or memoranda of insurance on "request made in a record" to any unit owner or holder of a security interest.[96] The insurer may not cancel or refuse to renew the policy until 30 days after notice of the proposed cancellation or nonrenewal has "been mailed to the association, each unit owner and each holder of a security interest to whom a certificate or memorandum of insurance has been issued at their respective last known addresses."

[b] Alteration Agreements

Many common interest communities require their individual owners or tenant/shareholders to sign an alteration agreement before making significant changes to their units or apartments. These agreements often require proof of insurance from both the resident and the contractors who will be working for the resident.

The New York City Bar, for example, has drafted a form agreement for cooperative corporations that states a tenant/shareholder is required to deliver to the corporation a copy of his or her applicable insurance policies or, at the option of the corporation, a certificate evidencing that insurance, and must also deliver, or cause each of his or her contractors and subcontractors to deliver, to the corporation the insurance policies required by the agreement—including workers' compensation, commercial general liability, comprehensive automobile liability, and umbrella liability policies—or again, at the option of the corporation, certificates of that insurance.[97] An exhibit to the agreement requires that before beginning any work, detailed certificates of insurance have to be furnished to the corporation showing that the required insurance is in full force and the premiums due have been paid, and the certificates are required to provide that the insurance may not be cancelled, terminated, or modified without ten days' written advance notice to the corporation.[98] The notice of cancellation or modification is an especially important mandate because, as noted above, the cooperative corporation, even if named as an additional insured under these policies, is not entitled

96. Uniform Common Interest Ownership Act § 3-113(g) (2008).

97. *Alteration Agreement for Cooperative Apartment*, § 3.d (NYC Bar Ass'n), available at: http://www2.nycbar.org/RealEstate/Forms/Coop_Condo_%20Form_Alteration_Agreement_Coops_Commentary10.pdf.

98. *Alteration Agreement for Cooperative Apartment*, Exhibit C (NYC Bar Ass'n), available at: http://www2.nycbar.org/RealEstate/Forms/Coop_Condo_%20Form_Alteration_Agreement_Coops_Commentary10.pdf. Note that under the standard commercial general liability policy, if cancellation is for non-payment of the premium, that notice has to be mailed or delivered *at least ten days* before the effective date of cancellation. Therefore, the vendor may not know its policy is about to be cancelled in order to give the cooperative corporation ten days' advanced written notice of the cancellation. Generally, however, that time period in the policy is expanded by an endorsement mandated by state law.

to notice of cancellation under the standard commercial general liability policy issued to another party.

[c] The Association

Experts agree that it is critically important for common interest community associations to collect certificates of insurance from any vendor working on the property.[99] The certificates can serve to protect the interest of the association if there is a claim because the association will then know what coverage is in place and who to contact. The association needs to remember that the certificate is evidence of insurance at the time it is issued.[100] The policy may no longer be in effect when a claim arises. If, for example, the policy is cancelled, the association would ordinarily get no notice of the cancellation. The association could include a requirement in its contract with a vendor that it be notified in writing of any modification or cancellation of vendor policies, but that obligation would be imposed on the vendor, not the insurer, which is not a party of the contract between the vendor and the association.

One issue that arises with certificates of insurance is whether a certificate that names a party as an additional insured guarantees that there actually is coverage for that party. A few courts take the position that a carrier that issues a certificate of insurance—either itself or through its agent[101]—that names a particular party as an additional insured may be estopped from denying coverage to that party when the party has reasonably relied on the certificate to its detriment.[102] Most courts, however, taking note of the patent disclaimers in the typical certificate, hold that one cannot justifiably rely on those certificates and that those who take

99. *See* Levine, *Certificates of Insurance for Vendors: What We Should Have and From Who We Should Collect Them* (2014), available at: http://ebmg.com/2014/06/certificates-of-insurance-for-vendors-what-we-should-have-and-from-who-we-should-collect-them/; Braten, *Why Certificates of Insurance are so Important to Community Associations*, available at: https://rosenbaumpllc.com/1391-2/.

100. *See, e.g.*, 10 Ellicott Square Court Corp. v. Mt. Valley Indem. Co., 634 F.3d 112, 122 (2d Cir. 2010) (certificate of insurance is not conclusive proof that contract exists).

101. That the carrier or its agent issued the certificate is a key point, because often the broker for the service provider issues the certificate and the carrier has neither actual nor constructive knowledge of it. *See* 1200 Grand St. Condo. Ass'n v. 1200 Grand St. Urban Renewal LLC (*In re* Tarragon Corp.), 2013 Bankr. LEXIS 1676 (Bankr. D.N.J. Apr. 16, 2013) (insurer argued that insurance broker that issued certificate of insurance was not its agent, but rather agent of insured and, therefore, was not dispositive of question of whether particular party was additional named insured as listed in certificate; court concluded it did not need to resolve that question at that point in the case).

102. Sevenson Envtl. Servs., Inc. v. Sirius Am. Ins. Co., 74 A.D.3d 1751, 1753, 902 N.Y.S.2d 279, 281 (2010). *Compare* Mt. Hawley Ins. Co. v. Robinette Demolition, Inc., 374 Ill. Dec. 36, 994 N.E.2d 973, 983 (Ill. App.), *app. den.*, 377 Ill. Dec. 765, 2 N.E.3d 1046 (Ill. 2013) (that certificate of insurance was issued by agent for named insured rather than for insurer was not dispositive).

certificates of insurance at face value do so at their own risk.[103] Therefore, if an association wants proof that it has been named as an additional insured on policies of its service providers, it needs to ask for copies of those polices. Additionally, without the actual policy or a list of its exclusions, the association will not know of pertinent exclusions, including the one for work performed for a common interest community.[104] In an abundance of caution, it can also contact the insurance company to confirm that the policy is in effect and that it is named as an additional insured.

[8] Retaining Copies of Expired Policies

Common interest communities often dispose of old documents in their files on a periodic basis. This process may be initiated by the community association management company and may even be one of the services for which the contract between it and the association provides. When the documents are culled, should the association retain old commercial general liability policies? The answer is that there is no harm in retaining old policies, and there may be a benefit. For example, certain injuries—those caused by dangerous substances, for instance—may occur over a long period of time, and there may be coverage for them under long-expired policies issued by carriers with whom the association no longer contracts.[105] Because membership on the governing boards can change frequently, there may be no one on the board that even remembers that the association once contracted with a different carrier. One expert recommends keeping expired copies of policies for at least five years after their expiration and preferably ten years.[106]

---

103. Via Net v. TIG Ins. Co., 211 S.W.3d 310, 314 (Tex. 2006); Ann Taylor, Inc. v. Heritage Ins. Servs., 259 S.W.3d 494, 499 (Ky. App. 2008). *See also* G.E. Tignall & Co. v. Reliance Nat'l Ins. Co., 102 F. Supp. 2d 300, 304 (D. Md. 2000). *Compare* Mt. Hawley Ins. Co. v. Robinette Demolition, Inc., 374 Ill. Dec. 36, 994 N.E.2d 973, 984 (Ill. App.), *app. den.*, 377 Ill. Dec. 765, 2 N.E.3d 1046 (Ill. 2013) (where endorsement made all "persons or organizations where required by written contract" additional insureds, agreement between named insured and contractor requiring former to include latter and others reasonably required by latter, as additional insureds, together with certificate of insurance satisfied policy requirement that there be written contract requiring insured to name additional insureds).

104. *See* § 2.13, *supra.*

105. *See, e.g.*, Rubenstein v. Royal Ins. Co. of Am., 44 Mass. App. Ct. 842, 843, 694 N.E.2d 381, 382 (1998) (insured owned property for over 60 years and during that time purchased insurance from six different companies; after property was sold, oil leak was discovered and insured brought declaratory judgment action against those various insurance companies, seeking declaration that they had duty to defend and indemnify).

106. Wick, *Record Retention Means Future Protection*, Common Ground (CAI July/Aug 1990). *See also* Porter, *Records Retention Guide for Homeowners Associations* (CAI Ledger Quarterly 1990) (retention of insurance policies and claims paid records is board administrative decision; recommending retaining claims paid records for five years).

When an association sues an insurer, it has the initial burden of showing coverage,[107] and that is more difficult to do without the policy. It is often held that a copy of the policy needs to be attached to the complaint in a suit against the insurer,[108] although where the policy cannot be produced, courts generally will allow evidence of its contents to be introduced.[109] Gathering and introducing that evidence takes time and is an additional expenditure. Clearly, it is best if the association can produce the actual policy.[110] Thus, there is nothing to be gained by disposing of old policies, and there may be a benefit to retaining them.

Record retrieval is as important as record retention. The association may have retained expired policies, but if no one can find them, they may as well have been destroyed. An expert asserts that it is the responsibility of the governing board to assure that records are adequately maintained.[111] The association should have a storage facility for important documents that is separate from any facility maintained by the management company and should not be in the home or garage of a member of the association, but in an area accessible to future board members,

107. *See, e.g.*, Borough of Sayreville v. Bellefonte Ins. Co., 320 N.J. Super. 598, 605, 728 A.2d 225, 228 (1998); Gold Fields Am. Corp. v. Aetna Cas. & Sur. Co., 173 Misc. 2d 901, 904, 661 N.Y.S.2d 948, 950 (1997) (policyholder has burden of proof on issue of existence of policy and its terms; where policyholder asserts it has lost policy, problem is for policyholder to address).

108. *See, e.g.*, Karaskiewicz v. Allstate Ins. Co. (*In re* Am. Arbitration Ass'n Arbitration), 109 Ill. App. 2d 370, 372, 248 N.E.2d 756, 758 (1969) (remanded to lower court with directions to strike complaint for failure to attach copy of insurance contract); State Farm Mut. Auto. Ins. Co. v. Jones, 98 Ga. App. 46, 56, 104 S.E.2d 725, 733 (1958) (pleadings in action against insurer required that copy of policy be attached or that petition allege language contained in policy).

109. *See, e.g.*, Rubenstein v. Royal Ins. Co. of Am., 44 Mass. App. Ct. 842, 846, 694 N.E.2d 381, 384 (1998) (existence of insurance policy is generally proven by documentary evidence; that policy has been lost or destroyed does not mean that its existence and contents may not be reconstructed from business records, underwriter's folios, or billings of insurer to insured); Borough of Sayreville v. Bellefonte Ins. Co., 320 N.J. Super. 598, 605, 728 A.2d 225, 228 (1998) (nothing in record suggested missing policies were different from others issued later that were available); Fraser v. Metropolitan Life Ins. Co., 165 Wash. 667, 669, 5 P.2d 978, 980 (1931) (where evidence was introduced that policy had been lost or mislaid and could not be found, form of policy was offered and received into evidence as testimony showed it was same form of policy as had been issued to insured). *See generally* Jones, *No Policy, No Problem? How Insureds are Finding Coverage Even Though They Can't Find Their Policies*, 50 Drake L. Rev. 611 (2002). The author notes that claims for breach of insurance agreements are based on allegations of a breach of a written contract and much of the information to complete the policy is unique to the specific insured: coverage limits, locations for which coverage is provided, and the period during which coverage exists. The written contract is, therefore, critical to determining the existence and scope of coverage.

110. One problem is that a court may allow use of a sample policy of the type that was apparently issued by the carrier at the time the policy in question was issued. *See, e.g.*, Gold Fields Am. Corp. v. Aetna Cas. & Sur. Co., 173 Misc. 2d 901, 906, 661 N.Y.S.2d 948, 951 (1997) (courts have permitted use of specimen policies to show what terms of policy at issue were). That policy, however, will not contain the information on the Declarations Page that may be critically important, for example, the limits of insurance. Additionally, use of a sample policy will not help determine the specific endorsements that were a part of the actual policy.

111. Porter, *Records Retention Guide for Homeowners Associations* (CAI Ledger Quarterly 1990).

either an offsite leased facility or a segregated and secure area that is part of the common areas of the community, for example, a clubhouse. It is also important that there be an index or cataloging system that makes it easy to find a specific document in the collection of retained material.

Record retention and retrieval can be made easier in the age of electronic documents. Documents can be scanned to create an electronic copy. That copy can be kept on the association computer with a backup retained on a flash drive. Community association managers often scan the insurance policies issued to the associations they manage and post them along with other documents on a website so that members of the association can view them. The association can retain the electronic copy of the policies each year. Storage of hardcopies of policies is a challenge as collectively the various policies can total several hundred pages each year. Electronic copies take up little space, but some of the same cautions that apply to hardcopies also apply to electronic ones. The sole electronic copy should not be in the possession of the management company. The association should have its own copy. When the electronic copies are on a flash drive, they should be kept in a common area to which all governing board members have access, not in the home of a board member.

§ 13.02 Who Is an Insured?

The standard commercial general liability policy states that "insured" means any person or organization qualifying as an insured under the policy. There are three categories of insureds. Insureds can be "named," "automatic," or "additional."[112]

[1] Named Insured

Under the standard commercial general liability policy, the named insured is the person or entity shown on the Declarations Page and any other person or entity qualifying as a named insured under the policy. The language distinguishes between an "insured" and the "named insured."[113] A "named insured" has a restricted meaning and does not apply to anyone other than those named in the policy, and the distinction between a "named insured" and a mere "insured" means a party that becomes an additional insured does not become a "named

112. *See generally* Kealy, *Understanding Named, Automatic, and Additional Insureds in the CGL Policy* (2014).

113. The policy says that throughout it, the words "you" and "your" refer to the named insured shown on the Declarations Page, and any other person or organization qualifying as a named insured under the policy. It then says that the word "insured" means any person or organization qualifying as such under Section II of the policy.

insured."[114] Some courts, however, have found that the entire policy applies to each additional insured just as it applies to the named insured.[115]

In a common interest community, the named insured would typically be the association or, in the case of a cooperative, the corporation that owns the building. While courts may look beyond the use of an appellation that is not the legal name of the named insured,[116] it is best for the legal name of the association as it appears in the governing documents to be the named insured stated on the Declarations Page, not a name by which the association may be popularly known.[117] One reason for that is that the association may be a part of a community that has layers of associations. For example, a community may consist of several condominium or townhouse associations, a recreation association, and a master or umbrella association, all with similar-sounding names. Each of these will have distinct responsibilities delineated in their respective governing documents. It is important for the Declarations Page to list the proper association as named insured.

---

114. EMC Ins. Cos. v. Mid-Continent Cas. Co., 884 F. Supp. 2d 1147, 1157–58 (D. Colo. 2012). *See also* Alexander v. Nat'l Fire Ins., 454 F.3d 214, 226–27 (3d Cir. 2006) (although term named insured is not defined in policy, Declarations Page listed condominium association as named insured and fact that someone—for example, condominium unit owner—may be additional insured does not mean that they are named insured as two terms are not interchangeable; named insured means named insured); 1300 Alki Condo. Owners Ass'n v. Hartford Cas. Ins. Co., 2004 U.S. Dist. LEXIS 32398 (W.D. Wash. Oct. 22, 2004) (where insurer contended "you" as used in exclusion encompassed all insureds while condominium association countered policy specifically defined pronoun "you" as "named insured," court found reasonable people could differ on whether use of word "you" contemplated individual unit owners named in endorsement and, therefore, policy was ambiguous and court construed it against carrier).

115. Prisco Serena Sturm Architects v. Liberty Mut. Ins. Co., 126 F.3d 886, 893 (7th Cir. 1997) (where named insured, was obligated to include others as additional insureds on its CGL policy, entire policy applied to each of them just as it applied to named insured). *See also* Wyner v. North Am. Specialty Ins. Co., 78 F.3d 752 (1st Cir. 1996) (where policy defined "you" as named insured shown on Declarations Page "and any other person or organization," court held that exclusions for property "you own, rent or occupy" extended to landlords as an additional insured).

116. *See* North American Acc. Ins. Co. v. Canady, 196 Okla. 105, 107–08, 163 P.2d 221, 223 (1945) (that insured when applying for insurance used adopted or business name, rather than real name, did not necessarily render policy void).

117. *Consider* QBE Ins. Corp. v. Creston Court Condo., Inc., 58 F. Supp. 3d 1137 (D. Or. 2014), in which a condominium project was developed by a company called Creston Court Condominium, Inc. and was subsequently governed by the Association of Unit Owners of Creston Court Condominium. The Declarations Page of the CGL policy listed "Creston Court Condominium" as the named insured, but there was no entity by that name. Instead, that was the name of the property. The court concluded "Creston Court Condominium" had to refer to an entity, not a building, and there were two entities to which it could refer: the developer or the association. The term was, therefore, ambiguous and the court held there was only one reasonable interpretation of it: the parties intended to refer to the association. The court noted the title of the policy was "Condominium Association Insurance Policy."

[2] Automatic Insureds

An automatic insured is a person or entity not identified by name on the Declarations Page but instead described in the policy as an insured by a relationship to the named insured. Where, for example, an insured under a policy included any person or organization to whom the named insured became obligated to include as an additional insured, that party was an "automatic insured" even though the policy itself did not name the party.[118]

[a] Limited Liability Companies and Trusts as Named Insured

Under the standard CGL, if the named insured is designated as a limited liability company (LLC), then the LLC is an insured, and so are its members, but only with respect to the conduct of the business of the LLC and its managers,[119] but only with respect to their duties as managers of the LLC.[120] To determine the meaning of "member" or "manager," one looks to the state's limited liability company statutes.[121]

If the named insured is designated as a trust, the trust is an insured and so are the trustees, but only with respect to their duties as trustees.[122] This reference to LLCs and trusts can be significant because, although uncommon, it is possible for a common interest community to be an LLC[123] or a trust.[124] The Uniform Common Interest Ownership Act, for instance, requires an association to be

118. Transcon. Pipe Line Corp. v. Nat'l Union Fire Ins. Co., 378 F. Supp. 2d 729, 738 (M.D. La. 2005).

119. *See* EMC Ins. Cos. v. Mid-Continent Cas. Co., 884 F. Supp. 2d 1147, 1157 (D. Colo. 2012) (for manager of limited liability company to be an "insured," entity for which she serves in that role must be "named insured" as shown on Declarations Page or must qualify as "named insured" under policy).

120. *See, e.g.*, ISO Form CG 00 01 12 07, § II.1.a.

121. Brown v. MR Group, LLC, 278 Wis. 2d 760, 764, 693 N.W.2d 138, 140 (2005) (when clause in standard CGL policy refers to manager or member of limited liability company, intent is for those words to mean same as defined in state's limited liability company statute).

122. *See, e.g.*, ISO Form CG 00 01 12 07, § II.1.e.

123. *See, e.g.*, Whitehouse Condo. Group, LLC v. Cincinnati Ins. Co., 569 Fed. Appx. 413 (6th Cir. 2014); Edgewood Manor Apt. Homes LLC v. RSUI Indem. Co., 782 F. Supp. 2d 716 (E.D. Wis. 2011).

124. The Massachusetts Condominium Act specifically authorizes condominiums to be organized as trusts. *See* Mass. G.L. c. 183A, § 1 ("organization of unit owners" is corporation, trust, or association owned by unit owners and used by them to manage and regulate a condominium). Trust ownership is rare but occasionally found in cooperative housing. *See* 2 Rohan & Reskin, *Real Estate Transactions: Cooperative Housing Law and Practice—Forms*, § 1.05[4][a][ii] (Matthew Bender, 2016) (trust form of cooperative ownership is found in Illinois but is prohibited in New York).

organized as a profit or non-profit corporation, trust, limited liability company, partnership,[125] or any other form of organization authorized by state law.[126]

[b] Corporation as Named Insured

Most common interest communities are organized as non-profit corporations. The standard CGL provides that if the named insured is designated as an organization other than a partnership, joint venture, or LLC, the organization is an insured as are its "executive officers" and directors,[127] but only with respect to their duties as officers or directors,[128] and probably only when they hold office during the term of the policy.[129] The policy also provides that the corporation's

125. It is rare for a residential common interest community to be organized as a partnership, but if it were, the standard CGL states that if the named insured is designated as a partnership or joint venture, the partnership or joint venture is an insured and so are its members, partners, and their spouses, but only with respect to the conduct of the business of the partnership or joint venture. ISO Form CG 00 01 12 07, § II.1.b.

126. Uniform Common Interest Ownership Act § 3-101.

127. *See* EMC Ins. Cos. v. Mid-Continent Cas. Co., 884 F. Supp. 2d 1147, 1157 (D. Colo. 2012) (for officer or director of corporation to be an "insured," entity for which she serves in that role must be "named insured" as shown on Declarations Page or must qualify as "named insured" under policy; only officers and directors of "named insured" are considered "insureds" under policy).

128. One commentary addresses scenarios in which the director of a private club might be considered to be engaged in her duties as a director. It says that picking up trash and straightening up the premises before and after board meetings would likely be within her duties, but entering the club premises during a weekend to straighten them up on her own initiative would not appear to be related to her role as a director unless the bylaws stated the activity was expected of directors. Finally, a director on the premises strictly as a guest at a social event would not be there as a part of her duties as a director, but if she were representing the club at the event in her official capacity it would be within those duties. *Officers and Directors Insureds under CGL Form?* (Summit Business Media, 2013). Directors and officers of common interest communities often find themselves in similar situations, especially because they live on the property. If a director stops to weed a flower bed in the common area, she is probably acting outside the scope of her duties as a director unless, perhaps, her duties include responsibility for landscaping. A director or officer who helps prepare a common area for an association sponsored party may well be acting in her official capacity, but that status may end when the party begins. *See* Villa Charlotte Bronte, Inc. v. Commercial Union Ins. Co., 487 N.Y.S.2d 314, 64 N.Y.2d 846, 476 N.E.2d 640 (1985) (insurer could be excused from defending officer of cooperative corporation sued for allegedly defamatory remarks if it could be established that officer was not acting on behalf of the corporation when he made those remarks).

129. *See* Truck Ins. Exch. v. Cassady, 2011 U.S. Dist. LEXIS 122052 (N.D. Ill. Oct. 21, 2011). In *Cassady* a condominium association brought suit for breach of fiduciary duties against the members of the initial governing board. Those board members had been appointed by the developer while the developer controlled the project. Almost two years after those board members had left office, the association obtained a policy with general liability and directors and officers liability coverage. The erstwhile board members sought coverage as directors for the association. The court said they were not insureds under the general liability coverage because they were not directors or officers when the policy was in effect. It noted that the directors and officers portion of the coverage applied to "any person who has been, now is, or shall become" an officer of an insured organization, but the general liability section does not contain language that extended coverage to past

stockholders are insureds, but only with respect to their liability as stockholders.[130] Typically, the only type of common interest community that would have stockholders is a residential cooperative.

What is the scope of the duties of an officer or director? The starting point for determining those duties would be the governing documents. Typically, the bylaws broadly describe the duties of officers and directors. One can also look to corporate law—statutory and judge made—of the applicable state. Finally, the day-to-day practice of the particular association may provide insight into the scope of those duties. In the end, the analysis will likely be fact driven. For example, in a Florida case a unit owner sued an officer and/or director of a condominium association who allegedly published a blog entry that defamed the plaintiff. In a separate declaratory action seeking coverage, the defendant argued he was insured under the association's CGL policy as an officer, director, and volunteer employee of the association. The insurer, however, noted that the underlying complaint alleged the defendant acted solely in his individual capacity, not on behalf of or authorized by the association and, because the defendant was not, therefore, acting within the scope of his duties as an officer, director, or volunteer worker of the association, he was not an insured under its policy. Taking a closer look at the underlying complaint, the court noted that the defendant was being sued based on his communications directed to persons who had an interest in the association—including unit owners—informing them of events relevant to an upcoming board election and of possible threats to the interests of the association. The court had nothing before it defining the duties of officers or directors and absent a contrary express definition of those duties, the court said there was a strong argument to be made that the duties included communication with unit owners about association business; thus, the defendant's actions potentially fell within the scope of his duties as an officer or director, so the potential for

---

officers. Thus, placed in the context of the entire contract, the general liability provision covered only then-current directors and officers.

130. *See, e.g.*, ISO Form CG 00 01 12 07, § II.1.d. *See* 426-428 W. 46th St. Owners, Inc. v. Greater NY Mut. Ins. Co., 847 N.Y.S.2d 896 (2007), in which the president of the cooperative corporation was also the general partner of a limited partnership that owned shares in the cooperative allocable to the proprietary leases of several apartments. The partnership rented one of its apartments to a tenant who was injured in a fall from an allegedly defective staircase. She sued the cooperative, its president, and the partnership. The court said that while the partnership might be liable to the tenant as her landlord for its negligence, the allegations of her complaint were extremely broad and could also implicate liability she was alleging that the partnership had as a shareholder. Additionally, the complaint could be read to implicate duties the cooperative president had in that role to investigate and perhaps ensure abatement of a potentially hazardous condition or violations about which he had knowledge. Thus, liberally construed, the claims against the partnership and cooperative president were "within the embrace of the policy," and both could potentially qualify as insureds.

coverage was sufficient to overcome the argument of the insurer for dismissal of the action seeking coverage.[131]

The Florida case raises an important question for common interest community associations. It is not unusual for an association director or officer to pursue his or her own agenda under color of his or her office. It is more likely to happen in a CIC than a business corporation because officers and directors in CIC associations are often unschooled in the duties and responsibilities of their office. That can result in costly litigation in which the association itself could be a party. The insurer called upon to defend one too many of these actions may refuse to renew the policy or demand higher premiums. An association might be able to minimize this risk by describing the duties of officers and directors in its documents with more specificity, a task that requires consultation with the association counsel.

It is not unusual for a resident in a common interest community to assist the association with an issue in an area in which he or she has special expertise. The governing board might formally appoint him or her to carry out a specific assignment and report back, or the president of the association might informally ask him or her to "take a look" at something. While the unit owner in those circumstances may be an agent of the board,[132] that status does not bring him or her within the "officers and directors" provision.[133]

[c] Volunteer Workers as Insureds

Under the standard CGL policy, volunteer workers may be automatic insureds. A "volunteer worker" is a person who is not an employee of the named insured and who "donates"[134] his or her work and acts at the direction of and within the

---

131. Int'l Vill. Ass'n v. AmTrust N. Am., Inc., 2015 U.S. Dist. LEXIS 79156 (S.D. Fla. June 17, 2015).

132. Note that there are state-specific endorsements that make agents of condominium or homeowners associations insureds. *See, e.g.*, ISO Form CG 01 65 11 85 (Commercial General Liability: Illinois Changes—Condominiums) (including as insured any agent of named insured while acting within scope of duties for named insured); ISO Form CG 01 20 07 98 (Commercial General Liability: Minnesota Changes—Townhouses) (including as insured any agent of named insured while acting within scope of their duties for named insured).

133. Martinez v. State Farm Lloyds, 2000 Tex. App. LEXIS 6008 (Tex. App. Corpus Christi Aug. 31, 2000) (finding "officers and directors" provision to be unambiguous and rejecting argument by unit owner that, because policy did not specifically exclude coverage for agents of board, it was ambiguous and should be construed in favor of coverage for him; holding that unit owner was not named insured under policy as agent of board while looking into vandalism and repair issues; finding that only board members were insureds, not their agents, and that to hold otherwise would mean board could add as many people as insureds under policy as it wished and at its sole discretion).

134. A North Carolina court said that "donate" means more than working without payment, otherwise the policy language that the work has to be without "fee, salary or other compensation" would be superfluous. The common everyday meaning of "volunteer," continued the court, is

scope of duties determined by the named insured,[135] without being paid a fee, salary, or other compensation by the named insured or anyone else for that work.[136] A volunteer worker is an insured, but only while performing duties related to the conduct of the business of the named insured.[137]

Volunteer workers are a common feature of common interest communities, especially those that are small or have limited funds. Association members volunteer their time for a variety of odd jobs on the property. Inevitably, concerns about liability arise should a volunteer be injured.[138] For the association, it is

---

characterized by lack of compensation *and* choice and free will. Therefore, to "donate" work under the terms of the CGL policy language requires the presence of choice and free will. North Carolina Farm Bureau Mutual Insurance v. Burns, 238 N.C. App. 72, 77–78, 767 S.E.2d 109, 112–13 (N.C. App. 2014) (eleven-year-old compelled by parental authority to sweep grain bin did not do so out of his own free will but out of obligation and obedience and, therefore, he did not donate his work). *See also* Newell v. Markel Corp., 2016 N.H. LEXIS 63 (N.H. June 28, 2016) (where alleged tortfeasor cleaned property of named insured without compensation but in exchange for tips from patrons, insurer argued work was not "donated" because benefit—tips—was obtained, but court concluded term "donates" was ambiguous and construed it in favor of coverage).

135. N. Am. Specialty Ins. Co. v. Pen Pals Prods., LLC, 789 F. Supp. 2d 1343, 1346 (M.D. Ga. 2011) (to be volunteer worker, worker must be acting at direction of and within the scope of duties determined by named insured). What does "direction" mean? *See* Newell v. Markel Corp., 2016 N.H. LEXIS 63 (N.H. June 28, 2016) (at least in context of unskilled labor, phrase "at your direction" can reasonably be read to mean something other than supervision or guidance; volunteer worker provision conditions coverage on worker conducting or performing activities at direction of named insured and within scope of duties for named insured and taken together, those two conditions foreclose action taken on one's own initiative and unrelated to agreed task and certainly foreclose any "frolic of his own").

136. *See, e.g.*, ISO Form CG 00 01 12 07, § V.20. What constitutes a "fee, salary, or other compensation?" In *Newell v. Markel Corp.*, 2016 N.H. LEXIS 63 (N.H. June 28, 2016), a cleaning service cleaned bathrooms on the property of the named insured. It was not compensated by the named insured but received tips from patrons of the facility. The insurer argued the cleaning service did not meet the definition of "volunteer worker" because the tips received from patrons amounted to compensation under the ordinary meaning of the word. The party injured by the alleged negligence of the cleaning service cited both a dictionary definition and case law that differentiated compensation and gratuities and contended compensation is for something owed, and not a gratuity or gift. The court concluded that although the insurer put forth a reasonable interpretation of the term "compensation," the injured party had identified an ambiguity by articulating another reasonable construction and, therefore, the court construed the term in favor of coverage.

137. *See, e.g.*, ISO Form CG 00 01 12 07, § II.2.a. *See* Crawford v. Guideone Mut. Ins. Co., 420 F. Supp. 2d 584, 600 (N.D. Tex. 2006) (stating in *dicta* that student member of university social club joined in action by student injured at university event "might possibly" have sought coverage for indemnity of his costs in defending that claim under "volunteer worker provision" based on state court findings that he acted in furtherance of mission under control of university).

138. In one unusual case, a member of the association volunteered his time to perform landscaping and related services to the common elements of his condominium association. He did the work with the knowledge and consent of, and sometimes at the direction of, the governing board or its property manager. The board became concerned about the potential liabilities to which the association might be exposed arising out of the defendant's service and decided to ask him to no longer assist with the landscaping. When the resident failed to abide by the board's wishes, the

important to consider the portion of the definition of volunteer worker that says that worker is one who "acts at the direction of and within the scope of duties determined by the named insured." One court has interpreted the language literally to mean that a person who might otherwise meet the definition of a volunteer worker but who acted at the direction of an *agent* of the named insured was not a volunteer worker.[139] Under that interpretation of the policy, a resident of a common interest community that performs volunteer work at the direction of the community association manager or building superintendent would not be a volunteer worker.

[d] Employees as Insureds

Employees of the named insured, other than either its executive officers,[140] if it is an organization other than a partnership, joint venture, or limited liability company, or its managers, if it is a limited liability company, are insureds, but only for acts within the scope of their employment by the named insured or while performing duties related to the conduct of the business of the named insured.[141] The term "employee" includes a "leased worker,"[142] meaning one leased to the named insured by a labor leasing firm under an agreement between those two parties to perform duties related to the conduct of the business of the named insured.[143] Neither the term "employee" nor "leased worker" includes a "temporary worker," which is someone furnished to the named insured to substitute for a permanent employee on leave or to meet seasonal or short-term workload conditions.[144]

The status of "leased workers" is particularly important to common interest communities because many of them—especially smaller communities—obtain their maintenance personnel from a firm that employs them and contracts for their services with the CIC association. It becomes important to establish whether that firm meets the definition of a "labor leasing firm," a term that is not defined in the policy. That topic is beyond the scope of this treatise, but fortunately there is an authoritative article that addresses it in depth.[145]

---

association sued him. Town in Country Condo. Ass'n v. Hinckley, 2016 Conn. Super. LEXIS 871 (Apr. 19, 2016).

139. Dry v. United Fire & Cas. Co., 420 S.W.3d 593, 596–97 (Mo. App. 2013).

140. An "executive officer" is someone holding any of the *officer* positions created by the charter, constitution, bylaws, or any other similar governing document of the named insured. ISO Form CG 00 01 12 07, § V.6.

141. *See, e.g.*, ISO Form CG 00 01 12 07, § II.2.a.

142. *See, e.g.*, ISO Form CG 00 01 12 07, § V.5.

143. *See, e.g.*, ISO Form CG 00 01 12 07, § V.10.

144. *See, e.g.*, ISO Form CG 00 01 12 07, § V.19.

145. Perlmutter, *The Law of "Leased Worker" and "Temporary Worker under a CGL Policy*, 45 Tort Trial & Ins. Prac. L.J. 761 (2010). The author describes various types of staffing-type

[e] Exception to Insured Status of Volunteer Workers and Employees

Neither an employee nor a volunteer worker is an insured for a "bodily injury"[146] or "personal and advertising injury"[147] to the named insured or to its partners, or to its members if it is a partnership, joint venture, or LLC.[148] An employee or a volunteer worker is also not an insured for a bodily injury or personal and advertising injury to a co-employee while in the course of his or her employment or performing duties related to the conduct of the business of the named insured or to other volunteer workers while performing duties related to the conduct of the business of the named insured.[149] In addition, neither an employee nor a volunteer worker is an insured for "property damage"[150] to property owned, occupied, or used by; rented to; in the care, custody, or control of; or over which physical control is being exercised for any purpose by the named insured, any employees

companies, discusses at length court decisions defining the phrase "labor leasing firm," and explains the import of state and federal statutory law to the determination. *See also* Cnty. of Maui v. Ace Am. Ins. Co., 2015 U.S. Dist. LEXIS 57229 (D. Haw. Apr. 30, 2015) (factors courts consider in determining whether someone is "leased worker" include whether worker is covered by named insured's workers' compensation insurance, whether worker can be considered independent contractor, and who paid worker's wages).

146. A "bodily injury" is defined as a bodily injury, sickness, or disease sustained by a person, including death resulting from bodily injury, sickness, or disease at any time. ISO Form CG 00 01 12 07, § V.3.

147. A "personal and advertising injury" is an injury, including consequential "bodily injury," arising out of false arrest, detention, or imprisonment; malicious prosecution; wrongful eviction from, wrongful entry into, or invasion of the right of private occupancy of a room, dwelling, or premises that a person occupies, committed by or on behalf of its owner, landlord, or lessor; oral or written publication of material that slanders or libels a person or organization or disparages the goods, products, or services of a person or organization; oral or written publication of material that violates a person's right of privacy; use of another's advertising idea; or infringing upon another's copyright, trade dress, or slogan. ISO Form CG 00 01 12 07, § V.14.

148. *See, e.g.*, ISO Form CG 00 01 12 07, § II.2.a.(1).(a). *See* Muller v. Colony Ins. Co., 57 So. 3d 341, 350 (La. App. 2010), *writ. den.*, 58 So. 3d 459 (La. 2011) (coverage is restricted or limited in that it does not extend to bodily injury to named insured).

149. An employee or a volunteer worker is also not an insured for a bodily injury or personal and advertising injury to the spouse, child, parent, brother, or sister of that co-employee or volunteer worker as a consequence of the course of his or her employment or performing duties related to the conduct of the business of the named insured or to other volunteer workers while performing duties related to the conduct of the business of the named insured. Additionally, an employee or a volunteer worker is not an insured for a bodily injury or personal and advertising injury to a co-employee or another volunteer worker, or to the spouse, child, parent, brother or sister of that co-employee or volunteer, for which there is any obligation to share damages with or repay someone else who must pay damages because of those injuries or for a bodily injury or personal and advertising injury arising out of his or her providing or failing to provide professional health care services. ISO Form CG 00 01 12 07, §§ II.2.a.(1).(b)–(d).

150. "Property damage" is defined as physical injury to tangible property, including all resulting loss of use of that property or loss of use of tangible property that is not physically injured. ISO Form CG 00 01 12 07, § V.17. Electronic data is not tangible property.

of the named insured, any volunteer workers, any partner or member of a named insured that is a partnership or joint venture, or any member of a named insured that is a limited liability company.[151]

[f] Real Estate or Community Association Manager as Insured

Anyone other than an employee or volunteer worker of the named insured or any organization, while acting as "real estate manager" for the named insured, is an insured.[152]

The term "real estate manager" has been used in the insurance industry as part of general liability policies since 1955,[153] yet the policies do not define "real estate manager." Courts give the phrase its obvious meaning: a real estate manager is a person or entity that manages real property for another.[154] The federal Fifth Circuit Court of Appeals expanded on that definition. It said that courts look to "whether the entity claiming additional insured status . . . undertook its claimed real estate management activity primarily in order to benefit the named insured—thus entitling it to coverage—or in pursuit of its own interests. [W]hen an entity undertakes management activity solely or primarily on behalf of others, and it owes duties to the property which derive from the duties owed to or by those it serves, it may claim coverage" as a real estate manager.[155]

---

151. *See, e.g.*, ISO Form CG 00 01 12 07, § II.2.a.(2).

152. *See, e.g.*, ISO Form CG 00 01 12 07, § II.2.b.

153. Sumitomo Marine & Fire Ins. Co. of Am. v. S. Guar. Ins. Co., 337 F. Supp. 2d 1339, 1359 (N.D. Ga. 2004).

154. QBE Ins. Corp. v. Creston Court Condo., Inc., 58 F. Supp. 3d 1137, 1151 (D. Or. 2014) (although policy did not define "real-estate manager," both parties agreed it had plain meaning: one who conducts, directs, or supervises another's real estate); Travelers Prop. Cas. Co. of Am. v. Liberty Mut. Ins. Co., 444 F.3d 217, 222 (4th Cir. 2006) (phrase "real estate manager" is not defined by policy and, therefore, should be given its ordinary meaning); California Union Ins. Co. v. City of Walnut Grove, 857 F. Supp. 515, 521 (S.D. Miss. 1994) (no Mississippi cases have construed term "real estate manager"; manager is one who conducts, directs, or supervises something, and real estate manager manages property for named insured and for benefit of that named insured); Brown v. MR Group, LLC, 278 Wis. 2d 760, 770, 693 N.W.2d 138, 143 (2005) ("real estate manager" is one who manages business affairs of certain real estate); Savoy v. Action Products Co., Inc., 324 So. 2d 921 (La. App. 1975), *cert. den.*, 329 So. 2d 463, 1976 La. LEXIS 4753 (La. 1976) (real estate manager is simply one who manages real estate for another). *See also* Sumitomo Marine & Fire Ins. Co. of Am. v. S. Guar. Ins. Co., 337 F. Supp. 2d 1339 (N.D. Ga. 2004) (entity that did not participate in sales, collection of rents, or other associated duties, and did not advertise, sell, manage, or build any homes, dwellings, or office buildings was not real estate manager as that term is understood in insurance and construction industries).

155. Western Alliance Ins. Co. v. Northern Ins. Co., 176 F.3d 825, 831–32 (5th Cir. 1999).

Courts have held that "mortgagees in possession,"[156] court-appointed "receivers,"[157] and even "common interest community developers"[158] may be real estate managers. On the other hand, "lessors,"[159] "lessees,"[160] and "construction managers"[161] have been held not to be real estate managers. Garage operators have also been found not to be real estate managers. In a Pennsylvania case, a condominium with a garage was owned by a real estate company that entered into a garage operating agreement with a company called Park America. Both

156. First National Bank of Palmerton v. Motor Club of America Insurance Co., 310 N.J. Super. 1, 708 A.2d 69, 72–73 (1997) (where after default, mortgagee assumed control of property and its representative took over management of property, it was real estate manager for named insureds who were mortgagors of property and, therefore, additional insured; under security agreement, in event of default mortgagee was given right to take possession and assume operation of the property, including leasing, collecting rent, repairing, and maintaining premises). Note that a mortgagee of a common interest community could qualify as a real estate manager under this reasoning, but not a mortgagee of an individual owner as the individual owners would not ordinarily be named insureds.

157. Fireman's Fund Insurance Co. v. Vordermeier, 415 So. 2d 1347, 1349–50 (Fla. 4th DCA), *pet. dis.*, 421 So. 2d 67 (Fla. 1982) (when receiver takes over management of real property during pendency of legal proceedings, ownership of property remains with title owners, but court appointed receiver as a matter of law manages property as representative of court for all interested parties, including owners and named insureds; mere fact that receiver may manage real property for creditors or other interested parties in addition to named insureds is not sufficient to defeat coverage). That a receiver can be a real estate manager and, therefore, an additional insured has implications for common interest communities because it is possible for them to be placed under receivership. *See, e.g.*, Uniform Common Interest Ownership Act § 2-119, comment 3 (there may be occasions when court of competent jurisdiction would order appointment of receiver for association), § 2-124 (where following catastrophe, governing board commences action seeking to terminate common interest community, during pendency of action, court may issue whatever orders it considers appropriate, including appointment of receiver); Fla. Stat. § 718.1124 (if association fails to fill vacancies on governing board sufficient to constitute quorum in accordance with bylaws, any unit owner may apply to circuit court for appointment of receiver to manage affairs of association).

158. *See* QBE Ins. Corp. v. Creston Court Condo., Inc., 58 F. Supp. 3d 1137, 1151 (D. Or. 2014) (developer responsible for supervising architectural design and repair and renovation work was real estate manager and insured for purposes of policy; insurer was free to draft policy to exclude developers acting as real estate managers from insured status, but did not do so).

159. California Union Ins. Co. v. City of Walnut Grove, 857 F. Supp. 515, 522 (S.D. Miss. 1994) (although lessor undertook to perform maintenance and/or repairs to leased premises, that undertaking did not qualify it as real estate manager); Olympic, Inc. v. Providence Washington Ins. Co., 648 P.2d 1008, 1013 n.9 (Alaska 1982) (rejecting argument that lessor qualified as real estate manager because lessor's rights under lease were not substantially different from affirmative duties required of every lessor). Note that whether a lessor is considered a real estate manager has implications for lessors of common interest communities subject to ground or recreational leases.

160. Savoy v. Action Products Co., Inc., 324 So. 2d 921, 924 (La. App. 1975), *cert. den.*, 329 So. 2d 463, 1976 La. LEXIS 4753 (La. 1976) (real estate manager may also be lessee, but not all lessees are real estate managers; lessee possesses for his or her lessor and not for him- or herself and must act as good administrator of lessor's property, but lessee does not as result of that performance become real estate manager, for those acts are merely affirmative duties required of every lessee).

161. Clarendon Am. Ins. Co. v. State Farm Fire & Cas. Co., 2013 U.S. Dist. LEXIS 880 (D. Or. Jan. 3, 2013) ("real estate manager" is one who conducts, directs, or supervises another's real estate as distinct from construction manager who conducts, directs, or supervises another's construction).

companies were sued by a person who fell in the garage. The insurer for Park America argued the garage operator was a real estate manager and, therefore, an insured under the property owner's policy. The court did not agree. Park America, concluded the court, ran a parking garage, not a real estate operation. It was not a real estate manager and, therefore, not an insured under the property owner's policy.[162] Finally, an association member acting on behalf of the governing board regarding an issue of property maintenance is not a real estate manager.[163]

The critical question for common interest communities is whether community association managers are considered to be real estate managers.[164] Following the basic definition of real estate manager enunciated by courts—an entity that manages real property for another—it would appear that CAMs are real estate managers. That may be why insurers have generally conceded that a CAM is a real estate manager.[165]

---

162. First Liberty Ins. Corp. v. Zurich Am. Ins. Co., 2013 U.S. Dist. LEXIS 23392 (E.D. Pa. Feb 20, 2013). *See also* Amerisure Mut. Ins. Co. v. Fed. Ins. Co., 2016 U.S. Dist. LEXIS 57175 (E.D. Mo. Apr. 29, 2016) (company managed parking garage, not real estate operation, where its responsibilities were primarily related to collection of parking revenue and cleaning of garage, with separate company managing most aspects of property itself).

163. Martinez v. State Farm Lloyds, 2000 Tex. App. LEXIS 6008 (Tex. App. Corpus Christi Aug. 31, 2000) (where unit owner, at request of governing board, conferred with community association manager regarding incidents of vandalism on property and resulting repairs, he was not acting as real estate manager for association).

164. National Fire & Marine Ins. Co. v. Hoene Springs Improvement Ass'n, 889 F. Supp. 362 (E.D. Mo. 1995) is case that raises some concern about who is an insured. A was person identified as an agent of a homeowners association, but neither an officer nor director. He was sued by a person injured at an event sponsored by the association. He sought coverage under the association's CGL policy, but the insurer argued the agent was not a named insured under the policy. The court held that the agent was not an insured under the policy because he was not a named insured nor did he fall within the class of insureds identified in the policy as insureds such as an officer, director or employee. It is not clear from the opinion what the agent's role was, but he could have been a manager.

165. *See* Great Am. Ins. Co. v. Sequoia Ins. Co., 2016 U.S. Dist. LEXIS 26551 (C.D. Cal. Mar. 1, 2016) (where party served as managing agent for homeowners association pursuant to written agreement, insurer defended managing agent under provision making real estate manager an insured); N. Sec. Ins. Co. v. Sandpiper Vill. Condo. Trust, 2008 Mass. Super. LEXIS 312, 24 Mass. L. Rep. 500 (Mass. Super. Ct. 2008) (insurer conceded that property manager for condominium was additional insured under provision making anyone acting as real estate manager an insured). *See also* 200 W. End Ave. Condominium v. Mt. Hawley Ins. Co., 2014 N.Y. Misc. LEXIS 5573 (Dec. 17, 2014) (according to employee for insurer, where Declaration Page identified association c/o management company, she assumed that was association's managing agent and was an insured); 426-428 W. 46th St. Owners, Inc. v. Greater NY Mut. Ins. Co., 847 N.Y.S.2d 896 (2007) (where partnership was shareholder in cooperative corporation and managing agent for building, court refused to find as matter of law that partnership was not real estate manager entitled to status as insured). *Compare* State Farm Fire & Cas. Co. v. Metro. Mgmt., 2007 U.S. Dist. LEXIS 99406 (D. Haw. Oct. 31, 2007) (management company apparently claimed insured status under policy provision extending insured status to real estate manager of named insured, but insurer did not concede that company was an insured and company made no showing that it was).

Even if a CAM—or anyone else—is considered a real estate manager, there are still two caveats to insured status. First, the CAM must be the real estate manager for the named insured. If the CAM or other entity is the real estate manager for an intermediary that is not a named insured, it will likely not be granted insured status.[166] Second, the CAM or entity must be acting as a real estate manager. If it acted in some other capacity, it again will likely not be granted insured status.[167] On the other hand, the fact that a party failed in its responsibilities as a real estate manager does not cause it to lose the status.[168]

[g] Newly Acquired or Formed Organization as Insured

Finally, any organization the named insured newly acquires or forms, other than a partnership, joint venture, or limited liability company, and over which it maintains ownership or majority interest, will qualify as a named insured if there is no other similar insurance available to that organization.[169] This coverage, however, is afforded only until the 90th day after that acquisition or formation or the end of the policy period, whichever is earlier.[170] The coverage can be eliminated by endorsement.[171]

---

166. *See* United States Fire Ins. Co. v. Aetna Cas. & Sur. Co., 1996 U.S. Dist. LEXIS 19445 (E.D. Pa. Dec. 27, 1996) (where general partnership was named insured and entity that was its managing partner contracted with third party to perform services at property owned by general partnership, for that third party to be real estate manager and, therefore, insured under policy, it would have to be acting as real estate manager for general partner, not managing partner).

167. *See, e.g.*, Russell v. Clapp, 201 S.W.3d 99 (Mo. App. 2006) (where manager of trailer park was watching television inside trailer home at time child was bitten by dog, television viewing could not be associated with or intended to benefit property owners and manager was not, therefore, engaged in property management activities for named insured property owners and, thus, was not an insured under policy).

168. *See* Travelers Prop. Cas. Co. of Am. v. Liberty Mut. Ins. Co., 444 F.3d 217, 223 (4th Cir. 2006), where the court said the fact that a real estate manager may have failed to make a repair would not cause it to lose coverage for liability imposed for that failure. The insurer could not rationally be contending, declared the court, that failure to perform as a real estate manager would lead to loss of insurance coverage. If actual performance of duties was required, in addition to a legal obligation to perform them, in order to meet the definition of "real estate manager," then purported negligence in performing as a real estate manager would mean the manager lacked coverage as an additional insured. That, observed the court, would lead to the absurdity that an insured would lose coverage in "precisely those circumstances for which it anticipated needing insurance."

169. *See, e.g.*, ISO Form CG 00 01 12 07, § II.3.

170. The coverage does not apply to bodily injury or property damage that occurred before the acquisition or formation of the organization and coverage does not apply to personal and advertising injury arising out of an offense committed before that acquisition or formation. Finally, no person or organization is an insured with respect to the conduct of any current or past partnership, joint venture or limited liability company that is not shown as a named insured on the Declarations Page.

171. *See, e.g.*, ISO Form CG 21 36 03 05 (Commercial General Liability: Exclusion—New Entities).

[3] Additional Insured

Endorsements to a CGL policy can add parties as additional insureds. The parties that would be of chief concern to a common interest community would be its residents and the developer.[172]

[a] Endorsement Adding Individual Association Members

There are standard ISO endorsements that add condominium unit owners[173] and townhouse owners[174] as insureds under limited conditions.[175] The former includes each individual unit owner of the insured association as an insured for liability arising out of ownership, maintenance, or repair of the portion of the premises not reserved for the exclusive use or occupancy of that unit owner.[176] The latter endorsement includes each individual townhouse owner as an insured for liability as a member of the townhouse association but not for any liability arising out of the ownership, maintenance, use, or repair of the property to which that owner has title. Unfortunately, that endorsement does not define "townhouse," but one definition of a townhouse development is one in which the individual owners have fee title to individual lots but indirect ownership of common areas that are owned by an association of which each lot owner is required to be a member.[177]

---

172. *See generally* Malecki, Gibson & Ligeros, *The Additional Insured Book* (International Risk Management Institute, Inc., 7th ed. 2014); Kealy, *Understanding Named, Automatic, and Additional Insureds in the CGL Policy* (2014); Mehta, *Additional Insured Status in Construction Contracts and Moral Hazard*, 3 Conn. Ins. L.J. 169 (1996/1997); Pomerantz, *Recognizing the Unique Status of Additional Named Insureds*, 53 Fordham L. Rev. 117 (1984).

173. *See, e.g.*, ISO Form CG 20 04 11 85 (Commercial General Liability: Additional Insured—Condominium Unit Owners).

174. *See, e.g.*, ISO Form CG 20 17 11 85 (Commercial General Liability: Additional Insured—Townhouse Associations).

175. Note that by endorsement, coverage for claims by association members might be excluded. *See* Northfield Ins. Co. v. Evian HPR, 2002 U.S. Dist. LEXIS 26684 (D.S.C. Aug. 27, 2002), *aff'd*, 2003 U.S. App. LEXIS 14064 (4th Cir. 2003) (endorsement excluded claims for bodily injury, property damage, personal and advertising injury, or medical expenses claims against *an insured* by association member).

176. *See* Boggs, *Understanding Legal Liability for Condominium Association and Unit Owners* (2011), available at: http://www.mynewmarkets.com/articles/180950/understanding-legal-liability-for-condominium-association-and-unit-owners (endorsement grants all unit owners additional insured status for liability arising out of any portion of premises not reserved for unit owner's exclusive use or occupancy and means that unit owner is an insured for any injury or damage on or caused by common element). *Consider* United States v. Wapinski Real Estate, 2000 U.S. Dist. LEXIS 193, at *8, n.2 (N.D. Ill. Jan. 7, 2000), where the condominium association policy provided coverage to the association and the unit owners "'but only with respect to liability arising out of the ownership, maintenance or repair of that portion of the . . . premises which is now owned solely by the unit owner.'" The court noted that the actions of the unit owner did not take place at, and had nothing to do with, the condominiums and concluded that it was clear on the face of the policy that it provided no coverage.

177. Breslau & O'Connor, *Subrogating Losses in Common Interest Communities.*

There are state-specific endorsements for condominium unit owners that are parallel to the generic endorsement but that add that the unit owner is an insured for liability arising out of ownership, maintenance, or repair of the portion of the premises not owned solely by the unit owner or out of the unit owner's *membership in the association*.[178] These endorsements conform the policy to a requirement derived from the Uniform Acts that a CGL policy include each individual owner as an insured person for liability arising out of his or her membership in the association.[179] Additionally, there are state-specific endorsements for townhouse association members.[180] There are also endorsements available for members of homeowners associations other than townhouse associations.[181]

Finally, there are endorsements that provide that an insured is any of the members of the named insured association, but only with respect to their liability for the activities of the association or activities they perform on behalf of the association.[182]

Condominium associations in Georgia and the companies that insure them should be aware of an interesting twist in the standard endorsement for condominiums in that state. It provides that all *agents* of the association and all unit owners and others entitled to *occupy* any unit "or other portion of the condominium" are insureds, but only for liability arising out of, or in connection with, use, ownership, maintenance, or repair of the common elements or other portion of

---

178. *See, e.g.*, ISO Form CG 01 41 03 11 (Commercial General Liability: Maryland—Condominiums); ISO Form CG 01 28 07 98 (Commercial General Liability: Minnesota Changes—Condominiums); ISO Form CG 26 37 06 95 (Commercial General Liability: Texas Changes—Condominiums); ISO Form CG 26 26 03 93 (Commercial General Liability: Washington Changes—Condominiums). Membership in the association does not make individual owners liable without fault. *See* Davis v. Riverside Court Condo. Ass'n Phase II, Inc., 154 So. 3d 643, 654 (La. App. 2014) (that insurance coverage includes each individual unit owner as additional insured does not create legal liability for each individual unit owner for any claim arising out of common elements; claimant must still prove liability of individual unit owner for particular claim relating to common elements or membership in association).

179. *See, e.g.*, Uniform Common Interest Ownership Act § 3-113(d)(1).

180. *See, e.g.*, ISO Form CG 26 23 10 05 (Commercial General Liability: Connecticut Changes—Townhouses); ISO Form CG 01 20 07 98 (Commercial General Liability: Minnesota Changes—Townhouses).

181. *See* the endorsement titled "Additional Insured—Homeowners Association Members," reading "WHO IS AN INSURED is amended to include as an additional insured each individual member of the insured Homeowners Association, but only with respect to liability arising out of the ownership, maintenance or repair of that portion of the premises which is not reserved for that member's exclusive use or occupancy." Quoted in Southern Owners Ins. Co. v. Cooperativa De Seguros Multiples, 143 So. 3d 439, 444 (Fla. 5th DCA 2014) (Sawaya, J., concurring in part, dissenting in part).

182. Northfield Ins. Co. v. Evian HPR, 2002 U.S. Dist. LEXIS 26684 (D.S.C. Aug. 27, 2002), *aff'd*, 2003 U.S. App. LEXIS 14064 (4th Cir. 2003) (specifically including unit owners as insureds for injuries resulting from activities of association protects unit owners from incurring costs of damages arising from any misfortune that may befall third parties present in common areas).

the condominium that the association has the responsibility to maintain.[183] The Georgia Condominium Act does not define "occupy," but long ago the United States Supreme Court, referencing *Webster's Dictionary*, said that it means "to hold in possession; to hold or keep for use; as to occupy an apartment."[184] A federal court in Tennessee added that to visit is not to occupy.[185] A New Jersey court reached a conclusion that would seem to have relevance to the concept of "occupy" in the Georgia condominium endorsement. It said that use of common areas by tenants, especially where those areas are unquestionably necessary for their use and enjoyment of their specific apartments, is effectively an occupation by them.[186] Taking that all together, it would seem that a tenant of a unit owner or a person residing with a unit owner for more than a visit would be an insured under the endorsement, and so might an entity that provides a service on the common property under an agreement with the association, for example, a company that operates a snack bar at a community club or a shop adjacent to tennis courts out of which an instructor operates and sells tennis equipment and attire.

[i] The Meaning of "Ownership, Maintenance, Use, or Repair"

A handful of cases have interpreted the phrase "ownership, maintenance, use, or repair."[187] In one of them the parties agreed that where a member of a homeowners association was accused of negligently supervising a child who drowned in the association swimming pool,[188] any potential liability she might have would

183. ISO Form CG 26 57 04 00 (Georgia Changes—Additional Insured—Condominium Associations).

184. Missionary Soc. v. Dalles, 107 U.S. 336, 343, 2 S. Ct. 672, 677, 27 L. Ed. 545, 547 (1883).

185. United States v. Burleson, 127 F. Supp. 400, 404 (D. Tenn. 1954).

186. Freygang v. Verona, 146 N.J. Super. 310, 316, 369 A.2d 959, 962 (1977). *See also* Den Gre Plastics Co. v. Travelers Indem. Co., 107 N.J. Super. 535, 545, 259 A.2d 485, 491 (1969) (that tenant insured had right to use of area where theft occurred, that it did actually make exclusive and continuous use of it, and that area was of such nature as to substantially lessen value of leasehold interest were plaintiff prohibited from its use, all showed insured did "occupy" that area within meaning of policy).

187. *Consider* Walker v. Farmers Ins. Exchange, 153 Cal. App. 4th 965, 971, 63 Cal. Rptr. 3d 507, 510 (2007) (where third party was struck and injured by garage door that was condominium common element when unit owner opened it with remote garage door opener, insurer refused to defend unit owner for liability arising from "use of garage door opener," but court found that, while it was not unreasonable for insurer to conclude that claimant sought damages based on independent negligent act of using garage door opener, there was possibility that unit owner would be liable on claim arising out of ownership, maintenance, or repair of common area).

188. Southern Owners Ins. Co. v. Cooperativa De Seguros Multiples, 143 So. 3d 439 (Fla. 5th DCA 2014). In *Southern Owners*, a resident in a homeowners association was sued in a wrongful death action for negligently supervising a child who drowned in the association pool. The defendant in that action then instituted a declaratory judgment action against the CGL insurer for the association seeking a determination that the insurer was required to defend and indemnify her in the underlying action pursuant to the standard endorsement. The parties agreed that any potential liability the defendant might have would not arise from maintenance or repair of the swimming pool and, therefore, the only question was whether she had potential liability arising from

not arise from maintenance or repair of the pool and, therefore, could only arise from its ownership. The lower court found there was coverage, but the appellate court noted the record was devoid of any documents or evidence showing the association member had any ownership interest in the common areas and, therefore, the lower court erred when it entered summary judgment in her favor. In a Texas case a property manager sued a unit owner claiming he physically assaulted her. The unit owner claimed coverage under the association policy as an additional insured because, he contended, he went to the manager's office to discuss repair and maintenance issues and, therefore, the injuries she received in the ensuing scuffle arose out of ownership, maintenance, or repair of the condominium common areas. The court would have none of it. The property manager's complaint alleged no liability that stemmed from property ownership, but rather facts supporting causes of action for assault, false imprisonment, and intentional infliction of emotional distress, none of which had any connection with anyone's ownership, maintenance, or repair of the common areas of the property. The court concluded there was no coverage under the policy endorsement.[189] Finally, a Louisiana court emphasized that while individual owners may be insured persons with respect to liability arising out of an ownership interest in the common elements, that does not create legal liability for each individual owner for any claim arising out of the common elements, the claimant still has to prove the liability of the individual owner for a particular claim relating to the common elements.[190]

---

ownership of the pool. The lower court found there was coverage. The appellate court, however, noted the record was devoid of any documents or evidence that would tend to reflect the defendant's specific ownership interest, if any, in the common areas. Absent an ownership interest in the pool, said the appellate court, she would not be entitled to coverage under association policy because her potential liability would arise, at most, out of her use of the pool and, although the right to use property is an *indicia* of ownership, it does not equate to ownership. Thus, because it is unclear from the record whether the defendant had an ownership interest in the community pool, it was error to enter summary judgment in her favor. If a person is a unit owner, then under condominium law, that person should be considered as an owner of common elements. *See* State Farm v. English Cove Assocs., 121 Wn. App. 358, 364–65, 88 P.3d 986, 990 (2004) (finding developer that retained ownership of unsold units was owner of common elements; chief incidents of ownership of property are right to its possession, use, and enjoyment, and to sell or otherwise dispose of it according to will of the owner and ownership in realty is not diminished because others also have interest in it; "own" includes undivided interest in property that entitles one to sell or otherwise dispose of that property as one chooses and does not require right to exclusive possession).

189. Martinez v. State Farm Lloyds, 2000 Tex. App. LEXIS 6008 (Tex. App.—Corpus Christi Aug. 31, 2000).

190. Davis v. Riverside Court Condo. Ass'n Phase II, Inc., 154 So. 3d 643, 654 (La. App. 2014) (lessee of unit owner was scalded by hot water in unit, but hot water for unit flowed through boiler that was part of common elements and served all units, therefore, unit owner was not liable).

[ii] Exclusive Use or Occupancy

Note that the basic condominium endorsement makes individual unit owners insureds, but not for liability arising out of the portion of the premises reserved for the *exclusive use or occupancy* of that unit owner. In a condominium, unit owners may have limited common elements, which are common elements reserved for the *exclusive use* of fewer than all the unit owners.[191] Typically, a limited common element is a balcony, patio, storage closet, or parking space reserved for the use of only a single unit owner. Insurers will deny coverage based on that exception.[192] The leading case on application of the exception is *Alexander v. Nat'l Fire Ins.*,[193] a decision by the federal Third Circuit Court of Appeals. It illustrates that the determination of the distinction between common elements and limited common elements reserved for exclusive use requires examination of the governing documents and state law.[194] In *Alexander* a deck collapsed and the owners of the unit to which the deck was attached were sued. They sought coverage from the association's insurer. The insurer argued the unit owners had exclusive use of the deck and it was, therefore, not a common element and they were not insureds. The court did not agree. After examining the definitions in the state condominium statutes and the governing documents of the association, it concluded that while the *surface* of the deck was a limited common element, the entire deck support structure was a common element and it was that support structure that collapsed. In light of *Alexander*, associations should review their

191. *See, e.g.*, Uniform Common Interest Ownership Act § 1-103(21) ("limited common element" means portion of common elements allocated by declaration or by operation of law for exclusive use of one or more, but fewer than all of units).

192. *See, e.g.*, AOAO Queen Emma Gardens v. Wai Hung Ma, 2013 Haw. App. LEXIS 192 (Haw. Ct. App. Apr. 5, 2013) (where tenant of condominium unit evidently fell from ledge outside unit and unit owner was sued for wrongful death, insurer reserved its right to deny coverage to unit owner under association policy if it was determined ledge outside unit was reserved for exclusive use or occupancy); Brown v. Am. W. Home Ins. Co., 2013 Tex. App. LEXIS 19 (Tex. App.—Dallas Jan. 3, 2013) (where unit owners sued association for improper maintenance and association counterclaimed for unauthorized alterations, repairs, and improvements defendants allegedly made to their patio and residence, insurer contended unit owners were not insureds under policy for purposes of counterclaim because it was not based on any damage to common elements, but arose from that portion of premises reserved for their exclusive use or occupancy).

193. Alexander v. Nat'l Fire Ins., 454 F.3d 214 (3d Cir. Pa. 2006).

194. *See also* Am. Family Ins. Co. v. Bergeson, 472 Fed. Appx. 604 (9th Cir. 2012). In *Bergeson*, a unit owner improperly installed a ceiling fan in the unit and rented the unit to a third party who died from carbon monoxide intoxication when the fan ignited the insulation above the unit. The unit owner claimed to be insured under the association's policy because liability arose out of their negligence as fractional owners of the ceiling and the fire occurred in the insulation to that ceiling, property not reserved for exclusive use or occupancy. However, the allegations in the underlying complaint concerned the ceiling fan, the electrical fixture into which it was connected, or the electrical wire powering it. Under the Declaration of Condominium and state condominium statutes, those components were all reserved for the exclusive use of the unit owner. There was, said the court, no causal relation or connection between liability and ownership, maintenance, or repair of the ceiling. Thus, the association policy did not cover the liability of the unit owner and the insurer had no duty to defend or indemnify.

documents with their attorneys to make sure the demarcation between common elements and those reserved for exclusive use or occupancy is clear.

The "exclusive use or occupancy" exception was found to be inapplicable by a Louisiana court.[195] While Louisiana is not one of the states listed as having adopted one of the Uniform Acts, the Louisiana Condominium Act borrows rather heavily from the Uniform legislation.[196] One of the provisions it borrowed requires that in the CGL policy each unit owner has to be an insured person under the policy with respect to liability arising out of his or her ownership of an individual interest in the common elements or membership in the association. This is an important requirement because it appears in all of the Uniform Acts,[197] including the Uniform Common Interest Ownership Act,[198] which governs all types of common interest communities. Therefore, the requirement has wide application.

In the Louisiana case, a woman visiting her parents' condominium slipped and fell on the front step area of that condominium. She sued the association's insurer. The insurer argued that coverage for an injury that occurred on the front step was excluded because it was an area reserved for the exclusive use or occupancy of the unit owners. The court first noted that if the front step was a limited common area, it was commonly owned even if limited in use. Under state law, said the court, the unit owners had to be insured with respect to any liability arising out their ownership interest in the common elements or membership in the association. The policy exception on which the insurer relied was in derogation of the statute to the extent it attempted to limit liability based on use of the property rather than ownership. The court did not decide the ultimate liability issue because a question of fact remained regarding whether the front step was actually a common element or part of the property of the unit owner. The court merely held that the policy did not clearly exclude the action.

The significance of the case is that in the states that require that each unit owner be an insured person with respect to liability arising out of his or her ownership of an individual interest in the common elements or membership in the association, the exception in the standard endorsement for premises reserved for "exclusive use or occupancy" of a unit owner would be inapplicable if other courts were to follow the Louisiana court. However, many courts do not agree with the rule in Louisiana that a policy must be reformed to conform it to any statutory requirements.[199] Those courts generally say common interest

195. Lussan v. State Farm Ins. Co., 659 So. 2d 830 (La. App. 1995).

196. Kratovil, *Declaration of Restrictions, Easements, Liens, and Covenants: An Overview of an Important Document*, 22 J. Marshall L. Rev. 69, 80 (1988) (Louisiana passed portions of UCA).

197. *See* Uniform Condominium Act § 3-113(d)(1); Uniform Planned Community Act § 3-113(d)(1); Model Real Estate Cooperative Act § 3-113(c)(1).

198. Uniform Common Interest Ownership Act § 3-113(d)(1).

199. *See, e.g.*, Royal Glen Condo. Ass'n v. S.T. Neswold & Assocs., 385 Ill. Dec. 137, 18 N.E.3d 137 (Ill. App. 2014) (while Illinois Condominium Property Act provides that no policy of property

community legislation is intended to govern the associations that govern those communities, not insurance companies, which are extensively regulated by state Insurance Codes.

While most courts reject application of common interest community legislation to insurers,[200] a policy argument can be made that supports the position taken by the Louisiana court. First, the insurer is certainly in the best position to understand and respond properly to legislative insurance mandates. Second, insurers already conform their policies to many of those mandates by state-specific endorsements and, therefore, know where to look for those requirements and how to modify their policies to meet them. Courts, it can be argued, should not impose an obligation on volunteer governing board members that requires an understanding of technical insurance law matters that they, as laypersons, likely do not have but that insurers certainly do have.

[iii] Liability as a Member of the Association

There do not appear to be many common interest community cases addressing the meaning of liability as a member of an association.[201] However, there are endorsements that add members of private clubs as insureds to the CGL policy of the club and some guidance may be found there. For example, in a New Jersey

---

insurance may be issued or delivered unless it meets minimum statutory requirements, that requirement does not to regulate business of insurance, but imposes insurance-related obligations on association and its board); Citizens Property Insurance Corp. v. River Manor Condominium Ass'n, Inc., 125 So. 3d 846, 853 (Fla. 4th DCA 2013) (insurance provision in Florida Condominium Act was not intended to impose mandatory obligation on insurance carriers); DiMillo v. Travelers Prop. Cas. Co. of Am., 789 F. Supp. 2d 194, 207 (D. Me. 2011) (failure of condominium association to purchase insurance required by state's Condominium Act would not give unit owner claim against insurer for coverage association did not purchase); Northfield Ins. Co. v. Evian HPR, 2002 U.S. Dist. LEXIS 26684 (D.S.C. Aug. 27, 2002), *aff'd*, 2003 U.S. App. LEXIS 14064 (4th Cir. 2003) (insurer had no responsibility to ensure condominium regime was properly insuring its property so as to meet its obligations under applicable state condominium law). *But see* Lawrence v. Commodore Commons Condo. Ass'n, 2000 Conn. Super. LEXIS 2359 (Conn. Super. Ct. Sept. 8, 2000) (plaintiff unit owner had status of insured where state statute required policies to include unit owners as insured persons with respect to liability arising out of their interest in common elements or membership in association and alleged legally sufficient claim for breach of the covenant of good faith and fair dealing against association's insurer for failure to pay claim).

200. *See* § 5.01[2], *supra*.

201. *But see* Land v. Auto-Owners Ins. Co., 511 Fed. Appx. 795 (10th Cir. 2013). The CGL policy had a "members endorsement" that that extended coverage under the policy to members of the homeowners association as additional insureds, but only with respect to their liability for the activities of the association or activities they performed on behalf of the association. A suit against one member alleged she had appointed her husband president of the association and that his actions on behalf of the association had violated the federal Racketeering Influenced and Corrupt Organizations Act. The defendants argued the wife was covered by the endorsement because the underlying complaint alleged damages covered by the policy. However, the court found the insurer had no duty to defend the wife because the allegations of the underlying complaint did not allege bodily injury or property damage caused by an occurrence and, therefore, did not fall within the scope of the CGL coverage.

case, residents of a neighborhood were eligible to become members of a beach club. The club had a CGL policy in which it was the only named insured. There was an "Additional Insured—Club Member" endorsement to the policy under which a member of the club was an insured but only with respect to their liability for activities of the named insured or activities they performed on behalf of the named insured. One club member injured another and sought coverage under the policy. The court carefully examined the endorsement. It began by noting the limiting terms of the provision—only with respect to—and concluded it made clear that the policy was not intended to cover every member pursuit at the club. The court read the portion of the endorsement that referred to "activities on behalf of the club" to include a member activity that was done for the benefit of the club at its request, for example, a membership drive. The second possibility for coverage, observed the court, arose under a type of vicarious liability. Because the club was incorporated—just as most common interest communities—it could enter into contracts, could be sued, and could be held liable for torts and breaches of contract. In light of that status, activities of the named insured had to refer to activities undertaken by the corporate entity, for example, when it entered into a service contract with a vendor. Therefore, when the endorsement provided coverage for member liability, that coverage would be invoked when a member was held vicariously liable for some activity undertaken by the club as a corporate entity.[202]

[iv] Notifying Association Members of the Endorsement

The residents of a common interest community likely have little understanding of insurance in general and even less about the association's coverage. They may assume, but do not know for a fact, that the association has liability coverage and very few residents will know if that policy has an endorsement that makes them additional insureds. Even if they learn of the Additional Insured endorsement and read it, they likely will not understand its meaning. Governing boards should make an effort to educate their residents about common interest community association insurance in general and specifically about their status as additional insureds. One way to do that would be to ask the broker or insurer to provide a written explanation of the endorsement that can be distributed to the residents.

[v] Coverage of Claims by Association Members

There is a distinction between the status of an association member as an additional insured and as a claimant. For example, the typical additional insured endorsement for a condominium association policy includes each individual unit owner of the insured association as an insured for liability arising out of ownership, maintenance, or repair of the portion of the premises not reserved for the

202. Lenox v. Scottsdale Ins. Co., 2005 U.S. Dist. LEXIS 48883 (D.N.J. May 5, 2005).

exclusive use or occupancy of that unit owner.[203] In those limited circumstances, the policy covers a *claim against* a unit owner. However, a unit owner can also be a claimant him- or herself. For example, if a unit owner slips and falls in the association parking lot, he or she may have a claim against the association and that claim would generally be covered regardless of whether the unit owner is an additional insured. The one exception may be for medical payments coverage for which there is an exclusion under which the insurer will not pay expenses for bodily injury to any insured, except a volunteer worker.[204] There do not appear to be any cases addressing whether that exclusion applies to a person who is an additional insured for limited purposes. Arguably, it should not apply when the individual owner is not the *subject of the claim*, but instead is the claimant.

[b] Developer

There are ISO endorsements that add the developer as an insured,[205] including state-specific endorsements.[206] The endorsements do not define "developer," but the term is generally understood to mean an entity that creates a common interest community.[207] Sometimes endorsements use the term "declarant," which generally means the same thing and is the term used in the Uniform Acts. California also uses that term and defines it as "the person or group of persons designated in the declaration as declarant, or if no declarant is designated, the person or group of persons who sign the original declaration or who succeed to special rights, preferences, or privileges designated in the declaration as belonging to the signatory of the original declaration."[208]

---

203. *See, e.g.*, ISO Form CG 20 04 11 85 (Commercial General Liability: Additional Insured—Condominium Unit Owners).

204. *See* § 13.07[4][a], *infra*.

205. *See, e.g.*, ISO Form CG 01 27 11 85 (Commercial General Liability: Condominiums).

206. *See, e.g.*, ISO Form CG 26 23 10 05 (Commercial General Liability: Connecticut Changes—Townhouses); ISO Form CG 01 65 08 05 (Commercial General Liability: Illinois Changes—Condominiums); ISO Form CG 01 41 03 11 (Commercial General Liability: Maryland—Condominiums); ISO Form CG 01 28 07 98 (Commercial General Liability: Minnesota Changes—Condominiums); ISO Form CG 01 20 07 98 (Commercial General Liability: Minnesota Changes—Townhouses); ISO Form CG 26 37 06 95 (Commercial General Liability: Texas Changes—Condominiums); ISO Form CG 26 26 03 93 (Commercial General Liability: Washington Changes—Condominiums).

207. *See, e.g.*, Fla. Stat. § 720.301(6) ("developer" means person or entity that creates community served by association or succeeds to rights and liabilities of person or entity that created community served by association, provided that such is evidenced in writing); 765 Ill. Comp. Stat. 605/2(q) ("developer" means any person who submits property legally or equitably owned in fee simple by developer, or leased to developer to provisions of Condominium Property Act, or any person who offers units legally or equitably owned in fee simple by developer, or leased to developer for sale in ordinary course of that person's business, including any successor or successors to developer's entire interest in property other than purchaser of individual unit).

208. Cal. Civ. Code § 4130. *See also* Uniform Common Interest Ownership Act § 1-103(14) (declarant is any person, or group of persons, acting in concert who as part of common promotional plan, offers to dispose of his or her interest in unit not previously disposed of).

Typically, these endorsements include the developer as an insured in the developer's capacity as a unit-owner—but only with respect to liability arising out of ownership, maintenance, or repair of the portion of the premises not owned solely by the developer—or the developer's membership in the association, and not for liability for acts or omissions *as a developer*. Thus, a developer does not qualify as a unit owner insured when the allegations against it are construction defects or misrepresentations in the marketing and sale of units as these are developer activities.[209] A successor to a developer may also be covered as an additional insured.[210]

[c] Association as Additional Insured on Other Policies

It is possible for a common interest community association to be an additional insured on policies issued to third parties, including a party with whom it contracts for services or an individual unit owner. Experts recommend that associations contracting for services obtain additional named insured status whenever possible.[211] Some associations require their members to have the association added as an additional insured on their homeowners policy. Associations, however, should note that by its terms, the association CGL policy is generally excess over any other primary insurance available to the association covering liability for damages arising out of the premises or operations to which the association has been added as an additional insured by endorsement.[212] Thus, for example, if the homeowners policy of an individual owner adds the association as an additional insured, then the CGL carrier for the association may no longer provide the primary coverage.[213] Any association that requires owners or vendors to include

209. *See, e.g.*, QBE Ins. Corp. v. Creston Court Condo., Inc., 58 F. Supp. 3d 1137, 1150 (D. Or. 2014) (where complaint in underlying action alleged construction defects and misrepresentations in marketing and sale of condominium units, which are developer activities, and there were no allegations in underlying complaint seeking to impose liability as unit owner, claims alleged liability arising out of acts or omissions as developer and, consequently, developer did not qualify for insured status as unit owner).

210. *See, e.g.*, Auto-Owners Ins. Co. v. Madison at Park West Prop. Owners Ass'n, 834 F. Supp. 2d 437, 441 (D.S.C. 2011).

211. Levine, *Certificates of Insurance for Vendors: What We Should Have and From Who We Should Collect Them* (2014), available at: http://ebmg.com/2014/06/certificates-of-insurance-for-vendors-what-we-should-have-and-from-who-we-should-collect-them/.

212. *See, e.g.*, ISO Form CG 00 01 12 07, § IV.4.b.(1).(b).

213. *Consider* Alexander v. Nat'l Fire Ins., 454 F.3d 214 (3d Cir. Pa. 2006). In *Alexander* the association was the named insured in a CGL policy and owners of a unit were named insureds in two policies issued to them. The court determined the association policy was primary. It noted that by substituting the association—as named insured—for "you" in a clause comparable to 4.b(1)(b), the policy read: "'This insurance is excess over . . . any other primary insurance available to [the Condominium Association] covering liability for damages arising out of the premises or operations for which [the Condominium Association has] been added as an additional insured by attachment of an endorsement.'" Thus, the association policy would only be excess if the unit owners' policies had an endorsement adding the association as an additional insured. Those policies, however, did not add the association as an additional insured by endorsement or in any other way and, therefore,

the association as an additional insured should discuss the implications with its broker.

§ 13.03 Bodily Injury (Coverage A)

Generally, "bodily injury" is a narrow term that encompasses only physical injuries to the body and the consequences of those injuries,[214] although as discussed below, some courts consider emotional harm as a bodily injury. Commercial general liability policies typically define "bodily injury" to mean bodily injury, sickness, or disease sustained by a person, including death resulting from bodily injury, sickness, or disease.[215] Under a commercial general liability policy, the carrier will pay sums the insured is legally obligated to pay as damages to which the coverage applies.[216] Coverage applies only if the bodily injury is caused by an "occurrence."[217] The occurrence has to take place in the "coverage territory"[218] and during the policy period.[219]

the association was primary. Finally, the court considered whether the unit owners' policies were also primary. They provided that their coverage would be excess over "other valid and collectible insurance except insurance written specifically to cover as excess over" them. The unit owners, said the court, had "other valid and collectible insurance" from the association CGL policy—under which they were additional insureds by endorsement—and therefore, because that policy was not specifically written to be excess to those issued to the unit owners, by the operation of the other insurance provisions in the three policies, the association's carrier was the sole primary insurer of the unit owners for the liability at issue.

214. Allstate Ins. Co. v. Diamant, 401 Mass. 654, 518 N.E.2d 1154 (1988).

215. *See, e.g.*, ISO Form CG 00 01 12 07, § V.3. Note that an endorsement can be added to a policy that includes "mental anguish or emotional distress" caused by bodily injury, sickness, or disease in the definition of bodily injury. *See, e.g.*, Essex Insurance Company Form MEIL 1216 07 10.

216. *See, e.g.*, ISO Form CG 00 01 12 07, § I.A.1.a.

217. *See, e.g.*, ISO Form CG 00 01 12 07, § I.A.1.b.(1).

218. The basic coverage territory is the United States and its territories and possessions, Puerto Rico, and Canada. *See, e.g.*, CG 00 01 12 07, § V.4.a. The coverage territory includes international waters or airspace, but only if the injury or damage occurs during travel or transportation between the United States and its territories and possessions, Puerto Rico, or Canada. *See, e.g.*, CG 00 01 12 07, § V.4.b. The coverage territory also includes any other part of the world if the injury or damage arises out of goods or products made or sold by the insured in the United States and its territories and possessions, Puerto Rico, or Canada, activities of a person whose home is in the United States and its territories and possessions, Puerto Rico, or Canada, but is away for a short time on the business of the insured, or a personal and advertising injury offense that take place through the Internet or similar electronic means of communication, provided the responsibility of the insured to pay damages is determined in a suit on the merits, in the United States and its territories and possessions, Puerto Rico, or Canada or in a settlement to which the carrier agrees. *See, e.g.*, CG 00 01 12 07, § V.4.c.

219. *See, e.g.*, ISO Form CG 00 01 12 07, §§ I.A.1.b.(1), (2). *See also* Heather Hill Villas Condo. Ass'n v. Am. Equity Ins. Co., 816 So. 2d 250 (Fla. 2d DCA 2002) (where in underlying action by association against unit owner, unit owner counterclaimed for alleged damages from excessive moisture in her condominium unit, dates in counterclaim were clearly outside term of coverage, and lower court correctly determined there was no coverage).

Bodily injury that occurs during the policy period includes any continuation, change, or resumption of that injury after the end of the policy period.[220] Damages because of bodily injury include those claimed by any person or organization for care, loss of services, or death resulting at any time from a bodily injury.[221] Generally, if an injury occurs during a prior period, any resulting damages should be covered under the policy in place at the time of the occurrence.

There is an important limitation on the coverage. It applies only if, prior to the policy period, no insured[222] and no employee[223] authorized by the named insured to give or receive notice of an occurrence or claim knew that the bodily injury had occurred, in whole or in part.[224] A bodily injury will be deemed to have been known to have occurred at the earliest time when any insured or any employee authorized to give or receive notice of an occurrence or claim reports all, or any part, of the bodily injury to the carrier or any other insurer, receives a written or verbal demand or claim for damages because of a bodily injury, or becomes aware by any other means that a bodily injury has occurred or has begun to occur.[225]

[1] Damages

CGL policies provide that the carrier will pay sums the insured is legally obligated to pay as "damages." They do not, however, define damages. Some courts say the term means a money judgment against the insured in a civil suit;[226] however, other courts view it as having a broader meaning.[227] Courts do not agree on the question of whether "damages" includes equitable remedies, for example,

220. *See, e.g.*, ISO Form CG 00 01 12 07, § I.A.1.c.

221. *See, e.g.*, ISO Form CG 00 01 12 07, § I.A.1.e.

222. "Insured" means anyone listed in section II.1 of the policy. For a discussion of who is an insured, see § 13.02, *supra*.

223. Employee includes a leased worker—meaning a person leased to the named insured by a labor leasing firm under an agreement to perform duties related to the conduct of the business of the named insured—but not a temporary one. *See, e.g.*, CG 00 01 12 07, § V.5 &10.

224. *See, e.g.*, ISO Form CG 00 01 12 07, § I.A.1.b.(3). If an insured or authorized employee knew, prior to the policy period, that the bodily injury occurred, then any continuation, change, or resumption of that bodily injury during or after the policy period is deemed to have been known prior to the policy period.

225. *See, e.g.*, ISO Form CG 00 01 12 07, § I.A.1.d.

226. *See, e.g.*, County of San Diego v. Ace Property & Casualty Ins. Co., 37 Cal. 4th 406, 33 Cal. Rptr. 3d 583, 118 P.3d 607 (2005).

227. *See, e.g.*, Desert Mt. Props. Ltd. P'ship v. Liberty Mut. Fire Ins. Co., 225 Ariz. 194, 201, 236 P.3d 421, 428 (Ariz. App. 2010), *aff'd*, 226 Ariz. 419, 250 P.3d 196 (Ariz. 2011) (no court action is required to create legal obligation and, therefore, coverage for sums insured becomes "legally obligated to pay as damages" may be triggered even absent civil suit against insured or court order requiring insured to make payment). Attorney's fees may constitute damages. *See* Ass'n of Apt. Owners of the Moorings v. Dongbu Ins. Co., 2016 U.S. Dist. LEXIS 110283 (D. Haw. Aug. 18, 2016). *See also* APL Co. v. Valley Force Ins. Co., 754 F. Supp. 2d 1084 (N.D. Cal. 2010).

an injunction.[228] Of course, a suit can seek both money damages and equitable relief. For example, in a common interest community case, the insurer argued that a request for injunctive/equitable relief did not constitute damages; however, the court pointed to allegations in the underlying complaint of past wrongs and injuries and an additional request for compensatory and statutory damages in an amount to be determined at trial and found there was a sufficient allegation of damages under the policy.[229] It is not unusual for common interest community associations to be sued for failure to carry out a duty allegedly mandated by its governing documents or by statutes, with the relief sought being an injunction.[230] Will the policy cover the costs of complying with a mandatory injunction? An association should discuss that question and the scope of coverage with its attorney and its broker.

Does an assessment levied by an association to pay a judgment against it constitute damages? In an unpublished California opinion, condominium unit owners argued a special assessment levied by the association to pay a judgment against the association constituted damages. The court, however, said that the duty of a carrier to indemnify its insured for sums the insured becomes legally obligated to pay as damages is limited to money judgments imposed by courts against the insured. The unit owners, noted the court, were not named as parties in the enforcement proceedings that resulted in the special assessment against them, and the fact that their contract with the association required them to contribute to its debts did not mean that a special assessment imposed for that purpose was a sum they were "legally obligated to pay as damages," as that term is defined in the standard commercial general liability policy.[231]

---

228. *See* State Farm Fire & Cas. Co. v. Metro. Mgmt., 2007 U.S. Dist. LEXIS 99406 (D. Haw. Oct. 31, 2007) (equitable relief, in form of injunction or otherwise—declaratory relief—does not constitute "damages" within meaning of insurance policy providing liability coverage); Cutler-Orosi Unified School Dist. v. Tulare County School etc. Authority, 31 Cal. App. 4th 617, 629, 37 Cal. Rptr. 2d 106, 113 (1994) (objectively reasonable insured would not conclude that costs of complying with federal court equitable order would be covered as damages). *Compare* Farmland Indus. v. Republic Ins. Co., 941 S.W.2d 505, 508 (Mo. 1997) (term "damages" is not rendered superfluous when given its ordinary meaning that includes equitable relief).

229. Toldt Woods Condos. Owner's Ass'n v. Madeline Square, LLC, 314 Wis. 2d 259, 757 N.W.2d 850 (2008).

230. *See, e.g.*, Willow Lake Residential Ass'n v. Juliano, 80 So. 3d 226 (Ala. App. 2010) (lot owners who cleared overgrown area of land immediately behind their home and erected series of steps mostly on common property sued association requesting that court permanently enjoin it from taking any action to remove steps or damage their property); Hobbs v. Weinkauf, 940 So. 2d 1151 (Fla. 2d DCA 2006) (injunction sought to require association to comply with statutory recordkeeping requirement); Wilson v. Playa De Serrano, 211 Ariz. 511, 123 P.3d 1148 (Ariz. App. 2005) (where association amended bylaws to declare community to be age-restricted community, resident sought declaratory judgment that age restriction was invalid and injunctive relief); Timmerman v. Board of Managers of the Anchorage Condominium, 212 A.D.2d 523, 622 N.Y.S.2d 320 (1995) (action seeking injunction to bar sitting board mounting any challenge to board election).

231. The Le Parc Cases, 2004 Cal. App. Unpub. LEXIS 4272 (Apr. 29, 2004).

[2] Occurrence

Commercial general liability policies cover an "occurrence." They typically define occurrence as an "accident."[232] They add that an accident includes continuous or repeated exposure to "substantially the same general harmful conditions." They do not, however, define "accident." Generally, common law determines what is, or is not, an accident for purposes of triggering coverage.[233] The meaning of the word has been the subject of countless court opinions and analyzed by the leading treatises on insurance law.[234] In general, an accident is an unforeseen event.[235] As a rule, the determination by a court of whether an event is an accident is based not on whether an act was intended, but whether the injury was intended.[236] However, courts may infer intent to injure where the harm is obvious, for example, battery.[237]

232. *See, e.g.*, ISO Form CG 00 01 12 07, § V.13.

233. https://www.irmi.com/online/insurance-glossary/terms/a/accident.aspx (noting that occasionally "accident" is defined in policy).

234. *See* 3 Jeffrey E. Thomas, *New Appleman on Insurance Law Library Edition* § 18.02[6] (Matthew Bender, 2017); Steven Plitt et al., *Couch on Insurance* § 129.3 (3d ed. Supp. 2015).

235. *See, e.g.*, Am. Family Mut. Ins. Co. v. Am. Girl, Inc., 268 Wis. 2d 16, 673 N.W.2d 65 (2004) (accident means event that takes place without one's foresight or expectation); Utica Mut. Ins. Co. v. Travelers Indem. Co., 223 Va. 145, 147, 286 S.E.2d 225, 226 (Va. 1982) (incident unexpected from viewpoint of insured); Hauenstein v. St. Paul-Mercury Indem. Co., 242 Minn. 354, 358–59, 65 N.W.2d 122, 126 (1954) (accident is unexpected, unforeseen, or undesigned happening or consequence from either known or unknown cause). *See also* Fed. Hill Homeowners Ass'n v. Cmty. Ass'n Underwriters of Am., Inc., 384 Fed. Appx. 209 (4th Cir. 2010) (where homeowners association issued disclosure packet containing information that allegedly caused plaintiff homeowner from being able to sell her property resulting in mental anguish for which she sued, there was an accident because mental anguish would not be natural and probable consequence of issuing disclosure packet; association was required by state law to produce disclosure packet at request of homeowner and packet contained information that was not extraordinary); Riverdale Peaks Homeowners Ass'n v. Auto-Owners Ins. Co., 2012 U.S. Dist. LEXIS 54180 (D. Colo. Apr. 18, 2012) (where suit against association member alleged retaliatory, dishonest, and criminal conduct and violations of violations of the federal Racketeer Influenced and Corrupt Organization Act and Colorado Organized Crime and Control Act, because there was no bodily injury or property damage caused by an occurrence); Brown v. Am. W. Home Ins. Co., 2013 Tex. App. LEXIS 19 (Tex. App.—Dallas Jan. 3, 2013) (where unit owners sued association and association counterclaimed alleging unit owners intentionally made certain alterations, repairs, and improvements to their residence without prior written consent, in violation of declarations, bylaws, and regulations of association, association insurer had no duty to defend unit owners even if insurer would otherwise have duty to defend unit owners because they were charged with liability as to the common elements, court found no duty to defend because counterclaim did not qualify as "occurrence); N.H. Ins. Co. v. RLI Ins. Co., 807 So. 2d 171 (Fla. 3d DCA 2002) (where resident of condominium fired three shots, at separate times, and injured three separate persons, killing two and wrongful act, if any, of association was allowing the perpetrator to reside in its community, trial court properly found there were three occurrences; dissent, however, countered that there was only one occurrence and that was permitting perpetrator's presence).

236. *See, e.g.*, Gruetzmacher v. Acuity, 393 F. Supp. 2d 860, 866 (D. Minn. 2005) (coverage is for unexpected bodily injury even where there was an intent to act).

237. *See generally* Monteleone, *Coverage Issues Under Commercial General Liability and Directors' and Officers' Liability Policies*, 18 W. New Eng. L. Rev. 47, 51–57 (1996).

When the insured intends to injure another, there is no accident, even though the insured did not foresee the extent of the injury.[238]

[3] Bodily Injury Claims against Common Interest Communities

Claims against common interest community associations for bodily injuries are not uncommon. Many of these cases are "slip and fall" accidents in which the injured person slips on a defective stair,[239] a wet surface,[240] ice or snow,[241] a misplaced object,[242] or some other defect to the premises.[243] Many associations

238. *See, e.g.*, Hartford Fire Ins. Co. v. Spreen, 343 So. 2d 649, 651 (Fla. 3d DCA 1977) (where insured swung at another, fact that he did not foresee or intend extent of harm inflicted did not convert admitted assault and battery into an accident).

239. *See, e.g.*, Griffin v. Dana Point Condominium Ass'n, 768 F. Supp. 1299 (N.D. Ill. 1991) (plaintiff's claim against condominium association stemmed from slip and fall she suffered on stairway in condominium building over which it was asserted association maintained control and had sole responsibility for care and maintenance); Paramount Ins. Co. v. Rosedale Gardens, Inc., 293 A.D.2d 235, 743 N.Y.S.2d 59 (2002) (resident of cooperative building slipped and fell down third-floor stairway); Morin v. Bell Court Condominium Ass'n, 223 Conn. 323, 612 A.2d 1197 (1992) (police officer responding to radio dispatch informing him of fire on premises of condominium association sustained injuries when he tripped on defective stair); Ruoff v. Harbor Creek Community Ass'n, 10 Cal. App. 4th 1624, 13 Cal. Rptr. 2d 755 (1992) (suit arising out of slip and fall on stairway in common area).

240. *See, e.g.*, 200 W. End Ave. Condominium v. Mt. Hawley Ins. Co., 2014 N.Y. Misc. LEXIS 5573 (Dec. 17, 2014) (worker slipped and fell while descending wet, slippery interior staircase); Thompson v. Poinciana Place Condo. Ass'n, 729 So. 2d 457 (Fla. 4th DCA 1999) (caretaker/house cleaner of unit owner slipped and fell in elevator—common element—on what appeared to be liquid soap and sued association); Janke v. Corinthian Gardens, Inc., 405 So. 2d 740 (Fla. 4th DCA 1981), *pet. den.*, 413 So. 2d 876 (Fla. 1982) (social guest of condominium unit owner sued association after he slipped and fell on wet condominium garage roof parking deck).

241. *See, e.g.*, Qian v. Toll Bros. Inc., 223 N.J. 124, 121 A.3d 363 (2015); Scrocca v. Ashwood Condominium Ass'n, 326 Ga. App. 226, 756 S.E.2d 308 (2014) (unit owner who fell on walkway and was injured sued condominium association); Solazzo v. Calverton Hills Homeowners Ass'n, Inc., 2014 N.Y. Misc. LEXIS 4417 (Oct. 1, 2014) (homeowners association sued for injuries allegedly sustained by plaintiff when he slipped and fell on ice in roadway owned by association); Pikul v. Villas Del Rey Condo. Ass'n, 2013 Ill. App. Unpub. LEXIS 2546 (2013) (condominium unit owner sued association claiming to have fallen on "unnatural accumulation of ice and slush in common area parking lot); Northfield Ins. Co. v. Evian HPR, 2002 U.S. Dist. LEXIS 26684 (D.S.C. Aug. 27, 2002), *aff'd*, 2003 U.S. App. LEXIS 14064 (4th Cir. 2003) (resident injured after slipping on walkway after irrigation sprinkler had run during night in freezing conditions creating sheet of ice on that walkway); Schoondyke v. Heil, Heil, Smart & Golee, Inc., 44 Ill. Dec. 802, 89 Ill. App. 3d 640, 411 N.E.2d 1168 (1980) (resident who fell on common sidewalk that had not been cleared of snow sued association).

242. *See, e.g.*, Maffeo v. Harbour Landing Condominium Ass'n, 1994 Conn. Super. LEXIS 2968 (Nov. 22, 1994) (condominium unit owner sued association claiming to have fallen on screwdriver left on common stairwell).

243. *See, e.g.*, Lloyd v. Pier W. Prop. Owners Ass'n, 470 S.W.3d 293 (Ark. App. 2015) (social guest or resident sued association after wooden guardrail attached to second-floor balcony collapsed, causing him to fall and sustain personal injuries); Wieder v. King Cole Condo. Ass'n, 109 So. 3d 1196 (Fla. 3d DCA 2013) (unit owner sued association after she fell when she caught her foot on carpet in her hallway that had buckled); Am. Family Ins. Group v. Bergeson, 2011 Ariz. App.

operate swimming pools and are sued for injuries suffered in those pools.[244] It is not uncommon for associations to sponsor social events, and actions can be brought against them for accidents that happen at those events. For example, a condominium association was sued for allowing illegal Fourth of July fireworks

Unpub. LEXIS 421 (2011) (wrongful death action brought against association by family of resident died from carbon monoxide poisoning, allegedly because ceiling fan in condominium unit had been installed improperly and caused ceiling insulation to combust); Balbert v. 302 96th St. Owners Corp., 77 A.D.3d 779, 909 N.Y.S.2d 535 (2010) (resident slipped and fell in lobby of cooperative building); Walker v. Farmers Ins. Exchange, 153 Cal. App. 4th 965, 63 Cal. Rptr. 3d 507 (2007) (association sued when unit owner was injured by garage door—common element—opened with remote garage door opener by another unit owner); Hayes v. Lakeside Vill. Owners Ass'n, 282 Ga. App. 866, 640 S.E.2d 373 (2006) (resident sued homeowners association after chair in common area in which he was seated collapsed and injured him); Simon v. Gables Plaza Condo. Ass'n, 892 So. 2d 553 (Fla. 3d DCA 2005) (resident sued association after tripping and falling in parking garage on mat on floor concealing broken tiles); Pekelnaya v. Allyn, 25 A.D.3d 111, 113, 808 N.Y.S.2d 590, 592 (2005) (passerby on sidewalk sued condominium association after being struck and seriously injured by section of chain-link fence that fell from roof of building); Denton v. Hahn, 2004 Tenn. App. LEXIS 605 (Tenn. Ct. App. Sept. 16, 2004) (resident of condominium sued association claiming she was injured when she caught her heel on threshold and/or in gap between threshold and concrete step); Roseman v. Town Square Ass'n Inc., 810 So. 2d 516 (Fla. 4th DCA 2001) (plaintiff sued condominium association after she was injured when front door of building closed quickly and struck her on back); Lotto v. Point East Two Condominium Corp. 702 So. 2d 1361 (Fla. 3d DCA 1997) (resident of condominium sued association after falling on large, uneven sidewalk crack); Sacker v. Perry Realty Servs., 217 Ga. App. 300, 457 S.E.2d 208 (1995) (owner of condominium unit sued association after she tripped over railroad tie used as parking space indicator that was out of place at time of accident); Porto v. Carlyle Plaza, Inc., 971 So. 2d 940 (3d DCA, 2007) (non-resident who crossed condominium property tripped and fell over a piece of metal protruding from association driveway sued association).

244. *See, e.g.*, First Specialty Ins. Corp. v. GRS Mgmt. Assocs., 2009 U.S. Dist. LEXIS 72708 (S.D. Fla. 2009) (homeowners association sued by swimmer who allegedly contracted viral infection from contaminants in water of community pool); Great Divide Ins. Co. v. Aoao Maluna Kai Estates, 492 F. Supp. 2d 1216 (D. Haw. 2007) (suit by family of child who drowned in swimming pool on association premises); Trailside Townhome Ass'n v. Acierno, 880 P.2d 1197, 1198 (Colo. 1994) (unit owner in townhome association sued association for injuries as result of diving into shallow water in swimming pool); Machin v. Royale Green Condominium Ass'n, 507 So. 2d 646 (Fla. 3d DCA 1987) (plaintiffs who rented condominium unit sued association after their son drowned in community swimming pool claiming association failed to comply with county code requirement that gate in swimming pool fence self-close or have spring lock); Hemispheres Condominium Ass'n v. Corbin, 357 So. 2d 1074 (Fla. 3d DCA 1975) (tenant of unit owner drowned in association swimming pool and spouse sued association). *Compare* Saga Bay Property Owners Association v. Askew, 513 So. 2d 691 (Fla. 3d DCA 1987), *rev. den.*, 525 So. 2d 876 (Fla. 1988) (association that owned property with lake used by residents and general public for recreational swimming, boating, and fishing was sued by parents of child who drowned in lake, but court held association was not liable in absence of unusual danger not generally existing in similar bodies of water or dangerous condition constituting trap). Associations should be aware that if a lifeguard provides care to a swimmer and further injures that person, the claim would likely fall under professional liability, not commercial general liability, coverage. .Associations that provide lifeguards, either as employees of the association or under contract with a swimming pool management company, need to discuss their coverage, and the coverage of any company with which the contract, with their broker.

to be ignited on its property and injuring bystanders.[245] Finally, property owners can be held liable under certain circumstances for injuries that are the result of criminal acts that occur on their property. Common interest community associations have been sued for those injuries.[246]

The discussion below addresses premises liability law broadly and the extent of the potential liability of associations under it. The purpose of the discussion is to raise issues, not to provide a comprehensive treatment of the subject. The law of premises liability is complex and varies from state to state. Additionally, community association law is relatively new and evolving, as is the relationship between it and tort law principles.[247] The only way for an association to determine the scope of its potential liability and its need for insurance coverage is to consult with its counsel.

A common claim in many lawsuits is emotional distress. Ordinarily it is combined with other causes of action. Claims for negligent or intentional infliction of emotional distress against common interest communities are not uncommon.[248]

245. *See* Colangelo v. Bay View Improvement Ass'n, 2013 Conn. Super. LEXIS 2496 (Conn. Super. Ct. Nov. 4, 2013). The case illustrates a tort law concept in which a defendant can be found liable without fault—strictly liable—where the plaintiff is injured as a result of an "ultrahazardous activity." *See generally* Restatement (Second) of Torts, § 364 (creation or maintenance of dangerous artificial conditions).

246. *See, e.g.*, Bradford Square Condo. Ass'n v. Miller, 258 Ga. App. 240, 573 S.E.2d 405 (2002) (unit owner sued association for wrongful death after she and her husband were attacked the association parking lot by three men who shot and killed the husband and stole the couple's automobile); N.H. Ins. Co. v. RLI Ins. Co., 807 So. 2d 171 (Fla. 3d DCA 2002) (where resident of condominium fired three shots, at separate times, and injured three separate persons, killing two, association was sued); Centeq Realty, Inc. v. Siegler, 899 S.W.2d 195 (Tex. 1995) (resident of condominium sued association after being attacked and kidnapped from parking garage); Phillips v. Parkside of Fountainbleau Condominium Ass'n, 634 So. 2d 1101 (Fla. 3d DCA 1994) (condominium unit owner assaulted by mugger in condominium parking lot brought suit against association); L.K. v. Water's Edge Ass'n, 532 So. 2d 1097 (Fla. 3d DCA 1988) (tenant sued condominium association for negligent failure to provide adequate security after she was sexually assaulted in her unit by intruder); Admiral's Port Condominium Ass'n v. Feldman, 426 So. 2d 1054 (Fla. 3d DCA 1983) (unit owner sued association after being mugged in parking lot).

247. Smith v. King's Grant Condominium, 418 Pa. Super. 260, 264, 614 A.2d 261, 267 (1992), *aff'd*, 537 Pa. 51, 640 A.2d 1276 (1994).

248. *See, e.g.*, Dubois v. Ass'n of Apt. Owners, 453 F.3d 1175 (9th Cir. 2006) (unit owner brought suit against association in dispute over pet); Ass'n of Apt. Owners of the Moorings v. Dongbu Ins. Co., 2016 U.S. Dist. LEXIS 110283 (D. Haw. Aug. 18, 2016) (unit owners brought claim for tortious infliction of emotional distress in connection with failure of association to repair and maintain their lanai roof, which caused water damage to interior of their unit); Walters v. Cowpet Bay W. Condo. Ass'n, 2015 U.S. Dist. LEXIS 13 (D.V.I. Jan. 2, 2015) (unit owner sued association over no pet rule); Kromenhoek v. Cowpet Bay W. Condo. Ass'n, 77 F. Supp. 3d 462 (D.V.I. 2014) (unit owner alleged intentional and negligent infliction of emotional distress by association in dispute over emotional support animal); Cohen v. Beachside Two-I Homeowners' Ass'n, 2005 U.S. Dist. LEXIS 28536 (D. Minn. Nov. 17, 2005), *aff'd*, 272 Fed. Appx. 534; 2008, *cert. den.*, 555 U.S. 945, 129 S. Ct. 417, 172 L. Ed. 2d 288 (2008) (allowing homeowner to raise negligent infliction of emotional distress claim against homeowners association as derivative of libel claim); Jones v. Jennings, 2016 Mich. App. LEXIS 1596 (Mich. App. Aug. 30, 2016) (resident of housing cooperative

The question, discussed below, is whether those claims are covered under a commercial general liability policy as "bodily injuries."

[a] Premises Liability

Premises liability is a theory of liability under which one who owns or occupies land owes a duty to those who come on the land, and if he or she breaches that duty, he or she incurs liability.[249] That liability is not based on ownership, but on possession and control. Generally, a possessor of land is one who occupies it with intent to control it or who has been in occupation of it with intent to control it, if no other person has subsequently occupied it with intent to control it, or who is entitled to immediate occupation of it, if no one else is in possession.[250]

The duty owed by the person in possession is based on the status of those who enter the land.[251] Under English common law brought forward to the United States, one who enters the land of another does so as an "invitee," a "licensee," or a "trespasser." The Restatement of Torts classifies invitees as either public invitees or business visitors.[252] A public invitee is one invited to enter or remain

---

brought suit for intentional infliction of emotional distress alleging other residents accused him of wrongdoing as director of cooperative corporation); Wood v. Granite Ridge Condo Ass'n, 2009 N.H. Super. LEXIS 76 (2009) (unit owner alleged negligent infliction of emotional distress by governing board as result of its maintenance decisions); Meadows Condo. Ass'n v. Redman, 2009 Conn. Super. LEXIS 2062 (Conn. Super. July 30, 2009) (unit owner alleged in counterclaim to associations' action that acts of association in allegedly withholding information from court and/or making false and misleading statements during foreclosure action were undertaken intentionally and with reckless disregard and constituted intentional infliction of emotional distress); Tai v. Crown View Manor I Condo. Ass'n, 2008 N.J. Super. Unpub. LEXIS 23 (App. Div. July 11, 2008) (unit owner sued association for infliction of emotional distress after receiving letter stating unit owner had been seen removing water jug from lobby); Papasodero v. Thayer & Assocs., 14 Mass. L. Rep. 684 (Mass. Super. 2002) (unit owner alleged intentional and/or negligent infliction of emotional distress by association because it published agenda notice stating his "bad debt" would be discussed at meeting).

249. *See, e.g.*, Ruoff v. Harbor Creek Community Ass'n, 10 Cal. App. 4th 1624, 1628, 13 Cal. Rptr. 2d 755, 758 (1992) (owner or occupier of real property has to exercise ordinary care in managing property and owes duty of care to persons who come on land).

250. Restatement (Second) of Torts, § 328E.

251. *See, e.g.*, Porto v. Carlyle Plaza, Inc., 971 So. 2d 940, 941 (Fla. 3d DCA 2007), *rev. den.*, 982 So. 2d 1178 (Fla. 2008) (duty of care owed by landowner depends on status of entrant on property); Sevigny v. Dibble Hollow Condo. Ass'n, 76 Conn. App. 306, 320, 819 A.2d 844, 854 (2003) (generally there is ascending degree of duty owed by possessor of land to persons on land based on their entrant status).

252. Restatement (Second) of Torts, § 332(1). Does a common interest community have "business visitors"? *See* Martinez v. Woodmar IV Condos. Homeowners Ass'n, 189 Ariz. 206, 941 P.2d 218 (1997) (condominium developments are businesses that could not be operated without common areas open to unit owners, their tenants, and their guests); O'Connor v. Village Green Owners Ass'n, 33 Cal. 3d 790, 796, 191 Cal. Rptr. 320, 324, 662 P.2d 427, 431 (1983) (condominium association was "business establishment" within meaning of state anti-discrimination law); Hemispheres Condominium Ass'n v. Corbin, 357 So. 2d 1074 (Fla. 3d DCA 1975) (association did not have same duty of guarding persons from harm that would apply to place providing public entertainment for profit).

on land as a member of the public for a purpose for which the land is held open to the public, and a business visitor is one invited to enter or remain on land for a purpose directly or indirectly connected with business dealings with the person in possession of the land.[253] Under the traditional hierarchy of duties, the person in possession of land owes the greatest duty to an invitee. He or she is subject to liability for physical harm caused to his or her invitees by a condition on the land if he or she knows of, or by exercise of reasonable care would discover,[254] the condition, and should realize that it involves an unreasonable risk of harm to those invitees, should expect they will not discover or realize the danger, or will fail to protect themselves against it, and fails to exercise reasonable care to protect them against it.[255]

A licensee is one privileged to enter or remain on land only by virtue of the consent of the person in possession.[256] Licensees include anyone whose presence on the land is solely for his or her own purposes,[257] in which the possessor has no interest, and to whom the privilege of entering is extended as a mere personal favor, members of the household of the person in possession—except boarders, paying guests, and servants, who are generally considered invitees—and social guests.[258] The person in possession is liable for physical harm suffered by a licensee by a condition on the land if he or she knows, or has reason to know, of the condition and should realize that it involves an unreasonable risk of harm to the licensee, and should expect the licensee will not discover or realize the danger, and fails to exercise reasonable care to make the condition safe, or to warn the

253. Restatement (Second) of Torts, §§ 332(2), (3). Are common areas "held open to the public"? The Connecticut Supreme Court concluded they are not. Morin v. Bell Court Condominium Ass'n, 223 Conn. 323, 335, 612 A.2d 1197, 1203 (1992) (that common areas of condominium complex are open to various condominium owners does not establish that they are, as matter of law, open to public; generally, premises have been considered open to public where some sort of public function or traditional business purpose is being served and public or business functions are conspicuously absent in private residence such as condominium building).

254. *See, e.g.*, Denton v. Hahn, 2004 Tenn. App. LEXIS 605 (Tenn. Ct. App. Sept. 16, 2004) (without evidence that condominium association had actual or constructive knowledge of existence of dangerous condition that caused resident to fall, it could not be held liable for injuries sustained).

255. Restatement (Second) of Torts, § 343. *See also* Restatement (Second) of Torts, § 341A (possessor of land is subject to liability to invitees for physical harm caused to them by failure to carry on activities with reasonable care for their safety, but only if he or she should expect they will not discover or realize danger, or will fail to protect themselves against it).

256. Restatement (Second) of Torts, § 330.

257. *See, e.g.*, Porto v. Carlyle Plaza, Inc., 971 So. 2d 940 (3d DCA, 2007) (non-resident who crossed condominium property while walking dog was uninvited licensee and association did not breach any duty of care owed to her); Morin v. Bell Court Condominium Ass'n, 223 Conn. 323, 612 A.2d 1197 (1992) (police officer responding to radio dispatch informing him of fire on association premises was licensee).

258. Restatement (Second) of Torts, § 330, comment h.

licensee of the condition and the risk involved, and the licensee does not know or have reason to know of the condition and the risk involved.[259]

The distinction between invitees and licensees differs from state to state. For example, some jurisdictions may consider social guests to be invitees.[260] Some courts adhere to the common-law dichotomy between invitees and licensees,[261] while others have abandoned it altogether in the face of increasingly subtle distinctions from which confusion has ensued.[262] In Colorado, the state supreme court attempted to reduce the significance of the categories,[263] only to have the legislature codify the common-law distinctions.[264] Thus, for one in possession of land to understand his or her potential liability, he or she must consult an attorney in that state.

There is somewhat more agreement about the third category of entrants to land: trespassers. The Restatement defines a "trespasser" as one who enters or remains on land in the possession of another without a privilege to do so created by the consent person in possession, or "otherwise."[265] Generally, the possessor of land is not liable to a trespasser for physical harm caused by failure to exercise reasonable care to put the land in a reasonably safe condition or to carry on activities so as not to endanger the trespasser.[266] More succinctly put, one in possession owes a duty to a trespasser not to cause willful, wanton, or deliberate injury.[267] A common exception is for children under the "attractive nuisance" doctrine.[268] The doctrine generally requires one in possession of land to use reasonable care to protect children from dangers of a condition attractive to them and that, because of their youth, they would not recognize. Once again, application of the doctrine may vary from state to state, and one needs to consult an attorney in that state to learn its parameters.

---

259. Restatement (Second) of Torts, § 342. *See also* Restatement (Second) of Torts, § 341 (possessor of land is subject to liability to licensees for physical harm caused to them by failure to carry on her activities with reasonable care for their safety but only if he or she should expect they will not discover or realize danger and do not know or have reason to know of activities of possessor and of risk involved).

260. *See* Wood v. Camp, 284 So. 2d 691 (Fla. 1973). *See also* Conn. Gen. Stat. § 52-557a (standard of care owed to social invitee shall be same as standard of care owed to business invitee).

261. *See, e.g.*, Lloyd v. Pier W. Prop. Owners Ass'n, 470 S.W.3d 293, 297 (Ark. App. 2015) (Arkansas courts adhere to common-law distinctions between duties owed to trespassers, licensees, and invitees); Post v. Lunney, 261 So. 2d 146 (Fla. 1972).

262. *See, e.g.*, Nelson v. Freeland, 349 N.C. 615, 507 S.E.2d 882 (1998); Mounsey v. Ellard, 363 Mass. 693, 297 N.E.2d 43 (1973).

263. Mile High Fence Co. v. Radovich, 175 Colo. 537, 489 P.2d 308 (1971).

264. Colo. Rev. Stat. § 13-21-115.

265. Restatement (Second) of Torts, § 329.

266. Restatement (Second) of Torts, § 333.

267. *See, e.g.*, Schofield v. Merrill, 386 Mass. 244, 435 N.E.2d 339 (1982); Nettles v. Your Ice, Inc., 191 S.C. 429, 4 S.E.2d 797 (S.C. 1939).

268. *See, e.g.*, Concrete Construction, Inc. of Lake Worth v. Pettersen, 216 So. 2d 221 (Fla. 1968); Walker v. Sprinkle, 267 N.C. 626, 148 S.E.2d 631 (1966); Staley v. Security Athletic Ass'n, 152 Colo. 19, 380 P.2d 53 (1963).

[i] Common Interest Communities as Owners or Occupiers

When does a common interest community association constitute the owner or occupier of land? The type of CIC has a bearing on the answer. In a residential cooperative, the cooperative corporation owns all the real property, and the residents are tenants under a proprietary lease. The cooperative corporation owes a duty for the common areas and, in some cases as discussed later,[269] for the individual apartments. In a condominium, the association by definition owns no real property, and the unit owners own their units outright. The common area is owned by the unit owners as tenants in common, although that common area in the case of a ground or recreation lease may be leased to the association. In either event, courts generally agree that the association occupies the common elements for purposes of liability.[270] There are some limited circumstances, again as discussed later, in which the association may have liability for an incident inside a unit. Finally, the demarcation of liability is clearest in the typical homeowners association where the association actually owns the common areas and the individual owners own their homes outright.

---

269. *See* § 13.03[3][a][vi], *infra*.

270. *See, e.g.*, Pekelnaya v. Allyn, 25 A.D.3d 111, 120, 808 N.Y.S.2d 590, 597 (2005) (condominium common elements are solely under control of governing board); Martinez v. Woodmar IV Condos. Homeowners Ass'n, 189 Ariz. 206, 208, 941 P.2d 218, 220 (1997) (characterizing condominium association as "owner or possessor of land"); Maffeo v. Harbour Landing Condominium Ass'n, 1994 Conn. Super. LEXIS 2968 (Nov. 22, 1994) (describing condominium association as possessor of common area). *See also* Jerdonek v. 41 W. 72 LLC, 143 A.D.3d 43, 48, 36 N.Y.S.3d 17, 21 (2016) (in keeping with vesting of exclusive control of condominium common elements in board of managers, it is well established that claim arising from condition or operation of common elements does not lie against owners of individual units but rather, proper defendant is board of managers; statute imposing obligations or liabilities on "owner" of real property does not give rise to claim against owners of individual condominium units where that claim arises from common elements or concerns duty not connected with any individual unit); Gittleman v. Woodhaven Condo. Ass'n, 972 F. Supp. 894, 902 (D.N.J. 1997) (managerial power of condominium association extends to aspects of dominion traditionally associated with ownership, for example, ability to lease or license use of common elements, to purchase insurance covering risks incidental to use of the common elements, and to sue third parties for damages to common elements); Porto v. Carlyle Plaza, Inc., 971 So. 2d 940, 941 (Fla. 3d DCA 2007), *rev. den.*, 982 So. 2d 1178 (Fla. 2008) (treating condominium association as possessor without addressing question); Sevigny v. Dibble Hollow Condo. Ass'n, 76 Conn. App. 306, 321, 819 A.2d 844, 854 (2003) (condominium association may be held to standard of care as to common areas under its control). *And see* Smith v. King's Grant Condominium, 418 Pa. Super. 260, 614 A.2d 261 (1992), *aff'd*, 537 Pa. 51, 640 A.2d 1276 (1994) (to apply tort principles to condominium, it is necessary to view association and its possession of common elements as entity separate and apart from unit owners and their possession of individual units, with each possessing definable, adjacent land interests); Janke v. Corinthian Gardens, Inc., 405 So. 2d 740, 742 (Fla. 4th DCA 1981), *pet. den.*, 413 So. 2d 876 (Fla. 1982) (parties agreed condominium association had duty to maintain and repair common area parking deck). *But see* Far Northwest Dev. Co., LLC v. Cmty. Ass'n of Underwriters of Am., Inc., 2006 U.S. Dist. LEXIS 79033 (W.D. Wash. Oct. 30, 2006) (condominium association does not own or occupy common elements and coverage could not, therefore, be precluded on basis of property damage exclusion).

[ii] The Status of the Common Interest Community and Duty

A common interest community association may have the duty any owner or occupier of premises has to those on the premises. That duty, as discussed above, would then be based on the status of the claimant. The duty may also be that of a landlord, the scope of which is addressed below. In the case of a cooperative, the corporation *actually is the landlord* because its residents occupy their apartments under a proprietary lease. However, even a homeowners or condominium association may be treated by courts as a landlord for purposes of determining duty. For example, the Arizona Supreme Court has specifically held that "with respect to common areas under its exclusive control, a condominium association has the same duties as a landlord."[271] Courts in other states agree.[272] They have also taken the same position with regard to homeowners associations.[273] Generally, if the association has the duty to its residents imposed on a landlord, or the residents are invitees, the same standard of care will apply.[274]

Regardless of the status of an association, it may by its actions,[275] or the governing documents, assume a duty that might not be imposed by common law. For example, an Illinois court said that while under that state's jurisprudence there was no common-law duty to remove snow or ice from a common area,

---

271. Martinez v. Woodmar IV Condos. Homeowners Ass'n, 189 Ariz. 206, 209, 941 P.2d 218, 221 (1997).

272. *See* Lloyd v. Pier W. Prop. Owners Ass'n, 470 S.W.3d 293, 299 (Ark. App. 2015) (association may be held to landlord standard of care as to common areas under its control even though it may, or may not, be typical landlord); Denton v. Hahn, 2004 Tenn. App. LEXIS 605 (Tenn. Ct. App. Sept. 16, 2004) (homeowners associations generally perform business functions that rest on landlord's shoulders in traditional landlord-tenant relationship); Sevigny v. Dibble Hollow Condo. Ass'n, 76 Conn. App. 306, 321, 819 A.2d 844, 854 (2003) (comparing relationship of unit owner and condominium association to that of tenant and landlord and stating association may be held to landlord's standard of care as to common areas under its control); Martinez v. Woodmar IV Condos. Homeowners Ass'n, 189 Ariz. 206, 941 P.2d 218 (1997) (comparing association to landlord); Francis T. v. Village Green Owners Ass'n, 42 Cal. 3d 490, 229 Cal. Rptr. 456, 723 P.2d 573 (1986) (association was, for all practical purposes, "landlord" and only one in position to maintain and secure common areas); Moody v. Cawdrey Assocs., 6 Haw. App. 355, 721 P.2d 708, 713–14 (1986) (relationship of condominium association and residential owner is analogous to that of landlord and tenant); Olar v. Schroit, 155 Cal. App. 3d 861, 202 Cal. Rptr. 457 (1984) (finding no distinction between landlord of a multiple-dwelling building and homeowners association). *But see* Frisch v. Bellmarc Mgt., Inc., 597 N.Y.S.2d 962, 966 (1993) (stating one would be "hard pressed" to find landlord tenant relationship between condominium unit owner and governing board).

273. *See* McMahon v. Pleasant Valley W. Ass'n, 952 A.2d 731 (Pa. Commw. 2008), *app. den.*, 599 Pa. 702, 961 A.2d 860 (2008) (comparing association to landlord by implication); Smolek v. K.W. Landscaping, 203 Ill. Dec. 415, 266 Ill. App. 3d 226, 639 N.E.2d 974 (1994) (relationship between homeowners association and homeowner was most akin to that of landlord and tenant).

274. *See, e.g.*, Maffeo v. Harbour Landing Condominium Ass'n, 1994 Conn. Super. LEXIS 2968 (Nov. 22, 1994).

275. *See* 6A Rohan, *Real Estate Transactions: Home Owner Associations and Planned Unit Developments—Law and Practice: Forms*, § 10.022[1] (Matthew Bender, 2017) (suggesting association might incur liability where it attempts to regulate an activity).

the association, by virtue of the provisions in its declaration of condominium and bylaws, assumed a duty for snow removal.[276] On the other hand, association guidelines for internal use that are not distributed to residents do not create a duty.[277]

[iii] The Tort Liability of a Landlord

The Restatement of Torts lays out the tort responsibilities of landlords. Generally, a landlord is not subject to liability to a tenant or others on the land with the consent of the tenant for physical harm caused by any dangerous condition that comes into existence *after* the tenant takes possession,[278] or by any dangerous condition, whether natural or artificial, that existed when the tenant took possession.[279] As a comment explains, the tenant acquires an estate in the land, and becomes the owner and occupier, subject to all of the liabilities of one in possession.[280] There are some exceptions. First, a landlord may be subject to liability for physical harm caused to a tenant and others on the land with the consent of the tenant by a condition of disrepair existing before or arising after the tenant has taken possession if the landlord contracted by a covenant in the lease or otherwise to keep the land in repair, any disrepair creates an unreasonable risk to persons on the land that performance of the agreement would have prevented, and the landlord failed to exercise reasonable care to perform the contract.[281]

276. Schoondyke v. Heil, Heil, Smart & Golee, Inc., 44 Ill. Dec. 802, 89 Ill. App. 3d 640, 411 N.E.2d 1168 (1980). *Accord* Taticek v. Homefield Gardens Condo. Ass'n, 2016 Mo. App. LEXIS 609 (Mo. App. June 21, 2016) (while condominium association had no duty to create reasonable rules and regulations, once it exercised power to create rules and regulations—specifically rules regarding dogs—and ensured enforcement of rules through "regular inspections of all buildings and vehicles" and hired management company for that purpose, association took it upon itself to enforce its rules and regulations and was potentially liable where dog owned by resident bit and seriously injured another resident); Lloyd v. Pier W. Prop. Owners Ass'n, 470 S.W.3d 293 (Ark. App. 2015) (where under bylaws, association exclusively reserved right and duty to maintain and repair the common areas, it assumed duty of reasonable care to perform its assumed duty); Qian v. Toll Bros. Inc., 223 N.J. 124, 121 A.3d 363 (2015) (where governing documents of homeowners association stated that governing board had affirmative and perpetual obligation and duty to cause common property and areas of common responsibility to be maintained according to accepted standards, association had responsibility to clear private sidewalks of accumulated snow and ice). *See also* Tressler v. Winfield Village Cooperative, Inc., 89 Ill. Dec. 723, 134 Ill. App. 3d 578, 481 N.E.2d 75 (1985) (handbook provided to residents and stating cooperative would arrange for snow removal could form basis for liability; however, liability for breach of covenant to remove snow arises only from failure to use due care in performing that covenant).

277. Dietch v. Carl Sandburg Vill. Home Owners Ass'n, 2015 Ill. App. Unpub. LEXIS 1167, *app. den.*, 396 Ill. Dec. 175, 39 N.E.3d 1001 (Ill. 2015) (while homeowners association Snow Removal Manual was concerned with the safety and protection of residents, it was not part of documents and was not distributed to residents; therefore, Manual did not create duty to clear snow and ice).

278. Restatement (Second) of Torts, § 355.

279. Restatement (Second) of Torts, § 356.

280. Restatement (Second) of Torts, § 356, comment a.

281. Restatement (Second) of Torts, § 357.

While the Restatement characterizes this as a minority rule, it is followed partially or completely by the five largest states.[282]

A landlord who leases a part of a property and retains control of any other part of it that the tenant is entitled to use as appurtenant to the portion leased is subject to liability to the tenant and others lawfully on the land with the consent of the tenant for physical harm caused by a dangerous condition on that part of the land retained in the control of the landlord, if the landlord by the exercise of reasonable care could have discovered the condition and the unreasonable risk involved and could have made the condition safe.[283] Two comments to the Restatement raise issues of relevance to common interest communities. One commentary notes that stairways, halls, elevators, and other common approaches to a lease property are provided not only for the use of the tenant but also for the use of those the tenant chooses to receive, but a tenant may have use of a yard in common with other tenants and if the purposes for that use do not include reception of licensees, a third person entering the yard at the invitation of a tenant is not lawfully there and the landlord is generally not liable to that person.[284]

Another comment discusses an exclusionary clause in a lease. It explains that an exclusionary clause could relieve a landlord of liability to a tenant for injury on the portion of the property over which the landlord retains control providing the clause does not violate the public policy of a state, but it does not affect the liability of the landlord to third persons—invitees or guests of the tenant—who are not parties to the lease contract nor in privity with it.[285] A Georgia appellate court considered exculpatory language in a recorded homeowners association covenant that said owners had the duty to continuously inspect the common

282. *See* Wallace v. Schrier, 107 So. 2d 754 (2d DCA 1958); Scholey v. Steele, 59 Cal. App. 2d 402, 138 P.2d 733 (1943); Ross v. Haner, 244 S.W. 231 (Tex. Civ. App. 1924), *aff'd*, 258 S.W. 1036 (1924). *See also* De Clara v. Barber Steamship Lines, 309 N.Y. 620, 628, 132 N.E.2d 871, 875 (1956) (*sine qua non* of liability in tort is retention by landlord of measure of occupation and control over leased premises although requisite reservation of control is not effected or accomplished by mere promise by landlord to make repairs at tenant's request); Alaimo v. Du Pont, 4 Ill. App. 2d 85, 91, 123 N.E.2d 583, 585 (1954) (landlord may be liable in tort for damages resulting from breach of the covenant to repair if covenant carries obligation to maintain premises in a safe or reasonably safe condition or is made under circumstances that indicated tort damages were to be recoverable for injuries resulting from breach or there is duty to repair apart from contract).

283. Restatement (Second) of Torts, § 360. A comment explains that the landlord is subject to liability to third persons entering the land, regardless of whether the tenant knows of the dangerous condition. If the tenant has knowledge of the dangerous condition, that may subject the tenant to liability, for example, for failure to warn third parties of the danger, but it will not relieve the landlord of liability for negligence in permitting the danger to exist. Restatement (Second) of Torts, § 360, comment a. *See* Martinez v. Woodmar IV Condos. Homeowners Ass'n, 189 Ariz. 206, 941 P.2d 218 (1997), specifically applying section 360 to a condominium association. *See also* Menendez v. Palms West Condo. Ass'n, 736 So. 2d 58, 62 (Fla. 1st DCA 1999) (association could not be liable on theory it failed to maintain safe conditions in common areas as criminal attack on resident did not occur in any common area).

284. Restatement (Second) of Torts, § 360, comment e.

285. Restatement (Second) of Torts, § 360, comment g.

areas and that they used the common areas "at their own risk and peril." The court said the wording of the covenant relieved the association of liability for an injury on the common areas by shifting the duty of care entirely to the owner using the common area.[286] It should be remembered, however, that the extent to which an exculpatory clause is valid, and not in violation of public policy will vary from state to state.

A landlord who leases a part of a property and retains control of any other part necessary to the safe use of the leased part is subject to liability to a tenant and others lawfully on the land with the consent of a tenant for physical harm caused by a dangerous condition on that part of the land retained in the control of the landlord, if the lessor by the exercise of reasonable care could have discovered the condition and the risk involved and could have made the condition safe.[287] A comment to the Restatement explains that the rule applies to maintenance of walls, roofs, and foundations and to any other part of a property the careful maintenance of which is essential to its safe use, for example, central heating, lighting, or a water system.[288] For instance, if leased property can only be safely used if heat or light is provided and the terms of the lease require the landlord to provide that service, the landlord is subject to liability for bodily harm caused by a failure to exercise reasonable care to maintain the service, not only to the tenant but also to those on the land with the consent of the tenant.[289]

Finally, a landlord who, by purporting to make repairs on the property while it is in the possession of a tenant, or by the negligent manner in making repairs has, as the tenant neither knows nor should know, made the property more dangerous for use or given it a deceptive appearance of safety is subject to liability for physical harm caused by the condition to the tenant or to others on the land with the consent of the tenant.[290]

[iv] Status of Residents and Their Tenants and Guests

A resident of a common interest community is generally considered an invitee when on the common areas.[291] Despite the fact that a resident is an invitee, he

286. Hayes v. Lakeside Vill. Owners Ass'n, 282 Ga. App. 866, 640 S.E.2d 373 (2006) (exculpatory clauses are valid and binding in Georgia and are not void as against public policy). *See also* Nido v. Ocean Owners' Council, 237 Va. 664, 378 S.E.2d 837 (1989) (where association bylaws provided association would not be liable for any for injury or damage to person or property resulting from electricity, water, snow, or ice that might leak or flow from any portion of common elements, court held unit owners voluntarily waived right to sue council for damage *originating* from common area).

287. Restatement (Second) of Torts, § 361.

288. Restatement (Second) of Torts, § 361, comment b.

289. Restatement (Second) of Torts, § 361, comment c.

290. Restatement (Second) of Torts, § 362.

291. *See, e.g.*, Sevigny v. Dibble Hollow Condo. Ass'n, 76 Conn. App. 306, 322, 819 A.2d 844, 855 (2003) (noting that courts of several states have analogized condominium unit owner's relationship with association as being akin to tenant's relationship to landlord with regard to common

or she lives on the property and would be expected to have a familiarity with it greater than that of the ordinary invitee. Does that affect the association's potential liability? In a Florida case, a court said that there is no "special legal duty" imposed on one who is a member of a condominium association or has an ownership interest in the common areas to report an unsafe condition to the association. A unit owner has, said the court, the same duty as anyone else, to look out for him- or herself in a reasonable manner. Thus, where an elevator was in an unsafe condition and a unit owner conceded she was aware of it well before it caused her to fall, a jury had a right to consider evidence of her failure to protect herself by reporting the condition when it determined the unit owner's own negligence.[292] Other courts have found that when an owner is familiar with an unsafe condition on the property and willingly encounters it, his or her comparative negligence is an appropriate consideration.[293]

Some courts reject application of traditional premises liability principles to common interest communities and hold that to the extent provisions of the documents creating the community prescribe the duties of the association to the owners and are consistent with public policy, those provisions control.[294]

---

areas, and that relationship involves same duty of care as that owed to invitee); Sacker v. Perry Realty Services, Inc., 217 Ga. App. 300, 301, 457 S.E.2d 208, 210 (1995) (owner of condominium unit was invitee of common area rather than mere licensee because there was clear mutuality of obligations and interests between unit owner and association); Maffeo v. Harbour Landing Condominium Ass'n, 1994 Conn. Super. LEXIS 2968 (Nov. 22, 1994) (occupancy of condominium unit reached by stairway that was part of common elements was a use connected with business purpose of association as possessor of that common area and, therefore, unit owner using common elements is invitee for purposes of premises liability); Admiral's Port Condominium Ass'n v. Feldman, 426 So. 2d 1054 (Fla. 3d DCA 1983); Pratt v. Maryland Farms Condominium Phase 1, Inc., 42 Md. App. 632, 637, 402 A.2d 105, 108 (1979), *cert. dis.*, 286 Md. 652, 408 A.2d 1042 (1980) (where child of unit owners climbed tree on common elements and was injured when he came in contact with uninsulated electrical wire parties concede, and court assumed, child was on property as invitee of association). *See also* Hayes v. Lakeside Vill. Owners Ass'n, 282 Ga. App. 866, 640 S.E.2d 373 (2006) (implying that residents of homeowners association were invitees without explicitly so stating); Bradford Square Condo. Ass'n v. Miller, 258 Ga. App. 240, 243, 573 S.E.2d 405, 408 (2002) (assuming, without explicitly stating, that unit owners are invitees); Smolek v. K.W. Landscaping, 203 Ill. Dec. 415, 266 Ill. App. 3d 226, 639 N.E.2d 974 (1994) (where homeowners association owned and maintained common area for use of its residents, it had duty to exercise reasonable care to keep premises over which it maintained control for common use of residents in reasonably safe condition).

292. Condominium Apartments Ass'n v. Trainor, 509 So. 2d 351 (Fla. 4th DCA 1987).

293. *See, e.g.*, Wieder v. King Cole Condo. Ass'n, 109 So. 3d 1196 (Fla. 3d DCA 2013) (where unit owner tripped over buckled carpet that she had seen and avoided several times, her familiarity with, and knowledge of, condition of carpet and decision to proceed to encounter that risk raise question whether she was comparatively negligent); Lotto v. Point East Two Condominium Corp. 702 So. 2d 1361 (Fla. 3d DCA 1997) (where unit owner admitted she had walked over severely cracked and somewhat uneven sidewalk more than 50 times previously and association acknowledged sidewalk had been in same condition for over three years, her decision to proceed to encounter risk raised question of whether she was comparatively negligent).

294. *See, e.g.*, Trailside Townhome Ass'n v. Acierno, 880 P.2d 119 (Colo. 1994) (definitions of terms describing entrants to land have no application to relationship between non-profit

It is common for individual homes in a common interest community to be leased to third parties. Generally, the duty owed by an association to those renters is the same as the duty it owes to its own members.[295] The relationship to the association of social guests of residents, however, is generally that of a licensee.[296]

Many common interest communities have clubhouses or other common facilities that are made available to individual owners for private events. In a Georgia case, for example, a homeowner rented the community clubhouse for a private event and a guest at the event was injured. The court said that even though the clubhouse was common property and the homeowner was an owner of all common property, the homeowner was a tenant of the association under the circumstances and a guest of the tenant/homeowner was an invitee of the association.[297]

[v] Criminal Acts by Third Parties and the Association's Duty

Generally, one who owns or occupies property may be liable to those who are victims of criminal acts by third parties while on the property.[298] Common interest community associations are no exception to that rule.[299] In general, courts hold associations liable when the criminal act is "foreseeable." Usually that means there have previously been similar acts.[300] If an association voluntarily assumes

---

corporation whose members were owners of lots in the townhome complex and those owners because owners had continuing right independent of association consent to make use of common areas by reason of their ownership of lots in community whereas trespassers, licensees, and invitees have no right to enter absent consent). *See also* Bradford Square Condo. Ass'n v. Miller, 258 Ga. App. 240, 246, 573 S.E.2d 405, 410 (2002) (duty of association to its members with regard to common elements of property may be circumscribed by terms of condominium instruments/contract, and court must look to terms of contract to determine its duties).

295. Hemispheres Condominium Ass'n v. Corbin, 357 So. 2d 1074 (Fla. 3d DCA 1975).

296. *See, e.g.*, Lloyd v. Pier W. Prop. Owners Ass'n, 470 S.W.3d 293 (Ark. App. 2015); Graveman v. Wind Drift Owners' Ass'n, 607 So. 2d 199 (Ala. 1992) (visitor of registered guest at condominium property was social guest and, therefore, licensee); Martinez v. Woodmar IV Condos. Homeowners Ass'n, 189 Ariz. 206, 941 P.2d 218 (1997). *But see* Colangelo v. Bay View Improvement Ass'n, 2013 Conn. Super. LEXIS 2496 (Conn. Super. Ct. Nov. 4, 2013) (guests of condominium unit owner were invitees of association when in common area); Fermin v. Woodland Hills Condo. # 1, Inc., 2007 Conn. Super. LEXIS 850 (Conn. Super. Ct. Mar. 29, 2007) (social guest of unit owner was an invitee of condominium association). *Compare* Bernstein v. Keystone Neighbourhood Co., 2015 U.S. Dist. LEXIS 127739 (D. Colo. Sept. 22, 2015) (where tenant who rented condominium unit from one association and slipped on snowy sidewalk owned by different association, there was at least genuine dispute of material fact as to whether tenant was invitee of association that owned sidewalk where accident occurred because two associations may have operated area in partnership).

297. Plantation at Lenox Unit Owners' Ass'n v. Lee, 196 Ga. App. 420, 395 S.E.2d 817, 819 (Ga. App. 1990). If the homeowner used the clubhouse with permission, but did not rent it, would the guest have been a licensee?

298. *See generally* Zinober, *Litigating the Negligent Security Case: Who's in Control Here?*, 44 Stetson L. Rev. 289 (2015); Mazun, *Condo Associations—New Cop on the Beat:* Martinez v. Woodmar IV Condominiums Homeowners Association, 73 St. John's L. Rev. 325 (1999).

299. *See, e.g.*, L.K. v. Water's Edge Ass'n, 532 So. 2d 1097 (Fla. 3d DCA 1988) (association was obligated to protect tenant from reasonably foreseeable criminal conduct).

300. *See, e.g.*, Menendez v. Palms West Condo. Ass'n, 736 So. 2d 58 (Fla. 1st DCA 1999) (while there was evidence that there had been a higher than average number of burglaries and assaults

a duty to provide security, however, the injured party generally does not have to show foreseeability.[301]

The liability of an association can extend to criminal activity that happens in a home that is not part of the property under its control. For example, in a particularly troubling case, a unit owner was burglarized, and she and her neighbors requested more exterior lighting. She installed her own exterior lighting after her second request went unanswered. The governing board decided the lighting had been installed without its permission in violation of the governing documents and directed the unit owner to remove the lighting.[302] The property manager told her she could not use the lights. Yielding to the pressure, the unit owner left the exterior lights off and was raped and robbed in her unit. The court found the unit

---

at condominium property and its vicinity, resident shot in unit failed to show association knew or should have known of similar attacks on other tenants or guests and general incidence of crime in area was not sufficient to put association on constructive notice of particular risk); Martinez v. Woodmar IV Condos. Homeowners Ass'n, 189 Ariz. 206, 941 P.2d 218 (1997) (duty to those using common areas with consent of association, its unit owners, and their tenants includes use of reasonable care to prevent harm from criminal intrusion and foreseeability of harm defines and limits scope of conduct necessary to fulfill that duty; where social guest of tenant was shot while on common area and there was evidence that association knew of incursion by gangs in parking lot and other common areas of its property, knew they engaged in drug dealing and other criminal activity, was warned by its own security guard of the need for 24-hour patrols, and had hired second guard for short period but terminated him because of expense considerations, there was sufficient evidence from which jury could find danger foreseeable and association negligent); Harper v. Tuscany Place Condominium Ass'n, 544 So. 2d 347 (Fla. 5th DCA 1989) (where resident was stabbed and sexually assaulted by assailant who apparently gained entrance to her bedroom through locked window facing parking lot and evidence showed prior incidents of *petit* theft, vandalism, burglary, and break-ins, court held foreseeability could not be established for violent crime with evidence of property crime); Moody v. Cawdrey Assocs., 6 Haw. App. 355, 721 P.2d 708 (1986) (if association or its managing agent has knowledge of criminal activities on its premises or in immediate neighborhood, association has duty to take reasonable measures, in view of existing circumstances, to protect owners from criminal acts of third parties); Olar v. Schroit 155 Cal. App. 3d 861, 202 Cal. Rptr. 457 (1984) (where resident was abducted from association parking lot and raped and alleged association had knowledge of vandalism and at least one burglary that had occurred on property and knew or should have known that project was located in high crime area, court held she stated cause of action for negligence sufficient to withstand demurrer); Admiral's Port Condominium Ass'n v. Feldman, 426 So. 2d 1054 (Fla. 3d DCA 1983) (evidence of similar crimes committed off premises and against persons other than landowner's invitees is not probative of foreseeability).

301. *See, e.g.*, Vazquez v. Lago Grande Homeowners Ass'n, 900 So. 2d 587 (Fla. 3d DCA 2004) (in gated community where employees of security company were not to admit visitors without permission of the unit owner, no evidence of prior crimes was required because of the voluntarily assumed duty; condominium association would properly be held liable where former husband of guest of unit owner shot and killed his ex-wife and injured unit owner).

302. *Compare* Hawkins v. Jamaicaway Place Condo. Trust, 409 Mass. 1005, 568 N.E.2d 1126 (1991) (where unit owner was attacked inside her unit, association was not negligent for having failed to install bars on windows of unit; unit owner made no effort to get association to install bars and could have installed them herself).

owner stated a cause of action for breach of the duty to take reasonable precautions to protect her from the foreseeable risk of crime.[303]

An association may be able to waive any duty to provide security in its governing documents. For example, in a Georgia case the husband of a couple living in a condominium was shot to death in the condominium parking lot. His wife brought a wrongful death action against the association contending it should have provided security gates, enhanced lighting, and security patrols. The Declaration of Condominium, however, provided that the association was not a provider of security and had no duty to provide any security on the property, and the obligation to provide security was solely that of each unit owner individually. Therefore, the association had no duty that it could have breached.[304]

[vi] Injury Occurring in an Area Reserved for a Resident

Generally, where an injury occurs on property owned and occupied by a resident, the association owes no duty, and has no liability, to the injured party.[305]

---

303. Francis T. v. Village Green Owners Ass'n, 42 Cal. 3d 490, 229 Cal. Rptr. 456, 723 P.2d 573 (1986). *See also* Camelot Club Condominium Ass'n v. Bonner, 207 Ga. App. 634, 428 S.E.2d 625 (1993) (where, in violation of policy, front gate attendant admitted unit owner's boyfriend to property without first obtaining her permission and boyfriend broke down front door to unit and raped unit owner, court decided association and its front gate attendant were insulated from liability because intervening criminal acts of boyfriend could not have been reasonably foreseen); Czerwinski v. Sunrise Point Condominium, 540 So. 2d 199 (Fla. 3d DCA 1989) (resident was sexually assaulted in her unit by intruder who gained access to premises by using ladder from unlocked storage room; where association had actual knowledge of nine other burglaries and rape and armed robbery committed in parking lot, fact that burglaries were different from crimes to persons, and that prior violent crimes occurred in common areas, not individual units, did not show lack of foreseeability and it was error for trial court to hold attack on unit owner was not foreseeable as matter of law). *Compare* Menendez v. Palms West Condo. Ass'n, 736 So. 2d 58, 62 (Fla. 1st DCA 1999) (association could not be liable on theory it failed to maintain safe conditions in common areas as criminal attack on resident did not occur in any common area, but in unit).

304. Bradford Square Condo. Ass'n v. Miller, 258 Ga. App. 240, 573 S.E.2d 405 (2002).

305. McMahon v. Pleasant Valley W. Ass'n, 952 A.2d 731 (Pa. Commw. 2008), *app. den.*, 599 Pa. 702, 961 A.2d 860 (2008) (in homeowners association where dogs of one homeowner went directly from property of that homeowner to that of adjacent homeowner and bit him while on his property and there was no allegation that association retained right to control lot on which dogs were kept, association did not have any duty nor did it assume duty to compel dog owner to maintain, control, and confine dogs on property of dog owner, or to prevent harm flowing from failure to control and confine dogs on property of their owner). *See also* Sandstrom v. De Silva, 206 Ill. Dec. 340, 268 Ill. App. 3d 932, 645 N.E.2d 345 (1994) (association was not owner of condominium unit and was not, generally, responsible for duties for which individual owners were obligated, including installation of smoke detector pursuant to state statute, within confines of respective units; court properly granted summary judgment to association in wrongful death action based on failure to maintain smoke detector in individual condominium unit); Gazdo Properties Corp. v. Lava, 149 Misc. 2d 828, 565 N.Y.S.2d 964, *app. dis.*, 150 Misc. 2d 1019, 579 N.Y.S.2d 305 (1991) (under state Multiple Dwelling Law and municipal Housing Maintenance Code, condominium governing board is not, by definition, an "owner" of each individual unit responsible for maintenance, repair, and correction of code violations within units; rather, owners of individual condominium units bear that responsibility); William B. May Co. v. Department of Health, 123

That conclusion can be based on ownership and/or possession, but also on the division of responsibilities set forth in the governing documents. However, there are circumstances in which a common interest community association could be liable for an injury happening within an individual unit. For example, the tenant in a condominium unit was scalded by her bathwater. The hot water for all units flowed through two boilers serving all the units. The hot water system was part of the central services for all units to which the unit owners lacked access or control and which constituted part of the common elements under the custody of the association. It, thus, was potentially liable for the tenant's injuries.[306]

The corporation that owns a housing cooperative building may have liability for injuries that happen inside an apartment if it has maintenance obligations for the apartment under the proprietary lease.[307] In New York, where the largest number of housing cooperatives are found, under the labor law an "owner" who may be liable to an injured worker includes owners in fee and those with an interest in the property and who fulfilled the role of owner by contracting to have work performed for their benefit. Thus, both a cooperative corporation—as fee owner of the building—and a tenant/shareholder in whose apartment an injury occurs—as one having an interest in the property and fulfilling the role of owner by contracting to have work performed—have potential liability.[308]

In homeowners associations and condominiums, there are often common areas that are reserved for the use of one resident or a small number of them. These are called limited common areas or elements. In a homeowners association they would be owned by the association, and in a condominium they are owned by all the unit owners as tenants in common. In a multi-story building, balconies are typically limited common areas reserved for the exclusive use of the resident

Misc. 2d 1010, 475 N.Y.S.2d 224 (1984) (neither management company nor condominium association was responsible to bring individual units in compliance with municipal code requiring owner, lessee, agent, or other person who manages or controls multiple dwelling to install window guards). *And see Is Your Condominium Unit Properly Insured?* (Association Times 2010) (association liability insurance generally provides coverage for injuries sustained in common areas and typically does not provide coverage for injury occurs in unit).

306. Davis v. Riverside Court Condo. Ass'n Phase II, Inc., 154 So. 3d 643 (La. App. 2014).

307. *See* 2 Rohan & Reskin, *Real Estate Transactions: Cooperative Housing Law and Practice—Forms*, § 8.02[1] (Matthew Bender, 2016) (where tort liability is asserted on basis of event within confines of individual apartment, existing lease and landlord-tenant principles have to be consulted to determine whether responsibility falls on individual tenant/shareholder, cooperative corporation, or both). *See also* Guryev v. Tomchinsky, 20 N.Y.3d 194, 957 N.Y.S.2d 677, 981 N.E.2d 273 (2012) (cooperative corporation as owner of building, including apartments where individual tenant/shareholders reside, may be "owner" with potential liability when contractor's employee is injured while performing construction work in individual apartment).

308. Paljevic v. 998 Fifth Avenue Corp., 2008 N.Y. Misc. LEXIS 8156 (2008), *aff'd in part, modified in part*, 65 A.D.3d 896, 885 N.Y.S.2d 65 (2009) (where plaintiff painter fell from ladder in kitchen of individual apartment and was injured, cooperative corporation was liable to plaintiff, but tenant/shareholder was entitled to protections of exemption for owner of one-family dwelling who did not direct work because tenant/shareholder did not hire plaintiff's employer and did not supervise, direct, or control way plaintiff did his work).

of the unit to which the balcony is attached. In a townhouse community, a patio or small yard might be a common area limited to the use of a single residence. These areas would be occupied, but not owned, by the resident to whose use they are reserved. In other words, the use may be limited, but the ownership remains in common.[309] Does the association then have any liability for an injury that occurs in a limited common area? What is the importance of the maintenance responsibilities assigned to the association?[310] It would seem that the resident to whom the limited common area is reserved would be the one occupying it for purposes of determining duty. The governing documents might require the resident to keep the area clean and free from debris but assign the responsibility for repairs to the association. Does that mean the unit owner could be liable to someone who slips on wet leaves on his or her balcony, but the association would be liable if someone were injured when he or she tripped over a broken tile? What is the result if the association has no duty to inspect the area and, indeed, has limited access to it? Does the resident breach a duty by failing to inform the association of the broken tile on "his" or "her" balcony? One commentary argues the resident should be held liable only when he or she retained some level of control over the common element, preserved some responsibility for its maintenance, and *unreasonably* relied on the association to fully provide for its maintenance.[311] While

---

309. *See* Boggs, *Understanding Legal Liability for Condominium Association and Unit Owners* (2011), available at: http://www.mynewmarkets.com/articles/180950/understanding-legal-liability-for-condominium-association-and-unit-owners (rules that apply to common elements apply to limited common elements, meaning association will most commonly be held financially responsible, although there are gray areas).

310. *Consider* Denton v. Hahn, 2004 Tenn. App. LEXIS 605 (Tenn. Ct. App. Sept. 16, 2004) (characterizing metal threshold over which resident tripped as general common element or limited common element would have little relevance as unit owner's responsibility under master deed to maintain premises in safe condition extended only to his or her unit and threshold was not part of unit because it extended beyond plane of unit's interior walls and must, therefore, necessarily be part of the common elements for which association had obligation to see that it was maintained in good repair and in safe condition).

311. Stanco, *The Proper Extent of Liability a Condominium Unit Owner Should Have For Injuries Caused By a Limited Common Element*, 19 St. John's J.L. Comm. 637, 639 (2005) (contending that where limited number of unit owners share in use of limited common element, they should only be held liable for any injury that it causes when it can be shown that they retained some level of control over that element, preserved some responsibility for its maintenance, and unreasonably relied on condominium governing board to fully provide for its maintenance). *See, e.g.*, Scrocca v. Ashwood Condominium Ass'n, 326 Ga. App. 226, 756 S.E.2d 308 (2014), where the resident of a condominium slipped on snow and ice on walkway in front of her home. The walkway was a limited common element. Under the Declaration, the unit owners had a duty to keep their walkways in a "neat, clean and sanitary condition," including removal of "extraneous foreign matter." The association, on the other hand, had the duty to maintain, keep in good repair, replace, and improve or alter those walkways. The court said snow and ice are extraneous foreign matter the removal of which was the obligation of unit owners. The association's responsibility was to keep walkways structurally sound; therefore, it had no duty to remove the snow and ice and no liability. It would appear by extension that any duty to non-residents to remove the snow and ice would have belonged to the unit owner, not the association.

that may be an appropriate analysis, it does not address all the potentialities, and neither do the cases. As one insurance expert acknowledges, assigning financial responsibility for an injury or accident that occurs on a limited common element is a little more complicated than when it occurs on general common elements or inside a unit.[312]

In one of the few cases to address this topic, the plaintiffs, a father and son, walked by a multi-story condominium building in Manhattan. A section of chain-link fence fell from the roof of the building and seriously injured them. The roof was designated a limited common element restricted to the use of the owners of two units,[313] but there was not apparently direct and exclusive access from the interior of those units and, instead, all unit owners had access to the roof, which could only be reached by way of a common interior stairway. The injured plaintiffs sued the association and all the unit owners individually. Apparently because all the unit owners had access to the roof, the court decided they were all "in the same legal position." It went on to find no basis to hold any of the unit owners personally liable, including the two for whom the roof was a limited common element. One commentary notes that the question remains whether liability might have been imposed if access to the roof had been limited to certain unit owners.[314] That is true, but another question also remains: why did the court not address the possible distinction between the unit owners for whom the roof was a limited common element and those for whom it was not?[315]

In a Louisiana case, the plaintiff was moving into a condominium unit before signing a lease-purchase agreement and slipped on a step leading from the unit down to the patio adjoining it. The step was a limited common element. The plaintiff sued the association, which denied that it owned the premises or had any control over it, and filed a third-party petition against the unit owner. The trial court found for the association because it did not have custody over the area where the accident occurred. The appellate court reversed. It said the question of control over the limited common elements was unclear, but it concluded that limited common elements were by definition part of the common elements and, therefore, any liability arising from them should be an insured risk under the association's policy. Apparently, it reached that conclusion because the unit

312. Boggs, *Understanding Legal Liability for Condominium Association and Unit Owners* (2011), available at: http://www.mynewmarkets.com/articles/180950/understanding-legal-liability-for-condominium-association-and-unit-owners.

313. The court said that each of those two unit owners was allotted a 50 percent ownership interest in the limited common element. If that actually were the case, the roof would not be a common element at all because by definition, a common element in a condominium is owned by *all the unit owners* as tenants in common. The designation of a common element as "limited" simply restricts its use but does not change its ownership.

314. Stanco, *The Proper Extent of Liability a Condominium Unit Owner Should Have for Injuries Caused by a Limited Common Element*, 19 St. John's J.L. Comm. 637, 639, 732 (2005).

315. Pekelnaya v. Allyn, 25 A.D.3d 111, 808 N.Y.S.2d 590 (2005).

owner, if liable, would be covered by the association policy for liability arising out of "ownership of an individual interest in the common elements or membership in the association." The court conceded that the association might not be liable for the limited use area but decided that made no difference to the plaintiff because the association was required by statute to maintain a policy insuring the defendant unit owner either as a unit owner or as a member of the association.[316] The case illustrates the confusion that arises with limited common areas. In this case the documents assigned responsibility for maintenance, upkeep, and repair of a limited use area to the individual unit owner to whom the area was reserved. Many would argue that clearly took the step out of the control of the association, and yet the court refused to concede that point.

In light of the confusion that can surround questions of control over common areas reserved for the use of one resident, or a small number of them, associations may want to ask their counsel to review and possibly clarify the governing documents.

[b] Infliction of Emotional Distress

The law surrounding infliction of emotional distress is complicated and fraught with nuisance. Basically, there are two causes of action based on infliction of emotional distress: intentional infliction, sometimes called "outrage," and negligent infliction. The Third Restatement of Torts describes "emotional harm" as impairment or injury to one's emotional tranquility.[317] It then provides that one who by extreme and outrageous conduct *intentionally or recklessly* causes severe emotional harm to another is subject to liability for that harm and, if it causes bodily harm, for that as well.[318] Next, it imparts the requirements for a negligence-based action. One whose *negligent conduct* causes serious emotional harm to another is subject to liability to that person if the conduct either places the other person in danger of immediate bodily harm and the emotional harm "results from that danger or the emotional harm occurs in the course of specified categories of activities, undertakings, or relationships in which negligent conduct is especially likely to cause serious emotional harm."[319] The specific parameters of the causes of action will vary from jurisdiction to jurisdiction. The insurance question is whether infliction of emotional harm is a "bodily" injury for purposes of a commercial general liability policy.

316. Blackwell v. Hanover Ins. Co., 551 So. 2d 47 (La. App. 1989).

317. Restatement of the Law (Third), Torts: Liability for Physical and Emotional Harm, § 45.

318. Restatement of the Law (Third), Torts: Liability for Physical and Emotional Harm, § 46.

319. Restatement of the Law (Third), Torts: Liability for Physical and Emotional Harm, § 47. *Consider* Peklun v. Tierra Del Mar Condo. Ass'n, 119 F. Supp. 3d 1361, 1366 (S.D. Fla. 2015) (Florida courts impose no *per se* special relationship between condominium association, along with its members, and respective owners).

Generally, courts hold that bodily injury includes claims for physical injury and excludes those for purely non-physical or emotional harm.[320] Most courts will find coverage for a claim for emotional distress accompanied by allegations of a specific physical injury, for example, ulcers or exacerbated hypertension.[321] A minority of courts, led by the New York Court of Appeals,[322] say that emotional distress is included in the definition of bodily injury.[323] Some carriers will add an endorsement to the policy that includes "mental anguish or emotional distress" caused by bodily injury, sickness, or disease to the definition of bodily injury.[324]

[4] Exclusions

The standard commercial general liability policy contains 17 exclusions to the bodily injury or property damage coverage, 11 of which apply to bodily injury.[325] The exclusions to bodily injury coverage that are most likely to apply to actions against common interest communities for bodily injury are discussed below.

One expert commentator says that in general, exclusions should be read with the insuring agreement, independently of every other exclusion; exceptions to exclusions do not create coverage; and if any one exclusion applies, there should be no coverage despite inferences that could be raised based on exceptions or qualifications contained in other exclusions.[326]

---

320. Farrell-Kolb, *General Liability Coverage for Claims of Emotional Distress—An Insurance Nightmare*, 45 Drake L. Rev. 981, 986 (1997). *See, e.g.*, Citizens Ins. Co. of Am. v. Leiendecker, 962 S.W.2d 446 (Mo. App. 1998) (common meaning of phrase "bodily harm, sickness or disease" is not ambiguous and refers to physical conditions of body and excludes mental suffering or emotional distress); Chatton v. National Union Fire Ins. Co., 10 Cal. App. 4th 846, 13 Cal. Rptr. 2d 318 (1992) (coverage under bodily injury clause of CGL policy is limited to physical injury to body and does not include non-physical, emotional, or mental harm); Allstate Ins. Co. v. Diamant, 401 Mass. 654, 518 N.E.2d 1154 (1988) ("bodily injury" is narrow term and encompasses only physical injuries to body, not emotional distress).

321. Monteleone, *Coverage Issues Under Commercial General Liability and Directors' and Officers' Liability Policies*, 18 W. New Eng. L. Rev. 47, 49 (1996). *See, e.g.*, Allstate v. Wagner-Ellsworth, 344 Mont. 445, 188 P.3d 1042 (2008) (phrase "bodily injury" in insurance policy includes mental or psychological injury accompanied by physical manifestations).

322. Lavanant v. General Acci. Ins. Co., 584 N.Y.S.2d 744, 745, 79 N.Y.2d 623, 626, 595 N.E.2d 819, 820 (1992) (coverage for "bodily injury" includes emotional distress resulting from negligent conduct of insured, where no physical injury or contact is involved; mental injury alone is covered). *See also* Sova v. Cove Homeowner's Ass'n, 102 So. 3d 863 (La. App. 2012) (claims for mental anguish have been held to be claims for bodily injury).

323. *See generally* Farrell-Kolb, *General Liability Coverage for Claims of Emotional Distress—An Insurance Nightmare*, 45 Drake L. Rev. 981, 989–93 (1997).

324. *See, e.g.*, Essex Insurance Company Form MEIL 1216 07 10.

325. *See, e.g.*, ISO Form CG 00 01 12 07, § I.A.2.

326. Johnson, *The Practical Art: On the Archaeology and Architecture of Liability Insurance Contracts*, 78 Def. Couns. J. 143, 164 (2011).

[a] Expected or Intended Injury

The first exclusion is for "expected or intended injury," and it bars coverage for bodily injury that is expected or intended from the standpoint of the insured[327] but does not apply to bodily injury that results from use of reasonable force to protect persons or property.[328] The application of this exclusion has been the subject of extensive and complex litigation. Discussion of those cases is beyond the scope of this discussion. Happily, the exclusion has been examined in depth by leading insurance law treatises[329] and by scholarly articles.[330]

[b] Contractual Liability

The "contractual liability" exclusion allows carriers to enforce the fortuity concept of insurance by excluding from coverage any agreements made by an insured to become liable after the insurance is in force and the liability is a certainty.[331] It proscribes coverage for bodily injury for which the insured is obligated to pay damages because of an assumption of liability in a contract or agreement.[332] The exclusion does not bar coverage for all contract liability[333] but only liability assumed in a hold harmless or indemnification agreement.[334] The exclusion

327. The exclusion can also apply when the underlying complaint alleges property damage. *See, e.g.*, Cambridge Mut. Fire Ins. Co. v. 1347-49 N. Sedgwick Condo. Ass'n, 2013 U.S. Dist. LEXIS 9750 (N.D. Ill. Jan. 23, 2013) (where unit owner sued condominium association alleging its governing board breached fiduciary duty by failing and refusing to address defects in building and hire plumber and by failing and refusing to forward to unit owner funds from association property insurer that were intended to reimburse unit owner for damages to its unit, claims were based on intentional conduct and coverage was excluded).

328. *See, e.g.*, ISO Form CG 00 01 12 07, § I.A.2.a.

329. *See* 3 Jeffrey E. Thomas, *New Appleman on Insurance Law Library Edition* § 18.03[2] (Matthew Bender, 2017).

330. *See, e.g.*, French, *Debunking the Myth That Insurance Coverage Is Not Available or Allowed for Intentional Torts or Damages*, 8 Hastings Bus. L.J. 65 (2012); Ingram, *The Expected or Intended Exclusion in Liability Insurance: What About Self-Defense?*, 42 Creighton L. Rev. 123 (2009); Ingram, *The "Expected or Intended" Exclusion Clause in Liability Insurance Policies: What Should It Exclude?*, 13 Whittier L. Rev. 713 (1992).

331. Am. Family Mut. Ins. Co. v. Am. Girl, Inc., 268 Wis. 2d 16, 673 N.W.2d 65 (2004).

332. *See, e.g.*, ISO Form CG 00 01 12 07, § I.A.2.b.

333. Some courts appear to believe otherwise. For example, a federal court applied the exclusion to a common interest community property management contract without mentioning whether that contract contained indemnification or hold harmless language. State Farm Fire & Cas. Co. v. Metro. Mgmt., 2007 U.S. Dist. LEXIS 99406 (D. Haw. Oct. 31, 2007) (where association sued its property manager and property manager claimed status as insured under association policy, court found that exclusion for coverage for liability for which insured is obligated to pay damages by reason of assumption of liability in contract or agreement applied because all claims by association arose, if at all, from manager's performance or non-performance of its obligations under its management contract with association).

334. *See* Am. Family Mut. Ins. Co. v. Am. Girl, Inc., 268 Wis. 2d 16, 48, 673 N.W.2d 65, 81 (2004) (contractually assumed liability exclusion applies where insured has contractually assumed liability of third party—as in indemnification or hold harmless agreements—and does not exclude

does not apply to liability for damages the insured would have had even without the contract or agreement assuming liability. It also does not apply to liability for damages the insured assumed in a contract or agreement that is an "insured contract," when the bodily injury happens after execution of that contract or agreement.[335] "Insured contract" is defined to include a contract for a lease of premises, an easement or license agreement, an obligation required by ordinance to indemnify a municipality, an elevator maintenance agreement, and the part of a contract or agreement pertaining to the business of the named insured pursuant to which the named insured assumes the tort liability of another to pay for bodily injury to a third person or organization.[336] Some policies may narrow the definition by eliminating agreements pertaining to the business of the named insured from the definition.[337]

The purpose of the "insured contract" exception to the exclusion is to provide coverage when a party with which the insured has contracted invokes an indemnification clause in that agreement. Common interest community associations may enter a number of contracts that may contain an indemnification clause and qualify for the exception. For example, the association may be a party to a ground or recreation lease. An association with a multi-story building likely has an elevator maintenance agreement. Associations also probably have several agreements that "pertain to its business," for example, a management contract

coverage for any and all liabilities to which insured is exposed under terms of contracts it makes generally); Olympic, Inc. v. Providence Wash. Ins. Co., 648 P.2d 1008, 1011 (Alaska 1982) (liability assumed by insured under contract refers to liability incurred when one promises to indemnify or hold harmless another, and does not refer to liability that results from breach of contract). *See generally* 3 Jeffrey E. Thomas, *New Appleman on Insurance Law Library Edition* § 18.03[3][a] (Matthew Bender, 2017).

335. For the purposes of liability assumed in an insured contract, reasonable attorney's fees and necessary litigation expenses are considered damages.

336. *See, e.g.*, ISO Form CG 00 01 12 07, § V.9. Tort liability means liability that would be imposed by law absent any contract or agreement. *See* Tremco, Inc. v. Mfrs. Ass'n Ins. Co., 832 A.2d 1120 (Pa. Super. 2003) (where manufacturer sold roofing products to contractor and contractor agreed in sales contract to indemnify and hold manufacturer, its officers, and employees harmless from any and all losses, costs, expenses, claims, demands, and suits for any bodily injury, court found language of contract bound contractor to assume liability for tort claims against manufacturer arising out of its negligence, and was, therefore, *apparently* an "insured contract").

337. *See, e.g.*, Western Heritage Ins. Co. v. Jacobs Dev. Corp., 2013 U.S. Dist. LEXIS 184369 (E.D.N.Y. Dec. 16, 2013), where a passerby tripped and fell on a sidewalk in front of multi-story residential building and sued the building owner, which filed a third-party complaint against the company that had provided concrete installation at the site. The building owner contended it was entitled to full contractual indemnity from that company based on a Subcontract Agreement Rider between the parties in which the company was required to defend, indemnify, and hold harmless the building owner, at its own expense, against all liability or claimed liability for bodily injury. The insurer for the company invoked the contractual liability exclusion, which omitted from the definition of "insured contract" an agreement pertaining to the business of the named insured. The court found that the Subcontract Agreement Rider did not meet the definition of an insured contract and, thus, did not fall within the exception to the exclusion. Therefore, the exclusion for contractual liability applied to the underlying claims against the insured company for contractual liability.

with a community association manager and agreements for building maintenance and lawn care. Anytime an association is considering entering a contract with an indemnification clause, it should consult the association counsel. When it has contracts with these clauses, it should discuss with its broker whether the agreements qualify as "insured contracts." It may be that the status of specific agreements can be addressed by endorsement.

[c] Liquor Liability

The liquor liability exclusion in the standard commercial general liability policy bars coverage for bodily injury for which "any insured"[338] may be held liable for causing or contributing to the intoxication of anyone;[339] for furnishing alcoholic beverages to a person under the legal drinking age or under the influence of alcohol; or for violation of any statute, ordinance, or regulation related to sale, gift, distribution, or use of alcohol.[340] The exclusion applies only if the named insured is in the *business* of manufacturing, distributing, selling, serving, or furnishing alcohol. The purpose of the exception is to provide "host liquor liability coverage"—previously provided by an endorsement added to the CGL policy—which covers a person or organization for functions or events incidental to the business of the named insured.[341] Common interest community associations might assume that the exception to the exclusion assures them coverage, but should not.

The damages in suits for negligently providing alcohol can be enormous. CICs need to determine the extent of their potential liability and whether they have coverage for that liability. The first step is to identify all the circumstances in which alcohol may be consumed on common property. Does the community have social events at which alcohol is served? Is it provided by the association,[342] or

338. If a common interest community rents space to an entity that sells liquor, is it covered by the tenant's liability policy? *See* Stanovich, *Legal Separation—The Severability Test in the CGL* (IRMI 2011) (asserting that landlord that rents property to liquor establishment and is additional insured on tenant's CGL policy would not have coverage as conduct by one insured bars coverage for all other insureds under same policy on claims arising from same occurrence and that rule applies even when insureds seeking coverage did not themselves participate in act for which coverage is excluded, even when their liability is premised on their own independent acts or omissions that would otherwise be covered).

339. Note that if the insured serves a single drink to a person who later becomes intoxicated, the insured could be said to have contributed to the intoxication. The insured is unlikely to be held liable for injuries caused by that person, but if it is sued, the insurer may not provide a defense. *See* Stanovich, *Raising the Bar—The Liquor Liability Exclusion in the CGL* (IRMI 2008), available at: https://www.irmi.com/articles/expert-commentary/liquor-liability-exclusion-in-the-cgl.

340. *See, e.g.*, ISO Form CG 00 01 12 07, § I.A.2.c.

341. *See* Stanovich, *Raising the Bar—The Liquor Liability Exclusion in the CGL* (IRMI 2008), available at: https://www.irmi.com/articles/expert-commentary/liquor-liability-exclusion-in-the-cgl.

342. If the association charges a fee to attend an event, some states may require that it obtain a liquor license. If these events are a regular occurrence, might the fact that the association profits from them and has a liquor license mean that it is in the business of selling, serving, or furnishing alcohol? What if it pays for the alcohol out of the assessments the residents pay to it? Is the

do residents bring their own drinks?[343] Is there a BYOB clubhouse or one with a full bar? Is there a common area that the association makes available to residents for parties?[344] Does the association own property—or in a condominium, do the unit owners own property as tenants in common—that is leased to a third party to operate a facility that serves alcohol?[345] The association should review with its attorney all the circumstances in which alcohol is provided. The law on liability for providing alcohol varies widely from state to state, and the association should know specifically what that potential liability is in their state. In a handful of states, liability is extended to "social hosts," but in most it is not,[346] although in some states liability arises for a social host when alcohol is served to an underage person.[347] After being briefed by counsel on its potential liability, the association should also confer with its broker who, with knowledge of the coverage, can advise how the coverage works or whether an endorsement would be required.

Once the association understands the potential extent of its liability, it needs to discuss with its broker whether it has coverage for that liability.[348] It should not assume that the liquor liability exclusion is inapplicable because it perceives that it is not in the *business* of selling, serving, or furnishing alcohol. A few courts

---

association indirectly selling alcohol? These are questions the association would need to direct to its attorney.

343. If the association holds a party but residents bring their own drinks or the party is catered, the association's potential liability may be reduced but not eliminated. Any caterer could be required to indemnify the association and provide the association with proof of insurance. The association needs to consult its counsel to learn the extent of its liability and the requirements for contracting with a caterer. *See generally* Wilson, *Do BYOB Establishments Need Liquor Liability Coverage?* (Insurance Agent, Feb. 2014).

344. Consider whether, if an association has a function room that it regularly leases to residents for parties and generates income from that practice, it might be considered to be "in the business" of serving alcohol? If that should pose a concern, the association could include an indemnification clause in the lease or require the lessee to obtain event insurance. Before taking either approach, it should consult the association attorney. The association could also ban alcohol from the facility or the common elements entirely. *See, e.g.*, Hidden Harbor Estates, Inc. v. Norman, 309 So. 2d 180, 182 (Fla. 4th DCA 1975) (holding there was nothing unreasonable about prohibiting use of alcohol in commonly owned areas).

345. A commentary notes that statutes may impose liquor liability on landlords for the actions of their tenants and that the landlord's CGL policy would provide it with coverage. Stanovich, *Raising the Bar—The Liquor Liability Exclusion in the CGL* (IRMI 2008), available at: https://www.irmi.com/articles/expert-commentary/liquor-liability-exclusion-in-the-cgl.

346. *See generally* Coppock, *Social Host Immunity: A New Paradigm to Foster Responsibility*, 38 Cap. U.L. Rev. 19 (2009) (reviewing common and statutory law of commercial and social host liquor liability).

347. For example, in South Carolina, there is no social host liability for serving alcohol to an adult. Garren v. Cummings & McCrady, Inc., 289 S.C. 348, 345 S.E.2d 508 (Ct. App. 1986). There is, however, social host liability for serving alcohol to an underage person. Marcum v. Bowden, 372 S.C. 452, 643 S.E.2d 85 (S.C. 2007).

348. *See, e.g.*, Rohan, Reskin & Sanchirico, *Recent Developments in the Field of Insurance for Condominium Projects*, 48 St. John's L. Rev. 1084, 1093 (1974) (consultation with insurance advisor might reveal need for coverage if common elements contain restaurant or other facility in which alcoholic beverages are sold).

have held that a non-profit entity that sells or serves alcohol is not in the business of doing so.[349] Most courts, however, find that a non-profit organization that regularly sells alcohol is "in the business" despite not being a profit-making venture,[350] and the fact that sale of alcohol generates little if any consistent revenues in excess of expenses does not necessarily matter to these courts.[351] For example, a private country club sought coverage and argued it was not in the business of selling, serving, or furnishing alcoholic beverages because it was a non-profit organization whose primary focus was the operation of a golf course and serving alcoholic was a service to its members that did not generate substantial revenue. The court responded that if the selling, serving, or furnishing of alcohol is a permanent, ongoing operation, the insured is in the business whereas when that conduct is infrequent or occasional, the insured is not in the business. It is irrelevant, said the court, whether the insured is a non-profit organization, the income from the sale of alcohol constitutes a major portion of the revenue, or the primary purpose of the organization is something other than the sale of alcohol.[352] On the other hand, a non-profit organization that holds an occasional event at which alcohol is sold and a small profit generated will likely be found not to be in the business of selling alcohol.[353] If an association concluded it might

349. *See, e.g.*, Newell-Blais Post #443, Veterans of Foreign Wars, Inc. v. Shelby Mut. Ins. Co., 396 Mass. 633, 636, 487 N.E.2d 1371, 1373 (1986) (non-profit organization incorporated for charitable purposes was not engaged in "business" of selling or serving alcoholic beverages within clear meaning of exclusion); Laconia Rod & Gun Club v. Hartford Acc. & Indem. Co., 123 N.H. 179, 459 A.2d 249 (N.H. 1984) (where private gun club argued liquor liability exclusion did not apply to it because it is not "in the business of" selling or serving alcoholic beverages as it did not make profit on beverages, as would a tavern, court held phrase "in the business of" was ambiguous; it had to interpret it in favor of club and hold that club was not "in the business of" selling or serving alcohol).

350. *See, e.g.*, Mustard v. Owners Ins. Co., 6 N.E.3d 1235, 1237 (Ohio App. 2014) (to determine whether liquor liability exclusion applies, focus should be on activity of insured, rather than its corporate status; phrase "in the business of" unambiguously includes activity of regularly selling liquor to generate significant revenues and, thus, because American Legion Post derived significant profits from systematic sale of alcoholic beverages to its members and their guests, it was in the business of selling or serving alcoholic beverages, regardless of how it used or reported that revenue and exclusion applied); McGriff v. United States Fire Ins. Co., 436 N.W.2d 859, 860 (S.D. 1989) (liquor lability exclusion applies to non-profit corporations, and term "engaged in the business" is not ambiguous; therefore, fraternal, non-profit organization that operates on-sale liquor establishment is not provided coverage by its general liability insurance policy).

351. *See* Sprangers v. Greatway Ins. Co., 182 Wis. 2d 521, 527–29, 514 N.W.2d 1, 2–4 (1994) (even though revenues from bar exceeded expenses in some years but not in others, VFW was in business of selling and serving alcoholic beverages as that phrase is used in policy and, therefore, it was excluded from coverage for liability arising from sale of alcoholic beverages to underaged person).

352. United States Fidelity & Guar. Co. v. Country Club, 119 N.C. App. 365, 371–72, 458 S.E.2d 734, 738–39 (1995).

353. *See, e.g.*, Mutual Serv. Cas. Ins. Co. v. Wilson Twp., 603 N.W.2d 151 (1999) (where township and its volunteer fire department sponsored annual fundraising event at which beer sales generated less than 2 percent of township's revenues, it was not in business of selling, serving, or furnishing alcoholic beverages and exclusion did not apply because township was non-profit

have liquor liability for which coverage is excluded, it can add coverage by an endorsement.[354]

[d] Workers' Compensation and Employer Liability

Coverage is excluded for any obligation an insured has under a workers' compensation law, disability benefits or unemployment compensation law, or any similar law.[355] The consensus of courts is that the exclusion is not limited to when workers' compensation or other benefits have actually been paid, but precludes coverage for liability derived from an obligation that *should have* been handled by a workers' compensation or similar claim.[356]

Another exclusion bars coverage for bodily injury to an employee of the insured that arises out of and in the course of employment by the insured or performing duties related to conduct of the business of the insured.[357] The exclusion also proscribes coverage for bodily injury to the spouse, child, parent, brother, or sister of that employee as a consequence of a bodily injury to an employee that arises out of and in the course of employment by the insured or performing duties related to conduct of the business of the insured. The exclusion applies whether the insured might be liable as an employer, or in any other capacity, and it applies to any obligation to share damages with or repay another who is required to pay damages because of the injury. It does not apply to liability the insured assumes under an "insured contract."

The term "employee" includes a "leased worker,"[358] meaning one leased to the named insured by a labor leasing firm under an agreement between those two parties to perform duties related to the conduct of the business of the named

---

organization that did not sell alcoholic beverages as part of permanent and ongoing commercial venture); County of Schenectady v. Travelers Ins. Co., 48 A.D.2d 299, 368 N.Y.S.2d 894 (1975) (where party was held on premises of community college sponsored by its Student Government Association, that association was not a business as it was not a profit-seeking organization and did not stand to realize any pecuniary gain from party and temporary nature of permit for sale of beer itself, with duration of only seven hours, satisfactorily dispelled any notion that business was being conducted). *See also* Sprangers v. Greatway Ins. Co., 182 Wis. 2d 521, 544, 514 N.W.2d 1, 9 (Wis. 1994) (stating in *dicta* that club serving alcoholic beverages only at its annual holiday party would not likely be excluded from coverage).

354. *See, e.g.*, ISO Form ISO Form CG 21 50 04 13.

355. *See, e.g.*, ISO Form CG 00 01 12 07, § I.A.2.d.

356. *See* Johnson v. Marciniak, 231 F. Supp. 2d 958, 960 (D.N.D. 2002). *See also* Brown v. Ind. Ins. Co., 184 S.W.3d 528, 534–35 (Ky. 2005) (every jurisdiction that has considered application of exclusion has held it precludes coverage when insured employer is exposed to tort liability solely because of its failure to procure policy of workers' compensation insurance).

357. *See, e.g.*, ISO Form CG 00 01 12 07, § I.A.2.e. *See* Kmart Corp. v. Securitas Sec. Servs. USA, 2012 U.S. Dist. LEXIS 191234 (N.D. Ga. Mar. 13, 2012) (employer's liability exclusion only bars coverage where injured party is employee of particular insured who is seeking protection under policy).

358. *See, e.g.*, ISO Form CG 00 01 12 07, § V.5.

insured.[359] Neither the term "employee" nor "leased worker" includes a "temporary worker," which is someone furnished to the named insured to substitute for a permanent employee on leave or to meet seasonal or short-term workload conditions.[360] A "volunteer worker" is a person who is not an employee of the named insured and who "donates"[361] his or her work and acts at the direction of and within the scope of duties determined by the named insured, without being paid a fee, salary, or other compensation by the named insured or anyone else for that work.[362] The exclusion should not apply to either temporary or volunteer workers, although the workers' compensation exclusion could. Associations that have either temporary or volunteer workers should discuss with their broker whether they have coverage for bodily injuries to those workers.

[e] Pollution Exclusion

The lengthiest exclusion is for bodily injury arising out of actual, alleged, or threatened discharge, dispersal, seepage, migration, release, or escape of pollutants.[363] A "pollutant" is any solid, liquid, gaseous, or thermal irritant or contaminant and includes smoke, vapor, soot, fumes, acids, alkalis, chemicals, and waste.[364]

The "pollution" exclusion is complex and has a number of exceptions. An explanation of its application is beyond the scope of this discussion. Fortunately, it is examined in considerable length by the leading insurance law treatises[365] and by scholarly articles.[366] One way to understand the scope of the pollution

359. *See, e.g.*, ISO Form CG 00 01 12 07, § V.10.

360. *See, e.g.*, ISO Form CG 00 01 12 07, § V.19.

361. A North Carolina court said that "donate" means more than working without payment, otherwise the policy language that the work has to be without "fee, salary or other compensation" would be superfluous. The common everyday meaning of "volunteer," continued the court, is characterized by lack of compensation *and* choice and free will. Therefore, to "donate" work under the terms of the CGL policy language requires the presence of choice and free will. North Carolina Farm Bureau Mutual Insurance v. Burns, 238 N.C. App. 72, 77–78, 767 S.E.2d 109, 112–13 (N.C. App. 2014).

362. *See, e.g.*, ISO Form CG 00 01 12 07, § V.20.

363. *See, e.g.*, ISO Form CG 00 01 12 07, § I.A.2.f. *Consider* Commodore Plaza Condo. Ass'n v. QBE Ins. Corp., 2013 U.S. Dist. LEXIS 192675 (S.D. Fla. May 20, 2013) (where underlying complaint alleged association failed to install roof tarps in timely and proper manner resulting in additional water and mold damage and workers it hired were removing asbestos containing materials improperly and without the proper qualifications, pollution exclusion was inapplicable because complaint did not allege damages were caused by fungus, bacteria, or asbestos).

364. *See, e.g.*, ISO Form CG 00 01 12 07, § V.15. Waste includes materials that are to be recycled, reconditioned, or reclaimed.

365. *See* 3 Jeffrey E. Thomas, *New Appleman on Insurance Law Library Edition* § 18.03[6] (Matthew Bender, 2017); Steven Plitt et al., *Couch on Insurance* §§ 127.14–.15 (3d ed. Supp. 2015).

366. *See, e.g.*, Meeks, *The Pollution Delusion: A Proposal for a Uniform Interpretation of Pollution in General Liability Absolute Pollution Exclusions*, 77 Geo. Wash. L. Rev. 824 (2009); Guiliano, *The Sudden and Accidental Exception to the Pollution Exclusion Solution?*, 13 Temp. Envtl. L. & Tech. J. 261 (1994).

exclusion is to forget about "pollution" in the usual sense. As one expert in the insurance field explains, the easiest way to think of the pollution exclusion is that it can apply to a *contaminant* and, therefore, if there is something that could contaminate something else, the pollution exclusion could apply.[367]

What common interest community associations need to know about the exclusion is that it does not just apply to industrial plants. Common interest communities can be liable for bodily injury by pollutants and can be denied coverage under the exclusion. For example, the employee of a community association management company sued a condominium association alleging it negligently failed to maintain its premises in a safe manner, free from a hazardous condition, specifically the presence of feces, raw sewage, and battery acid. The court found that battery acid qualified as an acid, and raw sewage and feces would be included in the definition of waste and, therefore, the insurer has no duty to defend or indemnify the association in the underlying litigation.[368]

Suits against associations often concern substances not considered to be "traditional" pollutants. As one federal circuit court noted, jurisdictions that have addressed the scope of the exclusion generally either apply it as written because they find it clear and unmistakable or narrow it to traditional environmental pollution, often because they find the terms of the exclusion to be ambiguous.[369] For example, an underlying personal injury action brought against a condominium association arose out of asbestos inhalation. The court decided that because the term "asbestos" was not specifically included within the definition of pollutants, there was an ambiguity that had to be resolved against the insurer, and summary judgment for the insurer on the question of its obligation to provide a defense and/or indemnify was properly denied.[370] In contrast, a homeowners association was sued after a swimmer contracted a viral infection from contaminants in the water of the community pool. The court said meaning of the term "pollutant" includes contaminants and, therefore, the pollution exclusion unambiguously applied.[371]

---

367. Connelly, *How Much Do You Know About Pollution Exclusions?* (Independent Agent, Feb. 2015).

368. Phila. Indem. Ins. Co. v. Yachtsman's Inn Condo Ass'n, 595 F. Supp. 2d 1319, 1321 (S.D. Fla. 2009).

369. Headwaters Res., Inc. v. Ill. Union Ins. Co., 770 F.3d 885, 889 (10th Cir. 2014).

370. Vill. Mall at Hillcrest Condo. v. Merrimack Mut. Fire Ins. Co., 309 A.D.2d 857, 766 N.Y.S.2d 70 (2003).

371. First Specialty Ins. Corp. v. GRS Mgmt. Assocs., 2009 U.S. Dist. LEXIS 72708 (S.D. Fla. 2009).

[f] Aircraft, Auto, or Watercraft and Mobile Equipment

The standard commercial general liability policy excludes coverage for a bodily injury that arises out of ownership, maintenance, use,[372] or entrustment to others of an aircraft, an auto, or a watercraft owned or operated by, or rented or loaned to, *any* insured.[373] "Auto" refers to a land motor vehicle, trailer, or semitrailer designed for travel on public roads, including any attached machinery or equipment or any other land vehicle subject to a compulsory or financial responsibility law or other motor vehicle insurance law in the state where it is licensed or principally garaged but does not include "mobile equipment.[374] "Mobile equipment" includes a vehicle maintained for use solely on or next to premises owned or rented by the named insured.[375] However, self-propelled vehicles with permanently attached equipment designed primarily for snow removal or road maintenance are not mobile equipment but are considered to be autos.[376] Mobile equipment also does not include any land vehicles subject to a compulsory or financial responsibility law or other motor vehicle insurance law in the state where it is licensed or principally garaged. Those vehicles are considered to be autos.

The exclusion applies even if claims against any insured allege negligence or other wrongdoing in supervision, hiring, employment, training, or monitoring of others by that insured when the occurrence that caused the bodily injury involved ownership, maintenance, use, or entrustment to others of an aircraft, auto, or watercraft owned or operated by or rented or loaned to *any* insured.

There are a number of exceptions to the exclusion. It does not apply to watercraft ashore on premises owned or rented by the named insured or that the named insured does not own that is less than 26 feet long and not being used to carry persons or property for a fee. It also does not apply to the parking of an auto on, or on the ways next to, premises the named insured owns or rents, provided that auto is not owned by or rented or loaned to the named insured or any insured. The exclusion does not apply to liability assumed under any insured contract

372. The word "use" includes operation and loading or unloading. The phrase "loading or unloading" means handling of property after it is moved from the place where it is accepted for movement into or onto an aircraft, watercraft, or auto; while it is in or on an aircraft, watercraft, or auto; or while being moved from an aircraft, watercraft, or auto to the place where it is finally delivered, but does not include movement of property by means of a mechanical device, other than a hand truck, not attached to the aircraft, watercraft, or auto. *See, e.g.*, ISO Form CG 00 01 12 07, § V.11.

373. *See, e.g.*, ISO Form CG 00 01 12 07, § I.A.2.g. *Consider* Robinson v. Transportation Ins. Co., 881 S.W.2d 218 (Tex. App.—Houston 1st Dist. 1994) (policy excludes claims arising out of operations of insured's own automobiles and has, according to insurer, generally been used to cover valet parking situation).

374. *See, e.g.*, ISO Form CG 00 01 12 07, § V.2.

375. *See, e.g.*, ISO Form CG 00 01 12 07, § V.12.

376. *See, e.g.*, ISO Form CG 00 01 12 07, § V.12.f.

for ownership, maintenance, or use of aircraft or watercraft. "Insured contract" is defined to include a contract for a lease of premises; an easement or license agreement; an obligation, required by ordinance, to indemnify a municipality; an elevator maintenance agreement; and the part of a contract or agreement pertaining to the business of the named insured pursuant to which the named insured assumes the tort liability of another to pay for bodily injury to a third person or organization.[377] Finally, the exclusion is inapplicable to a bodily injury arising out of operation of machinery or equipment attached to, or part of, a land vehicle that would qualify as mobile equipment if it were not subject to a compulsory or financial responsibility law or other motor vehicle insurance law.

While mobile equipment is excepted from the definition of auto, there is a separate exclusion regarding it. Under that exclusion, coverage is barred for bodily injury arising out of transportation of mobile equipment by an auto owned or operated by or rented or loaned to any insured or use of it in, or while in practice for, or while being prepared for, any prearranged racing, speed, demolition, or stunting activity.[378]

[g] Personal and Advertising Injury

There is an exclusion that says simply that "this insurance" does not apply to bodily injury that arises out of personal and advertising injury.[379] "Personal and advertising injury," of course, is Coverage B of the policy and is defined as an injury arising out of false arrest, detention, or imprisonment; malicious prosecution; wrongful eviction from, wrongful entry into, or invasion of the right of private occupancy; slander, libel, or trade disparagement; violation of the right of another to privacy; use of the advertising idea of someone else; or infringement of the copyright, trade dress, or slogan of someone else.[380] Thus, as explained by one commentary, "this insurance" means Coverage A and, therefore, a bodily injury that arises out of one of the named personal and advertising injury offenses is not insured under Coverage A and the injury would not be covered twice and thereby entitled to application of two limits rather than one.[381] A claimant who suffers a heart attack from being falsely arrested or imprisoned would be, explains the commentary, an example of a consequential bodily injury under Coverage B.

377. *See, e.g.*, ISO Form CG 00 01 12 07, § V.9.

378. *See, e.g.*, ISO Form CG 00 01 12 07, § I.A.2.h.

379. *See, e.g.*, ISO Form CG 00 01 12 07, § I.A.2.o.

380. *See, e.g.*, CG 00 01 12 07, § V.14.

381. Dykes, *Send in the B Team: Insurance Coverage for Personal and Advertising Injury*, 27 Utah Bar J. 24, 25 (2014).

§ 13.04 Property Damage (Coverage A)

The purpose of property damage coverage is to insure against liability for damage to the property of others for which the insured is liable. It does not cover damage to the property of the insured.[382] A common interest community association should, therefore, be aware that the policy may cover damage to the property of its residents for which it is responsible.[383]

There are two parts to the definition of property damage. First, it means *physical injury* to tangible property including any resulting loss of its use.[384] The Illinois Supreme Court explained that tangible property suffers a *physical* injury when it is "altered in appearance, shape, color or in other material dimension," but it does not experience *physical* injury if it suffers intangible damage, for example, diminution in value as a result of the failure of a component.[385] The concept is illustrated by a case in which a common interest community association dredged a creek on neighboring land and was subsequently the subject of an enforcement action for violation of wetlands regulations. The association paid almost $300,000 in fines and costs to create and implement a restoration plan.

---

382. *See* State Farm Fire & Cas. Co. v. Metro. Mgmt., 2007 U.S. Dist. LEXIS 99406 (D. Haw. Oct. 31, 2007) (clearly, purpose of owned property exclusion is to prevent liability coverage designed to protect an insured from third-party claims from being turned into first-party property coverage for losses to insured's own property; under exclusion claims by association for failure of manager to turn over records and funds belonging to association would be barred); Porter v. Clarendon Nat'l Ins. Co., 76 Mass. App. Ct. 655, 660, 925 N.E.2d 58, 62, *rev. den.*, 457 Mass. 1103, 928 N.E.2d 950 (2010) ("own, rent, or occupy" exclusion is common to commercial general liability policies and prevents insured from using general liability policy as property insurance); State Farm v. English Cove Assocs., 121 Wn. App. 358, 360–61, 88 P.3d 986, 988 (2004) (owned property exclusion is intended to prevent general liability policy from providing first-party benefits to insured).

383. *See, e.g.*, 1300 Alki Condo. Owners Ass'n v. Hartford Cas. Ins. Co., 2004 U.S. Dist. LEXIS 32398 (W.D. Wash. Oct. 22, 2004) (finding coverage when condominium association paid for damage to individual units caused by defects in sprinkler system that was common element).

384. *See, e.g.*, ISO Form CG 00 01 12 07, § V.17.a. All loss of use is deemed to occur at the time of the physical injury that caused it. *Consider* United States Fire Ins. Co. v. Meridian of Palm Beach Condo. Ass'n, 700 So. 2d 161, 162 (Fla. 4th DCA 1997), *pet. den.*, 717 So. 2d 535 (Fla. 1998) (CGL policy covers damage caused by building flaws or deficiencies, but not for those flaws or deficiencies; lower court erred in determining policy provided coverage for defective workmanship and construction by insured).

385. Traveler's Ins. Co. v. Eljer Mfg., 258 Ill. Dec. 792, 197 Ill. 2d 278, 301–02, 757 N.E.2d 481, 496 (2001) (term "physical" limits word "injury" in policy definition of "property damage," and phrase "physical injury" does not include intangible damage to property, such as economic loss and, therefore, diminution in value of whole, resulting from failure of component to perform as promised, does not constitute physical injury). *See also* Phibro Animal Health Corp. v. National Union Fire Ins. Co., 446 N.J. Super. 419, 437, 142 A.3d 761, 771 (2016); Cunningham v. Universal Underwriters, 98 Cal. App. 4th 1141, 1155, 120 Cal. Rptr. 2d 162, 173 (2002) (coverage for claims alleging damage to or loss of use of *tangible* property means there is no coverage for loss of use of intangible property rights and tangible property refers to things that can be touched, seen, and smelled, and as matter of law interference with non-possessory interest in land of another does not satisfy that definition).

It sought coverage for sums for which it became liable. The insurer conceded that real property is tangible property but disputed whether a "physical injury" took place. The court noted that the dredging resulted in significant changes to the condition of the creek, and the fact that a restoration plan was required to reverse that result supported the conclusion that the property had been "physically injured."[386]

The standard commercial general liability policy does not define "tangible property," but courts have said it is "that which is capable of being handled, touched, or physically possessed."[387] The standard policy specifically states that electronic data is not tangible property.[388] The limitation of property damage to physical injury to tangible property generally means the basic coverage does not apply to purely economic losses, meaning lost profits, goodwill, or loss of investment.[389] Economic losses from alleged conversion or breach of a fiduciary duty are also generally not considered property damage.[390]

---

386. Oak Ford Owners Ass'n v. Auto-Owners Ins. Co., 510 F. Supp. 2d 812, 815–17 (M.D. Fla. 2007) (noting word "injury" is not defined in policy; stating that item need not be completely destroyed to be rendered damaged; holding that dredging from creek and depositing fill on it bank constituted property damage under CGL policy).

387. Lamar Truck Plaza, Inc. v. Sentry Ins., 757 P.2d 1143, 1144 (Colo. App. 1988) (purely economic losses—lost profits or investment—are not included in definition of "tangible property"). *See also* Graber v. State Farm Fire & Casualty Co., 244 Mont. 265, 269, 797 P.2d 214, 216 (Mont. 1990). *But see* Dietrich v. Travelers Ins. Co., 551 So. 2d 64, 66 (La. App. 1989) (Louisiana Supreme Court equates "tangible property" with "corporeal property"; thus although right to benefits payable under health and disability policy may be intangible, actual benefits that would have been payable constitute tangible property, that is money).

388. Electronic data means information, facts, or programs stored as or on, created or used on, or transmitted to or from computer software. It includes systems and applications software, hard or floppy disks, CD-ROMS, tapes, drives, cells, data processing devices, or any other media used with electronically controlled equipment.

389. Johnson, *The Practical Art: On the Archaeology and Architecture of Liability Insurance Contracts*, 78 Def. Couns. J. 143, 162 (2011). *Consider* Land v. Auto-Owners Ins. Co., 511 Fed. Appx. 795 (10th Cir. 2013) (conclusory allegations of property damage in underlying complaint alleging physical injury to or loss of use of tangible property insufficient; insured failed to show that underlying suit challenging propriety of assessment of, and attempts to collect, homeowners fees, alleged property damage).

390. State Farm Fire & Cas. Co. v. Metro. Mgmt., 2007 U.S. Dist. LEXIS 99406 (D. Haw. Oct. 31, 2007) (where association sued its property manager and property manager claimed status as insured under association policy, court found allegations against management company did not constitute physical injury to any tangible property; association claimed manager breached fiduciary and refused to turn over records and funds of association, thus causing association pecuniary, or economic, losses; however, purely economic losses, unaccompanied by physical injury to tangible property or loss of use of that property, do not constitute property damage; courts have generally held that claim for conversion or the unauthorized exercise of control over another person's property is not claim for property damage; claim for economic losses resulting from breach of fiduciary duty generally do not constitute property damage).

The second meaning of property damage is loss of use of tangible property not physically injured.[391] An Oregon appellate court explained this portion of the coverage. The owner of a building alleged that inadequate window assemblies caused a delay in completion and occupancy of its building, with resulting loss of rental income. The court said the delay in completion and occupancy was an injury that constituted loss of use of tangible property that had not been physically injured or destroyed and that was property damage for which coverage clearly applied.[392]

Under a commercial general liability policy, the carrier will pay sums the insured is legally obligated to pay as damages to which the coverage applies.[393] Coverage applies only if the property damage is caused by an "occurrence."[394] The occurrence has to take place in the "coverage territory"[395] and during the policy period.[396] Additionally, the coverage applies only if, prior to the policy period, no insured[397] and no employee[398] authorized by the named insured to give

391. *See, e.g.*, ISO Form CG 00 01 12 07, § V.17.b. These losses of use are deemed to occur at the time of the occurrence that caused them.

392. Milgard Mfg., Inc. v. Continental Ins. Co., 92 Ore. App. 609, 613, 759 P.2d 1111, 1112 (1988) (injury, however, came squarely within policy exclusion).

393. *See, e.g.*, ISO Form CG 00 01 12 07, § I.A.1.a.

394. *See, e.g.*, ISO Form CG 00 01 12 07, § I.A.1.b.(1).

395. The basic coverage territory is the United States and its territories and possessions, Puerto Rico, and Canada. *See, e.g.*, CG 00 01 12 07, § V.4.a. The coverage territory includes international waters or airspace, but only if the injury or damage occurs during travel or transportation between the United States and its territories and possessions, Puerto Rico, or Canada. *See, e.g.*, CG 00 01 12 07, § V.4.b. The coverage territory also includes any other part of the world if the injury or damage arises out of goods or products made or sold by the insured in the United States and its territories and possessions, Puerto Rico, or Canada; activities of a person whose home is in the United States and its territories and possessions, Puerto Rico, or Canada, but is away for a short time on the business of the insured; or a personal and advertising injury offense that take place through the Internet or similar electronic means of communication, provided the responsibility of the insured to pay damages is determined in a suit on the merits, in the United States and its territories and possessions, Puerto Rico, or Canada or in a settlement to which the carrier agrees. *See, e.g.*, CG 00 01 12 07, § V.4.c.

396. *See, e.g.*, ISO Form CG 00 01 12 07, §§ I.A.1.b.(1) & (2). *See also* Porter v. Clarendon Nat'l Ins. Co., 76 Mass. App. Ct. 655, 659, 925 N.E.2d 58, 62, *rev. den.*, 457 Mass. 1103, 928 N.E.2d 950 (2010) (where condominium association built retaining wall and paved two parking spaces on abutting property some time before 2000 and retaining wall and parking spaces remained on that property until abutter sued in 2004, trespass occurred continuously, for duration policies in effect from October 1, 2000, to October 1, 2003); Heather Hill Villas Condo. Ass'n v. Am. Equity Ins. Co., 816 So. 2d 250 (Fla. 2d DCA 2002) (where in underlying action by association against unit owner, unit owner counterclaimed for alleged damages from excessive moisture in her condominium unit, dates in counterclaim were clearly outside term of coverage and lower court correctly determined there was no coverage).

397. "Insured" means anyone listed in section II.1 of the policy. For a discussion of who is an insured, see generally § 13.02, *supra*.

398. Employee includes a leased worker—meaning a person leased to the named insured by a labor leasing firm under an agreement to perform duties related to the conduct of the business of the named insured—but not a temporary one. *See, e.g.*, CG 00 01 12 07, § V.5 &10.

or receive notice of an occurrence or claim knew that the property damage had occurred, in whole or in part.[399]

Property damage that occurs during the policy period and was not, prior to that period, known to have occurred by any insured or any employee authorized by the named insured to give or receive notice of an occurrence or claim includes any continuation, change, or resumption of that injury after the end of the policy period.[400] Property damage will be deemed to have been known to have occurred at the earliest time when any insured or any employee authorized to give or receive notice of an occurrence or claim reports all, or any part, of the property damage to the carrier or any other insurer, receives a written or verbal demand or claim for damages because of a bodily injury, or becomes aware by any other means that property damage has occurred or has begun to occur.[401]

When property damage has been continuous or progressive it can be difficult to determine when it first occurred. Courts have employed numerous theories to address the question, the most common of which are the manifestation, exposure, injury-in-fact, and continuous injury theories. Exposition of these legal concepts is beyond the scope of this discussion; however, the leading insurance law treatises[402] and scholarly journals[403] have devoted considerable attention to the subject.

[1] Damages

CGL policies say the carrier will pay sums the insured is legally obligated to pay as "damages." They do not, however, define damages. Some courts say the term means a money judgment against the insured in a civil suit;[404] however, other courts view it as having a broader meaning.[405] For example, a federal court

399. *See, e.g.*, ISO Form CG 00 01 12 07, § I.A.1.b.(3). If an insured or authorized employee knew, prior to the policy period, that the property damage occurred, then any continuation, change, or resumption of that damage during or after the policy period is deemed to have been known prior to the policy period.

400. *See, e.g.*, ISO Form CG 00 01 12 07, § I.A.1.c.

401. *See, e.g.*, ISO Form CG 00 01 12 07, § I.A.1.d.

402. *See* 3 Jeffrey E. Thomas, *New Appleman on Insurance Law Library Edition* § 18.02[5] (Matthew Bender, 2017); Steven Plitt et al., *Couch on Insurance* § 126.32–.40 (3d ed. Supp. 2015).

403. *See, e.g.*, Grand, *Nailing Down Occurrence Triggers for Property Damage in the Wake of Redevelopment—Why a Distinction Should Be Made Between First and Third Party Policies*, 68 La. L. Rev. 605 (2008); Goodman, *Insurance Triggers as Judicial Gatekeepers in Toxic Mold Litigation*, 57 Vand. L. Rev. 241, 263–69 (2004); Dykhouse & Falik, *Trigger of Coverage: The Business Context, The Plain Language, and American Home Products*, 16 Conn. L. Rev. 497 (1984).

404. *See, e.g.*, County of San Diego v. Ace Property & Casualty Ins. Co., 37 Cal. 4th 406, 33 Cal. Rptr. 3d 583, 118 P.3d 607 (2005).

405. *See, e.g.*, Desert Mt. Props. Ltd. P'ship v. Liberty Mut. Fire Ins. Co., 225 Ariz. 194, 201, 236 P.3d 421, 428 (Ariz. App. 2010), *aff'd*, 226 Ariz. 419, 250 P.3d 196 (Ariz. 2011) (no court action is required to create legal obligation and, therefore, coverage for sums insured becomes "legally obligated to pay as damages" may be triggered even absent civil suit against insured or court order requiring insured to make payment). *See also* Ass'n of Apt. Owners of the Moorings v. Dongbu

in Washington state concluded there was coverage when a condominium association paid for damage to individual units caused by defects in a sprinkler system that was a common element. The unit owners did not sue the association to recover for the damages, and it is not clear from the opinion that they even formally requested that the association pay for the damage, but it did pay and sought coverage from its insurer.[406]

Courts do not agree on the question of whether "damages" includes equitable remedies, for example, an injunction.[407] Of course, a suit can seek both money damages and equitable relief. For example, in a common interest community case, the insurer argued that a request for injunctive/equitable relief did not constitute damages; however, the court pointed to allegations in the underlying complaint of past wrongs and injuries and an additional request for compensatory and statutory damages in an amount to be determined at trial and found there was a sufficient allegation of damages under the policy.[408] It is not unusual for common interest community associations to be sued for failure to carry out a duty allegedly mandated by its governing documents or by statutes, with the relief

---

Ins. Co., 2016 U.S. Dist. LEXIS 110283 (D. Haw. Aug. 18, 2016) (damage to individual unit caused by failure of association to repair and maintain common element lanai roof resulting in water damage to interior of unit constituted property damage and that damage, as awarded to unit owner in arbitration, was "property damage" to which insurance applied); Pepper Mill Condo. Ass'n v. Hartford Fire Ins. Co., 71 Pa. D. & C.4th 54 (Pa. Dist. 2005) (where condominium association sought coverage for emergency expenses incurred to excavate in search of potential survivors of wreckage of collapsed parking deck, insurer argued those expenses were not sums insured became legally obligated to pay as damages because of bodily injury or property damage, but court denied summary judgment to insurer).

406. 1300 Alki Condo. Owners Ass'n v. Hartford Cas. Ins. Co., 2004 U.S. Dist. LEXIS 32398 (W.D. Wash. Oct. 22, 2004). The court said that it had to decide whether or not the Washington Condominium Act required the association to undertake the repairs and that the parties agreed that the association had to be legally obligated to pay for any damages before liability coverage commenced under the policy. The court analyzed two statutes. The first is found in the various Uniform Acts and the common interest community legislation in many states. It requires a condominium association to maintain liability insurance that covers all occurrences commonly insured against for property damage "arising out of or in connection with the use, ownership, or maintenance of the common elements." The second statute obligates an association to repair any portion of the condominium for it is required to maintain liability insurance. The court said that the damage to the individual units arose out of the failure of the sprinklers, a common element, and the association assumed responsibility for the damage as required by the second statute; therefore, the association acted under a legal duty and the insurer had to provide coverage unless otherwise excluded.

407. *See* State Farm Fire & Cas. Co. v. Metro. Mgmt., 2007 U.S. Dist. LEXIS 99406 (D. Haw. Oct. 31, 2007) (equitable relief, in form of injunction or otherwise—declaratory relief—does not constitute "damages" within meaning of insurance policy providing liability coverage); Cutler-Orosi Unified School Dist. v. Tulare County School etc. Authority, 31 Cal. App. 4th 617, 629, 37 Cal. Rptr. 2d 106, 113 (1994) (objectively reasonable insured would not conclude that costs of complying with federal court equitable order would be covered as damages). *Compare* Farmland Indus. v. Republic Ins. Co., 941 S.W.2d 505, 508 (Mo. 1997) (term "damages" is not rendered superfluous when given its ordinary meaning which includes equitable relief).

408. Toldt Woods Condos. Owner's Ass'n v. Madeline Square, LLC, 314 Wis. 2d 259, 757 N.W.2d 850 (2008).

sought being an injunction.[409] Will the policy cover the costs of complying with a mandatory injunction? An association should discuss that question and the scope of coverage with its attorney and its broker. It is also suggested that before the policy is accepted by the association or its designated representative, those issues be included by endorsement, if not already incorporated into the body of the CGL policy and if not prohibited by law.

Does an assessment levied by an association to pay a judgment against it constitute damages? In an unpublished California opinion, condominium unit owners argued a special assessment levied by the association to pay a judgment against the association constituted damages. The court, however, said that the duty of a carrier to indemnify its insured for sums the insured becomes legally obligated to pay as damages is limited to money judgments imposed by courts against the insured. The unit owners, noted the court, were not named as parties in the enforcement proceedings that resulted in the special assessment against them and the fact that their contract with the association required them to contribute to its debts did not mean that a special assessment imposed for that purpose was a sum they were "legally obligated to pay as damages," as that term is defined in the standard commercial general liability policy.[410]

Are attorney's fees damages? Several courts have found that they are. In one, an arbitrator awarded fees and costs to unit owners that sued their condominium association for failing to repair the common element roof over their unit. The award was confirmed by a state court. A federal court said the association became legally obligated to pay the attorney's fee award when the state court confirmed the arbitration award and the property damage at issue constituted property damage to which the insurance applied. Because the fee award was restitutive payment to the unit owners and flowed from their property damage—but for their property damage, they would not have pursued arbitration and been awarded fees—the arbitrator's award of attorney's fees was covered by the policy and had to be reimbursed to the association by the carrier.[411]

---

409. *See, e.g.*, Willow Lake Residential Ass'n v. Juliano, 80 So. 3d 226 (Ala. App. 2010) (lot owners who cleared overgrown area of land immediately behind their home and erected series of steps mostly on common property sued association requesting that court permanently enjoin it from taking any action to remove steps or damage their property); Hobbs v. Weinkauf, 940 So. 2d 1151 (Fla. 2d DCA 2006) (injunction sought to require association to comply with statutory recordkeeping requirement); Wilson v. Playa De Serrano, 211 Ariz. 511, 123 P.3d 1148 (Ariz. App. 2005) (where association amended bylaws to declare community to be age-restricted community, resident sought declaratory judgment that age restriction was invalid and injunctive relief); Timmerman v. Board of Managers of the Anchorage Condominium, 212 A.D.2d 523, 622 N.Y.S.2d 320 (1995) (action seeking injunction to bar sitting board mounting any challenge to board election).

410. The Le Parc Cases, 2004 Cal. App. Unpub. LEXIS 4272 (Apr. 29, 2004).

411. Ass'n of Apt. Owners of the Moorings v. Dongbu Ins. Co., 2016 U.S. Dist. LEXIS 110283 (D. Haw. Aug. 18, 2016). *See also* APL Co. v. Valley Force Ins. Co., 754 F. Supp. 2d 1084 (N.D. Cal. 2010).

[2] Occurrence

Commercial general liability policies cover an "occurrence," typically defined as an "accident."[412] They add that an accident includes continuous or repeated exposure to "substantially the same general harmful conditions." They do not, however, define "accident." Generally, common law determines what is, or is not, an accident for purposes of triggering coverage.[413] The meaning of the word has been the subject of countless court opinions and analyzed by the leading treatises on insurance law.[414] In general, an accident is an unforeseen event.[415] As a rule, the determination by a court of whether an event is an accident is based not on whether an act was intended but on whether the injury was intended.[416] However,

---

412. *See, e.g.*, ISO Form CG 00 01 12 07, § V.13.

413. https://www.irmi.com/online/insurance-glossary/terms/a/accident.aspx (noting that occasionally "accident" is defined in policy).

414. *See* 3 Jeffrey E. Thomas, *New Appleman on Insurance Law Library Edition* § 18.02[6] (Matthew Bender, 2017); Steven Plitt et al., *Couch on Insurance* § 129.3 (3d ed. Supp. 2015). *Consider* Willing v. Cmty. Ass'n Underwriters of Am., Inc., 2007 U.S. Dist. LEXIS 48543 (W.D. Wash. July 5, 2007), where the underlying suit was brought against developers who also served on the board of a condominium association. The association sued them as developers for construction defects and as directors for breach of fiduciary duty based on a conflict of interest in their dual roles. The insurer for the association argued the underlying litigation did not allege "property damage caused by an occurrence" against the developers in their capacity of directors. The court, however, concluded there was evidence property damage occurred because the defendant failed to maintain and repair the condominium, in violation of their fiduciary duties. There was sufficient evidence to show the association sued for conduct covered by the policy, thereby triggering the duty to defend.

415. *See, e.g.*, Am. Family Mut. Ins. Co. v. Am. Girl, Inc., 268 Wis. 2d 16, 673 N.W.2d 65 (2004) (accident means event that takes place without one's foresight or expectation); Utica Mut. Ins. Co. v. Travelers Indem. Co., 223 Va. 145, 147, 286 S.E.2d 225, 226 (Va. 1982) (incident unexpected from viewpoint of insured); Hauenstein v. St. Paul-Mercury Indem. Co., 242 Minn. 354, 358–59, 65 N.W.2d 122, 126 (1954) (accident is unexpected, unforeseen, or undesigned happening or consequence from either known or unknown cause). *See also* Fed. Hill Homeowners Ass'n v. Cmty. Ass'n Underwriters of Am., Inc., 384 Fed. Appx. 209 (4th Cir. 2010) (where homeowners association issued disclosure packet containing information that allegedly caused plaintiff homeowner from being able to sell her property resulting in mental anguish for which she sued, there was an accident because mental anguish would not be natural and probable consequence of issuing disclosure packet; association was required by state law to produce disclosure packet at request of homeowner, and packet contained information that was not extraordinary); N.H. Ins. Co. v. RLI Ins. Co., 807 So. 2d 171 (Fla. 3d DCA 2002) (where resident of condominium fired three shots, at separate times, and injured three separate persons, killing two and wrongful act, if any, of association was allowing the perpetrator to reside in its community, trial court properly found there were three occurrences; dissent, however, countered that there was only one occurrence and that was permitting perpetrator's presence). *And see* Land v. Auto-Owners Ins. Co., 511 Fed. Appx. 795 (10th Cir. 2013) (underlying suit alleging violation of federal Racketeering Influenced and Corrupt Organizations Act (RICO) and comparable state law by association president in seeking to collect payment of various assessments did not allege bodily injury or property damage caused by occurrence as defined in policy).

416. *See, e.g.*, Gruetzmacher v. Acuity, 393 F. Supp. 2d 860, 866 (D. Minn. 2005) (coverage is for unexpected injury even where there was an intent to act). *See also* State Auto Prop. & Cas. Ins. Co. v. Highland Terrace Counsel of Co-Owners, Inc., 2015 U.S. Dist. LEXIS 59663 (W.D. Ky. May 7, 2015) (where unit owner sued condominium association over its decision to levy special assessment

courts may infer intent to injure where the harm is obvious, for example, battery.[417] When the insured intends to injure another, there is no accident, even though the insured did not foresee the extent of the injury.[418]

A common complaint by unit owners that sometimes evolves into a lawsuit is that the association has failed to fulfill its duties to maintain the property. For example, in one case a condominium unit owner alleged the association failed to address a raw sewage backup problem. The unit owner sued the association for breach of fiduciary duty/constructive fraud/actual fraud and also sought declaratory relief requiring the association pursuant to the state's Condominium Property Act to repair or replace the drainage pipes. The insurer for the association refused to defend it because it argued that failure and refusal to perform certain actions was not an unexpected, unintended, and unusual event, and therefore not an occurrence. The court agreed. The underlying complaint demonstrated the association was aware of the sewage backups, and they continued for more than one year after the unit owner identified problems with the plumbing and drainage system that violated building code requirements and the association took limited action that proved unsuccessful. Therefore, the court found the insurer had no duty to defend the association because under those facts, there was no occurrence alleged in the complaint against the association.[419]

A Colorado federal court reached the opposite conclusion. The plaintiff unit owner in the underlying suit alleged the association, despite repeated demands, failed or refused to remedy roof drainage problems of interior leakage from overhead plumbing defects. The unit owner sued the association, and the CGL

---

and alleged association elected its governing board violation of its bylaws, passed special assessment in violation of master deed, assessed non-incurred expenses, assessed more costs than were actually incurred, denied plaintiff access to limited common elements in violation of bylaws, and failed to maintain capital replacement fund in violation of master deed, court held none of conduct alleged in complaint was accidental; all allegations involved intentional acts or omissions, not accidents, and insurer was not required to provide defense). *And see* State Farm Fire & Cas. Co. v. Metro. Mgmt., 2007 U.S. Dist. LEXIS 99406 (D. Haw. Oct. 31, 2007) (where association sued its property manager for refusing to turn over association records and funds and property manager claimed status as insured under association policy, court found alleged acts of management company were not in any way accidental; management company intentionally refused to turn over its records and funds in response to repeated demands by association and, therefore, injury claimed by association—interference with its right to possession of those records and funds—was necessarily "expected result" of alleged acts of manager).

417. *See generally* Monteleone, *Coverage Issues Under Commercial General Liability and Directors' and Officers' Liability Policies*, 18 W. New Eng. L. Rev. 47, 51–57 (1996).

418. *See, e.g.*, Hartford Fire Ins. Co. v. Spreen, 343 So. 2d 649, 651 (Fla. 3d DCA 1977) (where insured swung at another, the fact that he did not foresee or intend extent of harm inflicted did not convert admitted assault and battery into an accident).

419. Cambridge Mut. Fire Ins. Co. v. 1347-49 N. Sedgwick Condo. Ass'n, 2013 U.S. Dist. LEXIS 9750 (N.D. Ill. Jan. 23, 2013) (underlying complaint contained no allegations of negligence).

insurer refused to defend it. The carrier took the position that the claims in the underlying complaint were premised entirely on a breach of contractual duty to maintain the common elements and, because "accident" requires an element of fortuity and a breach of contract is not fortuitous, there was no coverage. The court, however, said in a conclusory statement that the factual allegations in the underlying complaint implied that some property damage was caused by water leakage and drainage problems that occurred after storms and that was sufficient to show property damage caused by an occurrence and trigger the carrier's defense obligation.[420]

[3] Exclusions

The standard commercial general liability policy contains 17 exclusions that apply to bodily injury or property damage coverage.[421] Three of them apply only to bodily injury. Eight of the exclusions apply to both bodily injury and property damage, and those that are significant to common interest communities are discussed in the section on bodily injury.[422] Six of the exclusions apply to property damage.

[a] Exclusions Unlikely to Apply to Common Interest Communities

Most of the exclusions to the property damage coverage have little or no application to common interest communities. For example, there is an exclusion for property damage to the product of the named insured arising out of it or any part of it.[423] The product of the insured means goods or products—other than real property[424]—manufactured, sold, handled, distributed, or disposed of by the named insured or others trading under its name, or a person or organization whose business or assets it has acquired.[425] Obviously, the exclusion applies to commercial ventures. Two other exclusions—recall of products, work, or

---

420. Beauvallon Condo. Ass'n v. Granite State Ins. Co., 2011 U.S. Dist. LEXIS 69606 (D. Colo. June 29, 2011).

421. *See, e.g.*, ISO Form CG 00 01 12 07, § I.A.2.

422. *See* §§ 13.03[4][a] (expected or intended injury exclusion), 13.03[4][b] (contractual liability exclusion), 13.03[4][c] (liquor liability exclusion), 13.03[4][e] (pollution exclusion), 13.03[4][f] (aircraft, auto or watercraft and mobile equipment exclusion).

423. *See, e.g.*, ISO Form CG 00 01 12 07, § I.2.k.

424. *See* Toldt Woods Condos. Owner's Ass'n v. Madeline Square, LLC, 314 Wis. 2d 259, 757 N.W.2d 850 (2008), where a developer's construction work damaged the property of an adjacent condominium association. The developer's insurer invoked the "damage to your product" exclusion. The court, however, held the exclusion was not applicable to a third-party property damage claim, as it fell under the exception for real property.

425. *See, e.g.*, ISO Form CG 00 01 12 07, § V.21.

impaired property[426] and damage to impaired property or property not physically injured[427]—also appear to apply primarily to commercial ventures.

The "damage to your work" exclusion applies to property damage to "your work" arising out of it or any part of it and included in the products-completed operations hazard.[428] "Your work" means work or operations performed by the named insured,[429] or on its behalf, and materials, parts, or equipment furnished in connection with the work or operations and includes warranties or representations made about the fitness, quality, durability, performance, or use of the work and providing of, or failure to provide, warnings or instructions.[430] The possibility that the exclusion could apply to a residential common interest community is limited by the fact that it specifically does not apply if the damaged work, or

426. *See, e.g.*, ISO Form CG 00 01 12 07, § I.2.n. This exclusion bars coverage for damages claimed for any loss, cost, or expense incurred by the named insured or others for the loss of use, withdrawal, recall, inspection, repair, replacement, adjustment, removal, or disposal of the product of the named insured; the work of the named insured; or impaired property if the product, work, or property is withdrawn or recalled from the market or from use because of a known or suspected defect, deficiency, inadequacy, or dangerous condition. The exclusion has been raised in at least one common interest community case. In *Porter v. Clarendon Nat'l Ins. Co.*, 76 Mass. App. Ct. 655, 925 N.E.2d 58, *rev. den.*, 457 Mass. 1103, 928 N.E.2d 950 (2010), a condominium association constructed a retaining wall and parking spaces on the property of an adjacent landowner. The landowner sued the association for trespass. The insurers argued that because the association built the retaining wall that, under the exclusion, the damages were caused by its work and not covered. The court noted that the exclusion to proscribe repair or replacement costs for faulty workmanship by the insured that it has been contracted or otherwise hired to perform and the reason for the exclusion is that general liability coverage is for tort liability for physical damages to others, not contractual liability economic loss because the product or completed work is not that for which it bargained. Because an abutter to the association, with no contractual or other business relationship with it, sought trespass damages, the exclusion did not apply.

427. *See, e.g.*, ISO Form CG 00 01 12 07, § I.2.m. This exclusion proscribes coverage for property damage to *impaired* property or property that has not been physically injured, that arises out of a defect, deficiency, inadequacy, or dangerous condition in the product or work of the insured or a delay or failure by the named insured or anyone acting on behalf of the named insured to perform a contract or agreement in accordance with its terms. "Impaired property" is defined as tangible property, other than the product or work of the named insured, that cannot be used or is less useful because incorporates the product or work of the insured that is known, or thought, to be defective, deficient, inadequate, or dangerous or the named insured has failed to fulfill the terms of a contract or agreement if the property can be restored to use by repair, replacement, adjustment, or removal of the product or work of the named insured or fulfilling the terms of the contract or agreement. *See, e.g.*, ISO Form CG 00 01 12 07, § V.8. The exclusion does not apply to loss of use of other property that arises out of sudden and accidental physical injury to product or work of the named insured after it has been put to its intended use.

428. *See, e.g.*, ISO Form CG 00 01 12 07, § I.2.l.

429. One court, faced with determining the scope of an association's operations, first turned to its Covenants, Conditions, and Restrictions, which it said provided the greatest amount of information about what was considered to be the "operations" of the association. It also examined the bylaws. The court also considered a state statute that provided a homeowners association was responsible for repairing, replacing, or maintaining the common area. Phila. Indem. Ins. Co. v. Lakeside Heights Homeowners Ass'n, 110 F. Supp. 3d 965, 971–72, 975 (N.D. Cal. 2015).

430. *See, e.g.*, ISO Form CG 00 01 12 07, § V. 22.

work out of which the damage arose, was performed on behalf of the association by a subcontractor.

[b] Damage to Property

The "damage to property" exclusion is frequently raised in claims by common interest communities. A primary purpose of the exclusion is to prevent the policy from being converted to first-party property insurance, that is, a policy that covers damage to the property of the insured.[431]

[i] Damage to Property Owned, Rented, or Occupied

The part of the exclusion bars coverage for damage to property owned,[432] rented, or occupied[433] by the named insured,[434] including costs or expenses incurred by the named insured, or any other person, organization, or entity, to repair, replace,

431. *See* State Farm Fire & Cas. Co. v. Metro. Mgmt., 2007 U.S. Dist. LEXIS 99406 (D. Haw. Oct. 31, 2007) (clearly, purpose of owned property exclusion is to prevent liability coverage designed to protect an insured from third-party claims from being turned into first-party property coverage for losses to insured's own property; under exclusion claims by association for failure of manager to turn of records and funds belonging to association would be barred); Porter v. Clarendon Nat'l Ins. Co., 76 Mass. App. Ct. 655, 660, 925 N.E.2d 58, 62, *rev. den.*, 457 Mass. 1103, 928 N.E.2d 950 (2010) ("own, rent, or occupy" exclusion is common to commercial general liability policies and prevents insured from using general liability policy as property insurance); State Farm v. English Cove Assocs., 121 Wn. App. 358, 360–61, 88 P.3d 986, 988 (2004) (owned property exclusion is intended to prevent general liability policy from providing first-party benefits to insured).

432. *See, e.g.*, State Farm v. English Cove Assocs., 121 Wn. App. 358, 88 P.3d 986 (2004) (where condominium association sued insured developer for breaches of both contract and various warranties based on numerous alleged construction defects and developer still owned about one-fourth of units and, therefore, had undivided interest in common areas, owned property exclusion applied as developer had undivided ownership interest in damaged property).

433. In *Porter v. Clarendon Nat'l Ins. Co.*, 76 Mass. App. Ct. 655, 925 N.E.2d 58, *rev. den.*, 457 Mass. 1103, 928 N.E.2d 950 (2010), the condominium association was found liable for trespass on the property of an abutting property owner. The trespass occurred when the association built a retaining wall and paved two parking spaces on that adjacent property. The insurers argued the "own, rent, or occupy" exclusion applied because the association *occupied* the disputed land by continuously trespassing on it. The court did not agree. It said the exclusion means that the policy was intended to cover only liability of the insured to third parties, not damage to property of the insured, so where the damage caused by the trespass was to property of a third party, not property of the insured association, the exclusion was not applicable.

434. *See* Alexander v. Nat'l Fire Ins., 454 F.3d 214, 226–27 (3d Cir. 2006) (although term "named insured" is not defined in policy, Declarations Page listed condominium association as named insured and fact that someone—for example, condominium unit owner—may be additional insured does not mean that they are named insured as two terms are not interchangeable; named insured means named insured). *Compare* Wyner v. North Am. Specialty Ins. Co., 78 F.3d 752 (1st Cir. 1996), where a restaurant rented space. It had a CGL policy under which it was the named insured and that named its landlord as an additional insured. The restaurant allegedly improperly altered and damaged portions of the building that were not owned, rented, or occupied by it. The landlord sought coverage under the policy. The insurer sought to bar coverage based on the property damage exclusion. The issue was whether the landlord and an additional insured was "you" for purposes of the exclusion for property "you own." The policy defined "you" as the named insured shown on the Declarations Page "and any other person or organization." The court held that

enhance, restore, or maintain that property for any reason, including preventing injury to a person[435] or damage to the property of another.[436] The exclusion does not apply to property damage, other than by fire, to premises, including the contents of those premises, rented to the named insured for seven or fewer consecutive days.[437]

[A] Cooperatives and Homeowners Associations

For purposes of the property damage exclusion it is clear that a cooperative corporation owns all the property. Thus, if there is damage to any of the property for which the cooperative is liable, including to the individual apartments, the exclusion should apply. A homeowners association owns the common property, and the individual homeowners own their residences with perhaps a surrounding yard. The exclusion should then apply when there is damage to the common area, but probably not when the association is liable for causing damage to an individual residence.[438]

[B] Condominium Associations

Condominium associations, however, present a potential conundrum. Courts generally appear to treat condominium associations as the owners of common elements,[439] but in fact, they are not. By definition,[440] the common elements are owned by the unit owners as tenants in common. One federal court, taking note of that fact, decided coverage could not, therefore, be precluded on basis of the

---

the exclusions for property "you own, rent or occupy" extended to the landlords as an additional insured.

435. *Consider* Pepper Mill Condo. Ass'n v. Hartford Fire Ins. Co., 71 Pa. D. & C.4th 54 (Pa. Dist. 2005) (for purposes of insurer's motion for summary judgment, condominium association sufficiently demonstrated that emergency expenses incurred to excavate in search of potential survivors of wreckage of collapsed parking deck were not included in exclusionary clause; costs to excavate in search of potential survivors were not mentioned or alluded to in exclusionary clause, and "prevention of injury" relates back to restorations and repairs portion of clause; insured was not attempting to repair, replace, enhance, restore, or maintain its collapsed parking deck to prevent injury; rather, it was attempting to locate possible survivors of wreckage).

436. *See, e.g.*, ISO Form CG 00 01 12 07, § I.2.j.(1). Some policies may also have a "subsidence" exclusion. *See, e.g.*, Phila. Indem. Ins. Co. v. Lakeside Heights Homeowners Ass'n, 110 F. Supp. 3d 965, 968–69 (N.D. Cal. 2015) (CGL policy excluded coverage for bodily injury, property damage, personal injury, or advertising injury caused by, resulting from, attributable or contributed to, or aggravated by subsidence of land as result of landslide, mudflow, earth sinking, or shifting resulting from operations of named insured or any subcontractor of named insured).

437. *See* A ISO Form CG 00 01 12 07, § III.6 regarding separate limits of insurance applied to damage to premises rented to the named insured.

438. *1300 Alki Condo. Owners Ass'n v. Hartford Cas. Ins. Co.*, 2004 U.S. Dist. LEXIS 32398 (W.D. Wash. Oct. 22, 2004), discussed below, reaches that conclusion for a condominium and its reasoning would seem to apply to a homeowners association.

439. *See* § 13.03[3][a][ii], *supra*.

440. *See, e.g.*, Uniform Common Interest Ownership Act § 1-103(10) (common interest community is not a condominium unless undivided interests in common elements are vested in unit owners).

Property Damage exclusion where the association was the named insured.[441] Under that reasoning, would a condominium association as named insured be indemnified if it were found liable for damage to the common elements in an action by a unit owner? It seems likely the CGL carrier would seek to invoke the exclusion, especially given that the association would have a property policy that covers damages to the common elements and the association would be the named insured under that policy despite the fact that it does not own the common elements.[442] Could, perhaps, the association be considered to occupy the common elements even if it does not own them?[443]

Does the exclusion apply when a defect in the common elements of a condominium causes damage to individual units? A federal court in Washington said no. A condominium building had a sprinkler system that was a common element. The system experienced two failures. The first was because of a defect in the system; the second was caused by a nail that pierced a pipe during the original construction of the building. The failures caused water damage to two units. The association paid for the damage and submitted a claim to its liability insurer. The insurer invoked the "owned property exclusion." It argued that the exclusion applied because the unit owners whose property was damaged were insured under the policy, and they owned and occupied the damaged property. The unit owners were insureds under a typical endorsement under which individual unit owners are insureds, "but only for liability arising out of the ownership, maintenance or repair of that portion of the premises which is not reserved for that unit-owner's exclusive use or occupancy." The exclusion applies to property "you own, rent, or occupy," so the question was whether "you" referred to all insureds or only the named insured, which was the association. The insurer contended "you" encompassed all insureds. The association countered that, as is usually the case, the policy defined the pronoun "you" as the "named insured." The court said reasonable people could differ on whether use of the word "you" contemplated the individual unit owners named in the endorsement and, therefore, there was an ambiguity in the policy that it would construe against the carrier. It granted

441. *See* Far Northwest Dev. Co., LLC v. Cmty. Ass'n of Underwriters of Am., Inc., 2006 U.S. Dist. LEXIS 79033 (W.D. Wash. Oct. 30, 2006) (condominium association does not own or occupy common elements and coverage could not, therefore, be precluded on basis of property damage exclusion where association was named insured). *See also* Willing v. Cmty. Ass'n Underwriters of Am., Inc., 2007 U.S. Dist. LEXIS 48543 (W.D. Wash. July 5, 2007) (rejecting argument that association owned and occupied common property because it held "incidents of ownership" including obligation to maintain, repair, and insure common elements and finding owned property exclusion inapplicable because condominium was not property owned by association).

442. *See* § 10.02[2], *supra*.

443. *See* Willing v. Cmty. Ass'n Underwriters of Am., Inc., 2007 U.S. Dist. LEXIS 48543 (W.D. Wash. July 5, 2007) (suggesting in *dicta* that association could occupy property by maintaining offices on premises).

summary judgment to the association and awarded damages to it in the amount it paid to repair the units.[444]

[C] Separation of Insureds Clause

The standard commercial general liability policy includes a "separation of insureds" clause, also called a "severability of interests" clause. It provides that, except with respect to the Limits of Insurance, and any rights or duties specifically assigned to the first named insured, the coverage applies as if each named insured were the only one, and separately to each insured against whom a claim is made or a suit is brought.[445] The clause could be significant for a community association that has a claim for damage to its property when there is more than one *named insured* on the policy. For example, a community association management company might be a named insured along with the association. If an employee of the management company damages association property while on the premises, and the association makes a claim against the company for the repair of the property, the policy would initially appear to exclude coverage. That is because the exclusion proscribes coverage for damage to property "you"—that is, the named insured—own, rent, or occupy. However, when the separation of insureds clause is read in conjunction with that exclusion, the *management company* would have coverage because "property you own" means only property owned by the company and not the property owned by the association. That is because the exclusion would be read as if the management company were the only named insured under the policy.[446]

---

444. 1300 Alki Condo. Owners Ass'n v. Hartford Cas. Ins. Co., 2004 U.S. Dist. LEXIS 32398 (W.D. Wash. Oct. 22, 2004). *See also* Ass'n of Apt. Owners of the Moorings v. Dongbu Ins. Co., 2016 U.S. Dist. LEXIS 110283 (D. Haw. Aug. 18, 2016) (damage to individual unit caused by failure of association to repair and maintain common element lanai roof resulting in water damage to interior of unit constituted property damage and that damage was "property damage" to which insurance applied; no discussion of exclusion). *And see* Cambridge Mut. Fire Ins. Co. v. 1347-49 N. Sedgwick Condo. Ass'n, 2013 U.S. Dist. LEXIS 9750 (N.D. Ill. Jan. 23, 2013), where a unit owner sued the association because of sewage backups that damaged its unit and were allegedly caused by inadequate and improperly maintained common element plumbing. The insurer denied coverage because the complaint did not allege an accident and because it contended an intentional acts exclusion applied. That fact that it did not raise the property damage exclusion suggests it may not have believed it was applicable, although the liability policy was a Business Owners Liability Coverage Form, so is also possible that any property damage exclusion was different from that in the standard CGL policy and, therefore, inapplicable.

445. *See, e.g.*, ISO Form CG 00 01 12 07, § IV.7.

446. Based on hypothetical in Bobotek, *Are You a "You"? Don't Ignore CGL Policies' Separation of Insureds Clause* (May 2, 2016), available at: http://www.policyholderpulse.com/2016/05/02/dont-ignore-cgl-policies-separation-insureds-clause/.

[ii] Other Categories of Property

There are five other categories of property damage that are excluded from coverage. Property damage to premises the named insured sells, gives away, or abandons is proscribed if the property damage arises out of any part of those premises.[447] The exclusion does not apply if the premises are the work of the named insured[448] and were never occupied, rented, or held for rental by the named insured.

Damage to property loaned to the named insured is not covered.[449] However, the exclusion does not apply to property damage, other than by fire, to premises, including the contents of those premises, rented to the named insured for seven or fewer consecutive days.[450]

Coverage is excluded for damage to *personal* property in the care, custody, or control of the insured. [451] This exclusion, however, is inapplicable to property damage, other than by fire, to premises, including the contents of those premises, rented to the named insured for seven or fewer consecutive days.[452]

Coverage for property damage to the particular part of real property on which the named insured, or any contractors or subcontractors working directly or indirectly on its behalf are performing operations, is excluded if that property damage arises out of those operations. [453] The exclusion was inapplicable where a builder sought coverage for damage suffered to the property of an adjacent condominium association.[454] It also did not apply to incidental damages to items

447. *See, e.g.*, ISO Form CG 00 01 12 07, § I.2.j.(2).

448. The work of the named insured is referred to as "your work" and is defined as work or operations performed by the named insured or on its behalf and materials, parts, or equipment furnished in connection with the work or operations. *See, e.g.*, ISO Form CG 00 01 12 07, § V.22. One court, faced with determining the scope of an association's operations first turned to its Covenants, Conditions, and Restrictions, which it said provided the greatest amount of information about what was considered to be the "operations" of the association. It also examined the bylaws. The court also considered a state statute that provided a homeowners association was responsible for repairing, replacing, or maintaining the common area. Phila. Indem. Ins. Co. v. Lakeside Heights Homeowners Ass'n, 110 F. Supp. 3d 965, 971–72, 975 (N.D. Cal. 2015).

449. *See, e.g.*, ISO Form CG 00 01 12 07, § I.2.j.(3).

450. *See* A ISO Form CG 00 01 12 07, § III.6 regarding separate limits of insurance applied to damage to premises rented to the named insured.

451. *See, e.g.*, ISO Form CG 00 01 12 07, § I.2.j.(4).

452. *See* A ISO Form CG 00 01 12 07, § III.6 regarding separate limits of insurance applied to damage to premises rented to the named insured.

453. *See, e.g.*, ISO Form CG 00 01 12 07, § I.2.j.(5). *See also* Oak Ford Owners Ass'n v. Auto-Owners Ins. Co., 510 F. Supp. 2d 812 (M.D. Fla. 2007) (exclusion applies to property damage *arising from and during* performance of operations and does not apply to off-premises property damage arising from *completed* work).

454. Toldt Woods Condos. Owner's Ass'n v. Madeline Square, LLC, 314 Wis. 2d 259, 757 N.W.2d 850 (2008) (builder claimed coverage for damages on adjacent property that arose out of construction on builder's property; allegations were not limited to property on which builder was performing operations, and damage to property exclusion was not applicable to third-party property damage claim).

in a unit that a condominium association did not undertake to repair.[455] Finally, where a common interest community association dredged a creek and deposited the fill on the creek bank, the exclusion applied because the property damage to the creek and its bank arose out of performance of dredging operations by the named insured, the association.[456]

There is no coverage for property damage for the particular part of any property that has to be restored, repaired, or replaced because the work of the named insured was incorrectly performed on it.[457] The work of the named insured is referred to as "your work" and is defined as work or operations performed by the named insured or on its behalf and as materials, parts, or equipment furnished in connection with the work or operations.[458] This part of the exclusion does not apply to property damage included in the "products-completed operations hazard."[459]

[c] Electronic Data

Damages that arise out of the loss of, loss of use of, damage to, corruption of, inability to access, or inability to manipulate electronic data are excluded.[460] "Electronic data" is defined as information, facts, or programs stored as or on, created or used on, or transmitted to or from computer software. It includes systems and applications software, hard or floppy disks, CD-ROMS, tapes, drives, cells, data processing devices, or any other media used with electronically controlled

455. Commodore Plaza Condo. Ass'n v. QBE Ins. Corp., 2013 U.S. Dist. LEXIS 192675 (S.D. Fla. May 20, 2013) (claims in underlying complaint for alleged damages to personal property, HVAC components, interior doors and frames, components of electrical system, components of plumbing system, kitchen countertop materials, cabinets, bookshelves, appliances, vanities, wall mirrors and materials underneath, bathroom tile and materials underneath, kitchen tile and materials underneath, and drywall and associated materials would not be excluded by property damage exclusion because neither association—or its contractors and subcontractors—undertook to repair damage to roof, windows, and screens and exclusion did not exclude damages to any property on which insured was not performing work).

456. Oak Ford Owners Ass'n v. Auto-Owners Ins. Co., 510 F. Supp. 2d 812 (M.D. Fla. 2007) (existence of coverage turned on whether damage arose out of ongoing or completed work; insurer contended damage occurred during dredging while insured argued negative environmental impact occurred after work was completed and exclusion did not apply; court found dredging and removing of the fill, which constituted property damage, occurred during project and, therefore, property damage to creek arose during dredging operations and costs incurred were excluded from coverage).

457. *See, e.g.*, ISO Form CG 00 01 12 07, § I.2.j.(6).

458. *See, e.g.*, ISO Form CG 00 01 12 07, § V.22.

459. *See* Phila. Indem. Ins. Co. v. Lakeside Heights Homeowners Ass'n, 110 F. Supp. 3d 965, 977 (N.D. Cal. 2015) (agreeing with insurer that purpose of products-completed operations hazard provision is to allow coverage for damage arising under exclusion j, which precludes recovery for damages arising from incorrect work and that products-completed operations hazard provision dictates when subcontractor exception to faulty-workmanship exclusion applies).

460. *See, e.g.*, ISO Form CG 00 01 12 07, § I.2.p.

equipment. Commercial *property* policies may include electronic data coverage as additional coverage.[461] Under electronic data coverage, an insurer will pay the cost to replace or restore electronic data that has been destroyed or corrupted by a covered cause of loss.[462] Associations concerned about coverage for electronic data coverage should discuss it with their broker.

§ 13.05 Products-Completed Operations Hazard

One confusing coverage is "products-completed operations hazard" (PCOH).[463] Not only is it complex and its application the subject of much disagreement among the courts, but also it is not readily apparent from a quick review of the standard commercial general liability policy. It is also often excluded from insurance policies.[464]

[1] Finding the Products-Completed Operations Hazard Coverage

In the typical commercial general liability policy three coverages are clearly marked and placed in their own sections: bodily injury and property damage (Coverage A), personal and advertising injury liability (Coverage B), and medical payments (Coverage C). PCOH coverage is not so easily found. There is no single section of CGL policies that specifically explains the coverage.[465] Courts agree that PCOH is part of the standard CGL policy,[466] but where is it? To find the coverage, one must look in at least four different places. First, the Declarations Page typically has a box labeled "Limits of Insurance." In that box, there will be a row that reads "products-completed operations aggregate limit." Next to it will be a line that, if products-completed operations hazard coverage applies, will be filled in with the word "included."

Next, products-completed operations hazard is mentioned in the exclusion of coverage for property damage for the particular part of any property that has

461. *See* § 10.16[6], *supra*.

462. *See, e.g.*, ISO Form CP 00 17 06 07, § A.4.f.(2); ISO Form CP 00 10 06 07, § A.4.f.(2).

463. Stanovich, *The Hazards of Products and Completed Operations: Understanding the Fundamentals* (IRMI 2006), available at: https://www.irmi.com/articles/expert-commentary/the-hazards-of-products-and-completed-operations (any type of coherent explanation as to how PCOH coverage actually works is usually lacking).

464. Phila. Indem. Ins. Co. v. Lakeside Heights Homeowners Ass'n, 110 F. Supp. 3d 965, 977 (N.D. Cal. 2015) (association emphasized that it specifically purchased PCOH coverage).

465. Kneisel & Cooke, *The Products-Completed Operations Hazard: When Coverage Exists, Just What Is Covered?*, 2009 Construction Law Update § 6.02 (Aspen Publishers, Inc. 2009).

466. *See, e.g.*, Am. Home Assur. Co. v. AGM Marine Contractors, Inc., 379 F. Supp. 2d 134, 137 (D. Mass. 2005), *aff'd*, 467 F.3d 810 (1st Cir. 2006) (PCOH, when properly construed as subpart of entire policy, describes coverage within policy for same type of injuries or damages covered by rest of policy; nothing in PCOH provision dispenses with requirement that occurrence cause damage).

to be restored, repaired, or replaced because the work of the named insured was incorrectly performed on it.[467] The exclusion then says it is inapplicable to property damage included in the "products-completed operations hazard."[468] There are two other exclusions that mention the PCOH. First, there is an exclusion to property damage coverage to the work of the named insured arising out of it or any part of it, and included in the products-completed operations hazard, but the exclusion is inapplicable if the damaged work or the work out of which the damage arises was performed on behalf of the named insured by a subcontractor.[469] Second, there is an exclusion for medical payments coverage for expenses for bodily injury included within the "products-completed operations hazard."[470]

The products-completed operations hazard is also mentioned in the section on "Limits of Insurance." The general aggregate limit shown on the Declarations Page is the most the carrier will pay for the total of medical expenses (Coverage C), bodily injury, or property damage (Coverage A) other than for damages because of bodily injury or property damage that is included in the products-completed operations hazard and personal and advertising injury (Coverage B).[471] The PCOH aggregate limit shown on the Declarations Page is the most the carrier will pay for damages because of bodily injury and property damage included in the products-completed operations hazard.[472]

Finally, the definitions section of the standard CGL policy has a definition of "products-completed operations hazard."[473]

[2] The Definition of Products-Completed Operations Hazard

The phrase "products-completed operations hazard" is defined in the standard commercial general liability policy. Under the definition it includes bodily injury and property damage that occurs away from premises the named insured owns

467. *See, e.g.*, ISO Form CG 00 01 12 07, § I.2.j.(6).

468. *See* Phila. Indem. Ins. Co. v. Lakeside Heights Homeowners Ass'n, 110 F. Supp. 3d 965, 977 (N.D. Cal. 2015) (agreeing with insurer that purpose of products-completed operations hazard provision is to allow coverage for damage arising under exclusion j, which precludes recovery for damages arising from incorrect work and that products-completed operations hazard provision dictates when subcontractor exception to faulty-workmanship exclusion applies).

469. *See, e.g.*, ISO Form CG 00 01 12 07, § I.2.l.

470. *See, e.g.*, ISO Form CG 00 01 12 07, § I.C.2.f.

471. *See, e.g.*, CG 00 01 12 07, § III.2.

472. *See, e.g.*, CG 00 01 12 07, § III.3.

473. *See, e.g.*, ISO Form CG 00 01 12 07, § V.16.

or rents,[474] and arising out of "your work" or "your product."[475] "Your work" is work or *operations* performed by the named insured or on its behalf and materials, parts, or equipment furnished in connection with that work or operations and also includes warranties or representations made at any time regarding the fitness, quality, durability, performance, or use of the work and providing of or failure to provide warnings or instructions.[476] "Operations" performed by the named insured is an important part of the definition of "your work." What constitutes the "operations" of a common interest community? One court, faced with determining the scope of an association's operations, first turned to its Covenants, Conditions, and Restrictions, which it said provided the greatest amount of information about what was considered to be the "operations" of the association. It also examined the bylaws and considered a state statute that provided a homeowners association was responsible for repairing, replacing, or maintaining the common area.[477]

"Your product" is defined to mean any goods or products, other than real property, manufactured, sold, handled, distributed, or disposed of by the named insured, others trading under the name of the named insured, or a person or organization whose business or assets the named insured has acquired, and containers—other than vehicles—materials, parts, or equipment furnished in connection with those goods or products. It also includes warranties or

474. Stanovich, *The Hazards of Products and Completed Operations: Understanding the Fundamentals* (IRMI 2006), available at: https://www.irmi.com/articles/expert-commentary/the-hazards-of-products-and-completed-operations (bodily injury or property damage that takes place on named insured premises is not within products-completed operations hazard although that can be amended by endorsement called "Products-Completed Operations Hazard Redefined"—ISO Form CG 24 07—which changes definition by removing requirement that bodily injury or property damage take place away from premises of named insured for claim to be included within products-completed operations hazard).

475. *See, e.g.*, ISO Form CG 00 01 12 07, § V.16. There are exceptions for products still in the physical possession of the named insured and work abandoned or not yet completed. Work that may need service, maintenance, correction, repair, or replacement, but is otherwise complete, is treated as completed. Products-completed operations hazard does not include bodily injury or property damage that arises out of transportation of property, unless injury or damage arises out of a condition in or on a vehicle not owned or operated by the named insured, and that condition was created by loading or unloading of that vehicle by any insured. It also does not include injury arising out of the existence of tools, uninstalled equipment, or abandoned or unused materials. A final exception is for products or operations for which the classification, listed on the Declarations Page or in a policy schedule, states that products-completed operations are subject to the general aggregate limit. *See* Goodwin v. Wright, 100 Wn. App. 631, 635–36, 6 P.3d 1, 4 (2000) (purpose of products-completed operations hazard coverage is to insure against the risk that the product or work, if defective, may cause bodily injury or damage to property of others after it leaves hands of insured).

476. *See, e.g.*, ISO Form CG 00 01 12 07, § V.22.

477. Phila. Indem. Ins. Co. v. Lakeside Heights Homeowners Ass'n, 110 F. Supp. 3d 965, 971–72, 975 (N.D. Cal. 2015).

representations made at any time regarding the fitness, quality, durability, performance, or use of the product and providing or failing to provide warnings or instructions, but does not include vending machines or other property rented to or located for the use of others but not sold.[478]

[3] Common Interest Communities and Products-Completed Operations Hazard

Ordinarily, one might think of products-completed operations hazard coverage as being for the benefit of manufacturers and contractors.[479] However, one expert commentary recommends common interest community associations should consider the coverage if they make or sell products—for example, crafts, food, or beverages[480]—have an in-unit maintenance service program, or perform work for others.[481] The coverage might apply in other circumstances. For instance, a homeowners association governing board approved a project to dredge over three miles of a creek in an attempt to alleviate flooding to individual properties in the community. Members of the association performed the work without any contractors or subcontractors. It turned out that the project violated regulations prohibiting removal of fill and placement of fill in wetland areas and tree lines. The association settled with the regulatory agencies and agreed to a costly restoration plan. It sought coverage from its liability carrier for sums for which it became liable as a result of the dredging project. The insurer contended three exclusions barred coverage. One of them was the exclusion of coverage for property damage for the particular part of any property that has to be restored, repaired, or replaced because the work of the named insured was incorrectly performed. That is the exclusion to which products-completed operations hazard is an exception. The court found the exception applied because it was undisputed that the work on the creek was completed when the association stopped dredging it. The court agreed that the exclusion, but for the PCOH coverage, would proscribe coverage for property damage to the creek for which restoration was required; however, the PCOH provided an exception to that exclusion when property damage arose

478. *See, e.g.*, ISO Form CG 00 01 12 07, § V.21.

479. *See, e.g.*, 3 *New Appleman Law of Liability Insurance* § 16.02[2][a] (Matthew Bender, 2016) (noting that most manufacturers' and general contractors' high-dollar losses fall within scope of products-completed operations hazard).

480. But note that food consumed on the premises of the named insured would not be included within the products-completed operations hazard. Stanovich, *The Hazards of Products and Completed Operations: Understanding the Fundamentals* (IRMI 2006), available at: https://www.irmi.com/articles/expert-commentary/the-hazards-of-products-and-completed-operations (bodily injury or property damage that takes place on named insured premises is not within products-completed operations hazard although that can be changed by endorsement).

481. Treese & Rosenberry, *Insurance: How Community Associations Protect Themselves*, at 45 (CAI Press 2013).

out of completed work. Unfortunately for the association, another exclusion did apply.

The PCOH, however, is not a broad grant of coverage. A California homeowners association attempted to bring a claim under the products-completed operations hazard coverage. The HOA and owners of property within the community sued a county government over a landslide, subsidence, and earth movement that damaged the property of the HOA and the individual owners. The county cross-claimed against the HOA and owners for, *inter alia*, negligence based on its private irrigation system. The county contended the system produced excessive overwatering and/or irrigation leaks that saturated the property and that it was improperly repaired. The irrigation system, said the county, was a substantial factor in causing the damages. The HOA sought coverage from its commercial general liability carrier. The insurer invoked a "subsidence" exclusion providing the policy did not apply to property damage caused by, resulting from, attributable or contributed to, or aggravated by the subsidence of land as a result of landslide, mudflow, earth sinking, or shifting resulting from operations of the named insured. The HOA, on the other hand, argued there was products-completed operations coverage for any negligent past performance of irrigation repair work. The subsidence exclusion, according to the HOA, did not exclude the broader range of potential liabilities insured against by PCOH coverage. The insurer responded that the purpose of the PCOH provision is to allow coverage for damage arising under the exclusion that otherwise precludes recovery for damages arising from incorrect work. The court agreed with the insurer and noted that the HOA failed to explain how the PCOH provision applied to override the subsidence exclusion. The language of the subsidence exclusion was clear, said the court, and unlike the incorrect work exclusion, it did not mention that it was subject to the products-completed operations hazard.[482]

§ 13.06 Personal and Advertising Injury Liability (Coverage B)

Coverage B under a standard commercial general liability policy provides coverage for "personal and advertising injury liability."[483] Coverage B has been described as "inarguably far more complicated" than Coverage A for bodily injury and property damage.[484]

A "personal and advertising injury" is defined as an injury arising out of one or more of seven specified "offenses."[485] Those offenses are false arrest, detention,

482. Phila. Indem. Ins. Co. v. Lakeside Heights Homeowners Ass'n, 110 F. Supp. 3d 965 (N.D. Cal. 2015).

483. *See, e.g.*, CG 00 01 12 07, § I.B.

484. Dykes, *Send in the B Team: Insurance Coverage for Personal and Advertising Injury*, 27 Utah Bar J. 24, 25 (2014).

485. Many courts say that the word "offense" does not limit coverage to a particular cause of action or claim. *See, e.g.*, McCormack Baron Mgmt. Servs., Inc. v. American Guar. & Liab. Ins.

or imprisonment; malicious prosecution; wrongful eviction from, wrongful entry into, or invasion of the right of private occupancy; slander, libel, or trade disparagement; violation of the right of another to privacy; use of the advertising idea of someone else; and infringement of the copyright, trade dress, or slogan of someone else.[486] The Massachusetts Supreme Judicial Court explained that within insurance law, "bodily injury" and "personal injury" are not synonymous. The latter is broader and includes not only physical injury but also "any affront or insult to the reputation or sensibilities of a person."[487]

Under standard CGL policy, the carrier will pay the amount the insured becomes legally obligated to pay as damages for a personal and advertising injury.[488] The policy provides that the carrier has the duty to defend the insured against a suit seeking those damages but does not have to defend any suit to which the insurance does not apply. It also states that the carrier may investigate any offense and settle any resulting claim or suit. A "suit" is a civil proceeding, including arbitration, to which the insured is either required to consent or submits with the consent of the carrier and any other alternative dispute resolution proceeding in which damages are claimed and to which the insured submits with the consent of the carrier.[489]

The typical policy adds several caveats to the coverage. First, the amount the carrier will pay for damages is limited as described in the section in the policy

Co., 989 S.W.2d 168 (Mo. 1999) (term "offense" does not restrict coverage to specific formal causes of action or claims and did not defeat right to defense where insured was sued for statements alleging "insubordination" of employee and asking that employer fire that employee).

486. *See, e.g.*, CG 00 01 12 07, § V.14. *Consider* Sova v. Cove Homeowner's Ass'n, 102 So. 3d 863, 872 (La. App. 2012) (claims of harassment and invasion of privacy and allegations suggesting malicious prosecution and slander would not be subject to coverage as "advertising injury" as claims for advertising injury require that occurrence that caused injury be committed in course of advertising good, product, or service of association). *See also* State Farm Fire & Cas. Co. v. Metro. Mgmt., 2007 U.S. Dist. LEXIS 99406 (D. Haw. Oct. 31, 2007) (to be covered, "advertising injury" has to occur in course of advertising insured's products or services; where condominium association sued its management company for breach of contract, breach of the duty of good faith and fair dealing, and breach of fiduciary duty and also sought declaration that it was entitled to terminate management contract, none of its allegations involved any tort defined in policy as personal injury and, therefore, coverage for personal injury was not implicated).

487. Allstate Ins. Co. v. Diamant, 401 Mass. 654, 518 N.E.2d 1154 (1988).

488. *See, e.g.*, CG 00 01 12 07, § I.B.1.a. In an unpublished California opinion, condominium unit owners argued a special assessment levied by the association to pay a judgment against it constituted damages. The court, however, said that the duty of a carrier to indemnify its insured for sums the insured becomes legally obligated to pay as damages is limited to money judgments imposed by courts against the insured. The unit owners, noted the court, were not named as parties in the enforcement proceedings that resulted in the special assessment against them, and the fact that their contract with the association required them to contribute to its debts did not mean that a special assessment imposed for that purpose was a sum they were "legally obligated to pay as damages," as that term is defined in the standard commercial general liability policy. The Le Parc Cases, 2004 Cal. App. Unpub. LEXIS 4272 (Apr. 29, 2004).

489. *See, e.g.*, CG 00 01 12 07, § V.18.

titled "Limits of Insurance."[490] That section says the amount stated on the Declarations Page and the rules of the section establish the maximum amount the carrier will pay. Second, the policy provides that the right and duty of the carrier to defend end when it has used up the applicable limit of insurance in the payment of judgments or settlements.[491] Third, coverage applies to personal and advertising injury caused by an offense arising out of the "business" of the insured,[492] but only if it was committed in the "coverage territory" and during the policy period.[493] The basic coverage territory is the United States and its territories and possessions, Puerto Rico, and Canada, but may include international waters or airspace,[494] or in some cases anywhere in the world.[495]

[1] False Arrest, Detention, or Imprisonment

The first of the personal and advertising injuries for which coverage is provided is false arrest, detention, or imprisonment.[496] False imprisonment is a common-law tort. Generally, a person is liable for false imprisonment when he or she acts intending to confine someone else within boundaries he or she fixes, the act directly or indirectly results in the confinement of that person,[497] and that

490. *See, e.g.*, CG 00 01 12 07, § I.B.1.a.(1).

491. *See, e.g.*, CG 00 01 12 07, § I.B.1.a.(2).

492. The Declarations Page of a CGL policy will have a place that states the "business description" of the insured, which, in the case of a condominium, will be "condominium association." What is the "business" of a condominium or any common interest community? *Consider* Maffeo v. Harbour Landing Condominium Ass'n, 1994 Conn. Super. LEXIS 2968 (Nov. 22, 1994) (business of condominium development can be said to be residence and use of units and of common elements by unit owners; occupancy of unit reached by stairway that was part of common elements of development was a use connected with business purpose of association as possessor of that common area).

493. *See, e.g.*, CG 00 01 12 07, § I.B.1.b.

494. The coverage territory includes international waters or airspace, but only if the injury or damage occurs during travel or transportation between the United States and its territories and possessions, Puerto Rico, or Canada. *See, e.g.*, CG 00 01 12 07, § V.4.b.

495. The coverage territory includes any other part of the world if the injury or damage arises out of goods or products made or sold by the insured in the United States and its territories and possessions, Puerto Rico, or Canada, activities of a person whose home is in the United States and its territories and possessions, Puerto Rico, or Canada, but is away for a short time on the business of the insured; or a personal and advertising injury offense that take place through the Internet or similar electronic means of communication, provided the responsibility of the insured to pay damages is determined in a suit on the merits, in the United States and its territories and possessions, Puerto Rico, or Canada or in a settlement to which the carrier agrees. *See, e.g.*, CG 00 01 12 07, § V.4.c.

496. *See, e.g.*, CG 00 01 12 07, § V.14.a.

497. False imprisonment requires that any restraint be total, not mere obstruction of the right to go where the plaintiff pleases. Pine Cone Harbour Condo. Ass'n v. Nationwide Mut. Ins. Co., 1993 U.S. Dist. LEXIS 21429 (W.D. Va. Oct. 19, 1993), *aff'd*, 30 F.3d 130 (4th Cir. 1994). In *Pine Cone Harbour* the plaintiffs in the underlying action were unit owners who sued their condominium association alleging it violated fair housing laws by refusing to allow them to construct a wheelchair ramp to access their unit unless they also agreed to build an additional set of stairs. The association

person is conscious of the confinement or is harmed by it.[498] A citizen's arrest without lawful cause is actionable false imprisonment.[499] False arrest has been described as a species of false imprisonment,[500] and that is logical as any false arrest is a restraint of liberty, which is the crux of false imprisonment.[501] Common interest communities are sued for false imprisonment,[502] and the possibility of being sued for false arrest or false imprisonment probably increases in a community with security guards.[503] A false arrest, detention, or imprisonment can involve an assault or battery, coverage for which may be barred under an exclusion that may also limit the extent of the coverage for false arrest, detention, or imprisonment.[504]

---

sought coverage of the action as a false detention or imprisonment. The court, however, said that the allegations in the underlying complaint stated neither that the plaintiffs were detained against their will nor that they were imprisoned in their condominium unit. The complaint stated that the plaintiffs rarely left their home, but not that leaving was impossible and, therefore, the insurer had no duty to cover or defend.

498. Restatement (Second) of Torts, § 35(1).

499. *See* Moojedi v. Sierra Village Homeowners Ass'n, 2002 Cal. App. Unpub. LEXIS 10514 (Nov. 15, 2002) (although someone will be liable for false imprisonment if she has taken active part in bad faith to bring about unlawful arrest of another, bad faith is not an element of that tort; only mental state required to be shown to prove false imprisonment is intent to confine, or to create similar intrusion). *See also* Fraser v. County of Maui, 855 F. Supp. 1167 (D. Haw. 1994).

500. Mitchell v. City of Boston, 130 F. Supp. 2d 201, 214 (D. Mass. 2001).

501. False arrest and false imprisonment are sometimes combined. *See, e.g.*, Fraser v. County of Maui, 855 F. Supp. 1167, 1179 (D. Haw. 1994) (under Hawaii tort law, to maintain action for false arrest or false imprisonment plaintiff must show detention or restraint against one's will and unlawfulness of that detention or restraint); Moojedi v. Sierra Village Homeowners Ass'n, 2002 Cal. App. Unpub. LEXIS 10514 (Nov. 15, 2002) (third cause of action alleged false arrest and false imprisonment).

502. *See, e.g.*, Johnston v. Carriage House I-Enfield Ass'n, 2016 Conn. Super. LEXIS 1956 (Conn. Super. Ct. July 11, 2016) (plaintiff unit owners sued association for false imprisonment alleging their physical liberty was restrained against their will); Galpern v. Rizzo, 2011 N.Y. Misc. LEXIS 1217, 2011 NY Slip Op. 30691(U) (N.Y. Sup. Ct. Mar. 11, 2011) (condominium unit owners brought claim against association for false imprisonment because their handyman was arrested for trespassing while passing out leaflets at complex on their behalf). *See also* Radcliffe v. Avenel Homeowners Ass'n, 2013 U.S. Dist. LEXIS 21422 (E.D.N.C. Feb. 12, 2013) (resident sued homeowners association for, *inter alia*, false imprisonment). *And see* Martinez v. State Farm Lloyds, 2000 Tex. App. LEXIS 6008 (Tex. App.—Corpus Christi Aug. 31, 2000) (property manager sued resident of condominium for false imprisonment after he allegedly physically assaulted her in her office).

503. *See, e.g.*, Payne v. Parkchester N. Condos., 134 F. Supp. 2d 582, 583 (S.D.N.Y. 2001) (resident of condominium unit sued association for false arrest and imprisonment after incident in which building security guards pepper-sprayed, handcuffed, and arrested him); Hollender v. Trump Village Cooperative, Inc., 461 N.Y.S.2d 765, 58 N.Y.2d 420, 448 N.E.2d 432 (1983) (resident of housing cooperative sued cooperative corporation after security guards ordered group of young people of which she was a part to disperse and, when she objected, summoned police who, at insistence of one guard, placed her under arrest).

504. *Consider* 101 Ocean Condo. Homeowners Ass'n v. Century Sur. Co., 407 Fed. Appx. 129 (9th Cir. 2010), where a condominium resident sued the association alleging assault, battery, and negligence. The policy expressly excluded coverage when any actual or alleged injury arose out of any combination of an assault or battery-related cause and a non-assault or battery-related

[2] Malicious Prosecution

Personal and advertising injury encompasses an injury arising out of a "malicious prosecution."[505] Malicious prosecution is a common-law tort action that is one of three causes of action the Restatement of Torts groups under the classification of "unjustifiable litigation." It is defined by the Restatement as the initiation or procurement by a private person of the institution of criminal proceedings against another who is not guilty of the offense charged without probable cause and primarily for a purpose other than that of bringing an offender to justice and the proceedings terminate in favor of the accused.[506] It does not include judicially imposed sanctions for filing a frivolous lawsuit.[507]

A second form of unjustifiable litigation is called "wrongful use of civil proceedings" The Restatement describes it as taking an active part in the initiation, continuation, or procurement of civil proceedings against another without probable cause, and primarily for a purpose other than securing proper adjudication of the claim in which the proceedings are based and in which the proceedings terminated in favor of the person against whom they were brought except when they were *ex parte*.[508] As can be seen, malicious prosecution and wrongful use of civil proceedings are similar and indeed, in many states, the courts have in effect combined the two—usually under the appellation malicious prosecution—fully or partially.[509]

---

cause or any actual or alleged injury arose out of a chain of events that included assault or battery, regardless of whether assault or battery was the initial or precipitating event or a substantial cause of injury. The association argued the plaintiff in the underlying action *could* have asserted a false imprisonment claim on the facts alleged, and that the possibility of that claim gave rise to the potential for coverage under the policy and the carrier, therefore, had a duty to defend. The court was unimpressed. It said that under the plain language of the policy the insurer had no duty to defend when an independent cause of action, even if otherwise covered, was alleged in combination with an assault or battery claim and, even if false imprisonment had been alleged as a separate claim, that injury would have arisen out of a chain of events including an assault or battery, so the exclusion would apply.

505. *See, e.g.*, ISO Form CG 00 01 12 07, § V.14.b.

506. Restatement (Second) of Torts, § 653. *See* Hollender v. Trump Village Cooperative, Inc., 461 N.Y.S.2d 765, 58 N.Y.2d 420, 448 N.E.2d 432 (1983) (in malicious prosecution action, it is for one who brings suit to establish that criminal proceeding allegedly instigated by defendant terminated in favor of accused). *Consider* Sova v. Cove Homeowner's Ass'n, 102 So. 3d 863 (La. App. 2012) (when absence of malice is established, want of probable cause is negated and action for malicious prosecution will not lie; where party has communicated to counsel all facts bearing on case of which she has knowledge, or could have ascertained by reasonable diligence and inquiry, and has acted on advice received honestly and in good faith, there is no malicious prosecution; finding association relied on counsel).

507. William J. Templeman Co. v. Liberty Mut. Ins. Co. , 249 Ill. Dec. 65, 316 Ill. App. 3d 379, 735 N.E.2d 669 (2000).

508. Restatement (Second) of Torts, § 674.

509. *See, e.g.*, Jordan v. Deese, 317 S.C. 260, 452 S.E.2d 838 (1995) (malicious prosecution involves institution or continuation of original judicial proceedings, either civil or criminal); Hubbard v. Beatty & Hyde, Inc., 343 Mass. 258, 178 N.E.2d 485 (1961) (improper institution of

The third form of unjustifiable litigation is called "abuse of process." It is defined as the use of a legal process, whether criminal or civil, against another primarily to accomplish a purpose for which it is not designed.[510] It is often confused with malicious prosecution and, in fact, is sometimes referred to as "malicious abuse of process."[511] However, abuse of process applies to misuse of the legal process after it has been issued as compared to malicious prosecution, which is malice in causing the process to issue.[512]

Even where there is a clear distinction between the three actions, the elements that define each of them and the defenses to them will vary from state to state. To further confuse matters, courts are divided over what coverage for "malicious prosecution" means in commercial general liability policies. Some courts hold that "malicious prosecution" is unambiguous and only a suit for that offense as defined in state law is covered by the policy.[513] Other courts find that the term "malicious prosecution" as used in the standard commercial general liability policy is ambiguous and construe it in favor of coverage because, as the federal Ninth Circuit Court of Appeal said, "[t]here is no reason, given the overlap between malicious prosecution and abuse of process . . . why persons who purchase insurance covering the cost of defending against the one claim would not also expect the contract to cover the cost of defending against the other."[514]

bankruptcy proceedings); Nassif v. Goodman, 203 N.C. 451, 166 S.E. 308 (1932) (action for malicious prosecution of civil action will not lie unless there is seizure of property or some special damage).

510. Restatement (Second) of Torts, § 682.

511. *See, e.g.*, Sietins v. Joseph, 238 F.Supp.2d 366 (D. Mass. 2003); Wright v. Harris, 160 N.C. 542, 76 S.E. 489 (1912). The two actions, however, may actually be combined. *See* Hinkle v. State Farm Fire & Cas. Co., 308 P.3d 1009, 1013 (N.M. App. 2013) (New Mexico Supreme Court combined abuse of process and malicious prosecution into single cause of action called malicious abuse of process).

512. *See* Barnette v. Woody, 242 N.C. 424, 88 S.E.2d 223 (1955). *See generally* Getzoff, *Dazed and Confused in Colorado: The Relationship Among Malicious Prosecution, Abuse of Process, and the Noerr-Pennington Doctrine*, 67 Colo. L. Rev. 675 (1996); Bretz, *Abuse of Process—A Misunderstood Concept*, 20 Clev. St. L. Rev. 401 (1971).

513. *See* Parker Supply Co. v. Travelers Indem. Co., 588 F.2d 180, 182–83 (5th Cir. 1979) (Alabama recognizes differences between actions for malicious prosecution, abuse of process, and wrongful attachment or garnishment, and only suit against insured for offense of malicious prosecution would create obligation for insurer to defend and indemnify; no coverage where complaint in underlying suit stated action for abuse of process rather than for malicious prosecution); Heil Co. v. Hartford Accident & Indem. Co., 937 F. Supp. 1355 (E.D. Wis. 1996) (common-law torts of malicious prosecution and abuse of process are separate and distinct, and allegation of abuse of process is not synonymous with malicious prosecution; abuse of process is not enumerated as covered offense in policy and is defined differently than covered offense of malicious prosecution and complaint alleging former did not, therefore, trigger duty to defend insured).

514. Lunsford v. American Guar. & Liab. Ins. Co., 18 F.3d 653, 656 (9th Cir. 1994). *See also* Northwestern Nat'l Casualty Co. v. Century III Chevrolet, 863 F. Supp. 247 (W.D. Pa. 1994), where the court discussed the statutory replacement of the common-law cause of action of malicious prosecution with "wrongful use of civil proceedings," an action similar to the Restatement action by the same name. The court concluded an action under the statute would be covered by a policy

Additionally, California courts hold there is no obligation to indemnify *or defend* an insured in a claim for malicious prosecution because malice is an element of the tort and it is against the state's public policy to indemnify an insured against liability for his or her own willful wrong.[515] Other states do not have the same public policy, and their courts note that while the standard commercial liability policy excludes coverage for intentional acts, it also explicitly provides coverage for acts of malicious prosecution, an offense that requires proof of intent and that creates an inherent ambiguity construed in favor of coverage.[516]

Given the uncertainty over the scope of coverage and meaning of "malicious prosecution," both as used in commercial general liability policies and as interpreted under state law,[517] associations should discuss with their broker and attorney the extent of their potential liability and the scope of their coverage for it.

Common interest communities definitely have exposure to allegations of malicious prosecution or abuse of process because of legal actions they need to take. They generally are considered to have a fiduciary responsibility to enforce their documents and to collect assessments or maintenance fees, and to do so they may need to bring a legal action. That may result in either a counterclaim or a subsequent independent action.[518] Indeed, associations are frequently the subject of claims for malicious prosecution or abuse of process, although rarely with success, when they seek to collect past due assessments or maintenance fees.[519] The same claims may be brought when an association sues a unit owner

---

providing coverage for malicious prosecution. Even if the insurer were correct that the statutory and common-law actions were different, the court found ambiguity in the policy language. It said that had the insurer intended to limit coverage to claims of common-law malicious prosecution, it should have specified common-law malicious prosecution, not including statutory actions, and absent that language, the ambiguity would be construed in favor of the insureds.

515. State Farm Fire & Casualty Co. v. Drasin, 152 Cal. App. 3d 864, 867, 199 Cal. Rptr. 749, 751 (1984).

516. *See, e.g.*, Titan Indem. Co. v. Riley, 641 So. 2d 766 (Ala. 1994).

517. *See, e.g.*, Thompson v. Md. Cas. Co., 84 P.3d 496, 503 (Colo. 2004) (elements of malicious prosecution are defendant contributed to bringing prior action against plaintiff, prior action ended in favor of plaintiff, no probable cause, malice, and damages); QSP, Inc. v. Aetna Cas. & Sur. Co., 256 Conn. 343, 361, 773 A.2d 906, 919 (2001) (to bring action for malicious prosecution plaintiff must show initiation of action by defendant against plaintiff, action was instituted with malice, action was instituted without probable cause to believe it would succeed, and action terminated in plaintiff's favor; where there is a settlement, it is routine for courts to deny that lawsuit has terminated in favor or either party).

518. Note that a counterclaim for malicious prosecution is generally barred because of the requirement that the prior proceeding terminate in favor of the party that was the defendant in it. *See, e.g.*, Reichler v. Tillman, 21 N.C. App. 38, 203 S.E.2d 68 (1974).

519. *See, e.g.*, Dubois v. Ass'n of Apt. Owners, 453 F.3d 1175 (9th Cir. 2006) (unit owner alleged association was liable for abuse of process for initiating state proceedings against him to collect attorney's fees and to foreclose on his property, but court held association initiated those proceedings for their intended purpose); Neil v. Kovitz Shifrin Nesbit, 2014 U.S. Dist. LEXIS 136696 (N.D. Ill. Sept. 27, 2014) (in response to association's debt collection litigation, unit owner brought claim for abuse of process; because under Illinois law, claim for abuse of process can only proceed where

to enforce restrictive covenants.[520] A variety of other circumstances may lead to an action for malicious prosecution or abuse of process against a common interest community including a malpractice claim against the association attorney,[521]

plaintiff has suffered actual arrest or seizure of property—"special injury"—and plaintiff did not allege any special injury, abuse of process claim failed); Lautman v. 2800 Coyle St. Owners Corp., 2014 U.S. Dist. LEXIS 72703 (E.D.N.Y. May 23, 2014) (tenant/shareholder brought action against his landlord cooperative alleging malicious abuse of process and malicious prosecution in connection with allegedly unlawful attempts to collect rent and related fees from him; court found abuse of process claim failed to allege any improper purpose for initiation of the summary non-payment proceedings, but rather that cooperative initiated non-payment proceedings for purposes of claiming rent arrears and having plaintiff removed for failure to pay rent, which is precisely purpose for which those proceedings were created; malicious prosecution claim failed because cooperative's action did not terminate favorably to tenant/shareholder because cooperative voluntarily discontinued its action); Cohen v. Beachside Two-I Homeowners' Ass'n, 2005 U.S. Dist. LEXIS 28536 (D. Minn. Nov. 17, 2005), *aff'd*, 272 Fed. Appx. 534; 2008, *cert. den.*, 555 U.S. 945, 129 S. Ct. 417, 172 L. Ed. 2d 288 (2008) (refusing to allow unit owner to add claim of abuse of process against association based on assertion that collection of unauthorized fees was clear purpose of foreclosure action because unit owner presented no evidence to support that collection of fees was ulterior motive behind foreclosure action); Kurtz v. Hubbard, 362 Ill. Dec. 528, 973 N.E.2d 924 (Ill. App. 2012) (condominium unit owner filed suit against association for, *inter alia*, malicious prosecution relating to "wrongfully" recording lien against title to her home); Lakeshore View Homeowners' Ass'n v. Tu, 2010 Cal. App. Unpub. LEXIS 6540 (Cal. App. Aug. 17, 2010) (where association filed suit against unit owner for foreclosure of lien, breach of Covenants, Conditions, and Restrictions, unit owner filed cross-complaint for, *inter alia*, abuse of process); 25 Van Zant St. Condo., Inc. v. Calvary Chapel of Norwalk, Inc., 2010 Conn. Super. LEXIS 1518 (Conn. Super. June 22, 2010) (where association brought action to foreclosure lien based on failure of unit owner to pay various common charges, assessments, fees, interest, and penalties, unit owner counterclaimed alleging abuse of process in that association commenced foreclosure action as result of personal *animus* and/or desire for retribution; court held that allegation of personal *animus*, spite, or desire for retribution, even when viewed in its most favorable light, failed to establish that primary purpose of foreclosure action was anything other than securing foreclosure to satisfy debts owed—proper purpose under law—and, thus, counterclaim was insufficient as matter of law); Meadows Condo. Ass'n v. Redman, 2009 Conn. Super. LEXIS 2062 (Conn. Super. July 30, 2009) (where association brought foreclosure action against unit owner to recover unpaid condominium fees and charges, unit owner counterclaimed for "vexatious litigation"); Sydney Warburton v. Feldsott, 2007 Cal. App. Unpub. LEXIS 5361 (Cal. App. June 29, 2007) (unit owners unsuccessfully brought actions for abuse of process and malicious prosecution against association attorneys and property manager for allegedly "unwarranted" collection action); Valois, Inc. v. Thorne, 86 A.2d 530 (Ct. App. D.C. 1951) (where cooperative corporation brought suit against resident alleging she was in default in payment of rent, she counterclaimed for malicious abuse of process).

520. *See, e.g.*, Ritchey v. Villa Nueva Condominium Ass'n, 81 Cal. App. 3d 688, 146 Cal. Rptr. 695 (Cal. App. 1978) (where association brought suit against unit owner for violation of bylaw restricting occupancy to persons 18 years of age and older, unit owner subsequently commenced action seeking damages for malicious prosecution and abuse of process).

521. *See, e.g.*, Guerrero v. Windsor Square Homeowners Ass'n, 2001 Cal. App. Unpub. LEXIS 1426 (Cal. App. Nov. 21, 2001) (after association sued its former attorney for legal malpractice, attorney then sued association for malicious prosecution and abuse of process; court found for association on both claims).

disagreements with the developer,[522] zoning challenges,[523] and actual criminal prosecutions.[524]

[3] Wrongful Eviction or Entry

Personal and advertising injury includes "wrongful eviction" from, "wrongful entry" into, or invasion of the right of private occupancy of a room, dwelling, or premises that a *person occupies*,[525] that is committed by or on behalf of the owner, landlord, or lessor of those premises.[526]

[a] Wrongful Eviction

In the narrowest sense "wrongful eviction" would mean ouster of a tenant by a landlord from leased premises in violation of the applicable state laws governing eviction.[527] The California Supreme Court has recognized the tort of "wrongful eviction," which it describes as a breach of the covenant of quiet enjoyment

522. *See, e.g.*, Green Trees Dev. v. Silver Meadows Condo. Ass'n, 1999 Conn. Super. LEXIS 2438 (Conn. Super. Sept. 8, 1999) (developer sued homeowners association alleging that filing of *lis pendens* was for improper purpose and constituted abuse of process; court found that developer failed to allege any specific facts that association filed *lis pendens* for primary purpose other than that which it was intended to accomplish or that it falsely represented any fact to public or that it was filed improperly; when process is used for legal purpose intended, ulterior motive to obtain incidental benefit is excluded from definition of process abuse).

523. *See, e.g.*, Anchorage Joint Venture v. Anchorage Condominium Ass'n, 670 P.2d 1249 (Colo. App. 1983) (where association sought judicial review of variance granted to nearby property, but complaint was dismissed for failure to join indispensable party, and appellant subsequently brought action against association for, *inter alia*, abuse of process, court held association had constitutionally protected right to institute its proceeding).

524. *See, e.g.*, Payne v. Parkchester N. Condos., 134 F. Supp. 2d 582, 583 (S.D.N.Y. 2001) (resident of condominium sued association for malicious prosecution after incident in which building security guards pepper-sprayed, handcuffed, and arrested him); Fraser v. County of Maui, 855 F. Supp. 1167 (D. Haw. 1994) (condominium unit owner sued her association over her citizen's arrest by resident manager of association; court found manager had probable cause and that there was no evidence that she was brought before official or tribunal whose function it was to determine whether she was guilty of harassment or whether she would be held for a later determination of guilt or innocence).

525. Courts generally hold that use of the word "person" means there is no coverage for a claim by an organization. *See, e.g.*, 47 Mamaroneck Ave. Corp. v. Hartford Fire Ins. Co., 50 A.D.3d 952, 857 N.Y.S.2d 610 (2008) (where plaintiff in underlying action was corporation, not natural person, any invasion of its leasehold was not covered by definition of personal and advertising injury); Mirpad, LLC v. California Ins. Guarantee Ass'n, 132 Cal. App. 4th 1058, 34 Cal. Rptr. 3d 136 (2005) (no coverage for claim for wrongful eviction of organizations—for example, corporation—because coverage is only extended under policy to claim by natural person).

526. *See, e.g.*, ISO Form CG 00 01 12 07, § V.14.c.

527. *See, e.g.*, Titan Holdings Syndicate, Inc. v. City of Keene, 898 F.2d 265, 272 (1st Cir. 1990) (action not properly considered one for wrongful eviction where there was no allegation of tenant-landlord relationship).

accomplished by "intentionally annoying acts" designed to force a tenant to vacate.[528] Courts also describe the phrase as meaning "a claim based on the removal of a person who asserts a right to occupy particular premises,"[529] or a non-trespassory invasion of the interest of another in the private use and enjoyment of land.[530] Some courts view "wrongful eviction" broadly. For example, an Arkansas court reviewed a case in which an African-American female was barred from playing tennis at a country club. She brought a civil rights action against the club, which turned to its commercial general liability for coverage. The insurer argued there was no coverage under the "wrongful eviction" clause of the policy because the term is limited to interference with the enjoyment of property by a tenant and the plaintiff in the underlying action was a mere licensee and not a tenant. Thus, no eviction occurred and no duty to defend arose under the policy. The court disagreed because it concluded the word "eviction" was ambiguous as used in the policy. Construing the word liberally in favor of the insured and strictly against the insurer, the court held the underlying complaint sufficiently stated a cause of action within the policy coverage to give rise to a duty to defend.[531] While the acts described in most cases would be considered intentional, the Alaska Supreme Court said that where intentional acts are excluded and wrongful eviction is covered, the exclusion is inapplicable because a wrongful eviction may be either intentional or unintentional.[532]

[b] Constructive Eviction

The elements of constructive eviction have been described as causing premises to become untenantable as the result of malfeasance or nonfeasance, abandonment of the premises because of their unsatisfactory condition, and a reasonable opportunity was provided to correct the problem before the plaintiff abandoned

528. Barkett v. Brucato, 122 Cal. App. 2d 264, 264 P.2d 978 (Cal. App. 1953). *See also* Barragan v. Deutsche Bank Nat'l Trust Co., 2015 U.S. Dist. LEXIS 74625 (C.D. Cal. June 9, 2015) (tort of "wrongful eviction" is usually applied in cases where landlord engages in self-help or otherwise behaves badly toward tenants in effort to get them to leave, but can also refer to eviction of tenant or *purchaser* and be based in contract).

529. American Hardware Ins. Group v. West One Auto. Group, Inc., 167 Ore. App. 244, 252, 2 P.3d 413, 417 (2000).

530. Continental Ins. Co. v. Bones, 596 N.W.2d 552, 559 (Iowa 1999).

531. Insurance Co. of North America v. Forrest City Country Club, 36 Ark. App. 124, 128, 819 S.W.2d 296, 298 (1991).

532. Tush v. Pharr, 68 P.3d 1239, 1249 (Alaska 2003).

the premises.[533] Constructive eviction apparently constitutes an injury for which there is coverage under the standard commercial general liability policy.[534]

Actions for constructive eviction have been brought against common interest communities based on noise,[535] secondhand smoke,[536] failure to maintain the property,[537] rule enforcement,[538] and foreclosing a lien for non-payment of

533. Coach Run Condo., Inc. v. Furniss, 136 Conn. App. 698, 706, 47 A.3d 413, 418 (2012). *See also* Stevens v. Hollywood Towers & Condo. Ass'n, 836 F. Supp. 2d 800, 813 (N.D. Ill. 2011) (generally, there is no cause of action for constructive eviction unless tenant surrenders possession of premises within reasonable time); Cunningham v. Universal Underwriters, 98 Cal. App. 4th 1141, 1152, 120 Cal. Rptr. 2d 162, 170–71 (2002) (eviction is constructive if landlord engages in acts that render premises unfit for occupancy for purpose for which it was leased, or deprives tenant of beneficial enjoyment of premises; however, there is no constructive eviction if tenant continues in possession of premises regardless of extent to which she may be disturbed in beneficial enjoyment).

534. *See* Gerchick, *Insurance Coverage for Constructive Eviction*, 21 Cal. Real. Prop. J. 22 (2003).

535. *See, e.g.*, O'Connor v. Bd. of Managers/Trustees of the 24 Norman St. Condo. Ass'n, 2006 U.S. Dist. LEXIS 61199 (E.D. Va. Aug. 28, 2006) (unit owner claimed she was unable to sell, rent, or occupy her unit because of disruptive activity and noise of renters occupying unit above and, as result, her creditors foreclosed on property; unit owner brought action for constructive eviction against association for its failure to enforce bylaw provision prohibiting nuisances); Baum v. Coronado Condominium Ass'n, 376 So. 2d 914 (Fla. 3d DCA 1979) (unit owners filed action against condominium association seeking injunction to abate nuisance caused by noise from uninsulated and uncovered portion of lobby above their unit).

536. *See, e.g.*, Schuman v. Greenbelt Homes, Inc., 212 Md. App. 451, 69 A.3d 512 (2013) (resident sued cooperative housing association for breach of implied covenant of quiet enjoyment based on secondhand cigarette smoke entering his patio and home from neighboring apartment).

537. *See, e.g.*, Admiral Indem. Co. v. Travelers Cas. & Sur. Co. of Am., 881 F. Supp. 2d 570 (S.D.N.Y. 2012) (unit owner sued condominium association for constructive eviction from part of unit due to faulty repairs that damaged greenhouse attached to unit); Pedalino v. Woodhill Green Condominium, Inc., 38 Misc. 3d 1223(A), 969 N.Y.S.2d 805 (2013) (condominium unit owner sued association asserting that pipe below her unit in common area crawl space had been leaking and burst, causing water and mold damage to her unit); Coach Run Condo., Inc. v. Furniss, 136 Conn. App. 698, 47 A.3d 413 (2012) (unit owner alleged she vacated unit because association had substantially failed to perform its maintenance obligations); Hunter v. Rittenhouse Square Condo. Ass'n, 2010 Ohio Misc. LEXIS 21876 (Ohio C.P. Oct. 21, 2010) (condominium unit owner brought suit against association based on alleged existence of mold that accumulated from water leak into unit for, *inter alia*, constructive eviction); Geffcken v. D'Andrea, 2006 Cal. App. Unpub. LEXIS 1681 (Feb. 27, 2006) (homeowners sued their homeowners association and others for, *inter alia*, constructive eviction based on alleged exposed to mold mycotoxins at their residence); Smith v. Glen Cove Apts. Condos. Master Ass'n, 847 So. 2d 1107 (Fla. 4th DCA 2003) (tenants of unit owners in condominium brought class action against association alleging that association failed to maintain common element roofs causing city to condemn buildings resulting in "constructive and wrongful eviction").

538. *See, e.g.*, Murphree v. Tides Condo. at Sweetwater by Del Webb Master Homeowners' Ass'n, Inc., 2014 U.S. Dist. LEXIS 43560 (M.D. Fla. Mar. 31, 2014) (unit owner sued condominium and master association and alleged constructive eviction/foreclosure based on alleged harassment by community association manager in dispute over right of unit owner to display American flags); Stevens v. Hollywood Towers & Condo. Ass'n, 836 F. Supp. 2d 800 (N.D. Ill. 2011) (unit owners sued condominium association for, *inter alia*, constructive eviction for refusing request for accommodation for emotional support animal).

assessments.[539] Is a common interest community subject to an action for constructive eviction? Typically, only a landlord could be liable for constructive eviction. Is the relationship between a CIC association and its residents that of a landlord and tenant? In a residential cooperative, the residents can be considered tenants because their right to occupancy is usually based on a proprietary lease between the parties. However, the "tenants" are usually also shareholders in the corporation that is the "landlord." Nonetheless, a number of courts, especially in New York, find that tenant/shareholders are in effect tenants.[540]

The relationship between condominium or homeowners associations and their member residents is, or at least should be, clear. The members own their units or homes outright. Thus, many courts state emphatically that the individual owners cannot bring a constructive eviction suit against their association because the relationship between them and their association is not one of landlord/tenant.[541] Some courts are less certain. For example, in a federal court action, unit

539. *See, e.g.*, Board of Mgrs. of Brightwater Towers Condominium v. Cheskiy, 109 A.D.3d 944, 971 N.Y.S.2d 349 (2013) (condominium board commenced action against unit owner to foreclose lien issued for non-payment of common charges, and unit owner counterclaimed alleging, in essence, constructive eviction).

540. *See, e.g.*, Granirer v. Bakery, Inc., 54 A.D.3d 269, 863 N.Y.S.2d 396 (2008); Leventritt v. 520 East 86th Street, Inc., 266 A.D.2d 45, 698 N.Y.S.2d 20, 21 (1999). *See also* Schuman v. Greenbelt Homes, Inc., 212 Md. App. 451, 69 A.3d 512 (2013) (resident sued cooperative housing association for breach of implied covenant of quiet enjoyment based on secondhand cigarette smoke entering his patio and home from neighboring apartment; court accepted, without deciding, that landlord-tenant relationship existed between parties, but held that as smoke did not create nuisance, cooperative had not violated implied covenant of quiet enjoyment). *But see In re* Robertson, 147 B.R. 358 (1992) (relationship between cooperative and cooperator is not same as between landlord and tenant under New Jersey law regardless of occupancy agreement defining it as such). *See generally* 2 Rohan & Reskin, *Real Estate Transactions: Cooperative Housing Law and Practice—Forms*, § 8.04 (Matthew Bender, 2016).

541. *See, e.g.*, Board of Mgrs. of Brightwater Towers Condominium v. Cheskiy, 109 A.D.3d 944, 971 N.Y.S.2d 349 (2013) (where condominium board commenced action against unit owner to foreclose lien issued for non-payment of common charges and unit owner counterclaimed alleging, in essence, constructive eviction, appellate court held counterclaims sounding in constructive eviction should have been dismissed because answer failed to adequately plead existence of landlord-tenant relationship between parties); Coach Run Condo., Inc. v. Furniss, 136 Conn. App. 698, 47 A.3d 413 (2012) (where, in response to action by association to foreclose lien for assessments, unit owner alleged she vacated unit because association had substantially failed to perform its maintenance obligations, court acknowledged that, had unit owner been common-law tenant, rather than owner of condominium unit, she might have been able to invoke doctrine of constructive eviction, but found that supplemental general principles of law applicable to interpretation of common interest ownership act did not include common-law doctrine of constructive eviction); Hunter v. Rittenhouse Square Condo. Ass'n, 2010 Ohio Misc. LEXIS 21876 (Ohio C.P. Oct. 21, 2010) (condominium unit owner brought suit for, *inter alia*, constructive eviction; court dismissed claim because relationship between association and plaintiff unit owner was not one of landlord/tenant); Katz v. Board of Mgrs., 83 A.D.3d 501, 921 N.Y.S.2d 228 (2011) (causes of action for constructive eviction and breach of the implied warranty of habitability against condominium

owners sued their condominium association over its alleged refusal to accommodate the need of one of them for an emotional support animal. They contended the actions of the association deprived them of their use and enjoyment of their home—forcing them to sell it—and amounted to a constructive eviction. The court said constructive eviction resulted from the failure of a *landlord* to keep the premises in a tenantable condition, and it was unclear whether state law recognized constructive eviction in the context of condominium ownership. It concluded, however, that even if constructive eviction were available, there is generally no cause of action for it unless the tenant surrenders possession *within a reasonable time* and the plaintiffs waited more than one year from the time they alleged the association refused to agree to their requested accommodations before they sold their unit.[542] Other courts have either allowed claims for constructive eviction against associations to go forward[543] or made no comment on the efficacy of the action.[544]

association were unavailing absent landlord/tenant relationship between parties). *See also* Pedalino v. Woodhill Green Condominium, Inc., 38 Misc. 3d 1223(A), 969 N.Y.S.2d 805 (2013) (where condominium unit owner sued association asserting that pipe below her unit in common area crawl space had been leaking and burst, causing water and mold damage to her unit, court noted that cause of action sounded in breach of quiet enjoyment, which requires tenant to demonstrate either actual or constructive eviction and, because condominium constitutes real property, unit owner is not tenant and, therefore, plaintiff had no cognizable claim against association for breach of covenant of quiet enjoyment).

542. Stevens v. Hollywood Towers & Condo. Ass'n, 836 F. Supp. 2d 800 (N.D. Ill. 2011) (dismissing claim because complaint showed significant gap between request for certain accommodations and sale of condominium unit and having waited so long to move, plaintiffs waived any right they may have had to bring claim for constructive eviction).

543. *See, e.g.*, Elekima v. Abbey Rd. Condo. Ass'n, 331 Ga. App. 357, 771 S.E.2d 63 (2015) (where condominium association filed complaint against unit owner seeking to foreclose on liens arising from unpaid assessments, unit owner filed separate action against association for constructive eviction alleging it had wrongfully locked him out of premises; appellate court decided allegations that association towed vehicles, erased parking numbers from parking spaces, changed gate codes, and cut off water supply could support constructive eviction claim if actions were beyond scope of lawful lien foreclosure process); Smith v. Glen Cove Apts. Condos. Master Ass'n, 847 So. 2d 1107 (Fla. 4th DCA 2003) (where over 100 tenants of unit owners in condominium brought class action against association alleging that, because association failed to maintain common element roofs, city condemned buildings resulting in "constructive and wrongful eviction" through that condemnation order, appellate court found that although tenants had separate leasing agreements with different landlords and association was not a party to those leases, trial court abused its discretion in denying motion of tenants for class certification).

544. *See, e.g.*, Baum v. Coronado Condominium Ass'n, 376 So. 2d 914 (Fla. 3d DCA 1979) (where unit owners filed action against condominium association seeking injunction to abate nuisance caused by noise from uninsulated and uncovered portion of lobby above their unit, trial court found that to permit that condition to exist would constitute constructive eviction of plaintiffs from their unit and appellate court held that unit owners presented case for abatement of nuisance).

[c] Wrongful Entry or Invasion of the Right of Private Occupancy

The meaning of the phrase "invasion of the right of private occupancy" is subject to great disagreement.[545] One Federal Circuit Court of Appeals has explained the various views of state courts. A number of state courts have found the disputed language unambiguous, said the federal appellate panel, while a smaller, but not insignificant, number of courts have held that an invasion of the right of private occupancy is ambiguous and has to be construed liberally.[546] Among the former, there are three approaches. Those courts say the right of private occupancy is limited to offenses similar to eviction or wrongful entry that include violation of a possessory interest in real property;[547] is only available in the landlord-tenant context; or requires a physical invasion, for example, a trespass. Those courts that construe "invasion of the right of private occupancy" liberally find it includes trespass and nuisance.[548] Similarly, some courts hold "wrongful entry" includes trespass or nuisance,[549] while others conclude neither action is a wrongful entry.[550]

---

545. One federal court found it could apply to allegations against a homeowners association of restraint of trade by imposition of an age restriction. Lime Tree Village Community Club Ass'n v. State Farm Gen. Ins. Co., 980 F.2d 1402, 1407 (11th Cir. 1993) (complaint alleging association "contracted, combined and/or conspired" for purpose and with effect of imposing unreasonable restraint on trade in market of private occupancy, purchase, and ownership of residential real property through imposition of age restriction potentially fell within policy coverage as damages arising from unintended invasion of right of private occupancy).

546. New Castle County v. Nat'l Union Fire Ins. Co., 243 F.3d 744, 750–54 (3d Cir. 2001).

547. *Consider* Mortgage Express, Inc. v. Tudor Ins. Co., 278 Neb. 449, 465, 771 N.W.2d 137, 151 (2009) (insured argued lien constituted "invasion of the right to private occupancy," but court held security interest did not interfere with legal right to occupy premises and did not, therefore, fit within definition of personal injury).

548. *See, e.g.*, Kitsap County v. Allstate Ins. Co., 136 Wn. 2d 567, 590–92, 964 P.2d 1173, 1185 (1998) (it would seem apparent that plain, ordinary, and popular meaning that average purchaser of insurance would ascribe to phrase "other invasion of the right of private occupancy" would include trespass on or against right to use premises or land that is secluded from the intrusion of others; agreeing that nuisance claim was equivalent to claim for other invasion of right of private occupancy).

549. *See, e.g.*, Titan Holdings Syndicate, Inc. v. City of Keene, 898 F.2d 265 (1st Cir. 1990) (wrongful entry closely resembles tort of trespass; claims of liability for bodily injury or property damage arising from loud and disturbing noises during night and from unduly bright night lighting are not excluded from coverage afforded and claims of liability for interference with quiet enjoyment and use of home fell within personal injury coverage); Kitsap County v. Allstate Ins. Co., 136 Wn. 2d 567, 592, 964 P.2d 1173, 1185 (1998) (agreeing that claim for nuisance was equivalent to claim for wrongful entry); Millers Mut. Ins. Ass'n v. Graham Oil Co., 218 Ill. Dec. 60, 282 Ill. App. 3d 129, 668 N.E.2d 223, *app. den.*, 219 Ill. Dec. 567, 168 Ill. 2d 598, 671 N.E.2d 734 (1996) (wrongful entry can be reasonably construed to include all trespassory invasions to real property and is at least ambiguous, requiring construction in favor of the insured; therefore, allegations of unauthorized seepage and migration of gasoline onto property of adjoining neighbor were sufficient to bring underlying complaint within personal injury coverage).

550. *See, e.g.*, Whiteville Oil Co. v. Federated Mut. Ins. Co., 889 F. Supp. 241 (E.D.N.C. 1995), *aff'd*, 87 F.3d 1310 (4th Cir. 1996) (assertion that trespass is to be equated with "wrongful entry"; thus, invoking personal injury coverage is incorrect under law of North Carolina; nuisance is not

[i] Nuisance

The Restatement defines a nuisance as a non-trespassory invasion of the interest of another in the private use and enjoyment of land,[551] and says that one is liable for a nuisance if, but only if, his or her conduct is a legal cause of an invasion of the interest of another in the private use and enjoyment of land, and the invasion is either intentional and unreasonable or unintentional and otherwise actionable under the rules controlling liability for negligent or reckless conduct, or those for abnormally dangerous conditions or activities.[552] The definition of nuisance, it should be noted, varies from state to state.[553] Suits charging common interest communities with nuisance are not uncommon. These suits have been based on faulty maintenance,[554] rule-making,[555] failing to prevent secondhand smoke from

---

a personal injury offense). *See generally* Bowman & Hofer, *The Fallacy of Personal Injury Liability Insurance Coverage for Environmental Claims*, 12 Va. Envtl. L.J. 393 (1993) (contending that to equate wrongful entry or eviction and related torts with trespass or nuisance is serious fallacy because wrongful entry or eviction is narrow cause of action in tort for violation of personal right not to be forcefully or wrongfully evicted from possession or occupancy of real property, whereas trespass and nuisance are broad causes of action in tort for interference with property rights).

551. Restatement (Second) of Torts, § 821D.

552. Restatement (Second) of Torts, § 822.

553. *See, e.g.*, Stevens v. Hollywood Towers & Condo. Ass'n, 836 F. Supp. 2d 800 (N.D. Ill. 2011) (Illinois law defines private nuisance as substantial invasion of interest of another in use and enjoyment of his or her land and that invasion must be either intentional or negligent, and unreasonable; what constitutes nuisance is incapable of any exact or comprehensive definition; however, typically, nuisance occurs when property owner uses its own property in manner that results in non-trespassory invasion of interest of another in use and enjoyment of his or her own land); Schuman v. Greenbelt Homes, Inc., 212 Md. App. 451, 464–65, 69 A.3d 512, 520 (2013) (nuisance is interference with enjoyment of property when that interference is substantial and unreasonable such that it would be offensive or inconvenient to normal person); Berenger v. 261 W. LLC, 93 A.D.3d 175, 182, 940 N.Y.S.2d 4, 11 (2012) (claim of private nuisance arises from interest in use and enjoyment of property and elements of common-law claim are interference substantial in nature, intentional in origin, unreasonable in character, with property right to use and enjoy land, caused by conduct in acting or failure to act); Taygeta Corp. v. Varian Assocs.; 436 Mass. 217, 763 N.E.2d 1053 (2002) (actionable nuisance occurs when property owner creates, permits, or maintains condition or activity on property that causes substantial and unreasonable interference with use and enjoyment of property of another); Pub. Serv. Co. v. Van Wyk, 27 P.3d 377 (Colo. 2001) (adopting Restatement); Baum v. Coronado Condominium Ass'n, 376 So. 2d 914 (Fla. 3d DCA 1979) (anything that annoys or disturbs one in free use, possession, or enjoyment of her property or that renders its ordinary use or occupation physically uncomfortable may become nuisance and may be restrained).

554. *See, e.g.*, Pedalino v. Woodhill Green Condominium, Inc., 38 Misc. 3d 1223(A), 969 N.Y.S.2d 805 (2013) (where unit owner alleged pipe below her unit in common area crawl space had been leaking and burst, causing water and mold damage to her unit she sued association for, *inter alia*, nuisance); Smith v. King's Grant Condo., 537 Pa. 51, 640 A.2d 1276 (1994) (common sewer line backed up into condominium unit and caused sewage to enter and damage it).

555. *See, e.g.*, Stevens v. Hollywood Towers & Condo. Ass'n, 836 F. Supp. 2d 800, 812 (N.D. Ill. 2011) (unit owners alleged association rules interfered with ability to use common areas of property).

infiltrating homes,[556] and failing to abate noise.[557] In a homeowners association or a condominium, the association can commit nuisance by invading the interest of individual unit or homeowners in the portion of the property they own. Can an association invade the interest of a resident in a limited common area, that is, an area the resident does not own but for which he or she has the exclusive use? The Restatement provides that mere occupancy is sufficient for one to recover for invasion of the interest in the use and enjoyment of land,[558] but there are decisions that appear to be to the contrary.[559] Can a housing cooperative be liable for invasion of the interest of a tenant/shareholder in his or her apartment? Courts generally hold a leasehold interest is a sufficient one for the tenant to bring a nuisance action.[560]

The exact parameters of nuisance will vary from state to state, as will coverage for nuisance claims under the language of the standard commercial general liability policy. Common interest communities should, therefore, discuss their potential liability and coverage with their counsel and broker.

[ii] Trespass

The Restatement of Torts provides that someone is liable for trespass if he or she intentionally enters land in the possession of another, causes a thing or a third person to enter, remains on the land, or fails to remove from the land a thing that he or she is under a duty to remove.[561] Additionally, entry is a trespass whether harm is caused to any legally protected interest of the person in possession. A comment explains that someone, without him- or herself entering land, may invade the interest of another in its exclusive possession by throwing, propelling, or placing a thing either on or beneath the surface of the land or in the airspace

---

556. *See, e.g.*, Schuman v. Greenbelt Homes, Inc., 212 Md. App. 451, 464–65, 69 A.3d 512, 520 (2013).

557. *See, e.g.*, Berenger v. 261 W. LLC, 93 A.D.3d 175, 940 N.Y.S.2d 4 (2012) (unit owner sued association for nuisance arising out of alleged emanations of noise and glycol—liquid antifreeze—from cooling tower located on roof of condominium building); McEneaney v. Chestnut Hill Realty Corp., 38 Mass. App. Ct. 573, 650 N.E.2d 93 (1995) (nuisance action brought by unit owner against association over noise and vibrations in his unit from air conditioning chiller system that was in place in common area of building); Baum v. Coronado Condominium Ass'n, 376 So. 2d 914 (Fla. 3d DCA 1979) (action by unit owners against association for nuisance based on noise from uninsulated flooring in lobby above unit).

558. Restatement (Second) of Torts, § 821E, comment d.

559. *See, e.g.*, Connerty v. Metro. Dist. Com., 398 Mass. 140, 495 N.E.2d 840 (1986) (status of licensee insufficient for recovery under nuisance).

560. *See, e.g.*, BNT Co. v. Baker Precythe Dev. Co., 151 N.C. App. 52, 564 S.E.2d 891 (2002); Gilbert v. Thierry, 319 Mass. 492, 66 N.E.2d 712 (1946).

561. Restatement (Second) of Torts, § 158.

above it.[562] Ultimately, trespass is defined by state law, and its meaning may vary from state to state.[563]

Allegations of trespass against common interest communities are fairly common. Often the purported trespass is actual entry by a person representing the association.[564] Sometimes, however, the alleged trespass is by a thing or object.[565]

562. Restatement (Second) of Torts, § 158, comment i. The comment says that it is an actionable trespass to fire projectiles or to fly an advertising kite or balloon through the air above the land of another, even though no harm is done to the land or the enjoyment of it. Further, the foreign matter need not be thrown directly and immediately on the land of another. For example, someone who piles sand close to his boundary that by force of gravity alone slides down onto neighboring land, or builds an embankment the dirt from which is washed on adjacent lands during ordinary rainfalls, commits trespass.

563. *See, e.g.*, Berenger v. 261 W. LLC, 93 A.D.3d 175, 181, 940 N.Y.S.2d 4, 10 (2012) (trespass is invasion of right to exclusive possession of land, and includes entry of substance onto that land and does not require intent to produce damaging consequences, merely intent to perform act that produces unlawful invasion); DiPasquale v. Costas, 186 Ohio App. 3d 121, 147, 926 N.E.2d 682, 703, *app. den.*, 126 Ohio St. 3d 1513, 930 N.E.2d 332 (2010) (elements of trespass are unauthorized intentional act and entry on land in possession of another); Plotkin v. Club Valencia Condominium Ass'n, 717 P.2d 1027 (Colo. App. 1986) (trespass is any entry on real estate of another without invitation or permission of person lawfully entitled to possession of that real estate, including landlord).

564. *See, e.g.*, Speights-Carnegie v. Blackstone Condo. Ass'n, 2016 U.S. Dist. LEXIS 61385 (N.D. Ill. May 10, 2016) (where court order authorized association to take possession of condominium unit in January, but allegedly it entered property in prior November and rented it to third party, unit owner brought claim for trespass); Blinn v. West Shore Villas of Naples Owners' Ass'n, 182 So. 3d 686 (Fla. 2d DCA 2015) (homeowner sued association for trespass regarding wires and equipment supporting electrical meters on his property); Willow Lake Residential Ass'n v. Juliano, 80 So. 3d 226 (Ala. App. 2010) (homeowners contended association trespassed on their property on three occasions when it was entered by property manager, employee of property manager, and two board members); Campaniello v. Board of Mgrs. of 225 E. 57th St. Condominium, 21 Misc. 3d 226, 863 N.Y.S.2d 340 (2008) (resident claimed that association trespassed when it disconnected hookup to ventilation system); Plotkin v. Club Valencia Condominium Ass'n, 717 P.2d 1027 (Colo. App. 1986) (unit owner sued condominium association alleging it, without their permission or authorization, entered unit and relocated storage locker on balcony). *See also* Fountain Valley Chateau Blanc Homeowner's Ass'n v. Department of Veterans Affairs, 67 Cal. App. 4th 743, 79 Cal. Rptr. 2d 248 (1998) (homeowners association sued homeowner seeking to require removal of items it considered to be fire hazard, and homeowner brought claim for trespass predicated on association's use of threat of litigation to gain entry to his home and force him to throw out various of his personal belongings).

565. *See, e.g.*, Auburn's Gameday Ctr. at Magnolia Corner Owners Ass'n, Inc. v. Murray, 138 So. 3d 317 (Ala. App. 2013) (unit owners sued condominium association for trespass based on water flow from patio into their basement); Schuman v. Greenbelt Homes, Inc., 212 Md. App. 451, 475, 69 A.3d 512, 526 (2013) (unit owner sued association alleging that secondhand smoke that entered his unit amounted to trespass; court noted that intangible intrusions like smoke, odor, light, and noise are not typically actionable under trespass theory); Berenger v. 261 W. LLC, 93 A.D.3d 175, 940 N.Y.S.2d 4 (2012) (unit owner sued association for trespass arising out of alleged emanations of noise and glycol—liquid antifreeze—from cooling tower located on roof of condominium building); Porter v. Clarendon Nat'l Ins. Co., 76 Mass. App. Ct. 655, 655–56, 925 N.E.2d 58, 59, *rev. den.*, 457 Mass. 1103, 928 N.E.2d 950 (2010) (trespass claim against condominium association arose out

Common interest community associations frequently have a need to gain entry to premises occupied by their members, especially when there are shared boundaries that are common areas for which the association has maintenance responsibilities. Associations need to ascertain their legal right of entry. Under the Restatement, one may enter or remain on land with consent.[566] "Consent" is defined as willingness in fact for conduct to occur and may be manifested by action or inaction and need not be communicated to the actor.[567] The Restatement provides that one who effectively consents to conduct of another intended to invade his or her interests cannot recover in tort for that conduct or harm resulting from it.[568] Consent is effective when it is by one who has capacity to consent or by a person empowered to consent for him or her, and it is for the particular conduct or substantially the same conduct.[569] Consent can be conditional or restricted as to time or area, in which case it is only effective within the limits of the condition or restriction and if one exceeds the consent, it is not effective for the excess.[570]

For some common interest communities, the right of access may be provided by statute. Many states include a right of access in their *condominium* enabling legislation, although the right may be circumscribed.[571] For example, under Florida law, condominium associations have the irrevocable right of access to each unit during reasonable hours, when needed for "maintenance, repair, or replacement of any common elements or of any portion of a unit to be maintained by the association pursuant to the declaration or as necessary to prevent damage to the common elements or to a unit."[572] The UCIOA provides that generally an

---

of misplaced retaining wall and construction of two parking spaces on property abutting property of insured association). *See also* Lofts at Albert Hall Condo. Ass'n v. Vintage Oaks II, 2014 U.S. Dist. LEXIS 113485 (M.D.N.C. Aug. 15, 2014) (causing water to flow onto property of another can give rise to cause of action for trespass).

566. Restatement (Second) of Torts, § 167.

567. Restatement (Second) of Torts, § 892(1). The Restatement adds that when words or conduct are reasonably understood by another to be intended as consent, they constitute apparent consent and are as effective as consent in fact. Restatement (Second) of Torts, § 892(2).

568. Restatement (Second) of Torts, § 892A(1).

569. Restatement (Second) of Torts, § 892A(2).

570. Restatement (Second) of Torts, §§ 892A(3), (4).

571. Illinois and New York have fairly broad grants of access. 765 Ill. Comp. Stat. 605/18.4(j) (powers and duties of board of managers include access to each unit from time to time as may be necessary for maintenance, repair, or replacement of any common elements or for making emergency repairs necessary to prevent damage to common elements or to other units); N.Y. Real Prop. Law § 339-i(5) (unit owners have irrevocable right, to be exercised by board of managers, to access to each unit from time to time during reasonable hours to extent necessary for operation of property, or for making emergency repairs necessary to prevent damage to common elements or to another unit or units). Texas, on the other hand, appears to limit the association's access to emergency situations. Tex. Prop. Code § 82.102(a)(16) (unless otherwise provided by declaration, association, acting through its board, may enter unit for *bona fide* emergency purposes when conditions present imminent risk of harm or damage to common elements, another unit, or occupants).

572. Fla. Stat. § 718.111(5)(a).

association is responsible for maintenance, repair, and replacement of the common elements and that each unit owner has to afford to the association, and to its agents or employees, access through his or her unit when reasonably necessary for those purposes.[573] However, few states, other than those that have enacted the UCIOA, grant a statutory right of entry for cooperatives or homeowners associations,[574] and the California Davis-Stirling Common Interest Development Act, which governs all types of common interest communities, makes no mention of association access. In the case of cooperatives, no statutory right may be needed as the cooperative generally owns the entire building and the residents are in effect "tenants." The cooperative corporation is the landlord and should have a right of access to its property.

Even where there is no statutory grant of access, the governing documents often address the right of an association to have access to units. For example, in a homeowners association, the Covenants, Conditions, and Restrictions or a similar document may grant an association access to individual homes or to lots under prescribed circumstances.[575] Similarly, the proprietary lease or occupancy agreement between each resident and a cooperative corporation may enshrine the right of entry, although it may also place limitations on it. Generally, courts hold that a grant of access in the association documents constitutes consent to entry.[576]

The documents may not only bestow a right of entry on the association but also bar claims of trespass. For example, the bylaws of a New York condominium required unit owners to maintain and repair their units and if they breached that duty, the association had a right to enter the unit or appurtenant limited common

573. Uniform Common Interest Ownership Act § 3-107(a).

574. Fla. Stat. § 719.104(1) (cooperative association has irrevocable right of access to each unit from time to time during reasonable hours when necessary for maintenance, repair, or replacement of any structural components of building or of any mechanical, electrical, or plumbing elements necessary to prevent damage to building or to another unit).

575. *See, e.g.*, Lloyd v. Pier W. Prop. Owners Ass'n, 470 S.W.3d 293, 301 (2015) (bylaws provided that governing board could enter any unit when necessary in connection with maintenance for which board was responsible); Phila. Indem. Ins. Co. v. Lakeside Heights Homeowners Ass'n, 110 F. Supp. 3d 965, 971 (N.D. Cal. 2015) (documents provided that where any lot was maintained as nuisance or fire or safety hazard, association had right to enter that lot, correct offensive or hazardous condition, and recover its costs). Note that in a homeowners association consisting of detached single-family homes, the need for entry by the association insurer would be rare.

576. *See, e.g.*, Willow Lake Residential Ass'n v. Juliano, 80 So. 3d 226, 248–49 (Ala. App. 2010) (where covenants granted association permanent and perpetual non-exclusive easement appurtenant, over, across, through, and on each lot and dwelling to provided ingress to and egress from each lot and dwelling and inspect them to determine compliance with covenants, homeowners impliedly agreed to covenants when they purchased their lots and consented to entry on their land by association; party who has consented to entry on his or her land by homeowners association cannot maintain action for trespass when entry conforms to that consent).

elements to abate or cure the breach "without thereby being deemed guilty or liable in any manner of trespass."[577]

Consent may not be relevant in emergencies. For example, the Restatement says that conduct that injures another does not make the actor liable, even though the injured party did not consent to the conduct, if an emergency makes it necessary—or apparently necessary—in order to prevent harm to that party. In that case, one may act before there is opportunity to obtain consent and the actor has no reason to believe that injured party, if he or she had the opportunity to consent, would decline.[578] Similarly, some commentators have suggested application of the doctrine of necessity to common interest communities, under which a party acting to prevent or mitigate the effects of an impending disaster would not be held liable for damage to property in the effort.[579]

Where there are common areas reserved for the exclusive use of a homeowner, but owned by the association or the owners as tenants in common, does the owner for whom that use is reserved have a possessory interest that can be the subject of trespass? A Colorado court rejected the argument of a condominium association that it could not trespass on a balcony that was a limited common element because the unit owner was not entitled to its possession.[580]

Whether an association believes it has a right of entry to the property of its members by statute, its documents, or common law, it must be wary of exceeding the parameters of any implied consent. An association should consult its counsel to determine the extent of its right of entry and any procedures that it should implement to protect itself from allegations of trespass. For example, when it has a right to enter "during reasonable hours," as in the Florida statute, it should consider discussing with its attorney rules that define reasonable hours as well as those that prescribe notice in non-emergency circumstances.

[4] Defamation or Disparagement

Coverage is provided under the standard commercial general liability policy for an injury arising out of an oral or written "publication" of material that slanders or libels a person or organization or disparages the goods, products, or services[581]

---

577. Campaniello v. Board of Mgrs. of 225 E. 57th St. Condominium, 21 Misc. 3d 226, 323–33, 863 N.Y.S.2d 340, 345 (2008) (in light of bylaws, unit owner's trespass claim failed).

578. Restatement (Second) of Torts, § 892D.

579. *See* Poliakoff, *Conflicting Rights in Condominium Living*, 53 Fla. B.J. 756, 759 (1980).

580. Plotkin v. Club Valencia Condominium Ass'n, 717 P.2d 1027, 1028 (Colo. App. 1986).

581. *Consider* Chimera Inv. Co. v. State Farm Fire & Cas. Co., 268 Fed. Appx. 793, 798 (10th Cir. 2008) (slander of services provision would not provide coverage to insured for slandering its own services as liability is, by definition, obligation owed to third party, not to one's self; appellant argued management company slandered association's "services," but court found that because management company was purporting to act on behalf of association, that distinction would make no difference).

of a person or organization.[582] This language provides coverage for two types of injuries. Communication of material that slanders or libels a person or organization is defamation. Disparagement of the goods, products, or services of a person or organization is trade libel or disparagement.

Quarrels among residents of common interest communities or between residents and governing boards are notoriously ferocious and vicious. All manner of accusations and innuendos fly.[583] Those are often followed by claims of slander, which is spoken defamation, or libel, which is written defamation. However, contrary to the belief of many laypersons, the epithets and insults that accompany the typical squabble rarely rise to the level of defamation as it is legally defined.[584] That, of course, does not mean that CIC associations are not sued for defamation.[585] The basis of these actions have included informing members of a community about a debt a resident owes to the association,[586] statements made in a

582. *See, e.g.*, ISO Form CG 00 01 12 07, § V.14.d.

583. Jones v. Jennings, 2016 Mich. App. LEXIS 1596 (Mich. App. Aug. 30, 2016), illustrates the type of disputes that generate charges of defamation. There was a disagreement between residents of a housing cooperative about an elevator renovation project that had taken place while the plaintiff served on the governing board. At a finance committee meeting a resident raised issues about the bid process. At another meeting residents made comments suggesting that there was a problem with the elevator contract and that the plaintiff was responsible for them. One resident laughed about the idea of anyone signing the contract that had been entered regarding the renovations. The plaintiff claimed the comments were defamatory. The court did not agree. It said the comments constituted protected, "hyperbolic expressions of opinion regarding whether plaintiff and the board of directors had adhered to bidding practices in contracting for the project, properly prepared a capital plan, or generally understood what they were doing."

584. *See, e.g.*, Loch Sheldrake Beach & Tennis Inc. v. Akulich, 141 A.D.3d 809, 815, 36 N.Y.S.3d 525, 532 (2016) (at meeting of tenant/shareholders one shareholder was described as "immoral," "out to destroy the fabric of the universe," and "700 pound gorilla," but these alleged defamatory statements were insufficient to state cause of action as they were opinions, not facts); Bridgers v. Wagner, 80 A.D.3d 528, 915 N.Y.S.2d 265 (2011) (email to cooperative governing board stating that plaintiffs had made unapproved renovations to their apartment was not defamatory); Barner v. Kroehle, 2006 Ohio App. LEXIS 5555 (Ohio App. Oct. 26, 2006) (former president of condominium association described unit owner who was delinquent in paying maintenance fees as "deadbeat" and said because he had not paid his maintenance fees, he could not attend governing board meetings; court concluded that in context entire statement appeared to be gossip, rather than fact, and based on totality of circumstances was non-defamatory opinion as matter of law and could not be basis for defamation claim).

585. *See, e.g.*, Admiral Indem. Co. v. Travelers Cas. & Sur. Co. of Am., 881 F. Supp. 2d 570 (S.D.N.Y. 2012) (in underlying action, tenant/shareholder sued cooperative corporation alleging, *inter alia*, defamation by building manager); Fieldston Prop. Owners Ass'n, Inc. v. Hermitage Ins. Co., Inc., 920 N.Y.S.2d 763, 16 N.Y.3d 257, 945 N.E.2d 1013 (2011) (association sued in underlying action by neighboring entity that alleged false statements were made about its right to access its property from adjacent public streets and that assert cause of action for "injurious falsehood").

586. *See* Lautman v. 2800 Coyle St. Owners Corp., 2014 U.S. Dist. LEXIS 72703 (E.D.N.Y. May 23, 2014) (claim against cooperative corporation and others based on alleged publication to other tenant/shareholders of statements regarding false rent arrears owed by plaintiff); Wood v. Granite Ridge Condo Ass'n, 2009 N.H. Super. LEXIS 76 (2009) (unit owner claimed association defamed her by publishing in its minutes that she did not pay her association fees); Cohen v. Beachside Two-I Homeowners' Ass'n, 2006 U.S. Dist. LEXIS 44978 (D. Minn. June 29, 2006), *aff'd*, 272

community blog about an alleged rule violation,[587] a dispute between the association and a resident,[588] and letters sent by attorneys for a homeowners association regarding allegations a resident wrongfully denied the association access through her property to an adjacent slope over which it had maintenance obligations.[589]

[a] Defamation

Defamation is a communication that tends to so harm the reputation of another that it lowers him or her in the estimation of the community or deters third persons from associating or dealing with him or her.[590] Note that it is not always necessary that a communication cause actual harm to someone's reputation or deter others from associating or dealing with him or her; the general tendency to have that effect may be sufficient for a statement to be defamatory.[591] Often a communication is considered defamatory because it tends to expose another to hatred, ridicule, or contempt.[592] Imputation of certain physical and mental

---

Fed. Appx. 534 (8th Cir.), *cert. den.*, 555 U.S. 945, 129 S. Ct. 417, 172 L. Ed. 2d 288 (2008) (homeowner sued association for defamation based on governing board minutes that stated an unnamed unit owner had not paid assessments and association had elected to proceed to foreclosure); Papasodero v. Thayer & Assocs., 14 Mass. L. Rep. 684 (Mass. Super. 2002) (unit owner alleged he was defamed by publication of an agenda notice that stated his "bad debt" would be discussed at regularly scheduled meeting of governing board). *See also* Barner v. Kroehle, 2006 Ohio App. LEXIS 5555 (Ohio App. Oct. 26, 2006) (unit owner sued former president of condominium association claiming she defamed him by saying he had not paid his maintenance fees).

587. *See* Walters v. Cowpet Bay W. Condo. Ass'n, 2015 U.S. Dist. LEXIS 13 (D.V.I. Jan. 2, 2015) (unit owner brought defamation action against association, association president, and another unit owner who published a community blog after association president emailed letter to plaintiff and blog publisher stating plaintiff had violated "no dogs" policy and, subsequently, discussions on plaintiff's pet ownership appeared on Internet blog).

588. *See* Willow Lake Residential Ass'n v. Juliano, 80 So. 3d 226 (Ala. App. 2010) (homeowner alleged letter informing other owners of his dispute with homeowners association was defamatory); Davidson v. Seneca Crossing Section II Homeowner's Ass'n, 187 Md. App. 601, 979 A.2d 260 (2009) (minutes of association meeting recorded concerns that plaintiff homeowner had been nominated for governing board after having allegedly assaulted someone at meeting and had history of threatening residents). *See also* Villa Charlotte Bronte, Inc. v. Commercial Union Ins. Co., 487 N.Y.S.2d 314, 64 N.Y.2d 846, 476 N.E.2d 640 (1985) (plaintiff in underlying action sued cooperative corporation and president and vice president of corporation over allegedly defamatory remarks).

589. *See* Healy v. Tuscany Hills Landscape & Recreation Corp., 137 Cal. App. 4th 1, 39 Cal. Rptr. 3d 547 (2006).

590. Restatement (Second) of Torts, § 559. Publication of the allegedly defamatory information to a third party is generally an essential element of the action. *See, e.g.*, Sova v. Cove Homeowner's Ass'n, 102 So. 3d 863 (La. App. 2012) (insurer showed there was no factual support for homeowners claim of defamation against association as notices regarding rule violations and assessments of fines and penalties were sent directly to homeowner so publication element of defamation action could not be established; mere filing of liens by association could not be basis for defamation).

591. Restatement (Second) of Torts, § 559, comment d. *See also* Knapp v. Post Printing & Publ'g Co., 111 Colo. 492, 144 P.2d 981 (1943).

592. Restatement (Second) of Torts, § 559, comment b.

attributes—disease or insanity—may be defamatory.[593] Traditional examples of defamation are allegations of crime, affliction of a "loathsome" disease, lack of chastity, and impropriety or inadequacy in one's trade or profession. Defamation is determined by state law, and its application and specific meaning varies widely from state to state.[594] One aspect of defamation on which there is consensus is that the truth of the statement is an absolute defense.[595]

[b] Trade Libel or Disparagement

Trade libel or disparagement is encompassed by what the Restatement of Torts calls "injurious falsehood" and describes as communication of a false statement harmful to the interests of another by one intending for publication of the statement to result in harm and who either recognizes or should recognize that it is likely to harm and knows the statement is false or acts in reckless disregard of its truth or falsity.[596] More specifically, the liability for this form of injurious falsehood extends to communication of matter disparaging the quality of the land, chattels, or intangible things of another, that one should recognize as likely

---

593. Restatement (Second) of Torts, § 559, comment c.

594. *See, e.g.*, Sletten & Brettin Orthodontics, LLC v. Cont'l Cas. Co., 782 F.3d 931, 936 (8th Cir. 2015) (in Minnesota, plaintiff pursuing defamation claim has to prove that defendant made false and defamatory statement about plaintiff, in unprivileged publication to third party, that harmed plaintiff's reputation in community); Jones v. Jennings, 2016 Mich. App. LEXIS 1596 (Mich. App. Aug. 30, 2016) (to establish viable defamation claim, plaintiff must prove false or defamatory statement concerning plaintiff, unprivileged publication to third party, fault amounting to at least negligence on part of publisher, and either actionability of statement irrespective of special harm—defamation *per se*—or existence of special harm caused by publication—defamation *per quod*); Sova v. Cove Homeowner's Ass'n, 102 So. 3d 863, 873 (La. App. 2012) (defamation involves invasion of interest in reputation and good name and to maintain a cause of action for defamation, plaintiff must prove defamatory words, publication, falsity, malice, actual or implied, and resulting injury); Barner v. Kroehle, 2006 Ohio App. LEXIS 5555 (Ohio App. Oct. 26, 2006) (elements of defamation action are that defendant made false and defamatory statement concerning another, statement was published, plaintiff was injured, and defendant acted with required degree of fault); QSP, Inc. v. Aetna Cas. & Sur. Co., 256 Conn. 343, 356, 773 A.2d 906, 916 (2001) (*prima facie* sowing of defamation requires defamatory statement, statement identified plaintiff to reasonable third person, statement was published to third person, and plaintiff's reputation suffered injury as result of defamatory statement).

595. Restatement (Second) of Torts, § 581A. *See, e.g.*, Wood v. Granite Ridge Condo Ass'n, 2009 N.H. Super. LEXIS 76 (2009) (where unit owner claimed association defamed her by publishing in its minutes that she did not pay her association fees, she could not succeed on claim because she does not dispute that she stopped paying association fees and association did not, therefore, publish *false* and defamatory statement); Cohen v. Beachside Two-I Homeowners' Ass'n, 2006 U.S. Dist. LEXIS 44978 (D. Minn. June 29, 2006), *aff'd*, 272 Fed. Appx. 534 (8th Cir.), *cert. den.*, 555 U.S. 945, 129 S. Ct. 417, 172 L. Ed. 2d 288 (2008) (truth and substantial truth are defenses to defamation claim); Barner v. Kroehle, 2006 Ohio App. LEXIS 5555 (Ohio App. Oct. 26, 2006) (true statement cannot provide basis for defamation action, and statement need not be literally true in every detail; it is sufficient imputation is substantially true; statement that plaintiff did not pay maintenance fees was true and not defamatory).

596. Restatement (Second) of Torts, § 623A.

to result in pecuniary loss through the conduct of a third person in respect to interests in the property of the other party.[597] The tort of disparagement is distinguished from defamation by the fact that it focuses on economic consequences of an injurious statement rather than on damage to reputation.[598] This form of injurious falsehood is covered by the standard commercial general liability policy.

[c] Slander of Title

Another form of injurious falsehood is commonly called "slander of title." The Restatement describes it as communication of a false statement disparaging the property rights in land, chattels, or intangible things of another that the person making the communication should recognize as likely to result in pecuniary harm to the other through the conduct of third persons in respect to the interests in the property of the other party.[599] Slander of title is most commonly associated with aspersions cast on the ownership of land that prevent the owner from selling or leasing it. It is thus sometimes raised by owners in common interest communities whose property is subjected to a lien for unpaid assessments by the association.[600]

---

597. Restatement (Second) of Torts, § 626. The Connecticut Supreme Court noted that the terminology is somewhat confusing, for example, false communications that damage or tend to damage the reputation of the quality of goods or services may be described as "disparagement," "product disparagement," "trade libel," or "slander of goods," while those that impugn title to goods or to real property are usually denominated "slander of title" even though "slander" connotes oral and "libel" written communication, but "trade libel" and "slander of title" are used without regard to the manner of publication. QSP, Inc. v. Aetna Cas. & Sur. Co., 256 Conn. 343, 358–59, 773 A.2d 906, 917 (2001) (defamation or disparagement of goods and services may be considered trade libel and is recognized by Connecticut and New York courts as species of defamation). *See also* Hartford Casualty Ins. Co. v. Swift Distribution, Inc., 59 Cal. 4th 277, 290, 172 Cal. Rptr. 3d 653, 661, 326 P.3d 253, 260 (2014) (confusion surrounds tort of commercial disparagement because not only is its content blurred and uncertain, but so is its name and shifting names have led counsel and courts into thinking they were dealing with different bodies of law).

598. Thompson v. Md. Cas. Co., 84 P.3d 496, 506 (Colo. 2004). *See also* Hartford Casualty Ins. Co. v. Swift Distribution, Inc., 59 Cal. 4th 277, 289, 172 Cal. Rptr. 3d 653, 660, 326 P.3d 253, 259 (2014) (defamation concerns damage to reputation of a person or business, disparagement concerns damage to reputation of products, goods, or services).

599. Restatement (Second) of Torts, § 624.

600. *See, e.g.*, Kurtz v. Hubbard, 362 Ill. Dec. 528, 973 N.E.2d 924 (Ill. App. 2012) (where association brought action against unit owner for possession of her condominium unit and judgment for assessments and subsequently recorded lien against that unit, court held that association's lien statements should only receive protection from tort liability if it was determined they were not made with knowledge as to their falsity or with reckless disregard as to their truth or falsity; reversing dismissal of unit owner's slander of title claim); Wilton v. Mountain Wood Homeowner's Ass'n, 18 Cal. App. 4th 565, 22 Cal. Rptr. 2d 471 (Cal. App. 1993) (litigation privilege protected publication of assessment liens by association from action for slander or disparagement of title). *See also* Kalian at Poconos, LLC v. Saw Creek Estates Cmty. Ass'n, 275 F. Supp. 2d 578 (M.D. Pa. 2003) (developer alleged association disparaged its title to unimproved lots to prospective third-party purchasers by claiming that developer was required to pay various association fees, assessments, and other charges on lots and by placing and/or threatening to place liens on any lots sold

It has also been asserted where an association has recorded a notice of violation of covenant restrictions,[601] when an association filed a *lis pendens* on property a developer was in the process of marketing,[602] and in one case, a claim for slander of title was based on imposition of an age restriction.[603]

Almost all courts hold that, because the policy covers disparagement of "goods, products or services," and title to real property is none of those, slander of title is not covered by the standard commercial general liability policy.[604] Some

for non-payment of fees, assessments, and other charges; court dismissed slander of title claim because developer failed to adequately allege publication of alleged slanderous statements to third party); Brown v. Spring Valley Homeowners Ass'n, 2016 S.C. App. Unpub. LEXIS 406 (S.C. App. June 29, 2016) (act of recording lien against homeowner's property for unpaid *fines* constituted publication of a false statement for purposes of slander of title as restrictive covenants provide that any unpaid *periodic assessments* would constitute lien on property, but there was no similar provision for unpaid fines in governing documents; neither nominal damages nor attorney's qualified as special damages required to meet elements to bring slander of title action).

601. *See, e.g.*, California Riviera Homeowners Ass'n v. Superior Court, 48 Cal. App. 4th 1886, 56 Cal. Rptr. 2d 564 (1996) (where, pursuant to authorization in CC&R's, association recorded Notice of Violation of Restrictions on property of plaintiff for failure to comply with ten-foot set-back requirement of covenants, property owner filed action against association and two of its officers for, *inter alia*, slander of title, but court found that because recording of notice was specifically authorized by documents, association was protected by litigation privilege).

602. Green Trees Dev. v. Silver Meadows Condo. Ass'n, 1999 Conn. Super. LEXIS 2438 (Conn. Super. Sept. 8, 1999) (developer did not allege anywhere in its complaint that allegations in *lis pendens* were false and its subsequent inability to convey clear title, resulting in loss of sale, could not alone state cause of action for slander of title).

603. Lime Tree Village Community Club Ass'n v. State Farm Gen. Ins. Co., 980 F.2d 1402 (11th Cir. 1993) (complaint alleged association slandered or disparaged title to properties by declaring to third parties that plaintiffs had no right to sell or lease their properties to families with children or any family without member over age of 55).

604. *See, e.g.*, Nationwide Mut. Ins. Co. v. Lake Caroline, Inc., 515 F.3d 414, 420 (5th Cir. 2008) (policy expressly limits coverage to slander of person or organization or disparagement of good, product, or service and slander of title claims pertain only to real property, which is neither person, organization, good, product, nor service and, therefore, slander of title claims do not trigger coverage under policies that limit coverage to slander of person or organization or disparagement of a good, product, or service); Mortgage Express, Inc. v. Tudor Ins. Co., 278 Neb. 449, 464, 771 N.W.2d 137, 150 (2009) (slander of title claim did not fall within definition of personal injury because title to real estate is neither good, product, nor service); Thompson v. Md. Cas. Co., 84 P.3d 496, 506 (Colo. 2004) (while tort of disparagement is often construed as encompassing claim for slander of title, policy limits disparagement coverage to include only disparagement of "goods, products, or services" and because title to real property does not fall within category of either "goods, products, or services," slander of title claim, standing alone, did not trigger duty to defend); Bank One, N.A. v. Breakers Dev., 208 Wis. 2d 230, 559 N.W.2d 911 (Wis. App. 1997) (no coverage for slander of title claim as reasonable insured would not believe that terms goods or products were meant to include real estate titles). *See also* Etchison v. Westfield Ins. Co., 2006 U.S. Dist. LEXIS 71467 (N.D. W. Va. Sept. 29, 2006) (title to real property does not meet definition of goods, products, or services); Kickham Group v. American Nat'l Fire Ins. Co., 1997 U.S. Dist. LEXIS 23733 (N.D. Tex. Sept. 24, 1997) (title to real property does not meet definition of "services," and policy did not encompass claim of slander of title; therefore, damages based on slander of title were not covered by CGL Policy).

courts, however, have required liability carriers to defend actions for slander of title.[605]

[d] Public Figure

When a public official or public figure sues for defamation in regard to his or her conduct, fitness, or role in that capacity, a high burden of proof is imposed. The plaintiff public figure or official has to show that the defendant knew the statement at issue was false and defamed the plaintiff or acted in reckless disregard of the truth and defamatory nature of that statement.[606] The U.S. Supreme Court imposed this burden to protect freedom of speech and the robust public debate essential to a free society.[607] A person allegedly defamed by a common interest association or its agents might not be a public figure or official in the larger society, but may be a public figure within that community. Those persons are called "limited purpose public figures," and the same high standard of proof applies to them as plaintiffs in a defamation action. If courts determine a controversy to be of sufficient *public concern*, an otherwise private person may be found to be a limited purpose public figure.[608]

The phrase "public concern" is not readily defined and has to be determined on a case-by-case basis.[609] Officers and governing board members of common interest communities may be considered limited purpose public figures,[610] as may candidates for those offices.[611] The description could also be applied to those

605. *See, e.g.*, Lime Tree Village Community Club Ass'n v. State Farm Gen. Ins. Co., 980 F.2d 1402, 1406–07 (11th Cir. 1993) (where, based on allegations of underlying complaint, homeowners association could be held liable for unintended slander of title, court found allegations on their face claimed damages for personal injury constituting occurrence falling within policy coverage and concluded insurer had duty to defend, but expressed no opinion on whether or not, if plaintiffs in underlying case recovered from association, insurer would be required to indemnify).

606. Restatement (Second) of Torts, § 580A.

607. New York Times Co. v. Sullivan, 376 U.S. 254, 84 S. Ct. 710, 11 L. Ed. 2d 686 (1964).

608. Smith, *Dragged into the Vortex: Reclaiming Private Plaintiffs' Interests in Limited Purpose Public Figure Doctrine*, 89 Iowa L. Rev. 1419 (2004).

609. McIntyre v. Jones, 194 P.3d 519 (Colo. App. 2008).

610. *See, e.g.*, Martin v. Comm. for Honesty & Justice, 101 P.3d 123 (Wyo. 2004) (one who attains membership on governing board of community association voluntarily chooses to assume position that, by its nature, has significant probability that he or she will be required to participate in issues of community concern and must accept consequences of status of limited public purpose public figure; director who participated in termination of professional manager was limited public figure). *But see* Jones v. Jennings, 2016 Mich. App. LEXIS 1596 (Mich. App. Aug. 30, 2016) (noting that parties agreed plaintiff residential cooperative board member constituted private figure although alleged defamation concerned board issue).

611. *See, e.g.*, Gulrajaney v. Petricha, 381 N.J. Super. 241, 885 A.2d 496 (2005) (plaintiff candidate for governing board claimed defamation and argued that since condominium was private development with private governing body, he was private figure, but court found held that for plaintiff to recover damages for defamation, he would have to show, by clear and convincing evidence, that defendant was motivated by actual malice, standard applied when plaintiff is public figure); Verna v. Links at Valleybrook Neighborhood Ass'n, 371 N.J. Super. 77, 852 A.2d 202 (2004) (where

who serve on association committees or to community association managers. One commentator contends CIC residents who are outspoken activists may be limited purpose public figures.[612]

[e] Conditional Privileges

There are a number of "conditional privileges" that serve as defenses to an action for defamation. Two of them are of particular importance to common interest communities. The first of these is the "common interest privilege." The Restatement of Torts says that an occasion makes a publication conditionally privileged if circumstances lead any one of several persons who have a common interest in a particular subject matter correctly or reasonably to believe that there is information that another who shares that common interest is entitled to know.[613] A comment to the Restatement explains that under this privilege, tenants in common, other co-owners of land or chattels, corporate officers, and fellow shareholders are conditionally privileged to communicate among themselves matter defamatory of others that concerns their common interests.[614] Another comment makes

---

plaintiff board candidate claimed that "candidate audit" distributed by board that listed his rule violations, said they remained unresolved, and that he was not in good standing and entitled to vote defamed him; court held that as candidate for election plaintiff "thrust himself into spotlight" that justified viewing him as public figure for limited purpose of his candidacy).

612. *See* MacGregor, *Florida Condominium Law Manual*, § 5.09[8] (LexisNexis Matthew Bender, 2018). *But see* Tai v. Crown View Manor I Condo. Ass'n, 2008 N.J. Super. Unpub. LEXIS 23 (July 11, 2008) (declining to address whether unit owner activist was limited purpose public figure because applicability of qualified privilege was not dependent on that finding).

613. Restatement (Second) of Torts, § 596. *See, e.g.*, Davidson v. Seneca Crossing Section II Homeowner's Ass'n, 187 Md. App. 601, 645–46, 979 A.2d 260, 286 (2009) (minutes of association meeting that recorded concerns that plaintiff homeowner had been nominated for position on governing board and had allegedly assaulted someone at meeting and had history of threatening residents were entitled to qualified privilege; court found meeting attendants shared common interest of electing qualified and competent members to governing board); Tai v. Crown View Manor I Condo. Ass'n, 2008 N.J. Super. Unpub. LEXIS 23 (July 11, 2008) (after plaintiff unit owner was allegedly observed removing water jug from building lobby, association representative wrote letter to plaintiff about incident and provided copies to members of governing board, association attorney, and property manager; court found letter to be privileged because it was written in connection with common interest of protecting association and sent only to those persons with corresponding interest and duty to protect association); Cohen v. Beachside Two-I Homeowners' Ass'n, 2006 U.S. Dist. LEXIS 44978 (D. Minn. June 29, 2006), *aff'd*, 272 Fed. Appx. 534 (8th Cir.), *cert. den.*, 555 U.S. 945, 129 S. Ct. 417, 172 L. Ed. 2d 288 (2008) (where homeowner sued association for defamation based on governing board minutes that stated he had not paid assessments and association had elected to proceed to foreclosure, association was entitled to common interest qualified privilege regarding communications in meeting minutes because governing board, management company, and homeowners shared common interest in their townhome community and failure of some homeowners to pay their monthly assessments directly impacted entire community; homeowners had general right to be kept informed by governing board of financial status of their community).

614. Restatement (Second) of Torts, § 596, comment d. *But see* Papasodero v. Thayer & Assocs., 14 Mass. L. Rep. 684 (Mass. Super. 2002), where the court considered a similar conditional privilege for publication of defamatory material that is reasonably necessary to protect or further a legitimate business interest. The condominium association in the case argued it should have that

two points of relevance to common interest communities. First, the privilege is based on the fact that one is entitled to learn from his or her associates what is being done in a matter in which he or she has an interest in common with them. Second, the communication need not be made at an official meeting or take the form of any official action on the part of the group or its representatives, as a purely private communication between members of a group may be privileged.[615] The common interest privilege has been applied to defamation actions against common interest community associations.[616] For example, an Alabama court said that communication among the directors of a homeowners association and its members about an ongoing dispute that could result in an increase in dues was the type of intra-organizational communication that was protected.[617] A related privilege applies to statements made by members of the governing board in the course of discharging their duties to the association.[618]

Another conditional privilege that could apply to common interest communities concerns reports of official proceedings or public meetings. The Restatement says that the publication of defamatory matter about someone in a report of an official action or proceeding or of a meeting open to the public dealing with a matter of public concern is privileged "if the report is accurate and complete or a

---

privilege for publishing an agenda listing a discussion at a governing board meeting of the plaintiff unit owner's "bad debt." It argued that in conducting the business of the association, it prepared an agenda to allow board members to prepare for discussion of agenda items. The court, however, raised the possibility that the privilege would not apply where the agenda was distributed to all unit owners, not just to members of the governing board.

615. Restatement (Second) of Torts, § 596, comment c.

616. *See, e.g.*, Abraham v. 257 Central Park West, Inc., 2015 N.Y. Misc. LEXIS 283 (Jan. 16, 2015) (plaintiff tenant shareholder sent letter to building residents alleging abusive behavior toward him by building superintendent, and in response cooperative board sent letter to tenant/shareholders stating that plaintiff was shown on videotape orally abusing and physically assaulting superintendent; plaintiff claimed letter defamed him, but court found that qualified common interest privilege was defense where board distributed its letter in response to plaintiff's letter and residents, if they previously had not shared interest with board in incident, surely shared that interest after plaintiff disseminated his letter). *See also* McIntyre v. Jones, 194 P.3d 519, 530 (Colo. App. 2008) (former governing board member who wrote letter to board stating that recently hired bookkeeper had previously been discharged for incompetence, insubordination, and withholding records and books from review and that she had enriched herself from association funds had qualified privilege to publish those statements, but abused and lost privilege because he acted with reckless disregard for truth by failing to investigate facts fully). *See also* Erdberg v. Freeman, 90 Misc. 2d 797, 396 N.Y.S.2d 315 (1977) (tenants and landlord of apartment building constitute group with common interest in its security and quality as residence and communication among members of that group for purpose of advancing that interest, made in good faith and published only to properly interested persons, are protected from action for defamation by qualified privilege).

617. Willow Lake Residential Ass'n v. Juliano, 80 So. 3d 226 (Ala. App. 2010) (letters to homeowners from association informed them about progress of dispute between plaintiff homeowner and association, and costs of that dispute were not defamatory).

618. *See, e.g.*, Black v. Green Harbour Homeowners' Ass'n, 19 A.D.3d 962, 963–64, 798 N.Y.S.2d 753, 754 (2005).

fair abridgement of the occurrence reported."[619] However, the privilege does not extend to a report of a private meeting that is not open to the general public nor to a report of a meeting that does not address matters of *public concern*, although it is open to the public. Thus, for the privilege to apply to a common interest community, it would need to argue that its meetings are open to the public within the community and the issues discussed are of concern to the public within that community just as discussions at a city council meeting are of concern to the public in that municipality. Certainly, courts and commentators have noted the similarity of community associations to municipal governments.[620] On the other hand, at least one court has explicitly refused to find that alleged defamation was a matter of "public concern" because it related to governance of a homeowners association.[621]

[5] Violation of Right of Privacy

Personal and advertising injury includes an injury arising out of communication of material that violates the right of a person to privacy.[622] The right of privacy can be invaded by unreasonable intrusion on the seclusion of another,[623]

619. Restatement (Second) of Torts, § 611. *See, e.g.*, Dubois v. Ass'n of Apt. Owners, 453 F.3d 1175, 1181 (9th Cir. 2006) (condominium resident alleged association defamed him in course of investigations by Hawaii Civil Rights Commission and Honolulu Police Department investigations, and at a Circuit Court hearing arising out of disputes with association and his neighbors; court found resident failed to make out a *prima facie* case of defamation because statements were made to officials whose duty it was to record them, and published to people with interest in investigations and proceedings and, therefore, covered by qualified privilege).

620. *See* Hyatt & Stubblefeld, *The Identity Crisis of Community Associations: In Search of the Appropriate Analogy*, 27 Real Prop. & T. J. 589 (1993); Rosenberry, *Condominium and Homeowner Associations: Should They Be Treated Like "Mini-Governments?,"* 8 Zoning & Plan. L. Rep. 153 (1985); Ellickson, *Cities and Homeowner's Associations*, 130 U. Pa. L. Rev. 1519 (1982). *See also* Chantiles v. Lake Forest II Master Ass'n, 37 Cal. App. 4th 914, 45 Cal. Rptr. 2d 1 (1995) (homeowners association may act as second municipal government). *Compare* Goldberg v. 400 E. Ohio Cond. Ass'n, 12 F. Supp. 2d 820 (N.D. Ill. 1998) (that condominium association may perform governmental functions does not show that it acts as state); Midlake on Big Boulder Lake Condo. Ass'n v. Cappucio, 449 Pa. Super. 124, 673 A.2d 340 (Pa. Super. 1996).

621. McIntyre v. Jones, 194 P.3d 519 (Col. App. 2008). *Compare* Martin v. Comm. for Honesty & Justice, 101 P.3d 123 (Wyo. 2004) (members of association should have same rights as citizens of municipality to criticize or comment on actions of their elected representatives; dispute over firing of manager was of great importance to owners and, at its essence, political and public).

622. *See, e.g.*, ISO Form CG 00 01 12 07, § V.14.e (oral or written publication, in any manner, of material that violates person's right of privacy).

623. Under this version of the action, someone who *intentionally* intrudes on the solitude or seclusion of another—or his or her private affairs or concerns—is subject to liability for invasion of privacy if the intrusion would be "highly offensive" to a reasonable person. Restatement (Second) of Torts, § 652B. The plaintiff must be the person whose seclusion was invaded. *See* Neil v. Kovitz Shifrin Nesbit, 2014 U.S. Dist. LEXIS 136696 (N.D. Ill. Sept. 27, 2014) (unit owner failed to state claim for intrusion on seclusion where she alleged association attorney contacted third parties and her roommates and attempted to interfere with relationship with her tenant as activities alleged all involve contact with third parties, not actions that intruded on unit owner's own seclusion).

appropriation of the name or likeness of another,[624] giving unreasonable publicity to the private life of another,[625] or publicity that unreasonably places another in a false light before the public.[626] Even where the "public" is not large, the existence of a special relationship between the plaintiff and recipients of the information might be enough to satisfy the public disclosure requirement.[627] Sharing membership in a common interest community should constitute a "special relationship."

Comments to the Restatement of Torts say that an invasion may be perpetrated when one insists on entering the home of another over the objection of that person,[628] but that there is no liability for examination of a *public record*

---

624. Appropriating the name or likeness of another for one's own *use or benefit* constitutes an invasion of privacy. Restatement (Second) of Torts, § 652C. This form of the action is not likely to be of concern to common interest communities because it usually involves use of the name or likeness for commercial purposes, generally to advertise a business or product. Restatement (Second) of Torts, § 652C, comment b.

625. There is the potential for liability under this version of the action when someone gives publicity to a matter concerning the private life of another if the matter publicized is of a kind that would be "highly offensive" to a reasonable person and is not of "legitimate concern" to the public. Restatement (Second) of Torts, § 652D. Note that a person can voluntarily place him- or herself in the public eye, by engaging in public activities, or by assuming a prominent role in institutions or activities that have general economic, cultural, social, or similar public interest. In that event, the person cannot complain when given publicity that he or she has sought, even though it may be unfavorable. Restatement (Second) of Torts, § 652D, comment e.

626. "False light" liability arises when someone communicates matters about someone else that places that person before the public in a false light, the false light in which that other person was placed would be "highly offensive" to a reasonable person, and the perpetrator had knowledge of or acted in reckless disregard of the falsity of the matter and the false light in which the other person would be placed. Restatement (Second) of Torts, § 652E. *See, e.g.*, Straub v. Scarpa, 967 So. 2d 437 (Fla. 4th DCA 2007) (where unit owner who was candidate for election to governing board sent letter to members of association decrying financial decisions of sitting board, she did not invade privacy of plaintiff board member because letter did not place board member in false light as it neither mentioned his name nor describe him and it was not "highly offensive" to reasonable person). *See also* Jones v. Jennings, 2016 Mich. App. LEXIS 1596 (Mich. App. Aug. 30, 2016) (plaintiff, member of governing board, sued other residents of housing cooperative for false light invasion of privacy; court said to maintain that action plaintiff would have to show that defendants broadcast to public in general, or to large number of people, information that was unreasonable and highly objectionable by attributing to plaintiff characteristics, conduct, or beliefs that were false and placed plaintiff in false position; court found plaintiff failed to show false statement by defendants concerning plaintiff and to establish question of material fact regarding whether defendants promulgated any information that was unreasonable and highly objectionable). The information on which a false light claim is based need not be defamatory, but if it is, invasion of privacy will provide an alternative or additional remedy. Restatement (Second) of Torts, § 652E, comment b.

627. Neil v. Kovitz Shifrin Nesbit, 2014 U.S. Dist. LEXIS 136696 (N.D. Ill. Sept. 27, 2014). *Compare* Cohen v. Beachside Two-I Homeowners' Ass'n, 2005 U.S. Dist. LEXIS 28536 (D. Minn. Nov. 17, 2005), *aff'd*, 272 Fed. Appx. 534; 2008, *cert. den.*, 555 U.S. 945, 129 S. Ct. 417, 172 L. Ed. 2d 288 (2008) (conclusion by trial court that distribution of governing board minutes to small common interest community of about 50 households in small geographic area was not to "public at large" was not clearly erroneous or contrary to law).

628. Restatement (Second) of Torts, § 652B, comment b.

concerning him or her.[629] Are documents an association is required to maintain by statute or its governing documents "public records"?

Common interest communities, or their agents or officers, are subject to accusations of invasions of privacy surprisingly often, although they are rarely successfully. The complaints have been based on disclosing "private" information,[630] disclosing non-payment of maintenance fees,[631] placing a lien on the plaintiff's

629. Restatement (Second) of Torts, § 652B, comment c.

630. *See, e.g.*, Walters v. Cowpet Bay W. Condo. Ass'n, 2015 U.S. Dist. LEXIS 13 (D.V.I. Jan. 2, 2015) (alleging invasion of privacy through public disclosure of private facts and false light against association and governing board apparently based on disclosure by association president of email to another unit owner who maintained community blog stating that plaintiff unit owner had violated "no dogs" policy); Kromenhoek v. Cowpet Bay W. Condo. Ass'n, 77 F. Supp. 3d 462 (D.V.I. 2014) (where unit owner submitted letter from her physician diagnosing her with anxiety disorder and containing information about qualifications of her emotional support animal and association president shared contents of her documents with some association members including one who maintained community blog, unit owner sued association and governing board for, *inter alia*, invasion of privacy through public disclosure of private facts and false light); Zopatti v. Rancho Dorado Homeowners Ass'n, 2010 U.S. Dist. LEXIS 132532 (S.D. Cal. Dec. 15, 2010), *aff'd*, 533 Fed. Appx. 777 (2013), *cert. den.*, 571 U.S. 1238, 134 S. Ct. 1500; 188 L. Ed. 2d 377 (2014) (unit owner alleged disclosure of her medical information to certain individuals constituted invasion of her privacy); Neil v. Kovitz Shifrin Nesbit, 2014 U.S. Dist. LEXIS 136696 (N.D. Ill. Sept. 27, 2014) (where unit owner alleged association attorney disclosed baseless debt collection demand notices to fellow employee and her work supervisors, she stated claim for false light invasion of privacy); Fontell v. Hassett, 2011 U.S. Dist. LEXIS 113500 (D. Md. Oct. 3, 2011) (allegations of complaint that collection and legal actions taken against unit owner by association were "openly discussed and communicated" during open board of directors meetings and that meeting minutes were "publicly posted online on the website" and available for unrestricted public review by association members and other third parties lacked "legitimate business need for information" did not articulate how dissemination of that information constituted tortious behavior); Holcomb v. Oso Valley Greenbelt Ass'n, 2008 Cal. App. Unpub. LEXIS 9009 (Cal. App. Oct. 30, 2008) (unit owner successfully sued association for invasion of privacy based on disclosure by property manager of private information about him to insurer without authorization); Cohen v. Beachside Two-I Homeowners' Ass'n, 2005 U.S. Dist. LEXIS 28536 (D. Minn. Nov. 17, 2005), *aff'd*, 272 Fed. Appx. 534; 2008, *cert. den.*, 555 U.S. 945, 129 S. Ct. 417, 172 L. Ed. 2d 288 (2008) (unit owner alleged invasion of privacy by publication of private facts based on minutes from two governing board meetings that stated by inference that unit owner was delinquent in paying his assessments and that were allegedly sent to members of community); Papasodero v. Thayer & Assocs., 14 Mass. L. Rep. 684 (Mass. Super. 2002) (where unit owners claimed association published agenda notice regarding their bad debt and distributed that agenda indiscriminately and allegedly disseminated information regarding debt capable of being interpreted as indication that unit owner was having serious financial trouble, court denied summary judgment to association as genuine issues of material fact existed as to damage to privacy interests of unit owner); Seaphus v. Lilly, 691 F. Supp. 127 (N.D. Ill. 1988) (allegation that unit owner's privacy was invaded when his unlisted telephone number was obtained by other unit owner; simple disclosure of private information to one other person is insufficient to state claim for invasion of privacy).

631. *See, e.g.*, Barner v. Kroehle, 2006 Ohio 5569, 2006 Ohio App. LEXIS 5555 (Ohio App. Oct. 26, 2006) (disclosure of non-payment of his maintenance fees was not invasion of unit owner's privacy as it was not private matter because information concerning who had or had not paid their maintenance fees was available to all owners of units as provide in bylaws; unit owner's own disclosure of non-payment undermined any claim that disclosure of that information was "highly

unit,[632] entering a unit,[633] interfering with the right to "use, enjoy and possess an interest" in a condominium unit, [634] making public accusations of misconduct,[635] photographing the unit owner's visitors,[636] approving changes to neighboring

---

offensive" and objectionable to reasonable person of ordinary sensibilities); Mushkat v. Pickawillany Condominium, 1981 Ohio App. LEXIS 11014 (Ohio App. 14, 1981) (where community newsletter included copy of minutes of meeting of governing board stating that board voted to initiate foreclosure proceedings against plaintiff unit owners, plaintiffs alleged minutes invaded their rights of privacy and exposed them to public ridicule, but court found where verbatim printing of minutes without embellishment or opinion contained no highly offensive language and made no accusations, publicized matters complained of fell short of standard that they be highly offensive and objectionable to reasonable person of ordinary sensibilities).

632. *See, e.g.*, Sova v. Cove Homeowner's Ass'n, 102 So. 3d 863 (La. App. 2012) (unit owner alleged invasion of privacy by association apparently by "unlawfully" causing lien to be placed on his property); Kurtz v. Hubbard, 362 Ill. Dec. 528, 973 N.E.2d 924 (Ill. App.), *app. den.* 366 Ill. Dec. 77, 979 N.E.2d 878 (Ill. 2012) (where association recorded lien against plaintiff's condominium unit, she alleged claim in connection with recording of lien, claiming association willfully or with gross negligence placed plaintiff in false light before community by recording lien contents of which it knew to be false).

633. *See, e.g.*, Acacia on the Green Condo. Ass'n v. Gottlieb, 2009 Ohio App. LEXIS 4143 (Ohio App. Sept. 17, 2009), *app. den.*, 124 Ohio St. 3d 1493, 922 N.E.2d 228 (2010) (in counterclaim to suit filed by association seeking injunction to prevent renovations in violation of rules without permit from association, unit owner claimed association invaded his privacy when its maintenance supervisor entered unit with permission of contractor as supervisor did not enter without consent of occupant and condominium Declaration granted association right to enter units where rule had been breached); Edgewater Townhouse Homeowner's Ass'n v. Holtman, 256 Mont. 182, 845 P.2d 1224 (1993) (association assessed unit owners for new heating systems and appellee refused to pay or allow access to his unit for installation, but after neighbor reported running water in his unit, association declared emergency requiring entry into unit and authorized plumber to fix leak and install new heating system while unit owner was absent; in subsequent suit by association, unit owner counterclaimed for, *inter alia*, invasion of privacy evidently based on unauthorized entry).

634. *See, e.g.*, Trombello v. Blue Sky Harbor Ltd. P'ship, 250 Wis. 2d 353, 639 N.W.2d 801 (2001) (where complaint alleged association and its officers seriously interfered with right of plaintiff unit owner to use, enjoy, and possess interest in condominium unit, nothing in it remotely suggested violation of privacy rights and absent any evidence that the plaintiff sought recovery for any "bodily injury," "property damage," or "personal injury," trial court properly concluded insurer had no obligation to defend or indemnity defendant).

635. *See, e.g.*, Jones v. Jennings, 2016 Mich. App. LEXIS 1596 (Mich. Ct. App. Aug. 30, 2016) (member of governing board of cooperative sued fellow tenant/shareholders alleging false light invasion of privacy because they accused him of bribery and taking kickbacks in elevator renovation project; court concluded plaintiff failed to establish question of material fact regarding whether defendants promulgated information that was unreasonable and highly objectionable by attributing characteristics, conduct, or beliefs to plaintiff that were false and placed him in false position).

636. *See, e.g.*, King v. Metcalf 56 Homes Ass'n, 385 F. Supp. 2d 1137 (D. Kan. 2005) (tenant of unit in homeowners association sued association for invasion on seclusion based on photographs taken of her visitors and family members and recording and photographing of vehicles and their license plate numbers; court concluded that because plaintiff's guests were undoubtedly readily observable to public eye and photographs were apparently not taken from non-public vantage point or using some type of magnifying lens, there was no evidence from which it could be inferred that anyone intruded into plaintiff's privacy).

property that allowed the interior of plaintiff's unit to be seen,[637] allowing installation of wood flooring in a unit above,[638] failing to abate noise from mechanical room equipment,[639] and attempting to enforce a "no pet" rule.[640]

A Florida court explained why judges may be hesitant to find invasions of privacy in matters concerning governance of common interest communities when it said: "In a residential community governed by a homeowners association, vigorous debate over community expenditures is a value to be encouraged, not a pathway to litigation. To encourage tort litigation in a case such as this is to stifle discussion and place political power in the hands of those wealthy and aggressive enough to finance a lawsuit."[641]

[6] Advertising

The standard commercial general liability policy provides coverage for an injury arising out of use by the insured of the advertising idea of another in its "advertisement,"[642] and infringement of the copyright, trade dress, or slogan of another in the insured's "advertisement."[643] "Advertisement" is defined as a notice—including material placed on the internet—broadcast or published to the general public, or specific parts of a market, about the goods, products, or services of the insured to attract customers or supporters.[644]

[7] Exclusions

There are 16 exclusions in the standard commercial general liability policy to the personal and advertising injury coverage. Several of them relate to business

---

637. *See, e.g.*, O'Shea v. Lesser, 308 S.C. 10, 416 S.E.2d 629 (S.C. 1992) (fact that as result of improvements approved by association, neighbors could see into portion of appellant's home was not so blatant or shocking as to constitute invasion of her right to privacy).

638. *See, e.g.*, Baldwin v. Vill. Walk Condo., Inc., 2010 Conn. Super. LEXIS 3027 (Conn. Super. Ct. Nov. 19, 2010) (where unit owner alleged association committed acts of intrusion on her seclusion by condoning installation of wood flooring in unit above her, association's actions did not constitute invasion of privacy).

639. *See, e.g.*, Cathedral Hill Tower Condo. Ass'n v. Garbar, 2012 Cal. App. Unpub. LEXIS 4888 (June 29, 2012) (unit owner asserted cause of action in cross-complaint for invasion of privacy that alleged association's refusal to adequately maintain, repair, and/or replace antiquated and defective and dangerous mechanical room equipment that produced excess heat and noise violated right to privacy in unit).

640. Dubois v. Ass'n of Apt. Owners, 453 F.3d 1175, 1181 (9th Cir. 2006) (invasion of privacy claim brought against association based on "no pet" restriction; action dismissed for lack of standing).

641. Straub v. Scarpa, 967 So. 2d 437, 439 (Fla. 4th DCA 2007).

642. *See, e.g.*, ISO Form CG 00 01 12 07, § V.14.f.

643. *See, e.g.*, ISO Form CG 00 01 12 07, § V.14.g.

644. *See, e.g.*, ISO Form CG 00 01 12 07, § V.1.

ventures: quality or performance of goods,[645] wrong description of prices,[646] media and internet businesses,[647] and unauthorized use of the name or product of another.[648] These are generally not relevant to residential common interest communities

[a] Knowing Violation of Rights

The first exclusion to coverage for personal and advertising injury is for injury caused by, or at the direction of, the insured with knowledge the act would violate another's rights and inflict personal and advertising injury.[649] Many of the injuries for which the standard commercial general liability policy specifically provides coverage are "intentional torts," for example, false arrest, false imprisonment, wrongful eviction, wrongful detention, malicious prosecution, libel, and slander.[650] Does that mean that one who, for instance, falsely imprisons another, has knowledge the act would violate another's rights and inflict injury? If so, is coverage proscribed by the exclusion? One commentary notes that because it is difficult to conceive of torts like malicious prosecution or false arrest as "accidental," courts set a very high bar for the exclusion when it comes to carriers arguing it relieves them of the duty to defend, and those courts often say it applies only to intentional and knowing infliction of injury, not to injury resulting from reckless or negligent behavior.[651]

A number of courts that have examined policies that provide coverage for personal injury torts—false imprisonment, malicious prosecution, defamation—and exclude it for injury expected or intended by the insured have concluded that the exclusion creates an ambiguity where the policy provides coverage for a

645. *See, e.g.*, ISO Form CG 00 01 12 07, § I.B.2.g (coverage does not apply to personal and advertising injury that arises out of failure of goods, products, or services to conform with any statement of quality or performance made in advertisement by insured).

646. *See, e.g.*, ISO Form CG 00 01 12 07, § I.B.2.h (no coverage for personal and advertising injury arising out of wrong description of price of goods, products, or services stated in advertisement by insured).

647. *See, e.g.*, ISO Form CG 00 01 12 07, § I.B.2.j (no coverage for personal and advertising injury committed by insured whose business is advertising, broadcasting, publishing, telecasting, designing, or determining content of websites for others, or internet search, access, content, or service provider).

648. *See, e.g.*, ISO Form CG 00 01 12 07, § I.B.2.l (no coverage for personal and advertising injury arising out of unauthorized use of name or product of another in email address, domain name or metatag of insured, or any other similar tactics to mislead potential customers of that other party).

649. *See, e.g.*, ISO Form CG 00 01 12 07, § I.B.2.a.

650. Stanback v. Westchester Fire Ins. Co., 68 N.C. App. 107, 115, 314 S.E.2d 775, 779 (1984). *See also* Flocco v. State Farm Mut. Auto. Ins. Co., 752 A.2d 147 (D.C. 2000) (false arrest, false imprisonment, wrongful eviction, wrongful detention, malicious prosecution, libel, and slander are clearly intentional torts).

651. Dykes, *Send in the B Team: Insurance Coverage for Personal and Advertising Injury*, 27 Utah Bar J. 24, 26 (2014).

tort that can be committed either intentionally or unintentionally and, therefore, because the policy provides a specific coverage by name, it must be excepted from the exclusion.[652] Some courts that have considered the "knowing violation of rights" exclusion have reached the same conclusion,[653] while others have applied the exclusion to tort actions for which coverage is specifically provided.[654] Courts will also consider the allegations of the underlying complaint and whether a covered tort can be committed either with or without a knowing violation of rights and find a duty to defend.[655] Courts also say that an insurer has the burden of

---

652. *See, e.g.*, Tush v. Pharr, 68 P.3d 1239, 1249 (Alaska 2003) (where policy explicitly covered injuries arising out of wrongful eviction and did not differentiate between intentional and negligent wrongful eviction, it had to be deemed excepted from intentional acts exclusion); Flocco v. State Farm Mut. Auto. Ins. Co., 752 A.2d 147 (D.C. 2000) (where policy specifically provided coverage for intentional torts and purportedly attempted to exclude intentional torts in intentional acts exclusion, apparent conflict between coverage and exclusion had to be resolved in favor of insured); Knowles v. United Servs. Auto. Ass'n, 113 N.M. 703, 708, 832 P.2d 394, 399 (1992) (where policy excluded coverage for injury or damage expected or intended by insured and underlying claim was for wrongful eviction, insurer argued policy covered only negligent wrongful eviction and not wrongful eviction resulting from intentional acts; court held clause excluding coverage for "expected or intended" harm was repugnant to that offering coverage for wrongful eviction, and, therefore, ineffective to preclude coverage); Stanback v. Westchester Fire Ins. Co., 68 N.C. App. 107, 115, 314 S.E.2d 775, 779 (1984) (where policy explicitly covered intentional torts while excluding acts committed by or at direction of insured with intent to cause personal injury, apparent conflict between coverage and exclusion had to be resolved in favor of coverage; allegations of intentional infliction of mental anguish and malicious prosecution were not excluded from coverage).

653. *See, e.g.*, Regent Ins. Co. v. Strausser Enters., 902 F. Supp. 2d 628, 641–42 (E.D. Pa. 2012) (if malicious prosecution requires proof of improper motive or actual malice and, thus, all malicious prosecution claims would fall within "knowing violation" exclusion, then insurer would effectively have promised never to defend against malicious prosecution claim; finding ambiguity regarding coverage for malicious prosecution because person of reasonable intelligence who read Coverage B, "knowing violation" exclusion, and definition of "personal and advertising injury" could reasonably conclude policy never covers malicious prosecution or always covers it and under Pennsylvania law, ambiguous provisions in insurance contracts are interpreted in favor of insured); Doyle v. Country Mut. Ins. Co., 380 Ill. Dec. 320, 8 N.E.3d 490, 498 (2014) (if policy did not cover wrongful evictions, despite expressly listing it as covered, because resulting harm was "expected or intended from the standpoint of the insured," two reasonable and competing interpretations of policy would exist and if policy contains competing interpretations, and both interpretations are reasonable, court must construe policy in favor of insured). *See also* Park Univ. Enters. v. Am. Cas. Co. of Reading, 314 F. Supp. 2d 1094, 1110 (D. Kan. 2004) (rejecting argument that policy excluded coverage for advertising injury caused by or at direction of insured with knowledge that act would violate rights of another and inflict personal and advertising injury).

654. *See, e.g.*, Singer v. Colony Ins. Co., 147 F. Supp. 3d 1369, 1378 (S.D. Fla. 2015) (even if underlying complaint sufficiently established personal and advertising injury resulting from false imprisonment, malicious prosecution, libel, slander, or invasion of privacy, insurer had no duty to defend because policy excludes coverage for personal and advertising injury where insured knowingly violated rights of another); Allied World Natl. Assur. Co. v. Great Divide Ins. Co., 140 A.D.3d 103, 108–09, 32 N.Y.S.3d 72, 76 (2016) (allegations of tortious interference whether through defamatory or disparaging statements arguably stated offense within scope of coverage for personal and advertising injury liability; however, exclusion for "knowledge of falsity" presents bar to coverage).

655. *See, e.g.*, Sletten & Brettin Orthodontics, LLC v. Cont'l Cas. Co., 782 F.3d 931, 936 (8th Cir. 2015) (where policy provided coverage for defamation, but excluded coverage for intent-to-injure

establishing application of an exclusion and that it does not meet that burden by pointing to *unproven and disputed* allegations in the very complaint it is called on to defend.[656]

[b] Publishing Material with Knowledge of Its Falsity

The standard commercial general liability policy bars coverage for personal and advertising injury that arises out of oral or written publication of material, when done by, or at the direction of, the insured with knowledge it is false.[657] Some courts find it doubtful that the exclusion applied to injuries other than libel, slander, and invasion of privacy.[658] How the exclusion applies is problematic. Courts may hold that when the underlying complaint alleges intentional conduct—for example, fraud or defamation—coverage is excluded,[659] but if the cause of action does not require proof of knowing or intentional conduct, the exclusion is inapplicable.[660]

---

acts, coverage was provided for defamation in general as intentional act, but excluded coverage for defamation committed with intent to injure; exclusion makes sense because defamation is often committed without intending injury); Norfolk & Dedham Mut. Fire Ins. Co. v. Cleary Consultants, Inc., 81 Mass. App. Ct. 40, 958 N.E.2d 853 (2011) (exclusion must be understood as applying only to intentional and knowing infliction of injury, and not to injury resulting from reckless or negligent behavior; allegations of invasion of privacy fell well within range of reckless misconduct, leaving it possible for insured to be found liable based on something less than intentional and knowing infliction of injury and, therefore, exclusion does not negate duty to defend); Kubit v. MAG Mut. Ins. Co., 210 N.C. App. 273, 708 S.E.2d 138 (2011) (central question is whether underlying complaint alleges any facts permitting conclusion that insured did not know statements were violating rights and inflicting personal and advertising injury and where complaint specifically alleged defamation cause of action in which statements were made negligently or with knowledge that they were false, and/or with reckless disregard as to whether or not they were false, complaint contained allegations that fell within exclusion and allegations that arguably did not fall within exclusion, and insurer had duty to defend defamation claim).

656. *See, e.g.*, KM Strategic Mgmt., LLC v. Am. Cas. Co. of Reading, PA, 156 F. Supp. 3d 1154 (C.D. Cal. 2015) (where underlying complaint alleged disparagement and there was at least possibility of coverage because, despite allegations of intentional acts, conduct of insured might be shown to have been merely reckless or negligent, "knowing violation" exclusion did not excuse denial of duty to defend).

657. *See, e.g.*, ISO Form CG 00 01 12 07, § I.B.2.b.

658. *See, e.g.*, Adolfo House Distrib. Corp. v. Travelers Prop. & Cas. Ins. Co., 165 F. Supp. 2d 1332, 1341 (S.D. Fla. 2001) (finding it questionable as to whether exclusion applies to all advertising injuries, or only to libel, slander, and invasion of privacy).

659. *See, e.g.*, Thompson v. Md. Cas. Co., 84 P.3d 496, 499 (Colo. 2004) (where complaint alleged that insureds disparaged services of plaintiff by interfering with ability to develop and sell real property, insurer had no duty to defend because complaint alleged insureds knew that their disparaging statement was false, and, as a consequence, knowledge-of-falsity exclusion provision precluded coverage); Altivia Corp. v. Greenwich Ins. Co., 161 S.W.3d 52 (Tex. App.—Houston 4th Dist. 2004) (to extent statements allegedly libelous or slanderous were false and malicious and made with knowledge of their falsity, they were outside scope of coverage).

660. Cent. Mut. Ins. Co. v. StunFence, Inc., 292 F. Supp. 2d 1072, 1082 (N.D. Ill. 2003) (because assertions of intentional and willful conduct need not have been proved for claimant to recover damages for trademark infringement, exclusion did not apply); Bay Elec. Supply, Inc. v. Travelers

[c] Publishing Material Prior to the Policy Period

Under the third exclusion, there is no coverage for personal and advertising injury that arises out of oral or written publication of material when the first publication occurred before the beginning of the policy period.[661]

[d] Criminal Acts

The standard CGL policy proscribes coverage for personal and advertising injury that arises out of a criminal act committed by, or at the direction of, the insured.[662]

[e] Contractual Liability and Breach of Contract

Two exclusions in the standard CGL concern contractual liability. The first excludes coverage for personal and advertising injury for which the insured assumed liability in a contract or agreement,[663] but does not apply to liability for damages the insured would have absent the contract or agreement.[664] Second, there is no coverage for personal and advertising injury that arises out of a *breach* of contract.[665]

Lloyds Ins. Co., 61 F. Supp. 2d 611, 619 (S.D. Tex. 1999) (where knowledge was not requirement for finding of liability in underlying action, insurer failed to carry its burden of demonstrating that knowledge of falsity exclusion barred coverage). *See also* Nationwide Mut. Ins. Co. v. Lake Caroline, Inc., 515 F.3d 414 (5th Cir. 2008) (under Mississippi law "knowledge of falsity" exclusions do not apply to conduct constituting "gross and reckless disregard of the truth"); Cincinnati Ins. Co. v. E. Atl. Ins. Co., 260 F.3d 742, 745 (7th Cir. 2001) (where underlying claim was for tortious interference, which can be alleged as either negligent or intentional tort, because insured could be found liable even if knowledge of falsity was not shown, there was duty to defend).

661. *See, e.g.*, ISO Form CG 00 01 12 07, § I.B.2.c. *See* Villa Charlotte Bronte, Inc. v. Commercial Union Ins. Co., 487 N.Y.S.2d 314, 64 N.Y.2d 846, 476 N.E.2d 640 (1985) (insurer would only be excused based on exclusion from defending officer of cooperative corporation sued for allegedly defamatory remarks if dates of alleged remarks could be shown, it could be established whether he was acting on behalf of corporation when he made them, and whether pre-policy statements were same as or similar to those made after inception of policy).

662. *See, e.g.*, ISO Form CG 00 01 12 07, § I.B.2.d.

663. One commentary warns of a "trap" in the exclusion. Dykes, *Send in the B Team: Insurance Coverage for Personal and Advertising Injury*, 27 Utah Bar J. 24, 27, n.3 (2014). The author notes that indemnity provisions are extremely common in contracts. Under Coverage A, if the insured assumes the tort liability of another party to pay damages to a third party that arise from a bodily injury or from property damage, the carrier will reimburse for those indemnity costs. However, under the Coverage B exclusion, if the insured agrees to indemnify another party for damages caused by injury resulting from the advertising injury of the other party, the carrier will not reimburse the insured for the indemnity costs. The author warns insureds to be wary of signing agreements indemnifying others for claims that could give rise to personal or advertising injury and also to avoid the use of the phrase "personal injury" in indemnity agreements when what is meant is *bodily* injury.

664. *See, e.g.*, ISO Form CG 00 01 12 07, § I.B.2.e.

665. *See, e.g.*, ISO Form CG 00 01 12 07, § I.B.2.f. There is an exception that would rarely apply to residential common interest communities for an implied contract to use the advertising idea of another in advertisement of the named insured. An advertisement is a notice broadcast or

[f] Infringement of Copyright, Patent, Trademark, or Trade Secret

Coverage is excluded for personal and advertising injury that arises out of infringement of copyright, patent, trademark, trade secret, or other intellectual property rights, although the exclusion does not apply to infringement of copyright, trade dress, or slogan,[666] in the insured's advertisement. [667]

While most litigation over intellectual property rights involves commercial ventures, residential common interest communities are not immune from violation of those rights. Trademark or trade name infringement actions against them are rare but not unheard of.[668] The fact that they are affected by trademark

---

published to the general public or specific markets about the goods, products, or services of the named insured to attract customers or supporters. *See, e.g.*, ISO Form CG 00 01 12 07, § V.1.

666. *See* Land's End at Sunset Beach Cmty. Ass'n v. Aspen Specialty Ins. Co., 2017 U.S. Dist. LEXIS 163457 (M.D. Fla. Oct. 3, 2017) (exclusion bars coverage for trademark infringement but expressly permits coverage for slogan infringement, and it would make little sense for court to allow phrase to serve as trademark and also conclude it was slogan).

667. *See, e.g.*, ISO Form CG 00 01 12 07, § I.B.2.i. *See also* Land's End at Sunset Beach Cmty. Ass'n v. Aspen Specialty Ins. Co., 2017 U.S. Dist. LEXIS 163457 (M.D. Fla. Oct. 3, 2017) (exception under which other intellectual property rights do not include use of another's advertising idea in "your advertisement" did not apply to trademark infringement, but only to infringement of other intellectual property rights).

668. *See* Land's End at Sunset Beach Cmty. Ass'n v. Aspen Specialty Ins. Co., 2017 U.S. Dist. LEXIS 163457 (M.D. Fla. Oct. 3, 2017) (corporation that operated hotels and resorts in Alaska and owned trademark for "Land's End" alleged Florida condominium association used that phrase in advertising its short-term rental services); Islander East Rental Program v. Ferguson, 917 F. Supp. 504 (S.D. Tex. 1996), *aff'd*, 145 F.3d 359 (5th Cir. 1998), *cert. den.*, 525 U.S. 932, 119 S. Ct. 341, 142 L. Ed. 2d 281 (1998) (rental management company sued condominium association of similar name alleging, *inter alia*, servicemark and trademark infringement and misappropriation of trade secrets); Showtime/The Movie Channel, Inc. v. Covered Bridge Condominium Ass'n, 693 F. Supp. 1080 (S.D. Fla. 1988), *vacated and remanded*, 895 F.2d 711 (11th Cir. 1990) (plaintiff producer of private, commercial-free, pay television entertainment services sued association for, *inter alia*, violation of Federal Communications Act and trademark infringement after association discontinued contract with plaintiff and refused to obtain authorization for receipt of plaintiff's services or to make any payments for programming, but allegedly intercepted and appropriated to its own use plaintiff's satellite cable programming through satellite reception dish antenna installed on its premises and distributed that programming to all its unit owners; court found both violation of Federal Communications Act and trademark infringement); Ritter v. Farrow, 355 Wis. 2d 577, 851 N.W.2d 471 (2014) (appellant found guilty of trade name infringement argued on appeal that lower court erred by denying motion to require joinder of condominium association known by that trade name and individual condominium unit owners; association argued court erroneously denied its motion to intervene); Ocean House, Inc. v. Seabury Hous. Assocs., 1990 Me. Super. LEXIS 42 (Feb. 13, 1990) (where landmark hotel was converted by defendant to condominium ownership and was given name to which plaintiff claimed to have acquired exclusive right, plaintiff brought statutory claim under state trademark protection law seeking injunction to stop further use by defendants of that name); Wawa, Inc. v. Commons at Wawa, Inc., 1989 U.S. Dist. LEXIS 10382 (E.D. Pa. Aug. 30, 1989) (where plaintiff used term "Wawa" to refer to its various food products and convenience stores, while defendant used it to refer to its condominium development, plaintiff sued for trademark infringement and court ordered defendant to include disclaimer disaffirming any connection to plaintiff in its stationery, advertising, and promotional material). *See also* Holiday Inns, Inc. v. Holiday Out in America, 481 F.2d 445 (5th Cir. 1973) (famous hotel chain sued

and trade name issues is confirmed by the fact that common interest communities have themselves found the need occasionally to sue others over use of trade names.[669]

Typically, before litigation over intellectual property rights is initiated, the association will receive a "cease and desist" letter from the attorney of the party that believes itself wronged. Because of the exclusion from coverage, the association needs to forward that letter immediately to its attorney and discuss with the attorney its potential liability and whether the exception to the exclusion might apply.

[g] Electronic Chatrooms or Bulletin Boards

There is no coverage for personal and advertising injury that arises out of an electronic chatroom or bulletin board hosted or owned by the insured, or over which it exercises control.[670] A common interest community may have networking sites or blogs where comments are made that are defamatory or invade the privacy of others. Even though a suit for defamation or invasion of privacy might otherwise be covered by the standard commercial general liability policy, this exclusion would bar coverage.

[h] Pollution

There are two exclusions that concern pollution. First, coverage is proscribed for personal and advertising injury that arises out of the actual, alleged, or threatened discharge, dispersal, seepage, migration, release, or escape of pollutants at any time.[671] A "pollutant" is any solid, liquid, gaseous, or thermal irritant or contaminant, and includes smoke, vapor, soot, fumes, acids, alkalis, chemicals, and waste.[672] The second exclusion bars coverage for any loss, cost, or expense

owner of campground facilities that sold lots in campground as condominiums and managed their rental for trademark and service mark infringement).

669. *See, e.g.*, Bd. of Dirs. of Sapphire Bay Condos. W. v. Simpson, 129 Fed. Appx. 711 (3d Cir. 2005) (affirming judgment in favor of condominium governing board in its suit against owner of unit in complex for common-law trademark-related claims arising from unauthorized use of its trade name and service mark; plaintiff board claimed defendant had no right to register domain name *sapphirebaycondos.com* or to operate website at that domain claiming to be official website of association); Tortoise Island Homeowners Ass'n v. Tortoise Island Realty, Inc., 790 So. 2d 525 (Fla. 5th DCA), *rev. dis.*, 804 So. 2d 331 (Fla. 2001) (association sued realty company for infringement and dilution of its trade name; appellate court reversed decision of trial court that quality of association's trade name was not threatened by defendant's use of it); Lion's Head Homeowners Ass'n v. White Bridge Rd. Assocs., 1985 Tenn. App. LEXIS 3424 (Aug. 28, 1985) (association sued owner of apartment complexes to enjoin it from using name "Lion's Head" and appellate court affirmed issuance of injunction prohibiting defendants from using or continuing to use that name).

670. *See, e.g.*, ISO Form CG 00 01 12 07, § I.B.2.k.

671. *See, e.g.*, ISO Form CG 00 01 12 07, § I.B.2.m.

672. *See, e.g.*, ISO Form CG 00 01 12 07, § V.15. Waste includes materials that are to be recycled, reconditioned, or reclaimed.

that arises out of any request, demand, order, or statutory or regulatory requirement that any insured or others test for, monitor, clean up, remove, contain, treat, detoxify, or neutralize, or respond in any way to, or assess the effects of, pollutants or any claim or suit by or on behalf of a governmental authority for damages because of testing for, monitoring, cleaning up, removing, containing, treating, detoxifying, or neutralizing, or responding in any way to, or assessing the effects of, pollutants.[673]

[i] Distribution of Material in Violation of Certain Statutes

The final exclusion is quite narrow and bars coverage for personal and advertising injury that arises directly or indirectly out of any action or omission that violates, or is alleged to violate, the federal Telephone Consumer Protection Act (TCPA)[674] or the CAN-SPAM Act of 2003.[675] Additionally, there is no coverage for personal and advertising injury that arises directly or indirectly out of any action or omission that violates, or is alleged to violate, any other statute, ordinance, or regulation that prohibits or limits sending, transmitting, communicating, or distributing material or information.[676] This would include state statutes, of which there are many.[677]

The TCPA[678] in general prohibits making a call using any automatic telephone dialing system or an artificial or prerecorded voice to any telephone number assigned to a cellular telephone service,[679] or initiating any telephone call to any residential telephone line using an artificial or prerecorded voice to deliver a message without the prior express consent of the called party.[680] It also generally bans using any telephone facsimile machine, computer, or other device to send, to a telephone facsimile machine, an unsolicited advertisement.[681] A common interest community could violate the Act if it places prohibited calls to collect overdue assessments or other debts.[682]

---

673. *See, e.g.*, ISO Form CG 00 01 12 07, § I.B.2.n.

674. *See, e.g.*, ISO Form CG 00 01 12 07, § I.B.2.p.(1).

675. *See, e.g.*, ISO Form CG 00 01 12 07, § I.B.2.p.(2).

676. *See, e.g.*, ISO Form CG 00 01 12 07, § I.B.2.p.(3).

677. *See* Erickson, *Disfavored Advertising: Telemarketing, Junk Faxes and the Commercial Speech Doctrine*, 11 Comm. L. & Pol'y 589, 592 (2006).

678. 47 U.S.C.S. § 227. *See generally* Erickson, *Disfavored Advertising: Telemarketing, Junk Faxes and the Commercial Speech Doctrine*, 11 Comm. L. & Pol'y 589 (2006).

679. 47 U.S.C.S. § 227(b)(1)(A)(iii).

680. 47 U.S.C.S. § 227(b)(1)(B).

681. 47 U.S.C.S. § 227(b)(1)(C).

682. *See, e.g.*, Mangiaracina v. Orange Lake Country Club, Inc., 2015 U.S. Dist. LEXIS 19289, 26 Fla. L. Weekly Fed. D 1 (M.D. Fla. Feb. 18, 2015) (refusing to dismiss action against condominium association for, *inter alia*, violation of TCPA based on calls made on its behalf to cellphones of timeshare owners for purposes of collection of balance allegedly owed on consumer timeshare account). *Compare* Soulliere v. Cent. Fla. Invs., Inc., 2015 U.S. Dist. LEXIS 36858 (M.D. Fla. Mar. 23, 2015) (summary judgment granted to homeowners association in action for violation of TCPA

The CAN-SPAM Act[683] seeks to thwart "nuisance e-mail" by prohibiting commercial advertisement email senders from deceiving recipients about its source or subject matter, requiring senders to provide and comply with an opt-out mechanism in their emails, and requiring senders of unsolicited commercial email to provide a valid physical address and proper notification that the message is an advertisement.[684] To the extent they use email at all, common interest community associations send notice and information to their members who have willingly provided their email addresses, so generally, they should not run afoul of the Act.

§ 13.07 Medical Payments (Coverage C)

The third category of coverage under the standard commercial general liability policy is for medical payments.[685] The primary purpose of this coverage—often called "MedPay"—is to pay for injuries sustained by the general public while on the premises of the insured or otherwise exposed to its operations.[686] Under the standard policy language, the carrier will pay "medical expenses" for "bodily injury"—meaning bodily injury, sickness, or disease sustained by a person, including death resulting from any of them[687]—caused by an "accident" on premises owned or rented by the named insured, on ways next to those premises, or because of the operations of the named insured.[688] There are three provisos. First, the accident has to take place in the "coverage territory" and during the policy period.[689] The basic coverage territory is the United States and its territories and possessions, Puerto Rico, and Canada, but may include international

based on calls made to cell phone using automatic telephone dialing system in attempt to collect past due maintenance and tax payments on timeshare account owed to association).

683. 15 U.S.C.S. § 7701, *et seq.*

684. Arora, *The CAN-SPAM Act: An Inadequate Attempt to Deal with a Growing Problem*, 39 Colum. J.L. & Soc. Probs. 299, 300 (2006).

685. *See, e.g.*, ISO Form CG 00 01 12 07, § I.C.

686. Zurich Am. Ins. Co. v. Ainsworth, 18 So. 3d 9, 11 (Fla. 3d DCA 2009). *See generally* Johnson, *The Practical Art: On the Archaeology & Architecture of Liability Insurance Contracts*, 78 Def. Couns. J. 143, 154 (Apr. 2011).

687. *See, e.g.*, ISO Form CG 00 01 12 07, § V.3. *See also* Clifford v. Church Mut. Ins. Co., 2015 U.S. Dist. LEXIS 138271 (S.D. Ohio Sept. 30, 2015) (denying claim under medical expense coverage for sexual assault/battery because plaintiffs failed to sufficiently show they were entitled to recover under policy for "bodily injury").

688. *See, e.g.*, ISO Form CG 00 01 12 07, § I.C.1. What are the "operations" of an insured association? One court, faced with determining the scope of an association's operations first turned to its Covenants, Conditions, and Restrictions, which it said provided the greatest amount of information about what was considered to be the "operations" of the association. It also examined the bylaws. The court also considered a state statute that provided a homeowners association was responsible for repairing, replacing, or maintaining the common area. Phila. Indem. Ins. Co. v. Lakeside Heights Homeowners Ass'n, 110 F. Supp. 3d 965, 971–72, 975 (N.D. Cal. 2015).

689. *See, e.g.*, ISO Form CG 00 01 12 07, § I.C.1.a.(3).(a).

waters or airspace,[690] or in some cases anywhere in the world.[691] Second, the expenses must be incurred[692] and reported[693] to the insurer within one year of the date of the accident.[694] Finally, the injured person has to submit to examination—at the expense of the insurer—by physicians of the carrier's choice as often as it reasonably requires.

The policy requires the named insured to see to it that the insurer is notified as soon as practicable of an "occurrence"[695] or offense that could result in a claim.[696] Can an injured party submit a claim directly to the insurer? The policy does not specify the method of reporting an occurrence,[697] but in one case where an injured person requested payment of medical expenses, the insurer refused to

---

690. The coverage territory includes international waters or airspace, but only if the injury or damage occurs during travel or transportation between the United States and its territories and possessions, Puerto Rico, or Canada. *See, e.g.*, CG 00 01 12 07, § V.4.b.

691. The coverage territory includes any other part of the world if the injury or damage arises out of goods or products made or sold by the insured in the United States and its territories and possessions, Puerto Rico, or Canada; activities of a person whose home is in the United States and its territories and possessions, Puerto Rico, or Canada, but is away for a short time on the business of the insured; or a personal and advertising injury offense that take place through the Internet or similar electronic means of communication, provided the responsibility of the insured to pay damages is determined in a suit on the merits, in the United States and its territories and possessions, Puerto Rico, or Canada or in a settlement to which the carrier agrees. *See, e.g.*, CG 00 01 12 07, § V.4.c.

692. *See* Gausepohl v. Towne Props., Inc., 2014 U.S. Dist. LEXIS 96676 (E.D. Ky. July 15, 2014) (insurer correctly advised claimant that bills had to be incurred and reported to it within one year of accident).

693. The policy language generally does not specify the method of "reporting" the expenses. Where the CGL carrier for the alleged tortfeasor asked the injured person to provide it with "explanation of benefit" forms from his insurance carrier, which had already made payments, the court found that providing the requested information within one year of the incident was a sufficient report to the CGL insurer. Donald v. Liberty Mut. Ins. Co., 18 F.3d 474 (7th Cir. 1994).

694. *See, e.g.*, ISO Form CG 00 01 12 07, § I.C.1.a.(3).(b). *See* Colonial Woods Condo. v. Hanover Ins. Co., 245 A.D.2d 329, 665 N.Y.S.2d 102 (1997) (in early 1992 claimant was injured when she slipped and fell on snow and ice on premises of condominium, and in July she requested reimbursement of $300 in medical expenses, but association did not notify carrier of claim until November of 1993 when claimant's attorney informed it lawsuit was planned; court found that delay of, at minimum, 16 months, in notifying insurer was unreasonable as matter of law). *See also* Bates v. Vt. Mut. Ins. Co., 157 N.H. 391, 399, 950 A.2d 186, 192 (2008) (medical payments coverage is occurrence based and, therefore, insurer cannot deny coverage for late reporting of medical expenses unless it showed it had been prejudiced); Salerno v. Atlantic Mut. Ins. Co., 198 Ariz. 54, 60, 6 P.3d 758, 764 (Ariz. App. 2000) (late notice of medical expenses claim will not bar recovery absent actual prejudice). *Compare* Brenegan v. Fireman's Fund Ins. Co., 2015 Cal. App. Unpub. LEXIS 2022 (Mar. 23, 2015). In *Brenegan* the court said the medical expenses provision was not the typical claims-made policy clause, but it was analogous to one because it contained a reporting element essential to coverage. Coverage is triggered not by the accident, but by reporting medical expenses within one year of the accident. The notice-prejudice rule does not apply to claims-made policies and because a medical expenses clause makes notice an element of coverage, application of the rule would materially alter the risk of the insurer.

695. An "occurrence" is an accident. *See, e.g.*, ISO Form CG 00 01 12 07, § V.13.

696. *See, e.g.*, ISO Form CG 00 01 12 07, § IV.2.a.

697. Donald v. Liberty Mut. Ins. Co., 18 F.3d 474 (7th Cir. 1994).

pay benefits without a request from its insured to do so.[698] On the other hand, in case in which a condominium unit owner sent the association's insurance company a letter advising it of a fall she took on common property, a claims specialist for the company responded and advised her the policy would cover the expenses of reasonable medical treatment she received as a result of her fall up to $5,000.[699] No mention was made in the case of whether the association contacted the insurer; however, as the unit owner would appear to have been considered an insured because the fall happened on common property, notification by the association may have been unnecessary. Ordinarily, residents of a common interest community will not be aware of the medical payments coverage and are not, therefore, likely to submit a claim. However, if an association is concerned about residents potentially filing frivolous claims, or there has been a history of such claims, and the association is concerned about a possible increase in premiums or cancellation of the policy as a result, it should explore document amendments with the association attorney that would require owners to submit claims through the association and allow the association to refuse to submit a claim it deems frivolous on behalf of a unit owner.

[1] Coverage

Coverage C applies under three circumstances. The first is when bodily injuries are caused by an accident on premises owned or rented by the named insured. Second, there is coverage when bodily injuries are caused by an accident on "ways"[700] next to those premises. Finally, Coverage C applies when bodily injuries are caused by an accident because of the operations of the named insured.

[a] Premises Owned or Rented by the Named Insured

The part of the coverage for bodily injuries caused by accidents on premises owned or rented by the named insured takes on some twists and turns in common interest communities. In a housing cooperative, the cooperative corporation owns all the real property, although it could also be the lessee of that property. Coverage C should, therefore, apply to bodily injuries to anyone—including tenant/shareholders—anywhere on the property, including in the individual apartments, unless otherwise excluded. In a homeowners association, the association typically owns, or may lease, common areas—recreational facilities, opens space, roads, and sidewalks—while the association members usually own their homes,

698. Schmalfeldt v. N. Pointe Ins. Co., 469 Mich. 422, 424, 670 N.W.2d 651, 652 (2003).

699. Gausepohl v. Towne Props., Inc., 2014 U.S. Dist. LEXIS 96676 (E.D. Ky. July 15, 2014). *See also* Walker v. Farmers Ins. Exchange, 153 Cal. App. 4th 965, 968, 63 Cal. Rptr. 3d 507, 509–10 (2007) (after association reported injury to its carrier around September, insurer paid injured unit owner $5,000 under coverage for medical expenses after request in October from claimant's attorney).

700. *See* § 13.07[1][b], *infra*.

and any yard, outright in fee simple. In that case the "premises owned or rented" portion of the coverage would only apply when an accident occurred to anyone, including an association member unless otherwise excluded, on the association property. However, in some associations, for example, townhouse or zero lot line communities, there may be a yard reserved for the exclusive use of the owner of a particular home, but the yard is owned by the association. In that case, coverage should apply when an accident occurred to anyone, including an association member unless otherwise excluded, in that yard.

Condominiums present a bit of a riddle in application of the "premises owned or rented by the named insured" portion of the coverage. By definition, a condominium association, although it is the named insured, owns no property.[701] Each member of the association owns an individual unit, and all the property that is not a unit is owned collectively by the unit owners as tenants in common. Therefore, there can be no accidents on premises owned or rented by the named insured. Nonetheless, many courts describe the association as the owner of the common elements,[702] and insurers appear to treat condominium associations in effect as the owners of common elements.[703] Therefore, the "premises owned or rented" portion of the coverage should apply when an accident occurs to anyone, including a unit owner unless otherwise excluded, on the common property. However, most condominiums also have "limited common elements," which are common elements reserved for the exclusive use of fewer than all the unit

701. *See* Uniform Condominium Act § 1-130, Comment 5 (unless ownership interest in common elements is vested in owners of units, project is not a condominium).

702. *See* Harbor House Condominium Ass'n v. Massachusetts Bay Ins. Co., 915 F.2d 316 (7th Cir. 1990) (saying that association owned common areas of condominium building). *See also* Crystal Colony Condo. Ass'n v. Aspen Specialty Ins. Co., 2014 U.S. Dist. LEXIS 39543 (S.D. Fla. Mar. 21, 2014); Raintree Vill. Condo. No. 11 Ass'n v. Great Am. Ins. Co., 2013 U.S. Dist. LEXIS 134907 (M.D. Fla. Sept. 20, 2013); Ass'n of Apt. Owners of Imperial Plaza v. Fireman's Fund Ins. Co., 2013 U.S. Dist. LEXIS 69933 (D. Haw. May 16, 2013); Seagate Towers Condo. Ass'n v. QBE Ins. Corp., 2012 U.S. Dist. LEXIS 188462 (S.D. Fla. Nov. 16, 2012); Palma Vista Condo. Ass'n of Hillsborough County v. Nationwide Mut. Fire Ins. Co., 2010 U.S. Dist. LEXIS 118262 (M.D. Fla. Oct. 7, 2010); Beverly Hills Condo. 1-12 v. Aspen Specialty Ins. Co., 2007 U.S. Dist. LEXIS 28999 (S.D. Fla. Jan. 31, 2007); Longpoint Condo. Ass'n v. Allstate Ins. Co., 2005 U.S. Dist. LEXIS 43917 (N.D. Fla. June 1, 2005); Pioneer Tower Owners Ass'n v. State Farm Fire & Cas. Co., 880 N.Y.S.2d 885, 12 N.Y.3d 302, 908 N.E.2d 875 (2009); Walker v. Farmers Ins. Exchange, 153 Cal. App. 4th 965, 63 Cal. Rptr. 3d 507 (2007); Sunbreaker Condominium Ass'n v. Travelers Ins. Co., 79 Wn. App. 368, 370, 901 P.2d 1079, 1080 (1995).

703. In what appears to be the only appellate opinion concerning Coverage C and a common interest community, the insurer paid medical expenses to a unit owner injured in a slip and fall in a common area, apparently without raising any question about the ownership of the common area. Gausepohl v. Towne Props., Inc., 2014 U.S. Dist. LEXIS 96676 (E.D. Ky. July 15, 2014) (where claimant slipped and fell at her condominium complex allegedly because faulty sprinkler system came on at non-scheduled time and wet common area surface without warning, court agreed that insurance company for association properly paid medical expenses reported within one year of accident).

owners.[704] Typically, a limited common element is a balcony, patio, storage closet, or parking space reserved for the use of a single unit owner. In that case, coverage should apply when an accident occurs to anyone, including the unit owner to whom the limited common element is reserved, unless otherwise excluded.

[b] Ways Next to the Premises of the Named Insured

Coverage for injuries caused by an accident on "ways next to" premises owned or rented by the named insured requires a determination of the meaning of "ways next to." A Florida court said that construction of the term includes "considerations of whether public or commonly held property separates the way in question from the designated premises."[705] In that case the insured rented a building in a shopping center located on a public highway. Between that highway and the shopping center parking lot were a swale, a sidewalk, and another swale. The highway did not abut or touch the parking lot or the rented premises of the insured in the shopping center. The accident occurred on the highway. The court declined to find coverage within the meaning of the term "ways next to premises" and chose instead to follow cases that hold that a claim arising from an accident on a way that is not contiguous to or touching the insured premises is excluded from coverage.

[c] The Operations of the Named Insured

To establish whether there is coverage for bodily injuries caused by an accident allegedly because of the operations of the named insured, the meaning of "operations of the named insured" has to be determined. A Colorado court held that "operations" as used in a medical payments provision means "the process or series of acts actively engaged in by the insured . . . on behalf of its business."[706] Thus, under this aspect of the medical expenses coverage, there is no requirement that the injury occur on premises owned or rented by the named insured or on ways next to those premises so long as the accident was because of the operations of the named insured.

---

704. *See, e.g.*, Uniform Common Interest Ownership Act § 1-103(21) ("limited common element" means portion of common elements allocated by declaration or by operation of law for exclusive use of one or more, but fewer than all of units).

705. Zurich Am. Ins. Co. v. Ainsworth, 18 So. 3d 9, 12 (Fla. 3d DCA 2009).

706. Merrell v. Republic Western Ins. Co., 931 P.2d 577, 579 (Colo. App. 1997) (generally accepted meaning of "operations" involves series of actions to effect certain purpose, for example, whole process of planning for and managing business and refers to only those activities actively engaged in by business for its "certain purpose," that is, for benefit of that business; where business of insured was to rent and lease equipment, those activities might include locating, selecting, and delivering equipment to customers or advertising, customer assistance, promotions, and employee decisions, but activities of others concerning equipment rented or leased by it would not be activities actively engaged in by it for the benefit of its business and, therefore, injury suffered by claimant while using machinery leased from insured at site away from that of insured was not covered).

[2] Meaning of "Accident"

The coverage is for bodily injuries that are caused by an accident. The policy, however, does not define "accident." One commentary says the term is generally understood to mean that the event that caused an injury can be traced to a definite time and place and was not expected or intended from the point of view of the insured or the injured person, so that the fact that someone was injured by an intentional act of a third party should not prevent medical payments coverage.[707] There is disagreement over whether "intended" means intent to act or intent to injure. Some courts hold there is an accident when an insured did not intend for there to be an injury,[708] while others conclude a deliberate act is not an accident regardless of whether injury was intended.[709]

[3] Covered Payments

The carrier will make payments regardless of fault,[710] but those payments will not exceed the applicable limit of insurance.[711] The insurer will pay *reasonable* expenses for first aid administered at the time of an accident. It will also pay

---

707. *Commercial General Liability Form Medical Payments Coverage* (Summit Business Media, 2013).

708. *See, e.g.*, Std. Constr. Co. v. Md. Cas. Co., 359 F.3d 846, 851 (6th Cir. 2004) (deliberate act with unforeseen and unintended consequences fell within definition of "occurrence," which is an accident, as matter of law); State Farm Fire & Cas. Co. v. CTC Dev. Corp., 720 So. 2d 1072, 1075–76 (Fla. 1998) (if resulting damages are unintended, they are accidental even though original acts were intentional; where insured did not intend to inflict injury on victim by intentional act, and act was not so inherently injurious that injury was certain to follow from it, that act as contributing cause of injury would be regarded as accidental).

709. *See, e.g.*, Fire Ins. Exchange v. Superior Court, 181 Cal. App. 4th 388, 392–93, 104 Cal. Rptr. 3d 534, 538–39 (2010) (where insured intended all of acts that resulted in injury, event may not be deemed an "accident" merely because insured did not intend to cause injury; term "accident" refers to nature of act giving rise to liability, not to intent of insured to cause harm). *See also* Smolker v. Pac. Villas Homeowners Ass'n, 2007 Cal. App. Unpub. LEXIS 2155 (Mar. 19, 2007), where unit owners claimed to have been injured in the common areas of the condominium building when the insureds opened doors and walked in the common hallway causing the spread of a noxious substance. The court said walking down the common area hallway and opening doors were not accidents. The conduct was intentional, whether or not the insureds expected or intended that conduct to cause harm. Therefore, without an accident, there was no coverage.

710. *See, e.g.*, Heimerl v. Waverly Beach, Inc., 273 Wis. 2d 784, 680 N.W.2d 832 (2004) (payments made under medical expense provisions are completely independent of liability on part of insured).

711. *See, e.g.*, ISO Form CG 00 01 12 07, § I.C.1.b. Coverage C, then, is subject to the general aggregate policy limit, meaning that if that limit is exhausted by claims under the other coverages, the insurer has no further obligations under Coverage C, even if no other medical payment claims have been made during the policy period. *Commercial General Liability Form Medical Payments Coverage* (Summit Business Media, 2013). *Compare* Atkins v. Metro. Junior Baseball League, Inc., 61 Va. Cir. 155 (2003) (nowhere in policy is anything said about payments provided for under one coverage of policy being applied to, or deducted from, payments provided for under different coverage of policy).

necessary medical, surgical, x-ray, and dental services—including prosthetic devices—and ambulance, hospital, professional nursing, and funeral services. The medical expense limit will be stated on the Declarations Page and typically is a small amount, often merely $5,000 per person.[712]

One treatise contends that because the medical expenses coverage typically has no "other insurance" clause, it is unclear whether the coverage is primary or excess to other applicable coverages, including non-liability insurance of the injured party, for example, health insurance.[713] Note that the typical policy does have an "other insurance" clause in its commercial general liability conditions section that specifically applies to Coverage A and B, but does not mention Coverage C.[714] An endorsement can be added to a policy that makes the medical payments coverage excess over any other available insurance.[715]

[4] Exclusions

Medical payments coverage in the standard commercial general liability policy has seven exclusions. The first five have some relation to common interest communities. Under the sixth exclusion, the carrier will not pay for expenses for bodily injury included within the "products-completed operations hazard,"[716] a provision that has limited application to CICs.[717] The seventh exclusion incorporates the exclusions of Coverage A. Note that if coverage is being sought under Coverage A itself, the Coverage C exclusions do not apply.[718]

---

712. *See* Donald v. Liberty Mut. Ins. Co., 18 F.3d 474, 478 (7th Cir. 1994) (applicable limit of insurance for Coverage C was $5,000); Gausepohl v. Towne Props., Inc., 2014 U.S. Dist. LEXIS 96676 (E.D. Ky. July 15, 2014) (policy provided $5,000 in no-fault medical payment coverage); Heimerl v. Waverly Beach, Inc., 273 Wis. 2d 784, 680 N.W.2d 832 (2004) (medical expenses under provision were $5,000 per person). The amount may be larger and may be modified by endorsement. *See, e.g.*, Brenegan v. Fireman's Fund Ins. Co., 2015 Cal. App. Unpub. LEXIS 2022 (Mar. 23, 2015) (Declarations Page showed medical expenses limit of $10,000, but endorsement modified that to $20,000 for any one person).

713. 2 *New Appleman Law of Liability Insurance* § 9.08[2] (Matthew Bender, 2016). *But see* Gausepohl v. Towne Props., Inc., 2014 U.S. Dist. LEXIS 96676 (E.D. Ky. July 15, 2014), where the insurer took the position that it would cover medical payments of a condominium unit owner injured on common elements up to $5,000 in excess of any other health insurance she might have. No mention was made in the opinion of whether there was an "other insurance" clause in the medical payments coverage or whether the insurer had correctly interpreted the policy.

714. *See* ISO Form CG 00 01 12 07, § IV.4.

715. For example, Western World Insurance Group has an endorsement that replaces the standard Coverage C. Although the coverage is substantially the same as in the ISO standard CGL policy, it adds that the insurance is excess over any other available insurance. Form WW456, § 1.c.

716. *See, e.g.*, ISO Form CG 00 01 12 07, § I.C.2.f.

717. *See* ISO Form CG 00 01 12 07, § V.16 for the definition of "products-completed operations hazard."

718. *See* Kmart Corp. v. Securitas Sec. Servs. USA, 2012 U.S. Dist. LEXIS 191234 (N.D. Ga. Mar. 13, 2012).

[a] An Insured

The carrier will not pay expenses for bodily injury to any insured except "volunteer workers."[719] Under the standard policy, an "insured" is any person or organization qualifying as an insured under the policy. For a common interest community, that can mean the residents in certain circumstances. For example, if the named insured is designated as an organization other than a partnership, joint venture, or LLC, the organization is an insured as are its "executive officers" and directors, but only with respect to their duties as officers or directors, and its stockholders are insureds, but only with respect to their liability as stockholders.[720]

Additionally, in condominiums a *unit owner* is an insured, but only with respect to liability arising out of ownership, maintenance, or repair of that portion of the premises not reserved for his or her exclusive use or occupancy.[721] In a townhouse community, each individual townhouse owner is an insured, but only with respect to liability as a member of the association and not with respect to any liability arising out of ownership, maintenance, use, or repair of the property to which the individual owner has title.[722] Pursuant to these definitions of "an insured," it has been argued that when an owner is injured on common property, the exclusion for insureds applies.[723]

A volunteer worker is an insured, but only while performing duties related to the conduct of the business of the named insured.[724] A "volunteer worker" is a person who is not an employee of the named insured and who "donates" his or her work and acts at the direction of and within the scope of duties determined by the named insured, without being paid a fee, salary, or other compensation by the named insured or anyone else for that work.[725] Clearly, there are circumstances in which the resident of a common interest community would be considered a volunteer worker.

Anyone while acting as "real estate manager" for the named insured is an insured.[726] That means a community association manager is an insured under the policy.

---

719. *See, e.g.*, ISO Form CG 00 01 12 07, § I.C.2.a.

720. *See, e.g.*, ISO Form CG 00 01 12 07, § II.1.d.

721. *See, e.g.*, ISO Form CG 20 04 11 85 (Additional Insured—Condominium Unit Owners).

722. *See, e.g.*, ISO Form CG 20 17 11 85 (Additional Insured—Townhouse Associations).

723. *How Well Do You Know Condo Insurance Exclusions?* (2017), available at: http://www.propertycasualty360.com/2017/05/10/how-well-do-you-know-condo-insurance-exclusions?t=coverage-issues&slreturn=1494455183. The contrary argument is that the definition of owners as insureds is intended to address their potential vicarious liability for claims related to ownership, maintenance, repair, or the condition of the common elements. When an owner is injured on the common elements, the injury is not about their "liability arising out of ownership, maintenance, or repair" and should not be excluded from coverage.

724. *See, e.g.*, ISO Form CG 00 01 12 07, § II.2.a. *See* § 13.02[2][c], *infra*.

725. *See, e.g.*, ISO Form CG 00 01 12 07, § V.20. For a discussion of who is an insured, see § 13.02, *infra*.

726. *See, e.g.*, ISO Form CG 00 01 12 07, § II.2.b.

[b] Employees

Ordinarily, an employee of the named insured is an insured, but only for acts within the scope of his or her employment by the named insured or while performing duties related to the conduct of the business of the named insured.[727] That would bring employees within the exclusion for bodily injury to any insured discussed above, at least while the employee is preforming his or her duties. Additionally, under the second policy exclusion, the carrier will not pay expenses for bodily injury to a person *hired to do work* for, or on behalf of, *any* insured.[728] A person "hired to do work" could be an employee but could also be an independent contractor.[729] Any insured encompasses the association as the named insured but also, as discussed above, could include a resident or the community association manager. Sometimes a common interest community will have maintenance personnel regularly on site who are employees of a business with which the CIC association contracts. Those personnel should be excluded from medical payments coverage as persons hired to do work for, or on behalf of, an insured.

Note that the language of the exclusion does not explicitly limit its application to a hired person while that person is preforming his or her duties. The exclusion also applies to a person hired to do work for, or on behalf of, a tenant of any insured.[730] That would appear to extend the exclusion to a person hired to do work for, or on behalf of, a tenant/shareholder in a cooperative.

[c] Workers' Compensation and Similar Laws

The "workers' compensation" exclusion encompasses employees and others. Under the exclusion, the carrier will not pay expenses for bodily injury to anyone, whether or not an employee of *any insured*, if benefits for that bodily injury are payable, or have to be provided, under a workers' compensation, disability benefits, or a *similar* law.[731] There is also a workers' compensation exclusion under Coverage A for bodily injury,[732] but the Coverage C exclusion is broader. It applies to any person, whether or not an employee of any insured. Thus, it could apply to a delivery person injured on the premises of the insured, for whom the

727. *See, e.g.*, ISO Form CG 00 01 12 07, § II.2.a. *See* § 13.02[2][d], *infra.*

728. *See, e.g.*, ISO Form CG 00 01 12 07, § I.C.2.b.

729. *See, e.g.*, Nationwide Mut. Ins. Co. v. American Reliance Ins. Co., 1996 U.S. Dist. LEXIS 7214 (E.D. Pa. May 24, 1996) (where there was disputed issue of fact whether plaintiff in underlying action was employee of insured at time of accident or independent contractor, there was no dispute that plaintiff was "doing work for" insured at time of accident; summary judgment granted to insurer on medical payments coverage).

730. Apparently, some carriers interpret the "hired person" exclusion to exclude tenants of an insured; however, one authority notes that the exclusion actually refers to someone hired to do work by an insured or hired by a tenant of any insured, and that does not mean tenants are excluded from medical payments coverage. *Medical Payments under CGL Form—Tenants Covered?* (Summit Business Media, 2013).

731. *See, e.g.*, ISO Form CG 00 01 12 07, § I.C.2.d.

732. *See, e.g.*, ISO Form CG 00 01 12 07, § I.2.d.

insured has no workers' compensation obligation, if that person's injuries are compensable under workers' compensation by a policy that person's employer would be obligated to maintain.[733] The extent of the exclusion will depend on the applicable state laws. Volunteer workers, for example, are covered for medical expense payments even if they would otherwise be excluded as an insured, but if benefits for their bodily injury "are payable or have to be provided" under workers' compensation or similar law, will medical expense coverage be excluded for them even if a common interest community has no workers' compensation policy? Because workers' compensation laws vary from state to state, associations need to discuss the scope of coverage and reach of the workers' compensation exclusion with their broker and/or their attorney.

[d] Injury on "Normally Occupied" Premises

Under another policy exclusion, the carrier will not pay expenses for bodily injury to a person injured on the part of premises owned or rented by the named insured that the injured person "normally occupies."[734] This provision is intended to exclude coverage for tenants, although it should be noted that it refers to part of the premises a person "normally occupies." It does not limit that habitation to occupancy under a lease. Thus, the exclusion should apply to a subtenant or a person occupying a part of the premises with a tenant's permission but in violation of a lease. In some circumstances it could apply to residents of a condominium or homeowners association. Note that the exclusion does not appear to be limited to an injury caused by a defect to the premises. The medical payments coverage applies to a bodily injury caused by an accident because of the operations of the named insured. Apparently, therefore, if a person is injured on property he or she normally occupies that is owned by the named insured and the injury was caused by the operations of the named insured—for example, the negligence of a maintenance worker—the exclusion applies.

Key to interpreting the exclusion is the meaning of the phrase "normally occupy." Does it encompass only the part of a premises to which a person has exclusive use, or does it extend to areas that person traverses in his or her daily routine? One commentary opines that if a tenant in an apartment building owned by the named insured were injured in a common area, for example, a parking lot, the exclusion would not apply.[735] On the other hand, a New Jersey court held that "use of the common areas by tenants, especially where they are unquestionably necessary for their use and enjoyment of their specific apartments, is an effective occupation by them [and] . . . therefore . . . common space used by residential

733. *Commercial General Liability Form Medical Payments Coverage* (Summit Business Media, 2013).

734. *See, e.g.*, ISO Form CG 00 01 12 07, § II.2.c.

735. *Commercial General Liability Form Medical Payments Coverage* (Summit Business Media, 2013).

tenants" is included in the area "occupied" by them.[736] Moreover, a number of courts have held that "occupy" means to possess, to have in possession or use, or to use.[737]

[i] Cooperatives

In a cooperative, the exclusion would certainly apply to the tenant/shareholders as they "normally occupy" a part of the premises—their apartment—that is owned by the named insured, the cooperative corporation. At the same time, it would not apply to them if they are injured on a part of the premises that they do not *normally occupy*. If "normally occupy" can be interpreted to mean "normally use," the exclusion would apply to parts of the property a tenant/shareholder might use on a regular basis: hallways, stairs, elevators, and maybe even a lobby and recreation room.

[ii] Homeowners Associations

Typically, in a homeowners association, a home, and perhaps any yard surrounding it, is owned by a member of the association. The exclusion should not, therefore, apply to residents of an HOA or to their tenants when they are within the part of the premises they own or lease because it only excludes coverage when they are injured on the part of the premises owned or rented by the *association*. The association usually owns recreational areas and open space and perhaps streets and sidewalks. Coverage for a person injured in those areas—presuming he or she does not "normally occupy them—should not be excluded whether that person is a member of the association, a tenant of a member, or a visitor to the community. In townhouse or zero lot line communities there may be yards reserved for the exclusive use of the owner of a particular home but owned by the association. If the homeowner can be said to "normally occupy" that yard, the exclusion should be triggered to bar coverage when the homeowner is injured in that yard.

---

736. Freygang v. Verona, 146 N.J. Super. 310, 315–16, 369 A.2d 959, 962–63 (1977) (interpreting rent control ordinance).

737. Missionary Soc. v. Dalles, 107 U.S. 336, 343, 2 S. Ct. 672, 677, 27 L. Ed. 545, 547 (1883) (citing *Webster's Dictionary* for definition that to occupy means to hold in possession, or to hold or keep for use, as to occupy apartment); Den Gre Plastics Co. v. Travelers Indem. Co., 107 N.J. Super. 535, 545, 259 A.2d 485, 491 (1969) (holding that fact insured had right to use of an area, that it did actually make exclusive and continuous use of it, and that area was of such a nature as to substantially lessen value of plaintiff's leasehold interest were plaintiff prohibited from its use, all showed plaintiff occupied that area within meaning of transportation policy); Grillo v. State, 209 Md. 154, 160, 120 A.2d 384, 388 (1956) (while "occupy" means to hold in possession; to hold or keep for use, court could not agree that private home where members of club regularly met could be considered as being regularly occupied by that club). *Compare* United States v. Burleson, 127 F. Supp. 400, 404 (D. Tenn. 1954) (to visit is not to occupy); Paulson v. Rogis, 247 Iowa 893, 895, 77 N.W.2d 33, 35 (1956) (occupy generally refers to actual possession to exclusion of everyone else, but does not necessarily include residence).

[iii] Condominiums

A condominium presents more difficult questions. A condominium association does not actually own real property. In a condominium, by definition, all the property that is not an individually owned unit is owned by all the unit owners as tenants in common. Therefore, condominium unit owners do not "normally occupy" premises owned or rented by the named insured, that is the association. Assuming the common areas are treated as owned by the association, the exclusion should not apply to unit owners when in common areas unless they are considered to "normally occupy" those common elements. If normally occupy means "normally use," the exclusion would apply to parts of the property unit owners might use on a regular basis: hallways, stairs, elevators, and perhaps a lobby or a recreation room.[738]

One type of common element that a unit owner should definitely be considered to "normally occupy" is a limited common element reserved for the exclusive use of that unit owner.[739] Balconies, patios, storage closets, and parking spaces are examples of these limited common elements. That a common element is limited does not, however, change its ownership. Therefore, if a unit owner is injured while on a limited common element reserved to his or her use, he or she has probably been deemed to have been hurt on premises he or she normally occupies and, therefore, there would be no medical expense coverage.

[e] Athletics Activities

Under the athletic activities exclusion, the carrier will not pay expenses for bodily injury to a person injured while practicing, instructing, or participating in any physical exercises, games, sports, or athletic contests.[740] This is a broadly worded exclusion that has significance for common interest communities, which often have facilities or open space that residents use for recreation or exercise. The exclusion would bar medical expense coverage for any injury connected to exercise or recreation.[741] Note that there is no exception for an injury that is unrelated to the athletic activity and would not have occurred but for a dangerous condition on the property. The policy also does not define "physical exercises."

---

738. *Consider* Smolker v. Pac. Villas Homeowners Ass'n, 2007 Cal. App. Unpub. LEXIS 2155 (Mar. 19, 2007), where an insurer argued that if common areas were insured premises under the homeowner's policy of a defendant unit owner, that policy excluded plaintiff injured unit owners from coverage, because they were "regular residents" of the insured premises. The plaintiffs did not challenge that interpretation.

739. *See, e.g.*, Uniform Common Interest Ownership Act § 1-103(21) ("limited common element" means portion of common elements allocated by declaration or by operation of law for exclusive use of one or more but fewer than all of units).

740. *See, e.g.*, ISO Form CG 00 01 12 07, § I.C.2.e.

741. One commentary offers as an example of the exclusion a person injured while playing basketball or softball at a picnic on the grounds of the insured, explaining that the injured person's health insurance should provide the coverage. *Commercial General Liability Form Medical Payments Coverage* (Summit Business Media, 2013).

A person injured while taking a brisk walk for exercise on a jogging trail through the community would apparently be barred from receiving medical expenses, but the same person using the same trail on a brisk walk to visit a neighbor may well be eligible for medical expense coverage.

[f] Coverage A Exclusions

Under the final exclusion, the carrier will not pay expenses for bodily injury excluded under Coverage A.[742] These exclusions include expected or intended injury; liquor liability; pollution; aircraft, auto, or watercraft;[743] mobile equipment; and war.

[5] Recovery against Insurer by Injured Party

Generally, an injured party cannot bring an action against the carrier for the insured because the former is not a party to the contract. In some states a "direct action statute" allows an injured party who obtains a judgment against the insured—known as a judgment creditor—to sue the insured's carrier directly,[744] and in a few states the injured party can sue that insurer without first obtaining a judgment against the insured.[745]

There is an exception to the general rule for intended third-party beneficiaries of the insurance contract. Under Coverage C, the liability of the insurer to pay medical expenses to a claimant is not dependent on the negligence of the insured—the policy specifically says the insurer will make payments *regardless of fault*—and, therefore, the insurer can be considered to be directly liable to that third-party claimant.[746] Thus, many courts allow a direct action by an injured

742. *See, e.g.*, ISO Form CG 00 01 12 07, § I.C.2.g. *See* Founders Ins. Co. v. Cortes-Garcia, 2012 U.S. Dist. LEXIS 89969 (M.D. Fla. June 28, 2012) (where Coverage A included assault and/or battery/negligent hiring exclusion, it applied to medical payments coverage as well); Colony Ins. Co. v. Griffin, 2007 U.S. Dist. LEXIS 86783 (M.D. Ala. Nov. 26, 2007) (Coverage C of policy provides that medical payments need not be made when any of Coverage A exclusions apply and Coverage A exclusions specifically included assault and battery exclusion; therefore, policy unambiguously provided that assault and battery exclusion was applicable to Coverage C).

743. *See, e.g.*, Robinson v. Transportation Ins. Co., 881 S.W.2d 218 (Tex. App.—Houston 1st Dist. 1994) (policy excludes claims arising out of operations of insured's own automobiles).

744. *See, e.g.*, Cal. Ins. Code § 11580(b)(2); N.Y. Ins. Law § 3420(a)(2).

745. *See, e.g.*, La. Rev. Stat. § 22:1269(B)(1) (listing six circumstances in which action can be brought directly against insurer); Wisc. Stat. § 632.24.

746. Walter & Cory, *The Circumvention of Mississippi's Prohibition of Direct Actions*, 66 Miss. L.J. 493, 503–04 (1997). *See also* Certain Underwriters at Lloyds v. Waveblast Watersports, Inc., 2014 U.S. Dist. LEXIS 189072 (S.D. Fla. Apr. 3, 2014) (to require injured party to obtain settlement or verdict based fault of insured before seeking or obtaining medical payments contradicts explicit terms of Coverage C as it provides insurer will make medical payments regardless of fault). *And see* Alexander v. W.F. Shuck Petroleum Co., 2009 Conn. Super. LEXIS 2096 (Conn. Super. Ct. Aug. 3, 2009), for a decision extensively reviewing the holdings and reasoning of courts across the country. The *Alexander* court found an injured party could bring an action directly against the insurer.

claimant without first having obtained a judgment against the insured.[747] There are, however, courts that do not permit direct suits against insurers by an injured party.[748]

[6] Medical Payments Exclusion

There is an ISO endorsement that in effect removes Coverage C from a standard commercial general liability policy.[749] The exclusion applies to premises specifically identified in the endorsement. It provides that medical payments coverage does not apply, and none of the references to it in the Coverage Part apply. The endorsement adds a clause to the supplementary payments provision of the CGL policy under which the carrier will pay, in the case of any claim it investigates or settles, or any suit against an insured that it defends, expenses sustained by the insured for first aid administered at the time of an accident for bodily injury to which the policy applies.

The endorsement may run afoul of statutory requirements. For example, under the Uniform Common Interest Ownership Act, an association is required

747. *See, e.g.*, Cain v. Griffin, 849 N.E.2d 507, 515 (Ind. 2006) (as third-party beneficiary, injured party could sue insurer directly to enforce medical payment coverage provision of contract); Heimerl v. Waverly Beach, Inc., 273 Wis. 2d 784, 680 N.W.2d 832 (2004) (when insurer agrees to pay medical expenses for bodily injury caused by accident on premises of its insured, injured person may sue insurer directly to recover those expenses); Harper v. Wausau Ins. Corp., 56 Cal. App. 4th 1079, 1090, 66 Cal. Rptr. 2d 64, 70 (1997) (express language of Coverage C plainly indicates it is meant to directly confer benefit on third parties who are injured on owner's property, and payment is premised on happening of event and is not premised on fault; insurer undertook separate and direct obligation to pay medical expenses of any persons injured on owner's property regardless of negligence, and, thus, payments were plainly intended to directly benefit injured party and were not incidental or remote and as intended third-party beneficiary, injured party had right to enforce contract). *See also* Donald v. Liberty Mut. Ins. Co., 18 F.3d 474, 481 (7th Cir. 1994) (weight of authority suggests that medical payment provisions regarding injured third parties are third-party beneficiary contracts; holding that insured party was third-party beneficiary of policy and was not barred from bringing suit directly against insurer to recover the medical payment benefits provided by Coverage C). *And see* Alexander v. W.F. Shuck Petroleum Co., 2009 Conn. Super. LEXIS 2096 (Conn. Super. Ct. Aug. 3, 2009) (discussing cases on point from several jurisdictions and deciding to adopt majority view that injured party can bring direct action against insurer under medical payments clause of insured's policy).

748. *See, e.g.*, Schmalfeldt v. N. Pointe Ins. Co., 469 Mich. 422, 426, 670 N.W.2d 651, 653 (2003) (patron of insured bar injured in fight could not directly sue bar's insurer for medical expenses; insurance contract benefitted insured and injured party was merely incidental beneficiary who was not entitled to enforce contract); Trouten v. Heritage Mut. Ins. Co., 632 N.W.2d 856 (2001); Zegar v. Sears Roebuck & Co., 211 Ill. App. 3d 1025, 1032, 570 N.E.2d 1176, 1180, 156 Ill. Dec. 454 (1991) (absent express or clearly implied right to sue insurer directly for medical expenses under Coverage C, injured party could not maintain action to recover medical expenses directly from insurer at least until after settlement, adjudication, or release of claim against insured had been secured).

749. *See, e.g.*, ISO Form CG 21 35 10 01. The form has a schedule that will describe the location of the premises or the classifications to which the exclusion applies. It may simply state "all locations of the named insured." If no entry appears on the schedule, the information required to complete the endorsement will be shown on the Declarations Page as applicable to the endorsement.

to maintain liability insurance, *including medical payments insurance*, in an amount determined by the governing board, but not less than any amount specified in the Declaration.[750]

§ 13.08 Duty to Defend

Commercial general liability policies provide both indemnity and a defense when an insured is sued. The duty of the insurer to defend its insureds is a critically important component of the coverage of the policy.

[1] The Significance of the Duty to Defend

Coverage in a standard commercial general liability policy includes two facets: the duty of the carrier to defend its insured when the insured is a defendant in a lawsuit and its duty to indemnify the insured if damages are ultimately assessed in that lawsuit.[751] The duty to defend is an obligation that is independent from the duty to pay claims under the policy.[752] Businesspeople, for whom risk management is an important part of their planning, will likely be well aware of the significance of the duty to defend. Other policyholders, however, may think of liability insurance as principally providing coverage for damages they may incur if they are sued. They may not consider the importance or even be aware of the duty to defend.[753] That may be true of the volunteer members of common interest community governing boards, many of whom have very little knowledge of business or of insurance.

In fact, the duty to defend may be the more important part of the coverage for insureds who are never the subject of a major claim. A defendant can prevail in a legal action and yet incur substantial expenses in the process.[754] Moreover, even though a defendant may lose, defense costs sometimes dwarf the damages

750. Uniform Common Interest Ownership Act § 3-113(a)(2).

751. Morgan Int'l Realty v. Dade Underwriters Ins. Agency, 617 So. 2d 455, 457 (Fla. 3d DCA 1993). *See also* Monteleone, *Coverage Issues Under Commercial General Liability and Directors' and Officers' Liability Policies*, 18 W. New Eng. L. Rev. 47, 58 (1996) (insurer's obligation under typical CGL policy is two-fold: to defend insured in any lawsuit or proceeding alleging covered claim, and to indemnify insured for any insurable damages arising from covered claim).

752. Henning v. Contl Cas. Co., 254 F.3d 1291, 1295 (11th Cir. 2001). *See also* Morgan Int'l Realty v. Dade Underwriters Ins. Agency, 617 So. 2d 455, 457 (Fla. 3d DCA 1993) (duty to defend is distinct from and broader than duty to indemnify).

753. Powers, *Advantages of the One-Client Model in Insurance Defense*, 45 N.M.L. Rev. 79, 80 (2104) (noting that the average automobile owner may not have given much thought to fact that her policy would provide defense if she were sued, and her main impetus for buying insurance may have been legal requirement to carry coverage).

754. Jerry, *The Insurer's Right to Reimbursement of Defense Costs*, 42 Ariz. L. Rev. 13 (2000) (as percentage of total claims costs, expense of providing defenses to insureds is considerable and according to industry data, approximately 14 percent of expenditures on claims is attributable to defense costs).

the defendant has to pay.[755] This can be particularly true for common interest community associations because, unlike commercial businesses that may be defendants in multi-million dollar actions—for example, products liability or pollution disasters—much of the litigation involving CIC associations derives from dissatisfied residents whose potential damages, should they succeed, are relatively small. Additionally, many of the suits that residents bring against their associations are dubious, albeit just shy of frivolous. For common interest communities, the threat of sustaining significant defense costs may exceed that of substantial damages. For that reason, as one commentator observes, they need to know whether they can rely on the duty to defend and to what extent.[756] To that end, this section provides a broad overview of the issues that arise with the duty to defend.

Unfortunately, the standard commercial general liability policy provides little guidance on the defense obligations of carriers. For example, as one commentary observes, it does not address to what extent an insurer has to defend when covered and uncovered claims are asserted in the same complaint, the right of the insurer to control the defense, or whether the duty to defend continues through appeals.[757] These questions are left to courts to decide.

[2] Insuring Agreements

The insuring agreements for bodily injury and property damage (Coverage A) and personal and advertising injury liability (Coverage B) mirror one another in the standard commercial general liability policy. Combining them, they provide that the carrier has the *right*[758] and duty to defend the insured against any suit seeking damages because of bodily injury, property damage, or personal and advertising injury to which the policy applies, but has no duty to defend the insured against a suit seeking damages because of bodily injury, property damage, or personal and advertising injury to which the policy *does not* apply.[759] "Suit" is defined as a civil proceeding in which damages because of either bodily injury, property damage, or personal and advertising injury to which the policy applies are alleged and includes arbitration in which damages are claimed and to which the insured

755. Pine Cone Harbour Condo. Ass'n v. Nationwide Mut. Ins. Co., 1993 U.S. Dist. LEXIS 21429 (W.D. Va. Oct. 19, 1993), *aff'd*, 30 F.3d 130 (4th Cir. 1994) (underlying suit against association was settled for relatively small amount; however, association incurred substantial legal fees in its defense of action for which insurer disclaimed liability and refused to defend).

756. Monteleone, *Coverage Issues Under Commercial General Liability and Directors' and Officers' Liability Policies*, 18 W. New Eng. L. Rev. 47, 58 (1996).

757. Jerry, *The Insurer's Right to Reimbursement of Defense Costs*, 42 Ariz. L. Rev. 13, 20 (2000).

758. The "right" to defend means the insurer generally has control over any litigation against its insured in order to protect its financial interests. *See* McCormack Baron Mgmt. Servs., Inc. v. American Guar. & Liab. Ins. Co., 989 S.W.2d 168, 170, n.2 (Mo. 1999).

759. *See, e.g.*, CG 00 01 12 07, §§ I.A.1, B.1.

has to submit or submits with the consent of the carrier or any other alternative dispute resolution proceeding in which damages are claimed and to which the insured submits with the consent of the insurer.[760]

The carrier may, at is discretion, investigate any occurrence—meaning an accident—or offense and settle any claim or suit that may result, but its right and duty to defend ends when it has used up the applicable limit of insurance in the payment of judgments or settlements under Coverages A or B or medical expenses under Coverage C.[761] It is important for an insured to know if expenses of litigation are in addition to payment for liability or part of the amount of liability. In the latter case, the amount available for payment of damages, judgments, and settlements is eroded. The insured needs to confer with its broker to determine how the limits are structured. Many policies provide that supplementary payments—which, as discussed immediately below, include expenses of defense—will not reduce the limits of insurance.[762] In that case, the expenses of litigation are in addition to payment for liability and do not erode the limits of coverage.

[3] Supplementary Payments

The carrier will pay for any claim it investigates or settles, or any suit against an insured that it defends:

- All expenses it incurs;[763]
- Bail bonds;[764]
- Bonds to release attachments, but only for amounts within the applicable limit of insurance;[765]
- All reasonable expenses incurred by the insured at the request of the insurer to assist it in the investigation or defense of the claim or suit;[766]
- Court costs taxed against the insured in a suit, but not including attorney's fees or expenses taxed against the insured;
- Prejudgment interest awarded against the insured on the part of any judgment the carrier pays;[767] and

760. *See, e.g.*, CG 00 01 12 07, § V.18.
761. *See, e.g.*, CG 00 01 12 07, §§ I. A.1.a.(2), B.1.a.(2).
762. *See, e.g.*, CG 00 01 12 07, § I.1 (supplementary payments).
763. These expenses would be subject, however, to the limits of the policy.
764. The carrier will pay up to $250 for the cost of bail bonds that are required because of accidents or traffic law violations that arise out of the use of any vehicle to which bodily injury coverage applies, but it does not have to furnish bonds.
765. The carrier does not have to furnish the bonds.
766. This includes actual loss of earnings up to $250 a day because of time taken off from work.
767. If the insurer makes an offer to pay the applicable limit of insurance, it will not pay any prejudgment interest based on the period of time after that offer.

- Interest on the full amount of any judgment that accrues after its entry, and before the insurer has paid, offered to pay, or deposited in court the part of the judgment that is within the applicable limit of insurance;[768]

These payments do not reduce the limits of insurance.

If the carrier defends an insured against a suit and an indemnitee of the insured—meaning a person or organization held harmless by agreement[769]—is also named as a party to that suit, the insurer will defend the indemnitee if six conditions are met.[770] First, the suit against the indemnitee has to seek damages for which the insured has assumed the liability of that indemnitee in a contract or agreement that is an *insured contract*. "Insured contract" is defined to include a contract for a lease of premises; an easement or license agreement; an obligation, required by ordinance to indemnify a municipality; an elevator maintenance agreement; and the part of a contract or agreement pertaining to the business of the named insured pursuant to which the named insured assumes the tort liability of another to pay for bodily injury to a third person or organization.[771] Some policies may narrow the definition by eliminating agreements pertaining to the business of the named insured from the definition.[772]

Next, the policy has to apply to the liability assumed by the insured. Third, the obligation to defend—or cost of defense of—that indemnitee has to also have been assumed by the insured in the same insured contract. Then, no conflict can appear to exist between the interests of the insured and of the indemnitee in the allegations of the suit and the information the carrier knows about the occurrence. Penultimately, the indemnitee and insured have to ask the insurer

768. *See, e.g.*, CG 00 01 12 07, § I.1 (supplementary payments).

769. https://www.irmi.com/term/insurance-definitions/indemnitee.

770. *See, e.g.*, CG 00 01 12 07, § I.2 (supplementary payments).

771. *See, e.g.*, ISO Form CG 00 01 12 07, § V.9. Tort liability means liability that would be imposed by law absent any contract or agreement. *See* Tremco, Inc. v. Mfrs. Ass'n Ins. Co., 832 A.2d 1120 (Pa. Super. 2003) (where manufacturer sold roofing products to contractor and contractor agreed in sales contract to indemnify and hold manufacturer, its officers, and employees harmless from any and all losses, costs, expenses, claims, demands, and suits for any bodily injury, court found language of contract bound contractor to assume liability for tort claims against manufacturer arising out of its negligence, and was, therefore, *apparently* an "insured contract").

772. *See, e.g.*, Western Heritage Ins. Co. v. Jacobs Dev. Corp., 2013 U.S. Dist. LEXIS 184369 (E.D.N.Y. Dec. 16, 2013), where a passerby tripped and fell on a sidewalk in front of multi-story residential building and sued the building owner, which filed a third-party complaint against the company that had provided concrete installation at the site. The building owner contended it was entitled to full contractual indemnity from that company based on a Subcontract Agreement Rider between the parties in which the company was required to defend, indemnify, and hold harmless the building owner, at its own expense, against all liability or claimed liability for bodily injury. The insurer for the company invoked the contractual liability exclusion that omitted from the definition of "insured contract" an agreement pertaining to the business of the named insured. The court found that the Subcontract Agreement Rider did not meet the definition of an insured contract and, thus, did not fall within the exception to the exclusion. Therefore, the exclusion for contractual liability applied to the underlying claims against the insured company for contractual liability.

to conduct and control the defense of the indemnitee against the suit, and they have to agree the insurer is permitted to assign the same counsel to defend both of them. Finally, the indemnitee has to agree in writing to cooperate with the carrier in the investigation, settlement, or defense of the suit; immediately send it copies of any demands, notices, summonses, or legal papers received in connection with that suit; notify any other insurer whose coverage is available to it; and cooperate with the insurer in coordinating other applicable insurance available to it as well as providing the insurer with written authorization to obtain records and other information related to the suit and conduct and control the defense of the indemnitee.

As long as the six conditions are met, attorney's fees incurred by the carrier in defense of the indemnitee, necessary litigation expenses incurred by it, and necessary litigation expenses incurred by the indemnitee at the request of the insurer will be paid as supplementary payments. Those payments will not be deemed damages for bodily injury or property damage and will not reduce the limits of insurance. The obligation of the carrier to defend an indemnitee of the insured and pay attorney's fees and necessary litigation expenses as supplementary payments ends when the insurer has used up the applicable limit of insurance in the payment of judgments or settlements or the policy conditions imposed on indemnitees or the terms of the required agreement with the insurer are no longer met.

[4] Determining the Duty to Defend

The most often repeated statement in the law of liability insurance is that the duty of an insurer to defend its insured is broader than its duty to indemnify.[773] As the Wisconsin Supreme Court explained, the duty to defend is broader than the duty to indemnify because the former arises from allegations contained in the complaint, whereas the latter is supported by fully developed facts and, thus, a carrier may be obligated to defend claims it ultimately may not be obligated to indemnify.[774]

One expert says courts follow one of two approaches to determine whether an insurer has a duty to defend. In many jurisdictions, the courts follow the four- or eight-corners rule under which the allegations within the complaint are compared to the policy terms and the insurer owes a defense only if the allegations are within the coverage.[775] Generally, these courts do not allow consideration

773. *See, e.g.*, Western Alliance Ins. Co. v. Northern Ins. Co., 176 F.3d 825, 829 (5th Cir. 1999); EMC Ins. Cos. v. Mid-Continent Cas. Co., 884 F. Supp. 2d 1147, 1155 (D. Colo. 2012) (duty to defend is triggered more easily than is duty to indemnify); Phila. Indem. Ins. Co. v. Yachtsman's Inn Condo Ass'n, 595 F. Supp. 2d 1319, 1322 (S.D. Fla. 2009); Henly v. Phillips Abita Lumber Co., 971 So. 2d 1104, 1109 (La. App. 2007).

774. Toldt Woods Condos. Owner's Ass'n v. Madeline Square, LLC, 314 Wis. 2d 259, 757 N.W.2d 850 (2008).

775. Jerry, *The Insurer's Right to Reimbursement of Defense Costs*, 42 Ariz. L. Rev. 13, 22 (2000). *See, e.g.*, Phila. Indem. Ins. Co. v. Yachtsman's Inn Condo Ass'n, 595 F. Supp. 2d 1319, 1323

of extrinsic facts.[776] Other courts adopt the "potentiality rule" under which an insurer has an obligation to defend if a complaint raises a potential for coverage.[777] Under the "potentiality rule" insurers are generally expected to consider actual facts beyond the pleadings in determining their obligation to defend.[778]

(S.D. Fla. 2009) (Florida courts make determination as to whether insurer's duty to defend insured exists by looking to allegations contained within four corners of complaint in underlying action against insured and court must apply language of policy to facts of underlying complaint); Henly v. Phillips Abita Lumber Co., 971 So. 2d 1104, 1109 (La. App. 2007) (issue of whether liability insurer has duty to defend civil action against its insured is determined by application of "eight-corners rule" under which insurer must look to "four corners" of plaintiff's petition and "four corners" of its policy to determine whether it owes that duty); Crawford v. Guideone Mut. Ins. Co., 420 F. Supp. 2d 584, 593 (N.D. Tex. 2006) (under Texas law, court determines insurer's duty to defend by following "Eight Corners" or "Complaint Allegation" rule under which court examines only allegations in underlying complaint for which duty is sought and policy to determine whether duty to defend exists); Brown v. MR Group, LLC, 278 Wis. 2d 760, 766, 693 N.W.2d 138, 140 (2005) (insurer has duty to defend suit whenever complaint alleges facts that, if proven to be true, would lead to insurer's liability pursuant to policy and to determine whether duty exists, court compares factual allegations within four corners of complaint to terms of the policy). *See also* State Farm Fire & Cas. Co. v. Metro. Mgmt., 2007 U.S. Dist. LEXIS 99406 (D. Haw. Oct. 31, 2007) (under "complaint allegation rule, allegations of complaint in underlying lawsuit dictate whether or not insurer has duty to defend; however, in determining whether coverage exists under liability policy, Hawaii courts do not look merely at label that litigant places on claim, but at underlying facts alleged in pleadings). *See generally* Stempel, *Enhancing the Socially Instrumental Role of Insurance: The Opportunity and Challenge Presented by the ALI Restatement Position on Breach of the Duty to Defend*, 5 U.C. Irvine L. Rev. 587, 592 (2015).

776. *See, e.g.*, Heather Hill Villas Condo. Ass'n v. Am. Equity Ins. Co., 816 So. 2d 250 (Fla. 2d DCA 2002) (general rule is that duty to defend is determined solely by allegations of complaint against insured not by actual facts).

777. Jerry, *The Insurer's Right to Reimbursement of Defense Costs*, 42 Ariz. L. Rev. 13, 23 (2000). *See, e.g.*, Lime Tree Village Community Club Ass'n v. State Farm Gen. Ins. Co., 980 F.2d 1402, 1405 (11th Cir. 1993); Phila. Indem. Ins. Co. v. Lakeside Heights Homeowners Ass'n, 110 F. Supp. 3d 965, 970 (N.D. Cal. 2015) (insurer must defend insured in suit that potentially seeks damages within policy coverage); Crawford v. Guideone Mut. Ins. Co., 420 F. Supp. 2d 584, 593 (N.D. Tex. 2006) (duty to defend arises when third party sues insured on allegations that, if taken as true, potentially state cause of action within policy terms); Insurance Co. of N. Am. v. Hilton Hotels U.S.A., 908 F. Supp. 809, 814, n.2 (D. Neb. 1995), *aff'd*, 110 F.3d 715 (9th Cir. 1997) (duty to defend rule provides that insurer must defend any suit brought against its insured that potentially seeks damages within coverage of policy; thus, if facts are alleged that, if proven, would give rise to duty to indemnify, insurer must defend).

778. *See, e.g.*, Nationwide Mut. Ins. Co. v. Lake Caroline, Inc., 515 F.3d 414, 418 (5th Cir. 2008) (under Mississippi law, insurer's duty to defend action against its insured is measured by allegations in plaintiff's pleadings, and only if pleadings state facts that bring injury within coverage of policy is insured required to defend; however, exception to that rule exists when insurer is presented with extrinsic facts, of which it has knowledge or could obtain knowledge by means of reasonable investigation, that trigger coverage under policy); Alexander v. Nat'l Fire Ins., 454 F.3d 214, 218, 221 (3d Cir. Pa. 2006) (in determining whether insurance company has duty to defend under terms of its policy, court is not limited to facts and allegations contained within four corners of underlying complaint, and facts outside complaint may trigger duty to defend as insureds expect coverage and defense benefits to be determined by nature of claim against them, not fortuity of how plaintiff phrased complaint); Phila. Indem. Ins. Co. v. Lakeside Heights Homeowners Ass'n, 110 F. Supp.

In the evaluation of the duty to defend, doubts are generally resolved in favor of the insured.[779] Additionally, the general rule is that if there is a possibility of liability for any covered claim in the complaint, the carrier has a duty to defend the entire lawsuit, even though other allegations are not covered.[780]

[5] The Carrier's Options When Its Insured Is Sued

When its insured is sued, the carrier has four options. It can refuse to defend, defend unconditionally, defend under a reservation of its rights, or seek a declaratory judgment on its obligation to defend. If the insurer is not going to defend, it must promptly notify the insured of that fact.[781] Insurers are usually reluctant to

---

3d 965, 970 (N.D. Cal. 2015) (facts extrinsic to complaint give rise to duty to defend when they reveal possibility that claim may be covered by policy).

779. *See, e.g.*, Lime Tree Village Community Club Ass'n v. State Farm Gen. Ins. Co., 980 F.2d 1402, 1405 (11th Cir. 1993) (duty to defend is determined by examining allegations in complaint filed against insured and if they leave any doubt as to duty to defend, question has to be resolved in favor of insured); Toldt Woods Condos. Owner's Ass'n v. Madeline Square, LLC, 314 Wis. 2d 259, 757 N.W.2d 850 (2008) (complaint is construed liberally in favor of insured, and insured is entitled to benefit of all reasonable inferences from facts pled in complaint and, additionally, doubts over whether coverage exists because of incomplete or ambiguous information in complaint are resolved in favor of insured); Altaf v. Hanover Square Condominium Asso. No. 1, 136 Ill. Dec. 257, 188 Ill. App. 3d 533, 541, 544 N.E.2d 1032, 1036 (1989) (complaint must be liberally construed and all doubts resolved in favor of insured).

780. Toldt Woods Condos. Owner's Ass'n v. Madeline Square, LLC, 314 Wis. 2d 259, 757 N.W.2d 850 (2008). *See also* Phila. Indem. Ins. Co. v. Yachtsman's Inn Condo Ass'n, 595 F. Supp. 2d 1319, 1322 (S.D. Fla. 2009) (where complaint against insured alleges any facts that actually, or even potentially, fall within scope of coverage under policy, insurer is obligated to defend entire suit); Altaf v. Hanover Square Condominium Ass'n No. 1, 136 Ill. Dec. 257, 188 Ill. App. 3d 533, 540–41, 544 N.E.2d 1032, 1036 (1989) (insurer has duty to defend action brought against insured if complaint alleges facts within, or potentially within, coverage and duty to defend applies where complaint alleges several causes of action or theories of recovery against insured, even if only one or some of them are within policy coverage). *Consider* 101 Ocean Condo. Homeowners Ass'n v. Century Sur. Co., 407 Fed. Appx. 129 (9th Cir. 2010), where a condominium resident sued the association alleging assault, battery, and negligence. The policy expressly excluded coverage when any actual or alleged injury arose out of any combination of an assault or battery-related cause and a non-assault or battery-related cause or any actual or alleged injury arose out of a chain of events that included assault or battery, regardless of whether assault or battery was the initial or precipitating event or a substantial cause of injury. The association argued the plaintiff in the underlying action *could* have asserted a false imprisonment claim on the facts alleged, and that the possibility of that claim gave rise to the potential for coverage under the policy and the carrier, therefore, had a duty to defend. The court was unimpressed. It said that under the plain language of the policy the insurer had no duty to defend when an independent cause of action, even if otherwise covered, was alleged in combination with an assault or battery claim and, even if false imprisonment had been alleged as a separate claim, that injury would have arisen out of a chain of events including an assault or battery, so the exclusion would apply.

781. Ashland Window & Housecleaning Co. v. Metropolitan Casualty Ins. Co., 269 A.D. 31, 35, 53 N.Y.S.2d 677, 680 (1945) (when insurer wishes on proper grounds to disclaim liability, it must inform insured promptly of that intention and liberate latter to make defense in his or her own behalf). *Accord* Commercial Standard Ins. Co. v. Blankenship, 40 F. Supp. 618, 620 (D. Tenn. 1941); Zak v. Fidelity-Phenix Ins. Co., 34 Ill. 2d 438, 444, 216 N.E.2d 113, 116 (1966).

simply refuse to defend because a wrongful refusal exposes them to liability for breach of contract, and possibly for bad faith, which may carry punitive damages.[782] If the insurer does refuse to defend, the insured can seek a declaratory judgment from a court regarding that duty.

A reservation of rights by the insurer—which is usually in the form of a letter to the insured—is its notice that there may not be coverage under the policy for a claim against the insured. It allows the insurer to investigate to determine whether coverage exists without waiving the right to later deny coverage.[783] The insurer may *defend* under reservation of rights, which is a warning to the insured that the insurer is not conceding it has duties to the insured under the policy. An insured may object to the reservation of rights, and generally if it does not, it is considered to have consented to defense under reservation. In addition to asserting its reservation of rights, an insurer may ask the insured to enter into a non-waiver agreement. Reservation of rights letters can present particular problems for common interest communities. The person who receives it may be the community association manager or an officer of the association—probably the secretary—who collects the association mail. That person may not recognize the import of the letter and may file it without informing the governing board members. This is yet another reason why associations should have either an insurance committee or a governing board member designated to handle all insurance matters. The governing board should set out clear procedures for the manager and all board members and officers under which any communications from an insurer or broker are submitted to that committee or individual. The goal would be to have those communications reviewed by someone with an understanding of insurance. When the communication is a reservation of rights, that person will probably want to consult the association attorney to determine its scope and whether the association should raise objections to it. If the insurer is asking the association to enter into a non-waiver agreement, advice of counsel is definitely needed.

The insurer can also seek a declaratory judgment from a court regarding its duty to defend.[784] Obviously, that involves an expense, so the company will probably not take that course when the potential liability is modest. The insured should not assume that if the insurer agrees to defend under a reservation of rights, it will not subsequently seek a declaratory judgment.[785]

782. Shreve, *Determining an Insurer's Duty to Defend*, 74 Ala. Law. 238, 239 (2013).

783. https://www.irmi.com/online/insurance-glossary/terms/r/reservation-of-rights.aspx.

784. Once the underlying liability has been determined, any declaratory judgment action is subject to dismissal because when the underlying case has been dismissed without liability for the insured, the insurer is no longer facing imminent injury. Omega Dedicated v. Cowpet Bay W. Condo. Ass'n, 2015 U.S. Dist. LEXIS 12 (D.V.I. Jan. 2, 2015).

785. *See, e.g.*, Phila. Indem. Ins. Co. v. Lakeside Heights Homeowners Ass'n, 110 F. Supp. 3d 965, 967 (N.D. Cal. 2015) (carrier initially agreed to defend homeowners association with full reservation of rights and subsequently filed complaint for declaratory judgment seeking declaration that it did not owe duty to defend or indemnify association in underlying action).

[6] The Insurance Defense Attorney

Generally, the insurance company selects the attorney who will represent the insured. The attorney may be "in house"[786]—that is, an employee of the insurer—or more likely one of a number of attorneys in private practice with whom the company regularly contracts to represent its policyholders. The relationship between the attorney, the insurance company that hires him or her, and the insured is widely called "tripartite" because counsel, the insurer, and the insured have to interrelate during the representation.[787] While it is generally said that counsel employed or hired by an insurance carrier to represent one of its insureds has to represent that insureds with undivided loyalty,[788] the possibility for conflicts of interest are obvious. For example, a conflict can arise when there are multiple defendants covered by the same carrier and adverse interests develop, for example, crossclaims between those defendants.[789] In the case of common interest communities, the association is the named insured on a commercial general liability policy, but the community association manager and the members of the association are usually additional insureds. It is not at all unusual for a plaintiff to sue the association, its management company, and individual association members in the same suit. These defendants can have conflicting defenses. Many cases are settled before trial, and that presents another possibility for conflicts. For instance, an association might want to settle within the policy limits because it fears a verdict that exceeds the limits, while the carrier wants to hold out for a lower settlement offer or wants to go to trial in hopes of avoiding liability altogether or discouraging similar lawsuits.[790]

---

786. Jerry, *The Insurer's Right to Reimbursement of Defense Costs*, 42 Ariz. L. Rev. 13, 14–15 (2000) (some insurers have promoted use of in-house staff counsel to defend claims filed against policyholders, as opposed to retaining outside counsel, and while that practice has not been without controversy, it has been upheld in almost all cases where it has been challenged).

787. *See generally* Abramovsky, *The Enterprise Model of Managing Conflicts of Interest in the Tripartite Insurance Defense Relationship*, 27 Cardozo L. Rev. 193 (2005); Bryant, *Loyalty Divided? The Ethical Considerations of the Tripartite Relationship in Insurance Defense Litigation*, 29 Okla. City U.L. Rev. 889 (2004); Brown, *Conflicts of Interest Between Insurer and Insured: When Is Independent Counsel Necessary*, 22 J. Legal Prof. 211 (1997/1998).

788. Bassett, *Three's A Crowd: A Proposal to Abolish Joint Representation*, 32 Rutgers L. J. 387, 430 (2001). *Compare* State Farm Mut. Auto. Ins. Co. v. Hansen, 357 P.3d 338, 340 (Nev. 2015) (Nevada is dual-representation state in which insurer-appointed counsel represents both insurer and insured); Finley v. Home Ins. Co., 90 Haw. 25, 32, 975 P.2d 1145, 1152 (1998) (absent express agreement specifying identity of lawyer's client or clients, lawyer hired by insurer to defend its insured may be held to have client-lawyer relationship with insured alone or with both insured and insurer; however, under rules of professional conduct, retained counsel solely represents insured when conflict arises between interests of insurer and insured).

789. Brown, *Conflicts of Interest Between Insurer and Insured: When Is Independent Counsel Necessary*, 22 J. Legal Prof. 211, 218–19 (1997/1998).

790. Bassett, *Three's A Crowd: A Proposal to Abolish Joint Representation*, 32 Rutgers L. J. 387, 431 (2001).

There are some circumstances in which the insured may have a say in who is retained to provide the defense. For example, in Florida a liability insurer is not permitted to deny coverage based on a particular defense unless it provides written notice of reservation of rights to assert a coverage defense to the named insured and gives written notice to the named insured of its refusal to defend, obtains a non-waiver agreement from the insured, or retains independent counsel *mutually agreeable* to the parties.[791] In a landmark decision, a California appellate court held that when an insurer provides its own counsel but reserves its right to assert non-coverage at a later date, there is a conflict of interest between the insurer and insured, and the insured has a right to independent counsel paid for by the insurer.[792] That holding was subsequently curtailed by other California courts that require more than a mere reservation of rights. Instead, there has to be specific evidence of an actual conflict of interest.[793]

Because of the possibility of conflicts of interest and the differences in state law, an association that is concerned about the representation it is receiving from a carrier-appointed counsel should consult the association attorney to discuss its rights. The association attorney probably has limited familiarity with the issues that arise concerning insurance defense counsel. These matters are beyond the scope of the treatise, but fortunately there are insurance law resources that treat it in depth.[794] There are also many excellent law review articles on the issue.[795]

---

791. Fla. Stat. § 627.426(2).

792. San Diego Fed. Credit Union v. Cumis Ins. Society, Inc., 162 Cal. App. 3d 358, 361, 208 Cal. Rptr. 494, 496 (1984). *See also* State Farm Mut. Auto. Ins. Co. v. Hansen, 357 P.3d 338, 341 (Nev. 2015) (counsel may not represent both insurer and insured when their interests conflict and no special exception applies; *Cumis* rule under which insurer has to satisfy its contractual duty to provide counsel by paying for counsel of insured's choosing is appropriate for Nevada). *And see* Scioneaux, *Louisiana Recognizes the Insurance Policyholder's Entitlement to Select Independent Counsel, Now What?: A Legislative Proposal*, 81 Tul. L. Rev. 537 (2006).

793. 2 *New Appleman Law of Liability Insurance* § 6.04 (Matthew Bender, 2016); Brown, *Conflicts of Interest Between Insurer and Insured: When Is Independent Counsel Necessary*, 22 J. Legal Prof. 211, 213 (1997/1998).

794. *See* 3 Jeffrey E. Thomas, *New Appleman on Insurance Law Library Edition* §§ 16.04, 17.02 (Matthew Bender, 2017); Steven Plitt *et al.*, *Couch on Insurance* § 202.34–.37 (3d ed. Supp. 2015). One treatise has a concise but very helpful over view in just two chapters. *See* 2 *New Appleman Law of Liability Insurance* §§ 6.04, 6.05 (Matthew Bender, 2017)

795. *See, e.g.*, Powers, *Advantages of the One-Client Model in Insurance Defense*, 45 N.M.L. Rev. 79 (2014); Fischer, *The Professional Responsibilities of Cumis Counsel Retained for the Policyholder but Not Subject to Insurer Control*, 43 Tort, Trial & Insurance Practice Law Journal 173 (2008); Abramovsky, *The Enterprise Model of Managing Conflicts of Interest in the Tripartite Insurance Defense Relationship*, 27 Cardozo L. Rev. 193 (2005); Bryant, *Loyalty Divided? The Ethical Considerations of the Tripartite Relationship in Insurance Defense Litigation*, 29 Okla. City U.L. Rev. 889 (2004); Brown, *Conflicts of Interest Between Insurer and Insured: When Is Independent Counsel Necessary*, 22 J. Legal Prof. 211 (1997/1998); Silver, *Does Insurance Defense Counsel Represent the Company or the Insured?*, 72 Tex. L. Rev. 1583 (1994); Machanic, *Insurance Defense Counsel: Who is the Client?*, 43 Fed'n Ins. & Corp. Couns. Q. 45 (1992); O'Malley, *Ethics Principles for the Insurer, the Insured, and Defense Counsel: The Eternal Triangle Reformed*, 66 Tul. L. Rev.

[7] Recoupment of Defense Costs by the Carrier

The average member of a common interest community governing board may be surprised to learn that the liability carrier for the association may be able to recoup its defense costs from the association. The standard commercial general liability policy says nothing about the right of the carrier to reimbursement of defense costs for defending non-covered claims.[796] However, the majority rule allows recoupment of the costs of defense when a court subsequently decides the insurer advanced costs under a reservation of rights for an *uncovered* claim.[797] A minority of courts take a different view.[798]

§ 13.09 Commercial General Liability Conditions

The standard commercial general liability policy requires the insured to notify the carrier of an event—an "occurrence"—that might result in a claim. Then, the insured must also give notice of an actual claim by a third party. It also imposes a number of conditions on the liability of the carrier and conditions, for example, the "other insurance" and "separation of insureds" clauses that may benefit insured parties.

[1] Duties in the Event of Occurrence or Offense

The named insured is required to "see to it" that the insurer is notified "as soon as practicable" of an occurrence—meaning an accident[799]—or offense that *could* result in a claim.[800] Under this language, the fact that a particular occurrence may

---

511 (1991); Holmes, *A Conflicts-of-Interest Roadmap for Insurance Defense Counsel: Walking an Ethical Tightrope Without a Net*, 26 Willamette L. Rev. 1 (1989).

796. Jerry, *The Insurer's Right to Reimbursement of Defense Costs*, 42 Ariz. L. Rev. 13, 21 (2000).

797. Foggan, *Insurer Recoupment of Defense Costs: Why the Restatement Adopts the Wrong Approach*, 68 Rutgers U. L. Rev. 193 (2015).

798. *See* Michael M. Marick, *An Insurer's Right to Recover Non-Covered Defense Costs and Indemnity Payments*, at 9–12 New Appleman on Insurance: Critical Current Issues in Insurance Law (July 2007). The appendix to the article has a 50-state survey of the law on recoupment.

799. *See, e.g.*, ISO Form CG 00 01 12 07, § V.13. "Accident" includes continuous or repeated exposure to substantially the same general harmful conditions.

800. *See, e.g.*, ISO Form CG 00 01 12 07, § IV.2.a. *See* Queens Blvd.- 40th Owners Corp. v. Stonington Ins. Co., 2012 N.Y. Misc. LEXIS 3861 (2012) (where accident occurred in February and insured did not notify insurer until following August, about six months after underlying action was served on it, late notice was unreasonable as matter of law); Balbert v. 302 96th St. Owners Corp., 77 A.D.3d 779, 909 N.Y.S.2d 535 (2010) (where resident slipped in fell in lobby of cooperative building in June, and cooperative did not notify insurer until following May, 11-month delay between occurrence and notice was unreasonable in light of fact that cooperative was aware of accident on date that it occurred, and was aware resident had been removed by ambulance in stretcher, had undergone surgery, and was subsequently seen walking with cane); Paramount Ins. Co. v. Rosedale Gardens, Inc., 293 A.D.2d 235, 743 N.Y.S.2d 59 (2002) (where cooperative resident fell and was injured on property and removed by ambulance in May, suit was filed in December, and insurer was notified in January, notice was insufficient).

not in the end result in a claim will generally not relieve the insured of the duty of timely notice.[801] To the *extent possible*, the notice should include how, when, and where the occurrence or offense took place; names and addresses of any injured persons and witnesses; and the nature and location of any injury or damage that arose out of the occurrence or offense. The association should keep a record of the claim it has filed and obtain a written acknowledgment from the insurer that it has received notice of the claim.[802]

[2] Duties in the Event of a Claim or Suit

If a claim is made, or a suit is brought, against any insured, the named insured is required to record the specifics of the claim or suit and the date it was received immediately and notify the carrier "as soon as practical."[803] The named insured is responsible to "see to it" that the carrier receives *written* notice of the claim or suit.[804] In other words, if a common interest community association notifies its broker of a claim or suit and the broker fails to transmit notice to the carrier, the *association* has failed to comply with the policy.[805] On the other hand, if the association notifies an *agent for the insurer*, that notice is deemed notice to the company.

A "suit" is a *civil* proceeding in which damages are alleged.[806] It includes arbitration, or any other alternative dispute resolution proceeding, in which damages are claimed and to which the insured is required to submit or does so with the consent of the insurer.

The named insured—and any other involved insured—is required to send the insurer copies of any demands, notices, summonses, or legal papers it receives related to the claim or suit immediately;[807] to authorize the insurer to obtain

801. 39 W. 29th St. Owners v. Lig Ins., 2011 N.Y. Misc. LEXIS 3461 (July 11, 2011).

802. *Board of Directors' Guide: Condominium Insurance—Including Fidelity Bonds*, at 6 (Hawaii Real Estate Commission 1996).

803. *See, e.g.*, ISO Form CG 00 01 12 07, § IV.2.b.

804. *See* Ainslie et al., *Business Insurance Law and Practice Guide*, § 2.08[7][a] (Matthew Bender, 2016) (where policy does not prescribe method of notice, notice mailed to office of carrier within state, when notice is in fact received, will suffice).

805. *See, e.g.*, Berkley Reg'l Ins. Co. v. Phila. Indem. Ins. Co., 600 Fed. Appx. 230 (5th Cir. 2015) (notice by condominium association to broker was insufficient notice to carrier); Board of Mgr. of Sagamore Hills Condominium v. Hometown Ins. Agency of L.I., Inc., 2009 N.Y. Misc. LEXIS 6046 (2009) (where condominium association claimed to have notified its broker of letter from attorney stating he had been retained to represent injured resident and of subsequent summons and complaint and only notice of latter was forwarded to insurer two months after receipt, whether association may have been unaware that notice provided to its broker was insufficient was no excuse at all).

806. *See, e.g.*, ISO Form CG 00 01 12 07, § V.18.

807. *See* Pennsylvania Threshermen & Farmers' Mut. Casualty Ins. Co. v. Thornton, 244 F.2d 823, 825 (4th Cir. 1957) (policy requirement that insured *immediately* turn over to insurer any summons or complaint served has been interpreted to mean, not instantaneously, but within reasonable time and what is reasonable is fact question to be determined in each case according to surrounding

records and other information; to cooperate with the insurer in its investigation or settlement of the claim or defense;[808] and to assist the insurer on its request in enforcing any right against anyone that may be liable to the insured because of injury or damage to which the policy may also apply.[809]

In compliance with its obligation to cooperate with the insurer in its investigation of the claim, an association may be asked to provide the insurer with copies of minutes that relate to the claim or suit. Minutes can present a problem for common interest communities. Experts warn that the contents of board minutes should be limited.[810] Other than basic introductory information—the name of the organization; the date, time, and place of the meeting; the determination of a quorum; and the announcement of compliance with any meeting notice requirements—the minutes should state no more than the motions made and seconded and the results of the vote on each motion. Nonetheless, well-meaning association secretaries persist in making the minutes a narrative account of meetings. They include not only the discussion surrounding motions but also discussion that took place without a proper motion having ever been made. That presents a danger for the association.[811] The minutes can be used to prove the association was aware of an accident.[812] Under the rules of evidence, records of regularly

circumstances). *See also* Am. Nat'l Fire Ins. Co. v. Nat'l Union Fire Ins. Co., 277 Ill. Dec. 767, 343 Ill. App. 3d 93, 104, 796 N.E.2d 1133, 1142 (2003) (additional insured had obligation to immediately send carrier for named insured copies of any demands, notices, summonses or legal papers it received in connection with underlying suit).

808. *See generally* Giles, *Rethinking the Cooperation Clause in Standard Liability Insurance Contracts*, 161 U. Pa. L. Rev. 585 (2013).

809. *See, e.g.*, ISO Form CG 00 01 12 07, § IV.2.c.

810. *See, e.g.*, 6A Rohan, *Real Estate Transactions: Home Owner Associations and Planned Unit Developments—Law and Practice: Forms*, § 7A.04[2][c] (Matthew Bender, 2016).

811. *See, e.g.*, Cohen v. Beachside Two-I Homeowners' Ass'n, 2006 U.S. Dist. LEXIS 44978 (D. Minn. June 29, 2006), *aff'd*, 272 Fed. Appx. 534 (8th Cir.), *cert. den.*, 555 U.S. 945, 129 S. Ct. 417, 172 L. Ed. 2d 288 (2008), where the association was sued for defamation based on the contents of the minutes of meetings of the governing board. The minutes contained a narrative discussion of the failure of the plaintiff to pay maintenance fees. The court found that for the most part the narrative was substantially true and, therefore, not actionable. However, the minutes for one meeting stated that the plaintiff's property had been purchased by a bank when in fact the bank had sent the association a check drawn from the tax escrow account of the plaintiff to satisfy a lien against the property. The governing board mistakenly assumed the bank had purchased the property, but that mistaken assumption did not, said the court, render the statement substantially true for purposes of the law of defamation.

812. *See, e.g.*, Board of Mgr. of Sagamore Hills Condominium v. Hometown Ins. Agency of L.I., Inc., 2009 N.Y. Misc. LEXIS 6046 (2009), where an elderly resident slipped and fell on the condominium property in March. In January of the *following year* an attorney for the injured resident advised the association that he had been retained to represent her. The association received service of the summons and complaint the following month. The association forwarded them to its broker who apparently did not deliver them to the insurer until April, more than one year after the accident. The association argued it had no reason to believe a claim would be asserted against it until the January letter from the attorney. The court, in finding the insurer had no duty to defend or indemnify because it established it did not receive notice of the accident until more than one year later, pointed to the testimony of the association president and the board minutes. Together

conducted business activity are generally admissible in court as an exception to the hearsay rule.[813] Additionally, before they ever reach a courtroom, the minutes may be examined by the carrier and found to provide a basis for denying a claim. For example, in a case in which an association was sued by the family of a child who drowned in its swimming pool, the board minutes stated the pool gate needed repair. Minutes from a June meeting said the gate would be repaired in June, and yet minutes of the July meeting said that damage to the gate from misuse and poor original construction would be repaired as soon as possible because the "non-closing" gate constituted "a liability exposure to homeowners."[814] Regardless of whether this information would ultimately have harmed the association's defense or threaten its insurance coverage, it would have been better for it had the minutes lacked the narrative.

Insurers need to realize that there is a difference between the minutes of the association and those of the governing board. Governing boards meet regularly, usually once or twice a month. The association is the organization made up of all the residents and ordinarily has one annual meeting at which the members of the governing board are elected. Occasionally there are special association meetings. When an insurer requests minutes, it should specify whether it wants board or association minutes. It should also consider that a committee appointed by the governing board—for example, an insurance committee—may have minutes that are material to the claim.

Insurance carriers may not be aware of other documents that may be beneficial to them. For example, some associations produce and post "board reports" or "meeting summaries." When they are prepared by an association board member or director, they may constitute official association records. Similarly, a newsletter that purports to represent the views of the association governing board may also be considered an official record. A carrier when requesting documents would be wise to inquire whether the association produces these or similar documents. Associations, on the other hand, should not produce board reports or meeting summaries at all, should make sure any newsletter is "unofficial," and should be careful about the content of any written communication to unit owners about claims against it.[815]

---

they showed the association was aware of the accident when it occurred and that the injured resident had been taken from the accident scene by ambulance to a hospital where she was treated for a broken hip.

813. Uniform Rules of Evidence Act, Rule 803(6). The federal rules and those of the states are similar to the Uniform Act. *See also* Meadows Condo. Ass'n v. Redman, 2009 Conn. Super. LEXIS 2062 (Conn. Super. July 30, 2009) (board minutes should be taken as best evidence of actions actually taken by board).

814. Great Divide Ins. Co. v. Aoao Maluna Kai Estates, 492 F. Supp. 2d 1216, 1224 (D. Haw. 2007).

815. *See, e.g.*, Encino Park W. Homeowners Ass'n v. Truck Ins. Exch., 2007 Cal. App. Unpub. LEXIS 6354 (Aug. 3, 2007) (memorandum from HOA board of directors to unit owners referring

[3] Failure to Notify Insurer

Breaching a notice clause defeats the right of an insured to recover under the policy.[816] Notice to the insurer, whether of an occurrence or a claim or suit, has to be "as soon as practicable." What does "as soon as practicable" mean? The Federal Fifth Circuit Court of Appeals called "as soon as practicable" "roomy words," not to be given effect on an arbitrary time table.[817] Courts say "as soon as practicable" requires notice "within a reasonable time," which is generally determined by the facts and circumstances of each case.[818]

[a] Belief That No Claim Will Be Asserted

Sometimes associations fail to notify the insurer of an occurrence because the governing board or officers believe, based on conjecture or statements made to them, that no claim would be asserted against the association. That is a mistake.[819] The standard policy language requires notice of an occurrence or offense

---

to "stylish upgrading that has taken place" used by insurer to prove release signed on behalf of association was not executed under "economic duress").

816. Country Mut. Ins. Co. v. Livorsi Marine, Inc., 305 Ill. Dec. 533, 222 Ill. 2d 303, 312, 856 N.E.2d 338, 343 (2006).

817. Young v. Travelers Ins. Co., 119 F.2d 877, 880 (5th Cir. 1941).

818. *See, e.g.*, Country Mut. Ins. Co. v. Livorsi Marine, Inc., 305 Ill. Dec. 533, 222 Ill. 2d 303, 311–12, 856 N.E.2d 338, 343 (2006) (policy condition requiring notice as soon as practicable is interpreted to mean within reasonable time, and whether notice has been given within reasonable time depends on facts and circumstances of each case); Sagendorf v. Selective Ins. Co. of Am., 293 N.J. Super. 81, 94, 679 A.2d 709, 716 (1996) (phrase "as soon as practicable" has been construed in New Jersey to mean within reasonable time, which depends on facts and circumstances of particular case, and is ordinarily factual issue for resolution by jury unless facts are undisputed and different inferences cannot reasonably be drawn therefrom; mere lapse of time is not determinative); Fireman's Fund Ins. Co. v. Valley Manufactured Products Co., 765 F. Supp. 1121, 1123 (D. Mass. 1991), *aff'd*, 960 F.2d 143 (1st Cir. 1992) (where policy called for written notice of occurrence "as soon as practicable" after its happening, insured was required to notify insurer within reasonable time and what is a reasonable time is question of fact, unless basic facts are undisputed, in which case it becomes question of law).

819. *See, e.g.*, Board of Mgrs. of the 1235 Park Condominium v. Clermont Specialty Mgrs., Ltd., 68 A.D.3d 496, 891 N.Y.S.2d 340 (2009) (where worker on association property fell from ladder while installing water tank on roof of building and association immediately learned of accident but did not notify insurer because employer of worker informed association on day of accident that worker was not admitted to hospital, did not sustain any serious injuries, and was expected to return to work on following day, that single phone call did not constitute adequate inquiry into circumstances of accident and its outcome and, as matter of law, could not have caused association to reasonably believe there was no reasonable possibility of claim against it); 426-428 W. 46th St. Owners, Inc. v. Greater NY Mut. Ins. Co., 847 N.Y.S.2d 896 (2007), *aff'd*, 55 A.D.3d 480, 867 N.Y.S.2d 385 (2008) (where building superintendent of cooperative building discovered tenant on floor and she allegedly fell from nearby defective staircase, and cooperative did not notify its insurer for approximately ten months after the incident, shortly after receiving tenant's summons and complaint, apparent failure to inquire into tenant's condition and hospitalization, did not, as matter of law, render excuse for failure to notify unreasonable, but was factor for consideration by trier of fact; because there were mitigating factors bearing on issue of reasonableness, summary judgment for insurer on issue of notice was denied); Paramount Ins. Co. v. Rosedale Gardens,

that "may result in a claim." While a reasonable belief in lack of liability may excuse the insured from providing notice to the carrier,[820] the volunteer board members rarely possess the legal knowledge to assess whether an occurrence or offense could possibly lead to a claim.[821] This judgment is better left to the broker or association attorney.

[b] Notification Provided by Community Association Manager

Often in common interest communities, the community association manager is delegated the responsibility of providing notice to insurers. The fact that the CAM has a duty to notify the insurer of an occurrence does not relieve the association of its duty under the policy to "see to it" that the insurer receives notification because the insurer is not a party to, nor is it bound by, any agreement between an association and its manager.[822]

When the CAM is delegated the responsibility to provide notice to insurers, it is important for the association and the CAM to have clear procedures to be followed and for the governing board to monitor the course of process. For example, in one case, an electrician working in a condominium building fell

---

Inc., 293 A.D.2d 235, 743 N.Y.S.2d 59 (2002) (where property manager learned of accident, but gave no notice to insurer because after examining site he did not see or hear any further substantiation of anything having occurred and injured resident had made "unsubstantiated" complaints of lead poisoning and he, therefore, doubted validity of claims of accident, particularly because after accident, possibility of lawsuit was never raised, court said notice requirement did not exempt occurrences, that in estimation of insured, did not portend probable liability; noting manager was aware injured resident was taken from scene in ambulance). *See also* 39 W. 29th St. Owners v. Lig Ins., 2011 N.Y. Misc. LEXIS 3461 (July 11, 2011) (where tenant was burglarized and cooperative corporation provided no notice to insurer eight months after burglary when tenant sued cooperative for negligence and breach of contract, cooperative could not rely on statement of investigating officer that burglary was "inside job" that would not result in liability to building; insured was required to make further inquiry into circumstances surrounding subject incident, and assumption that other parties would bear ultimate responsibility for loss is insufficient, as matter of law, to excuse untimely notice).

820. *See, e.g.*, 426-428 W. 46th St. Owners, Inc. v. Greater NY Mut. Ins. Co., 847 N.Y.S.2d 896 (2007), *aff'd*, 55 A.D.3d 480, 867 N.Y.S.2d 385 (2008) (reasonable belief in non-liability may excuse or explain delay in giving notice, but good faith belief in non-liability must be reasonable in light of all of circumstances and it may be relevant to issue of reasonableness whether and to what extent insured inquired into circumstances of accident or occurrence).

821. *See, e.g.*, Balbert v. 302 96th St. Owners Corp., 77 A.D.3d 779, 780, 909 N.Y.S.2d 535, 537 (2010) (where resident who was attorney and member of cooperative board of directors slipped and fell in lobby, was removed by ambulance after accident, underwent surgery, and was seen walking with cane after accident, cooperative failed to demonstrate good faith belief in non-liability so as to excuse its failure to timely serve notice of occurrence based on its belief that injured resident would not sue because she was board member).

822. *See* Paramount Ins. Co. v. Rosedale Gardens, Inc., 293 A.D.2d 235, 743 N.Y.S.2d 59 (2002) (duty of cooperative corporation to report accident to insurer was not discharged by notification to managing agent because, whatever may have been the arrangement between cooperative and manager regarding reporting of incidents to insurer, it was not binding on insurer, which, pursuant to policy, was entitled to notice "as soon as practicable from insured or anyone acting for it).

while descending a wet, slippery interior staircase. The CAM and the association each had a liability policy obtained from different carriers, but through the same broker. On receipt of the complaint, the CAM notified the broker. The broker notified the insurer for the association and then advised the CAM that the insurer for the association had been notified and would provide coverage to her as well. The insurer for the CAM was not notified until one year later. The court said no explanation, reasonable or otherwise, was offered as to why the carrier for the CAM was not notified at or about the same time as the association's insurer and held that the former had no duty to defend and indemnify.[823] The insurer who did not receive notice could well have been the carrier for the association and, given the loose process, the association probably would not have known that its insurer had no notice until it was too late. The case, therefore, underscores the need for a clear notification procedure. The standard CGL policy requires *written* notice, so one part of the procedure could be that the governing board, or a designated officer or director, obtain and file a copy of the written notice and also obtain and file *written* confirmation of receipt of notice by the insurer.

[c] Notification and Association Members as Additional Insureds

Typically, members of a common interest community association are additional insureds for limited purposes.[824] What happens if there is an "occurrence" and the association fails to notify the insurer, but an association member is sued over that occurrence and promptly notifies the insurer of the suit? Can the insurer deny coverage based on the failure of the association to notify it of the occurrence?

The first thing to observe about the notice requirement is that the policy provides "*you* must see to it that we are notified as soon as practicable of an 'occurrence' or an offense which may result in a claim" [825] and "[i]f a claim is made or 'suit' is brought against any insured, *you* must . . . [n]otify us as soon as practicable"[826] (emphasis supplied). At its very beginning, the policy explains that "you" refers to the named insured shown on the Declarations Page, and any other person or organization qualifying as a named insured under the policy. Thus, the notice obligation belongs to the named insured. Some courts, therefore, find that an additional insured is not denied coverage when the named insured fails to notify the insurer of an occurrence.

For example, in an Illinois case, a builder was an additional insured on a commercial general liability policy issued to a subcontractor. An employee of the subcontractor was injured on a job site. The subcontractor did not notify the insurer of the accident. Almost two years later the employee sued the builder.

823. 200 W. End Ave. Condominium v. Mt. Hawley Ins. Co., 2014 N.Y. Misc. LEXIS 5573 (Dec. 17, 2014).

824. *See* § 13.02[3][a], *supra*.

825. *See, e.g.*, ISO Form CG 00 01 12 07, § IV.2.a.

826. *See, e.g.*, ISO Form CG 00 01 12 07, § IV.2.b.(2).

The insurer was notified of the suit but denied coverage because it did not receive notice of the accident "as soon as practicable." The court, however, said only the subcontractor, as the named insured, had a duty to provide notice of the occurrence.[827] Nothing in the notice requirement, noted the court, made coverage for an additional insured contingent on compliance by the named insured with its duty to notify, and as the builder notified the insurer of the lawsuit, it was entitled to coverage as an additional insured.[828] Under the ruling by the Illinois court, an association member who is an additional insured and who notifies the association insurer of a lawsuit against him or her could still be covered even though the association failed to notify the insurer of the precipitating occurrence. Unfortunately, not all courts agree with that holding.[829]

What if the association member, aware of his or her potential liability, notifies the association insurer of an accident? The association member may well not have that opportunity. Many association members are unfamiliar with the coverage carried by the association, and even fewer are aware of the possibility that they may be an additional insured under the association policy. Some courts hold that an additional insured who was unaware of the policy or his or her status as an additional insured is barred from coverage by the failure of the named insured to give timely notice of an occurrence.[830] Others say that a claimant is entitled to provide notice to the insurer within a reasonable time after learning of the existence of the policy and obtaining possession of it.[831]

From a practical standpoint, an association can avoid having its members face the complex legal wrangling over notice. If there is the potential for liability of a member of the association in that status, then there is also a possibility of liability for the association itself. When there is an injury on the property,

827. *See also* Am. Nat'l Fire Ins. Co. v. Nat'l Union Fire Ins. Co., 277 Ill. Dec. 767, 343 Ill. App. 3d 93, 104, 796 N.E.2d 1133, 1142 (2003) (additional insured could not have violated notice requirements because they specifically required named insured to notify carrier of occurrence or claim).

828. Mt. Hawley Ins. Co. v. Robinette Demolition, Inc., 374 Ill. Dec. 36, 994 N.E.2d 973, 981 (Ill. App.), *app. den.*, 377 Ill. Dec. 765, 2 N.E.3d 1046 (Ill. 2013).

829. *See, e.g.*, Capital Rental Equipment Co. v. Pacific Indem. Co., 193 F. Supp. 897 (W.D. Tex. 1961) (where owner of crane responsible for accident in underlying wrongful death action may have been additional insured under policy issued to trucking company that was on site at time of accident, failure of crane owner to give notice of accident to insurer for trucking company barred coverage).

830. *See, e.g.*, Barrington Consol. High School v. American Ins. Co., 11 Ill. App. 3d 180, 296 N.E.2d 62 (1973), *rev'd on other grounds*, 58 Ill. 2d 278, 319 N.E.2d 25 (1974) (where school—named insured—failed to give notice of injury to student, that failure bound teacher as additional insured, even though she had no knowledge of policy). *See also* Navigazione Alta Italia v. Columbia Casualty Co., 256 F.2d 26 (5th Cir. 1958).

831. *See, e.g.*, American Liberty Ins. Co. v. Soules, 288 Ala. 163, 258 So. 2d 872 (1972) (where accident involving son of insured was not reported to carrier that issued homeowner's policy to parents until almost one year later when attorney advised family that policy would provide coverage to son as additional insured, lower court properly found notice was given as soon as practicable under all circumstances).

the association can confer with its attorney and/or its broker on the question of whether the incident should be reported to the insurer. The attorney can advise the association whether he or she believes any association members are potentially liable, and the association can call the policy—and any additional insured endorsement—to the attention of those members.

Association members who are additional insureds need to be aware that another duty in the event of a claim or suit would apply to them. The standard CGL policy says the named insured, *and any other involved insured*, is required to send the insurer copies of any demands, notices, summonses, or legal papers it receives related to the claim or suit immediately.[832] An additional insured who failed to comply with that requirement was properly barred from coverage by the carrier for the named insured.[833]

[d] Notice-Prejudice Rule

Even if an insured fails to provide notice "as soon as practicable," the insurer may be barred from disclaiming coverage because it was not prejudiced by the late notice. This "notice-prejudice" rule is the law in most states by either court decision[834] or statute.[835] Whether prejudice is presumed when notice is found to be late is a matter about which the courts do not agree.[836] What constitutes prejudice

832. *See, e.g.*, ISO Form CG 00 01 12 07, § IV.2.c.

833. Am. Nat'l Fire Ins. Co. v. Nat'l Union Fire Ins. Co., 277 Ill. Dec. 767, 343 Ill. App. 3d 93, 104, 796 N.E.2d 1133, 1142 (2003) (additional insured had obligation to immediately send carrier for named insured copies of any demands, notices, summonses, or legal papers it received in connection with underlying suit). *See also* Pennsylvania Threshermen & Farmers' Mut. Casualty Ins. Co. v. Thornton, 244 F.2d 823, 825 (4th Cir. 1957) (policy requirement that insured *immediately* turn over to insurer any summons or complaint served has been interpreted to mean, not instantaneously, but within reasonable time and what is reasonable is fact question to be determined in each case according to surrounding circumstances).

834. *See, e.g.*, PAJ, Inc. v. Hanover Ins. Co., 243 S.W.3d 630, 636–37 (Tex. 2008) (insured's failure to timely notify its insurer of claim or suit does not defeat coverage if insurer was not prejudiced by delay); Moe v. Transamerica Title Ins. Co., 21 Cal. App. 3d 289, 302, 98 Cal. Rptr. 547, 555 (1971) (breach of notice clause by insured may not be asserted by insurer unless it was substantially prejudiced by it). *Compare* Sisters of Divine Providence v. Interstate Fire & Casualty Co., 72 Ill. Dec. 731, 117 Ill. App. 3d 158, 162, 453 N.E.2d 36, 38 (1983) (prejudice, or lack of it, is not factor that determines coverage; rather, determination is based on standard of reasonableness, and prejudice to insurer is but one factor taken into consideration in making determination of reasonableness of notice).

835. *See, e.g.*, N.Y. Ins. Law § 3420(a)(5) (no policy or contract insuring against liability for injury to person or property may be issued or delivered unless it contains in substance provision stating that failure to give any notice required to be given by that policy within time prescribed will not invalidate any claim made by insured, injured person, or any other claimant, unless failure to provide timely notice has prejudiced insurer).

836. *See, e.g.*, Moe v. Transamerica Title Ins. Co., 21 Cal. App. 3d 289, 302, 98 Cal. Rptr. 547, 555 (1971) (prejudice is not presumed as matter of law, and insurer has burden of proving actual prejudice and not just mere possibility of prejudice); Tiedtke v. Fidelity & Casualty Co., 222 So. 2d 206, 209 (Fla. 1969) (effect of prejudice in delayed notice cases is that while prejudice to insurer

is also a matter of considerable debate.[837] Ordinarily, for example, where the insured does not notify the carrier until *after* a jury verdict against it, the notice will be considered insufficient because the insurer has lost valuable rights in the interim and clearly has been prejudiced.[838] However, even when notice is not given until after a default judgment has been entered against the insured, courts may be hesitant to find prejudice.[839] Additionally, while the notice may be late from the insured, the insurer may be barred from disclaiming coverage when it delays unreasonably in notifying its insured of its disclaimer.[840] An association may be able to gain the benefit of the notice-prejudice rule if it fails to provide notification, but likely not without protracted and costly litigation, especially if the potential liability in the underlying suit is great. It makes much more sense to discuss any potential claim promptly with the association attorney and broker and to notify the insurer of any actual claim or suit filed against it in a timely manner.

[4] Voluntary Payments by Insured

Under a provision of the standard commercial general liability policy on duties in the event of occurrence, offense, claim, or suit, *no insured* may—except at the expense of that insured—voluntarily make a payment, assume any obligation, or incur any expense—other than for first aid—without the consent of the

---

is presumed, if insured can demonstrate that insurer has not been prejudiced, insurer will not be relieved of liability merely by showing that notice was not given "as soon as practicable").

837. *See* American Mut. Liab. Ins. Co. v. Beatrice Cos., 924 F. Supp. 861, 871 (N.D. Ill. 1996) (where damages are at issue, prejudice inquiry revolves around whether critical evidence has been lost, insurer had sufficient opportunity to investigate claims, and insurer had chance to settle claim and avoid liability altogether).

838. *See, e.g.*, Berkley Reg'l Ins. Co. v. Phila. Indem. Ins. Co., 600 Fed. Appx. 230 (5th Cir. 2015) (insurer prejudiced as matter of law).

839. *See, e.g.*, Chimera Inv. Co. v. State Farm Fire & Cas. Co., 268 Fed. Appx. 793 (10th Cir. 2008). In *Chimera* an insured association did not provide timely notice as required under the policy. In fact, the insurer did not receive notice until almost a year after the lawsuit had been filed and judgment by default had been entered. The trial court concluded that non-compliance with the notice provision could defeat coverage with a showing of substantial prejudice to the insurer and that there was unquestionably substantial prejudice. The appellate court, however, said that notwithstanding the surface appeal of the rationale that a liability insurer not notified of an action against its insured until after a default judgment has been entered has necessarily been prejudiced by the untimely notice, it found "significant obstacles" to affirming the judgment on that basis as the correct resolution under Utah law of the issues raised in opposition to the trial court ruling was less than clear.

840. *See, e.g.*, Public Serv. Mut. Ins. Co. v. 66 Overlook Terrace Corp., 209 A.D.2d 343, 619 N.Y.S.2d 18 (1994) , *app. dis.*, 631 N.Y.S.2d 290, 85 N.Y.2d 1032, 655 N.E.2d 403 (1995) (where insured failed to give notice of potential claim until 15 months after tort plaintiff first complained, insurer was nonetheless estopped from disclaiming coverage because of unreasonable delay in notifying insured of disclaimer). *See also* 233 E. 17th St., LLC v. L.G.B. Dev., Inc., 78 A.D.3d 930, 913 N.Y.S.2d 110 (2010).

insurer.[841] The effect of this proscription is that the insured must get the consent of the insurance company before making any defense expenditure and, if he or she does not, he or she has to bear the expense him- or herself. Many policies do not specify *written* consent, but it is a good idea to have the consent in writing. If the insured fails to obtain consent—or the insurer denies consent was given—many courts will require that the insurer be prejudiced by that failure before they will relieve the carrier of the duty to pay.[842] Obviously, it is better for the insured to obtain distinct, written consent from the insurance company for an expenditure than to litigate the question of prejudice.

The voluntary payment proscription uses the words "no insured"; therefore, it would apply to the member of an association who is an additional insured.[843]

Common interest community associations need to be especially mindful of the voluntary payments clause. In the commercial setting, a company presented with a claim will handle it as an "arm's length" business matter. That may not be the case in a community association. The claimant and members of the governing board are by definition neighbors and may be friends. If, for example, an elderly resident slips in the building lobby on a wet floor, her distraught friend who happens to be the president of the association may "assume an obligation" on behalf of the association that a business entity would not.

Similarly, if a common interest community were to believe itself liable for damages to the property of its residents, its governing board might make expenditures to expedite repairs in response to the needs of neighbors who might well be personal friends for whom the board members have a personal concern and whom they would not want to face in court. Would these expenditures come under the voluntary payments clause? An Arizona case provides an answer. A development company, apparently anticipating lawsuits by owners of homes in two subdivisions it developed over settlement and drainage problems, sent a notice of claim to its commercial general liability carrier saying it had already spent $640,000 in repairs and that more repairs were needed. The insurer, relying on the voluntary payments clause, argued the repair costs were not covered because the insured undertook the repairs voluntarily, without its consent. On appeal, the insurer did not contest that the voluntary payments clause would only bar coverage if it had been prejudiced but contended the developer made the repairs without asserting defenses it could have raised had the homeowners sued and did not obtain releases from the homeowners after the repairs were

841. *See, e.g.*, ISO Form CG 00 01 12 07, § IV.2.d. *See* Clarendon Am. Ins. Co. v. Bayside Rest., LLC, 567 F. Supp. 2d 1379, 1389 (M.D. Fla. 2008) (insured breached policy when it assumed obligation to make settlement agreement without consent of insurer).

842. *See, e.g.*, Hernandez v. Gulf Group Lloyds, 875 S.W.2d 691, 692 (Tex. 1994) (insurer may escape liability on basis of settlement-without-consent exclusion only when insurer is actually prejudiced by insured's settlement with tortfeasor).

843. Am. Nat'l Fire Ins. Co. v. Nat'l Union Fire Ins. Co., 277 Ill. Dec. 767, 343 Ill. App. 3d 93, 104–05, 796 N.E.2d 1133, 1142 (2003).

completed. The appellate court did not address whether the insured had breached the voluntary payments clause and held there was sufficient evidence from which the jury could conclude that the insurer was not prejudiced by the actions of the development company.[844]

[5] Legal Actions against the Insurer

Under the standard commercial general liability policy, no one may join the insurer as a party or otherwise bring it into a suit—which by definition includes arbitration or other alternative dispute resolution proceedings[845]—asking for damages from an insured or sue the insurer under the policy without first complying with all of the terms of the policy.[846] The policy allows that a person or organization may sue the insurer to recover on an agreed settlement,[847] or on a final judgment against an insured, but the insurer will not be liable for damages that are not payable under the terms of the policy or that exceed the applicable limit of insurance.

May an association member sue the association insurer? In a Connecticut case a condominium unit owner sued the association's liability insurer claiming it breached the implied covenant of good faith and fair dealing by unreasonably failing, refusing, or neglecting to pay a claim. The insurer argued the unit owner was not an insured under the policy and was not entitled to enforce it. The unit owner countered that under Connecticut's Uniform Common Interest Ownership Act, each unit owner was an insured person under the association policy with respect to liability arising out of his or her interest in the common elements or membership in the association.[848] The court agreed. It found the plaintiff had sufficiently alleged that he was an insured under the policy, that the insurer

---

844. Desert Mt. Props. Ltd. P'ship v. Liberty Mut. Fire Ins. Co., 225 Ariz. 194, 207, 236 P.3d 421, 434 (Ariz. App. 2010).

845. *See, e.g.*, ISO Form CG 00 01 12 07, § V.18.

846. *See, e.g.*, ISO Form CG 00 01 12 07, § IV.3.

847. An agreed settlement is a settlement and release of liability signed by the carrier, the insured, and the claimant or the legal representative of the claimant. *Consider* Henning v. Contl Cas. Co., 254 F.3d 1291 (11th Cir. 2001), where a resident of a condominium sued the association for negligent failure to obtain proper insurance after her claim against another resident for injuries she suffered when she was struck by a motorized cart being driven by that resident was denied by the insurer for the association. The insurer refused to defend the association and denied coverage for the claim for negligent procurement. The plaintiff and her association settled the claim, and the association consented to judgment against it in exchange for the plaintiff's agreement not to seek to execute the judgment, but rather to pursue any rights the association might have against its insurer. The trial court granted summary judgment to the insurer based on the clause barring coverage for settlements to which the insurer is not a party. However, the appellate court reversed as that clause was not a proper basis for its decision because the insurer refused to defend its insured or participate in settlement.

848. Note that commercial general liability policies issued to common interest communities likely have an endorsement with similar language.

unreasonably withheld payment of a claim, and that he alleged a legally sufficient claim for breach of the covenant of good faith and fair dealing.[849]

[6] Other Insurance

When there is other "valid and collectible" insurance available to the insured for a loss covered under Coverages A—bodily injury and property damage liability—or B—personal and advertising injury liability—the standard CGL policy provides limitations on the obligations of the insurer.[850] In general, the CGL policy is primary,[851] and when it is, the obligations of the insurer are not affected unless any of the other insurance is also primary, in which case the insurer will share with all other insurance by a method prescribed in the policy.[852] Under that formula, if all other insurance allows contribution by equal shares, the insurer will follow that method in which each insurer contributes equal amounts until it has paid its applicable limit of insurance, or no loss remains, whichever comes first.[853] However, if any of the other insurance does not allow contribution by equal shares, then the insurer will contribute by limits, in which case the share of each insurer will be based on the ratio of its applicable limit of insurance to the total applicable limits of all insurers.

There are several circumstances in which the CGL policy becomes excess coverage. A few of those circumstances have application to common interest communities. The CGL policy is excess over any other insurance—whether primary, excess, contingent, or on any other basis—purchased by the named insured to cover its liability as a tenant for property damage to premises rented to it.[854] An association that is party to a ground or recreation lease may have this type of policy. The association's CGL policy is also excess over any other insurance when the loss arises out of the maintenance or use of aircraft, autos, or watercraft to the extent the loss is not subject to exclusion.[855]

849. Lawrence v. Commodore Commons Condo. Ass'n, 2000 Conn. Super. LEXIS 2359 (Conn. Super. Ct. Sept. 8, 2000).

850. *See, e.g.*, ISO Form CG 00 01 12 07, § IV.4. An example of other insurance would be an association directors and officers policy. *See, e.g.*, Admiral Indem. Co. v. Travelers Cas. & Sur. Co. of Am., 881 F. Supp. 2d 570 (S.D.N.Y. 2012), where the CGL carrier for a cooperative sued the D&O carrier, which had disclaimed coverage for an underlying action in which a resident had sued the cooperative. *See generally "Other Insurance" Clause Dictates Insurer's Obligations* (Community Association Law Reporter 2011).

851. *See, e.g.*, Fieldston Prop. Owners Ass'n, Inc. v. Hermitage Ins. Co., Inc., 920 N.Y.S.2d 763, 16 N.Y.3d 257, 945 N.E.2d 1013 (2011) (where it was possible that both CGL and D&O policies covered underlying injurious falsehood claims, based on Other Insurance clauses, CGL policy was primary and CGL carrier had duty to provide defense to entirety of complaints). *Accord* Admiral Indem. Co. v. Travelers Cas. & Sur. Co. of Am., 881 F. Supp. 2d 570 (S.D.N.Y. 2012).

852. *See, e.g.*, ISO Form CG 00 01 12 07, § IV.4.a.

853. *See, e.g.*, ISO Form CG 00 01 12 07, § IV.4.c.

854. *See, e.g.*, ISO Form CG 00 01 12 07, § IV.4.b.(1).(a).(iii).

855. *See, e.g.*, ISO Form CG 00 01 12 07, § IV.4.b.(1).(a).(iv). *See* CG 00 01 12 07, § I.A.2.g (aircraft, auto, or watercraft exclusion).

Finally, the association CGL policy is excess over any other primary insurance available to the association covering liability for damages arising out of the premises or operations to which the association has been added as an additional insured by endorsement.[856] In other words, if the homeowner's policy of an individual owner adds the association as an additional insured, then the CGL carrier for the association may no longer provide the primary coverage.[857] Some associations require their members to have the association added as an additional insured on their homeowner's policy. Any association that has that requirement—or is contemplating adopting it—should discuss the implications with its broker.

When the association CGL is excess, the carrier has no duty under the bodily injury and property damage liability or personal and advertising injury liability coverages to defend the insured against any suit if any other insurer has a duty to defend in that suit, but if no other insurer defends, the association CGL carrier will undertake to do so, while retaining the rights of the insured against those other insurers.[858] When the association CGL policy is excess over other insurance, the carrier for the association will pay only its share of the amount of a loss that exceeds the sum of the total amount that all other insurance would pay for the loss absent the association CGL policy and the total of all deductible and self-insured amounts under all the other insurance.[859] The association's CGL carrier will then share any remaining loss with any other insurance that is not described in the excess insurance clause and was not bought specifically to apply in excess of the Limits of Insurance shown on the Declarations Page of the association CGL policy.[860]

---

856. *See, e.g.*, ISO Form CG 00 01 12 07, § IV.4.b.(1).(b).

857. *Consider* Alexander v. Nat'l Fire Ins., 454 F.3d 214 (3d Cir. Pa. 2006). In *Alexander* the association was the named insured in a CGL policy, and owners of a unit were named insureds in two policies issued to them. The court determined the association policy was primary. It noted that by substituting the association—as named insured—for "you" in a clause comparable to 4.b(1)(b), the policy read: "'This insurance is excess over . . . any other primary insurance available to [the Condominium Association] covering liability for damages arising out of the premises or operations for which [the Condominium Association has] been added as an additional insured by attachment of an endorsement.'" Thus, the association policy would only be excess if the unit owners' policies had an endorsement adding the association as an additional insured. Those policies, however, did not add the association as an additional insured by endorsement or in any other way and, therefore, the association was primary. Finally, the court considered whether the unit owners' policies were also primary. They provided that their coverage would be excess over "other valid and collectible insurance except insurance written specifically to cover as excess over" them. The unit owners, said the court, had "other valid and collectible insurance" from the association CGL policy—under which they were additional insureds by endorsement—and therefore, because that policy was not specifically written to be excess to those issued to the unit owners, by the operation of the other insurance provisions in the three policies, the association's carrier was the sole primary insurer of the unit owners for the liability at issue.

858. *See, e.g.*, ISO Form CG 00 01 12 07, § IV.4.b.(2).

859. *See, e.g.*, ISO Form CG 00 01 12 07, § IV.4.b.(3).

860. *See, e.g.*, ISO Form CG 00 01 12 07, § IV.4.b.(4).

[7] Separation of Insureds

The standard commercial general liability policy includes a "separation of insureds" clause, also called a "severability of interests" clause.[861] If the CGL policy does not include this provision, then Fannie Mae requires an endorsement that prevents an insurer from denying a unit owner's claim because of negligent acts of a common interest community association or of other unit owners.[862] Severability of interests guarantees the policy will cover a suit brought against one insured by another insured.[863]

The separation of insureds clause provides that, except with respect to the Limits of Insurance, and any rights or duties specifically assigned to the first named insured,[864] the coverage applies as if each named insured were the only one,[865] and separately to each insured against whom a claim is made or a suit is brought.[866] Under these "severability of interests" clauses the policy is construed

---

861. *See generally* Richmond & Black, *Expanding Liability Coverage: Insured Contracts and Additional Insureds*, 44 Drake L. Rev. 781 (1996).

862. *Fannie Mae Selling Guide*, § B7-4-01 (Aug. 30, 2016).

863. Woodward, *What Does "Separation of Insureds" Mean—Part 1* (International Risk Management Institute, June 2001), available at: https://www.irmi.com/articles/expert-commentary/what-does-separation-of-insureds-mean-part-1.

864. One expert explains that the meaning of these clauses is first that the separate application of the policy coverages to each insured does not include the limits of insurance. In other words, each insured does not have a separate amount of insurance that is equal to the policy limits; rather, all insureds share the limits. Additionally, application of insurance to each named insured as if it were the only named insured means each named insured becomes, effectively, the first named insured with respect to its own coverage although there remains only one first named insured under the policy. Woodward, *What Does "Separation of Insureds" Mean—Part 1* (IRMI 2001), available at: https://www.irmi.com/articles/expert-commentary/what-does-separation-of-insureds-mean-part-1. *See, e.g.*, Mt. Hawley Ins. Co. v. Robinette Demolition, Inc., 374 Ill. Dec. 36, 994 N.E.2d 973, 980 (Ill. App.), *app. den.*, 377 Ill. Dec. 765, 2 N.E.3d 1046 (Ill. 2013) (named insured alone under policy had duty to provide notice of occurrences, and nothing in exception to separation of insureds provision changed terms of the policy to make coverage for additional insureds contingent on compliance by named insured with its duty under notice provision).

865. One commentary observes that, because the named insured is considered "you" under the typical CGL policy preamble, this portion of the clause has been interpreted to mean that when a named insured seeks coverage, policy provisions that refer to "you," and to any other persons or organizations that have insured status because of their relationship to "you," are to be read as if any other named insured under the policy did not exist. Bobotek, *Are You a "You"? Don't Ignore CGL Policies' Separation of Insureds Clause* (May 2, 2016), available at: http://www.policyholderpulse.com/2016/05/02/dont-ignore-cgl-policies-separation-insureds-clause/.

866. *See, e.g.*, ISO Form CG 00 01 12 07, § IV.7. *See also* Mt. Hawley Ins. Co. v. Robinette Demolition, Inc., 374 Ill. Dec. 36, 994 N.E.2d 973, 980 (Ill. App.), *app. den.*, 377 Ill. Dec. 765, 2 N.E.3d 1046 (Ill. 2013) (by language of separation of insureds clause, insurer recognizes obligation to additional insureds distinct from its obligation to named insured); 233 E. 17th St., LLC v. L.G.B. Dev., Inc., 24 Misc. 3d 1210(A), 890 N.Y.S.2d 371 (2009), *aff'd*, 78 A.D.3d 930, 913 N.Y.S.2d 110 (2010) (where general contractor for demolition and construction job and employee of subcontractor was injured on work site and sued general contractor and property owner—additional insured on contractor's CGL policy—insurer disclaimed coverage because general contractor failed to obtain hold harmless agreement from its subcontractor, which was condition precedent to coverage

to mean that it should be read as if each insured were the only insured and, thus, if an exclusion uses the term "the insured," courts generally interpret the phrase as referring only to the insured against whom a claim is being made under the policy,[867] while if an exclusion uses the phrase "any insured," a court may conclude application of the separation of insureds clause has no effect on the exclusion and a claim made against any insured is excluded.[868]

The separation of insureds clause could be significant for a community association if, for example, the community association management company is a named insured along with the association. For example, if an employee of the management company damages association property while on the premises, and the association makes a claim against the management company for the repair of the property, the policy would initially appear to exclude coverage. That is because a standard exclusion proscribes coverage for damage to property "you"—that is, the named insured—own, rent, or occupy. However, when the separation of insureds clause is read in conjunction with that exclusion, the *management company* would have coverage because "property you own" means only property

---

under policy, but court said fact that primary insured had breached condition precedent under which coverage was voided, was not sufficient to disclaim coverage for additional insured because each individual insured had to be treated as if it had separate policy of its own with insurer). *See generally* Nation, *Coverage Granted Under Separation of Insureds Clause* (Feb. 11, 2016), available at: http://www.floridainsuranceblog.com/2016/02/articles/bad-faith/coverage-granted-under-severability-of-insureds-clause/ (noting possibility of application of separation of insureds clause where one insured has intentionally caused damage to insured property and other insured did not).

867. Bobotek, *Are You a "You"? Don't Ignore CGL Policies' Separation of Insureds Clause* (May 2, 2016), available at: http://www.policyholderpulse.com/2016/05/02/dont-ignore-cgl-policies-separation-insureds-clause/ (in context of policy exclusions, "the insured" means insured who seeks coverage; thus, exclusion for damage to property in care, custody, or control of insured limits coverage only for insured who actually had care, custody, or control of damaged property, but if another insured were to be held liable for same damage, exclusion would not apply to that other insured); Woodward, *What Does "Separation of Insureds" Mean—Part 2* (IRMI 2002), available at: https://www.irmi.com/articles/expert-commentary/what-does-separation-of-insureds-mean-part-2 (majority of courts hold that references to "the insured" are to be construed very differently from references to "an insured" or "any insured" and within context of policy exclusions "the insured" means insured who is looking for coverage; exclusion of damage to property in care, custody, or control of "the insured, for example, only limits coverage for "the insured" who actually has care, custody, or control of damaged property while if another insured were to be held liable for that same damage, exclusion would not apply to that other insured).

868. Stanovich, *Legal Separation—The Severability Test in the CGL* (IRMI 2011), available at: http://www.irmi.com/expert/articles/2011/stanovich06-cgl-general-liability-insurance.aspx. *Compare* Taylor v. Admiral Ins. Co., 187 So. 3d 258 (Fla. 3d DCA 2016), *rev. den.*, ___ So. 3d___ (Fla. Oct. 10, 2016) (where employee of named insured was injured at event sponsored by her employer, her suit against additional insureds was not barred by employer's liability exclusion because, pursuant to separation of insureds clause, neither additional insured was her employer and each was separately insured and subject to claims by their non-employee; exclusion's use of term "*any insured*," when read in conjunction with severability clause, created class of insureds who were excluded from coverage—employers of injured claimant—and others who were not in class of excludable insureds—non-employers of injured claimant—but against whom claim could be asserted and coverage was not precluded).

owned by the company, and not the property owned by the association, because the exclusion would be read as if the management company were the only named insured under the policy.[869]

[8] Transfer of Rights of Recovery against Others to the Insurer

When the insured has the rights to recover all or part of any payment the insurer has made under the policy, those rights are transferred to the insurer and the insured is prohibited from doing anything after the loss to impair those rights. Additionally, at the request of the insurer, the insured must bring suit—which by definition includes arbitration or other alternative dispute resolution proceedings[870]—or transfer those rights to the insurer and help it enforce them.[871] This clause of the policy addresses subrogation, although it does not use the term.

[9] Nonrenewal

The standard policy provides that if the carrier decides not to renew the policy, it will mail or deliver *written* notice of that nonrenewal to the first named insured shown in the Declaration Page no fewer than 30 days before the expiration date.[872] When that notice is mailed, proof of mailing constitutes sufficient proof of notice. In other words, if the insurer can prove it mailed the notice of nonrenewal, an argument by the insured that it did not *receive* the notice is generally to no avail.

In many states, the policy language on renewal is modified by a mandatory endorsement conforming the policy to state law. These endorsements often increase the minimum time before the expiration date in which the insurer is required to send a notice of nonrenewal.[873]

[10] Common Policy Conditions

All commercial general liability policies include a common policy conditions form. The standard form addresses policy cancellation, changes to the policy, examination of the books and records of the named insured,[874] inspections and

---

869. Based on hypothetical in Bobotek, *Are You a "You"? Don't Ignore CGL Policies' Separation of Insureds Clause* (May 2, 2016), available at: http://www.policyholderpulse.com/2016/05/02/dont-ignore-cgl-policies-separation-insureds-clause/.

870. *See, e.g.*, ISO Form CG 00 01 12 07, § V.18.

871. *See, e.g.*, ISO Form CG 00 01 12 07, § IV.8.

872. *See, e.g.*, ISO Form CG 00 01 12 07, § IV.9.

873. *See, e.g.*, ISO Form IL 02 70 09 12, § C.1 (California Changes—Cancellation and Nonrenewal); ISO Form CG 02 20 03 12 § D (Florida Changes—Cancellation and Nonrenewal); ISO Form IL 02 75 11 13, § B (Texas Changes—Cancellation and Nonrenewal Provisions for Casualty Lines and Commercial Package Policies).

874. That provision states that the carrier may examine and audit the books and records of the named insured as they relate to the policy at any time during the policy period, and up to three years afterward. *See, e.g.*, IL 00 17 11 98, § C.

surveys, premiums, and transfer of rights and duties under the policy. These conditions apply to all coverage parts.[875]

[a] Policy Cancellation

The standard conditions form provides that the first named insured shown on the Declarations Page may cancel the policy by mailing or delivering to the insurer advance *written* notice of cancellation.[876] The insurer will send the first named insured any premium refund that is due, and that refund may be less than pro rata.[877]

The insurer may cancel the policy by mailing or delivering *written* notice of cancellation to the first named insured.[878] If cancellation is for non-payment of the premium, that notice has to be mailed or delivered at least ten days before the effective date of cancellation. If the cancellation is for any other reason, the notice has to be mailed or delivered at least 30 days before the effective date of cancellation. The insurer will mail or deliver the notice to the last mailing address of the named insured known to it.[879] The notice will state the effective date of cancellation, and the policy period ends on that date. [880] The insurer will send premium refunds due, if any, to the first named insured; however, cancellation will be effective even if the insurer has not made or offered a refund.[881] Any refund will be pro rata. When notice is mailed, proof of mailing is sufficient proof of notice.[882] The standard policy form requirements and procedures for cancellation are substantially changed by state law and regulation in virtually every state. In order to determine the cancellation laws and procedures that the insurer must follow in each state, one has to examine and become familiar with the state-specific cancellation and nonrenewal endorsement attached to the policy.[883]

[b] Changes

Under the standard common policy conditions, the policy is declared to be all the agreements between the insurer and the named insured.[884] This includes the

875. Hartford Ins. Co. v. BellSouth Telecomms., Inc., 824 So. 2d 234, 236 (Fla. 4th DCA 2002).
876. *See, e.g.*, IL 00 17 11 98, § A.1.
877. *See, e.g.*, IL 00 17 11 98, § A.5.
878. *See, e.g.*, IL 00 17 11 98, § A.2.
879. *See, e.g.*, IL 00 17 11 98, § A.3.
880. *See, e.g.*, IL 00 17 11 98, § A.4.
881. *See, e.g.*, IL 00 17 11 98, § A.5.
882. *See, e.g.*, IL 00 17 11 98, § A.6.
883. *See* § 13.11[1], *infra*.
884. *See, e.g.*, IL 00 17 11 98, § B. *See* Builders Mut. Ins. Co. v. Pickens, 2013 U.S. Dist. LEXIS 101410 (E.D. Tenn. July 18, 2013) (pursuant to Changes clause, insured was charged with knowledge that agent lacked authority to alter policy terms, and his estoppel argument, therefore, failed as matter of law); Patel v. Northfield Ins. Co., 940 F. Supp. 995, 999 (N.D. Tex. 1996) (Changes provision constitutes integration clause and, therefore, affidavit could not be accepted into evidence to create factual dispute on issue of intent of the parties regarding assault and battery endorsement).

application, which when attached to the policy becomes part of it. With the consent of the insurer, the first named insured may make changes to the terms of the policy, but those terms can only be amended or waived by an endorsement issued and signed by the insurer and made a part of the policy.

The changes clause can seriously affect rights to coverage. For example, in a California case, a company claimed additional insured status. It relied on an endorsement that provided an organization would be an additional insured while acting as any agent for, or on behalf of, the named insured, but the coverage would only be granted on written request of the *insured.* The company argued that the coverage trigger for an additional insured was when "the insured," rather that the "named insured," made a written request to the insurer. The company said it had indeed made a written request to the insurer. The court, however, citing the change clause, said that only the named insured had authority to request changes to the policy, and reading that clause in conjunction with the special endorsement for additional insureds, it was clear that the company had no standing to make written requests to the insurer to be named as an additional insured under the policy.[885]

[c] Inspections and Surveys

The standard conditions form provides that the carrier has the right to make inspections and surveys at any time, to provide the named insured reports on the conditions it finds, and to recommend changes.[886] The insurer, however, is not obligated to make any inspections, surveys, reports, or recommendations, but if it does, they relate only to insurability and the premiums to be charged. The insurer does not make safety inspections or undertake to perform the duty of another to provide for the health or safety of workers or the public and does not warrant that conditions are safe or healthful or comply with laws, regulations, codes, or standards.[887] The conditions under this part of the form apply not only to the insurer but also to any rating, advisory, rate service, or similar organization that makes insurance inspections, surveys, reports, or recommendations.[888]

Accord 3139 Props., LLC v. First Specialty Ins. Corp., 2007 U.S. Dist. LEXIS 41912 (D. Haw. June 8, 2007).

885. Boeing Co. v. Continental Casualty Co., 157 Cal. App. 4th 1258, 69 Cal. Rptr. 3d 322 (2007).

886. *See, e.g.*, IL 00 17 11 98, § D.1.

887. *See, e.g.*, IL 00 17 11 98, § D.2. The condition does not apply to inspections, surveys, reports, or recommendations the insure makes related to certification, under state or municipal statutes, ordinances, or regulations, of boilers, pressure vessels, or elevators. *See* IL 00 17 11 98, § D.4. *And see* Clarendon Am. Ins. Co. v. Bayside Rest., LLC, 567 F. Supp. 2d 1379, 1388 (M.D. Fla. 2008) (language of condition is clear: insured is not to rely on inspection conducted by third party at behest of insurer).

888. *See, e.g.*, IL 00 17 11 98, § D.3. The condition does not apply to inspections, surveys, reports, or recommendations the insure makes related to certification, under state or municipal statutes, ordinances, or regulations, of boilers, pressure vessels, or elevators.

[d] Premiums

Under the standard common policy conditions, the first named insured shown on the Declarations Page is responsible for payment of all premiums, and the carrier is the payee for any return premiums it pays.[889]

[e] Transfer of Rights and Duties under the Policy

The standard common policy conditions provide that the rights and duties of the named insured under the policy may not be transferred—that is, assigned—without the written consent of the insurer except in the case of death of an individual named insured.[890] An issue that arises is whether that clause prohibits assignment of claims. The Kentucky Supreme Court explained the divide among the courts on that question. The majority rule, said the court, is that an anti-assignment clause "is unenforceable once an insured occurrence takes place because at that point the insured is entitled to recovery under the policy; that right is a chose in action; a chose in action is a form of personal property; the anti-assignment provision amounts to a restraint upon the alienation of this property right; and, a restraint upon the alienation of property is in opposition to public policy."[891] On the other hand, the minority view—followed most notably in Texas—is that "the unambiguous language of an anti-assignment clause . . . should be enforced as written" and no assignments permitted without the consent of the insurer.[892]

---

889. *See, e.g.*, IL 00 17 11 98, § E.

890. *See, e.g.*, IL 00 17 11 98, § F.

891. Wehr Constructors, Inc. v. Assur. Co. of Am., 384 S.W.3d 680, 682–83 (Ky. 2012) (adopting majority view). *See, e.g.*, Action Auto Stores v. United Capitol Ins. Co., 845 F. Supp. 417, 423 (W.D. Mich. 1993) (only transfer and assignment of right prior to loss is prohibited, not assignment of accrued cause of action); Givaudan Fragrances Corp. v. Aetna Cas. & Sur. Co., 442 N.J. Super. 28, 38, 120 A.3d 959, 965 (2015) (once liability of insurer has become fixed assignment of rights to collect under policy is not a transfer of actual policy but of right to claim of money). *And see* Lime Tree Assocs., LLC v. Burlington Ins. Co., 2014 U.S. Dist. LEXIS 165794 (D.N.J. Nov. 25, 2014) (where individual was injured on apartment complex property owned by insured and after incident, insured merged into LLC and over two years later, injured party sued LLC, court held that absent explicit language prohibiting assignment of policy through merger, it would not deprive surviving corporation of protection bargained and paid for by merged corporation); 1200 Grand St. Condo. Ass'n v. 1200 Grand St. Urban Renewal LLC (*In re* Tarragon Corp.), 2013 Bankr. LEXIS 1676 (Bankr. D.N.J. Apr. 16, 2013) (where rights were assigned to association by consent order only assignment that could have occurred was assignment of claim, not general rights under policy; association would not incur actual loss until judgment fixed amount).

892. Wehr Constructors, Inc. v. Assur. Co. of Am., 384 S.W.3d 680, 685 (Ky. 2012). *See, e.g.*, Keller Founds., Inc. v. Wausau Underwriters Ins. Co., 626 F.3d 871, 875 (5th Cir. 2010) (Texas courts diverge from majority position and enforce non-assignment clauses even for assignments made post-loss). *See also* Bambrick, *In re Katrina Canal Breaches Litigation: The Louisiana Supreme Court Defies the Majority in Upholding Prohibitions on Postloss Assignments of Insurance Policies*, 86 Tul. L. Rev. 1345 (2012).

§ 13.10 Limits of Insurance

The standard commercial general liability policy provides that the limits of insurance shown on the Declarations Page and the rules of the policy establish the maximum amount the carrier will pay no matter the number of insureds, claims made or suits brought, or persons or organizations that make claims or bring suits.[893] The Declarations Page typically lists six specific limits: the general aggregate limit, products-completed operations aggregate limit, personal and advertising injury limit, each occurrence limit, damage to premises rented to the named insured limit, and the medical expense limit. Some policies may add a "professional incident" limit.

The general aggregate limit shown on the Declarations Page is the most the carrier will pay for the total of medical expenses (Coverage C), bodily injury, or property damage (Coverage A) other than for damages because of bodily injury or property damage that is included in the products-completed operations hazard and personal and advertising injury (Coverage B).[894] The products-completed operations aggregate limit shown on the Declarations Page is the most the carrier will pay for damages because of bodily injury and property damage included in the products-completed operations hazard.[895]

Subject to the general aggregate limit, the personal and advertising injury limit shown on the Declarations Page is the most the insurer will pay under Coverage B for the total of all damages because of all personal and advertising injury borne by any one person or organization.[896]

Subject to the general aggregate limit or products-completed operations aggregate limit, whichever is applicable, the "each occurrence" limit shown on the Declarations Page is the most the insurer will pay for the total of damages under the bodily injury or property damage coverage (Coverage A) and medical expenses (Coverage C) because of all bodily injury and property damage that arise out of any one occurrence.[897] An "occurrence" is an accident, including continuous or repeated exposure to substantially the same general harmful conditions.[898] Subject to the each occurrence limit, the damage to premises rented to the named insured limit shown on the Declarations Page is the most the insurer will pay under bodily injury or property damage coverage (Coverage A) for damages because of property damage to any one premises, while rented to the named insured, or in the case of damage by fire, while rented to the named insured or

893. *See, e.g.*, CG 00 01 12 07, § III.1.
894. *See, e.g.*, CG 00 01 12 07, § III.2.
895. *See, e.g.*, CG 00 01 12 07, § III.3.
896. *See, e.g.*, CG 00 01 12 07, § III.4.
897. *See, e.g.*, CG 00 01 12 07, § III.5.
898. *See, e.g.*, CG 00 01 12 07, § V.13.

temporarily occupied by the named insured with permission of the owner.[899] Also subject to the each occurrence limit, the medical expense limit shown on the Declarations Page is the most the carrier will pay under the medical expense coverage (Coverage C) for all medical expenses because of bodily injury sustained by any one person.[900]

The limits of insurance apply separately to each consecutive annual period and to any remaining period of fewer than 12 months, commencing with the beginning of the policy period shown on the Declarations Page, unless the policy period is extended after issuance for an additional period of less than 12 months, in which case the additional period will be deemed part of the last preceding period for purposes of determining the limits of insurance. The association needs to be aware that the limits can change when the policy is renewed. As part of an annual insurance audit, the governing board should review the limits on the renewal policy with its broker.

Understanding the different policy limits in a CGL policy can be a formidable task for an insured. There are different policy limits for different coverages under the policy. Most CGL policies have at least four different types of limits. Consider as an example a CGL policy with the following limits noted on its Declarations Page:

General Aggregate Limit	$1,000,000
Products/Completed Operations Aggregate Limit	Included
Personal and Advertising Injury Limit	$500,000 (Any One Person or Organization)
Each Occurrence Limit	$500,000
Damages to Premises Rented to You Limit	$100,000 (Any One Premise)
Medical Expense Limit	$5,000 (Any One Person)

The General Aggregate Limit is the most the insurer will pay under the policy, no matter how many claims there are or the value of the claims within the policy period. For example, using the example above, assume there were three events, that is occurrences, that happened during the policy period. First, a visitor slips and falls on common property and claims $300,000 in damages. Next, the maintenance staff of the association replaces electrical equipment causing $600,000 in damages to an adjacent property. Finally, a misrepresentation compares the

899. *See, e.g.*, CG 00 01 12 07, § III.6.
900. *See, e.g.*, CG 00 01 12 07, § III.7.

property to other properties in the area and causes $400,000 damages to one of them. Remember that the General Aggregate Limit is $1,000,000.

Assume that there are no exclusions or other limits that apply, except the General Aggregate Limit. Putting aside the Per Occurrence Limit for the moment, the first two occurrences would be covered because they fall within the $1 million limit. This leaves only $100,000 for any other occurrences during the policy term. Therefore, the third event would only be covered for the $100,000 left under the policy.

Now apply the Each Occurrence Limit to the same three occurrences that happen in the policy term. First, one has to understand that the Each Occurrence Limit may sometimes be equal to the General Aggregate Limit, and in other policies it might be less than the General Aggregate Limit, as is the case in this example. It is also important to recognize that the most the insurer will pay for any One Occurrence is the limit noted in "Each Occurrence Limit," which in this example is $500,000. Therefore, no matter how large the claim or judgment might be for a single occurrence under the policy, the most the insurer would pay under this policy would be $500,000.

In the example of the three occurrences, the first occurrence of $300,000 would be paid in full. The second occurrence is a claim for $600,000. It exceeds the $500,000 Each Occurrence Limit and, therefore, only $500,000 would be paid on that claim. That leaves a balance of $200,000 under the policy for any further claims in the policy period. The third occurrence would be limited not only by the General Aggregate Limit—$1 million—but also by the Personal and Advertising Limit of $500,000. The claim is worth $400,000, but there is only $200,000 left under the policy's General Aggregate Limit and that is all the insurer will pay under the policy.

Finally, it should be remembered that a common interest community may carry excess insurance to pay covered claims that *exceed* the limits of the primary policy.

§ 13.11 Endorsements

An "endorsement"—also called a "rider"—is a separate form attached to a policy that modifies it. An endorsement may add to, or exclude from, coverage provided in the main policy or change some other aspect of the policy. It is generally said that an endorsement is subject to, and governed by, all relevant terms of the primary policy unless otherwise stated.[901] The typical commercial

901. LCS Corr. Servs. v. Lexington Ins. Co., 800 F.3d 664 (5th Cir. 2015); Penthouse Owners Ass'n, Inc. v. Certain Underwriters, 612 F.3d 383, 386 (5th Cir. 2010) (endorsement controls policy insofar as it enlarges, modifies, or restricts terms of policy and if there is any conflict between it and

general liability policy issued to a common interest community association may have as many as 15 or 20, or even more, endorsements. One commonly finds the following endorsements: service of suit clause, nuclear energy liability exclusion, employment-related practices, total pollution exclusion with hostile fire exception, exclusion of certified acts of terrorism, asbestos exclusion, and lead exclusion. There will also invariably be endorsements modifying the cancellation procedures, conforming them to state law, and adding individual owners as insureds under the policy. Finally, in a number of states there are endorsements that incorporate state law on common interest communities.

[1] Endorsements Specifically for Common Interest Communities

There are over a dozen standard endorsements that are specifically for common interest communities. Some of these may be used in any state, but others are specifically designed to conform the policy to state law.

[a] Endorsements Applicable for Any State

There is a standard endorsement that amends the definition of "insured" in Section II of the standard commercial general liability policy to include as an insured each individual unit owner, but only for liability that arises out of ownership, maintenance, or repair of the portion of the premises not reserved for that unit owner's exclusive use or occupancy.[902] There is another standard endorsement that makes the same amendment for "townhouse associations" that provides each individual townhouse owner is included as an insured, but only for liability as a member of the townhouse association and for any liability that arises out of the ownership, maintenance, use, or repair of the real property to which the owner has title.[903]

---

policy, endorsement controls in construing contract expressly where provisions of endorsement are more specific); Transcon. Ins. Co. v. Wash. Pub. Utils. Dist. Util. Sys., 111 Wn. 2d 452, 462, 760 P.2d 337 (1988).

902. *See* ISO Form CG 20 04 11 85 (Commercial General Liability: Additional Insured—Condominium Unit Owners).

903. *See* ISO Form CG 20 17 10 93 (Commercial General Liability: Additional Insured—Townhouse Associations).

Another standard endorsement for condominiums modifies the CGL policy more broadly.[904] First, it provides that the developer is an insured in its capacity as a unit owner, but only for its liability arising out of ownership, maintenance, or repair of the portion of the premises not owned solely by it or its membership in the association; however, coverage for the developer does not apply to liability for acts or omissions as a developer. Next, all other unit owners are also insureds, but only for their liability arising out of ownership, maintenance, or repair of that portion of the premises not owned solely by them or out of their membership in the association. The endorsement provides the insurer may cancel the policy by mailing or delivering to the first named insured, and each unit owner to whom certificates of insurance have been issued, written notice of cancellation at least 30 days before the effective date of cancellation. Additionally, the insurer waives any rights the "transfer of rights of recovery against others to us" condition may give it against any unit owner—including the developer—and household members, the association, and members of the governing board for acts or omissions within the scope of their duties for the association; however, the insurer reserves its right to recover against the developer for acts or omissions for which it may be liable in its capacity as a developer. Finally, the endorsement provides that no act or omission by any unit owner, unless acting within the scope of his or her authority on behalf of the association, will void the policy or be a condition to recovery.

[b] State-Specific Endorsements

There are state-specific endorsements applicable to common interest communities in a number of states that conform the policy to state law. Typically, these endorsements add unit owners—including developers—as insureds under the policy; provide that no act or omission by a unit owner, unless acting within the scope of his or her authority on behalf of the association, will be a condition to recovery; and waive the insurer's rights under the "transfer of rights of recovery against others to us" condition.

904. *See* ISO Form CG 01 27 11 85 (Commercial General Liability: Condominiums).

There are endorsements available in Connecticut,[905] Georgia,[906] Illinois,[907]

---

905. The Connecticut endorsement provides that the developer is an insured in its capacity as a unit owner, but only for liability arising out of ownership, maintenance, repair, or use of the portion of the premises not owned solely by it or membership in the association; however, the coverage for the developer does not apply to liability for acts or omissions as a developer. The endorsement also makes each individual unit owner an insured, but only for liability that arises out of his or her membership in the association or ownership, maintenance, repair, or use of the portion of the premises not owned solely by him or her. Next, the endorsement states that the association CGL policy is primary over any other insurance available to a unit owner, with an exception, and that if the association policy is primary, the carrier's obligations are not affected unless any of the other insurance is also primary in which case it will share with all that other insurance by a method prescribed in the policy. The endorsement also provides that no act or omission by a unit owner—unless acting within the scope of his or her authority on behalf of the association—will void the policy or be a condition of recovery. The carrier also waives its rights under the "transfer of rights of recovery against others to us" condition against any unit-owner—including the developer—and any household members, the association, and members of the governing board for acts or omissions within the scope of their duties for the association; however, it reserves its right to recover against the developer for acts or omissions for which the developer may be liable in that capacity. Finally, if the insurer decides not to renew the policy, it is required under the endorsement to mail or deliver to the named insured shown on the Declarations Page and to each unit owner and each holder of a security interest to whom it issued a certificate or memorandum of insurance, written notice of nonrenewal that states the specific reason for that nonrenewal. The notice must be mailed or delivered not less than 60 days before the expiration date and will be sent to the respective mailing addresses last known to the insurer. If notice is mailed, proof of mailing constitutes sufficient proof of notice. The endorsement also provides that the first named insured shown on the Declarations Page may cancel the policy by mailing or delivering advance written notice of cancellation to the insurer. The insurer may cancel the policy by mailing or delivering written notice of cancellation at least 60 days before the effective date of cancellation to the named insured and to each unit owner and each holder of a security interest to whom it issued a certificate or memorandum of insurance. If the policy has been in effect for fewer than 60 days, and is not a renewal of a policy the insurer issued, it may cancel it for any reason, but if it has been in effect for 60 days or more, or is a renewal of a policy the insurer issued, it may only cancel for one or more prescribed reasons. It may not cancel policies in effect for 60 days or more or renewal policies for any reason other than the reasons described in the endorsement. The insurer will mail or deliver its notice to the named insured's last mailing address known to it, and the notice will state the specific reason for cancellation and the effective date of cancellation. The policy period ends on that date. If the policy is cancelled, the carrier will send the first named insured any premium refund due. If the insurer cancels, the refund will be pro rata, but if the first named insured cancels, the refund may be less than pro rata. Cancellation is effective even if the carrier has not made or offered a refund. When notice is mailed, proof of mailing constitutes sufficient proof of notice. ISO Form CG 26 19 10 05 (Connecticut Changes—Condominiums).

906. The Georgia endorsement merely amends the definition of who is an insured. It provides that all agents of the association and all unit owners and others entitled to occupy any unit "or other portion of the condominium" are insureds, but only for liability arising out of, or in connection with, use, ownership, maintenance, or repair of the common elements or other portion of the condominium that the association has the responsibility to maintain. ISO Form CG 26 57 04 00 (Georgia Changes—Additional Insured—Condominium Associations).

907. The Illinois endorsement provides that the developer is an insured in its capacity as a unit owner, but only for its liability arising out of ownership, maintenance, or repair of the portion of the premises it does not solely own; however, the insurance does not apply to liability for its acts or omissions as a developer. Additionally, each other unit owner and secured party of the condominium is an insured, but only with respect to liability arising out of ownership, maintenance, or repair of the portion of the premises not owned solely by the unit owner. Finally, any agent of the association and any employee or agent of a management agency is an insured while acting within

Maryland,[908] Minnesota,[909] Texas,[910] and Washington[911] that apply to condominium

---

the scope of their duties for the association; however, there are limitations on that status. Under the endorsement, the insurer waives any rights the "transfer of rights of recovery against others to us" condition may give it against any unit owner or members of the unit owner's household, the association, and members of the governing board for acts or omissions within the scope of their duties for the association. Unit owners waive any rights of subrogation under the policy against the association and the board of directors. ISO Form CG 01 65 08 05 (Illinois Changes—Condominiums).

908. Under the Maryland endorsement the developer is an insured in its capacity as a unit owner, but only for its liability arising out of ownership, maintenance, or repair of that portion of the premises not owned solely by it or its membership in the association, and the coverage does not apply to liability for acts or omissions as a developer. Each other unit owner is also an insured, but only for his or her liability that arises out of ownership, maintenance, or repair of that portion of the premises not owned solely by the unit owner or out of his or her membership in the association. The endorsement adds that the insurer waives any rights that the "transfer of rights of recovery against others to us" condition may give it against any unit owner—including the developer—and household members, the association, and members of the governing board for acts or omissions within the scope of their duties for the association. The insurer, however, does reserve the right to recover against the developer for acts or omissions for which it may be liable in its capacity as a developer. Finally, the endorsement adds that no act or omission by any unit owner, unless acting within the scope of his or her authority on behalf of the association, will void the policy or be a condition to recovery under it. ISO Form CG 01 41 03 11 (Maryland—Condominiums).

909. Under the Minnesota endorsement, a "declarant," as defined in the Minnesota Common Interest Ownership Act is an insured in its capacity as a unit owner, but only with respect to liability arising out of ownership, existence, use, or management of the portion of the premises not owned solely by it; however, this coverage does not apply to liability for acts or omissions as a declarant. Each other unit owner or owner of a security interest is also an insured, but only for liability that arises out of ownership, existence, use, or management of the portion of the premises not owned solely by the unit owner or that arises out of membership in the association. Finally, with prescribed limitations, any agent of the association, and any employee or agent of a management agent is an insured, while acting within the scope of their duties for the association. Next, the insurer waives any rights that the "transfer of rights of recovery against others to us" condition may give it against any unit owners—including a declarant—and household members, the association, and members of the governing board for acts or omissions within the scope of their duties for the association. However, the carrier reserves it right to recover against a declarant for liability for acts or omissions as a declarant. The endorsement adds to the policy that no act or omission by any unit owner or owner of a security interest—unless acting within the scope of the unit owner's authority on behalf of the association—will be a condition to recovery. Finally, the endorsement sets forth the requirements for cancelling the policy. ISO Form CG 01 28 02 96 (Minnesota Changes—Condominiums).

910. Under the Texas endorsement, the developer is an insured in its capacity as a unit owner, but only for its liability arising out of ownership, maintenance, or repair of the portion of the premises not owned solely by the developer or its membership in the association; however, this coverage does not apply to liability for acts or omissions committed in its capacity as a developer. Each other unit owner is also an insured, but only for his or her liability arising out of ownership, maintenance, or repair of the portion of the premises not owned solely by the unit owner or out of his or her membership in the association. Additionally, no act or omission by a unit owner, unless acting within the scope of his or her authority on behalf of the association, will be a condition to recovery. Finally, the insurer waives any rights the "transfer of rights of recovery against others to us" condition may give it against any unit owner—including the developer—and household members, the association, and members of the governing board for acts or omissions committed within the scope of their duties for the association; however, it reserves the right to recover against the developer for acts or omissions for which the developer may be liable in its capacity as a developer. ISO Form CG 26 37 06 95 (Texas Changes—Condominiums).

911. The Washington endorsement provides that the developer is an insured in its capacity as a unit owner, but only for its liability arising out of ownership, maintenance, or repair of the portion

associations. For Connecticut[912] and Minnesota,[913] there are endorsements applicable to townhouses. In Utah[914] and Nevada,[915] there are endorsements for common interest communities or associations.

---

of the premises not owned solely by it or its membership in the association; however, this coverage does not apply to liability for acts or omissions committed in its capacity as a developer. Each other unit owner is also an insured, but only for his or her liability arising out of ownership, maintenance, or repair of the portion of the premises not owned solely by the unit owner or out of his or her membership in the association. Next, the policy is declared to be primary over any other insurance available to unit owners with one exception, and when the policy is primary, the obligations of the carrier are not affected unless any of the other insurance is also primary in which case it will share with all that other insurance by a prescribed method. The endorsement also states that no act or omission by a unit owner, unless acting within the scope of his or her authority on behalf of the association, will void the policy or be a condition to recovery under it. Finally, the insurer waives any rights the "transfer of rights of recovery against others to us" condition may give it against any unit owner—including the developer—household members and lessees of the unit owner, the association, and members of the governing board for acts or omissions committed within the scope of their duties for the association; however, the insurer reserves the right to recover against the developer for acts or omissions for which it may be liable in its capacity as a developer. ISO Form CG 26 26 03 93 (Washington Changes—Condominiums).

912. ISO Form CG 26 23 10 05 (Connecticut Changes—Townhouses). The content of the endorsement is substantially the same as that of the Connecticut condominium endorsement.

913. ISO Form CG 01 20 07 98 (Minnesota Changes—Townhouses). The content of the endorsement is nearly identical to that of the Minnesota condominium endorsement except that it conforms the policy to the Minnesota Common Interest Ownership Act.

914. The Utah endorsement provides that each individual unit owner or lot owner of an insured association is an insured, but only for liability that arises out of that owner's ownership interest in the common elements and facilities or membership in the association and maintenance, repair, or replacement of common elements and facilities. The endorsement adds that no act or omission by any individual owner, unless acting within the scope of his or her authority on behalf of the association, voids the policy or is a condition to recovery. It also adds that the insurer waives any rights the "transfer of rights of recovery against others to us" condition may give it against any individual owner and anyone residing with an owner, if the owner resides in the unit or on the lot. ISO Form CG 01 47 11 13 (Utah Changes—Common-Interest Associations).

915. The Nevada endorsement provides that each individual unit owner is an insured, but only for liability that arises out of his or her interest in the common elements or membership in the association. Next, the endorsement states the CGL policy is primary over any other insurance available to a unit owner, with an exception, and that when the association CGL policy is primary, the obligations of the insured are not affected unless any of the other insurance is also primary in which case the carrier will share with all that other insurance by the method prescribed in its policy. Under the endorsement, no act or omission by any unit owner, unless acting within the scope of his or her authority on behalf of the association, will void the policy or be a condition to recovery under it. Additionally, the carrier waives any rights the "transfer of rights of recovery against others to us" condition may give it against any unit-owner or member of his or her household. Finally, the endorsement addresses nonrenewal and cancellation of the policy. If the carrier decides not to renew the policy, it will mail or deliver written notice of the nonrenewal to the association, to each unit owner, and to each holder of a security interest to whom it has issued a certificate or memorandum of insurance, at their last known addresses, no fewer than 30 days before the expiration date. The insurer may cancel the policy by mailing or delivering written notice of the cancellation to the association, to each unit owner, and to each holder of a security interest to whom it issued a certificate or memorandum of insurance, at their last known addresses, at least 30 days before

[2] State-Specific Cancellation and Nonrenewal Endorsements

State insurance laws and regulations govern the right of insurers to cancel or to refuse to renew insurance policies. There are endorsements that conform policies to those requirements, and they vary from state to state. These endorsements may be amended from time to time to conform to changes in the law of a particular state or changes filed by an insurer with the insurance regulators to incorporate revisions to the policy. Endorsements for policy renewal and cancellations replace a portion of the common policy conditions that is found in a form separate from, but included with, every commercial general liability coverage form.[916]

It is important to remember that each state mandates the terms for cancellation and nonrenewal. Generally, under the standard common policy conditions form, if cancellation is for non-payment of the premium, notice of cancellation has to be mailed or delivered to the insured at least 10 days before the effective date of cancellation. If the cancellation is for any other reason, the notice has to be mailed or delivered at least 30 days before the effective date of cancellation.[917] State-specific endorsements typically link cancellation to the length of time the policy has been in effect. The California standard endorsement, for example, has one requirement for policies in effect 60 days or fewer and another for policies in effect for more than 60 days and limits the reasons on which an insurer may base cancellation.[918] The Texas endorsement, in conformance with the state's Uniform Condominium Act, provides that if the policy covers a *condominium association*, and there is at least one residence or the Declaration conforms with the Act, written notice of cancellation will be provided to the first named insured 30 days before the effective date of cancellation and will also be provided to each unit owner to whom the insurer issued a certificate or memorandum of insurance.[919] Connecticut, Minnesota, and Nevada also have endorsements that

---

the effective date of cancellation. ISO Form CG 26 19 04 94 (Nevada Changes—Common-Interest Communities).

916. For a discussion of the generic policy provisions on cancellation, see § 13.09[9][a], *supra.*

917. *See, e.g.*, ISO Form IL 00 17 11 98, § A.2.

918. Under the standard endorsement for California, if the CGL policy has been in effect for *60 days or less*, and is not a renewal of a policy that the carrier has previously issued, the carrier may cancel it by mailing or delivering to the first named insured and to the producer—agent or broker—of record, advance written notice of cancellation. The notice, which must state the reason for cancellation, has to be mailed of delivered at least ten days before the effective date of cancellation if the carrier cancels for either non-payment of the premium or fraud, or thirty days before the effective date of cancellation, if it cancels for any other reason. If the policy has been in effect for *more than 60 days*, or it is a renewal of a policy the carrier issued, it may cancel the policy only on occurrence, after the effective date of the policy, of one or more prescribed circumstances. *See* ISO Form IL 02 70 09 12, § A (California Changes—Cancellation and Nonrenewal).

919. ISO Form IL 02 75 11 13, § A.2.a (Texas Changes—Cancellation and Nonrenewal Provisions for Casualty Lines and Commercial Package Policies). When notice is mailed, proof of mailing is sufficient proof of notice.

address cancellation of CGL policies issued to common interest communities,[920] and there is a non-state-specific endorsement for condominiums generally.[921]

Many state-specific endorsements address nonrenewal and modify the language in the standard policy.[922] The endorsement for Florida provides that generally, if the carrier elects not to renew the policy, it will mail or deliver written notice, stating the reason for nonrenewal, to the first named insured shown on the Declarations Page, and to the producer of record at least 60 days, but not more than 120 days, before expiration or the anniversary date.[923] The New York standard endorsement imposes notice requirements to the insurer if it "conditionally" renews a policy, which might include a change of limits, a change in type of coverage, reduction of coverage, increase of the deductible, addition of an exclusion, or, with certain exceptions, an increase in premiums of greater than 10 percent.[924]

[3] Mandatory State-Specific Endorsements

In order to conform policies to state law regarding matters other than cancellation or nonrenewal, there are endorsements that must be added to commercial general liability policies. For example, in New York there are required endorsements concerning the insuring agreements and duties in the event of a claim,[925] the insuring agreements and suits against the carrier,[926] the duty of the insurer to defend its insured,[927] and premium audits.[928] Texas endorsements address failure of the insured to comply with notice requirements,[929] an exclusion for personal

920. *See* ISO Form CG 26 19 10 05 (Connecticut Changes—Condominiums); ISO Form CG 26 23 10 05 (Connecticut Changes—Townhouses); ISO Form CG 01 28 02 96 (Minnesota Changes—Condominiums); ISO Form CG 01 20 07 98 (Minnesota Changes—Townhouses); ISO Form CG 26 19 04 94 (Nevada Changes—Common-Interest Communities).

921. The endorsement provides the insurer may cancel the policy by mailing or delivering to the first named insured and each unit owner to whom certificates of insurance have been issued written notice of cancellation at least 30 days before the effective date of cancellation. ISO Form CG 01 27 11 85 (Commercial General Liability: Condominiums).

922. *See* § 13.09[9], *supra.*

923. ISO Form CG 02 20 03 12 § D (Florida Changes—Cancellation and Nonrenewal).

924. *See* ISO Form IL 02 68 11 05, § C.2 (New York Changes—Cancellation and Nonrenewal).

925. ISO Form CG 01 63 01 96 (New York Changes Commercial General Liability Coverage Form); ISO Form CG 01 63 09 99 (New York Changes Commercial General Liability Coverage Form).

926. ISO Form CG 01 63 07 11 (New York Changes—Commercial General Liability Coverage Form).

927. ISO Form CG 01 63 04 86 (New York Changes—Amendatory Endorsement).

928. ISO Form CG 01 04 12 04 (New York Changes—Premium Audit).

929. ISO Form CG 01 03 10 93 (Texas Changes—Conditions Requiring Notice); ISO Form CG 01 03 10 06 (Texas Changes).

and advertising injury,[930] pesticide and herbicide application,[931] and experience rating modification.[932]

[4] State-Specific Risk-Related Endorsements

There are a number of state-specific endorsements that are risk related. These address a wide variety of risks including liquor liability.[933] In New York, there are endorsements concerning corporal punishment,[934] products/completed operations liability,[935] owners and contractors protective liability,[936] transfer of duties when a limit of insurance is used up,[937] and legal actions against the insurer.[938] Exclusions for employment-related practices[939] and abuse or molestation[940] are addressed by Texas endorsements. There is a very specific risk-related endorsement for Illinois about scaffolding requiring the City of Chicago be named as an additional insured.[941]

[5] Motor Vehicles

Common interest community associations need to take inventory of any vehicles they own or lease or that are used for association business. That includes personal vehicles of the community association manager, association employees, and residents used to conduct any association business. It also includes golf carts and maintenance equipment, for example, rider lawn mowers. The association should then discuss that inventory with its broker to determine whether it has coverage

930. ISO Form CG 01 03 10 00 (Texas Changes).

931. ISO Form CG 01 56 04 13 (Texas Changes—Pesticide or Herbicide Applicator—Limited Pollution Coverage).

932. ISO Form CG 01 13 12 04 (Texas Changes—Experience Rating Modification).

933. *See* ISO Form CG 26 22 03 11 (Michigan Changes—Liquor Liability); ISO Form CG 26 03 04 09 (New York Changes—Liquor Liability Coverage Form); ISO Form CG 26 01 04 13(Washington Changes—Amendment of Liquor Liability Exclusion); ISO Form CG 26 02 04 13 (Washington Changes—Amendment of Liquor Liability Exclusion Exception for Scheduled Premises or Activities).

934. *See, e.g.*, ISO Form CG 26 06 10 93 (New York Changes—Corporal Punishment).

935. *See, e.g.*, ISO Form CG 26 11 04 09 (New York Changes—Products/Completed Operations Liability Coverage Form).

936. *See, e.g.*, ISO Form CG 26 04 07 11 (New York Changes—Owners and Contractors Protective Liability Coverage Form).

937. *See, e.g.*, ISO Form CG 26 21 10 91 (New York Changes—Transfer of Duties When a Limit of Insurance Is Used Up).

938. *See, e.g.*, ISO Form CG 26 24 08 92 (New York Changes—Legal Action Against Us).

939. *See, e.g.*, ISO Form CG 26 39 04 99 (Texas Changes—Employment-Related Practices Exclusion).

940. *See, e.g.*, ISO Form CG 26 46 04 99 (Texas Abuse or Molestation Exclusion).

941. *See* ISO Form CG 26 57 04 00 (Illinois Changes—Additional Insured—City of Chicago—Scaffolding).

for any liability the association might incur if one of those vehicles is involved in an accident.

[a] Auto Exclusion

The standard commercial general liability policy excludes coverage for a bodily injury that arises out of ownership, maintenance, use,[942] or entrustment to others of an "auto owned or operated by, or rented or loaned to, *any* insured."[943] "Auto" refers to a land motor vehicle, trailer, or semitrailer designed for travel on public roads, including any attached machinery or equipment or any other land vehicle subject to a compulsory or financial responsibility law or other motor vehicle insurance law in the state where it is licensed or principally garaged, but does not include "mobile equipment.[944] "Mobile equipment" includes a vehicle maintained for use solely on or next to premises owned or rented by the named insured.[945] However, self-propelled vehicles with permanently attached equipment designed primarily for snow removal or road maintenance are not mobile equipment but are considered to be autos.[946] Mobile equipment also does not include any land vehicles subject to a compulsory or financial responsibility law or other motor vehicle insurance law in the state where it is licensed or principally garaged. Those vehicles are considered to be autos.

[b] Commercial Automobile Policy

If an association *owns or leases* vehicles that meet the definition of "auto," it probably needs a commercial automobile policy.[947] One danger to an association that owns or leases vehicles is that it could be liable for "negligent entrustment." Liability for negligent entrustment of a motor vehicle arises when one entrusts a vehicle to another knowing that person is unfit to use it properly.[948] The

942. The word "use" includes operation and loading or unloading. The phrase "loading or unloading" means handling of property after it is moved from the place where it is accepted for movement into or onto an aircraft, watercraft, or auto, while it is in or on an aircraft, watercraft, or auto, or while being moved from an aircraft, watercraft, or auto to the place where it is finally delivered, but does not include movement of property by means of a mechanical device, other than a hand truck, not attached to the aircraft, watercraft, or auto. *See, e.g.*, ISO Form CG 00 01 12 07, § V.11.

943. *See, e.g.*, ISO Form CG 00 01 12 07, § I.A.2.g. *Consider* Robinson v. Transportation Ins. Co., 881 S.W.2d 218 (Tex. App.—Houston 1st Dist. 1994) (policy excludes claims arising out of operations of insured's own automobiles and has, according to insurer, generally been used to cover valet parking situation).

944. *See, e.g.*, ISO Form CG 00 01 12 07, § V.2.

945. *See, e.g.*, ISO Form CG 00 01 12 07, § V.12.

946. *See, e.g.*, ISO Form CG 00 01 12 07, § V.12.f.

947. Treese & Rosenberry, *Insurance: How Community Associations Protect Themselves*, at 47 (CAI Press 2013).

948. *See, e.g.*, Doyle v. Hasbro, Inc., 884 F. Supp. 35 (D. Mass. 1995), *aff'd*, 103 F.3d 186 (1st Cir. 1996); Tucker v. United States, 385 F. Supp. 717 (D.S.C. 1974).

association needs to discuss with its attorney a risk management plan for vehicles it owns or leases. The plan should address who will be permitted to use an association vehicle and under what circumstances. It should also have a recordkeeping component in which the association confirms that anyone who is permitted to use an association vehicle is properly licensed, carries his or her own insurance coverage, and does not have a record of moving violations or accidents that would mark him or her as an unsafe driver.

[c] Hired Auto and Non-Owned Auto Liability Endorsement

A "Hired Auto and Non-Owned Auto Liability Endorsement" is generally required for common interest communities because individuals—principally managers or members of the governing board—use their personal vehicles to conduct the business of the association. It provides coverage for liability for use of rented or loaned automobiles used by the association and applies if, for example, an employee uses his or her own car on an errand for the association and is involved in an accident that results in damage exceeding is or her personal auto limit. The endorsement can be added to the commercial general liability policy or, if the association has a commercial automobile policy, it can be added to that policy.[949] Any additional premium is listed in a schedule at the beginning of the typical endorsement, and the schedule may also contain a specific limit of insurance. The endorsement provides coverage that is excess of other valid and collectible insurance coverage.[950]

Typically, the endorsement states that the bodily injury or property damage under Coverage A applies to bodily injury or property damage that arises out of the maintenance or use of a hired auto by the named insured or its employees in the course of the business of the named insured or that arises out of the use of any non-owned auto in the business of the named insured by any person other than the named insured.[951] A "hired auto" is defined as any auto leased, hired, or borrowed by the named insured, but does not include any auto the named insured leases, hires, or borrows from any of its employees or from any of its executive officers. A "non-owned auto" is defined as one the named insured does not own, lease, hire, or borrow that is used in connection with its business. The endorsement modifies the definition of who is an insured.[952] For purposes of the endorsement, in addition to the named insured, an insured includes anyone using a hired auto with the permission of the named insured. An executive officer of

949. Treese, *Under Cover* (CAI 2006) (noting that hired and non-owned vehicle endorsement will provide excess coverage for third parties injured by community association manager while in a car and conducting business on behalf of association).

950. Treese & Rosenberry, *Insurance: How Community Associations Protect Themselves*, at 47 (CAI Press 2013).

951. *See, e.g.*, ISO Form CG 04 19 11 85.

952. In the policy, the definition of who is an insured is found in ISO Form CG 00 01 12 07, § II.

the named insured is also included as an insured while using a non-owned auto in the business of the named insured.

[6] Liquor Liability

The "liquor liability" exclusion in the standard commercial general liability policy bars coverage for bodily injury for which "any insured" may be held liable for causing or contributing to the intoxication of anyone, for furnishing alcoholic beverages to a person under the legal drinking age or under the influence of alcohol, or for violation of any statute, ordinance, or regulation related to sale, gift, distribution, or use of alcohol.[953] The exclusion applies only if the named insured is in the *business* of manufacturing, distributing, selling, serving, or furnishing alcohol. The purpose of the exception is to provide "host liquor liability coverage"—previously provided by an endorsement added to the CGL policy—which covers a person or organization for functions or events incidental to the business of the named insured.[954] Many associations will conclude that, because they do not consider themselves to be *in the business* of manufacturing, distributing, selling, serving, or furnishing alcohol, the exclusion does not apply to them. As discussed previously, that may not be a correct assumption.[955]

[a] Expansion of the Liquor Liability Exclusion

Common interest communities need to be alert to any endorsements added to the policy that broaden the liquor liability exclusion.[956] For example, a common standard endorsement provides that coverage is excluded for bodily injury or property damage for which any insured may be held liable for causing or contributing to the intoxication of any person, including causing or contributing to intoxication of any person because alcoholic beverages were permitted to be brought on the premises of the named insured, for consumption on those premises, for furnishing alcohol to someone under the legal drinking age or under the influence of alcohol, or violation of any statute, ordinance, or regulation that relates to sale, gift, distribution, or use of alcohol.[957] The exclusion applies even if the claims against any insured allege negligence or other wrongdoing in supervision, hiring, employment, training, or monitoring of others by that insured or providing or failing to provide transportation for any person that may be under

953. *See, e.g.*, ISO Form CG 00 01 12 07, § I.A.2.c.

954. *See* Stanovich, *Raising the Bar—The Liquor Liability Exclusion in the CGL* (IRMI 2008), available at: https://www.irmi.com/articles/expert-commentary/liquor-liability-exclusion-in-the-cgl.

955. *See* § 13.03[4][c], *supra*.

956. In 2013, the Insurance Services Office amended some endorsements on liquor liability and adopted others. A full discussion of the amendments and new endorsements is beyond the scope of this discussion, but is available elsewhere. *See* Powell, *Further Erosion in the Host Liquor Liability Coverage* (Insurspective, Oct. 2015); Kinney, *Liquor Liability Coverage Changes under New ISO Forms* (Independent Agent, May 2013).

957. *See* ISO Form CG 21 50 04 13.

the influence of alcohol if the occurrence that caused the bodily injury or property damage involved one of the actions prescribed as a basis for the exclusion. The exclusion, however, only applies if the named insured manufactures, sells, or distributes alcohol, serves, or furnishes alcoholic beverages for a charge, whether or not that requires a license and whether or not it is for the purpose of financial gain or livelihood, serves or furnishes alcohol without charge, if a license is required, or permits anyone to bring any alcohol on its premises for consumption on those premises.

Note that the endorsement completely eliminates the "in the business" caveat of the standard policy. As one commentator observes, the endorsement broadens the exclusion significantly because under it there is no coverage for serving or furnishing alcoholic beverages if a charge is made or if a license is required, and it removes coverage for what might be expected to be a host liquor risk.[958] For example, if the social committee of a homeowners association holds a St. Patrick's Day dinner at the community clubhouse for which it charges a fee and green beer is served with the dinner, there would be no coverage. Even if the social committee allows guests to bring their own alcoholic refreshments, there would be no coverage because under the endorsement, the exclusion applies when the association allows anyone to bring any alcohol on its premises for consumption on those premises.

If the policy has the broad liquor liability endorsement and the carrier will not remove it, the association can ask for a version of the endorsement that provides coverage limited to declared premises or activities.[959] That endorsement provides the exclusion does not apply to bodily injury or property damage that arises out of selling, serving, or furnishing alcohol at the specified activity described in a schedule or permitting anyone to bring any alcohol on the premises described in a schedule, for consumption on the premises described in the schedule.[960] This endorsement will allow an association to obtain coverage for specific events, for example, an annual Fourth of July picnic or Christmas party.

[b] Liquor Liability Coverage

Liquor liability coverage can be purchased in a stand-alone policy.[961] It can also be added to the commercial general liability policy by endorsement. A standard endorsement simply deletes the liquor liability exclusion from the policy.[962] Note

958. Stanovich, *Raising the Bar—The Liquor Liability Exclusion in the CGL* (IRMI 2008), available at: https://www.irmi.com/articles/expert-commentary/liquor-liability-exclusion-in-the-cgl.

959. *See* Powell, *Further Erosion in the Host Liquor Liability Coverage* (Insurspective, Oct. 2015) (urging that agents should be vigilant to presence of endorsement on any CGL and should make named insured aware of its presence and degree to which social distribution of adult beverages is limited).

960. *See* ISO Form CG 21 51 04 13.

961. *See, e.g.*, ISO Form CG 00 33 04 13.

962. *See* ISO Form CG 24 08 10 93 and ISO Form CG 24 08 11 85.

that if an insurer agrees to provide coverage for liquor liability, it may insist on adding an assault and battery exclusion to the policy.[963]

[7] Swimming Pools

Many common interest community associations operate swimming pools. They need to be alert to endorsements that would affect coverage for their liability for injuries that occur at a pool. Some insurers may add an endorsement that completely excludes coverage for bodily injury, property damage, or personal and advertising injury that arises out of the ownership, operation, maintenance, existence, or use of a swimming pool.[964] Note that by excluding coverage for property damage that arises out ownership, operation, maintenance, existence, or use, the endorsement would appear to preclude coverage if, for example, a leak in a pool damaged neighboring property. Also, when the endorsement bars coverage for *personal and advertising injury* that arises out of the ownership, operation, maintenance, existence, or use of a swimming pool, it refers to false arrest, detention, or imprisonment; malicious prosecution; wrongful eviction from, wrongful entry into, or invasion of the right of private occupancy; slander, libel, or trade disparagement; violation of the right of another to privacy; use of the advertising idea of someone else; or infringement of the copyright, trade dress, or slogan of someone else.[965]

Other exclusions may be narrower. For instance, a federal court in Hawaii examined an endorsement in an association policy that read, "This insurance does not apply to 'bodily injury,' 'personal and advertising injury' or medical payments arising out of the ownership, maintenance, operation or use of a swimming pool unless the swimming pool is fenced with a self-locking gate and meets or exceeds all local governing codes and regulations."[966] A child drowned in the association pool, and the insurer sought a declaration that it had no duty to defend or indemnify the association because it allegedly did not maintain functioning self-locking, self-latching, or self-closing gates at the time of the drowning. There was evidence that at the time of the incident, the spring mechanism on the pool gate was not functioning to automatically close the gate. Nonetheless, the court held that the swimming pool exclusion did not bar coverage because the exception to the exclusion was met, that is, the pool was fenced with a self-locking gate that met or exceeded all local governing codes and regulations. To be a *self-locking gate*, noted that court, a gate did not need to automatically swing

963. National Fire & Marine Ins. Co. v. Hoene Springs Improvement Ass'n, 889 F. Supp. 362, 365 (E.D. Mo. 1995) (carrier's policies required inclusion of assault and battery endorsement whenever alcohol was served).

964. *See, e.g.*, Form CGL 1709 03 01 (exclusion applies whether use is authorized or unauthorized).

965. *See, e.g.*, CG 00 01 12 07, § V.14.

966. Great Divide Ins. Co. v. Aoao Maluna Kai Estates, 492 F. Supp. 2d 1216, 1219 (D. Haw. 2007).

into closed position when released from an open position; in other words, it did not need to be *self-closing*.

Associations that operate swimming pools need to be aware that even if there is no swimming pool exclusion, when a swimmer is injured by a contaminant in the pool, courts may say that the meaning of the term "pollutant" includes contaminants and, therefore, the standard pollution exclusion applies.[967]

[8] Exclusion of Claims by Member of Association

A South Carolina federal court examined a "member endorsement" that does not appear to be widely employed for common interest community associations. It proscribed coverage for "'bodily injury,' 'property damage,' 'personal and advertising injury,' or medical expenses claims against an insured by an association member."[968] The policy also included a version of the standard endorsement—the "covered persons endorsement"—that made any association members "an insured," but only with respect to their liability for association activities or activities they performed on behalf of the association.[969] A unit owner slipped and fell on an icy walkway on the common elements. He sued the association, which claimed coverage under its commercial general liability policy. The insurer sought a declaratory judgment that it had no duty to defend or indemnify because of the member endorsement. In response, the association argued that the member endorsement conflicted with the defined duties set forth in the basic policy and with the definition of covered persons in the covered persons endorsement. The court said the member endorsement limited the coverage to protect the unit owners only from third-party suits. It found for the insurance company and entered a declaratory judgment on behalf of the insurer that it was under no duty to defend or indemnify the association.[970]

[9] Volunteer Workers and Employees

Under the standard CGL policy, volunteer workers and employees may be automatic insureds. A volunteer worker—one who "donates" his or her work and acts

967. First Specialty Ins. Corp. v. GRS Mgmt. Assocs., 2009 U.S. Dist. LEXIS 72708 (S.D. Fla. 2009) (association was sued after swimmer contracted viral infection from contaminants in water of community pool).

968. The endorsement added that association members included current or former members of the association.

969. There is a standard ISO endorsement that is the same. *See* ISO Form CG 20 02 11 85 (modifying CGL policy to include as "an insured" any members of named insured, but only with respect to their liability for activities of named insured or activities they perform on behalf of named insured). *See also* Lenox v. Scottsdale Ins. Co., 2005 U.S. Dist. LEXIS 48883 (D.N.J. May 5, 2005) (coverage for member liability would be invoked when member is held vicariously liable for some activity undertaken by named insured; "on behalf of" includes member activity done for benefit of named insured at its request).

970. Northfield Ins. Co. v. Evian HPR, 2002 U.S. Dist. LEXIS 26684 (D.S.C. Aug. 27, 2002), *aff'd*, 2003 U.S. App. LEXIS 14064 (4th Cir. 2003).

at the direction of and within the scope of duties determined by the association without being paid[971]—is an insured, but only while performing duties related to the conduct of the business of the association.[972] Similarly, an association employee is an insured, but only for acts within the scope of his or her employment by the association or while performing duties related to the conduct of its business.[973] The status of volunteer workers and employees as insureds under the standard CGL policy may be eliminated by endorsement.[974] If this endorsement is added to the policy, the association needs to discuss the extent to which association members who perform volunteer work might be covered under the standard endorsement making association members insureds for liability arising out of their membership in the association,[975] and whether there are options for obtaining coverage for employees if the associations wants that coverage. The association also probably needs to confer with its attorney to determine the extent to which it has uncovered liability as a result of the endorsement removing volunteer workers and employees as insureds.

[10] Total Pollution Exclusion

The standard commercial general liability policy contains an exclusion for bodily injury or property damage arising out of actual, alleged, or threatened discharge, dispersal, seepage, migration, release, or escape of pollutants.[976] That exclusion can be broadened by a "total pollution exclusion" endorsement. There are a number of standard forms of this endorsement. One is very simple: it replaces the lengthy pollution exclusion in the policy with "this insurance does not apply to pollution."[977] Another endorsement adds a definition of pollutants to that endorsement.[978] One expert labels the total pollution provision one of the three

971. *See, e.g.*, ISO Form CG 00 01 12 07, § V.20.

972. *See, e.g.*, ISO Form CG 00 01 12 07, § II.2.a. Note that the endorsement also modifies the exclusion in ISO Form CG 00 01 12 07, § I.A.2.g. to make it applicable to employees or volunteer workers when operating aircraft, autos, or watercraft in either the course of their employment or while performing duties related to the conduct of the business of the named insured.

973. *See, e.g.*, ISO Form CG 00 01 12 07, § II.2.a.

974. *See, e.g.*, ISO Form CG 21 37 10 01, § A. (paragraph 2.a. of section II—Who Is An Insured—does not apply).

975. *See, e.g.*, ISO Form CG 20 04 11 85 (Commercial General Liability: Additional Insured—Condominium Unit Owners); ISO Form CG 20 17 11 85 (Commercial General Liability: Additional Insured—Townhouse Associations).

976. *See, e.g.*, ISO Form CG 00 01 12 07, § I.A.2.f. *Consider* Commodore Plaza Condo. Ass'n v. QBE Ins. Corp., 2013 U.S. Dist. LEXIS 192675 (S.D. Fla. May 20, 2013) (where underlying complaint alleged association failed to install roof tarps in timely and proper manner, resulting in additional water and mold damage, and workers it hired were removing asbestos-containing materials improperly and without the proper qualifications, pollution exclusion was inapplicable because complaint did not allege damages were caused by fungus, bacteria, or asbestos).

977. ISO Form CG 21 49 09 99.

978. ISO Form CG 21 49 01 96.

GCL endorsements everyone should avoid.[979] He adds that if the insured is unable to convince the carrier to remove the endorsement—a feat he considers nearly impossible—two substitute endorsements offer a bit more coverage. First, the "Total Pollution Exclusion with a Hostile Fire Exception" provides an exception for bodily injuries or property damage that arise out of heat, smoke, or fumes from hostile fires with certain enumerated exceptions.[980] Second, there is a "Total Pollution Exclusion with a Building Heating, Cooling and Dehumidifying Equipment Exception and a Hostile Fire Exception" that provides an exception to the exclusion for bodily injury (1) sustained in a building that is or was at any time owned or occupied by, or rented or loaned to, any insured and caused by smoke, fumes, vapor, or soot produced by or originating from equipment used to heat, cool, or dehumidify the building, or equipment used to heat water for personal use, by the occupants or guests of the building or (2) that arises out of heat, smoke, or fumes from a hostile fire with certain enumerated exceptions.[981]

One caution about all the various pollution exclusions is that experts say that many insurance agents and brokers know little about them.[982] This is likely true for insurance professionals that specialize in coverage for common interest communities. The agents and brokers that probably have the most experience with and knowledge of pollution exclusions handle liability coverage for manufacturing and industrial concerns. If the association's broker is not able to answer its questions about pollution exclusions, it should ask the broker to consult with a colleague or seek assistance from the association attorney.

If a common interest community association is forced to accept any of these total pollution exclusions, it may be wise to confer with the association attorney to determine the extent to which it is exposed to uncovered liability. If the attorney advises that, because of the peculiar circumstances the association faces, it needs coverage for pollution, the association can explore with its broker purchase of an environmental liability policy.[983] It may also be advisable to consult with other brokers to determine if the association may be able to purchase a more comprehensive policy.

979. Boggs, *Three CGL Endorsements Every Insured Should AVOID* (July 2009), available at: http://www.mynewmarkets.com/articles/102583/three-cgl-endorsements-every-insured-should-avoid.

980. *See* ISO form CG 21 55 09 99. *See also* ISO Form CG 21 55 03 97 (defining "hostile fire" to mean one that becomes uncontrollable or breaks out from where it was intended to be).

981. *See* ISO Form CG 21 65 12 04. *See also* ISO Form CG 21 65 09 99 (Total Pollution Exclusion with a Building Heating Equipment Exception and a Hostile Fire Exception).

982. Connelly, *How Much Do You Know About Pollution Exclusions?* (Independent Agent, Feb. 2015) (for most agents "pollution exclusion" calls to mind "hazardous waste disposal facility," and many agents may not understand total or absolute pollution exclusion because insurance educators typically concentrate on seven exceptions to that exclusions).

983. *See generally* Doering, *Understanding Environmental Impairment Liability* (Society of Environmental Insurance Professionals 2001).

[11] Limitation of Coverage to Designated Premises or Projects

Common interest community associations should be alert to inclusion of a "designated premises" endorsement. The standard version of the endorsement provides a schedule on which specific premises or projects can be listed. Typically, the schedule states that if it is left blank, then the information needed to complete the endorsement will be shown on the Declarations Page—in other words, the designated premises will be the location of the named insured shown on the Declarations Page. The endorsement then provides that coverage under the policy only applies to bodily injury, property damage, personal and advertising injury, and medical expenses arising out of ownership, maintenance, or use of the premises shown in that schedule, and operations necessary or incidental to those premises, or the project shown in the schedule.[984]

One insurance expert asserts that the endorsement is most often seen when the insured is "real-estate based" with a specific location, for example, condominium associations or apartments.[985] Insurers argue the intent of the endorsement is to transform an underlying CGL policy, which insured against risks from business operations, into a premises liability policy that insures only risks related to use of the premises.[986] Courts, for their part, often hold that language in a designated premises endorsement has to be clear and unequivocal to convert a CGL policy into a premises liability policy.[987]

Use of the endorsement is controversial. A commentator describes it as a "messy endorsement" and says agents should fight it whenever an underwriter wants to attach it because there are too many potential situations in which it is unclear whether there will be coverage or not.[988] Another observer says that court interpretations of the endorsement have not been uniform, adding uncertainty for claim professionals.[989]

---

984. *See, e.g.*, ISO Form CG 21 44 07 98.

985. Boggs, *Three CGL Endorsements Every Insured Should AVOID* (July 2009), available at: http://www.mynewmarkets.com/articles/102583/three-cgl-endorsements-every-insured-should-avoid. *See also* Wilson, *Just How Restrictive is a Designated Premises Endorsement?* (Independent Agent, Aug. 2016) (endorsement is designed for premises-only exposures: restaurants or apartment complexes).

986. *See, e.g.*, Indiana Ins. Co. v. Royce Realty & Mgmt., 371 Ill. Dec. 866, 990 N.E.2d 1244, 1251 (Ill. App.), *app. den.*, 374 Ill. Dec. 566, 996 N.E.2d 13 (Ill. 2013).

987. *See, e.g.*, C. Brewer & Co. v. Marine Indem. Ins. Co. of Am., 135 Haw. 190, 193, 347 P.3d 163, 166 (Haw. 2015).

988. Wilson, *Just How Restrictive is a Designated Premises Endorsement?* (Independent Agent, Aug. 2016). *See also* Boggs, *Three CGL Endorsements Every Insured Should AVOID* (July 2009), available at: http://www.mynewmarkets.com/articles/102583/three-cgl-endorsements-every-insured-should-avoid (agent faced with designated premises endorsement should make every effort to have it removed to avoid possible coverage gap).

989. Duane & Rajbanshi, *The Designated-Premises Endorsement* (2010), available at: http://www.propertycasualty360.com/2010/08/02/the-designated-premises-endorsement. *See also* Indiana Ins. Co. v. Royce Realty & Mgmt., 371 Ill. Dec. 866, 990 N.E.2d 1244, 1248 (Ill. App.), *app. den.*, 374 Ill. Dec. 566, 996 N.E.2d 13 (Ill. 2013) (senior claims specialist for insurer testified that

A Massachusetts case illustrates the problems the endorsement can make for common interest community associations.[990] In that case a Cape Cod restaurant decided to participate in a concert sponsored by one of its vendors in another part of the state. The restaurant rented a bus to transport its employees and its guests to the venue where it hosted a tailgate party. When employees of the restaurant tried to start a gas grill, it exploded and injured a guest. In the ensuing suit against the restaurant, the carrier disclaimed coverage based on the designated premises endorsement. The court rejected the contention that the event was unconnected to the business of the insured, but noted that the language of the endorsement required that any injury arise from an activity necessary or incidental to the *premises*, not just the business. The policy as amended by the endorsement only provided coverage when there was a causal connection between the event giving rise to the injury and the designated premises. In this case, said the court, the event occurred far from the premises and served no purpose related to the premises, as distinct from the business. Thus, there was no coverage under the policy.[991] One need only substitute "homeowners association" for "restaurant" to see how the designated premises endorsement could harm an association.

It is also possible that the endorsement could apply to a new common interest community being developed in phases. For example, consider a development in which one phase is completed and control of the association is transferred to the individual owners. The association purchases commercial general liability coverage with a designated premises endorsement, and on the schedule to the endorsement the only premises listed is that of the completed phase. During the term of the policy, another phase is completed and the association takes over responsibility for it. Are the premises of that phase excluded from coverage under the association CGL policy? One commentator says, "there is no coverage for a new location until the insurer is notified and the location is added."[992] That suggests there would be no coverage for the newly added phase.

There are circumstances in which a designated premises endorsement might benefit a common interest community. A housing cooperative, for example, was sued when a passerby tripped outside a ground floor restaurant on a sidewalk that was not level. She sued the cooperative. The restaurant had subleased the space from a tenant/shareholder of the cooperative. The restaurant had commercial liability coverage that named the cooperative as an additional insured. The cooperative sought coverage under that policy, which had a designated premises endorsement. Relying on the endorsement, the cooperative argued the trip and

---

she was uncertain about effect of endorsement on policy and that in more than 20 years as adjuster, she had never seen it).

990. United States Liab. Ins. Co. v. Harbor Club, Inc., 24 Mass. L. Rep. 78 (Mass. Super. 2008).

991. *See also* Union American Ins. Co. v. Haitian Refugee Ctr., 858 So. 2d 1076 (Fla. 2003).

992. Boggs, *Three CGL Endorsements Every Insured Should AVOID* (July 2009), available at: http://www.mynewmarkets.com/articles/102583/three-cgl-endorsements-every-insured-should-avoid.

fall accident occurred on a sidewalk that was the premises covered under the endorsement. The court said the sidewalk outside the restaurant would necessarily be used for access to it, and thus, by implication, would be considered part of the "use of the premises" or "operations necessary or incidental to those premises." Thus, the court refused to dismiss the cooperative's third-party complaint against the insurer that sought a declaration that the insurer had to defend and indemnify it in the underlying personal injury action.[993]

§ 13.12 Association Policy Content Checklist

When the association reviews its commercial general liability policy, the checklist below provides some important questions it should ask about that policy.

- ☐ Is the name of the association as it appears on the Declarations Page the legal name of the association in its governing documents? Is the management company the named insured? See § 13.01[4].
- ☐ Is there an endorsement adding members of the association as additional insureds? See § 13.02[3][a].
- ☐ Will the policy cover the costs of complying with a mandatory injunction against the association? See §§ 13.03[1], 13.04[1].
- ☐ Do the contracts the association has with service providers qualify as "insured contracts" under the policy? See § 13.03[4][b].
- ☐ Does the liquor liability exclusion apply to the association, and does it need an endorsement to add coverage? See §§ 13.03[4][c], 13.11[6].
- ☐ How does the property damage exclusion apply to the association? See § 13.04[3][b].
- ☐ Does the policy cover malicious prosecution as it is defined in the state in which the association is located? See § 13.06[2].
- ☐ Does the medical payments coverage apply to injuries that occur on limited common areas? See § 13.07[1][a].
- ☐ In a cooperative, does the medical payments coverage exclusion for employees apply to a person hired to do work for, or on behalf of, a tenant/shareholder? See § 13.07[4][b].

993. Stein v. 1394 Hous. Corp., 31 Misc. 3d 1224(A), 929 N.Y.S.2d 203 (2011).

- ☐ How does the medical payments exclusion for bodily injury to a person injured on the part of premises owned or rented by the named insured that the injured person "normally occupies" apply to the association? *See* § 13.07[4][d].
- ☐ From whom will the insurer accept notice under the policy? See § 13.09[3].
- ☐ If the association requires its members to have the association added as an additional insured on their homeowner's policies, does the association commercial general liability policy provide primary coverage? See § 13.09[6].
- ☐ If there are vehicles used for association business, what coverage related to them is excluded under the policy and is there a Hired Auto and Non-Owned Auto Liability endorsement added to the policy? See § 13.11[5].
- ☐ If the association has a swimming pool, is there an endorsement that affects coverage for liability associated with swimming pools? See § 13.11[7].
- ☐ Is there an endorsement added to the policy that eliminates volunteer workers and employees from insured status? See § 13.11[8].
- ☐ Is there a total pollution exclusion, and how does it potentially leave the association open to uncovered liability? See § 13.11[10].
- ☐ Is there a "designated premises" endorsement added to the policy? What affect does it have on the association's coverage? See § 13.11[11].

Chapter 14

Directors and Officers Liability Insurance

§ 14.01 Introduction: Essential Coverage

Director and officers (D&O) liability insurance is a relatively new form of coverage.[1] It was created after the stock market crash of 1929 and the resulting securities laws passed in the 1930s.[2] Lloyd's of London first introduced the coverage and for many years was the only source for it.[3] D&O insurance was originally designed to protect directors from liability in shareholder suits at a time when corporations were not allowed to indemnify directors.[4] Initially, it had few policyholders. However, in the 1960s changes in securities laws increased potential liability for corporate directors. D&O insurance then began to protect directors and officers from derivative lawsuits.[5] It gained popularity in the 1970s and in the 1980s came to be an increasingly common form of coverage.[6] In the early 1960s Lloyd's remained the only market for D&O insurance; however, with an increase in the perceived need for the coverage, many large insurers began to offer it.[7]

1. Dobiac, *I Came, I Saw, I Underwrote: D&O Liability Insurance's Past Underwriting Practices and Potential Future Directions*, 14 Conn. Ins. L.J. 487, 518 (2008); Johnston, *Corporate Indemnification and Liability Insurance for Directors and Officers*, 33 Bus. Law. 1993, 2012 (1978) (D&O insurance is relatively new form of liability insurance; although policies have been marketed since 1950s, coverage received little attention until mid-1960s).

2. Romano, *What Went Wrong with Directors' and Officers' Liability Insurance?*, 14 Del. J. Corp. L. 1, 4 (1989).

3. Monteleone & Conca, *Directors and Officers Indemnification and Liability Insurance: An Overview of Legal and Practical Issues*, 51 Bus. Law 573, 574 (1996).

4. Romano, *What Went Wrong with Directors' and Officers' Liability Insurance?*, 14 Del. J. Corp. L. 1, 4 (1989).

5. Dobiac, *I Came, I Saw, I Underwrote: D&O Liability Insurance's Past Underwriting Practices and Potential Future Directions*, 14 Conn. Ins. L.J. 487, 488 (2008).

6. Quinn & Levin, *Directors and Officers Liability Insurance: Probable Directions in Texas Law*, 20 Rev. Litig. 381, 411 (2001). *See also* Clark v. General Accident Ins. Co. PR., 951 F. Supp. 559 (D.V.I. 1997) (D&O liability insurance became common after rash of litigation against corporate directors and officers in mid-1980s).

7. Romano, *What Went Wrong with Directors' and Officers' Liability Insurance?*, 14 Del. J. Corp. L. 1, 15 (1989).

D&O insurance has come to be considered essential in the corporate world. Today, the insurance is designed to protect directors and officers—as well as the corporation that has to indemnify them—from losses that arise out of claims made by "outsiders."[8] It also has often come to be referred to as a form of "executive liability" insurance, although that is a broader term and encompasses other coverages.[9] One consequence of the relatively recent advent of D&O coverage is that there are a limited number of appellate decisions interpreting it,[10] and as a result courts may need to rely on decisions rendered in other jurisdictions.[11]

NOTE: The brokers from whom associations obtain policies have to put forth a special effort to familiarize themselves with the policies available, and associations have to be prepared to ask pertinent questions of their brokers.

One expert calls D&O insurance one of the most important policies in any association's financial portfolio and yet also one of the most overlooked and misunderstood.[12] Observers agree that the first thing to understand about D&O insurance is that there is no standard policy form.[13] For other forms of

8. Mount Hawley Ins. Co. v. FSLIC, 695 F. Supp. 469, 484 (C.D. Cal. 1987).

9. Quinn & Levin, *Directors and Officers Liability Insurance: Probable Directions in Texas Law*, 20 Rev. Litig. 381, 384 (2001) (executive liability insurance is broader concept than D&O insurance and includes employment practices liability insurance, fiduciary liability insurance—designed to address liability exposures under federal Employee Retirement Income Security Act (ERISA)—kidnap/ransom insurance, and specialized executive insurance; noting that one leading D&O carrier titles one of its package policies "Executive Protection Policy" and that policy includes D&O insurance).

10. Kokinda, *D&O Liability Insurance: There Are Exclusions, and Then There Are Exclusions*, 28-10 ABIJ 46 (2010) (because of lack of standardization and relatively short history of usage, interpretative precedents of D&O policies tend to be limited); Quinn & Levin, *Directors and Officers Liability Insurance: Probable Directions in Texas Law*, 20 Rev. Litig. 381, 385 (2001); Romano, *What Went Wrong with Directors' and Officers' Liability Insurance?*, 14 Del. J. Corp. L. 1, 29 (1989) (until mid-1980s there were very few cases involving D&O policies because insurers rarely litigated D&O contract disputes).

11. *See, e.g.*, Oak Park Calabasas Condominium Ass'n v. State Farm Fire & Casualty Co., 137 Cal. App. 4th 557, 564, 40 Cal. Rptr. 3d 263, 267 (2006) (observing that there are few California appellate decisions dealing with D&O policies, and consequently California courts often look to decisions of California federal courts and out-of-state cases in resolving coverage issues and interpreting policy provisions).

12. Bateman, *What Homeowner Associations Need to Know About Directors' & Officers' Liability* (2017), available at: https://communityassociationmanagement.com/c33-financial-matters/c37-insurance/what-homeowner-associations-need-to-know-about-directors-officers-liability/. *See also* Mosher, *Directors' and Officers' Insurance Don't Serve on the Board Without It* (Cooperator, 1997), available at: http://cooperator.com/articles/278/1/Directors039-and-Officers039-Insurance/Page1.html (many governing board members do not give D&O insurance much thought and do not realize association is subject to all rules faced by any other non-profit organization).

13. *Director and Officer Indemnification and Insurance—Issues for Public Companies to Consider* at 8 (July 15, 2013) (D&O insurance is not an "off the shelf" product"); Kokinda, *D&O Liability Insurance: There Are Exclusions, and Then There Are Exclusions*, 28-10 ABIJ 46 (2010) (D&O

coverage—particularly commercial property and general liability insurance issued to common interest communities—there are standard Insurance Service Office (ISO) policies that insurers issue to policyholders. D&O policies, however, differ from insurer to insurer. One commentary notes that while there are common elements in D&O policies, each insurer has different coverage formats.[14] Moreover, many insurance companies develop policies to address the needs of particular types of policyholders.[15] Indeed, there are, as discussed throughout this chapter, policies specifically designed to cover common interest communities. Small differences in policies—even a comma or semicolon—can mean that one policy provides coverage that another does not.[16]

§ 14.02 Legal Protections for Officers and Directors

Most common interest community directors and officers are not fully aware of all of the financial risks and liabilities to which they may be exposed.[17] There is no question that corporate officers and directors in general are at increasing risk of liability for actions taken in their official capacity. At the same time, the law affords them significant protection from liability.[18] Initially, corporate directors are generally not liable for their actions absent a crime, fraud, self-dealing, willful misconduct, or unjust enrichment.[19] Additionally, as discussed below, directors and officers of non-profit entities, including common interest communities, may have even greater protection. There may be exculpatory language in the governing

policies are not as standardized as others, for example, commercial general liability insurance); *D&O Insurance Policy Exclusions*, available at: https://www.connerstrong.com/resources/site1/news/1414CSB%20ER%20Policy%20Exclusions-2.pdf (there is no standard D&O insurance policy; each carrier has forms that differ from their competitors); Monteleone, *Coverage Issues Under Commercial General Liability and Directors' And Officers' Liability Policies*, 18 W. New Eng. L. Rev. 47, 62 (1996) (unlike standard CGL policy form, there is no single standard D&O policy form and policies vary from insurer to insurer and in many instances those variations are significant and material).

14. Kokinda, *D&O Liability Insurance: There Are Exclusions, and Then There Are Exclusions*, 28-10 ABIJ 46 (2010).

15. *Director and Officer Indemnification and Insurance—Issues for Public Companies to Consider* at 8 (July 15, 2013) (D&O insurance differs from one policy to next, and sometimes from one type of industry to next, depending on perception of litigation risks associated with certain industries).

16. *Director and Officer Indemnification and Insurance—Issues for Public Companies to Consider* at 8 (July 15, 2013) (minor wording changes can mean the difference between having and not having coverage, or having significantly more limited coverage).

17. Mistretta, *The Growing Importance of D&O Insurance: Avoiding Liability for Your Co-op & Condo Board Members* (Cooperator, Jan. 2014), available at: http://cooperator.com/articles/2729/1/The-Growing-Importance-of-DampO-Insurance/Page1.html.

18. *Directors and Officers Liability Survey: 2012 Summary of Results*, p. 3 (Towers Watson, 2013).

19. *See, e.g.*, Pelton v. 77 Park Ave. Condominium, 38 A.D.3d 1, 825 N.Y.S.2d 28 (2006); Sonny Boy, L.L.C. v. Asnani, 879 So. 2d 25 (Fla. 5th DCA 2004).

documents.[20] Most governing documents also provide for indemnification of directors for certain legal liabilities.[21]

[1] The Business Judgment Rule

Under the business judgment rule, if a board or an individual director acts in good faith and with a rational basis for a decision, the courts will not "second-guess" that decision and impose liability.[22] The rule generally applies to common interest communities,[23] although not all courts agree.[24] There are exceptions to application of the rule.[25] It does not protect actions taken in bad faith.[26] It also does not apply to *ultra vires* acts—that is, acts outside the scope of a board's authority.[27] The rule does not protect directors from a suit to enforce lawful contractual obligations of the association to a third-party.[28]

Governing boards often turn to professionals—community association managers, engineers, accountants, and attorneys—for guidance. Good faith reliance

---

20. *See, e.g.*, Breedy-Fryson v. Towne Estates Condo. Owners Ass'n, 2010 Del. Ch. LEXIS 37 (Feb. 25, 2010) (ordinarily, provision limiting personal liability of directors could be contained only in certificate of incorporation; however, in corporation subject to Unit Property Act—condominium enabling legislation—association codes of regulations could contain exculpatory provisions that address circumstances in which directors could be held liable for violating those regulations; under Declaration association and members of governing board had no liability to unit owners for any error of judgment or otherwise, except for willful misconduct or bad faith, and under Code of Regulations members of governing board were not liable to unit owners for any mistake of judgments, negligence, or otherwise except for their own individual willful misconduct or bad faith).

21. Winzenburg, *Condominium Law and Practice: Forms* § 49.04[7] (Matthew Bender & Company, 2007).

22. Sonny Boy, L.L.C. v. Asnani, 879 So. 2d 25 (Fla. 5th DCA, 2004); Hochman v. 35 Park West Corp., 741 N.Y.S.2d 261 (2002).

23. *See* LoRusso v. Brookside Homeowner's Ass'n, 17 A.D.3d 323, 793 N.Y.S.2d 96 (2005); Garcia v. Crescent Plaza Condominium Ass'n, Inc., 813 So. 2d 975 (Fla. 2d DCA 2002); Colorado Homes v. Loerch-Wilson, 43 P.3d 718 (Colo. App. 2001); Bennett v. Weimar, 975 P.2d 691 (Alaska 1999); Leppaluoto v. Warm Springs Hollow Homeowners Ass'n, 114 Idaho 3, 752 P.2d 605 (1988); Courts at Beachgate v. Bird, 226 N.J. Super. 631, 545 A.2d 243 (1988); Dockside Ass'n v. Detyens, 291 S.C. 214, 352 S.E.2d 714 (Ct. App.), *aff'd*, 294 S.C. 86, 362 S.E.2d 874 (S.C. 1987); Schwarzmann v. Association of Apt. Owners of Bridgehaven, 655 P.2d 1177 (Wash. App. 1982).

24. *See, e.g.*, Johnson v. Hobson, 505 A.2d 1313 (D.C. App. 1986); Noble v. Murphy, 612 N.E.2d 266 (Mass. App. 1993).

25. *See, e.g.*, McDaniel v. 162 Columbia Hgts. Hous. Corp., 25 Misc. 3d 1024, 1040, 886 N.Y.S.2d 562, 576 (2009) (absent breach of fiduciary duty, decisions of board of directors for cooperative housing corporation are entitled to deference under business judgment rule).

26. *See, e.g.*, Hunt v. Sharp, 202, A.D.2d 151, 608 N.Y.S.2d 188 (1994), *aff'd*, 626 N.Y.S.2d 57, 85 N.Y.2d 883, 649 N.E.2d 1201 (1995).

27. *See, e.g.*, Blumberg v. Albicocco, 12 Misc. 3d 1045, 820 N.Y.S.2d 711 (2006) (before reviewing any exercise of power under business judgment rule, court has to determine whether board had power it purported to exercise); Verna v. Links at Valleybrook Neighborhood Ass'n, 371 N.J. Super. 77, 852 A.2d 202 (2004).

28. Colony Beach & Tennis Club, Inc. v. Colony Beach & Tennis Club Ass'n (*In re* Colony Beach & Tennis Club Ass'n), 456 B.R. 545 (M.D. Fla. 2011).

on advice of a professional can bring board action within the business judgment rule. However, a board may not be able to rely on one of its members—or even a member of the association—who is a professional as the advice would not be unbiased.[29] On the other hand, when a director has a particular area of expertise, he or she may be limited in his or her ability to rely on advice from third parties within his or her area of expertise.[30]

Instead of the deference granted under the business judgment rule, some courts apply a reasonableness standard to governing board decisions, requiring a fact-intensive inquiry by a court.[31] For example, the Alaska Supreme Court rejected the business judgment rule and applied a reasonableness standard in a common interest community case.[32] While some courts may suggest there is a bright line distinction between the business judgment rule and the reasonableness standard, the difference is not always clear.[33]

[2] Corporate Law Statutes on Indemnification

Common interest community associations are nearly always incorporated under the non-profit corporation statutes of the state in which they are located. State laws authorize the corporation to indemnify officers and directors. Indemnify means to secure another against a future loss or recompense for a past one.[34] California,[35] Florida,[36] Illinois,[37] New York,[38] and Texas[39] all have indemnification statutes. These statutes authorize, but do not require, the corporation to indemnify officers and directors. Thus, the governing documents do not need to provide for indemnification, although they may,[40] and corporate bylaws often do.[41]

29. Wolinsky v. Kadison, 370 Ill. Dec. 205, 987 N.E.2d 971 (Ill. App. 2013) (advice of board members who were attorneys could not be considered unbiased and board, therefore, could not claim to have relied on advice of counsel).

30. Quinn & Levin, *Directors and Officers Liability Insurance: Probable Directions in Texas Law*, 20 Rev. Litig. 381, 400 (2001). *See generally* McCutcheon, *Professional Liability Insurance Issues for Lawyers Sitting on Corporate Boards*, 25 The Brief 8 (1996).

31. Nichols, *Reasonableness Standard Versus Business-Judgment Rule* (ABA 2012).

32. Bennett v. Weimar, 975 P.2d 691 (Alaska 1999).

33. Nichols, *Reasonableness Standard Versus Business-Judgment Rule* (ABA 2012) (some courts conflate business judgment and reasonableness standards and others appear to mislabel them).

34. *Ballentine's Law Dictionary* (LexisNexis 2010).

35. Cal. Corp. Code § 7237.

36. Fla. Stat. §§ 607.0850, 617.0831.

37. 805 Ill. Comp. Stat. 105/108.75.

38. NY CLS N-PCL § 722.

39. Tex. Bus. Org. Code § 2.101(16).

40. *Consider* NY CLS N-PCL § 721 (indemnification provided by statute is not to be deemed exclusive of any other rights to which director or officer may be entitled, whether contained in certificate of incorporation or bylaws).

41. *See, e.g.*, Owens Corning v. Nat'l Union Fire Ins. Co. of Pittsburgh, PA, 257 F.3d 484, 494 (6th Cir. 2001) (it is common for corporations to adopt bylaws requiring that they must reimburse directors for their costs).

The statutes vary from state to state, but the Illinois statute is fairly typical. It provides that a non-profit corporation may indemnify any person who was or is a party, or is threatened to be made a party to any threatened, pending, or completed action, suit, or proceeding, whether civil, criminal, administrative, or investigative, by reason of the fact that he or she is or was a director, officer, employee, or agent of the corporation. The indemnification is against expenses, including attorney's fees, judgments, fines, and amounts paid in settlement actually and reasonably incurred in connection with that action, suit, or proceeding providing that person acted in good faith and in a manner he or she reasonably believed to be in, or not opposed to, the best interests of the corporation.[42]

[3] Non-Profit Corporations Laws and Immunity

Statutes under a state's non-profit corporation law may provide some immunity to directors and officers of common interest communities.[43] However, many of these statutes apply only to directors and officers of organizations with 501(c) tax-exempt status. Another limitation on the state laws is that they may not apply to liability under a federal statute. For example, federal courts in Florida have held that the state statute providing immunity to officers and directors of non-profit corporations did not insulate condominium association directors from liability for violations of the Federal Fair Housing Act (FHA).[44]

[a] Immunity Statutes Not Requiring Federal Tax-Exempt Status

Some states have statutes that provide qualified immunity to officers and directors of non-profit corporations and do not limit the immunity to officers and directors of corporations with 501(c) tax-exempt status. For example, the North Carolina Nonprofit Corporation Act provides that anyone who serves as a director or officer of a non-profit corporation is generally immune individually from civil liability for monetary damages, *except to the extent covered by insurance*, for any act or failure to act arising out of his or her service.[45] The immunity does

42. 805 Ill. Comp. Stat. 105/108.75(a).

43. *See generally Developments in the Law—Nonprofit Corporations: VI. Special Treatment and Tort Law*, 105 Harv. L. Rev. 1677, 1687 (1992) (because most states passed their liability legislation hastily, in response to insurance crisis of 1980s, many of these laws are quite complicated and unclear).

44. Hous. Opportunities Project for Excellence, Inc. v. Key Colony No. 4 Condo. Assoc., 510 F. Supp. 2d 1003, 1014 (S.D. Fla. 2007) (where plaintiff unit owners alleged condominium directors enforced regulations that actively discriminated against families with children, state immunity statute could not be applied to bar federal cause of action). *See also* Sabal Palm Condos. of Pine Island Ridge Ass'n v. Fischer, 2014 U.S. Dist. LEXIS 32705 (S.D. Fla. Mar. 13, 2014) (where plaintiff unit owner sued association president after she was refused reasonable accommodation for service animal, state immunity statute could not bar federal cause of action claim under FHA).

45. N.C. Gen. Stat. § 55A-8-60(a). The immunity is personal to directors and officers and does not immunize the corporation against liability for acts or omissions of directors or officers. N.C. Gen. Stat. § 55A-8-60(b).

not apply if, *inter alia*, the officer or director compensated for services—other than reimbursement for expenses—was not acting within the scope of his or her official duties, was not acting in good faith, or derived an improper personal financial benefit from the transaction.

Wisconsin statutes provide qualified immunity for "volunteers" and directors and officers of non-profit corporations. Under one statute, a volunteer is generally not liable to any person for damages, settlements, fees, fines, penalties, or other monetary liabilities arising from any act or omission as a volunteer.[46] The term "volunteer" *could* include an officer or director of a common interest community as it is defined as simply "an individual, other than an employee of the corporation, who provides services to or on behalf of the corporation without compensation."[47] However, the statute adds that if the volunteer is a director or officer of the corporation, the granted immunity does not apply to an act or omission within the scope of the volunteers duties as a director or officer.[48] There is another statute that does apply to officers and directors. Under that statute, a director or officer is generally not liable to "the corporation, its members or creditors, or any person asserting rights on behalf of the corporation, its members or creditors, or any other person, for damages, settlements, fees, fines, penalties or other monetary liabilities arising from a breach of, or failure to perform, any duty resulting solely from his or her status as a director or officer . . . ."[49] There are a number of exceptions to the immunity including for material conflicts of interest, violations of criminal law, improper personal profits or benefits, and willful misconduct.

[b] Statutes Requiring Federal Tax-Exempt Status

A number of states have statutes in their non-profit corporation laws that provide limited immunity for officers and directors of non-profit corporations that qualify for federal tax-exempt status.[50] For example, the New York Not-For-Profit

---

46. Wis. Stat. § 181.0670(2).
47. Wis. Stat. § 181.0670(1).
48. Wis. Stat. § 181.0670(2)(c).
49. Wis. Stat. § 181.0855(1).
50. Cal. Corp. Code §§ 5047.5(b), (d) (no cause of action for monetary damages may arise against any person serving without compensation as director or officer of non-profit corporation on account of any negligent act or omission occurring within scope of that person's duties as director acting as board member or as officer acting in an official capacity when non-profit corporation was organized to provide religious, charitable, literary, educational, scientific, social, or other forms of public service exempt from federal income taxation under 501(c)(3) or 501(c)(6)); Colo. Rev. Stat. 13-21-115.7(2) (generally, any person who serves as director, officer, or trustee of non-profit corporation or non-profit organization—meaning corporation or organization listed as exempt organization in 501(c) (2), (3), (4), (5), (6), (7), (8), (11), or (19)—and who is not compensated will be immune from civil liability for any act or omission that results in damage or injury if he or she was acting within scope of his or her official functions and duties); Fla. Stat. § 617.0834(1) (officer or director of non-profit organization recognized under 501(c)(3), (4), or (6) or horticultural

Corporation Law has a fairly typical immunity statute that reads in part: "no person serving without compensation as a director, officer or trustee of a corporation, association, organization or trust described in section 501(c)(3) . . . shall be liable to any person other than such corporation, association, organization or trust based solely on his or her conduct in the execution of such office unless the conduct of such director, officer or trustee with respect to the person asserting liability constituted gross negligence or was intended to cause the resulting harm to the person asserting such liability."[51]

A New York court made quite clear that the protection of the statute was limited. The governing board members of a country club were sued for defamation. The lower court dismissed the action finding the plaintiff had failed to overcome the qualified immunity conferred on uncompensated officials of not-for-profit corporations by the statute. The appellate court, however, said the statute only granted immunity to officers of not-for-profit organizations described in 501(c)(3) and, because the country club was not one of those organizations, the members of its governing board were not entitled to the statutory protection.[52]

Subsequently, an Illinois court reached the same conclusion in a suit against a condominium association.[53] The Illinois statute provides that "no director or officer serving without compensation, other than reimbursement for actual expenses, of a corporation organized under [the Not-For-Profit Corporation Act] and exempt, or qualified for exemption, from taxation pursuant to Section 501(c) of the Internal Revenue Code of 1986 . . . shall be liable, and no cause of action may be brought, for damages resulting from the exercise of judgment or discretion in connection with the duties or responsibilities of such director or officer unless the act or omission involved willful or wanton conduct."[54] The directors of a condominium association were sued by the estate of a child who drowned in the community swimming pool. They asserted immunity under the statute. The court found the statute inapplicable. First, the statute required that the corporation be *organized* under the Not-For-Profit Corporation Act. However, the condominium was, said the court, not organized under that Act. Instead, the Declaration of

---

organization recognized under 501(c)(5) is generally not personally liable for monetary damages to any person for any statement, vote, decision, or failure to take action, regarding organizational management or policy by an officer or director); Miss. Code Ann. § 95-9-1 (liability exemption for volunteers of any department, institution, community volunteer organization, or any non-profit corporation designated under 501(c)(3), except agency established primarily for the recreational benefit of its stockholders or members).

51. N.Y. N-PCL § 720-a. The New York law, like other similar statutes, defines "compensation." It says a director, officer, or trustee is not considered compensated "solely by reason of payment of his or her actual expenses incurred in attending meetings or otherwise in the execution of such office."

52. Bernbach v. Bonnie Briar Country Club, 144 A.D.2d 610, 534 N.Y.S.2d 695 (1988).

53. Robinson v. LaCasa Grande Condominium Ass'n, 150 Ill. Dec. 148, 204 Ill. App. 3d 853, 562 N.E.2d 678 (1990).

54. 805 Ill. Comp. Stat. 105/108.70(a).

Condominium stated that it was organized under the state's Condominium Act. That is an interesting assertion because the court did not explain what it meant by "organized." It is true that a *condominium association*—and in some states a *homeowners association*—would be organized under the applicable common interest community enabling legislation, but the *corporation* would be created pursuant to a state corporations law. The exemption statutes typically refer to a *corporation* organized under corporations law. If that distinction is significant, it did not matter because the condominium would also have to be exempt from or qualify for exemption from taxation under Federal law—§ 501(c)—and the court found it was not.[55]

[4] State "Volunteer" Immunity Laws

In most states, the legislatures have enacted statutes affording "volunteers" with qualified tort immunity.[56] While these statutes might apply to officers and directors who "volunteer" to serve on the boards of common interest community associations, on close reading, they generally do not.[57]

For example, under North Carolina's "immunity from civil liability for volunteers" statute, a volunteer[58] who performs services for a "charitable organization"

---

55. The court specifically addressed the tax exemption for associations for the "promotion of social welfare." That exemption applies to "[c]ivic leagues or organizations not organized for profit but operated exclusively for the promotion of social welfare . . . and the net earnings of which are devoted exclusively to charitable, educational, or recreational purposes." 26 U.S.C. § 501(c)(4). "Homeowners associations" can qualify for that exemption. *See* Rev. Rul. 72-102, 1972-1 C.B. 149. However, they must meet three criteria: the association has to serve a community that bears a "reasonably, recognizable relationship to an area ordinarily identified as a governmental subdivision or unit," it must not conduct activities directed to exterior maintenance of any private residence, and its common areas or facilities have to be for the use and enjoyment of the general public. Rev. Rul. 74-99, 1974-1 C.B. 131. *See also* Rev. Rul. 80-63; 1980-1 C.B. 116. The *LaCasa Grande* court said that neither the condominium Declaration nor its bylaws provided for opening the common areas of the condominium to the public and, therefore, it was not exempt from taxation under 501(c)(4) and its directors were not exempt from liability under the Illinois Not For Profit Corporation Act. *See also* Ocean Pines Ass'n v. Comm'r, 672 F.3d 284 (4th Cir. 2012); Flat Top Lake Ass'n v. United States, 868 F.2d 108 (4th Cir. 1989).

56. *See* Hazen & Hazen, *Punctilios and Nonprofit Corporate Governance—A Comprehensive Look at Nonprofit Directors' Fiduciary Duties*, 14 U. Pa. J. Bus. L. 347, 412 (2012) (non-profit directors in most states may take advantage of limited immunity for volunteers); Biedzynski, *The Federal Volunteer Protection Act: Does Congress Want to Play Ball?*, 23 Seton Hall Legis. J. 319, 325 (1999) (statutes have been enacted to provide volunteers with qualified tort immunity).

57. *Consider* Wheelbarger v. Landing Council of Co-Owners, 471 S.W.3d 875, 886 n.5 (Tex. App.—Houston 1st Dist., 2015) (declining to address argument that Texas Charitable Immunity and Liability Act did not confer immunity on board members, because absent evidence demonstrating wrongful actions taken by individual board members, availability of immunity was irrelevant).

58. The term "volunteer" could in theory include a director of a common interest community association because it means "an individual, serving as a direct service volunteer performing services for a charitable, non-profit organization, who does not receive compensation, or anything of value in lieu of compensation, for the services, other than reimbursement for expenses actually incurred . . . ." N.C. Gen. Stat. § 1-539.11(2).

is not liable in civil damages for any acts or omissions resulting in any injury, death, or loss to person or property that arises from volunteer services rendered.[59] Unfortunately, another statute defines "charitable organization" to mean one with "humane and philanthropic objectives, whose activities benefit humanity or a significant rather than limited segment of the community without expectation of pecuniary profit or reward" and that is exempt from income taxation under either North Carolina statutes or § 501(c)(3) of the Internal Revenue Code.[60] In any event, if a volunteer has liability insurance coverage, that volunteer is deemed to have waived the statutory qualified immunity to the extent of indemnification by insurance for any negligence.[61]

The Florida Volunteer Protection Act initially appears as if it might provide immunity for common interest community association officers and directors, but it too contains a condition excluding applicability to them. Under the Act, anyone who volunteers to perform any service for any non-profit organization, including an officer or director, without compensation—except reimbursement for actual expenses—from the non-profit organization may, if certain conditions are met, be insulated from civil liability for any act or omission that results in personal injury or property damage.[62] "Non-profit organization," however, means any organization that is a governmental entity or is exempt from taxation pursuant to § 501 of the Internal Revenue Code.[63]

The Texas Charitable Immunity and Liability Act[64] is an exception to the general rule. It provides that a volunteer[65] of a "charitable organization" is immune from civil liability for any act or omission that results in death, damage, or injury if that volunteer was acting in the course and scope of his or her duties or functions, including as an officer or director.[66] The definition of "charitable organization" includes a "homeowners association" as defined by § 528(c) of the Internal Revenue Code.[67] That definition encompasses virtually all residential

59. N.C. Gen. Stat. § 1-539.10(a).

60. N.C. Gen. Stat. § 1-539.11(1).

61. N.C. Gen. Stat. § 1-539.10(b).

62. Fla. Stat. § 768.1355(1).

63. Fla. Stat. § 768.1355(1)(b)1.

64. Tex. Civ. Prac. & Rem. Code § 84.001, *et seq.*

65. A "volunteer" is someone who renders services for or on behalf of a charitable organization who does not receive compensation in excess of reimbursement for expenses incurred and includes a person serving as a director, officer, trustee, or direct service volunteer. Tex. Civ. Prac. & Rem. Code § 84.003(2).

66. Tex. Civ. Prac. & Rem. Code § 84.004(a).

67. Tex. Civ. Prac. & Rem. Code § 84.003(1)(C). The definition also includes a homeowners association that is exempt from federal income tax under 501(a) by being listed as an exempt organization in 501(c)(4). "Homeowners associations" can qualify for that exemption. *See* Rev. Rul. 72-102, 1972-1 C.B. 149. However, they must meet three criteria: the association has to serve a community that bears a "reasonably, recognizable relationship to an area ordinarily identified as a governmental subdivision or unit," it must not conduct activities directed to exterior maintenance

condominium and homeowners associations.[68] The statutory immunity does not apply to acts or omissions that are intentional, willfully negligent, or done with conscious indifference or reckless disregard for the safety of others.[69]

[5] The Federal Volunteer Protection Act

The federal Volunteer Protection Act (VPA)[70] grants qualified immunity to volunteers of non-profit and government organizations.[71] Under the VPA, if the negligence of a volunteer of a non-profit results in harm to another person, that person has no recourse directly from the volunteer who committed the wrongful act.[72] There appears to be an implied assumption that the VPA provides protection to directors and officers of common interest communities.[73] However, the legislative history of the Act belies that opinion. The report of the House Judiciary Committee on the proposed legislation expresses concern about the willingness of volunteers to "give of their time to charity" and of ability of charities to navigate the patchwork quilt of state laws that potentially protect them.[74] It mentions a number of groups by name: Big Brother/Big Sister Foundation, the American Diabetes Association, Habitat for Humanity, Little League Baseball, Girl Scouts, Boy Scouts, United Way, and meals-on-wheels programs. Nowhere in the report are common interest communities cited. A number of organizations testified before Congress on the proposed legislation, and none of them represented community associations.

The language of the Act itself suggests it is not intended to apply to common interest communities (CICs). The Act's stated purpose is "to promote the interests of social service program beneficiaries."[75] In adopting the Act, Congress found that "voluntary associations, social service agencies, educational institutions, and other civic programs, have been adversely affected by the withdrawal

---

of any private residence, and its common areas or facilities have to be for the use and enjoyment of the general public. Rev. Rul. 74-99, 1974-1 C.B. 131.

68. *See* 26 U.S.C. § 528(c).

69. Tex. Civ. Prac. & Rem. Code § 84.007(a).

70. 42 U.S.C. § 14501, *et seq. See generally* Biedzynski, *The Federal Volunteer Protection Act: Does Congress Want to Play Ball?*, 23 Seton Hall Legis. J. 319 (1999).

71. Hazen & Hazen, *Punctilios and Nonprofit Corporate Governance—A Comprehensive Look at Nonprofit Directors' Fiduciary Duties*, 14 U. Pa. J. Bus. L. 347, 413 (2012).

72. Baez, *Volunteers, Victims, and Vicarious Liability: Why Tort Law Should Recognize Altruism*, 48 U. Louisville L. Rev. 221, 253 (2009).

73. *See, e.g.*, Iannucci, *The ABC's of D&O: Insuring Your Board's Decisions* (Cooperator, Aug. 2011), available at: http://cooperator.com/articles/2291/1/The-ABC039s-of-DampO/Page1.html (discussing Volunteer Protection Act in context of community associations directors and officers and noting Act does not prohibit lawsuits against volunteers or provide any protection for non-profits).

74. House Report 105-101 (U.S. Government Printing Office, May 19, 1997).

75. 42 U.S.C. § 14501(b).

of volunteers from boards of directors."[76] The Act provides protection to volunteers of a "non-profit organization" or governmental entity.[77] A "non-profit organization" is either a 501(c)(3) tax-exempt organization[78]—a designation that would not apply to a common interest community—or an entity "organized and conducted for public benefit and operated primarily for charitable, civic, educational, religious, welfare, or health purposes."[79] All this may explain why a New York lawyer specializing in condominium and cooperative law referred to the Act in a journal article the year after its passage as "federal legislation that protects volunteers working for non-profit and governmental entities such as the Girl Scouts and Boy Scouts (as opposed to co-op and condominium entities) from civil liability."[80]

Even if the VPA were to apply to CIC directors and officers, the Act has a number of exceptions that water down its protection. First, the Act has no effect on the liability of the organization itself.[81] Second, the term "volunteer" includes persons serving as directors, officers, trustees, or direct service volunteers, but is limited to those individuals performing services for a non-profit organization or a governmental entity who do not receive compensation—other than reasonable reimbursement or allowance for expenses actually incurred—or anything of value in lieu of compensation in excess of $500 per year.[82] Third, it only relieves volunteers of liability for harm caused by an act or omission made on behalf of the organization or entity if:

- The volunteer was acting within the scope of his or her responsibilities at the time of the act or omission;
- The volunteer was, if appropriate or required, properly licensed, certified, or authorized by the appropriate authorities for the activities or practice in the state in which the harm occurred;
- The harm was not caused by willful or criminal misconduct, gross negligence, reckless misconduct, or a conscious, flagrant indifference to the rights or safety of the individual harmed; and

---

76. 42 U.S.C. § 14501(a).

77. 42 U.S.C. § 14503(a).

78. *See* 26 U.S.C. § 501(c)(3).

79. 42 U.S.C. § 14505(4). To be an eligible non-profit organization the entity must be one that does not practice any action that constitutes a "hate crime." *See* 28 U.S.C. § 534.

80. Siegler, *The Liability of Board Members*, 219 N.Y.L.J. No. 4 (Jan. 7, 1998).

81. 42 U.S.C. § 14503(c) (nothing in statute is to be construed to affect liability of any non-profit organization or governmental entity with respect to harm caused to any person). *See also* Baez, *Volunteers, Victims, and Vicarious Liability: Why Tort Law Should Recognize Altruism*, 48 U. Louisville L. Rev. 221, 253, 256 (2009) (VPA limits immunity solely to volunteers and provides no immunity from tort liability to non-profit organizations; under some circumstances, VPA will leave tort victim without any remedy against non-profit entity under doctrine of vicarious liability).

82. 42 U.S.C. § 14505(6). Generally, CIC directors and officers serve without compensation.

- The harm was not caused by operation of a motor vehicle, vessel, aircraft, or other vehicle for which the state requires the operator or owner have an operator's license or maintain insurance.[83]

Fourth, the limitations on the liability of a volunteer do not apply to any misconduct that constitutes a hate crime, a crime of violence, or an act of international terrorism for which the defendant has been convicted in any court, or that involves a sexual offense, as defined by applicable state law, for which the defendant has been convicted in any court, involves misconduct for which the defendant has been found to have violated a federal or state civil rights law, or where the defendant was under the influence of intoxicating alcohol or any drug at the time of the misconduct.[84] Fifth, the VPA does not protect a volunteer when a civil action is brought against him or her by the non-profit organization or a governmental entity.[85] And finally, while the VPA generally preempts inconsistent state laws,[86] state law may impose certain conditions. These conditions are:

- A requirement that non-profit organizations or governmental entities adhere to risk management procedures, including mandatory training of volunteers.
- The imposition of liability on an organization or entity for the acts or omissions of its volunteers to the same extent as an employer is liable for the acts or omissions of its employees.
- An elimination of a limitation of liability if the civil action was brought by an officer of a state or local government pursuant to state or local law.
- A modification on a limitation of liability making it applicable only if the non-profit organization or governmental entity provides a "financially secure source of recovery" for persons suffering harm as a result of actions taken by a volunteer on behalf of the organization or entity.[87]

83. 42 U.S.C. § 14503(a).

84. 42 U.S.C. § 14503(f).

85. 42 U.S.C. § 14503(b).

86. The VPA preempts state laws to the extent they are inconsistent with it, but it does not preempt laws that provide additional protection from liability. 42 U.S.C. § 14502(a). States may elect to make the VPA inapplicable to civil actions in their courts against a volunteer where all parties to the action are citizens of that state if the state enacts a statute that cites its authority to do so under the VPA, declares its intent to make the election, and contains nothing else. 42 U.S.C. § 14502(b). *See also* Baez, *Volunteers, Victims, and Vicarious Liability: Why Tort Law Should Recognize Altruism*, 48 U. Louisville L. Rev. 221, 253 (2009) (unless state adopts laws consistent with VPA or provisions with greater protections, VPA becomes law of that state).

87. 42 U.S.C. § 14503(d). A "financially secure source of recovery" may be an insurance policy, a risk pooling mechanism, equivalent assets, or alternative arrangements that satisfy the state that the organization or entity will be able to pay for losses up to a specified amount.

§ 14.03 The Need for D&O Coverage in Common Interest Communities

One reason CICs need D&O insurance is that the chances are the association's general liability policy does not include personal liability coverage for board members.[88] At the same time, the potential *liability* of directors and officers is probably not the primary reason associations need D&O insurance. A third reason an association generally needs D&O coverage is that the governing documents require the association to indemnify the officers and directors. In that case, the policy—subject to its terms—funds the mandate.[89]

NOTE: Directors and officers are more likely to be sued than they are to be sued successfully. The cost of defending some of the complex actions brought against those who govern associations can quickly soar.[90] Given those costs, knowledgeable residents of CICs will refuse to serve as directors or officers without D&O coverage, and that is a reason for an association to purchase coverage: without coverage, it may have no directors at all.[91]

---

88. Mistretta, *The Growing Importance of D&O Insurance: Avoiding Liability for Your Co-op & Condo Board Members* (Cooperator, Jan. 2014), available at: http://cooperator.com/articles/2729/1/The-Growing-Importance-of-DampO-Insurance/Page1.html. *See also* Hazen & Hazen, *Punctilios and Nonprofit Corporate Governance—A Comprehensive Look at Nonprofit Directors' Fiduciary Duties*, 14 U. Pa. J. Bus. L. 347, 413, n.343 (2012) (while some personal umbrella policies and homeowners insurance may cover non-profit board service, corporation-sponsored D&O insurance should be prerequisite to service on non-profit board).

89. Treese & Rosenberry, *Insurance: How Community Associations Protect Themselves*, at 50 (CAI Press 2013).

90. For example, one commentator examined cases involving common claims against CIC boards and found $280,000 in defense costs for an allegation of breach of fiduciary duty, $660,000 for a dispute over the validity of a board election, $170,000 for an allegation of wrongful termination, and $140,000 for a claim of discrimination. Davis, *Why Board Members Need Community Association D&O Liability* (Insurance Journal, Apr. 2, 2012), available at: http://www.insurancejournal.com/magazines/features/2012/04/02/241157.htm.

91. Meskin, *When Are You Not Covered by Your D&O Policy? Maintaining Proper Coverage* (Cooperator, Aug. 2008), available at: http://cooperator.com/articles/1673/1/When-Are-You-Not-Covered-By-Your-DampO-Policy/Page1.html (to attract the best and most talented people to serve as volunteer board members, it is imperative to provide them with insurance coverage to protect them from decision-making process they are involved in); Bateman, *What Homeowner Associations Need to Know About Directors' & Officers' Liability* (2017), https://communityassociationmanagement.com/c33-financial-matters/c37-insurance/what-homeowner-associations-need-to-know-about-directors-officers-liability/ (having appropriate D&O liability coverage could help attract board members because it allows them to make decisions without having to worry about costing community money and they know that if they make a decision that sparks a lawsuit, their D&O liability policy is going to defend them); Price & Schneider, *Nonprofit D&O Essentials: Homeowners, Condo Association Boards Beware* (Insurance Journal, Nov. 7, 2005), available at: http://www.insurancejournal.com/magazines/features/2005/11/07/62357.htm (directors and officers of non-profit association boards could end up paying steep price for their good citizenship if lawsuit

Claims against non-profits in general are rising. A 2013 survey revealed that 63 percent of its non-profit respondents reported a claim during the previous 10 years.[92] The same is true for common interest community association boards.[93] One commentary notes that CIC associations have more tasks and responsibilities, and more complex ones, than ever before and that governing boards made up of individuals who are not well-versed in running associations results in disputes over bylaws and covenants.[94] However, those disputes are only the tip of the iceberg. Besides disgruntled residents, D&O-related claims can come from creditors, other associations, and governmental agencies, and typical suits against board members can include allegations of mismanagement, self-dealing and conflicts of interest, actions beyond the authority granted in bylaws, violation of state or federal law, breach of fiduciary duty, failure of supervision, non-employment discrimination, breach of contract, wrongful termination or discipline, and wrongful foreclosure.[95]

One insurance industry expert raises another concern. If an association has no D&O policy, or a policy with inadequate coverage, the association will have to pay the defense costs of a lawsuit, as well as any judgment against it, and the source of funds to pay those expenses is the members of the association. Few associations will maintain a contingency fund for these expenses, so they will generally levy a special assessment to acquire the necessary funds. Some mortgage companies ask if there has been a special assessment in the community and may be reluctant to lend to prospective purchasers if the answer is yes, thus making it

comes calling and board does not have proper insurance coverage in place); Hedderman, *The Value of Directors and Officers Insurance: Cover Yourself* (New Jersey Cooperator, 2004), available at: http://njcooperator.com/articles/266/1/The-Value-of-Directors-and-Officers-Insurance/Page1.html (warning of dangers of serving on board lacking coverage and quoting attorney as wondering why any board member would want to be on that board if it is unwilling to buy D&O insurance).

92. *Directors and Officers Liability Survey: 2012 Summary of Results*, p. 3 (Towers Watson, 2013).

93. Mistretta, *The Growing Importance of D&O Insurance: Avoiding Liability for Your Co-op & Condo Board Members* (Cooperator, Jan. 2014), available at: http://cooperator.com/articles/2729/1/The-Growing-Importance-of-DampO-Insurance/Page1.html (board members face increasing risk of personal liability for any actual or alleged breach of duty, neglect, error, misstatement, misleading statement, act, or omission in performance of their duties).

94. Price & Schneider, *Nonprofit D&O Essentials: Homeowners, Condo Association Boards Beware* (Insurance Journal, Nov. 7, 2005), available at: http://www.insurancejournal.com/magazines/features/2005/11/07/62357.htm (with broader range of activities in modern, upscale subdivision, increase in activities means more things to supervise and more potential for claims against association and board for failing to act prudently).

95. Mistretta, *The Growing Importance of D&O Insurance: Avoiding Liability for Your Co-op & Condo Board Members* (Cooperator, Jan. 2014), available at: http://cooperator.com/articles/2729/1/The-Growing-Importance-of-DampO-Insurance/Page1.html; Davis, *Why Board Members Need Community Association D&O Liability* (Insurance Journal, Apr. 2, 2012), available at: http://www.insurancejournal.com/magazines/features/2012/04/02/241157.htm.

more difficult for residents to sell their homes.[96] Additionally, by either statute[97] or the governing documents, a special assessment may require the approval of a majority—maybe even a super-majority—of the members of the association. If the majority of the members disapproved of the actions that brought about the litigation, they may refuse to approve any special assessment and send the association into a fiscal crisis.

Finally, experts note that D&O coverage is relatively inexpensive. It can range, depending on the size of the community and specific risk factors, from $700 to $2,100 for a stand-alone policy.[98]

NOTE: Failing to purchase a D&O policy to save money would be a foolish decision when a D&O premium can be less than 5 percent of the overall insurance budget for an association.

---

§ 14.04 Association's Obligation to Obtain Liability Insurance

Commercial property and general liability insurance are required for common interest community associations because of state law mandates, the governing documents, or the practical need to meet the Fannie Mae guidelines. D&O insurance, however, is generally not mandated. Nonetheless, it is considered "must have" coverage by experts.[99]

---

96. Bateman, *What Homeowner Associations Need to Know About Directors' & Officers' Liability* (2017), available at: https://communityassociationmanagement.com/c33-financial-matters/c37-insurance/what-homeowner-associations-need-to-know-about-directors-officers-liability/.

97. *See, e.g.*, Cal. Civ. Code § 5605(b) (board may not impose special assessments that in aggregate exceed 5 percent of budgeted gross expenses of association for that fiscal year without approval of majority of quorum of members at member meeting or election). *See also* Uniform Common Interest Ownership Act § 3-123 (if executive board determines by two-thirds vote that special assessment is necessary to respond to emergency, it becomes effective immediately in accordance with terms of that vote, otherwise assessment is effective only if executive board follows statutory procedures for ratification of budgets and unit owners do not reject proposed assessment).

98. Bateman, *What Homeowner Associations Need to Know About Directors' & Officers' Liability* (2017), available at: https://communityassociationmanagement.com/c33-financial-matters/c37-insurance/what-homeowner-associations-need-to-know-about-directors-officers-liability/. *See also* Iannucci, *The ABCs of D&O: Insuring Your Board's Decisions*, at 25 (Cooperator, 2011), available at: http://www.ihginsurance.com/Documents/Pdf/ABCs_of_DO_Cooperator.pdf (premiums can start around $1,200 and increase depending on number of units as well as other risk factors); Hedderman, *The Value of Directors and Officers Insurance: Cover Yourself* (New Jersey Cooperator, 2004), available at: http://njcooperator.com/articles/266/1/The-Value-of-Directors-and-Officers-Insurance/Page1.html (typical D&O premium is around $1,000 for condominium association and $1,500 for residential cooperative).

99. Treese & Rosenberry, *Insurance: How Community Associations Protect Themselves*, at 50 (CAI Press 2013) (noting that D&O insurance can fund governing document requirement that association indemnify officers and directors).

[1] State Law

A great many states have either adopted one of the Uniform Acts or modeled their common interest community legislation partially on those Acts. The Uniform Common Interest Ownership Act has requirements that are paralleled in all the other Uniform Acts. It provides that an association may carry any insurance it considers appropriate to protect the association or the unit owners.[100] More specifically, an association may provide for indemnification of its officers and executive board and maintain directors and officers liability insurance subject to limitation by any "other provisions" of the Uniform Common Interest Ownership Act (UCIOA).[101]

A few non–Uniform Act states address D&O insurance in their common interest community legislation. Florida law on condominiums,[102] for example, authorizes associations to obtain and maintain liability insurance for directors and officers. The Illinois Condominium Property Act authorizes associations to obtain "adequate and appropriate kinds of insurance,"[103] and states that the Declaration of Condominium may require the association to carry any insurance, including coverage to protect the officers or directors of the association.[104] Moreover, the Act provides for directors and officers liability coverage to be obtained at a level the governing board deems reasonable unless the coverage is dictated by the Declaration or bylaws.[105] The coverage has to extend to all contracts and other actions taken by the board members in their official capacity as directors and officers, but has to exclude actions for which the directors are not entitled to indemnification under the Not For Profit Corporation Act[106] or the Declaration and bylaws. The coverage has to include, but not be limited to, defense of non-monetary actions, breach of contract, and decisions related to the placement or adequacy of insurance and also include as insureds past, present, and future board members while acting in their capacity as members of the board. A

100. Uniform Common Interest Ownership Act § 3-113(c) (1982). In 2008, the words "in any event" were deleted from the subsection.

101. Uniform Common Interest Ownership Act § 3-102(a).

102. Fla. Stat. § 718.111(11)(e).

103. 765 Ill. Comp. Stat. 605/18.4.

104. 765 Ill. Comp. Stat. 605/12(d).

105. 765 Ill. Comp. Stat. 605/12(a)(3)(D).

106. *See* 805 Ill, Comp. Stat. 105/108.75 (indemnification of officers, directors, employees, and agents).

handful of other non–Uniform Act states—Hawaii,[107] Indiana,[108] Oregon[109]—have comparable legislation.

[2] Governing Documents

The governing documents may not mention D&O insurance, but they may require the association to indemnify the officers and directors. When that is the case, the association can avoid funding that obligation out of association funds by obtaining D&O coverage.[110]

[a] Requirement for Coverage

Two highly regarded experts on common interest community law urge that the governing documents should include provisions obligating an association to indemnify officers and directors and that the duty to indemnify should be supported by a requirement to obtain and maintain comprehensive liability insurance, including officers and directors liability insurance.[111] That wise counsel notwithstanding, the documents in many associations—especially older ones—may not address D&O coverage at all.

[b] Prohibition on D&O Insurance

It is possible that the governing documents will in effect bar the association from obtaining D&O insurance. For example, the Restatement on Servitudes offers a hypothetical in which the Declaration of a condominium association prohibits

---

107. Under the Hawaii Condominium Property Act, unless the declaration or bylaws provide otherwise, the association is required to purchase and at all times maintain directors and officers liability coverage. Haw. Rev. Stat. § 514B-143(a). The governing board has to obtain directors and officers liability coverage at a level deemed reasonable by the board, if not otherwise limited by the declaration or bylaws. Haw. Rev. Stat. § 514B-143(a)(4). That is reinforced by a statute that says subject to the declaration and bylaws, an association, even if unincorporated, may provide for indemnification of its officers, board, committee members, and agents, and maintain directors and officers liability insurance. Haw. Rev. Stat. § 514B-104(a)(14).

108. Under legislation governing condominiums, policies required by the condominium instruments may be obtained by the association, including officers and directors liability coverage. Ind. Code § 32-25-8-9(c).

109. Under the Oregon Condominium Act, subject to the declaration and bylaws, and whether or not the association is unincorporated, it may provide for indemnification of its officers and executive board, as may be limited by statute—*see* Or. Rev. Stat. § 61.218 (3)(d)—and maintain D&O liability insurance. Or. Rev. Stat. § 100.405(4)(o). The Oregon Planned Community Act states that unless the declaration or bylaws provide otherwise, the association may provide for indemnification of its officers and directors and maintain liability insurance for directors and officers. Or. Rev. Stat. § 94.630(1)(p).

110. Treese & Rosenberry, *Insurance: How Community Associations Protect Themselves*, at 50 (CAI Press 2013).

111. Hyatt & Stubblefield, *Community Association Boards Should Minimize Potential Liability*, Prob. & Prop. 25, 27 (May/June 1987).

payment of compensation to directors or officers, including payment for liability insurance.[112] Under those circumstances, no one might be willing to serve as an officer or director and, while there may be no significant opposition in the community to changing the Declaration to allow the association to purchase insurance, there is no provision for amendment in the Restatement example. The Restatement concludes that under those circumstances the owners holding a majority of the voting power should be able to amend the Declaration for that purpose. It is rare for there to be no method for amending the governing documents, but it is common for documents to require a super-majority for amendments. Thus, the hypothetical posited by the Restatement could become a real crisis for an association.

[3] Fannie Mae Requirements

Fannie Mae requires that common interest communities have a number of different types of insurance coverage, but makes no mention of D&O insurance.

§ 14.05 Locating and Obtaining the Proper Coverage

There are several regrettable truths about common interest communities that can result in poor decisions about D&O insurance. First, boards of directors often have very little knowledge of insurance in general,[113] and likely even less understanding of D&O coverage.[114] Second, a board may choose an insurance agent who has little knowledge of CICs and their insurance needs, and even less knowledge of D&O coverage. Third, in obtaining D&O coverage, CICs usually rely on the advice of the same broker who provides their other policies and who may or may not have very much understanding of D&O coverage for CICs. Fourth, if a board relies on anyone other than the insurance broker, it is usually the community association manager, who again, may have little understanding of D&O coverage even if he or she knows a great deal about property and

---

112. Restatement (Third) of Property: Servitudes, § 6.10, illustration 4.

113. Blanch, *Community Association Boards Need to Know and Understand the Exclusions and Requirements in their Association Insurance Policies* (Apr. 28, 2014) (attorney specializing in community association law finds that associations often acquire policies with little thought about their provisions other than cost of premiums).

114. A 2012 survey of D&O policyholders showed that of the responding non-profit organizations—a category that included more than CICs—18 percent were unsure how their primary D&O program was structured. *Directors and Officers Liability Survey: 2012 Summary of Results*, p. 11 (Towers Watson, 2013). Those respondents would be the more sophisticated purchasers of insurance, so the level of ignorance among non-respondents could be expected to be much higher. *Consider* Cmty. Ass'n Underwriters of Am. v. Queensboro Flooring Corp., 2014 U.S. Dist. LEXIS 90939 (M.D. Pa. July 3, 2014) (in discovery request for D&O policy by association member suing association, association responded that its general liability carrier had not issued any D&O policy, but that it would inquire with its umbrella carrier to determine if D&O policy had been issued).

liability insurance.[115] Fifth, boards rarely consult the association attorney about insurance matters, and even if they do, many association attorneys know little more about CIC insurance than community association managers. As discussed elsewhere,[116] D&O insurance is unique, specialized, and highly complex. There are considerable differences among the policies available in the marketplace, and a minimum level of knowledge and expertise is required to assess those differences and determine the coverage that is best for a particular community.

Experts agree there is a great range in the quality of D&O policies and that searching for the best is worth the effort.[117] CICs need to be wary because they may be offered a policy that was originally drafted for use by profit-making corporations and then was "cut and pasted" to produce a "nonprofit D&O form."[118] Thus, many authorities recommend stand-alone policies tailored for community associations rather than generic endorsements to a general liability policy.[119] These policies generally have broader coverage for a premium that is not significantly greater.[120] One estimate of the cost is around $1,500 for $1 million of coverage for a 100-unit CIC.[121] The question is: how does an association find quality D&O coverage?[122]

---

115. In *Prudential-LMI Commer. Ins. Co. v. Meadowood Condo. Ass'n*, 1992 U.S. Dist. LEXIS 11461 (E.D. Pa. July 31, 1992), the association obtained a general liability policy that included D&O coverage from the plaintiff insurer. In the insurer's action seeking a declaratory judgment that it had no duty to defend or indemnify the association and the directors under the policy, the condominium manager, "admitted that she had no idea what the policy did or did not cover when it was purchased because she did not read it." If the association relied on the manager for assistance in securing D&O coverage, it clearly did so in vain.

116. *See* § 14.07, *infra.*

117. *See, e.g.*, Winzenburg, *Condominium Law and Practice: Forms* § 49.04[7] (Matthew Bender & Company, 2007).

118. Davis, *Professional Liability and Governance Exposures: A Closer Look* (Nonprofit Risk Management Center 2017), available at: https://www.nonprofitrisk.org/resources/articles/professional-liability-and-governance-exposures-a-closer-look/.

119. *See, e.g.*, Tegan, *Directors' & Officers' Liability: What Homeowner Associations Need to Know*, p. 2 (Ian H. Graham Ins., June 8, 2012); Meskin, *When Are You Not Covered By Your D&O Policy? Maintaining Proper Coverage* (Cooperator, Aug. 2008), available at: http://cooperator.com/articles/1673/1/When-Are-You-Not-Covered-By-Your-DampO-Policy/Page1.html.

120. *See, e.g.*, Hedderman, *The Value of Directors and Officers Insurance: Cover Yourself* (New Jersey Cooperator, 2004), available at: http://njcooperator.com/articles/266/1/The-Value-of-Directors-and-Officers-Insurance/Page1.html.

121. *D&O Liability Insurance For Co-op & Condo Board Members* (July 10, 2013), available at: http://www.mackoul.com/blog/do-liability-insurance-for-co-op-condo-board-members/.

122. The International Risk Management Institute, Inc. (IRMI) offers a comprehensive analysis of more than 300 available D&O policies by company and category. IRMI says its "D&O Coverage Guide contains a comprehensive, user-friendly analysis of the major and minor provisions found within D&O policy forms, and is packed with numerous, practical tips on how to negotiate broader versions of these provisions." *See* http://www.irmi.com/products/store/directors-and-officers-liability-maps.aspx. The National Association of Corporate Directors (NACD), which appears to be concerned with directors of *for-profit* corporations, has an director liability and insurance resource center. *See* https://www.nacdonline.org/insights/resource_center.cfm?ItemNumber=30692.

[1] Finding a Broker

The first step in obtaining D&O coverage is to find an insurance professional who is familiar with D&O insurance for CICs. In large urban areas with many condominiums and homeowners associations (HOAs), there will be companies that specialize in CICs or have one or more employees who do. A community association manager would almost certainly know the names of those companies and their reputation in the community. The ideal is to find someone who is a "specialist" in D&O coverage for CICs.[123] At the same time, if the broker who obtains other liability insurance for the association also obtains the D&O policy, it should make it more likely that the coverages will be coordinated.[124]

Some brokers will have a "Community Insurance and Risk Management Specialist" (CIRMS) designation. This a credential awarded by the Community Associations Institute (CAI). CAI is a national organization for common interest communities with chapters throughout the country. Its membership includes owners, managers, management firms, attorneys who specialize in community association law, and companies, including insurers and agents or brokers, that provide products and services to associations. CAI says the CIRMS designation "recognizes a demonstrated high level of competency within the risk management profession."[125] Designees are required to have five years' experience in the community association insurance field and "satisfactory legal and ethical standing in the industry." The CIRMS designation, however, is evidence of a general level of competency in the insurance field but not necessarily a specific knowledge of D&O coverage.

As is the case whenever a professional is being hired, the client needs to be prepared to ask questions to determine the professional's experience and level of expertise. Some of the questions are rather basic:

- Does the broker specialize in common interest communities?
- How many community associations does the broker work with?
- How much experience does the broker have with D&O coverage for CICs?
- Does the broker know which companies offer policies specifically for non-profit organizations or CICs?
- Does the broker have any specialized training in understanding D&O insurance?[126]

---

123. *See* Meskin, *When Are You Not Covered by Your D&O Policy? Maintaining Proper Coverage* (Cooperator, Aug. 2008), available at: http://cooperator.com/articles/1673/1/When-Are-You-Not-Covered-By-Your-DampO-Policy/Page1.html (to make the most of their D&O coverage, associations must use a "specialist").

124. Iannucci, *Discussing D&O Insurance: 10 Things You Need to Know* (Cooperator, 2007), available at: http://cooperator.com/articles/1509/1/Discussing-DampO-Insurance/Page1.html.

125. *See* http://www.caionline.org/career/designations/Pages/cirms.aspx.

126. *See generally* Meskin, *When Are You Not Covered by Your D&O Policy? Maintaining Proper Coverage* (Cooperator, Aug. 2008), available at: http://cooperator.com/articles/1673/1/When-Are-You-Not-Covered-By-Your-DampO-Policy/Page1.html.

One company that is a large provider of D&O coverage designed specifically for CICs has a checklist of questions it suggests clients ask about D&O policies. To be sure, the questions are intended to compare its products favorably with others, but nonetheless, the questions are valid ones to ask. They include:

- Does the definition of "insured" extend beyond current directors and officers and include past, present, and future directors? Does it include committee members or volunteers?
- Does the policy provide a defense to claims and lawsuits rather than reimbursement of costs?
- Are libel and slander covered?
- Are claims seeking non-monetary loss covered?
- Is failure to maintain or obtain adequate insurance covered?
- Is there coverage for the community association manager?[127]

If the broker does not know the answers to these questions, he or she probably lacks the knowledge needed to help an association obtain the D&O coverage it needs. Of course, no matter how well informed the broker is about D&O insurance, if no one asks any questions of him or her, the governing board will not know what kind of coverage they have. This happens all too often as demonstrated in a case where coverage was denied because of an exclusion unknown to the association. At trial the broker acknowledged familiarity with the policy terms at the time that it was purchased, including the exclusion at issue. The court noted that since the association's broker knew of the exclusion when the insurance was first purchased, the association was charged with that knowledge.[128] While some might say the broker should explain the coverage to the client, all any association has to do is ask. Brokers are there to answer questions from policyholders.

[2] Being Prepared for Questions from the Broker

One expert commentary identifies key points for consideration by brokers who secure D&O coverage for common interest community associations.[129] If an association is aware of these issues before meeting with a broker, it will be better prepared to provide requested information and address any concerns. Brokers are told to be sure to have a copy of the bylaws to review.[130] They should also

---

127. http://www.ihginsurance.com/sites/ihg/riskmanagement/Pages/Article16.aspx (no longer in print).

128. Prudential-LMI Commer. Ins. Co. v. Meadowood Condo. Ass'n, 1992 U.S. Dist. LEXIS 11461 (E.D. Pa. July 31, 1992).

129. Price & Schneider, *Nonprofit D&O Essentials: Homeowners, Condo Association Boards Beware* (Insurance Journal 2005), available at: http://www.insurancejournal.com/magazines/features/2005/11/07/62357.htm.

130. The commentary also says the broker should make certain the bylaws comply with relevant state laws, although that should be in the purview of an attorney.

make sure the association is properly certified as a non-profit. A broker should determine if there are prior or pending claims, disputes, or lawsuits. The commentary notes the association would be covered for a claim or settlement going forward, subject to the applicable statute of limitations, but only if there was no prior knowledge. Brokers are also advised to be alert to lingering issues with disgruntled board members and to consider the possibility of owners who believe they have been discriminated against. Finally, if a community is relatively new, brokers are told to look for developer involvement in the association as the developer may still own units that are unsold.

[3] Limit of Liability

Once the agent has helped the association select the appropriate policy, the amount of coverage and the deductible need to be determined. Often the limit of liability is $1 million for all claims first made in the policy period.[131] However, there can be variations on the limit, so it is important to determine whether the limit applies for all claims during the policy period or is applied on some other basis, for example, per claim. Whether the usual $1 million is a sufficient amount of coverage depends on a number of factors:

- How long is the policy period?
- Is the association, because of its size or the amenities it manages, more likely to be the subject of larger claims than the ordinary association?
- Does the policy cover persons other than current officers and directors—for example, the community association manager or former directors and officers—thereby increasing the pool of persons who might seek coverage and reducing the amount available to the sitting directors and officers?[132]
- Are defense costs included in the limit?

[4] Defense Costs

Defense costs *are* typically included within the limit of liability. Policies in which the limit of liability available for paying losses is reduced by defense costs are

131. Stoeckert, *The Insurance Puzzle: Making Sense of Premiums and Policies* (Apr. 2012), available at: http://cooperator.com/articles/2418/1/The-Insurance-Puzzle/Page1.html (generally, a common interest community building will have $1 million of coverage). *See, e.g.*, Landing Council of Co-Owners v. Fed. Ins. Co., 247 F. Supp. 3d 802 (S.D. Tex. 2017) (not-for-profit organization's insurance policy had maximum aggregate limit of liability of $1 million); Petro v. Travelers Cas. & Sur. Co. of Am., 54 F. Supp. 3d 1295, 1297 (N.D. Fla. 2014) ($1 million annual aggregate limit per claim); Board of Mgrs. of the Schaefer Landing N. Condominium v. Continental Cas. Co., 2011 N.Y. Misc. LEXIS 6252 (Dec. 16, 2011).

132. *Directors and Officers Liability* (Summit Business Media, 2013) (when policy covers large number of insureds, aggregate policy limits available to each individual insured may be severely diluted and policy limits deemed adequate for handful of corporate directors and officers may be inadequate for larger and more liberally defined population of insureds).

called "defense within limits" (DWL) policies and are also referred to as "self-liquidating,"[133] "wasting," "cannibalizing," or "self-consuming."[134] They have the potential to shrink dramatically, or even totally exhaust, the liability limit. For example, an action in which the directors are charged with discrimination will generally require counsel with special expertise and probably costly expert witnesses. A highly complex case that goes up on appeal could have a tab for defense costs in the hundreds of thousands. Two major discrimination suits during the policy period could leave little to cover the claim itself. For this reason, defense costs should pay in addition to or outside of the policy limits as that leaves the full limit to pay any judgment.

[5] Deductibles

The standard deductible is $1,000. Some experts argue that is too low and that a $10,000 deductible would be more appropriate.[135] The size of the deductible is, of course, within the discretion of the governing board; however, it is usually determined by the insurer. There may be a choice of deductibles, which in turn will change the overall premium. Many boards simply choose the lowest deductible without discussion. That may be because the board members consider a small deductible to be superior protection against loss. It may also be because they do not know enough about insurance to give the question due consideration or to appreciate any alternative. One alternative is to choose a larger deductible, create an insurance contingency, and fund it from the savings realized by the lower premium. That allows the association to retain some of its money and earn interest on it. If there is a claim, the deductible amount can be paid out of the fund. If the association is fortunate enough to have no claims, eventually the fund will exceed the amount of the deductible, at which point the association could further increase the deductible or use the interest on the fund and the premium savings for other needs.

---

133. *See, e.g.*, Emerald Bay Community Ass'n v. Golden Eagle Ins. Corp., 130 Cal. App. 4th 1078, 31 Cal. Rptr. 3d 43 (2005) (association carried $1 million *self-liquidating* directors and officers liability policy and $10 million excess/umbrella policy).

134. Munro, *Defense Within Limits: The Conflicts of "Wasting" Or "Cannibalizing" Insurance Policies*, 62 Mont. L. Rev. 131, 133 (2001).

135. Hedderman, *The Value of Directors and Officers Insurance: Cover Yourself* (New Jersey Cooperator, 2004), available at: http://njcooperator.com/articles/266/1/The-Value-of-Directors-and-Officers-Insurance/Page1.html. *See also* Head, *Love Those Deductibles!*, available at: https://nonprofitrisk.org/resources/articles/love-those-deductibles/ (recommending organizations choose largest deductibles they can safely afford because it lowers long-run average loss costs, motivates staff and management to operate safely, and leads to best allocation of overall insurance budget).

[6] Stand-Alone Policy or Endorsement

D&O coverage is offered as both an endorsement to other policies and a stand-alone policy. The latter is often recommended by experts.[136] One warns associations that an endorsement to a package policy—one, for example, providing commercial property and general liability insurance—may cost as little as $150 to add, but for the price it often does not afford much coverage.[137] If the association is offered D&O coverage in an endorsement, it needs to ask the broker to compare its coverage with that of a stand-alone policy.

ISO has a generic endorsement for condominiums, cooperatives, and associations,[138] and specific endorsements for 11 states.[139] A cursory review of reported decisions in which a D&O policy for a common interest community was at issue reveals the majority of them to have stand-alone policies,[140] although a substantial number had an endorsement to a general liability insurance policy.[141]

---

136. *See, e.g.*, Iannucci, *The ABCs of D&O: Insuring Your Board's Decisions*, at 25 (Cooperator, 2011), available at: http://www.ihginsurance.com/Documents/Pdf/ABCs_of_DO_Cooperator.pdf (cooperatives and condominiums should purchase stand-alone policy as opposed to endorsement added to larger package policy).

137. Bateman, *What Homeowner Associations Need to Know About Directors' & Officers' Liability* (2017), available at: https://communityassociationmanagement.com/c33-financial-matters/c37-insurance/what-homeowner-associations-need-to-know-about-directors-officers-liability/ (D&O endorsements typically state what they cover in first two paragraphs and then next three pages consist of exclusions).

138. *See* ISO Form BP 17 24 01 10.

139. The states are Alaska, Colorado, Connecticut, Illinois, Minnesota, Missouri, Montana, New Hampshire, New Mexico, Pennsylvania, and Virginia. In some cases, there is more than one endorsement for a state.

140. *See, e.g.*, Salisbury West Condo. Trust v. Travelers Cas. & Sur. Co., 2013 U.S. Dist. LEXIS 167496 (D. Mass. Oct. 15, 2013); Hess v. Travelers Cas. & Sur. Co. of Am., 2013 U.S. Dist. LEXIS 23281 (N.D. Ill. Feb. 20, 2013); Commodore Plaza Condo. Ass'n v. QBE Ins. Corp., 2013 U.S. Dist. LEXIS 5195 (S.D. Fla. Jan. 14, 2013); Beauvallon Condo. Ass'n v. Granite State Ins. Co., 2011 U.S. Dist. LEXIS 69606 (D. Colo. June 29, 2011); Lumbermens Mut. Cas. Co. v. Dadeland Cove Section One Homeowners' Ass'n, 2007 U.S. Dist. LEXIS 78319 (S.D. Fla. Oct. 11, 2007), *aff'd*, 295 Fed. Appx. 361 (11th Cir. 2008); Marquez Knolls Property Owners Ass'n, Inc. v. Executive Risk Indemnity, Inc., 153 Cal. App. 4th 228, 62 Cal. Rptr. 3d 510 (2007); 30 W. 15th St. Owners Corp. v. Travelers Ins. Co., 165 A.D.2d 731, 563 N.Y.S.2d 784 (1990); Board of Managers of Yardarm Condo. II v. Federal Ins. Co., 247 A.D.2d 499, 669 N.Y.S.2d 332 (1998).

141. *See, e.g.*, Riverdale Peaks Homeowners Ass'n v. Auto-Owners Ins. Co., 2012 U.S. Dist. LEXIS 54180 (D. Colo. Apr. 18, 2012) (Commercial General Liability form included Habitational Association Directors and Officers Liability Endorsement); Oak Ford Owners Ass'n v. Auto-Owners Ins. Co., 510 F. Supp. 2d 812 (M.D. Fla. 2007) (CGL policy included D&O endorsement); Hollingsworth v. Landing Condos. of Waukesha Ass'n, 353 Wis. 2d 553, 846 N.W.2d 34 (2014); Pulliam v. Travelers Indem. Co., 403 S.C. 332, 743 S.E.2d 117 (Ct. App. 2013); 116 Commonwealth Condominium Trust v. Aetna Cas. & Sur. Co., 433 Mass. 373, 742 N.E.2d 76 (2001) (describing directors and officers liability endorsement to general liability insurance policy); Altaf v. Hanover Square Condominium Ass'n No. 1, 136 Ill. Dec. 257, 188 Ill. App. 3d 533, 544 N.E.2d 1032 (1989); N. Sec. Ins. Co. v. Sandpiper Vill. Condo. Trust, 2008 Mass. Super. LEXIS 312 (2008).

While it should be easy enough to distinguish an endorsement from a stand-alone policy, one insurer contended its policy was an endorsement form that merely extended the protections of the general policy to the directors and officers of the insured condominium. Then Federal District Judge Sonia Sotomayor was unconvinced. She said the D&O policy was on its face a "separate and distinct agreement, with its own declarations page, terms and exclusions."[142] There really should not be any confusion over whether a document is an endorsement or not. Endorsements are usually identified as such at the top of the first page and include a statement explaining what "this endorsement" does and advising the policyholder to read it carefully.

There are reasons the insurer might want the court to view a D&O policy as merely an endorsement. An endorsement is a document in writing that is attached to and modifies a policy.[143] The policy and endorsement have to be read together and construed to give effect to all their provisions.[144] Thus, the policy remains in effect except as modified by the endorsement. When conflict between the policy and an endorsement cannot be resolved, the endorsement controls.[145]

---

142. Hotel Des Artistes v. Transamerica Ins. Co., 1994 U.S. Dist. LEXIS 7800 (S.D.N.Y. June 10, 1994).

143. 1 Jeffery E. Thomas, *New Appleman on Insurance Law Library Edition* § 1.07[8] (LexisNexis 2023).

144. *See, e.g.*, United Services Auto. Ass'n v. McCray, 348 So. 2d 6 (Fla. 3d DCA 1977) (policy should be construed according to entirety of its terms and as amplified by any endorsement); Dairyland Ins. Co. v. Implement Dealers Ins. Co., 294 Minn. 236, 199 N.W.2d 806 (1972) (endorsements attached to insurance contract are part of contract; endorsements and policy must be construed together, and should be construed, if possible, to give effect to all provisions, but where provisions in the body of the policy conflict with endorsement, endorsement governs). Many states have a statute on construction of policies that addresses the status of endorsements. The language of these statutes is quite similar. *See, e.g.*, Alaska Stat. § 21.42.230 (insurance contracts must be construed according to entirety of their terms and conditions as set out in policy and amplified, extended, or modified by rider, endorsement, or application that is part of policy); Fla. Stat. § 627.419(1) (every insurance contract is to be construed according to entirety of its terms and conditions as set forth in policy and as amplified, extended, or modified by any application, rider, or endorsement); Ga. Code Ann. § 33-24-16 (every insurance contract is to be construed according to entirety of its terms and conditions and as amplified, extended, or modified by any rider, endorsement, or application made part of policy); La. Rev. Stat. § 22:881 (every insurance contract is to be construed according to entirety of its terms and conditions as set forth in policy, and as amplified, extended, or modified by any rider, endorsement, or application attached to or made part of policy); Okl. Stat. tit. 36, § 3621 (every insurance contract is to be construed according to entirety of its terms and conditions as amplified, extended, or modified by any rider, endorsement, or application attached to and made part of policy).

145. *See, e.g.*, Fireman's Fund Ins. Co. v. Reliance Ins. Co., 291 F. Supp. 618 (D. Or. 1968) (policy endorsements become part of insurance contract and must be construed with it and under ordinary circumstances, where conflict exists between provisions of policy and of endorsement, latter must control; it is presumed each clause of main policy and of endorsements was inserted to accomplish some specific purpose, and it is not proper to assume that clause is without meaning); Manchester Ins. & Indem. Co. v. Universal Underwriters Ins. Co., 5 Ill. App. 3d 847, 285 N.E.2d

The endorsement is read as if the provisions of the policy to which it is attached are set forth in the endorsement.[146] Thus, a definition in the policy that is not modified by the endorsement should apply to the endorsement. In the case before Judge Sotomayor, the insurer might have benefited from application of a definition, exclusion, or condition that appeared in the general policy, but not the D&O policy.

[7] Policy Packages

Some insurers offer "packages" for common interest communities that bundle coverages.[147] For example, one company has created what it calls "V3 CAPP+," which is a package program for condominiums, homeowner associations, and cooperatives.[148] It is currently available in about 20 states. It is a multi-line policy that includes property, crime/fidelity, general liability, and directors and officers insurance. The D&O coverage includes enhancements for crisis management expense and privacy event protection to address emerging risks. When an association is offered a package, it may not need to take the whole package or nothing as the insurer that writes the packages may be willing to get another specialized insurer to accept the D&O risk. In other words, when offered a package, the association should carefully review the D&O coverage with its broker and if better coverage is available with a stand-alone policy, it should ask the broker to work to obtain that coverage.

185 (1972) (if there is conflict in meaning between endorsement and body of policy, endorsement controls); Inter-Insurance Exchange v. Westchester Fire Ins. Co., 25 Wis. 2d 100, 130 N.W.2d 185 (1964) (where provisions of rider or endorsement are irreconcilable, rider must control; policy and endorsements must be read together and only where irreconcilable conflict exists should resort be had to rule that endorsement should abrogate or nullify policy provisions). One federal court articulated the reason the endorsement controls: it is the later expression of the party's intent. The court added that an endorsement does not need to be handwritten to control the policy; it controls even if it is stamped or typewritten. It does not matter that the endorsement is, just like the policy, a printed form. B. L. Ivey Constr. Co. v. Pilot Fire & Casualty Co., 295 F. Supp. 840 (N.D. Ga. 1968) (when endorsement or rider and policy conflict, former controls latter, since it is later expression of intent).

146. 2 Holmes & Rhode's, *Holmes's Appleman on Insurance 2d* § 5.1 (West, 1996).

147. *See, e.g.*, Lime Tree Village Community Club Ass'n v. State Farm Gen. Ins. Co., 980 F.2d 1402 (11th Cir. 1993) (policy afforded association both comprehensive business liability insurance and Directors and Officers liability insurance). *See also* Kittansett Club v. Phila. Indem. Ins. Co., 2012 U.S. Dist. LEXIS 127939 (D. Mass. Sept. 10, 2012) (insurer issued "Flexi Plus Five" policy containing D&O liability insurance and employment practices liability insurance to golf club organized as non-profit corporation). *See also* Huntingdon Ridge Townhouse Homeowners Ass'n v. QBE Ins. Corp., 2009 U.S. Dist. LEXIS 108558 (M.D. Tenn. Nov. 20, 2009) (commercial property and D&O insurance combined in one policy).

148. *See V3 Launches Community Association Package Program* (Insurance Journal, May 27, 2015), available at: http://www.insurancejournal.com/news/national/2015/05/27/369573.htm.

[8] Excess Policy[149]

Typically, the limit of liability for a D&O policy issued to a common interest community is $1 million for all claims first made in the policy period. Whether that is sufficient coverage is a matter an association should discuss with its broker and the association attorney. The insurer may be willing to increase the limit, but in any event an association can purchase additional coverage with an "excess policy."[150] Generally, excess liability insurance merely provides an increase in the limit of insurance over the amount provided by the underlying policy, as opposed to an umbrella policy, which may provide both an increased limit of insurance and differences in coverage.[151] It is not uncommon for the excess coverage to be issued by the insurer that issued the underlying or primary coverage. That raises a concern. If that insurer becomes insolvent, the association has little or no coverage. Assuming the policy is issued by an admitted insurer, the association will have to rely on the state guaranty fund to pay a claim and the fund has a statutory limit, which is substantially below the limit of liability of the primary insurer. If the excess and primary insurer are the same company, the fund may or may not pay under both policies.

§ 14.06 Retaining Copies of Expired Policies

Common interest communities often dispose of old documents in their files on a periodic basis. This process may be initiated by the community association management company and may even be one of the services for which the contract between it and the association provides. When the documents are culled, should the association retain old D&O liability policies? The answer is that there is no harm in retaining old policies, and there may be a benefit. One expert recommends keeping expired copies of policies for at least 5 years after their expiration and preferably 10 years.[152]

When an association sues an insurer, it has the initial burden of showing coverage,[153] and that is more difficult to do without the policy. It is often held that a copy of the policy needs to be attached to the complaint in a suit against

149. *See generally* Kokinda, *Excess and DIC Side A D&O Insurance: An Answer to Management's Wishes?*, 28-6 ABIJ 40 (2009).

150. Stoeckert, *The Insurance Puzzle: Making Sense of Premiums and Policies* (Apr. 2012), available at: http://cooperator.com/articles/2418/1/The-Insurance-Puzzle/Page1.html (associations can buy up to $200 million in umbrella coverage in addition to initial D&O coverage).

151. *Excess Liability Insurance and Umbrella Insurance for Homeowner Associations*, available at: http://dandavisins.com/excess-liabilityumbrella/.

152. Wick, *Record Retention Means Future Protection*, Common Ground (CAI July/Aug. 1990). *See also* Porter, *Records Retention Guide for Homeowners Associations* (CAI Ledger Quarterly 1990) (retention of insurance policies and claims paid records is board administrative decision; recommending retaining claims paid records for five years).

153. *See, e.g.*, Borough of Sayreville v. Bellefonte Ins. Co., 320 N.J. Super. 598, 605, 728 A.2d 225, 228 (1998); Gold Fields Am. Corp. v. Aetna Cas. & Sur. Co., 173 Misc. 2d 901, 904, 661

the insurer,[154] although where the policy cannot be produced, courts generally will allow evidence of its contents to be introduced.[155] Gathering and introducing that evidence takes time and is an additional expenditure. Clearly, it is best if the association can produce the actual policy.[156] Thus, there is nothing to be gained by disposing of old policies, and there may be a benefit to retaining them. That is especially true with D&O policies because there is no standard policy, and that can make proving the contents without the policy that much more difficult.[157]

Associations should remember that D&O policies provide coverage for claims made during the policy period.[158] Once a claim is made, it essential to retain the policy until the claim is resolved and the insurer has paid it. It can be many years before a claim is settled or a judgment rendered. If the insurer refuses to pay and the association has to sue, it will sue for breach of the policy that was in effect when the claim was first made even though it was issued many years earlier.

N.Y.S.2d 948, 950 (1997) (policyholder has burden of proof on issue of existence of policy and its terms; where policyholder asserts it has lost policy, problem is for policyholder to address).

154. *See, e.g.*, Karaskiewicz v. Allstate Ins. Co. (*In re* Am. Arbitration Ass'n Arbitration), 109 Ill. App. 2d 370, 372, 248 N.E.2d 756, 758 (1969) (remanded to lower court with directions to strike complaint for failure to attach copy of insurance contract); State Farm Mut. Auto. Ins. Co. v. Jones, 98 Ga. App. 46, 56, 104 S.E.2d 725, 733 (1958) (pleadings in action against insurer required that copy of policy be attached or that petition allege language contained in policy).

155. *See, e.g.*, Rubenstein v. Royal Ins. Co. of Am., 44 Mass. App. Ct. 842, 846, 694 N.E.2d 381, 384 (1998) (existence of insurance policy is generally proven by documentary evidence; that policy has been lost or destroyed does not mean that its existence and contents may not be reconstructed from business records, underwriter's folios, or billings of insurer to insured); Borough of Sayreville v. Bellefonte Ins. Co., 320 N.J. Super. 598, 605, 728 A.2d 225, 228 (1998) (nothing in record suggested missing policies were different from others issued later that were available); Fraser v. Metropolitan Life Ins. Co., 165 Wash. 667, 669, 5 P.2d 978, 980 (1931) (where evidence was introduced that policy had been lost or mislaid and could not be found, form of policy was offered and received into evidence as testimony showed it was same form of policy as had been issued to insured). *See generally* Jones, *No Policy, No Problem? How Insureds are Finding Coverage Even Though They Can't Find Their Policies*, 50 Drake L. Rev. 611 (2002). The author notes that claims for breach of insurance agreements are based on allegations of a breach of a written contract and much of the information to complete the policy is unique to the specific insured: coverage limits, locations for which coverage is provided, and the period during which coverage exists. The written contract is, therefore, critical to determining the existence and scope of coverage.

156. One problem is that a court may allow use of a sample policy of the type that was apparently issued by the carrier at the time the policy in question was issued. *See, e.g.*, Gold Fields Am. Corp. v. Aetna Cas. & Sur. Co., 173 Misc. 2d 901, 906, 661 N.Y.S.2d 948, 951 (1997) (courts have permitted use of specimen policies to show what terms of policy at issue were). That policy, however, will not contain the information on the Declarations Page that may be critically important, for example, the limits of insurance or whether an extended discovery period was elected. Additionally, use of a sample policy will not help determine the specific endorsements that were a part of the actual policy.

157. Note that the broker of record should—and is required to—retain a copy of the policies issued for a prescribed time period.

158. Quinn & Levin, *Directors and Officers Liability Insurance: Probable Directions in Texas Law*, 20 Rev. Litig. 381 (2001).

Record retrieval is as important as record retention. The association may have retained expired policies, but if no one can find them, they may as well have been destroyed. An expert asserts that it is the responsibility of the governing board to assure that records are adequately maintained.[159] The association should have a storage facility for important documents that is separate from any facility maintained by the management company and should not be in the home or garage of a member of the association, but in an area accessible to future board members, either an offsite leased facility or a segregated and secure area that is part of the common areas of the community, for example, a clubhouse. It is also important that there be an index or cataloging system that makes it easy to find a specific document in the collection of retained material.

Record retention and retrieval can be made easier in the age of electronic documents. Documents can be scanned to create an electronic copy. That copy can be kept on the association computer with a backup retained on a flash drive. Community association managers (CAMs) often scan the insurance policies issued to the associations they manage and post them along with other documents on a website so that members of the association can view them. The association can retain the electronic copy of the policies each year. Storage of hardcopies of policies is a challenge as collectively the various policies can total several hundred pages each year. Electronic copies take up little space, but some of the same cautions that apply to hardcopies also apply to electronic ones. The sole electronic copy should not be in the possession of the management company. The association should have its own copy. When the electronic copies are on a flash drive, they should be kept in a common area to which all governing board members have access, not in the home of a board member.

§ 14.07 Distinguishing D&O from Other Forms of Insurance

Even though D&O insurance has become commonplace, it remains a unique line of insurance that is highly specialized. Coverage options, terms, and conditions often vary widely from one policy and insurer to the next.[160] The typical property and liability coverages purchased by common interest communities use standard ISO forms, but many carriers of D&O insurance write their own

159. Porter, *Records Retention Guide for Homeowners Associations* (CAI Ledger Quarterly 1990).

160. Mistretta, *The Growing Importance of D&O Insurance: Avoiding Liability for Your Co-op & Condo Board Members* (Jan. 2014), available at: http://cooperator.com/articles/2729/1/The-Growing-Importance-of-DampO-Insurance/Page1.html.

specialized policy.[161] Indeed, one commentary says a "standard" D&O policy is "a misnomer."[162]

D&O coverage is offered by a relatively few companies compared to other insurance lines.[163] A 2012 survey, for example, showed 65 carriers offering D&O policies, and most of them were affiliates of major companies, for example, AIG or Travelers.[164]

Several features make D&O insurance different from other insurance:

- Generally, D&O policies provide "all-risk" coverage rather than limiting coverage to specifically named perils.
- Many carriers draft their own polices instead of using a standard ISO form, making for more variety in policy language.
- The coverage may be found in a stand-alone policy or an endorsement to a commercial liability policy.
- The policies are almost always "claims-made."

[1] Commercial General Liability Insurance

Commercial general liability (CGL) insurance protects an insured from liability—including defense costs—for bodily injury, property damage—meaning liability for damage to the property of others for which the insured is liable—and personal and advertising injury, encompassing liability for false arrest, detention, or imprisonment; malicious prosecution; wrongful eviction from, wrongful entry into, or invasion of the right of private occupancy; slander, libel, or trade disparagement; violation of the right of another to privacy; use of the advertising idea of someone else; or infringement of copyright, trade dress, or slogan. Under the standard CGL, if the name insured is designated as an organization—other than a partnership, joint venture, or LLC—the organization is an insured as are its "executive officers" and directors, but only with respect to their duties as officers or directors, and probably only when they hold office during the term of the policy. The typical D&O policy will have an exclusion for some or all of these perils and to the extent it does not, its "other insurance" clause will render it excess insurance to any CGL policy providing this type of coverage.

---

161. Davis, *Professional Liability and Governance Exposures: A Closer Look* (Nonprofit Risk Management Center 2017), available at: https://www.nonprofitrisk.org/resources/articles/professional-liability-and-governance-exposures-a-closer-look/.

162. Kokinda, *D&O Liability Insurance: There Are Exclusions, and Then There Are Exclusions*, 28-10 ABIJ 46 (2010).

163. Dobiac, *I Came, I Saw, I Underwrote: D&O Liability Insurance's Past Underwriting Practices and Potential Future Directions*, 14 Conn. Ins. L.J. 487, 518 (2008); Romano, *What Went Wrong with Directors' and Officers' Liability Insurance?*, 14 Del. J. Corp. L. 1, 15–16 (1989).

164. *Directors and Officers Liability Survey: 2012 Summary of Results*, Appendix A, at 22–39 (Towers Watson, 2013).

[2] Crime/Fidelity Insurance

For common interest communities, a crime/fidelity policy indemnifies the association for loss of money, securities, or other property because of acts of fraud, dishonesty, forgery, theft, larceny, embezzlement, misappropriation, or criminal acts by its directors, officers, committee members, association employees, volunteers, and managing agents.[165] A D&O policy is generally written in conjunction with a crime/fidelity policy but provides different coverage.[166] It is *not* designed to cover risks arising from moral turpitude or a want of integrity and, indeed, typically has a dishonesty exclusion.[167] Nonetheless, many associations mistakenly believe that when money is taken by a board member, employee, or volunteer, that coverage is available under their D&O policy.[168] As one commentary notes, a D&O policy and a crime/fidelity policy are actually mutually exclusive, as once the loss is proven for purposes of recovery under the latter, the dishonesty exclusion in the former is triggered as to the "dishonest" officer or director.[169] D&O insurance, on the other hand, generally purports to cover *good faith* errors and omissions, as well as *negligence*.[170]

[3] Errors and Omissions Insurance

There are basically two types of professional liability insurance: errors and omissions (E&O) and directors and officers (D&O). An E&O policy provides liability insurance for professionals—for example, lawyers, doctors, accountants, and community association managers—and is commonly referred to as malpractice insurance. It protects professionals against claims arising out of alleged errors and omissions in performance of covered services conducted within the scope of their profession.[171] Some confusion can arise because the term "E&O" is

165. Meskin, *A Funny Thing Happened on the Way to the Bank: Fraud in the Community Association* (Katzman & Korr: Legal News Tailored for Community Associations 2008). *See also* Branson, *Fidelity Bond Insurance: Protection Against Condo Crime* (Cooperator, 2014), available at: http://cooperator.com/articles/2823/1/Fidelity-Bond-Insurance/Page1.html.

166. Hedderman, *The Value of Directors and Officers Insurance: Cover Yourself* (New Jersey Cooperator, 2004), available at: http://njcooperator.com/articles/266/1/The-Value-of-Directors-and-Officers-Insurance/Page1.html.

167. Quinn & Levin, *Directors and Officers Liability Insurance: Probable Directions in Texas Law*, 20 Rev. Litig. 381, 384 (2001).

168. Meskin, *When Are You Not Covered By Your D&O Policy? Maintaining Proper Coverage* (Cooperator, Aug. 2008), available at: http://cooperator.com/articles/1673/1/When-Are-You-Not-Covered-By-Your-DampO-Policy/Page1.html.

169. Monteleone & Conca, *Directors and Officers Indemnification and Liability Insurance: An Overview of Legal and Practical Issues*, 51 Bus. Law 573, 602 (1996) (many D&O policies provide that dishonesty exclusion applies severally and thus will not preclude coverage for individual whose culpability may have been less than dishonest).

170. Quinn & Levin, *Directors and Officers Liability Insurance: Probable Directions in Texas Law*, 20 Rev. Litig. 381, 385 (2001).

171. 4 Jeffery E. Thomas, *New Appleman on Insurance Law Library Edition* § 25.01[1] (LexisNexis 2023).

sometimes used in connection with the coverage associations obtain for officers and directors;[172] however, instead of providing coverage for performance of professional services, D&O insurance generally covers claims against an insured's directors or officers based on their actions as directors or officers.[173]

§ 14.08 The Application: Preparation and Accuracy

Applications for D&O coverage usually call for more detailed information than do those for other types of policies. There is, therefore, probably an increased possibility of misinformation. Applicants need to work closely with their broker to be certain the information provided is accurate. One commentary notes that innocent misrepresentations appear to happen most often either because the insured represents a fact about which he or she is mistaken or there is a miscommunication with the insurer.[174] A good faith misrepresentation may be based on an incorrect assumption, undiscovered fact, or forgotten detail, or the applicant may misinterpret a question, fail to mention a fact that he or she wrongly assumes the insurer already knows, or does not read the application carefully. Sometimes the insurer claims pertinent information has been omitted, but its questions were not clear. In general, the insured is not obligated to volunteer information for which the insurer did not ask.[175]

The first question for common interest communities to answer regarding insurance applications is who will contact the broker to make the application and sign it? It may be an officer of the CIC[176] or the CAM. In many cases the manager will be the person best equipped to answer the questions on the application; however, if the CAM omits information from the application, even if none of the officers or directors is aware of that information, the association will likely be bound by the failure of the CAM to supply the requested information

172. *See, e.g.*, Fed. Ins. Co. v. Evian Horizontal Prop. Regime, 126 Fed. Appx. 589 (4th Cir. 2005) (condominium association had errors & omissions coverage for its officers and directors); 34th Ave. Apt. Corp. v. Nationwide Mut. Ins. Co., 283 A.D.2d 604, 725 N.Y.S.2d 98 (2001) (cooperative had Directors and Officers Errors or Omissions Liability Endorsement).

173. 4 Jeffery E. Thomas, *New Appleman on Insurance Law Library Edition* § 25.01[1] (LexisNexis 2023).

174. Barnes, *Against Insurance Rescission*, 120 Yale L.J. 328, 334 (2010).

175. Quinn & Levin, *Directors and Officers Liability Insurance: Probable Directions in Texas Law*, 20 Rev. Litig. 381, 477 (2001) (unless insurer clearly asks question, insured has no duty of disclosure in application process, even if insured thinks information might be relevant).

176. In a curious argument, an association contended an application was "blank" because it was never signed by it, but only its agent. Therefore, it argued, any misrepresentations in the application could not be attributed to it. The application was signed by the president of the association. The court characterized the association's contention as raising "troubling agency concerns," by which it probably meant that the association could only act through its agents and the authority of the president of an organization to bind it is not generally a matter of dispute. The court found that any misrepresentation in the application was "squarely and unequivocally" that of the association. Caribbean I Owners' Ass'n v. Great Am. Ins. Co., 600 F. Supp. 2d 1228 (S.D. Ala. 2009).

and coverage may be denied or the policy rescinded.[177] The CAM may also omit information of which officers and directors have knowledge so, if the CAM represents the CIC, the governing board should obtain a copy of the application and review it for accuracy.[178] It may be that the CAM provided incomplete[179] or incorrect information to the broker,[180] or the broker may have obtained inaccurate data from a prior application.

An insurer will rarely investigate the information in an application when it is submitted. Instead, when the insured notifies the insurer of a claim, the D&O insurer will probably scrutinize the application for possible misrepresentations, specifically looking for indications that the circumstances that gave rise to the claim were known to the insureds at the time of the application and should have been disclosed.[181] Thus, the fact that the insurer accepts the application and issues a policy does not mean it accepts the information supplied on the application as true. That burden falls on the insured at the time the application is submitted.

[1] Policy Provisions Regarding Applications

The application will typically be addressed in a couple of policy provisions. D&O policies will generally have a definition of "application" and a "warranties and covenants" clause that may or may not include a "severability" provision. Policies may also have an "entire agreement" clause stating that the named insured agrees that the policy, consisting of the application, coverage parts, and all endorsements listed on the Declarations Page, constitutes the entire contract between the parties.[182]

---

177. Gotham Condominium v. Firstservice Residential, 2015 N.Y. Misc. LEXIS 287 (Feb. 2, 2015) (management company for condominium association failed to disclose information on application for directors and officers insurance, and as result carrier declined coverage for litigation subsequently commenced by unit owners against association).

178. The governing board should remember that the manger is its agent, and it will, therefore, generally be bound by the actions of the manager on behalf of the association. *See, e.g.*, Biscayne Cove Condo. Ass'n v. QBE Ins. Corp., 971 F. Supp. 2d 1121, 1126 (S.D. Fla. 2013).

179. A new manager may well lack the complete history of prior losses that need to be reported or a complete picture of the needs of the particular association.

180. *See, e.g.*, Towers Condo. Ass'n v. C.E. Brathwaite & Assocs., 40 V.I. 33 (1999) (manager signed application prepared by broker without providing any additional information; application lacked information about prior claim, and manager professed to have no awareness of that prior claim).

181. Monteleone, *Coverage Issues Under Commercial General Liability and Directors' and Officers' Liability Policies*, 18 W. New Eng. L. Rev. 47, 64 (1996). See also Barnes, Against Insurance Rescission, 120 Yale L.J. 328, 335–36 (2010) (reviews of reported innocent misrepresentation cases and anecdotal experiences of practitioners suggest that insurers seldom discover innocent misrepresentations until after insured suffers loss).

182. *See, e.g.*, Continental Casualty Company Community Association Policy (G-145170-A), § XXI.

[a] "Application" Defined

A typical policy definition of "application" is all signed, written applications including any attachments and materials submitted with them, for the current policy and for any policy in an uninterrupted series of policies issued by the insurer of which the current one is a renewal or replacement, all of which are deemed attached to the policy and incorporated into it.[183] There are several aspects of the definition of which to take note. First, only written documents constitute the application. Anything the applicant and broker discuss that is not put in writing is not considered part of the application. Second, the application includes not only the initial application but any renewal applications as well.[184] Next, the application includes any attachments and materials submitted with the initial or any renewal application. Finally, all these documents are considered to be incorporated into the policy. Thus, not only is the application a part of the policy—which is how applications are generally interpreted—but so are documents submitted with it. Thus, when the insurer asks for documents to be submitted at the time of application, a common interest community association needs to be sure those documents are accurate.[185] For example, if the insurer were to ask for a copy of the governing documents, the association would need to make sure the copy it supplied included all amendments to the documents.

[b] Warranties and Covenants

The "warranties and covenants" clause states that the insureds warrant and agree that as a condition to the obligations of the insurer under the policy, the statements and representations made in the application are the statements and representations of the insureds and are true. It will also typically say that the policy was issued in reliance on the truth of those statements and representations,[186] and that if any statement or representation in the application is untrue, the policy is "void and of no effect whatsoever."[187] This language attempts to convert representations into warranties by having the applicant agree that the representations are material.[188]

---

183. *See, e.g.*, Non-Profit Management and Organization Liability Insurance Policy § II.A.

184. *Directors and Officers Liability (D&O) Insurance Dictionary* (Willis Towers Watson, 2012) (renewal application is typically shorter than main form application and does not usually require warranty that no potential claims or circumstances exist).

185. *See generally* 3 *New Appleman Law of Liability Insurance* § 22.09[2][f] (rev. ed., Matthew Bender, 2017).

186. *See, e.g.*, Non-Profit Management and Organization Liability Insurance Policy § VI.1.

187. *See, e.g.*, Non-Profit Management and Organization Liability Insurance Policy § VI.2.

188. Quinn & Levin, *Directors and Officers Liability Insurance: Probable Directions in Texas Law*, 20 Rev. Litig. 381, 473 (2001) (any statement that application is attached to policy, when false, sometimes defeats substance of warranty and makes it impossible for insurer to enforce it).

While that language of the clause raises the possibility that an innocent error or omission will void coverage, states generally require that any misrepresentation actually be material to the risk before they will allow the insurer to avoid liability under the policy.[189] The materiality of misrepresentations is, as one authority has said, "a confusing area of the law, [because] it varies both from state to state and among types of policies."[190]

[c] Severability

A critically important part of a D&O policy is the severability provision. It prevents the insurer from imputing the knowledge of the person who signed the application to any other insured.[191] Without it, a misstatement on the application can render coverage void for all the insureds, even those who had no knowledge of the misstatement.[192] Some insurers include a severability provision within the policy, but others do not. When there is no severability provision, the applicant should ask for an endorsement to the policy adding it.[193]

Under a severability provision, when any statement or representation in the application is untrue, the clause that voids the policy is limited in its application. First, it only applies to any insured person who had knowledge or information as of the *policy inception date* of the facts that were not truthfully disclosed.[194] In other words, even though untrue information was supplied in the application, an innocent officer or director—one who lacked knowledge or information of the untruths—retains coverage. Additionally, if that innocent officer or director obtains knowledge or information of the facts that were not truthfully disclosed *after* the commencement of the policy, his or her coverage remains intact. Second, the clause that voids the policy does not apply to the insured organization—that is, the association—even if it or the person who signed the application had knowledge or information as of the policy inception date of the facts that were

189. *See generally* 3 *New Appleman Law of Liability Insurance* § 22.09[2][a] (rev. ed., Matthew Bender, 2017).

190. Quinn & Levin, *Directors and Officers Liability Insurance: Probable Directions in Texas Law*, 20 Rev. Litig. 381, 474 (2001). *See also* Barnes, *Against Insurance Rescission*, 120 Yale L.J. 328, 353 (2010) (what modern insurer must prove to obtain rescission varies among jurisdictions).

191. Monteleone & Conca, *Directors and Officers Indemnification and Liability Insurance: An Overview of Legal and Practical Issues*, 51 Bus. Law 573, 586 (1996) (insurer seeking to rescind entire policy based on misrepresentations in application has to prove that each and every insured director and officer had knowledge of that misrepresentation).

192. *Directors and Officers Liability (D&O) Insurance Dictionary* (Willis Towers Watson, 2012) (where it is later determined that at time application was signed, an insured knew or should have known of existence of potential claim or circumstance likely to lead to claim, insurer may seek to rescind or revoke entire policy as to all insureds).

193. *Directors and Officers Liability (D&O) Insurance Dictionary* (Willis Towers Watson, 2012) (insurers whose policies do not provide severability are typically willing to consider adding it).

194. *See, e.g.*, Non-Profit Management and Organization Liability Insurance Policy § VI.2.a.

not truthfully disclosed.[195] The severability provision typically adds that whether an insured person had knowledge or information is determined without regard to whether he or she actually knew the application contained an untrue statement or representation. In other words, it does not matter whether the association, or the person with the authority to sign the application, knew, should have known, or did not know that there was a misrepresentation on the application or that information was withheld.

[2] Common Application Questions

Applications for D&O insurance ask for a great deal of information. Most of the information can be supplied by a community association manager familiar with the community, but some requires answers from the officers and directors or others. Some of the answers are used to determine the premium.[196] Information typically requested includes:

- General information about the association, including its name, physical address, and mailing address.
- Whether the association is a condominium, homeowners association, cooperative, timeshare, or master association.
- Whether the association has a community association manager and, if so, general information about the manager.
- Some details about the community including the name of the developer, the completion date if the project is not completed, when the association was established, the number of units, their value, and whether the developer controls the governing board.
- Whether there is any commercial occupancy, the percentage of commercial occupancy, and whether there are specific commercial uses, for example, bars or schools.
- The community amenities, for example, clubs, golf courses, or marinas, and whether those amenities are open to the general public.
- Whether there is a rental pool and if so, what percentage of units participate in it.
- The community's financial status, specifically whether there is a positive or negative fund balance and whether the association has been in receivership or bankruptcy, has levied a special assessment, has adequate reserves,

195. *See, e.g.*, Non-Profit Management and Organization Liability Insurance Policy § VI.2.b.

196. The amenities will generally be a factor in determining the premium. *See* Hedderman, *The Value of Directors and Officers Insurance: Cover Yourself* (New Jersey Cooperator, 2004), available at: http://njcooperator.com/articles/266/1/The-Value-of-Directors-and-Officers-Insurance/Page1.html (premium is generally based on number of units and various other factors such as commercial components, employees, and extraordinary recreational facilities such as golf courses, boat slips, piers, or horse trails).

or has unit owners who are more than 90 days delinquent in paying their assessments. In some cases, a year-end financial statement may be required to be submitted with the application.

- Whether there are renovation projects planned or in progress.
- Whether the association has armed security services or salaried employees.
- The association's claims history and prior insurance, including the premium and deductible of that prior insurance and whether the association has had a D&O policy cancelled.
- Whether anyone who is to be insured by the policy is aware of possible claims.
- The requested limit of liability and the requested deductible.

[3] Avoiding Misrepresentations

The association needs to be careful to avoid misrepresentations. A wrong answer, even an innocent one, may be a misrepresentation that in some cases is grounds to rescind the contract or, at a minimum, reduce the coverage available. That applies to all the questions in the application.

[a] Possible Claims

The application will generally include a warning that no coverage will be provided for a claim when the possibility of that claim should have been disclosed.[197] Thus, the language that asks about knowledge of possible claims needs to be carefully examined. Observers generally agree that the most significant aspect of main form applications is that they expressly ask about potential claims or circumstances that could lead to claims and that when the applicant identifies potential claims or circumstances on the application, the policy typically will not cover them.[198]

The question about possible claims might be subjective: does anyone have knowledge of anything he or she *has reason to believe* could result in a claim? It could be objective: does anyone have knowledge of anything that *could reasonably* result in a claim? Under the objective language, an innocent, good faith omission might still be considered a misrepresentation. The application will almost certainly make the question about possible claims applicable to *anyone* to be insured. That may mean more than the officers and directors. It could include the community association manager,[199] as well as members of committees currently in

197. The application may limit the prohibition so that it only applies to those actually failing to make the required disclosure.

198. *Directors and Officers Liability (D&O) Insurance Dictionary* (Willis Towers Watson, 2012).

199. *See, e.g.*, Gotham Condominium v. Firstservice Residential, 2015 N.Y. Misc. LEXIS 287 (Feb. 2, 2015) (where management company for condominium association failed to disclose threatened litigation by unit owners on application for D&O insurance, carrier declined coverage for litigation subsequently commenced by unit owners against association).

existence. In a large association, for example, there may be a landscape committee whose members are aware of a potential claim by the landscaping company or an employee of the company that is as yet unknown to the governing board. All the persons who may be insured need to be polled about the possibility of a claim. The question may ask about claims that would be covered *under the policy* or may be more open ended and simply ask about *any possible claim*. Arguably in the latter circumstance, even claims that would not be covered by the proposed policy need to be revealed to avoid making a misrepresentation.

Applications generally use vague language about possible claims: does anyone have knowledge or information that *might* or that *could* give rise to a claim? As one commentary notes, the interpretation given to words like "might" will determine the breadth and scope of any inquiry and resulting response to the question. For example, if the person answering the questions construes "might" as "could possibly," the query broadens as virtually any act, error, or omission *could possibly* give rise to a claim.[200]

There is usually a statement above the signature line on an application that says the person who signs it on behalf of the organization declares that the answers in it are true and correct and that "thorough efforts" were made to obtain sufficient information from each insured to allow for "proper and accurate" completion of the application. The application, however, does not explain what would constitute "thorough efforts" to discover whether *any potential insureds* had knowledge of possible claims. Should each prospective insured be informally interviewed or polled, or should copies of the entire application be distributed to them for individual review?[201] Should a written, signed response be obtained from each of them? An abundance of caution would dictate that all potential insureds state in writing that they do or do not have knowledge of possible claims.

A New York case demonstrates how easily an association can lose coverage because of the question about possible claims.[202] A tenant/shareholder in a residential cooperative was denied permission to sell his interest to a particular buyer. He wrote a letter to the governing board asking that it revisit its decision and threatening "unpleasant actions"—and vaguely mentioning the state Attorney General—if he did not hear from the board by a specific date. Subsequently the corporation submitted a signed application for a D&O insurance policy. The application asked if "the undersigned, or any individual proposed for this insurance, [was] aware of any fact, circumstance or situation involving the organization . . . which he/she has reason to believe might result in any future claim which would fall within the scope of the proposed insurance?" The corporation

200. Caraccio, *Void Ab Initio: Application Fraud as Grounds for Avoiding Directors' and Officers' Liability Insurance Coverage*, 74 Calif. L. Rev. 929, 976 (1986).

201. Caraccio, *Void Ab Initio: Application Fraud as Grounds for Avoiding Directors' and Officers' Liability Insurance Coverage*, 74 Calif. L. Rev. 929, 970 (1986).

202. 2575 Owners Corp., 1998 U.S. Dist. LEXIS 18822 (S.D.N.Y. Dec. 2, 1998).

answered "no," and neither disclosed the letter from the disgruntled tenant/shareholder nor its threat of "unpleasant action." A few weeks later the corporation and its directors were sued by the would-be buyers for alleged discrimination in the denial of the sale. After discovering the tenant/shareholder's letter, the insurer denied coverage, contending the directors knew of, and failed to disclose, the litigation risk when the application was signed.

The court said the case boiled down to the question of whether a reasonable director who received that letter would have perceived some material risk of litigation and concluded the answer was "yes." The letter directly challenged the decision of the board, alleged specific injuries to both the tenant/shareholder and the buyers, and threatened further unpleasant actions, including resort to legal channels, for example, the Attorney General. The court acknowledged that the letter did not expressly threaten a suit but, nonetheless, it carried a warning that any reasonable director would have perceived and clearly raised a sufficient threat of risk to fall within the scope of the application question. Moreover, the fact that it was the *buyers*, not the *tenant/shareholder*, who ultimately sued was of "no moment," because the buyer's lawsuit was based largely on the same facts as those discussed by the tenant/shareholder in his letter and was inherent in any potential suit he might have brought.

The facts of the New York case are worth relating in detail because they serve as a warning of how little it could take for an insurer to decide the application failed to disclose a possible claim and, based on that failure, successfully deny coverage. It has to be conceded that another court faced with similar facts might well reach an entirely different conclusion, but one cannot depend on that. Many common interest community directors will, no doubt, find the reasoning of the New York case bewildering. After all, they receive vague threats all the time. A condominium unit owner troubled by a neighbor's loud music "has had it" and "will take matters into her own hands" if the association does not act. A resident in a community of detached homes wonders when the board will enforce the landscaping rules being widely flouted and what she has to do to get the board to do its job. In a residential cooperative, a tenant/shareholder complains at every meeting about the "gross incompetence" of the property management company and says that if the board will not fire the company, she is going to "look into her options." Do these "threats" have to be disclosed on an application for D&O coverage? Is disclosure required even if the "threats" are spoken and not in writing? What about the gadfly resident that most every common interest community seems to have who for years has complained about nearly everything and who no one takes seriously anymore? In light of the New York decision, the safe answer would be to list anything on the application that even remotely sounds like a possible claim, keeping in mind the broad definition of "claim."[203] The best avenue would be to consult the association counsel.

203. *See* § 14.12[1], *infra*.

[b] Adequacy of Reserve Funds

There are some questions that may require careful consideration and in answering them the association is probably best served by erring on the side of full disclosure. For example, if the application asks whether "adequate" or the "proper amount of" reserves have been set aside, the association may not be able to easily answer the question. Reserves are calculated for a component by dividing the replacement cost of that component by its remaining useful life. Determining the replacement cost obviously requires an estimate of future inflation. However, neither the useful life of a component nor future inflation can be estimated with any certainty. Some states have statutory requirements for reserve funding,[204] but many do not.[205] Even where there is no statutory requirement, the governing documents may require the association to establish reserve funds and even specify the components to be included. Nonetheless, associations generally have some discretion in determining the components for which they will create reserves. Some associations reserve for relatively inexpensive components, but others decide they will cover the expense with a special assessment or surplus funds they maintain in a contingency account. Some make the same decision for more expensive components where there is no specific requirement that they reserve funds for that purpose. A budget prepared by a community association management firm will usually include a breakdown of reserve funds, showing annual contributions to the fund for each component and the amount the fund will contain at the end of the component's useful life. If an association has any doubt about the answer to a question about reserves, it should probably submit a copy of its most recent budget along with the application.

[c] Receivership

When an application asks about receivership, the insurer undoubtedly wants to know if the association is experiencing financial difficulty. However, there are circumstances in which a receiver may be appointed for an association that is in good financial condition. For example, the Maryland Homeowners Association Act includes a statute providing that if a homeowners association fails to fill vacancies on its governing body sufficient to constitute a quorum, three or more lot owners may petition a court to appoint a receiver to manage the affairs of the association.[206] Florida law has a similar provision for condominiums with an insufficient number of directors to constitute a quorum, and also provides for

---

204. *See, e.g.*, Cal. Civ. Code §§ 5510–5580; Minn. Stat. § 515B.3-114.

205. *See, e.g.*, Ariz. Rev. Stat. § 33-1242(A)(2) (subject to provisions of declaration association may adopt and amend budgets for revenues, expenditures, and reserves); O.C.G.A. § 44-3-220, *et seq.* (Georgia Property Owners' Association Act); Md. Code Ann. § 5-6B-01, *et seq.* (Maryland Cooperative Housing Corporation Act); R.I. Gen. Laws § 34-36.1-3.02(a)(2) (subject to provisions of declaration, association, even if unincorporated, may adopt and amend budgets for revenues, expenditures, and reserves).

206. Md. Real Prop. Code Ann. § 11B-111.5(a).

appointment of receivers after a natural disaster or to lease out an abandoned unit.[207] The Uniform Common Interest Ownership Act allows an association to have a receiver appointed to assist in collecting assessments.[208] Depending on how a question about receivership is worded, the association that had a receiver appointed in one of these circumstances might need to acknowledge that appointment or risk making a misrepresentation, even though the insurer is probably not asking about appointment of a receiver for non-financial reasons.

NOTE: The association should probably make the purpose of the appointment clear in the application so that the insurer is not left with a misperception.

[d] Commercial Uses

Questions about commercial uses may be too broad to be easily answered. For example, the question may not distinguish between commercial uses that are governed by the association and those that occupy the same property. In a high-rise building, for instance, the bottom floor may consist of retail space owned by the development company, or a successor, and rented to tenants. The second and third floors may consist of professional offices also owned by the development company, or a successor, and rented to tenants. Beginning at the fourth floor, there may be residential condominium units governed by the association that is the insured entity. The top floor may be a restaurant with a bar, also owned by the development company, or a successor, and rented to a tenant. In this situation, must the association inform the insurer of these commercial uses even though they are completely separate from the association? Again, full disclosure with an explanation is probably the best course.

[e] Community Amenities

An application that asks about community amenities may provide a check-off list of specific amenities, but it may also ask for disclosure of any other amenities not on the list. The association should include on its list any feature of the community that is at all similar to the listed amenities. A lengthy list of "amenities" about which the insurer has no concern is preferable to one the insurer might consider to be a misrepresentation by omission.

[f] Security Services or Salaried Employees

Inquiries about armed security services or salaried employees may be problematic. For example, an association may be located in a gated community governed

207. *See* Fla. Stat. §§ 718.1124, 718.117(7)(a), and 718.111(5)(b)4.
208. *See* UCIOA § 3-116(l).

by a master association that employs a security service. The security personnel may have access to weapons, but not actually be armed and the association may not be aware of that fact. Were there to be a lawsuit concerning the conduct of the security personnel, the defendant, in addition to the security company, would likely be the master association, not the association applying for coverage. Once again, to avoid possible misrepresentation (and maybe a higher premium), the association should ask the master association if the security personnel are armed, and then disclose that there is an armed or unarmed security service in the community that is not employed by the association and over which it has no supervisory control. Similarly, there may be salaried employees on the association property but who are employed by a company with which the association contracts for services. In an abundance of caution, the association should probably disclose that there are salaried employees working on the property, but state that they are employed and paid by a third party. A question about employees may also ask about volunteers. "Volunteer" in this context probably means residents who occasionally do odd jobs—for example, change light bulbs in, or make minor repairs to, the common property—for which they are not compensated.

[4] Reviewing the Application

When reviewing the application before signing, the association should ensure the name of the entity is its "legal name," that is, the name that appears in its document of creation.[209] While some may say that it is not necessary for the entire governing board to review the completed application before it is signed and submitted, experts in D&O insurance say that directors should always be given an opportunity to review the application.[210] One reason would be that one director might catch a mistake that other directors miss. The governing board may lack the knowledge to select appropriate D&O coverage without professional assistance from an insurance broker or a knowledgeable association attorney or manager, but it can take responsibility for reviewing the application to ensure it contains accurate answers to the questions asked. The signature line of the application will probably call for the signature of the "authorized representative" of the association. It may even provide that an attorney or community association manager may be the authorized representative.

---

209. For a condominium, the document of creation will be the Declaration of Condominium or, in some states, the master deed; in a homeowners association that document will be the recorded covenants called the Declaration of Covenants and Restrictions or something similar; and in a cooperative, the document will be the articles of incorporation.

210. Sagalow, *Directors and Officers Liability Insurance: A Guide for Directors, Professional Edition*, at 67, available at: http://innovationinsurancegroup.com/wp-content/uploads/2014/07/D_O_Handbook_Professional_Edition.pdf (warning that too often directors are not walked through application by knowledgeable guide and may not be aware of misrepresentations or omissions).

§ 14.09 Basic D&O Insurance Coverage

The basic D&O insurance coverage will be illustrated throughout this chapter by comparing two policies. The first is actually an endorsement prepared by the Insurance Services Organization (ISO) that modifies the ISO Business Owners Coverage Form[211] and is titled "Business Owners: Condominiums, Co-Ops, Associations—Directors and Officers Liability Endorsement."[212] The second policy is the Travelers stand-alone policy called the Non-Profit Management and Organization Liability Insurance Policy (NPMOLIP).[213] It is a policy that is commonly provided to common interest communities. It should be remembered that D&O coverage is different from other coverages—for example, commercial property and commercial general liability insurance—in which there are widely used standard ISO policies. The insurers that offer D&O coverage often eschew standardized policies and, therefore, there can be significant differences between policies issued by different companies. Therefore, the examples of policy language cited in the chapter are just that, examples. One always has to check the language of the specific policy at issue.

Remember that the policy consists of the Declarations Page, the insuring agreement, the definitions, extensions, the discovery period, exclusions, conditions and limitations, and warranties, as well as any endorsements.[214] Moreover, the application is a part of the insurance contract.

[1] Directors and Officers Direct Coverage—Side A

In general, D&O insurance is said to cover good faith errors and omissions and negligence.[215] Standard coverage is in two parts. The first "provides personal coverage, reimbursing the individual directors and officers for un-indemnified payments."[216] This is commonly referred to as "Side A coverage." Even though

---

211. The policy combines commercial property and general liability coverage.

212. ISO Form BP 17 24 01 10.

213. Travelers Non-Profit Management and Organization Liability Insurance Policy, CIRI 72001. Travelers is a preferred policy among brokers, so it serves as a useful example for this discussion.

214. Treese & Rosenberry, *Insurance: How Community Associations Protect Themselves*, at 14 (CAI Press 2013).

215. Quinn & Levin, *Directors and Officers Liability Insurance: Probable Directions in Texas Law*, 20 Rev. Litig. 381, 385 (2001).

216. Romano, *What Went Wrong with Directors' and Officers' Liability Insurance?*, 14 Del. J. Corp. L. 1, 9 (1989). *See also* Quinn & Levin, *Directors and Officers Liability Insurance: Probable Directions in Texas Law*, 20 Rev. Litig. 381 (2001) (policy provides coverage to director or officer if corporation has not already paid, reimbursed, or indemnified him or her); Dobiac, *I Came, I Saw, I Underwrote: D&O Liability Insurance's Past Underwriting Practices and Potential Future Directions*, 14 Conn. Ins. L.J. 487, 491 (2008) (Side A is individual coverage meant to indemnify corporate officers for any sums for which they become liable to pay and often includes policy

this is the *directors and officers* portion of D&O coverage, it is actually rarely implicated. Claims arise under Side A in limited circumstances. It applies when the corporation is bankrupt or insolvent or the amounts are paid to settle a derivative action.[217] It also applies when the bylaws or state law does not allow indemnity, or the governing board decides the actions of the officer or director were outside the indemnity obligations of the insured organization.[218]

[2] Organization Reimbursement Coverage—Side B

The second part of the standard coverage provides "company reimbursement." It "reimburses the corporation for legally valid indemnification payments made to directors and officers for covered losses."[219] This is called "Side B coverage." It does not insure the business entity against its own misconduct, but against indemnifying the directors and officers for their liability.[220] Payments under Side B coverage are triggered when the organization incurs an obligation to indemnify.[221] While Side B protects the corporate entity, it is best not referred to as "entity coverage," because there is a third coverage, Side C, that is not considered part

---

language restricting indemnification to circumstances where firm is not permitted to indemnify officer directly).

217. Baker & Griffith, *The Missing Monitor in Corporate Governance: The Directors' & Officers' Liability Insurer*, 95 Geo. L.J. 1795, 1802 (2007). *See also* Ackerman, *A Common Law Approach to D&O Insurance "In Fact" Exclusion Disputes*, 79 U. Chi. L. Rev. 1429, 1432 (2012) (Side A coverage is most important when organization is insolvent, does not indemnify, or is prohibited from indemnifying, its executives); Griffith, *Uncovering a Gatekeeper: Why the SEC Should Mandate Disclosure of Details Concerning Directors' And Officers' Liability Insurance Policies*, 154 U. Pa. L. Rev. 1147, 166 (2006) (when company is not legally permitted to indemnify its directors and officers—for example, in case of derivative suit settlements—insurer will pay pursuant to Side A coverage).

218. Kokinda, *Excess and DIC Side A D&O Insurance: An Answer to Management's Wishes?*, 28-6 ABIJ 40 (2009).

219. Romano, *What Went Wrong with Directors' and Officers' Liability Insurance?*, 14 Del. J. Corp. L. 1, 9 (1989).

220. Quinn & Levin, *Directors and Officers Liability Insurance: Probable Directions in Texas Law*, 20 Rev. Litig. 381, 416 (2001); Johnston, *Corporate Indemnification and Liability Insurance for Directors and Officers*, 33 Bus. Law. 1993, 2013 (1978) (corporate reimbursement only covers corporation's obligation to indemnify its directors and officers, not any liability corporation itself may have to plaintiff in any given action). *See also* Baker & Griffith, *The Missing Monitor in Corporate Governance: The Directors' & Officers' Liability Insurer*, 95 Geo. L.J. 1795, 1802 (2007) (Side B coverage protects corporation itself from losses resulting from its indemnification obligations to individual directors and officers). *And see* Clark v. General Accident Ins. Co. PR., 951 F. Supp. 559 (D.V.I. 1997) (where under "coverage B" insurer agreed to "pay on behalf of the named insured all loss which the named insured shall be required or permitted by law to pay as indemnity to any director or officer because of any civil claim," association was not covered except to extent that it might indemnify its directors and officers for covered loss incurred by them).

221. Griffith, *Uncovering a Gatekeeper: Why the SEC Should Mandate Disclosure of Details Concerning Directors' and Officers' Liability Insurance Policies*, 154 U. Pa. L. Rev. 1147, 1165 (2006).

of the standard coverage[222] but that is the only one of the three that is typically called "entity coverage" in the insurance industry.[223]

[3] Necessity of Suit against Director or Officer

Generally, if an officer or director is *not* sued, the first two coverages would not apply.[224] For example, a tenant/shareholder brought a suit alleging the board of directors of her cooperative refused to allow her to sublease her apartment, but no directors or officers were named as defendants in the action. The policy limited recovery to those instances where an officer or director was entitled to indemnification from the corporation or was obligated to pay an amount based on his or her legal liability for an actual or asserted wrongful act. The court said no showing could be made that the underlying action fit within the coverage, because no directors or officers were named as defendants in it and, therefore, the cooperative corporation was not entitled to defense and indemnification.[225]

---

222. Dobiac, *I Came, I Saw, I Underwrote: D&O Liability Insurance's Past Underwriting Practices and Potential Future Directions*, 14 Conn. Ins. L.J. 487, 491 (2008) (Sides A and B coverage are generally referred to as "standard coverage").

223. Skilling, *Coverage for Ill-Gotten Gains?: Discussing the (Un)Insurability of Restitution and Disgorgement*, 72 Wash. & Lee L. Rev. 1077, 1084 (2015) (Side C coverage is commonly referred to as "entity" coverage and applies to claims against company itself); Baker & Griffith, *The Missing Monitor in Corporate Governance: The Directors' & Officers' Liability Insurer*, 95 Geo. L.J. 1795, 1802 (2007).

224. The D&O policy does not cover the costs of an action a director or officer brings against other directors or officers or the association over actions by them that may have wronged the plaintiff. *See, e.g.*, Brooks-Mccollum v. State Farm Ins. Co., 2009 U.S. Dist. LEXIS 106802 (D. Del. Nov. 10, 2009) (D&O coverage did not provide any benefits to insured—director seeking indemnification for expenses in pursuing litigation against other directors and association—against whom no claim has been brought, nor did it provide coverage to insured who filed action).

225. 34th Ave. Apt. Corp. v. Nationwide Mut. Ins. Co., 283 A.D.2d 604, 725 N.Y.S.2d 98 (2001). *See also* Medical Mut. Ins. Co. v. Indian Harbor Ins. Co., 583 F.3d 57, 59 (1st Cir. 2009) (extending coverage to situations in which directors and officers are not themselves actual targets of claims made would transmogrify D&O policies into comprehensive corporate liability policies, and that is contrary to both letter and spirit of D&O policy at issue); State Auto Prop. & Cas. Ins. Co. v. Highland Terrace Counsel of Co-Owners, Inc., 2015 U.S. Dist. LEXIS 59663 (W.D. Ky. May 7, 2015) (as no directors were named as defendants in underlying litigation, no claims were made against them and, without claims against directors, there was no need for indemnification); Am. Sec. Bank & Trust Co. v. Progressive Cas. Ins. Co., 2011 U.S. Dist. LEXIS 68231 (M.D. Tenn. June 24, 2011) (D&O policies exist to fund indemnification covenants that protect corporate directors and officers from personal liability, not to protect corporation by which they are employed and, therefore, policies do not extend coverage to situations in which directors and officers are not themselves actual targets of the claims made and to do so would violate intent of D&O policy and run counter to usual, natural, and ordinary meaning of policy language); American Continental Ins. Co. v. American Casualty Co., 86 Cal. App. 4th 929, 940, 103 Cal. Rptr. 2d 632, 640, n.8 (2001) (corporations often are held vicariously liable for torts of their directors and officers, yet where tort victim elects to bring claims against corporation, but not individual directors or officers, those claims are insufficient to justify coverage under directors and officers liability policies, which typically extend coverage only to directors and officers); Buckingham Apartments, Ltd. v. Liberty Mut. Ins. Co., 124 A.D.2d 774, 508 N.Y.S.2d 493 (1986).

[4] Acting within Scope of Duties

Coverage under a D&O policy is only extended to persons in their capacities as directors and officers.[226] To that end, a policy may define an "insured" to include directors and officers "while acting within the scope of their duties for" the association.[227] More likely, the policy will provide that it covers claims arising out of wrongful acts and will define "wrongful acts" as being committed by an insured person in his or her insured position or capacity for the insured organization.[228] No matter how it accomplishes it, the D&O policy only provides coverage for actions or omissions of officers and directors while they were acting as officers or directors.[229]

For example, two neighbors are standing outside their homes arguing about their favorite sports teams and one neighbor becomes so angry he punches the other. Even assuming the D&O policy had no exclusions barring coverage for intentional bodily injury, the fact that the person who threw the punch happened to serve on the association governing board would not implicate the policy because he was not acting in his role as a director.

The duties of the officers and directors may be addressed in any applicable common interest community enabling legislation. For example, the Uniform Common Interest Ownership Act provides that what it calls the "executive board" acts on behalf of the association.[230] It has a long list of the powers and duties of the association. These include adopting and amending bylaws and rules; adopting and amending budgets; collecting assessments for common expenses; investing funds of the association; hiring and discharging managing agents and other employees, agents, and independent contractors; instituting, defending, or

226. Plitt, Maldonado & Rogers, 9A *Couch on Insurance 3d* § 131:32 (Thomson/West, 2005 with 2016 supp.) (to be within coverage, officer or director must be sued solely because he or she was officer or director and was discharging duties to corporation when actionable conduct arose). Quinn & Levin, *Directors and Officers Liability Insurance: Probable Directions in Texas Law*, 20 Rev. Litig. 381, 412 (2001) (line between being director and something else—for example, stockholder—can be difficult to draw, and courts usually err on side of protecting insureds); Johnston, *Corporate Indemnification and Liability Insurance for Directors and Officers*, 33 Bus. Law. 1993, 2015 (1978) (insuring clause only covers losses from wrongful acts by directors and officers "in their respective capacities," meaning insurer may deny coverage if it believes director or officer was acting in some other capacity or for his or her own account).

227. *See* N. Sec. Ins. Co. v. Sandpiper Vill. Condo. Trust, 24 Mass. L. Rep. 500 (Mass. Super. Ct. 2008).

228. *See, e.g.*, ISO Form BP 17 24 01 10, § H.8.

229. *See, e.g.*, Far Northwest Dev. Co., LLC v. Cmty. Ass'n of Underwriters of Am., Inc., 2007 U.S. Dist. LEXIS 28355 (W.D. Wash. Apr. 16, 2007), *rev'd on other grounds*, 297 Fed. Appx. 694 (9th Cir. 2008) (where complaint alleged that sole officer and director of association who was also managing partner of development company was, as developer, responsible for water intrusion that resulted from number of construction defects, that was not damage for which he as director/officer, was legally liable).

230. Uniform Common Interest Ownership Act. § 3-103(a). Otherwise, the section only specifies one board duty: adopting a budget. Uniform Common Interest Ownership Act. § 3-103(c).

intervening in litigation, arbitration, mediation, or administrative proceedings in its own name on behalf of itself or two or more unit owners on matters affecting the community; making contracts and incurring liabilities; regulating the use, maintenance, repair, replacement, and modification of common elements; and making additional improvements to the common elements.[231]

Even if there is no applicable enabling legislation, the governing documents—usually the bylaws—usually specify the powers and duties of officers and directors. Indeed, the Uniform Common Interest Ownership Act provides that the bylaws of an association must specify the powers and duties of directors and officers.[232] An association should review its documents to identify what powers and duties are given to the directors and officers and confer with its broker and attorney to determine if the description of powers and duties is sufficient for purposes of D&O coverage.

Attorneys who serve on governing boards need to consider the scope of duties. For instance, if an attorney offers legal advice to his or her colleagues on the board, is he or she acting within the scope of his or her duties to the association? One commentary on D&O insurance says a lawyer/director may in some circumstances face questions about whether the D&O policy or his or her malpractice insurance policy applies.[233]

[5] Organization Direct Coverage—Side C

Side C coverage is said to be the least common type of D&O insurance.[234] It reimburses the *organization* for judgments against itself, even if the officers or

231. Uniform Common Interest Ownership Act. § 3-102(a). Other duties stated in that provision are acquiring, holding, encumbering, and conveying in its own name any right, title, or interest to real estate or personal property, granting easements, leases, licenses, and concessions through or over the common elements, imposing and receiving any payments, fees, or charges, imposing charges for late payment of assessments and fines for violations of the documents, providing for indemnification of officers and directors and maintaining directors and officers liability insurance, assigning the right to future income, exercising any other powers conferred by the documents, that may be exercised in by organizations of the same type, or any other powers necessary and proper for the governance and operation of the association, requiring that disputes be submitted to nonbinding alternative dispute resolution as a prerequisite to commencement of a judicial proceeding, and suspending any right or privilege of a unit owner that fails to pay an assessment

232. Uniform Common Interest Ownership Act. § 3-106(a)(3).

233. Quinn & Levin, *Directors and Officers Liability Insurance: Probable Directions in Texas Law*, 20 Rev. Litig. 381, 401 (2001). *See generally* McCutcheon, *Professional Liability Insurance Issues for Lawyers Sitting on Corporate Boards*, 25 The Brief 8 (1996).

234. Dobiac, *I Came, I Saw, I Underwrote: D&O Liability Insurance's Past Underwriting Practices and Potential Future Directions*, 14 Conn. Ins. L.J. 487, 491 (2008). *But see* Ackerman, *A Common Law Approach to D&O Insurance "In Fact" Exclusion Disputes*, 79 U. Chi. L. Rev. 1429, 1432–33 (2012) (majority of organizations purchase all three types of coverage, but substantial minority opts for only Sides A and B coverage). An interesting historical note is that Sides A and B coverage can be traced to the original Lloyd's of London D&O form, while Side C coverage is a newer development. Griffith, *Uncovering a Gatekeeper: Why the SEC Should Mandate Disclosure*

directors are not also named defendants.[235] Some insurers will require a higher retention or deductible for Side C coverage than for the other coverages.[236] For non-profit corporations, Side C may provide coverage for many kinds of claims other than those not specifically excluded,[237] whereas in publicly held for-profit corporations, the coverage is often limited to securities claims.[238] The D&O policy likely has an "other insurance" clause that makes it excess to any other insurance. Thus, Side C coverage will generally only be triggered after the limits of any other policy—for example, a CGL policy—have been exhausted. Additionally, in the case of a CGL policy, the D&O policy will probably exclude coverage for some or virtually all of the perils insured against in that CGL policy. Therefore, if the association is paying for Side C coverage, it should discuss with its broker precisely what additional coverage it is receiving for that payment.

[6] Endorsements

An endorsement can change either the Declarations Page or the body of the policy by making additions or deletions. As many as 30 to 50 endorsements may be added to a D&O policy form.[239] It is important to be aware of an oddity in D&O policies identified by one commentary: endorsements often come first, frequently appearing before the standardized body of the policy.[240] No matter where they appear, they have the same effect: they change the policy.

---

of Details Concerning Directors' and Officers' Liability Insurance Policies, 154 U. Pa. L. Rev. 1147, 1164 (2006)

235. Ackerman, *A Common Law Approach to D&O Insurance "In Fact" Exclusion Disputes*, 79 U. Chi. L. Rev. 1429, 1432 (2012). *See also* Dobiac, *I Came, I Saw, I Underwrote: D&O Liability Insurance's Past Underwriting Practices and Potential Future Directions*, 14 Conn. Ins. L.J. 487, 491–92 (2008) (Side C protects corporation from risk of shareholder litigation to which corporate entity is itself a party).

236. Griffith, *Uncovering a Gatekeeper: Why the SEC Should Mandate Disclosure of Details Concerning Directors' and Officers' Liability Insurance Policies*, 154 U. Pa. L. Rev. 1147, 1167 (2006) (insurer may insist on higher retention amount for Side C claims and significant coinsurance percentage).

237. *See, e.g.*, 360 Condo. B Ass'n v. United States Liab. Ins. Co., 2012 U.S. Dist. LEXIS 193086 (S.D. Fla. Dec. 20, 2012) (policy provided insurer would pay on behalf of organization all loss it became legally obligated to pay on account of any claim first made against it during policy period or extended reporting period, if exercised, for wrongful act taking place before or during policy period).

238. 4 Jeffery E. Thomas, *New Appleman on Insurance Law Library Edition* § 26.05[1] (LexisNexis 2023).

239. Kokinda, *D&O Liability Insurance: There Are Exclusions, and Then There Are Exclusions*, 28-10 ABIJ 46 (2010) (multiple amendments may apply to same basic coverage clause, creating increased potential uncertainty and ambiguity).

240. Quinn & Levin, *Directors and Officers Liability Insurance: Probable Directions in Texas Law*, 20 Rev. Litig. 381, 415 (2001).

§ 14.10 The Declarations Page

The Declarations Page is not merely informational. It contains vitally important data that defines the scope of coverage. Keep in mind that a stand-alone policy will have its own Declarations Page while an endorsement will be listed in the Declarations Page of the policy to which it is attached. The endorsement may include basic information—the named insured, the limit of liability, the deductible,[241] and the pending or prior litigation date—with other information left to the Declarations Page of the primary policy.[242]

At the top of the Declarations Page will be the name of the insurer, the type of policy, and policy number. The policy itself will likely be a standard form, so the policy number is not likely to appear on it. The policy number is generally needed to submit a claim.

Next, the Declarations Page will identify the name of the insured organization and its address. The name of the insured as it appears on the Declarations Page should be the legal name of the association in the governing documents, not a name by which it is popularly known.[243] It is also important in a CIC to take into account any layers of associations. For example, a community may consist of several condominium or townhouse associations, a recreation association, and a master or umbrella association, all with similar sounding names. Each of these will have distinct responsibilities spelled out in their respective governing documents. It is important to determine that the Declarations Page lists the proper association as named insured.[244]

---

241. The deductible amount may be different for different parts of the coverage.

242. *See* ISO Form BP 17 24 01 10.

243. *Consider* Far Northwest Dev. Co., LLC v. Cmty. Ass'n of Underwriters of Am., Inc., 2006 U.S. Dist. LEXIS 79033 (W.D. Wash. Oct. 30, 2006), where the policy was issued to the "Somerset Village Townhomes Condominium," rather than the association. It was argued that the condominium was merely a building and, therefore, not a legal entity capable of owning anything. The court found it clear that the intent of the parties was to provide coverage to the association and, therefore, the association was the named insured regardless of the Declarations Page. *See also* Atain Specialty Ins. Co. v. Thousand Oaks Prop. Owners Ass'n, 2015 U.S. Dist. LEXIS 181490 (S.D. Tex. June 29, 2015), where the court said the association was "Thousand Oaks Property Owners Association, Inc. a/k/a Thousand Oaks Homeowners Association."

244. Note that courts may look beyond the actual name listed on the Declarations Page to the intent of the parties. *See, e.g.*, El-Ad 250 West LLC v. Zurich Am. Ins. Co., 2016 N.Y. Misc. LEXIS 1239, 2016 NY Slip Op. 30595(U) (N.Y. Sup. Ct. Mar. 30, 2016) (if policy inaccurately recites party for whom it was intended, that coverage for subject risk would be available, that intended insured could receive coverage, despite not being named in policy; equitable reformation of policy could be employed to correct obvious inadvertent misidentification of named insured). Courts will not, however, ignore the fact that an entirely different entity is the named insured. In *Board of Mgrs. of the Schaefer Landing N. Condominium v. Continental Cas. Co.*, 2011 N.Y. Misc. LEXIS 428 (Sup. Ct., Feb. 18, 2011), condominium unit owners sued the governing board of their association. The board sought coverage from an insurer that issued *umbrella* liability policies from 2001 to 2010. The carrier responded that the polices were issued to a risk-purchasing company, and the board and the association were not listed as insureds on any of those policies, with one exception. Indeed, the

The address will likely be that of the community association management company. That is generally best because the management company address is a business office, and someone will be in that office on weekdays to examine the mail. No one keeps regular business hours in most common interest communities; in fact, the officers and directors may have another residence and, therefore, spend considerable time away from the property. Of course, if the management office address is on the Declarations Page, the association governing board needs to make sure the manager gives the board immediate notice of any correspondence from the insurer.

The Declarations Page will also state the policy period.[245] That needs to be checked carefully. It may be for one year or multiple years.[246] When the D&O coverage is added by endorsement, the period of the main policy governs unless it is specifically stated in the endorsement that the coverage period is different from the main policy coverage period.[247]

The limit of liability will appear on the Declarations Page and will likely state that it is inclusive of defense costs, a fact that may not be prominently stated in the policy. However, the policy *will* in all likelihood *define* "defense costs."

The Declarations Page will state the premium paid for the policy period, any premium for a "discovery period," and the length of the discovery period.[248] The deductible, or retention, will also be found on the Declarations Page together with when it applies and when it does not.

---

association did not exist until 2005. Thus, the only coverage at issue was under the one policy issued in the name of the association.

245. *See generally* Sagalow, *Directors and Officers Liability Insurance: A Guide for Directors, Professional Edition*, at 16, available at: http://innovationinsurancegroup.com/wp-content/uploads/2014/07/D_O_Handbook_Professional_Edition.pdf (retroactive or prior acts date is starting point for coverage, that is, first date in which covered wrongful acts may occur and if retroactive date is concurrent with inception date of policy, for any claim to be covered, both wrongful acts alleged and claim arising out of those acts have to occur during policy period).

246. *See, e.g.*, Citrus Course Homeowners Ass'n v. Great Am. Ins. Co., 2016 U.S. Dist. LEXIS 10199 (C.D. Cal. Jan. 7, 2016) (HOA insured under D&O policy from claims initiated against it for period of one year). *See generally* Ross, *Director and Officer Liability: Protecting Corporate Directors and Officers: Insurance and Other Alternatives*, 40 Vand. L. Rev. 775, 777, n.15 (1987) (while three-year policy terms once were common, today few carriers are willing to extend coverage beyond one year).

247. *See* Clark v. General Accident Ins. Co. PR., 1996 U.S. Dist. LEXIS 20809 (D.V.I. Mar. 5, 1996), where the D&O coverage was added by endorsement to another policy that constituted one policy with continuous coverage for three years. The D&O endorsement did not state that its coverage was not for the same period as the main policy. The insurer pointed to a statement in the upper left corner of the endorsement that the effective period was for January of 1989 through January of 1990. The court said that, assuming the intent of the insurer was to provide three separate D&O policies, "each with a coverage period of one year, the policy was inartfully drawn." The court concluded that it would be difficult to glean the intent to limit the D&O coverage to one year from the language of the endorsement. Another court might reach a different conclusion, but the lesson of the case is that if a D&O endorsement is added to a principal policy with a multi-year term, the policyholder needs to establish definitively the term of the D&O coverage.

248. For discussion of discovery periods, see § 14.13, *infra*.

The insured may have a folder full of information from or about the insurer with addresses for the company, but the address for giving the company notice is the one stated on the Declarations Page. Use of another address allows the company to contend it did not receive notice, and with some justification, as notice sent to the wrong address may not be forwarded, and in the case of a claim, even if it is forwarded, it may not provide notice within the prescribed period.

Usually the last item of information on the Declarations Page is the list of attached endorsements. In order to understand the coverage provided by the policy it is critical for an association to discuss the endorsements with its broker as they add or subtract coverage found in the policy.

§ 14.11 The Insuring Agreement

The insuring agreement describes the party's rights and duties and the coverage the policy provides.[249] D&O insurance is generally "all-risk" coverage, meaning it is not limited to covering certain named risks, but covers all claims for wrongful acts not specifically excluded.[250] The insuring language tends, therefore, to be broad. While there is a great deal of variety in D&O policies, their insuring agreements are, as one observer notes, remarkably similar.[251] For that reason, when comparing policies, the fact that the insuring agreements may be nearly identical does not mean the coverage is the same. The definitions and exclusions—which can vary greatly from policy to policy—can render the coverage of one D&O policy very different from that of another.

[1] Liability for Loss

An insuring agreement generally states the insurer will *pay on behalf of the insureds* any loss an insured person becomes "legally obligated to pay"[252] as the result of a claim first made during the policy period, or any extended reporting or discovery period, for a wrongful act.[253]

The ISO D&O endorsement has three insuring agreements. The first is for "Management Liability" and provides the insurer will pay on behalf of an insured

---

249. 1 Jeffery E. Thomas, *New Appleman on Insurance Law Library Edition* § 1.07[5] (LexisNexis 2023).

250. 4 Jeffery E. Thomas, *New Appleman on Insurance Law Library Edition* § 26.05[2] (LexisNexis 2023).

251. Quinn & Levin, *Directors and Officers Liability Insurance: Probable Directions in Texas Law*, 20 Rev. Litig. 381, 419 (2001).

252. In one case an insurer argued that "legally obligated to pay" refers to tort liability, not to damages for breach of contract. The court, however, concluded the phrase would encompass any obligation that was binding and enforceable under law, whether pursuant to contract or tort liability. Sigma Chi Corp. v. Westchester Fire Ins. Co., 587 F. Supp. 2d 891, 896 (N.D. Ill. 2008).

253. Non-Profit Management and Organization Liability Insurance Policy § I.A. The policy only covers losses as a result of any claim "first made" and "reported in writing" to the company during the policy period.

person any loss the insured person becomes legally obligated to pay as a result of a claim first made against that person during the policy period or during any extended reporting period except to the extent the association has indemnified that person for the loss.[254] This is what is known as "Side A" coverage, and in a policy not specifically designed for common interest community associations, may refer to payment on behalf of directors or officers as opposed to on behalf of "an insured person." In the ISO endorsement, the insuring agreement labeled "Association Reimbursement" states that the insurer will pay on behalf of the association any loss for which it has indemnified an insured person, as permitted or required by law, and which the insured person becomes legally obligated to pay as a result of a claim first made against him or her during the policy period or any extended reporting period.[255] This is "Side B" coverage, and in a policy not specifically designed for common interest community associations, rather than refer to the association, it will probably refer to the named insured. In either event, the association is only covered to the extent that it may indemnify its directors and officers—or any other insured—for a covered loss incurred by them.[256] Side B coverage is essential because most governing documents provide for indemnification of directors for certain legal liabilities.[257]

Finally, under the ISO endorsement insuring agreement for "Association Liability," the carrier will pay on behalf of the association any loss the association becomes legally obligated to pay as a result of a claim first made against it during the policy period or during any extended reporting period.[258] This is called "Side C" coverage and without it, the policy does not provide coverage directly to the association for defense of claims against it.[259]

Note that the Side C coverage applies to claims made against the named insured, in other words, the association. A California association sought coverage under a policy that provided coverage for losses arising from a claim first made against the named insured where the underlying suit was against all the members of the association. The insurer denied coverage because the claim was not "made" against the association, that is, the association was not the named defendant. The court, however, found that the association had a statutory right to

---

254. *See* ISO Form BP 17 24 01 10 § A.1.a. The insurance, however, applies only to a claim that arises out of a wrongful act committed by the *insured person* that occurs on or after the retroactive date, if any, and before the end of the policy period.

255. *See* ISO Form BP 17 24 01 10 § A.2. The insurance, however, applies only to a claim that arises out of a wrongful act committed by the *insured person* that occurs on or after the retroactive date, if any, and before the end of the policy period.

256. Clark v. General Accident Ins. Co. PR., 951 F. Supp. 559 (D.V.I. 1997).

257. Winzenburg, *Condominium Law and Practice: Forms* § 49.04[7] (Matthew Bender & Company, 2007).

258. *See* ISO Form BP 17 24 01 10 § A.3. The insurance, however, applies only to a claim that arises out of a wrongful act committed by the *association* that occurs on or after the retroactive date, if any, and before the end of the policy period.

259. Clark v. General Accident Ins. Co. PR., 951 F. Supp. 559 (D.V.I. 1997).

defend an action against its members and the claim was, therefore "made against" the association under the terms of the policy.[260] The statute to which the court referred provides that an association has standing to institute, defend, settle, or intervene in litigation, arbitration, mediation, or administrative proceedings in its own name as the real party in interest and without joining with it the members in action that pertain to enforcement of the governing documents, damage to the common area, damage to a separate interest that the association is obligated to maintain or repair, or damage to a separate interest that arises out of, or is integrally related to, damage to the common area or a separate interest that the association is obligated to maintain or repair.[261] Some states have similar statutes.[262]

Note that as a "claims-made" policy, the coverage is for claims made during the policy period even though the wrongful act on which the claim is made may have happened before the policy period. Some policies will make this explicit. Others will contain a cutoff date—which should appear on the Declarations Page—under which coverage only applies when the wrongful act is committed on or after that date and before the end of the policy period.[263] The "pay on behalf" language typically found in D&O policies means the company must pay a covered loss once the insured becomes legally obligated to pay it, rather than after the insured has paid it.[264] The definitions of "claim," "loss," "insured," and "wrongful act" are needed to fully understand the scope of coverage. These are discussed below.[265]

---

260. Mkt. Lofts Cmty. Ass'n v. Nat'l Union Fire Ins. Co., 2015 U.S. Dist. LEXIS 100691 (C.D. Cal. July 30, 2015). The court also found that the term "made against" to be ambiguous in part because it could reasonably be read to cover a complaint in which an association has a statutory right to defend and which names the members of the association as defendants in an apparent improper attempt to circumvent the association's interest.

261. Cal. Civ. Code § 5980.

262. *See, e.g.*, 765 Ill. Comp. Stat. 605/9.1(b) (governing board has standing and capacity to act in representative capacity in relation to matters involving common elements or more than one unit, on behalf of the unit owners, as their interests may appear); Tex. Prop. Code § 82.102(a)(4) (unless otherwise provided by declaration, association, acting through its board, may institute, defend, intervene in, settle, or compromise litigation or administrative proceedings in its own name on behalf of itself or two or more-unit owners on matters affecting condominium). *See also* Fla. R. Civ. P. 1.221 (homeowners or condominium association, after control is obtained by homeowners or unit owners other than developer, may institute, maintain, settle, or appeal actions or hearings in its name on behalf of all association members concerning matters of common interest to those members).

263. *See* ISO Form BP 17 24 01 10 § A.1.a.

264. 4 Jeffery E. Thomas, *New Appleman on Insurance Law Library Edition* § 26.05[3] (LexisNexis 2023).

265. *See* § 14.12, *infra*.

[2] Defense

Some policies do not require the insurer to provide a defense;[266] however, a usual second part of the insuring agreement addresses defense of suits. Typically, the defense portion of the insuring agreement begins by stating that the insurer has the "right and duty" to defend any claim covered by the policy.[267] It may add that a defense will be provided even for claims that are groundless, false, or fraudulent,[268] or it may state that the insurer has no duty to defend against a claim to which the insurance does not apply.[269] The policy may also explicitly state that the insurer's duty to defend terminates on exhaustion of the limit of liability. A stand-alone policy will almost certainly require the insured to cooperate in the defense and agree not to settle the claim, incur defense cost, or admit liability without the written consent of the insurer. It will also allow the insurer to settle a claim—with the consent of the insured—and address the consequences when an insured withholds consent. The standard ISO endorsement only says it may settle any claim with the consent of the insured[270] and discusses lack of consent in a separate section.[271]

Instead of a duty to defend, a policy may provide that the insurer will pay defense costs.[272] Some of these policies require the carrier to advance defense

266. Munro, *Defense Within Limits: The Conflicts of "Wasting" Or "Cannibalizing" Insurance Policies*, 62 Mont. L. Rev. 131, 133 (2001) (some D&O policies contain no duty to defend and leave defense costs entirely to insured). In the early years of D&O insurance, a duty to defend was not included in policies. Sagalow, *Directors and Officers Liability Insurance: A Guide for Directors, Professional Edition*, at 41, available at: http://innovationinsurancegroup.com/wp-content/uploads/2014/07/D_O_Handbook_Professional_Edition.pdf (historically, D&O policies have been written without duty to defend provisions).

267. *See, e.g.*, Non-Profit Management and Organization Liability Insurance Policy § I.B.

268. Fireman's Fund Ins. Co. v. Univ. of Ga. Ath. Ass'n, 288 Ga. App. 355, 654 S.E.2d 207, 209 (2007) (where policy imposes duty to defend even if allegations are groundless, false, or fraudulent, courts look to allegations of complaint to determine whether liability covered by policy is asserted).

269. *See* State Auto Prop. & Cas. Ins. Co. v. Highland Terrace Counsel of Co-Owners, Inc., 2015 U.S. Dist. LEXIS 59663 (W.D. Ky. May 7, 2015) (where underlying suit was brought only against association, it contended that because policy defined "wrongful act" to include acts attributed to both association and its directors, it was entitled to defense in underlying action, but court, citing provision stating insurer had no duty to defend suits as result of wrongful acts not covered by coverage form, insurer was not required to provide coverage under D&O policy and because it was not required to provide coverage, it did not need to provide defense).

270. *See* ISO Form BP 17 24 01 10 § A.4.

271. *See* ISO Form BP 17 24 01 10 § F.

272. Ackerman, *A Common Law Approach to D&O Insurance "In Fact" Exclusion Disputes*, 79 U. Chi. L. Rev. 1429, 1454 (2012) (noting that smaller organizations often have D&O policies that include duty to defend, while larger entities tend to have policies that instead include duty to advance defense costs in which insured control its own defense of claims and carrier periodically advances sums to insured for cost of that defense with carrier retaining right to "associate" with defense meaning it is entitled to obtain certain information, to consent to settlement, to specify list of defense counsel from which insured must choose, and to control cost of defense in some

costs while under others the insured is reimbursed when the claim is settled.[273] One expert recommends the former, noting that the latter requires the *insured* to pay all costs, including attorney's fees, out of pocket and wait for repayment, and that can be ruinous for non-profits like CICs because D&O litigation can be prolonged and costly to defend.[274]

The most often repeated statement in the law of liability insurance is that the duty of an insurer to defend its insured is broader than its duty to indemnify.[275] As the Wisconsin Supreme Court explained, the duty to defend is broader than the duty to indemnify because the former arises from allegations contained in the complaint, whereas the latter is supported by fully developed facts and, thus, a carrier may be obligated to defend claims it ultimately may not be obligated to indemnify.[276] The extent of the duty to defend varies from jurisdiction to jurisdiction. The general rule is that the duty arises when the allegations against the insured state a claim potentially within the scope of the policy's coverage.[277] In

ways including by negotiating with defense counsel and monitoring counsel to reduce unnecessary discovery or motion practice).

273. *But see* Clark v. Travelers Cas. Ins. Co. of Am., 2015 U.S. Dist. LEXIS 114877 (C.D. Cal. Aug. 28, 2015) (D&O policy did not provide for duty to defend and stated carrier would not be called to assume charge of settlement or defense of any claim or suit brought, or proceeding instituted against, any insured; court did not decide whether insurer would have duty to reimburse defense costs at some later date).

274. Davis, *Professional Liability and Governance Exposures: A Closer Look* (Nonprofit Risk Management Center 2017), available at: https://www.nonprofitrisk.org/resources/articles/professional-liability-and-governance-exposures-a-closer-look/.

275. *See, e.g.*, Western Alliance Ins. Co. v. Northern Ins. Co., 176 F.3d 825, 829 (5th Cir. 1999); EMC Ins. Cos. v. Mid-Continent Cas. Co., 884 F. Supp. 2d 1147, 1155 (D. Colo. 2012) (duty to defend is triggered more easily than is duty to indemnify); Phila. Indem. Ins. Co. v. Yachtsman's Inn Condo Ass'n, 595 F. Supp. 2d 1319, 1322 (S.D. Fla. 2009); Henly v. Phillips Abita Lumber Co., 971 So. 2d 1104, 1109 (La. App. 2007).

276. Toldt Woods Condos. Owner's Ass'n v. Madeline Square, LLC, 314 Wis. 2d 259, 757 N.W.2d 850 (2008).

277. Ackerman, *A Common Law Approach to D&O Insurance "In Fact" Exclusion Disputes*, 79 U. Chi. L. Rev. 1429, 1450 (2012). *See, e.g.*, Lime Tree Village Community Club Ass'n v. State Farm Gen. Ins. Co., 980 F.2d 1402 (11th Cir. 1993) (where homeowners filed suit over changes in age restrictions, insurer argued it had no duty to defend because underlying complaint alleged only excluded intentional acts, but court found duty to defend turned on grounds for liability expressed by allegations of fact in underlying complaint under which liability could be based on unintended slander of title or unintended restraint of trade, grounds other than intentional acts and discrimination and if facts alleged show any basis for imposing liability that falls within policy coverage, insurer has duty to defend). *See also* Land v. Auto-Owners Ins. Co., 511 Fed. Appx. 795 (10th Cir. 2013) (where owner in homeowners association alleged president engaged in illegal debt-collection efforts in violation of federal Racketeering Influenced and Corrupt Organizations Act (RICO) and comparable state law, lower court held complaint alleged deceptive or criminal intent and as result allegations were plainly within policy, but appellate court found that in looking beyond conclusory allegations of fraud and conspiracy, factual allegations of underlying complaint clearly alleged president committed negligent acts, errors, omissions, or breaches of duty directly related to management of premises—covered wrongful acts—and did not fall solely and entirely within policy exclusions); Villa Charlotte Bronte, Inc. v. Commercial Union Ins. Co., 487 N.Y.S.2d 314, 64 N.Y.2d 846, 476 N.E.2d 640 (1985) (vice president of cooperative was entitled to defense on

most states, if any one claim might be covered, the insurer has to defend against all the claims, while in others the carrier has to defend even if the complaint does not allege a covered claim.[278] A broad duty to defend provision may be incorporated into the policy as previously noted, because some policies provide that the duty applies even if any of the allegations against the insured are groundless, false, or fraudulent.

Courts have held that a D&O insurer has to defend when there is an allegation in a suit against the directors of a common interest community that they breached a fiduciary duty. For example, a suit was brought alleging directors of a cooperative governing board breached fiduciary duties owed to the corporation and to the individual shareholders when they approved a surcharge on the maintenance of tenants who sublet their apartments. The insurer sought to avoid its duty to defend. The court agreed with the insurer that the complaint "largely asserted" intentional wrongdoing by the directors. However, the court added that there was no "patent inconsistency" between a negligence theory and the acts and omissions alleged. It noted that the second cause of action asserted the directors breached their fiduciary duties by improperly conducting a shareholders' meeting and by arbitrarily and capriciously imposing unreasonable charges. Harm caused by arbitrary and capricious acts need not, said the court, be intentional, and the allegation, if proven, could support a finding that the directors acted negligently. Because claims were asserted that suggested a reasonable possibility of coverage under the D&O policy, the insurer was obligated to defend the action unless a policy exclusion applied or the action was otherwise exempted from coverage.[279]

[3] The Meaning of "Claims-Made"

Almost all D&O policies are "claims-made."[280] Other policies a community association purchases will be "occurrence" policies, meaning they protect the "policy holder against occurrences that happen during the policy period and for which

---

allegedly defamatory statements that underlying complaint charged him with making on behalf of corporation because insurer could only be excused from defense if, under language of exclusion, it could establish, as matter of law, that there was no possible factual or legal basis on which insurer might eventually be obligated to indemnify insured under any provision contained in policy and it could not do so at summary judgment stage of proceedings before several factual issues were resolved).

278. Ackerman, *A Common Law Approach to D&O Insurance "In Fact" Exclusion Disputes*, 79 U. Chi. L. Rev. 1429, 1451–52 (2012)

279. Hotel Des Artistes v. Transamerica Ins. Co., 1994 U.S. Dist. LEXIS 7800 (S.D.N.Y. June 10, 1994). *See also* N. Sec. Ins. Co. v. Sandpiper Vill. Condo. Trust, 24 Mass. L. Rep. 500 (Mass. Super. Ct. 2008) (where condominium unit owner alleged negligence and breach of fiduciary duty in complaint, under terms of Directors and Officers Liability Endorsement duty to defend was triggered).

280. 4 Jeffery E. Thomas, *New Appleman on Insurance Law Library Edition* § 26.02 (LexisNexis 2023).

claims may arise later."[281] In contrast, a D&O policy provides coverage for covered claims made against an insured during the policy period, even though any breach of duty and causal process that gives rise to the claim may have ended long before the policy period.[282] In other words, "regardless of the date of the original occurrence giving rise to the lawsuit against the insured, only claims filed with the insurer during the policy period will be covered."[283] Obviously, to fully understand the meaning of "claims-made," one must know the meaning of the word "claim." That is discussed below.[284]

The nature of claims-made coverage makes it essential that a CIC association continuously renew its D&O coverage because claims may be made years after the alleged wrongdoing happened and if a policy is purchased only for the year in which that alleged wrongdoing happened and not renewed for subsequent years, a later claim based on prior wrongdoing would not be covered.[285] D&O policies issued to CICs may include a "pending and prior litigation date" exclusion in which the insurer is not liable to pay for a loss connected to a claim based on, arising out of, resulting from, or in any way involving litigation on or prior to the stated date.[286] However, the policies generally do not have a "prior acts" exclusion, which would exclude claims first made during the policy period for alleged wrongdoing that occurred before the policy was in force.[287]

---

281. Am. Auto. Ins. Co. v. Murray, 658 F.3d 311, 323, n.8 (3d Cir. Pa. 2011) (claims-made policy protects against claims made during life of a policy as opposed to occurrence policy, which protects against occurrences that happen during policy period and for which claims may arise later); Township of Center v. First Mercury Syndicate, 117 F.3d 115, 118 (3d Cir. 1997) (claims-made policy, as opposed to occurrence policy, protects against claims made during life of policy, rather than against occurrences that happen during policy period and for which claims may arise later).

282. Quinn & Levin, *Directors and Officers Liability Insurance: Probable Directions in Texas Law*, 20 Rev. Litig. 381, 457 (2001) (when any alleged injury occurred is irrelevant to coverage; instead, when claim was first presented to insured is what is important). *See, e.g.*, Hotel Des Artistes v. Transamerica Ins. Co., 1994 U.S. Dist. LEXIS 7800 (S.D.N.Y. June 10, 1994) (finding that it was irrelevant that triggering event of claims—approval by cooperative board of sublet surcharge—occurred prior to effective date of policy as policy plainly stated it was "claims made").

283. Caraccio, *Void Ab Initio: Application Fraud as Grounds for Avoiding Directors' and Officers' Liability Insurance Coverage*, 74 Calif. L. Rev. 929, 951 (1986). *See also* Ackerman, *A Common Law Approach to D&O Insurance "In Fact" Exclusion Disputes*, 79 U. Chi. L. Rev. 1429, 1433 (2012) (D&O policies are "claims made," meaning they cover all claims made against insured during period policy is effective, regardless of whether those acts that led to liability occurred during policy period).

284. *See* § 14.12[1], *infra*.

285. 4 Jeffery E. Thomas, *New Appleman on Insurance Law Library Edition* § 26.02 (LexisNexis 2023)

286. Non-Profit Management and Organization Liability Insurance Policy § IV(5). The "pending and prior litigation date" will be found on the Declarations Page.

287. 4 Jeffery E. Thomas, *New Appleman on Insurance Law Library Edition* § 26.02 (LexisNexis 2023).

§ 14.12 Definitions: Understanding Common Terms

The definition section will often follow immediately after the insuring agreement. The section will typically include definitions for a dozen or more terms. Four definitions—"claim," "insured person," "loss," and "wrongful act"—are required to understand the insuring clause and are found in virtually all D&O policies. These definitions are discussed below. The remaining commonly found definitions apply to other specific parts of the policy and are discussed where applicable. It is important to recognize that some D&O coverage exclusions can be found within the definitions.[288] One commentary cautions that definitions in insurance policies "are very much like definitions in mathematics: every word means something, every difference is significant, and small differences can have large financial consequences."[289]

[1] Claim

The definition of "claim" seems to be one aspect of D&O policies that is similar in many of them.[290] Almost all policies include four actions in the definition of "claim."[291] The first is a written demand for monetary damages.[292] The second is a civil proceeding commenced by service of a complaint or similar pleading. The third is a criminal proceeding commenced by return of an indictment. The fourth is a formal administrative or regulatory proceeding commenced by filing of a notice of charges, formal investigative order, or similar document. Some policies may specifically include a proceeding before the federal Equal Employment Opportunity Commission, or a similar state or local entity, for a "wrongful employment practice." The definition requires that one of these actions occur. It is not enough that an insured is aware of an alleged injury.[293]

---

288. Kokinda, *D&O Liability Insurance: There Are Exclusions, and Then There Are Exclusions*, 28-10 ABIJ 46 (2010).

289. Quinn & Levin, *Directors and Officers Liability Insurance: Probable Directions in Texas Law*, 20 Rev. Litig. 381, 420–21 (2001).

290. *But see* 3 *New Appleman Law of Liability Insurance* § 22.05[7] (rev. ed., Matthew Bender, 2017) (asserting that there is no "standard" definition of "claim" and it is, therefore, necessary to examine that term closely when evaluating D&O policies).

291. *See generally* Quinn & Levin, *Directors and Officers Liability Insurance: Probable Directions in Texas Law*, 20 Rev. Litig. 381, 462 (2001) (courts tend to construe concept of "claim" fairly narrowly while attorneys who argue D&O cases would probably privately agree that term is complex one, and perhaps even ambiguous).

292. Note that some policies also include a written demand for "non-monetary" relief. *See, e.g.*, Medical Mut. Ins. Co. v. Indian Harbor Ins. Co., 583 F.3d 57, 61 (1st Cir. 2009). Most policies specifically designed for common interest communities, however, appear to omit demands for non-monetary relief from the definition of "claim." *See also* 3 *New Appleman Law of Liability Insurance* § 22.05[7] (rev. ed., Matthew Bender, 2017).

293. Titan Indem. Co. v. Williams, 743 So. 2d 1020 (Miss. App. 1999).

In cases concerning common interest communities, many of the actions that are brought seek to establish the rights of the members of the association, to prohibit the governing board from taking certain action, or to force it to take action. If the policy does not include non-monetary actions within its definition of "claim," these types of suits will likely not be covered under the policy. An association needs to discuss with its broker whether the policy covers non-monetary claims and, if there is doubt, can request an endorsement that specifically defines a claim as a demand for monetary or non-monetary relief.

[a] Written Demand

One commentary describes the first action—a written demand—as "the weakest possible statement that can constitute a claim."[294] The commentary observes that courts have determined that a letter from a lawyer suggesting a client is considering bringing a lawsuit, a threat to bring a lawsuit,[295] or a claim that a wrongful act has occurred are not claims as none is a written demand for monetary damages.[296] One Federal Circuit court observed in interpreting a D&O policy definition that a claim that a wrongful act has occurred is different from a claim for payment *on account of* a wrongful act. The definition does not refer to a claim that wrongdoing occurred but a demand for a discrete amount of money owed to the claimant on account of the alleged wrongdoing.[297] A claimant must

294. Quinn & Levin, *Directors and Officers Liability Insurance: Probable Directions in Texas Law*, 20 Rev. Litig. 381, 460 (2001).

295. *But see* Deer Oaks Office Park Owners Ass'n v. State Farm Lloyds, 2012 U.S. Dist. LEXIS 19240 (W.D. Tex. Feb. 15, 2012) (where letter from unit owner's attorney used word "demand," it placed association on notice that unit owner asserted a right and where letter further warned that attorney had been asked to pursue litigation if satisfactory settlement could not be reached and concluded by saying that if the attorney had not heard any response by specified date, client has instructed attorney to file suit, court found that under any construction, letter constituted claim). One commentary notes that the "demand" letter in *Deer Oaks* did not appear to demand anything in particular. LaCroix, *D&O Insurance: When is a Claim First Made?* (2012), available at: http://www.dandodiary.com/2012/02/articles/d-o-insurance/do-insurance-when-is-a-claim-first-made/. Consider a Florida statute that makes it a precondition of filing a petition for mandatory non-binding arbitration of a condominium dispute that the respondent be given notice of intent to file an arbitration petition "or other legal action" absent resolution of the dispute. Fla. Stat. § 718.1255(4)(b)3. Could that constitute a written demand, or is it merely a threat to bring a legal action?

296. *See, e.g.*, Cal. Union Ins. Co. v. Am. Diversified Sav. Bank, 914 F.2d 1271 (9th Cir. 1990), *cert. den.*, 498 U.S. 1088, 111 S. Ct. 966, 112 L. Ed. 2d 1052 (1991) (term "claim" should not be interpreted so broadly as to include request from regulatory agency to comply with regulations where agency did not directly threaten recipient of letter with liability, made no money demand, and did not demand or challenge something as of right); Hyde v. Fidelity & Deposit Co. of Am., 23 F. Supp. 2d 630, 633 (D. Md. 1998) (notice of wrongful act does not rise to level of claim; claim must be something more than notice).

297. MGIC Indem. Corp. v. Home State Sav. Ass'n, 797 F.2d 285 (6th Cir. Ohio 1986) (mere potential for claims is not enough to meet condition imposed by policy). *See also* Mt. Hood, LLC v. Travelers Cas. & Sur. Co. of Am., 2009 U.S. Dist. LEXIS 16775 (D. Or. Mar. 3, 2009) (demand for monetary relief that preceded filing of lawsuit constituted claim).

press his or her own claim. If a person tells an insured that someone else may make a claim or that they themselves will make one, that is not a claim.[298]

[b] Administrative Proceeding

The fourth of the actions that can constitute a claim is a formal administrative or regulatory proceeding. The definition of "claim" requires a notice of charges, formal investigative order, or "similar document." Is a subpoena issued by a regulatory body a claim? That may depend on the specific facts and circumstances around the subpoena, as well as whether a subpoena is similar to a notice of charges or a formal investigative order.

[c] Arbitration

One action that the language of the typical policy does not explicitly include in the definition of "claim" is *arbitration*.[299] In some common interest communities, the governing documents may require that disputes between individual owners and the association be submitted to arbitration. Indeed, Colorado specifically provides that the declaration, bylaws, or even the rules of a common interest community association *may* specify situations in which disputes *must* be submitted to binding arbitration.[300] Similarly, Illinois allows the declaration or bylaws of a condominium association to "require mediation or arbitration of disputes in which the matter in controversy has either no specific monetary value or a value of $10,000 or less," other than disputes involving levying and collection of assessments or arising out of violations of the declaration, bylaws, or rules and regulations of the association.[301] Depending on the wording of an arbitration clause in the governing documents, it may also apply to disputes involving individual board members.

In some cases, state law may mandate arbitration. For example, Florida law *requires* certain enumerated disputes to be submitted to mandatory *non-binding* arbitration.[302] The arbitration is conducted by an arbitrator employed by the state agency that regulates condominiums, cooperatives, and homeowners associations. It is initiated by a petition to the agency, and that petition must include a demand for relief.[303]

---

298. Quinn & Levin, *Directors and Officers Liability Insurance: Probable Directions in Texas Law*, 20 Rev. Litig. 381 (2001) (claim has not yet been made when one person tells insured corporation that someone else may make claim or, indeed, that they *will* make claim). Note that any of these "non-claims" may still be sufficient to constitute awareness of a possible claim for purposes of the application for insurance.

299. Quinn & Levin, *Directors and Officers Liability Insurance: Probable Directions in Texas Law*, 20 Rev. Litig. 381, 460 (2001).

300. Colo. Rev. Stat. § 38-33.3-124(3).

301. 765 ILCS 605/32.

302. Fla. Stat. § 718.1255.

303. Fla. Stat. § 718.1255(4)(a).

Could a petition for arbitration constitute either a "written demand for monetary damages" or a "civil proceeding commenced by service of a complaint or similar pleading"? California has an article in its Civil Code titled "Alternative Dispute Resolution Prerequisite to Civil Action."[304] Under one provision of that article, neither associations nor their members may file a court action to enforce the governing documents, the applicable corporation law, or the state's Davis-Stirling Common Interest Development Act unless the parties "have endeavored to submit their dispute to alternative dispute resolution,"[305] Alternative dispute resolution means "mediation, arbitration, conciliation, or other nonjudicial procedure that involves a neutral party in the decision making process."[306] Again, will the procedure by which alternative dispute resolution is initiated be considered a "civil proceeding commenced by service of a complaint or similar pleading"?

[d] Modifying Words

It is important to check the language defining "claim" for modifying words. For example, in some policies, "claim" is defined as any of the four actions against an "insured," and insured includes the association.[307] In other policies actions may only meet the definition of "claim" when they are brought against "insured persons" as opposed to the association.[308] The First Circuit Court of Appeals considered a D&O policy with this language.[309] The underlying suit was brought against a corporation. The policy required that a claim be "made against" an insured person. The court said that for a judicial complaint to be "made against" a person, it had to be filed in court and identify the person as a defendant in the action. The corporation observed that the underlying complaint consisted "largely of allegations of misconduct on the part of its directors and officers." The court responded that the policy was not implicated because, no matter the conduct the complaint described, it was not a claim "made against" any of the directors or officers who were the "insured persons."

---

304. Cal. Civ. Code § 5925, *et seq.*

305. Cal. Civ. Code § 5930(a).

306. Cal. Civ. Code § 5925(a).

307. *See* Non-Profit Management and Organization Liability Insurance Policy § II(B).

308. *See, e.g.*, ISO Form BP 17 24 01 10 § H(1)(b), which limits the definition of "claim" to a written demand for monetary damages or civil, criminal, or administrative proceedings against any "insured person." The definition of "insured person" does not include the association. *See* ISO Form BP 17 24 01 10 § H(5).

309. Medical Mut. Ins. Co. v. Indian Harbor Ins. Co., 583 F.3d 57 (1st Cir. 2009) (prayer for injunctive relief against company that incidentally refers to agents of that company does not qualify as claim made against those agents because it does not demand relief from them in their personal capacities; although agents can be enjoined to extent company itself is enjoined, as corporate representatives, they cannot be held legally liable in their personal capacities unless and until they are joined as parties).

The definition of "wrongful act" is important to understanding the meaning of the term "claim" because to meet the definition of "claim," the action usually must be for a wrongful act as defined by the policy. The definition will generally include an appeal from any of these actions.

[2] Insured Person

The definition of "insured person" is obviously critical. A broad definition is recommended,[310] although it should be remembered that the critical "Insured versus Insured" exclusion is triggered when one insured person brings a claim against another.[311]

The policy may simply define the phrase "insured person" to mean former, present, or future directors, officers, trustees,[312] employees, or volunteers of the association.[313] Some policies modify the words "directors and officers" with the phrase "while acting within the scope of their duties for" the association.[314]

---

310. Davis, *Professional Liability and Governance Exposures: A Closer Look* (Nonprofit Risk Management Center 2017), available at: https://www.nonprofitrisk.org/resources/articles/professional-liability-and-governance-exposures-a-closer-look/. The author notes that if the organization is not a named insured, and its only coverage is reimbursement of what it pays to indemnify directors and officers for claims made against them, "there are serious unaddressed exposures."

311. *See* § 14.14[2], *infra*. *See generally How to Soften the Insured vs. Insured Exclusion in Your Client's D&O Insurance Policy* (AmWins Group, Inc. 2015) (adding employees to definition of "insured" as extension of coverage can also implicate insured vs. insured exclusion).

312. There are a number of circumstances in which a common interest community might have trustees. Some cooperatives are under trust ownership in which the members of the governing board are trustees. 2 Rohan & Reskin, *Cooperative Housing Law and Practice—Forms*, § 105[4][a][ii] (Matthew Bender, 2023). Massachusetts law provides for creation of condominium trusts in which the governing board consists of trustees. Mass. G.L. c. 183A, § 8(i). Florida allows for an individual to be appointed as a termination trustee to govern the association during the process of terminating a condominium and then, after dissolution, to conclude the affairs of the association. Fla. Stat. § 718.117(13). The Uniform Common Interest Ownership Act specifically provides that an insurance trustee may hold any insurance proceeds in trust. UCIOA § 3-113(e). States that have not adopted the Uniform Act also provide for insurance trustees to be appointed. *See, e.g.*, 765 Ill. Comp. Stat. 605/12(g) (insurance proceeds for loss must be payable to association or to insurance trustee designated by association for that purpose; insurance trustee or association must hold any insurance proceeds in trust for unit owners and secured parties as their interests may appear).

313. There are some differences between the NMOLIP and ISO language. The former has a definition that includes persons who were, now are, or will become duly elected or appointed directors, trustees, or officers of any insured organization or employees, committee members, or volunteers of any insured organization that is a non-profit entity. *See* Non-Profit Management and Organization Liability Insurance Policy § IV(2)(I). The reference to a "non-profit entity" excludes employees of a community association management firm's employees from the definition. The ISO language simply defines "insured person" as any former, present, or future director, officer, trustee, employee, or volunteer of the association. *See* ISO Form BP 17 24 01 10, § H(5). The ISO phrasing omits reference to committee members, although they may be considered to be volunteers as, indeed, are board members because they are generally uncompensated.

314. *See* N. Sec. Ins. Co. v. Sandpiper Vill. Condo. Trust, 24 Mass. L. Rep. 500 (Mass. Super. Ct. 2008).

[a] "Duly" Elected or Appointed Officers or Directors

Many D&O policies define "insured persons" to include "duly elected or appointed" directors or officers or members of "duly constituted" committees.[315] Thus, to determine whether an individual is insured, it must be ascertained whether he or she was "duly" elected or appointed or a member of a "duly constituted" committee. Unfortunately, what policies do not define is "duly." The federal Eleventh Circuit Court, however, has said that the lack of definition of that word is not determinative. It held that "duly" could be given the dictionary definition. Thus, "duly elected" means through "regular and proper channels" of corporate governance.[316] The federal court for the Southern District of New York has agreed and suggested that one indication a person has not been duly elected or appointed would be a violation of a company's bylaws.[317]

Almost all common interest communities are incorporated and, therefore, the bylaws would be the first place to look to determine whether a director or officer was "duly elected or appointed."[318] Those bylaws should be consistent with the requirements for electing directors and officers set forth in the non-profit incorporation statutes of the state of incorporation. In many states, CIC legislation says little if anything about electing directors and officers, leaving the applicable non-profit incorporation statute to govern.[319]

In some states, CIC legislation requires the bylaws to provide for election of officers.[320] The officers may then be elected by either the directors or members of the association. Typically, the bylaws will provide for the board to elect or

---

315. *See, e.g.*, Non-Profit Management and Organization Liability Insurance Policy § II(G). *See also* Walsh v. Truck Ins. Exch. Co., 2003 Cal. App. Unpub. LEXIS 373 (Cal. App., Jan. 13, 2003), where a condominium unit owner argued that by using the term "duly," the policy incorporated by reference all governing documents into the insurance contract. The court characterized the argument as bordering on frivolous and said it could find nothing in the contract language to support that sweeping interpretation.

316. Sphinx Int'l, Inc. v. Nat'l Union Fire Ins. Co., 412 F.3d 1224, 1228 (11th Cir. 2005) (interpreting policy in context of "insured vs. insured" exclusion).

317. Julio & Sons Co. v. Travelers Cas. & Sur. Co. of Am., 684 F. Supp. 2d 330, 337 (S.D.N.Y. 2010).

318. It would, however, be advisable to examine other governing documents and any association rules and regulations for any requirements that may relate to election or appointment of directors and officers.

319. *See, e.g.*, NY CLS Co-op Corp § 14 (cooperative corporation has power to adopt and amend bylaws, consistent with law and its certificate of incorporation, including manner of voting, election, appointment, removal, powers, duties, terms and compensation of officers, directors, and committees); S.C. Code Ann. § 27-31-160(a) (bylaws must necessarily provide for form of administration).

320. *See, e.g.*, Ind. Code Ann. §§ 32-25-8-2(3)–(5) (bylaws must provide for election of president from among board of directors, and election of secretary and treasurer); NY CLS Real P §§ 339-v(c)–(e) (bylaws must provide for at least election of a president from among board of managers and election of secretary and election of treasurer). Note that in these statutes, the president must be a board member to be "duly elected."

appoint officers. Other states *require* the governing board to elect officers, usually a President, Secretary, and Treasurer.[321] When the board elects the officers, the minutes of the board meeting at which officers were elected should be sufficient proof that an election was "through regular and proper channels of corporate governance."

The association is created by the developer—also called the "declarant"—before any individual residences are sold and, therefore, the developer initially holds all the votes in the association and elects the governing board. At some point, control of the association must be transferred to those who have purchased the individual residences. Some states provide for a gradual transfer in which there is a period of joint control with purchasers able to elect a prescribed percentage of board members.[322] Because litigation by newly unit owner–controlled associations against developer-controlled boards and their directors is quite common, failure to meet the election requirements of the transfer of control statutes could be an issue.[323]

A handful of states have detailed requirements for conducting elections for directors.[324] These requirements are in effect superimposed on any bylaw directives in a state's non-profit incorporation statutes.[325] Failure to follow the requirements may call into question whether a director or officer was "duly elected or

321. *See, e.g.*, Nev. Rev. Stat. Ann. § 116.3106.1(b) (bylaws must provide for election by governing board of president, treasurer, secretary, and any other officers bylaws specify and specify qualifications of officers).

322. The Uniform Common Interest Ownership Act, for example, provides that no later than 60 days after 25 percent of the units that may be created are conveyed to unit owners other than a declarant, at least one member and not less than 25 percent of the members of the governing board must be elected by unit owners other than the declarant and no later than 60 days 50 percent of the units that may be created are conveyed to unit owners other than a declarant, not less than 33 percent of the members of the executive board must be elected by unit owners other than the declarant. UCIOA § 3-103(e). States adopting the UCIOA have included that provision in their Acts. *See, e.g.*, Colo. Rev. Stat. § 38-33.3-303(6). Florida, a non-UCIOA state, has a similar transfer of control procedure. Fla. Stat. § 718.301.

323. For example, if the developer is supposed to allow the purchaser unit owners to elect board members, is a board "duly elected"?

324. *See, e.g.*, Cal. Civ. Code § 5105 (requiring CIC association to adopt rules specify qualifications for board candidates, procedures for the nomination of candidates, qualifications for voting, and selection of election inspectors); Cal. Civ. Code § 5115 (setting forth voting procedures including ballot requirements); Cal. Civ. Code § 5120 (providing mandatory ballot counting procedures); Fla. Stat. § 718.112(2)(d)4. (bylaws must provide that board election may be by written ballot or voting machine and that proxies may not be used); Nev. Rev. Stat. Ann. § 116.31034.11 (requiring election of directors by secret written ballot and prescribing method of counting ballots); Nev. Rev. Stat. Ann. § 116.311 (prescribing voting procedures).

325. In some cases, a CIC statute will explicitly make its provisions superior to those of non-profit incorporation statutes. *See, e.g.*, Fla. Stat. § 718.111(2). However, even absent an explicit statement on the applicability of non-profit incorporation statutes, CIC legislation would take precedence under the maxim of statutory construction that a specific statute governs over a general one when there is a conflict.

appointed." Minutes of an association meeting at which an election took place should provide evidence of whether proper procedures were followed.

In a few states, CIC statutes restrict who may serve as a director or officer. For example, in Nevada common interest communities, directors elected after termination of the period of declarant control must be unit owners,[326] but association officers are not required to be unit owners unless the governing documents provide otherwise, and no one may serve as either a director or officer whose spouse or parent or child, by blood, marriage, or adoption, performs the duties of a community manager for the association.[327] Under Florida law a person who is delinquent in paying any fee or fine owed to the association, or who has been convicted of a felony, is not eligible to serve on a condominium board of directors.[328] Georgia law governing property owners' associations defines who is a considered a "lot owner" when the governing documents require directors and officers to be lot owners.[329] The Georgia Condominium Act states that if the condominium instruments provide that any member of the board of directors, or any officer of the association, has to be a unit owner, then the term "unit owner" includes, unless the condominium instruments otherwise provide, any shareholder, director, officer, partner in, or trustee of any person who is, either alone or in conjunction with any other person or persons, a unit owner.[330]

[b] "Duly Constituted" Committees

Whether a committee was "duly constituted" will also be determined by reference to the bylaws and possibly other governing documents or association rules. Often, the bylaws will say little more than that the president or board may appoint committees from time to time. Authority to appoint committees may be found in CIC[331] or non-profit incorporation statutes,[332] but in any event, is probably

326. Nev. Rev. Stat. § 116.31034.1.

327. Nev. Rev. Stat. § 116.31034.9.

328. Fla. Stat. § 718.112(2)(d)2. Note that the statute requires the bylaws to include these proscriptions and if they do not, they are deemed to do so.

329. Ga. Code § 44-3-229.

330. Ga. Code § 44-3-104.

331. NY CLS Co-op Corp § 14 (in addition to powers and rights set out in not-for-profit corporation law cooperative corporation has power to appoint committees). *See also* Colo. Rev. Stat § 38-33.3-303(3)(b) (association committees are to be appointed pursuant to governing documents, or if they contain no applicable provisions, pursuant to corporation law).

332. *See, e.g.*, Fla. Stat. § 617.0825(1) (unless articles of incorporation or bylaws otherwise provide, board of directors, by resolution adopted by majority, may designate from among its members an executive committee and one or more other committees); 805 Ill. Comp. Stat. 105/108.40(a) (if articles of incorporation or bylaws so provide, majority of directors may create one or more committees and appoint directors or other persons as board designates, to serve); Tex. Bus. Org. Code § 22.219 (board of directors may designate and appoint one or more committees that do not have authority of board in management of corporation, and membership may be limited to directors).

an inherent power of a corporation. The bylaws of large CICs may provide for standing committees. These may include a social committee, a budget or audit committee, an insurance committee, a rule enforcement committee, and an architectural review board.[333] There are a few instances in which state CIC legislation provides for appointment of committees for specific purposes and prescribes who may serve on the committee.[334] While these statutes are rare, when the status of a committee, or committee member, is in question, it is imperative to determine whether a statute governs that status. When the board appoints committees, the minutes of the board meeting at which the committee was created, or appointments were made, should be sufficient proof that the committee is "duly constituted."

[c] Volunteers

D&O policies do not generally define "volunteer." Usually policies mention both committee members and volunteers, suggesting a difference between them. Sometimes a definition will omit any reference to committee members but include volunteers.[335] In that case, committee members would arguably come under the term "volunteer." Generally, a volunteer would be a resident acting on behalf of the association at the specific direction of the board or an officer, most likely the president. For example, a resident with professional knowledge of heating and air conditioning equipment might be appointed as a volunteer to negotiate with a contractor for installation of a new heating and air conditioning system and to supervise the installation. Another example of an individual volunteer would be a retired accountant who agrees to review the association's books and accounts. To be certain that the volunteer is actually considered to be one for purposes of the definition of "insured person," the appointment should be memorialized in the board minutes, even if the appointment is made solely by the president or some other officer.

---

333. Architectural review boards are common in subdivisions governed by a homeowners or condominium association. These boards are charged with enforcing rules on the appearance of homes and building of accessory structures.

334. *See, e.g.*, Fla. Stat. § 720.305(2)(b) (homeowners association may not impose fine or suspend use of common areas and facilities for rule violation unless "committee of at least three members appointed by the board who are not officers, directors, or employees of the association, or the spouse, parent, child, brother, or sister of an officer, director, or employee" approves fine or suspension); NY CLS Co-op Corp § 17 (after members vote to dissolve cooperative corporation, corporation must appoint committee of three members who will liquidate its assets, pay its debts and expenses, and divide net assets among members, patrons, or stockholders); NY CLS Co-op Corp § 75 (cooperative corporation must have annual audit of its operations that may be made by auditing committee of three members of corporation who are not directors, officers, or employees.

335. *See, e.g.*, ISO Form BP 17 24 01 10, § H.5.

[d] Community Association Managers

Some experts emphasize the need for the property or community association manager to be an insured under an association D&O policy.[336] A few policies explicitly include a CAM within the definition of "insured persons," but most do not. When the CAM is omitted from the list defining "insured persons," the manager is not an insured person unless some other part of the policy brings the manager within the coverage.[337] When the D&O coverage is through an endorsement to a general liability policy, there may be language in the policy that makes the manager an insured, although that is highly unlikely. In a stand-alone policy, an endorsement may specifically modify the policy definition of an insured to include the manager, or more likely a management firm or organization.[338] Usually the definition will include a director, officer, or employee of that management firm or organization. Whether the manager is defined as an insured in the main policy or an endorsement, it is important to check for modifying language. The definition may apply only to a management firm under a *written* contractual agreement with the association and only while performing services for the association identified in the agreement. Associations need to be alert to the fact that if the CAM is an insured, the policy may address the limits of liability when there is coverage under the D&O policy and another liability policy.[339] Finally, some associations may directly employ a community association manager in which case the manager would be insured as an employee if the definition includes employees of the association within the definition of "insured persons." When the manager is an insured, the association should discuss with its broker, and perhaps the

---

336. Worley, *Not Your Grandfather's Policy: Changing Times Require a New Look at Condo Insurance* (Chicago Cooperator, 2011), available at: http://chicagocooperator.com/article/not-your-grandfathers-policy.

337. *See* N. Sec. Ins. Co. v. Sandpiper Vill. Condo. Trust, 24 Mass. L. Rep. 500 (Mass. Super. Ct. 2008) (where policy was unambiguous in that manager was not named insured, thereby failing to qualify as person insured). *See also* N. Sec. Ins. Co. v. Sandpiper Vill. Condo. Trust, 2008 Mass. Super. LEXIS 312 (2008), where the policy provided that an "insured person" was a director or officer or "you." The court concluded the property manager did not fall within the definition of "you" because the policy prescribed—as most do—that the words "you" and "your" referred to the named insured shown on the Declarations Page and any other person or organization that qualified as a named insured under the policy. The sole named insured was the condominium trust, that is, the association.

338. *See* Iannucci, *Discussing D&O Insurance: 10 Things You Need to Know* (Cooperator, 2007), available at: http://cooperator.com/articles/1509/1/Discussing-DampO-Insurance/Page1.html (managing agent's endorsement can be purchased or provided to include coverage for property manager).

339. For example, a Travelers endorsement provides that if any claim against a manager or director, officer, or employee of a manager gives rise to coverage under the D&O policy and any other liability policy issued by the insurer or one of its affiliates, the maximum aggregate limit of liability under all those policies, including defense costs, from that claim may not exceed $1 million, subject to the remaining limits of those policies. *See* Amended Definition of Insured to Include Property Manager (CIRI 70064).

association attorney, the implications for the Insured versus Insured exclusion and for the limits of liability.

[e] Developer

Common interest community associations are typically created by a development company—also called the "declarant"—before any individual residences are sold. The developer initially owns all the units or lots and, therefore, holds all the votes in the association. Thus, the development company "elects" the governing board whose members are usually employees or affiliates of the company.[340] Is the development company or the directors it appoints considered insureds? That question may be largely academic. One expert says that most insurance companies will not write a D&O policy on an association if a developer is still involved with the community.[341] That is an understandable avoidance of risk. The developer appointed directors will ordinarily act at the direction of the development company and in its interests, despite the fact that those directors generally have a fiduciary obligation to act in the interest of the association.[342] The insurer will not want to indirectly insure the development company.[343] The development company will most likely carry its own insurance.

The control of the association will eventually be transferred to those who have purchased the individual residences. This may happen all at once. If the developer retains control until all residences are sold, all the developer-appointed directors will be replaced at one time with those elected by residents. The transfer may also occur gradually with the number of directors elected by the residents increasing as the number owned by the developer decreases. One commentary

340. *See, e.g.*, Far Northwest Dev. Co., LLC v. Cmty. Ass'n of Underwriters of Am., Inc., 2007 U.S. Dist. LEXIS 28355 (W.D. Wash. Apr. 16, 2007), *rev'd on other grounds*, 297 Fed. Appx. 694 (9th Cir. 2008) (individual was managing member of development company and served as sole officer and director of homeowners association from date of its formation until approximately nine months later).

341. Bateman, *What Homeowner Associations Need to Know About Directors' & Officers' Liability* (2017), https://communityassociationmanagement.com/c33-financial-matters/c37-insurance/what-homeowner-associations-need-to-know-about-directors-officers-liability/. *But see* Far Northwest Dev. Co., LLC v. Cmty. Ass'n of Underwriters of Am., Inc., 2007 U.S. Dist. LEXIS 28355 (W.D. Wash. Apr. 16, 2007), *rev'd on other grounds*, 297 Fed. Appx. 694 (9th Cir. 2008) (policy whose period began before first unit was sold provided coverage for directors and executive officers of association; parties agreed that individual who was managing partner of development company as well sole officer and director of the homeowners association from date of its formation was insured).

342. *See, e.g.*, Uniform Common Interest Ownership Act § 3-103(a) (in performance of their duties, officers and members of executive board appointed by declarant must exercise degree of care and loyalty to association required of trustee).

343. It is not uncommon for associations, once they come under the control of the residents, to sue the development company and the directors and officers it appointed over construction defects. *See, e.g.*, Truck Ins. Exch. v. Cassady, 2011 U.S. Dist. LEXIS 122052 (N.D. Ill. Oct. 21, 2011).

suggests that even after control of the governing board is partially transferred to residents, an insurer may exclude coverage for the developer.[344] Any exclusion could extend to developer appointed board members.[345]

[f] Extended Coverage

D&O policies typically extend coverage to estates, heirs, and marital estates, meaning spouses. These extensions may be added by endorsement but are often found in the main policy.

Marital estate or spousal coverage is necessary because, when named in a lawsuit, directors and officers may shield assets by transferring them to spouses, and plaintiffs' attorneys, recognizing this tactic, may name spouses in suit papers.[346] One commentary points out that the extended coverage protects the spouse of an "insured person" when a suit is brought against community property or property held jointly.[347] Typical policy language provides the insurer will cover a loss arising from any claim made against the "lawful spouse"[348] of an insured person for claims that arise solely out of his or her capacity as the spouse of that insured person, including claims that seek damages recoverable from marital community property, property jointly held, or property transferred from the insured person to the spouse.[349] The coverage does not apply to a claim for an actual or alleged wrongful act of the spouse; it only applies when the actions of the "insured person" caused the claim.[350]

Policies also provide for coverage of claims that arise out of the wrongful acts of an insured person made against the estate, heirs, or legal representatives of a deceased insured person and a legal representative of that insured person in the

---

344. Bateman, *What Homeowner Associations Need to Know About Directors' & Officers' Liability* (2017) https://communityassociationmanagement.com/c33-financial-matters/c37-insurance/what-homeowner-associations-need-to-know-about-directors-officers-liability/.

345. *See* Treese & Rosenberry, *Insurance: How Community Associations Protect Themselves*, at 49 (CAI Press 2013) (association governing boards should be aware of policy in which developer board members are not insureds). *See also* Mt. Hood, LLC v. Travelers Cas. & Sur. Co. of Am., 2009 U.S. Dist. LEXIS 16775 (D. Or. Mar. 3, 2009), where the policy had an endorsement limiting coverage for actions of association governing board members who were also managing members of the developer. It provided the insurer would not be liable for any losses in connection with any claim brought against those directors after the end of the policy year in which he or she ceased to serve on the association board.

346. https://www.irmi.com/term/insurance-definitions/spousal-coverage.

347. *Executive Risk/Directors' and Officers' Insurance*, available at: http://www.scottsimmonds.com/bank-insurance-coverage/executive-riskdirectors-officers-insurance/.

348. The marital status may be derived by reason of statute, common law, or other law of any applicable jurisdiction in the world.

349. Non-Profit Management and Organization Liability Insurance Policy § III.B; ISO Form BP 17 24 01 10, § A.1.b.

350. *Executive Risk/Directors' and Officers' Insurance*, available at: http://www.scottsimmonds.com/bank-insurance-coverage/executive-riskdirectors-officers-insurance/.

event of incompetency, insolvency, or bankruptcy.[351] This extension only applies to claims if, and to the extent that, absent death, incompetency, insolvency, or bankruptcy of the insured person, the claim would have been covered according to all applicable policy terms, conditions, and exclusions. In other words, the coverage does not apply to wrongful acts of an estate, heirs, or legal representatives.

[g] Courtesy Defense

The purpose, of course, of the definition of "insured persons" is primarily to limit the persons for whom the insurer must provide coverage. That does not, however, prevent the insurer from extending coverage to those who do not appear to meet the definition. For example, in a California case, a condominium unit owner sued the governing board, its individual members, and owners of two upstairs units. She contended the owners of the upstairs units had been given permission by the board to remove carpet and padding, and that the board then failed to enforce its rules, causing the plaintiff to suffer an increase in noise and reduction in the value of her unit. The insurer defended the board and its members, but also decided to extend a "courtesy defense" to the offending unit owners.[352] The plaintiff then brought an action against the insurer, alleging breach of the covenant of good faith and fair dealing, and aiding and abetting a breach of fiduciary duty in its decision to extend the courtesy defense. Ultimately, the court held the plaintiff lacked standing to sue the association's insurer. However, it also ruled on the plaintiff's motion to disqualify the defendants' counsel because the joint representation created a conflict and breached the board's fiduciary duty to the plaintiff. The court denied the motion.[353]

351. ISO Form BP 17 24 01 10, § A.1.c. A policy may also contain a provision stating that the bankruptcy or insolvency of an insured will not relieve the insurer of its obligations under the policy. In *Hollingsworth v. Landing Condos. of Waukesha Ass'n*, 353 Wis. 2d 553, 846 N.W.2d 34 (2014), condominium unit owners sued several directors for breach of their fiduciary duties. The directors filed for bankruptcy and were dismissed from the underlying case. The D&O insurer disclaimed coverage, arguing that because the directors no longer were parties to the underlying action, they could incur no personal liability and there, thus, could be no loss under the policy. The court rejected that argument. It acknowledged that the directors were dismissed before being found liable, but, said the court, the harm the unit owners alleged was because of the director's wrongful acts and could have ripened into a compensable loss but for the bankruptcy. Under the policy, the insurer agreed that its obligation would remain when an insured would be obligated to pay because of a legal liability, but instead sought bankruptcy protection.

352. It is not clear from the opinion whether the insurer was also offering to cover any loss the non-insured unit owners might suffer, but it almost certainly was not, because when insurers offer what they call a "courtesy defense," it usually means they are contesting liability and providing a defense under a reservation of rights.

353. Walsh v. Truck Ins. Exch. Co., 2003 Cal. App. Unpub. LEXIS 373 (Cal. App., Jan. 13, 2003) (noting that unit owner defendants who were alleged to have acted with board permission or on its advice might have claims for indemnity against board members, who were insureds, and there was at least potential for coverage of those claims).

Because the California court dismissed the case on the procedural grounds of standing, it did not resolve the substantive question: does the definition "insured person" limit to whom the insurer may provide a defense? Could the association have sued the insurer for breach of contract for providing the courtesy defense? Certainly, the association, as a party to the contract, would have standing. It would also arguably have the damages—or at least potential damage—that a breach of contract action requires. The damages would result from the fact that any additional money spent in defending the individual unit owners would be subtracted from the limit of liability and, therefore, reduce the amount available for coverage of the defense and any liability of the association and the actual insured persons. Additionally, the additional money spent by the insurer on the defense of the individual unit owners could be the basis for the insurer to raise the premium.

[3] Loss

The concept of "loss" is critical to comprehending D&O policies.[354] The definitions of "loss" can vary greatly among policies, but all will have inclusions and exclusions. It is critically important to examine the definition for fine distinctions. Virtually all policies define "loss" to include damages, judgments, settlements, and defense costs, but they generally do not define "damages," "judgments," or "settlements."[355] Damages may be limited to "compensatory" damages.[356] Many insurers will employ the definition to exclude coverage for fines or penalties.[357]

Sometimes residents of common interest communities bring actions for a determination of whether they or the association is responsible for the

---

354. Quinn & Levin, *Directors and Officers Liability Insurance: Probable Directions in Texas Law*, 20 Rev. Litig. 381, 420 (2001). *See also* Skilling, *Coverage for Ill-Gotten Gains?: Discussing the (Un)Insurability of Restitution and Disgorgement*, 72 Wash. & Lee L. Rev. 1077, 1102 (2015) (because D&O policies provide coverage only for loss resulting from covered claim based on wrongful act, definition of "loss" is critical to determining scope of coverage).

355. Skilling, *Coverage for Ill-Gotten Gains?: Discussing the (Un)Insurability of Restitution and Disgorgement*, 72 Wash. & Lee L. Rev. 1077, 1102 (2015) (words "damages," "judgments," and "settlements" are usually not defined in policy and that is especially problematic in context of coverage for restitution and disgorgement because whether there is coverage will often turn on whether restitution and disgorgement fall within policy definition of "loss").

356. *See* ISO Form BP 17 24 01 10, § H.7. *Consider* Kittansett Club v. Phila. Indem. Ins. Co., 2012 U.S. Dist. LEXIS 127939 (D. Mass. Sept. 10, 2012) (restitution payments made to fulfill preexisting obligation were not losses resulting from wrongful act in breach of that obligation). *Compare* N. Sec. Ins. Co. v. Sandpiper Vill. Condo. Trust, 2008 Mass. Super. LEXIS 312 (2008) (insurer argued coverage was only for "damages," and underlying unit owner sought restitution, not damages; however, court found that contested assessment was within amount sought by the unit owner and, therefore, underlying claim was one for damages, as that word was used in policy).

357. Monteleone & Conca, *Directors and Officers Indemnification and Liability Insurance: An Overview of Legal and Practical Issues*, 51 Bus. Law 573, 598 (1996) (most insurers use definition of "loss" to set forth exclusion for fines or penalties).

maintenance and repair of a particular component of the property. In one case, money an association had to pay as a result of a declaratory judgment finding it responsible to pay for repair to common elements was held not to be damages under a D&O policy.[358]

The policy may specifically include pre-judgment and post-judgment interest in the meaning of "judgments. Some policies will define "defense costs" to include *reasonable* costs, charges, and expenses including attorney's fees for defending or *investigating* a claim[359] but exclude from the definition salaries of officers or employees.[360] Generally, defense costs include those incurred in an appeal. Notice that in those policies that modify costs, charges, and expenses with the word "reasonable," the insurer is in effect reserving the right to contest the amount of those costs, charges, and expenses.

Some definitions of "loss" will specify that it applies to claims against any insured,[361] while others will limit the definition to claims against prescribed persons.[362] Many policies will specifically define "loss" to require a claim for "wrongful acts."

[a] Legal Obligation to Pay

Most, though not all, policies define "loss" in terms of an amount someone is or becomes "legally obligated to pay." The "someone" can be important. For example, in the NPMOLIP loss means the total amount—exceeding any retention—*any insured* becomes legally obligated to pay. The policy specifically defines "insured" to include both the insured organization—the association—and the insured persons.[363] On the other hand, in an Ohio case the "someone" legally obligated was the directors and officers. The policy added that loss included an

358. Huntingdon Ridge Townhouse Homeowners Ass'n v. QBE Ins. Corp., 2009 U.S. Dist. LEXIS 108558 (M.D. Tenn. Nov. 20, 2009) (D&O policy provided coverage for losses insured became legally obligated to pay as *damages* and where court in underlying action did not award damages, but determined floor trusses were common element for which association was responsible to repair under its covenants and bylaws, policy did not cover any repair expenses association might have incurred as result of that determination as they would not be damages).

359. *See, e.g.*, Non-Profit Management and Organization Liability Insurance Policy § II.J. *Compare* ISO Form BP 17 24 01 10, § H(7), which includes "claims expenses" in the definition of "loss" and defines that term to embrace *reasonable and necessary* fees including those for attorneys and experts as well as the premium for appeal, attachment, or similar bonds. ISO Form BP 17 24 01 10, § H(3). Would a supersedes bond for an interlocutory appeal be considered a loss?

360. *See* MGIC Indem. Corp. v. Home State Sav. Assoc., 797 F.2d 285, 286 (6th Cir. Ohio 1986). The Non-Profit Management and Organization Liability Insurance Policy § II(J) excludes salaries, wages, overhead, or benefit expenses of an insured person.

361. Non-Profit Management and Organization Liability Insurance Policy § II(J).

362. MGIC Indem. Corp. v. Home State Sav. Assoc., 797 F.2d 285 (6th Cir. Ohio 1986) (claim or claims made against directors and officers).

363. Non-Profit Management and Organization Liability Insurance Policy § II(G).

amount for which the entity was required to indemnify the directors or officers or for which it had, to the extent permitted by law,[364] indemnified them.[365]

[b] Attorney's Fees

Does any of the language defining loss serve to incorporate a plaintiff's attorney's fees in a civil proceeding that an insured defendant is ordered to pay? In many cases this question would be academic. Under the "American rule," parties to a lawsuit pay their own attorney's fees absent a statute or contract clause providing otherwise. In litigation between a common interest community and a resident of that community, the question may not be academic because quite a few states have a statute allowing the prevailing party to be awarded fees in actions to enforce the governing documents or even the applicable state common interest community enabling law.[366] Even where there is no statute, the governing documents may provide for fees to the prevailing party.[367] Under the ISO D&O endorsement "loss" includes legal fees and costs awarded pursuant to judgments. Other policies define "loss" to mean "any amount" or the "total amount," less any retention, an insured becomes "legally obligated to pay." All this language should bring an award of attorney's fees within the meaning of loss. Any limitation on defense costs to a reasonable amount should not apply to an award of

---

364. Skilling, *Coverage for Ill-Gotten Gains?: Discussing the (Un)Insurability of Restitution and Disgorgement*, 72 Wash. & Lee L. Rev. 1077, 1084–85 (2015) (most policies provide that "loss" does not include coverage for matters uninsurable under applicable law and insurers often use that limitation to deny coverage for claims that are restitutionary in nature).

365. MGIC Indem. Corp. v. Home State Sav. Assoc., 797 F.2d 285, 286 (6th Cir. Ohio 1986).

366. *See, e.g.*, Cal. Civ. Code § 5975 (in action to enforce governing documents, prevailing party shall be awarded reasonable attorney's fees and costs); Conn. Gen. Stat. § 47-278(a) (declarant, association, unit owner, or any other person subject to Uniform Common Interest Ownership Act may bring action to enforce right granted or obligation imposed by Act, declaration, or bylaws, and court may award reasonable attorney's fees and costs); Md. Real Prop. Code Ann. § 11-113(c) (if any unit owner fails to comply with Condominium Act, declaration, or bylaws, he or she may be sued for damages caused by that failure or for injunctive relief, or both, by council of unit owners or by any other unit owner, and prevailing party is entitled to award for counsel fees as determined by court); Fla. Stat. § 719.303(1) (each unit owner and association shall be governed by and comply with Cooperative Act, cooperative documents, documents creating association, and association bylaws; actions for damages or for injunctive relief, or both, for failure to comply with these provisions may be brought by association or by unit owner against association, unit owner, or directors and prevailing party is entitled to recover reasonable attorney's fees; unit owner prevailing in action between association and unit owner may, in addition to recovering reasonable attorney's fees, recover additional amounts as determined by court to be necessary to reimburse unit owner for his or her share of assessments levied by association to fund its expenses of litigation); Tex. Prop. Code § 82.161 (if anyone subject to Texas Uniform Condominium Act violates it, declaration, or bylaws, any person or class of persons adversely affected by that violation has claim for appropriate relief and prevailing party in action to enforce declaration, bylaws, or rules is entitled to reasonable attorney's fees and costs of litigation from non-prevailing party).

367. *See* 6A Patrick J. Rohan, *Real Estate Transactions: Home Owner Associations and Planned Unit Developments—Forms* § 8.29 (Matthew Bender, 2016).

the opponent's attorney's fees for two reasons. First, the policy language usually connects the word "reasonable" to the *costs of defending* a claim, not to any attorney's fees awarded. Indeed, the ISO endorsement lists "claims expenses"—meaning, *inter alia*, attorney's fees incurred in the defense of a claim—and fees awarded pursuant to a judgment as two types of losses. If the latter type of loss included attorney's fees for the insured's defense, the phrase "claims expenses" would be rendered superfluous, an interpretation that courts abjure. To put it most simply, an award of fees and the cost of defending a claim are two entirely separate things. Second, many statutes providing for fees in CIC litigation only allow for the award of *reasonable* fees. If the judge has determined what fees are reasonable, the insurer would be hard put to substitute its judgment of reasonable for that of a judge.

[c] Punitive Damages

At one time, it was customary for the definition of "loss" in D&O policies to explicitly exclude punitive or exemplary damages.[368] Many policies, including those designed for common interest communities, continue to incorporate that exclusion.[369] However, some policies now drop it. Quite a few courts, indeed a majority, hold that a policy providing coverage for "all sums an insured becomes legally obligated to pay"—language typically found in D&O policies—includes coverage for punitive damages.[370] Other polices specifically state that a loss includes punitive or exemplary damages "to the fullest extent permitted by any applicable law."[371] The "applicable law" varies from state to state.

---

368. 4 Jeffery E. Thomas, *New Appleman on Insurance Law Library Edition* § 26.06[5] (LexisNexis 2023).

369. *See, e.g.*, Pulliam v. Travelers Indem. Co., 403 S.C. 332, 344, 743 S.E.2d 117, 123 (Ct. App. 2013) (because policy clearly excluded punitive damages, D&O endorsement did not cover those damages).

370. *See, e.g.*, Fluke Corp. v. Hartford Accident & Indem. Co., 102 Wn. App. 237, 7 P.3d 825 (2000) (where insurer agreed to pay sums insured became legally obligated to pay as damages, under majority rule, policy language by its express terms unequivocally covered not only award of compensatory damages but of punitive damages as well); Abbie Uriguen Oldsmobile Buick v. United States Fire Ins. Co., 95 Idaho 501, 511 P.2d 783 (Idaho 1973) (where policy provided company promised to pay on behalf of insured all sums insured was legally obligated to pay as damages and made no distinction between actual and punitive damages, absent any public policy to the contrary, punitive damages would be covered); Scott v. Instant Parking, Inc., 105 Ill. App. 2d 133, 245 N.E.2d 124 (1969) (punitive damages are part of "all sums" insured became liable to pay, and thus were covered by express wording of policy); Lazenby v. Universal Underwriters Ins. Co., 214 Tenn. 639, 383 S.W.2d 1 (1964) (where policy provides company will pay on behalf of insured all sums insured becomes legally obligated to pay as damages, most courts interpret that language to provide coverage for both compensatory and punitive damages; average policyholder reading that language would expect to be protected against all claims, not intentionally inflicted).

371. Of course, no matter what the policy says, if the applicable law prohibits coverage for punitive damages, no coverage can be provided. The question of the insurability of punitive damages has been evolving fairly rapidly and bears monitoring. *See generally* French, *Debunking the Myth*

The courts are split over whether there can be insurance coverage for punitive damages.[372] While many bar coverage for punitive damages, the majority hold that coverage can be obtained unless those damages are expressly excluded under the policy.[373] Even where coverage is allowed, however, it may be limited to policies that expressly or specifically include it.[374] Other very specific limitations may be imposed by statute.[375] There are, however, notable exceptions in important states. The largest state in the Union, California, still holds that its public policy proscribes indemnification for punitive damages.[376] New York public policy also broadly bans coverage for punitive damages.[377] In some states the prohibition

That Insurance Coverage Is Not Available or Allowed for Intentional Torts or Damages, 8 Hastings Bus. L.J. 65 (2012) (majority of courts now hold that policyholder can obtain coverage for punitive damages unless they are expressly excluded).

372. Plitt, Maldonado & Rogers, 12 *Couch on Insurance 3d* §§ 172:33, 172.35 (Thomson/West, 2005 with 2016 supp.). *See also* Skilling, *Coverage for Ill-Gotten Gains?: Discussing the (Un)Insurability of Restitution and Disgorgement*, 72 Wash. & Lee L. Rev. 1077, 1088 (2015) (there is substantial split among courts as to whether punitive damages arising out of accident, or awarded for gross, malicious, wanton, or reckless conduct, are covered under terms of liability policies).

373. French, *Debunking the Myth That Insurance Coverage is Not Available or Allowed for Intentional Torts or Damages*, 8 Hastings Bus. L.J. 65, 70, 92 (2012). *See also* Skilling, *Coverage for Ill-Gotten Gains?: Discussing the (Un)Insurability of Restitution and Disgorgement*, 72 Wash. & Lee L. Rev. 1077, 1089 (2015) (some courts have held that when there is no provision in policy specifically excluding punitive damages, there can be coverage for them).

374. *See, e.g.*, Haw Rev. Stat. § 431:10-240 (coverage under any policy issued in Hawaii is not to be construed to provide coverage for punitive or exemplary damages unless specifically included); Mont. Code Ann. § 33-15-317(1) (insurance coverage does not extend to punitive or exemplary damages unless expressly included by contract of insurance).

375. *See, e.g.*, Nev. Rev. Stat. § 681A.095 (carrier may insure against legal liability for exemplary or punitive damages that do not arise from wrongful act of the insured committed with intent to cause injury to another); Va. Code Ann. § 38.2-227 (it is not against state's public policy for anyone to purchase insurance providing coverage for punitive damages arising out of death or injury of any person as result of negligence, including willful and wanton negligence, but excluding intentional acts).

376. PPG Industries, Inc. v. Transamerica Ins. Co., 20 Cal. 4th 310, 84 Cal. Rptr. 2d 455, 975 P.2d 652 (1999) (public policy prohibits indemnification for punitive damages); City Products Corp. v. Globe Indemnity Co., 88 Cal. App. 3d 31, 151 Cal. Rptr. 494 (1979) (public policy of state prohibits insurance covering punitive damages; policy behind punitive damages would be frustrated by permitting party against whom they are awarded to pass liability onto carrier).

377. Home Ins. Co. v. American Home Products Corp., 75 N.Y.2d 196, 550 N.E.2d 930 (1990) (New York public policy precludes insurance indemnification for punitive damage awards, whether punitive damages are based on intentional actions or those that, while not intentional, amount to gross negligence, recklessness, wantonness, conscious disregard of rights of others, or conduct so reckless as to amount to that degree of disregard); Rental & Management Assocs. v. Hartford Ins. Co., 155 Misc. 2d 547, 588 N.Y.S.2d 982 (1992) (public policy of New York prohibits insurance indemnification for punitive damages, whether foundation for award is intentional conduct, gross negligence, recklessness, wantonness, or conscious disregard of rights of others).

is by statute.[378] Florida,[379] Illinois,[380] and Pennsylvania[381] hold to the general rule prohibiting coverage for punitive damages, but apply an exception when the insured is only *vicariously* liable for those damages.[382] The law on insurance of punitive damages has been evolving, so it is important to check current statutes and case law in a given jurisdiction to determine the status of the law.[383]

[d] Multiple Damages

There are many laws that allow for awards of "multiple damages," most popularly "treble damages." Policies exclude the "multiple" part of multiple damage awards from the definition of "loss," meaning there is coverage for the base amount, but not the multiplied portion of the loss. However, some polices will provide that a loss includes multiple damage awards "to the fullest extent permitted by any applicable law."[384] Courts may treat multiple damages as the functional equivalent of punitive damages and, thus, not permit them to be covered "under applicable law."[385] Also, generally excluded from the definition of "loss" are taxes, fines or penalties, and "matters uninsurable under" the applicable law.

---

378. *See, e.g.*, Utah Code Ann. § 31A-20-101(4) (no insurer may insure or attempt to insure against punitive damages).

379. U.S. Concrete Pipe Co. v. Bould, 437 So. 2d 1061, 1064 (Fla. 1983) (Florida public policy prohibits liability insurance coverage for punitive damages assessed against person because of his or her own wrongful conduct, but does not preclude coverage of punitive damages when insured is not personally at fault, but is merely vicariously liable for another's wrong).

380. Scott v. Instant Parking, Inc., 105 Ill. App. 2d 133, 245 N.E.2d 124 (1969).

381. Pennbank v. St. Paul Fire & Marine Ins. Co., 669 F. Supp. 122 (W.D. Pa. 1987) (public policy does not permit tortfeasor who is personally guilty of wanton misconduct to shift burden of punitive damages to insurer; however, Pennsylvania law does not preclude recovery of punitive damages from insurer where insured is only vicariously liable for those damages).

382. The exception may also be found in a statute. For example, under Kansas law, it is not against the state's public policy to obtain insurance covering liability for punitive damages assessed against an insured for acts or omissions, intentional or otherwise, of the insured's employees, agents, or servants, or of any other person or entity for whose acts the insured is vicariously liable, without the actual prior knowledge of the insured. Kan. Stat. Ann. § 40-2,115(a).

383. It should be kept in mind that a statutory change may not govern the policy at issue if it is found to retroactively impair the obligations of contract.

384. *See, e.g.*, Cieslewicz v. Mutual Service Casualty Ins. Co., 84 Wis. 2d 91, 267 N.W.2d 595 (Wis. 1978) (where insurer promised in policy to pay all sums insured became legally obligated to pay as damages because of bodily injury, there could be no serious dispute that treble damage award was sum insured was legally obligated to pay as damages).

385. *See, e.g.*, Rental & Management Assocs. v. Hartford Ins. Co., 155 Misc. 2d 547, 588 N.Y.S.2d 982 (1992), *aff'd*, 206 A.D.2d 288, 614 N.Y.S.2d 513 (1994), where a property manager was sued by a former tenant for unlawful eviction. The tenant was awarded treble damages pursuant to statute. The court said that damages were trebled under the statute to punish and deter—as is the case with punitive damages—and allowing insurance coverage would weaken the deterrent and water down the punishment. The court cautioned that the relationship of landlords and tenants was a "special territory" and that a different outcome might be appropriate in other cases where

[e] Appellate Bonds

One commentary notes that D&O policies typically say nothing about the cost of bonds in the appellate process.[386] On the one hand, this is an esoteric matter; on the other, it can become very concrete as some bonds can be very costly. The chances are that no one in a common interest community association will give any consideration as to whether the policy covers bonds when seeking coverage. Still, it is worth asking the association broker if the costs of appellate bonds are included in the coverage.

[4] Wrongful Act

The fourth of the key definitions provides the meaning of "wrongful act." D&O policies typically only pay a claim that arises out of a *wrongful act* by an insured in his or her official capacity.[387]

A layperson may think of "wrongful" as meaning intent to do harm: a criminal act or at least one that is morally reprehensible. The typical D&O policy definition of "wrongful act," however, is much broader. For example, a policy examined by a Federal Circuit court defined the phrase as:

> "any actual or alleged error, misstatement, misleading statement, act or omission or neglect or breach of duty by the Directors or Officers in the discharge of their duties solely in their capacity as Directors or Officers of the Association, individually or collectively, or any matter claimed against them solely by reason of their being Directors or Officers of the Association."[388]

Note that this definition, similar to other D&O definitions, specifically includes acts generally not *intended* to do harm: errors, misstatements, and neglect.

The last part of the definition, "solely by reason of their being directors or officers," is intended, according to one commentary, to include circumstances in

---

treble damages applied. *Compare* Kittansett Club v. Phila. Indem. Ins. Co., 2012 U.S. Dist. LEXIS 127939 (D. Mass. Sept. 10, 2012) (where treble damages allowed by statute were compensatory, not punitive, they were not excluded from definition of "loss" as "penalties" and would be covered under policy if no exclusion applied).

386. Quinn & Levin, *Directors and Officers Liability Insurance: Probable Directions in Texas Law*, 20 Rev. Litig. 381, 428 (2001).

387. Hollingsworth v. Landing Condos. of Waukesha Ass'n, 353 Wis. 2d 553, 846 N.W.2d 34 (2014) (D&O policies generally are issued to protect directors and officers from third-party claims made against them while acting in that capacity).

388. MGIC Indem. Corp. v. Home State Sav. Assoc., 797 F.2d 285, 287 (6th Cir. Ohio 1986). *See also* Mkt. Lofts Cmty. Ass'n v. Nat'l Union Fire Ins. Co., 2015 U.S. Dist. LEXIS 100691 (C.D. Cal. July 30, 2015) (alleged failure by association to follow through on promise to pay parking fee constituted "omission" and, therefore, "wrongful act" for purposes of policy).

which directors and officers are sued merely because of their position rather than for any specific conduct.[389]

Breach of contract is ordinarily not considered a wrongful act. Courts have said that performance of a contractual obligation is a voluntarily accepted debt, not a loss resulting from a *wrongful* act within the meaning of a D&O policy.[390] In any event, as discussed below,[391] policies often have a "breach of contract" exclusion.

Some policies may not include the word "negligent" in their definitions of wrongful act or use it to modify "act, error, and omission." One commentary notes that when negligent *is used* to modify "act, error, and omission," courts hold the definition does not encompass intentional or other non-negligent wrongdoing.[392] Where a policy covered "negligent acts, errors, omissions or breach of

389. Johnston, *Corporate Indemnification and Liability Insurance for Directors and Officers*, 33 Bus. Law. 1993, 2017 (1978). *See also* 3 *New Appleman Law of Liability Insurance* § 22.05[9][a] (rev. ed., Matthew Bender, 2017) (where policy includes within definition of "wrongful act," matter claimed against directors or officers solely as result of their capacity as directors or officers, lawsuit naming director as defendant based on his or her status as director of insured corporation is covered, even if it does not allege that director committed wrongful conduct otherwise falling within purview of definition).

390. August Entm't, Inc. v. Phila. Indem. Ins. Co., 146 Cal. App. 4th 565, 579, 52 Cal. Rptr. 3d 908, 917 (Cal. App. 2007) (noting that D&O policies limit coverage for directors and officers to liability arising from errors committed in their official capacity and that officer acting in an official capacity cannot be held liable for breach of corporate contract while officer who breaches contract in individual capacity is excluded from coverage because he or she was not acting in any official capacity). *See also* Sauter v. Houston Cas. Co., 168 Wn. App. 348, 360, 276 P.3d 358, 364 (2012); Oak Park Calabasas Condominium Ass'n v. State Farm Fire & Casualty Co., 137 Cal. App. 4th 557, 40 Cal. Rptr. 3d 263 (2006).

391. *See* § 14.14[10], *infra*.

392. 4 Jeffery E. Thomas, *New Appleman on Insurance Law Library Edition* § 26.06[3] (LexisNexis 2023). *See, e.g.*, Forest Meadows Owners Ass'n v. State Farm Gen. Ins. Co., 569 Fed. Appx. 523 (9th Cir. 2014) (where alleged misconduct of association was firing of employee in violation of specific state and federal employment laws, and policy defined "wrongful acts" to mean any negligent acts, errors, omissions, or breach of duty directly related to operations of association, firing was intentional act that did not qualify as negligence and did not, therefore, fall within policy); Far Northwest Dev. Co., LLC v. Cmty. Ass'n of Underwriters of Am., Inc., 2009 U.S. Dist. LEXIS 34521 (W.D. Wash. Apr. 22, 2009), *aff'd*, 362 Fed. Appx. 861 (9th Cir. 2010) (property damage at issue was "expected or intended" from standpoint of insured director, thereby precluding coverage as director was not simply negligent); Sova v. Cove Homeowner's Ass'n, 102 So. 3d 863, 874 (La. App. 2012) (where association member sued homeowners association alleging it "negligently" executed affidavit and caused lien to be filed creating cloud on his title, court found insurer made *prima facie* showing that association purposefully and intentionally filed liens as privilege to secure payment of fines and penalties levied against him and, thus association did not commit "wrongful acts" that would trigger coverage). *But see* Volney Residence, Inc. v. Atlantic Mut. Ins. Co., 195 A.D.2d 434, 600 N.Y.S.2d 707 (1993) (cooperative corporation—as well as past and present directors—was sued in Federal RICO action in which individual defendants were alleged to have intentionally committed acts of self-dealing and fraud; although policy covered claims arising from *negligent* acts, errors, or omissions, or breach of duty, court held policy could be understood to cover any breach of duty by directors or officers, not exclusively negligent breaches).

duty," an insured California condominium association argued that "negligent" only modified the word immediately following it: "acts." The insurer countered that "negligent" modified the serial terms following it and contended courts interpreting similar language have held the term "negligent" modifies all the words following it, whether they are separated by commas or the disjunctive word "or." The court rejected the association's construction, noting that a previous court had said that interpretation would mean the policy covered every "negligent act" and *every* "error or omission," whether those errors or omissions were negligent or intentional. The court found that result would lead to coverage that violated public policy.[393]

The definition of "wrongful act" can be employed to limit coverage to actions taken in discharge of organizational duties,[394] although the definition of "insured person" may serve that purpose as well.[395] In some policies, that limitation is exceedingly clear, for example, "discharge of their duties solely in their capacity as . . . ." Similar but a bit less precise is the ISO phrase "in their insured position or capacity for the association"[396] modifying acts by an insured person and the NPMOLIP language of "in their respective capacities as such"[397] that modifies acts of insured persons.

Some definitions, like the one quoted above, define "wrongful act" to include *anything* claimed against an insured person solely by reason of serving in that

---

393. Oak Park Calabasas Condo. Ass'n v. State Farm Fire & Cas. Co., 2006 Cal. App. Unpub. LEXIS 1456 (Cal. App., Feb. 21, 2006). The condominium in *Oak Park* had recovered almost $5 million under its earthquake coverage for damages suffered in the Northridge earthquake. It hired a contractor to repair the damage and agreed to pay the contractor with the insurance proceeds, but subsequently refused to pay a substantial portion of the money. The contractor and individual unit owners sued the condominium association. The association sought coverage from the appellee, its D&O carrier, which coincidentally also had provided the association's earthquake coverage. The court said that if the association's construction of the policy were correct, an association could enter a reconstruction, remodeling, or renovation contract, decide not to pay the bill, and shift the obligation to the insurer. "No rational insurer," observed the court, "would wish to undertake such an insuring obligation." Additionally, the court concluded that were it to rule for the association, the association would enrich itself by forcing the carrier to pay twice for the same property loss. The court refused to countenance that result. *See also* Able Roofing, LLC v. Vill. at Quail Creek Condo. Ass'n, 2012 Ohio Misc. LEXIS 19617 (Mar. 1, 2012) (breach of contract does not constitute negligent act, error, omission and is not, therefore, wrongful act under policy for which insurer must provide coverage).

394. Skilling, *Coverage for Ill-Gotten Gains?: Discussing the (Un)Insurability of Restitution and Disgorgement*, 72 Wash. & Lee L. Rev. 1077, 1084 (2015) (typically, concept that insured individuals are covered only for actions taken in insured capacity is included in the definition of "director," "officer," or "wrongful acts"); Monteleone & Conca, *Directors and Officers Indemnification and Liability Insurance: An Overview of Legal and Practical Issues*, 51 Bus. Law 573, 599 (1996) (defense to coverage under D&O policies relating to "insured capacity" may arise from definition of "wrongful act").

395. *See* N. Sec. Ins. Co. v. Sandpiper Vill. Condo. Trust, 24 Mass. L. Rep. 500 (Mass. Super. Ct. 2008).

396. *See* ISO Form BP 17 24 01 10, § H.8.a.

397. Non-Profit Management and Organization Liability Insurance Policy § II.S.

insured position or capacity.[398] This "anything" is distinct from an "error, misstatement, misleading statement, act or omission or neglect or breach of duty." It is designed to apply to situations where there is a claim against an insured person and the claim is not based on any alleged wrongdoing, but is an action requesting equitable relief. Most likely the action would seek to enjoin the conduct of the insured person.[399] For example, a resident of a homeowners association might sue the association and directors, asking the court to prohibit them from enforcing a particular covenant or from taking action that would subject him or her to increased fees or assessments.

Notice that the definition usually includes "actual or alleged" acts or omissions[400] or acts or omissions "committed or attempted or allegedly committed or attempted."[401]

The definition of "wrongful act" may apply to the association or, as in the case of the ISO endorsement, there may be a separate definition for the association.[402]

The definition of "wrongful act" will probably include "wrongful employment practices." When it does, there will also be a definition of "wrongful employment practices." Generally, wrongful employment practices include wrongful dismissal, discharge, or termination; employment-related misrepresentation; violation of employment laws; sexual or workplace harassment; employment discrimination; wrongful failure to employ or promote; wrongful discipline; wrongful reference; failure to provide adequate workplace or employment policies and procedures; illegal retaliation; and breach of an implied employment contract. The exact list of wrongful employment practices will vary slightly from policy to policy.

Sometimes there will be a specific exception to the definition of "wrongful act" that applies when an insured person acts in a position or capacity in any entity other than the association, even though the association has directed or requested that insured person to serve in that other position or capacity. Even if the definition of "wrongful act" omits this exception, there will often be an exclusion containing similar language.[403] This can be a significant exception or exclusion. It is not at all uncommon for a common interest community to be part of a larger community or a recreational association and to appoint one or more

398. *See* ISO Form BP 17 24 01 10, § H.8.a.

399. 4 Jeffery E. Thomas, *New Appleman on Insurance Law Library Edition* § 26.06[3] (LexisNexis 2023).

400. *See* ISO Form BP 17 24 01 10, § H(8)(a).

401. Non-Profit Management and Organization Liability Insurance Policy § II.S.

402. *See* ISO Form BP 17 24 01 10, § H.8.b.

403. *See, e.g.*, ISO Form BP 17 24 01 10, § B.j (barring coverage for claim arising out of any wrongful act committed or allegedly committed by any insured person serving in any position or capacity in any organization or association other than association even if association directed or requested that person to serve in that other position or capacity); Non-Profit Management and Organization Liability Insurance Policy § IV.7 (proscribing coverage for wrongful acts by any insured person as director, officer or employee of any entity other than insured organization, even if that service is directed or requested by insured organization).

of its directors to serve on the board of the master or recreational association. It is also not uncommon for the association to specifically direct how its director is to vote on matters that come before the other association. From the standpoint of the director, the hope would be that the master or recreational association has its own D&O policy.

§ 14.13 Discovery or Extended Reporting Period

D&O policies nearly always include a discovery or extended reporting period.[404] This extends the period of coverage during which an insured can report a claim based on an alleged wrongful act committed during the original policy period.[405] The association must pay an additional premium to obtain the extension.[406] The amount of that premium will be found on the Declarations Page. The primary purpose of the extension is to protect the association against a potential gap in coverage if the policy is cancelled or not renewed.[407] It does not extend the policy period or change the scope of coverage.[408]

Typically, the right to elect an extension only applies when the insurer cancels or refuses to renew. If an association acts to end the coverage, there is no right to an extension, although the insurer may offer one. One commentary recommends that before exercising the right to extended coverage, the insured should determine whether, in fact, the insurer has cancelled or refused to renew the policy.[409] For example, if an offer to renew is based on terms significantly different from those

404. Quinn & Levin, *Directors and Officers Liability Insurance: Probable Directions in Texas Law*, 20 Rev. Litig. 381, 458 (2001) (some policies use term "extended reporting period" and others "discovery period").

405. Romano, *What Went Wrong with Directors' and Officers' Liability Insurance?*, 14 Del. J. Corp. L. 1, 11 (1989). *See also* Quinn & Levin, *Directors and Officers Liability Insurance: Probable Directions in Texas Law*, 20 Rev. Litig. 381, 458 (2001) (extended reporting period provides insured with period of time in which to report claims that come in after termination date of policy if wrongful act was allegedly committed before effective date of termination).

406. Quinn & Levin, *Directors and Officers Liability Insurance: Probable Directions in Texas Law*, 20 Rev. Litig. 381, 458 (2001) (extended reporting periods must be purchased); Caraccio, *Void Ab Initio: Application Fraud as Grounds for Avoiding Directors' and Officers' Liability Insurance Coverage*, 74 Calif. L. Rev. 929, 951 (1986) (most policies allow insured to extend coverage for limited period on payment of additional premium).

407. Romano, *What Went Wrong with Directors' and Officers' Liability Insurance?*, 14 Del. J. Corp. L. 1, 11 (1989) (extension provisions often come into play when insurer has exercised its cancellation right).

408. Quinn & Levin, *Directors and Officers Liability Insurance: Probable Directions in Texas Law*, 20 Rev. Litig. 381, 469 (2001) (purchase of extended reporting period does not increase policy limits, unless that is explicitly specified, or otherwise change policy terms and conditions).

409. Ross, *Director and Officer Liability: Protecting Corporate Directors and Officers: Insurance and Other Alternatives*, 40 Vand. L. Rev. 775, 789 (1987).

of the expiring policy, courts may treat the offer as in effect a refusal to renew, triggering the right to exercise the discovery or extended reporting period.[410]

The association usually has to give the insurer written notice of its election of the extended reporting period.[411] The notice must typically be given or received within 30 days of either the end of the policy period or effective date of cancellation.[412] The association may be required to include the full premium for the extension with the notice or "promptly when due." If the association is unclear whether an offer to renew is effectively a refusal to renew and it would have elected the extended reporting period were that the case, it should probably make the election within the prescribed time period to avoid an argument by the insurer that the right to elect has been waived. If, however, it is later determined that the insurer did in effect refuse to renew the policy, failure by the insured to notify the insurer may not prevent that insured from electing the extended reporting period.[413]

The right of the association to invoke the extension may not be absolute. For example, the NPMOLIP does not allow the association the right to extend if the insurer cancels or refuses to renew the policy because the association has not paid the premium or has not complied with the terms and conditions of

410. *See, e.g.*, Continental Casualty Co. v. Allen, 710 F. Supp. 1088, 1094 (N.D. Tex. 1989) (renewals must be on same terms and conditions as prior policy; finding that policy offered was completely different from prior policy and was, therefore, nonrenewal of prior policy); Kemmerer Engineering Co. v. Continental Casualty Co., 253 Cal. App. 2d 188, 61 Cal. Rptr. 94 (Cal. App. 1967) (where insurer offered to renew coverage, but with doubling of premium, increase in deductible from $1,000 to $7,500, and reduction in policy from three years to one year, offer to renew—conditioned on acceptance by insured of materially new and different terms—amounted to refusal to renew existing policy of insurance within meaning of extended coverage clause). *See also* American Casualty Co. v. FDIC, 822 F. Supp. 1525 (W.D. Okla. 1992) (where proffered renewal policy included new endorsements providing 90-day discovery, "insured vs. insured" exclusion, reorganization/cessation of business provision, question of fact existed as to whether parties agreed and understood that offer constituted renewal).

411. Quinn & Levin, *Directors and Officers Liability Insurance: Probable Directions in Texas Law*, 20 Rev. Litig. 381, 458 (2001) (insureds must elect to use their extended reporting periods soon after they receive notice of termination).

412. *But see* Quinn & Levin, *Directors and Officers Liability Insurance: Probable Directions in Texas Law*, 20 Rev. Litig. 381, 469 (2001) (time frame for exercising extended reporting period may be 10 days; if option must be exercised within 10 days of notice of nonrenewal, option would probably have to be exercised before underlying policy expired).

413. *See* American Casualty Co. v. FDIC, 822 F. Supp. 1525, 1527–28 (W.D. Okla. 1992) (if parties did not agree to different terms in proffered renewal policy and insurer was required to give notice of refusal to renew, right to exercise discovery option was not barred by waiver, estoppel, or laches); Continental Casualty Co. v. Allen, 710 F. Supp. 1088 (N.D. Tex. 1989) (discovery option is not triggered until insurance company gives at least 30 days' notice of nonrenewal or termination and any discussions regarding new terms with insurance agent were not sufficient to meet insurer's affirmative duty to give notice; insured did not waive right to exercise discovery option as requisite notice of nonrenewal was never provided).

the policy.[414] In contrast, the ISO endorsement grants the right to purchase an extended reporting period if the endorsement is cancelled or not renewed for any reason or if the insurer renews or replaces it with insurance that has a later retroactive date or does not apply to wrongful acts on a claims-made basis.[415]

The extended reporting period can be for a relatively long period of time.[416] One year is common. The ISO endorsement provides that the extended reporting period starts with the end of the policy period and lasts three years.[417] The length of the period may be stated in the policy or on the Declarations Page.

The extension does not increase or reinstate the limit of liability.[418] The available limit is whatever remains of the amount of coverage available under the original policy. In other words, if the aggregate limit of liability in the policy was $1 million and the insurer had paid out half of that amount at the time the policy was cancelled or not renewed, then the available coverage during the period of extension would be $500,000.

Although the most likely scenario in which an association would seek to invoke the discovery or extended reporting period is that the insurer has cancelled or refused to renew the policy, there will be rare situations in which the association decides to discontinue coverage but wants the extension. One example would be if the common interest community is terminated.[419] In that event, the association may want coverage for its former officers and directors for claims arising after the termination based wrongful acts allegedly committed during the policy period. Ideally, the extension would last as long as any applicable statute of limitations.[420]

---

414. Non-Profit Management and Organization Liability Insurance Policy § III(C)(1).

415. ISO Form BP 17 24 01 10, § G(1).

416. Quinn & Levin, *Directors and Officers Liability Insurance: Probable Directions in Texas Law*, 20 Rev. Litig. 381, 458 (2001) (extended reporting periods of up to one year or longer are not uncommon).

417. ISO Form BP 17 24 01 10, § G(2).

418. Quinn & Levin, *Directors and Officers Liability Insurance: Probable Directions in Texas Law*, 20 Rev. Litig. 381, 469 (2001) (extended reporting period does not increase policy limits unless that is explicitly specified).

419. Many states have statutes governing termination of CICs and the distribution of their assets. *See, e.g.*, Uniform Common Interest Ownership Act § 2-118 (termination of common interest community). CICs are almost always incorporated as non-profit corporations. Therefore, the corporation also needs to be terminated and that process will be governed by state law on non-profit corporations. The various statutes will address the rights of creditors, including judgment creditors.

420. *See* Quinn & Levin, *Directors and Officers Liability Insurance: Probable Directions in Texas Law*, 20 Rev. Litig. 381, 468 (2001), discussing cessation of business by a for-profit entity.

§ 14.14 Exclusions

The typical D&O policy has 12 to 15 exclusions. Some are standard and will be found in almost any policy, and others will not. It is important to be aware that exclusions are not only found in the section of the policy titled "exclusions"[421]—for example, policy definitions can also contain language that has the effect of excluding coverage.[422]

One commentary notes that because the grant of coverage in D&O policies is usually very broad, the policy exclusions in a sense define the coverage more than any other part of the policy.[423] That is one reason experts advise common interest community associations to examine the exclusions in their policies with care to determine if they bar coverage for protection associations need.[424] Another reason to review the exclusions carefully is that insurers may be open to negotiations about eliminating some of them.[425]

The exclusions most likely to be of concern to community associations are discussed below. Those commonly found in D&O policies block coverage for bodily injury and emotional distress; pollution; violation of the federal Employee Retirement Income Security Act or similar federal, state, or local laws; pending and prior litigation; actions by an insured against another insured; conduct occurring while a person serves in a position or capacity in an association other than the named insured association; breach of contract; dishonesty or fraud; and an improper gain. Two other frequent exclusions prohibit coverage for property damage and failure to purchase or maintain adequate insurance. Some polices will also exclude claims for personal and advertising injury or selection or direction of a contractor who is liable for a construction defect. Before determining which exclusions apply to the policy, it is critical to check the endorsements. An

---

421. Monteleone & Conca, *Directors and Officers Indemnification and Liability Insurance: An Overview of Legal and Practical Issues*, 51 Bus. Law 573, 607 (1996).

422. Kokinda, *D&O Liability Insurance: There Are Exclusions, and Then There Are Exclusions*, 28-10 ABIJ 46 (2010). *See also* Monteleone & Conca, *Directors and Officers Indemnification and Liability Insurance: An Overview of Legal and Practical Issues*, 51 Bus. Law 573, 607 (1996).

423. Monteleone & Conca, *Directors and Officers Indemnification and Liability Insurance: An Overview of Legal and Practical Issues*, 51 Bus. Law 573, 598 (1996). *See also* 3 *New Appleman Law of Liability Insurance* § 22.06[1] (rev. ed., Matthew Bender, 2017) (insuring agreements in D&O policies are written to cover claims arising out of "wrongful acts," and that term is defined so broadly that scope of coverage is determined to large degree by exclusions).

424. Davis, *Why Board Members Need Community Association D&O Liability* (Insurance Journal, Apr. 2, 2012), available at: http://www.insurancejournal.com/magazines/features/2012/04/02/241157.htm.

425. 3 *New Appleman Law of Liability Insurance* § 22.05[1] (rev. ed., Matthew Bender, 2017).

endorsement can add or *subtract* an exclusion. It can also exclude coverage for a peril particular to the association, for example, specific litigation.[426]

The prefatory language to exclusions is particularly important.[427] It may be narrow, barring coverage of losses *for* a specified peril. It may also be "all-encompassing omnibus language, precluding all loss 'based upon, arising out of, or any way relating to'" the named peril.[428] The phrase "arising out of" is generally construed very broadly by courts.[429] One treatise explains that when exclusions are preceded by the word "for," they apply to direct claims brought by or on behalf of those suffering an injury while those beginning with the phrases "based on, arising out of, or attributable to," would exclude not only direct claims but also subsequent ones, for example, shareholder derivate suits for mismanagement.[430] As discussed below,[431] the broader prefatory language is of special concern to common interest communities when the policy excludes a claim that arises out of property damage or a breach of contract. Finally, the end of the section on exclusions ordinarily includes "imputation" language. It is important to check for that provision and examine its exact wording.

426. *See, e.g.*, One James Plaza Condo. Ass'n v. RSUI Grp., Inc., 2015 U.S. Dist. LEXIS 161460 (D.N.J. Dec. 1, 2015) (D&O policy including "Specific Litigation" exclusion under insurer was not liable to make any payment for loss arising out of or in connection with any claim made against any insured alleging, arising out of, based on, or attributable to, directly or indirectly, in whole or in part, and litigation by certain named unit owners).

427. Monteleone & Conca, *Directors and Officers Indemnification and Liability Insurance: An Overview of Legal and Practical Issues*, 51 Bus. Law 573, 607 (1996) (recommending policyholder read preamble language to particular exclusion very carefully to ascertain its breadth).

428. *D&O Insurance Policy Exclusions*, available at: https://www.connerstrong.com/resources/site1/news/1414CSB%20ER%20Policy%20Exclusions-2.pdf (broader preamble can substantially expand exclusion's preclusive effect, and accordingly, it is critically important to consider not only what exclusions policy contains but also how exclusions are worded and what terms and conditions accompany them).

429. *See* Windt, *Insurance Claims & Disputes: Representation of Insurance Companies and Insureds*, § 11:22A (5th ed. West, 2012) (if exclusion is written to eliminate coverage for injuries arising out of or occurring by reason of certain events, it is enough that theory of liability alleged arises out of or exists by reason of events or causes listed in exclusion). *See, e.g.*, VierraMoore, Inc. v. Cont'l Cas. Co., 940 F. Supp. 2d 1270, 1281 (E.D. Cal. 2013) (under California law, term "arising out of" and similar broadly defined clauses require only slight connection or incidental relationship between injury and excluded risk); Eastpointe Condo. I Ass'n v. Travelers Cas. & Sur. Co. of Am., 664 F. Supp. 2d 1281, 1288 (S.D. Fla. 2009), *aff'd*, 379 Fed. Appx. 906 (11th Cir. 2010) (phrase "arising out of" is broader in meaning than term "caused by," and means originating from, having its origin in, growing out of, flowing from, incident to, or having connection with and requires some causal connection or relationship, but not proximate cause in legal sense).

430. Sagalow, *Directors and Officers Liability Insurance: A Guide for Directors, Professional Edition*, at 25, available at: http://innovationinsurancegroup.com/wp-content/uploads/2014/07/D_O_Handbook_Professional_Edition.pdf.

431. *See* §§ 14.14[7][b], [10], *infra*.

[1] Dishonesty

The "dishonesty" exclusion has, as one treatise notes, potential applicability to many D&O claims and is, therefore, frequently relied on by carriers.[432] The exclusion is, in fact, a broad bar to coverage.[433] It usually encompasses fraud, criminal acts, or willful violations of statutes or regulations.[434] Virtually all D&O policies exclude coverage for fraud, dishonesty, and deliberate criminality,[435] although there is a great deal of variety in the policy exclusion language from one carrier to the next. For example, not all policies include an intent requirement.[436] Some polices will defend directors and officers until a criminal act is proven.[437]

The basic ISO endorsement states it does not apply to a loss resulting from a claim "arising out of any dishonest, malicious, fraudulent or deliberately criminal act or any willful violation of any statute or regulation."[438] In contrast, the NPMOLIP provides the company will not be liable to make any payment for a loss in connection with a claim made against any insureds brought about, or contributed to, by any "deliberately fraudulent or dishonest act or omission or any purposeful violation of any statute or regulation" by the insured.[439] When

432. 4 Jeffery E. Thomas, *New Appleman on Insurance Law Library Edition* § 26.07[3][a] (LexisNexis 2023).

433. *See, e.g.*, Johnston, *Corporate Indemnification and Liability Insurance for Directors and Officers*, 33 Bus. Law. 1993, 2018 (1978) (where policy excludes any claim against insureds based on or attributable to their gaining in fact of any personal profit or advantage to which they were not legally entitled, language is so broadly written that it excludes virtually any kind of case where directors or officers are held liable for conflicts of interest or self-dealing). *See also* Bisceglia, *Practical Aspects of Directors' and Officers' Liability Insurance—Allocating and Advancing Legal Fees and the Duty to Defend*, 32 UCLA L. Rev. 690, 701 (1985) ("active and deliberate dishonesty" exclusion has been criticized for vagueness; exclusion raises question, how bad does conduct have to be to qualify as actively and deliberately dishonest and where does active and deliberate dishonesty fit in negligence-gross negligence-recklessness-intentional wrongdoing continuum?).

434. *See, e.g.*, Riverdale Peaks Homeowners Ass'n v. Auto-Owners Ins. Co., 2012 U.S. Dist. LEXIS 54180 (D. Colo. Apr. 18, 2012) (claims for relief in underlying action were based on allegations of retaliatory, dishonest, and criminal conduct and were, therefore, plainly within policy exclusions and insurer had no legal duty to defend association in that action).

435. Quinn & Levin, *Directors and Officers Liability Insurance: Probable Directions in Texas Law*, 20 Rev. Litig. 381, 432 (2001). *See also* Kokinda, *D&O Liability Insurance: There Are Exclusions, and Then There Are Exclusions*, 28-10 ABIJ 46, 67 (2010) (all standard D&O policies exclude dishonesty).

436. 3 *New Appleman Law of Liability Insurance* § 22.06[2][b][i] (rev. ed., Matthew Bender, 2017) (some exclusions require proof of deliberate conduct, and others do not contain any intent requirement).

437. Iannucci, *The ABCs of D&O: Insuring Your Board's Decisions*, at 25 (Cooperator, 2011), available at: http://www.ihginsurance.com/Documents/Pdf/ABCs_of_DO_Cooperator.pdf.

438. ISO Form BP 17 24 01 10, § B(a).

439. Non-Profit Management and Organization Liability Insurance Policy § IV(10).

the modifier "deliberately" is used, the insurer will generally have a more difficult time denying coverage.[440]

There is a common misunderstanding that D&O coverage applies to theft by an insured or a claim that a governing board negligently allowed a board member or manager to steal association's funds. However, theft of association funds by a board member or a manager is a deliberately fraudulent and dishonest act to which the dishonesty exclusion applies.

Careful attention to detail is required to determine the scope of the dishonesty exclusion. For instance, a South Carolina court considered a policy that excluded coverage for damages resulting from dishonest, fraudulent, criminal, or malicious acts or errors or omissions committed by or with the knowledge of any insured.[441] In the underlying action, condominium unit owners alleged the developer-controlled association had placed the interests of the developer ahead of the owners when it failed to properly inspect or maintain the property or establish a reserve fund. They also filed a declaratory judgment action seeking a determination of whether the D&O policy issued to the association covered the claims alleged against the association in their underlying suit. The court concluded that, while the act of placing the developer's interests before the owners might constitute a breach of fiduciary duty, it did not allege any dishonest, fraudulent, criminal, or malicious action and, therefore, the exclusion did not bar coverage for the claims.

Even though an underlying complaint may allege bad faith by the directors—conduct that would likely fit within most dishonesty exclusions—claims that might be proved by demonstrating directors acted negligently would not be excluded.[442] However, the fact that directors claim to have been merely negligent is not conclusive. For example, property owners in a common interest community sued members of the association's board of directors alleging they used their positions for self-dealing and to facilitate a takeover by a gaming corporation that sought to build a casino in or near the neighborhood. Among the specific claims were that the directors, breached their common-law duty of loyalty and fiduciary duty to the association, acted in bad faith, engaged in intentional misconduct and knowing violation of the governing documents, and committed illegal, oppressive, and/or fraudulent acts. To forestall application of the dishonesty exclusion, the directors contended that the claims for breach of fiduciary duty and breach of duty of care involved mere negligent acts and breaches of

440. Kokinda, *D&O Liability Insurance: There Are Exclusions, and Then There Are Exclusions*, 28-10 ABIJ 46, 67 (2010).

441. *See* Pulliam v. Travelers Indem. Co., 403 S.C. 332, 343, 743 S.E.2d 117, 122 (Ct. App. 2013).

442. Hotel Des Artistes v. Transamerica Ins. Co., 1994 U.S. Dist. LEXIS 7800 (S.D.N.Y. June 10, 1994).

duty. The court, however, found that within the context of the complaint, those claims communicated fraud, dishonesty, bad faith, and self-dealing. The breaches alleged, therefore, fell squarely within the exclusion for "dishonest, fraudulent, criminal or malicious" acts, and there was a result of no coverage under the D&O policy.[443]

In addition to the list of excluded acts, some, but not all, dishonesty exclusions contain triggers for application of the exclusion. The triggering language may be "in fact,"[444] "adjudicated," "judgment or other final adjudication," or "finding in any judicial or other proceeding or a written admission or statement under oath." If the policy requires that a determination be made in a "non-appealable judgment of the underlying action," it precludes the insurer from bringing a separate action to determine whether the exclusion applies and allows the insured to exhaust court remedies before protection is excluded.[445]

[a] Final Adjudication

A policy may require a judgment or some *final adjudication* establishing that the identified conduct actually occurred.[446] For example, under the NPMOLIP, the Dishonesty exclusion does not apply unless a "judgment or other final adjudication" adverse to the insured establishes a "deliberately fraudulent or dishonest act or omission or purposeful violation."[447] Where the policy excludes coverage when the insured is "adjudged guilty of criminal acts," a trial or some other adjudication is required. The carrier does not have the prerogative to determine that an insured has committed a crime.[448]

---

443. State Farm Fire & Cas. Co. v. Anderson, 2013 U.S. Dist. LEXIS 57837 (S.D. Miss. Apr. 23, 2013).

444. 4 Jeffery E. Thomas, *New Appleman on Insurance Law Library Edition* § 26.07[3][a] (LexisNexis 2023) (policies may require that identified conduct occurred "in fact."). *See also* Kokinda, *D&O Liability Insurance: There Are Exclusions, and Then There Are Exclusions*, 28-10 ABIJ 46 (2010) (when general terminology is used such as "in fact" to describe excluded conduct, insurer is in better position to decide when revealed facts have triggered conduct exclusion, which may occur during investigation and before any court proceeding); Johnston, *Corporate Indemnification and Liability Insurance for Directors and Officers*, 33 Bus. Law. 1993, 2018 (1978) (phrase "in fact" indicates that insured will not be denied coverage merely because of allegation of personal profit or advantage, but only if he or she in fact gained profit or advantage, although it is unclear how that determination is to be made).

445. Kokinda, *D&O Liability Insurance: There Are Exclusions, and Then There Are Exclusions*, 28-10 ABIJ 46, 67 (2010).

446. One commentary notes this condition lessens the application of the exclusion because shareholder litigation is almost always settled and, therefore, not adjudicated in the proceeding for which the coverage is sought. Baker & Griffith, *The Missing Monitor in Corporate Governance: The Directors' & Officers' Liability Insurer*, 95 Geo. L.J. 1795, 1805 (2007).

447. Non-Profit Management and Organization Liability Insurance Policy § IV.10.

448. Quinn & Levin, *Directors and Officers Liability Insurance: Probable Directions in Texas Law*, 20 Rev. Litig. 381, 434 (2001).

[b] Broader Triggering Language

Some D&O policy forms adopt another type of trigger, invoking the exclusion if there is a finding in any judicial or other proceeding or a written admission or statement under oath—not just a final adjudication—by the insured that establishes the requisite conduct occurred. This approach may require more proof than the "in fact" trigger, but may be held to allow the insurer to invoke the exclusion even if the underlying claim is settled.[449]

[2] Insured versus Insured

The Insured versus Insured exclusion (also sometimes called "one versus one" exclusion)[450] is intended—as the name suggests—to proscribe coverage for claims between parties that are both insured by the same D&O policy. The point is to prevent collusive lawsuits.[451] More specifically, the purpose has been described as avoiding collusive claims by insured corporations that try to "'recoup corporate losses by attributing them to the wrongdoing of directors and officers who, if insured, have nothing to lose by taking the blame.'"[452] Another purpose of the exclusion is to bar coverage for fights between board members,[453] which can be contentious in business corporations but seriously vicious in common interest communities.

Early versions of D&O policies did not bar claims between one insured and another.[454] The exclusion was developed in the 1980s in response to claims asserted by banks against their own officers in order to access the proceeds of

---

449. 4 Jeffery E. Thomas, *New Appleman on Insurance Law Library Edition* § 26.07[3][a] (LexisNexis 2023).

450. *How to Soften the Insured vs. Insured Exclusion in Your Client's D&O Insurance Policy* (AmWins Group, Inc. 2015); Monteleone & Conca, *Directors and Officers Indemnification and Liability Insurance: An Overview of Legal and Practical Issues*, 51 Bus. Law 573, 605 (1996).

451. Plitt, Maldonado & Rogers, 9A *Couch on Insurance 3d* § 131:32 (Thomson/West, 2005 with 2016 supp.).

452. Willson v. Vanderlick (*In re* Cent. La. Grain Coop., Inc.), 467 B.R. 390, 394 (Bankr. W.D. La. 2012). *See also How to Soften the Insured vs. Insured Exclusion in Your Client's D&O Insurance Policy* (AmWins Group, Inc. 2015). The article explains that the exclusion prevents a company from pursuing a risky business strategy knowing that if its plan fails and causes losses, it could recoup those losses by having one executive sue another, claiming that she disagreed with the strategy and insisting that the insurer indemnify the company for the negligent acts of management. Similarly, without the exclusion, a common interest community association governing board could decide not to fund a reserve and then, when a major component of the property needs replacing, a director who supported reserve funding could sue the other directors in hopes of obtaining the funds needed for the project from the insurer.

453. Carleton & Markovich, *Modern Interpretation and Application of the Insured v. Insured Exclusion* (Professionals', Officers' and Directors' Liability Committee Newsletter 2015), available at: http://www.skarzynski.com/siteFiles/files/2015PODLSummer_premium_authcheckdam.pdf; *D&O Insurance Policy Exclusions*, available at: https://www.connerstrong.com/resources/site1/news/1414CSB%20ER%20Policy%20Exclusions-2.pdf.

454. 4 Jeffery E. Thomas, *New Appleman on Insurance Law Library Edition* § 26.07[3][d] (LexisNexis 2023).

their policies.[455] While there are now over three decades of case law interpreting the exclusion, its application exclusion remains highly fact specific, and it is therefore difficult to predict how courts—and insurers[456]—may interpret it, especially where there is no controlling precedent in a particular jurisdiction.[457]

In the typical medium to large for-profit corporation, the exclusion may not be implicated very often, although when it is invoked by insurers it is often challenged, making it one of the most litigated of the provisions in D&O policies.[458] In small to medium-size common interest communities, the exclusion has the potential to hinder, if not entirely block, coverage of claims by individual owners against sitting directors. The reason is the definition of "insured persons." Policies ordinarily define an "insured person" to include any former, present, or future elected or appointed directors, trustees, officers, employees, committee members, or volunteers.[459] This broad definition has the potential to severely limit the coverage of the policy.[460] In a smaller CIC, that definition may encompass most of the residents. It should be noted that many D&O policies define "insured persons" as "duly elected or appointed" directors or officers or as members of "duly

455. *How to Soften the Insured vs. Insured Exclusion in Your Client's D&O Insurance Policy* (AmWins Group, Inc. 2015).

456. Consider, for example, a case in which an association sued its property management firm alleging it had failed to obtain an extension of surety bond coverage for the association. The management company crossclaimed against the association's former directors alleging that, if it was liable to the association, the directors were liable for their failure to direct the company to obtain the extension. The association's D&O insurer concluded the crossclaims against the directors were covered by the policy, although the property management company was apparently an insured under the policy. VierraMoore, Inc. v. Cont'l Cas. Co., 940 F. Supp. 2d 1270 (E.D. Cal. 2013).

457. Carleton & Markovich, *Modern Interpretation and Application of the Insured v. Insured Exclusion* (Professionals', Officers' and Directors' Liability Committee Newsletter 2015), available at: http://www.skarzynski.com/siteFiles/files/2015PODLSummer_premium_authcheckdam.pdf.

458. *See How to Soften the Insured vs. Insured Exclusion in Your Client's D&O Insurance Policy* (AmWins Group, Inc. 2015) (Insured versus Insured exclusion is one of most heavily litigated provisions of D&O policies).

459. There are some differences between the NMOLIP and ISO language. The former has a definition that includes persons who were, now are, or will become duly elected or appointed directors, trustees, or officers of any insured organization or employees, committee members, or volunteers of any insured organization that is a non-profit entity. *See* Non-Profit Management and Organization Liability Insurance Policy § IV.2.I. The reference to a "non-profit entity" excludes employees of a community association management firm's employees from the definition. The ISO language simply defines "insured person" as any former, present, or future director, officer, trustee, employee, or volunteer of the association. *See* ISO Form BP 17 24 01 10, § H.5. The ISO phrasing omits reference to committee members, although they may be considered to be volunteers as, indeed are board members because they are generally uncompensated.

460. *Directors and Officers Liability* (Summit Business Media, 2013) (large population of insureds can expand Insured versus Insured exclusion to apply to individuals who otherwise may not have been contemplated by that exclusion; many not-for-profit and association policy forms expand "insured" definition to include all employees and even some non-employees—for example, volunteers—and thus, when policy contains Insured versus Insured exclusion, its coverage could be severely restricted in suits by employees against officers and directors).

constituted" committees,[461] and, therefore, to determine whether an individual qualifies as an insured for purposes of the Insured versus Insured exclusion, it must be ascertained whether he or she was "duly elected or appointed" or a member of "duly constituted" committee.[462]

It is important to read any Insured versus Insured exclusion carefully as they are not all alike. For example, a policy held by a Florida association excluded coverage for any claim made against *any insured* brought by or on behalf of *any insured.*[463] Other versions of the exclusion may bar coverage of claims against directors and officers brought by the organization or any insured.[464]

[a] Derivative Action Exception

A common exception to the Insured versus Insured exclusion is for "'a shareholder's derivative action brought on behalf of the Company by one or more shareholders who are not Insured Persons and make a Claim without the cooperation or solicitation of any Insured Person or the Company.'"[465] The U.S. Supreme Court long ago explained that stockholders' derivative suits are actions to enforce a corporate claim and are one of the remedies equity designed for those situations in which the management declines to take the proper and necessary steps to assert the rights the corporation has; stockholders are then allowed to institute the suit the management should have initiated had it performed its duty.[466] The Delaware Supreme Court subsequently observed that the nature of these actions is two-fold: first, the action is the equivalent of a suit by the shareholders to compel the corporation to sue and second, it is a suit by the corporation, asserted by the shareholders on its behalf.[467]

---

461. *See, e.g.*, Non-Profit Management and Organization Liability Insurance Policy § II.G.

462. For discussion of the definition of "insured person," see § 14.12[2], *supra*.

463. Marbella Condo. Ass'n v. RSUI Indem. Co., 2017 U.S. Dist. LEXIS 12363 (S.D. Fla. Jan. 30, 2017).

464. Sagalow, *Directors and Officers Liability Insurance: A Guide for Directors, Professional Edition*, at 27–28, available at: http://innovationinsurancegroup.com/wp-content/uploads/2014/07/D_O_Handbook_Professional_Edition.pdf.

465. BancInsure, Inc. v. FDIC, 796 F.3d 1226, 1231 (10th Cir. 2015). *See also* Kiewit Diversified Group v. Federal Ins. Co., 999 F. Supp. 1169, 1171 (N.D. Ill. 1998) (Insured versus Insured exclusion stated insurer would not be liable for loss on account of any claim made against any insured person brought or maintained by or on behalf of any insured except claim that was derivative action brought or maintained on behalf of insured organization by one or more persons who were not insured persons and who brought and maintained claim without the solicitation, assistance, or participation of any insured).

466. Meyer v. Fleming, 327 U.S. 161, 167, 66 S. Ct. 382, 386, 90 L. Ed. 595, 600 (1946).

467. Aronson v. Lewis, 473 A.2d 805, 811 (Del. 1984). *See also* Cooney, *A Modality for Accountability to Shareholders: The American Way?*, 28 Okla. City U.L. Rev. 717, 718 (2003) (derivative lawsuit is one in which shareholder derives right to sue from corporation; shareholder brings suit in attempt to redress violations of corporation as entity and cause of action actually belongs to corporation; however, shareholders initiate derivative suits when their corporation fails to assert

Does the exception apply in common interest communities? For residential cooperatives, the answer would seem clearly to be yes. They are generally formed as corporations with tenant/shareholders who have the same right to bring a derivative action as any other shareholder.[468] The answer is less certain for condominiums and homeowners associations.

While condominiums and homeowners associations typically are incorporated, they are usually formed under non-profit corporation statutes and have members, but no shareholders. Nonetheless, many courts find that members of condominium and homeowners associations may bring derivative actions. Courts in some states—for example, California,[469] Florida,[470] and Massachusetts[471]—agree by implication.[472] In other states, most notably New York[473] and Illinois,[474]

claim; while individual shareholder may initiate derivative lawsuit, because it is actually brought on behalf of corporation, any recovery inures to corporation, rather than shareholder).

468. Claman, *Derivative Lawsuits Co-ops Can Have Them Dismissed* (Cooperator, 1995), available at: https://cooperator.com/article/derivative-lawsuits (cooperative is generally organized as business corporation, and its shareholders have same rights as shareholders in other New York business corporations to initiate shareholder derivative lawsuits).

469. *See, e.g.*, Gantman v. United Pacific Ins. Co., 232 Cal. App. 3d 1560, 284 Cal. Rptr. 188 (1991) (member of non-profit corporation is prohibited from instituting or maintaining action in right of the corporation unless action is derivative suit). *See also* San Simeon Condo. Ass'n v. 2006, 2008 Cal. App. Unpub. LEXIS 6105 (July 29, 2008) (association member failed to meet statutory requirements for bringing derivative suit).

470. Rogers & Ford Constr. Corp. v. Carlandia Corp., 626 So. 2d 1350, 1354 (Fla. 1993) (actions with respect to common areas or common elements of condominiums have been brought as either class actions or derivative actions, or by unit owner joined by condominium association and/or other unit owners).

471. *See, e.g.*, Cigal v. Leader Dev. Corp., 408 Mass. 212, 219, 557 N.E.2d 1119, 1123 (1990) (claims for failing to collect common charges from units owned by developer and negligent construction of common areas were ones only association could raise; as unit owners were seeking recovery of funds properly owing to association, they could not assert their claims except through derivative suit); Sea Pines Condo. III Ass'n v. Steffens, 61 Mass. App. Ct. 838, 845, 814 N.E.2d 752, 760, n.17 (2004), *rev. den.*, 442 Mass. 1112, 816 N.E.2d 1223, 2004 Mass. LEXIS 872 (2004) (when condominium association holds capacity to bring suit under condominium statute, individual unit owners typically may appear as parties only in derivative capacity).

472. *Consider* McMillan v. Ryan Jackson Props., LLC, 232 N.C. App. 35, 753 S.E.2d 373 (2014) (where unit owners brought negligence action derivatively on behalf of condominium association, court did not dispute right of owners generally to bring derivative actions); Smith v. Ridgeview Homeowner's Ass'n, 2011 Minn. App. Unpub. LEXIS 441 (Minn. Ct. App. May 9, 2011) (conceivably, applying related corporate-law principles, unit owner might have considered derivative lawsuit to enforce rights of association against allegedly deficient contractor with whom association contracted to repair common area patios).

473. *See, e.g.*, Caprer v. Nussbaum, 36 A.D.3d 176, 189, 825 N.Y.S.2d 55, 67 (2006) (same factors that caused courts to fashion derivative action procedure for shareholders apply to condominium unit owners).

474. *See, e.g.*, Goldberg v. Astor Plaza Condo. Ass'n, 361 Ill. Dec. 346, 971 N.E.2d 1, 15 (Ill. App. 2012), *app. den.*, 366 Ill. Dec. 75, 979 N.E.2d 876 (Ill. 2012) (although right to sue over damages to common elements belongs exclusively to association, unit owners do not usurp that right by bringing derivative suits on association's behalf against third parties; rather, they are simply

the courts have definitively held that members of common interest community associations may bring derivative actions.[475] Generally, these courts are untroubled by any lack of authorization for derivative suits in their state's non-profit corporations laws.[476] However, the courts in the states of Washington[477] and Maine[478] have refused to recognize the right of members of non-profit organizations to bring derivative actions because there is no statutory sanction for them.

Clearly, to determine whether members of common interest community associations may bring derivative actions, one must examine the statutory and case law of the particular jurisdiction in which they are located. Any enabling legislation should also be appraised. The Uniform Common Interest Ownership Act, for instance, provides that a unit owner may bring an action to enforce a right granted or obligation imposed by the declaration or bylaws.[479] Some states—for

acting as arms of association to exercise that associational right); Bd. of Dirs. v. Mob Ventures, LLC, 296 Ill. Dec. 700, 359 Ill. App. 3d 991, 996, 836 N.E.2d 115, 120 (2005) (while condominium association has exclusive standing to assert claim against third party, unit owners have remedy of filing derivative action against governing board if it fails to assert their claim against that third party). *See also Illinois Condominium Law* § 16.16 (IICLE 2010) (while derivative action is standard method for unit owners to seek relief for damage to condominium association, unit owners also may sue individually if they can allege separate and distinct injury or injury existing independently of harm to association).

475. *See, e.g.*, Kirtley v. McClelland, 562 N.E.2d 27 (Ind. App. 1990); Hannewald v. Fairfield Communities, Inc., 651 S.W.2d 222, 225 (Tenn. App. 1983) (finding that members of membership corporation—including members of property owners' association—have standing to bring derivative suit on behalf of corporation even though they are not "shareholders" in true sense).

476. *See, e.g.*, Caprer v. Nussbaum, 36 A.D.3d 176, 189, 825 N.Y.S.2d 55, 67 (2006) (condominium unit owners are entitled to same consideration by the courts as litigants in those situations in which courts have historically allowed derivative actions to proceed, independent of any statutory authority); Kirtley v. McClelland, 562 N.E.2d 27 (Ind. App. 1990) (absence of statutory procedure for initiating derivative action by not-for-profit corporation when one has been affirmatively provided for for-profit corporations does not require conclusion that statutory authorization is required; court of general jurisdiction has inherent equitable power unless statute either explicitly or by necessary implication provides otherwise and, thus, as Not-for-Profit Corporation Act does not expressly bar derivative actions by members of a non-profit corporation and nothing indicates legislative intent to preclude courts from exercising equitable jurisdiction over actions initiated by members of non-profit corporation, derivative remedy is available and minority members of unit owner's association had standing to sue).

477. *See* Lundberg v. Coleman, 115 Wn. App. 172, 60 P.3d 595 (2002), *rev. den.*, 150 Wn. 2d 1010, 79 P.3d 446 (2003) (nothing in Nonprofit Corporation Act expressly authorized derivative suits and, therefore, right of directors/trustees to bring derivative actions on behalf of non-profit corporation has not been adopted).

478. *See* America v. Sunspray Condo. Ass'n, 61 A.3d 1249 (Me. 2013) (where action was brought derivatively on behalf of condominium association alleging its board failed to enforce smoking ban rule, but Maine Nonprofit Corporation Act did not expressly provide for derivative action on behalf of non-profit corporation, court refused to infer that derivate actions were authorized when legislature did not so provide by statute).

479. Uniform Common Interest Ownership Act § 4-117(a).

example, California[480] and Florida[481]—have similar laws. Do they in effect authorize derivative actions?

Finally, when the exception applies to derivative actions brought without the cooperation, assistance, or solicitation of any insured person, what constitutes "cooperation, assistance, or solicitation"? Policies do not define those terms. One commentary asks if compliance by a director with a request by a shareholder for an internal investigation of an officer would be considered excluded assistance by the insured if a claim is ultimately brought against that officer?[482]

[b] Declarant-Appointed Directors

The association generally comes into existence when the CIC is being created. Therefore, the developer—also called the "declarant"—initially holds all the votes in the association and appoints the governing board. These directors are either employed by or in some other way affiliated with and controlled by, the development corporation. It is quite common for an association to sue the developer-appointed board that governed it before the individual owners took control of the association. The Insured versus Insured exclusion is likely to be invoked by the D&O insurer to bar coverage to the developer appointed directors. For example, in an Illinois case,[483] a condominium association sued the developer and the initial members of the association board of directors. The directors were sued for breach of their fiduciary duties to the association in connection with construction defects. The directors tendered their defense to the liability insurer, considering themselves to be additional insureds under the association policy. The policy provided both general liability and directors and officers liability coverage. The court quickly found there was no coverage under the general liability portion of the policy because the policy became effective almost two years after the directors relinquished their positions. On the other hand, the D&O portion of the policy, like many D&O policies, covered *former*

480. Cal. Civ. Code § 5975 (covenants and restrictions in declaration may be enforced by any owner of separate interest, unless declaration states otherwise and governing document other than declaration may be enforced by owner of separate interest against association).

481. Fla. Stat. § 718.303(1) (actions for damages or injunctive relief, or both, for failure to comply with declaration, documents creating condominium association, or association bylaws, may be brought by unit owner against directors designated by developer, for actions taken by them before control of association is assumed by unit owners other than developer and any director who willfully and knowingly fails to comply with those documents); Fla. Stat. § 720.305(1)(c) (actions at law or in equity, or both, to redress alleged failure or refusal to comply with governing documents or rules of homeowners association may be brought by any member against any director or officer association who willfully and knowingly fails to comply with those documents).

482. Kokinda, *D&O Liability Insurance: There Are Exclusions, and Then There Are Exclusions*, 28-10 ABIJ 46, 47 (2010).

483. Truck Ins. Exch. v. Cassady, 2011 U.S. Dist. LEXIS 122052 (N.D. Ill. Oct. 21, 2011).

directors. However, said the court, the Insured versus Insured exclusion unambiguously barred coverage for the defendants in the underlying action.[484]

[c] Combined Insured and Non-insured Parties

When there are multiple plaintiffs in the underlying action and at least one of them is *not* an insured, does the Insured versus Insured exclusion still apply? In general, the answer is yes. For example, two condominium unit owners sued their association and an individual insured—apparently, an officer and/or director of the association—over installation of "non-compliant windows." One of the plaintiffs was a former president of the association and, therefore, remained insured under the policy. The insurer invoked the exclusion, and the defendants in the underlying action sued seeking coverage. They argued that the presence of a non-insured as a plaintiff in the underlying action prevented application of the exclusion. The court did not agree. From its inception, said the court, the underlying action involved claims by both an insured and an individual not insured under the policy, and the exclusion, therefore, operated to bar coverage for the entire suit.[485] Courts generally appear to agree with that view of the exclusion,[486] although different interpretations tend to emerge when the insured status of the plaintiffs changes when one is added or removed from pending litigation.[487] That is a topic beyond the scope of this discussion, but when it arises associations and their attorneys need the counsel of an attorney knowledgeable about D&O insurance law. They also need to be aware of two other possible complications. First, the Insured versus Insured exclusion may have an exception for suits brought *independently* of a former director—or other insureds—and without their active participation. Second, an allocation provision in the policy may determine how the court applies the exclusion. An allocation clause addresses allocation of losses

484. The policy excluded coverage for any claims brought or maintained by or on behalf of an insured organization. The exclusion prevented coverage because the association—the insured organization—brought the underlying action.

485. Marbella Condo. Ass'n v. RSUI Indem. Co., 2017 U.S. Dist. LEXIS 12363 (S.D. Fla. Jan. 30, 2017) (while measure of damages in underlying claim may have been different because plaintiffs in that action owned separate units, claims asserted were brought on behalf of both together and stemmed from same alleged installation of non-compliant glass). One commentator criticizes the opinion as elevating form over substance because the claims in the underlying action could have been brought as separate actions, and the claims of the non-insured party did not depend on those of the insured person. LaCroix, *Insured vs. Insured Exclusion: No Coverage When Claim Includes Both Non-Insured and Insured Claimants* (2017), available at: http://www.dandodiary.com/2017/02/articles/d-o-insurance/insured-vs-insured-exclusion-no-coverage-claims-includes-non-insured-insured-claimants/.

486. Jerry's Enters. v. United States Specialty Ins. Co., 845 F.3d 883 (8th Cir. 2017); Sphinx International, Inc. v. National Union Fire Insurance Company of Pittsburgh, Pennsylvania, 412 F.3d 1224 (11th Cir. 2005); PowerSports, Inc. v. Royal & Sunalliance Insurance Company, 307 F. Supp. 2d 1355 (S.D. Fla. 2004).

487. *See, e.g.*, Level 3 Communications, Inc. v. Federal Insurance Company, 168 F.3d 956 (7th Cir. 1999); Bodewes v. Ulico Cas. Co., 336 F. Supp. 2d 263 (W.D.N.Y. 2004).

when, in a single claim, there are both losses that are covered and losses that are not covered.

[d] Successors of the Association

Some policies provide that the Insured versus Insured exclusion applies to any person or entity that succeeds to the interest of the insured organization.[488] This is often raised in the corporate setting when a business is in bankruptcy, and cases addressing that issue can, therefore, be helpful in understanding that policy language.[489]

A condominium case illustrates how the successor provision may apply in the common interest community context. The treasurer of a condominium association was accused of misappropriation of association funds. The association made a claim for the alleged loss with its crime/fidelity insurer, which paid the claim in exchange for a written assignment of all of the association's rights and claims against the treasurer. The insurer, standing in the shoes of the association, sued the treasurer to recover the funds. The treasurer demanded that the D&O carrier defend him in that suit. After the crime/fidelity insurer took a voluntary dismissal, the treasurer brought an action against the D&O carrier seeking reimbursement for the defense costs and attorney's fees he incurred in the suit that had been dismissed. The D&O insurer argued that it owed no duty to defend the treasurer in that suit because it fell within the Insured versus Insured exclusion as the crime/fidelity insurer had succeeded to the interests of the association. The court agreed. The assignment to the crime/fidelity insurer of the association's claims against the treasurer meant that the crime/fidelity insurer succeeded to the interest of the association for purposes of the exclusion.[490]

[e] Prior Insureds

Courts have refused to allow the exclusion to be invoked to preclude coverage where a party in the underlying action was an insured but is no longer. For example, former employees sued their former employer for wrongful discharge. They were insureds for purposes of the employer's policy while they were employed

488. Even without specific mention of successors, some courts have applied the exclusion to receivers for the insured organization because the receiver "stands in the shoes" of the organization and if the exclusion applies to it, it should also apply to the receiver. Sagalow, *Directors and Officers Liability Insurance: A Guide for Directors, Professional Edition*, at 28, available at: http://innovationinsurancegroup.com/wp-content/uploads/2014/07/D_O_Handbook_Professional_Edition.pdf.

489. *See generally* Vance & Berman, *Last in Line; Do "Insured vs. Insured" Exclusions Apply to Assignees in Assignment for the Benefit of Creditors?*, 23 Am. Bankr. Inst. J. 12 (2004); Palmore, *"Insured vs. Insured" Exclusions in Director and Officer Liability Insurance Policies: Is Coverage Available When Chapter 11 Trustees and Debtors-In-Possession Sue Former Directors and Officers?*, 9 Bank. Dev. J. 101 (1992).

490. Great Am. Ins. Co. v. Primo, 2017 Tex. LEXIS 212 (Feb. 24, 2017).

but not after the termination. The court said that, because the policy was "claims made," the determination of the status of an injured party in the "insured v. insured" context had to be made as of the time the claim was made. It was irrelevant whether the plaintiffs were insureds at the time of the alleged wrongful act.[491]

However, policies often specifically define "insureds" to include *former* officers and directors, thus making the Insured versus Insured exclusion applicable.[492] For example, the NPMOLIP definition includes those who *were*, now are, or will become duly elected or appointed directors or officers.[493] The ISO endorsement simply defines "insured person" as any *former*, present, or future director or officer of the association.[494] Some policies may narrow the definition by stating that an insured is one who was a director or officer when the wrongful act at issue took place.[495] Additionally, the exclusion itself may modify its application to former directors and officers by an exception for claims brought by any past director or officer who has not served in that capacity for at least a prescribed number of years before the date of the claim at issue was first made.[496] One reason insurers may include this time buffer is that former officers and directors are less likely to sue for problems created before they left office.[497] Common interest communities should keep in mind that "volunteers" and committee members may also be defined as insureds, and it would be beneficial if any time buffer applied to them as well.

491. Township of Center v. First Mercury Syndicate, 117 F.3d 115 (3d Cir. 1997) (when underlying actions were brought against employer, and hence by time claims were made, plaintiffs were no longer employed by it and it would be difficult to imagine circumstance, short of conspiracy to defraud, in which wrongful discharge suit, brought by former employee, could be perceived as constituting collusive act, therefore, under facts of case ex-employees/plaintiffs were not insureds within meaning of exclusion).

492. *See, e.g.*, Biltmore Associates, LLC v. Twin City Fire Ins. Co., 572 F.3d 663, 669 (9th Cir. 2009) (holding that coverage for claims brought by company against former officers and directors was barred by Insured versus Insured exclusion).

493. Non-Profit Management and Organization Liability Insurance Policy § IV(2)(I).

494. *See* ISO Form BP 17 24 01 10, § H(5).

495. Pulliam v. Travelers Indem. Co., 403 S.C. 332, 344, 743 S.E.2d 117, 123 (Ct. App. 2013) (insurer invoked exclusion against seven respondents in underlying action who had previously served as board members and were, therefore, insureds under policy and could not participate in underlying lawsuit; however, court found wrongful acts alleged occurred during time period when none of those members were serving on board).

496. *See* Marbella Condo. Ass'n v. RSUI Indem. Co., 2017 U.S. Dist. LEXIS 12363 (S.D. Fla. Jan. 30, 2017) (three years). *See also How to Soften the Insured vs. Insured Exclusion in Your Client's D&O Insurance Policy* (AmWins Group, Inc. 2015) (carriers will frequently provide coverage for claims brought by former insureds that have not held any executive position for stated period of time, usually two years or more).

497. *How to Soften the Insured vs. Insured Exclusion in Your Client's D&O Insurance Policy* (AmWins Group, Inc. 2015).

[f] Non-collusive Actions

Some courts have taken the position that the Insured versus Insured exclusion should not apply where the underlying action is clearly not collusive.[498] In other words, these courts look to the substance of the underlying claim and the understood purpose of the exclusion. This interpretation would often prove favorable to CICs because a claim by a former director of an association against the current board members could be, but is unlikely to be, collusive. Similarly, an action against officers or directors by a member of the association who is considered an insured by virtue of being a committee member is probably not collusive.

Unfortunately for those seeking coverage, other courts reject that interpretation. Instead, they invoke basic rules of contract interpretation under which courts are generally prohibited from looking to extrinsic evidence to defeat the meaning of plain contract language.[499] In other words, absent ambiguity, the court should not look beyond the four corners of the contract. Two directors of a condominium association were boxed into the four corners of a policy when they were sued by their association.[500] The directors sought coverage from the D&O insurer, but the company denied it based on the Insured versus Insured exclusion. The court noted that the insurer did not suggest that the directors colluded with the association and conceded that in the context of the underlying action, the association and directors were true adversaries. However, the court concluded that simply because the underlying lawsuit was not collusive did not mean it could disregard the plain language of the policy.

[g] Application of Exclusion in Small Communities

The potential problem with the Insured versus Insured exclusion for small to medium-size common interest communities is that, especially in those with fewer than 100 individual owners, many, if not most, of those owners will have served at one time on the governing board or a committee. Thus, it is easy to imagine a scenario in which a great many claims by individual owners would be barred by the exclusion. This is illustrated by a Texas case in which a crossclaim was filed in an underlying case by a unit owner who had been a member of the governing board but apparently was not at the time the D&O insurer denied coverage based on the Insured versus Insured exclusion. She raised claims against the board for

---

498. *See, e.g.*, Township of Center v. First Mercury Syndicate, 117 F.3d 115 (3d Cir. 1997) (where it is clear that underlying action is not collusive, exclusion has not precluded coverage); Fidelity and Deposit Co. of Maryland v. Zandstra, 756 F. Supp. 429, 432 (N.D. Cal. 1990) (it was clear beyond doubt that party's involvement in underlying actions was not collusive and, therefore, "insured v. insured" exclusion did not preclude coverage).

499. *See, e.g.*, Sphinx Int'l, Inc. v. Nat'l Union Fire Ins. Co., 412 F.3d 1224 (11th Cir. 2005) (exclusion rationale does not trump its text); Stratton v. Nat'l Union Fire Ins. Co., 2004 U.S. Dist. LEXIS 17613 (D. Mass. Sept. 3, 2004).

500. Lee v. Nat'l Union Fire Ins. Co., 2014 U.S. Dist. LEXIS 194904 (C.D. Cal. July 9, 2014).

mishandling insurance proceeds from damages caused by a hurricane and subsequent fire that damaged several buildings, for failing to repair the buildings, for having them demolished without appropriate consent of all owners, and for otherwise not following the declaration and bylaws. The association raised no counter argument to the insurer, and the court granted the insurer summary judgment on the ground that the Insured versus Insured exclusion applied.[501]

In some cases, an exception for derivative actions would apply, but not always. In others, the "independence" exception might be invoked. However, courts generally hold that the *insured* bears the burden of proving an exception to an exclusion.[502] If the burden falls on the insured, how will he or she show the independence of the claim and that it was brought "totally" without solicitation, assistance, participation, or intervention of any association officer or director as generally required under the exception to the exclusion? How heavy a burden will a court impose? The fact is that in many residential CICs the residents interact and socialize regularly. It is easy to imagine one individual owner discussing his or her complaint against the association with a friend and neighbor who just happens to also be a member of the governing board. Is that "assistance, participation, or intervention"?

Because of the damaging potential of the Insured versus Insured exclusion for small common interest communities, they should discuss with their broker policies that limit or even omit the exclusion. One observer suggests that if a policyholder is unable to obtain a satisfactory modification to the Insured versus Insured exclusion—or eliminate it—a "Side A" Differences in Conditions (DIC) policy without the exclusion may be purchased, and this excess coverage will drop down to fill the coverage gap.[503] If the association seeks a DIC policy that omits the Insured versus Insured exclusion, it needs to make certain that the policy clearly covers the gap, because if there is an ambiguity, the DIC insurer will most likely deny coverage. The policyholder also needs to remember that Side A covers directors and officers directly rather than pays the association for its indemnification of them.

---

501. Landing Council of Co-Owners v. Fed. Ins. Co., 2013 U.S. Dist. LEXIS 127989 (S.D. Tex. Sept. 9, 2013).

502. *See, e.g.*, Bldg. Specialties, Inc. v. Liberty Mut. Fire Ins. Co., 712 F. Supp. 2d 628 (S.D. Tex. 2010) (insurer bears burden of establishing that policy exclusion constitutes avoidance or affirmative defense to coverage and once insurer demonstrates exclusion arguably applies, burden shifts to insured to show that claim does not fall within exclusion or that it comes within an exception to exclusion); U.S. Fid. & Guar. Co. v. B & B Oil Well Serv., 910 F. Supp. 1172 (S.D. Miss. 1995) (most courts have held that burden is on insured to prove that sudden and accidental exception in pollution exclusion applies); Smith v. State Farm Fire & Cas. Co., 656 N.W.2d 432 (2003) (once insurer shows application of exclusion clause, burden of proof shifts to insured because exception to exclusion "restores" coverage for which insured bears burden of proof).

503. *How to Soften the Insured vs. Insured Exclusion in Your Client's D&O Insurance Policy* (AmWins Group, Inc. 2015).

[3] Entity versus Insured Exclusion

A variation on the Insured versus Insured exclusion often found in policies designed for non-profit organizations including common interest communities is called the "entity versus insured" exclusion. It bars claims brought by the insured organization—the association—against other insureds, so there is no coverage for the defense or settlement of claims by the organization against its officers and directors.[504] Claims brought by an insured individual against another insured individual, however, are not proscribed.[505] One court noted that where the exclusion barred coverage of any claim made brought *by or on behalf* of the insured organization against any individual insured, there was no distinction between suits brought by the condominium association as the party in interest and suits brought by it as a representative and, action by the association against directors for breaching their fiduciary duties to it was not covered by the D&O policy.[506]

The ISO endorsement has a variation on the entity versus insured exclusion. It says the policy does not apply to a loss resulting from a claim brought by or on behalf of the association or any insured person in any capacity. It provides for two exceptions: derivative actions brought on behalf of the association by one or more unit owners who are not insureds and who bring the claim without solicitation, assistance,[507] or participation of an insured and claims arising out of a wrongful employment practices act.[508]

[4] Property or Community Association Manager

Policies may have an exclusion for claims brought against the manager. For example, in one case the policy provided the insurer would not be liable to pay any loss of the property manager based on, directly or indirectly arising out of, or in any

504. *See* http://www.insurancejournal.com/news/national/2012/05/25/248979.htm quoting *Directors and Officers Liability (D&O) Insurance Dictionary* (Willis Towers Watson, 2012). *See, e.g.*, Non-Profit Management and Organization Liability Insurance Policy § IV.6. The NPMOLIP exclusion bars coverage for any loss connected to any claim against any insured "brought or maintained by or on behalf" of the association unless it is "brought and maintained totally independently of, and totally without the solicitation, assistance, participation, or intervention of any officer, director or trustee" of the association. Note that this exclusion may be removed from the policy by an endorsement specifically designed for that purpose. *See* Travelers Non-Profit Change Endorsement (CIRI 70004).

505. LaCroix, *D&O Insurance: Thinking About the Insured vs. Insured Exclusion* (2016), available at: http://www.dandodiary.com/2016/06/articles/d-o-insurance/do-insurance-thinking-about-the-insured-vs-insured-exclusion/.

506. Lee v. Nat'l Union Fire Ins. Co., 2014 U.S. Dist. LEXIS 194904 (C.D. Cal. July 9, 2014).

507. *But see* Julio & Sons Co. v. Travelers Cas. & Sur. Co. of Am., 684 F. Supp. 2d 330 (S.D.N.Y. 2010) (when shareholders bringing derivative action on behalf of insured organization are themselves insureds, derivative exception is inapplicable).

508. ISO Form BP 17 24 01 10, § B.k. The exception to the exclusion that would allow a person defined as in insured to bring a claim arising out of wrongful employment practices would seem to apply to circumstances in which a former officer, for example, brought an action for wrongful discharge. That exception would not be relevant in the CIC context.

way involving any claim brought by, or derivatively on behalf of, the association against a property manager or an employee of the manager.[509] This is in effect an "entity versus insured" exclusion, albeit applying only to a specific insured. Obviously, the reason for including the exclusion is that the manager is an insured under the policy. As discussed previously,[510] it is not common for managers to be insured under a D&O policy issued to a common interest community. If the manager is an insured, the association needs to discuss with its broker the import of adding a manager exclusion. The exclusion, however, may be incorporated into any endorsement that adds the manager as an insured. For example, there is an "Amended Definition of Insured to Include Property Manager" endorsement that can be added to the NPMOLIP, and it excludes coverage for a claim brought or maintained by or on behalf of the association against the manager and any of its directors, officers, or employees.

NOTE: Given the fact that the manager may not be covered by the association's D&O coverage questions, the association should make sure the manager has an errors & omissions policy.

[5] Illegal Profit

All standard D&O policies exclude illegal remuneration.[511] The customary language of the "illegal" or "personal" profit exclusion bars coverage for claims involving the gain of any profit, remuneration, or advantage to which the insured was not "legally entitled."[512] In policies specifically designed for common interest communities, the exclusion may proscribe damages arising out of any transaction of the insured from which the insured will gain any personal profit or advantage not shared equitably by the association members.[513]

Many—but not all[514]—policies modify the standard language to bar the gain *in fact* of any profit, remuneration, or advantage.[515] The words "in fact" have caused confusion. As one commentary notes, questions arise over whether allegations of

509. VierraMoore, Inc. v. Cont'l Cas. Co., 940 F. Supp. 2d 1270 (E.D. Cal. 2013).

510. *See* § 14.12[2][d], *supra.*

511. Ackerman, *A Common Law Approach to D&O Insurance "In Fact" Exclusion Disputes*, 79 U. Chi. L. Rev. 1429, 1434 (2012) (exclusions barring coverage for wrongful acts from which insured personally profited are universal feature of D&O policies).; Kokinda, *D&O Liability Insurance: There Are Exclusions, and Then There Are Exclusions*, 28-10 ABIJ 46, 67 (2010).

512. ISO Form BP 17 24 01 10, § B.1.e.

513. *See, e.g.*, State Farm Fire & Cas. Co. v. Anderson, 2013 U.S. Dist. LEXIS 57837 (S.D. Miss. Apr. 23, 2013).

514. Ackerman, *A Common Law Approach to D&O Insurance "In Fact" Exclusion Disputes*, 79 U. Chi. L. Rev. 1429, 1434 (2012) (not all policies use "in fact" language; some personal profit exclusions set out more detailed requirements as to what kind of factual showing must be made to invoke exclusion).

515. *See, e.g.*, Non-Profit Management and Organization Liability Insurance Policy § IV.11.

personal profit in a complaint are sufficient for the insurer to invoke the exclusion or whether there must be a judicial determination of improper personal profit.[516] The commentary notes that courts have taken different approaches, with some finding the allegations of the complaint are sufficient, others requiring a judicial determination, and still others requiring something in between.[517]

The fact that the allegations in the underlying complaint may allege actions that could be considered negligent or a breach of fiduciary duties does not prevent application of the personal profit exclusion.[518]

At first blush, one might think this exclusion has far more application to for-profit corporations where directors or officers might engage in insider trading or accept bribes or improper gifts. In fact, the Illegal Profit exclusion simply takes on a different meaning in the common interest community context.

Association directors and officers may be prohibited from being paid or accepting gifts. In many states the bylaws are required to address what compensation, if any, officers and directors may receive,[519] and in response, the bylaws may bar compensation. In Florida officers and board members serve *without compensation* unless the bylaws provide *otherwise*.[520] Florida law also prohibits officers and directors from accepting gifts from anyone providing or proposing

516. *See* Ackerman, *A Common Law Approach to D&O Insurance "In Fact" Exclusion Disputes*, 79 U. Chi. L. Rev. 1429, 1430 (2012) (asking if carrier should be able to produce its own evidence of personal profit and if it can it deny coverage before underlying case is litigated or if it must wait until that case has concluded).

517. Ackerman, *A Common Law Approach to D&O Insurance "In Fact" Exclusion Disputes*, 79 U. Chi. L. Rev. 1429, 1436–45 (2012).

518. *See, e.g.*, State Farm Fire & Cas. Co. v. Anderson, 2013 U.S. Dist. LEXIS 57837 (S.D. Miss. Apr. 23, 2013) (where unit owners sued directors of condominium association and alleged self-dealing, breach of common-law duty of loyalty and fiduciary duty to association, bad faith, intentional misconduct, knowing violation of governing documents, and illegal, oppressive, and/or fraudulent acts, breaches alleged fell squarely within exclusion for damages arising out of any transaction of insured from which insured would gain any personal profit or advantage not shared equitably by condominium association members).

519. *See, e.g.*, 765 Ill. Comp. Stat. 605/18(a)(3) (bylaws must provide for compensation, if any, of members of board); Ohio Rev. Code Ann. § 5311.08(B)(1)(e) (unless otherwise provided by declaration, bylaws must provide for compensation of directors); Ore. Rev. Stat. § 100.415(1)(e)(D) (bylaws must provide for compensation, if any, of the directors); S.C. Code Ann. § 27-31-160(a) (bylaws must necessarily provide for, where proper, compensation of administrator or board of administration). *See also* N.Y. Co-op. Corp. § 62 (corporation may provide fair remuneration for its officers and directors and for members of its executive committee).

520. Fla. Stat. § 718.112(2)(a)1 (bylaws of condominium association must provide for compensation, if any, of officers and board members and unless otherwise provided in bylaws, officers, and board members serve without compensation); Fla. Stat. § 719.106(1)(a)1. (bylaws or other cooperative documents must provide for compensation, if any, of officers and board members and unless otherwise provided in bylaws, officers, and board members serve without compensation); Fla. Stat. § 720.303(12) (director, officer, or committee member of homeowners association may not directly receive any salary or compensation from association for performance of duties as director, officer, or committee member and may not in any other way benefit financially from service to association except for any fee or compensation authorized in governing documents or in advance by vote of a majority of voting interests).

to provide goods or services to the association.[521] The governing documents of any CIC could include a similar prohibition. Thus, if an officer or director is prohibited by statute or the governing documents from receiving compensation or gifts and accepts a gift or votes to compensate him- or herself,[522] the illegal remuneration exclusion will likely bar coverage for a resulting claim against that officer or director.

Unlike directors in large for-profit companies, CIC directors often vote on the approval of virtually every contract for goods and services supplied to the association. There is great opportunity for steering a contract in exchange for a personal benefit, a "kickback," or offer of a discount.[523] Also, it is not at all unusual for friends or family members to own or manage a business that provides the precise good or service the association is seeking. These personal gains or conflicts may be barred by state law. For example, in many states a corporate director's conflict of interest can render a contract void or voidable when the conflict is not disclosed in compliance with the law.[524] Some states specifically incorporate those statutes by reference into common interest community laws,[525] and in Illinois, limitations on self-dealing contracts are found in the Condominium

521. Fla. Stat. § 718.111(1)(a) (officer or director of condominium may not solicit, offer to accept, or accept anything or service of value for which consideration has not been provided for his or her own benefit or that of his or her immediate family, from any person providing or proposing to provide goods or services to association); Fla. Stat. § 719.104(8)(a) (officer or director of cooperative association may not solicit, offer to accept, or accept anything or service of value for which consideration has not been provided for his or her own benefit or that of his or her immediate family, from any person providing or proposing to provide goods or services to association); Fla. Stat. § 720.3033(3) (officer or director of homeowners association may not solicit, offer to accept, or accept any good or service of value for which consideration has not been provided for his or her benefit or for benefit of member of his or her immediate family from any person providing or proposing to provide goods or services to association and if board finds that any officer or director has violated this proscription, it must immediately remove that officer or director from office).

522. Any time a board takes vote that could result in a personal benefit to a director, that director should recuse him- or herself from the vote.

523. Ackerman, *A Common Law Approach to D&O Insurance "In Fact" Exclusion Disputes*, 79 U. Chi. L. Rev. 1429 (2012) (exclusion would prevent coverage of judgment against executive for accepting kickbacks from corporation's suppliers).

524. *See, e.g.*, Cal. Corp. Code § 7233(a) (no contract or other transaction between corporation and one or more of its directors, or between corporation and any domestic or foreign corporation, firm, or association in which one or more of its directors has material financial interest, is either void or voidable if material facts as to transaction, and director's interest are fully disclosed or known to members); Fla. Stat. § 617.0832(1) (no contract or other transaction between corporation and one or more of its directors or any other corporation, firm, association, or entity in which one or more of its directors are directors or officers or are financially interested will be either void or voidable if fact of that relationship or interest is disclosed or known to board of directors or committee or contract or transaction is fair and reasonable at time it is authorized).

525. *See, e.g.*, Cal. Civ. Code § 5350(a) (applying corporate conflict statute to all common interest community associations even those not incorporated); Fla. Stat. § 718.3026(3) (requiring disclosure of self-dealing contracts to association members and cancellation of contract by vote of members).

Property Act.[526] Failure to follow the requirements of those laws could result in the Illegal Remuneration exclusion barring coverage for a resulting claim.

Associations need to be wary of actions by the community association manager that could cause the exclusion to be invoked. In one case, for example, unit owners sued both their condominium association and its management company claiming the company collected premiums to pay for the association's insurance, overcharged for those premiums, and "pocketed" some of the money. The claim against the association was based on the manager being its agent. The insurer contended that to the extent the overcharging allegations claimed that the *association* collected money from unit owners to which it was not entitled, the Personal Profit exclusion applied. The court agreed.[527]

Finally, claims for wrongfully charging personal expenses to the association would be barred by the exclusion.[528] Ordinarily, common interest community associations have safeguards in place to avoid these misuses of association funds, but in small communities without professional management, abuses are possible.

[6] Investment Loss

An exclusion that will probably not be included in D&O policies specifically designed for non-profit organizations bars coverage for damages arising out of profits or losses resulting from any investment. It is understandable that insurers of for-profit corporations would not want to insure against suits contending the directors made a bad business decision. In one case, however, an insurer attempted to assert that the exclusion precluded coverage for suits by tenant/shareholders who sought damages for diminution in the value of their apartments or their shares in the cooperative. The court characterized the interpretation of the insurer as "highly implausible" and said it would bar coverage of virtually every suit by a shareholder against directors and officers of the cooperative. The exclusion did not relieve the insurer of the duty to defend the underlying suit.[529]

There is, however, a possible application of the Investment Loss exclusion to common interest communities. These communities typically have reserve funds

526. 765 Ill. Comp. Stat. 605/18(a)(16) (board of managers may not enter into contract with current board member or with corporation or partnership in which board member or member of board member's immediate family has 25 percent or more interest, unless notice of intent to enter contract is given to unit owners and unit owners are afforded opportunity by filing a petition for election to approve or disapprove that contract).

527. Parc Condo. Ass'n v. Travelers Cas. & Sur. Co. of Am., 2016 U.S. Dist. LEXIS 155779 (S.D. Tex. Mar. 31, 2016) (factual allegations on which association relied in seeking coverage concerned it, through management company, allegedly gaining profit, remuneration, or advantage to which it was allegedly not legally entitled and, thus insurer met its burden to prove exclusion applied and it had no duty to defend).

528. 3 *New Appleman Law of Liability Insurance* § 22.06[2][b][ii] (rev. ed., Matthew Bender, 2017).

529. Hotel Des Artistes v. Transamerica Ins. Co., 1994 U.S. Dist. LEXIS 7800 (S.D.N.Y. June 10, 1994).

for replacing major building components, for example, roofs and elevators, and for expensive maintenance like repainting a building. Depending on the size of the community, the funds can total hundreds of thousands or even millions of dollars. Most commonly, these monies are invested in certificates of deposit, currently paying little interest. Some governing boards will invest in bonds.[530] There is little guidance—in common interest community enabling legislation or governing documents—on investment of association funds, although the basic fiduciary obligation directors owe provides some parameters.[531] A comment to the Uniform Common Interest Ownership Act explains that the drafters of the Act concluded that investment standards governing investment of reserves or other association funds did not need to be included in the Act because boards are usually very conservative when investing association funds.[532] Nonetheless, a governing board could decide to make risky investments and then be subject to suit. An Investment Loss exclusion would bar coverage for that suit.

[7] Bodily or Personal Injury and Property Damage

One commentary asserts that if one were to ask a D&O claims analyst or adjuster which claims are most often rejected, he or she would answer claims seeking "bodily injury and/or property damages."[533] Most D&O policies include exclusions for loss from claims arising from bodily injury or property damage, because those perils are typically insured under a CGL policy.[534] CGL policies also usually cover "personal injury," so losses arising from them may also be excluded from D&O coverage. Both the ISO endorsement and NPMOLIP contain these exclusions.

---

530. *See* Uniform Common Interest Ownership Act § 3-102, comment 12 (anecdotal evidence suggests that reserves of most common interest community associations are invested in cash or short-term bond funds).

531. *See generally Are You a Prudent Investor?* (Becker & Poliakoff 2012).

532. *See* Uniform Common Interest Ownership Act § 3-102, comment 12.

533. Meskin, *When Are You Not Covered by Your D&O Policy? Maintaining Proper Coverage* (Cooperator, Aug. 2008), available at: http://cooperator.com/articles/1673/1/When-Are-You-Not-Covered-By-Your-DampO-Policy/Page1.html.

534. Quinn & Levin, *Directors and Officers Liability Insurance: Probable Directions in Texas Law*, 20 Rev. Litig. 381, 432 (2001) (exclusions for bodily injury, emotional distress, property damage, invasions of privacy, wrongful entry, wrongful eviction, false arrest, false imprisonment, malicious prosecution, and defamation are designed to eliminate overlapping coverage between D&O policies and general or homeowners liability policies); *D&O Insurance Policy Exclusions*, available at: https://www.connerstrong.com/resources/site1/news/1414CSB%20ER%20Policy%20Exclusions-2.pdf (D&O policies are built with presumption that they are just part of policyholder's overall program of insurance and they, therefore, generally contain exclusions to preclude coverage for claims that are typically covered by other types of insurance).

The ISO endorsement states that the insurance does not apply to any loss resulting from any claim for bodily injury,[535] mental or emotional distress,[536] or property damage[537] or any claim arising out of personal and advertising injury.[538] The NPMOLIP provides that the insurer will not be liable to make any payment for loss in connection with any claim made against any of the insureds for bodily injury, sickness, disease, or death of any person, or any damage to or destruction of any tangible property including loss of its use or mental anguish or emotional distress.[539]

[a] Bodily Injury

Generally, "bodily injury" is a narrow term that encompasses only physical injuries to the body and the consequences of those injuries.[540] However, remember that D&O policy exclusions for bodily injury often include broad prefatory language. For example, the policy may proscribe coverage for losses based on, arising from, or in consequence of any bodily injury. Under that language, coverage for a claim based on the typical slip and fall accident would be barred,[541] but so also could be claims *related* to the bodily injury.[542]

535. ISO Form BP 17 24 01 10, § B.b.

536. ISO Form BP 17 24 01 10, § B.c. There is an exception for circumstances in which allegations of mental or emotional distress are made in a claim arising from a wrongful employment practices act, a term defined in the policy as wrongful dismissal, discharge or termination of employment, breach of any implied employment contract, employment-related misrepresentation, violation of any federal, state or local statute, regulation, ordinance or common law concerning employment or discrimination in employment, sexual or other illegal workplace harassment, wrongful failure to employ or promote, wrongful reference, discipline, or deprivation of a career opportunity, failure to adopt adequate workplace or employment policies and procedures; or, illegal retaliatory treatment. ISO Form BP 17 24 01 10, § H.9.

537. ISO Form BP 17 24 01 10, § B.d.

538. ISO Form BP 17 24 01 10, § B.n.

539. Non-Profit Management and Organization Liability Insurance Policy § IV.1. The exclusion for mental anguish or emotional distress does not apply to any claim for Wrongful Employment Practices.

540. Citizens Ins. Co. of Am. v. Leiendecker, 962 S.W.2d 446 (Mo. App. 1998) (common meaning of phrase "bodily harm, sickness or disease" is not ambiguous and refers to physical conditions of body and excludes mental suffering or emotional distress); Chatton v. National Union Fire Ins. Co., 10 Cal. App. 4th 846, 13 Cal. Rptr. 2d 318 (1992) (coverage under bodily injury clause of CGL policy is limited to physical injury to body and does not include nonphysical, emotional or mental harm); Allstate Ins. Co. v. Diamant, 401 Mass. 654, 518 N.E.2d 1154 (1988). *See generally* Farrell-Kolb, *General Liability Coverage for Claims of Emotional Distress—An Insurance Nightmare*, 45 Drake L. Rev. 981, 986 (1997).

541. *See, e.g.*, Fed. Ins. Co. v. Evian Horizontal Prop. Regime, 126 Fed. Appx. 589 (4th Cir. 2005) (where unit owner sued association after fall on common area walkway for bodily injury by negligent, willful, wanton, careless, and grossly negligent acts, all claims alleged unmistakably arose from bodily injury and were, therefore, excluded).

542. *See, e.g.*, Henning v. Contl Cas. Co., 254 F.3d 1291 (11th Cir. 2001) (appellant was injured when struck by motorized cart driven by resident of community and association's professional

Commercial general liability policies typically define "bodily injury" to mean bodily injury, sickness, or disease sustained by a person, including death resulting from bodily injury, sickness, or disease.[543] Some courts consider emotional harm as a bodily injury.[544] However, even if a court excepts emotional distress from the meaning of bodily injury, some D&O policies exclude losses resulting from any claim for emotional distress, so coverage would still be excluded.

[b] Property Damage

The exclusion in D&O policies for property damage is generally tersely stated, and policies do not define "property damage." One can, however, look to commercial general liability policies for the meaning of property damage.[545] Indeed,

---

liability policy excluded coverage for claims based on, arising out of, or in any way involving any actual or alleged bodily injury; although appellant argued her claim was not for personal injury, but for negligent failure to obtain insurance after CGL carrier disclaimed coverage, court held that because claim was based on underlying personal injury claim, exclusionary clause applied); Salisbury West Condo. Trust v. Travelers Cas. & Sur. Co., 2013 U.S. Dist. LEXIS 167496 (D. Mass. Oct. 15, 2013) (where unit owners in underlying suit sought damages for "lasting personal injury to safety, health and welfare" caused by flooding at their unit and policy excluded claims arising out of, directly or indirectly resulting from, in consequence of, or in any way involving bodily injury, sickness, mental anguish, emotional distress, disease or death of any person, term "arising out of" required only slight or incidental link between injury and risk and served to bar coverage).

543. *See, e.g.*, ISO Form CG 00 01 12 07, § V.3. Note that an endorsement can be added to a policy that includes "mental anguish or emotional distress" caused by bodily injury, sickness, or disease in the definition of "bodily injury." *See, e.g.*, Essex Insurance Company Form MEIL 1216 07 10.

544. Most courts will find coverage for a claim for emotional distress accompanied by allegations of a specific physical injury, for example ulcers or exacerbated hypertension. Monteleone, *Coverage Issues Under Commercial General Liability and Directors' and Officers' Liability Policies*, 18 W. New Eng. L. Rev. 47, 49 (1996). A minority of courts say that emotional distress is included in the definition of "bodily injury." *See, e.g.*, Sova v. Cove Homeowner's Ass'n, 102 So. 3d 863 (La. .App. 2012) (claims for mental anguish have been held to be claims for bodily injury); Lavanant v. General Acci. Ins. Co., 584 N.Y.S.2d 744, 745, 79 N.Y.2d 623, 626, 595 N.E.2d 819, 820 (1992) (coverage for "bodily injury" includes emotional distress resulting from negligent conduct of insured, where no physical injury or contact is involved; mental injury alone is covered).

545. In CGL policies there are two parts to the definition of "property damage." First, it means *physical injury* to tangible property including any resulting loss of its use. *See, e.g.*, ISO Form CG 00 01 12 07, § V.17.a. *See also* Oak Ford Owners Ass'n v. Auto-Owners Ins. Co., 510 F. Supp. 2d 812 (M.D. Fla. 2007) (dredging from creek and depositing fill on bank brought about significant changes that constituted physical injury and, therefore, property damage); Traveler's Ins. Co. v. Eljer Mfg., 258 Ill. Dec. 792, 197 Ill. 2d 278, 301-02, 757 N.E.2d 481, 496 (2001) (tangible property suffers *physical* injury when it is "altered in appearance, shape, color or in other material dimension," but it does not experience *physical* injury if it suffers intangible damage; term "physical" limits word "injury" in policy definition of "property damage" and phrase "physical injury" does not include intangible damage to property, such as economic loss and, therefore, diminution in value of whole, resulting from failure of component to perform as promised, does not constitute physical injury). Policies generally do not define "tangible property," but courts have said it is "that which is capable of being handled, touched, or physically possessed." Lamar Truck Plaza, Inc. v. Sentry Ins., 757 P.2d 1143, 1144 (Colo. App. 1988) (purely economic losses—lost profits or investment—are not included in definition of "tangible property"). *See also* Graber v. State Farm Fire &

when D&O coverage is added by endorsement to a CGL, the property damage definition in the primary policy will probably apply.[546] It is important to keep in mind that D&O policies cover *claims against an insured*, not property damage. The purpose, therefore, of the Property Damage exclusion is to bar *claims related* to property damage.

When the allegations of an underlying complaint are solely and entirely within the Property Damage exclusion, there is no coverage.[547] The "arising out of" language in many policies will bring claims that flow from property damage within the exclusion.[548] Claims only tangentially related to property damage, however, are generally not barred from coverage.[549] For example, a condominium

---

Casualty Co., 244 Mont. 265, 269, 797 P.2d 214, 216 (Mont. 1990). *But see* Dietrich v. Travelers Ins. Co., 551 So. 2d 64, 66 (La. App. 1989) (Louisiana Supreme Court equates "tangible property" with "corporeal property," thus although right to benefits payable under health and disability policy may be intangible, actual benefits that would have been payable constitute tangible property, that is money). The second meaning of property damage is loss of use of tangible property not physically injured. *See, e.g.*, ISO Form CG 00 01 12 07, § V.17.b. These losses of use are deemed to occur at the time of the occurrence that caused them.

546. *See, e.g.*, Oak Ford Owners Ass'n v. Auto-Owners Ins. Co., 510 F. Supp. 2d 812 (M.D. Fla. 2007) where the association policy included CGL coverage, which covered property damage, and a D&O endorsement, which excluded coverage for property damage. The court interpreted the exclusion by examining the definition of "property damage" in the CGL policy.

547. Beauvallon Condo. Ass'n v. Granite State Ins. Co., 2011 U.S. Dist. LEXIS 69606 (D. Colo. June 29, 2011). *See also* Scharf v. Federal Ins. Co., 261 A.D.2d 257, 690 N.Y.S.2d 265 (1999) (genesis of underlying claim that sought to compel cooperative corporation directors to restore building to habitability after devastating fire was property damage caused by that fire and was, therefore, excluded from coverage under property damage exclusion).

548. *See, e.g.*, Commodore Plaza Condo. Ass'n v. QBE Ins. Corp., 2013 U.S. Dist. LEXIS 5195 (S.D. Fla. Jan. 14, 2013). In *Commodore Plaza* a hurricane damaged a townhouse roof. The association sent workers into the house, and they caused additional damages. The association also failed to keep the house clean and sanitary and dropped debris inside it, causing damages to the walls, ceilings, and roof. These actions, along with inadequate extermination, in turn caused a rodent infestation. Finally, the association failed to install roof tarps in a timely and proper manner resulting in additional water and mold damage. The townhouse owner sued the association. The D&O carrier denied coverage based on the property damage exclusion. The court held that all of the complained of actions in the underlying complaint flowed from the hurricane property damage.

549. *See, e.g.*, Landing Council of Co-Owners v. Fed. Ins. Co., 2013 U.S. Dist. LEXIS 127989 (S.D. Tex. Sept. 9, 2013) (where underlying action alleged association, in violation of Texas Condominium Act and in breach of documents, failed to assess for common expenses, including security, claim appeared to be separate and independent of hurricane damage and was covered); Pulliam v. Travelers Indem. Co., 403 S.C. 332, 342, 743 S.E.2d 117, 122 (Ct. App. 2013) (where unit owners, in action concerning construction defects, alleged association failed to inform them of conflict of interest in developer-controlled association and, thereby breached fiduciary duty, court concluded unit owners did not allege physical injury to tangible property constituting property damage); Clark v. General Accident Ins. Co. PR., 1996 U.S. Dist. LEXIS 20809 (D.V.I. Mar. 5, 1996) (where unit owners sued over handling of insurance proceeds after their unit was damaged by hurricane, the claims they asserted were not based on or attributable to injury to or destruction of any tangible property; while hurricane and damage it wrought formed part of background to suit, underlying action did not seek to recover for physical injury to and destruction of property caused by that hurricane). *See also* Admiral Indem. Co. v. Travelers Cas. & Sur. Co. of Am., 881 F. Supp. 2d 570, 577, n.5 (S.D.N.Y. 2012) (where in underlying action by owner against association

property was damaged by a hurricane. It was eventually terminated and the common elements sold. Unit owners sued arguing that the condominium was not properly terminated and the association lacked authority to sell the common elements. The insurer contended these claims arose out of the damage caused by the hurricane, but the court said that hurricane property damage did not cause the association to make decisions outside of its range of authority nor lead to the process for terminating the condominium and, thus, the Property Damage exclusion did not apply.[550]

The Property Damage exclusion is of particular significance to common interest community associations because their purpose is largely property maintenance and repair, and claims based on those duties are not uncommon. Indeed, associations have argued the Property Damage exclusion renders a D&O policy illusory and violates public policy. One court, however, responded that the fact that the primary responsibility of an association was related to operation and maintenance of tangible property did not mean the Property Damage exclusion barred coverage for all claims that might be asserted against it. There were other claims, said the court, that could be asserted against the association that would not fall within the Property Damage exclusion and might, therefore, be covered by a D&O policy.[551] Another court said that while it understood that the association believed the exclusion was unfair given its line of business, the court had to presume that the association read the policy and understood its contents and that, had it not wished to enter into an policy containing a broad exclusion for claims arising from property damage, it could have negotiated a change to the exclusion or obtained coverage from a different insurer.[552]

NOTE: Associations should establish how a general exclusion for claims arising out of property damage or a more specific one added by endorsement might limit its coverage. In the case of an endorsement, the association may be able to convince the insurer not to add it to the policy. It can also discuss with its broker the possibility of obtaining coverage for claims arising out of property damage.[553]

over damage allegedly caused by it to owner's property, one claim was for defamation against building manager, court, in *dicta*, rejected insurer's contention that defamation claim was not covered because it arose from original property damage and stated that harm from property damage was very different from that from defamation and insurer cited no case where "property damage" exclusion excluded defamation claim).

550. Landing Council of Co-Owners v. Fed. Ins. Co., 247 F. Supp. 3d 802 (S.D. Tex. 2017).

551. Eastpointe Condo. I Ass'n v. Travelers Cas. & Sur. Co. of Am., 379 Fed. Appx. 906 (11th Cir. 2010).

552. Landing Council of Co-Owners v. Fed. Ins. Co., 2013 U.S. Dist. LEXIS 127989 (S.D. Tex. Sept. 9, 2013).

553. *See* Edlin, *Common Interest Communities in North Carolina*, at 272 (N.C. Bar Ass'n Found. 2013) (association will want to make sure coverage includes claims arising out of or related to damage to property association is obligated to maintain as one of its main functions is to maintain property). *Consider* Far Northwest Dev. Co., LLC v. Cmty. Ass'n of Underwriters of Am., Inc.,

[i] Exclusion Applied to Failure to Repair

Actions alleging a governing board has failed to repair property are not uncommon. Coverage for these suits under a D&O policy is likely barred by the property damage portion of the exclusion. For example, the owner of a commercial condominium unit sued after the association failed to remedy plumbing leaks that damaged the property and the leaks caused the unit owner to lose tenants and rent. The court held that the allegations of the underlying complaint were solely and entirely within the Property Damage exclusion and the insurer, therefore, had no duty to defend.[554] Similarly, claims for negligence based on failure to clean up and repair property after a hurricane and to exercise reasonable care to preserve the value of one unit owner's property were not covered.[555] The same result was reached in cases in which the association allegedly failed to repair property after a fire.[556] Diminution in the value of the property resulting from the failure of an association to repair it would also come within the exclusion.[557]

Disputes over whether property is the maintenance responsibility of the association or the individual owner are common. In a fairly typical suit, a townhouse owner brought an action against the homeowners association seeking a determination that floor trusses were common elements and that, under the governing

2007 U.S. Dist. LEXIS 28355 (W.D. Wash. Apr. 16, 2007), *rev'd on other grounds*, 297 Fed. Appx. 694 (9th Cir. 2008) (policy covered property damage caused by occurrence that took place during policy period in coverage territory). In *Far Northwest* a director was sued for, *inter alia*, failure to disclose, failure to investigate, failure to maintain and repair the condominiums, and failure to provide adequate reserves. The lower court held those failures did not cause the property damage alleged. The appellate court reversed and said the acts of the director caused some of the property damage and, as a result, those acts, if merely negligent, were covered under the policy.

554. Beauvallon Condo. Ass'n v. Granite State Ins. Co., 2011 U.S. Dist. LEXIS 69606 (D. Colo. June 29, 2011).

555. Landing Council of Co-Owners v. Fed. Ins. Co., 2013 U.S. Dist. LEXIS 127989 (S.D. Tex. Sept. 9, 2013) (negligence claims based on failure to clean up and repair property after hurricane and to exercise reasonable care to preserve value of unit owner's property clearly arose from property damage related to hurricane and were subject to property damage exclusion).

556. Scharf v. Federal Ins. Co., 261 A.D.2d 257, 690 N.Y.S.2d 265 (1999) (genesis of underlying claim that sought to compel cooperative corporation directors to restore building to habitability after devastating fire was property damage caused by that fire and was, therefore, excluded from coverage under property damage exclusion). Board of Managers of Yardarm Condo. II v. Federal Ins. Co., 247 A.D.2d 499, 669 N.Y.S.2d 332 (1998) (where underlying complaint alleged governing board was negligent in failing to rebuild condominium in timely manner after fire damaged it, property damage exclusion clearly and unequivocally applied to that claim, which was indirectly, if not directly, related to property damage caused by fire).

557. Pulliam v. Travelers Indem. Co., 403 S.C. 332, 341, 743 S.E.2d 117, 122 (Ct. App. 2013). In *Pulliam* condominium unit owners sued their association. Before the association was created, the developer completed construction of the project and made repairs. The plaintiffs alleged the association failed to adequately inspect, repair, and maintain the common elements. The court noted the association did not exist at the time of the initial construction or repairs, so it could not be sued for defective construction or repairs. Assuming any subsequent further deterioration of the faulty construction or repairs could be attributed to inaction by the association, it would at most constitute diminution in the value of the property which would be specifically included in the definition of "property damage" for purposes of the exclusion.

documents, the association was required to repair them. The court found the carrier was not obligated to indemnify for losses related to the underlying action because it was clearly related to physical property damage to the townhouse floor truss system.[558] The actual physical damage should generally be covered by the association's property policy. What is excluded from D&O coverage is a suit over the failure to accept responsibility for the repairs.

NOTE: Because suits are brought against officers or directors for failure to maintain the property, it is important for associations to determine whether the Property Damage exclusion applies to those claims. If so, the association should ask its broker to obtain coverage for them.

[ii] Breach of Fiduciary Duty Claims

When an association has allegedly failed to maintain the property, one cause of action brought against it will likely be for breach of a fiduciary duty. Two cases out the federal Southern District from Florida decided only a few years apart demonstrate that courts can apply the law differently to similar facts.

In the first case, members of a homeowners association sued for breach of fiduciary duty for failure to maintain the property after the association failed to act to prevent the common areas from deteriorating and then, contrary to the advice of an engineer that it hired, made repairs using inferior materials. The association sought coverage from its D&O insurer, but the insurer invoked the Property Damage exclusion. The court said a homeowners association exists primarily to protect the fiduciary interests of its members in the common areas of the community. Therefore, any breach of fiduciary duty would likely result in property damage, making it "nonsensical" to say that D&O coverage excludes property damage. The exclusion, averred the court, only proscribed coverage for damage that should be covered by general liability insurance, for example, damage by a fire, but the loss in the case before the court was property damage that arose from a claim for breach of fiduciary duty: the exact scenario, concluded the court, the policy covered.[559]

A Texas federal court sided partly with that Florida decision.[560] In the Texas case there was a breach of fiduciary claim in the underlying action. One basis for the claim was that after a hurricane damaged the property, the governing board

558. Huntingdon Ridge Townhouse Homeowners Ass'n v. QBE Ins. Corp., 2009 U.S. Dist. LEXIS 108558 (M.D. Tenn. Nov. 20, 2009).

559. Lumbermens Mut. Cas. Co. v. Dadeland Cove Section One Homeowners' Ass'n, 2007 U.S. Dist. LEXIS 78319 (S.D. Fla. Oct. 11, 2007), *aff'd*, 295 Fed. Appx. 361 (11th Cir. 2008) (to whatever little extent property damage exclusion muddied coverage issue, if at all, court was compelled to resolve ambiguity in favor of insured).

560. Landing Council of Co-Owners v. Fed. Ins. Co., 2013 U.S. Dist. LEXIS 127989 (S.D. Tex. Sept. 9, 2013).

failed to collect assessments because it had an undisclosed interest in selling the property. That claim, said the court, could have arisen independent of the hurricane and was not, therefore, barred by the Property Damage exclusion. On the other hand, a claim that the board breached its fiduciary duty by mismanaging insurance proceeds received as a result of the hurricane could not have arisen but for that hurricane and was not covered.

In the second Florida case, a condominium unit owner sued her association after two hurricanes struck the building. The plaintiff in that underlying action brought a breach of fiduciary duty claim alleging the association failed to properly maintain, repair, and replace the building's roof and air conditioning units, and that, as a result, water infiltrated the building and caused extensive damage to her unit. The court said the claim depended on the existence of property damage and the Property Damage exclusion, therefore, applied to the breach of fiduciary duty claim.[561]

An Illinois federal court agreed with the later Florida decision.[562] In that case the association sued the developer over construction defects. The developer responded by suing the members of the association's board of directors for breach of fiduciary duties, charging them with allowing the alleged defects to occur and continue and failing to make necessary repairs, remediation, or replacements. The insurer said the construction defects were within the Property Damage exclusion. The court concluded the breach of fiduciary duty claim clearly originated from the construction defects alleged in the association suit against the developer and that the exclusion was not limited to claims for construction defects *directly caused* by an insured. The insurer had no duty to defend the directors.

[iii] Failure to Establish Reserve for Repairs

The establishment of a reserve fund for repair or replacement of major components of a common interest community property is a good business practice and required by law in some states. Failure to establish a reserve may be a basis for a suit by unit owners against the association and governing board. However, even though that claim would clearly be related to property damage, the failure itself to establish a reserve would not result in physical damage to tangible property, but in more money having to be spent from the pockets of unit owners to make the repairs than might have otherwise been required and that, as one court said, was economic, not property, damage.[563]

561. Eastpointe Condo. I Ass'n v. Travelers Cas. & Sur. Co. of Am., 379 Fed. Appx. 906 (11th Cir. 2010).

562. Hess v. Travelers Cas. & Sur. Co. of Am., 2013 U.S. Dist. LEXIS 23281 (N.D. Ill. Feb. 20, 2013).

563. Pulliam v. Travelers Indem. Co., 403 S.C. 332, 342, 743 S.E.2d 117, 122 (Ct. App. 2013). In *Pulliam* unit owners also alleged the association failed to inform them of the conflict of interest in a developer-controlled association and thereby breached a fiduciary duty. The court concluded that the unit owners did not allege physical injury to tangible property constituting property damage.

[iv] Related Tangible Property Exclusion

Common interest community associations should be aware of a related exclusion that is added by endorsement by some carriers for policies issued to associations. The exclusion concerns damage, destruction, loss of use, or deterioration of tangible property.[564] In the few cases in which the exclusion has been examined, it has been given broad application.

In a New York case, unit owners sued their condominium association and its board for failure to disclose needed repairs resulting from construction defects and failure to cure a water infiltration problem that resulted in significant water intrusion and leaks into individual units. The D&O policy included an endorsement titled "Not For Profit Community Associations" that provided the insurer would not be liable to pay any loss connected with any claim based on, directly or indirectly, arising out of, or in any way involving any construction defect or damage to tangible property, loss of use, or destruction or deterioration of, any tangible property, or failure to supervise, repair, or maintain tangible property. The court said the underlying action arose directly from property damage resulting from alleged construction defects and failure to repair or maintain the building and, therefore, the insurer had made a *prima facie* showing that there was no coverage under the policy. The association argued that a breach of fiduciary duty claim fell outside the scope of the exclusion, but the court found that even that claim arose from the underlying assertion that the plaintiffs' damages were caused by, among other things, defective construction of the building and failure to repair those defects.[565]

Not all breach of fiduciary duty claims may be excluded. For example, in an Oregon case, the underlying suit alleged a developer-appointed director participated in selling residences with knowledge of construction defects and failed to inform the members of the association of those defects, allegedly leading to severe property damage. A second allegation was that the director breached his fiduciary duty by helping the developer avoid paying its share of monthly expenses, maintenance and repair costs, and its contributions to reserves. The insurer raised the tangible property exclusion, but the court said the breach of

---

See also Hess v. Travelers Cas. & Sur. Co. of Am., 2013 U.S. Dist. LEXIS 23281 (N.D. Ill. Feb. 20, 2013) (plaintiff in underlying action alleged directors failed to establish proper reserve fund to address costs incurred and to be incurred for repairing alleged construction defects; court observed that underlying complaint explicitly tied reserve-fund issue to core allegations about construction defects and there was found no duty to defend).

564. *See, e.g.*, Travelers Endorsement Form CIRI-70007 (Amended BI/PD Exclusion). The endorsement excludes coverage for any claim for or arising out of damage, destruction, loss of use, or deterioration of any tangible property including without limitation construction defects, improper soil testing, inadequate or insufficient protection from soil or groundwater movement, soil subsidence, mold, toxic mold, spores, mildew, fungus, or wet or dry rot.

565. Board of Mgrs. of the Schaefer Landing N. Condominium v. Continental Cas. Co., 2011 N.Y. Misc. LEXIS 6252 (Dec. 16, 2011).

fiduciary duty was not barred because it could be interpreted to be unrelated to the construction defects.[566]

In a Texas case,[567] condominium unit owners sued their association after three units they owned were damaged in a hurricane. The plaintiffs in the underlying action alleged the association retaliated against them in response to attempts to communicate with it about repairs to the units and the damage caused by the Hurricane Ike. The court said that but for the hurricane damage, the alleged retaliation would not have occurred and, therefore, the claim arose out of the hurricane damage and was barred under the tangible property damage exclusion. The unit owners also alleged the association failed to properly insure the property, but the court said that claim too concerned the consequences of any failure after the hurricane damage and was excluded. A third allegation was that the management company, as agent for the association, collected premiums to pay for the association's insurance and overcharged for the premiums. This claim, concluded the court, concerned conduct that occurred before the hurricane and was unrelated to the damage caused by it. The exclusion, therefore, did not apply.

[c] Personal and Advertising Injury

Under a standard commercial general liability policy, coverage is provided for "personal and advertising injury liability."[568] A "personal and advertising injury" is defined as an injury arising out of one or more of seven specified "offenses."[569] Those offenses are false arrest, detention, or imprisonment; malicious prosecution; wrongful eviction from, wrongful entry into, or invasion of the right of private occupancy;[570] slander, libel, or trade disparagement;[571] violation of the right

566. Mt. Hood, LLC v. Travelers Cas. & Sur. Co. of Am., 2009 U.S. Dist. LEXIS 16775 (D. Or. Mar. 3, 2009).

567. Parc Condo. Ass'n v. Travelers Cas. & Sur. Co. of Am., 2016 U.S. Dist. LEXIS 155779 (S.D. Tex. Mar. 31, 2016).

568. *See, e.g.*, CG 00 01 12 07, § I.B.

569. Many courts say that the word "offense" does not limit coverage to a particular cause of action or claim. *See, e.g.*, McCormack Baron Mgmt. Servs., Inc. v. American Guar. & Liab. Ins. Co., 989 S.W.2d 168 (Mo. 1999) (term "offense" does not restrict coverage to specific formal causes of action or claims and did not defeat right to defense where insured was sued for statements alleging "insubordination" of employee and asking that employer fire that employee).

570. Note that "wrongful foreclosure" in one of the causes of action most often brought against common interest communities. Davis, *Why Board Members Need Community Association D&O Liability* (Insurance Journal, Apr. 2, 2012), available at: http://www.insurancejournal.com/magazines/features/2012/04/02/241157.htm. If that action falls under the meaning of "personal injury," it will be excluded from coverage.

571. A D&O policy may have an exclusion specifically for claims of libel and slander. *See, e.g.*, York Golf & Tennis Club v. Tudor Ins. Co., 845 A.2d 1173, 1175 (Me. 2004) (D&O policy provided that insurer was not liable for losses arising out of claims for libel or slander).

of another to privacy; use of the advertising idea of someone else; or, infringement of the copyright, trade dress, or slogan of someone else.[572]

Not all of the injuries classified as "personal and advertising" are of concern to common interest community association directors and officers; however, claims for false imprisonment,[573] malicious prosecution,[574] and defamation[575] are not infrequent in common interest communities. The threat of these actions may dissuade association members from serving as directors or officers, so it is incumbent on the association to determine if the coverage is excluded in the D&O policy and if it is available elsewhere. The standard CGL provides that if the name insured is designated as an organization other than a partnership, joint venture, or LLC, the organization is an insured as are its "executive officers" and directors,[576] but only with respect to their duties as officers or directors,[577] and

572. *See, e.g.*, CG 00 01 12 07, § V.14. *Consider* Sova v. Cove Homeowner's Ass'n, 102 So. 3d 863, 872 (La. .App. 2012) (claims of harassment and invasion of privacy and allegations suggesting malicious prosecution and slander would not be subject to coverage as "advertising injury" as claims for advertising injury require that occurrence that caused injury be committed in course of advertising good, product, or service of association). *See also* State Farm Fire & Cas. Co. v. Metro. Mgmt., 2007 U.S. Dist. LEXIS 99406 (D. Haw. Oct. 31, 2007) (to be covered, "advertising injury" has to occur in course of advertising insured's products or services; where condominium association sued its management company for breach of contract, breach of the duty of good faith and fair dealing, and breach of fiduciary duty and also sought declaration that it was entitled to terminate management contract, none of its allegations involved any tort defined in policy as personal injury and, therefore, coverage for personal injury was not implicated).

573. *See, e.g.*, Radcliffe v. Avenel Homeowners Ass'n, 2013 U.S. Dist. LEXIS 21422 (E.D.N.C. Feb. 12, 2013); Johnston v. Carriage House I-Enfield Ass'n, 2016 Conn. Super. LEXIS 1956 (Conn. Super. Ct. July 11, 2016); Galpern v. Rizzo, 2011 N.Y. Misc. LEXIS 1217, 2011 NY Slip Op. 30691(U) (N.Y. Sup. Ct. Mar. 11, 2011); Martinez v. State Farm Lloyds, 2000 Tex. App. LEXIS 6008 (Tex. App.—Corpus Christi Aug. 31, 2000).

574. *See, e.g.*, Dubois v. Ass'n of Apt. Owners, 453 F.3d 1175 (9th Cir. 2006); Neil v. Kovitz Shifrin Nesbit, 2014 U.S. Dist. LEXIS 136696 (N.D. Ill. Sept. 27, 2014); Cohen v. Beachside Two-I Homeowners' Ass'n, 2005 U.S. Dist. LEXIS 28536 (D. Minn. Nov. 17, 2005), *aff'd*, 272 Fed. Appx. 534; 2008, *cert. den.*, 555 U.S. 945, 129 S. Ct. 417, 172 L. Ed. 2d 288 (2008); Kurtz v. Hubbard, 362 Ill. Dec. 528, 973 N.E.2d 924 (Ill. App. 2012); Valois, Inc. v. Thorne, 86 A.2d 530 (Ct. App. D.C. 1951).

575. *See, e.g.*, Lautman v. 2800 Coyle St. Owners Corp., 2014 U.S. Dist. LEXIS 72703 (E.D.N.Y. May 23, 2014); Wood v. Granite Ridge Condo Ass'n, 2009 N.H. Super. LEXIS 76 (2009); Cohen v. Beachside Two-I Homeowners' Ass'n, 2006 U.S. Dist. LEXIS 44978 (D. Minn. June 29, 2006), *aff'd*, 272 Fed. Appx. 534 (8th Cir.), *cert. den.*, 555 U.S. 945, 129 S. Ct. 417, 172 L. Ed. 2d 288 (2008); Willow Lake Residential Ass'n v. Juliano, 80 So. 3d 226 (Ala. App. 2010); Davidson v. Seneca Crossing Section II Homeowner's Ass'n, 187 Md. App. 601, 979 A.2d 260 (2009).

576. *See* EMC Ins. Cos. v. Mid-Continent Cas. Co., 884 F. Supp. 2d 1147, 1157 (D. Colo. 2012) (for officer or director of corporation to be an "insured," entity for which she serves in that role must be "named insured" as shown on Declarations Page or must qualify as "named insured" under policy; only officers and directors of "named insured" are considered "insureds" under policy).

577. One commentary addresses scenarios in which the director of a private club might be considered to be engaged in her duties as a director. It says that picking up trash and straightening up the premises before and after board meetings would likely be within her duties, but entering the club premises during a weekend to straighten them up on her own initiative would not appear to be related to her role as a director unless the bylaws stated the activity was expected of directors.

probably only when they hold office during the term of the policy. For example, in an Illinois case,[578] a condominium association brought suit for breach of fiduciary duties against the members of the initial governing board. Those board members had been appointed by the developer while the developer controlled the project. Almost two years after those board members had left office, the association obtained a policy with general liability and directors and officers liability coverage. The erstwhile board members sought coverage as directors for the association. The court said they were not insureds under the general liability coverage because they were not directors or officers when the policy was in effect. It noted that the directors and officers portion of the coverage applied to "any person who has been, now is, or shall become" an officer of an insured organization, but the general liability section did not contain language that extended coverage to past officers. Thus, placed in the context of the entire contract, the general liability provision covered only then-current directors and officers.

Setting aside the specific facts and policy provisions in the Illinois case, its general lesson is that there may be gaps in coverage. The CGL policy may not cover a former director against claims for personal and advertising injury liability while the D&O policy may exclude coverage for *all* claims of personal and advertising injury liability. It is incumbent on associations to discuss these potential gaps in coverage and to make certain, in particular, that there is coverage for former directors and officers.

[8] Development/Construction

Some D&O policies will include an exclusion for design or construction. For example, in one case an exclusion barred coverage for claims for wrongful acts based on, arising out of, directly or indirectly resulting from, in consequence of, or in any way involving development, planning, or landscaping of any real property, the exercise of any development rights with respect to any real property, any actual or alleged violation of any federal, state, local, or common-law rule, law, regulation, or ordinance respecting the environment or environmental conservation, in connection with any development, planning or landscaping of

---

Finally, a director on the premises strictly as a guest at a social event would not be there as a part of her duties as a director, but if she were representing the club at the event in her official capacity it would be within those duties. *Officers and Directors Insureds under CGL Form?* (Summit Business Media, 2013). Directors and officers of common interest communities often find themselves in similar situations, especially because they live on the property. If a director stops to weed a flower bed in the common area, she is probably acting outside the scope of her duties as a director unless, perhaps, her duties include responsibility for landscaping. A director or officer who helps prepare a common area for an association sponsored party may well be acting in her official capacity, but that status may end when the party begins. *See* Villa Charlotte Bronte, Inc. v. Commercial Union Ins. Co., 487 N.Y.S.2d 314, 64 N.Y.2d 846, 476 N.E.2d 640 (1985) (insurer could be excused from defending officer of cooperative corporation sued for allegedly defamatory remarks if it could be established that officer was not acting on behalf of the corporation when he made those remarks).

578. Truck Ins. Exch. v. Cassady, 2011 U.S. Dist. LEXIS 122052 (N.D. Ill. Oct. 21, 2011).

real property, or the design, construction, renovation, or rehabilitation of any building, structure, or other improvement on any real property.[579]

Clearly that exclusion could be of significant concern to common interest community associations. Renovating or rehabilitating buildings and landscaping property are frequent association endeavors. Additionally, many homeowners associations regulate the use of property of their residents through architectural restrictions and/or architectural review committees.[580] For example, in one association the governing documents regulated construction of structures that obstructed the view from other lots. Association members sued the association because they had sought its assistance in resolving a dispute over a patio they enclosed that blocked a neighbor's view and the association sided with the other property owner. The plaintiffs asserted claims for fraud, breach of fiduciary duty, and breach of duty to act in good faith. The D&O insurer invoked the design or construction exclusion, but the court said the exclusion concerned "design, construction, renovation or rehabilitation" of a structure by the insured. The association, said the court, had nothing to do with designing or constructing or renovating or rehabilitating any structure and its only "wrongful acts" were confined to a written determination, and related activities, connected to a dispute between two of its members. The claims arose from the alleged improper conduct of the association in resolving a dispute between its members, and those claims, held the court, were clearly covered by the policy.[581]

[9] Builder/Developer

Associations should be alert to the inclusion in the policy of a "Builder/Developer Exclusion." In a Texas case, the exclusion was added to the D&O policy by endorsement. It provided that the insurer would not be liable to make any payment for losses or claims expenses in connection with any claim made against any insured based on, arising out of, directly or indirectly resulting from, or in consequence of, any claim made by or against any builder or developer. In the underlying action, several development companies sued a property owners' association alleging that, in violation of its bylaws, it had wrongfully failed to provide them with the correct number of voting ballots and to properly construct roads and maintain certain road maintenance fees. The insurer invoked the exclusion.

579. *See also* ISO Form BP 17 24 01 10, § B.p (coverage does not apply to any loss resulting from any claim arising out of wrongful acts in selection or direct or indirect supervision of any contractor or subcontractor liable or alleged to be liable for any defect in construction at any premises insured under policy).

580. *See* Elmore, *Directors and Officers Liability Insurance for Community Associations* (2014), available at: http://www.ksnlaw.com/blog/directors-officers-liability-insurance-community-associations/ (stating that D&O policy may be triggered where association architectural review refuses request from resident to proceed with plans for modification or construction to her unit or home).

581. Marquez Knolls Property Owners Ass'n, Inc. v. Executive Risk Indemnity, Inc., 153 Cal. App. 4th 228, 62 Cal. Rptr. 3d 510 (2007).

The court held that the allegations in the underlying action all fell squarely within the exclusion and the insurer had no duty to defend or indemnify.[582]

Associations, particularly those that are new construction, should be concerned about this exclusion. Litigation between associations and development companies is very common. Usually it is a construction defect suit brought by the association against the developer. The developer will sometimes counterclaim against the association and its directors and officers. A similar scenario can occur when an established community employs a builder for renovations or additions. Construction defect litigation is often protracted and costly. If a broad exclusion for "claim made by or against any builder or developer" applies, the association will likely find itself paying a considerable amount of attorney's fees out of pocket. Associations, especially in newly constructed communities, should discuss with their broker removing any "Builder/Developer Exclusion" they find in the D&O policy.

Another type of "Builder/Developer Exclusion" was mentioned in a South Carolina case. It applied to the failure of any insured to enforce the rights of the association against the builder, sponsor, or developer of the property designated in the Declaration. This exclusion bars coverage not for suits directly against a builder or developer, but principally for actions against the governing board for failing to sue the builder or developer or to exercise any other rights—statutory or contractual—that may exist to protect the association. In the South Carolina case, the court concluded the exclusion did not apply to an action by unit owners alleging failure establish a reserve fund and to warn of conflicts of interest.[583]

[10] Breach of Contract

One of the top five claims faced by common interest community associations is breach of contract.[584] A standard exclusion in D&O policies bars coverage for breaches of contract. These exclusions typically proscribe coverage for losses resulting from any claim for liability under, or breach of, any oral, written, or implied contract or agreement, or for liability of others assumed by the insured under that contract or agreement.[585] Some exclusions may more broadly state that they bar coverage for claims in "any way related" to any actual or alleged liability under any contract or agreement.[586] Note also that some policies will

---

582. Atain Specialty Ins. Co. v. Thousand Oaks Prop. Owners Ass'n, 2015 U.S. Dist. LEXIS 181490 (S.D. Tex. June 29, 2015).

583. Pulliam v. Travelers Indem. Co., 403 S.C. 332, 343–44, 743 S.E.2d 117, 123 (Ct. App. 2013).

584. Davis, *Why Board Members Need Community Association D&O Liability* (Insurance Journal, Apr. 2, 2012), available at: http://www.insurancejournal.com/magazines/features/2012/04/02/241157.htm.

585. ISO Form BP 17 24 01 10, § B.m; Non-Profit Management and Organization Liability Insurance Policy § IV.9.

586. PNY Techs., Inc. v. Twin City Fire Ins. Co., 2014 U.S. Dist. LEXIS 96489 (D.N.J. July 16, 2014), *aff'd*, 607 Fed. Appx. 155 (3d Cir. 2015).

limit application of the exclusion to claims brought under a specific insuring agreement in which case the exclusion does not apply to claims brought under other insuring agreements.[587] Additionally, some D&O policies will specifically provide coverage for costs and expenses incurred in *defending* breach of contract claims.[588]

The purpose of the exclusion is to prevent policyholders from shifting separate, voluntarily undertaken contractual obligations to the insurer, for example, one should not be able to borrow money, fail to repay the debt, and then shift the repayment obligation to an insurer.[589]

Typically, there are two exceptions to the exclusion. The first applies if the insured would have been liable absent the contract or agreement. The second is for allegations of liability or breach of contract or agreement made in a claim arising out of a wrongful employment practices act. Additionally, some policies will have an exception for defense costs.[590] That can be a very beneficial exception for the insured because, while the Breach of Contract exclusion may ultimately allow the insurer to avoid indemnification, considerable defense costs can amass before that determination is made.

Courts have said that any *defenses* to contractual liability are not relevant to the operation of the exclusion.[591] Thus, for example, even if a contract is found invalid, if liability is alleged under that contract, the Contractual Liability exclusion would still apply.[592]

[a] Scope of the Exclusion

Disagreement surrounds the scope of the exclusion. Insurers contend the exclusion applies very broadly and excludes any claims for liability that would not lie "but for" the existence of an underlying contract or agreement while insureds usually counter that it is more limited and applies strictly to claims based on the

---

587. *See, e.g.*, Sigma Chi Corp. v. Westchester Fire Ins. Co., 587 F. Supp. 2d 891, 898 (N.D. Ill. 2008) (where underlying claim was based on refusal of insured to honor contracts, breach of contract exclusion was inapplicable because although management liability policy did exclude coverage for breach of contract liability, exclusion was limited to claims covered, in whole or in part, under Insuring Agreement A, Directors' and Officers' Liability, but parties agreed that claims were based on provisions from A.3, Company Liability section of the policy, not from directors and officers liability provisions).

588. 3 *New Appleman Law of Liability Insurance* § 22.06[2][j] (rev. ed., Matthew Bender, 2017).

589. LaCroix, *D&O Insurance: The Contract Exclusion* (2009), available at: http://www.dandodiary.com/2009/03/articles/d-o-insurance/do-insurance-the-contract-exclusion/ (expansive reading given certain exclusionary language in cases suggests that more narrowly constructed exclusion would more appropriately address concern that provision was originally intended to address).

590. *See, e.g.*, Citrus Course Homeowners Ass'n v. Great Am. Ins. Co., 2016 U.S. Dist. LEXIS 10199 (C.D. Cal. Jan. 7, 2016) (contract exclusion clause stated it did not apply to costs of defense).

591. PNY Techs., Inc. v. Twin City Fire Ins. Co., 2014 U.S. Dist. LEXIS 96489 (D.N.J. July 16, 2014), *aff'd*, 607 Fed. Appx. 155 (3d Cir. 2015).

592. PNY Techs., Inc. v. Twin City Fire Ins. Co., 607 Fed. Appx. 155 (3d Cir. 2015).

contract itself.[593] The interpretation of the exclusion can be affected by the prefatory language. If instead of excluding claims "arising from," "resulting from," or "in any way related to" a contract, the exclusion is "for" liability under any contract or agreement, it would likely receive the narrower construction put forward by insureds.[594]

In any event, the breadth of the exclusion is much debated, and courts have applied different tests in evaluating it.[595] A detailed exploration of that topic is beyond the scope of this treatise; fortunately, there are resources available on the topic.[596] It is enough here to take note that many courts interpret the exclusion broadly and apply it to tort and other claims that "arise" out of contractual liability.[597]

One federal court concluded the exclusion covers any claim that would not exist but for liability under a contract or agreement. It then offered a helpful hypothetical. A homeowner hires a carpet cleaner. While the carpet cleaner is working, the homeowner backs out of her garage and collides with the carpet cleaner's truck. The carpet cleaner would have a tort claim against the homeowner for negligence. An insurer might argue a Contractual Liability exclusion applied because, but for the carpet-cleaning contract, the truck would not have been parked in the homeowner's driveway. However, said the court, the exclusion does not bar coverage for claims that would not exist but for a contract, but rather claims that would not exist but for contractual liability—in other words, but for a breach of a contract. The carpet cleaner's negligence claim would not

593. Cousins Submarines, Inc. v. Fed. Ins. Co., 2013 U.S. Dist. LEXIS 17306 (E.D. Wis. Feb. 8, 2013).

594. *See generally* LaCroix, *D&O Insurance: Contract Exclusion Precludes Coverage for Negligent and Fraudulent Misrepresentation Claims* (2012), available at: http://www.dandodiary.com/2012/08/articles/d-o-insurance/do-insurance-contract-exclusion-precludes-coverage-for-negligent-and-fraudulent-misrepresentation-claims/ (policy forms using narrower "for" wording are superior from perspective of policyholder, particularly if carriers whose policies have broader wording choose to try to apply that exclusion to preclude wide swath of claims, including claims for fraudulent inducement and negligent misrepresentation; contending "for" wording is much closer to original purposes for inclusion of contract exclusion).

595. Fed. Ins. Co. v. KDW Restructuring & Liquidation Servs., LLC, 889 F. Supp. 2d 694, 701 (M.D. Pa. 2012).

596. *See generally* LaCroix, *D&O Insurance: The Contract Exclusion* (2009), available at: http://www.dandodiary.com/2009/03/articles/d-o-insurance/do-insurance-the-contract-exclusion/.

597. *See, e.g.*, Spirtas Co. v. Fed. Ins. Co., 521 F.3d 833, 834–37 (8th Cir. 2008) (finding that claims of conversion and unjust enrichment arose from contractual liability and thus fell under the contractual-liability exclusion at issue); Callas Enters., Inc. v. Travelers Indem. Co. of Am., 193 F.3d 952, 955–57 (8th Cir. 1999) (finding that claims of trademark infringement and defamation arose out of contractual liability); Fed. Ins. Co. v. KDW Restructuring & Liquidation Servs., LLC, 889 F. Supp. 2d 694, 708 (M.D. Pa. 2012) (fraudulent inducement and negligent misrepresentation claims were based on and arose from liability under contracts where they arose from same essential facts and circumstances as those that underlay breach of contract claims).

fall within the exclusion, because it would exist even if both parties to the carpet-cleaning contract had fulfilled all of their obligations under that contract.[598]

[b] Governing Documents as Contracts under the Exclusion

The Contracts exclusion takes on particular importance for common interest community associations.[599] Courts generally consider the governing documents—the Declaration of Condominium or Covenants, Conditions and Restrictions (CC&Rs) in a homeowners association—to be contracts.[600] Articles of incorporation and bylaws are also considered contracts.[601] A cooperative proprietary lease—or occupancy agreement—like any other lease, would seem clearly to be a contract. All these documents impose obligations on directors and officers. A violation of those obligations would be a breach of contract,[602] and the D&O insurer may, therefore, invoke the Breach of Contract exclusion.[603] An associa-

598. Zayed v. Arch Ins. Co., 932 F. Supp. 2d 956, 964-65 (D. Minn. 2013).

599. *See generally* Treese & Rosenberry, *Insurance: How Community Associations Protect Themselves*, at 49 (CAI Press 2013) (association governing boards should be aware of exclusion for contractual indemnity, for example, tortious interference or breach of contract).

600. Fort Pierce Indus. Park Phases II, III & IV Owners Ass'n v. Shakespeare, 379 P.3d 1218, 1223 (Utah 2016) (restrictive covenants should be construed under same principles used to interpret contracts); Bixeman v. Hunter's Run Homeowners Ass'n of St. John, Inc., 36 N.E.3d 1074, 1077 (Ind. App. 2015) (Declaration is tantamount to contract); Schwartzott v. Etheridge Prop. Mgmt., 403 S.W.3d 488, 498 (Tex. App.—Houston 14th Dist. 2013) (condominium declarations are treated as contracts); Town Houses at Bonnet Shores Condo. Ass'n v. Langlois, 45 A.3d 577, 583 (R.I. 2012) (finding it appropriate to apply laws of contract construction when reviewing declaration); Cusimano v. Port Esplanade Condominium Association, Inc., 55 So. 3d 931, 936 (La. App. 2011) (rules of contract interpretation apply to interpretation of condominium declaration); Cantonbury Heights Condo. Ass'n v. Local Land Dev., LLC, 273 Conn. 724, 734, 873 A.2d 898, 904 (2005) (declaration operates in nature of contract in that it establishes rights and obligations of parties); Nordic Inn Condo. Owners Ass'n v. Ventullo, 151 N.H. 571, 575, 864 A.2d 1079, 1084 (2004) (condominium association legal documents constitute contract that governs legal rights between association and property owners). *Compare* Bowles v. Schilling, 581 N.W.2d 192 (Iowa App. 1998) (for purposes of determining applicable statute of limitations, declaration covenant constitutes property interest rather than contract). *See generally* Glazer & Goetz, *Florida Community Association Law: Contracts Clause Application in an Ever-Changing Legislative Landscape*, 89 Fla. Bar J. 46 (2015) (Declarations of condominium, cooperative documents, and declarations of covenants and restrictions are contracts between community associations and their members).

601. *See* Personal Industrial Bankers, Inc. v. Citizens Budget Co. of Dayton, 80 F. 2d 327 (6th Cir. 1935), *cert. den.*, 298 U.S. 674, 56 S. Ct. 939, 80 L. Ed. 1396 (1936) (charter of corporation constitutes contract between corporation and its shareholders). *See also* Airgas, Inc. v. Air Products & Chemicals, Inc., 8 A.3d 1182, 1188 (Del. 2010).

602. *See, e.g.*, Beauvallon Condo. Ass'n v. Granite State Ins. Co., 2011 U.S. Dist. LEXIS 69606 (D. Colo. June 29, 2011) (where underlying complaint alleged association failed or refused to remedy problems with unit, unit owner brought claim for breach of contract, i.e., condominium declaration).

603. *See, e.g.*, Atain Specialty Ins. Co. v. Thousand Oaks Prop. Owners Ass'n, 2015 U.S. Dist. LEXIS 181490 (S.D. Tex. June 29, 2015) (where association was sued for improperly issuing voting ballots and failing to properly construct roads and maintain road maintenance fees, all allegedly in violation of its bylaws, insurer argued breach of contract exclusion applied because bylaws are contractual in nature; court did not address that exclusion because it decided case on a different one).

tion should determine, through consultation with its broker and/or association counsel, whether the exclusion might indeed be applied to claims based on an alleged breach of governing documents. If the answer is "yes," it should discuss with its broker whether there might be coverage under its commercial general liability policy and/or work with its broker to obtain D&O coverage for these claims, because they are not uncommon.

While the governing documents are generally viewed as contracts, they are in fact—especially in the case of Declarations of Condominium and CC&Rs—much more. Unlike ordinary contracts, Declarations of Condominium and CC&Rs are almost always recorded documents and considered covenants running with the land.[604] Although they constitute an agreement between the association and its members, that agreement is almost always drafted unilaterally by the development company that creates the community association.[605] The members of the association "agree" to the governing documents in the same way the owner of a single-family home "agrees" to deed restrictions, by purchasing the property. Both become bound by covenants that restrict their property and were recorded in the public records prior to their purchase of that property. Because they buy with notice of and subject to the covenants, courts sometimes say those covenants may have a degree of unreasonableness.[606]

The distinction between recorded governing documents and ordinary contracts may be the basis of an argument against application of the Contract exclusion to breaches of common interest community governing documents. If the purpose of the exclusion is to bar coverage for a voluntarily assumed—and then breached—duty, the "voluntary assumption" of a duty imposed by association governing documents is different from that in an ordinary contract. In most contracts one party agrees to provide a service or product to another party who agrees to pay for it. When officers and directors assume a duty to follow and enforce the governing documents of their association, they do not negotiate over whether to accept that duty. The governing documents are already in place.

The exception for circumstances in which there would have been liability absent the contract may come into play because the governing documents often reflect language found in statutes governing CICs. For example, the Uniform

604. *See, e.g.*, Association of Owners of Regency Park Condominiums v. Thomasson, 878 S.W.2d 560 (Tenn. App. 1994); Courts at Beachgate v. Bird, 226 N.J. Super. 631, 545 A.2d 243 (1988); Pepe v. Whispering Sands Condo. Ass'n, 351 So. 2d 755, 757–58 (Fla. 2d DCA 1977).

605. *See, e.g.*, Club Envy of Spokane, LLC v. Ridpath Tower Condo. Ass'n, 184 Wn. App. 593, 604, 337 P.3d 1131, 1136 (2014) (condominium declaration is document unilaterally creating type of real property).

606. *See, e.g.*, Ridgely Condo. Ass'n v. Smyrnioudis, 105 Md. App. 404, 660 A.2d 942 (1995), *aff'd*, 343 Md. 357, 681 A.2d 494 (1996); Bluffs of Wildwood Homeowners' Ass'n v. Dinkel, 96 Ohio App. 3d 278, 644 N.E.2d 1100 (1994); Preston Tower Condominium Assoc. v. S.B. Realty, Inc., 685 S.W.2d 98, 102 (Tex. App. 1985); Hidden Harbour Estates, Inc. v. Basso, 393 So. 2d 637 (Fla. 4th DCA 1981).

Common Interest Ownership Act provides that associations are responsible for maintenance, repair, and replacement of the common elements.[607] That obligation is often repeated in the governing documents. Thus, while the failure of the directors to maintain the common elements may be a breach of contract, the directors could be liable absent the contract for failure to carry out a statutory obligation.

Although the exclusion may proscribe coverage for losses resulting from any claimed breach of contract, in a claim by condominium unit owners that arguably resulted from breach of a contract between the association and a third party, the insurer conceded coverage. In that California case, a condominium association contracted with a builder to repair structural damage caused by an earthquake. The association refused to pay all the amounts due under the contract, and the builder recorded a mechanic's lien on the complex. It then filed an action against the association and the unit owners for, *inter alia*, breach of written contract and foreclosure of the mechanic's lien. Several unit owners filed cross-complaints alleging the association had been negligent in its handling of the builder's claims and had breached a number of duties to the owners. The D&O insurer denied coverage for the breach of contract claims, but accepted defense of the association and its board of directors in the unit owner's cross-complaints. The court did not comment on that decision because the cross-complaints were resolved in another action.[608] It did, however, reject the association's argument that the exclusion did not apply. The court said that if that were the case, "any condominium association could choose to enter a reconstruction, remodeling or renovation contract with a contractor, then decide not to pay the bill, thus shifting the obligation to its insurer." That would be untenable and lead to a type of risk that would be virtually impossible to underwrite.[609]

[11] Failure to Maintain Insurance

Some polices will exclude coverage for a loss resulting from any claim arising out of actual or alleged failure—or omission by any insured—to "effect or maintain insurance."[610] The purpose of the exclusion—also called the FTMI exclusion—is to avoid having the D&O policy become a substitute for liability and property insurance coverage, and it applies to a failure to maintain sufficient coverage, as

607. Uniform Common Interest Ownership Act § 3-107(a).

608. Oak Park Calabasas Condominium Ass'n v. State Farm Fire & Casualty Co., 137 Cal. App. 4th 557, 40 Cal. Rptr. 3d 263 (2006).

609. Oak Park Calabasas Condominium Ass'n v. State Farm Fire & Casualty Co., 137 Cal. App. 4th 557, 565, 40 Cal. Rptr. 3d 263, 268 (2006) (it would be literally impossible, from actuarial standpoint, to set appropriate premiums to guard against risk that association would enter into multi-million-dollar construction contracts, and then not pay for that construction work).

610. *See, e.g.*, ISO Form BP 17 24 01 10, § B.i.

well as failure to obtain a policy at all.[611] One large insurance broker calls this exclusion anachronistic and says it has largely been phased out by all but a few carriers.[612]

This exclusion should be of particular concern to directors and officers of common interest community associations because either by statute or the governing documents they often have an obligation to obtain certain insurance coverage for the association, principally property and general liability insurance.[613] Association members have sued over the failure of a board to obtain coverage at all or to obtain adequate coverage.

Unfortunately, there are few reported decisions interpreting the "failure to maintain insurance" exclusion. One of those cases concerned a condominium association.[614] A unit owner sought to recover for property damage to his unit that resulted from a fire that began in an adjacent unit. He sued the association and its directors alleging they failed to obtain insurance that would fully insure replacement costs, to pursue the underlying property claim with diligence, and to oversee the insurer's response to claims made under the policy. The insurer invoked an exclusion for claims based on or attributable to any wrongful act in procuring, effecting, and maintaining insurance, or with respect to amount, form, conditions, or provisions of the insurance. The association and directors sued the insurer for coverage and argued that the allegations in the underlying complaint regarding the purported failure to assist the unit owner in his claim, to push the insurer to act with dispatch, and to monitor adjustment of the claim were not subject to the exclusion. The court did not agree. It said those allegations, when read in the context of the complaint as a whole, did relate to "procuring, effecting and maintaining" insurance and, therefore, came within the language of exclusion. The insurer had no duty to defend.

In one case of note the E&O insurer for a community association management company refused to defend the company when associations sued it for

---

611. Bateman, *What Homeowner Associations Need to Know About Directors' & Officers' Liability* (2017), available at: https://communityassociationmanagement.com/c33-financial-matters/c37-insurance/what-homeowner-associations-need-to-know-about-directors-officers-liability/ (failure to procure claim can occur when governing board approves policy and property or risk is underinsured, in which case, board could be held liable failure to procure correct insurance); Johnston, *Corporate Indemnification and Liability Insurance for Directors and Officers*, 33 Bus. Law. 1993, 2020 (1978) (shareholder derivative action brought against directors and officers for failing to maintain adequate insurance coverage on property destroyed by fire would be barred from coverage by exclusion).

612. *D&O Insurance Policy Exclusions*, available at: https://www.connerstrong.com/resources/site1/news/1414CSB%20ER%20Policy%20Exclusions-2.pdf.

613. Treese & Rosenberry, *Insurance: How Community Associations Protect Themselves*, at 49 (CAI Press 2013) (association governing boards should be aware of lack of coverage for wrongful insurance purchase claims).

614. Altaf v. Hanover Square Condominium Ass'n No. 1, 136 Ill. Dec. 257, 188 Ill. App. 3d 533, 544 N.E.2d 1032 (1989).

failure to obtain insurance for them.[615] The exclusion in that case was for damages arising out of "failure or inability to maintain adequate levels or types of insurance." The CAM had contracts with homeowners associations obligating it to obtain insurance for them. One HOA sued the CAM alleging it failed to purchase D&O coverage for it as required by the parties' contract. Another HOA sued the CAM claiming it had made late premium payments on the HOA liability policy and ultimately allowed the coverage to lapse. The E&O carrier invoked the exclusion and refused to defend the CAM. The CAM argued the exclusion referred to damages arising out of its own failure to maintain insurance coverage for itself and, therefore, the policy did not exclude coverage for either underlying claim. The court rejected that argument. The exclusion, it concluded, meant that failure to maintain insurance of *any kind*—whether for itself or for others—was excluded from coverage.[616] The exclusion did not differentiate between types of insurance or for whom insurance is maintained. The CAM also contended that there was a distinction between failure to maintain insurance—the wording of the exclusion—and failure to procure it. Therefore, in the case in which it failed to procure D&O coverage for its HOA, the CAM argued the exclusion did not apply. Again, the court disagreed. It concluded that the CAM did not succeed in providing insurance coverage for its HOA client and, thus, it failed to maintain insurance within the meaning of the policy.

A Georgia appellate court reached a different conclusion.[617] The exclusion in that case proscribed coverage for claims based on, attributable to, arising out of, in consequence of, or in any way related to, failure of the insured to effect or maintain insurance. An employee of the University of Georgia Athletic Association whose job it was to obtain disability insurance for student athletes failed to obtain that coverage for a football player who requested it. The insurer contended the exclusion applied. The court found the exclusion to be ambiguous. It could exclude coverage for failure to procure, obtain, or continue insurance, regardless of the type of insurance, the circumstances giving rise to the duty to procure, obtain, or continue insurance, or the type of damages a plaintiff claims to have sustained by the failure of the insured. On the other hand, it could be concluded that the exclusion was limited to failure to obtain and maintain the kinds of insurance an organization like the insured would typically have—for example, property hazard and premises liability coverage—rather than student-

615. Management Specialists, Inc. v. Northfield Ins. Co., 117 P.3d 32 (Colo. App. 2004).

616. *See also* VierraMoore, Inc. v. Cont'l Cas. Co., 940 F. Supp. 2d 1270, 1279 (E.D. Cal. 2013) (where underlying action arose out of alleged failure of property manager to ensure that association had effective surety bond coverage in event that its common area construction phases were not completed pursuant to terms of development agreements, association's claims against manager fell squarely within scope of exclusion; rejecting argument that exclusion should be limited to manager's failure to maintain bond for itself rather than for association or any other third parties).

617. Fireman's Fund Ins. Co. v. Univ. of Ga. Ath. Ass'n, 288 Ga. App. 355, 654 S.E.2d 207 (2007).

athlete disability insurance. Because the exclusion was susceptible of more than one reasonable construction, it was ambiguous and the court construed it against the insurer. It concluded the claim potentially came within the policy and the Failure to Maintain Insurance exclusion did not justify the refusal of the insurer to defend.

These cases illustrate that the specific language of "failure to maintain insurance" exclusions can be quite different and so too can be the interpretations courts place on that language. However, no matter the particular language or the interpretation a court might give it, common interest community associations should seek policies that omit the exclusion or ask to have it removed by endorsement. That, however, may not avoid a Coverage exclusion. Because the duty to obtain insurance coverage is often found in the governing documents and a failure to abide by the documents is usually conceived of as a breach of contract, an action for failure to maintain insurance may be excluded from coverage by the Breach of Contract exclusion, which is common to most D&O policies.

[12] Directors or Officers Serving Another Organization

An exclusion that receives little attention, but has significance for common interest communities, bars coverage for wrongful acts by a director or officer while serving in some capacity in another organization. The NPMOLIP, for example, provides that the insurer is not liable for losses for any claim made against any insured for wrongful acts by any insured person as a director, officer, or employee of any entity other than the insured organization, even if that service is directed or requested by the insured organization.[618] The exclusion in the ISO endorsement is broader. It excludes coverage for any loss resulting from any claim that arises out of any wrongful act committed, or allegedly committed, by any insured person while serving in *any position or capacity* in any organization or association other than the association, even if the association directed or requested that person to serve in that position or capacity.[619]

Either version of the exclusion could apply in a community with layers of associations. Consider, for example, a planned community divided into three parts: a multi-story condominium building, a group of townhouses, and a neighborhood of zero lot line attached villas. Each part has its own association. A recreation association manages a swimming pool and tennis courts that serve the entire community. The governing board of each of the primary associations appoints one of its directors to also serve as a director of the recreation association. If there is a claim against one of those directors for a wrongful act committed in her capacity as a director of the recreational association, the exclusion

618. Non-Profit Management and Organization Liability Insurance Policy § IV.7.
619. *See, e.g.*, ISO Form BP 17 24 01 10, § B.j.

could bar coverage by the D&O policy of her primary association. She would then need to look to any coverage provided by the recreation association.

An association in a community with layers of associations needs to discuss the exclusion with its broker. It should determine how, if at all, the exclusion applies and how its directors can be protected when serving on the board of another related association. Ultimately, of course, the governing board of the other association should be responsible for making sure its officers and directors have coverage. However, in the common interest community setting where officers and directors—unlike those in business corporations—may be unsophisticated, it behooves the primary association to assess the coverage afforded one of its directors serving another association in any capacity. The reason is simply practical. It is difficult to convince residents of common interest communities to serve on governing boards. Should a director ever suffer an uninsured loss, finding residents to serve may become even more difficult.

[13] For-Profit Subsidiary

D&O policies issued to non-profit organizations may include an exclusion for any payment for losses in connection with any claim made against any insured related to the ownership, control, management, or operations of any *for-profit* subsidiary of the insured organization.[620] For many common interest communities, the exclusion will be of no consequence. Some CICs, however, operate country clubs or recreational facilities that are profit-making. If those operations are under an organization considered a subsidiary of the CIC association, the exclusion could apply. Associations that operate profit-making facilities should, therefore, discuss application of the exclusion with their broker. If it does apply, an endorsement can generally be added to the policy making the profit-making entity an insured organization and typically the exclusion has an exception for any for-profit subsidiary that is itself an insured organization pursuant to an endorsement to the policy.

[14] Prior Claim

A standard exclusion in D&O policies is for claims reported during a prior policy or prior policy period.[621] For example, under the NPMOLIP, coverage is excluded for a claim based on, arising out of, directly or indirectly resulting from,

620. Non-Profit Management and Organization Liability Insurance Policy § IV.12. The exclusion says the insurer is not liable to pay for a loss connected with any claim made against any insureds "based upon, arising out of, directly or indirectly resulting from, in consequence of, or in any way involving" the ownership, control, management, or operations of any for-profit subsidiary of the insured organization.

621. *See generally* Monteleone & Conca, *Directors and Officers Indemnification and Liability Insurance: An Overview of Legal and Practical Issues*, 51 Bus. Law 573, 603–04 (1996) (purpose of exclusion for claims for which directors or officers were entitled to indemnity and/or payment by reason of having given notice of any circumstance that might give rise to claim under any policy or

in consequence of, or in any way involving any fact, circumstance, or situation that has been the subject of any notice given under any other policy of which the current one is a renewal or replacement.[622] The ISO endorsement states that there is no coverage for a claim that arises out of the same facts, wrongful acts, or "interrelated wrongful acts," alleged or contained in any claim that has been reported, or in any circumstances of which notice has been given during a prior policy period of the current policy or under any policy of which the current one is a replacement.[623]

A prior claim can involve a threat to sue. For example, a unit owner had an ongoing dispute with his condominium association over an elevator he wanted to install in his two-story commercial condominium unit. Eventually, the unit owner sued the association. The D&O insurer for the association contended there was no coverage because a letter from the unit owner's attorney had given the association notice of the claim before the policy effective date. The letter traced multiple complaints by the unit owner about the association and attributed monetary losses to it. The letter said the unit owner had asked the attorney to pursue litigation if a satisfactory settlement could not be reached and concluded by saying that if the attorney had not heard a response back from the association by a certain date, the attorney had been instructed to file suit. The court said that "under any construction," the letter constituted a claim, and because the association had notice of the claim before the effective date of the policy, the claim fell outside of the policy and the insurer had no duty to defend.[624] One observer doubts the precedential value of the case because, unlike the typical D&O policy, there was no definition of "claim" in the policy and additionally, the letter on which the court relied did not appear to demand anything in particular of the association.[625]

The question that arises with application of the exclusion is what is an interrelated claim? A condominium case illustrates the analysis that is applied. A condominium association notified a cable company in 2010 that it was terminating the cable agreement to which the development company had previously agreed. The cable company filed suit against the association that same year. The following year the association obtained a D&O policy and during the term of the policy, the association membership voted to terminate the cable contract pursuant to a Florida statute permitting cancellation of contracts entered into by developers.

---

policies term of which has expired prior to inception date of current policy is to ensure there can be no inappropriate "stacking" of serial D&O policies to apply to single loss).

622. Non-Profit Management and Organization Liability Insurance Policy § IV.2.

623. ISO Form BP 17 24 01 10, § B.g. 6. The term "interrelated wrongful act" is defined as all causally connected wrongful acts. ISO Form BP 17 24 01 10, § H.6.

624. Deer Oaks Office Park Owners Ass'n v. State Farm Lloyds, 2012 U.S. Dist. LEXIS 19240 (W.D. Tex. Feb. 15, 2012).

625. LaCroix, *D&O Insurance: When is a Claim First Made?* (2012), available at: http://www.dandodiary.com/2012/02/articles/d-o-insurance/do-insurance-when-is-a-claim-first-made/.

During that policy period, the cable company filed a second suit against the association. The insurer refused to defend or indemnify the association because it said the unit owner vote to cancel the policy was an interrelated wrongful act with the prior notification by the association of termination of the cable agreement. The court agreed. The two claims were sufficiently related to relieve the insurer of the duty to defend the association against the second claim. The court noted that the claims involved the same parties and the same set of contracts. Further, they arose from an ongoing conflict between the parties. The court, therefore, held as a matter of law that the second claim was not covered under the policy.[626]

[15] Pollution

Liability policies of all types today exclude coverage for pollution-related claims. D&O policies are no different. The ISO endorsement bars coverage for claims arising out of actual, alleged, or threatened discharge, dispersal, seepage, migration, release, or escape of pollutants at any time as well as requests, demands, orders, or statutory or regulatory requirements that an insured or others test for, monitor, clean up, remove, contain, treat, detoxify or neutralize, or in any way respond to, or assess the effects of, pollutants.[627] It also excludes claims made or suits brought by or on behalf of any governmental authority for damages because of testing for, monitoring, cleaning up, removing, containing, treating, detoxifying or neutralizing, or in any way responding to, or assessing the effects of, pollutants.

The NPMOLIP excludes coverage for a claim based on, arising out of, directly or indirectly resulting from, in consequence of, or in any way involving actual, alleged, or threatened discharge, release, escape, or disposal of pollutants into or on real or personal property, water, or the atmosphere; any direction or request that the insured test for, monitor, clean up, remove, contain, treat, detoxify, or neutralize pollutants; or any voluntary decision.[628]

These exclusions are considered "absolute" because they do not include the much-litigated "sudden and accidental" language.[629]

---

626. 360 Condo. B Ass'n v. United States Liab. Ins. Co., 2012 U.S. Dist. LEXIS 193086 (S.D. Fla. Dec. 20, 2012) (that claims were filed about one year apart was not dispositive in claims-made policy).

627. ISO Form BP 17 24 01 10, § B.o.

628. Non-Profit Management and Organization Liability Insurance Policy § IV.3.

629. 3 *New Appleman Law of Liability Insurance* § 22.06[2][g] (rev. ed., Matthew Bender, 2017). One form of pollution exclusion bars coverage for a loss arising out of the release pollutants except when the discharge is "sudden and accidental." *See generally Sudden and Accidental Pollution Coverage*, available at: https://b-h-a.com/sudden-accidental-coverage/. After 1986, the standard pollution exclusion in commercial general liability policies was referred to as an "absolute pollution exclusion." It omits the "sudden and accidental" language and removes coverage for most pollution events but is not in fact "absolute." *See* https://www.irmi.com/term/insurance-definitions/absolute-pollution-exclusion.

Residential common interest community associations may believe pollution exclusions do not concern them and mainly apply to industry. They would be wrong. For example, a condominium association had an employee spray an insecticide on the property to exterminate pests. However, residents became ill and the property was evacuated. Unit owners brought suit against the association and certain of its directors. Initially, the court note that the insecticide appeared to have been an ordinary household product and there was a question about whether it was a pollutant within the meaning of the policy.[630] However, in the end, the court determined the damages arose out of the dispersal of a pollutant and the Pollution exclusion applied. There was no coverage under the policy, and the insurer was not required to defend the underlying action.[631]

[16] Civil Rights Law Violations

Some policies exclude coverage for claims for violation of any civil rights law. That exclusion has serious consequences for common interest communities.[632] Discrimination suits against associations and their directors are fairly common. Actions have been brought over alleged discrimination based on race,[633] religion,[634] disability,[635] and familial status.[636] While these suits are rarely successful, the cost of defending them is usually considerable as special legal expertise is required.

Civil rights laws are not all federal. State statutes and even city ordinances may prescribe civil rights. Those laws may be broader and more comprehensive than federal law. Additionally, not all discrimination violates civil rights laws.

---

630. Prudential-LMI Commer. Ins. Co. v. Meadowood Condo. Ass'n, 1992 U.S. Dist. LEXIS 1990 (E.D. Pa. Feb. 24, 1992).

631. Prudential-LMI Commer. Ins. Co. v. Meadowood Condo. Ass'n, 1992 U.S. Dist. LEXIS 11461 (E.D. Pa. July 31, 1992).

632. Treese & Rosenberry, *Insurance: How Community Associations Protect Themselves*, at 49 (CAI Press 2013) (association governing boards should be aware of exclusion for discrimination and civil rights claims).

633. *See, e.g.*, Robinson v. Section 23 Prop. Owner's Ass'n, 2014 U.S. Dist. LEXIS 122055 (M.D. Fla. Sept. 2, 2014); Reeves v. Carrollsburg Condominium Unit Owners Assoc., 1997 U.S. Dist. LEXIS 21762 (D.D.C. Dec. 18, 1997) (alleged racial discrimination *and* sexual harassment); Pinchback v. Armistead Homes Corp., 689 F. Supp. 541 (D. Md. 1988), *aff'd*, 907 F.2d 1447 (4th Cir. 1990), *cert. den.*, 498 U.S. 983, 111 S. Ct. 515, 112 L. Ed. 2d 527 (1990).

634. Sassower v. Field, 752 F. Supp. 1182 (S.D.N.Y. 1992), *cert. den.*, 507 U.S. 1043, 113 S. Ct. 1879, 123 L. Ed. 2d 497 (1993) (alleged discrimination based on religion and marital status).

635. *See, e.g.*, Morgan v. Fairway Nine II Condo. Ass'n, 2015 U.S. Dist. LEXIS 38040 (D. Idaho Mar. 24, 2015); Donovan v. Woodbridge Maint. Ass'n, 2015 U.S. Dist. LEXIS 32977 (E.D. Cal. Mar. 16, 2015); Weiss v. 2100 Condo. Ass'n, 941 F. Supp. 2d 1337 (S.D. Fla. 2013); Solodar v. Old Port Cove Lake Point Tower Condo. Ass'n, 2013 U.S. Dist. LEXIS 104996 (S.D. Fla. July 26, 2013); Jacobs v. Concord Village Condominium X Ass'n, Inc. 2004 U.S. Dist. LEXIS 4876 (S.D. Fla., Feb. 17, 2004); Shapiro v. Cadman Towers, Inc., 51 F.3d 328 (S.D.N.Y. 1995).

636. *See, e.g.*, Fair Hous. Ctr. of the Greater Palm Beaches, Inc. v. Sonoma Bay Cmty. Homeowners Ass'n, 2015 U.S. Dist. LEXIS 133906 (S.D. Fla. Oct. 1, 2015); United States v. Tropic Seas, Inc., 887 F. Supp. 1347 (D. Haw. 1995).

A frequent claim against common interest community associations is "selective enforcement."[637] That is an accusation that the association is enforcing its rules against some residents and not others.[638] While selective enforcement is discriminatory, it would not constitute a civil rights violation where the target did not fall into one of the protected classifications, for example, race, religion, or gender.

An exclusion for claims based on a violation of any civil rights law, including discrimination on account of race, religion, sex, or age, may not apply to related claims. A homeowners association and its officers and directors, for example, were sued over an age restriction. The governing documents originally limited occupancy to adults and children age 16 or over. The documents were subsequently amended to make the community one limited to adults age 55 or over. The change was adopted to conform the documents to federal law. The amendment was challenged by a group of homeowners, and among their objections were claims for slander or disparagement of title and restraint of trade. The insurer contended these claims were "creative ways" to in effect allege violations of state and federal anti-discrimination laws. The court was unimpressed. It found the claims did not fall within the exclusion, and the insurer had a duty to defend.[639]

Associations that require sales of residences to be approved by the governing board need to be especially attentive to their coverage for discrimination claims. For example, if a board denies an applicant based on a criminal history, the Office of General Counsel of the United States Department of Housing and Urban Development has issued an opinion that the action may violate the federal Fair Housing Act.[640]

---

637. *See, e.g.*, White Egret Condominium, Inc. v. Franklin, 379 So. 2d 346 (Fla. 1979); Dunlap v. Bavarian Village Condominium Ass'n, 780 P.2d 1012 (Alaska 1989); Board of Managers of Ocean Terrace Towne House Condominium v. Lent, 148 A.D.2d 408, 538 N.Y.S.2d 824 (1989); Franklin v. Spadafora, 388 Mass. 764, 447 N.E.2d 1244 (1983).

638. Elmore, *Directors and Officers Liability Insurance for Community Associations* (2014), available at: http://www.ksnlaw.com/blog/directors-officers-liability-insurance-community-associations/ (claims often submitted under D&O policy include those of discrimination against board for inequitable enforcement or application of association rules and regulations; these claims may arise where board has expressed, or appeared to express, preference for particular group of owners, or has clearly treated certain group of owners in inferior manner as compared to another group).

639. Lime Tree Village Community Club Ass'n v. State Farm Gen. Ins. Co., 980 F.2d 1402 (11th Cir. 1993).

640. Office of General Counsel Guidance on Application of Fair Housing Act Standards to the Use of Criminal Records by Providers of Housing and Real Estate-Related Transactions (HUD Apr. 4, 2016). The opinion says a policy or practice that restricts access to housing based on criminal history has a disparate impact on individuals of a particular race, national origin, or other protected class. That makes it unlawful under the federal Fair Housing Act if it is not necessary to serve a substantial, legitimate, non-discriminatory interest or if that interest could be served by another, less discriminatory, practice. A tailored policy that only excludes those with certain types of convictions may be acceptable if it accurately distinguishes between criminal conduct that suggests a demonstrable risk to resident safety and/or property, and criminal conduct that does not.

Absent an exclusion, a D&O policy may cover claims for housing discrimination or sexual harassment,[641] but it is important for associations to specifically ask for a policy that covers these claims and to make certain there is no applicable exclusion.[642]

[17] Claims Related to "Service Animals"

In common interest communities with rules restricting or prohibiting pets, residents with disabilities are increasingly challenging those proscriptions. It is illegal under the federal Fair Housing Act (FHA) to refuse to make a "reasonable accommodation" in rules, policies, practices, or services, when it may be needed to afford an equal opportunity to use and enjoy a dwelling. Pursuant to that, or to state laws, residents seek the right to maintain a "service" or "emotional support" animal. A "service animal" is one trained to do work or perform tasks for the benefit of a person with a disability. The meaning of "emotional support" animal is less clear. Governing boards in common interest communities encounter a complex legal minefield when residents insist on their right to a service or emotional support animal. First, the board has an obligation to enforce any pet restrictions in its governing documents, while it also must obey the FHA and any applicable state law. Second, the law on what boards must do and what they are prohibited from doing in response to a request for a reasonable accommodation is complex and evolving. A great deal has been written about the law requiring accommodations for service or emotional support animals.[643]

Suits against associations and individual directors over failure to provide a reasonable accommodation are now fairly common.[644] The cost to defend them can be considerable. Officers and directors would expect that these suits would

641. Iannucci, *Discussing D&O Insurance: 10 Things You Need to Know* (Cooperator, 2007), available at: http://cooperator.com/articles/1509/1/Discussing-DampO-Insurance/Page1.html.

642. Mosher, *Directors' and Officers' Insurance Don't Serve on the Board Without It* (Cooperator, 1997), available at: http://cooperator.com/articles/278/1/Directors039-and-Officers039-Insurance/Page1.html.

643. *See, e.g.*, Huss, *Re-evaluating the Role of Companion Animals in the Era of the Aging Boomer*, 47 Akron L. Rev. 497 (2014); Luck, *Advocating Emotional-Support Animals in No-Pets Housing*, 48 Clearinghouse Rev. 38 (2014); Waterlander, *Some Tenants Have Tails: When Housing Providers Must Permit Animals to Reside in "No-pet" Properties*, 18 Animal L. 321 (2012); Ligatti, *No Training Required: The Availability of Emotional Support Animals as a Component of Equal Access for the Psychiatrically Disabled under the Fair Housing Act*, 35 T. Marshall L. Rev. 139 (2010); Ligatti, *No Training Required: The Availability of Emotional Support Animals as a Component of Equal Access for the Psychiatrically Disabled under the Fair Housing Act*, 35 T. Marshall L. Rev. 139 (2010); Huss, *No Pets Allowed: Housing Issues and Companion Animals*, 11 Animal L. 69 (2005).

644. *See, e.g.*, Dubois v. Ass'n of Apt. Owners, 453 F.3d 1175 (9th Cir. 2006); Prindable v. Ass'n of Apt. Owners of 2987 Kalakaua, 304 F. Supp. 2d 1245 (D. Haw. 2003); Fowler v. Paradise Lakes Condo. Ass'n, 133 So. 3d 576 (Fla. 2d DCA 2014); *In re* Kenna Homes Coop. Corp., 210 W. Va. 380, 557 S.E.2d 787 (2001).

be covered by the D&O carrier, but that might not be the case. One attorney has written about a case in which a condominium association responded to a request from a unit owner for a reasonable accommodation with specific inquiries about the nature of the accommodation and the disability. The unit owner sued the association alleging its inquiries were discriminatory. The association filed a claim under its D&O policy for its legal costs and defense, but the carrier said the policy specifically excluded coverage for any claims related to assistance animals.[645] That exclusion was probably added by an endorsement. The warning for associations with pet restrictions is that they need to ask whether the policy will cover these claims and if it will not, they should negotiate to have claims related to decisions on service and emotional support animals included.

[18] Money Damages Limitation

As discussed earlier, the definition of "loss" can serve to limit coverage.[646] Additionally, some policies may have a specific exclusion proscribing coverage of claims for anything *other* than money damages.[647] This exclusion can be detrimental to common interest communities.[648] For example, a Massachusetts condominium was sued by a unit owner who sought an injunction that would allow him access to the adjoining unit and common areas to connect a gas line to his unit. His complaint had a request for costs and attorney's fees, but it did not ask for monetary damages. The D&O insurer denied coverage because the policy excluded coverage for anything other than money damages. The court found for the insurer. It said that under the exclusion there was no coverage for an action for injunctive relief that did not seek money damages and that a complaint for purely equitable relief that included counts seeking costs or attorney's fees was not one seeking money damages.[649] Another Massachusetts decision distinguished that holding where the underlying complaint by a condominium unit owner sought

645. Blanch, *Community Association Boards Need to Know and Understand the Exclusions and Requirements in their Association Insurance Policies* (Apr. 28, 2014), available at: https://www.floridahoalawyerblog.com/community-association-boards-n/#:~:text=In%20an%20effort%20to%20avoid%20encountering%20costly%20experiences,they%20are%20under%20the%20impression%20they%20have%20paid.

646. *See* § 14.12[3] *infra.*

647. *See, e.g.*, Oak Park Calabasas Condominium Ass'n v. State Farm Fire & Casualty Co., 137 Cal. App. 4th 557, 40 Cal. Rptr. 3d 263 (2006).

648. Treese & Rosenberry, *Insurance: How Community Associations Protect Themselves*, at 49 (CAI Press 2013) (non-monetary damages form bulk of association liability claims, and association governing boards should be aware of exclusion for them). *See also* Bateman, *What Homeowner Associations Need to Know About Directors' & Officers' Liability* (2017), available at: https://communityassociationmanagement.com/c33-financial-matters/c37-insurance/what-homeowner-associations-need-to-know-about-directors-officers-liability/ (if governing board in lakefront community decides to remove large, established trees and unit owner who objects cannot establish price on loss in value of real estate value and any claim would be non-monetary and excluded).

649. 116 Commonwealth Condominium Trust v. Aetna Cas. & Sur. Co., 433 Mass. 373, 742 N.E.2d 76 (2001). *See also* Walpole v. Le Petit Theatre Du Vieux Carre, 2012 U.S. Dist. LEXIS 670

restitution that included recovery of a $1,000 assessment. That claim, concluded the court was one for damages, as that word was used in the policy.[650]

The Maine Supreme Court considered a case involving a country club with facts that would be familiar to common interest communities. A dispute arose over a governing board election. Two persons were initially deemed to have been elected to the board, but after a recount, they were removed from office. They sought an injunction requiring the club to seat them. The D&O insurer contended it had no duty to defend because the complaint sought injunctive relief and not monetary damages. The court agreed that the exclusion for claims for relief in "any form other than money damages" applied as the underlying complaint did not request monetary damages; however, because a court could grant relief not requested if the plaintiff was entitled to that relief, the allegations in the underlying complaint had to be examined to determine whether they would support an award of damages even though damages were not requested. The court found no basis for non-monetary damages to be awarded and no duty to defend.[651]

NOTE: When disputes arise in common interest communities, the resulting litigation often seeks an injunction to either prohibit the governing board from acting or require it to act. Although neither the association nor the board members will suffer a financial loss if the plaintiffs prevail, the cost of defending these suits can be considerable and, therefore, if the policy excludes coverage for claims for anything other than money damages, an association should discuss with its broker eliminating the exclusion.

[19] Imputation or Severability of Exclusions Provision

D&O policies almost invariably address whether the actions of one insured person can be imputed to another, but one commentary recommends checking to be sure that is true of the policy in question.[652] The "imputation" language will generally be found at the end of the section on exclusions.[653] Policies commonly issued to CICs will almost certainly preclude imputation. The language, however, may be quite different. For example, the NPMOLIP says that "no fact pertaining to or knowledge or information possessed by any" insured person will, for purposes

(E.D. La. Jan. 4, 2012) (no duty to defend against claim for injunction to prohibit enforcement or operation of amendments to bylaws).

650. N. Sec. Ins. Co. v. Sandpiper Vill. Condo. Trust, 24 Mass. L. Rep. 500 (Mass. Super. Ct. 2008).

651. York Golf & Tennis Club v. Tudor Ins. Co., 845 A.2d 1173 (Me. 2004).

652. Kokinda, *D&O Liability Insurance: There Are Exclusions, and Then There Are Exclusions*, 28-10 ABIJ 46, 67 (2010).

653. *Directors and Officers Liability (D&O) Insurance Dictionary* (Willis Towers Watson, 2012) (most D&O policies automatically include statement about severability either at beginning or end of exclusions section, or directly underneath exclusions relating to wrongful conduct).

of applying any exclusion, be imputed to any other insured person. On the other hand, the ISO endorsement states that a "wrongful act" committed by an insured person will not, for purposes of applying the exclusions in the endorsement, be imputed to another "insured person." Thus, the ISO endorsement requires an examination of the definition of "wrongful act," which in general is any "actual or alleged error, misstatement, misleading statement, neglect or breach of duty, omission or act." The NPMOLIP would seem broader as it precludes any fact pertaining to any insured person from being imputed to another insured person. It also prohibits any knowledge or information possessed by an insured person from being imputed to another insured person.

Note that both the NPMOLIP and the ISO endorsement refer only to insured persons. The former says that facts pertaining to or knowledge or information possessed by an officer, director, or trustee of association *will be imputed* to the association for purposes of applying any exclusion. The ISO endorsement contains no similar language, but it also only limits imputation between insured persons. It is typical for policies to prescribe the parties whose actions will be imputed to the organization.[654] It is significant that the NPMOLIP does not impute facts pertaining to, or knowledge or information possessed by, committee members, volunteers, or community association managers to the association. In some CICs members of a committee or volunteers may have more involvement in—and knowledge of—the actions that form the basis of the underlying claim than board members or officers. There are CICs where the manager dominates the association and functions more like a CEO than a staff support person. Policies issued to profit-making corporations generally provide for imputation between a CEO and the corporation.

The imputation provision can lead to more complicated litigation. For example, because there is generally no imputation between insured persons, some directors, officers, committee members, or volunteers may be excluded from any coverage and receive no defense from the insurer while others are defended. The association may come within an exclusion by virtue of imputation from a single officer or director. All the members of a duly appointed committee may be excluded from coverage under the NPMOLIP by virtue of their status as insured persons because of imputation to them. On the other hand, under the NPMOLIP, the knowledge of those committee members would not be imputed to the association and the association may then avoid application of an exclusion.

654. Kokinda, *D&O Liability Insurance: There Are Exclusions, and Then There Are Exclusions*, 28-10 ABIJ 46, 67 (2010).

§ 14.15 Claims

The requirements for notifying the insurer of claims against an insured and the duties the policy imposes on the insured when there is a claim are critically important parts of the policy.

[1] Duties of Insured

The principal duties of the insured when there is a claim against it are to notify the insurer promptly and to cooperate fully in the investigation and settlement of the claim. Compliance with these duties is mandatory. When a common interest community believes that there is a covered claim against it, the designated board member or management company should discuss with its broker the extent of its responsibilities under the policy and, when it has doubts about requests from the insurer, it should discuss them with its attorney without delay.

[a] Notice of Claim

All D&O policies require that the insured give notice of a claim, but the requirements for that notice vary from policy to policy. D&O coverage is almost always provided in a "claims-made" policy. There are two basic types of claims-made policies. The first, and less common, is the *pure* claims-made policy. Under it, the insured has to report any claim to the insurer promptly, but not necessarily during the policy period.[655] Coverage is triggered when the insured receives a claim within the policy period but is conditioned on prompt notice to the insurer.[656] D&O coverage, however, is usually provided under a "claims-made and reported" policy. It requires that the claim against the insured be made during the policy period *and* that it be reported to the insurer during that period, or any extended reporting or discovery period provided under the policy.[657] Even though pure claims-made policies are uncommon, one commentator notes that they are more frequently used with D&O coverage and that it may be difficult for ordinary policyholders to determine the type of policy that has been issued to them.[658] An association should, therefore, discuss with its broker the specific notice requirements of its policy.

---

655. Bernstein, *The Ins and Outs of Claims-Made Policies* (Insurance Journal 2005), available at: http://www.insurancejournal.com/magazines/features/2005/10/03/61167.htm.

656. Quinn & Levin, *Directors and Officers Liability Insurance: Probable Directions in Texas Law*, 20 Rev. Litig. 381, 457 (2001) (policy does not require that insured give notice to insurer of claim within policy period, but only that insured receive claim within policy period to trigger coverage; trigger rules and notice rules generally are not the same).

657. *See* https://www.irmi.com/term/insurance-definitions/claims-made-and-reported-policy (claims-made and reported policy is one in which claim must be both made against insured and reported to insurer during policy period for coverage to apply).

658. Bernstein, *The Ins and Outs of Claims-Made Policies* (Insurance Journal 2005), available at: http://www.insurancejournal.com/magazines/features/2005/10/03/61167.htm (pure "claims-made" is less common but more frequently used in D&O coverage).

Claims-made and reported policies are unfavorable to an insured because it can be difficult to report a claim during the policy period if it was made late in that policy period.[659] To address that concern, many policies provide a "post-policy" reporting window. For example, the NPMOLIP states that if during the policy period—or any additional discovery period that is applicable—any claim is first made against any insured, the insureds, as a condition precedent to the right to reimbursement under the policy, are required to give the insurer *written* notice of the claim *as soon as practicable*, but in no event later than 30 days after expiration of the policy, or any discovery period if applicable.[660]

Policies may contain some specific reporting requirements. The ISO endorsement, for instance, says that if a claim is received by any insured, the named insured has to immediately record the specifics of the claim and the date received and notify the insurer *as soon as practicable*.[661] The endorsement also places the burden on the insured to make sure the notice reaches the insurer when it says the named insured has to "see to it" that the insurer *receives written notice* of the claim as soon as practicable. Other polices may simply require notice within a prescribed number of days after a claim is first made.[662]

It is also important to understand that under a "claims-made" policy, claims made during the policy period—assuming they are "covered" claims—are covered, even if the triggering event may have occurred during a prior policy period, assuming the policy provides for a "retroactive date." The insured, therefore, needs to maintain continuous coverage. If there is any lapse in coverage, insurers will not provide "retroactive coverage." Under a "claims-made" policy, when an insured receives a claim within the policy period, coverage is triggered, irrespective of when the actual triggering event occurred, but coverage is also conditioned on prompt notice to the insurer.

Complaints filed in lawsuits are often amended, and that may have implications for notice. For example, in a Florida condominium case,[663] the underlying complaint filed by a unit owner alleged the association failed to maintain and repair the property after a hurricane. The D&O insurer denied coverage and disclaimed any duty to defend pursuant to a Property Damage exclusion. Over a year later, the plaintiff in the underlying action amended her complaint adding

---

659. https://www.irmi.com/term/insurance-definitions/claims-made-and-reported-policy.

660. Non-Profit Management and Organization Liability Insurance Policy § V.B.1. The policy also states that, except as otherwise provided in it, all notices must be in writing and given by mail, prepaid express courier, or facsimile properly addressed and are effective on receipt. Non-Profit Management and Organization Liability Insurance Policy § V.B.3.

661. ISO Form BP 17 24 01 10, § E.2.

662. Sagalow, *Directors and Officers Liability Insurance: A Guide for Directors, Professional Edition*, at 27–33, available at: http://innovationinsurancegroup.com/wp-content/uploads/2014/07/D_O_Handbook_Professional_Edition.pdf.

663. Eastpointe Condo. I Ass'n v. Travelers Cas. & Sur. Co. of Am., 664 F. Supp. 2d 1281, 1287 (S.D. Fla. 2009), *aff'd*, 379 Fed. Appx. 906 (11th Cir. 2010).

allegations of fiscal mismanagement. The association later sued the D&O insurer for breach of contract. The court said that when the insurer denied coverage based on the specific allegations of the original complaint, it had no continuing duty to monitor the litigation for possible amendments that could potentially bring the claims within the scope of coverage. Instead, the association was obligated, under the notice of claim requirement of the policy, to give the insurer notice of the amended claim as soon as practicable if it sought to bring the new allegations outside the scope of the insurer's prior denial of coverage.

[i] Sufficiency of Notice

What constitutes sufficient notice of a claim? A commentary notes that few cases address the question, but that generally, the more vague the notice, the less probable courts are to find that an insured has given coverage-triggering notice.[664] At the same time, courts do not expect policyholders to be prescient or insurance law experts. When an insurer believes that a notice is improper, it may have to inform the insured of the inadequacy before a court will allow it to disclaim coverage for insufficiency of notice.[665] One recommendation is that an insured simply send the insurer the written demand, complaint, indictment, or notice of an administrative proceeding.[666]

[ii] Meaning of "as Soon as Practicable"

The obvious question about the notice is what does "as soon as practicable" mean? There is, unfortunately, no definitive answer. As one insurance treatise explains, the analysis of whether notice was indeed given as soon as practicable is fact-driven and based on the "totality of the circumstances," including a determination of the earliest possible moment at which the insured *could* have reported the claim.[667] A New Jersey federal court provided some clarity. It said that the clock on notice should begin to run not when a complaint is filed, but when the

664. Quinn & Levin, *Directors and Officers Liability Insurance: Probable Directions in Texas Law*, 20 Rev. Litig. 381, 462–63 (2001) (probability that court will deem proper notice to have been given is directly proportional to details provided in that notice; disclosures in renewal application probably do not constitute notice of claim).

665. Quinn & Levin, *Directors and Officers Liability Insurance: Probable Directions in Texas Law*, 20 Rev. Litig. 381, 479 (2001) (insurers may be estopped from denying claim or from placing it in particular year if they do not give insured timely and accurate information about their intent).

666. Quinn & Levin, *Directors and Officers Liability Insurance: Probable Directions in Texas Law*, 20 Rev. Litig. 381, 462-63 (2001) (probability that court will deem proper notice to have been given is directly proportional to details provided in that notice; disclosures in renewal application probably do not constitute notice of claim).

667. 5 Jeffery E. Thomas, *New Appleman on Insurance Law Library Edition* § 4.04[4][b] (LexisNexis 2023). In a cooperative case, notice of claim given over one year after the underlying action was instituted and was litigated to verdict was "palpably unreasonable." Scharf v. Federal Ins. Co., 261 A.D.2d 257, 690 N.Y.S.2d 265 (1999).

insured was served and that notifying the insurer within two weeks of receipt of service was sufficient notice.[668]

One commentary recommends that when a claim comes in, "it should be dispatched to the insurer that same day if possible."[669] It goes on to point out that any additional information that is required can be provided later, and that it does not matter to an insurer if it receives information in bits and pieces.

Ordinarily, even if an insured fails to provide notice "as soon as practicable," the insurer may be barred from disclaiming coverage when it was not prejudiced by the late notice. That is the rule in most states either by court decision[670] or statute.[671] However, in many states, courts do not apply the rule to claims-made policies,[672] and D&O policies are generally claims-made.

[iii] Notice and Common Interest Communities

A question that arises in common interest communities is: who provides the notice? Often the CAM is delegated the responsibility of providing notice to insurers.[673] The fact that the CAM has a duty to notify the insurer of a claim does not relieve the association of its duty under the policy to "see to it" that the insurer receives notification, because the insurer is not a party to, nor is it bound by, any agreement between an association and its manager.[674] When the CAM is delegated the responsibility to provide notice to insurers, it is important for the

668. NL Indus. v. Commercial Union Ins. Co., 926 F. Supp. 446, 455 (D.N.J. 1996) (noting that timeliness of investigation insurer would have to perform to defend against claims varies with type of claim).

669. Quinn & Levin, *Directors and Officers Liability Insurance: Probable Directions in Texas Law*, 20 Rev. Litig. 381 (2001).

670. *See, e.g.*, PAJ, Inc. v. Hanover Ins. Co., 243 S.W.3d 630, 636–37 (Tex. 2008) (insured's failure to timely notify its insurer of claim or suit does not defeat coverage if insurer was not prejudiced by delay); Moe v. Transamerica Title Ins. Co., 21 Cal. App. 3d 289, 302, 98 Cal. Rptr. 547, 555 (1971) (breach of notice clause by insured may not be asserted by insurer unless it was substantially prejudiced by it). *Compare* Sisters of Divine Providence v. Interstate Fire & Casualty Co., 72 Ill. Dec. 731, 117 Ill. App. 3d 158, 162, 453 N.E.2d 36, 38 (1983) (prejudice, or lack of it, is not factor that determines coverage; rather, determination is based on standard of reasonableness, and prejudice to insurer is but one factor taken into consideration in making determination of reasonableness of notice).

671. *See, e.g.*, N.Y. Ins. Law § 3420(a)(5) (no policy or contract insuring against liability for injury to person or property may be issued or delivered unless it contains in substance provision stating that failure to give any notice required to be given by that policy within time prescribed will not invalidate any claim made by insured, injured person, or any other claimant, unless failure to provide timely notice has prejudiced insurer).

672. 3 *New Appleman Law of Liability Insurance* § 22.05 (rev. ed., Matthew Bender, 2017).

673. Loria, *The Course of an Insurance Claim: From Filing to Finishing* (Cooperator, Aug. 2011), available at: http://cooperator.com/articles/2294/1/The-Course-of-an-Insurance-Claim/Page1.html (managing agent usually sends broker incident report, although sometimes those who have suffered claim contact broker directly).

674. *See* Paramount Ins. Co. v. Rosedale Gardens, Inc., 293 A.D.2d 235, 743 N.Y.S.2d 59 (2002) (duty of cooperative corporation to report accident to insurer was not discharged by notification to managing agent because, whatever may have been arrangement between cooperative and manager

association and the CAM to have clear procedures to be followed and for the governing board to monitor the course of the process. One reason to have procedures is that knowledge of a claim may be derived by a letter from an attorney to the association, and that letter may not be received by anyone on the governing board, but by the management company.[675] The procedures should require the manager to immediately notify the board of a letter that may constitute a claim. Even if the manager is the one to report the claim, the governing board members should be given immediate notice of it by the manager.

One reason common interest community associations may not provide timely notice of a claim is that the members of the governing board assume the claim is not covered under the policy.[676] That is a serious mistake. The association should discuss any potential claim with its broker. Brokers will typically notify any insurer whose policy *might* cover the claim.[677] Associations should remember, however, that discussing a potential claim with the broker is not deemed notice to the insurer. Notice must be given to the insurer, whether by the broker on behalf of the association or by the association directly to the insurer.

[iv] Multiple Claims

Multiple lawsuits can arise out of the same wrongful act or acts. How does that affect notice? In one condominium case a unit owner sued the directors and officers of the association in 1992 over alleged failures to repair common property and the handling of insurance proceeds after a hurricane. The insurer was notified of that claim in March 1992. A prior 1991 suit against the officers and directors by another unit owner also concerned the handling of insurance proceeds.

---

regarding reporting of incidents to insurer, it was not binding on insurer that, pursuant to policy, was entitled to notice "as soon as practicable from insured or anyone acting for it").

675. Loria, *The Course of an Insurance Claim: From Filing to Finishing* (Cooperator, Aug. 2011), available at: http://cooperator.com/articles/2294/1/The-Course-of-an-Insurance-Claim/Page1.html.

676. *See, e.g.*, Citrus Course Homeowners Ass'n v. Great Am. Ins. Co., 2016 U.S. Dist. LEXIS 10199 (C.D. Cal. Jan. 7, 2016). In *Citrus Course*, the association sought to foreclose assessment liens against the developer in a non-judicial proceeding after the developer stopped paying its assessments. The developer brought an action for a temporary restraining order to enjoin the foreclosure proceedings in April and the next month amended its complaint to add causes of action for breach of contract, unjust enrichment, conversion. The association's D&O policy required notice no later than 90 days after the end of a policy period. The association did not notify its D&O insurer of the claim until March of the following year, and the insurer denied coverage because the notice was late. The association argued it reasonably believed the developer's action fell under the contract exclusion until it received a settlement demand from the developer in February of that year. The court sided with the insurer. The association became aware of the complaint in April, the policy period ended in May, and the association had up to 90 days after the end of the policy period to provide notice. Notice the following March was untimely.

677. Meskin, *When Are You Not Covered by Your D&O Policy? Maintaining Proper Coverage* (Cooperator, Aug. 2008), available at: http://cooperator.com/articles/1673/1/When-Are-You-Not-Covered-By-Your-DampO-Policy/Page1.html (one reason that the bodily injury or property damage claims are commonly rejected by D&O insurers is that community managers and insurance agents tend to submit claims to every insurer, letting insurance companies deny claim).

The insurer was notified of that action in July of 1991. It denied coverage for the 1992 suit because the policy was claims-made, and the claim had not been submitted within the coverage period. The court said that notice of the wrongful act had been given with the first suit in 1991. That notice encompassed the subsequent 1992 action as well, because the same allegedly wrongful acts led to it. In effect, said the court, by giving notice that handling of the proceeds of the insurance might lead to lawsuits being filed, the insured stated a claim to be defended in any lawsuit arising from those wrongful acts, even though other wrongful acts might become implicated.[678]

Policies generally address multiple claims. The ISO endorsement, for example, provides that all claims arising out of the same wrongful act or "interrelated wrongful acts" committed by one or more insured persons are considered a single claim.[679] "Interrelated wrongful act" simply means all causally connected wrongful acts.[680]

[b] Notice of Potential Claim

D&O policies typically provide for notice to be given of *potential* claims. For example, the ISO endorsement states that in the event of a wrongful act that *could* result in a claim, the named insured has to "see to it" that the insurer is notified *as soon as practicable* of a "wrongful act" that might result in a claim, and to the extent possible, the notice should include how, when, and where the wrongful act took place, the names and addresses of any person involved in the specific wrongful act, including names and addresses of potential claimants, particulars about the reasons for anticipating a claim may result from a specific wrongful act, the nature of the alleged or potential damages arising from the wrongful act, and the circumstances by which the insureds first became aware of the specific wrongful act.[681] Another part of the endorsement provides that a claim is deemed to be first made on the date notice of the wrongful act was first reported pursuant to the notice requirements.[682]

---

678. Clark v. General Accident Ins. Co. PR., 1996 U.S. Dist. LEXIS 20809 (D.V.I. Mar. 5, 1996).

679. ISO Form BP 17 24 01 10, § A.4.

680. ISO Form BP 17 24 01 10, § I.6. *Consider* Citrus Course Homeowners Ass'n v. Great Am. Ins. Co., 2016 U.S. Dist. LEXIS 10199 (C.D. Cal. Jan. 7, 2016) (where initial complaint was filed in April and amended following month, notice to insurer in March of next year was untimely; had notice mandate been measured from the date of May amended complaint, March notice would have come within next policy period; however, date of the amended complaint was immaterial because all claims involving same wrongful act or related wrongful acts were considered single claim and deemed to have been first made on earliest date on which it was made to insured).

681. ISO Form BP 17 24 01 10, § E.1.

682. ISO Form BP 17 24 01 10, § A.4. *See, e.g.*, Mt. Hood, LLC v. Travelers Cas. & Sur. Co. of Am., 2009 U.S. Dist. LEXIS 16775 (D. Or. Mar. 3, 2009) (tender of defense of demand for monetary damages gave notice of possible claim during policy period where suit was filed after policy period).

The NPMOLIP states that if during the policy period insureds become aware of any wrongful act that may subsequently give rise to a claim and give *written notice* to the insurer *as soon as practicable* during the policy period—or any applicable discovery period—then any claim subsequently made against the insureds that arises out of that wrongful act will be deemed to have been made during the policy period.[683] The notice is required to articulate the full particulars of the nature of the potential claim, the date of the wrongful act, the persons involved, and the reasons for anticipating a claim.

While the language of the "notice of potential claims" is written as a mandate, it benefits the insured by allowing notice during the policy period of acts that may ripen into a claim at some later time. As one observer notes, the insured can report, during the policy period, circumstances that might give rise to future claims and if those claims ultimately are made—even if after expiration of the policy—they are deemed to have been made at the time the notice was provided.[684]

Because of the provisions of these notice of potential claim clauses, one expert commentary recommends that when an insured discovers that its directors or officers may have done something wrong—but no claim has been brought—that fact should be reported to the insurer as soon as possible and further, insureds should provide their D&O insurers with specific "possibility reports" near the end of a policy period.[685] Insureds need, however, to consider the potential negative consequences of providing the insurer with an extensive "laundry list" of potential claims. There are several: if the list is submitted before the insured receives notice of cancellation or nonrenewal, it will almost certainly precipitate cancellation; the list can be used by a subsequent insurer for substantial exclusions from coverage; and, if an event on the list predates the policy period and the insurer can prove the insured knew of, but did not disclose, that event on the policy application, it may be grounds for declaring the policy void.[686]

The principal dispute that arises over notices of potential claims is the sufficiency—that is, the specificity—of the notice.[687] As one commentary observes, there are a number of questions about the notice requirements. For example, how full and detailed does the description of the wrongful act have to be, and

683. Non-Profit Management and Organization Liability Insurance Policy § V.B.2.

684. Monteleone & Conca, *Directors and Officers Indemnification and Liability Insurance: An Overview of Legal and Practical Issues*, 51 Bus. Law 573, 588 (1996) (if insured becomes aware of circumstances that may give rise to claim and properly reports those circumstances to D&O insurer during policy period, term of policy can be effectively extended to respond to claim involving those circumstances even if claim is first made after expiration of policy).

685. Quinn & Levin, *Directors and Officers Liability Insurance: Probable Directions in Texas Law*, 20 Rev. Litig. 381, 458 (2001).

686. Caraccio, *Void Ab Initio: Application Fraud as Grounds for Avoiding Directors' and Officers' Liability Insurance Coverage*, 74 Calif. L. Rev. 929, 947 (1986) (noting also that if prior carrier successfully denies coverage for list on ground that stated events are too vague or general to constitute reported claims, insured will be left with sizable gaps in protection).

687. 3 *New Appleman Law of Liability Insurance* § 22.08[1] (rev. ed., Matthew Bender, 2017).

what if the insured identifies four claimants but more turn up in a subsequent lawsuit?[688] An association should, therefore, consider seeking the assistance of its attorney in preparing the notice and should be careful to include the information the policy requires to be included with the notice.[689]

[c] Cooperation

A standard clause in any insurance policy, including D&O policies, requires the cooperation of the insured. Cooperation clauses are typically very straightforward. The ISO endorsement, for example, says that the named insured, and any other involved insured, has to cooperate with the insurer in the investigation or settlement of the claim.[690] The endorsement adds that the named insured, and any other involved insured, has to assist the insurer, on its request, in enforcement of any right against any person or organization that may be liable to the insured because of wrongful acts to which the policy may also apply.[691] The NPMOLIP has two clauses that address cooperation. The first is in the conditions section of the policy and simply states that the insured has to give the insurer any cooperation that it may reasonably require.[692] Cooperation is also mentioned in the part of the insuring agreement on defense coverage where the policy says the insureds agree to provide the insurer with all assistance and cooperation the insurer reasonably requests[693]

Very few cases have interpreted cooperation clauses in the context of D&O insurance, although there is extensive case law on these clauses in commercial general liability policies to which one might turn for explication. In general, denial of coverage by an insurer extinguishes any duty to cooperate.[694] An insured, on learning of a claim against it, may want to immediately consult and retain counsel, even before notifying the insurer of the claim. It may do so because it needs an explanation of its potential coverage, because it anticipates conflicts of

688. Quinn & Levin, *Directors and Officers Liability Insurance: Probable Directions in Texas Law*, 20 Rev. Litig. 381, 465 (2001). The authors also wonder about a notice that describes some of consequences of a wrongful act that has already occurred, misses a few or speculates about the future results of a wrongful act, but misses a causal chain.

689. However, one commentary says that under the language of potential claims clauses, it will be difficult for an insurer to contend that an early fragmentary report did not constitute a sufficient one. Quinn & Levin, *Directors and Officers Liability Insurance: Probable Directions in Texas Law*, 20 Rev. Litig. 381, 458 (2001).

690. ISO Form BP 17 24 01 10, § E.3.c.

691. ISO Form BP 17 24 01 10, § E.3.d.

692. Non-Profit Management and Organization Liability Insurance Policy § V.B.1.

693. Non-Profit Management and Organization Liability Insurance Policy § I.B. Additionally, the policy says the insureds agree that in the event of a claim they will do nothing that may prejudice the position of the insurer or its potential or actual rights of recovery.

694. Fed. Ins. Co. v. Hawaiian Elec. Indus., 1995 U.S. Dist. LEXIS 22594 (D. Haw. Dec. 14, 1995).

interest with the insurer. Another good reason to retain competent and knowledgeable counsel is that the claim needs to be properly worded so that it falls within the coverage under the policy. Merely retaining counsel should not violate the Cooperation clause.[695]

A clause allowing the insurer to examine the insured under oath (Examination Under Oath—EUO) is standard in many types of policies, particularly property policies.[696] However, it is not typically found in D&O policies. Nonetheless, an insurer may ask to "interview" an insured. If an insured refuses to submit to an interview, has the Cooperation clause been breached? A Pennsylvania federal court held that a former president and director breached his duty to cooperate by refusing to submit to an interview and by failing to disclose information and documents reasonably requested by the insurer.[697] Given that holding, a director or officer should seek advice of counsel before refusing to submit to an interview. The question is, which attorney? The association attorney represents the entity, not individual directors or officers.[698] If an individual director or officer is seeking direct Side A coverage for a non-indemnified payment and asks for the guidance of the association's attorney, the attorney would probably be considered to be providing direct representation to that person. That raises ethical "dual representation" issues for the association attorney. The attorney *may* be able to directly represent an individual officer or director, but under the Rules of Professional Conduct of the state in which he or she is licensed, he or she may need consent from the association to that dual representation.[699]

NOTE: Regardless of any requirement in the applicable Rules of Professional Conduct, the attorney should always obtain consent for dual representation.

695. NL Indus. v. Commercial Union Ins. Co., 926 F. Supp. 446, 456 (D.N.J. 1996) (under New York law, where conflicts of interest between insurer and its insured arise, insured is entitled to select its counsel, whose reasonable fee is paid by insurer).

696. *See generally* Knoll, *Examination Under Oath: The Insurance Companies Best Friend*, 16 Forum 777 (1981).

697. Bogatin v. Federal Ins. Co., 2000 U.S. Dist. LEXIS 8632 (E.D. Pa. June 21, 2000).

698. Restatement (Third) of the Law Governing Lawyers § 96 (Representing an Organization as Client) (when employed or retained to represent organization, lawyer represents interests of that organization); Taylor, *Who Does "Our" Attorney Represent Anyway?* (Association Times, Oct. 2006) (association counsel represents corporate entity).

699. *See, e.g.*, Restatement (Third) of the Law Governing Lawyers § 131 (Conflicts of Interest in Representing an Organization) (attorney may not represent both organization and director or officer when there is substantial risk that representation of either would be materially and adversely affected by duties to other unless all affected clients consent to representation under applicable limitations and conditions).

[d] Documents and Information

D&O policies sometimes simply require the insured to provide the insurer with all the information it reasonably requests or requires.[700] Other policies will be more specific. For example, the ISO endorsement requires the named insured, and any other involved insured, to immediately send the insurer copies of any demands, notices, summonses, or legal papers received in connection with the claim and authorize the insurer to obtain records and other information.[701] When the policy requires the insured to provide information *requested* by the insurer, the insurer generally has to show a diligent effort to obtain information to prove a breach by the insured.[702]

An association should anticipate that a D&O insurer will request copies of the governing documents and of minutes of board meetings. Minutes can present a problem for common interest communities. Experts warn that the contents of board minutes should be limited.[703] Other than basic introductory information—the name of the organization, the date, time, and place of the meeting, the determination of a quorum, and the announcement of compliance with any meeting notice requirements—the minutes should state no more than the motions made and seconded and the results of the vote on each motion. Nonetheless, well-meaning association secretaries persist in making the minutes a narrative account of meetings. They include not only the discussion surrounding motions but even discussion that took place without a proper motion having ever been made. That presents a danger for the association and its officers and directors because information in the minutes may undermine their defense[704] but also because the insurer may find a basis in the minutes to deny coverage.

---

700. Non-Profit Management and Organization Liability Insurance Policy §§ I.B, V.B.1.

701. ISO Form BP 17 24 01 10, § E.3.

702. National Union Fire Ins. Co. v. Cagle, 68 F.3d 905, 912 (5th Cir. 1995) (insurer cannot claim breach of cooperation clause because insured failed to voluntarily produce pertinent information).

703. *See, e.g.*, 6A Rohan, *Real Estate Transactions: Home Owner Associations and Planned Unit Developments—Law and Practice: Forms*, § 7A.04[2][c] (Matthew Bender, 2016).

704. For example, a statement in the minutes about liability could prove detrimental to the coverage. *Consider* Cohen v. Beachside Two-I Homeowners' Ass'n, 2006 U.S. Dist. LEXIS 44978 (D. Minn. June 29, 2006), *aff'd*, 272 Fed. Appx. 534 (8th Cir.), *cert. den.*, 555 U.S. 945, 129 S. Ct. 417, 172 L. Ed. 2d 288 (2008), where the association was sued for defamation based on the contents of the minutes of meetings of the governing board. The minutes contained a narrative discussion of the failure of the plaintiff to pay maintenance fees. The court found that for the most part the narrative was substantially true and, therefore, not actionable. However, the minutes for one meeting stated that the plaintiff's property had been purchased by a bank when in fact the bank had sent the association a check drawn from the tax escrow account of the plaintiff to satisfy a lien against the property. The governing board mistakenly assumed the bank had purchased the property, but that mistaken assumption did not, said the court, render the statement substantially true for purposes of the law of defamation.

[e] Settlement

The ISO endorsement simply says that no insured may, except at the cost of that insured, voluntarily make a payment, assume any obligation, or incur any expense without the written consent of the insurer.[705] The NPMOLIP provides that the insureds agree not to settle any claim, incur any defense costs, or otherwise assume any contractual obligation or admit any liability with respect to any claim without the written consent of the insurer, which will not be unreasonably withheld. Additionally, the policy provides that the insurer is not liable under the policy for any settlement, defense costs, assumed obligation, or admission to which it did not consent.[706]

The language of the NPMOLIP was applied in a condominium case in which the insurer had provided the association and its directors a defense. The association governing board wanted to settle the suit. It retained its own attorney and instructed him that if the insurer did not consent to a proffered settlement offer, or otherwise settle the case within 24 hours, the plaintiffs' settlement offer was to be accepted immediately. The attorney sent a letter to the insurer informing it of the recent settlement offer and demanding that it immediately confirm complete coverage or settle the case, otherwise the association intended to terminate the insurer's defense and settle the case on its own to mitigate further damages. The insurer responded that it would not agree to assume full financial responsibility for the settlement but would contribute a portion. The association then terminated the insurer's defense and executed a settlement agreement with the plaintiffs in the underlying action. The court said that under the policy terms, the association agreed not to settle any claim or admit any liability without the written consent of the insurer, and it was undisputed that it did settle the underlying lawsuit without that consent. Because the association entered into a settlement agreement without the consent of the insurer, and to the substantial prejudice of its rights under the policy, the court held the association breached the policy and there was no coverage under its terms.[707]

---

705. ISO Form BP 17 24 01 10, § E.4. Does settlement without consent violate the cooperation clause? *See* Quinn & Levin, *Directors and Officers Liability Insurance: Probable Directions in Texas Law*, 20 Rev. Litig. 381, 471 (2001) (carriers may argue that insured has violated cooperation clause if it settles without carrier consent, but courts appear skeptical of argument if that settlement was non-collusive and insurer had problems with coverage). *See also* Wojtunik v. Kealy, 2011 U.S. Dist. LEXIS 36229 (D. Ariz. Mar. 31, 2011) (under Arizona law, cooperation clause only forbids non-consensual settling of claims for which insurer has unconditionally assumed liability and insured defended under reservation of rights may enter into reasonable, non-collusive settlement with claimant without breaching cooperation clause to protect itself from personal liability).

706. Non-Profit Management and Organization Liability Insurance Policy § I.B.

707. Petro v. Travelers Cas. & Sur. Co. of Am., 54 F. Supp. 3d 1295 (N.D. Fla. 2014). The court noted that the insurer had retained defense counsel and provided a fully funded, though conditional, defense, which the association accepted for over four years before rejecting it on the eve of trial. Although, said the court, the association was not required to accept the insurer's conditional

[2] Recommendations for Avoiding Claims

One large wholesale broker with extensive experience in addressing the needs of non-profit organizations including common interest community associations has several recommendations for avoiding claims against directors and officers.[708] First it recommends using experienced professionals: attorneys specializing in community association law to, for example, review and update bylaws;[709] experienced and credentialed property managers; and an accountant with whom the association consults regularly.

The second suggestion is that board members be required to read and understand the bylaws and that meetings, though informal, follow the procedures and rules.[710] That might seem obvious, but it is surprising how often officers and directors are unaware of the contents of the governing documents and even the rules they and prior boards have adopted. Failure to follow those documents and rules can result in unnecessary litigation.

The next recommendation is that prospective board members should be made aware of what the position entails, should be required to read the governing documents before taking office, and should be provided training as a group in their duties and responsibilities. For example, at the first meeting after election of new board members, the board should review the governing documents and each board member should receive his or her own copy. Informed board members are less likely to find themselves the object of lawsuits,[711] and fortunately training is widely available in most communities. Organizations like the Community

---

defense at the outset, the fact is that it did accept it and no material change in the terms of the defense were shown that justified the belated rejection. The insurer's refusal to accept the association's ultimatum on the eve of trial was not a wrongful refusal to defend. Instead, the association arranged a settlement without the participation of the insurer and unilaterally chose to terminate the defense which, under the policy, it had agreed not to do.

708. *7 Simple Steps to Help Avoid Common Non-Profit Community Association Directors' & Officers' Liability Claims* (Ian H. Graham Insurance), available at: bing.com/ck/a?!&&p=1fdb1902d47bc7b0JmltdHM9MTY4Njk2MDAwMCZpZ3VpZD0zZjdjYjgzZC03YmRiLTZlYzMtMmRhYS1hYTg1N2FiNzZmOTQmaW5zaWQ9NTE4NA&ptn=3&hsh=3&fclid=3f7cb83d-7bdb-6ec3-2daa-aa857ab76f94&psq=7+Simple+Steps+to+Help+Avoid+Common+Non-Profit+Community+Association+Directors'+%26+Officers'+Liability+Claims&u=a1aHR0cHM6Ly93d3cuaWhnaW5zdXJhbmNlLmNvbS9nZXRtZWRpYS8zMDQzYmViYS1lNTIxLTQyZTEtYmFhMC01NzJjYzc3MGU2YWYvNy1TaW1wbGUtU3RlcHMtdG8tQXZvaWQtRE8tQ2xhaW1zLnBkZg&ntb=1. The company is Ian H. Graham Insurance, and since 1982 it has served more than 5,000 insurance brokers representing over 42,000 community association clients.

709. It is recommended that the association counsel periodically review and update the documents, that changes be made following the proper procedure, and that the board be updated on new laws affecting associations.

710. It is also recommended that association members be required to acknowledge receipt of bylaws.

711. *See generally* Price & Schneider, *Nonprofit D&O Essentials: Homeowners, Condo Association Boards Beware* (Nov. 7, 2005), available at: http://www.insurancejournal.com/magazines/features/2005/11/07/62357.htm (frequent difficulty in common interest communities is that people

Associations Institute as well as local law firms and management companies offer training seminars for association officers and directors.

Another recommendation reflects one of the most serious problems in common interest communities: important decisions are often made in an emotionally charged, contentious atmosphere. Thus, the brokerage firm cautions against allowing emotions and personalities to get in the way of decision-making. One way to accomplish that is to have a chair who is skilled in managing meetings. In the typical common interest community, the officers are also board members and the president chairs the board meetings. The person who is president may be right for the job because he or she has the time and necessary knowledge, but may not be effective at managing meetings. Unless the governing documents specifically require that board meetings be chaired by the president, there is no reason that another board member cannot chair meetings. When the association is facing a meeting in which a particularly controversial topic will be discussed, it should contemplate having the association attorney present and designating him or her to chair the event. A well-run meeting during which residents feel they are heard and their concerns are considered is less likely to result in litigation.

The final recommendation is that the association maintain good records. Proper board meeting minutes leave no doubt about the action taken. Associations should also record communications with members, vendors, insurers, counsel, property managers, and anyone else. When communications are oral, it is easy to forget what was said and what commitments were made. In many common interest communities, there is considerable turnover in the governing board membership. The person who had an unrecorded discussion may no longer serve on the board, or even live in the community, when questions are raised about that discussion. For example, one claim often brought against associations is that their rules are not uniformly enforced. In too many communities, rules are informally interpreted. One board member tells a resident that the no pet rule does not apply to fish while another board member tells a different resident it applies to dogs but not "in door" cats. Sometimes these interpretations are made without even reading the text of the rule. Challenges to rule enforcement can be minimized if the board has a firm policy that requires that requests for interpretations of the rules be submitted in writing and that responses be made in writing after review by the entire board at a meeting. Assuming the written record shows consistent enforcement by the board, it will be difficult for a resident to mount a serious challenge. Of course, the association needs to be careful in the wording of any written response because it would be subject to discovery in a lawsuit and could reveal wrongful behavior. It would be wise for the association to seek guidance from the association counsel before adopting an interpretation of its rules.

---

running for and being elected to governing boards are not always well-versed in running associations and that results in many disputes over bylaws and covenants).

§ 14.16 Other Insurance

The "other insurance" clause takes on particular importance in D&O policies because at least two other policies that common interest communities almost always maintain—commercial general liability and crime/fidelity insurance—may be subject to it. The other insurance clause in a D&O policy is typically an "excess clause."[712] For example, the NPMOLIP states that if any loss otherwise covered under it is insured under any other valid and collectible policy or policies, then it applies only in excess of the amount of any deductibles, retentions, and limits of liability under that other insurance, whether that other insurance is stated to be primary, contributory excess, contingent, or otherwise unless that other insurance is written specifically excess of the D&O policy by reference in that other policy to the policy number of the D&O policy.[713] Simply put, under this language, when there is other insurance, that other policy defends and pays first.[714]

Early policies often had an exclusion that was in effect an "other insurance" clause.[715] For example, a policy would bar coverage for a claim insured by another valid policy or policies except in respect to any excess beyond the amount or amounts of payments under that other policy or policies.[716]

A difficulty that arises with Other Insurance clauses is that the other policies may also have Other Insurance clauses; in fact, they may have clauses with nearly identical language. Courts will generally attempt to give effect to the language of the policies except when they are inconsistent—for instance, where both claim to be excess over any other policy—in which case the general rule is that the provisions are mutually repugnant,[717] the clauses are disregarded, and the losses are prorated among the insurance companies.[718]

---

712. Quinn & Levin, *Directors and Officers Liability Insurance: Probable Directions in Texas Law*, 20 Rev. Litig. 381, 471 (2001). However, an "other insurance" clause might also state that the D&O policy is null and void, or inapplicable, up to the limits of the other policy or that the coverage provided by the D&O policy is "complementary" and each insurer shares the loss on a pro rata basis up to its own limit of liability. 3 *New Appleman Law of Liability Insurance* § 22.08[4] (rev. ed., Matthew Bender, 2017).

713. Non-Profit Management and Organization Liability Insurance Policy § V.K.

714. Quinn & Levin, *Directors and Officers Liability Insurance: Probable Directions in Texas Law*, 20 Rev. Litig. 381, 471 (2001). *See, e.g.*, Fieldston Prop. Owners Ass'n, Inc. v. Hermitage Ins. Co., Inc., 920 N.Y.S.2d 763, 16 N.Y.3d 257, 945 N.E.2d 1013 (N.Y. 2011) (where CGL policy stated it was primary and under other insurance clause in D&O policy, it was excess, CGL insurer had primary duty to defend on behalf of its insured and generally would have no entitlement to contribution from excess insurer).

715. 3 *New Appleman Law of Liability Insurance* § 22.08[4] (rev. ed., Matthew Bender, 2017).

716. Monteleone & Conca, *Directors and Officers Indemnification and Liability Insurance: An Overview of Legal and Practical Issues*, 51 Bus. Law 573, 603 (1996).

717. Monteleone & Conca, *Directors and Officers Indemnification and Liability Insurance: An Overview of Legal and Practical Issues*, 51 Bus. Law 573, 603 (1996) (often, other policy will contain identical other insurance provision, thereby creating "mutual repugnancy").

718. 3 *New Appleman Law of Liability Insurance* § 22.08[4] (rev. ed., Matthew Bender, 2017).

Sometimes insurers will change the other insurance clause when they renew the policy. For example, in one condominium case, the initial Other Insurance clause in the CGL policy explicitly made its coverage primary. The clause in the D&O policy clearly made its coverage excess. When the CGL policy was renewed, its Other Insurance clause was changed to make it all but identical to the one in the D&O policy. Prior to that change, a unit owner brought suit over property damage that was allegedly caused by repair work by the association to the exterior of the building. The D&O insurer disclaimed coverage based on a Property Damage exclusion. The CGL carrier agreed to defend under its policy and later sued the D&O insurer arguing there was coverage under its policy. The court found that only the CGL policy provided coverage. It rejected the argument that a change in the Other Insurance clause in the CGL policy made after a potentially covered occurrence and the onset of litigation could apply. The CGL insurer, concluded the court, had a primary policy and the D&O company had an excess policy during the policy periods in which the initial occurrence happened, the initial claims were made, and the litigation began and the CGL insurer, therefore, became obligated to defend the underlying action before the policy with the revised Other Insurance clause ever went into effect.[719]

§ 14.17 No Action Clause; Suits against the Insurer

A standard clause in insurance policies addresses legal actions against the insurer. These provisions are called "no action" clauses. Typically, they provide that no action will lie against the insurer unless, as a condition precedent, the insureds have fully complied with all of the terms of the policy.[720] In a common interest community, this applies to the association and to the individuals who are insureds under the policy. Thus, a director denied coverage will not be able to bring suit against the insurer if he or she relied on the association to give notice of an underlying claim and it failed to do so.

The No Action clause generally also states that no action against the insurer may be brought until the amount of the insured's obligation to pay has been

719. Admiral Indem. Co. v. Travelers Cas. & Sur. Co. of Am., 881 F. Supp. 2d 570 (S.D.N.Y. 2012).

720. Non-Profit Management and Organization Liability Insurance Policy § V.H. This clause has been invoked to prevent an insured from suing the insurer where the insured settled without the insurer's consent in violation of the policy. LaCroix, *D&O Insurance: Insured That Settled Underlying Claim Without Insurer's Consent Cannot Sue the Insurer for Breach of Contract or Bad Faith* (2015), available at: http://www.dandodiary.com/2015/04/articles/d-o-insurance/do-insurance-insured-that-settled-underlying-claim-without-insurers-consent-cannot-sue-the-insurer-for-breach-of-contract-or-bad-faith/ (contending that if policyholder cannot, because of no action clause, sue insurer for breach of contract where insurer declined to consent to settlement of underlying claim, there is no way for policyholder to argue that insurer unreasonably refused to consent). *Compare* First Fidelity Bancorporation v. National Union Fire Ins. Co., 1990 U.S. Dist. LEXIS 14468 (E.D. Pa. Oct. 23, 1990).

finally determined either by judgment against an insured after *actual* trial or by written agreement of the insured, the claimant, and the insurer. Courts generally enforce this precondition rather vigorously,[721] although they may allow a declaratory judgment action to determine coverage.[722]

Another portion of a No Action clause may state that no person or organization has any right under the policy to join the insurer as a party to any action against the insureds to determine the insurer's liability, nor may the insurer be impleaded by the insureds or their legal representatives. "Implead" means to "bring a new party into an action."[723]

Even if the conditions of a No Action clause are met, many courts hold that members of a common interest community association lack standing to bring suit against the D&O insurer because they are not parties to the policy.[724]

721. *See, e.g.*, Haxton v. CNA Financial Corp., 1990 U.S. App. LEXIS 19764 (6th Cir. Nov. 2, 1990) (courts have recognized validity of no action clauses; under no action clause, claim for coverage had not ripened because condition precedent of judgment or settlement establishing the amount of obligation had not been met); S & S Healthcare, Inc. v. Virginia Sur. Co., 1998 U.S. Dist. LEXIS 21810 (W.D. Va. Dec. 21, 1998) (holding that no action clause prohibited insured from bringing any action against insurer concerning underlying cases until after amount of any obligation of insured to plaintiffs was fully and finally determined; contention that settlement was impossible without insurer's involvement did not change outcome as fact that settlement would be more readily attained did not authorize court to rewrite agreed on terms of contract; noting terms of no action policy allowed insured to be indemnified in settlement if written agreement was entered into by claimant, insured, and insurer). *But see* First Fidelity Bancorporation v. National Union Fire Ins. Co., 1990 U.S. Dist. LEXIS 14468 (E.D. Pa. Oct. 23, 1990) (denying summary judgment to insurer based on no action clause where insured alleged insurer unreasonably withheld consent to settlement in violation of policy and there was genuine dispute as to whether withholding of consent was unreasonable or otherwise amounted to breach of contractual obligations).

722. *See, e.g.*, Eureka Federal Sav. & Loan Ass'n v. American Casualty Co., 873 F.2d 229, 233 (9th Cir. 1989) (declining to apply no action clause to bar action by insureds for declaration of liability limits, especially when insureds seek to facilitate settlement negotiations by establishing policy limits). *Accord* Wilbanks Secs., Inc. v. Scottsdale Ins. Co., 2016 U.S. Dist. LEXIS 144761 (W.D. Okla. Oct. 19, 2016) (no action clause did not bar declaratory judgment regarding duty of insurer to defend insured in underlying arbitration); Cardin v. Pacific Employers Ins. Co., 745 F. Supp. 330 (D. Md. 1990). *But see* Zaborac v. American Casualty Co., 663 F. Supp. 330, 333 (C.D. Ill. 1987) (declaratory judgment action seeking to resolve rights and liabilities of parties under directors and officers liability insurance policy barred by no action clause that expressly prohibited insureds from bringing action until underlying claims had been determined).

723. https://www.irmi.com/term/insurance-definitions/implead.

724. *See, e.g.*, Walsh v. Truck Ins. Exch. Co., 2003 Cal. App. Unpub. LEXIS 373 (Cal. App. 1st Dist. Jan. 13, 2003).

§ 14.18 Association Policy Content Checklist

When the association reviews its directors and officers liability policy, the checklist below provides some important questions it should ask about that policy.

- ☐ Does the policy include a "Warranties and Covenants" clause? See § 14.08[1][b]. Does that clause incorporate a "severability" of insureds provision? See § 14.08[1][c].
- ☐ Has the "possible claims" question in the application been thoroughly and accurately answered? See § 14.08[3][a].
- ☐ Does the policy include "Side C" coverage? See §§ 14.09[5], 14.11[1].
- ☐ Is the association correctly identified on the Declarations Page? See § 14.10.
- ☐ Does the policy require the insurer to defend the association? See § 14.11[2]. Are defense costs included within the limit of liability? See § 14.04[4].
- ☐ Does the definition of "claim" include non-monetary damages? See § 14.12[1]. Is there a specific exclusion for non-monetary damages? See § 14.14[18].
- ☐ Are committee members, volunteers, community association managers, and *prior* officers and directors included within the definition of "insured person"? See §§ 14.12[2][b], [c], and [d].
- ☐ What is included within the definition of "loss"? See § 14.12[3].
- ☐ Does the meaning of "wrongful acts" include only *negligent* acts, errors, or omissions? See § 14.12[4].
- ☐ Has the discovery or extended reporting period been elected by the insured? See § 14.13.
- ☐ How broad is the "dishonesty" exclusion? See § 14.14[1].
- ☐ Is there an "Insured versus Insured" exclusion? See § 14.14[2]. Does it include a "shareholder derivative action" exception? See § 14.14[2][a].
- ☐ Instead of, or in addition to, an "Insured versus Insured" exclusion, is there an "entity versus insured" exclusion? See § 14.14[3].
- ☐ Is the community association manager an insured, or is there a specific exclusion for the manager? See §§ 14.12[2][d], 14.14[4].

- [ ] Is there a Property Damage exclusion, and is it prefaced by "arising out of" or similar broad language? See § 14.14[7][b]. Is coverage excluded for claims arising out of failure to repair property? See § 14.14[7][b][i].
- [ ] Is there an exclusion for "personal and advertising injury"? See § 14.14[7][c].
- [ ] Does the policy contain a "design or construction" exclusion? See § 14.14[8].
- [ ] Does the exclusion for losses resulting from any claim for liability under, or breach of, any oral, written, or implied contract or agreement include broad "arising out of" or similar language that expands the proscription? See § 14.14[10]. Is an endorsement available that will except breaches of the governing documents from the exclusion? See § 14.14[10][b].
- [ ] Is coverage for failure to maintain insurance excluded? See § 14.14[11].
- [ ] Do officers or directors of the association also serve on the board of a related association—for example, a recreation or master association—and if so is coverage for them excluded under a "serving another organization" exclusion? See § 14.14[12].
- [ ] If the association operates a profit-making venture, is coverage for losses in connection with any claim made against any insured related to the ownership, control, management, or operations of that venture excluded? See § 14.14[13].
- [ ] Does the policy contain a specific exclusion for claims related to "service animals" or a broadly worded exclusion of civil rights claims? See §§ 14.14[16], [17].
- [ ] How and when must the insured report a claim to the insurer? See § 14.15[1][a].
- [ ] Under the "other insurance" clause, is the D&O policy excess to other liability policies, or is there a conflict between it and the clauses of any of those policies? See § 14.16.

Chapter 15

Crime/Fidelity Insurance

§ 15.01 Introduction

The term "crime policy" is relatively new. The policy was previously called a "fidelity bond"[1] or "fidelity policy,"[2] and one frequently still sees those terms used. The coverage may be referred to by several other names including "employee dishonesty" insurance, "employee dishonesty bond," or "crime fidelity" insurance.[3]

As one of the leading treatises on insurance law notes, the crime policy was patterned after financial institution bonds.[4] The commercial crime policy, however, is designed to serve the needs of organizations other than financial institutions.[5]

Crime policies indemnify the insured against a loss that arises from a lack of integrity, fidelity, or honesty of employees or others who hold positions of trust.[6] The insurer is only liable for a loss sustained by the insured. A crime policy basically provides property—first-party insurance—coverage for perils omitted from commercial property policies. For common interest communities, the policy indemnifies the association for loss of money, securities, or other property

1. Although the term "fidelity bond" today refers to an insurance policy, historically it was a "suretyship," a three-party agreement in which the surety guarantees to one party the honesty of another party. *See generally* 10 Jeffrey E. Thomas, *New Appleman on Insurance Law Library Edition* §§ 110.01[1], [6][b] (Matthew Bender, 2023).

2. Branson, *Fidelity Bond Insurance: Protection Against Condo Crime* (Cooperator, 2014), available at: http://cooperator.com/articles/2823/1/Fidelity-Bond-Insurance/Page1.html.

3. *Fidelity Insurance*, available at: http://www.davis-stirling.com/tabid/1664/default.aspx.

4. 10 Jeffrey E. Thomas, *New Appleman on Insurance Law Library Edition* § 120.01 (Matthew Bender, 2023).

5. https://www.irmi.com/term/insurance-definitions/commercial-crime-policy. *See also* Price & Wear, *Claims Made and Insurance Coverage Available for Losses Arising Out of or Related to Electronic Data*, Tort Trial & Insurance Practice L.J. 51, 65 (2015) (commercial crime policies provide coverage for losses arising from activities like employee dishonesty and forgery or alteration while fidelity bond is special type of crime policy that covers many of same risks, only tailored to needs of financial institution policyholders).

6. Resolution Trust Corp. v. Moskowitz, 845 F. Supp. 247, 250 (D.N.J. 1994); Bralko Holdings, Ltd. v. Insurance Co. of North America, 193 Mich. App. 157, 162, 483 N.W.2d 929, 931 (1992); Ronnau v. Caravan Int'l Corp., 205 Kan. 154, 158, 468 P.2d 118, 122 (Kan. 1970).

because of acts of fraud, dishonesty, forgery, theft, larceny, embezzlement, misappropriation, or criminal acts by directors, officers, committee members, association employees, volunteers, and managing agents.[7] It does not cover the imprudent use or investment of association funds.[8]

While a crime policy is generally not a liability policy, there are limited circumstances in which it does provide liability coverage. For example, if an insured is sued for refusing to pay any instrument, on the basis that it was forged or altered, the insurer will pay for any reasonable legal expenses incurred and paid in that defense.[9]

Residents of common interest communities, including those who serve on governing boards, may mistakenly believe that if a board member steals associations funds, the directors & officers (D&O) policy will cover the loss. However, D&O insurance primarily protects directors and officers from liability *they* may incur from conduct in their official capacity.[10] Additionally, the standard D&O policy has exclusions that would bar coverage for theft by an officer or director.

[1] The Need for Coverage and Scope of the Problem

While employee theft is an enormous problem and results in huge losses annually, one expert observes that many residents of common interest communities believe that their associations are very unlikely to be the victim of fraud or embezzlement.[11] After all, they know their neighbors, the manager, and the building maintenance person. It is just not possible that any of them would take something from the association. In fact, however, fraud is often committed by an insider.[12] Common interest community associations are said to be inherently vulnerable to

7. Meskin, *A Funny Thing Happened on the Way to the Bank: Fraud in the Community Association* (Katzman & Korr: Legal News Tailored for Community Associations 2008). *See also* Branson, *Fidelity Bond Insurance: Protection Against Condo Crime* (Cooperator, 2014), available at: http://cooperator.com/articles/2823/1/Fidelity-Bond-Insurance/Page1.html.

8. *See* March, *Guarding the VAULT* (Common Ground 1993), available at: https://www.caionline.org/LearningCenter/ResLib/Pages/1377.aspx (policy will not protect boards from their lack of knowledge, experience, or willingness to listen to experts).

9. ISO Form CR 00 23 11 15. § A.2.

10. *See* Quinn & Levin, *Directors and Officers Liability Insurance: Probable Directions in Texas Law*, 20 Rev. Litig. 381 (2001) (D&O policy provides coverage to director or officer if corporation has not already paid, reimbursed, or indemnified him or her); Dobiac, *I Came, I Saw, I Underwrote: D & O Liability Insurance's Past Underwriting Practices and Potential Future Directions*, 14 Conn. Ins. L.J. 487, 491 (2008) (D&O coverage indemnifies corporate officers for any sums for which they become liable to pay and often includes policy language restricting indemnification to circumstances where firm is not permitted to indemnify officer directly).

11. Meskin, *A Funny Thing Happened on the Way to the Bank: Fraud in the Community Association* (Katzman & Korr: Legal News Tailored for Community Associations 2008).

12. Horkovich, Reeves & Andrews, *Insurance Coverage for Employee Theft Losses: A Policyholder Primer on Commonly Litigated Issues*, 29 U. Mem. L. Rev. 363, 364 (1999) (84% of worst frauds were committed by employees).

fraud and employee theft,[13] and dishonesty and theft are an association's largest exposure to crime.[14] Maintenance personnel may pilfer supplies. A manager may conspire with a vendor to submit inflated invoices and split the overstated payments.[15] Sometimes a small association saves money by hiring a resident to manage its business, only to find later that the trusted neighbor has embezzled its funds by misusing its credit card or writing fraudulent checks. As one expert has said, "it is too easy to steal from most community associations."[16]

The seriousness of the problem of theft from common interest communities is illustrated by one recent case in which nearly $400,000 was diverted from the account of a New York residential cooperative corporation by the management company.[17] The cooperative sued its accountant for failing to discover the unauthorized transfers, demonstrating that having professional assistance in managing community funds is not sufficient risk management. Insurance coverage is essential.

[2] The Policy

Crime coverage is widely available. The Insurance Services Office (ISO) provides basic standard commercial crime policies. Some insurers may use them without modification. Others use a filing made with a state insurance department independent of ISO or use limited parts of the ISO form.[18] Large insurance companies, for example, Hartford, Chubb, and Travelers, fall into the latter category.[19]

---

13. Meskin, *A Funny Thing Happened on the Way to the Bank: Fraud in the Community Association* (Katzman & Korr: Legal News Tailored for Community Associations 2008). *See also Protecting Community Association Funds* (CAI 1996). The article recounts several examples of losses suffered by common interest community associations by officers. These include a former treasurer and president of an association arrested on charges that he embezzled about $50,000 during his three-year term and another former treasurer pleading no contest to charges that he embezzled more than $10,000 during his term in office.

14. *Fidelity Insurance*, available at: http://www.davis-stirling.com/tabid/1664/default.aspx.

15. Horkovich, Reeves & Andrews, *Insurance Coverage for Employee Theft Losses: A Policyholder Primer on Commonly Litigated Issues*, 29 U. Mem. L. Rev. 363, 364 (1999). A manager may also create fictitious vendors, submit invoices from those vendors to the association, and then deposit the payment check into a personal bank account. *Protecting Community Association Funds* (CAI 1996).

16. March, *Guarding the VAULT* (Common Ground 1993).

17. Jefferson Apts., Inc. v. Mauceri, 52 Misc. 3d 1012, 36 N.Y.S.3d 789 (2016). *See also* Cedar Lake Homeowners Ass'n v. Northwest Empire Cmty. Mgmt., 2015 U.S. Dist. LEXIS 174503 (D. Or. Nov. 13, 2015) (officer of management company stole over $160,000 from association). *And see Protecting Community Association Funds* (CAI 1996). The article relates two incidents of manager embezzlement. In one a community association manager was sentenced for embezzling $7,070 from an association and in another former manager of three condominium associations in disappeared after allegedly embezzling about $300,000.

18. Austin, *Crime Insurance—The Other Property Policy*, at 2 (2009), available at: http://austinstanovich.com/pdf/Articles/Crime-the-other-property-policy-4-09.pdf.

19. Austin, *Crime—Getting More Out of the Policy* (2010), available at: https://www.irmi.com/articles/expert-commentary/crime-getting-more-out-of-the-policy.

This chapter will discuss the standard ISO Commercial Crime Policy and use it to illustrate the typical coverage, and sometimes contrast it with the Travelers Crime Policy. Crime coverage may be provided by a stand-alone policy or be incorporated into either an association's commercial property or commercial general liability policy.[20]

The basic ISO policy comes in two forms: the Loss Sustained Form and the Discovery Form. The two are largely the same. Because the Loss Sustained Form is probably the more commonly used,[21] it is cited in the discussion below with the differences between it and the Discovery Form noted. There is one fundamental difference between the two forms. The Loss Sustained Form provides coverage for claims for losses that were both sustained and discovered during the policy period[22] or that are sustained during the policy period and discovered within one year of the end of that period.[23] Under the Discovery Form, it does not matter when the loss occurred.[24] It provides for payment of losses discovered during the policy period even though they were not necessarily sustained during that particular period.[25]

The type of policy recommended for common interest communities is called "commercial blanket," meaning it covers all employees collectively as opposed to a policy that covers employees by name or position.[26]

---

20. *See, e.g.*, Mt. Lodge Ass'n v. Crum & Forster Indem. Co., 210 W. Va. 536, 558 S.E.2d 336, 340 (2001) (condominium association purchased commercial general liability policy which included employee dishonesty section intended to protect insured from theft of property or money by employees); Mansion Hills Condo. Ass'n v. Am. Family Mut. Ins. Co., 62 S.W.3d 633, 635 (Mo. App. 2001) (condominium association had coverage for employee dishonesty under its business and property insurance policy for additional premium and by separate endorsement); Southeast Bakery Feeds v. Ranger Ins. Co., 974 S.W.2d 635, 637 (Mo. App. 1998) (commercial crime coverage, including employee dishonesty coverage form, was added to commercial general liability policy).

21. Eubank, *It's Criminal What Agents DON'T Know About Crime Insurance*, at 6 (2014), available at: http://www.independentagent.com/Education/Webinars/SiteAssets/Pages/live-webinars/2014%20Crime%20Webinar%20Handout.pdf.

22. *The Basics of Commercial Crime Insurance*, available at: https://www.marsh.com/us/services/financial-professional-liability/insights/basics-of-commercial-crime-insurance.html.

23. Kowatch, *1998 ISO Commercial Crime Revisions: ISO Introduces Discovery-Based Crime Policy* (The Rough Notes Magazine 1998), available at: http://www.roughnotes.com/rnmagazine/1998/august98/08p42.htm (loss sustained coverage is very similar to occurrence-based general liability coverage).

24. *The Basics of Commercial Crime Insurance*, available at: https://www.marsh.com/us/services/financial-professional-liability/insights/basics-of-commercial-crime-insurance.html.

25. Kowatch, *1998 ISO Commercial Crime Revisions: ISO Introduces Discovery-Based Crime Policy* (The Rough Notes Magazine 1998), available at: http://www.roughnotes.com/rnmagazine/1998/august98/08p42.htm (retroactive date is required to avoid overlap with previous loss sustained coverage and no losses that actually occurred before retroactive date are covered by existing policy, regardless of when they are reported; if no retroactive date has been shown on the Declarations Page, policy effective date becomes retroactive date by default).

26. Scarr, *Fidelity Bonding* (Common Ground 1990) (blanket coverage is more appropriate for community associations because it provides broader coverage and is easier to administer).

[3] Resources

Crime coverage is complex and not as well understood as property and liability insurance. This chapter discusses the basics about commercial crime insurance as well as particular concerns for common interest communities; however, in-depth analysis is beyond its scope. Fortunately, there are resources available that examine this coverage more extensively. The leading insurance law treatises devote considerable attention to fidelity bonds and crime policies.[27] There are also works devoted exclusively to analyzing commercial crime coverage.[28]

An excellent resource is the Fidelity Law Association (FLA), founded in 1994.[29] Its members are employed in fidelity claims handling or underwriting of licensed insurance and reinsurance companies, the American Insurance Association, the Insurance Services Office, Inc., and the Surety and Fidelity Association of America. FLA receives expertise and guidance from lawyers, accountants, and professional fidelity claim adjusters. It publishes the *Fidelity Law Journal*, which contains articles that examine some of the finer points of the law of this recondite coverage. The articles are available at the journal's website.[30]

[4] The Insurance Broker and Crime Coverage

Crime coverage is specialized and has evolved over recent years. In order to obtain adequate coverage, associations should conduct a proper assessment of their needs by employing a knowledgeable insurance professional to assist them in meeting those needs. Associations must take initiative in the process, because generally, that insurance professional—usually the broker—does not have a duty to anticipate the association's needs or to inform it about optional coverage that may be available.

[a] Identifying Coverage Needs and Experienced Brokers

There are significant differences in the available crime policies.[31] A common interest community needs a procedure that assures the crime coverage it obtains meets

27. Steven Plitt et al., *Couch on Insurance* §§ 160.1–160.121 (3d ed. Supp. 2015); 10 Jeffrey E. Thomas, *New Appleman on Insurance Law Library Edition* §§ 111.01–137.06 (Matthew Bender, 2023).

28. Kain & Glovach, *Annotated Commercial Crime Policy*, 542 (2d ed. ABA 2006).

29. *See* http://www.fidelitylaw.org/.

30. The FLA has published the *Fidelity Law Journal* since 1995, and all of the articles from volume I (1995) through volume XXI (2015) are available online in PDF format. *See* https://www.fidelitylaw.org/content.aspx?page_id=22&club_id=638640&module_id=533272.

31. Austin, *Crime—Getting More Out of the Policy* (2010), available at: https://www.irmi.com/articles/expert-commentary/crime-getting-more-out-of-the-policy (it is possible to have coverage proposals from two or more insurers that have different coverage terms and conditions and while those differences may be subtle, they should be identified and understood before binding coverage; risk management professionals need to understand crime exposures and coverages available to determine what is best for any insured organization).

it needs as well as any statutory requirements or the mandates of its governing documents. This can be accomplished by appointing a member of the governing board or an insurance committee to investigate the association's requirements and the coverage available. The designated director or insurance committee will need to examine the peculiar needs of the association with a person knowledgeable about insurance. That person is broadly referred to as an insurance producer, and finding him or her is the first task.

The general public uses the terms "agent" and "broker" interchangeably; however, in the insurance industry, and in law, they have specific meanings.[32] An "agent" represents the insurance company. The agent may be an employee of a particular company, may have a contract to work exclusively for one company, or have contracts with several insurers.[33] A "broker" is independent and usually is considered the agent of the insured.[34] The broker is not limited to obtaining coverage from a single company. The association needs a broker who will find the best coverage available. Insurance for common interest communities is a "niche market"—a specialty—and the association needs to work with a broker who specializes in it.[35] One way to find a broker who has the requisite knowledge is to look for one with the Community Insurance & Risk Management Specialist Designation from the Community Associations Institute. The designation is available to brokers with five years' experience as a practitioner in the community association insurance industry.

Associations need to remember that if insurance for common interest communities is a niche market, crime coverage is a specialty within it. Commentators warn that this is an insurance area often glossed over by agents and brokers,[36] and that there is much confusion over how different forms of crime coverage work. It is critically important, therefore, to work with a broker who understands the available coverage and how it relates to the needs of common interest communities.

---

32. *But see* UBS Fin. Servs. v. Thompson, 94 A.3d 176 (Md. App. 2014) (Maryland eliminated distinction between terms "insurance agent" and "insurance broker").

33. *See, e.g.*, Ramirez v. State Farm Mut. Auto. Ins. Co., 2016 U.S. Dist. LEXIS 5245 (N.D. Ind. Jan. 15, 2016).

34. *See, e.g.*, Ga. Cas. & Sur. Co. v. Valley Wood, Inc., 336 Ga. App. 795 (2016).

35. Stoeckert, *The Insurance Puzzle; Making Sense of Premiums and Policies* (Cooperator, Apr. 2012), available at: http://cooperator.com/articles/2418/1/The-Insurance-Puzzle/Page1.html; *Understanding Homeowner Association Insurance*, available at: http://www.hindmansanchez.com/resources/article/understanding-homeowner-association-insurance (association should only work with broker who is experienced in handling association insurance and one way to determine that is to ask about level of experience of broker and how many associations he or she currently insures). *See also* Hennessey, *Condominium Management*, 48 St. John's L. Rev. 1064, 1070 (1974) (insuring condominiums creates more difficult problems than many insurance agents and most businesspeople appreciate and, therefore, association is well advised to employ knowledgeable and experienced insurance broker who will be able to recommend best and most economical policies that provide requisite coverage).

36. Austin, *Crime—Getting More Out of the Policy* (IRMI 2010), available at: https://www.irmi.com/articles/expert-commentary/crime-getting-more-out-of-the-policy.

One expert warns that because the premiums for crime coverage are small, so are the commissions and, therefore, some brokers have limited patience for spending time on it.[37] However, associations typically obtain all—or nearly all—of their policies from one broker in a package. The premiums for that package of policies yield a healthy commission. If the broker is reluctant to spend a few hours helping the association to find the crime coverage it needs, it is probably time to find a different broker.

It is generally recommended that associations interview at least two or three brokers.[38] It is critically important to assess whether the broker is one that will actively protect the interests of the association.[39] When the designated director or insurance committee interviews brokers, it will also want to determine the services the broker routinely provides. For example, will the broker participate in an annual review of the association's coverage?[40]

[b] Obtaining Requested Coverage

While the association may place heavy reliance on the skill and knowledge of the broker, the broker's obligations to the association, or any insured, are circumscribed by long-standing principals of agency. The broker has limited responsibilities to the insured.

The average layperson has little or no understanding of insurance and relies heavily on the assistance of an insurance agent. Yet, agents and brokers generally have no duty to anticipate the needs of their customers, to advise them about the adequacy of coverage obtained, or to inform them of optional coverage that may

---

37. Meskin, *Writing Condominium and Homeowners' Association Insurance* (2008), available at: http://www.propertycasualty360.com/2008/09/01/writing-condominium-and-homeowners-association-insurance.

38. Lent, *The ABC's of Insuring Your Co-op or Condo; Common Terms and Options for Insurance* (Cooperator, Aug. 2014), available at: http://cooperator.com/articles/2818/1/The-ABCs-of-Insuring-Your-Co-op-or-Condo/Page1.html; *Understanding Homeowner Association Insurance*, available at: http://www.hindmansanchez.com/resources/article/understanding-homeowner-association-insurance (it is customary to get two or three bids or proposals from different brokers before acquiring policy). *See also* Green, *Shopping for Insurance; What Do Boards Need to Know?* (Cooperator, Aug. 2011) (recommending comparing services of at least three insurance brokers).

39. *See, e.g.*, Mt. Lodge Ass'n v. Crum & Forster Indem. Co., 210 W. Va. 536, 558 S.E.2d 336, 340 (2001) (after insurer denied condominium association's claim, its broker sent detailed letter to insurer in support of claim leading insurer to reconsider). The facts of one case illustrate a particularly egregious example of a broker that failed to properly protect the interests of its client. The broker secured a CGL policy for a homeowners association. Shortly after renewal of the policy, the insurer added two endorsements to it that reduced the coverage without notifying the broker or the association. An underwriter subsequently sent copies of the endorsements to the broker, and the broker admitted it had copies of both endorsements in its office files, but its spokesperson could not recall if copies had been sent to the association and acknowledged he had not spoken to anyone at the association about the endorsements. National Fire & Marine Ins. Co. v. Hoene Springs Improvement Ass'n, 889 F. Supp. 362, 365–66 (E.D. Mo. 1995). Fortunately for the association, the court in effect refused to enforce the endorsements.

40. For considerations regarding annual review, see generally Ch. 2, *supra*.

be available.[41] Conversely, the applicant for coverage has an obligation to specify the coverage and terms he or she requires.[42] When an applicant for insurance requests specific coverage, courts usually hold the agent or broker has a duty of reasonable care to procure that coverage,[43] as long as he or she has agreed to obtain that particular coverage.[44] Courts will find a duty to advise if the insured can show a "special relationship" between the parties.[45] Failure of an agent or broker to exercise the required care may result in liability.[46] However, agents or

41. *See* Emerson Elec. Co. v. Marsh & McLennan Cos., 362 S.W.3d 7, 13 (Mo. 2012) (neither agents nor brokers have duty to advise insured on its insurance needs or on availability of particular coverage, unless they specifically agree to do so); Houck v. State Farm Fire & Cas. Ins. Co., 366 S.C. 7, 12, 620 S.E.2d 326, 330 (S.C. 2005) (generally agent has no duty to advise insured at point of application, absent express or implied undertaking to do so); Baggett v. Summerlin Ins. & Realty, Inc., 354 N.C. 347, 554 S.E.2d 336 (2001) (agent did not have duty to point out exclusions in written policy where those exclusions did not negate particular coverage specifically requested by plaintiffs).

42. City Blueprint & Supply Co. v. Boggio, 3 So. 3d 62, 65–66 (La. App. 2008); Sinex v. Wallis, 611 A.2d 31, 33 (Del. Super. 1991); Kenyon v. Larsen, 205 Neb. 209, 217, 286 N.W.2d 759, 784 (1980).

43. Star Spa Servs. v. Robert G. Turano Ins. Agency, Inc., 595 F. Supp. 2d 519 (M.D. Pa. 2009). *See also* Traina Enters. v. Cord & Wilburn, Inc. Ins. Agency, 289 Ga. App. 833, 838, 658 S.E.2d 460, 464 (2008) (jury could find agent negligently misrepresented extent of coverage where insured requested renewal of existing policy that included vital coverage for particular business, agent told insured renewal policy had been obtained, agent expressly noted that coverage sought was included in renewal policy, and agent did not advise insured of change in coverage letter received from insurer).

44. *See, e.g.*, Avery v. Diedrich, 301 Wis. 2d 693, 734 N.W.2d 159 (2007).

45. *See* Tiara Condo. Ass'n v. Marsh, USA, Inc., 991 F. Supp. 2d 1271, 1281 (S.D. Fla. 2014) (exception to general rule of no duty to advise applies when broker encourages and engages in "special relationship" with client thereby triggering enhanced duty of care to advise the client about amount of coverage prudently needed to meet its complete insurance needs; evidence of special relationship includes representations by broker about its expertise and about breadth of coverage obtained, length and depth of relationship, extent of broker's involvement in client's decision-making about insurance needs, information volunteered by broker about insurance needs, and payment of additional compensation for advisory services); Schweitzer v. Am. Family Mut. Ins. Co., 16 N.E.3d 982 (Ind. App. 2014); Garnerville Holding Co. v. Kaye Ins. Assocs., 309 A.D.2d 541, 765 N.Y.S.2d 317 (2003), *app. den.*, 780 N.Y.S.2d 311, 2 N.Y.3d 705, 812 N.E.2d 1261 (2004).

46. *See, e.g.*, Sitaram, Inc. v. Bryan Ins. Agency, Inc., 104 So. 3d 524 (La. App.), *writ den.*, 103 So. 3d 375 (La. 2012); Seascape of Hickory Point Condo. Ass'n v. Associated Ins. Servs., 443 So. 2d 488 (Fla. 2d DCA 1984) (where condominium association contacted broker seeking to purchase insurance to cover its seawall in event of storm damage, but was told seawall insurance was not available, only to discover after suffering loss that coverage was available, court held association sufficiently alleged relationship between parties from which it could be said broker owed duty to exercise reasonable care in rendering advice on insurance matters because broker held itself out as professional insurance planner, had served association's insurance needs for several years, and association sought specific advice). *See also* Anthony v. Indep. Ins. Advisors, Inc., 56 V.I. 516 (2012) (association sued brokers and others over procurement of policy from insurer who was declared insolvent less than one month after policy was obtained and four months before property was damaged by hurricane and parties reached settlement). *Compare* Garcia v. Omaha Prop. & Cas. Ins. Co., 933 F. Supp. 1064, 1070 (S.D. Fla. 1995), *aff'd*, 95 F.3d 58 (11th Cir. 1996) (regardless of any duty on agent, there is no liability for negligence in failing to procure coverage that is unavailable).

brokers have been held not to be liable for failure to procure coverage mandated by common interest community laws.[47]

[5] Requirement That Associations Obtain Crime Coverage

For almost all common interest community associations, fidelity/crime coverage is a necessity. For some, their governing documents mandate that they maintain the coverage. Also, in many states, associations are required by statute to have the coverage in place. Finally, lenders and Fannie Mae expect associations to obtain crime coverage.

[a] Governing Documents

Many community associations are required by their documents—declaration, articles, or bylaws[48]—to carry "fidelity insurance" or a "fidelity bond."[49] These documents were often drafted before the term "crime insurance" was commonly used and, therefore, the coverage to which they refer is in fact found in a standard commercial crime policy.[50] The mandate stated in the documents may be brief and vague, especially in older documents. For example, it may state that the governing board must require that any officer, agent, or employee of the association who handles or is responsible for association funds has to furnish an adequate fidelity bond, with the amount determined by the board and the premium paid by the association.[51] In comparison, the Declaration in one condominium required the association to carry a blanket fidelity bond for anyone who either handled or was responsible for funds held or administered by the association, whether or not

47. *See, e.g.*, Royal Glen Condo. Ass'n v. S.T. Neswold & Assocs., 385 Ill. Dec. 137, 18 N.E.3d 137 (Ill. App. 2014) (where Illinois law provided no policy was to be issued to or renewed for condominium associations unless it met statutory requirements, that law imposed obligations on condominium associations and their boards, not on insurance producers; statute did not impose duty on association's insurance broker giving rise to statutory cause of action).

48. Perkins & Grennan, *Coverage for Losses Resulting from Association Property Manager Dishonesty*, XVII Fid. L.J. 77, 83 (2011).

49. *What Is Fidelity Insurance and Why Your Association Needs It*, available at: http://www.hindmansanchez.com/resources/newsletter/what-fidelity-insurance-and-why-your-association-needs-it/.

50. The terms "fidelity bond," "fidelity insurance," and "crime insurance" are used interchangeably. *See generally* 10 Jeffrey E. Thomas, *New Appleman on Insurance Law Library Edition* § 110.01[1] (Matthew Bender, 2023). Nonetheless, when the governing documents require a "fidelity bond," the governing board, in an abundance of caution may, after consulting with the association counsel, want to memorialize in the minutes or by resolution that on advice of counsel and/or the association's broker, it obtained a crime policy in substitution for a bond. That should bring the board within the protection of the "business judgement rule" under which courts will generally not substitute their judgment for that of the governing board. *See* 6A Rohan, *Real Estate Transactions: Home Owner Associations and Planned Unit Developments—Law and Practice: Forms*, § 7.08[7] (Matthew Bender, 2023); 2 Rohan & Reskin, *Real Estate Transactions: Cooperative Housing Law and Practice—Forms*, § 9.03[9][d][i] (Matthew Bender, 2023).

51. Perkins & Grennan, *Coverage for Losses Resulting from Association Property Manager Dishonesty*, XVII Fid. L.J. 77, 83–84 (2011).

they received compensation for their services.[52] The bond was required to name the association as obligee, and include a provision for 30 days' written notice to the association, lenders, and loan servicers of cancellation or substantial modification of the bond.

More recently drafted documents will often have more specific requirements. For instance, condominium bylaws recorded in 2007 required the governing board to maintain "blanket fidelity insurance," to the extent reasonably available, for all association officers, directors, managers, trustees, employees, and volunteers and for anyone else who handled or was responsible for funds held or administered by the association, whether or not they received compensation for their services.[53] The bylaws also stated that if the board delegated some or all of the responsibility for handling funds to a managing agent, that managing agent was to be covered by its own policy that had to provide the same coverage as that of the policy maintained by the board and had to name the association as an additional insured. The total amount of coverage required by the bylaws was the amount sufficient to cover the maximum funds—including reserve funds—that would be in the custody of the association or managing agent at any time while the policy was in force, but at least equal the total of three months' aggregate assessment on all units in the condominium plus any reserves. Finally, the policy was to include waivers by the insurer of all defenses based on the exclusion of persons serving without compensation from the definition of "employees," or similar terms or expressions.

Because the language of crime coverage mandates can vary and because it may be found in any of several documents, governing boards need to carefully review their documents to determine the extent of the coverage they are required to maintain for the association.[54] The members of the governing board need to realize that they have a duty of at least ordinary care, if not a fiduciary obligation, to protect the interests of the association and, therefore, while they can delegate some research and clerical matters—for example, organizing a meeting with the broker—they cannot delegate the responsibility of obtaining the proper coverage for the association and cannot delegate the duty to review, to ask questions, and to employ the due diligence required to understand insurance.[55] Thus, while the community association manager (CAM) may have more knowledge about crime coverage than the members of the board, handing over responsibility

52. Humphrey Place Condo. Ass'n v. Snipes, 2005 Conn. Super. LEXIS 792 (Conn. Super. Ct. Mar. 17, 2005).

53. Perkins & Grennan, *Coverage for Losses Resulting from Association Property Manager Dishonesty*, XVII Fid. L.J. 77, 85 (2011).

54. *Fidelity Insurance*, available at: http://www.davis-stirling.com/tabid/1664/default.aspx (boards should check association governing documents to determine what minimums in amount of coverage may be required).

55. Meskin, *The Community Association Insurance Puzzle: What Boards MUST DO and MUST AVOID to Assemble the Puzzle* 13–14 (Community Association Living, CAI Austin 2012).

for obtaining coverage to the CAM does not fulfill their duties, especially given that documents and statutes place the responsibility squarely on the association, which acts through the governing board.

[b] Statutory Requirements

The Uniform Common Interest Ownership Act (UCIOA) provides that beginning no later than the time of the first conveyance of a unit to a person other than a declarant, the association has to maintain fidelity insurance, to the extent reasonably available and subject to reasonable deductibles.[56] A few states—some that have adopted the UCIOA and some that have not—address fidelity insurance and, interestingly, only one—Nevada[57]—has updated the language to call the policy one for "crime." Other statutes address "fidelity insurance" or "fidelity bonds, but the coverage to which they refer is in fact generally found in a standard a commercial crime policy.[58]

Of the five largest states, all but New York have some statutory provision mentioning fidelity insurance. All the California statute does is mention fidelity coverage. The California Davis-Stirling Common Interest Development Act, which governs all types of residential common interest communities, does not specifically require that associations obtain any insurance but does mandate an annual budget report that includes a summary of the association's insurance policies including fidelity.[59]

Florida has separate acts governing condominiums, cooperatives, and homeowners associations. Each requires that associations maintain insurance or fidelity bonding of anyone who controls or disburses association funds, that the policy

---

56. Uniform Common Interest Ownership Act § 3-113(a)(3). A comment to the UCIOA explains that fidelity insurance typically protects against loss of money or physical property as a result of criminal behavior and that common claims under fidelity policies are for employee dishonesty, embezzlement, forgery, robbery, computer fraud, wire transfer fraud, counterfeiting, and other criminal acts. Uniform Common Interest Ownership Act § 3-113, comment 4.

57. Nevada has adopted the Uniform Common Interest Ownership Act and, thus, has a statute requiring that beginning no later than the first conveyance of a unit to a person other than a declarant, the association has to maintain, to the extent reasonably available, and subject to reasonable deductibles, property, liability, and "crime" insurance. Nev. Rev. Stat. § 116.3113.1.

58. The terms "fidelity bond," "fidelity insurance," and "crime insurance" are used interchangeably. *See generally* 10 Jeffrey E. Thomas, *New Appleman on Insurance Law Library Edition* § 110.01[1] (Matthew Bender, 2023). Nonetheless, when an applicable statute requires a "fidelity bond," the governing board, in an abundance of caution may, after consulting with the association counsel, want to memorialize in the minutes or by resolution that on advice of counsel and/or the association's broker, it obtained a crime policy in substitution for a bond. That should bring the board within the protection of the "business judgement rule" under which courts will generally not substitute their judgment for that of the governing board. *See* 6A Rohan, *Real Estate Transactions: Home Owner Associations and Planned Unit Developments—Law and Practice: Forms*, § 7.08[7] (Matthew Bender, 2023); 2 Rohan & Reskin, *Real Estate Transactions: Cooperative Housing Law and Practice—Forms*, § 9.03[9][d][i] (Matthew Bender, 2023).

59. Cal. Civ. Code § 5300(b)(9).

or fidelity bond cover the maximum funds that will be in the custody of the association or its management agent at any one time, and that the association bear the cost. [60] In all three laws, the phrase "persons who control or disburse funds of the association" includes, but is not limited to, those individuals authorized to sign checks, and the President, Secretary, and Treasurer of the association.

The Illinois Common Interest Community Association Act is in effect a homeowners association law. It mandates fidelity insurance for associations with 30 or more units.[61] A policy has to provide coverage for persons who control or disburse association funds for the maximum amount of coverage commercially available or reasonably required to protect funds in the custody or control of the association. Additionally, under the Illinois Condominium Property Act the bylaws of a condominium with 30 or more units have to provide that the association will obtain and maintain fidelity insurance covering persons who control or disburse association funds.[62] The association has to pay for the fidelity insurance unless the contract between it and a management company provides otherwise. The association is required to obtain the maximum amount of coverage available to protect funds in its custody or control, plus the association reserve fund. Finally, associations with six or more *dwelling units* are required to obtain and maintain a fidelity bond covering persons, including the managing agent and its employees who control or disburse association funds.[63] The bond must be for the maximum amount of coverage available to protect funds in the custody or control of the association, plus the association reserve fund.[64]

The pertinent Texas condominium statute provides that, unless the declaration states otherwise, an association *may* purchase insurance and fidelity bonds it considers appropriate or necessary.[65] Similarly, Texas law authorizes property owners' associations to purchase insurance and fidelity bonds the governing board considers appropriate or necessary.[66]

60. Fla. Stat. § 718.111(11)(h) (condominiums); Fla. Stat. § 719.106(1)(k) (cooperatives); Fla. Stat. § 720.3033(5) (homeowners associations). Only the statute governing homeowners associations allows for waiver of the coverage requirement. It provides that if annually approved by a majority of the voting interests present at a properly called meeting of the association, the association may waive the requirement of obtaining a policy or bond for all those who control or disburse funds of the association.

61. 765 Ill. Comp. Stat. 160/1-55.

62. 765 Ill. Comp. Stat. 605/18(g).

63. 765 Ill. Comp. Stat. 605/12(a)(3)(A).

64. The bond has to be in the full amount of association funds and reserves in the custody of the association or management company. 765 Ill. Comp. Stat. 605/12(a)(3)(C).

65. Tex. Prop. Code § 82.102(18).

66. Tex. Prop. Code § 204.010(a)(15) (authorization may be changed by restrictions, articles of incorporation, or bylaws); Tex. Prop. Code § 215.005(17) (applicable to "master mixed-use" property owners' associations).

Eleven other states—Colorado,[67] Delaware,[68] Hawaii,[69] Idaho,[70] Louisiana,[71] Maryland,[72] Massachusetts,[73] Ohio,[74] Vermont,[75] Virginia,[76] and Nevada[77]—and Puerto Rico have statutes addressing fidelity coverage for common interest communities. In some of these states, there are specific requirements about the *amount of coverage* that has to be maintained. For example, the Louisiana statute mandates in an amount equal to the lesser of $1 million or the amount of reserve balances of the association plus one-fourth of the total annual association assessment.[78] Maryland requires the amount of the coverage to be equal to at least the lesser of three months' worth of gross annual assessments and the total amount held in all investment accounts at the time the fidelity insurance is issued or $3 million.[79] However, some associations may have considerable non-assessment income, often generated from renting common areas, and if these associations follow the statutory formulations, their coverage may be inadequate, so they should treat the statutory formula as a guide and discuss coverage limits with their brokers.

Associations need to carefully compare any governing document requirements with statutory mandates. Obviously, the association has to comply with statutory mandates. The documents, however, could impose additional requirements. A knowledgeable broker will be aware of statutory obligations, but not the provisions of the documents, so the association needs to discuss those requirements with its broker.

[c] Lenders and Fannie Mae

Lenders that provide mortgages to purchase individual homes or units in common interest communities are, of course, concerned about the viability of their collateral. If an association is the victim of an embezzlement scheme and suffers a significant uninsured loss, its only source of revenue to replace the stolen funds

67. Colo. Rev. Stat. § 38-33.3-306(3)(a)(I); Colo. Rev. Stat. § 38-33.3-313.
68. Del. Code Ann. tit. 25, § 81-313(a).
69. Haw. Rev. Stat. § 514B-143(a).
70. Idaho Code § 55-1505(2)(j)(2).
71. La. Rev. Stat. § 9:1123.113(A).
72. Md. Code Ann., Corps & Ass'ns § 5-6B-27(c)(1) (cooperatives); Md. Code Ann., Real Prop. § 11-114.1(c)(1) (condominiums); Md. Code Ann., Real Prop. § 11B-111.6(c)(1) (homeowners associations).
73. Mass. G.L. ch. 183A, § 10(h).
74. Ohio Rev. Code Ann. § 5311.081(B)(19) (condominiums); Ohio Rev. Code Ann. § 5312.06(D)(16) (planned communities).
75. Vt. Stat. Ann tit. 27A, § 3-113(a).
76. Va. Code § 55-79.81(B) (condominiums; Va. Code § 55-514.2(B) (property owners associations).
77. Nev. Rev. Stat. § 116.3113.1.
78. La. Rev. Stat. § 9:1123.113(B).
79. Md. Code Ann., Real Prop. § 11-114.1(e)(1).

is the members of the association. The governing board will be forced to levy a special assessment on the members of the association. Special assessments have the potential to affect the resale value of homes because buyers may shy away from communities that levy them, especially if that community has a reputation for poor financial controls. Thus, most lenders require associations to obtain commercial crime coverage by making it a condition of a loan to purchase a home or unit.[80]

Lenders also require crime coverage because Fannie Mae mandates it. The lender that does not comply with Fannie Mae guidelines cannot sell a mortgage to it. Fannie Mae requires fidelity/crime insurance for all condominium and cooperative projects with some exceptions.[81] One exception is for projects of 20 units[82] or fewer or that would need fidelity/crime insurance coverage of $5,000 or less based on the Fannie Mae formula. Also, Fannie Mae says it will accept state coverage requirements in place of its own.

Under the Fannie Mae requirements, a common interest community association has to have blanket fidelity/crime insurance coverage for anyone who either handles or is responsible for funds that it holds or administers, whether or not that individual receives compensation for services, including coverage for a management agent.[83] The insurance policy must name the association as the insured, and the premiums *should* be paid as a common expense by the association. A management agent that handles funds for the common interest community (CIC), says Fannie Mae, *should* additionally be covered by its *own* fidelity/crime insurance policy. The association policy has to cover the maximum funds in the custody of the association or its management agent at any time while the policy is in force. No coverage, however, is required if the maximum estimated funds are less than or equal to $5,000. A lesser amount of coverage is acceptable if the association legal documents require it, or another source acceptable to the lender verifies that the CIC and any management company adhere to one or more prescribed financial controls.[84] Even when one or more of the financial controls is in place,

80. *See* Humphrey Place Condo. Ass'n v. Snipes, 2005 Conn. Super. LEXIS 792 (Conn. Super. Ct. Mar. 17, 2005) (lender approved application for mortgage loan on condition that association either obtain fidelity bond on its officers and directors or employee dishonesty provision in its insurance policy; employee for lender testified that most lenders require that condominium associations obtain fidelity bonds).

81. *Fannie Mae Single Family Selling Guide* § B7-4-02 (Mar. 29, 2016). "Fidelity/crime insurance" is defined by Fannie Mae as a type of insurance that a condominium or planned unit development homeowners association or a cooperative corporation obtains to protect itself against economic loss from dishonest acts of anyone who either handles—or is responsible for—funds that the association or corporation holds or administers, whether or not that individual receives compensation for services. *Fannie Mae Single Family Selling Guide* § E-3-06 (May 31, 2016).

82. The *Selling Guide* does not define "unit."

83. *Fannie Mae Single Family Selling Guide* § B7-4-02 (Mar. 29, 2016).

84. One financial control is that separate bank accounts are maintained for the working account and the reserve account, each with appropriate access controls, and the bank in which funds are deposited sends copies of the monthly bank statements directly to the association. A

the coverage has to equal *at least* the total of three months of assessments on all units in the project, unless this calculated amount is less than or equal to $5,000, in which case no coverage is required. Finally, the policy has to include a provision that calls for at least ten days' written notice to the association or insurance trustee before it can be cancelled or substantially modified for any reason.

The Fannie Mae requirement of three months of assessments should be considered an absolute minimum.[85] An association's potential loss could far exceed that amount. Consider a condominium association with 100 units that charges a monthly assessment of $500 per unit. Three months of assessments would total $150,000. Ordinarily, the most that would be in its operating account at the beginning of the month when it receives the assessments is $50,000 plus any carryover from the previous month because the assessment is based on budgeted expenses. By the end of the month, the association typically has spent nearly all of the $50,000. However, the budget almost always includes insurance premiums. Unless the association finances the premiums, the funds to pay the premiums will accumulate during the year. If the premiums for all the policies are $100,000, then that amount will be in the association's account in the month before the premiums are due. The association may also have income from leasing a portion of the common elements—in this hypothetical, $5,000 a month—and that would not be included in the "three months of assessments" formulation. Finally, the association has reserves for maintenance of $250,000 and a contingency fund of $50,000. Therefore, in the beginning of the month before its insurance premiums are due, the association would have $405,000 in its accounts. That, however, is not the limit of its risk because embezzlement can occur over time. If someone embezzled $2,000 a month over two years and then emptied the association's bank accounts when they contained the $405,000, the loss would exceed $453,000, more than three times three months of assessments. Thus, using the Fannie Mae formula would leave the association underinsured.

[d] Policies That Conflict with Requirements on Associations

As discussed above, in many states, common interest community legislation imposes requirements for fidelity/crime coverage. The governing documents of a common interest community association may also require the association to

---

second financial control is that the management company maintains separate records and bank accounts for each association that uses its services, and the company does not have the authority to draw checks on, or transfer funds from, the reserve account of the association. Finally, two members of the board of directors have to sign any checks written on the reserve account. *See generally* 6A Rohan, *Real Estate Transactions: Home Owner Associations and Planned Unit Developments—Law and Practice: Forms*, § 11A.06[2][b] (Matthew Bender, 2023); March, *Guarding the VAULT* (Common Ground 1993).

85. *Fidelity Insurance*, available at: http://www.davis-stirling.com/tabid/1664/default.aspx (if association documents do not prescribe minimum coverage amount, associations should, at a minimum, carry coverage amounts required by Fannie Mae).

obtain insurance with specifically prescribed coverage. Finally, Fannie Mae has detailed crime coverage mandates. What happens if a policy issued to an association fails to meet any of the requirements?

One expert commentator contends that the terms of coverage will likely be governed by the mandates of statutes or regulations, and not the language of the policy itself when there is a conflict between them.[86] Some courts agree and hold that insurers are required to provide coverage as mandated under the state's common interest community statutes, and that any policy provision contrary to an applicable statute may be reformed.[87] However, many more courts—including in Florida[88] and Illinois[89]—disagree and conclude that statutory requirements do not to regulate the business of insurance, but impose insurance-related obligations on associations.[90] Nonetheless, a policy argument can be made that supports the minority view. First, the insurer is certainly in the best position to understand and respond properly to legislative insurance mandates. Second, insurers already conform their policies to many of those mandates by state-specific endorsements and, therefore, know where to look for those requirements and how to modify their policies to meet them. Courts, it can be argued, should not impose an obligation on volunteer governing board members that requires an understanding of technical insurance law matters that they, as laypersons, likely do not have but that insurers certainly do have.

Insurance requirements in association governing documents clearly apply to the association itself and not to an insurer who is not a party to those documents.[91] Under the Fannie Mae guidelines, lenders or servicers are obligated to assure that associations obtain policies that meet those guidelines. If a policy fails to meet the requirements, the consequence is that Fannie Mae will not purchase or securitize mortgages for the purchase of individual homes in the community.

86. Perkins & Grennan, *Coverage for Losses Resulting from Association Property Manager Dishonesty*, XVII Fid. L.J. 77, 100–01 (2011).

87. Lussan v. State Farm Ins. Co., 659 So. 2d 830, 833 (La. App. 1995) (insurer must provide coverage as mandated under statutes); Blackwell v. Hanover Ins. Co., 551 So. 2d 47, 50 (La. App. 1989). *See also* Mahogany Run Condo. Ass'n v. ICG Realty Mgmt. Corp., 40 V.I. 404, 409 (1999) (condominium insurance statute overrode provisions in any insurance policy to contrary).

88. Citizens Property Insurance Corp. v. River Manor Condominium Ass'n, Inc., 125 So. 3d 846, 850 (Fla. 4th DCA 2013) (although insurers—not condominium associations—issue or renew policies, "Florida Condominium Act" regulates condominiums, not insurance companies). *See also* Windward on Lake Conway Condo. Ass'n v. United Nat'l Ins. Co., 2015 U.S. Dist. LEXIS 153915, at *15, n. 9 (M.D. Fla. Nov. 13, 2015).

89. Royal Glen Condo. Ass'n v. S.T. Neswold & Assocs., 385 Ill. Dec. 137, 18 N.E.3d 137 (Ill. App. 2014).

90. *See, e.g.*, Northfield Ins. Co. v. Evian HPR, 2002 U.S. Dist. LEXIS 26684 (D.S.C. Aug. 27, 2002), *aff'd*, 2003 U.S. App. LEXIS 14064 (4th Cir. 2003) (insurer had no responsibility to ensure association was properly insured so as to meet its obligations under state condominium law).

91. Perkins & Grennan, *Coverage for Losses Resulting from Association Property Manager Dishonesty*, XVII Fid. L.J. 77, 100 (2011).

Neither Fannie Mae nor a lender originating a loan can force an insurer to change its policy to conform to the Fannie Mae guidelines.

[6] Policy in the Name of Community Association Management Company

Some states specifically address crime coverage for community association management companies. These include Alaska,[92] California,[93] Colorado,[94] Connecticut,[95] Georgia,[96] Hawaii,[97] Illinois,[98] Louisiana,[99] Nevada,[100] and Virginia.[101] A few of those states allow for the policy issued to the management company to be the coverage for the association. For example, under Alaska law, if the board of directors of a community association allows a "broker"—which includes community association management—to exercise control over its fees or funds, that broker has to provide evidence to the state that he or she is covered by a blanket fidelity insurance bond either in the name of the broker with the association as an additional insured or in the name of the association with the broker as an additional insured.[102] Georgia regulations require a fidelity bond or fidelity insurance policy that names the community association as an additional named

92. Alaska Stat. § 08.88.173(a).

93. Before entering into or renewing a contract with an association, the manager is required to disclose to the board whether the manager's fidelity insurance, or that of his or her employer, covers the current year's operating and reserve funds of the association. The requirement, however, does not compel an association to require a common interest development manager to obtain or maintain fidelity insurance. Cal. Bus. & Prof. Code § 11504(d), repealed effective January 1, 2019.

94. Anyone employed as an independent contractor by an association with 30 or more units to manage a common interest community has to obtain and maintain fidelity insurance in an amount not less than two months' current assessments plus reserves, as calculated from the current association budget, unless the association names that person as an insured employee in its required contract of fidelity insurance. Colo. Rev. Stat. § 38-33.3-313(11). *See also* 4 Colo. Code R. 725-7 (D-10) (every active licensed CAM company and licensed sole proprietorship must have in effect a crime fidelity insurance policy covering dishonest acts of all employees in CAM company or sole proprietorship; coverage for each common interest community managed must not be less in aggregate than two months of current assessments plus reserves, as calculated from current budget of community, or such higher amount as common interest community may require in its bylaws or management contract with CAM; policy may have deductible of no greater than 1 percent of face value of policy and insurer must pay claims on first dollar basis).

95. Conn. Gen. Stat. § 20-460(a).

96. Ga. Comp. R. & Regs. § 520-1-.06(3).

97. Haw. Rev. Stat. § 514B-143(a)(3)(B).

98. 765 Ill. Comp. Stat. 160/1-55 (homeowners associations); 765 Ill. Comp. Stat. 605/18(g) (condominiums).

99. La. Rev. Stat. § 9:1123.113(C).

100. Nev. Rev. Stat. § 116A.620.1(k)(1). Under a parallel rule, management agreements are required to state which party will maintain fidelity bond coverage and whether either contracting party has to be named as an additional insured under any required insurance. Nev. Admin. Code § 116A.325.1(k).

101. Va. Code § 54.1-2346(D).

102. Alaska Stat. § 08.88.173(a).

insured.[103] A Louisiana condominium statute provides that when the managing agent maintains its own bond or equivalent form of insurance, the association is in compliance with the statutory requirements for association coverage as long as the managing agent's bond or equivalent form of insurance itself meets the statutory requirements and the association is named as an additional insured.[104]

Other states address the status of the association. Connecticut law requires managers of common interest communities to obtain a fidelity bond that names the association as obligee.[105] The Illinois Condominium Property Act provides that the bylaws must provide that management companies responsible for funds held or administered by an association have to maintain and furnish to the association a fidelity bond and that the association is the direct obligee of any fidelity bond.[106] Under Hawaii law, a condominium association has standing to make a loss claim against the management company fidelity bond as a party covered under the bond.[107]

In some cases, the association governing documents may require the association to be an additional insured on the management company's crime policy.[108] Whether required by statute or the governing documents, when the association is an additional insured, it may believe it has adequate coverage. However, an association needs to discuss with its broker whether that is the case or it needs its own policy. Experts recommend associations have their own policies.[109]

The first concern about a policy issued to the management company is that when the standard commercial crime policy uses the words "you" and "your," it refers to the named insured shown on the Declarations Page. Therefore, if the association is an additional insured, its coverage may be limited when, for example, the policy provides the insurer will pay for a loss that results directly from forgeries or alterations made or drawn by or drawn on "you" or made or drawn by someone acting as "your" agent.[110] Unless the association is construed to be the named insured, the coverage would not apply.[111]

---

103. Ga. Comp. R. & Regs. § 520-1-.06(3)(a).

104. La. Rev. Stat. § 9:1123.113(C).

105. Conn. Gen. Stat. § 20-460(b). *See also* Conn. Agencies Regs. § 20-461-4.

106. 765 Ill. Comp. Stat. 605/18(g).

107. Haw. Rev. Stat. § 514B-143(a)(3)(B).

108. Perkins & Grennan, *Coverage for Losses Resulting from Association Property Manager Dishonesty*, XVII Fid. L.J. 77, 85 (2011).

109. *See, e.g.*, 2 Rohan & Reskin, *Real Estate Transactions: Cooperative Housing Law and Practice—Forms*, § 12.02[2][e] (Matthew Bender, 2023).

110. Because most policies are designed to cover theft of management company monies by management company employees, their policies ordinarily would not cover the funds of a third party, for example, a common interest community association. *Fidelity Insurance*, available at: http://www.davis-stirling.com/tabid/1664/default.aspx.

111. An endorsement might be added providing that the coverage applies equally to the named and any additional insured. State insurance law may also affect the status of an additional insured, a matter the broker should be able to address.

There are a number of other concerns for associations. As one commentary observes, while management companies should carry their own coverage, there are significant potential problems when an association relies on the management company's coverage to protect it from losses that result from the dishonest acts of management principals or management company employees.[112] The association governing board needs to remember that although the management company may have contractual obligations to the association, it is the board that has the duty to the association to obtain the coverage mandated by the governing documents or statute.[113] Should the management company's policy prove inadequate to meet those requirements, that association almost certainly has no recourse against the company, the insurer, or its broker unless, perhaps, one of them actively and fraudulently misled it.

One concern is that when a policy is carried by the management company and in its name, the association has no insurable interest and cannot directly collect from the insurer.[114] If an employee of the management company steals from the association, the insurer will pay claims to the management company,[115] not the association,[116] and the association will have to rely on the company to

---

112. *Fidelity Insurance*, available at: http://www.davis-stirling.com/tabid/1664/default.aspx. *See also Board of Directors' Guide: Condominium Insurance—Including Fidelity Bonds*, at 13 (Hawaii Real Estate Commission, 1996) (discussing case in which association was denied coverage under policy of management company).

113. Meskin, *The Community Association Insurance Puzzle: What Boards MUST DO and MUST AVOID to Assemble the Puzzle* at 13–14 (Community Association Living, CAI Austin 2012).

114. However, as one expert commentary observes, assignees of insureds under fidelity policies may step into the shoes of an insured and recover for direct loss suffered by the assignor/insured, when the loss occurred before the assignment, and this is generally true even if the policy forbids assignment of the insured's rights under the policy because of the public policy disfavoring restraints on the alienability of personal property. Cornett & Kent, *Who Can Recover Under a Fidelity Policy?*, XX Fid. L.J. 139, 176 (2014). Thus, the association could press the management company to assign it the rights to a claim. *But see Board of Directors' Guide: Condominium Insurance—Including Fidelity Bonds*, at 13 (Hawaii Real Estate Commission, 1996) (where association sought coverage under policy of management company after being assigned right of recovery by that company, insurer denied coverage based on its lack of consent to that assignment). Associations also might consider a clause in the management contract under which the management company agrees to cooperate fully with the association resolving any theft of association funds by a management company employee, including assigning any claim to the association. The advisability and specific language of any such clause need to be discussed, of course, with the association counsel.

115. Of course, for the insurer to pay a claim, the insured must have suffered a loss. When an employee of the management company steals funds belonging to one of the associations the company manages, there may be no basis for the insurer to pay unless it can be shown that the loss was suffered by the company or the association was an insured. *See, e.g.*, Towne Management Corp. v. Hartford Acci. & Indem. Co., 627 F. Supp. 170 (D. Md. 1985) (where owner of property management company took money from client of that company, company itself suffered no loss).

116. However, the association might be able to collect directly from the insurer if it first obtains a judgment against the management company. For example, in *Cedar Lake Homeowners Ass'n v. Northwest Empire Cmty. Mgmt.*, 2015 U.S. Dist. LEXIS 174503 (D. Or. Nov. 13, 2015), an employee

reimburse it.[117] Recognizing this issue, a Hawaiian law requires managing agents to act "promptly and diligently" to recover from the insurer, if the fraud or dishonesty of its employees causes a loss to an association, and apply the proceeds, if any, to reduce the loss to the association.[118]

Another basis under which coverage can be denied to the association is when a principal of the management company is the person whose conduct causes the loss. Typically, coverage is excluded under those circumstances. This specific problem has arisen and been litigated.[119]

The association probably has no control over the application process when the management company applies for coverage. If the company provides untruthful information on its application for coverage, the policy may be void through no fault of the association. For example, in a Virginia federal District Court case, a company that managed homeowners associations obtained a crime policy. On the application for coverage the President of the company answered a question about whether bank accounts were reconciled by someone not authorized to deposit or withdraw from those accounts. The President answered "yes." In fact, the chief financial officer for the company—who was also the son of the President—reconciled accounts *and* had authority to deposit or withdraw funds. He embezzled over $2 million from association accounts. The insurer conceded that, but for the misstatement on the application, it would be required to pay the

---

of the insured management company stole a substantial amount of money from the association. It sued the company and obtained a judgment. The association then brought a garnishment action against insurer. The court concluded that the management company held and was legally liable for the association funds, and the theft of the funds caused the company to suffer a direct loss. As garnishor, the association stood in the shoes of the management company. The insurer could, therefore, be ordered to pay the association directly for the loss.

117. *Fidelity Insurance*, available at: http://www.davis-stirling.com/tabid/1664/default.aspx. However, the associations could be added as "Joint Loss Payees." *See also* 175 East 74th Corp. v. Hartford Acci. & Indem. Co., 435 N.Y.S.2d 584, 51 N.Y.2d 585, 416 N.E.2d 584 (1980) (client of property management company whose funds were converted by employee of management company could not bring action directly against insurer).

118. Haw. Rev. Stat. § 514B-132(a)(4).

119. *See* Three Garden Village Ltd. P'ship v. U.S. Fid. & Guar. Co., 567 A.2d 85 (Md. 1989) (where sole shareholder, director, and officer of property manager misappropriated money from accounts of clients, there was no coverage; when dishonesty that causes loss is that of person who is only officer, director, and shareholder of insured, decisions are nearly uniform in holding that standard commercial blanket bond does not provide coverage because embezzling employee is *alter ego* of insured). *Compare* E. Attucks Cmty. Hous., Inc. v. Old Republic Sur. Co., 114 S.W.3d 311, 321 (Mo. App. 2003), where a property management company obtained fidelity coverage to indemnify it against theft, forgeries, and other defalcations committed by its employees in its management of a not-for-profit low-income housing project. The president and sole stockholder of the insured stole money from the account of the housing project. The insurer contended that by definition the president was not an employee, but the "alter ego" of the company and that the company could not, in effect, recover for its own conduct. The trial court agreed and granted summary judgment to the insurer. The appellate court, however, reversed because the company had a board of directors. Whether the president was under the control and direction of that board was key to determining if he was the *alter ego* of the company. That issue had not been resolved.

policy limit. However, because of the misstatement, the insurer argued it was entitled to rescission of the policy. The court agreed.[120] In the end, $3 million was diverted from the accounts of 400 homeowners associations. Unless those associations had their own coverage for the losses,[121] their only hope for retrieving the lost funds was to receive a portion of the $2 million in restitution ordered by a criminal court.

Finally, when a management company provides services to more than one association, the governing board of any one association would not know if the coverage is sufficient without full financial knowledge of the reserves and assessments of all the associations the company manages.[122] Georgia and Connecticut have addressed this concern by requiring the management company to have a separate policy for each association it manages.[123] Hawaii takes a different approach. It requires that if more than one association suffers a loss, the managing agent has to divide the proceeds among the associations in proportion to the loss of each association.[124] That does not protect the association when the management company policy provides inadequate limits of coverage, but it at least assures that what coverage is available will be equitably distributed.

[7] Funds in Possession of the Community Association Management Company

One increased risk for common interest community associations occurs when the community association management company commingles the funds for the associations it manages either with its own funds or with the funds of other associations. In states that regulate management companies, this practice is usually prohibited.[125] If there are no state regulations, any protection from commingling

120. Perkins & Grennan, *Coverage for Losses Resulting from Association Property Manager Dishonesty*, XVII Fid. L.J. 77, 102–03 (2011), discussing *Kroger Management Group, Inc. v. Continental Casualty Co.*, an unreported federal court decision.

121. Note that if an association had its own policy, it is possible that only the management company would know who reconciles the accounts. The association could, therefore, have to rely on the company's answer to the question of whether bank accounts were reconciled by someone not authorized to deposit or withdraw from those accounts. Under the facts of the *Kroger* case, the association policy could be subject to rescission for the misstatement.

122. *Fidelity Insurance*, available at: http://www.davis-stirling.com/tabid/1664/default.aspx.

123. Conn. Gen. Stat. § 20-460(g) (separate bond has to be provided for each association for which community association manager provides management services that include handling of funds); Ga. Comp. R. & Regs. § 520-1-.06(3)(c) (manager has to maintain separate fidelity bond or insurance policy for each community association for which it provides community association management services and collects, maintains, controls, has access to, or disburses community association funds or alternate fidelity coverage acceptable to Georgia Real Estate Commission).

124. Haw. Rev. Stat. § 514B-132(a)(4).

125. *See, e.g.*, Alaska Stat. § 08.88.351(5) (licensee may not commingle funds of community association with funds of another community association or with its own funds); Cal. Civ. Code § 5380(d) (managing agents are prohibited from commingling funds of association with their own money, or with the money of others that agent receives or accepts, unless certain requirements are met); 4 Colo. Code R. 725-7(E-6) (money belonging to others received by CAM or CAM company

of association funds would need to be addressed in the management contract. Associations should review their contracts with the association attorney to access their content and to have the attorney draft any necessary language to add addressing the protection of the association's funds.

[8] The Application

The first question for common interest communities to answer with regard to insurance applications is who will contact the agent or broker to make the application and sign it? It may be an officer of the CIC[126] or the CAM. In many cases the manager will be the person best equipped to answer the questions on the application; however, if the CAM represents the CIC, the governing board should obtain a copy of the completed application and review it for accuracy.[127] The CAM may have provided incorrect information to the agent,[128] or the agent may have obtained inaccurate data from a prior application.[129]

The contents of the application—or omissions from it—are important because misrepresentations in the application may be a basis for the insurer to

---

has to be segregated into each respective common interest community's bank account); Ga. Comp. R. & Regs. § 520-1-.08(4) (brokers who manage community associations may maintain designated accounts separate from their other trust or escrow accounts); Nev. Rev. Stat. § 116A.630(13) (except as required under collection agreements, community manager has to maintain various funds of client in separate financial accounts in name of the client and ensure that association is authorized to have direct access to those accounts); Va. Code § 54.1-2353(A) (common interest community manager owes a fiduciary duty to associations to which it provides management services with respect to handling funds or the records of each association; all funds deposited with common interest community manager shall be handled in fiduciary capacity and kept in separate fiduciary trust account or accounts; funds shall be property of association and shall be segregated for each depository in records of common interest community manager in manner that permits funds to be identified on association basis).

126. In a curious argument, an association contended an application was "blank" because it was never signed by it, but only its agent. Therefore, it argued, any misrepresentations in the application could not be attributed to it. The application was signed by the President of the association. The court characterized the association's contention as raising "troubling agency concerns," by which it probably meant that the association could only act through its agents and the authority of the President of an organization to bind it is not generally a matter of dispute. The court found that any misrepresentation in the application was "squarely and unequivocally" that of the association. Caribbean I Owners' Ass'n v. Great Am. Ins. Co., 600 F. Supp. 2d 1228 (S.D. Ala. 2009).

127. The governing board should remember that the manager is its agent, and it will, therefore, generally be bound by the actions of the manager on behalf of the association. *See, e.g.*, Biscayne Cove Condo. Ass'n v. QBE Ins. Corp., 971 F. Supp. 2d 1121, 1126 (S.D. Fla. 2013).

128. *See, e.g.*, Towers Condo. Ass'n v. C.E. Brathwaite & Assocs., 40 V.I. 33 (1999) (manager signed application prepared by broker without providing any additional information; application lacked information about prior claim and manager professed to have no awareness of that prior claim).

129. *See, e.g.*, Lexington Vil. Condominium v. Scottsdale Ins. Co., 2013 N.Y. Misc. LEXIS 5745 (Nov. 29, 2013), *aff'd*, 2016 N.Y. App. Div. LEXIS 664 (Feb. 3, 2016), where the agent included building square footage on an application obtained from an application for the prior policy and that information later proved to be incorrect.

deny coverage or, more accurately, rescind the policy.[130] The standard commercial crime policy specifically states that the policy is void in any case of fraud by the named insured as it relates to the policy *at any time* and is also void if the named insured or any other insured, at any time, intentionally conceals or misrepresents a material fact about the policy, the property covered under it, or the interest of the named insured in the property covered under the policy.[131] What happens if the CAM, for example, signs the application and is, unbeknown to the association, embezzling funds from it? There is authority supporting the proposition that a misrepresentation on an application by the manager about his or her own dishonesty would not be imputed to the association.[132]

When coverage is obtained from a particular carrier and then renewed year after year, the application may have been completed many years ago.[133] That presents a potential problem for common interest communities because, with turnover in the membership of the governing board, no board member may know what information is in the application and whether it was accurate originally or remains accurate.

[9] Application Questions

There are standard questions on crime coverage applications and others that particular insurers will ask. To illustrate the types of questions associations can expect, two common applications are compared. One is the Travelers Commercial

130. *See, e.g.*, Towers Condo. Ass'n v. C.E. Brathwaite & Assocs., 40 V.I. 33 (1999), where a representative of the condominium signed an application the agent filled in based on information previously supplied. The agent allegedly did not ask if the condominium had suffered any losses in the interim, which in fact it had. The insurer refused coverage because the failure to disclose that loss on the application constituted a material misrepresentation by the condominium association. The court said that when the association representative signed the application it constituted a failure by the association to disclose information pertaining to its prior loss. However, an issue of material fact remained as to whether the agent was negligent in its handling of the application and whether the association had an obligation to ascertain if the information given was current and accurate as of the date the application was signed. Additionally, there was also an issue of fact regarding whether the failure to disclose was made with intent to deceive. *See generally* Wood & Hurtado, *Don't Get Robbed of Your Fidelity Coverage*, 9 Enforce 12 (2011), available at: http://www.andersonkill.com/Custom/PublicationPDF/PublicationID_1062_Dont-Get-Robbed-of-Your-Fidelity-Coverage.pdf (application process is critical component in obtaining effective fidelity insurance, and insurers often looks back to representations made in application process for basis to denying claim or rescission of policy).

131. ISO Form CR 00 23 11 15, § E.1.d.

132. Horkovich, Reeves & Andrews, *Insurance Coverage for Employee Theft Losses: A Policyholder Primer on Commonly Litigated Issues*, 29 U. Mem. L. Rev. 363, 391 (1999) (generally, policyholder's misrepresentation of material fact on fidelity bond application renders it void *ab initio*; however, that principle has been challenged successfully when person completing application is wrongdoer and courts have refused to impute misrepresentation to corporate policyholder).

133. Lexington Vil. Condominium v. Scottsdale Ins. Co., 2013 N.Y. Misc. LEXIS 5745 (Nov. 29, 2013), *aff'd*, 2016 N.Y. App. Div. LEXIS 664 (Feb. 3, 2016) (application over a decade old).

Crime Coverage Application.[134] The other is a Non-Profit Community Associations Directors' & Officers' Liability (D&O) and Crime & Fidelity Insurance Application used by a large insurance agency.[135]

One question that does not appear on applications is: what requirements do your governing documents contain regarding crime coverage? The savvy broker will be aware that there may be requirements in the documents and will want copies of them. Nonetheless, when applying for crime coverage, the association should provide copies of the pertinent document provisions to the broker and discuss with him or her the fact that the coverage has to conform to the document mandates. The members of the governing board should remember that as a general rule, brokers do not have an obligation to anticipate all the coverage needs of a client. The client has an obligation to inform the broker of its needs. Moreover, it is the governing board that is ultimately responsible to the members of the association to obtain coverage that conforms to the documents and protects the association's assets.

[a] Basic Information

The basic information requested by an application for crime coverage includes the year the project was established, information about the community association management company, the number of association employees, and total number of individuals who are authorized to handle funds. An application specifically designed for common interest communities will probably ask whether the applicant is a condominium, homeowners association, or cooperative. Applications used for applicants generally will instead ask for a description of the operations of the applicant. An application may also ask for the applicant's Standard Industrial Classification (SIC) code number. If that is needed, the broker assisting the association should be able to supply it. Information about any current crime policy and whether the applicant has sustained any crime-related losses in the past three years are also commonly asked questions.

[b] Financial Information

Ordinarily, the application will have a section labeled either financial information or internal controls and procedures. This section will likely ask about the applicant's revenue, net income, and total assets. One commentator notes that crime coverage insures what the association "owns" and that is a "moving target"; therefore, an accounting has to be done to determine what the association has in all accounts and investments, taking into account "windfall deposits," for

134. *See* https://www.travelers.com/iw-documents/apps-forms/crime-non-financial-institutions/cri-1100w-ind.pdf.

135. *See* https://www.ihginsurance.com/Our-Products/Crime-Fidelity.

example, insurance proceeds and special assessments, that go beyond the usual fees accumulated by associations.[136]

The application typically asks how often the association has a financial statement prepared. It will also probably ask whether any statement is prepared by an Independent Certified Public Accountant, an internal bookkeeper, the management company, or someone else and whether it is in the form of an audit, review, or compilation. These are types of financial statements. The application may ask specific questions about outside auditors that are generally more applicable to businesses. For example, have the outside auditors stated there are material weaknesses in systems of internal controls, how did the applicant respond, and has the applicant implemented all material recommendations of any auditor? Some applications will require that the most recent annual financial statement be attached to the application when submitted, at least for limit requests of a significant amount.

Common interest community associations need to be aware of any requirements for financial statements. Some states have statutes mandating preparation of particular financial statements by persons with particular qualifications.[137] The Uniform Common Interest Ownership Act, on the other hand, has no similar requirement and explains that it rejects any proposal that requires records to be maintained in accordance with "generally accepted accounting principles" because for too many associations that would be an unnecessary and burdensome requirement.[138] Many states take the same approach. Certainly, if there *are* statutory requirements for financial statements and an association fails to meet those requirements, an insurer might refuse to issue a policy to the association. Could it also deny a claim on that basis that the association would have prevented a loss had it followed the statutory mandate? Another possible concern arises in associations that have "financial statements" prepared by volunteer association members. These persons may be—or have been before retiring—accountants or auditors or they may be individuals with some limited knowledge of accounting.

---

136. Meskin, *Writing Condominium and Homeowners' Association Insurance* (2008), available at: http://www.propertycasualty360.com/2008/09/01/writing-condominium-and-homeowners-association-insurance.

137. *See, e.g.*, Cal. Civ. Code § 5305 (unless governing documents impose more stringent standards, review of financial statement of community association must be prepared in accordance with generally accepted accounting principles by licensee of the California Board of Accountancy for any fiscal year in which gross income to association exceeds $75,000); Fla. Stat. § 718.111(13) (with some exceptions and opportunity for waiver, condominium associations must prepare complete set of financial statements in accordance with generally accepted accounting principles that, based on association's total annual revenues, must be either compiled financial statement, reviewed financial statement, or audited financial statement); Fla. Stat. § 719.104(4) (same; cooperatives); Fla. Stat. § 720.303(7) (same; homeowners associations); Tex. Prop. Code § 82.114(c) (condominium associations must annually obtain independent audit of records performed by certified public accountant if required by bylaws or vote of board of directors or majority vote of members of association).

138. Uniform Common Interest Ownership Act § 3-118, comment 3.

What if the insurer asks for a financial statement, and the association presents one of these member-prepared statements? If information in it proves inaccurate, does that constitute fraud that under the policy is grounds for it to be treated as void or voidable?

The financial information section of the application will also probably ask about the association's procedures, for example, is a countersignature required on all checks issued by the association and if so, is the countersignature only required for checks over a certain amount?[139] Another possible question is whether the association uses a positive pay service with its bank in which the association electronically shares its check register of all written checks with the bank so that the bank only pays checks listed in that register, with exactly the same specifications as listed in the register.[140] Applications also routinely ask whether bank accounts are regularly reconciled and whether the person who does so is someone who is not authorized to deposit or withdraw from the accounts.[141] Whether the management company has discretionary authority over association reserve funds and whether the governing board regularly reviews bank statements and reserve fund balances are two other common questions.[142] Depending on how the management company handles the finances of the association, only the company may be able to answer some of these questions. The association needs to consider that its policy could be rendered void by a material misstatement in the answer to a financial information question supplied by the management company. It should consider discussing with its counsel whether this is a matter that might be addressed in the management contract.

[c] Practices and Controls

The Travelers application asks a number of questions about the practices of the applicant. These include whether there is a software security system in place to detect fraudulent computer use by employees, agents, or outsiders and whether passwords and access codes are changed regularly and when users are terminated. It also asks whether the applicant has a fraud policy, a code of ethics, and a

139. Statutes or governing documents may require that checks issued by the association be signed by more than one officer or director. *See, e.g.*, Cal. Civ. Code § 5510(a) (in community association, signatures of at least two persons, who must be directors, or one officer who is not director and one who is director, required for withdrawal of moneys from reserve accounts).

140. The positive pay system can dramatically reduce check fraud.

141. In a case in which that applicant answered "yes" to that question, but after a loss the insurer showed the answer was false, the court granted rescission of the policy. *See* Perkins & Grennan, *Coverage for Losses Resulting from Association Property Manager Dishonesty*, XVII Fid. L.J. 77, 102–03 (2011), discussing *Kroger Management Group, Inc. v. Continental Casualty Co.*, an unreported federal court decision.

142. A review of association finances may be required by statute. *See, e.g.*, Cal. Civ. Code § 5500(a) (unless governing documents impose more stringent standards, governing board of community association has to review current reconciliation of association operating accounts on at least quarterly basis).

conflict of interest policy. There are enquiries about whether the premises have guards, alarm systems, or controlled access. The application also asks if there is an art collection or other valuable collectibles.

[d] Requested Limit of Coverage

Applications ask the applicant to state its desired limits of coverage. Associations need to recognize that unlike a commercial general liability or directors & officers policy where one can only speculate about the potential loss, the loss that needs to be covered by a crime policy can be calculated with some specificity. Except for a loss that occurs over time, it is basically the maximum amount of funds of the association at any point in time. Unless there is a state law mandate for the amount of coverage or an association implements prescribed protective financial controls, Fannie Mae requires policies to cover the maximum funds in the custody of the association at any time while the policy is in force. If the association accepts a package policy with set limits, those limits may bear no relation to the actual potential liability of the association or to the Fannie Mae requirements.[143]

Experts recommend minimum coverage of three months of total monthly dues plus the total amount in reserves.[144] That amount, it should be noted, is a *minimum*. Associations need to take two facts into consideration. First, losses can occur over time and could exceed the Fannie Mae requirement or three months of dues plus the reserves. Second, the amount at risk is a "moving target."[145] It can change over time. As one commentary notes, as funds are removed from or added to reserves, the association needs to adjust the coverage limit or give itself enough of a cushion to avoid being underinsured, because fluctuations can occur during the policy period.[146] Also, budgets and reserve balances change annually,

143. Meskin, *A Funny Thing Happened on the Way to the Bank: Fraud in the Community Association* (Katzman & Korr: Legal News Tailored for Community Associations 2008).

144. *See, e.g.*, McKuen, *It Pays to Know Insurance Requirements for Associations* (Chicago Tribune, Mar. 12, 2004), available at: http://articles.chicagotribune.com/2004-03-12/business/0403120250_1_liability-insurance-condominium-associations-policies. *See also* March, *Guarding the VAULT* (Common Ground 1993) (factors in determining limits of coverage include amount of funds at risk, both operating and reserves, how large special assessment would need to be to replace funds, financial controls used by association and manager, and financial reporting requirements, including audits).

145. Meskin, *Writing Condominium and Homeowners' Association Insurance* (2008), available at: http://www.propertycasualty360.com/2008/09/01/writing-condominium-and-homeowners-association-insurance (crime coverage insures what association "owns" and that is "moving target"; therefore, accounting has to be done to determine what association has in all accounts and investments, taking into account "windfall deposits," for example, insurance proceeds and special assessments, that go beyond usual fees accumulated by associations). *See also* McKuen, *It Pays to Know Insurance Requirements for Associations* (Chicago Tribune, Mar. 12, 2004), available at: http://articles.chicagotribune.com/2004-03-12/business/0403120250_1_liability-insurance-condominium-associations-policies.

146. Insurance that protects you from crime, employee dishonesty, and fidelity fraud, available at: https://abipdx.com/condominium/crime-fidelity-fraud/.

so if the policy has a multi-year period, the association needs to discuss with the broker annual adjustments to the limits of coverage.[147]

Finally, there are a host of protective financial controls that associations can implement that will substantially reduce the risk of loss.[148] An association that has stringent controls may decide it does not need more than the minimum coverage required by Fannie Mae, any applicable state law, or its governing documents. Before making that decision, however, the association should consider that the cost of crime coverage is usually quite low. Obtaining a lesser amount of coverage because the risk has been reduced by the implementation of financial controls may not save the association much in premiums. It might, therefore, be worth obtaining more than the minimum amount of coverage even after the association has put controls into effect.

[10] Declarations Page

At the beginning of the policy are pages denominated the Commercial Crime Policy Declarations, also known as the Declarations Page, "dec page," or "dec sheet." The Declarations state essential terms of the policy in abbreviated form.[149] To a large extent, the data in the Declarations is based on information supplied by the insured in its application for coverage. The policy provides that it is void in any case of fraud by the named insured as it relates to the policy at any time and is also void if the named or any other insured, *at any time*, intentionally conceals or misrepresents a material fact about the policy, the property covered under it or the interest of the named insured in the property covered under the policy.[150] This is significant because the basic rule of law is that if one party is induced to enter a contract by a fraudulent or material misrepresentation by the other party, and the first party was justified in his or her reliance, the contract is "voidable."[151] Of course, insurance law is rarely that simple. The general rule has been modified in many states. For example, in some states the insurer may be required to show *intent* to deceive or defraud before it can avoid the policy, while in others fraud or a misrepresentation that is without intent to deceive but *material* to the risk of loss is sufficient.[152] Whether a matter is material and whether the insurer justifiably relied on it are much litigated questions and beyond the scope of this discussion. If an association wants to know the law in its particular state, it needs to consult an attorney, but the principal thing an association needs to know is that the governing board should carefully scrutinize the Declarations—and the

147. *Fidelity Insurance*, available at: http://www.davis-stirling.com/tabid/1664/default.aspx.

148. *See, e.g.*, Majewski, *When Numbers Lie* (Ledger Quarterly 1995); *Protecting Community Association Funds* (CAI 1996); March, *Guarding the VAULT* (Common Ground 1993).

149. Midwestern Indem. Co. v. Brooks, 779 F.3d 540 (8th Cir. 2015) (terms stated on Declarations Page are subject to refinement and definition in body of policy).

150. ISO Form CR 00 23 11 15, § E.1.d.

151. Restatement (Second) of Contracts, § 164(1).

152. *See generally* 4 *New Appleman Law of Liability Insurance* § 38.03 (Matthew Bender, 2023).

application on which it is based—to insure the information is accurate. Anything that might not be completely accurate should be called to the attention of the broker. It is far better to have a discussion about possible inaccuracies at the outset than to engage in costly litigation later.

The Declarations Page includes important information. This information generally includes the name of the named insured, the policy period, whether the coverage is written as primary or excess, the applicable insuring agreements or coverages, the amount of the deductible, the amount of the premium, and identification of the attached endorsements.

[a] Named Insured

In a common interest community, the named insured would typically be the association or, in the case of a cooperative, the corporation that owns the building. The name of the insured as it appears on the Declarations Page should be the legal name of the association in the governing documents, not a name by which it is popularly known.[153] It is also important in a CIC to take into account any layers of associations. For example, a community may consist of several condominium or townhouse associations, a recreation association, and a master or umbrella association, all with similar sounding names. Each of these will have distinct responsibilities and property interests spelled out in their respective governing documents. It is important to determine that the Declarations Page lists the proper association(s) as named insured.

The standard commercial crime policy provides that if more than one insured is named on the Declarations Page, the first named insured will act for itself and for every other insured for all purposes of the policy, and if the first named insured ceases to be covered, then the next named insured becomes first named insured.[154]

[b] Policy Period

The term of the policy—policy period—will be stated on the Declarations Page. The period may be one year or multiple years.[155] Ordinarily, policyholders renew

---

153. *Consider* Far Northwest Dev. Co., LLC v. Cmty. Ass'n of Underwriters of Am., Inc., 2006 U.S. Dist. LEXIS 79033 (W.D. Wash. Oct. 30, 2006), where the policy was issued to the "Somerset Village Townhomes Condominium," rather than the association. It was argued that the condominium was merely a building and, therefore, not a legal entity capable of owning anything. The court found the clear intent of the parties was to provide coverage to the association and, therefore, the association was the named insured regardless of the Declarations Page.

154. ISO Form CR 00 23 11 15, § E.1.l.(1).

155. *See* 175 East 74th Corp. v. Hartford Acci. & Indem. Co., 435 N.Y.S.2d 584, 51 N.Y.2d 585, 416 N.E.2d 584 (1980) (three-year term). *Consider* Three Garden Village Ltd. P'ship v. U.S. Fid. & Guar. Co., 567 A.2d 85 (Md. 1989) (policy had no expiration date, but remained in effect unless and until cancelled by either party; premium was calculated for, and remained fixed for, three-year period, but was payable in annual installments).

coverage with the same insurer for a number of years. When the insurer issues separate policy documents and each refers to terms, conditions, and losses under that particular policy, it is strong evidence that the original policy and subsequent renewal policies were intended to be separate and distinct contracts.[156] The significance of a renewal policy being treated as a separate and distinct contract for the period of time covered is that the insurer is generally held liable up to the limit of liability for *each policy period.*

[c] Insuring Agreements and Limits of Coverages

The typical Declarations Page for a commercial crime policy will list the insuring agreements—coverages—and then provide a space beside each of them for a limit insurance to be enumerated. If no limit insurance is identified for a particular coverage, that coverage is not provided by the policy,[157] unless it is listed as included. When fewer than all the coverages in the policy are listed on the Declarations Page, the policy often only provides employee theft coverage.

The standard commercial crime policy provides that the most the insurer will pay for all loss that results directly from an occurrence is the applicable limit of insurance shown on the Declarations Page.[158] Additionally, if any loss is covered under more than one insuring agreement or coverage, the most the insurer will pay for that loss will not exceed the largest limit of insurance available under any one of those coverages.

The limits of insurance are usually the same for each coverage provided, and for common interest communities it may range from $100,000 to $500,000,[159] although under one crime insurance program specifically designed for common interest communities the limits start at $10,000 and can be increased up to $5 million.[160] The amount shown on the Declarations Page should coincide with the amount of coverage requested at the time the association applied for coverage. It should also reflect current conditions. If the coverage limits listed on the Declarations Page were carried forward from a previous policy, as is often the case, are

156. A.B.S. Clothing Collection v. Home Ins. Co., 34 Cal. App. 4th 1470, 1484, 41 Cal. Rptr. 2d 166, 173 (1995).

157. The ISO Commercial Crime Policy Declarations form says that coverage is only provided if an amount is shown opposite a specified insuring agreement and if the amount is left blank or "Not Covered" is inserted, that insuring agreement and any other reference to it in the policy are deleted. ISO Form CR DS 02 08 13. Similarly, the Travelers Crime Policy provides if the words "Not Covered" are inserted opposite any specified insuring agreement, or if no amount is included in the limit of insurance, that insuring agreement and any other reference to it are deemed to be deleted from the policy. Travelers Crime Declarations CRI-2001.

158. ISO Form CR 00 23 11 15, § B.

159. *See, e.g.*, E. Attucks Cmty. Hous., Inc. v. Old Republic Sur. Co., 114 S.W.3d 311, 315 (Mo. App. 2003) (crime policy with employee dishonesty coverage in amount up to $225,000). *See also* Scarr, *Fidelity Bonding* (Common Ground 1990) (most associations insured by author's agency carry between $50,000 to $200,000 in coverage).

160. *See* http://www.distinguished.com/site/programs/community-associations/crime/.

those limits still sufficient?[161] Budgets and reserve balances change annually, so it is recommended that boards review the limits of coverage each year and make necessary adjustments to ensure sufficient coverage.[162]

[d] Deductible

The deductible is stated on the Declarations Page. The standard Commercial Crime Policy in effect explains the meaning of deductibles when it says that the insurer will not pay for a loss resulting directly from an occurrence unless the amount of loss exceeds the deductible, and that it will then pay the amount of loss that exceeds the deductible, up to the limit of insurance.[163] On the standard ISO Commercial Crime Policy Declarations, a separate deductible is stated for each insuring agreement—coverage—and, therefore, different deductibles could apply to each coverage.[164] For common interest communities, however, the deductible is usually the same for all the coverages and can be small, anywhere from $250 to $2,500.[165]

The popular Travelers Crime Policy does not use the term "deductible" in its policy. Instead, it has a "single loss retention," the amount of which is also listed on the Declarations Page.[166] The Travelers policy provides that the insurer will not pay the insured for any single loss unless the amount of the single loss exceeds the single loss retention.[167] If more than one single loss retention applies to the same single loss, only the highest one is applied. The policy also provides that no single loss retention applies to any legal expenses paid to the insured solely under the forgery or alteration coverage.

[e] Premium

The premium is the consideration paid to secure insurance protection or coverage.[168] For common interest community associations, the premiums for crime

161. McKuen, *It Pays to Know Insurance Requirements for Associations* (Chicago Tribune, Mar. 12, 2004), available at: http://articles.chicagotribune.com/2004-03-12/business/0403120250_1_liability-insurance-condominium-associations-policies (as renewals go on, amount of association funds and reserves may fluctuate).

162. *Fidelity Insurance*, available at: http://www.davis-stirling.com/tabid/1664/default.aspx.

163. ISO Form CR 00 23 11 15, § C.

164. ISO Form CR DS 02 08 13.

165. *See, e.g.*, E. Attucks Cmty. Hous., Inc. v. Old Republic Sur. Co., 114 S.W.3d 311, 315 (Mo. App. 2003) (crime policy with deductible of $1,000).

166. *See* https://www.travelers.com/iw-documents/apps-forms/crime-non-financial-institutions/cri-2001.pdf.

167. Travelers Crime Policy CRI-3001, § V.B.2.

168. State Farm Mut. Auto. Ins. Co. v. United States, 200 F. Supp. 324 (S.D. Ill. 1961), *rev'd on other grounds*, 314 F.2d 363 (7th Cir. 1963) ("insurance premium" may be defined as agreed price for assuming and carrying risk, consideration paid insurer for undertaking to indemnify insured against specified peril); Brownsville Fabrics, Inc. v. Gulf Ins. Co., 550 S.W.2d 332, 338 (Tex. Civ. App.—Corpus Christi 1977).

coverage are typically modest, often between $500 and $1,000.[169] When the policy period is for more than one year, the premium is usually paid in annual installments.[170]

The standard commercial crime policy provides that the first named insured shown on the Declarations Page is the one responsible for payment of all premiums and will be the payee for any return premiums the insurer pays.[171] Thus, when the association is the first named insured, as typically it would be, the association, not its community association manager, broker, or anyone else it assigns to pay the premium, is responsible to assure that the payment is made.

[11] Retaining Expired Policies

Common interest communities often dispose of old documents in their files on a periodic basis. This process may be initiated by the community association management company and may even be one of the services for which the contract between it and the association provides. When the documents are culled, should the association retain old property policies?

A commercial crime policy may have a term of one year or more. Three-year terms are not unusual. However, covered losses can be discovered months or years after the precipitating incident. Retention of crime policies can be particularly important because the conduct they cover can occur over a number of years before it is discovered and because the policies cover losses discovered after the policy term ends. A New York residential cooperative corporation, for example, was the victim of unauthorized fund transfers by its management company over an approximately two-and-one-half-year period.[172] The Loss Sustained Form standard commercial crime policy coverage is for claims for losses that were both sustained and discovered during the policy period[173] or that were sustained during the policy period and discovered *within one year* of the end of that period.[174]

---

169. *See* Scarr, *Fidelity Bonding* (Common Ground 1990) (most associations insured by author's agency pay annual premiums of $100 to $300).

170. Three Garden Village Ltd. P'ship v. U.S. Fid. & Guar. Co., 567 A.2d 85 (Md. 1989) (premium was calculated for, and remained fixed for, three-year period, but was payable in annual installments).

171. ISO Form CR 00 23 11 15, § E.1.s. Note that under the Discovery Form, this clause is identical, but has a different designation. *See* CR 00 22 11 15, § E.1.r.

172. Jefferson Apts., Inc. v. Mauceri, 52 Misc. 3d 1012, 36 N.Y.S.3d 789 (2016). The first unexplained transfer occurred in January of 2010 at which time over $34,000 was transferred from the account of the cooperative to the management company. The last identified unexplained transfer occurred in May of 2012 when $20,000 was transferred to a company owned by an employee of the management company.

173. *Loss Sustained and Loss Discovered: The Difference Between the Two Main Crime Coverage Forms*, available at: http://www.lanierupshaw.com/2014/02/loss-sustained-and-loss-discovered-the-difference/.

174. Kowatch, *1998 ISO Commercial Crime Revisions: ISO Introduces Discovery-Based Crime Policy* (The Rough Notes Magazine 1998), available at: http://www.roughnotes.com/rnmagazine

Under the Discovery Form of the standard commercial crime policy, it does not matter when the loss occurred. It provides for payment of losses discovered during the policy period even though they were not necessarily sustained during that particular period.[175]

If a claim is made after the policy period ends, the process will be easier if the association maintains records of the policies it previously had in place, the name of the carrier, and the time period of each policy. When an association sues an insurer, it has the initial burden of showing coverage,[176] and that is more difficult to do without the policy. It is often held that a copy of the policy needs to be attached to the complaint in a suit against the insurer,[177] although where the policy cannot be produced, courts generally will allow evidence of its contents to be introduced.[178] Gathering and introducing that evidence takes time and is an additional expenditure. Clearly, it is best if the association can produce the

/1998/august98/08p42.htm (loss sustained coverage is very similar to occurrence-based general liability coverage).

175. Kowatch, *1998 ISO Commercial Crime Revisions: ISO Introduces Discovery-Based Crime Policy* (The Rough Notes Magazine 1998), available at: http://www.roughnotes.com/rnmagazine/1998/august98/08p42.htm (retroactive date is required to avoid overlap with previous loss sustained coverage, and no losses that actually occurred before retroactive date are covered by existing policy, regardless of when they are reported; if no retroactive date has been shown on the Declarations Page, policy effective date becomes retroactive date by default).

176. *See, e.g.*, Borough of Sayreville v. Bellefonte Ins. Co., 320 N.J. Super. 598, 605, 728 A.2d 225, 228 (1998); Gold Fields Am. Corp. v. Aetna Cas. & Sur. Co., 173 Misc. 2d 901, 904, 661 N.Y.S.2d 948, 950 (1997) (policyholder has burden of proof on issue of existence of policy and its terms; where policyholder asserts it has lost policy, problem is for policyholder to address).

177. *See, e.g.*, Karaskiewicz v. Allstate Ins. Co. (*In re* Am. Arbitration Ass'n Arbitration), 109 Ill. App. 2d 370, 372, 248 N.E.2d 756, 758 (1969) (remanded to lower court with directions to strike complaint for failure to attach copy of insurance contract); State Farm Mut. Auto. Ins. Co. v. Jones, 98 Ga. App. 46, 56, 104 S.E.2d 725, 733 (1958) (pleadings in action against insurer required that copy of policy be attached or that petition allege language contained in policy).

178. *See, e.g.*, Rubenstein v. Royal Ins. Co. of Am., 44 Mass. App. Ct. 842, 846, 694 N.E.2d 381, 384 (1998) (existence of insurance policy is generally proven by documentary evidence; that policy has been lost or destroyed does not mean that its existence and contents may not be reconstructed from business records, underwriter's folios, or billings of insurer to insured); Borough of Sayreville v. Bellefonte Ins. Co., 320 N.J. Super. 598, 605, 728 A.2d 225, 228 (1998) (nothing in record suggested missing policies were different from others issued later that were available); Fraser v. Metropolitan Life Ins. Co., 165 Wash. 667, 669, 5 P.2d 978, 980 (1931) (where evidence was introduced that policy had been lost or mislaid and could not be found, form of policy was offered and received into evidence as testimony showed it was same form of policy as had been issued to insured). *See generally* Jones, *No Policy, No Problem? How Insureds Are Finding Coverage Even Though They Can't Find Their Policies*, 50 Drake L. Rev. 611 (2002). The author notes that claims for breach of insurance agreements are based on allegations of a breach of a written contract, and much of the information to complete the policy is unique to the specific insured: coverage limits, locations for which coverage is provided, and the period during which coverage exists. The written contract is, therefore, critical to determining the existence and scope of coverage.

actual policy.[179] Thus, there is nothing to be gained by disposing of old policies, and there may be a benefit to retaining them.

One expert recommends keeping expired copies policies for at least five years after their expiration and preferably ten years.[180] Here is another reason for the association to have an insurance committee or governing board member designated to be responsible for insurance matters. That committee or board member can make sure expired policies are properly stored.

Record retrieval is as important as record retention. The association may have retained expired policies, but if no one can find them, they may as well have been destroyed. An expert asserts that it is the responsibility of the governing board to assure that records are adequately maintained.[181] The association should have a storage facility for important documents that is separate from any facility maintained by the management company and should not be in the home or garage of a member of the association, but in an area accessible to future board members, either an off-site leased facility or a segregated and secure area that is part of the common areas of the community, for example, a clubhouse. It is also important that there be an index or cataloging system that makes it easy to find a specific document in the collection of retained material.

Record retention and retrieval can be made easier in the age of electronic documents. Documents can be scanned to create an electronic copy. That copy can be kept on the association computer with a backup retained on a flash drive. Community association managers often scan the insurance policies issued to the associations they manage and post them along with other documents on a website so that members of the association can view them. The association can retain the electronic copy of the policies each year. Storage of hardcopies of policies is a challenge as collectively the various policies can total several hundred pages each year. Electronic copies take up little space, but some of the same cautions that apply to hardcopies also apply to electronic ones. The sole electronic copy should not be in the possession of the management company. The association should have its own copy. When the electronic copies are on a flash drive, they should be kept in a common area to which all governing board members have access, not in the home of a board member.

---

179. One problem is that a court may allow use of a sample policy of the type that was apparently issued by the carrier at the time the policy in question was issued. *See, e.g.*, Gold Fields Am. Corp. v. Aetna Cas. & Sur. Co., 173 Misc. 2d 901, 906, 661 N.Y.S.2d 948, 951 (1997) (courts have permitted use of specimen policies to show what terms of policy at issue were). That policy, however, will not contain the information on the Declarations Page that may be critically important, for example, the limits of insurance. Additionally, use of a sample policy will not help determine the specific endorsements that were a part of the actual policy.

180. Wick, *Record Retention Means Future Protection*, Common Ground (CAI July/Aug. 1990). *See also* Porter, *Records Retention Guide for Homeowners Associations* (CAI Ledger Quarterly 1990).

181. Porter, *Records Retention Guide for Homeowners Associations* (CAI Ledger Quarterly 1990).

[12] Covered Property

The standard commercial crime policy limits coverage to property that is owned or leased by the named insured or that is held by the named insured "in any capacity."[182] The policy also covers property for which the named insured is "legally liable," as long as the named insured was liable for it before the loss was sustained.[183] The policy adds that it is only for the benefit of the named insured and provides no rights or benefits to any other person or organization, meaning only the named insured may seek coverage under the policy.[184]

The purpose of this "ownership of property" clause is to make clear that although the named insured might be liable to a third party because of the conduct of an employee—which can include officers, directors, volunteer workers, and community association managers—its vicarious liability for that conduct is beyond the scope of coverage the policy provides.[185]

The clause is also of importance to common interest community associations for another reason. Under a crime policy, the covered property is either money, securities, or "other property." "Money" means currency, coins, and banknotes that are in current use and have a face value, traveler's checks and money orders that are held for sale to the public, and deposits in the account of the named insured at any financial institution.[186] "Securities" are negotiable and non-negotiable instruments or contracts that represent either money or property, including tokens, tickets, revenue, and other stamps in current use, and evidences of debt issued in connection with credit or charge cards that are not issued by the named insured, but not

182. ISO Form CR 00 23 11 15, §§ E.1.r.(1) & (2). Note that under the Discovery Form, this clause is identical but has a different designation. *See* CR 00 22 11 15, § E.1.p.

183. ISO Form CR 00 23 11 15, § E.1.r.(3).

184. *But see* Cedar Lake Homeowners Ass'n v. Northwest Empire Cmty. Mgmt., 2015 U.S. Dist. LEXIS 174503 (D. Or. Nov. 13, 2015), in which an Oregon federal court found that a theft of association funds by an employee of a management company was a direct loss to the company of covered property. The association sued the company over the theft by its employee and obtained a judgment. It then brought a garnishment action against insurer. The court said that the liability of the management company for the stolen funds arose from its management agreement with the association, which created a bailment. The liability attached prior to, and independent of, the theft. Moreover, even absent a bailment, the court said it would still conclude the company both held and was legally liable for the funds because the management agreement created an agency relationship in which the company acted as the agent of the association with respect to the funds and, therefore, assumed both contractual and fiduciary duties with respect to them. The association funds that were managed and controlled by the company fell squarely within the definition of "covered property." Thus, the court concluded that the management company held and was legally liable for the association's funds, and the theft of those funds caused the company to suffer a direct loss. The insurer cited to the language in the policy stating the insurance was only for the benefit of the named insured and provided no rights or benefits to any other person or organization. The court responded that provision did not preclude the association's action because, as garnishor, it stood in the shoes of the management company.

185. Kain & Glovach, *Annotated Commercial Crime Policy*, 542 (2d ed. ABA 2006).

186. ISO Form CR 00 22 11 15, § F.16. See ISO Form CR 00 22 11 15, § F.9, for the definition of "financial institution."

money.[187] "Other property" is tangible property, other than money and securities that have intrinsic value, but does not include computer programs, electronic data, or any property specifically excluded by the policy.[188]

Questions can arise about whether an association "owns" any of these types of property in its possession. Most, if not all, money in the possession of an association comes from its members by means of assessments levied by the governing board. Even though the association holds that money to operate the community on behalf of its members, there is probably little doubt that once it receives the money from its members, it owns it. The same is probably true of securities the association obtains. "Tangible property with intrinsic value" might be an exception, at least in a condominium where property is owned by the unit owners as tenants in common. Generally, however, condominium associations have an insurable interest in commonly owned property.[189] The "ownership of property" clause renders any ownership questions moot. Regardless of whether an association owns or leases covered property or even holds it in "any capacity," it is clearly "legally liable" for it. Indeed, association directors have a fiduciary duty to use property in the possession of the association for the good of the community.[190]

[13] Coverage Territory

The standard commercial crime policy covers losses sustained by the named insured that result directly from an occurrence that takes place within the United States of America—including its territories and possessions—Puerto Rico, and Canada.[191] Businesses who might sustain a loss outside these areas would need to address coverage for them, but for the typical common interest community association the territorial limitation will not be a factor in its coverage.

187. ISO Form CR 00 22 11 15, § F.22.

188. ISO Form CR 00 22 11 15, § F.18.

189. There appears to be an all but unspoken understanding that associations have an insurable interest by virtue of legislation or binding covenants. Moreover, the documents can be viewed as a contractual risk transfer that provides the association with an insurable interest. "Contractual risk transfer" is defined as "[t]he use of contractual obligations such as indemnity and exculpatory agreements, waivers of recovery rights, and insurance requirements to pass along to others what would otherwise be one's own risks of loss." *See* https://www.irmi.com/term/insurance-definitions/contractual-risk-transfer.

190. *See generally* 6A Rohan, *Real Estate Transactions: Home Owner Associations and Planned Unit Developments—Law and Practice: Forms*, § 7A.08[7] (Matthew Bender, 2023); 2 Rohan & Reskin, *Real Estate Transactions: Cooperative Housing Law and Practice—Forms*, § 9.03[1] (Matthew Bender, 2023).

191. ISO Form CR 00 23 11 15, § E.1.v. Note that under the Discovery Form, this clause is identical but has a different designation. *See* CR 00 22 11 15, § E.1.u.

§ 15.02 The Insuring Agreements

There are seven insuring agreements in the typical commercial crime policy: employee theft, forgery or alteration, inside the premises—theft of money and securities, inside the premises—robbery or safe burglary of other property, losses outside the premises, computer and funds transfer fraud, and money orders and counterfeit money.[192] Each insuring agreement provides coverage for a loss from an *occurrence* that is *discovered* by the named insured. Coverage is also limited to losses "resulting directly from an occurrence." The meanings of the words "occurrence," "discover," and "direct" are key to understanding the coverage provided by the policy.

In general, there are two types of crime policies: loss sustained and discovery. The Loss Sustained Form provides coverage for claims for losses that were both sustained and discovered during the policy period or that are sustained during the policy period and discovered within one year of the end of that period.[193] Under the Discovery Form, it does not matter when the loss occurred. It provides for payment of covered losses discovered during the policy period even though they were not necessarily sustained during that particular period.[194] The differences between the two forms arise in the definitions of "discovery" and "occurrence" and, therefore, the discussion below compares the language of the two forms.

[1] Discovery of Loss

The introductory language of the insuring agreements says the policy provides coverage for a loss that is *discovered* by the named insured. Therefore, the meaning of "discover" is an important part of determining the coverage. "Discover" is defined in the typical commercial crime policy as the time when the named insureds first *become aware* of facts that would cause a *reasonable person* to *assume* a loss of a type covered by the policy has been or will be incurred, regardless of when the act or acts causing or contributing to that loss occurred, even though the exact amount or details of loss may not then be known.[195] One commentator explains that if any circumstance arises or information comes to light

192. ISO Form CR 00 23 11 15, § A.

193. Kowatch, *1998 ISO Commercial Crime Revisions: ISO Introduces Discovery-Based Crime Policy* (The Rough Notes Magazine 1998), available at: http://www.roughnotes.com/rnmagazine/1998/august98/08p42.htm (loss sustained coverage is very similar to occurrence-based general liability coverage).

194. Kowatch, *1998 ISO Commercial Crime Revisions: ISO Introduces Discovery-Based Crime Policy* (The Rough Notes Magazine 1998), available at: http://www.roughnotes.com/rnmagazine/1998/august98/08p42.htm (retroactive date is required to avoid overlap with previous loss sustained coverage, and no losses that actually occurred before retroactive date are covered by existing policy, regardless of when they are reported; if no retroactive date has been shown on the Declarations Page, policy effective date becomes retroactive date by default).

195. ISO Form CR 00 23 11 15, § F.5.

that could eventually result in a claim, the insured has to contact the insurer with as much information as has been discovered and even if that information is incomplete, whether or not an actual claim has been filed, the insured has to notify the insurer of the potential loss.[196] Another writer, however, observes that actual subjective awareness of at least some facts that strongly suggest a loss has occurred are required.[197]

Discover also means the time when the named insured first receives notice of an actual or potential claim in which it is alleged that the named insured is liable to a third party under circumstances that, if true, would constitute a loss under the policy. In general, discovery clauses are strictly enforced.[198]

[a] Extended Discovery Period

Under the Loss Sustained Form of the standard commercial crime policy the insurer will pay for a loss that was sustained by the named insured before the effective date of cancellation of the policy that is discovered by the named insured no later than one year from the date of cancellation.[199] However, the extended discovery period terminates immediately on the effective date of any other policy the name insured obtains—whether from the same or another insurer—that replaces in whole or in part the coverage of the current policy, whether or not the other policy provides coverage for a loss sustained before its effective date.[200] The insurer will also pay for a loss the named insured suffers before the effective date of cancellation of the policy that the insured discovers no later than one year from the date of cancellation regarding any employee benefit plan.[201] The language of the Discovery Form of the standard commercial crime policy is the same as that of the Loss Sustained Form except that the time limit is no later than

196. Kowatch, *1998 ISO Commercial Crime Revisions: ISO Introduces Discovery-Based Crime Policy* (The Rough Notes Magazine 1998), available at: http://www.roughnotes.com/rnmagazine/1998/august98/08p42.htm.

197. Horkovich, Reeves & Andrews, *Insurance Coverage for Employee Theft Losses: A Policyholder Primer on Commonly Litigated Issues*, 29 U. Mem. L. Rev. 363, 367 (1999) (discovery requires actual subjective awareness by policyholder of at least some facts strongly suggesting that loss has occurred as result of employee dishonesty and courts have rejected arguments that it occurs at some earlier point when more vigilant hypothetical policyholder might have realized something was wrong).

198. Southeast Bakery Feeds v. Ranger Ins. Co., 974 S.W.2d 635, 640 (Mo. App. 1998).

199. *See, e.g.*, Karen Kane Inc. v. Reliance Ins. Co., 202 F.3d 1180, 1188 (9th Cir. 2000) (language of one-year discovery rule is quite plain and would appear to apply in straightforward fashion and is not subject to tolling); Southeast Bakery Feeds v. Ranger Ins. Co., 974 S.W.2d 635 (Mo. App. 1998) (where policy provided insurer would only pay for covered loss discovered no later than one year from end of policy period—September 1991—and insured did not submit notice of claim to insurer regarding forgery that occurred during policy period until almost three years after end of policy period, there was no coverage). *See generally* Konop, *The Loss Sustained Policy and Multiple Year Losses: Keeping it Simple*, XVIII Fid. L.J. 193 (2012).

200. ISO Form CR 00 23 11 15, § E.1.j.(1).

201. ISO Form CR 00 23 11 15, § E.1.j.(2).

60 days from the date of cancellation for losses in general and those in regard to any employee benefit plan.[202] The Travelers Crime Policy also has an extended discovery period. It provides the company will pay for a loss sustained prior to the effective date of cancellation *or termination* of the policy discovered by the insured no later than *90 days* from the date of cancellation *or termination.*[203] Note that the ISO policies apply the extended discovery period to a time after *cancellation* while the Travelers policy extended period applies to a time after cancellation *or termination.* In insurance law, "cancellation" refers to the termination, by either party, of an insurance policy *before* its expiration.[204]

[b] Suspicions of a Loss as Discovery of Loss

Words like "become aware" and "reasonable person" and "assume" should put an insured on notice that it is not sufficient to wait for definitive knowledge of a loss. If a reasonable person would assume there may have been a loss covered by the policy, even though the "details of loss may not then be known," a loss has been discovered for purposes of the policy. In other words, there does not need to be an actual loss to trigger the discovery provision, only the possibility of one.[205] Indeed, if facts known to a reasonable person raise a suspicion of loss, there may be an obligation to investigate those suspicions.[206] On the other hand, mere negligence by an insured in failing to discover a loss does not defeat coverage and indeed is one of the risks covered by crime insurance.[207]

Many courts agree that discovery takes place when an insured acquires enough knowledge—greater than mere suspicion—that would justify a reasonable and prudent person to believe a loss within policy coverage had taken place.[208] As the Second Circuit Court of Appeals has said, while an insured is not required to give notice of a loss based solely on a hunch or intuitive feeling that there had been misconduct, an insured cannot disregard known facts; when it learns facts

202. ISO Form CR 00 22 11 15, § E.1.j.

203. Travelers Crime Policy CRI-3001, § V.A.3.

204. *See* https://www.irmi.com/term/insurance-definitions/cancellation.

205. FDIC v. Oldenburg, 34 F.3d 1529, 1542 (10th Cir. 1994) (discovery occurs when insured becomes aware of facts that would cause reasonable person to assume that covered loss has been or will be incurred and language of policy definition of "discovery" clearly ties coverage to discovery of possible loss and does not require actual loss).

206. *See, e.g.*, Southeast Bakery Feeds v. Ranger Ins. Co., 974 S.W.2d 635, 640 (Mo. App. 1998) (discovery of loss clause is safeguard to insurer, imposing on insured reasonable effort to monitor its employees' work and faithfulness). *See also* FDIC v. St. Paul Cos., 634 F. Supp. 2d 1213 (D. Colo. 2008).

207. Horkovich, Reeves & Andrews, *Insurance Coverage for Employee Theft Losses: A Policyholder Primer on Commonly Litigated Issues*, 29 U. Mem. L. Rev. 363, 396 (1999) (courts have repeatedly held that negligence is no defense to coverage).

208. *See, e.g.*, Gulf USA Corp. v. Fed. Ins. Co., 259 F.3d 1049, 1059 (9th Cir. 2001); California Union Ins. Co. v. American Diversified Sav. Bank, 948 F.2d 556, 564 (9th Cir. 1991) (discovery of loss requires insured to have more than mere suspicion that covered loss has occurred; there must be discovery of both loss and dishonesty).

constituting alleged dishonesty, prior suspicions are converted to knowledge the insured cannot ignore and that constitutes discovery.[209]

To illustrate these concepts in the context of a common interest community association, consider the typical monthly governing board meeting. One of the first items on every agenda is a Treasurer's report. Month after month the report for an association shows $100,000 in reserves with small increases for interest, and then one month the reserve account has only $80,000 in it and no one seems to know on what the $20,000 was spent. The discrepancy might be a mere accounting error, but if it is not, a reasonable person might assume there is the possibility that something untoward has occurred. A court might hold that discovery happened when the governing board members became aware money was actually missing. The determination of discovery, however, is very much fact-based, and if the association has concerns about missing funds, it should confer with its broker and/or the association counsel. Of course, the reserve funds belong to the association and the board members have a fiduciary responsibility for them, so regardless of the insurance coverage, an investigation is warranted.[210]

[c] Common Interest Communities and Discovery

Common interest communities are generally organized as non-profit corporations and sometimes as unincorporated associations. An organization, whether incorporated or not, can only "become aware" of a fact or "receive notice" through persons acting on its behalf. The question is: who are those persons? In general, courts apply principles of agency law to determine whether someone's knowledge should be imputed to an entity that is a named insured.[211] Under those principles, the knowledge of officers and directors of an organization would certainly be attributed to it.[212] Moreover, under the standard commercial crime policy, if any insured, or officer, director, or trustee of that insured, has knowledge of any

---

209. Utica Mut. Ins. Co. v. Fireman's Fund Ins. Cos., 748 F.2d 118, 123 (2d Cir. 1984).

210. March, *Guarding the VAULT* (Common Ground 1993) (board members have fiduciary duty to protect, maintain, and enhance association assets including funds set aside for maintenance, upkeep, repair, and refurbishment and that is not just their legal responsibility, but moral and ethical one as well).

211. *See, e.g.*, Inryco, Inc. v. CGR Bldg. Systems, Inc., 780 F.2d 879, 883 (10th Cir. Wyo. 1986) (corporation is bound by knowledge acquired by or notice given to its agents or officers that is within scope of their authority); Ritchie Grocer Co. v. Aetna Casualty & Surety Co., 426 F.2d 499, 500 (8th Cir. 1970) (corporation must necessarily act through agents, and general rule is that knowledge of agent acquired in ordinary discharge of his or her duties for corporation is ordinarily to be imputed to principal). *See also* FDIC v. St. Paul Cos., 634 F. Supp. 2d 1213 (D. Colo. 2008) (notice to agent of corporation constitutes notice to corporation unless agent is acting adversely to corporation).

212. *See, e.g.*, California Union Ins. Co. v. American Diversified Sav. Bank, 948 F.2d 556, 563–64 (9th Cir. 1991) (discovery could occur if officer, director, general counsel, or some other person in position of responsibility became aware of facts that would cause reasonable person to assume covered loss had been or would be incurred).

information relevant to the policy, that knowledge is considered knowledge of *every* insured.[213] Many common interest community associations have a CAM and a bookkeeper or accountant, all of whom may have more knowledge of the association's finances than the officers and directors. Their knowledge can very likely be imputed to the association.[214] However, the knowledge of an officer, director, CAM, or other agent of the association it not attributable to it when that person is the one responsible for the loss, for example, the CAM embezzled association funds.[215]

[2] Occurrence

The standard commercial crime policy provides coverage for a loss sustained that results directly from an "occurrence." The meaning of "occurrence" differs between the Loss Sustained and Discovery Forms. Each form has a definition that applies to coverage for employee theft, another for forgery and alteration, and finally a third definition applicable to all other coverages.

[a] Loss Sustained Form

Under the Loss Sustained Form, in the case of coverage for employee theft, "occurrence" means an individual act, the combined total of all separate acts, whether or not related, or a series of acts, whether or not related, that are committed by an *employee*, acting alone or in collusion with others, during the policy period shown on the Declarations Page.[216] There are two exceptions to the last

213. ISO Form CR 00 23 11 15, § E.1.l.(2).

214. *See, e.g.*, E. Udolf, Inc. v. Aetna Casualty & Surety Co., 214 Conn. 741, 573 A.2d 1211 (1990) (knowledge of store manager and bookkeeper imputed to corporation).

215. *See, e.g.*, Southeast Bakery Feeds v. Ranger Ins. Co., 974 S.W.2d 635, 639 (Mo. App. 1998) (employee's undisclosed knowledge of his or her own unauthorized acts is not imputed to employer corporation and, therefore, discovery clause does not cover losses discovered by dishonest employee during discovery period, but only covers those losses timely discovered by named insured).

216. ISO Form CR 00 23 11 15 § F.17.a. *See* Madison Materials Co. v. St. Paul Fire & Marine Ins. Co., 523 F.3d 541 (5th Cir. 2008), *cert. den.*, 555 U.S. 1048, 129 S. Ct. 643, 172 L. Ed. 2d 613 (2008). In *Madison Materials*, the insured's financial officer embezzled almost $1.5 million from it over 10 years. The insured had an unbroken series of insurance contracts from the insurer that together span those ten years and submitted a claim for the full amount of the loss. The insurer concluded it only owed the limit of liability for the policy then in effect. In the subsequent suit by the insured the court said the issue was whether the prolonged embezzlement constituted a single occurrence. The policy in *Madison Materials* defined "occurrence" as "an act or series of related acts involving one or more 'employees.'" The court said the financial officer repeatedly committed related acts of embezzlement throughout the decade of coverage, but there was only one cause of the injury sustained and that was the dishonesty of the financial officer. Because there was only a single cause of injury and the policy stated that multiple related acts were to be treated as a single occurrence, there was only one occurrence of employee dishonesty over the ten-year period. The policyholder argued the definition of "occurrence" was ambiguous because it failed to state expressly that an occurrence could span multiple policy periods. The court disagreed. It acknowledged that other courts had found the language to be ambiguous, but it concluded that nowhere did the policy language state or even imply that acts committed outside of the policy

clause of the definition, and they are the conditions that apply to losses sustained during prior insurance issued by the same insurer or an affiliate[217] and to losses sustained during prior insurance issued by an unaffiliated insurer.[218] These conditions are only found in the Loss Sustained Form and govern settlement of claims for occurrences that bridge the policy periods of the existing and prior policies.

For forgery or alteration coverage "occurrence" means an individual act, the combined total of all separate acts, whether or not related, or a series of acts, whether or not related, that are committed by a *person*, acting alone or in collusion with others, *involving one or more instruments*, during the policy period shown on the Declarations Page.[219] The same two exceptions apply to this definition as apply to the definition applicable to employee theft.

For all other coverages, "occurrence" means an individual act *or event*, the combined total of all separate acts or *events*, whether or not related, or a series of acts or *events*, whether or not related, that are committed by a *person*, acting alone or in collusion with others, *or not committed by any person*, during the policy period shown on the Declarations Page.[220] The same two exceptions apply to this definition as apply to those applicable to employee theft and to forgery or alteration.

[b] Discovery Form

In the case of coverage for employee theft, for the Discovery Form, "occurrence" means either an individual act, the combined total of all separate acts, whether or not related, or a series of acts whether or not related that are committed by an *employee* acting alone or in collusion with others, during the policy period shown on the Declarations Page, *before that policy period, or both.*[221]

For forgery or alteration coverage, "occurrence" means an individual act, the combined total of all separate acts whether or not related, or a series of acts, whether or not related, committed by a *person* acting alone or in collusion with

period could be part of a "related acts" occurrence within that policy period. Karen Kane Inc. v. Reliance Ins. Co., 202 F.3d 1180 (9th Cir. 2000) is one of the cases to which the *Madison Materials* court referred when is noted that other courts had found "occurrence" to be ambiguous. In *Karen Kane*, the insurer issued three successive policies to the insured. During each those policy periods, an employee of the insured defrauded the company of just over $1.4 million. The scheme was discovered and reported to the insurer during the last of those policy periods. All the policies defined "occurrence" as "'all loss caused by, or involving, one or more employees, whether the result of a single act or series of acts.'" The insurer paid only the limit of insurance—$250,000—pursuant to the last of the three policies. The court found the term "occurrence" as defined in the policy was ambiguous regarding temporal limitation and, therefore, had to be construed in favor of liability.

217. ISO Form CR 00 23 11 15 § E.1.o.
218. ISO Form CR 00 23 11 15 § E.1.p.
219. ISO Form CR 00 23 11 15 § F.17.b.
220. ISO Form CR 00 23 11 15 § F.17.c.
221. ISO Form CR 00 22 11 15, § F.17.a.

others *that involves one or more instruments*, during the policy period shown on the Declarations Page, *before that period or both.*[222]

Finally, the Discovery Form defines "occurrence" for all the other coverages as an individual act or event, the combined total of all separate acts or events whether or not related, or a series of acts or events whether or not related, committed by a *person* acting alone or in collusion with others, *or not committed by any person*, during the policy period shown on the Declarations Page, *before that period or both.*[223]

[3] "Direct" Loss

The standard commercial crime policy provides coverage for losses sustained by the named insured that result *directly* from an occurrence.[224] The policy does not define "direct." It does exclude coverage for "indirect loss."[225] It defines "indirect loss" to include the inability of the named insured to realize income that it would have had if there had been no loss of money, securities or other property, payment of damages of any type for which the named insured is legally liable—but not compensatory damages that arise directly from a loss covered by the policy—and payment of costs, fees, or other expenses incurred by the named insured to establish either the existence or amount of a loss. The comparable exclusion in the popular Travelers Crime Policy is less wordy. It simply says the policy does not apply to indirect or consequential loss of any nature, including fines, penalties, or multiple or punitive damages.[226] In contrast to the ISO Commercial Crime Policy, the Travelers policy explicitly provides coverage for "claim expenses," which it defines as reasonable fees, costs, and expenses of outside accountants, attorneys, consultants, or experts retained by the insured to determine the amount and extent of loss covered under the policy.[227]

Both policies, therefore, explain "indirect" loss and then exclude it, but neither further clarifies the meaning of "direct." One commentary says that a direct loss is an actual loss to the insured, so that bookkeeping or theoretical losses that are not accompanied by a pecuniary loss would not be covered.[228] Moreover, commercial crime policies routinely provide that the policy is only for the benefit of the named insured and provide no rights or benefits to any other person or organization.[229] The purpose of this clause has been described as making

222. ISO Form CR 00 22 11 15, § F.17.b.
223. ISO Form CR 00 22 11 15, § F.17.c.
224. ISO Form CR 00 23 11 15. § A.
225. ISO Form CR 00 23 11 15. § D.1.g.
226. Travelers Crime Policy CRI-3001, § IV.L.
227. Travelers Crime Policy CRI-3001, § III.B.
228. Horkovich, Reeves & Andrews, *Insurance Coverage for Employee Theft Losses: A Policyholder Primer on Commonly Litigated Issues*, 29 U. Mem. L. Rev. 363, 372 (1999).
229. *See, e.g.*, ISO Form CR 00 23 11 15, §§ E.1.r.(3); Travelers Crime Policy CRI-3001, § V.A.5.

clear that although the named insured might be liable to a third party because of the conduct of an employee—which can include officers, directors, volunteer workers, and community association managers—its vicarious liability for that conduct is beyond the scope of coverage the crime policy provides.[230] As one court explained: "Employee dishonesty policies insure against the risk of property loss through employee dishonesty. . . . Liability policies, by contrast, require an insurer to discharge an obligation of the insured to a third party for some act of the insured or its employee . . . . Although employee dishonesty policies may cover the loss of third-party property in the possession of the insured . . . these polices do not serve as liability insurance to protect employers against tortious acts committed against third-parties by their employees."[231]

The distinction between the first-party property coverage of a crime policy and third-party liability coverage can be muddied because crime policies generally cover a loss of property that the insured *holds* or for which it is *legally liable* but does not own, for example, in the case of a bailment.[232] Thus, if a third party suffers a loss perpetrated by an employee of the insured, any obligation of the insured under a theory of vicarious liability could be covered as a direct loss.[233] Coverage is for the loss of the covered property, not for any liability asserted by a third party against the insured.[234] In other words, a *judgment* against a policyholder for the fraudulent behavior of its employee that is premised on theories of agency or vicarious liability can constitute a direct loss.[235] For example, an Oregon federal court found that a theft of association funds by an employee of a management company was a direct loss to the company.[236] The association sued the company and obtained a judgment. It then brought a garnishment action against the insurer. The court concluded that the management company held and

---

230. Kain & Glovach, *Annotated Commercial Crime Policy*, 542 (2d ed. ABA 2006). *See also* Montgomery, *The Alter Ego Type Defenses Reconsidered*, 13 Forum 528 (1978).

231. Lynch Props. v. Potomac Ins. Co., 140 F.3d 622, 629 (5th Cir. 1998). *See also* Vons Cos. v. Federal Ins. Co., 212 F.3d 489, 491 (9th Cir. 2000) (while direct loss to insured may be caused by its employee's theft of property for which it is legally liable—for example, where insured is bailee or trustee of property—there is no coverage for threat of vicarious liability for tort of employee that caused damage to third parties); 175 East 74th Corp. v. Hartford Acci. & Indem. Co., 435 N.Y.S.2d 584, 51 N.Y.2d 585, 416 N.E.2d 584 (1980) (that insured may be liable to third party for loss of money resulting from employee dishonesty does not transform policy covering insured against direct loss into one indemnifying against liability).

232. *See* CR 00 23 11 15, § E.1.r (property covered under policy is limited to property name insured owns or leases, held by named insured in any capacity, or for which named insured is legally liable); Travelers Crime Policy CRI-3001, § V.A.5 (property covered under policy is limited to property insured owns or leases, holds for others, or for which insured is legally liable).

233. Horkovich, Reeves & Andrews, *Insurance Coverage for Employee Theft Losses: A Policyholder Primer on Commonly Litigated Issues*, 29 U. Mem. L. Rev. 363, 372 (1999).

234. Cornett & Kent, *Who Can Recover Under a Fidelity Policy?* XX Fid. L. J 139, 140 (2014).

235. Horkovich, Reeves & Andrews, *Insurance Coverage for Employee Theft Losses: A Policyholder Primer on Commonly Litigated Issues*, 29 U. Mem. L. Rev. 363, 375 (1999).

236. Cedar Lake Homeowners Ass'n v. Northwest Empire Cmty. Mgmt., 2015 U.S. Dist. LEXIS 174503 (D. Or. Nov. 13, 2015).

was legally liable for the association's funds, and the theft of the funds, therefore, caused the company to suffer a direct loss. The insurer cited to the language in the policy stating the insurance was only for the benefit of the named insured and provided no rights or benefits to any other person or organization. The court said that provision did not preclude the association's action because, as garnishor, it stood in the shoes of the management company.[237]

[4] "Premises" Defined

There are three insuring agreements for which coverage is defined in terms of whether a loss or damages occurs inside or outside the "premises."[238] "Premises" is defined as the interior of that portion of any building the named insured occupies in conducting its business.[239] Courts have drawn a distinction between "on the premises" and "in the premises." For example, where a theft occurred on a concrete porch at the entry to a business, there was no coverage because the policy only covered a theft inside the premises. The inside of the premises began, said the court, at a recessed entrance door that was the point at which one passed from the exterior into the interior of the premises. Had the theft occurred when the person with the property had any part of his body through that doorway, it would, in the opinion of the court, have been covered by the policy.[240] Where the language "on the premises" is used, courts generally agree that a loss orchestrated by telephone or computer is only covered if the telephone or computer is on the premises of the insured.[241]

> **NOTE:** An endorsement can be added to the policy that expands the definition of "premises" to include the portion of the grounds entirely enclosed by a fence or wall.[242]

237. *See generally* Cornett & Kent, *Who Can Recover Under a Fidelity Policy?* XX Fid. L. J 139, 175-76 (2014) (judgment creditor of insured may, through judgment enforcement proceedings, take over right of insured to payment under policy; assignee of insured may also step into shoes of insured and recover for direct loss suffered by assignor/insured, if loss occurred before assignment).

238. CR 00 22 11 15, § A.3 (inside the premises—theft of money and securities); CR 00 22 11 15, § A.4 (inside the premises—robbery or safe burglary of other property); CR 00 22 11 15, § A.5 (outside the premises).

239. ISO Form CR 00 22 11 15, § F.19.

240. Singerman v. National Surety Corp., 196 So. 2d 291 (La. App. 1967). *See also* Fidelity & Deposit Co. v. Panitz, 142 Md. 300, 120 A. 713 (1923).

241. Bankmanagers Corp. v. Fed. Ins. Co., 712 F.3d 1163, 1164 (7th Cir. 2013) (fraud orchestrated from outside premises of financial institution is not covered); Private Bank & Trust Co. v. Progressive Cas. Ins. Co., 409 F.3d 814, 818 (7th Cir. 2005) ("on premises" requirement in standard blanket bonds is designed to exclude coverage for losses from fraud perpetrated by telephone or computer, except in rare instances where perpetrator phones or uses computer hook-up from property of bank itself or from property of custodian entrusted by bank to safeguard funds).

242. ISO Form CR 35 23 11 09.

[5] The Specific Coverages

The seven coverages themselves are the same in the Loss Sustained and Discovery Forms. The policy provides coverage for these risks when a limit of insurance is shown for them on the Declarations Page. Coverage applies to a loss sustained by the named insured that results directly from an occurrence that takes place any time—or in the case of the Loss Sustained Form, during the policy period shown on the Declarations Page[243]—and that is discovered by the named insured during the policy period shown on the Declarations Page or any extended period to discover a loss condition.[244] The substance of the Loss Sustained and Discovery Forms is essentially the same in the insuring agreements. To provide a comparison with the coverage of other policies, the Travelers Crime Policy—which is often used for non-profit organizations—is discussed.

[a] Employee Theft

A common interest community can be the victim of theft in myriad ways. For example, someone could embezzle association funds by generating and approving for payment a series of false and inflated invoices, or a maintenance person could make unauthorized charges on a charge card in the name of the association.[245] Under employee theft coverage, the carrier will pay for loss of, or damage to, money, securities, and other property that results directly from "theft" committed by an *employee*, whether identified or not, acting alone or in collusion with others.[246] The coverage includes forgery. The key to establishing the breadth of coverage is determining who constitutes an "employee" for purposes of the coverage, a topic discussed elsewhere.[247]

"Theft" is defined as unlawful taking of property to the deprivation of the insured.[248] What is an "unlawful taking"? One commentary contends the phrase

243. ISO Form CR 00 23 11 15, § A. There are two exceptions and they are found under the clauses titled "Loss Sustained During Prior Insurance Issued By Us Or Any Affiliate" and "Loss Sustained During Prior Insurance Not Issued By Us Or Any Affiliate." *See* ISO Form CR 00 23 11 15, §§ E.1.o & p.

244. In the Loss Sustained Form, the clause is found in ISO Form CR 00 23 11 15, § E.1.j. In the Discovery Form, the "Extended Period to Discover Loss" clause is found in ISO Form CR 00 22 11 15, § E.1.j. The clauses are different. The difference is discussed in § 15.02[1][a], *supra*.

245. Branson, *Fidelity Bond Insurance: Protection Against Condo Crime* (Cooperator, 2014), available at: http://cooperator.com/articles/2823/1/Fidelity-Bond-Insurance/Page1.html (noting case in which employee of subcontract valet service ran up long distance bills of $3,400).

246. ISO Form CR 00 23 11 15, § A.1. The state of mind of the employee—whether he or she acted with any intent to cause a loss—is, says one commentary, irrelevant, at least in terms of analyzing the stated coverage elements in those insuring agreements that focus on the term "theft." Reed, *Commercial Crime Coverage for the Twenty-First Century: Does A "Theft" Standard in Traditional Insuring Agreement (A) Broaden or Narrow Coverage for Employee Dishonesty?* XIV Fid. L.J. 137, 148 (2008).

247. For the meaning of "employee," see § 15.03, *infra*.

248. ISO Form CR 00 23 11 15, § F.23.

"appears to be unlimited in scope," and would certainly apply to embezzlement or larceny, but could also be expanded to encompass unlawful loans of money or property and any conduct in which an employee exercised control over money or property in a way that was not sanctioned by the employer and permanently deprives the employer of the property.[249]

"Money" is defined as currency, coins, and bank notes that are in current use and have a face value, traveler's checks and money orders that are held for sale to the public, and deposits in the account of the named insured at any financial institution.[250] "Securities" means negotiable and non-negotiable instruments or contracts that represent either money or property and includes tokens, tickets, revenue, and other stamps in current use and evidences of debt issued in connection with credit or charge cards that are not issued by the named insured but does not include money.[251] "Other property" is tangible property other than money and securities that has intrinsic value but does not include computer programs,[252] electronic data,[253] or any property specifically excluded by the policy.[254]

[i] Conditions

There are three policy conditions that are specifically applicable to the employee theft coverage. First, the insuring agreement terminates for any employee when the named insured or any of its partners, officers, directors, or trustees who are not in collusion with the employee learn of a theft, or any other dishonest act, committed by that employee, whether that act was committed *before* or after he or she became employed by the named insured.[255] Note that the New York

---

249. Reed, *Commercial Crime Coverage for the Twenty-First Century: Does A "Theft" Standard in Traditional Insuring Agreement (A) Broaden or Narrow Coverage for Employee Dishonesty?* XIV Fid. L.J. 137, 151 (2008). The author asserts that it is foreseeable that insureds will attempt to fit a number of different types of employee activities under the phrase "unlawful taking," and that the phrase provides the opportunity to argue that state criminal law and/or civil tort law on, for example, larceny, misappropriation, and similar "taking" crimes or torts, should apply to policy interpretation. This presents a cornucopia of possibilities as both civil and criminal "takings" vary widely from state to state.

250. ISO Form CR 00 23 11 15, § F.16. *See* ISO Form CR 00 23 11 15, § F.9, for the definition of "financial institution."

251. ISO Form CR 00 23 11 15, § F.22.

252. *See* ISO Form CR 00 23 11 15, § F.1.

253. *See* ISO Form CR 00 23 11 15, § F.6.

254. ISO Form CR 00 23 11 15, § F.18.

255. ISO Form CR 00 23 11 15, § E.2.a.(1). *See* Horkovich, Reeves & Andrews, *Insurance Coverage for Employee Theft Losses: A Policyholder Primer on Commonly Litigated Issues*, 29 U. Mem. L. Rev. 363, 389–91 (1999). The authors say that insurers sometimes argue this clause bars coverage for a loss if the insured was aware an employee had committed a dishonest act before the current one was discovered. The clause, they argue, places the risks of future losses from an employee who has engaged in known prior dishonest acts on the policyholder, not the insurer. The questions that arise are, say the authors, who in the insured organization has to "learn" of the dishonest or fraudulent act—for example, a director or mailroom clerk—and what constitutes a dishonest or fraudulent act. Courts, observe the authors, have placed limitations on the clause in at least

Department of Financial Services (DFS) has adopted a regulation that prohibits insurance companies from denying commercial crime coverage to those who employ individuals with criminal convictions, and other states are expected to follow.[256]

This condition can have implications for common interest communities. In a business setting, there will generally be someone who has authority to either immediately terminate an employee or at least bar him or her from access to company funds. In common interest communities, the CAM generally has access to association funds and is usually considered an employee under the policy.[257] The ability to terminate the CAM may well be defined by the management agreement. Does it allow termination for a dishonest act committed prior to execution of the agreement? If the contract can be terminated, most likely it will require a vote of the governing board. Pursuant to the policy language, any officer or director discovering a prior dishonest act by the CAM would need to immediately notify the board members and arrange for a board meeting, which can be delayed by notice requirements.[258] If it is unclear whether the contract can be terminated, does the board have policies in place to prevent the CAM from further access to association funds? Governing boards need to discuss with the association attorney their rights to terminate a management agreement and the necessary procedures on discovering a prior dishonest act. They should also consider conferring with the broker to determine how to address the needs of the association. For example, the language of the Travelers policy cancellation clause may be more favorable to associations. It provides that the policy terminates as to any employee *60 days*

four circumstances. First, the clause is inapplicable when previous dishonesty was hidden from the insured. Next, if the insured did not have an opportunity to fire the dishonest employee the clause does not apply. Third, mere suspicion or rumor of prior dishonesty by an employee is insufficient to invoke the clause. Finally, knowledge of inefficient business practices, accounting irregularities, or mistakes does not constitute discovery of prior dishonesty. The authors note some policies provide that discovery of a previous dishonest or fraudulent act has to be made by someone with authority to discharge the employee. For common interest communities, prior dishonest acts are more likely to be committed by the CAM or a director than by an employee. Only a majority of the governing board can terminate the contract with the CAM. Generally, a director can be removed only by the association membership, although that will depend on any applicable legislation and the governing documents. The association should consider discussing how its policy might be changed to reflect these facts.

256. Blosfield, *New York Issues First-in-Nation Regulation on Commercial Crime Insurance* (Insurance Journal 2017), available at: http://www.insurancejournal.com/news/east/2017/01/03/436865.htm.

257. *See* 15.03[9], *infra*.

258. By either statute or the governing documents, a governing board may be required to post notice of a meeting several days in advance. There may be a statutory or document provision allowing for emergency meetings without notice. If the association is incorporated, the applicable state laws governing corporations will likely have a provision governing emergency meetings. Insurance concerns aside, a governing board needs to know any requirements regarding notice and emergency meetings. There may be a need to amend the governing documents to allow for emergency meetings. All these are matters that should be discussed with the association attorney who can explain the current statutory and document requirements and draft any needed amendments to the documents.

after any management staff members—meaning members of boards of directors or trustees, officers, and risk managers[259]—become aware of any dishonest or fraudulent *non-employment*-related act committed during or prior to the employee's term of service to the insured.[260] At least in the case of a non-employment-related act, this language would permit the board time to make certain a quorum of the board was available and to post any required notice.

The insuring agreement in the standard commercial crime policy also terminates for any employee on the date specified in a notice mailed to the first named insured, and that date will be at least 30 days after the date of mailing.[261] The condition provides that the carrier will mail or deliver its notice to the last mailing address for the named insured known to it, and if the notice is mailed, proof of mailing is sufficient proof of notice.

The second condition concerns the territory to which the employee theft coverage applies. It provides that the carrier will pay for loss caused by an employee while that employee is temporarily outside the United States of America—including its territories and possessions—Puerto Rico, and Canada for a period of no more than 90 consecutive days.[262]

The third condition concerns "employee benefit plans." It provides that any employee benefit plan shown on the Declarations Page is an insured under the coverage for employee theft.[263] However, for a loss sustained or discovered by a plan, the language of the employee theft insuring agreement is replaced by a sentence that provides the insurer will pay for the loss of, or damage to, money, securities, and other property that results directly from fraudulent or dishonest acts committed by an employee, whether that employee is identified or not, and whether the employee acts alone or in collusion with others.[264] Note that the deductible otherwise applicable to coverage for employee theft does not apply to a loss sustained by an employee benefit plan.[265]

[ii] Exclusions

There are exclusions that are specifically applicable to employee theft coverage, but they have little or no application to common interest community associations.[266] There are, however, other exclusions that apply generally to theft that are discussed elsewhere.[267]

259. Travelers Crime Policy CRI-3001, § III.GG.
260. Travelers Crime Policy CRI-3001, § V.D.4.
261. ISO Form CR 00 23 11 15, § E.2.a.(2).
262. ISO Form CR 00 23 11 15, § E.2.b.
263. ISO Form CR 00 23 11 15, § E.1.h.
264. ISO Form CR 00 23 11 15, § E.1.h.(2).
265. ISO Form CR 00 23 11 15, § E.1.h.(5).
266. ISO Form CR 00 23 11 15, § D.2 (exclusions for losses from inventory shortages, trading, or warehouse receipts).
267. *See* § 15.04, *infra*.

[iii] The Travelers Crime Policy

The first insuring agreement in the widely used Travelers Crime Policy is labeled "fidelity" and has three parts. The initial part covers employee theft and is virtually identical to the coverage in the standard ISO coverage form.[268]

The second party of the fidelity coverage concerns employee benefit plans under the Employee Retirement Income Security Act of 1974 (ERISA).[269] Under this coverage, the insurance company will pay for direct loss of, or direct loss from damage to, money, securities, and other property that belong to an employee benefit plan, directly caused by a theft or forgery that is committed by a fiduciary, whether identified or not, acting alone or in collusion with others.[270] The definitions of the terms "money, securities, other property, theft, and forgery are substantially the same as those in the ISO policy. A "fiduciary" is any natural person who is a trustee, an officer, employee, or administrator of an employee benefit plan as well as any person, director, trustee, officer, or employee while handling money, securities, and other property belonging to an employee benefit plan.[271]

Finally, the Travelers Crime Policy provides coverage for employee theft of "client" property.[272] A "client" is an entity so designated by an endorsement to the policy for which the insured performs services pursuant to a written agreement, but only while that agreement is in effect.[273] This coverage would not ordinarily apply to a common interest community association. While associations in a residential community may be said to perform services for their members pursuant to a written agreement—the governing documents—they do not generally provide services to "entities." An exception could be for a master or recreational association. For example, a master association might provide maintenance of roads, water, and sewer pipes that service other associations. These associations should discuss whether "client property" coverage is applicable to them and needed.

Coverage for theft of client property can be added to the ISO Commercial Crime Policy. It adds to the employee theft insuring agreement that the carrier will pay for loss of or damage to money, securities, and other property[274] sustained by the client—meaning any entity for whom the named insured performs services

---

268. Travelers Crime Policy CRI-3001, § I.A.1 (company will pay insured for direct loss of, or direct loss from damage to, money, securities, and other property directly caused by theft or forgery committed by employee, whether identified or not, acting alone or in collusion with others).

269. *See* 29 U.S.C. § 1001, *et seq.*

270. Travelers Crime Policy CRI-3001, § I.A.2.

271. Travelers Crime Policy CRI-3001, § III.V.

272. Travelers Crime Policy CRI-3001, § I.A.3 (company will pay insured for direct loss of, or direct loss from damage to, money, securities, and other property sustained by client of insured, directly caused by theft or forgery committed by *identified* employee).

273. Travelers Crime Policy CRI-3001, § III.C.

274. "Other property" is tangible property other than money and securities that has intrinsic value but does not include computer programs, electronic data, or any property specifically excluded by the policy. ISO Form CR 00 23 11 15, § F.18.

under a written contract[275]—of the named insured that results directly from theft committed by an identified employee, acting alone or in collusion with others.[276] The endorsement also modifies the definition of "theft" to mean the unlawful taking of property to the deprivation of a client of the named insured.[277] The endorsement also changes the ownership of property condition. It provides that the property covered is limited to property that a client of the named insured owns or leases, holds for others in any capacity, or for which the client is legally liable, provided the client was liable for the property before the loss was sustained.[278] Nonetheless, the coverage is only for the benefit of the named insured and provides no rights or benefits to any other person or organization, including a client of the named insured. Additionally, any claim for loss has to be presented by the named insured. Finally, the policy has an "acts committed by your employees, managers, directors, trustees or representatives" exclusion,[279] but it does not apply to the coverage added by the endorsement.[280]

[b] Forgery or Alteration

An association can be the victim of forgery when, for example, a governing board member makes checks payable to him- or herself and forges the signatures of another board member.[281] The standard commercial crime policy generally covers a resulting loss, but not a loss that results when the insured cashes a forged check for someone.[282]

"Forgery" is defined as signing the name of another person or organization with the intent to deceive, but does not mean a signature that consists in whole or in part of one's own name signed with or without authority, in any capacity, for any purpose.[283] Thus, the signature that is illegible and does not represent the name of any known person is not a forgery.[284] "Alteration" is not defined

275. CR 04 01 08 13, § D.1.a.

276. CR 04 01 08 13, § A. Note that the definition of "occurrence" and the notice condition are the same as under the employee theft insuring agreement.

277. CR 04 01 08 13, § D.2.

278. CR 04 01 08 13, § C.2.

279. ISO Form CR 00 23 11 15, § D.1.c.

280. CR 04 01 08 13, § B.

281. Branson, *Fidelity Bond Insurance: Protection Against Condo Crime* (Cooperator, 2014), available at: http://cooperator.com/articles/2823/1/Fidelity-Bond-Insurance/Page1.html (loss by forgery or alteration happens when association documents and/or checks are forged, and this is growing crime because technology has made it easier to replicate documents/checks).

282. Eubank, *It's Criminal What Agents DON'T Know About Crime Insurance*, at 12 (2014), available at: http://www.independentagent.com/Education/Webinars/SiteAssets/Pages/live-webinars/2014%20Crime%20Webinar%20Handout.pdf.

283. ISO Form CR 00 23 11 15, § F.11.

284. French American Banking Corp. v. Flota Mercante Grancolombiana, S.A., 925 F.2d 603, 604 (2d Cir. 1991) (insured had burden of proving forgery, but offered no proof that signer of documents wrote someone else's name; where documents were signed in illegible script by unknown person, there was real possibility that signatures were by unauthorized person signing his own name,

in the policy, but courts employ a Uniform Commercial Code definition.[285] It defines "alterations" as "an unauthorized change in an instrument that purports to modify in any respect the obligation of a party, or . . . an unauthorized addition of words or numbers or other change to an incomplete instrument relating to the obligation of a party."[286]

Under the forgery or alteration coverage, the carrier will pay for a loss that results directly from forgery or alteration of checks,[287] drafts, promissory notes, or "similar written promises,"[288] orders or directions to pay a sum certain in "money"[289] that are made or drawn by or drawn on the named insured or made or drawn by one acting as the agent for the named insured or that are purported to have been so made or drawn.[290]

If the named insured is sued for refusing to pay any instrument listed in the forgery and alteration clause, on the basis that it has been forged or altered, and the named insured has the written consent of the carrier to defend against that suit, the carrier will pay for any reasonable legal expenses the named insured incurs and pays in that defense, and the amount it pays is in addition to the limit of insurance that applies to the forgery and alteration coverage.[291]

[i] Conditions

There are four policy conditions that apply specifically to the coverage for forgery or alteration. First, the deductible amount does not apply to any legal expenses under the forgery or alteration coverage.[292] Next, the carrier provides that it will treat signatures produced or reproduced electronically, mechanically, or by other means the same as handwritten signatures.[293] Thirdly, the named insured is required to include with a proof of loss any instrument involved in that loss or,

---

or simply scribbling no name); Ralston Bank v. Kansas Bankers Surety Co., 794 F. Supp. 896, 898 (D. Neb. 1992) (where signature was followed by word "cashier," there was no proof that person who wrote that was signing name of another organization as definition of "forgery" required).

285. *See, e.g.*, Metro Fed. Credit Union v. Fed. Ins. Co., 607 F. Supp. 2d 870, 880 (N.D. Ill. 2009) (citing Illinois UCC statute on alteration); Utica Mut. Ins. Co. v. Precedent Cos., LLC, 782 N.E.2d 470, 477 (Ind. App. 2003) (citing Indiana UCC statute on alteration).

286. Uniform Commercial Code § 3-407(a).

287. A "substitute check" as defined in the Check Clearing for the 21st Century Act is treated the same as the original it replaced.

288. *See* Travelers Cas. & Sur. Co. of Am. v. Baptist Health Sys., 313 F.3d 295 (5th Cir. 2002) (analyzing policy terms in commercial paper context).

289. "Money" is defined as currency, coins, and bank notes that are in current use and have a face value, traveler's checks and money orders that are held for sale to the public, and deposits in the account of the named insured at any financial institution. ISO Form CR 00 23 11 15, § F.16. See ISO Form CR 00 23 11 15, § F.9, for the definition of "financial institution."

290. ISO Form CR 00 23 11 15, § A.2.a.

291. ISO Form CR 00 23 11 15, § A.2.b.

292. ISO Form CR 00 23 11 15, § E.3.a.

293. ISO Form CR 00 23 11 15, § E.3.b.

if that is not possible, an affidavit that sets forth the amount and cause of loss.[294] Finally, territorial restrictions do not apply to the forgery or alteration coverage: the carrier will cover a loss sustained by the named insured that results directly from an occurrence that takes place anywhere in the world.[295]

[ii] The Travelers Crime Policy

The Travelers Crime Policy has a somewhat similar forgery or alteration coverage. Under it the insurer will pay for the insured's direct loss directly caused by forgery or alteration of, on, or in, any written "covered instruments" in three circumstances.[296] "Covered instruments" are checks, drafts, promissory notes, bills of exchange or similar written promises, and orders or directions to pay a sum certain in money.[297] The term also includes written instruments required in conjunction with any transaction involving any credit, debit, or charge card issued to the insured, its employees, or its "management staff members" for business purposes.[298] Members of boards of directors or trustees, officers, and risk managers are all considered "management staff members"[299] The policy provides coverage for a loss by forgery or alteration when a covered instrument is made by, drawn by, or drawn on, the insured, or purports to have been so made or drawn or is made or drawn by someone acting as the agent of the insured, or purports to have been so made or drawn.[300] Additionally, the insurer will reimburse the insured for reasonable legal defense expenses the insured has paid if it is sued for refusing to pay any written covered instrument under the forgery or alteration insuring agreement on the basis that it has been forged or altered.[301] Reimbursement is conditioned on receipt by the insured of prior written consent of the insurer to defend against the suit, and the amount of any legal expenses reimbursed is in addition to the applicable single loss limit shown on the Declarations Page for the forgery or alteration coverage.

The Travelers Crime Policy also includes "personal accounts protection," which can be added to the ISO Commercial Crime Policy by endorsement.[302]

---

294. ISO Form CR 00 23 11 15, § E.3.c.

295. ISO Form CR 00 23 11 15, § E.3.b.

296. Travelers Crime Policy CRI-3001, § I.B. The policy also provides that a signature that is a mechanical or electronic reproduction of a handwritten signature produced by a mechanical check-writing machine or a computer printer is treated the same as a handwritten one, but that an electronic signature is not treated the same as a mechanical or electronic reproduction of a handwritten signature and is not considered a forgery. Also, the term "check" includes a "substitute check" as defined in the Check Clearing for the 21st Century Act and will be treated the same as the original it replaced.

297. Travelers Crime Policy CRI-3001, § III.K.1.

298. Travelers Crime Policy CRI-3001, § III.K.2.

299. Travelers Crime Policy CRI-3001, § III.GG.

300. Travelers Crime Policy CRI-3001, § I.B.1.

301. Travelers Crime Policy CRI-3001, § I.B.2.

302. *See* § 15.02[9], *infra*.

[c] Inside the Premises—Theft of Money and Securities

Under the first of two "inside the premises" clauses, the carrier will pay for loss of money and securities inside the premises—meaning the interior of that portion of any building the named insured occupies in conducting its business[303]—or financial institution premises—meaning the interior of that portion of any building occupied by a financial institution as defined by the policy[304]—that results directly from a theft—meaning the unlawful taking of property to the deprivation of the insured[305]—committed by someone present inside the premises of the named insured or a financial institution or that results directly from disappearance or destruction.[306]

"Money" is defined as currency, coins, and bank notes that are in current use and have a face value, traveler's checks, and money orders that are held for sale to the public.[307] "Securities" means negotiable and non-negotiable instruments or contracts that represent either money or property and includes tokens, tickets, revenue, and other stamps in current use and evidences of debt issued in connection with credit or charge cards that are not issued by the named insured, but does not include money.[308]

The insurer will also pay loss from damage to the premises, or its exterior, that results directly from an actual or attempted theft of money and securities, if the named insured is the owner of the premises or is liable for damage to it.[309] It will also pay for loss of or damage to a locked safe, vault, cash register, cash box, or cash drawer that is located inside the premises that results directly from an actual or attempted theft of, or unlawful entry into, those containers.[310]

---

303. ISO Form CR 00 23 11 15, § F.19.

304. ISO Form CR 00 23 11 15, § F.10. *See* ISO Form CR 00 23 11 15, § F.9, for the definition of "financial institution."

305. ISO Form CR 00 23 11 15, § F.23.

306. ISO Form CR 00 23 11 15, § A.3.a. What does "disappearance" mean? *See* United States Smelting Refining & Mining Co. v. Aetna Casualty & Surety Co., 372 F. Supp. 489, 496 (S.D.N.Y. 1974) ("disappearance" was separately covered risk and where evidence showed gold and silver of insured was lost under unknown, puzzling, and baffling circumstances difficult to explain, court disagreed with insurer that only proof of existence and subsequent disappearance of gold and silver consisted of inventory records that were insufficient to prove disappearance); Columbiana County Bd. of Comm'rs v. Nationwide Ins. Co., 130 Ohio App. 3d 8.19, 719 N.E.2d 561, 568 (1998) (where funds were intentionally and knowingly converted into investments by treasurer, that conversion could not be likened to disappearance in that funds were traceable and recognizable and, while those funds might no longer be present at location of treasury of insured, they could not be said to have disappeared).

307. ISO Form CR 00 23 11 15, § F.16.

308. ISO Form CR 00 23 11 15, § F.22.

309. ISO Form CR 00 23 11 15, § A.3.b. In the case of a condominium, the association may not own covered property as the unit owners own the "common elements" as tenants in common, but the association would certainly be liable for damage to it. Homeowners associations and cooperative corporations will generally own or lease any covered property.

310. ISO Form CR 00 23 11 15, § A.3.b.

[i] Exclusions

There are exclusions that apply generally to theft that are discussed elsewhere.[311] One is particularly important to the "inside the premises" coverage. It bars coverage for a loss that results from theft or any other dishonest act committed by an employee, director, trustee, or "authorized representative" of the named insured.[312] That has the effect of limiting the inside the premises theft coverage to losses resulting from a theft committed by someone present inside the premises *other than* an employee, director, trustee, or authorized representative of the named insured. If that person colludes with an employee, director, trustee, or authorized representative, the exclusion applies.[313] A theft by someone who is an employee, director, trustee, or authorized representative must be covered, if at all, under the employee theft insuring agreement.

There are eight exclusions that apply specifically to the inside the premises coverage. First, a loss that results from accounting or arithmetical errors or omissions is not covered.[314] Coverage for a loss that results from giving or surrendering property in any exchange or purchase is proscribed.[315] Generally, a loss or damage that results from fire is not covered, no matter how it is caused, except for loss of or damage to money and securities and loss from damage to a safe or vault.[316] A loss of property that is contained in a money operated device is not covered except when an amount of money deposited in that device is recorded by a continuous recording instrument in it.[317] There is no coverage for loss of or damage to motor vehicles, trailers, semitrailers, or equipment and accessories attached to them.[318] When there is a loss from damage to the premises or its exterior, or to any safe, vault, cash register, cash box, cash drawer, or other property—meaning tangible property other than money and securities that has intrinsic value[319]—by vandalism or malicious mischief, it is not covered.[320] When the named insured, or anyone acting with the express or implied authority of the named insured, is induced by a dishonest act to voluntarily relinquish title to or possession of any property and a loss results, coverage for that loss is excluded.[321]

Finally, there is an exclusion concerning transfer or surrender of property. Under it, there is no coverage for a loss of or damage to property subsequent to

---

311. *See* § 15.04, *infra.*

312. ISO Form CR 00 23 11 15, § D.1.c.

313. 10 Jeffrey E. Thomas, *New Appleman on Insurance Law Library Edition* § 122.04[2] (Matthew Bender, 2023).

314. ISO Form CR 00 23 11 15, § D.3.a.

315. ISO Form CR 00 23 11 15, § D.3.b.

316. ISO Form CR 00 23 11 15, § D.3.c.

317. ISO Form CR 00 23 11 15, § D.3.d.

318. ISO Form CR 00 23 11 15, § D.3.e.

319. ISO Form CR 00 23 11 15, § F.18. "Other property" does not include computer programs, electronic data, or any property specifically excluded by the policy.

320. ISO Form CR 00 23 11 15, § D.3.g.

321. ISO Form CR 00 23 11 15, § D.3.h.

its transfer or surrender to a person or place that is outside the premises, or of financial institution premises, in two circumstances. The first is when the transfer or surrender was based on unauthorized instructions,[322] and the second is when it was as a result of a threat.[323] Those threats may include doing bodily harm, doing damage to property, introduction of a denial of service attack or virus, or other malicious instruction into a computer system, contaminating, polluting or rendering substandard the goods or products of the named insured, and disseminating, divulging, or using the confidential information of the named insured, the confidential or personal information of another person or organization, or weaknesses in the source code in a computer system.

[ii] The Travelers Crime Policy

The Travelers Crime Policy has a very similar provision. It states that the insurer will pay the insured for a direct loss of money or securities located inside the premises or a financial institution premises that is directly caused by a theft committed by a person present inside those premises;[324] or direct loss of money or securities located inside those premises directly caused by disappearance, damage, or destruction.[325]

[iii] Theft from Home of Officer or Director

In small common interest communities, there may be no office or other common area where property can be safely stored. It is not unusual for officers or directors in these associations to keep association money, stamps, and other property of value, including an association checkbook or credit card, in their homes.[326] Crime policies provide that the insurer will pay for loss of money and securities inside the premises—meaning the interior of that portion of any building the named insured *occupies* in conducting its business[327]—that results directly from a theft committed by someone present *inside the premises* of the named insured. If money is stolen from the home of an officer or director, is that home occupied by the association in conducting its business? Does the fact that an officer or director conducts business on behalf of the association in his or her home make his or her home the premises of the association?[328] These are questions that an

322. ISO Form CR 00 23 11 15, § D.3.f.(1).(a).

323. ISO Form CR 00 23 11 15, § D.3.f.(1).(b).

324. Travelers Crime Policy CRI-3001, § I.C.1.

325. Travelers Crime Policy CRI-3001, § I.C.2.

326. The UCIOA commissioners, for example, note that in smaller, self-managed associations, records may be kept by a unit owner. Uniform Common Interest Ownership Act § 3-118, comment 6.

327. ISO Form CR 00 23 11 15, § F.19.

328. In small associations, for example, the governing board meetings may take place around the President's dining room table. Before the meeting the Treasurer may write checks, reconcile the association bank statement, and prepare his or her report to the board at a desk in his or her spare

association should clarify with its broker. The association may need to seek an endorsement making clear that covered property in the home of an officer or director for purposes of conducting the business of the association is considered inside the premises of the association.[329]

[d] Inside the Premises—Robbery or Safe Burglary of Other Property

The second "inside the premises" clause concerns robbery and safe burglary. "Robbery" is defined in the policy as unlawful taking of property from the care and custody of a person by another who has caused or threatened to cause that person bodily harm or committed an obviously unlawful act witnessed by that person.[330] Safe burglary is the unlawful taking of property from within a locked safe or vault by someone who unlawfully entered the safe or vault, as evidenced by marks of forcible entry on its exterior,[331] or the unlawful taking of a safe or vault from inside the premises.[332] The "premises" means the interior of that portion of any building the named insured occupies in conducting its business.[333]

---

bedroom. The Secretary may handle correspondence and write up the minutes at his or her kitchen table.

329. If the broker believes the policy provides this coverage without an endorsement, it would be wise to get written confirmation of that from the insurance company itself. If the insurer is asked if the coverage is already in the policy and it confirms in a letter that the coverage is included within the policy issued, then that letter should be evidence that the coverage exists. Additionally, if when the association is seeking either new coverage or a renewal, it requests specific coverage in writing—in this case coverage when association property within the home of an officer or director—and the insurer responds that the policy provides that coverage, but then later denies a claim based on lack of coverage, the association should be able to sue the insurer for coverage under the policy and the insurer could be estopped to deny coverage.

330. ISO Form CR 00 23 11 15, § F.20.

331. Many, but not all, courts hold that there must be actual marks of forcible entry on the exterior of the safe itself, as opposed to signs of forced entry into the building, for there to be coverage. *See, e.g.*, Rosie O'Grady's Warehouse, Inc. v. Charter Oak Fire Ins. Co., 319 So. 2d 632, 633 (Fla. 1st DCA 1975) (where intruder forcefully entered premises by breaking window, but opened safe without force or violence and left no visible marks on doors of safe, there was no coverage because policy required that felonious entry into safe be made by actual force and violence leaving visible marks on safe doors); Hazuka v. Maryland Casualty Co., 183 Neb. 336, 339, 160 N.W.2d 174, 177 (1968) (where money was stolen from safe and there was evidence of forced entry into building, but no marks or fingerprints on front of steel safe, coverage was precluded because policy limited liability of insurer to losses sustained through forcible or violent entry into safe by use of actual force and violence of which there were visible marks). *Compare* Ferguson v. Phoenix Assurance Co., 189 Kan. 459, 461, 370 P.2d 379, 384 (1962) (while there were no visible marks on exterior of outer door of safe to show use of force or violence in gaining access, inner door did disclose marks of force and violence on its exterior; policy requirement that there be visible marks on exterior of all of doors to safe referred only to evidence of force and violence used in making felonious entry into safe, that is, it was merely evidentiary to show entry into safe by actual force and violence).

332. ISO Form CR 00 23 11 15, § F.21.

333. ISO Form CR 00 23 11 15, § F.19.

The insurer will pay for loss of, or damage to, other property—meaning tangible property other than money and securities that has intrinsic value[334]—inside the premises that results directly from an actual or attempted robbery of a custodian or inside the premises in a safe or vault that results directly from an actual or attempted safe burglary.[335] A custodian is the named insured or any employee[336] while having care and custody of property inside the premises.[337] If the insured has all-risk commercial property coverage, it would apply to the theft of tangible property and generally provide broader coverage.[338]

The insurer will also pay for loss from damage to the premises or its exterior that results directly from an actual or attempted robbery or safe burglary of other property, if the named insured is the owner of the premises or liable for damage to it,[339] and for loss of or damage to a locked safe or vault located inside the premises that results directly from an actual or attempted robbery or safe burglary.[340]

[i] Condition

There is a policy condition that specifically applies to the robbery or safe burglary coverage. The carrier will only pay up to $5000 for any single occurrence of loss or damage to manuscripts, drawings, or records of any kind, or the cost of reconstructing them or reproducing any information that is contained in them.[341]

---

334. ISO Form CR 00 23 11 15, § F.18. "Other property" does not include computer programs, electronic data, or any property specifically excluded by the policy.

335. ISO Form CR 00 23 11 15, § A.4.a.

336. The policy has a lengthy definition of "employee." *See* ISO Form CR 00 23 11 15, § F.7. The definition is critical to determining coverage under the policy and is discussed elsewhere. *See* § 15.03, *infra*.

337. ISO Form CR 00 23 11 15, § F.4. A custodian can also be a partner of the named insured or a member of the named insured. The term "member" has limited application to a common interest community association because it is defined as an owner of a limited liability company (LLC) represented by its membership interest. ISO Form CR 00 23 11 15, § F. 14. CICs are rarely organized as LLCs. A custodian is not anyone acting as a watchperson or janitor. A watchperson is someone the named insured retains specifically to have care and custody of property inside the premises and who has no other duties. ISO Form CR 00 23 11 15, § F.25.

338. *See* Eubank, *It's Criminal What Agents DON'T Know About Crime Insurance*, at 13(2014), available at: http://www.independentagent.com/Education/Webinars/SiteAssets/Pages/live-webinars/2014%20Crime%20Webinar%20Handout.pdf (robbery insuring agreement is rarely used because other property can be covered under special cause of loss form and that coverage is broader); Austin, *Crime Insurance—The Other Property Policy*, at 2 (2009), available at: http://austinstanovich.com/pdf/Articles/Crime-the-other-property-policy-4-09.pdf (theft is a covered peril within special form—all-risk—but is subject to dishonesty exclusion and to limitation under which accounts, bills, currency, food stamps, or other evidences of debt, money, notes, or securities are not covered property).

339. ISO Form CR 00 23 11 15, § A.4.b.

340. ISO Form CR 00 23 11 15, § A.4.c.

341. ISO Form CR 00 23 11 15, § E.4.b.(2). The same dollar limitation applies to loss of or damage to precious metals, precious or semiprecious stones, pearls, and furs, items that a common interest community is unlikely to possess.

[ii] Exclusions

There is an exclusion that bars coverage for a loss that results from theft or any other dishonest act committed by an employee, director, trustee, or "authorized representative" of the named insured.[342] That has the effect of limiting the inside the premises *robbery coverage* to losses resulting from an act committed by someone present inside the premises *other than* an employee, director, trustee, or authorized representative of the named insured. If that person has an accomplice who is an employee, director, trustee, or authorized representative, the exclusion applies.[343]

There are eight exclusions that apply specifically *to this coverage.* First, a loss that results from accounting or arithmetical errors or omissions is not covered.[344] Coverage for a loss that results from giving or surrendering property in any exchange or purchase is proscribed.[345] Generally, a loss or damage that results from fire is not covered, no matter how it is caused, except for loss of or damage to money and securities and loss from damage to a safe or vault.[346] A loss of property that is contained in a money operated device is not covered except when an amount of money deposited in that device is recorded by a continuous recording instrument in it.[347] There is no coverage for loss of or damage to motor vehicles, trailers, semitrailers or equipment and accessories attached to them.[348] When there is a loss from damage to the premises or its exterior, or to any safe, vault, cash register, cash box, cash drawer or other property—meaning tangible property other than money and securities that has intrinsic value[349]—by vandalism or malicious mischief it is not covered.[350] When the named insured, or anyone acting with the express or implied authority of the named insured is induced by a dishonest act to voluntarily relinquish title to or possession of any property and a loss results, coverage for that loss is excluded.[351]

Finally, there is an exclusion concerning transfer or surrender of property. Under it, there is no coverage for a loss of or damage to property subsequent to its transfer or surrender to a person or place that is outside the premises, or of financial institution premises, in two circumstances. The first is when the transfer or surrender was based on unauthorized instructions,[352] and the second is when

342. ISO Form CR 00 23 11 15, § D.1.c.

343. 10 Jeffrey E. Thomas, *New Appleman on Insurance Law Library Edition* § 123.04[1] (Matthew Bender, 2023).

344. ISO Form CR 00 23 11 15, § D.3.a.

345. ISO Form CR 00 23 11 15, § D.3.b.

346. ISO Form CR 00 23 11 15, § D.3.c.

347. ISO Form CR 00 23 11 15, § D.3.d.

348. ISO Form CR 00 23 11 15, § D.3.e.

349. ISO Form CR 00 23 11 15, § F.18. "Other property" does not include computer programs, electronic data, or any property specifically excluded by the policy.

350. ISO Form CR 00 23 11 15, § D.3.g.

351. ISO Form CR 00 23 11 15, § D.3.h.

352. ISO Form CR 00 23 11 15, § D.3.f.(1).(a).

it was as a result of a threat.[353] Those threats may include doing bodily harm, doing damage to property, introduction of a denial of service attack or virus, or other malicious instruction into a computer system, contaminating, polluting or rendering substandard the goods or products of the named insured, and disseminating, divulging, or using the confidential information of the named insured, the confidential or personal information of another person or organization or weaknesses in the source code in a computer system.

[iii] The Travelers Crime Policy

The Travelers Crime Policy has similar coverage that it breaks down into several parts. First, the company will pay the insured for a direct loss of, or direct loss from damage to, other property located inside the premises that is directly caused by an actual or attempted robbery.[354] It will also pay the insured for a direct loss of, or direct loss from damage to, other property located inside the premises in a safe or vault that is directly caused by an actual or attempted safe burglary.[355] Next, the company will pay for a direct loss by the insured from damage to the premises, or its exterior, that results directly from an actual or attempted theft, robbery, or safe burglary, if the insured is the owner of the premises, or is liable for damage to it.[356] Finally, the company will pay for a direct loss by the insured of, or loss from damage to, a locked safe, vault, cash register, cash box, or cash drawer located inside the premises that results directly from an actual or attempted theft, robbery or safe burglary, if the insured is the owner of the locked safe, vault, cash register, cash box, or cash drawer or is liable for damage to them.[357]

[iv] Robbery of Officer or Director

In small common interest communities, there may be no office or other common area where property can be safely stored. It is not unusual for officers or directors in these associations to keep association property of value in their homes.[358] Crime policies say the insurer will pay for loss of or damage to tangible property—other than money and securities—that has intrinsic value, and is inside the premises, that results directly from an actual or attempted robbery of a custodian, which is the named insured or any employee—which can include directors and

353. ISO Form CR 00 23 11 15, § D.3.f.(1).(b).

354. Travelers Crime Policy CRI-3001, § I.C.3.a.

355. Travelers Crime Policy CRI-3001, § I.C.3.b.

356. Travelers Crime Policy CRI-3001, § I.C.4.

357. Travelers Crime Policy CRI-3001, § I.C.5. In the case of a condominium, the association may not own covered property as the unit owners own the "common elements" as tenants in common, but the association would certainly be liable for damage to it. Homeowners associations and cooperative corporations will generally own or lease any covered property.

358. The UCIOA commissioners, for example, note that in smaller, self-managed associations, records may be kept by a unit owner. Uniform Common Interest Ownership Act § 3-118, comment 6.

officers—while having care and custody of property inside the premises. Premises means the interior of that portion of any building the named insured *occupies* in conducting its business.[359] If association property is taken in a robbery from the home of an officer or director, is that home occupied by the association in conducting its business? Does the fact that an officer or director conducts business on behalf of the association at home make her home the premises of the association?[360] These are questions that an association should clarify with its broker. The association may need to seek an endorsement making clear that covered property in the home of an officer or director for purposes of conducting the business of the association is considered inside the premises of the association.[361]

[e] Losses Outside the Premises

The fifth coverage is for a loss "outside the premises." The word "premises" is defined as the interior of that portion of any building the named insured occupies in conducting its business.[362] The carrier will pay for loss of money and securities *outside* the premises in the care and custody of a messenger—meaning the named insured, or any employee,[363] while having care and custody of property outside the premises[364]—or an armored motor vehicle company that results directly from theft—meaning the unlawful taking of property to the deprivation of the insured[365]—or from disappearance or destruction.[366]

---

359. ISO Form CR 00 22 11 15, § F.19.

360. In small associations, the governing board meetings may take place around the President's dining room table. Before the meeting the Treasurer probably writes checks, reconciles the association bank statement, and prepares his or her report to the board at a desk in his or her spare bedroom. The Secretary may handle correspondence and write up the minutes at his or her kitchen table.

361. If the broker believes the policy provides this coverage without an endorsement, it would be wise to get written confirmation of that from the insurance company itself. If the insurer is asked if the coverage is already in the policy and it confirms in a letter that the coverage is included within the policy issued, then that letter should be evidence that the coverage exists. Additionally, if when the association is seeking either new coverage or a renewal, it requests specific coverage in writing—in this case coverage for association property within the home of an officer or director—and the insurer responds that the policy provides that coverage, but then later denies a claim based on lack of coverage, the association should be able to sue the insurer for coverage under the policy and the insurer could be estopped to deny coverage.

362. ISO Form CR 00 23 11 15, § F.19.

363. The policy has a lengthy definition of "employee." *See* ISO Form CR 00 23 11 15, § F.7. The definition is critical to determining coverage under the policy and is discussed elsewhere. *See* § 15.03, *infra*.

364. ISO Form CR 00 23 11 15, § F.15. Messenger also means a relative of the named insured or any of partner or member of the named insured. The term "member" has limited application to a common interest community association because it is defined as an owner of a limited liability company (LLC) represented by its membership interest. ISO Form CR 00 23 11 15, § F. 14. CICs are rarely organized as LLCs.

365. ISO Form CR 00 23 11 15, § F.23.

366. ISO Form CR 00 23 11 15, § A.5.a.

"Money" is defined as currency, coins, and bank notes that are in current use and have a face value, traveler's checks and money orders that are held for sale to the public.[367] "Securities" means negotiable and non-negotiable instruments or contracts that represent either money or property and includes tokens, tickets, revenue and other stamps in current use and evidences of debt issued in connection with credit or charge cards that are not issued by the named insured, but does not include money.[368]

The carrier will also pay for loss of or damage to other property—meaning tangible property other than money and securities that has intrinsic value[369]—outside the premises in the care and custody of a messenger or an armored motor vehicle company that results directly from an actual or attempted robbery.[370] Robbery is unlawful taking of property from the care and custody of a person by another who has caused or threatened to cause that person bodily harm or committed an obviously unlawful act witnessed by that person.[371]

[i] Meaning of "Care and Custody" and of "Conveyed"

Two questions often arise when coverage is sought for a loss outside the premises. First, was the property at issue in the care and custody of the messenger? Second, was the property being "conveyed" by that messenger? Courts are divided on the first question. Some hold the property has to be in the personal, physical custody of the messenger for the coverage to apply.[372] Other courts say that actual custody is not required and that "protective custody," meaning reasonable attempts to protect and secure the insured property, is sufficient.[373] At one time, many policies referred to property outside the premises and "conveyed by a messenger" or "in transit." The standard ISO commercial crime policy no longer uses the word

---

367. ISO Form CR 00 23 11 15, § F.16.

368. ISO Form CR 00 23 11 15, § F.22.

369. ISO Form CR 00 23 11 15, § F.18. "Other property" does not include computer programs, electronic data, or any property specifically excluded by the policy.

370. ISO Form CR 00 23 11 15, § A.5.b.

371. ISO Form CR 00 23 11 15, § F.20.

372. *See, e.g.*, Cleveland Avenue Liquor Store, Inc. v. Home Ins. Co., 115 Ga. App. 864, 868, 156 S.E.2d 202, 205 (1967) (stolen or lost money has to be in immediate custody or possession of messenger at time of theft and that messenger must be conveying it rather than acting as custodian or repository; property left unprotected in car parked on public street was not in custody of messenger); Sansone v. American Ins. Co., 245 La. 674, 160 So. 2d 575 (1964) (messenger required to keep insured property in personal custody at all times).

373. *See, e.g.*, Deleson Steel Co. v. Hartford Ins. Group, 148 N.J. Super. 336, 339, 372 A.2d 663, 665 (1977) (payroll was under supervision and control of job superintendent of insured construction company when stolen, even though it was left unattended in locked van, where superintendent placed keys in his pocket and remained near where van was parked); Home Indem. Co. v. Desert Palace, 86 Nev. 234, 237, 468 P.2d 19, 21 (1970) (care and custody does not mean continuous, personal custody of messenger; property left in locked vehicle while employee of insured was conducting business for insured was in custody of that employee).

"conveyed," although some crime policies still refer to property "in transit."[374] Courts interpreting "conveyed" generally have held that property was not being conveyed by a messenger when that messenger was on a "frolic" of his or her own, substantially deviating from the reasonable course of carrying out the assigned delivery.[375] A common interest community association should be able to avoid protracted litigation over coverage by making certain that anyone entrusted with covered property outside the premises qualifies as a "messenger,"[376] retains the property in his or her personal custody until the assigned task is completed, and does not deviate from completion of that task to pursue personal matters.

[ii] Conditions

There are policy conditions that specifically apply to the robbery or safe burglary coverage. The first concerns a loss of money and securities in the care and custody of an armored motor vehicle company. The carrier will only pay for the amount of loss the named insured cannot recover under its contract with that company and from any insurance or indemnity carried by, or for the benefit of customers of, the company.[377] Additionally, the carrier will only pay up to $5,000 for any single occurrence of loss or damage to manuscripts, drawings, or records

---

374. *See, e.g.*, Travelers Crime Policy CRI-3001, § I.D (company will pay for loss of money or securities by theft, disappearance, damage, destruction, or robbery while property is in transit).

375. Deleson Steel Co. v. Hartford Ins. Group, 148 N.J. Super. 336, 342, 372 A.2d 663, 666 (1977). *See, e.g.*, Trad Television Corp. v. Hartford Acci. & Indem. Co., 35 N.J. Super. 36, 41, 113 A.2d 47, 50, *cert. den.*, 19 N.J. 330, 116 A.2d 827 (1955) (vice president of insured corporation had in his possession cash belonging to corporation to be delivered another officer, but before delivering it engaged in social activities and money was lost; insured failed adequately to prove that loss of money occurred while it was being conveyed by messenger); Sansone v. American Ins. Co., 245 La. 674, 160 So. 2d 575 (1964) (money entrusted to restaurant manager for deposit in bank was lost when manager had turned aside from function as messenger to engage in evening of social activities); O. K. Express Corp. v. Maryland Casualty Co., 10 A.D.2d 203, 205, 198 N.Y.S.2d 105, 107 (1960) (general manager for insured took company funds with him for safekeeping over weekend while engaged in social activities and, therefore, loss did not occur while money was being conveyed by messenger). *See also* State Liquor Stores v. United States Fire Ins. Co., 243 So. 2d 228, 232–33 (Fla. 1st DCA 1971) (president of insured was to convey funds from places of business to bank, but took money to his home at close of business on Saturday and intended to keep it until he could deposit it on following Monday morning; at time of robbery the money was not in the process of being conveyed). *Compare* Deleson Steel Co. v. Hartford Ins. Group, 148 N.J. Super. 336, 314, 372 A.2d 663, 666 (1977) ("conveyed" includes periods or instances of stops or non-motion reasonably necessary to accomplish insured operation as contemplated by parties; courts allow recovery when respite is merely minor deviation from reasonable course in accomplishing assigned mission); Home Indem. Co. v. Desert Palace, 86 Nev. 234, 238, 468 P.2d 19, 22 (1970) (examples of periods or instances of non-motion would include stops for traffic signals, necessary repairs or fuel, pickups or deliveries, and the like).

376. Messenger means an employee, which can include officers, directors, volunteers, and community association managers. For the definition of "employee," see § 15.03, *infra*.

377. ISO Form CR 00 23 11 15, § E.4.a. The same dollar limitation applies to loss of or damage to precious metals, precious or semiprecious stones, pearls, and furs, items that a common interest community is unlikely to possess.

of any kind, or the cost of reconstructing them or reproducing any information that is contained in them.[378]

[iii] Exclusions

There are exclusions that apply generally to theft that are discussed elsewhere,[379] and there are eight exclusions that apply specifically to this coverage. First, a loss that results from accounting or arithmetical errors or omissions is not covered.[380] Coverage for a loss that results from giving or surrendering property in any exchange or purchase is proscribed.[381] Generally, a loss or damage that results from fire is not covered, no matter how it is caused, except for loss of or damage to money and securities and loss from damage to a safe or vault.[382] A loss of property that is contained in a money-operated device is not covered except when an amount of money deposited in that device is recorded by a continuous recording instrument in it.[383] There is no coverage for loss of or damage to motor vehicles, trailers, semitrailers, or equipment and accessories attached to them.[384] When there is a loss from damage to the premises or its exterior, or to any safe, vault, cash register, cash box, cash drawer, or other property—meaning tangible property other than money and securities that has intrinsic value[385]—by vandalism or malicious mischief, it is not covered.[386] When the named insured, or anyone acting with the express or implied authority of the named insured is induced by a dishonest act to voluntarily relinquish title to or possession of any property and a loss results, coverage for that loss is excluded.[387]

Finally, there is an exclusion concerning transfer or surrender of property. Under it, there is no coverage for a loss of or damage to property subsequent to its transfer or surrender to a person or place that is outside the premises, or of financial institution premises, in two circumstances. The first is when the transfer or surrender was based on unauthorized instructions,[388] and the second is when it was as a result of a threat.[389] Those threats may include doing bodily harm, doing damage to property, introduction of a denial of service attack or virus,

---

378. ISO Form CR 00 23 11 15, § E.4.b.(2). The same dollar limitation applies to loss of or damage to precious metals, precious or semiprecious stones, pearls, and furs, items that a common interest community is unlikely to possess.

379. *See* § 15.04, *infra.*

380. ISO Form CR 00 23 11 15, § D.3.a.

381. ISO Form CR 00 23 11 15, § D.3.b.

382. ISO Form CR 00 23 11 15, § D.3.c.

383. ISO Form CR 00 23 11 15, § D.3.d.

384. ISO Form CR 00 23 11 15, § D.3.e.

385. ISO Form CR 00 23 11 15, § F.18. "Other property" does not include computer programs, electronic data, or any property specifically excluded by the policy.

386. ISO Form CR 00 23 11 15, § D.3.g.

387. ISO Form CR 00 23 11 15, § D.3.h.

388. ISO Form CR 00 23 11 15, § D.3.f.(1).(a).

389. ISO Form CR 00 23 11 15, § D.3.f.(1).(b).

or other malicious instruction into a computer system, contaminating, polluting, or rendering substandard the goods or products of the named insured, and disseminating, divulging, or using the confidential information of the named insured, the confidential or personal information of another person or organization, or weaknesses in the source code in a computer system. However, the exclusion does not apply to loss of money, securities, or other property while outside the premises in the care and custody of a messenger if the named insured either had no knowledge of any threat at the time the conveyance commenced or had knowledge of a threat at that time, but the loss was not related to it.[390]

[iv] The Travelers Crime Policy

The outside the premises coverage of the Travelers Crime Policy is similar, but not identical to, that of the ISO Commercial Crime Policy and is titled "In Transit." Under it, the insurer will pay the insured for a direct loss of money or securities that is directly caused by theft, disappearance, damage, or destruction *while in transit* outside the premises and in the care and custody of a messenger—including *while temporarily within the living quarters* of a messenger—or of an armored motor vehicle company.[391] The phrase "while temporarily within the living quarters" may be significant for common interest communities. There have, over the years, been cases in which a messenger took the property of his or her employer home over night or over a weekend, intending to deliver it later.[392] Questions can then arise about the status of the property and of the messenger while the property is in a private residence. Some common interest communities have no office or other common area where property can be safely stored. It is not unusual for officers or directors to keep association property in their homes temporarily pending its transfer or permanently, for that matter.[393] The Travelers policy makes clear that coverage applies when the property is temporarily in the home of a messenger. Associations that have an ISO Commercial Crime Policy and in which governing board members temporarily keep association property in their homes should discuss the extent to which the policy provides coverage during those temporary intervals.

The Travelers policy also provides coverage when the insured suffers a direct loss of, or the direct loss from damage to, its "other property"—meaning tangible property other than money and securities that has intrinsic value[394]—directly caused by an actual or attempted robbery *while in transit* outside the premises and

390. ISO Form CR 00 23 11 15, § D.3.f.(2).

391. Travelers Crime Policy CRI-3001, § I.D.1.

392. *See, e.g.*, State Liquor Stores v. United States Fire Ins. Co., 243 So. 2d 228, 232–33 (Fla. 1st DCA 1971) (president of insured was to convey funds from places of business to bank but took money to his home at close of business on Saturday).

393. The UCIOA notes that in smaller, self-managed associations, records may be kept by a unit owner. Uniform Common Interest Ownership Act § 3-118, comment 6.

394. Travelers Crime Policy CRI-3001, § III.KK.

in the care and custody of a messenger or an armored motor vehicle company.[395] Again, the insurer will also pay the insured for a direct loss of, or direct loss from damage to, the other property of the insured that is directly caused by an actual or attempted theft of that property *while it is temporarily within the living quarters* of a messenger.

The coverage under the "In Transit" insuring agreement begins immediately on receipt of the money, securities, or other property by the transporting party and ends immediately on delivery to the designated recipient or its agent.

[f] Computer and Funds Transfer Fraud

Computer-related crime is a growing problem. It can occur when someone uses the password of another on an off-premises computer to embezzle funds. For example, in one case, an association treasurer received an email containing a virus that purloined the ID and password to the association's bank account, allowing an electronic wire transfer that caused $147,000 to be wired to another bank.[396] The intent of the current standard commercial crime policy is that the policy cover only "hacking" incidents in which a fraudulent entry to a computer system or a change of data or a program in it results in a transfer of covered property.[397]

The standard commercial crime policy provides that the insurer will pay for a loss that results directly from a fraudulent entry of "electronic data"[398] or

---

395. Travelers Crime Policy CRI-3001, § I.D.2.

396. Branson, *Fidelity Bond Insurance: Protection Against Condo Crime* (Cooperator, 2014), available at: http://cooperator.com/articles/2823/1/Fidelity-Bond-Insurance/Page1.html.

397. Eubank, *It's Criminal What Agents DON'T Know About Crime Insurance*, at 15 (2014), available at: http://www.independentagent.com/Education/Webinars/SiteAssets/Pages/live-webinars/2014%20Crime%20Webinar%20Handout.pdf. *See, e.g.*, Universal Am. Corp. v. National Union Fire Ins. Co. of Pittsburgh, PA., 16 N.Y.S.3d 21, 23, 25 N.Y.3d 675, 680–81, 37 N.E.3d 78, 80 (2015) (finding no coverage for losses caused by authorized user's submission of fraudulent information into insured's computer system; language of policy unambiguously applied to losses incurred from unauthorized access to computer system of insured, and not to losses resulting from fraudulent content submitted to computer system by authorized users; term "fraudulent," while not defined, refers to deceit and dishonesty and intentional word placement of "fraudulent" before "entry" and "change" manifests intent to provide coverage for violation of integrity of computer system through deceitful and dishonest access). *See also* Apache Corp. v. Great Am. Ins. Co., 2016 U.S. App. LEXIS 18748 (5th Cir. Oct. 18, 2016) (where only "computer use" was email received by insured from criminals posing as vendor of insured with instructions to change vendor's payment information and to make all future payments to new bank account, email was part of fraudulent scheme, but was merely incidental to occurrence of authorized transfer of money; to interpret computer-fraud coverage as reaching any fraudulent scheme in which email communication was part of process would convert policy and make it one for general fraud).

398. "Electronic data" is information, facts, images, or sounds stored as or on, created or used on, or transmitted to or from computer software on data storage devices, including disks, CD-ROMs, tapes, drives, cells, data processing devices or any other media used with electronically controlled equipment. ISO Form CR 00 23 11 15, § F.6.

computer program into, or electronic data or "computer program"[399] within, any "computer system"[400] that is owned, leased, or operated by the named insured.[401] The coverage is for a fraudulent entry or fraudulent change that causes *money*,[402] securities,[403] or other property,[404] to be transferred, paid, or delivered or an account of the named insured to be debited or deleted. There is also coverage for a loss that results directly from a fraudulent instruction directing a financial institution to debit a "transfer account"[405] of the named insured and transfer, pay, or deliver money or securities from that account.[406]

"Fraudulent entry" or "fraudulent change" of electronic data or computer programs includes entry or change made by an employee acting, in good faith, on a fraudulent instruction received from a computer software contractor who has a written agreement with the named insured to design, implement, or service computer programs for a computer system covered under the insuring agreement for computer and funds transfer fraud.[407]

The insurer will only pay up to $5,000 for any one occurrence of loss of or damage to manuscripts, drawings, or records of any kind, or the cost of

---

399. A "computer program" is a set of related electronic instructions that direct operation and function of a computer or devices connected to it and that allow the computer or devices to receive, process, store, or send electronic data. ISO Form CR 00 23 11 15, § F.1.

400. A "computer system" is a computer, including Personal Digital Assistants (PDAs), and other transportable or handheld devices, electronic storage devices, related peripheral components, systems and applications software, and related communications networks by which electronic data is collected, transmitted, processed, stored, or retrieved. ISO Form CR 00 23 11 15, § F.2.

401. ISO Form CR 00 23 11 15, § A.6.a.(1).

402. Generally, "money" is defined as currency, coins, and bank notes that are in current use and have a face value, traveler's checks and money orders that are held for sale to the public, and deposits in the account of the named insured at any financial institution. Additionally, for purposes of the computer and funds transfer fraud coverage, it also means deposits in an account of the named insured at a financial institution. ISO Form CR 00 23 11 15, § F.16. A "financial institution" with regard to the computer and funds transfer fraud coverage is a bank, savings bank, savings and loan association, trust company, credit union, similar depository institution, insurance company, or stock brokerage firm or investment company. *See* ISO Form CR 00 23 11 15, § F.9.b.

403. "Securities" means negotiable and non-negotiable instruments or contracts that represent either money or property and includes tokens, tickets, revenue, and other stamps in current use and evidences of debt issued in connection with credit or charge cards that are not issued by the named insured, but does not include money. ISO Form CR 00 23 11 15, § F.22.

404. "Other property" is tangible property other than money and securities that has intrinsic value, but does not include computer programs, electronic data, or any property specifically excluded by the policy. ISO Form CR 00 23 11 15, § F.18.

405. A "transfer account" is one maintained by the named insured at a financial institution from which the transfer, payment, or delivery of money or securities can be initiated by means of computer, telefacsimile, telephone, other electronic instructions, or written instructions—other than those covered by the forgery and alteration insuring agreement—that establish conditions under which transfers are to be initiated by the financial institution through an electronic funds transfer system. ISO Form CR 00 23 11 15, § F.24.

406. ISO Form CR 00 23 11 15, § A.6.a.(2).

407. ISO Form CR 00 23 11 15, § A.6.b.

reconstructing them or reproducing any information contained in them.[408] Ordinarily, the policy only covers a loss that results directly from an occurrence taking place in the United States of America—including its territories and possessions—Puerto Rico, and Canada;[409] however, the computer and transfer funds fraud coverage is for an occurrence taking place anywhere in the world.[410]

[i] Exclusions

The computer fraud coverage is not intended to cover theft by an employee. To that end, a generally applicable exclusion provides that the policy does not cover a loss that results from theft, or any other dishonest act, committed by any of the employees, directors, trustees, or authorized representatives of the named insured unless specifically covered by the employee theft insuring agreement.[411] The exclusion was applied in a case in which the insured was a community association management company. An employee of the company stole substantial sums from the accounts of the associations the company managed. The insurer argued the loss was not covered under the computer fraud provision of the policy and the court, citing the exclusion, agreed. Any coverage would be pursuant to the employee theft provision.[412]

There are also exclusions that specifically apply to the insuring agreement for computer and funds transfer fraud. It does not cover any loss that results from a fraudulent entry of electronic data or computer program into, or change of electronic data or computer program within, any computer system owned, leased, or operated by the named insured by a person or organization with authorized access to that computer system, unless an employee acts in good faith on a fraudulent instruction.[413] There is also no coverage for either a loss that results from the use, or purported use, of credit, debit, charge, access, convenience, identification, stored-value, or other cards or the information contained on those cards,[414] or that results from giving or surrendering property in any exchange or purchase.[415] Unless otherwise covered under the insuring agreement for computer and funds transfer fraud, the policy does not cover a loss that results from an employee or financial institution acting on an instruction to transfer, pay, or deliver money,

408. CR 00 23 11 15, § E.5.a.

409. CR 00 23 11 15, § E.1.v. See CR 00 22 11 15, § E.1.u. for the same provision in the Discovery Form of the commercial crime policy.

410. CR 00 23 11 15, § E.5.b.

411. CR 00 23 11 15, § D.1.c.

412. Cedar Lake Homeowners Ass'n v. Northwest Empire Cmty. Mgmt., 2015 U.S. Dist. LEXIS 174503 (D. Or. Nov. 13, 2015). The opinion did not reveal any computer-related conduct by the employee. A prior opinion, however, disclosed that the U.S. Department of Justice charged the employee with wire fraud related to his theft and misappropriation. Cedar Lake Homeowners Ass'n v. Northwest Empire Cmty. Mgmt., 2015 U.S. Dist. LEXIS 140972 (D. Or. Aug. 21, 2015).

413. CR 00 23 11 15, § D.4.a. See CR 00 23 11 15, § A.6.b for the exception.

414. CR 00 23 11 15, § D.4.b.

415. CR 00 23 11 15, § D.4.c.

securities, or other property or debit or delete the account of the named insured when that instruction proves to be fraudulent.[416] Finally, there is no coverage for a loss, or a part of a loss, for which the proof of its existence or amount depends on an inventory computation or a profit and loss computation.[417]

[ii] The Travelers Crime Policy

The Travelers Crime Policy provides coverage for "funds transfer fraud." It simply states that the insurer will pay the insured for a direct loss of money and securities in a transfer account of the insured when the loss is directly caused by funds transfer fraud.[418] A transfer account is one maintained by the insured at a financial institution from which the insured is able to initiate the transfer, payment, or delivery of money or securities by electronic, telegraphic, cable, teletype, telefacsimile, or telephone instructions communicated directly or through an electronic funds transfer system or by written instructions that establish conditions under which transfers are to be initiated by the financial institution through an electronic funds transfer system.[419]

"Funds transfer fraud" is defined in three ways. First, it means an electronic, telegraphic, cable, teletype, or telephone instruction that is fraudulently transmitted to a financial institution directing it to debit a transfer account and to transfer, pay, or deliver money or securities from the account when the instruction purports to have been transmitted by the insured, but was actually fraudulently transmitted by someone else without the knowledge or consent of the insured.[420] Second, it means a fraudulent written instruction—except one covered under the forgery and alteration insuring agreement—that is issued to a financial institution that directs it to debit a transfer account and transfer, pay, or deliver money or securities from that account by use of an electronic funds transfer system at specified intervals or under specified conditions, when the written instruction purports to have been issued by the insured but was actually fraudulently issued, forged, or altered by someone else without the knowledge or consent of the insured.[421] Finally, funds transfer fraud means an electronic, telegraphic, cable, teletype, telefacsimile, telephone, or written instruction that is initially received by the insured purporting to have been transmitted by an employee, but that was in fact fraudulently transmitted by someone else without the consent the insured or the employee.[422]

416. CR 00 23 11 15, § D.4.d.
417. CR 00 23 11 15, § D.4.e.
418. Travelers Crime Policy CRI-3001, § I.G.
419. Travelers Crime Policy CRI-3001, § III.VV.
420. Travelers Crime Policy CRI-3001, § III.AA.1.
421. Travelers Crime Policy CRI-3001, § III.AA.2.
422. Travelers Crime Policy CRI-3001, § III.AA.3.

[g] Money Orders and Counterfeit Money

The final insuring clause in the standard ISO Commercial Crime Policy provides coverage for money orders and counterfeit money. Under it, the insurer will pay for a loss that results directly from the named insured having, in good faith, accepted either money orders issued by a post office, express company, or financial institution[423] that are not paid on presentation or counterfeit money[424] acquired during the regular course of business in exchange for money[425] or services.[426] The Travelers Crime Policy is substantially similar except that the issuer of any money order has to be located in the United States, its territories and possessions, Canada, or any other country in which the insured maintains physical premises.[427] Also, the ISO policy does not specify the country of origin of counterfeit money while the Travelers policy specifies that its coverage is provided for counterfeit money of the United States, its territories and possessions, Canada, or any other country in which the insured maintains physical premises.[428]

[6] Identity Fraud Expense

The ISO Commercial Crime Policy can be modified by endorsement to add "Identity Fraud Expense" coverage.[429] "Identity fraud" is defined as knowingly transferring or using, without lawful authority, a means of identification of the business of the named insured as shown on the Declarations Page or of any insured person—meaning any director, trustee, or employee of any insured[430]—with intent to commit, or to aid or abet someone else to commit, any unlawful activity constituting a violation of federal law or a felony under any applicable law.[431] The endorsement lists eight specific "expenses" that result directly from identity fraud for which the insurer will pay when incurred by either the named insured or any insured person.[432] One of those expenses is the reasonable attorney's fees required to defend lawsuits brought against the named insured by merchants, vendors, suppliers, financial institutions, or their collection agencies, to remove criminal or civil judgments wrongly entered against the named insured, and to challenge the accuracy or completeness of any information in a consumer

423. See ISO Form CR 00 23 11 15, § F.9, for the definition of "financial institution."

424. Counterfeit money is an imitation of money intended to deceive and to be taken as genuine. ISO Form CR 00 23 11 15, § F.3.

425. "Money" is defined as currency, coins, and bank notes that are in current use and have a face value, traveler's checks, and money orders that are held for sale to the public. ISO Form CR 00 23 11 15, § F.16.

426. ISO Form CR 00 23 11 15, § A.7.

427. Travelers Crime Policy CRI-3001, § I.E.1.

428. Travelers Crime Policy CRI-3001, § I.E.2.

429. *See* ISO Form CR 04 15 08 13.

430. *See* ISO Form CR 04 15 08 13, § E.3. A schedule incorporated into the endorsement can exclude any of these persons.

431. *See* ISO Form CR 04 15 08 13, E.2.

432. *See* ISO Form CR 04 15 08 13, A.

credit report for the named insured.[433] The insurer also will pay for reasonable expenses incurred with its written consent.[434]

Some experts question the value of identity theft coverage because typically—as is the case with both the Travelers policy and ISO endorsement—it does not cover the loss of money stolen from the insured, but only expenses incurred in resolving the identity theft.[435] Coverage for actual losses requires a separate specific policy.

[7] Claims Expenses

The standard ISO Commercial Crime Policy does not cover claims expenses. Indeed, the policy specifically excludes payment of costs, fees, or other expenses incurred in establishing either the existence or amount of a loss under the policy.[436]

The Travelers Crime Policy, on the other hand, does provide coverage for "claim expenses." It defines "claim expenses" as reasonable fees, costs, and expenses of outside accountants, attorneys, consultants, or experts retained by the insured to determine the amount and extent of loss covered under the policy, but does not include any of internal corporate fees, costs whether direct or indirect, or obligations or employee wages and salaries.[437] The reasonableness of expenses is determined by the company. It will pay for reasonable claim expenses that are incurred and paid by the insured to establish the existence, amount, and preparation of its proof of loss in support of a covered claim for loss under any coverages of the policy.[438] There are three conditions to this coverage. First, any claim expenses payable to the insured are only applicable to a covered loss that exceeds the "single loss retention" for the insuring agreement—coverage—that is the subject of a claim.[439] The single loss retention is an amount shown on the Declarations Page. The insurer will only pay for a single loss when it exceeds that amount.[440] Generally, a "single loss" means an act or series of related acts or events involving one or more persons, an act, acts, or events involving a person or group of persons acting together, whether identified or not, both during and before the policy period.[441] Second, claim expenses payable to the insured are in addition to the single loss limit shown on the Declarations Page for the insuring

433. *See* ISO Form CR 04 15 08 13, E.1.g.

434. *See* ISO Form CR 04 15 08 13, E.1.i.

435. Clarke, *Is ID Theft Insurance Worth Recommending to Agency Clients?* (Insurance Journal 2008), available at: http://www.insurancejournal.com/news/national/2008/10/09/94495.htm. The author notes that Travelers and AIG are the largest writers of group ID theft expense reimbursement policies. Non-group policies, says the author, typically cost $50 to $70 for $15,000 to $25,000 in coverage.

436. CR 00 23 11 15, § D.1.g.(3).

437. Travelers Crime Policy CRI-3001, § III.B.

438. Travelers Crime Policy CRI-3001, § I.I.

439. Travelers Crime Policy CRI-3001, § I.I.1.

440. Travelers Crime Policy CRI-3001, § V.B.2.

441. Travelers Crime Policy CRI-3001, § III.R.3.

agreement—coverage—that is the subject of a claim.[442] For example, if the single loss limit for employee theft shown on the Declarations Page is $500,000 and the insurer pays a claim in that amount, it will still pay the insureds claim expenses, although the claim expense single loss limit is typically a small amount, perhaps only $5,000. Finally, claim expenses payable to the insured will be paid at the same time as payment of the valid and collectible loss under the insuring agreement that is the subject of a claim.[443]

An endorsement can be added to a standard ISO commercial crime policy to add coverage for claim expenses.[444] Under that endorsement, the insurer will pay for reasonable costs, fees, or other expenses the named insured incurs and pays to an independent accounting, auditing, or other service that is used to determine the amount of loss covered under the policy. The most it will pay is the lesser of the limit of insurance or a percentage of the covered loss shown on a schedule in the endorsement, and the amount it pays is part of—not in addition to—the limit of insurance for the applicable coverage. The carrier will not pay if the amount of the covered loss does not exceed any deductible amount for the applicable coverage. Payment will only be made after settlement of a covered loss. Finally, the endorsement modifies the policy exclusion to bar coverage for payment of costs, fees, or other expenses incurred in establishing the existence—but not amount—of a loss under the policy. That makes the coverage under the ISO endorsement narrower than that provided by the Travelers policy.

[8] Computer Crime

The Travelers Crime Policy includes as a standard part of its coverage "computer crime." The first part of the coverage concerns "computer fraud." Computer fraud is the use of a computer to fraudulently cause a transfer of money, securities, or other property from inside the premises of the insured or a financial institution to a person—other than a messenger, meaning an employee, director, or officer of the insured[445]—outside those premises or to a place outside those premises.[446] The insurer will pay the insured for direct loss of, or direct loss from damage to, money, securities, and other property caused directly by computer fraud.[447]

The second part of the coverage is for computer program and electronic data restoration expenses.[448] Under this part of the coverage, the insurance company will pay the insured for reasonable restoration expenses incurred by the insured

---

442. Travelers Crime Policy CRI-3001, § I.I.2.
443. Travelers Crime Policy CRI-3001, § I.I.3.
444. *See* ISO Form CR 25 40 08 13.
445. Travelers Crime Policy CRI-3001, § III.HH.
446. Travelers Crime Policy CRI-3001, § III.E.
447. Travelers Crime Policy CRI-3001, § I.F.1.
448. Travelers Crime Policy CRI-3001, § I.F.2.

to restore or replace damaged or destroyed computer programs[449] or electronic data[450] stored within the computer system[451] of the insured when that damage or destruction is caused directly by a computer violation. A "computer violation" is a computer virus that is designed to damage or destroy a computer program or electronic data or vandalism by a natural person, including by an employee, who has gained unauthorized electronic access to the computer system of the insured.[452] Note that the unauthorized access is access to the computer system of the insured; therefore, the policy apparently does not cover restoration expenses when the vandalism is the result of unauthorized access to other computers that may be used to conduct the business of the insured. For example, in many common interest communities the association may not have a computer, but officers and directors conduct association business on their own computers. These associations may want to confer with their broker to determine whether computers owned by association officers and directors are eligible for restoration expense coverage. They should note that payment of reasonable restoration expense only applies to computer programs and electronic data that the insured owns or leases, or for which the insured is *legally liable*.

Restoration expenses are those reasonable costs incurred by the insured to reproduce computer programs or electronic data to allow restoration of the computer system to the level of operational capability existing immediately prior to a computer violation.[453] Among the expenses that are specifically excepted from restoration costs are internal corporate costs and expenses, including employee remuneration, any costs related to any legal action, expenses incurred for reconstruction of computer programs and electronic data when the insured knowingly used illegal copies of programs, and expenses incurred to design, update, or improve computer programs or electronic data or to perfect their operation or performance.

---

449. A "computer program" is a set of related electronic instructions that direct the operations and functions of a computer system, or devices connected to it, that enable the system or devices to receive, process, store, retrieve, send, create, or otherwise act on electronic data. Travelers Crime Policy CRI-3001, § III.F.

450. "Electronic data" means facts or information converted to a form that can be used in a computer system that does not provide instructions or directions to a computer system or that is stored on electronic processing media for use by a computer program. Travelers Crime Policy CRI-3001, § III.Q.

451. A "computer system" is a computer and all input, output, processing, storage, and communication facilities and equipment connected to the device. The operating system or application software are to be under the direct operational control of the insured. Travelers Crime Policy CRI-3001, § III.G.

452. Travelers Crime Policy CRI-3001, § III.H. A "computer virus" is a set of unauthorized instructions, programmatic or otherwise, directed solely against the insured that propagate themselves through the computer system or networks, provided the instructions were maliciously introduced by a natural person. Travelers Crime Policy CRI-3001, § III.I.

453. Travelers Crime Policy CRI-3001, § III.NN.

For purposes of the restoration expense coverage, a single loss involving computer program and electronic data restoration expense applies to reasonable restoration expense incurred by the insured between the time the insured discovers the damage or destruction and the time the computer program or electronic data is restored to the level of operational capability that existed immediately before the computer violation. Recurrence of the same computer virus after the computer program or electronic data has been restored is a separate single loss.

Payment of reasonable restoration expense only applies to computer programs and electronic data that the insured owns or leases, or for which the insured is legally liable and only if the insured is unable to reproduce the computer programs or electronic data from back-up data copies.

Payment of reasonable restoration expenses is made on completion of the restoration of the damaged or destroyed computer programs or electronic data. If a single loss is covered under both the computer fraud and restoration expenses coverages, only the retention for a single loss under the computer fraud coverage will apply and payment of and restoration expense will be part of, not in addition to, the single loss limit of insurance for computer fraud.

[9] Personal Accounts Protection

The Travelers Crime Policy includes as a standard part of its coverage "personal accounts protection." The coverage has two parts. First the insurer will pay the insured, on behalf of a management staff member, for a loss incurred by that management staff member that is directly caused by forgery or alteration of, on, or in any written covered personal instruments that are either drawn on personal accounts of the management staff member—or purported to have been so drawn—or made or drawn by one acting as an agent of the management staff member, or purport to have been so made or drawn.[454] Management staff members includes directors, trustees, and officers of the insured.[455] A "covered personal instrument" is a check, draft, promissory note, or similar written promise, orders, or directions to pay a sum certain in money, and written instruments required in conjunction with any transaction involving any credit, debit, or charge card issued to a management staff member for personal use.[456]

Under the second part of the personal account protection, the insurance company will reimburse the insured, on behalf of a management staff member,

454. Travelers Crime Policy CRI-3001, § I.F.1. A signature that is a mechanical or electronic reproduction of a handwritten signature produced by a mechanical check-writing machine or a computer printer is treated the same as a handwritten signature. An electronic signature, however, is not treated the same as a mechanical or electronic reproduction of a handwritten signature and is not a forgery under the personal accounts protection coverage. For purposes of the coverage, the term "check" includes a substitute check as defined in the Check Clearing for the 21st Century Act, and is treated the same as the original it replaced.

455. Travelers Crime Policy CRI-3001, § III.GG.

456. Travelers Crime Policy CRI-3001, § III.L.

for an identity fraud expense incurred by that management staff member as a direct result of any identity fraud.[457] The policy defines "identity fraud" as the act of knowingly transferring or using, without lawful authority, a means of identification of a management staff member with intent to commit, aid, or abet any unlawful activity constituting a violation of federal law or a felony in any applicable jurisdiction.[458] The policy lists seven "identity fraud expenses"[459] including reasonable attorney's fees that are incurred, with the prior written consent of the insurer, for defense of any lawsuits that are brought against a management staff member by financial institutions, merchants, other credit grantors, or their collection agencies, removal of any criminal or civil judgments wrongly entered against a member, or challenging the accuracy or completeness of any information in a consumer credit report.[460]

Coverage for personal accounts of specified persons can be added to the standard ISO Commercial Crime Policy by endorsement. The endorsement modifies the policy and applies to the forgery or alteration insuring agreement.[461] It includes a schedule for listing the names of persons to whom it applies and the applicable limit of insurance. The endorsement provides that each person named on the schedule is an insured under the coverage for forgery or alteration, but only for a loss involving covered instruments of that person's *personal account*. The coverage is subject to the limit of insurance shown on the Schedule, and that limit is part of, not in addition to, the limit shown on the Declarations Page.

§ 15.03 Definition of "Employee"

For two parts of the coverage of standard commercial crime policies, the definition of "employee" is critical.[462] The first is employee theft.[463] The second is loss of money or securities or loss of or damage to "other property"—meaning tangible property other than money and securities that has intrinsic value[464]—while outside the premises of the insured and in the care and custody of a "messenger,"[465] which means, *inter alia*, an employee.[466] To illustrate the meaning of "employee,"

457. Travelers Crime Policy CRI-3001, § I.F.2.

458. Travelers Crime Policy CRI-3001, § III.BB.

459. Travelers Crime Policy CRI-3001, § III.CC.

460. Travelers Crime Policy CRI-3001, § III.CC.6.

461. ISO Form CR 25 22 08 07.

462. *See generally* Koch, *Who is an Employee—Known or Unknown—Under the Crime Policy?*, I Fid. L.J. 5 (1995); Elliott, *Who is an Employee Under Fidelity Coverage*, 14 Forum 620 (1979).

463. *See, e.g.*, ISO Form CR 00 22 11 15, § A.1.

464. ISO Form CR 00 23 11 15, § F.18. "Other property" does not include computer programs, electronic data, or any property specifically excluded by the policy.

465. *See, e.g.*, ISO Form CR 00 23 11 15, § A.5

466. *See, e.g.*, ISO Form CR 00 23 11 15, § F.15. Note that the Travelers policy defines "messenger" as any management staff member, or relative thereof, any officer-shareholder, or any employee, duly authorized. Travelers Crime Policy CRI-3001, § III.HH. The term "management

the definition of the standard ISO Commercial Crime Policy is compared with that of the widely used Crime Policy of the Travelers Insurance Company.

[1] Basic Definition

Both policies initially define an "employee" as a natural person while in the service of the insured who is compensated by the insured directly by salary, wages, or commissions and who the insured has the *right to direct and control*[467] while that person is performing services for the insured.[468] Ultimately, in applying the definition, the determination of who qualifies as an employee is fact-driven.[469]

Note that in the typical crime policy, an employee of *any* insured is considered an employee of *every* insured.[470] Thus, if a common interest community association is an additional insured on the policy of its community association manager, anyone considered an employee of the association would also be considered an employee of the CAM, and *vice versa.*

Under the ISO policy a person is included in the definition of "employee" for the first 30 days immediately after termination, unless that termination was because of theft or any other dishonest act.[471] The Travelers policy expands the time frame to 60 days unless a termination is because of theft or *forgery* or any other dishonest act.[472]

[a] Association Officers and Directors[473]

The basic definition of "employee" would rarely apply to officers and directors in a common interest community because they are almost never compensated by the association. Yet experts agree that associations need coverage for the acts

---

staff member" includes members of the board of directors or trustees, officers, risk managers, and in-house general counsel. Travelers Crime Policy CRI-3001, § III.GG. An "officer-shareholder" is an officer who has a 25 percent or greater ownership interest in any one or more insureds. Travelers Crime Policy CRI-3001, § III.JJ.

467. *See* Bird v. Centennial Ins. Co., 11 F.3d 228, 233 (1st Cir. 1993) ("right to govern and direct" language materially limits definition of "employee" to those persons over whom corporate insureds have control).

468. ISO Form CR 00 23 11 15, § F.7.a.(1); Travelers Crime Policy CRI-3001, § III.S.1.

469. Three Garden Village Ltd. P'ship v. U.S. Fid. & Guar. Co., 567 A.2d 85, 109 (Md. 1989) (whether individual is employee within standard commercial fidelity bonds depends on facts of given case).

470. ISO Form CR 00 23 11 15, § E.1.l.(3); Travelers Crime Policy CRI-3001, § II.A.3.

471. ISO Form CR 00 23 11 15, § F.7.a.(1)(a).

472. Travelers Crime Policy CRI-3001, § III.S.1.a. Note that under the policy an employee is also any individual described as an employee in the policy while that person is on medical, military, or other leave of absence from the insured and coverage applies to that employee while on leave, regardless of whether he or she remains subject to the direction and control of the insured during the time of leave.

473. The reader should understand that a crime policy protects the association from loss and if officers and directors are "covered" under the policy, it means the *association* is covered for losses resulting from their acts. The association also will have a D&O policy that primarily covers directors and officers if a claim is made against them.

of officers and directors.[474] In the typical association, most directors are also officers. Associations usually have governing boards consisting of three to nine directors elected by the membership. The most common number of directors appears to be five. There are also usually four officers: President, Vice President, Secretary, and Treasurer. The officers are almost always chosen by the directors from among their own number. Thus, in many associations all but one director will be an officer. As explained below, policies generally expand the definition of "employee" to include directors in particular circumstances. However, associations need the definition of "employee" to apply broadly to its directors because, unlike in a large business corporation in which directors meet occasionally to set policy, the directors in a residential association do much of the work of the association. Some have access to its funds, and all probably have access to at least some covered property.[475] Officers who are uncompensated may be considered employees in some policies or may be added by endorsement to the definition of "employee." The particular language of policies and applicable endorsements regarding officers and directors is discussed in more detail below.[476]

[b] Independent Contractors

Crime policies specifically exclude independent contractors from the definition of "employee."[477] An insured has the duty to bring its claim within the policy coverage,[478] and where coverage is based on wrongdoing by an employee the

474. *Fidelity Insurance*, available at: http://www.davis-stirling.com/tabid/1664/default.aspx (associations need broadest possible coverage to include board members, committee members, managers, bookkeepers, and anyone else who may have access to association's money); *What Is Fidelity Insurance and Why Your Association Needs It*, available at: http://www.hindmansanchez.com/resources/newsletter/what-fidelity-insurance-and-why-your-association-needs-it/ (non-salaried board members do not meet definition of "employee" and to protect association from theft by those with access to assets, but not technically "employees," it needs endorsement to policy that expands definition of "employee" to include directors); Branson, *Fidelity Bond Insurance: Protection Against Condo Crime* (Cooperator, 2014), available at: http://cooperator.com/articles/2823/1/Fidelity-Bond-Insurance/Page1.html (definition of "employee" should be extended to cover non-compensated board members); Treese, *Risk Management Essential to Insurance Plan* (CAI 1995) (fidelity must be endorsed to provide for theft by non-compensated individuals such as board or committee members); Scarr, *Fidelity Bonding* (Common Ground 1990) (for associations, employee definition should be extended to cover directors and officers as well as salaried employees such as manager and bookkeeper).

475. Experts recommend that only a select group of people should handle the operating funds. These would include the management company or on-site manager, directors, president, and treasurer. March, *Guarding the VAULT* (Common Ground 1993).

476. *See* § 15.03[6], *infra*.

477. ISO Form CR 00 23 11 15, § F.7.b; Travelers Crime Policy CRI-3001, § III.S. Actually, the policies more broadly exclude agents and independent contractors or "representatives of the same general character" from the definition of "employee."

478. *See, e.g.*, Southeast Bakery Feeds v. Ranger Ins. Co., 974 S.W.2d 635, 638 (Mo. App. 1998) (under Missouri law insured has burden of showing by substantial evidence that its claim falls within coverage provided by insurance contract).

insured may have to show the wrongdoer was an employee. The insurer may respond that the person was actually an independent contractor. In general, an independent contractor is a person or entity with which an association contracts for services, for example, a landscaping company or community association manager. A legal definition of "independent contractor" is someone who contracts with another to do something for that other party, but who is not controlled by the other party or subject to the right of the other party to control the contractor's physical conduct in the performance of the undertaking.[479] That definition leaves considerable room for debate. The case involving a condominium association in the next subsection illustrates that fact. There is a large body of law on the question of whether someone is an independent contractor or an employee. That is a topic beyond the scope of this treatise, but it is one for which associations should seek the guidance of their counsel.

Because the conduct of independent contractors is not covered under an association policy, when the association hires an independent contractor it needs to insist that person or entity have insurance coverage naming the association as an additional insured. That coverage would include commercial general liability, workers' compensation, and crime/fidelity insurance.

[c] The Importance of Documenting Employee Status

Most businesses memorialize the status of service providers in contracts and other documents. Common interest community associations, however, are run by volunteers with varying levels of business experience. They may not properly document the status of those whom they engage to provide services. For example, a condominium association acted as its own general contractor to make renovations to the property. It hired an individual to act as construction manager. The association alleged the construction manager misappropriated funds and submitted an insurance claim. The insurer denied the claim, concluding the construction manager was an independent contractor.

The association apparently did not execute a clear contract with the construction manager. Instead there was a letter addressed to the president of the association that referred to a "professional services contract" for the manager. The letter, together with attachments, outlined the duties and compensation of the manager. The letter was signed by the association president but not the construction

479. Restatement of Agency (Second), § 2(3). *See, e.g.*, Mansion Hills Condo. Ass'n v. Am. Family Mut. Ins. Co., 62 S.W.3d 633, 637, n.3 (Mo. App. 2001) (office manager employed by "employment contractor" to staff condominium association office was not independent contractor because association controlled her daily work activities); Mt. Lodge Ass'n v. Crum & Forster Indem. Co., 210 W. Va. 536, 558 S.E.2d 336 (2001) (if association had right of control over manner in which "construction manager" performed his duties in that role, he was employee covered by policy at issue, but if association did not have that right of control, he was independent contractor not covered by policy).

manager. There were also documents disclosing a plan to pay the construction manager for his services in a series of installments, plus a possible bonus. The minutes of a governing board meeting showed that the board approved a plan to hire the construction manager to "work for the board." The trial court decided the construction manager was an independent contractor because the association had failed to retain control over him. The appellate court treated the letter as at least a part of a contract and reversed because it found the documents in evidence did not directly address the right to control and supervise the work of the construction manager. The court said it could not conclude that the lower court had before it a full picture of the relationship between the parties, and it remanded the case to that court for a full examination of the factual issues and for further development of the record as might be appropriate.[480]

The association could have avoided costly and protracted litigation had it properly executed an agreement establishing an employee and employer relationship between the parties. Here is a good example of why an association should consult its attorney before beginning a project that requires it to engage the services of others. The attorney could have explained the significance of the status of the construction manager, provided the association with an appropriate contract, and made sure it was properly executed. The attorney's fees the association would have expended for that guidance would have been a fraction of the over $50,000 they may have lost if the lower court ended up finding for the insurer.

[2] Temporary Workers

The second part of the definition in both the Travelers and standard ISO policies concerns temporary workers. Both policies define an "employee" to include a natural person temporarily furnished to the insured to substitute for a permanent employee who is on leave or to meet seasonal or short-term workloads while that temporary worker is subject to the direction and control of the insured and performing services for the insured.[481] The Travelers policy provides that the employee for whom the temporary worker is substituted must be on medical, military, or other leave of absence, and specifically excludes from the definition anyone with care and custody of property outside the premises of the insured.[482]

[3] Leased Workers

Leased workers are included in the definition of "employee." Both policies provide that a natural person—other than a temporary employee as described above—leased to the insured under a written agreement between the insured and a labor leasing firm for the purpose of performing duties related to the conduct

480. Mt. Lodge Ass'n v. Crum & Forster Indem. Co., 210 W. Va. 536, 558 S.E.2d 336 (2001).
481. ISO Form CR 00 23 11 15, § F.7.a.(2); Travelers Crime Policy CRI-3001, § III.S.2.
482. Travelers Crime Policy CRI-3001, § III.S.2.b.

of the business of the insured is an employee.[483] The Travelers policy adds the condition that the leased worker is an employee while subject to the direction and control of the insured.

What is a "labor leasing firm"? Policies do not define the term. There are endorsements added to commercial property policies that provide coverage for "employee dishonesty" and define "employee" to include a natural person employed by an "employment contractor," while that person is subject to the direction and control of the named insured and performing services for the named insured. In one case, the developer of a condominium community was hired by the association to manage the property and staff the condominium office. The developer provided the association with an on-site office manager who embezzled a considerable amount of money from the association. The association submitted a claim under its employee dishonesty coverage. The office manager was clearly not an employee of the association, so the issue was whether she was an employee of an "employment contractor," a term not defined in the policy. The insurer contended "employment contractor" was unambiguous and that its plain meaning referred to temporary employment services or agencies. The court did not agree. It found the term to be ambiguous and, construing it against the insurer, found that it could encompass the development company. A reasonable policyholder, said the court, might have assumed that "employment contractor" meant any third party who contracted to provide workers for another.[484] Would a court similarly find "labor leasing firm" to be an ambiguous phrase?

[4] Consultants

When the insured retains a former employee, director, or trustee as a consultant, both policies provide that person is an employee while he or she performs services for the insured.[485] The Travelers policy adds the condition that the consultant is an employee while subject to the direction and control of the insured.

[5] Interns

Under both policies, a guest student or intern who is pursuing studies or duties is considered an employee.[486] The Travelers policy requires that the guest student or intern be pursuing studies or duties in any office or premises of the insured and that he or she is an employee while subject to the direction and control of the insured and performing services for the insured.

483. ISO Form CR 00 23 11 15, § F.7.a.(3); Travelers Crime Policy CRI-3001, § III.S.3.
484. Mansion Hills Condo. Ass'n v. Am. Family Mut. Ins. Co., 62 S.W.3d 633 (Mo. App. 2001).
485. ISO Form CR 00 23 11 15, § F.7.a.(5); Travelers Crime Policy CRI-3001, § III.S.4.e.
486. ISO Form CR 00 23 11 15, § F.7.a.(6); Travelers Crime Policy CRI-3001, § III.S.4.f.

[6] Directors, Trustees, or Officers Considered as "Employees"

Some policies may omit directors entirely from the definition of "employee" or impose rigid restrictions on the circumstances in which they are considered employees. In the typical large business corporation, directors are policy makers who are not involved in the day-to-day operations of the insured. In a common interest community, especially a small one without professional management, the directors often have responsibility for day-to-day operations. Typically, the officers are also directors. It is important, therefore, that the association determine whether directors and/or officers are considered employees under the policy.

[a] Directors as Employees in Limited Circumstances

Both the standard ISO Commercial Crime Policy and the Travelers Crime Policy define "directors" or "trustees" of the insured as employees in specific circumstances. Under the Travelers policy a member of a board of directors or trustees is an employee while acting as a member of any elected or appointed committee of the insured—including any member of a committee—to perform specific, as distinguished from general, directorial acts on behalf of the insured.[487] The ISO policy is broader. It provides directors or trustees are employees while performing acts within the *scope of the usual duties of an employee* as well as acting as a member of any committee duly elected or appointed by resolution of the governing board to perform specific, as opposed to general, directorial acts on behalf of the insured.[488]

What are "the usual duties" of an employee? Policies do not define the phrase. The federal Fifth Circuit Court of Appeals explained that directors exercise their office only through the collective action of the board of which they are a member and that a director has no individual power of action. In comparison, an officer is usually elected to perform specific duties as agent of the corporation. There is nothing, however, said the court, to prevent a board from authorizing one of its members to act in an "officer-like capacity" for the corporation in a particular transaction. Thus, where officers were considered employees under the policy, a director who carried out the direction of the board was acting within the scope of the *usual duties of an officer*.[489] Extrapolating from that, if the board instructs a particular director to act in an "employee-like capacity," then the director could be said to be acting within the scope of the usual duties of an employee. Unfortunately, residential association boards rarely operate in

---

487. Travelers Crime Policy CRI-3001, § III.S.4.a.

488. ISO Form CR 00 23 11 15, § F.7.a.(8). The policy includes managers as employees under the same circumstances as directors or trustees, but defines "managers" as natural persons serving in a directorial capacity for a limited liability company. ISO Form CR 00 23 11 15, § F.13.

489. Federal Deposit Ins. Corp. v. Aetna Casualty & Surety Co., 426 F.2d 729, 738 (5th Cir. 1970).

that fashion. More commonly, a problem arises and the President asks a board member to take care of it or the only board member on the property at the time a problem arises takes the initiative to address it. Associations, therefore, may need to confer with the association attorney about any necessary amendments to the governing documents. As the Fifth Circuit Court noted, the duties of officers are usually specified. In common interest communities, the governing documents often broadly define the duties and responsibilities of the President, Vice President, Secretary, and Treasurer. An amendment to the governing documents might specify, in broad terms, the duties and responsibilities of members of the governing board generally, whether acting at the direction of the President or on their own initiative. When the question of the "usual duties of an employee" arises in court, judges accept the testimony of a witness who is an expert in the particular industry as sufficient evidence of those duties.[490] In drafting a document amendment regarding the duties and responsibilities of the association as carried out by members of the governing board the association can in effect incorporate "expert testimony" by conforming the amendment to the views of experts on the duties and responsibilities of common interest community associations.[491]

[b] Compensated Officers or Directors

The basic definition of "employee" is a natural person in the service of the insured who is compensated by the insured directly by salary, wages, or commissions and who the insured has the right to direct and control.[492] Thus, one way for an association to bring directors or officers under the definition of "employee" would be to provide them with a nominal compensation while performing services for the association. That, however, is problematic. The governing documents of residential associations may prohibit compensating directors.[493] Some states have laws addressing the issue. Of the five largest states, Texas and California have no pertinent statutes. In Florida, a director, officer, or committee member of a homeowners association may not directly receive any salary or compensation from the association for performance of his or her duties and may not *in any other way*

490. *See, e.g.*, Puget Sound Nat'l Bank v. St. Paul Fire & Marine Ins. Co., 32 Wn. App. 32, 39, 645 P.2d 1122, 1126 (1982) (expert testimony was relevant to factual determination of usual duties of typical employees of bank in question and supported conclusion that person at issue performed such duties and trial court properly concluded that losses due to those acts were within coverage of fidelity bonds).

491. *See, e.g.*, Hyatt, *Condominium and Homeowner Association Practice: Community Association Law* at 183–86 (American Law Institute 1981) (summary of association activities for which governing boards are responsible).

492. *See* Bird v. Centennial Ins. Co., 11 F.3d 228, 233 (1st Cir. 1993) ("right to govern and direct" language materially limits definition of "employee" to those persons over whom corporate insureds have control).

493. *See* 6A Rohan, *Real Estate Transactions: Home Owner Associations and Planned Unit Developments—Law and Practice: Forms*, § 7.08[5] (Matthew Bender, 2023).

benefit financially from service to the association; however, the prohibition does not bar any fee or compensation authorized in the governing documents or in advance by a vote of a majority of the voting interests.[494] For Florida condominiums and cooperatives, the bylaws may include a description of the compensation, if any, of officers and directors, but officers and directors have to serve without compensation unless the bylaws specifically so provide.[495] Illinois has essentially the same law for homeowners associations,[496] and its condominium legislation simply says the bylaws must provide for the compensation, if any, of the members of the board.[497] Under the New York Cooperative Corporations Law a cooperative corporation has the power to adopt and amend bylaws regarding, *inter alia*, compensation of its officers and directors,[498] while the New York Condominium Act says the bylaws have to provide for the compensation, if any, of the members of the governing board.[499] Thus, while associations may be able to compensate directors and/or officers, experts caution that if directors vote to compensate themselves without prior authorization, they could be subject to claims of breach of fiduciary duty or conversion.[500]

[c] Non-compensated Officers as Employees

The Travelers policy makes any natural person who is a "non-compensated officer" an employee. There is an endorsement to the ISO Commercial Crime Coverage Form that amends the definition of "employee" to include any non-compensated officers of the insured shown on a schedule on which officers can be listed by name or title.[501] Apparently, directors can be included in that endorsement. If that is not acceptable, non-compensated *directors* who do not already serve as officers could be designated as officers and would, thereby, be considered employees. For example, on a five-member board, the one director who would ordinarily not be an officer could be denominated the Second Vice President.

494. Fla. Stat. § 720.303(12).

495. Fla. Stat. § 718.112(2)(a) (condominiums); Fla. Stat. § 719.106(1)(a) (cooperatives).

496. 765 Ill. Comp. Stat. 160/1-25(c) (directors serve without compensation, unless community instruments indicate otherwise).

497. 765 Ill. Comp. Stat. 605/18(a)(3).

498. N.Y. Co-op. Corp. § 14(i).

499. N.Y. Real Prop. Law § 339-v(a).

500. 6A Rohan, *Real Estate Transactions: Home Owner Associations and Planned Unit Developments—Law and Practice: Forms*, § 7.08[5] (Matthew Bender, 2023); 2 Rohan & Reskin, *Real Estate Transactions: Cooperative Housing Law and Practice—Forms*, § 9.03[5] (Matthew Bender, 2023). *See, e.g.*, SantiEsteban v. Crowder, 92 A.D.3d 544, 939 N.Y.S.2d 28 (2012) (as bylaws contemplated vote of tenant/shareholders authorizing compensation, directors who paid themselves salary without that authorization breached their fiduciary duty).

501. ISO Form CR 25 08 10 10.

[d] The Alter Ego Doctrine

Under the "alter ego" doctrine the wrongdoing of the principal of the insured organization is considered the equivalent of the wrongdoing of the policyholder.[502] In other words, the principal, because he or she in effect controls the insured, is the insured, that is, constitutes its alter ego. Public policy does not allow an organization to collect insurance for the wrongdoing of its alter ego.[503] Moreover, crime policies specifically exclude coverage for wrongful acts of the insured,[504] although they almost never contain a specific alter ego exclusion.[505] An act of the alter ego of the insured is the act of the insured and, therefore, the exclusion applies when the wrongful acts are those of the alter ego. As the Fifth Circuit Court of Appeals explained: "A corporation can only act through its officers and directors. When one person owns a controlling interest in the corporation and dominates the corporation's actions, his acts are the corporation's acts. Allowing the corporation to recover for the owner's fraudulent or dishonest conduct would essentially allow the corporation to recover for its own fraudulent or dishonest acts."[506]

Typically, an alter ego is someone who has a majority interest in the insured organization. In a residential common interest community, generally no one resident has a majority interest, except when the developer controls the association prior to transferring control to the residents. However, there are cases in which a group of persons acting in concert have been considered the alter ego of an insured organization.[507] In small associations consisting of five, seven, or

502. Horkovich, Reeves & Andrews, *Insurance Coverage for Employee Theft Losses: A Policyholder Primer on Commonly Litigated Issues*, 29 U. Mem. L. Rev. 363, 385 (1999). The authors caution that the alter ego doctrine is not a hard and fast rule. Some courts have found coverage even though the dishonest actors essentially controlled the policyholder.

503. *See, e.g.*, California Union Ins. Co. v. American Diversified Sav. Bank, 948 F.2d 556, 566 (9th Cir. 1991).

504. ISO Form CR 00 23 11 15, § D.1.a.; Travelers Crime Policy CRI-3001, § IV.C.

505. Horkovich, Reeves & Andrews, *Insurance Coverage for Employee Theft Losses: A Policyholder Primer on Commonly Litigated Issues*, 29 U. Mem. L. Rev. 363, 385 (1999).

506. *In re* World Hospitality, Ltd., 983 F.2d 650, 962 (5th Cir. 1993). *Compare* Cedar Lake Homeowners Ass'n v. Northwest Empire Cmty. Mgmt., 2015 U.S. Dist. LEXIS 139033 (D. Or. Oct. 13, 2015) (where wrongdoer held 40 percent share in parent company of community association management firm and held positions of Director, Secretary, Vice President, and Chief Financial Officer, that person was not alter ego of firm because he was minority shareholder and was fired by majority shareholder after his misdeeds were discovered).

507. *See, e.g.*, Kerr v. Aetna Casualty & Surety Co., 350 F.2d 146, 154 (4th Cir. 1965) (where controlling shareholders of insured elected themselves its sole directors, and as directors elected themselves its chief executive officers, they may have, in their role as shareholders, had right to control themselves as officers, but that theoretical and unrealistic right of control did not make them "employees" of insured and fidelity insurance was not intended to cover fraud and dishonesty of those who are in effect sole stockholders as well as only directors of closely held corporation); Employer's Admin. Servs. v. Hartford Accident & Indem. Co., 147 Ariz. 202, 206, 709 P.2d 559, 563 (Ariz. App. 1985) (sole officers, directors, and shareholders of insured company misappropriated funds from it and insurer denied claim of company arguing those persons were alter egos of

nine members, all or a majority of the members might constitute the governing board and thus potentially subject the association to application of the alter ego doctrine.

[7] Volunteers

Under the Travelers policy, a "volunteer" is considered an employee while he or she is performing services for the insured and is subject to the direction and control of the insured.[508] The ISO policy makes no mention of volunteers.[509] Thus, for a volunteer to be an employee under the ISO policy, an endorsement has to be added. There is an ISO endorsement titled "Crime and Fidelity: Include Volunteer Workers Other Than Fund Solicitors as Employees" that amends the definition of "employee" to include any non-compensated natural person—other than a fund solicitor—while that person performs services for the insured that are usual to the duties of an employee.[510] This endorsement can be very important to common interest communities, especially small ones that lack professional management. The members of the governing board—from which the officers are typically selected—will generally operate the association and, because they often have employment and family responsibilities, they may turn to other residents to volunteer in the operation of the community. One resident might volunteer to act as bookkeeper or to hand deliver checks to a service provider. Another resident might deposit cash collected from a social event into the association bank account. Thus, CIC associations will want to determine whether their volunteers are treated as employees.

[8] Committee Members

Experts recommend that members of association committees have employee status.[511] This is important because some committees may have access to association

---

insured, not its employees; court agreed with insurer and said those persons were acting in concert and since together they constituted totality of officers, directors, and shareholders of insured, they were never subject to anyone's governance and direction and to allow insured company to recover on its claim would in essence be interpreting policy as allowing individual wrongdoers to insure themselves through their company, over which they had unbridled control, for their own intentional wrongdoing).

508. Travelers Crime Policy CRI-3001, § III.S.4.g.

509. *What Is Fidelity Insurance and Why Your Association Needs It*, available at: http://www.hindmansanchez.com/resources/newsletter/what-fidelity-insurance-and-why-your-association-needs-it/ (volunteers do not meet definition of "employee").

510. ISO Form CR 25 10 10 10.

511. *See, e.g.*, *What Is Fidelity Insurance and Why Your Association Needs It*, available at: http://www.hindmansanchez.com/resources/newsletter/what-fidelity-insurance-and-why-your-association-needs-it/ (committee members need status of employees if possible); *Fidelity Insurance*, available at: http://www.davis-stirling.com/tabid/1664/default.aspx (associations need broadest possible coverage to include committee members and anyone else who may have access to association money).

funds or other valuable property covered by a crime policy. The volunteer category may encompass those who serve on committees for the association; however, there is an ISO endorsement specifically designed for committee members titled "Crime and Fidelity: Include Chairperson and Members of Specified Committees as Employees."[512] The endorsement does exactly what its title says. It amends the definition of "employee" to include any natural person, whether or not compensated, while performing services for the named insured as chairperson or member of any committee named on a schedule incorporated into the endorsement. Note that it is the committee, not the individual member, who is listed on the schedule, thus allowing the membership of the committee to change during the policy term without any change in coverage.

[9] Association Attorney

The ISO policy makes no mention of attorneys. Experts agree that outside counsel are independent contractors and therefore specifically excluded from the definition of "employee."[513] In contrast, under the Travelers policy, an attorney retained by the insured, and any employee of that attorney, is considered an employee while performing legal services for the insured.[514] For the association attorney to be considered an employee under the ISO policy, an endorsement would need to be added. There is an endorsement that amends the definition of "employee" to include any natural person or group of persons named or described on the schedule to the endorsement.[515] Whether an association needs its attorney to be considered an employee is a matter it should discuss with the attorney and its broker.

[10] Community Association Manager

The community association management company is an independent contractor and under both policies, an independent contractor is not an employee.[516] However, managers often control the association checkbook and associations require protection from dishonest managers.[517] Associations need, therefore, to have an endorsement added to their policies that makes the manager an employee for

512. ISO Form CR 25 06 10 10.

513. 10 Jeffrey E. Thomas, *New Appleman on Insurance Law Library Edition* § 120.05[4] (Matthew Bender, 2023) (noting that outside counsel could be employee of insured if he or she is director who performs acts within scope of usual duties of employee).

514. Travelers Crime Policy CRI-3001, § III.S.5.

515. ISO Form CR 25 41 10 10 (Crime and Fidelity: Include Designated Persons or Classes of Persons as Employees).

516. ISO Form CR 00 23 11 15, § F.7.b; Travelers Crime Policy CRI-3001, § III.S.

517. Perkins & Grennan, *Coverage for Losses Resulting From Association Property Manager Dishonesty*, XVII Fid. L.J. 77, 82 (2011).

purposes of the coverage.[518] As discussed elsewhere, it is required by Fannie Mae and Freddie Mac guidelines, and by statute in some states, that managers be covered by an association crime policy.[519] There is an ISO endorsement that amends the definition of "employee" to include any natural person or group of persons named or described on the schedule to the endorsement.[520] However, another ISO form is the recommended method for adding managers as employees.[521] That is the Designated Agents as Employees Endorsement.[522]

The Designated Agents Endorsement modifies the policy and applies the insuring agreement for employee theft. It includes a schedule for listing the capacity of the agent and the limit of insurance. It amends the definition of "employee" to include a natural person, partnership, or corporation that the named insured appoints *in writing* to act as its agent in the capacity shown on the schedule.[523] That person or entity is an employee while acting on behalf of the named insured or while in possession of covered property. The only coverage applicable to the person or entity is theft.[524] The person or entity and the partners, officers, and employees of that person or entity are considered as collectively one employee for the purposes of the coverage, the endorsement adds, however, the "termination as to any employee" condition[525] applies individually to each of them.[526] The most the carrier will pay for a loss caused by an agent who is included as an employee by the endorsement is the limit of insurance that is shown in the schedule and that limit is part of, not in addition to, the limit shown on the Declarations Page for the employee theft insuring agreement.[527]

518. *What Is Fidelity Insurance and Why Your Association Needs It*, available at: http://www.hindmansanchez.com/resources/newsletter/what-fidelity-insurance-and-why-your-association-needs-it/ (association managers do not meet definition of "employee" and to protect association from theft by those with access to assets, but not technically "employees," it needs to purchase endorsement that expands definition of "employee" to include among others, management company agents); Branson, *Fidelity Bond Insurance: Protection Against Condo Crime* (Cooperator, 2014), available at: http://cooperator.com/articles/2823/1/Fidelity-Bond-Insurance/Page1.html (because definition of "employee" includes only those compensated by wages by association, it should also be extended to cover non-compensated community association managers).

519. *See* §§ 15.01[6][b]&[c], *supra*.

520. ISO Form CR 25 41 10 10 (Crime and Fidelity: Include Designated Persons or Classes of Persons as Employees).

521. Perkins & Grennan, *Coverage for Losses Resulting From Association Property Manager Dishonesty*, XVII Fid. L.J. 77, 98–99 (2011).

522. ISO Form CR 25 02 10 10.

523. ISO Form CR 25 02 10 10, § 1.

524. The policy specifically provides the person or entity is not covered for faithful performance of duty, even if the policy has been amended by endorsement to provide that coverage on other employees.

525. *See* § 15.02[5][a][i], *infra*.

526. ISO Form CR 25 02 10 10, § 2.

527. ISO Form CR 25 02 10 10, § 2.

Some carriers have developed their own endorsements that are specific to property managers. For example, Travelers has an endorsement that can be added to its crime policy that amends the definition of "employee" to include each natural person, partnership, or corporation the insured appoints by *written agreement* to act as its property manager provided the person or entity is shown on a schedule in the endorsement and is subject to the direction and control of the insured while performing services for it.[528] That person or entity, however, is only an employee while acting on behalf of the insured or while in the possession of the money, securities, or other property—meaning tangible property other than money or securities with intrinsic value[529]—of the insured. The designated property manager and partners, officers, and employees of that manager are considered to be collectively *one employee* except that the condition in the policy that specifies when the policy terminates as to any employee applies individually to each of them.[530]

§ 15.04 Exclusions

The standard ISO Crime Policy has 12 exclusions. It also has 16 exclusions that apply to specific insuring agreements—coverages—and these are discussed in conjunction with the specific coverages to which they apply. Of the 12 generally applicable exclusions, four—governmental action,[531] nuclear hazard,[532] pollution,[533] and war and military action [534]—are short, simple, and found in many other types of policies. These are not discussed below. One exclusion that is *not* in standard policies is negligence of the named insured. The fact that the financial controls of the insured failed and the insured was in some way negligent in adopting or implementing those controls is not a basis for excluding coverage.[535]

528. Travelers CRI 7132, § 2 (Include Designated Property Managers as Employees; Covered for Employee Theft Only Endorsement).

529. Travelers Crime Policy CRI-3001, § III.KK.

530. *See* Travelers Crime Policy CRI-3001, § V.D.4.

531. ISO Form CR 00 23 11 15, § D.1.f (no coverage for loss that results from seizure or destruction of property by order of governmental authority).

532. ISO Form CR 00 23 11 15, § D.1.i (no coverage for loss or damage that results from nuclear reaction or radiation, or radioactive contamination, however caused).

533. ISO Form CR 00 23 11 15, § D.1.j (no coverage for loss or damage caused by or that results from pollution as defined in policy).

534. ISO Form CR 00 23 11 15, § D.1.l (no coverage for loss or damage that results from war, including undeclared or civil war, warlike action by a military force—including action in hindering or defending against actual or expected attack—by any government, sovereign or other authority using military personnel or other agents, or insurrection, rebellion, revolution, usurped power, or action taken by governmental authority in hindering or defending against any of them).

535. Horkovich, Reeves & Andrews, *Insurance Coverage for Employee Theft Losses: A Policyholder Primer on Commonly Litigated Issues*, 29 U. Mem. L. Rev. 363, 395 (1999) (noting that

[1] Acts Committed by Named Insured

The first exclusion is for any loss that results from theft—meaning the unlawful taking of property to the deprivation of the insured[536]—or any "other dishonest act" committed by the named insured.[537] The policy defines "criminal" to include acts showing a lack of integrity or breach of trust.[538] When the named insured is an entity, rather than a person—as is the case in a common interest community—the named insured can only act through its agents,[539] and the exclusion would, therefore, appear to render theft coverage illusory as the acts of its agents would be its own acts and, therefore, excluded. However, the policy specifically provides that the insurer will pay for loss of, or damage to, money, securities, and other property that results directly from "theft" committed by an *employee* whether identified or not and whether acting alone or in collusion with others.[540] Therefore, the exclusion would not apply when a theft is committed by anyone that is an employee as defined in the policy.[541] The circumstances in which officers and directors of the association are considered employees is, thus, of particular import because otherwise their acts would be the acts of the association.[542]

[2] Employee Acts Prior to the Policy Period

The ISO Crime Policy excludes coverage for a loss caused by an employee if that employee committed theft—meaning the unlawful taking of property to the deprivation of the insured[543]—or *any other* dishonest act *before* the effective date of the policy and the named insured, or an officer, director, or trustee of the named insured—not in collusion with that employee—*learned* of the theft or "dishonest act" before the policy period as shown on the Declarations Page.[544]

---

insurance company, which will have asked about financial controls in its application for coverage, found those very same controls acceptable when it sold policy and took premium).

536. ISO Form CR 00 23 11 15, § F.23.

537. ISO Form CR 00 23 11 15, § D.1.a. Note that the exclusion also applies to theft or dishonest acts by partners or "members"—meaning an owner of a limited liability company—of the named insured; however, common interest communities are rarely formed as partnerships or limited liability companies.

538. *See* First Nat'l Bank Co. v. Insurance Co. of North America, 606 F.2d 760, 768 (7th Cir. 1979). *See also* Capital Bank & Trust Co. v. Gulf Ins. Co., 91 A.D.3d 1251, 1252, 937 N.Y.S.2d 463, 465 (2012) (dishonest must be given ordinary meaning and broadly includes acts that demonstrate want of integrity, breach of trust, or moral turpitude affecting official fidelity or character).

539. Stanford Univ. Hosp. v. Federal Ins. Co., 174 F.3d 1077, 1085 (9th Cir. 1999) (though corporation exists *sui generis* under law, it can conduct its affairs only through its officers and employees); Stop & Shop Cos. v. Federal Ins. Co., 136 F.3d 71, 74 (1st Cir. 1998) (while corporations have non-corporeal and independent existence, they can conduct their affairs only through their officers and employees).

540. ISO Form CR 00 23 11 15, § A.1.

541. For the meaning of "employee," see § 15.03, *supra*.

542. *See* § 15.03[6], *supra*.

543. ISO Form CR 00 23 11 15, § F.23.

544. ISO Form CR 00 23 11 15, § D.1.b.

The policy does not define the phrase "other dishonest act." Courts generally interpret "dishonest" broadly and say it is more comprehensive than "criminal" and includes acts showing a lack of integrity or breach of trust.[545]

[3] Acts of Employees, Directors, Trustees, or Representatives

The third policy exclusion is for a loss that results from theft—meaning the unlawful taking of property to the deprivation of the insured[546]—or any other dishonest act committed by an employee, director, trustee, or "authorized representative" of the named insured.[547] The purpose of the exclusion is, as one Federal Circuit court put it, "to place on the insured the risk of picking a faithless agent."[548] Another circuit court described the exclusion as barring coverage for misappropriation of funds by individuals or entities authorized by the insured to have access to its funds, that is, those whom the insured empowers to act on its behalf.[549] Because, as discussed below, the exclusion *does not apply* to the specific insuring agreement for employee theft, the effect of the exclusion is to bar coverage when a claim is brought under one of the other insuring agreements and that claim is for a loss that results from theft or any other dishonest act committed by an employee, director, trustee, or "authorized representative."

The exclusion applies whether the perpetrator acted alone or in collusion with others or while performing services for the named insured "or otherwise." The words "or otherwise" mean that the perpetrator does not have to be performing services on behalf of the named insured for the exclusion to apply.[550] For example, if an employee steals from the insured while "off the clock," the exclusion can still apply. The policy does not define the phrase "other dishonest act." Courts generally interpret "dishonest" broadly and say it is more comprehensive than "criminal" and includes acts showing a lack of integrity or breach of trust.[551] The policy also does not define "authorized representative." A key

545. *See* First Nat'l Bank Co. v. Insurance Co. of North America, 606 F.2d 760, 768 (7th Cir. 1979). *See also* Capital Bank & Trust Co. v. Gulf Ins. Co., 91 A.D.3d 1251, 1252, 937 N.Y.S.2d 463, 465 (2012) (dishonest must be given ordinary meaning and broadly includes acts that demonstrate want of integrity, breach of trust, or moral turpitude affecting official fidelity or character).

546. ISO Form CR 00 23 11 15, § F.23.

547. ISO Form CR 00 23 11 15, § D.1.c.

548. Stop & Shop Cos. v. Federal Ins. Co., 136 F.3d 71, 76 (1st Cir. 1998).

549. Stanford Univ. Hosp. v. Federal Ins. Co., 174 F.3d 1077, 1085 (9th Cir. 1999).

550. *See* Sehon, Stevenson & Co. v. Buckeye Union Ins. Co., 298 F. Supp. 1168, 1171 (S.D. W. Va. 1969) (obvious intent of defendant in using phrase "or otherwise" following phrase "while working" was to cover circumstance in which property was removed by employees after working hours and, while language might have been more explicit, to construe exclusionary clause to limit its effect to activities of employees during working hours would require distorted application of terms of clause and would require court to completely ignore phrase "or otherwise"). *See also* Century Indem. Co. v. Schmick, 351 Mich. 622, 88 N.W.2d 622 (1958).

551. *See* First Nat'l Bank Co. v. Insurance Co. of North America, 606 F.2d 760, 768 (7th Cir. 1979). *See also* Capital Bank & Trust Co. v. Gulf Ins. Co., 91 A.D.3d 1251, 1252, 937 N.Y.S.2d 463,

question for common interest communities is whether a community association manager, accountant, bookkeeper, or attorney is an authorized representative for purposes of the exclusion.

Broadly stated, an authorized representative is a person or company empowered to act on behalf of another.[552] For example, in one notable case the insured hired a tax service company. The insured deposited funds with that company, and the company remitted timely payments to taxing authorities on behalf of the insured. Executives of the tax service company diverted funds belonging to the insured for their own gain. The company itself was an authorized representative of the insured. The insured argued the exclusion should not apply because the individual executives behaved inconsistently with the interests of the company. The court, however, concluded that it was irrelevant whether the wrong was perpetrated for the benefit of the company or the individual actors.[553] That decision has two implications for common interest community associations. First, management companies, accounting firms, and law firms would all appear to meet the court's definition of "authorized representative." Second, wrongful acts of the employees of those entities would trigger the exclusion. For example, if an association retained a community association management company, the act of an individual employee of that company—not necessarily the particular manager for the association—would be the act of the management company as the authorized representative of the association.

The exclusion does not apply when the act is covered under the insuring agreement for employee theft, which, it should be noted, includes forgery.[554] The exception means that when there is a theft of money, securities, or *other property*—meaning generally tangible property that has intrinsic value[555]—is committed by someone considered to be an employee—which can include officers, directors, "volunteer" workers, or community association managers—the

465 (2012) (dishonest must be given ordinary meaning and broadly includes acts that demonstrate want of integrity, breach of trust, or moral turpitude affecting official fidelity or character).

552. *See, e.g.*, Stanford Univ. Hosp. v. Federal Ins. Co., 174 F.3d 1077, 1085 (9th Cir. 1999) (term "authorized representative" covers those who by authorization of insured are given access to and permitted to handle funds of insured); Florists' Mut. Ins. Co. v. Ludy Greenhouse Mfg. Corp., 521 F. Supp. 2d 661, 679 (S.D. Ohio 2007) (term "authorized representative" covers those who by authorization of insured are given access to and permitted to handle funds of insured); Colson Servs. Corp. v. Insurance Co. of N. Am., 874 F. Supp. 65, 68 (S.D.N.Y. 1994) (dictionary definition of "representative" is one that represents another as agent, deputy, substitute, or delegate usually being invested with authority of principal and authorized means endowed with authority, therefore, term "authorized representative" would encompass entity given authority by insured to act as its agent in choosing investments to make money held in account of insured).

553. Stop & Shop Cos. v. Federal Ins. Co., 136 F.3d 71 (1st Cir. 1998). *See also* Stanford Univ. Hosp. v. Federal Ins. Co., 174 F.3d 1077, 1086 (9th Cir. 1999) (under "authorized representative" exclusion, acts committed by officers or employees of authorized representative are encompassed by that exclusion regardless of their motivations or net effects).

554. ISO Form CR 00 23 11 15, § D.1.c.(2).

555. ISO Form CR 00 23 11 15, § F.18.

exclusion is inapplicable.[556] A loss that does not fit under the employee theft coverage can require threading a needle to determine whether or not there is coverage. For example, the third insuring agreement of the ISO Crime Policy covers a loss of money and securities—but not other property—inside the premises—meaning the interior of that portion of any building the named insured occupies in conducting its business[557]—that results directly from theft committed by any person present inside those premises. If the thief inside the premises is neither an employee, director, trustee, nor "authorized representative" of the named insured, then the exclusion would not apply. If, however, that thief has an employee of the named insured for an accomplice, then the loss results from the dishonest act of an employee in collusion with another and the exclusion does apply.

[4] Confidential or Personal Information

There is no coverage for a loss that results from disclosure or use of confidential or personal information of another person or organization.[558] "Confidential" can be equated with "private" or "secret."[559] The policy exclusion itself says that confidential or personal information includes, but is not limited to, patents, trade secrets, processing methods, customer lists, financial information, credit card information, health information, or any other type of information that is "non-public." This exclusion has the effect of eliminating coverage for identity theft or fraud,[560] although the coverage may be added by endorsement.[561]

No matter how either "personal" or "confidential" might be defined, there is no question that common interest community associations can have information about their residents that would arguably be considered confidential or secret. For example, associations routinely keep emergency contact information. Associations that require a background check of those seeking to purchase a home in the community will have received information—for instance, any criminal offenses committed by the applicant and the applicant's credit status—that would be considered confidential and personal. When associations provide the option to

---

556. For the meaning of "employee," see § 15.03, *supra.*

557. ISO Form CR 00 23 11 15, § F.19.

558. ISO Form CR 00 23 11 15, § D.1.d.(1).

559. *See* Retail Ventures, Inc. v. Nat'l Union Fire Ins. Co., 2010 U.S. Dist. LEXIS 140154 (S.D. Ohio Sept. 28, 2010), *aff'd*, 691 F.3d 821 (6th Cir. 2012) (although "confidential" has more than one definition, plain and ordinary meaning of "confidential information" is generally synonymous with private or secret).

560. *See* Eubank, *It's Criminal What Agents DON'T Know About Crime Insurance*, at 19 (2014), available at: http://www.independentagent.com/Education/Webinars/SiteAssets/Pages/live-webinars/2014%20Crime%20Webinar%20Handout.pdf (noting that commercial crime policies are not intended to cover potential losses created through unauthorized disclosure of information belonging to insured, and confidential information exclusion makes clear that policies do not cover identity theft). The Travelers policy, however, does provide identity theft coverage as a part of its personal accounts protection. *See* Travelers Crime Policy CRI-3001, § I.F.2.

561. *See* § 15.02[5], *supra.*

residents of having monthly maintenance fees automatically deducted from their bank accounts, the association, or more likely someone acting on their behalf, has the account numbers of those residents. There are at least two kinds of losses that could result from disclosure or use of confidential or personal information. The first would occur if the association were sued for defamation or invasion of privacy after personal or confidential information about a resident was disclosed. The second would be a theft from the account of a resident perpetrated by someone who obtained access to the account using information from the association. Both occurrences would be excluded from coverage of the crime policy, but could be covered by the association commercial general liability policy.[562]

A second part of the exclusion bars coverage for losses that result from disclosure of confidential or personal information of the named insured; however, this exclusion does not apply to a loss that is otherwise covered under the policy that results directly from the use of the confidential or personal information of the named insured.[563]

[5] Data Security Breach

There is no coverage for fees, costs, fines, penalties, or other expenses the named insured incurs that are related to access to or disclosure of confidential or personal information of another person or organization including, but not limited to, patents, trade secrets, processing methods, customer lists, financial information, credit card information, health information, or any other type of information that is non-public.[564]

[6] Indirect Loss and Legal Fees, Costs, and Expenses

Generally, the crime policy does not cover "indirect losses." Courts explain that under these policies a loss is the deprivation or dispossession of money or property of the insured, and indirect loss exclusions reinforce the conclusion that the policy is intended to insure against immediate harm from employee dishonesty, not for any obligations the insured might have to others as a result of that dishonesty.[565]

To implement the bar on coverage for indirect losses, an exclusion states that there is no coverage for a loss that is an indirect result of an occurrence covered

562. For more on commercial general liability, see Ch. 10, *supra*.

563. ISO Form CR 00 23 11 15, § D.1.d.(2).

564. ISO Form CR 00 23 11 15, § D.1.e.

565. Fireman's Fund Ins. Co. v. Special Olympics Int'l, Inc., 249 F. Supp. 2d 19 (D. Mass.), *aff'd*, 346 F.3d 259 (1st Cir. 2003) (courts interpreting fidelity policies have consistently concluded that insured does not suffer direct loss unless its assets, and not those of third party, are reduced because of wrongful conduct.). *See also* Tooling, Mfg. & Techs. Ass'n v. Hartford Fire Ins. Co., 693 F.3d 665 (6th Cir. 2012); Patrick Schaumburg Autos., Inc. v. Hanover Ins. Co., 452 F. Supp. 2d 857 (N.D. Ill. 2006).

by the policy.[566] There are three types of indirect losses that are specifically identified as excluded, though other indirect losses are also excluded. The first is for the inability of the named insured to realize income that it would have realized had there been no loss of or damage to money, securities, or other property.[567] The second concerns payment of damages of any type for which the named insured is legally liable, although the insurer will pay compensatory damages that arise directly from a loss covered under the policy.[568] Finally, payment of costs, fees, or other expenses incurred by the named insured to establish either the existence or amount of loss under the policy are not covered. [569] However, there is an ISO endorsement that can be added to the policy that modifies the exclusion to bar only coverage for payment of costs, fees, or other expenses incurred in establishing the existence—but not the amount—of a loss under the policy.[570] Under that endorsement, the insurer will pay for reasonable costs, fees, or other expenses the named insured incurs and pays to an independent accounting, auditing, or other service that is used to determine the amount of loss covered under the policy.

There is also an exclusion for fees, costs, and expenses the named insured incurs that are related to any legal action,[571] except when covered under the forgery or alteration insuring agreement.[572]

[7] Virtual Currency

There is no coverage for a loss that involves any kind of "virtual currency," whether actual or fictitious, including, but not limited to, digital currency, crypto currency, or any other type of electronic currency.[573]

§ 15.05 Generally Applicable Conditions

The standard commercial crime policy has both conditions that are generally applicable to the policy and those applicable to specific coverages. The latter are discussed with the coverages to which they apply.

---

566. ISO Form CR 00 23 11 15, § D.1.g.
567. ISO Form CR 00 23 11 15, § D.1.g.(1).
568. ISO Form CR 00 23 11 15, § D.1.g.(2).
569. ISO Form CR 00 23 11 15, § D.1.g.(3). The exclusion of ISO Form CR 00 23 11 15, § D.1.g.(3) is modified to read that the policy does not cover payment of costs, fees, or other expenses incurred to establish the existence of a loss.
570. *See* ISO Form CR 25 40 08 13.
571. ISO Form CR 00 23 11 15, § D.1.h.
572. *See* ISO Form CR 00 23 11 15, § A.2.b (if named insured is sued for refusing to pay any instrument listed in forgery and alteration clause, on basis that it has been forged or altered, and named insured has written consent of carrier to defend against that suit, carrier will pay for any reasonable legal expenses named insured incurs and pays in that defense).
573. ISO Form CR 00 23 11 15, § D.1.k.

[1] Additional Premises or Employees

The standard crime policy has conditions that apply when the named insured adds premises or hires additional employees.

[a] Additional Premises

The word "premises" is defined in the policy as the *interior* of the portion of any building the named insured occupies in conducting its business.[574] However, an endorsement can be added to the policy that expands the definition of "premises" to include the portion of the grounds *entirely* enclosed by a fence or wall.[575] For a common interest community, what does "occupies in conducting its business" mean? The policy defines neither "occupy" nor "business."[576]

For long-standing common interest communities, an addition to the premises would be rare; however, new communities are often developed in phases in which additional property is added to the community as the developer completes each phase. The UCIOA—and the laws of a number of states—specifically address development in phases. The UCIOA provides for "development rights," which means a right reserved by the Declarant—developer—in the Declaration creating the community to, *inter alia*, add real estate to a community or create units, common elements, or limited common elements within a community.[577] These development rights, explains a commentary to the Act, maximize the flexibility available to developers to adjust the size and mix of a project to demands of the marketplace, both before and after creation.[578]

A developer exercises any reserved development rights by recording a Declaration amendment assigning an identifying number to each new unit created and describing any common elements and limited common elements created.[579] The exact point at which an additional phase may be completed and added to a community cannot be predicted. Therefore, it is possible that an association can be formed and can have obtained a crime policy and then, during the term of that policy—especially a policy with a term of longer than one year—additional premises can be created. The standard policy provides that if, while the policy is

574. ISO Form CR 00 23 11 15, § F.19.

575. ISO Form CR 35 23 11 09.

576. The "business" of the insured should be set forth in the governing documents. *See, e.g.*, Hyatt, *Condominium and Homeowner Association Practice: Community Association Law* at 183–86 (American Law Institute 1981) (summary of association activities for which governing boards are responsible).

577. *See* Uniform Common Interest Ownership Act, § 1-103(16).

578. Uniform Common Interest Ownership Act, § 1-103, comment 15.

579. Uniform Common Interest Ownership Act, § 2-110(a). *See also* Uniform Common Interest Ownership Act, § 2-122, which allows an original Declaration in a planned community to reserve the right of the declarant to amend it subsequently to add a limited number of after-acquired parcels of real estate to the development.

in force, the association—as named insured—establishes any additional premises—other than by consolidation or merger with, or purchase or acquisition of assets or liabilities of, another entity—those premises are automatically covered under the policy without notice of the increase in the number of premises to the insurer, and without an additional premium, for the remainder of the term of the policy.[580] While no notification of the addition to the insurer is required, an association will want to discuss the addition with its broker so the broker has information that will be required at the time the policy is renewed, or coverage with a different carrier is sought, and so that the broker can consider the implications that any addition to the premises may have for policies providing other coverages.

[b] Additional Employees

If, while the crime policy is in force, the named insured hires additional employees—other than by consolidation or merger with another entity—those employees are automatically covered under the policy without notice to the insurer of the increase in the number of employees and without an additional premium for the remainder of the term of the policy.[581] Under the policy, the basic definition of an "employee" is a natural person while in the service of the insured who is compensated by the insured directly by salary, wages, or commissions and who the insured has the right to direct and control while that person is performing services for the insured.[582] However, the definition also includes others, for example, lease workers and consultants, and can be—and usually is—amended by endorsement to add non-compensated officers of the named insured or a community association manager.

[2] Consolidation of the Insured with Another Entity

The crime policy addresses the circumstances in which a named insured merges or consolidates with another entity.[583] Some may think this provision is inapplicable to common interest communities; however, CICs do occasionally merge or consolidate with other communities. While unusual, merger or consolidation happens enough that the UCIOA specifically provides for its implementation. It allows any two or more common interest communities that are of the same form of ownership to merge or consolidate into a single common interest community by agreement of the unit owners and, unless the agreement otherwise provides, the resulting community becomes the legal successor, *for all purposes*, of all of

580. ISO Form CR 00 23 11 15, § E.1.a.

581. ISO Form CR 00 23 11 15, § E.1.a.

582. ISO Form CR 00 23 11 15, § F.7.a.(1); Travelers Crime Policy CRI-3001, § III.S.1.

583. ISO Form CR 00 23 11 15, § E.1.e. The policy also addresses the circumstances in which a named insured purchases or acquires the assets or liabilities of another entity. That is an event unlikely to occur in a residential common interest community.

the preexisting communities.[584] Consolidation might occur because, for example, two or more small condominium communities are adjacent to one another and forming a single community under one association might be more efficient and economical.

The standard crime policy provides that if the named insured consolidates or merges with another entity, it has to give written notice to the insurer as soon as possible and obtain the written consent of the insurer to extend the policy coverage to the consolidated or merged entity.[585] The insurer may condition its consent on payment of an additional premium, but for the first 90 days following the effective date of any consolidation or merger, the coverage provided by the policy applies to the consolidated or merged entity as long as all occurrences causing or contributing to a loss involving the consolidation or merger takes place after the effective date of the consolidation or merger.[586]

[3] Policy Changes

The standard crime policy provides that it contains all the agreements between the named insured and the insurer. It authorizes the first named insured to make changes in the terms of the policy with the consent of the insurer, but those terms can only be amended or waived by an endorsement issued by the insurer and made a part of the policy.[587] The standard policy has been revised fairly frequently and provides that if the insurer adopts a revision that would broaden the coverage without an additional premium within 45 days before or during the policy period, the broadened coverage immediately applies to the policy.[588]

[4] Obligations of the Named Insured

The standard crime policy imposes specific obligations in the event of a loss and a general duty to cooperate with the insurer in all matters that pertain to the policy as stated in its terms and conditions.[589] One of the duties in the event of a loss is to cooperate with the insurer in its investigation and settlement of any claim.[590] Failure to comply with the duties in the event of a loss can be a basis for finding a violation of the cooperation clause. Those duties arise after the named insured discovers a loss of—or a *situation that could result* in a loss of or damage to—money, securities, or other property.

584. Uniform Common Interest Ownership Act, § 1-121(a).
585. ISO Form CR 00 23 11 15, § E.1.e.(1).
586. ISO Form CR 00 23 11 15, § E.1.e.(2).
587. ISO Form CR 00 23 11 15, § E.1.c.
588. ISO Form CR 00 23 11 15, § E.1.n.
589. ISO Form CR 00 23 11 15, § E.1.f.
590. ISO Form CR 00 23 11 15, § E.1.g.(3).

[a] Notice

The policy provides that any claim for loss covered under it has to be *presented by the named insured.*[591] After the named insured discovers a loss, or a situation that could result in a loss or damage to covered property, the named insured is required to notify the insurer of it "as soon as possible."[592] If the named insured has reason to believe that a loss, other than under the coverages for employee theft or forgery, involves a violation of law, the named insured is also required to notify local law enforcement authorities. The insured should consider that a claim might be covered by more than one policy. One expert commentary recommends making sure the broker confirms that all potentially responsible insurance companies have been notified within the respective notice periods, and then backing up the broker with direct notices of claim.[593]

It is not uncommon for insurers to deny a claim because the notice of loss was allegedly late. However, under the "notice-prejudice" rule, an untimely notice will not necessarily bar a claim unless the insurer is prejudiced by the delay.[594] Additionally, under the "adverse domination" doctrine, if a corporate policyholder is prevented from discovering wrongdoing and providing timely notice of it because the corporate officer charged with providing notice is the wrongdoer, knowledge of the wrongdoing is not imputed to the corporation through that wrongdoer and discovery of the wrongdoing is tolled until a non-wrongdoing officer first learns of it.[595]

591. ISO Form CR 00 23 11 15, §§ E.1.r. Note that under the Discovery Form, this clause is identical, but has a different designation. *See* CR 00 22 11 15, § E.1.p.

592. ISO Form CR 00 23 11 15, § E.1.g.(1). *See* Wood & Hurtado, *Don't Get Robbed of Your Fidelity Coverage*, 9 Enforce 12, 13 (2011), available at: http://www.andersonkill.com/Custom/PublicationPDF/PublicationID_1062_Dont-Get-Robbed-of-Your-Fidelity-Coverage.pdf (policies often specify that notice has to be given to company within 30 days of discovery of loss—and in some cases within as little as seven days); Horkovich, Reeves & Andrews, *Insurance Coverage for Employee Theft Losses: A Policyholder Primer on Commonly Litigated Issues*, 29 U. Mem. L. Rev. 363, 366 (1999) (some policies require that notice be sent within as few as seven days from discovery of loss).

593. Wood & Hurtado, *Don't Get Robbed of Your Fidelity Coverage*, 9 Enforce 12, 13 (2011), available at: http://www.andersonkill.com/Custom/PublicationPDF/PublicationID_1062_Dont-Get-Robbed-of-Your-Fidelity-Coverage.pdf.

594. *See generally* Zauderer & Mills, *At the Apex of the Arc of the Pendulum—Notice Prejudice Rule in Fidelity Cases*, IV Fid. L.J. 127 (1988). *See, e.g.*, Yacht Club on the Intracoastal Condo. Ass'n v. Lexington Ins. Co., 599 Fed. Appx. 875 (11th Cir. 2015) (that structure sustained additional damage because repairs were not made immediately and that certain repairs were undertaken before filing claim were evidence of prejudicial effect of passage of time and prejudice from inability of insurer to investigate prior to repairs).

595. Horkovich, Reeves & Andrews, *Insurance Coverage for Employee Theft Losses: A Policyholder Primer on Commonly Litigated Issues*, 29 U. Mem. L. Rev. 363, 371 (1999).

[i] Method of Providing Notice

Policyholders usually provide notice of a loss by calling the insurance "agent" that sold them the policy because that is who they know.[596] Generally, however, they do not know whether that "agent" is a representative of the insurer or a broker who is their representative.[597] When the policy covers commercial property, the party from whom it was obtained is usually a broker and notice to a broker is not notice to the insurer,[598] while notice to an agent of the insurer is. Any doubt can be avoided by providing notice directly to the insurer as well as to the agent or broker.[599] It is important for common interest community associations to realize that when the duty of submitting notice of a claim is delegated to the community association manager, failure of the manager to provide prompt notice of the loss will not excuse late notice.[600]

The standard crime policy does not specify that the notice be in writing. Nonetheless, it is advisable to provide notice in writing. First, written notice creates a record of the action of the insured that may be necessary if the insurer disputes having received prompt notice of the loss. Second, under state law written notice may provide the insured with certain protections.

---

596. *Consider* Hilton Head Resort Four Seasons Ctr. Horizontal Prop. Regime Council of Co-Owners, Inc. v. General Star Indem. Co., 357 F. Supp. 2d 885, 886 (D.S.C. 2005) (council asserted that it notified insurance agency from which it purchased policy several times, to no avail).

597. *See, e.g.*, Mitchell Buick & Oldsmobile Sales, Inc. v. National Dealer Services, Inc., 93 Ill. Dec. 71, 138 Ill. App. 3d 574, 582, 485 N.E.2d 1281, 1287 (1985) (it is generally recognized that broker acts as agent of insured rather than agent of insurance carrier).

598. *See, e.g.*, Southeastern Express Sys. v. Southern Guar. Ins. Co., 224 Ga. App. 697, 700, 482 S.E.2d 433, 435 (1997) (independent insurance agent or broker found to be agent of insured and notice to that agent did not constitute notice to insurer). *See also* Kendall Lakes Towers Condo. Ass'n v. Pac. Ins. Co., 2012 U.S. Dist. LEXIS 10749 (S.D. Fla. Jan. 30, 2012) (prompt notice to "producing agent"—party hired by insured and acting on its behalf—was not notice to carrier).

599. Experts recommend sending notice directly to the insurance company. Wood & Hurtado, *Don't Get Robbed of Your Fidelity Coverage*, 9 Enforce 12, 13 (2011), available at: http://www.andersonkill.com/Custom/PublicationPDF/PublicationID_1062_Dont-Get-Robbed-of-Your-Fidelity-Coverage.pdf (on discovery of theft or fraud, policyholder should immediately send notice of loss to its insurance broker and its insurer); Horkovich, Reeves & Andrews, *Insurance Coverage for Employee Theft Losses: A Policyholder Primer on Commonly Litigated Issues*, 29 U. Mem. L. Rev. 363, 366 (1999) (notice of event possibly covered by policy should be sent *to insurance company* as soon as possible after loss first is discovered).

600. Ridglea Estate Condo. Ass'n v. Lexington Ins. Co., 2005 U.S. App. LEXIS 16724 (5th Cir. Aug. 10, 2005) (that management neglected to have roofs inspected by expert at some reasonable time soon after hailstorm occurred did not serve to toll prompt notice provision in favor of association); Ridglea Estate Condo. Ass'n v. Lexington Ins. Co., 309 F. Supp. 2d 851 (N.D. Tex. 2004) (that association's manager may have been negligent in discovering damage or engaged in subsequent activities to blame damage on later-occurring storms—perhaps as cover-up for earlier negligence—did not work to benefit of association on notice issue). The governing board should remember that the manger is its agent, and it will, therefore, generally be bound by the actions of the manager on behalf of the association. *See, e.g.*, Biscayne Cove Condo. Ass'n v. QBE Ins. Corp., 971 F. Supp. 2d 1121, 1126 (S.D. Fla. 2013).

Written notice need not take any particular form.[601] A letter, or series of letters, to the insurer that briefly describes the loss is generally sufficient. Email can be used to provide notice;[602] however, if an association does not have its own email address—as is the case with many smaller associations—and notice is sent by an officer, board member, or the manager, it is a good idea to place a hardcopy of the notice—and the insurer's response—in the association files because board members, officers, and managers change and the association may not be able to access the electronic version of the notice in the future.

[ii] Notice Problems for Common Interest Communities

Meeting notice of loss requirements presents special concerns for common interest communities. First, who will provide the notice? In a business of any size there will likely be a person whose job responsibilities include handling insurance claims. That person is probably fairly familiar with the insurance coverage and claims procedures. A common interest community, however, is run by residents who volunteer to serve on the governing board with, in many cases, the assistance of a professional manager. The person who provides the notice will generally be either the manager or an officer of the corporation. Neither the officers nor the manager may have much experience with insurance claims. It would be advisable for one person to be assigned the responsibility of handling claims and to educate him- or herself on the process. Unfortunately, common interest community officers are often only in office for a few years. Thus, an association may turn to the manager to handle a claim. Ordinarily managers have some knowledge of insurance. The association, however, needs to monitor the progress of its claim. It should assign an officer or director to receive copies of all communications to or from the manager concerning the claim [603]

The membership on a common interest community governing board can change significantly in a short period of time. Decisions made by earlier boards can be reversed by later boards. Occasionally, a board will submit a claim to the insurer and, before the company makes a decision, a newly elected board will decide not to pursue the claim. If the claim is later resubmitted, will the notice be considered late? In one condominium case, notice of a claim was submitted

601. Horkovich, Reeves & Andrews, *Insurance Coverage for Employee Theft Losses: A Policyholder Primer on Commonly Litigated Issues*, 29 U. Mem. L. Rev. 363, 366 (1999) (notice of loss is brief statement to insurance company informing it that policyholder has discovered loss; notice need not contain details that still may be unknown to policyholder at that time).

602. Branson, *Fidelity Bond Insurance: Protection Against Condo Crime* (Cooperator, 2014), available at: http://cooperator.com/articles/2823/1/Fidelity-Bond-Insurance/Page1.html (insured can either call, email, fax, file lawsuit, or submit loss form obtained from broker to report loss to broker who will then notify insurance company).

603. The governing board should remember that the manger is its agent, and it will, therefore, generally be bound by the actions of the manager on behalf of the association. *See, e.g.*, Biscayne Cove Condo. Ass'n v. QBE Ins. Corp., 971 F. Supp. 2d 1121, 1126 (S.D. Fla. 2013).

in March, but the claim was withdrawn in September. Over two years later the association again notified the insurer of the claim. The insurer contended that filing, withdrawing, and resubmitting the claim constituted a breach of the prompt notice provision. The court found there was evidence tending to show the insurer was not prejudiced and it refused to grant summary judgment. Whether the notice was prompt was, concluded the court, a question for the jury.[604]

[b] Proof of Loss

Under the standard crime policy, the named insured has to provide the insurer with a detailed, sworn proof of loss within 120 days after discovering a loss or a situation that could result in a loss or damage to covered property.[605] Note that the policy provides that any claim for loss covered under it has to be "presented" by the named insured.[606]

There may be losses that could fall under either the crime policy or a commercial property policy. Insureds need to be aware that there is a difference in the proof of loss requirements between the standard versions of those two types of policies. Under basic commercial property policies, the insurer supplies the insured with the proof of loss form and the insured must send the insurer the signed, sworn proof of loss containing the information it requires within 60 days after its request.[607] Under the standard crime policy, however, the requirement to provide a proof of loss is not triggered by a request from the insurer. Rather, the clock on the 120-day limit in the crime policy begins to run on "discovery." Fortunately, the "notice-prejudice" rule generally applies to proofs of loss meaning generally that late submission of a proof of loss will not bar the claim unless the insurer was prejudiced by the delay.[608]

While the policy might appear to place the burden of obtaining or creating a proof of loss form on the insured, in practice the claims examiner for the insurer will generally provide a proof of loss form to the insured.[609] Typically, the

---

604. Palma Vista Condo. Ass'n of Hillsborough County v. Nationwide Mut. Fire Ins. Co., 2010 U.S. Dist. LEXIS 118262 (M.D. Fla. Oct. 7, 2010).

605. ISO Form CR 00 23 11 15, § E.1.g.(2). *See generally* Horkovich, Reeves & Andrews, *Insurance Coverage for Employee Theft Losses: A Policyholder Primer on Commonly Litigated Issues*, 29 U. Mem. L. Rev. 363, 369 (1999); Haase, *Proof of Loss in Fidelity Cases—Sufficiency & Requirements of Good Faith*, 12 Forum 980 (1977).

606. ISO Form CR 00 23 11 15, §§ E.1.r. Note that under the Discovery Form, this clause is identical, but has a different designation. *See* CR 00 22 11 15, § E.1.p.

607. *See* ISO Form CP 00 10 10 00, § E.3.a.(7); ISO Form CP 00 17 04 02, § E.3.a.(7).

608. *See generally* Horkovich, Reeves & Andrews, *Insurance Coverage for Employee Theft Losses: A Policyholder Primer on Commonly Litigated Issues*, 29 U. Mem. L. Rev. 363, 370 (1999) (as with untimely notices of loss, untimely proofs of loss have become increasingly subject to prejudice standard); Zauderer & Mills, *At the Apex of the Arc of the Pendulum—Notice Prejudice Rule in Fidelity Cases*, IV Fid. L.J. 127 (1988).

609. Branson, *Fidelity Bond Insurance: Protection Against Condo Crime* (Cooperator, 2014), available at: http://cooperator.com/articles/2823/1/Fidelity-Bond-Insurance/Page1.html.

form will ask for a detailed explanation of the claim and whether there is supporting documentation for the amount being claimed.[610] The policy refers to a "sworn" proof of loss,[611] but apparently proofs of loss need to be both signed by an "authorized individual" and *notarized*,[612] although failure to have the proof of loss signed may not be fatal to its validity.[613] The President of the association would probably be considered an "authorized individual" by virtue of the office. Any other officer or a director, and perhaps the community association manager, might also be considered an "authorized individual." It is probably advisable for the association to specifically authorize an individual or individuals to sign the proof of loss on behalf of the association and to do so by a formal vote of the governing board recorded in the minutes.[614] The policy requires an insured that has reason to believe that a loss—other than under the coverages for employee theft or forgery—involves a violation of law, has to notify local law enforcement authorities.[615] The proof of loss form will generally ask if there is a police report, and if there is, require it to be attached to the form when submitted.[616]

610. Branson, *Fidelity Bond Insurance: Protection Against Condo Crime* (Cooperator, 2014), available at: http://cooperator.com/articles/2823/1/Fidelity-Bond-Insurance/Page1.html. *See also* Horkovich, Reeves & Andrews, *Insurance Coverage for Employee Theft Losses: A Policyholder Primer on Commonly Litigated Issues*, 29 U. Mem. L. Rev. 363, 369 (1999) (proof of loss should explain circumstances surrounding loss and substantiate amount of loss in some detail).

611. ISO Form CR 00 23 11 15, § E.1.g.(2).

612. *See, e.g.*, Schupak Group v. Travelers Cas. & Sur. Co. of Am., 716 F. Supp. 2d 262, 268–69 (S.D.N.Y. 2010), *cert. den.*, 565 U.S. 1093, 132 S. Ct. 849, 181 L. Ed. 2d 549 (2011) (where insured failed to sign or swear to proof of loss submitted in support of its claim and failed to plead any facts demonstrating that its proof of loss included *required notarized signature*, insured's pleadings regarding proof of loss were insufficient to demonstrate plausible inference of adequate performance). *See also* Branson, *Fidelity Bond Insurance: Protection Against Condo Crime* (Cooperator, 2014), available at: http://cooperator.com/articles/2823/1/Fidelity-Bond-Insurance/Page1.html (proof of loss form will ask if it has been signed by authorized individual and notarized).

613. *See, e.g.*, Walker v. American Bankers Ins. Group, 108 Nev. 533, 536–37, 836 P.2d 59, 61 (1992) (one-page list of personal property destroyed and replacement cost for each item claimed fulfilled purpose of proof of loss requirement even though it was unsigned and unsworn); Sutton v. Fire Ins. Exchange, 265 Ore. 322, 325–26, 509 P.2d 418, 420 (1973) (where insured furnished all that policy required for proof of loss except that he did not affix his signature under oath to information furnished, jury could find that he substantially complied with requirement).

614. Governing boards usually have an organizational meeting once a year at which the officers are elected by the board members. At that meeting, the board could designate an officer or director—or the manager—to acts on its behalf for the coming year on insurance matters including signing proofs of loss and memorialize that designation in the minutes.

615. ISO Form CR 00 23 11 15, § E.1.g.(1).

616. Branson, *Fidelity Bond Insurance: Protection Against Condo Crime* (Cooperator, 2014), available at: http://cooperator.com/articles/2823/1/Fidelity-Bond-Insurance/Page1.html.

While the form may ask for specific detailed information, courts generally say that substantial compliance with the proof of loss requirements is sufficient.[617] Thus, a document, or group of documents, containing the necessary information may be considered a sufficient proof of loss even though not submitted with a standard proof of loss form.[618]

[c] Examination under Oath

The named insured is required to submit to Examination Under Oath (EUO) at the request of the insurer and to give the insurer a signed statement of its answers.[619] The purpose of an EUO is to determine whether a claim is just and should be paid.[620] The examination serves to protect the insurance company from fraud by allowing it to probe into the circumstances of a loss.[621] An EUO clause is more than a cooperation requirement. It requires an insured to perform specific duties, and compliance with a request under an EUO clause is not optional nor subject to determination of reasonableness by a trial court.[622] The insurer can

617. Walker v. American Bankers Ins. Group, 108 Nev. 533, 536–37, 836 P.2d 59, 61 (1992) (absent express forfeiture provision, failure to comply with proof of loss requirement does not preclude recovery, at least where insured complied substantially with requirement; one-page list of personal property destroyed and replacement cost for each item claimed fulfilled purpose of proof of loss requirement even though it was unsigned and unsworn as information was sufficient to enable insurer to investigate losses, estimate its rights and liabilities, and prevent fraud and unjust claims from being asserted); Sutton v. Fire Ins. Exchange, 265 Ore. 322, 325, 509 P.2d 418, 419 (1973) (substantial, as distinguished from strict, compliance of proof of loss requirement is all that is required and test of whether insured substantially complied with proof of loss requirement should be whether proof submitted by insured fulfilled purpose of proof of loss).

618. *See, e.g.*, Los Angeles Athletic Club v. United States Fidelity & Guaranty Co., 41 Cal. App. 439, 441, 183 P. 174, 175 (1919) (requirement for itemized statement of claim was as fully and satisfactorily made as it could be under circumstances, by affidavit of various officers and employees of insured that provided in detail all information as to nature and amount of alleged misappropriations that various witnesses possessed).

619. ISO Form CR 00 23 11 15, § E.1.g.(5). *See generally* Knoll, *Examination Under Oath: The Insurance Companies Best Friend*, 16 Forum 777 (1981).

620. Ransom v. Selective Ins. Co., 229 N.J. Super. 43, 46, 550 A.2d 1006, 1007 (1988); Gordon v. St. Paul Fire & Marine Ins. Co., 197 Mich. 226, 230, 163 N.W. 956, 957 (1917) (purpose of examination is to elicit facts based on which company may determine whether it will defend or adjust claim). *See also* Graham, *The Sworn Examination Under Oath in Insurance Investigations*, 26 Los Angeles Lawyer 26 (2003) (examination of an insured may be useful in resolving issues such as valuation of damaged or destroyed property or ascertainment of coverage under policy and if proof of loss is unclear or contains numerous inaccuracies, or fails to provide adequate documentation, EUO proceeding may assist in resolving outstanding questions).

621. Hart v. Mechanics & Traders Ins. Co., 46 F. Supp. 166, 169 (D. La. 1942) (through Examination Under Oath insurer is better able to determine its obligations and to protect itself against false claims).

622. Knowledge A-Z, Inc. v. Sentry Ins., 857 N.E.2d 411, 421 (Ind. App. 2006).

generally inquire about any information *relevant and material* to the claim or the insurance,[623] but an insured is not required to answer *immaterial* questions.[624]

[i] Demand for Examination under Oath

A requirement that an insured submit to a sworn examination is generally said not to be self-executing.[625] The insurer has to make a demand on the insured.[626] Usually, the insured is not required to do more than meet the specifics of that demand.[627] For a demand to be legally sufficient, it usually has to designate the time and place of the examination and the person before whom the examination is to be conducted. Typically, the insurer can defend itself in an action by its insured for failure to pay a claim by showing the insured failed to submit to a sworn examination. That defense, however, is generally unavailable to the insurer if its demand for an EUO lacks the requisite specificity.[628] A request for an EUO

---

623. *See, e.g.*, Stover v. Aetna Casualty & Surety Co., 658 F. Supp. 156, 160 (S.D. W. Va. 1987) (insurer has right to examine about any matter material to its liability limited by rule of reasonableness and specificity); Phillips v. Allstate Indem. Co., 156 Md. App. 729, 734, 848 A.2d 681, 689 (2004) (generally during EUO insurer may conduct searching examination, though all questions should be confined to matters relevant and material to loss which is determined in context of claim and investigation); Southern Guaranty Ins. Co. v. Dean, 252 Miss. 69, 76, 172 So. 2d 553, 556 (1965) (all matters are material in examination of insured that have bearing on insurance and loss). *See also* 200 Leslie Condo. Ass'n v. QBE Ins. Corp., 965 F. Supp. 2d 1386, 1397 (S.D. Fla. 2013), *aff'd*, 616 Fed. Appx. 936 (11th Cir. 2015) (demand for Examination Under Oath of representative with most knowledge about quantum of loss, cause of loss, maintenance history of buildings, preparation of and support for claim package, repairs/replacement of damaged property and any estimates for them, and whether repair and replacement of windows and sliding glass doors providing access to individual units was responsibility of association or its members presented subject areas of inquiry within scope of EUO clause permitting examination about any matter relating to policy or claim).

624. Phillips v. Allstate Indem. Co., 156 Md. App. 729, 734, 848 A.2d 681, 689 (2004).

625. Weber v. General Acci. Fire & Life Assurance Corp., 10 Ohio App. 3d 305, 307, 462 N.E.2d 422, 424 (1983).

626. Nicolai v. Transcontinental Ins. Co., 61 Wn. 2d 295, 297, 378 P.2d 287, 288 (1963) (numerous cases hold demand is prerequisite for Examination Under Oath). *See also* C-Suzanne Beauty Salon, Ltd. v. General Ins. Co., 574 F.2d 106 (2d Cir. 1978) (where insurer requested examination and set date for it, but did not further insist on its right to examine insureds and instead appeared to have decided to mark time silently until period for insured to bring suit expired, no proper demand was made).

627. *See, e.g.*, Summit Towers Condo. Ass'n v. QBE Ins. Corp., 2012 U.S. Dist. LEXIS 188510 (S.D. Fla. Apr. 26, 2012) (no dispute of fact existed over whether condominium association complied with demand for EUO where when association filed suit it had complied with request for EUO of named individual and there was no pending request to complete that EUO or to take additional EUOs).

628. Weber v. General Acci. Fire & Life Assurance Corp., 10 Ohio App. 3d 305, 307, 462 N.E.2d 422, 424 (1983). In *Weber*, the insurer sent a letter to the attorney for the insured requesting that the insured "'appear for the purpose of taking his examination under oath at a mutually agreeable time and place,'" but no additional communications were made by either party and the sworn examination was never conducted. The court said the notice of the Examination Under Oath was defective in two respects. First, apparently only the attorney received the letter, but because the policy was a

has to be made within a reasonable time.[629] Even though compliance with a demand for Examination Under Oath may be a condition to recovery under the policy, where it is impossible for the insured to comply with the condition, that failure generally does not operate to forfeit the policy.[630]

[ii] Common Interest Communities and Examinations

Common interest communities are ordinarily organized as non-profit corporations. Because a corporation can only act through its officers and agents, its officers, employees, and agents may be required to submit to Examinations Under Oath.[631] However, an insurance treatise cautions that the insured, not its counsel, has to submit to the examination.[632] Examination of officers or directors of a common interest community presents problems for both the CIC and the insurance company. First, unlike in a business corporation, officers and directors of a CIC are volunteers that may devote little time to the affairs of the CIC and often lack sophistication in commercial matters. They usually rely on the professional manager for guidance in business matters.[633] Second, officers and directors in a CIC generally serve a two- or three-year term of office. There are CICs, especially smaller ones, in which officers and directors serve many consecutive terms, but there are others in which there is frequent turnover in the directors and officers.

---

contract between the carrier and the insured, fairness required notice to be given to the insured as well as to his attorney. Next, the letter requesting a sworn examination was not reasonably specific, but was couched in precatory language and appeared to shift to the insured the responsibility of arranging the details of the examination. *See also* Roberto v. Hartford Fire Ins. Co., 177 F.2d 811, 815 (7th Cir. 1949) (policy stipulation for examination of insured is valid and performance of it is condition precedent for recovery providing time and place designated for examination are reasonable); Green v. St. Paul Fire & Marine Ins. Co., 691 F. Supp. 700, 703 (S.D.N.Y. 1988) (where no demand was made that former employee of insured corporation appear at specific time and place, he did not breach insurance policy by not appearing); Saft America, Inc. v. Insurance Co. of North America, 155 Ga. App. 500, 271 S.E.2d 641 (1980) (insurer failed to specifically designate time and place for examination as required under its own policy provisions and, therefore, summary judgment in its favor was error); Nicolai v. Transcontinental Ins. Co., 61 Wn. 2d 295, 297, 378 P.2d 287, 288 (1963) (demand must be explicit as to time and place for examination and as to person before whom it should take place).

629. Beckley v. Otsego County Farmers Cooperative Fire Ins. Co., 3 A.D.2d 190, 195, 159 N.Y.S.2d 270, 275 (1957) (timeliness of demand made almost four months after proofs of loss were filed was a question of fact that could not be determined on motion for summary judgment).

630. Roberto v. Hartford Fire Ins. Co., 177 F.2d 811, 815 (7th Cir. 1949).

631. Cozen, *Insuring Real Property*, § 22.02[1] (Matthew Bender & Co., 2015) (insurance company may request the insured to "cooperate" by making independent contractors voluntarily available for examination); Biller & Schillaci, *The Examination Under Oath—A Connecticut Overview*, 83 Conn. B.J. 289, 318 (2009) (employees and agents of insured may be examined).

632. 1 Jeffrey E. Thomas, *New Appleman on Insurance Law Library Edition* § 4.06[4][c] (Matthew Bender, 2023) (insureds are often represented by public adjusters or legal counsel, but insured, and not his or her representative, must submit to Examination Under Oath).

633. The insurer may seek to examine the manager under oath. *See, e.g.*, El Dorado Towers Condo. Ass'n v. QBE Ins. Corp., 717 F. Supp. 2d 1311 (S.D. Fla. 2010) (insurer requested Examinations Under Oath of property manager).

Thus, the officers and directors who were serving at the time of a loss may not be serving or even living in the community at the time the insurer wants to conduct an Examination Under Oath.[634] The sitting officers may not have served at the time of loss.[635] The best person available for the examination may not have held any office or even have been a resident of the community at the time of the loss.[636] Even if the persons who were serving at the time of the loss are still in office, or at least available, it is quite common for them to have little or no knowledge or useful information about the claim.

The CIC has an obligation to present a knowledgeable person for examination. If it produces someone who is unable to answer—or fails to prepare for—the questions put forward at the examination, a court may find that it did not fully comply with the policy requirement that its representative submit to examination.[637] Lack of preparation and knowledge can be so deficient as to constitute a failure to comply with the EUO requirement and, therefore, be a material breach the policy.[638]

---

634. *See, e.g.*, 200 Leslie Condo. Ass'n v. QBE Ins. Corp., 965 F. Supp. 2d 1386, 1397 (S.D. Fla. 2013), *aff'd*, 616 Fed. Appx. 936 (11th Cir. 2015) (while association president at time of hurricane would have been better candidate for EUO, he no longer resided at condominium at time of examination).

635. *See, e.g.*, Garden-Aire Vill. South Condo. Ass'n v. QBE Ins. Corp., 591 Fed. Appx. 868 (11th Cir. 2014) (association property suffered damage from hurricane in 2005 and later produced its president for Examination Under Oath, but he knew virtually nothing about claim, having come to association after hurricane and having made no effort to learn even most basic information about it); Oriole Gardens Condominiums, III v. Independence Casualty & Surety Company, 2012 U.S. Dist. LEXIS 29100 (S.D. Fla. Mar. 6, 2012) (association president submitted to EUO, but did not possess certain knowledge of information prior to his election); Citizens Prop. Ins. Corp. v. Mango Hill Condo. Ass'n 12, 54 So. 3d 578, 580 (Fla. 3d DCA 2011) (current president of condominium association who was not president when losses were incurred submitted to Examination Under Oath).

636. *See, e.g.*, 1231 Euclid Homeowners Ass'n v. State Farm Fire & Casualty Co., 135 Cal. App. 4th 1008, 1020, 37 Cal. Rptr. 3d 795, 804 (2006) (individual declared to be "person most knowledgeable" during discovery did not even live in community at time of earthquake that cause claimed loss).

637. In one case, for example, the sitting president, who was not in office at the time of the loss, submitted to an Examination Under Oath on behalf of the association. He did not look at any association minutes or records in preparation for the EUO, and his only preparation for the examination was a meeting with the association and brief review of the Proof of Loss. Although he did not refuse to answer any of the questions posed, he did not know the answer to many of them. The court found he did not reasonably prepare for the EUO and, therefore, did not adequately respond to the inquiries regarding matters relating to the insurance or the claim as required by the policy The association thus did not fully comply with the policy requirement that its representative submit to Examination Under Oath. 200 Leslie Condo. Ass'n v. QBE Ins. Corp., 965 F. Supp. 2d 1386, 1397 (S.D. Fla. 2013), *aff'd*, 616 Fed. Appx. 936 (11th Cir. 2015).

638. Biscayne Cove Condo. Ass'n v. QBE Ins. Corp., 971 F. Supp. 2d 1121, 1133 (S.D. Fla. 2013) (rejecting argument that person who testifies in EUO is not obligated to prepare or otherwise have information; where association "purposely presented" two witnesses who were not prepared for EUOs, refusal to produce witness who could respond amounted to willful disregard of post-loss obligation under policy and material breached of policy).

[d] Examination of Records

The named insured is required under the policy to keep records of all property covered under the policy so the insurer can verify the amount of any loss.[639] In the event of a loss it is the duty of the named insured to produce all "pertinent" records for examination by the insurer.[640] Failure to produce the requested records for examination may be the basis for denial of a claim. In a subsequent action on that claim, however, courts will generally be somewhat lenient if the insured has made a reasonable effort to comply—instead of being willfully uncooperative. The court will then either stay the action or dismiss it without prejudice to allow belated compliance.[641]

[i] Common Interest Communities and Records Production

Production of records can present problems for common interest community associations because they are operated by volunteers, albeit usually with the assistance of a professional community association manager. Nonetheless, an association may not maintain an effective filing system. Some documents may never end up in the files. Others may be removed and disposed of as unneeded. Documents may be in the hands of different officers who do not transfer them to the association files. Even if the association has good files, the person who maintains them may move away, leaving no one with knowledge of the filing system. At least in theory, if an association has professional management, its files are either in the possession of, or supervised by, the manager. That, however, may not guarantee a thorough filing system. Documents may be discarded or misfiled before the manager ever learns of them. Older—but still needed—files may be purged without the manager's knowledge. In small communities, the manager probably manages many other small projects and may only be on site a few times a month. All this means that an association may be thoroughly unprepared to respond to a records request.

The standard crime policy provides the insurer the right to "examine" records. All that should be required of the association is that it make records available on a reasonable basis. For example, where an CIC association through its president or attorney responded to repeated requests from the adjuster for a large number of documents and offered to make the documents available at the property or the

639. ISO Form CR 00 23 11 15, § E.1.t. Note that under the Discovery Form, this clause is identical, but has a different designation. *See* ISO Form CR 00 22 11 15, § E.1.s.

640. ISO Form CR 00 23 11 15, § E.1.g.(4).

641. *See* El-Ad Enclave at Miramar Condo. Ass'n v. Mt. Hawley Ins. Co., 752 F. Supp. 2d 1282 (S.D. Fla. 2010) (where association "amicably" attempted to coordinate production of documents and inquired whether insurer wanted copies of documents or wanted to inspect them personally and on two occasions parties agreed to dates for inspection of documents, there was disputed fact presented regarding whether association was in compliance with demands for documents; if insured has not demonstrated willful disregard of policy preconditions, courts either stay action or dismiss it without prejudice to allow belated compliance).

management offices, the insurer treated these offers as unresponsive and took the position that the association failed to respond to its requests to provide access to the requested records. The court did not directly address whether the insured had violated the cooperation requirement but appeared to accept that the insured had fully cooperated.[642]

A mere delay in producing documents may not breach the obligation to allow the insurer to examine the association records. For example, an insurer requested that an association produce unit owner files. The association claimed the files were confidential. The insurer offered a confidentiality agreement for any unit member files. Almost two years later the insurer was finally granted access to the unit owner files. The court said that summary judgment for the insurer based on failure to allow for examination of the files was unwarranted. The association offered an explanation for not producing the files and thus, the insurer failed to show as a matter of law that the association materially breached. The dispute over examination of the files was for a jury to decide.[643]

When the insurer's request appears to the association to be excessive or intrusive, it should consult with an experience insurance law attorney because many courts limit access to records by a rule of reasonableness and specificity and will prohibit the insurer from roaming at will through all of the financial records of the insured.[644]

[ii] Minutes

One set of records insurers often request is governing board or association minutes.[645] There is a difference between the minutes of the association and those of the governing board. Governing boards meet regularly, usually once or twice a month. The association is the organization made up of all the residents and ordinarily has one annual meeting at which the members of the governing board are elected. Occasionally there are special association meetings. When an insurer requests minutes, it should specify whether it wants board or association minutes.

---

642. Boardwalk Condo. Ass'n v. Travelers Indem. Co., 2007 U.S. Dist. LEXIS 48325 (S.D. Cal. July 3, 2007).

643. El Dorado Towers Condo. Ass'n v. QBE Ins. Corp., 717 F. Supp. 2d 1311 (S.D. Fla. 2010). *See also* Oriole Gardens Condominiums, III v. Independence Casualty & Surety Company, 2012 U.S. Dist. LEXIS 29100 (S.D. Fla. Mar. 6, 2012) (where record did not indicate what specific documents were outstanding, or whether they were relevant or necessary for insurer to investigate claim and association complied "to a certain degree" with its obligation to produce and disclose documents, there was question of fact for jury as to whether association satisfied its obligation and insurer was, therefore, not entitled to summary judgment for failure of association to comply with obligation to produce and disclose documents).

644. *See, e.g.*, Stover v. Aetna Cas. & Sur. Co., 658 F. Supp. 156, 160 (S.D. W. Va. 1987).

645. *See, e.g.*, Oriole Gardens Condominiums, III v. Independence Casualty & Surety Company, 2012 U.S. Dist. LEXIS 29100 (S.D. Fla. Mar. 6, 2012); Citizens Prop. Ins. Corp. v. Galeria Villas Condo. Ass'n, 48 So. 3d 188 (Fla. 3d DCA 2010).

Minutes can present a problem for common interest communities. Experts warn that the contents of board minutes should be limited.[646] Other than basic introductory information—the name of the organization, the date, time, and place of the meeting, the determination of a quorum, and the announcement of compliance with any meeting notice requirements—the minutes should state no more than the motions made and seconded and the results of the vote on each motion. Nonetheless, well-meaning association secretaries persist in making the minutes a narrative account of the meeting. They include not only the discussion surrounding motions but even discussion that took place without a proper motion having been made. Therein lies danger for the common interest community. Under the rules of evidence, records of regularly conducted business activity are admissible in court as an exception to the hearsay rule.[647] However, before they ever reach a courtroom, the minutes may be examined by the insurer and found to provide a basis for denying a claim,[648] or worse, evidence of fraud.

Insurance carriers may not be aware of other records that may be beneficial to them. For example, some associations produce and post "board reports" or "meeting summaries." When they are prepared by an association board member or director, they may constitute official association records. Similarly, a newsletter that purports to represent the views of the association governing board may also be considered an official record. These reports may be as useful to the insurer as the minutes. The carrier, therefore, when requesting records may very well inquire whether the association produces these or similar documents. Associations, on the other hand, should not produce board reports or meeting summaries at all, should make sure any newsletter is "unofficial," and should be careful about the content of any written communication about its claims to unit owners.

[iii] Governing Documents and Contracts

An association should anticipate that the insurer will want to inspect its governing documents and possibly contracts to which it is a party. For example, one insurer sought an association's Declaration of Condominium, condominium

646. *See, e.g.*, 6A Rohan, *Real Estate Transactions: Home Owner Associations and Planned Unit Developments—Law and Practice: Forms*, § 7A.04[2][c] (Matthew Bender, 2023).

647. Uniform Rules of Evidence Act, Rule 803(6). The federal rules and those of the states are similar to the Uniform Act. *See also* Meadows Condo. Ass'n v. Redman, 2009 Conn. Super. LEXIS 2062 (Conn. Super. July 30, 2009) (board minutes should be taken as best evidence of actions actually taken by board).

648. *Consider* Mt. Lodge Ass'n v. Crum & Forster Indem. Co., 210 W. Va. 536, 558 S.E.2d 336 (2001), where the insurer denied a claim under employee dishonesty coverage because it believed the "employee" was actually an independent contractor. The court decision mentions governing board minutes that state that the association's plan was for the board to hire a particular person to "work for" the "board as their construction manager." Whether the minutes had any bearing on the determination of the lower court to find for the insurer or the appellate court to reverse that decision is not clear. What is clear is that minutes do find their way into court, are taken seriously by judges, and can affect the rights of the association.

bylaws, and contracts for property management services for the prior seven years.[649] The association argued these requests were overbroad, ambiguous, and not relevant to adjustment of its claim. The court did not agree. It noted that these documents typically contain information bearing directly on a claim and the respective obligations of the insurer, the insured, and the residents who live within the insured units.

Property management contracts can be important. Under the standard crime policy, the acts of a CAM would not be covered unless an endorsement is added to the policy. The usual one is the Designated Agents Endorsement. It modifies the policy and applies the insuring agreement for employee theft. It includes a schedule for listing the capacity of the agent. It amends the definition of "employee" to include a natural person, partnership, or corporation that the named insured appoints in *writing* to act as its agent in the capacity shown on the schedule.[650] That person or entity is considered an "employee" of the association while acting on its behalf or while in possession of covered property, thus allowing the coverage for employee theft to be invoked. The management contract is the required *written appointment* of the CAM as agent of the association and also generally spells out the duties of the CAM. Therefore, it can determine when the CAM is acting on behalf of the association.

The insurer also may ask to examine other financial documents. For example, a condominium association acted as its own general contractor to make renovations to the property. It hired an individual to act as construction manager. It later alleged the construction manager misappropriated over $50,000 and submitted a claim under its employee dishonesty coverage. The insurer responded by requesting copies of the association's tax forms relating to the employment of the construction manager. The association had no tax records because it had neither withheld income taxes from, nor paid workers' compensation premiums for, the construction manager. The insurer denied the claim, stating that a key element in determining the status of the actor was whether or not the association paid taxes on his behalf.[651]

[e] Securing Rights of Recovery

The standard crime policy requires the named insured to secure all of its rights of recovery in the event of a loss against any person or organization responsible for that loss and to do nothing that would impair those rights.[652]

649. Citizens Prop. Ins. Corp. v. Galeria Villas Condo. Ass'n, 48 So. 3d 188, 191, n.3 (Fla. 3d DCA 2010).

650. ISO Form CR 25 02 10 10, § 1.

651. Mt. Lodge Ass'n v. Crum & Forster Indem. Co., 210 W. Va. 536, 558 S.E.2d 336 (2001).

652. ISO Form CR 00 23 11 15, § E.1.g.(6).

[5] Books, Records, Inspections, and Surveys

The standard crime policy grants the insurer the right to examine the books and records of the named insured and to conduct inspections and surveys.

[a] Books and Records

The named insured is required under the policy to keep records of all property covered under the policy so the insurer can verify the amount of any loss.[653] The policy also provides that the insurer may examine and audit the books and records of the named insured, as those books and records relate to the policy, at any time during the policy period and *up to three years* subsequent to it.[654]

[b] Inspections and Surveys

Under the standard crime policy, the insurer has the right to make inspections and surveys at any time, give reports on the conditions it finds to the named insured, and recommend changes.[655] The insurer, however, is not compelled to make inspections, surveys, reports, or recommendations, and any of those actions that it does undertake relate only to insurability and the premiums to be charged.[656] The policy provides the insurer does not make safety inspections or undertake to perform the duty of any person or organization to provide for the health or safety of workers or the public, and does not warrant that conditions are safe or healthful or comply with laws, regulations, codes, or standards.[657] The provisions regarding inspections and surveys apply not only to the insurer itself but also to any rating, advisory, rate service, or similar organization that makes insurance inspections, surveys, reports, or recommendations.[658]

[6] Valuation of Loss

The crime policy sets forth how losses are valued and paid based on whether the property is money, securities, or other property.[659]

---

653. ISO Form CR 00 23 11 15, § E.1.t. Note that under the Discovery Form, this clause is identical, but has a different designation. *See* ISO Form CR 00 22 11 15, § E.1.s.

654. ISO Form CR 00 23 11 15, § E.1.i.

655. ISO Form CR 00 23 11 15, § E.1.k.(1). *See, e.g.*, Great Am. Ins. Cos. v. Subranni (*In re* Tri-State Armored Servs.), 366 B.R. 326, 334 (D.N.J. 2007) (underwriter hired security firm to perform security survey of insured's facility and report recommended numerous improvements to security systems and procedures; subsequent security survey identified five areas of significant concern including access control, alarm coverage, liability storage, liability staging, and accountability).

656. ISO Form CR 00 23 11 15, § E.1.k.(2).

657. *See generally* Ingram, *Liability of Insurers for Negligence in Inspection of Insured Premises*, 50 Drake L. Rev. 623 (2002).

658. ISO Form CR 00 23 11 15, § E.1.k.(3).

659. ISO Form CR 00 23 11 15, § E.1.y. Note that under the Discovery Form, this clause is effectively identical, but has a different designation. *See* CR 00 22 11 15, § E.1.x.

[a] Money

"Money" is defined as currency, coins, and bank notes that are in current use and have a face value, traveler's checks and money orders that are held for sale to the public, and deposits in the account of the named insured at any financial institution.[660] The insurer pays for loss of money but only up to and including its face value.[661] It will, at the option of the named insured, pay for loss of money issued by any country other than the United States of America at the face value in the money issued by that country or in the United States of America dollar equivalent, determined by the rate of exchange published in *The Wall Street Journal* on the day the loss was discovered.

[b] Securities

"Securities" means negotiable and non-negotiable instruments or contracts that represent either money or property and includes tokens, tickets, revenue, and other stamps in current use and evidences of debt issued in connection with credit or charge cards that are not issued by the named insured, but does not include money.[662] The insurer pays for loss of securities, but only up to and including their value at the close of business on the day the loss was discovered.[663] At its option, the insurer may pay the market value of those securities or replace them in kind—in which event the named insured has to assign to all its rights, title, and interest in and to those securities to the insurer—or it may pay the cost of any Lost Securities Bond required in connection with issuing duplicates of the securities, but it will only be liable for payment of so much of the cost of the bond as would be charged for a bond having a penalty that did not exceed the lesser of the market value of the securities at the close of business on the day the loss was discovered or the limit of insurance applicable to the securities.

[c] Other Property

"Other property" is generally tangible property other than money and securities that has intrinsic value.[664] The insurer will pay for the loss of or damage to other property or loss from damage to the premises—meaning the interior of that portion of any building the named insured occupies in conducting its business[665]—or its exterior, for the replacement cost of the property without deduction for depreciation.[666] Any property that the insurer pays for or replaces becomes its

660. ISO Form CR 00 22 11 15, § F.16. See ISO Form CR 00 22 11 15, § F.9, for the definition of "financial institution."
661. ISO Form CR 00 23 11 15, § E.1.y.(1).
662. ISO Form CR 00 22 11 15, § F.22.
663. ISO Form CR 00 23 11 15, § E.1.y.(2).
664. ISO Form CR 00 22 11 15, § F.18.
665. ISO Form CR 00 22 11 15, § F.19.
666. ISO Form CR 00 23 11 15, § E.1.y.(3).(a).

property.[667] The insurer will not pay more than the least of the limit of insurance applicable to the lost or damaged property, the cost to replace the lost or damaged property with property of comparable material and quality and used for the same purpose, or the amount the named insured actually spends that is required to repair or replace the lost or damaged property.

The insurer will not pay on a replacement cost basis for any covered loss or damage to property until that property is actually repaired or replaced and unless the repair or replacement is made as soon as reasonably possible after the loss or damage.[668] If the property is not repaired or replaced, the insurer will pay on an actual cash value basis.

The insurer will, at the option of the named insured, pay for loss or damage to other property in the money of the country in which the loss or damage was sustained or in the United States of America dollar equivalent of the money of the country in which the loss or damage was sustained, determined by the rate of exchange published in *The Wall Street Journal* on the day the loss was discovered.[669]

[7] Joint Insureds and Payment of Loss

Under the standard commercial crime policy, the insurer will not pay more for a loss sustained by more than one insured than the amount it would have paid if all of the loss had been sustained by one insured.[670] Also, payment to the first named insured for a loss sustained by any insured, or payment to any "employee benefit plan" for a loss sustained by that plan, fully releases the insurer.[671]

[8] Loss Sustained during Prior Insurance

The Loss Sustained Form of the standard ISO Commercial Crime Policy contains two conditions regarding losses sustained during prior insurance.[672] The first applies when the prior policy was issued by the same insurer or any of its affiliates. The second applies when the prior policy was not issued by the same insurer or any of its affiliates. These conditions are omitted from the Discovery Form of the policy. Because prior policies may be important, they should be retained after they terminate. One expert recommends keeping expired copies policies for at least 5 years after their expiration and preferably 10 years.[673]

---

667. ISO Form CR 00 23 11 15, § E.1.y.(3).(d).
668. ISO Form CR 00 23 11 15, § E.1.y.(3).(b).
669. ISO Form CR 00 23 11 15, § E.1.y.(3).(c).
670. ISO Form CR 00 23 11 15, § E.1.l.(5).
671. ISO Form CR 00 23 11 15, § E.1.l.(6).
672. *See generally* Konop, *The Loss Sustained Policy and Multiple Year Losses: Keeping it Simple*, XVIII Fid. L.J. 193 (2012).
673. Wick, *Record Retention Means Future Protection*, Common Ground (CAI July/Aug. 1990). *See also* § 15.01[11], *supra*.

[a] Prior Policy Issued by Same Insurer or an Affiliate

If the named insured discovers a loss during the policy period that results directly from an occurrence that took place partly during that policy period and partly during the policy period or periods of any prior cancelled insurance that the same insurer or any of its affiliates issued to the named insured, or any *predecessor in interest*, and the current policy became effective at the time of cancellation of that prior insurance, the insurer will first settle the amount of loss the named insured sustained during the policy period of the current policy and then will settle the remaining amount of loss the named insured sustained during the policy period or periods of the prior insurance.[674]

If the named insured discovers a loss during the policy period that results directly from an occurrence that took place *entirely* during the policy period or periods of any prior cancelled insurance that the same insurer or any of its affiliates issued to the named insured, or any *predecessor in interest*, the insurer will pay for the loss, provided the current policy became effective at the time of cancellation of the prior insurance and the loss would have been covered under the current policy had it been in effect at the time of the occurrence.[675] When the current insurer pays for that loss, it will first settle the amount of loss that the named insured sustained during the most recent prior insurance and will then settle any remaining amount of loss sustained during the policy period or periods of any other prior insurance.

Whether the loss took place partly or entirely during the policy period or periods of any prior cancelled insurance, when the insurer settles the loss, the most it will pay for the entire loss is the highest single limit of insurance applicable during the period of loss, whether that limit was written under the current policy or under the prior insurance issued by it.[676] The insurer will apply the applicable deductible shown on the Declarations Page to the amount of loss sustained under the current policy, but if no loss was sustained under the current policy, it will apply the deductible shown on the Declarations Page to the amount of loss sustained under the most recent prior insurance.[677] If the deductible is larger than the amount of loss sustained under the current policy, or the most recent prior insurance, the insurer will apply the remaining deductible to the remaining amount of loss that was sustained during the prior insurance. It will not apply any other deductible that may have been applicable to that loss.

674. ISO Form CR 00 23 11 15, § E.1.o.(1).
675. ISO Form CR 00 23 11 15, § E.1.o.(2).
676. ISO Form CR 00 23 11 15, § E.1.o.(3).(a).
677. ISO Form CR 00 23 11 15, § E.1.o.(3).(b).

[b] Prior Policy *Not* Issued by Same Insurer or an Affiliate

If the named insured discovers a loss during the policy period that results directly from an occurrence that took place during the policy period of any prior cancelled insurance that was issued to the named insured or a predecessor in interest by *another* company, and the period of time to discover a loss under that insurance has expired, the insurer will pay for the loss under the current policy if the current policy became effective at the time of cancellation of the prior one and the loss would have been covered under the current policy had it been in effect at the time of the occurrence.[678] The most the insurer will pay for the entire loss is the lesser of the limits of insurance applicable during the period of loss, whether that limit was written under the current policy or the prior cancelled insurance.[679] The insurer will apply the pertinent deductible to the amount of loss sustained under the prior cancelled policy.[680]

If loss covered under this policy condition is also partially covered under the condition governing prior policies issued by the same insurer or an affiliate, the amount recoverable is part of, not in addition to, the amount recoverable under that condition.[681] Otherwise, the amount recoverable is part of, not in addition to, the limit of insurance applicable to the loss covered under the current policy and is limited to the lesser of the amount recoverable under the current policy as of its effective date or the prior cancelled insurance, had it remained in effect.[682]

[9] Other Insurance

The commercial crime policy has an "other insurance" clause.[683] Under the clause, if there is other valid and collectible insurance available to the named insured for a loss covered under the crime policy, the obligations of the insurer are limited based on whether the crime policy is primary or excess.

[a] Crime Policy as Primary Insurance

When the crime policy is written as primary insurance and the named insured has other insurance subject to the same terms and conditions as the crime policy, the insurer will pay its share of the covered loss meaning the proportion that the applicable limit of insurance shown on the Declarations Page bears to the total limit of all insurance covering the same loss.[684] If, on the other hand, the named

678. ISO Form CR 00 23 11 15, § E.1.p.(1).
679. ISO Form CR 00 23 11 15, § E.1.p.(2).(a).
680. ISO Form CR 00 23 11 15, § E.1.p.(2).(b).
681. ISO Form CR 00 23 11 15, § E.1.p.(3).(a).
682. ISO Form CR 00 23 11 15, § E.1.p.(3).(b).
683. ISO Form CR 00 23 11 15, § E.1.q. Note that under the Discovery Form, this clause is essentially identical, but has a different designation. *See* CR 00 22 11 15, § E.1.o.
684. ISO Form CR 00 23 11 15, § E.1.q.(1).(a).

insured has other insurance covering the same loss that is *not subject* to the same terms and conditions as the crime policy, the insurer will only pay for the amount of loss that exceeds either the limit of insurance and deductible amount of that other insurance—whether or not the named insured can collect on it—or the deductible amount shown on the Declarations Page, whichever is greater.[685] The payment for loss by the insurer is subject to the terms and conditions of its crime policy.

[b] Crime Policy as Excess Insurance

When the crime policy is written as excess over other insurance, the insurer will only pay for the amount of loss that exceeds the limit of insurance and deductible amount of the other insurance—whether or not the named insured can collect on it—and the payment by the insurer for a loss is subject to the terms and conditions of its crime policy.[686] However, if a loss covered under the crime policy is subject to a deductible, the insurer will reduce the deductible amount shown on the Declarations Page by the sum total of all other insurance combined with any deductible amount applicable to the other insurance.

[10] Transfer of Rights and Duties

The rights and duties of the named insured under the policy may not be transferred without the written consent of the insurer, except in the case of the death of an individual named insured.[687]

The named insured is required to transfer to the insurer all its rights of recovery against any person or organization for any loss it sustained and for which the insurer has paid or settled. The named insured also is required to do everything necessary to secure those rights and do nothing after a loss that impairs them.[688] The requirement to transfer rights of recovery is—though not so denominated—a subrogation provision, meaning it facilitates the ability of the insurer to obtain subrogation—recovery—from a party responsible for a loss its insured has suffered and for which the insurer has paid a claim.

[11] Recoveries

When either party to the policy recovers any portion of a loss from a responsible party, crime polices provide for the distribution of that recovery. The applicable provision describes how any recovery from a third party who was either

685. ISO Form CR 00 23 11 15, § E.1.q.(1).(b).

686. ISO Form CR 00 23 11 15, § E.1.q.(2).(a).

687. ISO Form CR 00 23 11 15, § E.1.w. Note that under the Discovery Form, this clause is identical, but has a different designation. *See* CR 00 22 11 15, § E.1.v.

688. ISO Form CR 00 23 11 15, § E.1.x. Note that under the Discovery Form, this clause is identical, but has a different designation. *See* CR 00 22 11 15, § E.1.w.

responsible or otherwise benefited from the dishonest activity is to be distributed.[689] The pertinent clause states that any recoveries, whether effected before or after any payment under the policy or whether made by the insurer or by the named insured, will be applied *net* of the expense of the recovery.[690] In other words, any expenses incurred in obtaining the recovery, which can be considerable as they usually include attorney's fees, are subtracted from the amount available for distribution. The order of distribution is first to the named insured in satisfaction of its covered loss that exceeds the amount paid by the insurer under the policy.[691] Next, the remainder goes to the insurer in satisfaction of amounts it paid in settlement of the claim.[692] After that, any undistributed funds will go to the named insured to cover its deductible.[693] If any funds remain, they are distributed to the named insured in satisfaction of any loss not covered under the policy.[694] In reality, the named insured is unlikely to receive an amount that covers either its deductible or uncovered losses because it is rare that there are sufficient recoveries to make both the insured and insurer whole.[695]

[12] Cancellation of the Policy

Either party may cancel the policy. The first named insured may cancel it merely by mailing or delivering advance written notice of cancellation to the insurer.[696] The insurer may cancel the policy by mailing or delivering written notice of cancellation to the first named insured.[697] That notice has to be mailed or delivered at least 10 days before the effective date of cancellation if the cancellation is for non-payment of premium or 30 days before the effective date of cancellation if the cancellation is for any other reason. The notice will be mailed or delivered to the last mailing address of the first named insured known to the insurer.[698] When the notice is mailed, proof of mailing is sufficient proof of notice.[699]

The notice will state the effective date of cancellation, and the policy period will end on that date.[700] When the policy is cancelled, the insurer will send the first

689. Kain & Glovach, *Annotated Commercial Crime Policy*, 574 (2d ed. ABA 2006).

690. ISO Form CR 00 23 11 15, § E.1.u.(1). Note that under the Discovery Form, this clause is identical but has a different designation. *See* CR 00 22 11 15, § E.1.t. Note also that recoveries do not include any recovery from insurance, suretyship, reinsurance, security, or indemnity taken for the benefit of the insurer or of original securities after duplicates of them have been issued. ISO Form CR 00 23 11 15, § E.1.u.(2).

691. ISO Form CR 00 23 11 15, § E.1.u.(1).(a).

692. ISO Form CR 00 23 11 15, § E.1.u.(1).(b).

693. ISO Form CR 00 23 11 15, § E.1.u.(1).(c).

694. ISO Form CR 00 23 11 15, § E.1.u.(1).(d).

695. Kain & Glovach, *Annotated Commercial Crime Policy*, 575 (2d ed. ABA 2006).

696. ISO Form CR 00 23 11 15, § E.1.b.(1).

697. ISO Form CR 00 23 11 15, § E.1.b.(2).

698. ISO Form CR 00 23 11 15, § E.1.b.(3).

699. ISO Form CR 00 23 11 15, § E.1.b.(6).

700. ISO Form CR 00 23 11 15, § E.1.b.(4).

named insured any premium refund due; however, the cancellation is effective even if the insurer has not made or offered any refund.[701] If the cancellation is by the insurer, the refund will be *pro rata*, but if it is by the first named insured, the refund may be less than *pro rata*.

Policy cancellation is regulated by the states under their laws and regulations. Therefore, there will generally be a state-specific endorsement added to the policy that modifies the cancellation conditions of the policy and conforms it to the requirements of the applicable state law. There are, for example, state-specific standard ISO endorsements for California,[702] Florida,[703] Illinois,[704] New York,[705] and Texas.[706]

In addition to modifying the cancellation provisions, these endorsements typically add requirements that apply when the insurer decides not to *renew* the policy. For example, the Illinois endorsement says that if the insurer decides not to renew or continue the policy, it will mail a written notice to the named insured and its agent or broker that states the reason for nonrenewal at least 60 days before the end of the policy period.[707] The New York endorsement addresses "conditional renewal." It provides that if the insurer conditionally renews the policy subject to a change of limits, a change in type of coverage, a reduction of coverage, an increased deductible, an additional exclusion, or increased premiums in excess of 10 percent, it will mail or deliver written notice to the first named insured at least 60, but not more than 120, days before the expiration date, or anniversary date if the policy is a continuous one, and the notice will include the specific reason or reasons for the conditional renewal, including the amount of any premium increase for conditional renewal and a description of any other changes.[708]

The sustained loss policy also provides that if it—or any of its coverages—is cancelled as to any insured, any loss sustained by that insured will only be covered if discovered by the named insured no later than *one year*—or 60 days in the case of the Discovery Form[709]—from the date of that cancellation.[710] However, the extended period to discover a loss terminates immediately on the effective date of any other insurance obtained by that insured that replaces in whole or in part the coverage afforded under the policy, whether or not that other insurance provides

701. ISO Form CR 00 23 11 15, § E.1.b.(5).

702. *See, e.g.*, ISO Form CR 02 49 09 12 (Crime and Fidelity: California Changes).

703. *See, e.g.*, ISO Form CR 02 06 02 12 (Crime and Fidelity: Florida Changes).

704. *See, e.g.*, ISO Form CR 02 02 10 10 (Crime and Fidelity: Illinois Changes).

705. *See, e.g.*, ISO Form CR 02 34 01 14 (Crime and Fidelity: New York Changes).

706. *See, e.g.*, ISO Form CR 02 47 10 10 (Crime and Fidelity: Texas Changes). Note that the Texas endorsement leaves the substance of the standard policy unchanged.

707. *See, e.g.*, ISO Form CR 02 02 10 10, § B.

708. *See, e.g.*, ISO Form CR 02 34 01 14, § B.2.

709. *See* CR 00 22 11 15, § E.1.I.(4).(a).

710. *See* ISO Form CR 00 23 11 15, § E.1.1.(4).(a).

coverage for a loss sustained before its effective date. Additionally, both forms provide that if the policy—or any of its coverages—is cancelled as to any insured, any loss sustained by that insured regarding any *employee benefit plan* will only be covered if discovered by the named insured no later than one year from the date of that cancellation.[711]

[13] Legal Action against the Insurer

The commercial crime policy includes conditions precedent to legal actions by the named insured and a contractual limitation period that are common to many types of policies.[712] First, the named insured is prohibited by the policy from bringing a legal action *involving loss* against the insurer unless it has complied with all the policy terms. Second, the named insured cannot bring an action involving loss until 90 days after it has filed a proof of loss with the insurer. Finally, the action has to be brought within two years from the date the named insured discovered the loss.[713] These limitations may not conform to state law. The policy provides that if any of these limitations is prohibited by law, it is amended to equal the minimum period of limitation provided by that law.

§ 15.06 The Stigma of Certain Claims

A crime policy is a form of property coverage, but an issue separate from the policies themselves distinguishes claims brought under them: stigma. When an insured has, for example, storm damage for which it seeks coverage, no one blames the insured for its loss. A claim under a crime policy, however, has the potential to damage the reputation of the insured. Businesses, for example, may choose not to submit a claim for fear that it will result in negative publicity for the company.[714] The fact that a high-ranking employee was able to embezzle funds can raise questions about a company's financial controls or the judgment exercised in its hiring process. If a company chooses not to submit a claim because it fears for its reputation, that is a business decision for it to make. For common interest community associations, it is a different matter. Certainly, a CIC could be damaged by negative publicity about a theft committed, for example, by an association officer. Potential buyers may avoid a community they fear is not careful with the funds it collects from its residents and that could depress property values. A CIC governing board, however, has less flexibility than the board of a business corporation. First, although common interest communities are subject

711. *See* ISO Form CR 00 23 11 15, § E.1.l.(4).(b); CR 00 22 11 15, § E.1.I.(4).(b).

712. ISO Form CR 00 23 11 15, § E.1.m.

713. On the meaning of "discovery," see § 15.02[1], *supra*.

714. Horkovich, Reeves & Andrews, *Insurance Coverage for Employee Theft Losses: A Policyholder Primer on Commonly Litigated Issues*, 29 U. Mem. L. Rev. 363, 364 (1999) (noting that some victims fail to use their fidelity insurance).

to federal income tax, they may elect to be treated as tax-exempt homeowners associations under the Internal Revenue Code,[715] a status that exempts most of their income from taxation but that also generally denies them deductions otherwise available,[716] for example, losses caused by theft.[717] Second, the governing board of an association has a fiduciary responsibility to its members. If it fails to recoup money taken from it that it held for the benefit of those members, it may be found to have breached its fiduciary duty.

For the most part, the process for a claim submitted under a crime policy is the same as it is under any other policy, with a few differences. Typically, under a commercial property policy the insured is required to provide the carrier with "prompt" notice of any loss or damage.[718] Crime policies dictate that after the named insured *discovers* a loss, or a situation that could result in a loss or damage to covered property, the named insured has to notify the insurer of it "as soon as possible."[719] "Discovery" triggers the obligation to provide notice, and it is generally defined to mean the time when the named insured first *become aware* of facts that would cause a *reasonable person* to *assume* a loss of a type covered by the policy has been or will be incurred, regardless of when the act or acts causing or contributing to that loss occurred, even though the exact amount or details of loss may not then be known.[720] This definition has been the subject of considerable interpretation by courts.[721]

One expert describes the usual process that an association can expect after it notifies the insurer of a claim. The insurer will appoint a claims examiner who will verify the coverage the association has in place by reviewing the underwriting file and will copy key documents and verify effective dates, limits, deductibles, and endorsements.[722] The claims examiner then generally sends an acknowledgment letter to the association that states that the claims examiner is handling the claim and invites the association to contact him or her with any questions or concerns about the coverage.

Under both commercial property and crime policies, the insured must submit a proof of loss. Basic commercial property policies provide that the insurer supplies the insured with the proof of loss form and the insured has to send the

715. *See* 26 U.S.C. § 528.

716. *See* 26 U.S.C. § 528(d)(1)(B) (only allowable deductions are those connected with production of gross income other than "exempt function income" meaning income from membership dues, fees, or assessments); § 528(d)(2)(B) & (C) (no operating loss or deductions under provisions for corporations allowed).

717. *See* 26 U.S.C. § 165(a) (deduction allowed for any loss sustained during taxable year and not compensated for by insurance or otherwise).

718. *See* ISO Form CP 00 10 06 07, § E.3.a.(2); ISO Form CP 00 17 06 07, § E.3.a.(2).

719. ISO Form CR 00 23 11 15, § E.1.g.(1).

720. ISO Form CR 00 23 11 15, § F.5.

721. *See* § 15.02[1], *supra.*

722. Branson, *Fidelity Bond Insurance: Protection Against Condo Crime* (Cooperator, 2014), available at: http://cooperator.com/articles/2823/1/Fidelity-Bond-Insurance/Page1.html.

carrier the signed, sworn proof of loss containing the information it requires within 60 days *after its request*.[723] In comparison, crime polices generally require the named insured to provide the insurer with a detailed, sworn proof of loss within 120 days after *discovering* a loss or a situation that could result in a loss or damage to covered property.[724] Crime policies generally do not say that the insurer will provide the insured with a proof of loss form, but in practice the claims examiner for the insurer will ordinarily provide a proof of loss form to the insured.[725]

After the insurance company has completed its investigation it may pay or deny the claim. If the insurer accepts liability it will issue a check—probably through the claims examiner—in exchange for a release by the association, which closes the claim and gives rights to the company to proceed against the accused for the money.[726] It should go without saying that the association should neither negotiate the check nor sign the release before its attorney has reviewed the matter. If the company has offered to pay less than the amount the association claimed, the attorney should be provided with documentation of the claim, which would include a copy of the proof of loss.

Of course, insurers often deny claims, which does not mean the association does not have a valid one. One commentary says that fidelity claims often are covered, but insurers nonetheless assert "shadowy defenses" to just say "no."[727] The defenses to coverage on which the insurer relies will be stated in a denial letter that the insurer prepares when it contends the loss does not qualify for coverage under the policy.[728] That letter needs to be forwarded to the association attorney who can determine if an attorney who specializes in insurance law is needed. Observers warn of some peculiarities in denial of claims under crime policies.[729]

723. *See* ISO Form CP 00 10 10 00, § E.3.a.(7); ISO Form CP 00 17 04 02, § E.3.a.(7).

724. ISO Form CR 00 23 11 15, § E.1.g.(2). *See generally* Haase, *Proof of Loss in Fidelity Cases—Sufficiency & Requirements of Good Faith*, 12 Forum 980 (1977).

725. Branson, *Fidelity Bond Insurance: Protection Against Condo Crime* (Cooperator, 2014), available at: http://cooperator.com/articles/2823/1/Fidelity-Bond-Insurance/Page1.html.

726. Branson, *Fidelity Bond Insurance: Protection Against Condo Crime* (Cooperator, 2014), available at: http://cooperator.com/articles/2823/1/Fidelity-Bond-Insurance/Page1.html.

727. Horkovich, Reeves & Andrews, *Insurance Coverage for Employee Theft Losses: A Policyholder Primer on Commonly Litigated Issues*, 29 U. Mem. L. Rev. 363, 364 (1999) (insured often must respond to barrage of defenses insurance companies typically interpose to even most clearly covered claims). *See also* Wood & Hurtado, *Don't Get Robbed of Your Fidelity Coverage*, 9 Enforce 12 (2011), available at: http://www.andersonkill.com/Custom/PublicationPDF/PublicationID_1062_Dont-Get-Robbed-of-Your-Fidelity-Coverage.pdf (most crime carriers and bonding companies read their policies narrowly, often far more narrowly than these policies warrant).

728. Branson, *Fidelity Bond Insurance: Protection Against Condo Crime* (Cooperator, 2014), available at: http://cooperator.com/articles/2823/1/Fidelity-Bond-Insurance/Page1.html.

729. *See generally* Wood & Hurtado, *Don't Get Robbed of Your Fidelity Coverage*, 9 Enforce 12 (2011), available at: http://www.andersonkill.com/Custom/PublicationPDF/PublicationID_1062_Dont-Get-Robbed-of-Your-Fidelity-Coverage.pdf (road to full recovery entails successfully resisting insurer's often overbroad assertion of coverage defenses).

For example, there is no "negligence" exclusion in the typical crime policy, but according to one authority insurance companies frequently prey on the guilt of the insured after a fraud loss by pointing to failures in financial controls even though those failures are not a legitimate reason to disclaim coverage.[730]

Not surprisingly, insurers search for ways to recoup money paid on claims and may look for those other than the principal perpetrator who may bear some degree of responsibility for a loss and examine all aspects of the roles they played in order to regain some of the money lost.[731] This can prove awkward for common interest community associations. Those most likely to come under the insurer's scrutiny are persons well known, perhaps personal friends, to the officers and directors of the association: fellow officers and directors, volunteer residents, maintenance personnel, and the community association manager. The standard crime policy, however, imposes some obligations on the insured association. First, there is a general duty to cooperate with the insurer in "all matters" that pertain to the policy,[732] and, in the event of a loss, to cooperate with the insurer in its investigation and settlement of any claim.[733] Next, the insured is to secure all rights of recovery against any person or organization responsible for that loss and to do nothing that would impair those rights.[734] The association, therefore, cannot simply refuse to cooperate with the insurer when it seeks recompense from persons known to the officers and directors of the association. If it has concerns about the extent to which it must cooperate with the insurer, the association needs to consult with its counsel. One question that will need to be addressed is whether anyone subject to legal action by the insurer has coverage under the association's D&O insurance. If the management company is the subject of the insurer's attention, there should be no reason for the association to hesitate in cooperating. One can expect a management company that routinely handles funds for others to be well prepared to defend its actions and insured to cover any liability.

730. Horkovich, Reeves & Andrews, *Insurance Coverage for Employee Theft Losses: A Policyholder Primer on Commonly Litigated Issues*, 29 U. Mem. L. Rev. 363, 395 (1999) (neither negligence, inattention, nor failure to discover what by diligence might have been discovered should defeat claims for loss caused by dishonesty).

731. Branson, *Fidelity Bond Insurance: Protection Against Condo Crime* (Cooperator, 2014), available at: http://cooperator.com/articles/2823/1/Fidelity-Bond-Insurance/Page1.html.

732. ISO Form CR 00 23 11 15, § E.1.f.

733. ISO Form CR 00 23 11 15, § E.1.g.(3).

734. ISO Form CR 00 23 11 15, § E.1.g.(6).

§ 15.07 Association Policy Content Checklist

When the association reviews its commercial crime policy, the checklist below provides some important questions it should ask about that policy.

- ☐ Is the policy a Loss Sustained Form or Discovery Form? What is the significance of the particular form to the association? See §§ 15.01[2], 15.02[1], 15.02[2].
- ☐ Does the policy provide the amount of coverage required by statute or its governing documents? See § 15.01[5].
- ☐ Does the policy provide limits of coverage that meet the association's needs, and in a renewal policy have the limits been updated to reflect changes in the association's assets? See §§ 15.01[9][d], 15.01[10][c].
- ☐ Is the policy issued in the name of the community association management company? If so, is the association an additional insured? Does the policy provide the association with sufficient coverage? See § 15.01[6].
- ☐ Is the name of the association as it appears on the Declarations Page the legal name of the association in the governing documents? See § 15.01[10][a].
- ☐ What coverage is shown on the Declarations Page? See § 15.01[10][c].
- ☐ How is "premises" defined in the policy and in any endorsement? See § 15.02[4].
- ☐ Do any rights the association has to terminate its contract with the community association management company affect coverage? See § 15.02[5][a][i].
- ☐ Is there coverage for employee theft of "client" property in the policy or added by endorsement? See § 15.02[5][a][iii].
- ☐ Does the policy cover theft or robbery of association covered property from the home of an officer or director? See §§ 15.02[5][c][iii], 15.02[5][d][iv].
- ☐ Who qualifies as a "messenger" for purposes of the "loss outside the premises" coverage? See § 15.02[5][e].
- ☐ Does the policy include "Identity Fraud Expense" coverage? See § 15.02[6].

- ☐ Are claims expenses covered by the policy or through an endorsement? See § 15.02[7].
- ☐ Is personal accounts protection needed by the association, and is it provided by the policy or an endorsement? See § 15.02[9].
- ☐ Are association officers and directors considered employees under the policy? See §§ 15.03[1][a], 15.03[6].
- ☐ Are volunteer workers for the association considered employees? See § 15.03[7].
- ☐ Is the community association manager considered an employee? See § 15.03[10].
- ☐ Are community association managers, accountants, bookkeepers, or attorneys "authorized representatives" for purposes of exclusion for a loss that results from theft or any other dishonest act committed by an authorized representative of the named insured. See § 15.04[3].
- ☐ If the community is being developed in phases, how does the condition on additional premises affect the association coverage? See § 15.05[1][a].
- ☐ What must the association do to meet the notice of loss requirement? See § 15.05[4][a][ii].
- ☐ Does a loss potentially fall under both the commercial property and crime policies? If so, the association needs to be aware of possible differences in the proof of loss requirements. See § 15.05[4][b].
- ☐ How does the policy treat losses sustained during prior insurance? See § 15.05[8].

INDEX